Instructional Practices

That Maximize Student Achievement

For Teachers, By Teachers

Third Edition

William B. Ribas, Ph.D.
Deborah A. Brady, Ph.D.
Jalene Tamerat, M.A.T., Ed.M.
Jennifer Antos Deane, Ph.D.
Colleen Billings, M.A.T.
Victoria Greer, Ph.D.

RIBAS ASSOCIATES AND PUBLICATIONS, INC.

© Copyright 2017 William B. Ribas

Published and distributed by Ribas Publications
596 Pleasant Street
Norwood, MA 02062
Website: ribasassociates.com
Phone: 781-551-9120

ISBN-13: 978-0-9976109-0-1

Book design and typestting by Jane Tenenbaum

Printed in Canada

AUTHOR BIOGRAPHIES

William B. Ribas, Ph.D.

Bill is has more than 36 years of experience as a paraprofessional, teacher, administrator, and consultant in a number of school districts. His teaching experience includes elementary, middle school, and high school. His administrative experience includes assistant principal, principal, director of pupil and personnel services, and assistant superintendent. Bill's other books include *Educator Supervision and Evaluation That Works* and *Inducting and Mentoring Educators New to the District*, which are published nationally and internationally. He has also published articles in a variety of practitioner journals.

Currently, Bill is the president of Ribas Associates and Publications, Inc., an educational consulting, training, and publishing company. The company is dedicated to the growth and development of paraprofessionals, teachers and administrators. Since the company's inception in 2002, Bill and the other Ribas Associates consultants have worked with over 110 urban, suburban, and rural school districts, helping educators raise student performance and better meet the needs of all students.

Deborah A. Brady, Ph.D.

With over thirty-five years in public and private education, Debby Brady has had experience as a teacher, administrator, and co-teacher. Deb has served as an assistant superintendent for teaching and learning in two districts for over 17 years. She has taught middle school, high school and college as an English, reading, and writing teacher and instructor. In addition, Deb has served as a director of a learning/writing center at Dean College, and as an adjunct professor at Lesley College, Assumption College, Worcester State College, and Fitchburg State College, where she taught both graduate and undergraduate courses in curriculum, reading, literacy, and writing. Deborah earned her doctorate at Lesley in educational studies. Her research focused on the impact of a standards-based curriculum on teaching, co-teaching, learning and assessment. Her special areas of interest include curriculum assessment, development, and improvement; instructional leadership and teacher evaluation; formative assessment and the effective use of feedback and data to improve instruction and student achievement; the gradual release of responsibility; effective data team development; and, literacy across the content areas and its assessment in reading, writing, speaking, listening, and accountable talk. Her initiatives as a district leader included: Instructional Rounds, MTSS-RTI, International Baccalaureate, teacher leadership, and Understanding by Design.

Jalene Tamerat, M.A.T., Ed.M.

Jalene Tamerat is a doctoral candidate in educational leadership and policy studies at Boston University. Prior to her pursuit of full-time graduate study, she worked in the Boston Public Schools for ten years, the last eight of those as a science teacher and teacher leader at the Josiah Quincy Upper School. At the Quincy Upper, in addition to her teaching duties, Jalene led groups of teachers through various school-based reform initiatives, including a comprehensive school quality review. Jalene also worked as part of a small team to develop the school's curriculum and practices for the adoption of the International Baccalaureate program, and supported the school through its first few years of implementation. Since 2014, Jalene has been working with Breakthrough Greater Boston to provide instructional coaching to aspiring science teachers.

Jalene received her B.A. in political science from the University of Massachusetts, Amherst, and holds master's degrees from Emmanuel College (M.A.T) and Harvard University (Ed.M., Education Policy and Management). In 2008, she earned administrative licensure through participation in the Greater Boston Principal Residency Network. Her research at Boston University involves the experience of urban teachers as global competence educators.

Jennifer Antos Deane, Ph.D.

Jenny Deane holds a doctorate from Boston College in curriculum and instruction with an emphasis on math and literacy education in elementary and middle school classrooms. While working in Braintree, Massachusetts, she was chosen Teacher of the Year. She was also a classroom teacher in North Reading and Needham, Massachusetts public schools. She worked as a mathematics resource teacher and presently works as the STEM coordinator in the Westborough Public Schools. Currently, she teaches mathematical problem-solving skills to elementary students. Jenny has been influential in developing materials and training teachers to extend and remediate mathematics and literacy teaching. She also assists teachers with integrating mathematics and literacy across the curriculum. She authored the article "Daily Journals Connect Mathematics to Real Life," which appeared in *The Journal of Mathematics Teaching in the Middle School*.

Colleen Billings, M.A.T.

Colleen Billings has been a district director of ESL programs and taught ESL and bilingual education for twenty-five years. She served on the Bilingual/ELL Advisory Council for the Massachusetts Department of Education. She served as a sheltered English immersion professional development coordinator for the Massachusetts Department of Elementary and Secondary Education. She currently works in Andover, Massachusetts public schools, where she teaches ESL and leads professional development workshops related to the academic needs of English learners. In addition, she teaches graduate level courses at The School of Education and Social Policy teacher education programs at Merrimack College.

Victoria Greer, Ph.D.

Dr. Greer began her career as a special education teacher in Nashville, Tennessee. She then became a school liaison supervisor, coordinating after school and summer programs in underserved communities in Nashville. In 2006 she became an instructional facilitator, providing teachers with professional development opportunities. Among the programs she provided were programs designed to close the achievement gap between special education and general education students. In 2009 she became the director of instruction for the city of Nashville. She presently serves as the assistant superintendent of student services for the Cambridge, Massachusetts Public Schools.

DEDICATIONS

To my parents, whose love of words and learning still speak to me.
  — Deborah Brady

To those who have significantly helped me along the way.
  - *My parents, for always believing in me and helping me achieve my fullest potential*
  - *Alan, my husband and best friend, for his unwavering support and his help putting things into perspective*
  - *My sisters, for the lifelong lessons they continue to teach me*
  - *Dr. Lillie Albert, my friend and mentor, for always encouraging me to take things one step further*
  — Jenny Deane

"To the foremost educators in my life: Patrick, Menelik, and my parents."
  — Jalene Tamerat

To Tom Ribas, a loving and devoted son, brother, uncle, and godfather. He's always there when you need him.
  — Bill Ribas

ACKNOWLEDGMENTS

The authors would like to thank the following educators for their contributions to this book.

1. A very special thank you to Dr. Scott Seider, associate professor, Boston University School of Education. Scott was one of the authors of the first and second editions for this book. He was unable to work on this edition because of his work and family demands. His contributions to those editions laid an important foundation for several chapters in this edition.

The other contributors are listed in alphabetical order.

2. Dr. Lillie Albert, associate professor, Boston College, Lynch Graduate School of Education, for her contributions to Chapter 4.
3. Ms. Beth Anderson, eighth-grade math teacher for Westborough Public Schools, for her contributions to chapter 6.
4. Ms. Donna Avery, seventh-grade math teacher for Westborough Public Schools, for her contributions to chapter 6.
5. Dr. Paul Ash, former superintendent, Lexington, Massachusetts, for serving as a reader on the earlier editions.
6. Ms. Jeannette Bastien, middle school teacher, Westfield, Massachusetts, for her contributions to Chapter 6.
7. Ms. Jeanelle Bradshaw, elementary school teacher, Boston, Massachusetts, for serving as a reader.
8. Ms. Mary Burchenal, high school teacher, Brookline, Massachusetts, for her contribution to Chapter 9.
9. Mr. Wayne Chatterton, high school teacher, Westwood, Massachusetts, for his contributions to Chapter 2.
10. Dr. William Conners, Retired Superintendent and Pre-K to 12 educational consultant, for serving as a reader on earlier editions.
11. Mr. Kevin Cousineau, Kindergarten Teacher, Holyoke, Massachusetts, for his contributions to Chapter 1.
12. Dr. Linda Denault, retired superintendent, pre-K to 12 educational consultant, and faculty member at Becker College, for serving as a reader on earlier editions.
13. Ms. Andrea Fowler, former elementary school teacher, Marblehead, Massachusetts, for her contributions to Chapter 9.
14. Ms. Lisa Freedman, special education teacher, Westwood, Massachusetts, for her contributions to Chapter 2.
15. Mr. Roger Grande, high school teacher, Brookline, Massachusetts, for his contributions to Chapter 1.
16. Mr. Brian Greenberg, Principal, Leadership Public Schools, Richmond, California, for his contributions to Chapter 2.
17. Ms. Elayne Gumlaw, retired director of curriculum and instruction, West Springfield, Massachusetts, for her help with the development of the "looking at student work" protocol and for serving as a reader.
18. Dr. Marilyn Gigliotti, retired assistant superintendent and principal and a pre-K to 12 educational consultant, for serving as a reader on earlier editions.

19. Mr. Kevin Higginbottom, supervisor of science and technology, grades K-12 Haverhill, Massachusetts, for his contributions to Chapter 3.

20. Mr. Richard Higgins, high school teacher, Weymouth, Massachusetts, for his contribution to Chapter 3.

21. Dr. David Hodgdon, former assistant superintendent of schools, for his comprehensive review of literature for several chapters.

22. Ms. Mindy LeBlanc, Montgomery County (Maryland) Public Schools, grades 3–5 math teacher, and Title One, Gifted and Talented, and grade four classroom teacher, for serving as a reader.

23. Ms. Laurie Levin, elementary mathematics curriculum leader, Needham, Massachusetts, for her contributions to Chapter 4.

24. Mr. Michael Mao, high school teacher, Westwood, Massachusetts, for his contributions to Chapter 5.

25. Dr. Gail Mayotte, Faculty of Supervision and Instruction, University of Notre Dame, for her contributions to Chapter 4.

26. Ms. Debbie Mercer, Teacher of the Gifted and Talented and Literacy Specialist, Brookline, Massachusetts, and pre-K to 12 educational consultant, for her contributions to Chapters 6, 9, and 11.

27. Ms. Marge Modena, technology specialist, Needham, Massachusetts, for her contributions to Chapter 4.

28. The Needham Public Schools for its contributions to Chapter 4.

29. Ms. Emily Parks, assistant superintendent, Westwood, Massachusetts, for her contributions to Chapters 2 and 5.

30. Mr. Dan Phelan, vice principal, Bellamy Middle School, Chicopee, Massachusetts, for his contributions to chapter 6.

31. Ms. Susan Plati, high school teacher, Brookline, Massachusetts, for her contributions to Chapter 9.

32. Ms. Carol Rosengarten, special education teacher, Westwood, Massachusetts, for writing the sections "Working With Special Education Students" found in earlier editions.

33. Ms. Rhonda Ruegar, former Principal, Oneida, New York, for serving as a reader in earlier editions.

34. Ms. Mitzi Sales, former middle school teacher, Rye, New York, for her contributions to Chapter 3.

35. Ms. Joyce Silberman, elementary teacher, Needham, Massachusetts, for her contributions to Chapter 6.

36. Dr. Sheila Cutler Sohn, educational consultant for elementary and middle school students in mathematics, science, organizational/study skills, and time management, for her contributions to Chapter 4.

37. Ms. Sharon Twomey, elementary teacher, Lawrence, Massachusetts, for her contributions to Chapter 1.

38. Mr. William Simmons, principal, Oneida, New York, for serving as a reader.

39. Ms. Jennifer Teahan, elementary teacher, for her contributions to Chapter 9.

40. Mr. Matthew Underwood, teacher, Francis Parker Charter School, Devens, Massachusetts, for his contributions to Chapter 8.

41. Dr. Chris Whitbeck, principal, Acton, Massachusetts, for his contributions to Chapter 1.

42. Ms. Melissa Williams, elementary teacher, Lawrence, Massachusetts, for her contributions to Chapter 1.

43. Dr. Amir Zarrimpar, MD, Ph.D., for his contributions to Chapter 8 in earlier editions.

CONTENTS

5 Questioning, Dipsticking, and In-the-Moment, "Short-Cycle" Formative Assessments That Target Mastery   213

6 Differentiating Instruction with a Connection to Universal Design for Learning   269

7 Student Motivation and Succeeding with Students from Poverty

8 The Brain and Student Learning

11 Job-Embedded Professional Development 517

Index of Topics and Names 581

INTRODUCTION

Objectives for the Introduction

After reading this introduction, the reader will be able to

a. explain the intended purpose of the authors in writing this book

b. describe the background of the authors and supporting professionals who contributed to the writing of this book

c. explain how readers use this book to increase their understanding and improve their implementation of strategies for:

1. universal pedagogy
2. content specific pedagogy
3. meeting the needs of students with disabilities, including Universal Design for Learning (UDL) and response to intervention (RtI)
4. working with students and families from poverty
5. meeting the needs of English language learners
6. social-emotional learning
7. student efficacy (growth mindset, incremental learning theory, learnable intelligence, elimination of deficit perspective)
8. collaborative models of professional learning as they relate to each of the 10 areas of effective teaching noted in Figure I.1

d. explain how readers can most effectively use this book to improve the level of achievement of all students

Purpose of the Book

The decision to write the first edition of this book stemmed from the frustration expressed to us by many of our teaching and administrative colleagues. Those educators described the difficulty they encountered in finding a book that incorporated into a single reference the current practice and research about teaching practices that lead to the highest levels of student achievement. For many of these educators, the time needed to read the literally hundreds of relevant books on topics such as the brain and learning; differentiated instruction; Universal Design for Learning; working with special education students; working with English language learners; questioning techniques; assessing student learning; planning; collaborating effectively with colleagues; working with parents, guardians, and families; classroom management; motivation; brain-based learning,; and the nature of intelligence would require a year's leave of absence just for professional reading. Few educators have such an opportunity. It was our objective to write a book that would do three things for educators:

1. Provide a single, comprehensive book that contains teacher-friendly information on the most current effective teaching practices that lead to the highest levels of student growth and achievement.

2. Provide numerous examples of effective teaching practices already in use by teachers.

3. Include in each chapter a reference list of sources that educators can use to study the topics in each chapter in greater depth.

Choosing the Authors for This Book

We, the six authors of the book, have expertise in a broad range of student grade levels and academic content areas. We have taught all elementary grades from two through five, middle school grades from six through eight, and high school grades from nine through twelve. Our content-specific teaching experience includes reading, writing, mathematics, science, technology, social studies, special education, and English language learning. One author is an experienced special education teacher and college instructor, and the other a gifted and talented teacher. We also have authors with experience in teaching in urban, suburban, and rural schools. One author took the lead on each chapter. However, in order to ensure that each chapter has relevance to elementary, middle, and high school teachers, all six of us read and gave input into each of the chapters at regular authors' meetings. All six of the authors have also worked as teacher trainers. Collectively, we have trained thousands of teachers and administrators in more than 150 school districts in the United States and Canada. Because we are aware that even our wide range of practical knowledge is not sufficient to write such a book, we enlisted additional educators with experience in teaching all grades and disciplines from preschool through grade 12, special education, English language learning, and many others to contribute classroom practices and to comment on drafts of the book. In total nearly 50 educators have worked on this book. The list of these contributors can be found on the preceding acknowledgement pages.

Because we are aware that even our wide range of practical knowledge is not sufficient to write such a book, we enlisted additional educators with experience in teaching all grades and disciplines from preschool through grade 12, special education, English language learning, and many others to contribute classroom practices and to comment on drafts of the book. In total nearly 50 educators have worked on this book.

Content-Specific Instructional Methods, Universal Instructional Methods, and Grade Level-Specific Instructional Methods

We believe that it is important for teachers to know the universal instructional practices that work in multiple disciplines and across grade levels. We further believe that it is important for teachers to know the content-specific instructional methods designed primarily for their specific disciplines and grade levels. In this book, we devote a chapter to each of the major areas of effective teaching practice. Within many of the chapters, we have embedded explanations and examples of many content-specific instructional methods for a variety of grade levels. In selecting examples for this book, we sought to have a representation of many disciplines and grade levels. Unfortunately, the scope of the book would not allow us to provide examples of each concept for every grade level and discipline.

Figure I.1 on the next page shows graphically the way in which this book was constructed. The "pin" wheel demonstrates the interrelationship between the body of current research and practice about effective teaching (center circle) and the 10 areas of effective teaching (the first circle outside of the center circle). We would have you think of this figure in the following way: If you were to look at the Assessing Student Learning spoke of the wheel, you would see that the knowledge and skills in the book on this topic are derived from the Proven Research and Practice (inner circle) on assessment of student learning. This interrelationship holds true for each of the 10 areas of effective teaching practice noted in the pin wheel.

Special Education and 504 Students

We purposely did not include a specific chapter on special education. The special education teachers and administrators who assisted with the writing of this book indicated that most of the information and skills described in Chapters 1 through 11 are directly relevant to the teaching of special needs students in the regular education classroom. To quote one special education teacher:

> The strategies we use for special needs students are the same strategies all students should receive. As teachers, we need to remember that for every student in our class who has an identified need that is written in an individual education plan (IEP), there are at least one or two other students in the class with the same need. The only reason they don't have IEPs is that their special need is either not as severe as the student on the IEP or it has not been identified.

Figure I.1

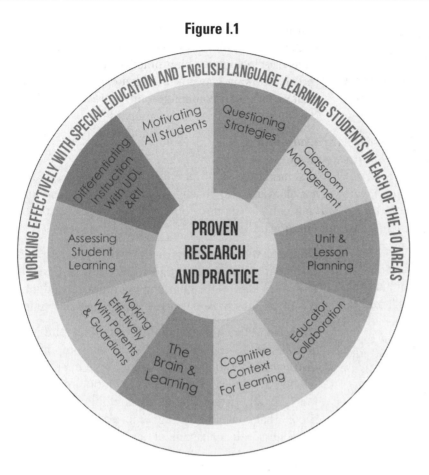

To assist educators in connecting students with special needs to the most beneficial strategies, we have included a brief special education essay at the end of each chapter. The essays are written by our special education author, with feedback from our general education authors. They explain how the concepts and strategies in each chapter can be used to maximize the learning of special education students. However, we remind all of our readers that these strategies are important for all students, not just those students with identified special needs.

English Language Learners

Along with teachers of special education students, teachers of students who are learning English as a second language indicated that many of the strategies contained in the book are the strategies teachers should use with second-language learners. In the chapter on differentiated instruction (Chapter 6), we briefly discuss the needs of English language learners. For example, a differentiated instruction lesson plan in a classroom with second-language learners should contain a list of the vocabulary words that the second-language learners need to be successful. This

list is typically more extensive than that which is needed by the students for whom English is their primary language. To assist educators with connecting English language learners in their classrooms to the most beneficial strategies, we have included a brief "English Language Learner" essay at the end of each chapter. These essays are written by our English language learning author. Each essay has also had feedback from our general education authors. They explain how the concepts and practices in each chapter can be used to maximize the learning of these students.

Universal Design for Learning

It was in 2008 that we began work on the 2010 edition of this book. It was at that time that we made the decision not to treat the instruction of special education students, students with 504s, and English language learners as separate entities. At that time, concepts such as Universal Design for Learning (UDL) and Positive Behavior Interventions and Supports (PBIS) were just beginning to gain broad recognition. The many years of work in these areas have proven that our decision not to separate these groups was the correct decision. To quote Meyer, Rose, and Gordon (2014, Chapter 4, Kindle edition), in their book *Universal Design for Learning*, "A core tenet of UDL is the understanding that what is 'essential for some' is almost always 'good for all.'" Kudos to our consulting educators on this book who made the same observation in the quote above as early as 2008.

Students from Poverty

The most recent U.S. Census reports that 21.1 percent of U.S. children live in poverty. Fortunately, we are learning more about how to meet the unique needs of these students in your schools. In Chapters 7, 8, and 9, we have brought in some of the key research related to working effectively with students from poverty and their parents/guardians. We have included a variety of practices that have led to higher levels of success for these students.

Social-Emotional Learning (a.k.a. Mental Health of Students and Staff)

Social-Emotional Learning is a comprehensive, well-organized collection of the teaching strategies that lead to higher student achievement and strong intrapersonal and interpersonal knowledge in students and staff. The five major areas are:

1. Self-Awareness
2. Self-Management
3. Social Awareness
4. Relationship Management
5. Responsible Decision-Making

The authors have addressed social-emotional learning in a comprehensive manner throughout this book. Because social-emotional learning should be weaved into everything a teacher does with students and colleagues, there is no single chapter on the topic. Below are selected examples of how teachers use this book to integrate social-emotional learning into all aspects of their teaching. Because of the inseparable relationship between social-emotional learning and all aspects of effective teaching, we provide a few examples below so teachers see the way in which they should view their teaching as opportunities for developing social-emotional learning.

Chapter 1 explains how teachers plan lessons in ways that address the multiple levels of student mastery. Making students aware of these stages of mastery facilitates awareness of their own learning styles and allows for increased self-management of their learning.

Chapter 2 explains the purpose of the cognitive context strategies in developing students' learning style self-awareness. Teachers learn to help students better manage their learning by replicating the strategies when working independently.

Chapter 3 addresses areas such as self-management, social awareness, and relationship management within the context of classroom management. The arrangement of student seating to promote student-to-student interaction, teacher physical proximity, use effective group work to develop interpersonal and intrapersonal skills, positively reinforcing appropriate social behavior, and building strong relationships with their students and among their students are explained in depth.

Chapter 4 addresses key aspects of teacher assessment and student self-assessment. Teachers and students learn to assess cognitive and social skills. It contains concrete, easy-to-use rubrics and criteria sheets for assessment and self-assessment that develop self-awareness, self-management, social awareness, relationship management, and responsible decision-making.

Chapter 5 contains questioning strategies that enable teachers to assess and develop students' cognitive skills and their self-awareness, self-management, and social awareness. Teachers learn to use partner work as a vehicle for developing all five areas of social-emotional learning.

Chapter 6 explains the ways in which teachers can differentiate instruction and use the practices of Universal Design for Learning to maximize students' cognitive, interpersonal, and intrapersonal learning.

Chapter 7 teaches strategies for building students' confidence as learners. It addresses key components of this process such as learnable intelligence, overcoming the deficit perspective, attribution retraining, incremental learning theory, and multiple intelligence theory that contribute to higher levels of student self-awareness, self-management, and social awareness.

Chapter 8 explains the key ways in which brain function impacts cognitive and social learning.

Chapter 9 contains strategies teachers use to develop strong relationships with families that engender effective family involvement. Teachers learn to help parents and guardians become effective partners in their children's development of self-awareness, self-management, social awareness, relationship management, and responsible decision-making.

Chapters 10 and 11 provide strategies for developing self-awareness, self-management, social awareness, relationship management, and responsible decision making within and among teachers. The chapters contain models for effective teacher collaboration that develop teacher awareness and skills in the five social-emotional areas when working with one another.

The special education essays and English language learning essays at the end of each chapter provide important understanding about these two groups of students. Teachers learn strategies that are unique to developing the cognitive, interpersonal, and intrapersonal skills of these students.

The Importance of Teaching

Since the days of Aristotle, it has been believed that skilled teachers cause students to achieve at higher levels than less-skilled teachers do. It is only in the last three decades that the work in value-added testing and other forms of growth testing has given us quantitative proof that the skill of the teacher correlates with the level of student achievement. Educators continue to discuss (and even debate) the correct use of this growth data, but it is almost universally accepted that this data is valuable and can be correlated to teacher performance. There have been well-documented issues of misuse of this data that must be avoided.

While family income remains the best predictor of absolute achievement, good instruction is 10 to 20 times more powerful in predicting student growth.

The following is statistical evidence that longitudinal, value-added growth assessment data has provided us about the impact of good teaching on student achievement. Stronge and Tucker (2000, p. 2) first described this evidence at the turn of the century when they looked at several years of longitudinal data from the Tennessee value-added testing system.

> When children, beginning in third grade, were placed with three high-performing teachers in a row, they scored, on average, at the 96th percentile on Tennessee's statewide mathematics assessment at the end of fifth grade.
>
> When children with comparable achievement histories starting in third grade were placed with three low-performing teachers in a row, their average score on the same mathematics assessment was at the 44th percentile."[1]

Robert Marzano tells us, in his book *The Art and Science of Teaching* (2007, p. 1),

> In the last decade of the 20th century, the picture of what constitutes an effective school became much clearer. Among the elements such as well-articulated curriculum and a safe and orderly environment, the one factor that surfaced as the single most influential component of an effective school is the individual teacher within that school.

We are in an era of educational accountability that is increasingly governed by state (provincial) laws and national legislation that requires quantitative proof of student achievement against set standards. This is creating pressure on teachers and schools to ensure that they are using the teaching practices that lead to the highest levels of student mastery. The good news is that we educators have a significant body of research and practice that enables us to choose those teaching practices that lead to the highest levels of student mastery. This book has synthesized the work contained in more than 800 current books, articles, and websites, and coupled them with the practical knowledge acquired by the almost 50 contributing educators to give teachers and administrators a concise, easy-to-use resource for teaching in ways that lead to the highest levels of student mastery.

The body of evidence supporting the relationship between effective classroom instruction and student achievement proves the power of teaching in positively influencing students' lives. In his article "The Revelations of Value-Added" (December 2004, p.10), Ted Hershberg, a professor of public policy at the University of Pennsylvania, writes, "While family income remains the best predictor of absolute achievement, good instruction is 10 to 20 times more powerful in predicting student growth." These studies prove that teachers have the power to improve the lives of students from any background or family circumstance. We believe this underscores the important role teachers and teaching play in the fabric of any society.

Advantages for Students and Teachers of Using the Strategies Contained in This Book to Teach for Mastery

Prior to and in the course of writing each edition of this book, we worked with thousands of teachers in more than 150 school districts. We found that teachers who work in districts

- that have well-constructed, standards-based curriculum
- in which all of the teachers have been trained in the research-based, universal, and content-specific instructional strategies that increase student mastery
- have been trained in effective parent, guardian, and family collaboration
- have been trained in effective collegial collaboration

report the following positive outcomes:

1. Students arrive at the start of the school year having been taught the same knowledge and skills

---

1   These findings first appeared in Sanders, W., and Rivers, J (1996).

regardless of who their teachers were in previous years.

2. Students arrive at the start of the year with higher levels of mastery of knowledge and skills acquired in their prior years of schooling. Not all students are at the application mastery or mastery levels on all knowledge and skills. Some students may even be only at the introductory level; however, overall, the knowledge and skill levels of each student are higher than they otherwise would have been.

3. Students have been taught learning strategies that enable them to learn more efficiently and effectively.

4. Students are more motivated to learn new knowledge and skills.

5. When standards are set at appropriate levels, teachers know what students are expected to master by the end of the year. Teachers may then focus on teaching that body of knowledge and skills. The teacher is no longer held accountable for poorly defined and limitless amounts of knowledge and skills. It is stressful for teachers when the expectation is that they will teach everyone everything!

6. Students achieve at higher levels on teacher, district, state (provincial), and national assessments.

7. Teachers experience greater levels of success and higher job satisfaction.

Districts may perform certain functions to assist teachers in ensuring that students reach the highest levels of mastery. First, curriculum mapping[2] maximizes the effectiveness and efficiency of teaching the curriculum standards at all levels. Second, appropriate levels of funding for staff enable districts to provide favorable class sizes, as well as support and enrichment programs. Third, high-quality professional development ensures that teachers have the highest level of competency on research-based effective practices. Curriculum mapping and funding levels are left for discussion in other books. We have written this book to provide each teacher with the universal teaching practices and content-specific teaching practices. As demonstrated above, the most important component in student achievement is the decisions teachers make on what strategy to use with each student at any particular moment during a lesson, unit, or the school year.

---

2   Curriculum mapping is a process made popular by Heidi Hayes Jacobs. It enables districts to "map" their curriculum to ensure that information and skills are taught as often as needed, thus avoiding over-teaching or gaps in teaching specific information and/or skills (Jacobs 1997).

Chapter-by-Chapter Overview

This book provides teachers with a comprehensive menu of proven, successful practices from which to choose.

Chapter 1: Standards-Based (Mastery-Based) Planning and Teaching

After reading this chapter, the reader will be able to

a. explain to a colleague the key components of standards-based (a.k.a. mastery-based) planning and teaching

b. explain to a colleague the levels of student mastery

c. write essential questions for units that frame the big ideas for a unit of study

d. write objectives for a lesson and unit in language that describes what the students will know and be able to do after the teaching is finished

e. write objectives for a lesson and unit in language that enables him/her to readily assess whether the objectives have been mastered

f   choose assessments that measure students' levels of mastery of the objectives during and at the conclusion of the lesson or unit

g. choose the activities that most efficiently and effectively result in student mastery of the objectives

Chapter 2: Creating a Cognitive Context for Learning

After reading this chapter, the reader will be able to

a. use mastery objectives to create a context that leads to deeper understanding and longer retention of independent facts as they appear in the lesson

b. use an agenda to tell students what they will do during the lesson and how to retain focus

c. use activators to show students how the knowledge and skills taught in the lesson connect to their previous learning

d. use summarizers to increase student mastery and retention of the knowledge and skills taught in the lesson

e. use other brain-based strategies for maximizing student learning, such as essential questions (a.k.a. important concepts), repetition, goal setting, teaching for transfer, brain breaks that embed learning, connecting to prior knowledge, connecting learning to the real world, chunking, and role plays/simulations

f. explain the impact of exercise, nutrition, and sleep on the brain

Chapter 3: The Social, Emotional, and Instructional Components of Classroom Management With a Section on the Effective Use of Homework)

After reading this chapter, the reader will be able to

a. explain the role of social–emotional development in effective classroom management
b. list the nine components of effective classroom management
c. develop classroom rules (a.k.a. behavior standards), routines, and expectations that maximize the level of respectful, on-task behavior
d. develop an effective homework routine with students and parents
e. enable students to work effectively in pairs and small groups
f. obtain students' attention at the start of the lesson, after group and partner activities, after interruptions, and after student attention has deteriorated
g. develop teacher-to-student and student-to-student relationships that proactively increase appropriate student behavior
h. set up a classroom structure that proactively maintains appropriate student behavior
i. develop a classroom management plan that includes a system of rewards and consequences for reinforcing respectful, on-task behavior
j. develop an individual contingency plan for a student who is unable to behave appropriately within the classroom management plan.

Chapter 4: Using Teacher-Made, Local, and State/Provincial, and National Assessments to Inform Instruction

After reading this chapter, the reader will be able to

a. use the principles of assessment for learning to develop quality assessments
b. use formative assessments effectively to support student achievement
c. use assessments effectively to support students' engagement
d. use assessment data to adjust, differentiate, and plan instruction
e. define the similarities and differences between diagnostic, formative, interim, benchmark, and summative assessments
f. create high-quality, authentic performance assessments
g. design assessments that use self-assessment or self-reflection
h. write rubrics and scoring guides to assess student products and performances and to guide students' learning

Chapter 5: Questioning, Dipsticking, and In-the-Moment "Short-Cycle" Formative Assessments That Target Mastery

After reading the chapter, the reader will be able to

a. use questions effectively
b. use student responses to assess their students' progress toward mastery
c. provide students with effective, actionable feedback
d. use formative assessment results to move all students toward mastery
e. use formative assessments to modify instruction to meet students' needs
f. increase the number of students who ask and answer questions
g. elevate the level of responses to oral and written questions

Chapter 6: Differentiating Instruction with a Connection to Universal Design for Learning

After reading the chapter, the reader will be able to

a. define the key components of differentiated instruction to a colleague
b. plan lessons that flexibly provide reteaching, practice, and extension as needed
c. manage differentiated activities in a single lesson
d. explain the connections between differentiated instruction and Universal Design for Learning
e. explain how Response to Intervention (RtI) supports differentiated instruction
f. use graphic organizers and other strategies that attend to various learning styles
g. use a variety of instructional strategies to differentiate instruction by content, process, and product

Chapter 7: Student Motivation and Succeeding with Students from Poverty

After reading the chapter, the reader will be able to

a. increase student motivation by
    i.   making learning relevant to students by connecting the curriculum to students' own lives, the real world, and previous learning
    ii. demonstrating our (the teachers') enthusiasm for the knowledge and skills we are teaching
    iii. making learning engaging
    iv. differentiating instruction to make the knowledge and skills accessible to all students
    v.   developing teacher-to-student and student-to-student relationships
    vi. demonstrating and developing in students a growth mindset related to life challenges

vii. better understanding the challenges of low-SES students
b. understand the challenges facing students from some low-SES homes and use strategies designed to help them overcome those challenges
c. implement classroom strategies that move students toward the belief that success is due more to effort and acquired strategies than to innate ability and luck
d. explain the key aspects of the following theories of intelligence and their relationship to student motivation:
  i. innate, single-entity intelligence (i.e., fixed mindset)
  ii. growth mindset (e.g., learnable intelligence)
  iii. multiple intelligences
  iv. attribution of intelligence
e. increase student motivation by creating the belief in students that they control their ability to "be smart"

Chapter 8: The Brain and Student Learning

After reading the chapter, the reader will be able to
a. explain the basics of brain anatomy and how the brain functions
b. explain the processes of memory creation and learning and how they are connected
c. explain how the brain functions in relation to learning math
d. explain how the brain functions in relation to reading and learning how to read
e. explain how the brain functions in relation to the arts and how the brain specifically benefits from arts engagement
f. distinguish between common neuro-myths and research-backed findings about the brain
g. use knowledge of learning and memory processes to optimize classroom experiences in all subject areas

Chapter 9: Working Effectively with Parents and Guardians (with a Section on Working with Families from Poverty)

After reading this chapter, the reader will be able to
a. use proactive communication to establish positive relationships with parents and guardians
b. conference effectively with parents and guardians
c. deal effectively with aggressive/overly assertive parents
d. maximize the engagement of uninvolved and low-socioeconomic status parents in their children's education
e. conduct a successful curriculum night presentation

Chapter 10: Co-Teaching: Developing High-Performing Teams

After reading the chapter the reader will be able to
a. identify and describe each of the models of co-teaching
b. identify the strengths and challenges of each co-teaching model
c. list the observable behaviors that identify successful co-teaching
d. explain how co-teaching brings added value to the classroom
e. develop a plan with a co-teacher for supporting their partnership and professional growth as educators in their use of data, their instruction, and their impact
f. develop a year-long plan and individual weekly lesson plans for co-teaching that selects and uses each teacher's capacity effectively, and that select models and instructional activities that support students' needs
g. develop a lesson plan with clear objectives for learning
h. explain the administrative support needed for co-teaching to her principal
i. develop a plan with a paraprofessional for working together for the year

Chapter 11: Job-Embedded Professional Development: Teacher-Led Collaborative Inquiry Groups and Professional Learning Communities (PLCs)

After reading the chapter, the reader will be able to work effectively within a collaborative group to improve teaching and learning by
a. working in a highly effective group that works collaboratively and establishes its group norms, sets collaborative goals, collects and analyzes data, researches and employs best practices
b. participating in a cycle of ongoing improvement
c. collaboratively solving classroom, curricular, school-based, and district-based concerns using a job-embedded and collaborative inquiry group, including
  i. learning community or professional learning community (PLC)
  ii. data teams
  iii. peer reflection teams including mentoring and coaching
  iv. peer-facilitated action research
  v. peer observation of teaching
  vi. lesson study group
  vii. creating common assessments
  viii. collaboratively assessing student work (CASW)
  ix. study groups for professional reading and research

Changing Practice

The book is designed to create permanent positive change in teacher performance. It provides teachers with direct instruction in the practices that lead to the highest levels of student learning. In Chapters 10 and 11, teachers learn to work collaboratively self- and peer-assessing, discussing practice, peer coaching, and co-teaching with one another with the intent of creating an environment of continuous improvement. Figure I.2 below demonstrates what has become known as the *professional development change cycle*. It is the road map for differentiated professional development. In Chapter 1, you will see the levels of mastery students flow through as they make their way to application mastery of new concepts. The same chart applies to teachers when they are learning new practices. Teachers move through the stages at varying rates and require varying levels of teaching and assistance to master new practices. This book follows the differentiated professional development model and provides all teachers with what they need to improve.

Figure I.2 The Professional Development Change Cycle

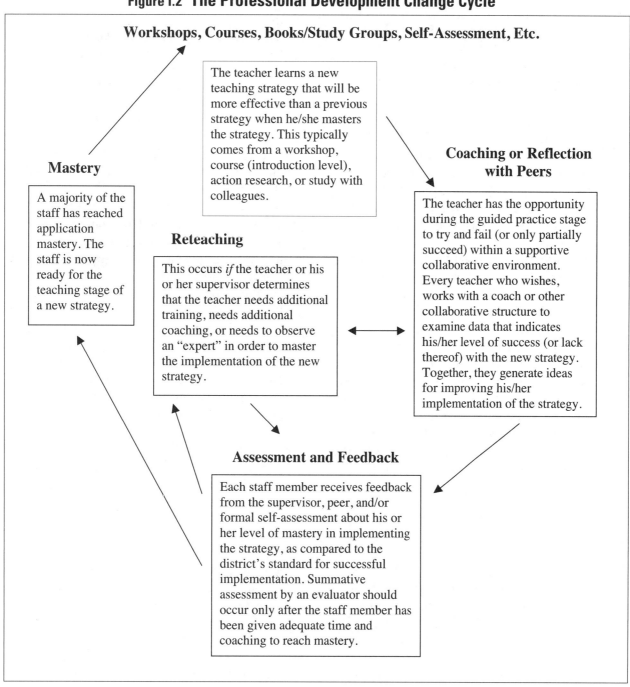

Workshops, Courses, Books/Study Groups, Self-Assessment, Etc.

The teacher learns a new teaching strategy that will be more effective than a previous strategy when he/she masters the strategy. This typically comes from a workshop, course (introduction level), action research, or study with colleagues.

Mastery

A majority of the staff has reached application mastery. The staff is now ready for the teaching stage of a new strategy.

Reteaching

This occurs *if* the teacher or his or her supervisor determines that the teacher needs additional training, needs additional coaching, or needs to observe an "expert" in order to master the implementation of the new strategy.

Coaching or Reflection with Peers

The teacher has the opportunity during the guided practice stage to try and fail (or only partially succeed) within a supportive collaborative environment. Every teacher who wishes, works with a coach or other collaborative structure to examine data that indicates his/her level of success (or lack thereof) with the new strategy. Together, they generate ideas for improving his/her implementation of the strategy.

Assessment and Feedback

Each staff member receives feedback from the supervisor, peer, and/or formal self-assessment about his or her level of mastery in implementing the strategy, as compared to the district's standard for successful implementation. Summative assessment by an evaluator should occur only after the staff member has been given adequate time and coaching to reach mastery.

References

Hershberg, T., Simon, V.A., and Lea-Kruger, B. "The Revelations of Value-Added." *The School Administrator* (December 2004): 10–14.

Hill, J.D. and Flynn, K.M. *Classroom Instruction That Works with English Language Learners*. Alexandria, VA: ASCD, 2006.

Marzano, R. *The Art and Science of Teaching: A Comprehensive Framework for Effective Instruction*. Alexandria, VA: ASCD, 2007.

Sanders, W.L. and Rivers, J.C. *Cumulative and Residual Effects of Teachers on Future Student Academic Achievement*. Knoxville, TN: University of Tennessee Value-Added Research and Assessment Center, 1996.

Stronge, J.H. and Tucker, P. *Teacher Evaluation and Student Achievement*. Washington, DC: National Education Association, 2000.

Students with Disabilities: Legal Requirements

Accountability in education has increased, and the requirement for school districts to ensure that all students, specifically those with exceptionalities, receive an education that aligns with that of students without exceptionalities. It is important for teachers to continue to expand their skills to meet the needs of the students entering their classrooms. In order to do that, it is imperative for teachers to understand the intent of the laws that were designed to afford students equal education under the law.

In 1975, Public Law 94-142, Education of All Handicapped Children Act, was enacted to ensure that children with disabilities were educated in public schools. Prior to P.L. 94-142, more than one million children with disabilities had been excluded from the educational system. The law had four purposes: (1) to ensure a "free appropriate public education (FAPE)," (2) to ensure the protection of the rights of children with disabilities and their parents, (3) to assist state and local school districts in providing an education for all children with disabilities, and (4) to assess and ensure the effectiveness of the efforts in educating children with disabilities (US Dept. of Education 2015).

The Individuals with Disabilities Education Act (IDEA) has been revised several times over the past 40 years to incorporate other acts, as well as to respond to the changes with the reauthorizations of the Elementary and Secondary Education Act (ESEA) of 1965. The two most impactful reauthorizations occurred in 2002 with the reauthorization that enacted No Child Left Behind and in 2012 with the development of "A Blueprint for Reform." Each reauthorization has brought broad and comprehensive revisions to the original laws and statues; however, there are two areas of IDEA that have remained unchanged with each reauthorization, and they are the provision for students with disabilities receiving a FAPE in the least-restrictive environment (LRE) (Latham 2014). These two areas have great implications for teachers and the skills needed to address the varying needs of the students in their classrooms.

While most educators understand the meaning of FAPE and LRE, very few understand the requirements and implications they have for teachers. It is imperative for teachers to understand that while teaching students with disabilities, the implementation of the student's individualized education plan (IEP) is a primary responsibility that is outlined in FAPE. The IEP ensures the appropriateness of the education. This is not just in regards to the goals outlined in the IEP, but it also encompasses the accommodations, modifications, and supplemental aids and supports. The responsibility to ensure that the IEP is implemented to the fullest has shifted with each reauthorization of IDEA and ESEA. In the past, it was the sole responsibility of the special education teacher and staff to ensure that the needs of students with disabilities were met and that they met the goals outlined in their IEP. However, this has transitioned to the expectation that students with disabilities will achieve at the same or similar levels as their non-disabled peers. Therefore, the responsibility to educate students with disabilities and implement their IEPs has become a dual responsibility of both general education and special education teachers and staff.

The focus to ensure that students with disabilities are educated in the LRE has challenged many educators' philosophies and practices regarding students with disabilities. IEP teams are required to ensure that removing a student with a disability from the general education classroom occurs only when the student is not successful. This is a shift from the past; while the LRE has always been a part of the law, the emphasis was not placed on ensuring that it was a primary consideration, which resulted in students with disabilities being removed and placed into separate classrooms—segregated from their non-disabled peers. Special education teachers and personnel were primarily responsible for the outcome of those students (Hodgkinson 2001). The shift back to ensuring that the LRE is a primary area addressed for students is resulting in general education and special education teachers sharing the responsibility for the outcomes of the students and those students spending the majority of their school day in the general education classroom.

These shifts make the "Working with Students with Disabilities" section at the end of each chapter imperative to expand teachers' skills not only to enable them to address the needs of students with disabilities, but also create classrooms that address the needs of all students.

Resources

Education for All Handicapped Children Act 1975. Pub. L. No. 94-142. US Department Of Education. http://www2.ed.gov/about/offices/list/osers/idea35/history/index_pg10.html.

Hodgkinson, H. "Educational Demographics: What Teachers Should Know." *Educational Leadership* 58, no. 4 (December 2000/January 2001): 6–11.

Latham, P. "At a Glance: Free and Appropriate Public Education (FAPE)." *Understood.org*. https:// www.understood.org/en/school-learning/your-childs-rights/basics-about-childs-rights/at-a-glance-free-and-appropriate-public-education.

English Language Learning: Current Trends

Current trends in teaching English learners include the examination of cultural perspectives, the study of linguistics, and the development of academic language across four language domains. Since the No Child Left Behind (NCLB) Act was passed in 2001, English as a Second Language (ESL) teachers are no longer the only educators accountable for the Limited English Proficient (LEP) or English language learner (ELL) subgroups. Schools and districts have adopted research-based instructional practices, such as those outlined in the work of Echevarria, Vogt, and Short (2013), which involve the development of academic language proficiency and literacy skills in all students (p. 13). Over thirty states have adopted the World Class Instructional Design and Assessment (WIDA) English Language Development Standards, which rely on features of academic language and levels of language proficiency in its framework (2013).

Researchers continue to support the theory that the process of acquiring a second language is similar to native language acquisition (Hill and Miller 2012). Essentially, learners listen and understand, then produce one-word expressions, then multi-word phrases, and then sentences. Eventually, they participate in extended discourse (p. 11).

In order to provide English learners with appropriate instruction, educators must study and learn the developmental levels of language proficiency. Table I.1 outlines the different stages of language acquisition children go through as they become proficient in a second language, characteristics of each stage, approximate time frame for each stage, and teacher prompts that are appropriate for each given stage. It is important to note that although all ELL students will pass through levels or stages of English language acquisition, the amount of time spent in each stage will vary from student to student (Hill and Flynn 2006). As you read each chapter and the article at the end of the chapter about teaching ELL students, you will see a reference to this chart from time to time.

Figure I.3 Stages of Language Acquisition

Stage	Characteristics	Approximate Time Frame	Teacher Prompts
Preproduction	*The student* • Has minimal comprehension • Does not verbalize • Nods "yes" and "no" • Draws and points	0–6 months	• Show me... • Circle the... • Where is...? • Who has...?
Early Production	*The student* • Has limited comprehension • Produces one- or two-word responses • Participates using key words and familiar phrases • Uses present tense verbs	6 months–1 year	• Yes/no questions • Either/or questions • One- or two-word answers • Lists • Labels
Speech Emergence	*The student* • Has good comprehension • Can produce simple sentences • Makes grammar and pronunciation errors • Frequently misunderstands jokes	1–3 years	• Why...? • How...? • Explain... • Phrasal or short-sentence answers
Intermediate Fluency	*The student* • Has excellent comprehension • Makes few grammatical errors	3–5 years	• What would happen if...? • Why do you think...?
Advanced Fluency	*The student* • Has a near-native level of speech.	5–7 years	• Decide if... • Retell...

Adapted from Krashen and Terrell (1983) in Hill, J.D., and Flynn, K.M. (2006). *Classroom Instruction That Works with English Language Learners*. Alexandria, VA: Association for Supervision and Curriculum Development (ASCD).

Resources

2012 Amplification of the English Language Development Standards, Kindergarten–12th Grade. Madison, WI: Board of Regents of the University of Wisconsin System/WIDA, 2013.

Echevarria, J., Vogt, M., and Short, D.J. *Making Content Comprehensible for English Language Learners; The SIOP Model*. Boston: Pearson, 2013.

Hill, J.D. and Flynn, K.M. *Classroom Instruction That Works with English Language Learners*. Alexandria, VA: ASCD, 2006.

Hill, J.D., Miller, K.B. *Classroom Instruction That Works with English Language Learners*, 2nd ed. Alexandria, VA: ASCD, 2012.

Standards-Based (Mastery-Based) Planning and Teaching

A Definition of Standards-Based (Mastery-Based) Teaching

Since the late 1990s, a movement toward standards-based or mastery-based teaching has become quite popular. This trend has generated some discussion and, at times, controversy. Although most now agree it is the most effective approach to teaching, the disagreements that exist are often fueled by the lack of a common understanding of the meaning of the words and phrases *high expectations, high standards, teaching the standards, teaching to mastery*, and others. Robert Marzano (2013, p. 82) described the confusion about terminology best when he said, "When I think about such constructs as learning targets, instructional objectives, learning goals, outcomes, education objectives, standards, and the like, I've come to the conclusion that besides having something to do with what students are supposed to know and be able to do, there's no consensus as to how these terms fit together." The first part of this chapter defines these words and phrases and the key components of what has come to be known as *standards-based* (a.k.a. *mastery-based*) teaching. We are aware that others may use different terms to mean the same thing. However, in order to provide a clear understanding throughout the book we have selected one term to represent each concept and stuck with it throughout the book.

The second part of the chapter describes a method for unit and lesson planning that results in the highest levels of student mastery.

The terms *standards-based teaching* and *mastery-based teaching* are often used interchangeably in the literature. In this book, we continue to use the terms interchangeably only as the title of the collective group of teaching methods that have been proven to ensure the highest level of student acquisition of usable knowledge and skills. Using this definition, we might argue that teachers have always taught for mastery. It would be hard to find an era in the history of education when it wasn't a teacher's wish to impart to students usable knowledge and skills. What we lacked, however, prior to the past decade was well-structured, specifically articulated, and coordinated standards (among and within disciplines) for curriculum (what we teach) and instruction (how we teach). Since 2010, many countries have developed a common national set of curriculum standards or guidelines for such standards (e.g., Common Core in the United States). We have also made significant strides in identifying an international body of research on effective teaching (as is contained in this book). These effective teaching strategies are often referred to as *instructional standards*.

The terms standards-based teaching and mastery-based *teaching are often used interchangeably in the literature. In this book, we continue to use the terms interchangeably only as the title of the collective group of teaching methods that have been proven to ensure the highest level of student acquisition of usable knowledge and skills.*

We define **curriculum standards** as the list of knowledge and skills that have been identified as important for students to acquire. Within the area of "skills," we include the higher-order thinking skills. The federal governments, state (or provincial) governments, and local school districts usually establish curriculum standards. Typically, these government entities include teachers on the committees that develop the standards. However, the average classroom teacher gives little or no direct input into the standards that are identified as important for students to learn. From the perspective of most teachers, the standards are established externally (by someone else).

The curriculum standards are the learning and behaviors students are expected to know and use. The curriculum standards typically contain the body of knowledge and skills that must be mastered. They articulate the level of quality and quantity of knowledge and skills that must be demonstrated to show mastery.

Contained within the curriculum standards we typically also find behavior standards. These include student behavior in the classroom (e.g., independent, group, or partner work), in other school locations, and at school events (e.g., walking to lunch, working in the library, or attending a school sporting event). In some instances, these standards are not contained in the curriculum standards but are set up as their own set of standards.

For each standard, we often have a series of benchmarks. These are the steps a student's learning follows to reach mastery on the standard. Like the rungs on a ladder, mastery of each benchmark brings the student closer to mastering the knowledge and skills that make up the specific standard. We use **scoring guides**[1] (rubrics and criteria sheets) to measure student growth against the benchmarks. Douglas Reeves (2003, p. 18) describes scoring guides as "very specific descriptions of student proficiency for an individual standard-based assessment."

Levels of Mastery

Grant Wiggins, in his article "How Good Is Good Enough?" (2013, p.4), describes mastery as follows:

> Mastery is effective transfer of learning in authentic and worthy performance. Students have mastered a subject when they are fluent, even creative, in using their knowledge, skills, and understanding in key performance challenges and contexts at the heart of that subject, as measured against valid and high standards.

In the next few paragraphs, we seek to "unpack" Wiggins' definition so teachers know the path students take to achieve mastery. Level of mastery is the level to which students have acquired the knowledge and skills identified in the standards on the path toward mastery described by Wiggins. We have found that mastery comes at six levels. The first level is **introduction** level of mastery (a.k.a. **exposure** level of mastery). A student is at the introduction level immediately after the knowledge and/or skill in the standard has been presented to him/her for the first time. At this level, there is no expectation that the student will be able to demonstrate mastery of the standard. The second level is **guided practice** level of mastery. At this level, the student is expected to demonstrate the knowledge or skill only with prompting from the teacher or another person who has mastered the standard. The third level is **immediate mastery** level of mastery. At

---

1   Scoring guides are described in depth in Chapter 4.

this level, the student can demonstrate the knowledge or skill of the standard independently, shortly after the teacher has presented the knowledge or skill of the standard. **Immediate application mastery** occurs when the student is able to use the knowledge and skill in an unfamiliar setting and/or in higher-order thinking skills shortly after the presentation of the concept. **Mastery** is achieved when the student can demonstrate the knowledge or skill after a period of time has passed since the standard was taught. **Application** mastery is the level at which the student can demonstrate mastery after a period of time, in an unfamiliar situation, and/or within a higher-order thinking skill.

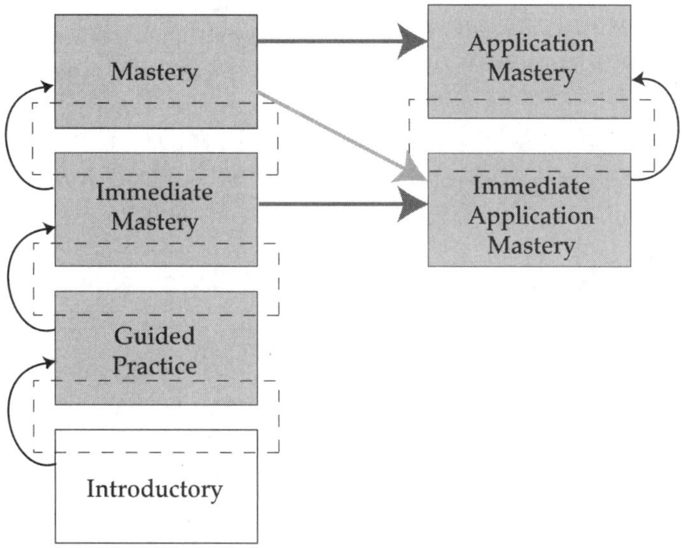

Figure 1.1 shows the typical progression students follow as they learn new knowledge and skills. It is important to note the following two factors that make teaching so complex:

1. All students *do not* follow the same path to application mastery.
2. All students *do not* move through these steps at the same pace.

You will note the dotted-line boxes that connect the levels of mastery. They represent the fact that the levels of mastery flow into one another, rather than being distinct lines that are crossed among the levels. For example, a student moving from guided practice to immediate mastery does so by straddling the two levels, not by taking a step across a line. Upon entering the guided-practice stage, a student may need a very high level of teacher guidance. As his or her mastery progresses, the level of guidance needed decreases until the student is able to complete the concept independently (immediate mastery). In some cases, a student is able to complete the skill independently but needs the reassurance that the teacher is readily accessible before he or she will attempt the skill on his or her own. Some people would consider this student at immediate mastery, while others would consider the student still at the upper end of guided practice.

To better understand the six levels of mastery, let's look at the example of teaching the following standard:

Students will be able to successfully complete a two-digit multiplication problem using clusters.

The students in the class are at the *introduction level of mastery*, the point at which the teacher has first presented all the steps to completing a two-digit multiplication example using clusters. Often, the next step in teaching this concept is to have the students complete one or more examples in class. Those students who can correctly complete an example with one or more prompts from the teacher or with the assistance of a peer are at the *guided practice level of mastery*. Those students who can correctly complete the example independently are at the *immediate mastery level*. Those students who can complete the assigned problem and the two-digit multiplication story problem given for extension are at the *immediate application mastery level*. Those students who can complete a two-digit multiplication algorithm two weeks[2] later are at the mastery level. Finally, those students who can write and solve their own two-digit multiplication story problem using a real-world setting two weeks later are probably at the *application mastery*[3] level. Transfer of knowledge to a real-world setting is an important part of the mastery process. We know transfer has occurred when students are able to do the following:

- apply the knowledge and skills in an unfamiliar setting
- apply the knowledge and skills in a real-world setting
- apply the knowledge and skills in activities that require higher-order thinking
- do all of the above after a period of time has passed since the teaching of the knowledge and skills

Figure 1.1

2 We use two weeks for the purpose of this example only. Differing periods of time may be more appropriate for various knowledge and skills.

3 Application mastery is similar to what Grant Wiggins and Jay McTighe refer to as *teaching for understanding* (Wiggins and McTighe 2011).

Expectations

An **expectation** is the level of mastery that the teacher believes a student or group of students can reach on a given standard. Setting high expectations is a two-step process. A teacher's *first step* is having the belief that the students can master the standard at the highest level. His or her *second step* is employing those teaching methods that result in the highest level of mastery. Figure 1.2 below shows the four quadrants of teacher standards and expectations we can fall into at any given time during our teaching. To ensure the highest levels of student mastery, we should always strive to be in quadrant 1. When operating in quadrant 1, we are

- teaching lessons that contain rigorous mastery objectives and holding students accountable for high standards
- teaching in ways that maximize the rate at which all students move up the levels of mastery shown in Figure 1.1; this means we are using high-quality corrective instruction (Guskey 2010, p. 3). Corrective instruction requires more than repeating the teaching more slowly. It includes teaching knowledge and/or skill in a different way that is better aligned with the learning styles of those learners who have not yet mastered the concept.

We are consistently assessing students' learning during the teaching and then differentiating instruction[4] to extend and remediate as needed. Although we always strive to teach in quadrant 1, this is not always possible due to factors that are sometimes

> *An expectation is the level of mastery that the teacher believes a student or group of students can reach on a given standard.*

within our control and factors that are not in our control, as discussed later in this chapter. We know we have slipped into quadrant 2 when large numbers of our students are doing poorly on our summative assessments. Whenever we give a test or quiz that large numbers of students fail, we should look back at the teaching and formative assessments we did prior to giving the test or quiz. Large numbers of failures should indicate the need to make changes in our instruction and assessment. This is a time when it is important to remind ourselves that what students learn is more important than what we teach.

It is a little more difficult to know when we have slipped into quadrant 3. This is the quadrant in which all of our students are achieving at high levels on our teacher-made tests and quizzes but doing poorly on the district, state (provincial), or national assessments. There are three reasons students do well on teacher-made assessments and poorly on these other assessments:

1. We are not teaching a rigorous enough curriculum.
2. We are not adequately assessing to ensure that students have moved from immediate mastery and immediate application mastery to mastery and application mastery.
3. The local curriculum we are teaching is not aligned with the state (provincial) and/or national standards.

Quadrant 4 is a place where few teachers ever reside. This is the quadrant in which the teacher is doing very little effective teaching or assessing. Classrooms with low levels of on-task student behavior, a "dumbed-down" curriculum, ineffective (or an absence of) teacher-made assessments,[5] and low student performance on district, state (provincial), or national assessments are typical characteristics of quadrant 4.

The level of mastery that students reach is influenced primarily by the following five factors:

1. The teacher's instructional skill level
2. The level of student motivation
   a. Those areas the teacher can impact
   b. Those areas the teacher cannot impact
3. The level of previous learning the students bring to the class (from home, school, or other environments)

Figure 1.2

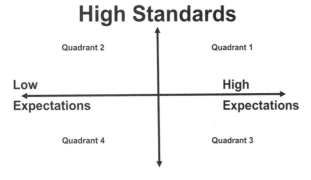

High Standards **and** Expectations

High Standards

Quadrant 2   Quadrant 1

Low   **High**
Expectations   **Expectations**

Quadrant 4   Quadrant 3

Low Standards

---

4   We discuss differentiating instruction in depth in Chapter 6.

5   Chapter 4 discusses effective classroom assessment.

4. The resources that the teacher has available to use in teaching the standards
5. The students' physical, cognitive, or emotional disabilities

The first factor, the teacher's instructional skill level, is completely within our control as teachers. We can always become more skillful at our teaching as a result of self-reflection, peer-facilitated reflection and collaboration, participation in workshops, reading of professional literature, and participation in other forms of professional development.

The second factor, student motivation, is partly within our control and partly influenced by factors outside of our control (e.g., home, peers, content to be learned, etc.). We have the ability to teach in ways that increase the level of student motivation.[6] We can work with parents, guardians, and families in ways that make them more effective participants in motivating students to work hard.[7] And, we can work within our classroom environment to increase the level of peer encouragement of hard work and high achievement. We can increase our skills in all of these areas with appropriate professional development and collegial collaboration.[8] We recognize that this still leaves important components (Nos. 3, 4, and 5 in the list above) out of the teacher's control; however, we believe that whatever the status of those factors not in our control, we can increase the level of student mastery in our classroom by increasing our effectiveness in those areas that *are* in our control.

For example, let's look briefly at the *resource* of class size. The size of classes in most schools is driven more by the availability of money for the school budget than by other factors. We believe that students will reach higher levels of mastery in a class of 15 versus a class of 35—if the previous factors Nos. 1, 2, and 3 are equal. We also believe that whether the class has 15 or 35 students, there are skills the teacher can use to increase the students' levels of mastery. The more skilled the teacher is, the higher the level of mastery that students can reach.

> *What students learn is more important than what we teach.*

Standards-Based Unit Planning and Standards-Based Lesson Planning

The way in which we do our planning is a window into our thinking about teaching. Some of us were trained to plan in a way that started with focusing on the activities we wanted to do with the students, a process called *activity-based planning*. For example, in activity-based planning, we start by asking ourselves questions such as the following:

1. What can I do to make my teaching interesting to the students?
2. In this unit, how can I use the lesson I really like and found effective or the book I really enjoy teaching?
3. Will I lecture to my students or do some cooperative activity I learned at a workshop last week?
4. If I do a cooperative activity, will I have the students in pairs or in groups?
5. If I put the students in groups, how many should be in each group?
6. How will I decide who will be in each group?

The questions above are an important part of any planning process; however, they should come at the end of our planning process, rather than at the beginning. Wiggins and McTighe (2011) refer to starting with these questions as one of the "twin sins,"[9] activity-oriented teaching. As we talk about in the following section, these questions should be the third step in our thinking.

Before we decide *how* we are going to teach, we need to be very clear as to *what* we want students to know and be able to do by the end of the unit or lesson. In setting mastery objectives, we must ensure they are clearly communicated to students in language they understand. Our next step is to choose assessments that tell us during and at the end of the lesson or unit what knowledge and skills each student has mastered. It is only then that we should turn our focus to structuring the activities for teaching the knowledge and skills. For many of us, planning in a way that focuses on student outcomes first, rather than classroom activities, requires a change in our thinking about teaching. Some of us have been so programmed to start with activities that we must consciously push

---

6 Chapter 7 contains an explanation of the ways in which teachers can motivate students who typically display low motivation.
7 Chapter 9 contains an explanation of ways in which teachers can get uninvolved parents to be more involved in their children's education.
8 We define *professional development* as workshops, courses, peer reflection and discussion (e.g., peer observing or lesson study), professional learning communities, self-reflection (e.g., reflection journals and other forms of classroom research), professional reading, and other techniques for improving our teaching skills.

9 The other "sin" is an overemphasis on delivering large amounts of content without considering the most effective and engaging means of delivery.

ourselves to invert this process each time we plan. Eventually, this shift in thinking becomes natural for all teachers.

Despite the efforts of Wiggins, McTighe, Ribas, and others, some teachers still approach planning through activities rather than standards. Thus, when adjusting to a new planning approach, they must push to invert each time they plan until their thinking about planning becomes natural and automatic. If teachers have recently engaged in preservice education, they have likely experienced mastery planning—what Mark O'Shea labels *standards-based planning* in his book *From Student to Success* (2005, p. 8) or what Wiggins and McTighe (2011) call **backward-design planning** (a.k.a., Understanding by Design, or UBD). All teachers, however, need ongoing support and professional development to keep their focus on standards-based planning.

Mastery-based planning (standards-based planning) is one area in which some newer teachers may initially be at an advantage over their more experienced colleagues. More teachers are entering the profession having trained in mastery planning during their preservice education. For these teachers, it is their initial training in the techniques of effective planning; therefore, there is no need to unlearn and relearn. The planning challenges for new teachers are still greater than those for veteran teachers, however, for three reasons. First, they do not have the experience to make fast and effective judgments about the activity-based questions listed previously once they have determined what they want students to know and to be able to do. Second, new teachers sometimes lack the repertoire of assessment techniques readily available to more veteran teachers. Third, a challenge shared by new teachers, experienced teachers new to a district, and teachers who change grades or subject levels is knowledge of the specific curriculum standards for the district at their teaching levels.

In this chapter, we will explain a simplified version of standards-based lesson and unit planning. The explanation and samples contained in this chapter will not go into planning a differentiated instruction and Universal Design for Learning lesson. The reason for this is that effective differentiation first requires a high level of skills in the areas of managing the differentiated instruction classroom, assessing student learning, effective classroom questioning, and strategies for differentiating by content, process, and product. Since these areas are addressed in Chapters 3, 4, 5, and 6, it

Before we decide how we are going to teach, we need to be very clear as to what we want students to know and be able to do by the end of the unit or lesson.

would be premature to try to address differentiated instruction during planning at this time. We will return to planning as it is done in a differentiated instruction and Universal Design for Learning classroom when we get to Chapter 6.

The Five Basic Steps for Standards-Based Planning

Step 1—Be certain that the concepts we are teaching are indeed in our district's curriculum standards.

Step 2—Be specific in our own minds about which standards and benchmarks we want the students to master by the end of the teaching time for which we are planning, and plan teaching that will lead to the mastery of these standards. Formulate mastery objectives for the lesson. If my class has English language learners, I should formulate English language learning mastery objectives for those students.[10]

Step 3— Plan assessments[11] that pre-assess student skills and knowledge on the topic and then effectively and frequently assess, both formatively and summatively, student mastery of the concepts in our district's standards. Be certain we have the scoring guides needed to assess the benchmarks identified for the lesson. Plan differentiated assessments, given that students will diverge in their level of mastery throughout the course of the lesson.

Step 4—Plan activities that maximize student mastery of the concepts and promote high student engagement. This should include the ways in which you will differentiate as students diverge in their levels of mastery.

Step 5—Self-reflect at the conclusion of each lesson to determine what parts of the lesson were successful and what parts should be revised the next time the lesson is taught.

There are many models for standards-based planning. Each of these models asks the teacher to use some form of the five steps when planning. Models such as Understanding by Design (UBD) and others follow these same basic steps. Below, we have specifically explained each of the steps.

10 At the end of chapter, you will find an essay that discusses how the concepts in this chapter can be applied to English language learners.

11 Chapters 4 and 6 will discuss differentiating assessments.

Step 1—Be certain that the concepts we are teaching are indeed in our district's curriculum standards. The first step is for the teacher to teach what is in the school's or district's curriculum standards. To do this, the teacher needs to have the standards readily available when planning. This step may sound rudimentary; however, in busy schools, the curriculum standards often become something we believe we are teaching but find, in fact, that we are not. We have often seen a similar dynamic related to districts' curriculum development and implementation that leads to poor performance on assessments of students' mastery of the standards. In these districts, a committee of teachers and administrators carefully and painstakingly develops the curriculum standards. Upon completion, the standards are given to all of the staff. Some districts conduct a considerable number of professional development programs about these standards, thereby ensuring that all the teachers know and are able to use the standards. Others do nothing more than distribute the documents to the teachers. Few districts go back to check the teachers' understanding and use of the specific curriculum standards in the years after they are released. Teachers often put the documents or computer files containing them in a "safe place," rarely to be opened again after their initial introduction. The teaching of these standards by teachers other than those on the development committee often drifts to topics and knowledge other than those in the standards. This tendency is not due to anyone's deliberate decision not to use the standards. Rather, it is due to the hectic pace of a teacher's day and year, which offers little time for reflection on the curriculum documents.

The gap between the district's curriculum standards and what is actually taught often becomes more pronounced as new staff members are hired into a district. Whether they're veteran teachers or teachers new to the profession, newly hired teachers often receive little or no training in the effective implementation of the standards. They are handed the documents and expected to implement them with little or no training. The training given to the entire staff at the implementation stage of the standards, when they are introduced, is designed to deepen the teachers' understanding of the context in which the standards are developed and to demonstrate the effective implementation of the standards. Teachers hired after this implementation stage may never receive this training. The lack of comprehensive training and understanding, such as that given during the implementation of the standards, leads to the teaching of concepts that are not in the standards or to teaching without adequate depth of the concepts in the standards. As a result, students perform poorly when those standards are assessed on state (provincial) or national assessments.

Another factor that contributes to lower student performance is the lack of clarity in the knowledge teachers receive as to which concepts within the curriculum are most important for students to master. Many state or provincial (and district) curriculum standards contain more knowledge and skills than teachers can teach to the level at which all students demonstrate mastery or application mastery during a specific lesson. Districts need to assist teachers in prioritizing this knowledge and these skills. The teacher should review the objectives in the lesson plan and determine which objectives are the highest priorities (these are often referred to as *power standards*) for the students to master, which objectives are lower priorities, and which objectives are merely interesting material connected to the topic but not priorities or high priorities. We define the terms *highest priority*, *priority*, and *connected*[12] as follows:

Highest-priority knowledge and skills (a.k.a. power standards) are those that will result in the highest level of (1) student achievement on local, state (provincial), and national assessments and (2) future school, career, and personal success. Thomas Armstrong, in his book *The Best Schools* (2006, pp. 2–13), states, "Educators want students to achieve academically so that they will be ready for something that will take place later (future academic challenges in elementary or secondary school, college, or jobs)." The objectives deemed to be highest priorities are the ones on which we should focus most of our instructional time and activities. Ideally, we would like to think of everything in the curriculum as a high priority. Unfortunately, factors out of the control of many teachers and administrators force this prioritizing.

Priority knowledge and skills are those that are important to ensure the students have reached at least the guided-practice level. We should, of course, strive to get students to mastery and application mastery in these areas. However, if time does not allow us to do this, then we have to make difficult choices about when to "move on." Hopefully, our district's curriculum spirals sufficiently that these students will have future opportunities to reach mastery in these areas.

---

12 Other books may use different terms for the priority of standards, such as *essential to know*, *important to know*, and *good to know*.

Connected knowledge and skills are those areas that don't fit in the previous two categories. It is fine to expose students to this body of knowledge and skills; however, we should not devote too much valuable instruction time to these concepts. Spending too much time on areas identified as connected but not priorities is often referred to as "going off on a tangent." In these times of high-stakes education, we cannot afford to devote valuable instructional time to tangents. As teachers, we all have our areas of high interest both to us and to students that we enjoy teaching. However, before spending large amounts of time on these areas, we should ask ourselves if this time is the most efficient and effective way to get the most students to the highest level of mastery on high-priority and priority standards.

> *Spending too much time on areas identified as connected but not priorities is often referred to as "going off on a tangent."*

Tangents and Teachable Moments

Teachers do, at times, capitalize on opportunities of student interest that come up in the lesson. They can take the teachers off the planned lesson for a brief period of time. We often refer to them as *teachable moments*. It is important to remember that teachable moments are different from tangents. **Teachable moments occur when we move into unplanned areas because this new direction will lead to higher levels of student mastery on the lesson and unit objectives. Tangents, on the other hand, are areas of interest that, if pursued, would detract from our primary goal of getting the highest number of students to the highest level of mastery on objectives for the lesson or unit as reflected in the curriculum standards.** Both teachable moments and tangents can be triggered by questions that indicate a high level of student interest. However, we must be cautious when pursuing those areas to ensure they will result in higher levels of student mastery of the curriculum. Teachable moments are a good thing, whereas tangents are to be avoided.

Step 2—Be specific in our own minds about which standards and benchmarks we want the students to master by the end of the teaching time for which we are planning. Plan teaching that will lead to the mastery of these standards. Formulate mastery objectives for the lesson. For example, if my class has English language learners, I should formulate English language learning mastery objec-

tives for those students. This second step means we must be clear about the specific knowledge and skills in those benchmarks that we want the students to know and be able to do at the end of the teaching time. The business community would call them the "deliverables": exactly what students will know and be able to do at the end of the lesson/unit that they did not know or could not do at its onset. As we visit schools, we see a lot of great instruction, preceded by hours of thoughtful planning. Unfortunately, this instruction either does not teach all the knowledge and skills identified in the curriculum as high priority, or the instruction

Figure 1.3

Prioritizing the Knowledge and Skills

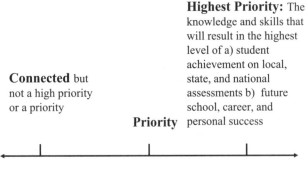

Highest Priority: The knowledge and skills that will result in the highest level of a) student achievement on local, state, and national assessments b) future school, career, and personal success

Connected but not a high priority or a priority

Priority

Least Instructional Time   Most Instructional Time

introduces the knowledge and skills in these areas without teaching them to mastery. This problem may be avoided by reviewing the curriculum standards documents, deciding which knowledge and skills are the highest priority for students to master at the highest levels, and focusing our planning there. We must hold a clear vision of what we want students to know and be able to do by the end of the teaching time. We must clearly communicate this to the students at the beginning, end, and at appropriate times throughout the lesson.

Step 3—Plan assessments that pre-assess student skills and knowledge on the topic and then effectively and frequently assess, both formatively and summatively, student mastery of the concepts in our district's standards. Be certain we have the scoring guides needed to assess the benchmarks identified for the lesson. We should differentiate our assessments to ensure they are valid

and reliable[13] for all of our students. The third step is to plan assessments that enable us to determine what students know and are able to do as relates to the material that has been determined as important in steps 1 and 2, discussed above. The assessment should include both formative and summative assessments. Formative assessments are the ways in which the teachers pre-assess knowledge and skills, as well as assess student progress toward mastery during the teaching. They also provide useful feedback to students designed to influence their achievement. Formative assessments typically include any pre-assessments we use to determine what the students already know about the skills and knowledge in the lesson or unit. They also use assessments throughout the lesson and unit to check student mastery levels and make instructional decisions.

> *The business community would call them the "deliverables:" exactly what students will know and be able to do at the end of the lesson/unit that they did not know or could not do at its onset.*

Summative assessments[14] are those assessments teachers use to assess the students' learning after the teaching is completed. Before we can assess a topic effectively, we must be clear in our own minds about our desired outcomes. It is only then that we will be able to effectively choose or create assessments that measure with validity and reliability what we want students to know and be able to do.

An example of the challenge in designing assessments that actually align with the mastery objectives involves two teachers with whom we worked. These teachers were teaching the same curriculum standards in the same district. The mastery objectives in the curriculum are listed below.

By the end of this unit, the students will be able to

a. given a diagram of a human skeleton, label at least 15 bones in the human body

b. explain the function of hinge, ball and socket, and glide joints in the human body

c. given a diagram of a human skeleton, identify at least one hinge, one ball and socket, and one glide joint

d. say and define in English the key vocabulary for the lesson, including *human*, *skeleton*, *bone*, *joint*, *hinge joint*, *socket joint*, and *glide joint* (English language learner mastery objective).

One teacher prepared an elaborate summative assessment that required students to first draw the skeleton. They then needed to cut pieces of paper to sizes that matched the labels they wished to write on those pieces of paper. They were asked to glue labels for the parts noted in objectives a, b, and c on the appropriate parts of the skeleton. The second teacher gave the students a choice of how best to label the parts noted above. They could either use the skeleton diagram she gave them or, for students who wished to draw, they could draw their own skeletons and label the parts. The teacher was careful to *guide* those students who would struggle with the act of drawing their own skeletons toward using the pre-drawn skeleton diagram.

After the assessment was given, both teachers brought the student work to a group of colleagues to discuss their assessment activities. The first teacher indicated that students spent a great deal of time trying to accurately draw the skeleton. Many of the drawings were of poor quality, and this made it difficult for the students to label the parts. Other students found it difficult to cut labels to the correct size, so they spent a great deal of time cutting the labels. It was difficult for the teacher to assess what the students knew of the standards stated above because their performance was hindered by their inability to draw, cut, and paste.

Upon discussion, it became apparent to the first teacher that her assessment more accurately assessed the students' ability to

- draw a human skeleton
- cut paper shapes to a size that matched the text for the appropriate label
- glue the labels neatly on the diagram

The students completing the first teacher's assessment did have a lot of fun and were actively engaged in the assessment; however, the activity did not effectively assess what students knew about the bones and joints of the human body. The second teacher's assessment gave an accurate representation of what the students knew or did not yet know about these concepts.

Step 4—Plan activities that maximize student mastery of the concepts and promote high student engagement. The activities we choose should be those that will lead to the highest number of students reaching the highest levels of mastery in the least amount of time. It is important here that we make the distinction between coverage and mastery.

---

13 We discuss in depth the concepts of validity and reliability in Chapter 4.
14 For more information, see Chapter 5 of this book.

Lecturing for 50 minutes will cover more material than providing engaging opportunities for students to interact with the material in the ways we identify throughout this book. However, what students master and retain in a 50-minute lecture is less than what they would master and retain through engaging teaching. It is important for all of us to remember that *how much is learned is more important than how much is taught.*

How much is learned is more important than how much is taught.

Step 5—Self-reflect at the conclusion of each lesson to determine what parts of the lesson were successful and what parts should be revised the next time the lesson is taught. Professional developers have increasingly become aware of the importance of teacher self-reflection and coaching in the development of new and veteran teachers. The importance of self-reflection and peer coaching was affirmed nearly 20 years ago in the 1999 Milken Family Foundation Report, *A Matter of Quality.* It quotes the National Center for Education Knowledge's *Profiles of Teachers in the US Survey* (1996), in which educators identified the five most valuable factors in developing competency to teach as follows:[15]

1.	Own teaching experience	92%
2.	Courses in the subject taught	73%
3.	Other teachers	72%
4.	Studying on one's own	43%
5.	Education methods courses	37%

We are seeing more and more districts moving toward the development of professional learning communities[16] to better access teacher self-reflection and teacher-to-teacher professional development. It is for this reason that we include question No. 5 in the planning process and in the lesson plan template in the next column. This step pushes us to analyze what we are teaching through the lens of another person.

Even when no other professional is in our room to observe with the purpose of helping us assess our practice (which usually is the case 95 to 99 percent of the time we are teaching), asking ourselves the following questions at the conclusion of the lesson helps to stimulate our self-reflection and improve our planning and teaching.

- What went well? Why did it go well? What did I learn that I can transfer to an area of my teaching that has been less successful?
- What did not go as well as I had planned? Why didn't it go well? What can I do next time to eliminate the issue? Who can I go to for ideas to address the issue as well as strategies to improve instruction?

We have distilled the recommended steps into the five-question lesson plan template presented in the box that follows. There are many variations of this template in mastery or backward-design planning; however, all contain the same basic concepts. For those of you interested in a more comprehensive template that specifically addresses differentiated instruction, please refer to the template in Chapter 6.

Lesson Planning Template

1. What is/are the district's curriculum standard(s) and/or the benchmarks from which these concepts are derived?

2. What do I want the students to know and be able to do by the end of the lesson (my mastery objectives, including language mastery objectives where appropriate)?

3. How will I formatively and summatively assess the students' level of mastery of these concepts?

4. What activities and sequence of activities in the lesson[17] will result in the highest levels of student mastery?

5. If a colleague were observing my class to give me ideas for improving the teaching of this lesson, what data could he or she gather that would be most helpful to me in improving the lesson?

---

1. What is/are the district's curriculum standard(s) and/or the benchmarks from which these concepts are derived? As stated earlier, this often appears to be a rudimentary step; however, our planning often strays from the actual curriculum standards as time passes after the adoption of those standards. In the following lesson plan and unit plan, you will see the improvement in the quality of the lesson plan

---

15 Teachers rated eight different professional development options as very valuable, somewhat valuable, not very valuable, not at all valuable, or not applicable. Teachers were permitted to give any of the ratings to more than one professional development option.

16 Chapters 10 and 11 contain information about co-teaching, professional learning communities, and other forms of professional development that involve structured self-analysis and self-reflection and/or structured colleague-facilitated analysis and reflection.

17 In Chapter 6, we expand this question to include the activities designed to address the learning needs and levels for mastery of a diverse group of learners.

when the teacher refocuses on the curriculum standards. Students are not going to do well on assessments if we are not teaching the curriculum objectives that the assessments were designed to assess.

2. What do I want the students to know and be able to do by the end of the lesson (my mastery objectives)? Mastery objectives (including language objectives when appropriate) describe the content (knowledge and skills) of the curriculum in terms of student products and performances that can be observed and, therefore, assessed. Words such as *know*, *think about*, and *understand* are not observable, so they are difficult to assess and should be avoided. Action verbs tend to have observable outcomes, for example: *describe, memorize, select, list, define, label, state, locate, identify, recite, match, rewrite, illustrate, apply, sew, paint, sketch,* and *name.* Using these words allow us to observe whether or not the student has reached mastery and, therefore, the level of mastery can be assessed formatively and summatively. Some words that may be used to articulate objectives related to higher-level thinking skills are *organize, summarize, dramatize, distinguish, interpret, appraise, judge, classify,* and *hypothesize.*[18] The revised edition of Bloom's Taxonomy is a wonderful reference containing many examples of action verbs that are observable and measureable (Anderson 2001).

A well-written curriculum typically contains objectives written in mastery form. Later in this chapter, we will examine a page from an eighth-grade curriculum in which the objectives are written in this way.

Mastery objectives should be communicated to the students at the start of a lesson or unit. Telling the students what they will be expected to know and be able to do by the end of the teaching provides a cognitive context[19] in which to understand the concepts presented. Students learn more efficiently when they know the goals and objectives of the lesson.

According to Marzano (May 2011), an ineffective teaching practice is "writing an objective on the board, mentioning it, and not returning to it." Since we tell the students the mastery objectives at the outset of the lesson, mastery objectives should be written in language that is easily understood by the students. Most curricula are written for adults, as they should be. The mastery objectives may, therefore, contain multiple concepts or language too complex for the students to understand. In those circumstances, we will need to divide the objectives into smaller parts that the students can understand. Students need to experience mastery objectives as "rigorous, bite-sized, and measureable" text that foreshadows what they will learn (Curtis 2011). **It is not enough to simply post mastery objectives and share them with students. The teacher must refer to the mastery objectives throughout the lesson/unit and at the conclusion of the lesson.** Using mastery objectives to frame the lesson or unit means actually referring to them and using them. For example, a teacher may use the mastery objectives as a "ticket to leave" summarizer, asking students to assess their learning in terms of the mastery objectives. Later in this chapter is a lesson plan from a unit on the Renaissance. You will see that the teacher has written several mastery objectives to teach about Machiavelli, a piece of the multiple-component standard that was written in the curriculum document.

In summary, mastery objectives are best used when students experience them as brackets for instruction. Successful mastery objectives describe the essential curriculum content to be learned, as well as provide an indication about the way in which mastery will be assessed. As we discussed, in order to be effective it is crucial that the mastery objectives be written and shared in language that is developmentally appropriate and accessible to students.

> *Mastery objectives (including language objectives when appropriate) describe the content (knowledge and skills) of the curriculum in terms of student products and performances that can be observed and, therefore, assessed.*

---

18 See Chapter 6 for more examples of words and phrases that can be used to create mastery objectives that reflect higher-order thinking skills.

19 Chapter 2 contains information on this and other strategies teachers use to develop a cognitive context for learning that increases students' levels of mastery.

Sample Mastery Objectives

Kindergarten

1. By the end of the lesson, students will be able to retell a short story and identify the beginning, middle, and end parts (language arts).
2. By the end of the lesson, students will be able to count, sort, and classify objects (math).
3. By the end of the lesson, students will be able to describe details and state similarities and differences among given objects (science).
4. By the end of the lesson, students will be able to identify water and land on a globe (social studies).

Rephrasing objective No. 1 in language students can understand:
    By the end of the lesson, you will be able to tell a story after I have told (or read) it to you. You will be able to tell me what part is the beginning, what part is the middle, and what part is the end of the story (language arts).

Grade 2

1. By the end of the lesson, students will be able to explain their reasons for an opinion about a story or an idea (language arts).
2. By the end of the lesson, students will be able to locate knowledge on a simple bar graph (math).
3. By the end of the lesson, students will be able to handle wiffle ball equipment safely (physical education).
4. By the end of the lesson, students will be able to explain a conclusion they reached based on their observations of a demonstrated experiment (science).

Rephrasing objective No. 1 in language the students can understand:
    By the end of the lesson, you will be able to tell me *why* you like or don't like a story I read to you (language arts).

Grade 5

1. By the end of the lesson, students will be able to draw outlines or graphic organizers (on paper or electronically) to organize their ideas (language arts).
2. By the end of the lesson, students will be able to write addition, subtraction, multiplication, and division problems from knowledge in the science and/or social studies curriculum (math).
3. By the end of the lesson, students will be able to perform an eight-measure solo on the recorder, on pitch, in rhythm, and with correct posture and hand technique (music).
4. By the end of the lesson, students will be able to use graphic-organizer software to visually represent collected data (science/computers).

Rephrasing objective No. 2 in language the students can understand:
    By the end of the lesson, you will be able to write addition, subtraction, multiplication, and division problems from the data in the social studies unit on immigration (math).

Grade 7

1. By the end of the lesson, you will be able to search a database and extract specific knowledge (computers).
2. By the end of the lesson, you will be able to create timelines using the designated timeline software (social studies/computers).
3. By the end of the lesson, you will be able to mix and use neutral colors with tempera paint (art).
4. By the end of the lesson, you will be able to demonstrate the laboratory safety and emergency procedures for the use of hot plates, eye-safety goggles, chemicals, laboratory glassware, and lab specimens (science) and explain the rationale behind each procedure.
5. By the end of the lesson, you will be able to create PowerPoint slides that use at least two different types of transitions (technology).

Grade 9

1. By the end of the lesson, you will be able to translate a restaurant menu and correctly pronounce all the items (foreign language).

2. By the end of the lesson, you will be able to write a convincing argument and support its claims with detailed evidence (language arts).
3. By the end of the lesson, you will be able to calculate the percent increase or decrease in different situations (math).
4. By the end of the lesson, you will be able to explain the major goals of the New Deal programs as they related to industry, workers, and farmers (social studies).
5. By the end of the lesson, you will be able to import, export, and link data among word-processing documents and other applications (technology).

Sample Language Mastery Objectives for English Language Learners[20]

Language objectives typically are written in one of three (or all three) skills areas. These include speaking and listening, reading, and writing.
1. By the end of the lesson, you will be able to orally define and say the English translation for the vocabulary words *human, skeleton, bone, joint, hinge joint, socket joint,* and *glide joint.*
2. By the end of the lesson, students will be able label these areas in English on a skeleton.
3. By the end of the lesson, students will be able to read the simplified English version sheet that explains parts of the human skeleton.

Information Services

By the end of the lesson, you will be able to:
1. Explain the different network classifications and terms.
2. Explain why an organization would implement a network system. Describe the historical and future evolution of network technologies.
3. In a given network environment, describe the components and topology used.
4. Explain the different types of communication systems.
5. Given the task of designing a network for a small organization housed in a multi-leveled building, research, document, and present why each topology may or may not be the best choice.

---

20 For more information about working with English language learners, see the relevant essays at the end of each chapter in this book.

3. How will I formatively and summatively assess the students' level of mastery of these concepts? Once the mastery objectives have been written and communicated to students, the teacher is ready to determine the criteria for success. These criteria and the evidence to be collected from students are the assessments that will determine how well the mastery objectives were met. Effective assessment includes techniques for both formative assessment (including pre-assessment, where appropriate) and summative assessment. According to two articles in *Educational Leadership*, identifying the purpose of the assessment is critical. "On-the-spot [formative] assessments help teachers make immediate instructional decisions; interim assessments identify where students are having difficulty and suggest instructional interventions; and end-of-year summative tests suggest how teachers can improve instruction the following year" (Chappius, Chappius, and Stiggins). Formative assessments are the ways in which teachers assess students' prior knowledge and progress toward mastery during the teaching. Students can use the feedback from formative assess-

Effective assessment includes techniques for both formative assessment (including pre-assessment, where appropriate) and summative assessment.

ments to identify where they are being successful and what remains to be accomplished to achieve mastery. When formative assessment is skillfully used, learning issues are immediately addressed. "This builds confidence that ultimate success is within reach" (Stiggins 2009). Formative assessments typically include any pre-assessments we use to determine what the students already know about the knowledge and skills in the lesson or unit, as well as what knowledge and skills they believe are important. After the pre-assessments, we use formative assessments that provide the functions noted above as "on the spot" and "interim."

Summative assessments are those assessments we use to assess the students' learning after the teaching is completed. These types of assessments involve judging final products or performances. In recent years, we have significantly improved our ability to assess students' products and performances. Of particular note is the wider implementation of criteria sheets and rubrics.

Chapters 4 and 5 provide comprehensive explanations of the most effective methods for assessing student learning.

4. What activities and sequence of activities in the lesson will result in the highest levels of student mastery?[21] Now that the mastery objectives have been written and the assessments developed and aligned with the objectives, we can create the most effective activities to teach the concepts we have identified. We select or design activities that will result in the highest levels of student mastery of the objectives. In choosing our activities, we should always remember: **How much students learn is far more important than how much we teach.**

> *When we know where we want to end up, we are better able to take the most efficient and effective route to get there.*

With the planning portion of the lesson complete, we are ready to begin teaching with an engaging activator designed to connect students to the lesson and in some cases serve as a pre-assessment. Each lesson should have a clear beginning, middle, and end. Most lessons should also provide an opportunity for teacher-guided practice and for independent student practice. Lessons should conclude with effective summarization of the knowledge and skills taught during the lesson. The specifics about the various instructional strategies we use in the lesson are discussed in depth in Chapters 2–9.

5. If a colleague were observing my class to give me ideas for improving the teaching of this lesson, what data could he or she gather that would be most helpful to me in improving the lesson?

Three Lesson Plans That Illustrate the Transformation of a Lesson from Activity-Based Planning to Standards-Based Planning

In the development of curriculum, unit planning should precede lesson planning. However, for the illustration of effective lesson planning, the authors have chosen to discuss lesson planning prior to addressing unit planning. We do this because, for most teachers, the majority of their time is devoted to lesson planning, as unit planning is typically done at the district (or in some cases the state, provincial, or even national) level by a representative group of teachers. After the discussion of lesson planning, we will move to unit planning.

Most of us learned in our pre-service training that all teaching requires lesson plans and unit plans. We learned that the definition of a lesson plan describes the block of time devoted to each lesson as a teaching activity that could be conducted in one class period in middle school and high school or in a single, contiguous time block in elementary school. The time block for lesson plans is no longer restricted to this definition, however. A single lesson plan may take several periods or larger blocks of time. In some cases, lesson plans interconnect in a way that makes it difficult to clearly determine when one lesson ends and another begins. Thinking about our teaching in lessons and units is helpful for effective planning; however, the time it takes to teach these lessons should be determined by the concepts in the curriculum that we need to teach, rather than by the period of time that the schedule allows for one class period.

To illustrate the difference between activity-based lesson planning and mastery-based lesson planning, we have included three plans for the same lesson. Each of these plans is a lesson in ninth-grade social studies that addresses the following state curriculum standard:

Ninth-grade history curriculum framework

Students will be able to describe the origins and development of the Renaissance, including the influence and accomplishments of Machiavelli, Michelangelo, Leonardo da Vinci, Raphael, Shakespeare, and Johannes Gutenberg. Students will be able to explain how these concepts relate to current events.

Lesson Plan 1 is written with an activity focus rather than a mastery focus. You will note that the bulk of the lesson plan talks about what the teacher and students *will do*. There is no specific identification of the knowledge or skills the students are expected to acquire as a result of this lesson, nor is there a specific identification of the district curriculum or benchmarks the lesson is designed to teach. Plans of this type result in lower levels of student mastery because the teacher and students are not sufficiently focused on the ultimate outcome of the lesson, which should be what students will learn. When we know where we want to end up, we are better able to take the most efficient and effective route to get there.

---

21 In Chapter 6, we expand this question to include the activities designed to address the learning needs and levels for mastery of a diverse group of learners.

Lesson Plan 1

Activity-Focused Planning

Objective: In groups, students will discuss a passage from Machiavelli's *The Prince*.

Steps to the Lesson

1. Sitting in groups, students will take a very brief self-assessment[22] (Machiavellian language simplified and disguised). In groups, students will discuss their responses to the questions. I will highlight one response from each group and allow for full-class exchange.

2. In groups, students will read a selection from *The Prince* aloud.

3. Students will answer the following questions (according to Machiavelli) in their groups:
   * Why should a prince be concerned with warfare?
   * Should a prince be cruel? Why or why not?
   * How should a prince utilize fear? Why?
   * How should a prince regard property?
   * Why did Machiavelli write *The Prince*?

4. As a whole group, students will discuss the question "Does the end justify the means?"

5. I will present a contemporary example for discussion.

6. Return to self-assessment. Connect questions to Machiavelli

---

22 The self-assessment given to the students and the passage from *The Prince* they were asked to read can be found after the sample lesson plans.

The time it takes to teach these lessons should be determined by the concepts in the curriculum that we need to teach, rather than by the period of time that the schedule allows for one class period.

Lesson Plan 2

Niccolo Machiavelli and Political Theory during the Renaissance

Unit: The Renaissance and Reformation

What are the district's curriculum standards and/or the benchmarks from which these concepts are derived?
Renaissance, Machiavelli, political theory, forming opinions

What do I want the students to know and be able to do by the end of the lesson (my mastery objectives)?
* comprehend the key ideas of Machiavelli (from *The Prince*)
* strengthen primary-source reading skills
* self-assess and critically analyze their own political theories and strengthen skills in defending their positions
* make Machiavelli relevant to today

How will I formatively and summatively assess the students' level of mastery of these concepts?
Students are presently working on their manor projects and will not be given homework on today's lesson. Students will be asked to reflect, at end of the lesson, on their personal political theories as they relate to Machiavelli's political theory.

What activities and sequence of activities in the lesson will result in the highest levels of student mastery?

1. Sitting in groups, students will take a very brief self-assessment (with Machiavellian language simplified and disguised). In groups, students will discuss responses. They will highlight one response from each group and allow for full-class exchange.
2. In groups, students will read selections from *The Prince* aloud.
3. Students will answer the following questions according to Machiavelli:
   * Why should a prince be concerned with warfare?
   * Should a prince be cruel? Why or why not?
   * How should a prince utilize fear? Why?
   * How should a prince regard property?
   * Why did Machiavelli write *The Prince*?

Lesson Plan 2 is for the same lesson. This lesson plan differs from Lesson Plan 1, in that the teacher used the five-question template as the structure for the lesson plan. However, the teacher has not received professional development in how to use the template to design standards-based lessons. The result of using the template is that the first part of the lesson plan talks about the learning that should take place rather than the activities. The wording of the objectives for learning, however, includes such terms as *comprehend* and *strengthen*, which are difficult to observe. You will also notice that the assessment question is answered with only a summative assessment. There is no indication of how the teacher will formatively assess during the teaching, so he or she may make instructional decisions.

4. Discuss as whole group. Present the question, "Does the end justify the means?" Present a contemporary example.

5. Return to self-assessment. Connect questions to Machiavelli.

If a colleague were observing my class to give me ideas for improving the teaching of this lesson, what data could s/he gather that would be most helpful to me in improving the lesson?

1. Did the lesson extend well (from personal to Machiavelli to contemporary)?

2. Was time managed well?

3. Was there enough time to manage content and understanding?

Lesson Plan 3 was written using the lesson-plan template after the teacher received training in standards-based planning.[23] The objectives are written in mastery form. The lesson plan contains both summative and formative assessments. The activities are designed to ensure that highest level of mastery of the objectives.[24]

---

23 Note that it is not our intent to imply that every individual teacher should write down this comprehensive a lesson plan for every lesson he or she teaches. This would not be possible for those teachers who teach four or five lessons in a single day. However, it is important that every teacher go through the process of thinking through each of his or her lessons using the five-question template.

24 As stated earlier, teachers can bring students to even higher levels of mastery when the teachers move from these mastery lesson plans to the type of differentiated instruction lesson plans. More information on this topic is available and explained in Chapter 6.

Lesson Plan 3

Niccolo Machiavelli and Political Theory during the Renaissance

Unit: The Renaissance and Reformation

What are the district's curriculum standards and/or the benchmarks from which these concepts are derived?

Ninth-grade history curriculum framework

Describe the origins and development of the Renaissance, including the influence and accomplishments of Machiavelli, Michelangelo, Leonardo da Vinci, Raphael, Shakespeare, and Johannes Gutenberg. Students will be able to explain how these concepts relate to current events.

What do I want the students to know and be able to do by the end of the lesson (my mastery objectives)?

By the end of this lesson, the students will be able to do the following:

- demonstrate orally or in writing comprehension of the following key ideas of Machiavelli (from *The Prince*):
  - The end justifies the means (or the end does not justify the means).
  - Using authority unjustly is not acceptable.
- strengthen the following primary-source reading skills:
  - identify orally or in writing a specific effect or acquire specific knowledge from a primary-source passage
  - articulate orally or in writing the realization that the author's ideas may not immediately reveal themselves
  - state orally or in writing the belief that their struggle to understand the author's ideas is worth it because the knowledge that is acquired is important
  - describe orally or in writing how the passage relates to their own lives and recent historical events
- describe orally or in writing their self-assessment and critical analysis of their own political theories as they relate to the key ideas from *The Prince* noted above
- demonstrate skills in defending a position (e.g., persuasive statements supported by evidence)
  - explain orally or in writing how Machiavelli's lessons are relevant to today's political events
  - demonstrate the behaviors of effective group work

English language learner mastery objectives:

1. Define and say in English the terms and phrases *the ends justify the means* (as it relates to political leadership), and *fear* (in the context of political oppression by a leader).

2. ELL students in language acquisition stages 1 through 3[25] will be able to read and comprehend the survey and Machiavelli passages provided in their native languages but discuss the concepts in English.

---

25 See the language acquisition stages found at the end of this book's Introduction.

3. ELL students in language acquisition stages 4 and 5 will be able to read and comprehend the survey and Machiavelli passages in English and discuss the concepts in English.

How will I formatively and summatively assess the students' level of mastery of these concepts?

1. "The Political Theory Self-Assessment," coupled with teacher observations of their work on the manor project, will help pre-assess the students' level of knowledge of the objectives above.

2. During the group discussions, the teacher will circulate around the room and listen to the discussions of the answers to the questions. The teacher will keep a running record of the students' comments as they demonstrate the knowledge and skills noted in the mastery objectives.

3. The verbal class reports from the groups will help the teacher assess the level of acquired student mastery of the knowledge and skills stated in the objectives above. I will collect the recorder sheets containing the group report.

4. Students will be asked to state in writing in their notebooks, at end of the lesson, how their personal political theories relate to Machiavelli's ideas.

What activities and sequence of activities in the lesson will result in the highest levels of student mastery?

1. Students will sit in the same groups with which they have been working on their manor research papers.

2. They will be assigned group jobs using a cooperative learning jobs grid.[26]

3. The teacher will do a brief check-in with the groups on the progress of their research papers.

4. Students will take a very brief self-assessment using Machiavellian language that has been simplified and disguised. See attached self-assessment.

5. In the groups,[27] they will discuss their responses to the self-assessment and prepare to report to the larger group on those discussions.

6. The teacher will discuss with the whole class one response from each group and allow for full-class exchange.

7. In groups, students will read selected paragraphs from *The Prince* aloud (see attached paragraphs).

8. Students will answer the following questions in each group according to how Machiavelli would answer the questions and prepare to report to the larger group on those discussions:
   a. Why should a prince be concerned with warfare?
   b. Should a prince be cruel? Why or why not?
   c. How should a prince utilize fear? Why?
   d. How should a prince regard property?
   e. Why did Machiavelli write *The Prince*?

8. The teacher will present the following question to the whole class for discussion in the groups: "Does the end justify the means?"

9. We will discuss the small group's answers to this question with the whole class.

10. The teacher will present contemporary examples of political situations and discuss how they apply to Machiavelli.

11. Students will return to the self-assessment survey and will connect the questions and comments from the assessment with the contemporary examples to Machiavelli.

12. In their groups, students will reflect on how their personal political theories relate to Machiavelli. These personal theories will be shared at the end of class or in the next class, depending on the time that is available.

If a colleague were observing my class to give me ideas for improving the teaching of this lesson, what data could he or she gather that would be most helpful to me in improving the lesson?

- Did the lesson result in connecting students' personal political theories to Machiavelli's ideas and to contemporary political events?
- Was the time managed well?
- Was time allocated appropriately throughout the lesson to teach the knowledge and skills noted in the objectives and to adequately assess to ensure student mastery?

---

26 Chapter 3 contains a description of the cooperative learning jobs grid.
27 Chapter 3 contains a description of the characteristics of effective group work.

Pre-Modern World History, Mr. Grande

Unit VII: The Renaissance and Reformation

Political Theory Self-Assessment

Mark a score of 1–5 for each statement.

1 = never true/strongly disagree
2 = rarely true/disagree
3 = somewhat true/generally agree
4 = frequently true/usually agree
5 = always true/strongly agree

1. _____ Nice people always get ahead eventually. Being kind will always earn someone's respect.
2. _____ It's better for people to fear you somewhat than to simply love you. People who love you may easily take advantage of you.
3. _____ The president should demonstrate that he is human too—that he may cry when people are hurt and that he may not always know the answer. Such a president will be loved by his fellow citizens.
4. _____ A good leader needs to be strong and well-respected, even if it means that the leader is feared by her people. No one will hate a leader who is feared.
5. _____ Peace is not worth it if you have to kill or act unjustly to obtain it.
6. _____ It is important to get what you need in life—more important than how you get it.
7. _____ The end justifies the means. If you have a good purpose, any way you go about accomplishing it is all right.
8. _____ Although it may be difficult sometimes, people should put their families first during difficult times.
9. _____ People should value their property above all else, as this will result in a secure society, even if it means having some conflict with people around them.
   _____ Total

Excerpts from *The Prince*, by Niccolo Machiavelli

Niccolo Machiavelli (1469–1527) was born in Florence as the son of a struggling lawyer. As a young boy, he received a solid humanist education and excelled in his studies. At age 25, he served the Republic of Florence, an Italian state, as a diplomat and political advisor. Although he mingled with many powerful people, his career was cut short when the Republic was overthrown in 1512. Machiavelli was jailed, tortured, and finally exiled. The following year, he wrote *The Prince*, which is Machiavelli's theory on the art of governance and, specifically, on the role of a prince. He wrote it to gain favor among rulers and be restored to a prominent political role.

Source: Machiavelli, N. *The Prince.* Marriott, W., trans. Retrieved: March 29, 2004 from http://www.constitution.org/mac/prince00.htm (original work published 1505).

That Which Concerns a Prince on the Subject of the Art of War

A prince ought to have no other aim or thought, nor select anything else for his study, than war and its rules and discipline; for this is the sole art that belongs to him who rules, and it is of such force that it not only upholds those who are born princes, but it often enables men to rise from a private station to that rank. And, on the contrary, it is seen that when princes have thought more of ease than of arms they have lost their states.... For among other evils which being unarmed brings you, it causes you to be despised, and this is one of those ignominies against which a prince ought to guard himself.... And therefore a prince who does not understand the art of war, over and above the other misfortunes already mentioned, cannot be respected by his soldiers, nor can he rely on them. He ought never, therefore, to have out of his thoughts this subject of war, and in peace he should addict himself more to its exercise than in war; this he can do in two ways, the one by action, the other by study.

CHAPTER XVII: Concerning Cruelty and Clemency, and Whether It Is Better to Be Loved Than Feared

Coming now to the other qualities mentioned above, I say that every prince ought to desire to be considered clement and not cruel. Nevertheless he ought to take care not to misuse this clemency. Cesare Borgia was considered cruel; notwithstanding, his cruelty reconciled the Romagna, unified it, and restored it to peace and loyalty.... Therefore a prince, so long as he keeps his subjects united and loyal, ought not to mind the reproach of cruelty; because with a few examples he will be more merciful than those who, through too much mercy, allow disorders to arise, from which follow murders or robberies. ... And of all princes, it is impossible for the new prince to avoid the imputation of cruelty, owing to new states being full of dangers. ...

Upon this a question arises: whether it be better to be loved than feared or feared than loved? It may be answered that one should wish to be both, but, because it is difficult to unite them in one person, is much safer to be feared than loved, when, of the two, either must be dispensed with...and as long as you succeed they are yours entirely; they will offer you their blood, property, life and children. ... For love is preserved by the link of obligation which, owing to the baseness of men, is broken at every opportunity for their advantage; but fear preserves you by a dread of punishment which never fails.

Nevertheless a prince ought to inspire fear in such a way that, if he does not win love, he avoids hatred; because he can endure very well being feared whilst he is not hated, which will always be as long as he abstains from the property of his citizens and subjects and from their women. But when it is necessary for him to proceed against the life of someone, he must do it on proper justification and for manifest cause, but above all things he must keep his hands off the property of others, because men more quickly forget the death of their father than the loss of their patrimony.

Activity for Standards-Based Lesson Plans

1. Read plans 1 and 3, above.

2. Describe the differences between the plans.

3. In what way does the planning in standards-based plan 3 better enable the teacher to ensure student mastery of the curriculum standards?

Standards-Based Unit Planning

As noted at the start of the lesson-planning section, units should be planned prior to lessons. We began with lesson planning for two reasons. First, more and more districts, states (provinces), and even countries are moving toward standardized curriculum units. In many to most instances, the units are written and teacher planning is at a lesson level. Second, it is important to understand the lesson level of planning before you can fully understand the unit level of planning. Once there is understanding of both levels, then the planning should start at the unit level. Once the unit is written, the individual lessons are constructed within the unit.

Essential questions and important concepts are large ideas that will ultimately encompass the specific learning contained in each individual lesson plan.

All unit planning should be based on the curriculum standards (a.k.a. curriculum frameworks or Common Core) that have been adopted by the state (province) or district. Some standards will be completely taught in a single unit. Other standards will spiral through several units. Those charged with developing the units of study must be well versed in the standards and have the standards document as their constant companion.

Standards-based unit plans are structured using six distinct parts:

1. Unit essential questions (a.k.a. important concepts)
2. Benchmarks
3. Standards addressed in the unit
4. Title list for individual lessons (this is only used if there are no pacing guides)
5. Assessments
6. Standards-based lessons

Essential Questions (Important Concepts)

Essential questions and important concepts are large ideas that will ultimately encompass the specific learning contained in each individual lesson plan. They differ from lesson mastery objectives and unit benchmarks. The ability to explain and apply essential questions typically requires mastery of specific mastery objectives like those we learned about in the previous section on mastery objectives. However, becoming an expert at writing mastery objectives is the means to the end. The end is the students' ability to articulate and apply the broader concept noted in the essential questions (important concepts). It is important to note that a unit may be designed to address a single essential question or more than one essential question. In the example unit below, the essential question is, "When faced with a scientific problem, how do scientists identify the problem and prepare a plan of inquiry for solving the problem?" You will note that essential questions are stated in terms of student behavior that demonstrates mastery.

Wiggins and McTighe (2011, p. 73) note the following characteristics for essential questions:

- cause genuine and relevant inquiry into the big ideas of the core content
- provoke deep thought, lively discussion, sustained inquiry, and new understanding, as well as more questions
- require students to consider alternatives, weigh evidence, support their ideas, and justify their answers
- stimulate vital, ongoing rethinking of big ideas, assumptions, and prior lessons
- spark meaningful connections with prior learning and personal experiences
- naturally recur, creating opportunities for transfer to other situations

We do not believe that the big ideas need to always be phrased in terms of a question. In some cases, it is clearer to the students if phrased as a statement. We refer to these statements as **important concepts**. What follows is an important concept that comes from the curriculum from which the standards-based lesson plan we read earlier in this chapter was derived. It is, "Students will be able to describe the origins and development of the Renaissance, including the names and influence of key artists, writers, soldiers, and political leaders, and explain how each relates to current events." As you can see, it is written in terms of observable behaviors to aid in constructing higher-order assessments to assess student understanding.

The following sample essential questions and important concepts were shared by some of the teachers we work with. You will note that the essential questions are written as questions and the important concepts are written as statements.

English Language Arts

- Why is writing history or a news article different from writing fiction?
- Identify words and phrases in stories or poems that suggest feelings or appeal to the senses.

Math

- How are ratios and rates used in everyday life? How would life be different without ratios and rates?
- How can the relationship between two quantities be represented visually?
- Explain why the sum or product of two rational numbers is rational; the sum of a rational number and an irrational number is irrational; and the product of a nonzero rational number and an irrational number is irrational.
- Solve real-life and mathematical problems involving angle measure, area, surface area, and volume.

History

- What is the purpose of government?
- Why do laws have to be interpreted?
- Analyze and compare and contrast primary and secondary sources, citing specific evidence from those sources.

Science

- Where does energy come from?
- How can energy be measured?

Technology

- Integrate multimedia and visual displays into presentations to clarify information, strengthen claims and evidence, and add interest.
- Describe and use network system hardware and software components.

Vocational

- Evaluate industries, organizations, and careers, based on multiple sources of research and information.
- How do I assess potential career pathways, including career ladders, and determine my areas of career interest?

Assessing the Knowledge and Skills Contained in Essential Questions (Important Concepts)

Essential questions are typically too broad to assess in interim assessments that measure less than what was learned in all of (or most of) a unit. That is because the comprehensiveness of the knowledge and skills needed to answer the questions typically requires the completion or near completion of the unit. As you will see below, it is when we get to the benchmarks that we have statements that more specifically guide the construction of our shorter-term interim assessments. Essential questions and important concepts are typically assessed with extensive assessments, such as end-of-unit tests, midterm and final exams, and/or course capstone projects. These assessments seek to assess the essential questions and important concepts for a full unit or a full course.

Benchmarks (a.k.a. Subconcepts in Some Districts)

The second part of the unit is listing the benchmarks that are addressed in the unit. Some standards can serve as benchmarks for the essential question (important concepts). However, if the standards are not specific enough, then the unit developers will need to write benchmarks. **The benchmarks are typically the component parts of the broader essential question or important concept. The reason we have benchmarks is to focus our development of lessons and interim assessments.** The benchmarks are still typically too broad to be taught in a single lesson (but not always). As mentioned above, the benchmarks also serve as guides for developing our interim assessments[28] within the units. In lessons, the mastery objectives are the road map for the dipsticking[29] that is done during the lesson. Below are some characteristics of benchmarks:

1. They are measureable. By this we mean you can construct an assessment that enables you to validly and reliably assess the benchmark. If you a find you are having difficulty determining an assessment for the benchmark, it is an indication that you need to revise the benchmark. Most essential questions (important concepts) are measured with end-of-unit exams, whereas benchmarks are assessed using quizzes or other shorter assessments that are the interim assessments leading up to the end of unit exam.

2. They are more specific than the essential questions (important concepts). Essential questions (important concepts) are driven by broad ideas. Benchmarks are driven by measureable "chunks" of information that may be learned over one to three hours of instruction.

---

28 Interim assessments are discussed in depth in the chapters on assessment (Chapter 4) and questioning (Chapter 5).
29 Dipsticking is described in Chapter 5.

3. Benchmarks typically encompass more than one mastery objective.
4. Benchmarks typically take a full lesson or more for students to learn the knowledge and skills contained in the benchmarks.

Essential Questions, Benchmarks, and Mastery Objectives: Which is Which?

The figure below shows the relationship between the three levels of learning in a unit of study. The assessment of the essential question comes after the students have mastered all the benchmarks. This may not come until the midpoint or the end of the unit. The benchmarks will be assessed when all the learning in that benchmark has been achieved. The mastery objectives are smaller bites of learning that will use free dipsticking or short interim assessments to determine student mastery. We should be assessing at all three levels of learning. It is, once again, important to note that some essential questions are specific enough to also serve as benchmarks, and some benchmarks are specific enough to serve as a mastery objective. We strongly suggest that unit developers not obsess over determining whether something is an essential question, a benchmark, or a mastery objective. These debates take up too much valuable time that is better spent on the content of the unit. A few minutes of healthy discussion is worthwhile. However, long discussions about whether a statement is an essential question, benchmark, or mastery objective divert from the important work of developing the units.

Figure 1.4

Essential Question/ Important Concept	Benchmarks	Mastery Objectives
Assessed at or near the end of the unit	Interim assessments that break up the content of the essential questions; these typically occur after one or more lessons.	Dipsticking and other assessments done several times during the lesson
Why is writing history or a news article different from writing fiction?	1. Students will be able to compare and contrast fiction and non-fiction. 2. Students will be able to compare and contrast the characteristics of a news article with those of a piece of fiction. 3. Students will be able to categorize a list of characteristics as either being associated with a news article, history passage, or a piece of fiction. 4. Students will be able to compare and contrast the purposes for writing news articles, history pieces, and fiction.	1. Students will be able to read a news article or history passage and explain the information contained in the article. 2. Students will be able to define the characteristics of a news article or history piece. 3. Students will be able to define the characteristics of fiction. 4. Students will be able to read several pieces of writing and determine which is a news article and which is fiction. 5. Students will be able to explain the purpose for writing news articles and history pieces. 6. Students will be able to explain the purpose for writing fiction. **ELL Mastery Objectives:** Students will be able to define the terms *history, news, article, fiction, non-fiction, compare, contrast, characteristic,* and *purpose*.

Role of Standards in Unit Development

The third component of the unit plan is listing the standards addressed in the unit. As mentioned above, some or all of the standards may be specific enough to serve as the benchmarks. Some may even be specific enough to serve as mastery objectives. We are frequently asked the question, "Shouldn't you start unit planning by knowing the standards you want to address in the unit?" The answer to that question is a definitive yes. Before you create your essential questions, you should have a list of the standards you wish to address. However, we sometimes find that as the essential questions and benchmarks are created, the following occurs:

- The unit will address additional standards we did not realize would also be addressed in the unit.
- The unit did not address one or more of the standards they originally thought would be addressed in this unit. They need either to do some revision of the essential questions and benchmarks or decide in what unit those standards will be addressed.

Shortly, after we explain each part of the unit plan, we will walk the reader through the steps to unit development and, hopefully, the role of standards will be clearer.

Why Write the Standards If We Already Identify the Essential Questions (Important Concepts), Benchmarks, and Mastery Objectives?

We identify the standards so we have a crosswalk between the standards and the units. Standards are created by districts, provinces (states), or countries to identify the important knowledge and skills a person needs to master in each discipline and across disciplines. Units, on the other hand, are what we create to "operationalize" the learning of the standards. A unit of study, particularly an interdisciplinary unit, may encompass a wide array of diverse standards. It is important, therefore, that we identify the standards that are addressed in each unit. As you can see in Figure 1.4, above, the standards addressed in the three levels of competencies (and the unit from which they come) most likely will incorporate history standards, reading standards, writing standards, and standards related to the development of higher-order thinking. Many of the standards addressed in this unit will probably also appear in other units as well.

Districts that have pacing guides do not need to have lesson lists in their units, since pacing is addressed in the guides.

What about Essential Questions (Important Concepts) and Benchmarks for English Language Learners?

We have found that it is most effective to identify the competencies for the English language learners at the lesson level. These should be clearly defined as ELL mastery objectives in the individual lessons. The essential question (important concepts) and benchmark learning levels typically encompass skills that can be mastered by English language learners once they have mastered the ELL mastery objectives in the individual lessons.

Planning the Pacing of a Unit

The next part we will discuss is the pacing of the unit. One way to help teachers pace is to provide a lesson list of the titles of the individual lessons with the estimated instructional time needed to teach each lesson. The other way is to create a pacing guide that shows the pace used to teach all the units and lessons during a year and through multiples school years. These structures give the teacher an understanding of the progression of the unit through the lesson phase so they can accurately plan the number of hours and classes devoted to each unit. These unit lesson lists and pacing guides are typically created in draft form at the outset of the curriculum development process. The reason for this is that unit developers are often unsure how best to "chunk" the competencies noted in the benchmarks until they develop the units and the specific lessons. For the teachers teaching the unit, it is important to plan the pacing of the unit. We will not go any further with the construction of pacing guides in this book. The scope of this book is not the development of multiyear district curricula. Our intent is to provide individual teachers a framework for developing units and lessons.

Lesson Lists

Districts that have pacing guides do not need to have lesson lists in their units, since pacing is addressed in the guides. However, for districts without pacing guides, lesson lists are important. As stated above, the lesson list will give the teacher the big picture of how lessons progress through the unit. It will also tell them how much time they should spend on each lesson. The collection of these individual lesson times tells teachers how much time they should spend on the unit.

Unit Assessments

The fifth part of the unit is the assessments. These should include both formative (pre-assessments, dipsticking, and interim classroom assessments) and summative assessments. Included in the unit are the quizzes, tests, and scoring guides (e.g., criteria sheets, rubrics, anchor papers, exemplars, and question lists) used to assess the benchmarks. Dipsticking and other single-lesson interim assessments are found in the lessons and not in the unit. The unit assessments only contain those that are too broad to be contained in a single lesson.

The scope of this chapter is not sufficient for us to provide all the assessments one would use with the unit below. Later in this chapter, we have included one example of a criteria sheet used to assess a benchmark related to collecting data. Chapters 4, 5, and 6 contain explanations of various types of assessments and the questioning practices one would include in the assessment section of a unit plan.

There are typically only a few essential questions (important concepts) in a unit.

The final part of the unit is the actual standards-based lessons designed to teach the benchmarks. The lesson plans are typically not contained in the unit itself (other than the lesson list, if one is used). The unit is the framework for the learning that will be contained in the lessons. A district curriculum guide will contain both the units and lessons.

Steps to Developing a Unit

Step 1: At the outset of unit development, the developers should have a list of the curriculum standards the unit is designed to teach. Each developer must be clear as to the knowledge and skill development that will be learned during the unit. As noted above, the list of standards may be modified later in the process when it becomes apparent that there are either additional standards addressed in the unit or that some of the standards originally listed will, in fact, be addressed in a different unit.

Step 2: Construct the essential questions and/or important concepts. As noted above, the essential questions or important concepts are overarching concepts learned through the unit. There are typically only a few essential questions (important concepts) in a unit. If during the development process you find you are coming up with a long list, then you will want to ask yourself if some of the items on your list are really benchmarks. Earlier in the chapter, we gave you Wiggins and McTighe's guidelines for essential questions (most of which also apply to important concepts). It is important to note that the line between an essential question and a benchmark is a gray area. There is no exact measure that will tell you if an essential ques-

tion that is written in observable language is actually a benchmark.

Step 3: This step is to change your essential questions into benchmarks. We chunk the learning needed to master what is stated in the essential questions into measureable parts. This is what is often referred to in business as "operationalizing" the broad ideas. The benchmarks turn our broad ideas into statements or questions that can be measured with a quiz or other interim assessment that addresses more than just a single mastery objective.

Step 4: Look at your preliminary list of standards, your list of essential questions (important concepts), and your benchmarks. Make certain they correspond to one another. For example, if you look at your benchmarks and realize additional standards are addressed, add those standards to your list of standards. If you look at your essential questions and realize there are pieces of learning not addressed in your benchmarks, then you may need to modify one or the other.

Step 4: Make your final list of standards.

Step 5: Construct your mastery objectives. Your mastery objectives should serve as the building blocks for each of your benchmarks. It is important to remember that some mastery objectives may address components of more than one benchmark. The mastery objectives will not be contained within the unit itself. Rather, they will be contained in the individual lessons. However, it is important to construct your mastery objectives at this time to guide your construction of assessments.

Step 6: Construct your assessments. You will need assessments that work on at least three levels: (1) dipsticking and other short interim assessments that can measure the level of student mastery of the mastery objectives, (2) longer interim assessments that assess the benchmarks, and (3) an assessment that measures all the knowledge and skills in the unit and mastery of the essential questions (important concepts). Assessments at this level are sometimes considered summative assessments and sometimes considered interim assessments. We choose not to enter that debate and just indicate that there should be an assessment that assesses the full unit of study.[30] As you will see in the

---

30 Since this is a section on unit planning, we will not address midterm and final exams.

next part, the lessons are their own entity and are not contained in the unit plan itself. The assessments at the end of unit and benchmark assessments will be contained in the unit plan, whereas the dipsticking and shorter interim assessments that measure the learning in a lesson will be contained in the lesson plan.

Step 7: Construct your lessons. The lessons will be constructed as described earlier in the chapter. As noted, the lessons are not contained in the unit itself because the unit serves as the road map from which the lessons will be constructed. Once lessons are constructed, they are typically appended to their respective units in the curriculum guide.

Sample Unit

The following excerpt is taken from a district curriculum document. The items in italics are addressed in the unit below. Following this page is an example of a mastery unit plan written to address several pieces of knowledge and some skills described in the cur-

riculum document. Districts beginning the curriculum development process will want to develop units using the format of the sample unit plan. Districts with curriculum that contain units not in standards-based form will want to revise these units to match the format of the sample unit plan. You will note below that this district had well-constructed science standards that could be used as the benchmarks. They were written in assessable form and with sufficient specificity to be assessed with interim assessments at various points during the lesson. You will also note that these science standards were constructed with the interdisciplinary writing skills (e.g., constructing, such as formulating and writing questions or taking notes on the salient knowledge), so there is no need to identify the standards from the writing curriculum. Therefore, in this unit you will see that the benchmarks and the standards are one and the same. In situations in which the standards are not this well constructed, benchmarks will need to be written and the standards listed separately.

Grade Eight—Force and Motion Waterwheels Unit[31]

Important Concept: At the conclusion of the unit, students will be able to explain and demonstrate how, when faced with a scientific problem, scientists identify the problem, as well as how they prepare and carry out a plan of inquiry for solving the problem.

Benchmarks and Science Curriculum Standards

Students will be able to

- Standard 2.b.: demonstrate the ability to design, perform, and analyze scientific experiments, including
  - acquiring from the books, the Internet, and other sources the prerequisite knowledge needed to formulate a research question about an area of inquiry
  - stating and writing an area of interest in the form of a question that leads to experimentation
  - formulating and writing questions that lead to experimentation
  - recognizing those questions about the topic that need experimentation to be answered and those questions that may be answered without experimentation
- Standard 2.c.: demonstrate independent use of the scientific method (stating an objective, forming a hypothesis, creating an experiment, and collecting and analyzing data to form a conclusion), including
  - defining and identifying the roles of trials, constants, and dependent and independent variables in experiments students design and perform
  - demonstrating the organizational skill of taking notes on the salient knowledge obtained from an experiment in a science notebook[32]
  - demonstrating organizational skills, including managing a science notebook, taking notes from a variety of resources, and data collection
  - constructing and interpreting data tables and flowcharts to present and understand collected data
  - describing trends in data even when patterns are not exact
  - using collected data to create a well-reasoned conclusion and generate questions and alternate procedures for further study, based on experimental outcomes
  - using the scientific method to create solutions to technological problems and realize that there is often more than one solution to such problems
- Standard 4.d.: demonstrate and describe key knowledge related to force and motion, including

---

31 The unit in the subsequent pages is based in part on information in the Public Schools of Brookline's (Brookline, MA) Science Learning Expectations for grade 8.

32 The criteria sheet used to teach the students the correct format for lab notebooks follows this plan.

- demonstrate and describe how forces acting on objects as "pushes" or "pulls" can either reinforce or oppose each other
- demonstrate and describe that all forces have magnitude and direction
- demonstrate and describe gravity
- demonstrate and describe the difference between speed and velocity
- Standard 1.b.: demonstrate the ability to work safely and thoughtfully in the laboratory situation, including
  - describing and following laboratory safety and emergency procedures regarding the use of heat sources, safety goggles, chemicals, and glassware
  - demonstrating the behaviors of effective group work, as described in the scoring guide for effective group work
  - demonstrating the correct set-up and clean-up procedures for a lab, including the safe handling of chemicals and equipment[33]

The Formative and Summative Assessments[34]

Pre-Assessment

1. The lesson will begin with students individually brainstorming on paper a list of their answers to the statement: *List everything you know about waterwheels.*
2. We will then do a large group share, with the teacher listing all the students' comments.
3. The papers will be collected and used as the basis for understanding the level of knowledge of each student.

Interim Assessments

1. Observe and assess using a running record of students' group work against the criteria for effective group work found in the rubric for lab group work.[35]
2. Observe and assess using a running record of each individual's contribution to the group, based on the criteria sheet, "My Contribution to Group Work."
3. Students will self-assess the group's performance and each member will self-assess his or her individual performance, based on the scoring guides noted in Nos. 1 and 2 above.
4. Observe and assess group performance on the task of constructing the waterwheel, using performance assessment rubric for the waterwheels. Students will be assessed at each of the three stages in the development of their waterwheels.
5. Observe and assess the students' use of the safety procedures during their lab work, using the district's required list of safety procedures.
6. Collect and assess each student's lab book, using the criteria sheet for lab books (see below).
7. Quiz on laboratory safety
8. Quiz on waterwheel background knowledge
9. Quiz on developing experimental design

Summative Assessment

1. The end-of-unit test

Pacing

Teachers should refer to the district pacing guides found in the district curriculum guides. The pacing guides indicate the approximate range of dates for the start and end of each unit and the approximate number of class periods that should be used to teach the unit.[36]

Lab Book Criteria Sheet

The following page criteria sheet is used to assess the students' entries into their lab journals.

---

33 Chapter 3 of this book contains a sample lesson plan for teaching middle school science students the routine for cleaning up after a lab.
34 We only included one assessment tool, the lab book criteria sheet, in the example. The explanation and construction of assessments is such a comprehensive topic that we decided to let it wait until we got to the chapters on assessment and questioning strategies (Chapters 4, 5, and 6) so as not to create confusion for the reader.
35 Readers can find examples of group work criteria in Chapter 4. Rubrics for assessing a working group's group work skills and the individual group work skills of its members can be found in Chapter 3.
36 Some districts have varied schedules among the district's schools. Some schools may have 50-minute periods while others may have 90-minute periods or longer. In those cases, we recommend that the pacing guides indicate the number of instructional hours that will be devoted to each unit rather than the number of periods.

WATERWHEELS: LAB BOOK CRITERIA

As you work on the waterwheel project, you will keep a detailed journal of your experience. The journal will have different types of entries in it: lab write-ups, drawings, plans, and reactions. Please use the knowledge below to guide your work.

My Lab Book entry is a
lab write-up—go to A.
drawing—go to B.
plan, reaction, or observation—go to C.

A. LAB WRITE-UP

- Does my lab have a title, question, hypothesis, materials list, procedure, data chart, data analysis, and conclusion?
- Is the hypothesis based on evidence or experience?
- Does my procedure clearly test my hypothesis?
- Is my procedure in step-by-step format?
- Is my data chart clearly labeled, and have I consistently used the proper units of measurement?
- Are my data analysis and conclusion both written in paragraph form?
- Does my data analysis report what happened and where errors might have been made?
- Does my conclusion answer my question and explain how the data supports or does not support my hypothesis?

B. DRAWING

- Is my drawing large enough to clearly show the detail that I want?
- Have I added written descriptions to make my drawing easier to understand?
- Do I need to show my drawing from different points of view to show what is happening in many places?
- Is my drawing detailed enough so that people can understand what I tried to show?

C. PLAN, REACTION, OR OBSERVATION

- Are these notes to myself? If they are, will I understand them later, and have I labeled them so that my teacher knows what they are?
- Are these brief reactions to a class question or homework thinking-problem? Have I labeled them and included the original question?

Reprinted with permission from Dr. Christopher Whitbeck.

Conclusion

Teaching for mastery begins with clarity about which knowledge and skills in the curriculum are the highest priorities, which are important, and which are connected but not essential. It next requires that teachers understand that mastery comes in stages (levels of mastery) and that students move through those stages at varying rates. It then proceeds to the effective construction of unit plans and lesson plans.

When teaching students to mastery, we need to clearly communicate to the students in developmentally appropriate language what they will know and be able to do at the end of the teaching. Next, we need to plan formative and summative assessments aligned with the objectives that enable us to determine each student's level of mastery. Finally, the activities we choose should focus student time on learning the highest-priority knowledge and skills.

Additional Sample Lesson Plans

You will note that two of the lesson plans below are for classes in which there are English language learners (fifth grade and middle school). These contains mastery objectives related to English language acquisition, in addition to the content mastery objectives. Those who wish to learn more about using English language acquisition objectives will want to read the essay on English language learning at the end of this chapter.

Also, as noted above, Chapter 6 contains models of differentiated instruction and Universal Design for Learning lesson plans, since the knowledge in Chapters 2–6 is a prerequisite for writing such plans.

Sample of a Kindergarten Lesson Plan

Learning Letters: Name Puzzles

Essential Question: What are letters and how do they relate to written and oral communication?
What district curriculum standard (and/or benchmark) does this lesson address?

Kindergarten Language Arts Curriculum Frameworks:

Standard 7 Beginning Reading—Students will explain the nature of written English and the relationship of letters and spelling patterns to the sounds of speech.
7.1 Identify uppercase and lowercase letters. Recognize that print is read from left to right in English.
7.3 Understand that written words are composed of letters that represent sounds.

What do I want the students to know and be able to do?
By the end of the class, the students will be able to
- state that names are made up of letters
- explain that the order of letters in their names is always the same
- connect the letter puzzle pieces together to make their names
- identify the letters in their names

How will I formatively and summatively assess the students' levels of mastery of these concepts?
1. Last week, the students were all pre-assessed on their ability to recognize and order letters.
2. During group work, I will circulate around the room and monitor students' work. At this time, I will take anecdotal notes.
3. I will work with individual groups for about five minutes each, checking their understanding and noting their levels of mastery using the letter-skills checklist.
4. Students self-assess their progress against an exemplar of their names.
5. Students peer-assess each other's work against an exemplar of their names.

What activities and sequence of activities in the lesson will result in the highest levels of student mastery?
1. Activate the lesson by writing sentences with children's names in them: "Emily likes red. Justin likes blue."
2. Tell the students that today they are going to put together their name puzzles. Arrange children in a circle so they can place their folders open flat on the floor in front of them, where I will be able to observe their work.
3. "I'm going to show you how to put together your name puzzle. Take out the letters that are in the envelope glued in your folder. Open your folder and lay it flat in front of you. Be sure you can see your name on the folder. Use the letter pieces to make your name. Put down the first letter first; then put down the next letter. Be sure the letters match exactly."
4. Demonstrate using one student's folder and puzzle pieces. Emphasize that each letter has to look the same as the letters written on the folder and face the way those letters do.
5. Using a pointer, point to each letter, demonstrating how to check letter by letter, saying the letters as I go: "E, E, m, m, i, i, l, l, y, y."
6. Show students how to mix up the letters so they can form the names again.
7. Have the students return to their tables with their name puzzles in front of them. Students will put together their names, mix up the letters, and make the names again three times.
8. When the students make their names easily, ask them to make a partner's name and check it.
9. Demonstrate how to put the name puzzle away by putting all the pieces back in the envelope, putting the envelope in the folder, and putting the folder in a box with the name on the folder facing up.

What knowledge about my teaching or the students would be most helpful to me in self-assessing my teaching in this lesson?
1. Did I provide adequate models and visuals for the ELL students?
2. Were the directions given in simple language that all students could understand?
3. Do I need to extend my wait time for all students to be able to respond to my questions?
4. Did all of the students participate in this activity?
5. How can I keep the noise level to a minimum?
6. Which students mastered the objectives?

Sample of a Second-Grade Lesson Plan

Balancing and Weighing: Equal-Arm Balance

Important Concept: Students will explain the purpose of having a system of weights and measures.
What district curriculum standard (and/or benchmark) does this lesson address?

Students will demonstrate that under certain conditions objects can be balanced (Standard 4B Benchmarks 14, 16, and 17).

- Make predictions based on past experiences with a particular material or object.
- Extend observations using simple tools—for example, a two-arm balance.
- Identify the observable properties, such as size and weight.

What do I want the students to know and be able to do?
By the end of the class, the students will be able to

- compare the weights of objects in one pail to those of objects in another
- explain why the objects balanced or did not balance
- complete the observation record sheet and write a reflection describing what they learned
- be able to work constructively in their cooperative learning groups by demonstrating the following:
  - use of a 12-inch voice
  - equitable distribution of the work
  - respect for the ideas expressed by their partners
  - absence of disruption to the work of the other groups
  - all members on task 100 percent of the time
  - each group member having a well-written record of the items he or she measured in the activities below, under certain conditions

How will I formatively and summatively assess the students' level of mastery of these concepts?
1. Begin the lesson with a series of recall and comprehension questions to pre-assess students' knowledge of the knowledge and skills in the objectives noted above.
2. During group work, I will circulate around the room and monitor students' work as it relates to the content and group dynamics objectives noted above. After circulating and clarifying any misconceptions, I will work with individual groups for a period of about five minutes each.
3. When I am working with groups, I will ask them questions about their "leveling the equal-arm balance" and make sure they understand everything.
4. Students will be recording their findings on their individual record sheets. The record sheets will be collected and checked for accuracy.
5. Students will do a written reflection indicating what they learned.

What activities and sequence of activities in the lesson will result in the highest levels of student mastery?
List the activities that will take place during the lesson.
1. Begin the lesson by activating and pre-assessing previous knowledge. I will ask a series of recall and comprehension questions that address the knowledge and skills in the objectives noted above.
2. Introduce lesson 6 in "Balancing and Weighing." Show the students Figures 6-3 and 6-4. Explain to them that in this activity they will be leveling and exploring with the equal-arm balance.
3. Introduce, distribute, and explain the worksheet that they will be using to record their findings.
4. Explain to students how they will make the measurements using the balancing scales. If needed, I will have two students come up and demonstrate how this is done after the explanation.
5. Supply students with additional materials to measure if such objects are not available at their desks.
6. Students will begin placing various objects in the pails and leveling them.
7. In the last five minutes of class, assign a writing activity. The students will reflect on what they have just experienced. Display various vocabulary words they will use in their writing.

What knowledge about my teaching or the students would be most helpful to me in self-assessing my teaching in this lesson?
1. Do you have any suggestions for ways that I could better manage the time to increase student mastery?
2. Did students all participate in their groups in ways that reflected the objectives for group work noted above?
3. Which students mastered the objectives?

Sample of a Fifth-Grade Lesson Plan

The Revolutionary War

Essential Question: Why did colonists seek independence from England?

What district curriculum standard (and/or benchmark) does this lesson address?
Grade 5 Learning Standards
The Revolution and the Formation of a Federal Government under the Constitution, 1775–1789

1. 5.17: Describe the major battles of the Revolution and explain the factors leading to American victory and British defeat. (H)
   - Lexington and Concord (1775)
   - Bunker Hill (1775)
   - Saratoga (1777)
   - Valley Forge (1777–1778)
   - Yorktown (1781)
2. S.3: Academic Interaction: English language learners (ELLs) will demonstrate comprehension and oral communication skills when using spoken English to answer the recall questions posed at the beginning of the lesson (FL 1, 2, 5, 6, 7; ELA 1, 2, 5).
3. R.3: Comprehension: ELLs will read English fluently and identify facts and evidence during the teacher-led reading of section 13.1 of Chapter 13 in *History Alive! America's Past* in order to interpret and analyze text (ELA 8, 11).
4. W.2: Writing: ELLs will write in English with clear focus, coherent organization, and sufficient detail when recording notes on the graphic organizer (ELA 19; FL 1).

What do I want the students to know and be able to do?
By the end of the class, the students will be able to
- compare and contrast the American and British forces at the beginning of the Revolutionary War
- explain why the American colonies were able to defeat Britain in the Revolutionary War
- be able to work constructively in their cooperative learning groups by demonstrating the following:
  - use of a 12-inch voice
  - equitable distribution of the work
  - respect for the ideas expressed by their group mates
  - absence of disruption to the work of the other groups
  - all members on task 100 percent of the time
  - each group member having a well-written copy of the notes noted in the activities list below

How will I formatively and summatively assess the students' level of mastery of these concepts?
1. I will begin the lesson with some recall and comprehension questions that will enable me to pre-assess students' prior knowledge of the mastery objectives below.
2. During group work, I will circulate around the room and monitor students' work as it relates to the content and group dynamics objectives noted above. After circulating and clarifying any misconceptions, I will work with individual groups for a period of about five minutes each.
3. When I am working with groups, I will ask them questions about their readings to make sure they understand the material.
4. Students will be filling in worksheets/graphic organizers to summarize what they are reading.

What activities and sequence of activities in the lesson will result in the highest levels of student mastery?
1. Introduce Chapter 13 in *History Alive! America's Past*. Read section 13.1 with the class. Explain **bold-faced** words. These words are defined in the glossary in the back of the book and appear on the social studies word wall.
2. Introduce Graphic Organizer Transparency 13: *Revolutionary War: Unequal Tug-of-War*.
3. Explain the homework.
4. Ask the following questions: What do you see here? Which aspects of our tug of war are shown in the drawing? Which aspects of our tug of war are not shown in the drawing? In what ways were the Continental Army and the British Army the same? In what ways were they different?
5. Tell students that the drawing represents the relationship between the American colonies and Britain

at the start of the Revolutionary War. The smaller team (American colonies) is making a determined effort to defeat the larger team (Britain) in a tug of war (Revolutionary War). Explain that the students will use this graphic organizer to learn about factors that allowed the American colonies to win the war.

6. Pass out reading notes. Tell students they will now read and take notes on how the seemingly weaker Continental Army defeated the British Army in the Revolutionary War. (Students were given guided practice on the strategies for content reading earlier in the week.)

7. Students will be placed in groups of three.

8. Students will begin reading sections 13.2–13.8 in the reading notes. After each two sections, we will regroup as a class and check answers. This process may take two days to complete.

9. During the last five minutes of class, summarize with a 3-2-1 and collect the packets.

If a colleague were observing my class to give me ideas for improving the teaching of this lesson, what data could s/he gather that would be most helpful to me in improving the lesson?

1. Do you have any suggestions for ways that I could better manage the time to increase student mastery?

2. Did students all participate in their groups in ways that reflected the objectives for group work noted above?

Sample of a Middle School Lesson Plan

Impressionist Painting Styles and Modern Translation of Landscape

Essential Question: What are the major styles of painting?
What district curriculum standard (and/or benchmark) does this lesson address?

1. 4.8: Create and prepare artwork for group or individual public exhibitions.

2. Use the appropriate vocabulary related to the methods, materials, and techniques students have learned and used in grades K–8.

3. 1.6: Create artwork that demonstrates an awareness of the range and purpose of tools.

4. 1.8: Maintain the workspace, materials, and tools responsibly and safely.

5. S.1: Vocabulary: English language learners (ELLs) will comprehend and communicate orally, using the English vocabulary words: *painting, strokes, slap-dash, Impressionist, French Salon, landscape, digital, image, photo,* and *camera* (FL 1, 2, 4, 5, 6, 7; ELA 4).

6. R.3: Comprehension: ELLs will read the pre-assessment and printed directions in English, identify facts and evidence in order to interpret the text, and complete the pre-assessment and the painting assignment.

7. W.2: Writing: ELLs will write a short statement in English about their favorite painter, maintaining a clear focus on their subject, using a coherent organization in each sentence, and listing three reasons why this painter is their favorite detail (ELA 19; FL 1).

What do I want the students to know and be able to do?
By the end of this class, the students will be able to

- demonstrate the short, slap-dash brush strokes characteristic to the time period and necessary to complete an Impressionist painting
- explain that landscape subject matter was typical of this style
- identify the difference between Impressionist brushstrokes and the more realistic style of the time used by the French Salon
- create a landscape image of some part of the school landscape by taking a digital camera and then translating the photo image into a painting in the Impressionist style

How will I formatively and summatively assess the students' level of mastery of these concepts?

1. Pre-assessment: Students will complete a Venn diagram, comparing and contrasting Impressionism with realism. They will be permitted to use both words and actual examples of brushstrokes.

2. During the creation of the painting, I will circulate and demonstrate the brushstrokes on the canvas.

3. Prior to painting, I will show examples of such painters as Manet, Monet, Renior, etc., to assess the students' level of understanding.

continued on next page

4. I will create a visual quiz to check students' understanding of Impressionist work and then create a practice sheet that will show their use of the different brushstrokes.

What activities and sequence of activities in the lesson will result in the highest levels of student mastery?
1. Students will complete the pre-assessment note above. This will also serve as an activator of the previous learning about Realist style.
2. I will give students the background knowledge and examples of Impressionist artwork and artists.
3. Students will write a short statement on which painter is their favorite and why.
4. In groups, the students will go outside and sketch eight thumbnails of landscapes they find interesting.
5. Upon choosing a final thumbnail, students will take digital images of their proposed Impressionist paintings.
6. After the digital images are printed, the students will grid the photo on a one-inch grid and then do the same to the canvas, but as a two-inch grid.
7. The student will consider questions such as
    *   Which colors are warm and which are cool?
    *   How do I figure the darks and lights of the image?
    *   How do I create the proper brushstrokes that resemble Impressionist styles?
8. Upon completion, students will show their works and explain the pros and cons of this particular style of painting.

What knowledge about your teaching or the students would be most helpful to you in self-assessing your teaching in this lesson?
1. Was the time well managed?
2. Was there enough time to teach the content and ensure student mastery?
3. Was there understanding of the time period versus modern techniques for capturing the traditional landscape?

Sample of a High School Lesson Plan

Automotive Technology: Charging and Electrical Circuits
Essential Question: What are the properties of electricity found in various types of vehicle engines?

What do I want the students to know and be able to do (mastery objectives)?
1. Students will be able to identify 12 electrical symbols.
2. Students will be able to draw the three types of electrical circuits (S, P, and SP).
3. Students will be able to use a DVOM to test a 12-volt circuit for power and continuity.
4. Students will be able to use a 12-volt test light to test a 12-volt circuit/fuse for power.
5. Students will be able to test the cranking amps of a starter.
6. Students will explain the safety issues involved in working on the electrical circuits and precautions one takes to avoid these issues.
7. Students will be able to identify the two circuits of a starting system.
8. Students will be able to identify the parts and operation of the charging circuit.
9. Students will be able to use the "snap circuit board" to create three circuits.
10. Students will be able to identify the two types of voltage regulators.
11. Students will be able to use OHMs Law to calculate (V, A, and R).
12. Students will be able to explain why a string of Christmas lights go out when one bulb is bad or missing.
13. Students will be able to explain why the engine starts when the ignition key is turned.
14. Students will be able to explain how a car battery stays charged and continually able to provide energy on demand.

What are the district curriculum standards and the state curriculum framework?
1. Distict Standard: Course level—M (1–2) from the automotive learning expectations
2. State Frameworks: Science and Technology/Engineering Technology/ Engineering—Power and Energy Systems (9–12)

3. Activator: Demonstrate a string of Christmas lights going out when a bulb is removed. Do you know why this happens?
4. Summarizer: Each student will have a different electrical part on their desk and they will identify it and explain to the class what it does in the automotive electrical circuit.

How will I formatively and summatively assess the students' levels of mastery?
1. Pre-assessment: Students will take a one-question quiz by listing everything they know about the function of electricity in a car starter.
2. Use physical proximity to observe students as they disassemble and reassemble a starter; then, bench test it to see if it works.
3. Activity sheet requiring students to identify the three types of circuits on a diagram
4. Physical proximity to observe students testing the electrical circuits

Describe the sequence of events in the lesson.
1. Direct instruction to introduce series and parallel circuits, using light board.
2. Direct instruction to introduce electrical circuit testing tools—12-volt test light,
3. DVOM, inductive amp meter.
4. Continue (from last unit) to introduce electrical symbols–OHM, diode, variable resistor.
5. Introduce the three types of circuits (S, P, and SP)
6. Lab—hand out snap electrical boards; groups will build the three types circuits and test them.
7. Summarize circuits and circuit testing.
8. Introduce charging circuits—parts and operation.
9. Introduction to charging system test equipment; direct instruction and demonstration on how to test for starter amperage.
10. Lab—groups will test customer cars for voltage output.
11. Introduce starting circuits: parts and operation; A/V—computer animation on the parts and operation of the charging and starting circuits.
12. Introduce starting system tests and equipment; direct instruction on the purpose of the starter and alternator.
13. Lab—groups will disassemble and reassemble a starter and then bench test it to see if it work.
14. Lab—students will perform a cranking amp test on a variety of customer vehicles.

Sample of a High School Lesson Plan

High School Academic Counseling

Important Concept: Students will demonstrate the interpersonal skills needed to function effectively in a 21st century work environment.
What district curriculum standard (and/or benchmarks) does this lesson address?

Academic Development
Standard I: Skills for Academic Self-Confidence, Learning, and Success
Benchmarks:
A1: Learners will develop and demonstrate academic skills for the 21st century.
A2: Learners will develop and demonstrate academic skills for career and life management.

What do I want the students to know and be able to do?

Sample School District School Counseling Program Learning Outcomes

By the end of the class, the students will be able to
- demonstrate increased academic confidence in their ability to master mathematics concepts in their mathematics classes
- 1.1.a: describe whether they believe success in mathematics is due more to effort or to innate ability
- 1.1.b: express the belief that success in mathematics is more than 50 percent due to effort
- 1.4: accept greater responsibility for their own success during mathematics class by demonstrating increased effort as measured by the classroom teacher

How will I formatively and summatively assess the students' level of mastery of these concepts?

Pre-Assessment(s)

1. The classroom mathematics teacher will be asked to complete the Checklist for Success in a High School Classroom found in Chapter 3 of the book *Instructional Practices that Maximize Student Achievement* (Ribas, Deane, Seider, 2017) for each student in the class during the week prior to the start of this unit. The classroom mathematics teacher will complete the assessment again for each student one month after the conclusion of the unit and each month thereafter. The results of these administrations of the checklist will be compared to determine the level of growth.

2. The students will each complete the "Personal Mathematics Learning Profile" found in Chapter 4 of the book *Instructional Practices That Maximize Student Achievement* (Ribas, Deane, and Seider 2017) on the first day of the unit. Students will complete the profile on the last day of the unit and again two months after the end of the unit. The results of these profiles will be compared to determine the level of growth.

Formative Assessment(s)

1. The teacher will circulate around the classroom during partner and group discussions and make a mental note of the comments students make that indicate their "beliefs" as to the causes of success and failure in general, and in mathematics specifically.

2. The teacher will circulate around the room and make a mental note of the responses students give to the intelligence inventory. These will be collected and reviewed after the class.

Summative Assessment(s)

1. At the end of the unit, the classroom mathematics teacher will be asked to complete the "Checklist for Success in a High School Classroom" found in Chapter 3 of the book *Instructional Practices That Maximize Student Achievement* (Ribas, Brady, Deane, and Tamerat, 2017) for each student in the class.

2. At the end of the unit, the students will each complete the "Personal Mathematics Learning Profile" found in Chapter 6 of the book *Instructional Practices That Maximize Student Achievement* (Ribas, Brady, Deane, and Tamerat 2017).

3. The pre-assessment and summative assessment administration of these documents will be compared.

What activities and sequence of activities in the lesson will result in the highest levels of student mastery?

1. Students will be assigned partners using the processing partner sheets given to them by the classroom teacher. The Thomas Edison quote, "Intelligence is 1 percent inspiration and 99 percent perspiration," will be projected on the overhead. The partners will be given three minutes to develop an explanation of this quote in their own words.

2. After the three minutes, the partners will be paired with another set of partners and asked to tell them their explanation of the quote.

3. Students will complete the intelligence inventory in Chapter 7 of the book *Instructional Practices That Maximize Student Achievement* (Ribas, Brady, Deane, and Tamerat 2017) as the questions relate to their "mathematics intelligence."

4. The classroom teacher will chart the students' answers to Question 5 on a sheet of chart paper.

5. The students will be divided into two groups and asked to stand on either side of the room. One group will be those students who indicated mathematics intelligence is 50 percent or more due to effort. The other group will be those who indicated mathematics intelligence is less than 50 percent due to effort.

6. The students in each group will be asked to defend their positions.

7. The intelligence inventories will be collected, reviewed by the teacher, and saved for future comparison.

8. The counselor will explain the "Personal Mathematics Learning Profile" found in Chapter 6 of the book *Instructional Practices That Maximize Student Achievement* (Ribas, et al. 2017). As part of the explanation, the counselor will define terms such as manipulative, distract, and any other terms he or she anticipates may be unfamiliar to the students.

9. The students will be asked to read through the document without writing on it and to ask any questions they have about items they do not understand.

10. The students will complete the profile for homework.

If a colleague were observing my class to give me ideas for improving the teaching of this lesson, what data could he or she gather that would be most helpful to me in improving the lesson?

As a guidance counselor, I only teach two or three periods each week. I get so focused on the lesson plan that I have trouble monitoring those students who are not on task. It would be helpful to me to know which students are off task at what times.

References

Anderson, L., Krathwohl, D., Airasian, P., Cruikshank, K., Mayer, R., Pintrich, P., Raths. J., and M. Wittrock, eds. *A Taxonomy for Learning, Teaching, and Assessing: A Revision of Bloom's Taxonomy of Educational Objectives*. New York: A. B. Longman, 2001.

Armstrong, T. *The Best Schools: How Human Development Research Should Inform Educational Practices*. Alexandria, VA: Association for Supervision and Curriculum Development, 2006.

Black, P.J. and Wiliam, D. "Assessment and Classroom Learning." *Assessment in Education Principles, Policies, and Practices* 5 no. 1(1998): 7–73.

Brookline Public Schools. "Learning Expectations Grades 7 and 8." Brookline, MA (public school internal document).

Chappuis, S. and Chappuis, J. "The Best Value in Formative Assessment." *Educational Leadership* (Dec. 2007/Jan. 2008): 14–18.

Chappuis, S. and Stiggins, R.J. "Classroom Assessment for Learning." *Educational Leadership* 60 (2002): 40–43.

Clymer, J. and Wiliam, D. "Improving the Way We Grade Science." *Educational Leadership* (Dec. 2006/Jan. 2007): 36–42.

Curtis, R. "Achievement First: Developing a Teacher Performance Management System That Recognizes Excellence." *The Aspen Institute Education and Society Program*. Accessed July 22, 2016. http://files.eric.ed.gov/fulltext/ED521072.pdf

Gregory, C. and Ribas, W. *Teacher Supervision and Evaluation That Works!!* 3rd ed. Westwood, MA: Ribas Publications, 2017.

Guskey, T.R. "Lessons of Mastery." *Educational Leadership* 68, no. 2 (2010): 3.

Hill, J.D. and Flynn, K.M. *Classroom Instruction That Works with English Language Learners*. Alexandria, VA: Association for Supervision and Curriculum Development, 2006.

Jacobs, H.H. *Mapping the Big Picture: Integrating Curriculum and Assessment K–12*. Alexandria, VA: Association for Supervision and Curriculum Development, 1997.

Machiavelli, N. *The Prince*. Translated by Marriott, W.K. Reprint of 1908 ed. *The Constitution Society*. Last updated November 11, 2011. http://www.constitution.org/mac/prince00.htm.

Marzano, R. "Objectives That Students Understand." *Educational Leadership* (May 2011): 86–87.

Marzano, R. "Targets, Objectives, Standards: How Do They Fit?" *Educational Leadership* 70, no. 8 (May 2013): 82–83.

Milken, L. *A Matter of Quality: A Strategy for Assuring the High Caliber of America's Teachers*. Santa Monica, CA: Milken Family Foundation, 1999.

O'Shea, M. *From Standards to Success*. Alexandria, VA: Association for Supervision and Curriculum Development, 2005.

Reeves, D. *Making Standards Work. How to Implement Standards-Based Assessments in the Classroom, School, and District*. 3rd ed. Englewood, CO: Advanced Learning Press, 2003.

Ribas, W., Brady, D., Deane, J., and Tamerat, S. *Instructional Practices That Maximize Student Achievement: For Teachers, By Teachers*. Westwood, MA: Ribas Publications, 2017.

Sanders, W.L. and Rivers, J.C. *Cumulative and Residual Effects of Teachers on Future Student Academic Achievement*. Knoxville, TN: University of Tennessee Value-Added Research and Assessment Center, 1996.

Stiggins, R. "Assessment FOR Learning in Upper Elementary Grades." *Phi Delta Kappan* 90, no. 6 (February 2009): 419–421. http://www.kappanmagazine.org/content/90/6.toc.

Strong, J.H. and Tucker, P. *Teacher Evaluation and Student Achievement*. Washington, DC: National Education Association, 2000.

Whitbeck, C. *Waterwheels: Lab Book Criteria*. Unpublished manuscript.

Wiggins, G. "How Good Is Good Enough?" *Educational Leadership* 71, no. 4 (December 2013/January 2014): 10–17.

Wiggins, G. *Educative Assessment: Designing Assessments to Inform and Improve Student Performance*. San Francisco: Jossey-Bass, 1998.

Wiggins, G. and McTighe, J. *Understanding by Design*. Expanded 2nd ed. Alexandria, VA: Association for Supervision and Curriculum Development, 2005.

Wiggins, G. and McTighe, J. *The Understanding by Design Guide to Creating High-Quality Units*. Alexandria, VA: Association for Supervision and Curriculum Development, 2011.

Bibliography of Related Readings

Alberti, S. "Making the Shifts." *Educational Leadership* 70, no. 4 (December 2012/January 2013): 24–27.

Barton, P.E. "National Education Standards: To Be or Not to Be?" *Educational Leadership* 67, no. 7 (April 2010): 22–29.

Black, P. and Wiliam, D. "Inside the Black Box: Raising Standards Through Classroom Assessment." *Phi Delta Kappan* 92, no. 1 (September 2010): 81–90.

Burns, M. "Go Figure: Math and the Common Core." *Educational Leadership* 70, no. 4 (December 2012/January 2013): 42–46.

Burns, M. "Snapshots of Student Misunderstanding." *Educational Leadership* 67, no. 5 (February 2012): 31–35.

Ceballos, P.T. "A Rural County Journeys to the Common Core." *School Administrator* 69, no. 11 (December 2012): 26–29.

Crawford, J.T. "Aligning Common Core, One Bite at a Time." *School Administrator* 69, no. 11 (December 2012): 19–23.

Cuban, L. "Standards vs. Customization: Finding the Balance." *Educational Leadership* 69, no. 5 (February 2012): 10–15.

Deddeh, H., Main, E., and Matzlaff, S. "Eight Steps to Meaningful Grading." *Phi Delta Kappan* 91, no. 7 (April 2010): 53–58.

Faulkner, V.N. "Why the Common Core Changes Math Instruction." *Phi Delta Kappan* 95, no. 2 (October 2013): 59–63.

Gallagher, K. "Reversing Readicide." *Educational Leadership* 67, no. 6 (March 2010): 36–41.

Gardner, N.S. and Powell, R. "The Common Core Is a Change for the Better." *Phi Delta Kappan* 95, no. 4 (December 2013/January 2014): 49–53.

Gianneschi, M. "One and the Same: College and Workforce Readiness." *School Administrator* 70, no. 5 (May 2013): 26–29.

Guskey, T.R., Swan, G.M., and Jung, L.A. "Grades That Mean Something: Kentucky Develops Standards-Based Report Cards." *Phi Delta Kappan* 93, no. 2 (October 2011): 52–57.

Guskey, T.R. "Lessons of Mastery Learning." *Educational Leadership* 68, no. 2 (October 2010): 52–57.

Himmele, W. and Persdees, H. "How to Know What Students Know." *Educational Leadership* 70, no. 1 (September 2012): 58–62.

Jung, L.A. and Guskey, T. "Grading Exceptional Learners." *Educational Leadership* 67, no. 5 (February 2010): 31–35.

Marzano, R. "High Expectations for All." *Educational Leadership* 68, no. 1 (September 2010): 82–85.

Marzano, R. "How to Show Student Learning." *Educational Leadership* 71, no. 2 (October 2013): 82–83.

McTighe, J. "LDC and UbD: Complementary Frameworks." EduCore (2013): 1–23.

McTighe, J. and Wiggins, G. "From Common Core Standards to Curriculum: Five Big Ideas." EduCore (2012): 1-12.

Phillips, V. and Wong, C. "Tying Together the Common Core of Standards, Instruction, and Assessments. *Phi Delta Kappan* 91, no. 5 (February 2010): 37–42.

Rollins, J.D. "An Early-Implementation District Promotes Staff Learning." *School Administrator* 69, no. 11 (December 2012): 20–21.

Sams, A. and Bergmann, J. "Flip Your Students' Learning." *Educational Leadership* 70, no. 6 (March 2013): 16–20.

Smith, M.W., Wilhelm, J., and Fredricksen, J. "The Common Core: New Standards, New Teaching." *Phi Delta Kappan* 94, no. 8 (May 2013): 45–48.

Turchi, L. and Thompson, A. "Shakespeare and the Common Core: An Opportunity to Reboot." *Phi Delta Kappan* 96, no. 1 (September 2013): 32–37.

Wiggins, G. "Seven Keys to Effective Feedback." *Educational Leadership* 70, no. 1 (September 2012): 11–16.

Wiggins, G. "Why We Should Stop Bashing State Tests." *Educational Leadership* 67, no. 6 (March 2010): 48–52.

Wiggins, G. and McTighe, J. *The Understanding by Design Guide to Creating High Quality Units*. Alexandria, VA: ASCD, 2011.

Willhoft, J.L. "Next-Generation Assessments Aligned to the Common Core." *School Administrator* 69, no. 11 (December 2012): 30–33.

Williams, C.S. "Just the Facts: Common Core State Standards." *Educational Horizons* (April/May 2012): 8–9.

William, D., Lee, C., Harrison, C. and Black, P.J. "Teachers Developing Assessment for Learning: Impact on Student Achievement." *Assessment in Education Principles, Policies, and Practices* 11, no. 1 (2004): 49–65.

Wolk, R. "Education: The Case for Making It Personal." *Educational Leadership* 67, no. 7 (April 2010): 16–21.

Students with Disabilities: Standards-Based Education

The discussion of standards-based education causes me to reflect on Horace Mann and the challenges he faced with the development of the first schools. Mann was determined to reform common schools to the point of making them superior to some of the best and most elite private schools. This is very similar to the current state of public education. Just as Mann used his position in government to persuade the residents of Massachusetts that the future of their state was tied to educating its neediest children, our current government has persuaded states in the nation that the future of our country is tied to the state of the public education system (Baines 2006).

New policies, expectations, and accountability measures have changed the way teachers teach and students learn. In addition, accountability measures such as No Child Left Behind (NCLB) and Common Core have changed the way schools view students with disabilities and how they provide special education services and supports to them (Devlin, et al. 2013). As standards-based education has evolved, students with disabilities have been affected. Standards-based education requires a depth of knowledge where students' foundational skills are imperative for their success in the classroom. A lack of those foundational skills or learning differences can greatly impact a student's ability to successfully access the curriculum.

The ability of general education teachers to differentiate instruction, implement appropriate accommodations, and collaborate with special education teachers in specially designing the instruction for students with disabilities ensures their success in this age of standards-based education. The *term differentiated instruction* is often referred to in regard to high-yield approaches to improve instruction for all students. However, one area that is often overlooked with differentiated instruction that greatly affects the diverse needs of students with disabilities is multiple intelligences (GENIUS 2002). Differentiated instruction and multiple intelligences will be further explored in Chapters 6 and 7.

Before one can plan and implement an accommodation, there must first be an understanding of what accommodations are. An accommodation changes how the student learns the material (Strom 2015); this is why planning for accommodations is so important.

Unfortunately, there has been very little preparation for general educators to learn how to implement accommodations. The best way to overcome this preparation gap is ongoing collaboration with the special education teacher (Thompson, et al. 2005).

Collaborative planning supports both types of educators in meeting the needs of all students. It supports general education teachers with understanding the impact of a student's disability on his or her classroom performance. It also helps the general education teacher embed student-specific accommodations into the lesson, and it gives the general education teacher the opportunity to learn how a specific accommodation can be implemented. Special education teachers also benefit from collaborative planning; it helps them better understand the content being taught and the expectation of mastery of that content. In addition, for students who are pulled out with the special education teacher for portions of the day, it will align the teaching that occurs in the general education setting with that in a separate setting.

Anticipating difficulties that specific students may have with a given concept, creating alternatives to the differentiated lesson, and planning student-specific accommodations are areas that a teacher should address while planning standards-based lessons (Beam 2009). As we learned in step 1 of the "Five Basic Steps for Standards-Based Planning" in Chapter 1, we must be certain that the concepts we are teaching are indeed in our district's curriculum standards. In planning for students with disabilities, an additional concept of this step is to ensure that the Individualized Education Plan (IEP) goals align with those standards. Determining goals that are aligned with the standards, and the need and type of accommodations for students with disabilities, occurs during the IEP meeting by the IEP team. Aligning the goals with the grade-level standards ensures that students' skills are being addressed from a curriculum-standard focus rather than a skill-deficit focus. The challenge for general education teachers is being intentional about implementing those accommodations throughout the lesson. As a teacher continues following steps 2 through 5, a question should be pondered at each step: "How and in what ways do I need to embed accommodations in the lesson so that my students can access the learning?" This is also a question that should be explored in collaborative planning sessions between the general education and special education teachers.

Many of the accommodations for individual students can also be used for multiple students or the entire student group. Choosing a lesson-planning template that is designed so that the planned accommodations can be thoughtful and reflected upon across the lesson—from communicating the mastery objective to assessing mastery of the objective—ensures better access and learning for the student. For example, if you are planning a summative assessment and there is

a testing accommodation, this is planned and thought out before the assessment occurs. Doing so not only decreases student test anxiety but also supports the teacher with managing instructional time.

Specially designed instruction (SDI) is a requirement under the Individuals with Disabilities Education Act (IDEA). SDI specifies the teaching strategies and methods used with students with disabilities based on their individual needs and the impact of their disabilities. SDI is delivered by a special education teacher and can occur in both the general education classroom and a separate classroom (Logsdon 2014).

Specially Designed Instruction (SDI) Examples

Basic Reading

General Education Teachers Provide	Special Education Teachers Provide SDI
graphic organizers	visual strategies, including word recognition and visual memory for words
prompting and cueing	auditory strategies, including language structure at the word, sentence, and text levels
recorded materials	mnemonic strategies
oral/visual presentation of materials above independent reading level	fluency strategies

Math

General Education Teachers Provide	Special Education Teachers Provide SDI
graph/vertical lined paper	model, lead, test
calculator/number line	touch-five-coin counting strategy
extended time	visual/picture cues/prompts
modified assignment (number)	time delay

Written Language

General Education Teachers Provide	Special Education Teachers Provide SDI
provide copies of notes	picture prompts/physical prompts
story starters	tactile kinesthetic tracing
scripted writing task (scaffold)	preview skills/pre-writing activity
color-coded direction words	guided practice

The standards-based education movement has influenced curriculum and instruction planning. It has also affected and changed the way in which students with disabilities are supported in the general education classroom. There is ongoing brain research to identify early indicators of when students may begin

to struggle. This will begin to play a part in planning and teaching the standards, specifically for students with dyslexia and language problems. Teachers can be successful with this evolving system of standards-based education and teaching students with disabilities by collaborating with special education and general education colleagues on planning and preparing lessons; placing greater focus and emphasis on embedding accommodations in planning and throughout the delivery of instruction; and better understanding what general education and special education teachers should provide to students with disabilities to ensure their success.

References

Beam, A.P. "Standards-Based Differentiation: Identifying the Concept of Multiple Intelligence for Use with Students with Disabilities." *TEACHING Exceptional Children Plus* 5, no. 4 (2009): 2–13.

Devlin, T., Feldhaus, C., and Bentrem, K.M. "The Evolving Classroom: A Study of Traditional and Technology-Based Instruction in a STEM Classroom." *Journal of Technology Education* 25, no. 1 (2013): 34–54.

Gardner, H. "Howard Gardner's Theory of Multiple Intelligences." *GENIUS*. January 1, 2002. http://www.cse.emory.edu/sciencenet/mismeasure/genius/research02.html.

Logsdon, A. "SDI Is Required by IDEA." *About.com*, last updated December 15, 2014. http://learningdisabilities.about.com/od/publicschoolprograms/g/sdidefinition.htm.

Strom, E. "Accommodations and Modifications: How They're Different." *Understood.org*, December 20, 2013. https://www.understood.org/en/learning-attention-issues/treatments-approaches/educational-strategies/accommodations-and-modifications-how-theyre-different.

Thompson, S.J., Morse A.B., Sharpe M., and Hall, S. "Accommodations Manual: How to Select, Administer, and Evaluate Use of Accommodations for Instruction and Assessment of Students with Disabilities," 2nd ed. Washington, DC: US Office of Special Education Programs. August 2005. http://www.osepideasthatwork.org/toolkit/accommodations_manual.asp.

English Language Learners and Teacher Collaboration

"New, rigorous content standards have increased the need for collaboration among all educators" (Honigsfeld and Dove, pp. 48–49), and have contributed to a shift in the responsibilities of both the ESL teacher and the general education teacher. ESL teachers are now encouraged to become more familiar with high-priority standards of subject-matter knowledge and skills, and content teachers are expected to become more familiar with linguistics and objectives that facilitate academic language learning. Many states and provinces now offer, and sometimes require, an ESL endorsement or certificate for content teachers and a subject-matter or general-education license for ESL teachers. This overlap in areas of expertise can benefit English learners by having consistent language experiences connected to curriculum standards. As content and ESL teachers work together to align their themes and lessons, they facilitate two processes for English learners: English language development and the acquisition of subject-matter knowledge and skills.

English Language Learners and Content and Language Standards

When a third-grade science teacher outlines a unit or lesson on the inheriting traits and provides the ESL teacher with the Science Standard, the ESL teacher can then share relevant language objectives and expectations from the district's English language proficiency (ELP) curriculum standards. Together, the two teachers can discuss scaffolding for different proficiency levels and approaches that consider varying educational backgrounds of students. The table below demonstrates the alignment of content and language standards.

Second-Grade Science: Unit on Life Cycles and Adaptations: Alignment of Curriculum Standards and Planning Considerations for English Learners		
Content Standard	Science Standard: *Determine characteristics of plants and animals that provide protection and assist in survival.*	
Language Standard	ELP Standard: *Identify science vocabulary and phrases, and apply them while participating in an inquiry-based task.*	
Tasks-Building Schema	(1) *Observe* photographs of children wearing a helmet to ride a bike, putting on sunscreen, building a snowman. Ask what do these children wear to protect themselves? What factor has made them wear these things? (2) *Read Aloud* Steve Jenkins' *What Do You Do When Something Wants to Eat You?*	
Task Directions for Proficiencies*	Pre-Production-Early Production: label, identify, match, classify words/phrases with pictures and real objects	Speech Emergence-Intermediate Fluency: discuss, describe, explain with phrases and sentences
Cultural Connections	Identify and use plants and animals that are native to students' home state, country, or region. Anticipate which plants and animals students may not have seen or heard of.	

* Refer to the "Stages of Second-Language Acquisition and Tiered Question" from the Introduction of this book.

English Language Learners and Academic Language

While English learners are still expected to rapidly acquire social language, or what Jim Cummins (2006) has considered basic interpersonal communication skills (BICS), experts in the field of second-language acquisition (SLA) have amplified Cummins' concept of cognitive academic language proficiency (CALP) to include specific language skills beyond vocabulary and phrases related to content topics. Linguists and educators in the field of language acquisition have not yet settled on one specific definition for academic language, but most now look at the language demand involved in reading, writing, speaking, and listening. They examine the function of language in each content area, and refer to multiple language features such as words, sentences, grammar, and extended discourse. Gottlieb explains that "the academic language needed for students to access disciplinary content and textbooks and successfully participate in activities and assessments involves knowledge and ability to use specific linguistic features associated with academic disciplines" (2014, p. 5).

Teaching Vocabulary Explicitly and in Context

Academic language is not limited to words and phrases, but it does include a range of essential vocabulary that does not come about in social contexts. Ask yourself, "How will I offer sufficient opportunities for my English learners to practice and learn new words and content-specific language needed to master curriculum information and skills in the curriculum standards?" Teachers can initiate a linguistic analysis of the vocabulary needed for all students to successfully learn and demonstrate understanding in lesson activities and assessments. For a lesson on plant and animal adaptation, teachers may choose to classify words into three tiers (Beck, McKeown, and Kucan 2013). This typically includes vocabulary identified for the native/near-native English speakers as well as additional words that may be unfamiliar to English learners.

Adaptations of Plants and Animals: Classifying and Categorizing Vocabulary		
Tier One: *familiar and easily supported with visuals, real objects, and act-out activities.*	**Tier Two:** *less familiar, more complex words that may be found in and taught with grade/age-appropriate text.*	**Tier Three:** *technical, and most complex words used in specific content*
thorn, prickly, claw, feathers, fur, quill, scale, horn	classify, poisonous, venom, scent, defense mechanism, predator, prey	camouflage, adaptation, trait, migration, hibernation, behavior

Beck, et. al. 2002 and 2013; Calderón 2011

Calderón recommends explicit pre-teaching and analyzing words before the content lesson (2011, p. 70). Word-study accommodations for English learners can be done within the general-education classroom and benefit all learners. Students with intermediate or advanced fluency and native English speakers can participate together in vocabulary analysis of tier-two and -three words. During that cooperative group analysis, the classroom teacher or ESL teacher can facilitate a homogeneous group of less proficient English learners in becoming familiar with relevant content words from tiers one and two. This word work can also be done with the ESL teacher during centers-based work, a warm-up activity, or in a small pull-out group. Students new to English will still need to participate with their peers in heterogeneous group work and tasks that employ content-specific vocabulary from tiers two and three.

As you prepare the complete vocabulary list for all learners, consider using student-friendly phrases to define in addition to dictionary definitions that sound "scientific." Mixed pairs or groups of native English speakers and English learners can create their own definitions and have them checked by a teacher. Word analysis can also involve labeling parts of speech, listing possible affixes, and composing context-rich sample sentences. Some students, including English learners, may need a visual connection to remember a word. Internet images are easy to copy and paste next to each term and many images are free. (Be sure to check your district's fair use policy.) Any student can create quick sketches and refer to them as the class discusses the terms. The total estimated time for vocabulary preview activities within the general-education classroom suggested here is approximately 15 minutes, but this will depend on the number and complexity of the terms and/or phrases. Students with lower English proficiency (i.e., speech-emergent level and earlier) will temporarily utilize posted word-picture walls or personal word journals that include some basic scientific phrases, or sentence frames such as "A ___ protects itself by ___" or "An animal uses its ___ for protection."

English Language Learners, Language Structure, Sentences and Extended Discourse

Since the Common Core State Standards are "based on rigorous content and application of knowledge through higher-order thinking skills" (CCSS 2012),

all students will need to participate in challenging activities and inquiry-based tasks in order to internalize and apply what they know and can do. The strategies mentioned here may be used with or without the ESL teacher present. They are language-based activities that require critical thinking, support content standards, and facilitate the participation of English learners of varying proficiency levels in general education classrooms.

Lessons that follow up word analysis involve learning activities and discussions that require new vocabulary, word/phrase lists, and sentence frames that employ those new words. Think about ways to contextualize the pre-taught vocabulary and continue your linguistic analysis by asking, "Which sentence structures do I expect my students to use during collaborative group work?" For example, in science and social studies, students may need to use the passive voice for conveying a more formal, school-like style or *register* in order to "sound scientific" or "like a news reporter." English learners do not learn this naturally and rely on explicit instruction from the ESL and content teachers to understand expectations, be successful in content-based tasks (Aguirre-Munoz 2010, p. 264), and practice language structures necessary for discourse and investigation.

One way for all students to anticipate expected responses is by analyzing questions. Pairs or small groups can spend a few minutes responding to a critical thinking question, prompt, or scenario. Students can categorize question starters or prompts as easy, difficult, or challenging. They will quickly decipher that questions starting with *do, does, did, is*, or *are* elicit a yes or no answer, while questions that start with *what, how*, and *why* require longer responses and usually more time. Other activities that motivate essential peer-to-peer interaction, extended discourse, and critical thinking involve inquiry-based prompts, hands-on investigations, or the development of open-ended dialogues for which student groups negotiate endings and outcomes.

Background Knowledge and Skills

When planning for each curriculum standard, it is beneficial for teachers to become aware of background knowledge, skills, and experiences students bring from home or other environments related to their culture, faith, and language. English learners are resourceful; they use what they know and can do (Cloud, Genesee, and Hamayan 2009, p. 9), and they have significant contributions to offer their learning community. English learners may even be experts in geography, weather, climate, math concepts, folktales, or content vocabulary with a cognate or connection to their home language(s). In another respect, awareness of students' background knowledge may also prevent cultural or social conflicts, misconceptions, or confusing contexts for students. This includes false cognates, political predispositions, idioms, cultural assumptions, or unfamiliar pop culture. We may make assumptions that the students we teach have common knowledge of topics. These might include folk tales, nursery rhymes, popular songs, famous personalities, American sports, foods, technology, or fashion. Planning for students with diverse background knowledge and experiences is essential for English learners' success in school and also assists any student who may have had unique life experiences.

References

Aguirre-Muñoz, Z., and Amabisca, A.A. "Defining Opportunity to Learn for English Language Learners: Linguistic and Cultural Dimensions of ELLs' Instructional Contexts." *Journal for the Education of Students Placed at Risk* 15, no. 3 (2010): 259–278.

Beck, I.L., McKeown, M. G., and Kucan, L. *Bringing Words to Life: Robust Vocabulary Instruction.* 2nd ed. New York: The Guilford Press, 2013.

Beck, I.L., McKeown, M.G., and Kucan, L. *Bringing Words to Life: Robust Vocabulary Instruction.* New York: The Guilford Press, 2002.

Calderón, M. *Teaching Reading and Comprehension to English Learners.* Bloomington, IN: Solution Tree Press, 2011.

Cloud, N., Genesee, G., and Hamayan, E. *Literacy Instruction for English Language Learners.* Portsmouth, NH: Heinemann, 2009.

Cummins, J. *Language, Power and Pedagogy: Bilingual Children in the Crossfire.* Buffalo, NY: Multilingual Matters Ltd., 2006.

Gottlieb, M. and Ernst-Slavit, G. *Academic Language in Diverse Classrooms: Definitions and Contexts.* Thousand Oaks, CA: Corwin, 2014.

Honigsfeld, A. and Dove, M.G. *Collaboration and Co-Teaching for English Learners: A Leader's Guide.* Thousand Oaks, CA: Corwin. 2015.

National Governors Association Center for Best Practices & Council of Chief State School Officers. (2010). *Common Core State Standards.* Washington, DC.

Creating a Cognitive Context for Learning

While Chapter 1 focused on the preparation and planning that we as educators need to do in order to begin the school day ready to serve as effective *teachers*, we will turn now in Chapter 2 to the steps we can take to help our students begin a class period, unit, or activity in the mindset of effective *learners*. Specifically, we will focus on the pedagogical strategies supported by research that we have used in our own classrooms to help our students more fully understand and then remember the information and skills they learn in class. These strategies fall into several categories: (1) strategies to consider before your students even enter your classroom; (2) strategies for effectively beginning a school year, unit, or class period; (3) strategies for maximizing learning; and (4) strategies for effectively concluding a unit or class period. Behind each one of these strategies is an explanation, from a cognitive perspective, of how each particular strategy supports student learning and retention. Some of these explanations we will discuss in great detail in this chapter; others we will touch upon briefly but withhold a full explanation of until Chapter 8, "The Brain and Student Learning."

Before They Walk through Your Classroom Door

As teachers, we like to hope that our students enter our classrooms each day healthy and ready to learn. We understand that there is a strong connection between the mind and the body, and that exercise, sleep, and nutrition all play important roles in proper brain functioning. Just as we would prepare a wall for paint by applying a primer, there are ways that students' brains can be "primed" for acquiring new material.

We begin this section by bringing your attention to the health-related behaviors that support the creation of a cognitive context for learning. We know that many of the suggestions we make here relate to activities that happen outside of school and are thus mostly out of teachers' control. Still, we urge you to support these healthful behaviors through clear, purposeful messaging about their benefits for both body and brain.

Exercise for Body and Mind

In this era of accountability, schools and educators are feeling tremendous pressure to allocate more and more of the school day to subjects such as math and language arts that are assessed through high-stakes testing. As a result, many schools are reducing or eliminating physical-education courses, and fewer than half of US schools today offer recess (Buscemi, et al. 2014). The rationale for these decisions is that all available time must be spent preparing students to succeed on the high-stakes assessments that lie ahead. While these decisions are made with the best of intentions, the research suggests that they are short-sighted. A 2011 synthesis of studies that looked at the effects of physical activity on academic and cognitive outcomes found a "significant and positive effect of physical activity on children's achievement and cognitive outcomes" (Fedewa and Ahn, p. 521). Likewise, Bracy (2005) cites a study by University of Minnesota researchers who found that students concentrate better on their schoolwork after recess. Why is exercise good for learning? Alomari, et al., (2013) explain that exercise increases the brain's level of BDNF (brain-derived neurotrophic factor), a chemical that plays a significant role in brain plasticity, or the ability of the brain to make and reorganize its neural connections. When individuals have low levels of BDNF, they have difficulty creating new memories or recalling old ones. It is for this reason that Harvard psychiatrist John Raty has referred to BDNF as "Miracle-Gro for the brain." In short, exercise and physical activity are necessary not just for physical health, but also for providing individuals with the chemicals in their brain that facilitate learning and memory.

Even in the absence of recess and sufficient physical education, there are some quick and easy ways that teachers can build movement into their classes each day. For example, in Chapter 8 we discuss the possibility of incorporating kinesthetically based activities to either jumpstart a lesson or reinforce content. Mid-lesson stretching breaks are another way to get students moving in a way that requires little

time and classroom space. All of this is to say that while the demands of greater accountability paired with strained resources can create a barrier to ensuring that students get a healthy dose of physical activity on a daily basis, we as educators can surely rely on our creative abilities to help our students reap the benefits of physical movement on learning.

Getting Enough Sleep

Parents and teachers have always told students that getting enough sleep is important. Today, there is a growing body of research that proves it. Sprenger (2005) reports on a study that found students who slept only six hours after a day of learning were able to remember much less about what they had learned than students who had slept eight hours. In drawing from research like this, the American Academy of Pediatrics issued a statement in 2014 suggesting that school districts start school no earlier than 8:30 a.m. to ensure that middle and high school students get a recommended eight and a half hours of sleep per night.

In Chapter 8 of this book, we describe the central role that sleep plays in the brain's creation of new neurons and in the development of long-term memory. There are socio-emotional benefits associated with getting adequate sleep as well. It is partially with this information in mind that a number of school systems across the country have been pushing back the start times of their high schools. Examples of such school systems include Arlington, Virginia; Milwaukee, Wisconsin; South Burlington, Vermont; and Tulsa, Oklahoma. Recently, researchers from the University of Minnesota's Center for Applied Research and Educational Improvement reported on the many academic benefits of a later school start time. Analyzing data from eight high schools in Colorado, Minnesota, and Wyoming, they found that a delayed morning resulted in improved test scores and attendance rates (McGuire 2015). Although this evidence is quite positive, we recognize that many, if not the majority of, school districts across the nation may not be in a position to switch to a later start because of real-life factors like transportation costs and schedules. Still, the moral of the story seems to be that students need to get their sleep. In Chapter 8 of this book, we discuss the impacts of insufficient sleep on the brain, as well as give a few tips for how students can get a more restful night's sleep. If your school is one that has an early start time (and even if it is not!), we recommend that you take regular opportunities to communicate the benefits of getting sufficient sleep each night to your students and their families.

Nutrition

While more about the effects of nutrition on the brain will be discussed in Chapter 8, it is enough to note here that there is clear evidence from educational research that good nutrition leads to students demonstrating better moods and behaviors (Jensen 2005). For this reason, it is crucial that students begin each day with a healthy breakfast. We know that, as with sleep, nutrition is an area of our students' lives that may be largely out of our control, except to send clear messages about best practices and why nutrition is important. In light of this apparent limitation, it is good to know that in some communities where nutrition may be more acutely at risk due to poverty and related issues, free and reduced-cost breakfast is often made available to students. This is particularly helpful, because both experts and conventional wisdom tell us that students who are hungry are less successful in the classroom. For example, Eric Jensen (2005, p. 36) tells us, "Students who show up in class with low blood sugar are likely to be tired, listless, and inattentive." We can recall from our own experience as teachers the differences in levels of student energy before the lunch period compared with after lunch.

Regardless of whether your students receive free or reduced breakfast at school, here is a small step you may be able to take to avoid a nutrition-related energy slump at any time of day: Jensen recommends, and we tend to agree with him, that in the absence of a school-wide "no eating or drinking in class" policy, that teachers consider the possibility of letting students bring snacks, or at least water, into class with them. Of course, there are inappropriate foods that students could bring to class with them, as well as inappropriate and distracting ways that students can eat such food. However, if there are clear expectations about the types of food that are permissible as well as the quiet, inconspicuous manner in which students are permitted to eat during class, the result may be a classroom of students who are cognitively better prepared for the content, materials, and instruction to which they are being exposed. (See Chapter 3 for establishing expectations.)

> *Students are better able to learn and retain information when their teacher explains at the outset of the lesson what information students will learn and what they will be expected to do with that information.*

Strategies for Beginning Class
Sharing Mastery Objectives

In Chapter 1, we discussed the use of mastery objectives in lesson and unit planning. To review briefly, mastery objectives list the information and skills of a given curriculum in language that describes student products and performances. You will notice that each chapter in this book begins with the mastery objectives for the learning we expect to occur upon reading that chapter.

What is the value of beginning each chapter in this way? The answer to this question varies for each reader. Some readers, upon acquiring this book, are willing to dive straight into each chapter with only the chapter's title for guidance. Other readers are more discerning. Before investing the time and energy to read a particular chapter in this book, they want to know precisely what they will get out of it. One reason we have included the mastery objectives at the outset of each chapter is for this second type of reader.

A second reason we have included mastery objectives at the outset of each chapter is to support *all* of our readers in learning and retaining the information presented in these chapters. How do mastery objectives provide this support? In *Accessing the General Curriculum*, Victor Nolet and Margaret McLaughlin (2005, p. 37) explain that "teachers can help their students learn and remember like experts when they are clear about the types of information they want their students to learn and make clear the manner in which the information will be used." In other words, students are better able to learn and retain information when their teacher explains at the outset of the lesson what information students will learn and what they will be expected to *do* with that information. In fact, Dean, et al., (2012) report that a recent study on the links between mastery objectives and student achievement found a positive effect on student achievement (a growth of 12 percentile points) when mastery objectives were employed. In a similar vein, this book's readers are better able to learn and retain the information in each chapter of this book when we include mastery objectives at the outset of each chapter.

In reading the earlier description of this book's two types of readers, it may have occurred to you that our students typically fall into these same two categories as well. Some students, upon entering our classrooms, are uninterested in discovering what the upcoming class period will hold. Whether out of a belief that *anything* we teach them will be useful or, in some cases, the opposite belief, some of our students feel no need for a preview of the learning that lies ahead. As is the case with readers of this book, however, there is a second group of students that feels differently. These are the students who, upon entering the classroom, immediately demand to know, "What are we doing today?" They might also fire questions at us like the following:

"Are we doing something fun?"
"Are we watching a video?"
"Can we go outside?"
"Are you collecting the homework?"
"Are we going over the homework?"
"Will there be time to review for the test tomorrow?"

The list of these types of questions could go on and on. For these students, the mastery objectives help to answer these questions. And for *all* students, the mastery objectives provide context for the information and skills they are about to learn. As mentioned above, such context increases the likelihood of students retaining this new learning in their long-term memories.

For middle school and high school teachers, our students are often advanced enough that we can simply share with the class our mastery objectives as they exist in our lesson plans. For elementary school teachers, we will likely need to translate the mastery objectives in our lesson plans into language more comprehensible to younger learners. Examples of such translations can be found in Chapter 1.

In what form should we share these mastery objectives? Different teachers utilize different strategies. Some teachers prefer to type up their mastery objectives for a particular unit and then distribute them to students as a handout upon beginning the unit. Students are expected to keep this handout in the front of their binders for the duration of the unit. This technique seems particularly suited to middle and high school teachers for whom a unit may last several weeks. Other teachers prefer to write the mastery objectives on a large sheet of flipchart paper or on a whiteboard in a location where students will notice them.

An additional point worth noting here is the strength of mastery objectives as an organizational tool. When going through daily the routines of our classes, it is ever so easy to venture off topic. Mastery objectives help us as teachers remain focused on what is most important in our lessons, reducing the likelihood that we spend valuable time on tangential items that might confuse our students or interfere with their mastery of important topics. Many of us are likely to recall a teacher from our past who struggled with keeping on topic in class. Posting mastery objectives so that they are visible to both students and the teacher help keep us all on track to meeting our objectives.

Sharing Daily Agendas

For those students who enter class needing to know, "What are we going to do today?" the mastery objectives provide only half of the answer. The mastery objectives essentially describe the finished product; they list the information that students in the class will hold and the skills they will be able to perform at the conclusion of the unit or lesson. The agenda, in contrast, describes the steps that the class will take to achieve these outcomes. A class agenda might be the following:

Figure 2.1

Agenda for February 6th, Period 3

1. *Noun Review* Do Now activity.
2. Collect and answer questions about last night's homework.
3. Record the definition of *adjective* in the "Grammar Terms" section of our notebooks.
4. Do the paper-bag activity with partners.
5. Practice finding adjectives in the sentences on the overhead projector.
6. Exit Ticket

As is the case with mastery objectives, middle and high school teachers will often be able to transcribe the agendas they share with their students word for word from their daily lesson plans. In contrast, the agendas that elementary school teachers share with their students may have to be "translated" into language more comprehensible to young learners.

Also similar to mastery objectives is our recommendation that teachers write their daily agendas on the whiteboard or on pieces of flipchart paper and then post these papers in easily visible spots on the front walls of their classrooms. Such a practice is in keeping with Nolet and McLaughlin's (2005, p. 40) recommendation that teachers "establish and keep schedules of classroom activities and events and provide systematic reminders for students of the sequence in which activities will occur." What is the value of keeping students informed about the sequence of activities within a given lesson or class period? First, in situations both inside and outside of school, most of us appreciate knowing what a particular meeting or engagement will involve. We generally expect our principals to provide us with an agenda at the start of faculty meetings, and we expect the same from our department heads prior to department meetings. If we don't know how many items are on the agenda or what topic is coming next, we may find it difficult to concentrate on the current topic of discussion. Instead, our mind is preoccupied with whether the meeting will end in time for us to make it to the dry cleaners or whether we are finally going to get to discuss new book orders for next year. Without an agenda, our students can become similarly preoccupied and unable to focus on the instruction that is taking place.

A second way in which an agenda supports student learning relates to Nolet and McLaughlin's mention of keeping students informed about the sequence of activities within a given class period. If you glance back at the sample agenda in Figure 2.1, you can see how providing students with an agenda better enables them to understand how the various pieces of a lesson fit together. In this sample lesson on adjectives, for example, the agenda reveals a logical sequence for learning. After the Do Now, students learn and write down the definition of *adjective* and then do the paper-bag activity, an activity in which students must reach into a lunch bag without looking and come up with five words that describe the object hidden inside. A partner then tries to guess the contents of the paper bag based on the five adjectives. Such an activity allows students to connect the definition of *adjective* that they have written in the "Grammar Terms" section of their notebooks with the descriptive words they come up with during the paper-bag activity. Finally, students will work as a class to identify the adjectives in sentences projected onto the front board. Such a lesson moves students from a *definition* to making a *connection* and finally to an *application*. Informing students of this sequence through a posted agenda allows them to better understand the way in which each of these separate activities fits into the teacher's larger goals—the mastery objectives. As we will discuss in more detail both later in this chapter and again in Chapter 8, students are better able to transfer information into their long-term memories when information "is presented in a meaningful context rather than as disparate bits of information" (Nolet and McLaugh-

The mastery objectives describe the finished product; they list information that students will hold and skills they will be able to perform at the conclusion of the unit or lesson. The agenda, in contrast, describes the steps that the class will take to achieve these outcomes.

lin 2005, p. 37). Posting both an agenda and mastery objectives can provide students with the context they need to transfer the content they are learning into their long-term memory.

Perhaps just as important for students as understanding the way in which different activities within a class period connect to each other is knowing the different *types* of activities that lie ahead. For example, in the lesson on adjectives, students in this class are engaged in some fairly standard "seat work." They are working independently to transcribe the definition of *adjective* into the "Grammar Terms" section of their notebooks. For students who are kinesthetic learners or who are dying to interact with their friends, such an activity can feel like a tedious one. By virtue of a posted agenda, however, those students itching for a more hands-on activity or the opportunity to work with a partner can see that such an activity is just a few moments away.

One example of a teacher utilizing the agenda to inform his or her students about the different types of activities ahead involves a young colleague of ours with a particularly chatty class of students. In essence, he had difficulty keeping them quiet long enough to provide any direct instruction himself. As a means of solving this problem, our colleague began writing in parentheses after each item on the daily agenda either "teacher talks" or "students talk." His goal in this modification was to help his students understand before the daily lesson had even begun that there would be some points in the lesson at which they would need to listen to his direct instruction and other points in the lesson at which he would solicit their thoughts and insights. While this young colleague of ours has since grown more adept at integrating his direct instruction and students' contributions, this slight modification to the agenda went a long way toward creating a more orderly environment during his class periods. His chatty students were better able to listen to what their teacher had to say when they could see on the agenda that several opportunities lay ahead for them to contribute to the class discussion.

Finally, posting an agenda also has the positive effect of keeping teachers and students "on track" over the course of a lesson or class period. At the end of the previous section, we discussed how, at times, it can be easy to deviate from our instructional plan as we spontaneously make connections to related and/or interesting ideas. Jackson and Zmuda (2014) remind us that "when you're in the weeds of daily instruction, you may lose sight of the larger purpose" (p. 20). As the agenda effectively represents what we believe the class should accomplish over the course of the period, it serves as a useful tool for ensuring that we meet our goals for the lesson. Though we may sometimes need to make adjustments to take advantage of a particularly astute question or to explain a particularly difficult concept, the agenda can also remind us not to linger unnecessarily on defining, for example, the term *adjective* at the expense of the paper-bag activity. And, ironically, we have found that posting an agenda can often lead to our students keeping *us* on track. While it is easy to forget to consult the lesson plan we have created for the day's lesson, posting the agenda involves our students in ensuring that we get through all of the necessary content for that particular class period. Somewhat to our surprise, students really do tend to keep us honest in regards to getting through the activities posted on the agenda. Whether it is because they know that they will need to complete all of these activities in order to successfully complete their nightly homework assignment or because they enjoy the opportunity to good-naturedly chastise their teacher, a good number of our students really do pay attention to the posted agenda and take steps to move the class along if they fear that we are in danger of not getting through the listed activities.

Educators now recognize that students become more focused, attentive learners throughout the class period when they understand precisely what they will be expected to do that night for homework.

Assigning Homework

In the previous section, we shared the point that students are more likely to store the content we are teaching them in their long-term memories when they are informed at the outset of the lesson of (1) what kind of information they will be learning and (2) what they will be expected to do with this information. Providing students with a lesson's mastery objectives allows them to see what kind of information they are about to learn as well as the various skills they will acquire. Providing students with the night's homework assignment *at the outset of the lesson* addresses the second point; such a strategy informs students what they will be expected to do with the information or skills they acquire.[1]

Providing students with their homework assignment at the beginning of a lesson is likely the opposite of what you recall from your own days as a student. Most of us remember our teachers announcing the homework assignment in the final moments of class or even as the bell signifying the end of the period was ringing. The advantage of such a strategy is that the teacher could adjust that evening's homework assignment based on how much content he or she had covered during the class period. However, educators now recognize that students become more focused, attentive learners throughout the class period when they understand precisely what they will be expected to do that night for homework. Such a benefit seems to outweigh the greater flexibility that comes with announcing the night's homework at the end of the class period or lesson.

Of course, one potential drawback to assigning homework at the beginning of the period is that our students may be tempted to try to start the homework assignment in class. There are a couple of responses to this issue. First, one question to ask is whether students are *able* to successfully complete the assigned homework. If so, then it is worthwhile for us to reflect upon the homework we are assigning. The purpose of homework, of course, is to help students synthesize and apply the learning they have done in class. If students are able to successfully complete a homework assignment in class, then there is likely some misalignment between the assignment and the learning they are supposed to be doing in class. Adjustments to either our instruction or our assignments may be necessary. If, on the other hand, students are incorrectly working on the homework during class, we suggest that teachers simply treat this behavior as a classroom management issue. In other words, we believe the appropriate response is for the teacher to redirect the behavior of this "early homework-doer" in the same way that we as teachers address students who are talking, passing notes, text messaging, etc.

Several of our elementary school colleagues have noted to us that assigning homework at the outset of a lesson may be a strategy better suited to middle and high school teachers than to elementary school teachers. Their reasoning is that younger children may find it alarming to be assigned homework for which they have not yet learned the information or skills necessary to complete it successfully. Our colleagues' point is well taken. Other elementary school teachers find

---

1   For students with some disabilities, the teacher will need to check to ensure that the assignment is written correctly. These students may be more likely not to write the assignment down or to transcribe it incorrectly. The special education teachers also note that when special needs students get their homework assignments correctly written, the special educators are better able to assist those students with the assignments.

the strategy of assigning homework at the outset of a lesson quite successful as long as the assignment is accompanied by a clear, reassuring explanation to students that they are about to learn the skills *right now* that are necessary to complete the evening's homework assignment.

In this section, we have discussed *when* in the course of a lesson or class period homework should be assigned. A final point about assigning homework concerns *where* the assignment itself should be written. As is the case with mastery objectives, different teachers have different strategies concerning this topic. Some teachers prefer to provide students on Monday morning with a handout listing the homework assignments for the entire week (or longer). Such a practice gives eager students the opportunity to work ahead if they so choose. Even for teachers who follow such a practice, however, we recommend listing the night's homework assignment either on a corner of the blackboard or on a second piece of flipchart paper hanging in the front of the classroom. The reasoning is the same as that behind posting the mastery objectives and agenda for a given class period: posting homework assignments, inspirational quotations, student work, etc., around the classroom serves as a stimulus that "feeds the brain." Posting the nightly homework assignment might be particularly useful in that a student who "spaces out" for a moment and finds himself or herself glancing at that evening's homework assignment will be reminded of the content or skills necessary to complete that assignment. Such a reminder will serve as a motivator for this student to refocus on the lesson at hand!

Activators

Activators are activities utilized at the beginning of a lesson or class period that either provide a brief review of the previous day's work or activate students' present knowledge of the topic to be taught in the upcoming lesson or class period. The most effective activators are those that accomplish both of these goals, effectively serving as a bridge that links the previous day's lesson and students' pre-existing knowledge to the lesson ahead. Activators also serve to give us a sense of how much information our students already know or remember about a particular topic, thereby serving as a quick pre-assessment for the lesson.

Give-One-Get-One

An example of an activator we often use is called Give-One-Get-One. In this activity, our students receive a sheet of paper with six to twelve boxes (see the following sample), and they are asked to write in *one* of the boxes a fact about the topic of the upcoming lesson that they already know. We then instruct students to circulate around the room for approximately five minutes, sharing their pieces of information with other students in the class and collecting information from their peers in return. They are to place the information they learn from their peers in the empty boxes contained on their handouts. At the end of this activity, students have filled in as many boxes as possible with information about the topic of the day's lesson. Below are examples of this activity used in various ways.

Example of a Give-One-Get-One

As noted in our mastery objectives, today we will learn about the causes of the Civil War. Write one fact you know about the causes of the Civil War in the box in the upper left-hand corner. When the teacher says "Circulate," approach a classmate and give your fact to that classmate. Then, write that classmate's fact in another box (if it is different than the one you have). Continue to trade information with classmates until either you fill up your box or the teacher asks you to stop.

Example of a Give-One-Get-One

Below is an example of the sheet after the activity is completed.

As noted in our mastery objectives, today we will learn about the causes of the Civil War. Write one fact you know about the causes of the Civil War in the box in the upper left-hand corner. When the teacher says "Circulate," approach a classmate and give your fact to that classmate. Then, write that classmate's fact in another box (if it is different than the one you have). Continue to trade information with classmates until either you fill up your box or the teacher asks you to stop.

The disagreement between the North and South about the abolition of slavery.	The South favored stronger states' rights. The North favored a stronger central government.
The South wanted the Northerners to aggressively enforce laws that required escaped slaves to be returned to their masters. Many Northerners openly disobeyed these laws.	The South had an agrarian society and the North had an industrial society. This led to disagreements about laws regulating and/or taxing trade.
The South had an active trade with England. England bought much of the cotton, tobacco, and other crops raised by Southern farmers. Since the South had very little industry, it wanted to purchase English manufactured goods without added costs due to tariffs.	

Other Examples of a Give-One-Get-One Include the Following:

In the box in the upper left-hand corner, write one piece of information you remember from yesterday's class. When the teacher says "Circulate," approach a student and give your fact to that student, and then write that student's fact in another box (if it is different from the one you have). Continue to do this with other students until either you fill up your boxes or the teacher asks you to stop.

In the box in the upper left-hand corner, write one of the common applications of physics we see in our everyday lives. When the teacher says "Circulate," approach a student and give your fact to that student, and then write that student's fact in another box (if it is different from the one you have). Continue to do this with students until you either fill up your boxes or the teacher asks you to stop.

K-W Activator

Another commonly used activator is referred to as a K-W Activator. The **K-W** stands for *Know* and *Want to Know*. This activity involves asking students to chart what they already know or think they know about a topic to be studied and the questions they have about the topic. This activator can be completed individually, in pairs, in small groups, or as a full-class brainstorming activity. The following is an example of a K-W Activator.

K-W Activator	
What I know about chemical reactions	What I want to know about chemical reactions

Cloze Activator

A cloze activity is an activator that can be used to assess students' existing knowledge of vocabulary terms, while previewing the new vocabulary that will be a part of that day's lesson. It is, essentially, a fill-in-the blank paragraph that students are to complete, often with the assistance of a word bank provided by the teacher. The following are two ways that a cloze activity might be used in a mathematics class. As you can see, in the second example, vocabulary words have been substituted for numerical values, and students are instructed to fill in the blanks for a multi-step algebra problem, this time, without a word bank.

Cloze Example No. 1 (Polynomials)

An _____ is a mathematical relationship that says one quantity is smaller than another. The inequality "6μ<18" reads 6 times a number _____ 18. The expression "18<6μ" reads 6 times a number _____ 18. The expression −17÷ reads the _____ of −17.

Word Bank:

is less than	*expression*	*absolute value*	*base*
reciprocal	*exponent*	*variable*	*cube*
less than	*inequality*	*monomial*	*opposite*
coefficient	*binomial*	*constant*	*trinomial*

Cloze Example No. 2 (Algebra)

Line 1: 3(__ × -3) + 4(_ × + _)

Line 2: = _ × - _ + 24× + 28

Line 3: = _ × + 24× - 9 + 28

Line 3: = 39× + __

The following are examples of additional ways that activators can be used to get students thinking about what they already know as they preview the day's lesson.

Example of an Agree/Disagree Activator

Literature and Justice
Mr. Seider
Illegal Immigration Unit

Anyone who wants to come to America should be allowed to come.

Strongly Agree	1	2	3	4	5	6	*Strongly Disagree*

If an undocumented worker is sick, he or she should be treated at a hospital.

Strongly Agree	1	2	3	4	5	6	*Strongly Disagree*

If an undocumented worker needs a costly heart transplant in order to survive, he or she should receive it.

Strongly Agree	1	2	3	4	5	6	*Strongly Disagree*

The children of undocumented workers should be allowed to attend a public school.

Strongly Agree	1	2	3	4	5	6	*Strongly Disagree*

Example of a "How Do You...?" Activator

Math 7
Ms. Sylvain

Think back to yesterday's lesson when we learned the process of graphing linear equations. In the space below, please explain, in order, each of the steps that you would take to graph the following:

$y = 10x+2$

Example of a "Create-Your-Own-Sentence" Activator

Earth Science 6
Ms. Levangie
Energy Unit
Word Bank

Hydro Power	Emissions	Nuclear Energy
Renewable Source	Carbon Footprint	Solar Power
Non-Renewable Source	Fossil Fuels	Wind Turbine

Write 5 different sentences using five of the words above.

1. _____

2. _____

3. _____

4. _____

5. _____

What is the value of activators? First, activators serve to connect new learning to students' previously held knowledge. This connection is crucial for helping students to commit this new information to their long-term memories. Nolet and McLaughlin (2005, p. 38) explain: "As information from the environment is detected through one of the senses, it is held briefly until it can be analyzed. This analysis involves matching the incoming stimulus with a recognizable pattern already stored in memory." While the topics of working and long-term memory will be discussed in greater depth in Chapter 8, it is clear from this explanation by Nolet and McLaughlin that the work of activators to connect new learning to previously held knowledge is a crucial ingredient in the act of learning.

Activators serve to connect new learning to students' previously held knowledge. This connection is crucial for helping students to commit this new information to their long-term memories.

A second way in which activators facilitate teaching and learning is by informing the teacher of any misconceptions about the previous day's content that a student or students may possess. It is important to discover these misconceptions as quickly as possible for two reasons. First, students who connect their new learning to these prior misconceptions may come away with even *more* confusion about the particular topic of study. Second, as will be discussed in greater detail in Chapter 8, it can be difficult for a student's brain to "unlearn" a misconception if this misconception is not quickly corrected. Imagine your own experiences in listening to music. Once you hear a song lyric incorrectly, it can feel nearly impossible to stop singing the song with that incorrect lyric inserted. The neurological reasoning behind this difficulty in "unlearning" information will be discussed in Chapter 8, but it is enough here to note that activators are an important tool for quickly catching and correcting students' misconceptions.

The Do Now

The Do Now was developed by Dr. Lorraine Monroe, the nationally recognized founding principal of the Frederick Douglass Academy in Central Harlem. The Do Now is a three- to four-minute activity that is already written on the blackboard or flipchart LCD paper, or projected from the time students enter the classroom at the beginning of a class period. It is called a Do Now because students are expected to begin working on this activity immediately upon entering the classroom and taking their seats. The Do Now often contains an activity that activates previous learning and sets the stage for the upcoming learning.

The Do Now is collected and/or assessed each day—perhaps with a check, check plus, or check minus grading system. Each of the examples of activators provided in this chapter could serve as an effective Do Now, as long as students are able to begin working on them upon entering the classroom.

One benefit of the Do Now is that it effectively serves as what Madeline Hunter once called a *sponge activity*. A sponge activity is an activity designed to soak up valuable class time that might otherwise be wasted. The Do Now can serve as an effective sponge activity because students are expected to begin working on their Do Now upon entering the classroom. This means that the teacher does not have to wait to start class until every student is present, and students have no excuse for standing around chatting as they wait for class to begin. Rather, each student in the class is expected to begin working immediately upon entering the classroom. As Lorraine Monroe notes, the Do Now allows for "bell-to-bell" teaching and learning.

While the ability of a Do Now to utilize two to three minutes of otherwise wasted class time may initially strike educators as "small potatoes," it is unquestionably the case that making good use of an additional two to three minutes a day, five days a week, over the course of an entire school year, can actually have a dramatic impact on a class's learning. Moreover, as is discussed in more detail in Chapter 8, the first 10–15 minutes of a class period represent the prime period for student learning in the entire class period (Laura Erlauer 2003). This research reveals the opening minutes of class to be all the more valuable for student learning and makes the Do Now that much more important a strategy for a teacher to utilize.

It should also briefly be noted that the Do Now has the capability of saving even more class time within a given period. One of the routines that we establish with our students is that they should put the previous night's homework on their desks prior to starting on the Do Now. Then, as students are working on their Do Nows, we move about the room taking attendance and checking off in our grade books which students have and have not completed the previous night's homework assignment. Such a practice allows us to avoid wasting instructional time later in the lesson taking attendance and checking on students' homework completion. More information about classroom routines and practices can be found in Chapter 3.

In a 2006 article from the *Project on School Innovation Newsletter*, high school math teacher Karen Crounse (2006) reports on her own innovative use of the Do Now. Students enter Crounse's class each day and begin working immediately on the Do Now—a math problem. After a few minutes, Crounse randomly selects one student to be the presenter of the day. That student may then choose another peer to be his or her "lifeline" to help prepare for the presentation. The two students go out into the hallway to organize their presentation while the rest of the class pairs up, exchanges Do Nows, and comes up with a question to ask the presenter. Finally, the presenter and his or her "lifeline peer" return to the classroom, present the problem (for a grade), and answer questions from the class. The entire class then turns in their Do Nows and proceeds with the day's lesson. Here, Crounse's students are not only learning math, but also practicing their presentation skills.

Strategies for Beginning a Unit
Goal-Setting

Dean, et al., write in *Classroom Instruction That Works* that "setting [goals] is the process of establishing a direction to guide learning" (2012, p. 3). A goal-setting activity that we have utilized in our classrooms with great success during the first week of the school year is a variation on a classic visioning exercise for nonprofit organizations called "The Cover Story" (COOL and Idealist Civic Engagement Curriculum 2015). For this activity, we ask our students to imagine that it is the end of the school year and the local newspaper is planning to devote an entire issue to our class. What would our students like the front page of this newspaper to look like? More specifically, what would they like the titles of the four or five front-page articles to say? Often, our first homework assignment of the school year is for students to come up with four or five possible article titles to bring with them to class the next day. We then divide our students into groups of four or five, provide pieces of flipchart paper and magic markers, and ask each group to take fifteen minutes to pool their ideas into a single front page. In an eleventh-grade English class, a final product might look something like the following example.

June 7, 2016 **The Newbury Gazette** **$2.00**

Students Ace SATs with Expert Vocabulary!
_____
_____
_____
_____
_____
_____
_____

Students Craft Brilliant Research Papers
_____
_____
_____
_____
_____
_____
_____

Entire Class Understands "Hamlet"
_____
_____
_____
_____
_____
_____

Students Avoid Grammar Mistakes: Receive As on Final Exams
_____
_____
_____
_____
_____
_____

Given additional time, students might choose to draw a front-page illustration or to write the opening sentence or two of each "story." Upon completing their front pages, each group takes a turn presenting its flipchart paper to the class. We then hang up each group's front page on a classroom wall where they remain for the rest of the school year, visible to our students from their seats.

For the rest of the year, when introducing a unit or activity, we try to connect this unit or activity with the learning goals that our students established for themselves during the first week of school. We literally walk over to the front pages on the wall and point out the goal that we believe this upcoming lesson addresses. What is the value of such a practice? Psychologist Mihaly Csikszentmihalyi (1990, p. 40) explains that "when information that keeps coming into awareness is congruent with personal goals, thought flows effortlessly....Attention can be freely invested to achieve a person's goals because there is no disorder to straighten out, no threat for the self to defend against." In other words, students are more focused, effective learners when they understand how a particular unit or lesson relates to their own goals.

Giving the Final Assignment First

Earlier in this chapter, we discussed the importance of sharing mastery objectives and homework assignments with students at the outset of a lesson. Similar to this practice is beginning a unit by handing out the assignment for the essay, project, or performance that students will be expected to complete as the final assessment of the unit. For example, prior to beginning a unit on short stories, we might hand out to students the final assignment of the unit: to write a four- to seven-page short story and then to write an analytic essay identifying three literary elements within the story. What is the value of providing this final assignment at the outset of the unit? Remember Nolet and McLaughlin's (2005, p. 37) explanation that "teachers can help their students learn and remember like experts when they are clear about the types of information they want their students to learn and make clear the manner in which the information will be used." Another example of how this might look in practice would be letting students know ahead of time that by the end of a unit on energy, they will be expected to carry out an experiment and then describe which

Teachers utilize essential questions to guide students' investigations of a particular topic of study. Therefore, these questions must be complex enough to serve as an appropriate frame for the topic of study and engaging enough to pique and hold students' interest.

of three materials is the best conductor of heat. This will better enable them to understand and retain the content that the unit seeks to convey by understanding precisely how the information they are learning will be useful to them in completing the unit's final assignment.

Essential Questions (a.k.a. Important Concepts)

In *Understanding by Design*, Grant Wiggins and Jay McTighe (2005, p. 26) explain that "essential questions are those that go to the heart of the discipline, recur naturally throughout one's learning and in the history of a field, [and] raise other important questions." Teachers utilize essential questions to guide students' investigations of a particular topic of study. Therefore, these questions must be complex enough to serve as an appropriate frame for the topic of study and engaging enough to pique and hold students' interest. For example, in a ninth-grade English class embarking upon a study of *The Odyssey*, the essential questions laid out at the start of the unit might include the following:

1. What is a hero?
2. Is Odysseus a hero?
3. Are there differences between the Ancient Greeks' definition of a hero and ours today?

As we read and discuss *The Odyssey* with our students, we keep these questions in mind and search for aspects of the plot and themes that contribute to our understanding of these questions. What is the value of such questions? According to Wiggins and Wilbur (2015, p. 11), these questions "foster the kinds of inquiries, discussions, and reflections that help learners find meaning in their learning and achieve deeper thought and better quality in their work".

An entire course can also utilize an essential question or questions. For example, a science teacher we know taught a biology class in which the overarching essential question was, "What does it mean to be alive?" In providing a broad lens for inquiry, such questions can be powerful tools for maintaining students' interest and engagement for the long duration of a course examining multiple life forms.

A natural question that arises for many teachers is how essential questions differ from mastery objectives. These pedagogical tools are similar but not identical; they strive to achieve the same purpose but through different means. In our previous section on mastery objectives, we explained that providing students at the outset of a unit with our expectations for what they will know and be able to do at the end of the unit leads them to be more focused, attentive learners and better able to transfer new information into their long-term memories. For example, a student who has been alerted at the start of a unit on *The Odyssey* that one of the class's mastery objectives is *identifying and explaining Homeric meter* will be better able to transfer this information into his or her long-term memory when the teacher points out examples of Homeric meter within the epic poem. Essential questions also work to increase the likelihood that students will transfer new information into their long-term memories; they support students in achieving this goal by providing a framework that connects all of the different pieces of a unit of study into a coherent whole. For example, the essential question for *The Odyssey*—"What is a hero?"—provides a structure through which a student can reflect upon the many different plotlines and themes running through *The Odyssey*: Odysseus making his way home over eighteen long years; Penelope fending off the suitors; and Telemachus setting out in search of his father. The essential question "What is a hero?" provides a framework for students to use in reflecting upon each of these plotlines and increases the likelihood that students will transfer each to their long-term memories. As we may recall from Nolet and McLaughlin's (2005) explanations of the brain and memory, information that is chunked together is more easily transferred to long-term memory than individual bits of information. While mastery objectives and essential questions both aim to support students in transferring skills and content to their long-term memories, they help students to accomplish this goal in different ways.

Word Splash

Another way to start a unit is with a word splash. A word splash involves handing out to students a sheet of paper with words related to the upcoming unit "splashed" all over the page. We ask students to take a look at all of the different words on the page and see if any look familiar. We ask students to write out definitions for the words they know and circle the words they don't know. Such an activity serves to activate students' prior knowledge about the upcoming unit. Moreover, if the teacher collects these word splashes, then they can serve as a valuable tool for assessing the level of prior knowledge with which different students in the class are beginning the particular unit.

Strategies for Maximizing Student Learning

Repetition

The way in which repetition strengthens connections along neural pathways in the brain will be explained in more detail in Chapter 8. For now, suffice to say that Nuthall (1999) found that students require at least four exposures to a particular piece of information in order to effectively incorporate that piece of information into their existing knowledge. Unfortunately, repetition can be boring for students and leads them to tune out or stop paying attention. One strategy for juggling this dilemma is to expose students to the same content but in different ways. For example, Willis (2005, p. 22) notes that if a science teacher wants to teach students about the diffusion of a gas, he or she could spend the first part of a class period *lecturing* or *explaining* about the concept of diffusion. Next, the teacher could release hydrogen sulfide (rotten egg smell) from a container and ask students to keep track of how long it takes for the gas to diffuse (i.e., for the room to start to smell like rotten eggs). In these two activities, the teacher has utilized repetition by exposing students twice to the concept of diffusion, but because the teacher utilized two different types of activities, students are unlikely to react with boredom.

Jensen (2005, p. 39) also advocates repetition but "under the guise of completely different approaches." In fact, he suggests three different strategies for exposing students to content before they have even formally started to study it. Specifically, Jensen advocates three strategies that he refers to as "pre-exposure," "previewing," and "priming." Pre-exposure involves exposing students to content weeks or even months before they will formally study it. For example, several weeks before students begin a unit on World War II, the teacher might hang a timeline of World War II up in the back of the classroom or perhaps play students a song composed by German composer Richard Wagner. Previewing, in contrast, involves helping students to access prior knowledge about a topic just minutes or hours before the start of a formal lesson. Several of the activators described earlier in this chapter could serve as examples of previewing activities. Finally, priming can occur either weeks or minutes before the start of a particular lesson. Priming involves exposing students to the vocabulary that they will hear over the course of a formal lesson. In a lesson about World War II, for example, the teacher might invoke vocabulary such as *appeasement* or *eugenics* several days before the unit actually begins. By utilizing this vocabulary and explaining its meaning, teachers will provide students with some useful repetition when these words come up again during the formal unit on World War II.

Teaching for Transfer

Transfer refers to the ability of students to take information they have learned in a classroom setting and apply it in a different context. A study in 1985 of adolescent street vendors in Brazil found that while these adolescents were extremely adept at doing the mathematics necessary to exchange money while conducting business, their accuracy dropped substantially when they were asked to demonstrate these *same skills* in a laboratory setting. In other words, these Brazilian adolescents had difficulty transferring their mathematical skills from one context to another. Grant Wiggins (2006, p. 3) writes, "Difficulty transferring what's been learned to a new situation is depressingly common. Students will not typically cue themselves to use all their prior learning or recognize how the 'new' situation reflects prior learning." For this reason, Wiggins contends that students must be taught *how* to transfer learning from one context to another. To accomplish this goal, he recommends that teachers deliberately design assessments that require transfer. For example, students should be asked to carry out a task such as solving a particular type of problem both in class and at home. Students need to be taught to expect "curve balls" in which they must apply something they have learned to a slightly different scenario or set of circumstances. Nolet and McLaughlin (2005) recommend that teachers scaffold transfer activities by leading students in a think aloud, modeling how previously acquired knowledge can be applied to new contexts. As we learned in Chapter 1, the ability to transfer the learning to an unfamiliar context is one of the characteristics of application mastery.

> *Students must be taught how to transfer learning from one context to another.*

Brain Breaks That Embed the Learning

While the workings of the brain will be described in greater detail in Chapter 8, it is important to explain here that amino acids in the brain such as serotonin and epinephrine serve as neurotransmitters. These are acids that transport information across neurons. According to Willis (2005, p. 23), "When the neurotransmitters are used up, memory efficiency drops rapidly. These neurotransmitters rebuild with time, so observe your students for the glazed or distracted signs of brain burn out, and try to prevent it with brain breaks before it occurs." According to Jensen (2005, p. 44), **learners need an approximately two- to five-minute brain break for every 15 minutes of instruction. These brain breaks allow new material to solidify in students' brains and the neurotransmitters to replenish themselves.** Willis recommends dividing a 60-minute class into four 15-minute chunks, with a brain break in between each chunk. A brain break does not mean that students sit and do nothing. On the contrary, Willis suggests that a brain break entail an activity that helps students to reflect on the new information they have just acquired. For example, Willis (p. 24) recommends giving students a piece of paper that they divide into four sections. At each 15-minute interval throughout the class, the teacher pauses instruction so that students can write down something they have learned so far. Another brain break might entail students making predictions about the rest of the lesson, reflecting on how the information they have learned will be useful, or writing down something that they are finding confusing. In Chapter 5, we will explain the use of processing partners. Processing partners are an excellent strategy for combining the brain break with movement.[2] Clearly, then, the brain break is not an opportunity for students to sit idly. Rather, the brain break represents a temporary pause in the lesson during which students can solidify what they have learned so far.

Images and Spatial Representations

In a classic educational study conducted in the 1970s, researchers exposed subjects to 10,000 pictures over five days. This means that subjects in this study saw one picture every 15 seconds for eight hours a day, for five straight days. At the conclusion of this five-day marathon, the researchers showed subjects a combination of pictures from those 10,000, as well as a number of new pictures. Amazingly, the subjects in the study were able to recognize pictures they had already seen with an 83 percent success rate. Although in Chapter 8 we explain that, generally speaking, our brains give precedence to visual stimuli over those received by other senses, this study demonstrates how powerful both our visual and spatial memory can be. Linn (2006) explains that part of the reason subjects

---

2   Movement doesn't need to be done every 15 minutes. It can be done every 30–35 minutes. Therefore, only some of the brain breaks should be done with processing partners.

in this study were able to remember the pictures so clearly is because people "code" images in their brain both visually and verbally. In other words, people not only remember the picture but actually "explain its content" to themselves in language as well. Thus, when they need to remember that image in the future, they have two different memories of it in their brains: a visual memory and a language-based memory.

For this reason, when teaching vocabulary to students, it is tremendously powerful to have students create flashcards on which they not only write out the word and its definition, but also create an image they associate with the word. Students who create both a language-based memory and an image-based memory of a particular vocabulary word are far more likely to remember the word in the future than students who only write out the word's definition.

Neural pathways in the brain actually become most efficient at carrying out a task or recalling a piece of information if the learner tries out several different possibilities and rules out the ones that don't work.

Students who have to memorize poems or speeches might take a cue from the ancient Greeks. According to Linn (2006, p. 284), "Orators memorized long speeches by associating elements of their speech with objects along a standard path through a cathedral, and retracing the objects on the path cued their memory for the speech." In other words, those ancient Greeks responsible for going from town to town reciting the story of *The Odyssey* managed to memorize many hundreds of pages of text by associating different parts of the story with different visual images. Students memorizing a poem or speech can utilize a similar technique as well.

Finally, along these same lines, Linn (2006, p. 288) reports that when individuals are reading a story, they "track the spatial location of the story's characters." In other words, as people read, they actually visualize the physical movements and paths charted by the story's characters. According to Linn, it is therefore very important that young children learning to read be exposed to stories that are particularly conducive to creating mental images and then taught how to imagine the narrative in their minds. A study by Glenberg, Gutierrez, Levin, Japuntich, and Kaschak (2004) found that young children who were taught how to read a passage and imagine the movements of the characters in the passage were better at remembering the events of the story and drawing inferences about the story than children who received no such training. A later article by Glenberg (2014) reflects on the substantial gains in reading comprehension in children who were instructed to move images on a computer screen as they read accompanying text. In short, then, teachers are well served to take advantage of students' very powerful visual and spatial memories.

Trial-and-Error Learning

While we are generally not proud of our mistakes, most of us understand how they can serve as powerful sources of learning. Brain-based research actually supports this idea. Specifically, Jensen (p. 53) explains that the neural pathways in the brain actually become most efficient at carrying out a task or recalling a piece of information if the learner tries out several different possibilities and rules out the ones that don't work. Imagine yourself starting a new job. During that first week of work, each evening you try a different route home in order to figure out the best route of all. By trying out several different options, you not only figure out the best route, but you also *understand* the geography between home and work far better than if someone had simply told you the best route at the outset. Learning works the same way. However, Jensen (p. 54) notes that there is one caveat to the effectiveness of trial-and-error learning: "We must make mistakes *and* get appropriate feedback to learn." Returning to the new job scenario for a moment: if you didn't have a clock or a speedometer in your car to clue you in to which route between home and work was the fastest, it wouldn't do you much good to try a different route each day. However, the feedback you got from your car's clock and speedometer made it easy to learn which route was the best of all. When encouraging students to learn by the trial-and-error method, teachers need to make sure that their students are equipped with the tools necessary to learn from their mistakes.

Quiz Early and Often

Particularly in this era of accountability, many of us likely feel that our students are tested *too* often. And there is no doubt that it is challenging to find time to teach our students everything we want them to know with all of the time devoted to lengthy standardized testing requirements. To the surprise of many teachers, however, research conducted in 2007 suggests that giving students frequent quizzes is good for their long-term learning. Glenn (2007, p. 3) reports that "when given regular quizzes, students are forced to retrieve facts from memory repeatedly, and they develop much deeper fluency in the material." For this reason, researchers have gone so far as to advocate that educators at all levels take a few minutes at the beginning or end of class to quiz students *several times a week*. The quizzes should not be long—just three or four questions—and preferably in short-answer format. This finding actually substantiates research reported by Marilee Sprenger in 2005, which found that college students who received frequent pop quizzes actually got higher grades on end-of-semester final exams than students who did not receive these pop quizzes. It seems, then, that utilizing the Do Now to give students short quizzes can be "a uniquely powerful method for implanting facts in students' memory" (Glenn, p. 2).

Tests

It is worth noting that despite research connecting frequent quizzes to increased fact retention, some studies paint a less than positive picture when it comes to the cognitive effects of testing. A 2013 study carried out by researchers at Harvard University, Brown University, and the Massachusetts Institute of Technology (MIT) found that increased student scores on the Massachusetts Comprehensive Assessment System (MCAS) exam had "almost no effect on students' performance on tests of fluid intelligence skills, such as working memory capacity, speed of information processing, and ability to solve abstract problems." Still, we educators understand that standardized tests are a reality in the current context of accountability, and we see the importance of formal assessments as a tool for better understanding levels of proficiency within our classrooms and as one that also gives a chance for our students to demonstrate what they know. That said, there are important ways that we can help our students best prepare for tests. Middle school educator Rick Wormeli (2007) argues that assigning students to "study" for a test for homework is far too vague an assignment to be effective. He explains that students should be assigned to study for a test by being asked "to categorize information, summarize, find three similarities and two differences between concepts, draw a mind-map, create a graphic organizer, write note-cards of facts about the topic, [or] create a chapter outline." Teachers who give their students explicit instructions about *how* to study for the upcoming test see much better grades on the test than teachers who give their students the vague directive to "study."

Actively Connect New Learning to Prior Knowledge

Earlier in this chapter, we discussed the importance of utilizing activators as tools to connect new learning to what is already understood. Elaborating on this concept, in Chapter 8 of this book, we describe how the brain builds upon existing neural pathways in the acquisition of new knowledge. Enabling these connections, of course, is crucial to helping students transfer new learning into their long-term memories. We raise the point here that teachers should continually help students create these connections between new learning and prior knowledge *throughout* a lesson or activity. For example, a teacher might begin a unit on the Cold War in the following way:

> "At the very end of our unit on World War II last week, we talked about the ways in which, as the war was ending, Russia and the United States began to see the possibility that they could become competitors instead of allies. In that way, the very end of World War II was also the start of the Cold War."

By explicitly connecting the new unit on the Cold War to the information on World War II that students have already committed to their long-term memories, this teacher is greatly increasing the likelihood that his or her students will transfer this new information about the Cold War into their long-term memories as well. This instructional technique is called *elaboration*. That is, "When the student is able to see how the old and new information are related, the connection between them is strengthened" (Nolet and McLaughlin 2005, p. 45). Nolet and McLaughlin recommend that educators keep the principles of elaboration in mind when creating instructional materials as well. For example, an elementary school math teacher creating a worksheet on regrouping numbers might include on the top half of the sheet a brief summary and sample problem from the previous day's lesson on carrying numbers. Helping students to see that both processes call for cross-column interaction within a multi-digit number enables these students to link their new knowledge of regrouping to their previously held knowledge of carrying, greatly increasing the likelihood that the new lesson on regrouping will "stick" (i.e., transfer to their long-term memories).

Chunking

The instructional strategies described in the preceding sections work to take advantage of the fact that students are more likely to transfer newly learned information into long-term memory if this new information can be connected to previously held knowledge. Nolet and McLaughlin (2000, p. 36) explain that "it also is possible to increase the amount of information that can be processed in working memory [and transferred to long-term memory] by chunking smaller bits of information into larger units." For example, many third-grade students learning their multiplication tables find it difficult to answer the question, "What is 7 × 4?" If asked to recite the 7s tables, however, these same students might be able to do so: "7, 14, 21, 28, 35, etc." In fact, such a child might choose to answer the initial question ("7 × 4") by simply reciting the 7s tables until arriving at the correct answer ("28"). How can elementary school students find it harder to remember the solution to "7 × 4" than all of the 7s tables chunked together? Nolet and McLaughlin (p. 37) explain that "chunking has the effect of simplifying the cognitive load by imposing meaning on otherwise disconnected bits of information." We expand on this concept in Chapter 8, but for now we would like you simply to understand that this aspect of learning and memory has important implications for structuring student learning. It is also important to note that "breaking [information] into small chunks is useful regardless of whether an experience involves students listening to a lecture, reading a section of a text, observing a demonstration, observing a video, and so on" (Marzano 2007, p. 34). In line with Willis's (2005) recommendation, we suggest that teachers offer students a brain break and a chance to review after every four to seven chunks of material to which students are exposed.

> *Teachers should continually help students create these connections between new learning and prior knowledge throughout a lesson or activity.*

Connecting Learning to the Real World

Students also need to be given assignments that have relevance to their lived experiences. One of the forefathers of American education, John Dewey (1897, pp. 230–231), wrote, "I believe that the school must represent present life—life as real and vital to the child as that which he carries on in the home, in the neighborhood, or on the playground." In other words, Dewey believed that motivating students to be engaged, attentive learners involves convincing them that their learning is connected to the goings-on of the real world. Here, we suggest several strategies for helping students to see that connection. In each of these examples of connecting learning to the real world, we describe teachers who are capitalizing on the point made by Jane McGeehan (1999) that the brain wants to know that new information or skills it is learning will be useful in the future. In other words, our students' brains are actually better able to learn and remember content that strikes them as important and relevant. The following activities and strategies

are those that we and other educators have found to strike such a chord with our students.

A colleague of ours who teaches at the high school level explained to us that, on the first day of school, he promises his students that he will always take the time to answer the question: "When are we ever going to use this?" And the lesson won't continue until he can answer that question to the class's satisfaction. Other teachers we know are even more proactive. One math teacher begins each unit by describing the different jobs that utilize the mathematical concepts found in the upcoming chapter. An English teacher we know begins a unit on poetry by citing Supreme Court justice John Stephens's contention that the best preparation for law school may be the study of poetry. After quizzing his students on possible connections between poetry and the law, he quotes English professor and attorney George Gopen, who says that "no other discipline so closely replicates the central question asked in the study of legal thinking: here is a text; in how many ways can it have meaning?"(Kennedy 1990, p. 6). These teachers recognize that engaging students in the content they are learning requires helping them to understand how this content is actually utilized in the "real world."

One way in which an elementary mathematics teacher connects learning to the real world is through having students write in a daily math journal. At night, each student brings home a notebook and writes about how he or she used mathematics beyond the classroom that day. In addition, the student is required to create a mathematical problem based upon how he or she used math that day. The following day, the students share their journal entries and problems with the rest of the class. Then, the entire class works together to solve each problem. As Albert and Deane (2000, p. 527) explain, "In this activity, students not only are given the opportunity to express and communicate their mathematical knowledge and creativity but are also exposed to collaborative learning situations in which they can experience multiple ways to solve a problem." By pushing students to reflect upon the "real world" application of skills they have just learned, this elementary school math teacher greatly increases the likelihood that her students will retain the information and skills they have acquired.

Developing "Real World" Assignments

Students are also motivated by assignments that they regard as real. Earlier in this chapter, we described a final assignment for a unit on short stories in which students wrote their own short stories and then completed an analysis of the literary elements within the short story. One year, as a means of shaking things up a bit, we assigned our students to write and illustrate children's stories and then to write their analysis of the literary elements found within their respective children's stories. Moreover, we explained to our students that, when the assignment was completed, we planned to donate their stories to a first-grade class at one of the local elementary schools. The reaction of our students was extremely positive. They loved the idea of local children actually benefiting from their assignment, and, though the process of writing, illustrating, and binding a children's story involved far more effort than had the more basic story-writing assignment of previous years, we heard far less complaining from our students. They were willing to do more work because they saw the work as real.

That same class of students regarded another assignment as real in a different way. Upon completing *The Odyssey*, we typically assign our students to write an essay addressing the question: "Was Odysseus a hero?" In order to shake things up again, however, we changed our assignment slightly. More specifically, we decided to put Odysseus on trial for the deaths of every member of his crew. The question became: "Is Odysseus guilty of murder?" We divided our students into two sides—one side prosecuting Odysseus for murder and the other side defending him—and assigned our students to write either an opening or closing statement that supported the side of the case to which they had been assigned. Though the form of the writing assignment and its topic were somewhat different than in previous years, the expectations for quality remained the same. Students were expected to find textual evidence to support their arguments and utilize all of the mechanics of good writing in making their cases. As in previous years, a rubric was provided to ensure that students understood what was expected of them. Rather than simply turning in the assignment, however, we took an additional two class periods to put Odysseus on trial. Each team assigned students to play either witnesses (characters from the story) or lawyers, and the entire team worked together to develop questions that they could pose to these witnesses to prove their side's claim about Odysseus's actions. On the day of the trial, several students for each side read their opening and closing state-

Reliance on the Internet for, say, recalling the steps of the scientific method would be less effective than actually writing out the steps by hand and then applying the steps to an experiment.

ments, and, in between, witnesses from both sides were called. At the conclusion of the trial, the legal studies teacher who had been recruited to serve as the judge rendered his verdict. Perhaps not surprisingly, in end-of-the-year course evaluations, students listed this activity as one of their favorites of the year. At its core, the writing assignment they completed was essentially the same as in previous years; however, placing that assignment within the context of a trial lent an authenticity to the project that motivated our students to focus more deeply on the content they were learning and, as a result, more successfully commit this content to their long-term memories.

Using Primary Source Materials

Another "real world" connection that motivates student learning is the use of primary source (i.e., real world) materials. For example, rather than assigning students to learn a vocabulary list photocopied from a textbook, we might bring in a recent article from *The New York Times* and ask students to read the article carefully, circling any words they don't immediately recognize. We can then put together our own vocabulary list from the circled words. What is the benefit of assembling a vocabulary list in this manner? Students can see firsthand that these words are utilized in the real world, as opposed to simply in a vocabulary textbook. Likewise, in a math class, students are far more motivated to understand concepts such as perimeter and area when their teacher brings in an actual blueprint for them to examine instead of relying on the diagram in their textbooks. In both of these examples, substituting a real-world artifact for a textbook excerpt allows students to see for themselves how the skill or concept they are learning plays out in the real world. See Chapter 1 for a specific example of a lesson that shows how a high school teacher used primary source material from the book *The Prince* by Machiavelli.

Newspaper articles as primary source materials can be valuable teaching tools at the elementary school level as well. One of our elementary school colleagues uses newspaper articles and *Time for Kids* in her mathematics class to help students develop number sense in a real-world context. This particular teacher chooses several appropriate sentences containing numbers. She then rewrites the sentences without the numbers and creates a "Number Bank" at the top of the sheet with the numbers that have been taken out. The students must fill in the missing blanks with the appropriate numbers. At the conclusion of the lesson, the teacher shows her students the original newspaper article and allows them to check their answers against the original sentences. In this way, her students can see how their number sense is developing as well as the ways in which numbers are utilized in everyday reading materials such as newspapers. An added benefit to using primary sources in the classroom is that these documents are said to help students achieve goals embedded in the Common Core State Standards (CCSS). According to a report published by the Library of Congress (2015), "Primary sources provide authentic materials for students to practice the skills required by the CCSS."

The Internet

While the Internet is, in no uncertain terms, a valuable instructional tool for accessing information and connecting our students to people and ideas, we must also consider how it might best be used within a cognitive context. Spitzer (2014, p. 81) notes that "using information technology in educational settings—from childcare to the classroom, to the lecture hall and beyond—may have benefits but also carries serious risks and side effects." In Chapter 8, we discuss how with the rise of new technologies and their growing ubiquity in our lives, our students may run the risk of experiencing negative effects on memory and processes of learning through sustained exposure to the Internet. Generally speaking, we know that students need multiple interactions with new material before it can be committed to memory. However, not all types of exposure to information are equal. A recent study that compared learning from books, magazines, journals, and Google found that of these formats, information from Google was the least likely to be retained in the memory (Spitzer, 2014). In addition, "Handwriting…is superior for memorizing anything from the shapes of characters to the content of a lecture" (p. 82). This evidence leads us to conclude that reliance on the Internet for, say, recalling the steps of the scientific method would be less effective than actually writing out the steps by hand and then applying the steps to an experiment. Similarly, consulting the Internet to find the formula for calculating volume would have a diminished chance of being encoded in the memory than would copying the formula in one's notebook and practicing the algorithm.

Few things are more motivating for students than the opportunity to hear firsthand about the ways in which the skills they are learning are actually applied in the real world.

Taking all of this into consideration, there are still a number of ways that the Internet can be used to enhance curriculum and enrich learning. For example, Angela McFarlane (2015, p. 26) recommends the use of computer-based and mobile technology to "facilitate individual, cooperative, and interactive work," as well as to "enable learners to revisit for repetition, consolidation, and reflection out of the classroom on things introduced in class." So while it may be unwise to rely *primarily* on the Internet to teach and reinforce curriculum-related ideas, it can serve as a useful supplement to other learning tools.

Guest Speakers

Even better than bringing in a real-world artifact is bringing in a "real-world" human being. For a unit on area and perimeter, for example, perhaps a friend of yours, the spouse of a teacher in your school, or the parent of a student in your class, is an architect. While our initial impulse might be to assume that such an architect would be too busy to visit our class for half an hour to explain his or her work, we have found quite the contrary; the various professionals we have invited into our classrooms have been excited and honored by the invitation to talk to a class full of students about the work that they do. Of course, few things are more motivating for students than the opportunity to hear firsthand about the ways in which the skills they are learning are actually applied in the real world.

We find that this strategy is most effective when the speaker is given information related to the purpose of the visit. For example, telling the architect the topics we teach that are reflected in architecture and asking the speaker to make these connections for the students will lead to a very productive experience. One of our colleagues recalls a time when she had a student's mother, a scientist, visit class to lead an activity where students extracted DNA from onion skin. Leading up to this activity, this teacher spent significant time with the parent discussing the objectives for the activity and how her demonstration could best contribute to their unit on cell structure. With proper planning and collaboration, the activity was a success, and her students consistently recalled that event as one of the most memorable of the year.

Role-Playing and Simulations

Another way in which we try to engage our students is through role-playing and simulations. A colleague of ours who teaches high school social studies uses a fantastic simulation to help students understand the Homestead Strike of 1892, during which factory workers at Andrew Carnegie's steel factory in Pittsburgh went on strike over the right to unionize, receive better pay, and have improved working conditions. In the simulation, approximately one third of the class takes the role of management, one third takes the role of skilled workers employed by Carnegie, and one third takes the role of unskilled workers employed by Carnegie. The simulation allows students to truly come to understand the competing goals, motivations, and concerns of these different groups and then to compare the resolution of their simulation to the violence and tragedy that actually ensued in 1892. Simulations such as this one engage students deeply in their learning.

> *If we truly feel that our subject area is utterly fascinating, our students will pick up on that enthusiasm and more willingly devote their energy and attention to understanding this subject matter.*

One of our elementary school colleagues uses a particular type of simulation throughout the school year. He divides his students into news teams, and they are expected each week to deliver a 10-minute news program to their classmates, utilizing the current events articles they have found for homework. By having his students role-play the work of newscasters, this teacher has discovered a particularly engaging way to teach his students (and have his students teach each other) about both current events and public speaking.

Conveying Passion and Enthusiasm

In this chapter, we have described several strategies that teachers use to increase their students' engagement and motivation for the content they are learning. Perhaps more obvious than some of the strategies already described, but unquestionably as important, is our own passion and enthusiasm for the content we are teaching. If we truly feel that our subject area—be it literature, physical education, world languages, or photography—is utterly fascinating and worth knowing, our students will pick up on that enthusiasm and more willingly devote their energy and attention to understanding this subject matter. This connection between enthusiasm and student achievement is supported by research from Rosenshine (1970), Armento (1978), and McConnell (1977). How does this work on a cognitive level? According to Marzano, "Teacher enthusiasm facilitates student achievement because animated behavior arouses the attending behavior of pupils" (2007, p. 101). In other words, showing passion for our subject matter to our students utilizes our

students' *emotional* learning system to support their more *academic* learning systems. While we will hold off until Chapter 8 to describe these different learning systems in detail, we can note here that students who are privy to their teachers' positive emotional responses to a particular subject matter are better able to focus their cognitive learning systems on learning and understanding this subject matter. For this reason, we recommend that teachers explicitly share their enthusiasm for their subject matter with their students as well as *what* they believe makes this subject matter so exciting. One of our colleagues who is a high school English teacher admitted to us that his students began teasing him midway through the year for claiming at the start of each unit or book, "This is my favorite one to teach. I think you're going to like this one best." Despite their good-natured teasing, our colleague's students are motivated by their teacher's enthusiasm to give authors like Shakespeare and Hawthorne a fair chance, instead of preemptively declaring them to be boring. His passion for these authors then plays a crucial role in his students' learning.

Of course, our larger goal is to get our students excited about the material they are learning. There is a cognitive reason behind this goal as well. Sprenger (2005, p. 23) explains that "excitory neurotransmitters are released when we feel excited. Norepinephrine starts a cascade of chemical responses that increase the intensity of the experience and the perception of it." To this end, Sprenger recommends doing anything and everything to try to get our students excited about learning: dress in a costume, play music, begin class with a story, or begin class with a dilemma for students to debate. Excited, engaged students are not just more fun; they're also better learners.

Issue Directions One Step at a Time[3]

In our discussion of activators and summarizers earlier in this chapter, we explained the process by which our students' brains commit new information to memory. To review briefly, newly received information is first held in our students' working memories and compared to information already stored in their long-term memories. If the new information can be connected to existing knowledge, this new information is much more easily transferred to our students' long-term memories than if no such connection can be made. In

---

3   Special education teachers indicate this can be particularly important for special needs students.

Accessing the General Curriculum, Nolet and McLaughlin (2005) explain that the capacity of our students' *working memories* is quite limited. Approximately seven units of information can be stored in the working memory at one time and only for about 10 to 20 seconds. For this reason, we as educators need to be strategic when providing our students with directions for accomplishing a particular activity or task.

For example, imagine a high school physical education teacher is instructing his or her students on the proper technique for shooting a foul shot in basketball. There are several different components that go into a successful foul shot: keeping one's knees bent, keeping one's eyes on the hoop, aiming for the back of the rim, properly positioning one's hands on the basketball, etc. A physical education teacher who simply describes each of these different components at once and then tells his or her students to "go to it" will almost certainly be disappointed when students begin practicing foul shots. In contrast, a physical education teacher who lists each of these different components on a blackboard, models each component, and has students practice each component in isolation before putting the entire routine together will likely meet with more success.

How would such a strategy work in an English classroom? Imagine we are teaching an activity involving a worksheet on semicolons, in which we would like students to read the sentences on the worksheet, decide whether or not a semicolon belongs in the sentence, add the semicolon if one is necessary, and, if not, expand the sentence in a manner that requires a semicolon. Rather than issuing all of those instructions at once and then trusting our students' working memories to keep all of that information straight, we are better served to divide our instructions into two or even three parts. First, we might ask our students to read through the sentences and circle those that require semicolons. When students have completed this task, we might ask them to pencil in the semicolon in the appropriate place for those sentences that are circled. Finally, we might instruct them to reread the sentences that they did not circle and add to them in such a way that they utilize a semicolon. Perhaps after issuing each step of these directions, we might then write that particular step on the blackboard. This teaching strategy acknowledges that students can only hold a limited amount of information in their working memories at one time.

> *Approximately seven units of information can be stored in the working memory at one time and only for about 10 to 20 seconds. For this reason, we as educators need to be strategic when providing our students with directions for accomplishing a particular activity or task.*

Finally, let us consider how this would look in a mathematics classroom. Because "doing" math often involves a multi-step process that must be accomplished in a particular sequence, it is fairly easy to see why issuing directions one step at a time would be of benefit to students. Imagine, for example, instructing students without prior knowledge of the order of operations to evaluate a multi-step expression like $2 + 3 \times 4$. In the absence of clear instructions to first calculate the product of 3×4, and then add 2, students may easily come up with an incorrect answer of 20, instead of the correct answer, 14.

Cognitive Coaching on Writing

In a 2007 article in *Educational Leadership*, educators Powell and Kusuma-Powell offer a five-step model for supporting students in improving their writing skills. First, students are instructed to clarify their goals on a particular writing assignment. They need to consider the question or assignment they have been given and consider what topics and strategies will most influence their intended audience. Next, the students identify success indicators. In other words, they decide which characteristics of effective writing or strategies of persuasive writing they will make sure to include in their pieces. Third, students anticipate approaches. They determine the content of their writing—the themes and topics they will include to support their theses. Fourth, students prioritize and organize. They organize their thoughts and decide upon the structure of their pieces. Finally, after students have pushed forward and developed drafts of their writing assignments, they reflect on how the previous steps of the process—clarifying, identifying, anticipating, and prioritizing— influenced their thinking and writing.

Cognitive Coaching on Reading

In a 2006 article for *Language Learner*, professor of education Timothy Rush offers a five-step process for supporting students from fourth grade through high school in improving their comprehension of textbooks. Rush first instructs students to open to the assigned chapter and then flip through the entire chapter, reading all of the bold-print headings and subheadings. This step allows the reader to gain a general sense of the chapter's content. Second, Rush instructs students to read the chapter's introduction to acquire an additional sense of what the content of the chapter will cover. Third, Rush directs students to flip through the chapter again. This time, the student pays attention to any graphic information embedded in the chapter: pictures, charts, figures, tables, graphs, etc. Fourth, Rush instructs the student to flip through the chapter one final time, reading the first and last sentence of each paragraph. Finally, the student returns to the first page of the chapter and reads the entire chapter from beginning to end. In this process laid out by Rush, one can see at work a number of the cognitive strategies described earlier in this chapter. The primary strategy at work is repetition. The student gains familiarity with the content of the chapter by flipping through the chapter several times. However, the student avoids boredom by focusing on a different aspect of the chapter with each pass. Moreover, the strategy outlined by Rush places special emphasis on visual and spatial images embedded in the chapter. Rush recognizes the ability of the student's mind to commit these images to memory before even starting to read the chapter in question.

Cognitive Coaching on Math

Nancy Protheroe (2007) details some key actions that teachers can take to support math achievement. To begin with, she urges teachers to engage in dialogue that involves routine questioning: "Teachers should present questions that stimulate students' curiosity and encourage them to investigate further" (p. 53). You may recall that earlier in this chapter we discussed how framing lessons around an essential question can serve as a method of growing student interest. Chapter 5 of this book discusses the benefits of questioning strategies in detail. A suggestion that we make here that is of particular benefit to math students would be also to incorporate routine questioning as part of regular classroom dialogue. And, of course, questions that engage students in higher-level thinking (found at a higher level on Bloom's Taxonomy[4]) are best for ensuring that deep mathematics learning is the result. Protheroe, in her description of math-oriented best practices, also describes the benefits of ensuring that students are actively engaged in math activities, rather than passively receiving information or observing other students solve problems. Optimally, this work should be done collaboratively, since "such opportunities appeal to the social nature of most children, while thinking through problems collaboratively makes it less likely that a student will get caught in a procedural dead end" (p. 54). A final recommendation is for

teachers to incorporate the frequent use of manipulatives in their instruction. As we discuss in Chapter 8, manipulatives allow for engagement in spatial reasoning and "bridge the conceptual links between concrete number knowledge and the more abstract symbolic understanding of letters and numerals" (Tokuhama-Espinosa 2011, p. 188).

Less Is More

In this chapter, we have suggested a number of strategies for supporting student learning that take advantage of recent advances in our understanding of memory. A final suggestion we have with regard to students, memory, and learning is one over which we as classroom teachers often do not have as much control as we would like—namely, the decision to favor a more in-depth study of a few topics over a more cursory study of many topics. Such an emphasis is more likely to result in students' understanding *and retaining* what they learn because of the greater ease with which they can transfer information into long-term memory when they can connect this information to previously held knowledge. One can see then how students are more likely to remember the content included in an in-depth study of one historical time period than a more cursory study of three historical periods. As Robert Fried (2001, p. 240) explains in *The Passionate Teacher*, "Students cannot dig deeply when they are rushing to get through quantities of stuff." Unfortunately, our autonomy as educators to determine the depth versus the breadth of the curriculum we cover is sometimes limited by high-stakes testing and state frameworks. One positive aspect of the recent adoption of the Common Core in many states is a curricular shift in favor of deep knowledge of a given topic. However, we know that many in education today struggle with the implementation of this relatively new set of standards, and that it may be some time before many classrooms master the ability to design their lessons and units to effectively emphasize depth over breadth.

In *The Passionate Teacher*, Fried (p. 242) asks teachers to consider the following question: "If the school board decreed that the final exam for any course had to be given a year after the course was completed, would that change how you teach?" For many of us, such a "late" final exam system would dramatically influence our teaching. We know that too many of our students spend the few nights before the final exam cramming information into their working memories, only to forget this information a few days later. And yet, if our goal is for students to truly under-

---

4   Chapter 5 contains a comprehensive description of effective questioning. Chapter 6 contains a chart describing Bloom's Taxonomy.

stand and retain the content of our courses beyond the final exam, then we should already be designing our curricula in such ways as to allow our students to dig deeply into the content we are teaching them and to hold on to what they uncover.

One way we can control the quality-versus-quantity struggle is to review the curriculum with an eye toward identifying the skills and information that are most important for our students to learn. In any curriculum, there are typically information and skills that we consider to be of the highest priority, those that are of a lower priority, and those that are connected but are not a priority.

We determine the level of importance of a particular skill or piece of information by asking ourselves, (a) what information and skills will result in the highest level of student achievement on the district, state, and national assessments, and (b) what information and skills will result in future scholastic, professional, and personal success.

Once we have determined how the various units and lessons within our curricula fit onto the continuum shown in Figure 2.2, we can then work to allocate our available instructional time accordingly. As can be seen in Figure 2.2, our "High Priority" lessons and units should receive the greatest allocation of instructional time, and those units or lessons that fall under "Connected but Not a Priority" should receive the least instructional time.

Self-Regulation

A recent study of eighth graders by University of Pennsylvania researcher Martin Seligman found that a student's level of self-discipline is a better predictor of academic achievement than a student's IQ. It is for this reason that Barry Zimmerman, a researcher at the City University of New York, believes that educators need to explicitly teach students how to become self-disciplined or, in his words, self-regulated. According to an article by Susan Black (2007) in the *American School Board Journal*, Zimmerman believes

that teaching students how to self-regulate consists of three phases: forethought, performance, and reflection. In the forethought phase, the student learns to set goals for him or herself and plan a strategy for actually achieving these goals. In the performance phase, the student learns to consider questions such as, "Do I need to study in a quiet place or in a place with background noise?" The student also needs to learn and practice how to defer immediate gratification (for example, watching television) in order to work toward a longer-term goal (for example, earning a place on the honor roll). Finally, in the self-reflection phase, the student considers how successful he or she has been in attaining the original goal. If the student has attained the goal, he or she must consider which steps were crucial to this process. If the student did not attain the goal, he or she must reflect upon the steps or behaviors that proved counterproductive. Zimmerman and Black report that, if students are carefully led through this three-phase process by a teacher or parent, they can dramatically improve their levels of academic achievement.

Strategies for the Close of Class

Summarizers

As might be guessed from its name, a summarizer serves the opposite function of an activator. While activators are intended to activate and gauge students' prior knowledge of a topic before studying it, summarizers are typically utilized at the *conclusion* of a lesson and provide an opportunity for students to summarize, synthesize, and demonstrate, *in their own words*, what they have learned.

We mentioned in the previous section that a common activator is the K-W Activator. Many educators utilize this activity as both an activator and a summarizer by adding either one or two columns to the teaching tool. A K-W-L Activator/Summarizer (**Know,**

Figure 2.2

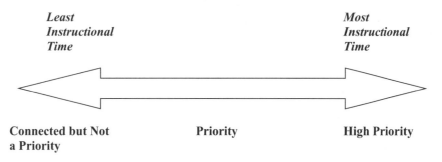

Least Instructional Time   *Most Instructional Time*

Connected but Not   **Priority**   **High Priority**
a Priority

Want to Know, and *Learned*) has an extra column for students to fill in at the conclusion of the unit. The additional column is labeled "What I Learned" and represents an opportunity for students to describe what they learned over the course of the unit or lesson.

Some teachers instruct students to fill in the "What I Learned" column as they proceed through the unit. Other educators utilize this column as a reflection activity to be completed at the unit's conclusion. Both strategies allow students the opportunity to express for themselves the learning that has taken place.

A teacher might also use the K-W-L as a summarizer by asking students to read over and reflect upon the thoughts and ideas they expressed at the unit's outset. Did everything they thought they knew about the topic turn out to be true? Did all of their "Want to Know" items get addressed? If not, we can reserve some class time for addressing any of these lingering "Want to Know" items. Demonstrating this commitment to the issues and questions that particularly inter-

est students heightens their motivation and effort level to understand the larger lesson or unit.

In *The Brain-Compatible Classroom*, Laura Erlauer (2003) recommends adding a fourth column to the K-W-L activity, creating the K-W-L-U Activator/Summarizer (**Know**, **Want to Know**, **Learned**, and **Used**). The following pages provide examples of several summarizers. The first is a bingo summarizer. At the end of a class period in which we have studied grammar, for example, we would hand out the sheet below and instruct students to fill in their bingo cards with words from the list. We then read out the definition of one of the eligible words. For example, for the term *pronoun*, we might call out, "A word that describes a noun!" Any student who has placed the term *pronoun* in one of his or her boxes can check off that term. The first student to get bingo—three terms in a row—wins (and perhaps earns a small prize). And then we start again. In this way, the bingo summarizer offers a fun and educational way to conclude a lesson.

Foundations 10

Mr. Seider

Bingo Summarizer

Independent Clause	*Dependent Clause*	*Simple Sentence*
Compound Sentence	*Complex Sentence*	*Compound-Complex Sentence*
Action Verb	*Helping Verb*	*Linking Verb*
Could Have	*Pronoun*	*Adjective*
Conjunction	*Subordinate Conjunction*	*Coordinating Conjunction*

Foundations 9   Literature Section

Character Types Summarizer

_____   I. What stories have we read in our Short Story unit?
_____   II. How many characters can you think of from these stories?
Put these characters into the appropriate box.

ROUND Character

| |
| |

FLAT Character

| |
| |

DYNAMIC Character

| |
| |

STATIC Character

| |
| |

K-W-L Activator/Summarizer

| | |
| | |

K-W-L-U Activator/Summarizer

Chemical Reactions

What I Know	What I Want to Know	What I Learned	How I Will Use This Learning

As you can see in the K-W-L-U example, the fourth column asks students to reflect upon how they will utilize the content or skills they have acquired over the course of the unit. Asking students to reflect upon this question of application increases the likelihood of students transferring their learning into their long-term memory systems. Why? In *Transformations: Leadership for Brain-Compatible Learning*, Jane McGeehan (1999) notes that the brain wants to know that the information it is learning will be useful in the future. In *How People Learn*, Bransford, Brown, and Cocking (1999, p. 7) report that "learners of all ages are more motivated when they can see the usefulness of what they are learning." In short, Erlauer's suggestion to add the "Usefulness" column to this activator/summarizer increases the likelihood that students will process and remember the learning they have engaged in throughout the lesson or unit.

Word Sort

Another summarizer that we often use to conclude class is a Word Sort. This activity is similar to the word splash that we use as an activator. In the Word Sort, we hand students a sheet of paper in which 10 terms

from the preceding lesson are listed. Rather than asking students to define these terms, we ask them to sort these terms into categories. For example, imagine that following a lesson on measurement, students received a sheet of paper with the following 10 terms:

Degrees   Celsius   Fahrenheit   Kelvin
Thermometer   Pounds   Ounces   Quarts
Grams   Meters

There are several different categories that students could create from such terms. One example is a "temperature" category that includes *degrees*, *Celsius*, *Fahrenheit*, *Kelvin*, and *thermometer*. Another possible category would be a "weight" category that includes *pounds*, *ounces*, and *grams*. There is generally no single correct answer on a Word Sort, but students demonstrate their understanding of the preceding lesson through their ability to recognize groupings that exist among a collection of terms.

$2 Summaries

This summarizer is a way to assess students' grasp of content-related vocabulary and understanding of a lesson's "big picture" by assigning a monetary value to individual words, and then having students write a $2 summary of what they learned in class. The example below uses science-related terms worth $0.25 each. Note that this summarizer can be used for any subject, and the value assigned to words (as well as the total) can be adjusted as needed.

Microbe = $0.25	Virus = $0.25
Spores = $0.25	Fungi = $0.25
Bacteria = $0.25	Yeast = $0.25
Mycelium = $0.25	Nucleus = $0.25
Membrane = $0.25	Unicellular = $0.25
Decomposer = $0.25	Reproduce = $0.25

Sample Test Question

This summarizer has students draw from what they have learned to create a sample test question related to the day's lesson. The questions should be fairly sophisticated (not to elicit a yes/no or one-word response), and, if done well, may be used as a lesson activator on the following day.

Frayer Model

The Frayer Model is a graphic organizer that summarizes students' understanding of a word or concept by having them identify its definition, describe its characteristics, and then provide examples and non-examples of the concept.

Frayer Model – Organisms	
DEFINITION	**CHARACTERISTICS**
EXAMPLES	**NON-EXAMPLES**

Here is an example of the Frayer Model after it has been completed.

Frayer Model – Organisms	
DEFINITION	**CHARACTERISTICS**
An organism is any living thing.	*An organism does or shows each of the characteristics of living things:* *1. Composed of cells* *2. Has levels of organization* *3. Uses energy* *4. Responds to its environment* *5. Adapts to its environment* *6. Grows* *7. Reproduces*
EXAMPLES	**NON-EXAMPLES**
Tree, human, bacteria, dog, broccoli, amoeba	*Fire, train, water, lightning, bed, car*

Paired and Group Verbal Fluency Summarizer

Two final examples of summarizers are the paired and group verbal-fluency activities. Both are activities for reviewing information that has been covered over the course of a class period or unit. In the paired verbal-fluency exercise, we put students into pairs. We choose one student from each pairing to go first (often with something silly, such as, "Whoever is wearing the darker shirt will go first!"). That student will speak for 30 seconds. In that time, the student will tell his or her partner everything he or she knows about the topic of discussion. The teacher stops the first student after 30 seconds and instructs the second student to pick up where the first left off. In other words, now the second student in each pairing must talk for 30 seconds about the topic at hand. We usually repeat the process so that both students end up speaking for one minute apiece on the topic about which they have just concluded learning. A variation of this activity is the group verbal-fluency summarizer. In this version of the activity, students are placed in groups of three or four, rather than groups of two. Students then go around the circle, speaking one by one for 30 seconds about the topic at hand. As a result, while each student only speaks for 30 seconds, they are all exposed to a full two minutes of review.

In the same way that activators can be valuable in alerting us to our students' misconceptions or misunderstandings of a particular topic, a summarizer can also be useful in alerting us to information or skills that our students have not yet acquired or mastered. For example, if none of our students reference diatomic molecules in the column under what they learned about chemical reactions, we might take this data as a clue that we did not cover this topic as thoroughly as originally intended. This information might lead us to extend the chemical equations unit an additional day to readdress the topic of diatomic molecules, or perhaps we will simply add in our notes for next year that this topic should be addressed more rigorously.

Finally, in this chapter's sections on activators and agendas, we have explained that students are better able to transfer information into their long-term memories when they understand how a particular piece of information relates to other information they have already learned about that same topic. Using a summarizer to reflect upon their learning gives students the opportunity to consider how new information they have acquired connects to previously held knowledge, and it also helps them to identify patterns and categories that provide structure to this newly acquired content. Both of these acts—linking new information to previous learning and categorizing new information—are crucial steps in transferring this newly learned content into students' long-term memories.

How Do You Know If They Get It?

If repetition involves exposing students to the same content multiple times, then recoding involves a student's ability to take content and explain it in his or her own words. After exposing students to content, one way to assess their mastery of this content is through their ability to recode the information they have learned. Sprenger (2005) identifies five different ways in which students can demonstrate their ability to recode content. Exemplification is the ability to explain an idea using specific examples. A student who learns about renewable energy sources might offer wind energy as an example of such a source. Classification is the ability to recognize how something fits into a particular category or grouping. A student who can describe the verb *jump* as an action verb and *was* as a linking verb is practicing classification. Identifying similarities and differences between two objects, characters, or events is another form of recoding. A student who has completed a unit on World War II might identify similarities between Hitler and Mussolini or perhaps between Roosevelt and Churchill. Inferring involves the ability to draw conclusions from the available information. The student who has completed a unit on World War II might be asked to make an inference about whether racism played a role in Truman's decision to drop the atomic bomb on the Japanese. Finally, Sprenger explains that one final form of recoding is nonlinguistic representation. This form of recoding involves expressing content in a form that does not involve language. Students might draw a picture, create a dance, or construct a model or graph. For example, a student who has just learned the Pythagorean Theorem ($A^2 + B^2 = C^2$) might be asked to draw a graphical representation of this theorem. In short, then, each of these five forms of recoding can be used to assess the extent to which students have learned and understand a particular lesson. If students are unable to recode successfully, more repetition (though in varied formats) may be necessary.

If repetition involves exposing students to the same content multiple times, then recoding involves a student's ability to take content and explain it in his or her own words.

Conclusion

The various strategies described in this chapter draw upon our understanding of learning, memory, and motivation to support student learning. More specifically, these strategies seek to create a context within our classrooms that maximizes our students' abilities to understand and retain the information and skills that we teach them. For many years, the education world considered student learning to be solely a function of each student's effort and intelligence. If students succeeded, it was because they were smart, studious, or both. If students were not succeeding, it was because they lacked either innate intelligence or the diligence to succeed. While innate intelligence, to some extent, and students' effort, to a much larger extent, do play roles in student achievement, we have also learned in recent years of the ways in which we as teachers can utilize structures, strategies, and activities to support student learning. While the abilities of our students to learn the information and skills we are teaching them is unquestionably affected by the effort they expend, there are also steps that we can take as educators to increase the likelihood that information and skills—when effort is expended—will "stick."

References

Albert, L. and Antos, J. "Daily Journals Connect Mathematics to Real Life." *Mathematics Teaching in the Middle School* 5, no. 8 (2000): 526–531.

Alomari, M.A., Khabour, O.F., Alzoubi, K.H., and Alzubi, M.A. "Forced and Voluntary Exercises Equally Improve Spatial Learning and Memory and Hippocampal BDNF Levels." *Behavioural Brain Research* 247 (2013): 34–39.

Armento, B. "Teacher Behavior and Effective Teaching of Concepts." Paper presented at the Annual Meeting of the American Association of Colleges for Teacher Education, Chicago (ERIC Document Reproduction Service, No. ED 153 949), 1978.

Black, S. "Easing ESL Students into Learning English Well." *Education Digest* 71, no. 1 (2005): 36–38.

Black, S. "The Search for True Grit." *American School Board Journal* 194, no. 4 (2007): 52–54.

Bracey, G. "The Cognitive Power of Monkey Bars." *Phi Delta Kappan.* 87 no. 3 (2005): 254.

Bransford, J., Brown, A., and Cocking, R., eds. *How People Learn: Brain, Mind, and Experience at School.* Washington, DC: National Academy Press, 1999.

Buscemi, J., Kong, A., Fitzgibbon, M.L., Bustamante, E.E., et al. "Society of Behavioral Medicine Position Statement: Elementary School-Based Physical Activity Supports Academic Achievement." *Transitional Behavioral Medicine* 4, no. 4 (December 2014): 436–438. doi 10.1007/s13142-014-0279-7. http://www.ncbi.nlm.nih.gov/pmc/articles/PMC4286548.

Cairn, R. "Primary Sources: At the Heart of the Common Core State Standards." *Teaching with Primary Sources*

Journal 5, no. 2 (Fall 2012): 2–4. http://www.loc.gov/teachers/tps/journal/common_core/article.html.

Carmichael, M. "Stronger, Faster, Smarter." *Newsweek*, March 26, 2007.

Carnes, E.R., Lindbeck, J.S., and Griffin, C.F. "Effects of Group Size and Advance Organizers on Learning Parameters When Using Microcomputer Tutorials in Kinematics." *Journal of Research in Science Teaching* 24 no. 9 (1987): 781–789.

Carrier, K. "Key Issues for Teaching English Language Learners in Academic Classrooms." *Middle School Journal* 37, no. 2 (November 2005): 4–9.

Clements-Davis, G.L., and Ley, T.C. "Thematic Preorganizers and the Reading Comprehension of Tenth-Grade World Literature Students." *Reading Research and Instruction* 31, no. 1 (1991): 43–53.

Checkley, K. "A is for Audacity: Lessons in Leadership from Lorraine Monroe." *Educational Leadership* 61, no. 7 (April 2004): 70–72.

Cook, G. "Killing PE is Killing Our Kids the Slow Way." *Education Digest* 71, no. 2 (October 2005): 25–32.

COOL and Idealist Civic Engagement Curriculum. "The Cover Story: A Fun Shared Visioning Activity." http://www.bhopal.net/old_studentsforbhopal_org/Assets/Cover-Story_Visioning_handout%5B1%5D.pdf.

Crounse, K. "Evaluating the Effectiveness of the Do Now Process." *Projects for School Innovation Newsletter*, May 2006.

Csikszentmihalyi, M. *Flow: The Psychology of Optimal Experience*. New York: Harper and Row, 1990.

Cusimano, A. *Learning Disabilities: There is a Cure*. Lonsdale, PA: Achieve Publications, 2001.

Dagler, C. "Clozes in the Mathematical Algebra." http://www.mrdagler.com/cloze.pdf.

Dean, C.B., Hubbell, E., Pitler, H., and Stone, B. *Classroom Instruction That Works: Research-Based Strategies for Increasing Student Achievement*, 2nd ed. Alexandria, VA: ASCD, 2012.

Deshler, D.D., Ellis E.S., and Lenz, B.K. *Teaching Adolescents with Learning Disabilities: Strategies and Methods*, 1st ed. Denver, CO: Love Pub Co., 1996.

Dewey, J. "My Pedagogic Creed" (1897). In The Essential Dewey, eds. Hickman L. and Alexander T., 229-235. Bloomington, IN: Indiana University Press, 1998.

Erlauer, L. *The Brain-Compatible Classroom*. Alexandria, VA: Association for Supervision and Curriculum Development, 2003.

Fedewa, A. L. and Ahn, S. "The Effects of Physical Activity and Physical Fitness on Children's Achievement and Cognitive Outcomes." *Research Quarterly for Exercise and Sport* 82, no. 3 (2011): 521–535.

Fried, R. *The Passionate Teacher*. Boston: Beacon Press, 2001.

Glenberg, A. "How Acting Out in School Boosts Learning." *Scientific American*, July 22, 2014. http://www.scientificamerican.com/article/how-acting-out-in-school-boosts-learning/.

Glenberg, A.M., Gutierrez, T., Levin, J.R., Japuntich, S., and Kaschak, M.P. "Activity and Imagined Activity Can Enhance Young Children's Reading Comprehension." *Journal of Educational Psychology* 96, no. 3 (2004): 424–436.

Glenn, D. "You Will Be Tested on This." *Chronicle of Higher Education* 53, no. 40 (2007): 15–17.

Hallowell, E, and Ratey, J. *Driven to Distraction: Recognizing and Coping with Attention Deficit Disorder From Childhood to Adulthood*. New York: Simon and Schuster, 1995.

Jackson, R., and Zmuda, A. "Four (Secret) Keys to Student Engagement." *Educational Leadership* 72, no. 1 (September 2014): 18–24. http://www.ascd.org/publications/educational-leadership/sept14/vol72/num01/Four-(Secret)-Keys-to-Student-Engagement.aspx.

Jensen, E. *Teaching with the Brain in Mind*. 2nd ed. Alexandria, VA: Association for Supervision and Curriculum Development, 2005.

Jones, F. *Tools for Teaching*. Santa Cruz, CA: Jones Publications, 2001.

Kennedy, X.J. *An Introduction to Poetry*. 7th ed. New York: HarperCollins Publishers, 1990.

Lavoie, R. *Understanding Learning Disabilities*. Boston: F.A.T. City Workshop, PBS Video, 1989.

Linn, M. "The Knowledge Integration Perspective on Learning and Instruction." In *The Cambridge Handbook of the Learning Sciences*, ed. Sawyer, R.K. New York: Cambridge University Press, 2006.

Marzano, R. *The Art and Science of Teaching: A Comprehensive Framework for Effective Instruction*. Alexandria, VA: Association for Supervision and Curriculum Development, 2007.

Marzano, R., Pickering, D., and Pollock, J. *Classroom Instruction that Works: Research-Based Strategies for Increasing Student Achievement*. Alexandria, VA: Association for Supervision and Curriculum Development, 2001.

McConnell, J. *The Relationship between Selected Teacher Behaviors and Attitudes and Achievement of Algebra Classes*. Paper presented at the Annual Meeting of the American Educational Research Association, New York (ERIC Document No. ED141118), 1977.

McFarlane, A. *Authentic Learning for the Digital Generation: Realising the Potential of Technology in the Classroom*. New York: Routledge, 2014.

McGeehan, J. *Transformations: Leadership for Brain-Compatible Learning*. Kent, WA: Books for Educators, Inc., 1999.

McGuire, K. "School Districts Mulling Chance for Teens to Sleep Later." *Star Tribune* (Minneapolis, MN), October 6, 2015. http://www.startribune.com/school-districts-mulling-chance-for-teens-to-sleep-later/298728971/.

Monroe, L. "Leadership for Excellence." *2000 SPANZ Conference Report*, presented March 28–April 1, 2000.

Monroe, L. *The Monroe Doctrine: An ABC Guide to What Great Bosses Do*. New York: Public Affairs, Inc., 2003.

Moore, D.W. and Readence, J.E. "A Quantitative and Qualitative Review of Graphic Organizer Research." *Journal of Educational Research* 78, no. 1 (1984): 11–17.

Naylor, G. *The Men of Brewster Place*. New York: Hyperion, 1995.

Nolet, V. and McLaughlin, M. *Accessing the General Curriculum: Including Students with Disabilities in Standards-Based Reform*. Thousand Oaks, CA: Corwin Press, Inc., 2000.

Nuthall, G. "The Way Students Learn: Acquiring Knowledge from an Integrated Science and Social Studies Unit." *Elementary School Journal* 99, no. 4 (1999): 303–341.

Powell, W. and Kusuma-Powell, O. "Coaching Students to New Heights in Writing." *Educational Leadership* 64 (Summer 2007): 1–5.

Protheroe, N. "What Does Good Math Instruction Look Like?" *Principal* 87, no. 1 (September-October 2007): 51–54.

Resnick, L. "From Aptitude to Effort: A New Foundation for Our Schools." *Daedalus* 124, no. 4 (1995): 55–62.

Rosenshine, B. "Enthusiastic Teaching: A Research Review." *School Review* 78, no. 4 (1970): 499–514.

Rush, T. "Five Steps for Effective Reading." *Language Learner* 1 no. 3 (2006): 10–11.

Schofield, J. "Internet Use in Schools: Promise and Problems," in *The Cambridge Handbook of the Learning Sciences*, ed. R.K. Sawyer. New York: Cambridge University Press, 2006.

Schwartz, D. and Heiser, J. "Spatial Representations and Imagery in Learning." In0 *The Cambridge Handbook of the Learning Sciences*, ed. Sawyer, R.K. New York: Cambridge University Press, 2006.

Spitzer, M. "Information Technology in Education: Risks and Side Effects." *Trends in Neuroscience and Education* 3, no. 3-4 (2014): 81–85. doi:10.1016/j.tine.2014.09.002.

Sprenger, M. *How to Teach So Students Remember*. Alexandria, VA: Association for Supervision and Curriculum Development, 2005.

Sprenger, M. *Learning and Memory: The Brain in Action*. Alexandria, VA: Association for Supervision and Curriculum Development, 1999.

Tokuhama-Espinosa, T. *Mind, Brain, and Education Science: A Comprehensive Guide to the New Brain-Based Teaching*. New York: W.W. Norton, 2011.

Tonn, J. "Later High-School Start Times a Reaction to Research." *Education Week* 25, no. 28 (2006): 5–17.

Trafton, A. "Even When Test Scores Go Up, Some Cognitive Abilities Don't." December 11, 2013. http://news.mit.edu/2013/even-when-test-scores-go-up-some-cognitive-abilities-dont-1211.

Wiggins, G. and McTighe, J. *Understanding by Design*, 2nd ed. Alexandria, VA: Association for Supervision and Curriculum Development, 2005.

Wiggins, G. "Transfer as the Goal of Education." *Perspectives* (September 2006).

Wiggins, G. and Wilbur, D. "How to Make Your Questions Essential." *Educational Leadership* 73, no. 1 (September 2015): 10–15.

Willis, J. "Sharpen Kids' Memory to Raise Test Scores." *Education Digest* 70, no. 7 (March 2005): 20–24.

Wormeli, R. "Spring Cleaning Our Teaching." *Middle Ground* 10, no. 4 (2007): 29–31.

Students with Disabilities: Executive Functioning, Memory, Chunking, Activators, and Homework

Children and teens with learning and attention issues, including learning disabilities (LD) and attention-deficit/hyperactivity disorder (ADD/ADHD), often struggle profoundly with intrinsic skills called *executive function*. Most people take for granted these skills that are used to navigate school, work, relationships, and daily life and fail to understand what it is like to lack certain executive skills. As classrooms continue to become more diverse with ranges of skills and needs, many students entering those classrooms are challenged in one or more of the executive functioning areas.

Executive function is a set of mental processes that help us connect past experiences with present action. It is used to perform basic activities, ranging from planning and organizing to managing time and space. Therefore, it is a major area that can affect the success of students' ability to engage successfully in learning or even be ready to begin to learn (National Center for Learning Disabilities 2013). Sharing daily agendas helps students anticipate the learning for the day, and supports their abilities to organize and prioritize the expected task and outcomes of the class. Students who struggle with executive function in the area of organizing and prioritizing often struggle with being independent learners. When teachers use daily agendas, they help students become independent learners. As students are able to anticipate shifts throughout the learning experience, including the learning focus and the mode of learning, they remain on-task, are better able to attend, can anticipate areas in which they may struggle, and solicit help before becoming frustrated.

One of the primary areas where students face organizational and prioritizing challenges is homework. The way homework is assigned can support students who struggle with executive functioning issues in the areas of organization and prioritizing. Using the suggested strategy of assigning homework at the beginning of class or on Monday for the entire week helps students know how to prioritize their time and work not only for that particular day and class, but also to help organize the week for all of their classes.

Another critical executive function for learning and school success is shifting or thinking flexibly. Students who have trouble shifting may struggle with changes in schedules, routines, content focus, or lesson delivery. They can often be viewed as rigid, stubborn, or single-minded (National Center for Learning Disabilities 2013). These students often challenge teachers the most. The students are often some of the brightest students in the class but, due to their inflexibility, it is often difficult to recognize how much they know and can do. There are a couple of strategies discussed in this chapter that, if used explicitly and in conjunction with one another, support this group of students.

Using strategies such as repetition and teaching for transfer supports students who struggle to shift and think flexibly throughout a lesson. Exposing students to the same content in various ways teaches flexible thinking and allows them to practice shifting the various ways of applying their knowledge. As you learned in the chapter, teaching for transfer is a very important skill for a teacher to execute for any student. However, for students who struggle with shifting or flexible thinking, teaching for transfer can make the difference in their overall educational success. As we have learned, this group of students often knows the information and has mastered the concepts; however, their inability to shift inhibits them from applying that knowledge across environments, and this often leads to underachievement and sometimes failure. Teaching for transfer is another way to embed the practice of shifting thinking into the class. It helps the student build his or her skills in this area over time and over concepts.

Working memory is a very important aspect of the learning process and will be dissected and discussed more in Chapter 8. Working memory plays a key role in our daily lives. It is the foundation that supports the other executive functions. In simple terms, working memory is the brain's Post-It note. Working memory helps us keep information in the mind while using the information to complete a task or execute a challenge. Working memory is like mental juggling. As information comes in, you are processing it at the same time you store it (National Center for Learning Disabilities 2013).

Using strategies such as brain breaks, chunking, and activators can support students who struggle with this executive function deficit. Brain breaks, chunking, and activators align very well together. In order for students who struggle with this executive function to maximize their full learning potential, the three should be used in conjunction with one another. For example, as you give students small chunks of instruction for 10 to 15 minutes throughout the class, you can use activator strategies during the breaks from instruction. Using the Know and Want to Know chart during a break allows students to reflect on their learning and take notes on things they already knew and what they wanted to learn. Their brain is getting a break from taking in new information, and they are intentionally reflecting on what they are learning and can connect the chunks of instruction together.

There are many strategies in this chapter that can support students who have deficits in their executive function skills. Since executive function skills are considered around-the-clock skills, they can make the difference between a student being ready and prepared to learn or not, and between a student acquiring skills and understanding or not. Therefore, using high-yield strategies, such as daily agendas, previewing homework assignments, activators, repetition, chunking, and teaching for transfer, creates a classroom that addresses the needs of all learners—including students with disabilities.

Resources

National Center for Learning Disabilities. "E-Book: Executive Function 101." *Understood.org*. 2013. https://www.understood.org/~/media/images/categorized/ebooks/executivefunction101ebook.pdf.

English Language Learners and Creating a Cognitive Context for Learning

Before They Walk into Your Classroom

It is beneficial for teachers to learn the ins and outs of the registration process and documents collected, because this will better prepare them to receive and welcome all new students, especially those who arrive after the school year has started. As part of their procedures, districts and charter schools will have a team or designees who welcome new families. Whether this is done at a parent information center or at the school, there is usually a procedure in which a school staff member conducts a survey or interview with the student, parent, or guardian. The registration process also includes the parent or guardian's completion of a home-language survey (HLS). This is a brief questionnaire that assists in the process of identifying students who may require an English language proficiency (ELP) assessment (see the essay on English learners at the end of Chapter 4). Having a conversation with the family about the student's educational history, including previous language learning, literacy skills in the home language, and any previous experience with literacy in English, will allow teachers to capitalize on what skills the student can use to learn English (Cloud, Genessee, and Hamayan, p. 37).

Below is a list of sample questions that might be asked when speaking with linguistically diverse families (in the home language, if necessary) and reviewed to gain valuable insight on a potential English learner's knowledge base, previous learning, emotional well-being, talents, and life experiences. Parents and guardians may become a little nervous about receiving so many questions, but most respond positively when they learn that the information gathered assists teachers in planning for diverse backgrounds, differentiating instruction, and providing accommodations for specific learning needs or for students who may have anxieties related to relocation and acculturation.

- Tell us about your child. What special talents and interests does your child have?

- What has your child enjoyed or not enjoyed about school?

- When did your child first attend school? Describe his or her experience in school and in learning to read or do math.

- How many hours per day and week did your child attend school? Were there any circumstances that prevented your child from attending school?

- When was the last day your child attended school? How does your child feel about his or her new school?

- (If not born in the United States) For how long has your child attended US schools?

- How would you describe your child's math, literacy, and knowledge base? How did your child's previous teacher describe your child's skills?

- How well does your child understand English? Describe your child's experience learning English.

- Would you like information on resources and other types of support offered by the community?

- Would you prefer to receive school-home communication in a language other than English?

After surveys, interviews, and initial assessments are completed, ELP results are communicated with the parent or guardian, and if the child qualifies to receive support for learning English, parents or guardians receive written notification. English learners may be placed in one of the following types of language support programs:

- A contained, grade-appropriate classroom in which the primary teacher carries an educator's license in bilingual education or ESL. This teacher may also be licensed in another content area, such as elementary education, reading, or, in middle and high schools, humanities, math, or science. Schools with larger populations of English learners generally offer contained language support classes, such as sheltered English instruction (SEI) or transitional bilingual education (TBE).

- A dual-language program in which all learners are learning a new language. This might be a one-way program in which the majority of students are learning English, or a two-way program in which there are two linguistically balanced groups of learners, with one group learning English and the other group learning the home language determined by the program's population.

- A general-education classroom in which the teacher or teachers are "qualified" to teach English learners because they have an ESL license, ESL/ELL endorsement, or have completed a state's required program for teaching English learners. ESL teachers provide English language development instruction based on the child's level of proficiency. This instruction may be offered in pull-out sessions that offer language- or content-based ESL or in co-taught lessons with the ESL and general education/content teacher.

- A separate setting, such as a mostly contained small-group environment based on an individualized education program. The ESL teacher may provide English language development (ELD) on a one-on-one basis, in a small-group setting or in co-taught lessons with the special education or general education teacher(s).

English Language Learners and Mastery Objectives

English learners must have access to and participate actively in age-appropriate, grade-level content objectives derived from the state curriculum frameworks or core standards. Selecting and writing one or two content objectives in student-friendly language, as well as posting and reviewing the objectives with students, are recommended practices for English learners (Echevarria, et al., pp. 26–17). This is done in the general-education, content-area, SEI, or content-based ESL classroom. The table below lists additional strategies for communicating content objectives to English learners at varying proficiency levels.

English Language Learners and the Communication of Content Objectives

Students New to Learning English	Students with Higher English Proficiency
• Match objectives with related visuals or graphics. • Briefly demonstrate or model what is to be mastered in the lesson. • Link **mastery objectives** to real-life objects, activities, questions, or conflicts. • Explain objectives with brief, simple English phrases with fewer technical content vocabulary words. • Offer a map of three to four steps to the lesson that lead to the objective(s) to be mastered. • Refer to the mastery objectives throughout the lesson. • Give each objective its own highlighted color or use different colored markers for each objective for emphasis so learners can follow the written steps of the lesson or activity.	• Write and explain objectives with comprehensible text, structures, and vocabulary. • Post what content, skill, and language is to be mastered in the lesson. • Link mastery objectives to meaningful or relevant activities, questions, or conflicts. • Explain objectives with comprehensible English that contextualizes content vocabulary and phrases. • Offer a list of steps to the lesson that lead to the objective(s) to be mastered. • Refer to the mastery objectives throughout the lesson.

English Language Learners and Using Agendas and Assigning Homework

The physical presence of an agenda and a sequence of events offer English learners a visual and mental roadmap for the lesson cycle. Often, English learners must rely on "what the rest of the class is doing" in order to figure out what is expected and what will happen next. The agenda items are written in comprehensible language, matched with visuals for students at pre-production or early-production levels. When agenda items are referred to often and used as part of lesson routines, English learners gain independence from their peers and develop confidence with the predictable structure. Moreover, students spend more time on learning content knowledge and aca-

demic language, and less time on having to figure out expectations and guessing where in the lesson they are and what comes next.

English learners need homework assignments written with comprehensible language, familiar vocabulary, and language structures appropriate to their proficiency and literacy levels. Hill and Miller suggest teachers plan time to explain the homework's task and purpose, and teach English learners to ask for clarification (2014, p. 122). It is important to remember that parental assistance and resources for homework may vary according to factors such as caretakers' work schedules and educational backgrounds, socioeconomic situations, transitional housing conditions, and availability of technological devices. Some parents of linguistically diverse students may be English learners themselves and find it challenging to assist their children with text-rich homework. In addition, the nature and/or process of doing homework or solving problems in the student's country of origin may be different from the American approach. Families of English learners should know the routine of assigning homework, and teachers can communicate expectations by sending home the policies and procedures in a language comprehensible to the parents.

English Language Learners and Activators and Summarizers

Learning content is a complex task for English learners in that they must acquire English while accessing, experiencing, and learning to master the same curriculum objectives as their English-proficient classmates. Teachers address the language needs of English learners when they use both language and content objectives to teach subject-matter knowledge and skills. The new language learned, whether it depends on academic vocabulary, structures, pragmatics, or grammar, should be included in activators and revisited in summarizers.

Activators and **summarizers** might assume that students in the same grade have some level of shared culture and school experiences. However, some English learners, such as those with limited or interrupted formal education, may lack the schemata and cultural context needed for an upcoming lesson or unit. Even if English learners succeed in acquiring language skills from a previous lesson, they might struggle to connect past learning to current lessons. It may also be challenging for them to remember content, academic vocabulary, sequence of events, and specific details. In these cases, teachers will need to actively demonstrate ways to make connections to prior knowledge and skills. Eliciting information and productive (oral and written) language from English-speaking classmates is one way to make connections while facilitating language learning. Here are three activities that can be used in the general-education classroom for students in grades 2–12* who have emergent speech to advanced fluency.

All students work in heterogeneous groups of three to four. They have a two-minute discussion about a question, a chapter read, a text heard, or findings from a previous lesson. Each student then writes for two to three minutes to record individual responses.

Activity 1, Activator: Peers share their writing aloud. English learners listen to and use the peers'

discourse and writing samples to activate past experiences, review plot events, or as study guides to prepare for the lesson ahead.

Activity 2, Activator: The general education teacher collects the writing, copies five samples (and removes student names) of exemplar work, and gives them to the ESL teacher. The samples are then used to introduce a content-based ESL lesson on academic vocabulary, sentence structure, or paragraph writing.

Activity 3, Summarizer: Students repeat the activity at the end of class based on the new text, information, or skill learned. The teacher records one group's discussion and collects its writing. The audio clip and writing samples can then be used to review and discuss new content learned. This follow up can take place either in a co-taught general education class or in a pull-out group with the ESL teacher.

This activity can be adapted for K–1 learners to have small groups look at and discuss student response pages that are based on letters, pictures, invented writing, or sequenced items.

Peers' productive language will sound less formal and use more familiar language structures. This will allow English learners to activate knowledge or summarize content through age-appropriate narrators and expected grade-level discourse. Other activators and summarizers that use peer-to-peer interaction might rely on pair work, cooperative completion of graphic organizers, dramatic dialogues, and group problem-solving prompts. Teachers can also record or have students record exemplar or rehearsed responses so that the information can be referred to and accessed during the new content lesson, if needed.

English Language Learners and Linking to the Real World

English learners use what they know and can do to figure out what is going on in the classroom. They often rely on multi-sensory experiences, such as listening to academic discourse while performing a task, linking visual images to define vocabulary words, or using graphic organizers to summarize new content and skills. Connecting learning to real-life situations and familiar people and locations helps English learners make connections between what they know and what they will learn (e.g., a physical or social context, audio prompts, the use of body language and gestures, social dialogue, and props). Many English learners may have been exposed to text and content, but did not actually demonstrate mastery of subject-matter knowledge or skills. These students and those who are unfamiliar with American educational topics will need additional socio-cultural contexts to help them develop background knowledge and make connections.

Resources

Cloud, N., Genesee, G., and Hamayan, E. *Literacy Instruction for English Language Learners*. Portsmouth, NH: Heinemann, 2009.

Echevarria, J., Vogt, M., and Short, D. *Making Content Comprehensible for English Learners: The SIOP Model*. Boston: Pearson, 2014.

Goldenberg, C. "Unlocking the Research on English Learners." *American Educator* 57, no. 2 (Summer 2013).

Hill, J.D. and Miller, K.B. *Classroom Instruction That Works with English Language Learners*. 2nd ed. Alexandria, VA: ASCD, 2012.

3

The Social, Emotional, and Instructional Components of Classroom Management

With a Section on the Effective Use of Homework

Objectives for the Chapter

After reading the chapter, the reader will be able to

a. Explain the role of social–emotional development in effective classroom management

b. list the nine components of effective classroom management

c. develop classroom rules (a.k.a. behavior standards), routines, and expectations that maximize the level of respectful, on-task behavior

d. develop an effective homework routine with students and parents

e. enable students to work effectively in pairs and small groups

f. obtain students' attention at the start of the lesson, after group and partner activities, after interruptions, and after student attention has deteriorated

g. develop teacher-to-student and student-to-student relationships that proactively increase appropriate student behavior

h. set up a classroom structure that proactively maintains appropriate student behavior

i. develop a classroom management plan that includes a system of rewards and consequences for reinforcing respectful, on-task behavior

j. develop an individual contingency plan for a student who is unable to behave appropriately within the classroom management plan

As Walker, Ramsey, and Gresham (2004) note in their article, a survey of teachers who are members of the American Federation of Teachers indicates that

Seventeen percent said they lost four or more hours of teaching time per week, thanks to disruptive student behavior; another 19 percent said they lost two or three hours. In urban areas, fully 21 percent said they lost four or more hours per week. And in urban secondary schools, the percentage (who report losing four or more hours of instruction) is 24 percent.

For the typical teacher who has between 20 and 30 hours a week of contact with students, this is a significant loss of instructional time over the course of the year. Even if we take the lowest figure (two hours) and multiply that by 38 weeks in a school year, we see a loss of 76 hours of instructional time. That is equal to more than three weeks of school!

Teachers have long been aware that effective and engaging instruction is an excellent means of avoiding classroom management issues; however, we also know that even the most engaging teacher will have classroom management issues unless he or she has an effective plan for classroom management.

There are many in-service programs designed to teach classroom management, as well as many online resources that address management strategies. One example for elementary teachers can be found at the website *I Love That Teaching Idea!* at ilovethatteach ingidea.com. Success of these in-service programs varies widely. Classroom management is one of the more difficult skills to teach teachers because it is so situational in nature. Landrum, Lingo, and Scott (2011), as well as Greene (2011), assert the importance of being proactive in classroom management rather than reactive. Predicting and solving problems before they occur is far more productive than addressing behaviors in the moment. Additionally, there are many variables and social structures (factors) that must be considered when developing a classroom management plan. In this chapter, we will look at the variables and social structures that must be considered when developing a classroom management plan. We will then look at specific steps we take when establishing such a plan. In the last part of the chapter, we will look at what we do with individual students who still disrupt even when we have a well-constructed and consistently implemented classroom management plan.

Variables to Consider When Constructing a Classroom Management Plan

Over the past 20 years, the authors of this book and other trainers who use this book have trained thousands of teachers in effective classroom management. The program described in this chapter has been used with preschool, elementary, middle school, and high school, as well as with undergraduate and graduate students. The key reason for the success of this program is that it explains all nine factors that must be addressed to have effective classroom management. It is a systematic approach to creating classrooms that are orderly, build a sense community, and develop children's intrinsic control of their behavior and achievement. These nine factors of classroom management include:

1. Beliefs
2. Relationships
3. Arranging classroom space and the teacher's proximity to students
4. Rules, routines, and expectations (including working effectively in partners and small groups)
5. Obtaining, maintaining, and regaining attention
6. Student self-assessment
7. Rewards and consequences
8. Engaging teaching
9. Teacher consistency

All nine of these factors must be evident in a classroom for there to be effective classroom management.

The key reason for the success of this program is that it explains all nine factors that must be addressed to have effective classroom management.

Each of these nine areas will be discussed in this chapter.

Factor 1: Beliefs

The first component to consider when constructing a classroom management plan is our (the teachers') belief system. One set of beliefs we have is about what constitutes appropriate student behavior. A second set of beliefs are about the best way to shape students' behavior. A third is the belief system of the students. The fourth set of beliefs is that of our teaching team. Students see many teachers in the course of a day. Even in elementary grades, students often interact with teachers in specialty areas such as art, music, and physical education, as well as at lunch or recess with other classroom teachers from their grade level. The fifth belief system is the school culture. Schools operate on different overt and covert cultural norms related to students. The sixth variable is the parenting beliefs in the school community. Parents' and guardians' education levels, socio-economic strata, religious beliefs, personal beliefs, personal experiences and cultural norms—all have an impact on the effectiveness of any classroom management plan. With all of these variables at play, it is little wonder that behavior management may be such a difficult area for teachers to master each and every year.

Teachers' Beliefs

Each of us operates with a belief system on two levels. The first is our cognitive-level conscious beliefs. This is what we learned in our pre-service and in-service training and through our experiences in working with students. The second level is our subconscious beliefs. This is how we react to students' behavior when we don't have the time to clearly reflect on a problem situation, weigh alternatives, and choose the best alternative based on our cognitive belief system. Our subconscious beliefs are the result of how we were parented, the classroom management we experienced as students, and a host of other factors (e.g., religion, culture, previous trauma). In the stress of the classroom, our subconscious beliefs may control our classroom management decisions as much or more than our cognitive beliefs.

There is a physiological reason for the domination of our subconscious beliefs. Our brain is made up of three primary parts: the *brain stem*, the *paleocortex*, and the *neocortex*. Frederic Jones, in his book *Tools for Teaching* (2013, p. 3859 of 8100, Kindle version), and Davis, Eshelman, and McKay, in their book *The*

Relaxation and Stress Reduction Workbook (2008), talk about the impact on our brain when we are confronted with a classroom discipline issue. Student misbehavior is stressful for teachers because it detracts from the learning the teacher is trying to achieve. Each student's misbehavior distracts the teacher and detracts from the teacher's learning goals. Not achieving one's goals is a stress producer for every person. Confronted with this stressful situation, we ideally would want to be able to calmly and rationally assess the situation, draw on our acquired knowledge, generate alternatives, assess each alternative, and select the alternative that is best suited to the situation at hand. To do this, we need to be operating in the higher level of our brain, the neocortex. Unfortunately, when confronted with a stressful situation, the brain's physiological response is to prepare for either flight, fight, or freeze. This response has been conditioned in us through millions of years of evolution. The blood leaves the neocortex and the paleocortex and flows to the brain stem and into large muscles. This move prepares us well to flee or fight. Or it can even cause us to freeze and not respond because the decision-making parts of our brain are impaired by lack of blood. It serves us poorly with solving complex problems such as discipline situations. We respond by avoiding, becoming aggressive, or resorting to conditioned responses, rather than using our cognitive belief system and problem-solving skills to deal with the situation.

> *In the stress of the classroom, our subconscious beliefs may control our classroom management decisions as much or more than our cognitive beliefs.*

When responding to behavior issues firmly, we need to be cognizant of whether we have a tendency to be **authoritative** or **authoritarian**. Ferlazzo (2012) describes the difference between these two behaviors as follows: "Being authoritarian means wielding power unilaterally to control someone, demanding obedience without giving any explanation for why one's orders are important. Being authoritative, on the other hand, means demonstrating control but doing so relationally through listening and explaining. Opting for the authoritative style will make students more likely to respect your authority—and probably more eager to cooperate."

Students' Beliefs

Students come to us from a broad range of parenting structures and previous classroom management structures. Each student has taken those varied experiences and integrated them into his or her personality. The result is an individual interpretation of various interpersonal interactions.

Prior conditioning at home and at school, coupled with students' innate **emotional intelligence**, results in each student responding differently to a situation. We often see patterns in student behavior; however, two students exhibiting the same behavior may be doing so for different reasons. This means that the teacher response that extinguishes the behavior in one student may not have the desired result in another student. Take, for example, two boys who may be constantly talking to each other in class.[1] One may come from a home in which the children hold status equal to or higher than the adults. He may be permitted to interrupt adults and choose to ignore adults when they are speaking. This student's belief is that talking to his neighbor during class is an entirely appropriate activity. The other student may come from a home in which he is required to listen to adults, not allowed to disagree or contradict adults, and certainly not allowed to interrupt an adult. In school, talking to his neighbor is a form of "pushing the envelope" and "walking on the wild side." For the second student, a firm look (or what we refer to later in the chapter as the *hairy eyeball*) may be sufficient to stop the behavior. For the other student, the look may only cause confusion.

Teaching Team's Beliefs

Classroom management plans work best when they are consistent among the teachers in a team (and in the school, which we will talk about next). By *teams*, we are referring to those teachers who have contact with the same students. In elementary schools with self-contained classrooms, the team includes the music, art, and physical education teachers. It includes teachers who may have lunch or recess duty when our students are at these activities. In middle schools, teams of teachers often share the same students, with each person teaching a different subject area. In high school, the team is often the teachers in the same department. Over the course of a high school career, a student will have four to six teachers from each department. A high level of consistency in classroom behavior expectations (and academic expectations) will make classroom management more effective for everyone. Later in this chapter, we will see a plan for teaching the expectations for cleaning up after a science lab. It would be significantly easier for

---

1 Jones's research (2007, p. 187) indicates that 80 percent of the student misbehavior in classrooms is students talking to their neighbors. Think how much easier classroom management would be if we could do away with this one behavior!

teachers to convey these expectations if all the science teachers established, taught, and consistently required the same expectations.

Students have spent many years figuring out the adults in their lives. By kindergarten, they have had six years of practice. By their senior year in high school, they have had 17 or 18 years of practice. They become very good at knowing what they can do with whom. This knowledge is evidenced by the ability students have developed to assess each teacher's behavior limits and "push the envelope" to those limits. One elementary principal with whom we worked could observe lines of students waiting for the bus from his office window without the students' seeing him. Even though the school had written behavior expectations for the bus lines, teachers would implement these expectations with varying consistency. Student behavior would vary, based on who was on duty. A middle school assistant principal with whom we worked who was the building "disciplinarian" was often in the position of monitoring the behavior of the repeat offenders from the various classes. He found marked improvement in the behavior of the students in all classes when the teachers began responding to inappropriate behaviors in a consistent fashion. He described with excitement the way in which a plan of common techniques for responding to inappropriate behavior, designed to address the behaviors of one or two students, resulted in the improved behavior of all the students.

In general, the more consistent the expectations and implementation of the expectations among the teaching team, the more effective each teacher will be in managing the classroom. Classroom management is one of those areas in which the consistent whole is more effective than the sum of the parts. Laurie Boyd (2012, p. 63) tells us that even teachers who are masters of classroom management incorporate the key features of the **building behavior management** plan into their classroom plans.

A very good exercise for a teaching team is to examine together their varying beliefs on student behavior. This can be achieved by having each person answer the following questions on his/her own.

1. When children behave in school, why do they behave?
2. When children misbehave in school, why do they misbehave?

The answers are then shared with the team. The team then discusses the similarities and differences in their answers.

Classroom management plans work best when they are consistent among the teachers in a team.

We have done this exercise with thousands of teachers during classroom management training and found in every group a wide range of answers. However, as the discussion progresses, the group's beliefs move closer together. This exercise has two objectives. The first is to create a larger foundation of common beliefs. The second is to understand where our beliefs may differ from those of our colleagues. We don't need to have a robotic consistency of beliefs to work effectively together to create an effective team plan for classroom management. However, we do need to identify our common beliefs and differences and develop a consistent set of rules, routines, and expectations.

School Culture

Each school has its own culture. In that culture, we should work to develop common expectations for student behavior; however, this is not always easy to do. There are many teachers in a school with many different sets of conscious and subconscious beliefs. The result is that even the best school-wide behavior plan will have gaps as a result of varying implementation. The goal of the school is to have common expectations and consistent implementation among the staff. This is one of those goals that schools never fully reach; however, constant effort from all staff toward this goal will result in more effective classroom management for all teachers.

An example of the value of school-wide behavior routines and expectations was observed in an urban district in a school located in the poorest neighborhood in the city. The governor of the state had come to present a successful achievement award to the school, which had previously been identified as underperforming and was placed under state monitoring. More than 1,000 students from grades K–8 and their teachers were gathered in the school gymnasium to hear the governor speak. The whispering, shuffling, and talking of more than 1,000 people added up to a significant level of noise. The superintendent stepped forward and raised his hand high over his head without speaking a word, and the entire gymnasium fell silent. The raised hand had become the signal for quiet in every classroom, in the entire school, and in the entire district!

It is important that we consider the culture in our school when crafting our classroom management plans. We want to have a plan that the administration supports and that is reasonably consistent with other teachers' plans. One author taught a workshop on classroom management to a group of teachers from several neighboring districts. In the workshop was a novice elementary music teacher who taught in two schools. Each time the trainer spoke about team consistency and school culture, he could see the teacher's frustration. At the break, the trainer asked the teacher what was frustrating him. He shared with the trainer that, in his district, the four elementary schools were built in a cluster on the same site. Each school had a different philosophy. Parents in that community could choose the school they wished their children to attend. He happened to be assigned to two schools with very different cultures related to student behavior. One school was "traditional." Most of the classrooms were arranged with students in rows. Students all passed through the halls in lines. The other school was an open concept school. There were large teaching spaces that several classes shared. Students flowed through the halls from one place to another without walking in lines. The students in that school called the teachers and the principal by their first names. The music teacher had tried to develop a classroom management plan that worked in both schools, but he ended up with one that did not work well in either school. The trainer spent some time with the teacher, modifying his single plan by turning it into two plans, one for each school. The teacher reported significant improvement when his classroom management plans matched the culture of each school.

We want to have a plan that the administration supports and that is reasonably consistent with other teachers' plans.

Fortunately, most of us don't have to work in more than one school culture at a time; however, this story does emphasize the importance of understanding the school culture and crafting a plan that is not inconsistent with that culture.

Parents and Guardians' Beliefs

The beliefs of parents and guardians as a group often correlate fairly closely with the school culture. The exception to this is when a school has been deemed in need of a significant change in its culture by a district initiative, an outside agency, or the parents themselves. In those cases, the school's stated culture and its operating culture will be separated by a fairly large gap. In these circumstances, it is important to be aware of both cultures and adjust our classroom plans as the culture of the building changes. The parents' culture might reflect the stated school culture, the operating school culture, or a completely different culture.

Within the parent and guardian group, there are significant numbers who have a belief system that is outside of the group's belief system. This is less the case in schools such as the ones described above, in which the parents get to match their belief system with the school's culture. Most school enrollments, however, are determined by geography. This leaves a greater likelihood that there will be parents with beliefs outside of the group belief system. This difference may be even more pronounced in cities and counties in which students are bused across neighborhood and community lines. In those cases, the socioeconomic, religious, and cultural differences tend to be greater than in schools that draw from a specific geographic neighborhood.

We worked with an assistant superintendent in an urban/suburban district with eight neighborhood schools. One school had a parent education level that was in the top 1 percent in the state. The parent income level was in the top 2 percent in the state. Across the district was another school in which more than 30 percent of the students were receiving free or reduced lunch, and many lived in public housing. In a third school, 20 percent of the student population was first- or second-generation Japanese American. In still another school, the population was 40 percent Jewish and 40 percent white Anglo-Saxon Protestant. Another school had a very large concentration of Chinese and Latino students who were predominantly Catholic and also had a growing Muslim community. These were all neighborhood schools with their own school cultures and some similarity in family beliefs about student behavior. All eight schools with their different cultures sent their ninth graders to a single high school. One can just imagine the multitude of parental belief systems and school cultures faced by the teachers of these ninth graders.

Factor 2: Classroom Management and Teacher-Student and Student-Student Relationships

A good relationship between the student and the teacher is a strong motivator for positive behavior. All of us can think back to some teacher or adult in our lives whom we genuinely respected and who genuinely liked and respected us, so much that it was important to us to please this person and keep his or her respect. This adult motivated us to work harder at our academics, at a sport, in our job, and/or on the appropriateness of our behavior. This person motivated us to try hard in any or all of these areas because we truly wanted his or her approval and respect. Being motivated by a good relationship is very different from being motivated by fear of consequences or punishment.

Robert Marzano (2007, p. 150) reviewed 100 studies related to classroom management. This meta-analysis found that "teachers who had high-quality relationships with their students had 31 percent fewer discipline problems, rule violations, and related problems over a year's time than did teachers who did not have high-quality relationships with their students."

School psychologist Allen Mendler, author of *Discipline With Dignity* (1999) and *As Tough As Necessary* (1997), writes in his book *Connecting With Students* (2001):

> Many educators wonder how they are going to find the time to build and sustain relationships with students when there are so many demands for achievement. In fact, successful educators realize that a strong relationship with students leads to better discipline in the classroom, which means more time for instruction. A 2013 study by Reichart and Hawley of "middle school boys and their teachers in the US, Canada, UK, and South Africa found that…varying degrees of resistance boys brought to the classroom were dissolved by a variety of relational gestures by teachers."

The following is a list of techniques for building relationships with students. We collected these ideas from our own teaching and from that of our colleagues.

- talking informally with students
- greeting students outside of school
- greeting students at the door when they enter class
- singling out students for conversations in the lunchroom
- commenting on important events in the students' lives
- complimenting students on important achievements outside of school
- making eye contact with individual students when talking to the group
- attending students' sporting events and performances

A good relationship between student and teacher is a strong motivator for positive behavior.

- being clear about expectations and enforcing rules consistently and fairly[2]
- making it clear to students in our words and behaviors that we are committed to helping them succeed
- making it clear to students that we enjoy our jobs and getting to work with them
- taking their insights and ideas seriously
- being willing to work with struggling students before and after school
- being passionate and enthusiastic about what we are teaching
- writing notes to students for good work done in or out of class
- making phone calls home to inform parents of good news!
- greeting students when we pass them in the hallway
- occasionally sharing stories from our own experiences as students
- taking a few moments of Monday class time to ask students about their weekends
- following the grading formula, *three compliments for every word of constructive criticism*
- making an effort to stand physically close to all students at different points in the class
- when working with seated students, getting down to their level so you are not looking down at them
- providing appropriate wait time so more students may successfully participate in class discussions
- being flexible about deadlines in genuine emergencies
- never using sarcasm to embarrass a student in front of the class
- whenever possible, handling disciplinary conversations in private
- sharing with individual students common interests you both share (e.g., soccer, jazz, NASCAR racing, gardening)
- smiling

Think again about that person who motivated you to work harder or behave better. How many of the above behaviors did that person exhibit?

---

2   "Schools can best encourage prosocial behavior by using consistent positive disciplinary practices that include clear expectations, discussions, and modeling" (Kidron and Fleishman, 2003, p. 91).

Student-to-Student Relationships within the Classroom

It is also important to establish a community of trust and care in our classrooms, as this goes hand in hand with building relationships with our students. Students need to know and understand that both their teacher and their classmates are going to do their best to take care of them throughout the year. Providing opportunities both for us and for our students to get to know one another, celebrating the successes of others, and helping students get through difficult times, are all critical components to creating a trusting and caring community. Mendler (2012, p. 27) tells of the role building student relationships and accountability plays in decreasing bullying.

In his book, *Relationship-Driven Classroom Management* (2003, p. 81), special educator John Vitto sums it up well with the following: "When students feel they belong, they are in a better position to learn; when they feel they do not belong, they often turn to misbehavior." Students who lack social skills are distracted from learning by the tremendous amount of energy they expend trying to fit in. Teachers cite **social skills deficits** as the most frequent cause of classroom behavior problems (Brophy and Good 2000). Marzano states, "The teacher must provide clear direction to students and generate an atmosphere in which all students feel valued and intellectually challenged" (Marzano 2011, p. 85).

Community building takes many forms in class-

When students feel they belong, they are in a better position to learn; when they feel they do not belong, they often turn to misbehavior.

rooms. Some teachers use activities known as community builders that are designed exclusively for the purpose of helping students get to know one another. An example of a community builder is Four Things We Have in Common. In this activity, students are placed in groups of four or five (see the eleven components of effective group work later in this chapter). Instead of giving the students an academic task, the teacher has them identify at least four things they all have in common. To complete this task, the group members must give the others information about their lives, such as number of siblings, place of birth, pets, favorite movie, etc., until they can find at least four things they all have in common. Through this process, the students get to know one another on a personal level.

Community building can also be achieved through the academic tasks. Later in this chapter, in the section on effective group work, we list some of the group social skills students need to develop to be socially successful in the classroom. We will learn about the cooperative learning jobs grid (see Factor 4: Rules, Routines, and Expectations later in this chapter). Structuring the jobs grid with criteria by which the students tell something about themselves is another way of building community. As the year progresses, different jobs grids can be used to learn different facts about one another. A more complete description of role definitions and responsibilities is found later in this chapter.

Table 3.1 Cooperative Learning Jobs Grid

Description Column	Activity 1	Activity 2	Activity 3	Activity 4
Oldest sibling	Leader	Gopher	Reporter	Scribe
Born the farthest from the school	Scribe	Leader	Gopher	Reporter
Oldest living relative	Reporter	Scribe	Leader	Gopher
Whoever is left	Gopher	Reporter	Scribe	Leader

It is also important that our classroom routines be structured with expectations that enhance rather than detract from the sense of community. For example, group work expectations should include expectations about tone of voice and types of comments that are off limits because of the detrimental effect they may have on relationships among students.

Student Ownership of the Class

The first way to help students feel ownership of the class is to follow this advice: **Don't do anything for students that they can do for themselves.** Instead, follow the lead of an elementary school colleague of ours who, each year, creates a job wheel that lists approximately twenty-five classroom responsibilities.

At the beginning of each week, she utilizes the job wheel to assign a responsibility to each member of the class. These jobs range from taking attendance to collecting homework to hanging up student work. Or consider the example of a high school science teacher we observed. By October the students started each lab by obtaining all the equipment from the appropriate storage area and setting it up for the lab. At the conclusion of the lab, they cleaned all the equipment and area, and then returned the equipment exactly where it belonged. All these tasks were done with little or no prompting by the teacher.

How does assigning students responsibilities within a classroom relate to creating an effective context for teaching and learning? In short, creating a classroom structure in which students play a role in the effective operation of the classroom sends the explicit message to students that they are active participants in what goes on inside the classroom. They are not there to sit passively and let the teacher do all of the work, but, rather, they have a role to play in making the classroom one in which effective teaching and learning can occur. Such a message may have a powerful impact not only on the jobs that students are assigned, but also on helping them to see their learning as a process in which they must take an active role rather than a passive one.

The second way to help students feel ownership of the class is to be clear with them about why the routines exist from the perspective of their own benefit, the benefit of other students, and the teacher's benefit. This can take many forms. Some teachers operate on the **democratic classroom** principle of allowing the students to establish the rules, routines, and expectations within reasonable parameters. Other teachers operate as "benevolent dictators." The teacher establishes the rules, routines, and expectations (see Factor 4: Rules, Routines, and Expectations later in this chapter) but gives students the opportunity to comment and offer suggestions for improvement. The teacher then modifies the classroom management plan if he/she feels the students' suggestions will indeed improve the overall classroom environment socially, emotionally, and/or academically.

Another way in which we help students take ownership of the class and their behavior is by requiring them to actively assess their own adherence to classroom routines. Later in this chapter, Factor

> *Marzano states that "desk arrangements should provide access to any student within four steps from where the teacher spends most of his time."*

6 looks at the ways in which teachers foster student self-assessment of their behavior.

Factor 3: Arranging the Classroom Space and the Teacher's Proximity to the Students

The way in which we arrange our classroom and place ourselves in the classroom can have a significant impact on students' behavior. Let's take, for example, a high school classroom in which the desks are arranged in rows, the students get to choose their seats, and the teacher primarily teaches from the front of the classroom. In this situation, the students who are the most prone to misbehavior tend to sit in the back of the room, placing themselves at the farthest point from the teacher. The most effective arrangement of classroom space would have those students close to the teacher. Teacher proximity to students is an excellent deterrent to inappropriate behavior. It also enables the teacher to use some of the more subtle attention moves (see Factor 5: Obtain, Maintain, and Regain Attention later in this chapter), such as a hand on the shoulder or a quick glance of the "hairy eyeball" to regain the attention of these students. In many classrooms, the "front of the room" changes during the lesson, so there is no consistent "front of the room." Therefore, teachers need to circulate to ensure close proximity to all students in order to minimize misbehavior and maintain attention.

For many years, teachers used proximity as a consequence. For example, once the student misbehaved, he or she was moved to the front of the room, or his or her desk was placed next to the teacher's desk. As discussed in the attention moves later in the chapter, this type of negative attention often achieved the desired result in the short term. The student stopped misbehaving. However, the embarrassment caused by this strategy often resulted in increased levels of misbehavior over the course of the year.

It is far more effective to arrange our classroom furniture and ensure that we move about the room while teaching in ways that insures close proximity to all students at various points in the lesson. This will proactively decrease acting-out behavior, rather than putting us in the position of reactively responding to inappropriate behavior. Marzano states that "desk arrangements should provide access to any student within four steps from where the teacher spends most of his time" (2007, p. 121). There are a variety of classroom arrangements that maximize the teacher's ability to remain in close proximity to the students. Some examples of this include the following:

Paired Rows

In this arrangement, student desks are positioned in pairs. This allows the teacher to position more students near the front of the room and enables all students to be looking forward. This also allows for easy partner support during the learning. For this to work effectively, the teacher needs to be sure to move between the rows during instruction so as not to spend a disproportionate amount of time in the proximity of those student pairs who are in the front of the room. In this arrangement, it is important to have both horizontal and vertical pathways for the teacher to ensure teacher proximity to all students.

Table Groups

In this setup, either the teacher uses tables in place of desks or the teacher arranges the desks into tables. Students are in groups of four or five. This setup enables the teacher to have quick and efficient group processing. It also creates more space for pathways for the teacher to circulate and ensures equal proximity to all students.

Double Horseshoe

In this setup (see next page), the desks are arranged in two horseshoes, with one inside the other. In this arrangement, the teacher teaches from the inside of the horseshoe. When inside the horseshoe, the teacher's proximity is never more than one desk and student away from any student.

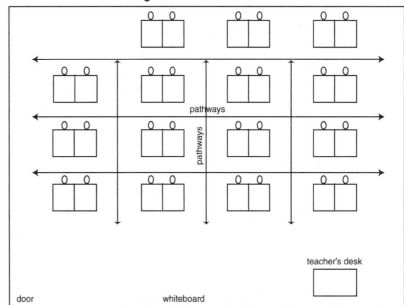

Figure 3.1 Paired Rows

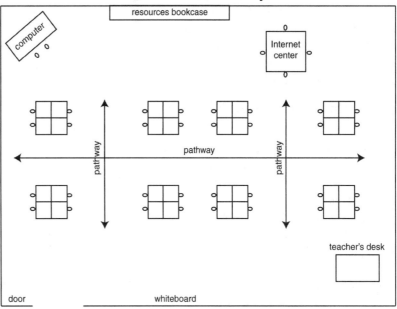

Figure 3.2 Table Groups

Figure 3.3 Double Horseshoe

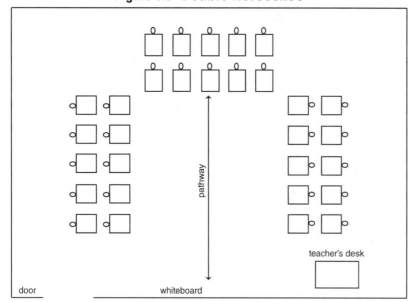

In any student arrangement, it is important that the teacher move throughout the room during the class period. We want to ensure an equitable distribution of teacher proximity to all students. In addition to preventing misbehavior, this type of proximity also enables the teacher to frequently formatively assess the seat work of all students.

Table Groups with Learning Centers

In elementary school classrooms with learning centers, and middle and high school classrooms with interest centers, it is important to place the centers for easy access with minimal disruption. Pathways to the centers should be unobstructed so other students are not disrupted by those going to the centers. Figure 3.2 is a middle or high school mathematics classroom with two interest centers. One is a computer workstation for accessing websites for mathematics enrichment, remediation, and application. The other is a table at which small groups of students can work together on mathematics problems that are real-life applications of the concepts taught in class.

At right is an elementary classroom configuration with several learning centers. In this classroom, the teacher has instructional times when all the students are in centers. As a result, the teacher needs enough centers to accommodate all the stu-

dents, and the centers need to be spaced so groups do not disturb one another. Teachers who only have space or furniture for two or three center areas can modify this setup by using some of the grouped desks as centers. For example, a table at the back and one on each side could contain three of the centers. The other four centers could be set up one at each of the four grouped desk tables.

Factor 4: Rules, Routines, and Expectations

In thinking about classroom management, we focus on three levels of behaviors. The first is our classroom **rules** (a.k.a. behavior standards). There tend to be only a few of these, and they are generally worded. We try to write rules/standards in terminology that is positive rather than focusing on the negative. Samples of rules/standards include the following:

1. We will treat everyone in the class with respect.
2. We will treat all school and personal materials and supplies in an appropriate manner.
3. We will support the learning and growth of all members of the class.
4. We will arrive to class on time with our materials, and we will complete our work in a timely manner.

Figure 3.4 Table Groups with Learning Center

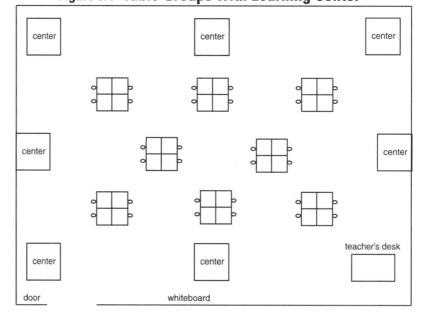

Rules/standards are often established on a school-wide basis. If they are not, then it is important that we start our work in developing our classroom management plans by creating the rules. These should be posted in a prominent place in the classroom. According to Marzano (2011):

> To provide academic direction, a teacher must have clear learning goals coupled with instruction and assessment that help students achieve those goals. To provide behavioral direction, the teacher must have well-designed rules and procedures[3] (usually established at the beginning of the school year) that s/he continually updates and reinforces throughout the year. In addition, these rules and procedures need to be the basis for interacting with students regarding behavior: When students follow the rules and procedure, the teacher thanks them; when they don't, the teacher reminds them of behavioral expectations (2007, p. 85).

In order to help students better understand and appreciate the rules, some teachers have the students brainstorm a list of behaviors (a.k.a. expectations) they think would be important to have in their classrooms. Students usually contribute a long list of fairly specific behaviors. As a class, students categorize these behaviors into four or five general rules. For example, the following expectations could all be categorized under the rule: *We will treat everyone with respect.*

1. I will listen when the teacher or another student is talking.
2. I will raise my hand when I have something to say in class.
3. I will ask permission if I would like to use another student's materials.
4. I will keep quiet when we are doing independent work.
5. I will make sure everyone is included when we are at lunch and recess.

After the class agrees on approximately five general rules, the students or the teacher creates a poster showing the rules, and students are asked to sign their names to the poster. In essence, they are signing a contract. There is a common understanding that if a student breaks a rule, s/he will face consequences that are also known and discussed ahead of time.[4]

After rules, the second level of our classroom management planning is the **routines** (a.k.a. behavior routines). These are specific tasks students must successfully complete to obey the rule. Classrooms have many routines. Examples of classroom routines include start of class, homework, answering/asking questions, and going the bathroom. Later in this chapter, you will see a comprehensive list of classroom routines and expectations one teacher developed for her classroom routine.

The third level is the **expectations** (a.k.a. behavioral expectations). These are the observable descriptions of the behaviors a student must exhibit to demonstrate successful implementation of the routine. McLeod, Fischer, and Hoover, in their book, *The Key Elements of Classroom Management* (2003, p. 79), warn us that "the student must be able to do what you are asking him to do." Our expectations should be behaviors that students can succeed in doing. Later in this chapter, you will see the specific expectations for one teacher's classroom routine for using the bathroom.

Starting Off Well

Teachers often start the year poorly with their classroom management because they fail to devote adequate time to teaching students the routines and expectations that *operationalize* the rules. Many teachers state and post their rules at the start of the year and never go beyond that point. The problem with this is that words may mean different things to different students based on their beliefs. The definition of *respect* may vary in different homes and in the classrooms of the various teachers the students had during prior years. The definition also changes for people as they enter different stages of their lives. Treating a person with *respect* means one thing to us when we are five years old, another when we are 10, another when we are 15, another when we are 20, and still another when we are 40. This is why it is important that we clearly state the routines and our expectations for the behaviors that lead to success in each routine. Respect is a good word for our rules, but it is not sufficiently observable for stating expectations.

Before a teacher can teach routines to students, he or she must have a clear and specific understand-

> *After rules, the second level of our classroom management planning is the routines (a.k.a. behavior routines).*

---

3 In this book, we use the term *routine* in the same way Marzano uses *procedure*.

4 Many middle school and high school teachers incorporate these rules into their classroom management plan, which they send home for parent and student signature.

ing of the expectations for each routine. For example, we were teaching a group of second-year high school teachers about developing routines. Several had expressed concern that the flow of the class was often interrupted by student requests to go to the bathroom. We asked each teacher to write down his or her expectations for bathroom use and the time he or she spent telling and/or teaching[5] the routines to students. Several gave a one-sentence explanation of routines, such as, "You must ask permission to use the bathroom in my class." All indicated they spent a minute or less telling students the bathroom routine and its expectations at the start of the school year. A series of questions was asked of one of the teachers who had given a single sentence as his bathroom expectation. As they stated an expectation, we wrote it down. Through this conversation, they realized there were, in fact, fifteen observable behavior expectations that made up what he expected for a successful classroom bathroom routine. The expectations listed were as follows:

1. No asking to go to the bathroom unless it is an emergency.
2. If you have a doctor-confirmed medical reason indicating you need to use the bathroom frequently, you should speak to me privately.
3. Emergency use is restricted to after the first ten minutes and before the last ten minutes of class.
4. You must raise your hand and ask permission.
5. You must sign out and include the time you leave.
6. You must walk directly to the door without detours and without talking to or touching anyone or anything.
7. You must go directly to the bathroom and directly back without disturbing any other classes along the way.
8. You may not take your backpack with you.
9. You must return in five minutes or less.
10. You must sign in and include the time you return.
11. You must walk directly to your seat without detours and without talking to or touching anyone or anything.

> *It soon became obvious to all that they needed to explicitly teach these behaviors to their classes. Students needed to know what was expected before they could correctly follow the routine.*

12. You must quietly check with a neighbor to see what you missed.
13. The first failure to follow these expectations means you lose independent bathroom privileges in this class for a week.
14. The second failure to do so means you lose independent bathroom privileges in this class for a month.
15. The third failure to do so means you will receive a discipline referral to the assistant principal.

It soon became obvious to all that they needed to explicitly teach these behaviors to their classes. Students needed to know what was expected before they could correctly follow the routine.

Below is a list of the specific routines and expectations that need to be thoroughly taught at the start of the school year. Put a check next to each routine for which you have already created specific expectations for your students. As you read through this list, you may write down any notes you wish to remember about any of the listed routines.

Beginning Class Routines and Expectations

____ entering the class
____ roll call, attendance (including procedures for tardiness)
____ seat work requirements when students first enter the class (e.g., Do Now expectations)
____ distribution of materials
____ sitting in assigned seats
____ procedure for checking and/or turning in homework
____ procedure for students absent the previous day to collect missed handouts and assignments and get caught up on missed material
____ writing down that night's homework assignment
____ materials students are expected to have with them in class each day

General Classroom Routines and Expectations

____ shared materials
____ teacher's desk
____ food and drinks (water)
____ gum
____ bathroom
____ distributing and collecting materials

---

5   We differentiate between the words *telling* and *teaching* in the following way. *Telling* is an activity done solely by the teacher. Tellers give out the requisite information but do not assess and ensure the students' level of understanding or mastery of the information (see Chapter 1 for an explanation of the levels of mastery). *Teaching* transfers a body of information in a way that maximizes understanding and retention. It includes an assessment of the students' understanding of the information and their mastery of any behavior required in the learning.

____ pencil sharpener
____ student storage, lockers, cubbies
____ dismissing class
____ lining up for assemblies, trips to library, or computer lab
____ attendance and tardiness
____ use of electronic devices in class

Routines and Expectations for Behavior During Independent and Group Work[6]

____ Is talk among students permitted?
____ If so, when and how?
____ identification of resources, such as Internet and dictionaries, and how they may be accessed during the work time
____ passing out and collecting of books, supplies
____ assigning tasks to the group members (e.g., leader, scribe, timekeeper, reporter)
____ interim checkpoints
____ teacher's signals for students' attention (see the section later in this chapter on obtaining and regaining student attention)
____ students' signals for obtaining the teacher's attention
____ activities to do when work is done
____ How does a student get help from the teacher?
____ How and when can a student get help from other students?
____ student participation
____ turning in work
____ when and how students return assignments when requested by the teacher
____ How does the teacher get back assignments after the student has them signed by parents (or in other situations)?
____ missed work
____ laboratory procedures
____ movement in and out of small groups
____ bringing materials to school
____ expected behavior in group[7]
____ what to do if you finish early
____ homework expectations and procedures
____ putting away supplies, equipment

____ cleaning up
____ organizing class materials

Expectations for Appropriately Completed Work

____ what headings used on papers
____ when students use pen, pencil, or word processor
____ Is writing on the backs of papers permitted?
____ What are the standards for neatness and legibility?
____ How is incomplete work handled?
____ How is late work handled?
____ When do students use manuscript, cursive, or typing?
____ What margins, fonts, and spacing (single- or double-spaced) are used?
____ Should "fringes" be cut off paper taken from spiral notebook?
____ spacing of written work (e.g., writing on every other line)
____ difference between draft quality and final copy quality

Grading Policies and Procedures

____ determining grades
____ recording grades
____ grading long assignments
____ closing date for grades
____ penalties for incomplete work
____ extra-credit work
____ keeping papers, grades, assignments
____ grading criteria
____ contracting for grades
____ rewrites and retests
____ makeup work policy (if absent)

Homework Routines[8]

____ When and where does a student write down assignments?
____ Who can assist a student?
____ What are the limits on the assistance others can give a student?
____ What Internet resources may a student use or not use (e.g., translations.com, Moodle, class website)?
____ How does a student get the homework assignment when absent?

6 Later in this chapter, we discuss the components needed for effective classroom work groups.
7 Monitoring the level of conversation during small group work that is on-task and off-task may be difficult when we are helping individual groups with their work. One technique we have used to teach the expectations for appropriate group discussions and, at times, to monitor that expectation, is to tape-record the work of some groups. Later in this section of this chapter, there is an explanation of how this may be done.
8 Later in this chapter, you will see examples of plans teachers use for establishing an effective homework routine.

_____ What are the plagiarism guidelines and penalties?

_____ What is the late-homework penalty system?

Other Routines and Expectations

_____ fire drills

_____ lunch procedures

_____ student helpers

_____ safety procedures

_____ out-of-seat policies

_____ consequences for misbehavior

_____ behavior in the computer lab, library, auditorium

_____ locker visits

_____ behavior in the halls

_____ medical emergencies

_____ expectations for when conflict arises

_____ behavior during tests

_____ expectations for how to address teacher and fellow students

Teaching Routines and Expectations

The time spent teaching routines and expectations is time well spent. Over the course of the year, a teacher will save a great deal of instructional time if s/he devotes adequate time at the start of the year to teaching routines and expectations.

In his book *Tools for Teaching*, Fred Jones states, "Research has repeatedly shown that the teachers with the best-run classrooms spend most of the first two weeks of the semester teaching their procedures and routines" (2013, p. 3359 of 8100, Kindle version).

We began this chapter by quoting a survey indicating the instructional time that is lost during a year due to student misbehavior. It makes a strong case for devoting sufficient time at the outset of the year to teaching routines. Teachers also typically find it is much easier to teach routines at the start of the year than it is to have students fall into bad habits that need to be broken prior to teaching the appropriate routines.

In our experience, poor classroom management only gets worse as the year progresses, causing an even greater loss of instructional time. In most cases, the time for student learning is far greater over the course of the year if the teacher adequately teaches the routines and expectations at the start of year and reteaches them whenever he/she notices a regression in students' compliance. Returning from a vacation or at the beginning of a term are good points at which to change seats or provide a "refresher" lesson on the rules, routines, and expectations.

Teaching Classroom Routines

It is never enough just to tell students our expectations for classroom routines. It is important that we *teach* the routines until the students master them, in the same way that we teach academic concepts until they are mastered. The following are the steps needed to effectively teach student classroom routines.

Over the course of the year, a teacher will save a great deal of instructional time if s/he devotes adequate time at the start of the year to teaching routines and expectations.

Step one in effectively teaching routines is to be clear about what it looks like when a student successfully completes the expectations for the routine and what it looks like when a student does not follow the expectations correctly. Wording the expectations in language that is observable will help you teach the expectation clearly. In the example above of the high school teacher's bathroom routine, we saw that at the expectation level, words such as *appropriate* were replaced with observable behaviors that the teacher could monitor and that students could use to monitor their own success.

Step two is to test the reality of the expectations for the routine. The teacher in the earlier example originally wanted no one to go to the bathroom. Upon reflection, he realized this was not a viable routine based on school policies.

Step three is to ensure that the routine you have planned is consistent with the expectations of the school and team.

Step four is to create a plan for teaching the routine. It will be helpful to model and/or role-play routines as part of teaching the routine. For example, if one of your expectations as an elementary educator is that students should make an effort to include others they see are being excluded during recess time, it would be helpful to have a few students role-play this scenario while the other students observe. After role-playing, the class might discuss other means by which to make sure everyone is included.

One high school teacher role-plays leaving the classroom to go to the bathroom, assigning himself the role of the student. The first time he shows the students how *not* to leave the class. He takes on the persona of the student by getting out of his chair and swaggering on a circuitous route around the room, before eventually getting to the door. On his way around, he pauses at the desks of a couple of his friends to make a comment or flip their books shut. This role-play always results in laughs from the students, as many of them can see themselves in his behaviors. He then role-plays the appropriate way one leaves the room to use the bathroom after receiving permission from the teacher.

Once a routine is taught, we need to expect students to consistently use it, and we should consistently assess students' success in carrying it out. We should look for opportunities to consistently reinforce successful performance of the routine. We should also be ready to reteach the routine if we see student performance regressing. One of the most important parts of establishing and maintaining good routines is consistent enforcement and reinforcement! The three most important things for teachers to remember when establishing effective classroom management are consistency, consistency, and consistency. Although there are too many classroom routines to post them all, it may be helpful to post those routines that are particularly important. For example, you may want to make a poster listing activities for students to complete when work is finished. You may also want to post a list of expectations for students engaged in collaborative work.

The three most important things for teachers to remember when establishing effective classroom management are consistency, consistency, and consistency.

Teacher Provisioning of Materials

It is important that we have all our materials prepared and ready at the start of class. If students are waiting for us to locate materials, the lesson loses its momentum, and this can lead to acting-out behavior. Effective teacher provisioning requires the following

1. We anticipate all the materials that will be needed for the lesson. This can include the obvious lesson materials, such as the books, activity sheets, paper, equipment for labs and demonstrations, and appropriate technology. It also includes expecting the unexpected. For example, this can include an extra bulb for the LCD projector, extra pencils for students who forget their own pencils, extra books for students who forgot their own, and even

a tissue for the student who sneezes and is without a tissue or handkerchief.

2. All the materials needed for the lesson are prepared prior to the lesson and placed in a location where they are readily available.

One of the advantages to being well provisioned is that students can then distribute materials or get their own materials. This frees the teacher to teach and/or facilitate appropriate behavior.

Routines and Expectations for Group Work

Many teachers struggle with getting students to work effectively in groups. Teachers who are unsuccessful at getting students to work effectively in groups often avoid doing group work. Unfortunately, we cannot adequately differentiate by content, process, and product unless students are able to work effectively in groups. Group work is also an important skill for life. Quinn (2012, p. 46) tells us, "Collaboration is included in every list of 21st century skills."

There are 11 areas of group work that teachers should address to have effective groups.

The first area is to remember to alert students to impending transitions. Students do not typically do well with surprises. They need some time to get physically and mentally ready for transitions.[9] Alert students to transitions, such as the time when group work will begin, when the group needs to shift activities, or when the group work will end. One way we do this is by indicating this information on our class agenda. Another is to provide students with verbal notice before the impending transition. The length of time we alert students prior to the transition will depend on how complex the transition will be. In some cases, the notice can be as little as two minutes. In other cases, it may need to be as much as five or ten minutes.

The second area of effective grouping is group size. Groups should be no larger than four or five students (or they can be as small as two students). In our experience, once groups exceed this limit, some students get lost and/or lose interest because they do not get adequate opportunity to participate.

9   This is true of all transitions and not just transitions in and out of group and partner work. Alerting students to an impending end of the class or expected classroom disruption makes them better prepared to respond appropriately.

This can lead to loss of learning by these students and, at times, misbehavior. Some people believe that in lower elementary grades, groups should have no more than three students.

All members of the group are responsible for monitoring themselves and others, following the basic group work expectations such as voice volume, good listening, courtesy, etc.

The third area is to assign jobs. A quick and efficient way to do this is to use the cooperative learning jobs grid.

Dean, Hubbell, Howard, and Pitler (2012, p. 37) tell us that "to foster positive interdependence, teachers must ensure that the workload of each individual is reasonably equal to the workload of other team members." Assigning jobs, as well as creating a system of individual accountability (see area eight on p. 98), are key components of ensuring reasonable equity in the workload. Figures 3.5 and 3.6 below are examples of cooperative learning jobs grids. When using the jobs grid, we start by putting the students into their groups. We then explain to the students that each student may only have one job at a time. Beginning with the top box, the students discuss the criteria and figure out who best fits the description in each description column box. Once the leader is established, he or she is out of the running for the scribe position

in the second description box. Once the scribe is set, the final two members of the group vie for the recorder position. The last person without a job is the gopher (this name is derived from the fact that he/she is the person to "go for" whatever is needed).

Each job has specific responsibilities. The leader's job is to ensure that the job gets done correctly in the time allowed. The leader must ensure that everyone contributes to accomplishing the task. This means that the leader must encourage the reticent to speak and contain any member who tries to disproportionately dominate the discussion. The scribe keeps notes as a record of the group's work. The notes must be legible enough so that the reporter can read them to give the group report or so others can copy the notes if that is required. The reporter gives the oral report of the group's work to the entire class.[10] The "gopher" is the one who gets any materials the group needs. He or she is the one who fetches the dictionary from the book-

---

10 Requiring the scribe to record notes that are neat enough for the reporter also makes the notes neat enough for the teacher to collect and review. At times, we will collect the group notes as a way of assessing the quality of the work done by the group.

Figure 3.5 Groups of Four Students

Description Column	Activity 1	Activity 2	Activity 3	Activity 4
Wearing the most red	Leader	Gopher	Reporter	Scribe
Traveled to the farthest place on summer vacation	Scribe	Leader	Gopher	Reporter
Most unusual pet at home	Reporter	Scribe	Leader	Gopher
Whoever is left	Gopher	Reporter	Scribe	Leader

Figure 3.6 Groups of Five Students

Description Column	Activity 1	Activity 2	Activity 3	Activity 4	Activity 5
Tallest	Leader	Timekeeper	Gopher	Reporter	Scribe
Shortest	Scribe	Leader	Timekeeper	Gopher	Reporter
Longest hair	Reporter	Scribe	Leader	Timekeeper	Gopher
Shortest hair	Gopher	Reporter	Scribe	Leader	Timekeeper
Whoever is left	Timekeeper	Gopher	Reporter	Scribe	Leader

case, goes to the library if research material is needed, or goes to the cabinet for the science lab equipment. He or she can also be designated as the person who gets the teacher if the group needs teacher assistance or goes to another group if the group needs peer assistance. In cases in which you have groups of five, a timekeeper can be added as the fifth job. If you only have four and need a timekeeper, then timekeeping can be assigned to the gopher or to one of the other job areas. All members of the group are responsible for monitoring themselves and others, following the basic group work expectations, such as voice volume, good listening, courtesy, etc. Later in this chapter, you will find methods for teaching students to do this monitoring.

Once the grid is set, the teacher has the jobs ready for four or five different activities. Since the students rotate through the jobs, there is little concern about fairness. Students typically find the initial placement in jobs by the randomly set descriptions more fair than when the teacher assigns the jobs. However, in circumstances when the teacher thinks it is best, the teacher may certainly assign the first set of jobs and then let the students rotate through the jobs during the next three activities. The cooperative learning jobs grid significantly reduces the time it takes to assign jobs each time there is a new activity and eliminates the bickering that may occur over who will do which job.

The fourth area of effective grouping challenges the notion that equity means spending equal amounts of time with each group. Some groups will need more of your time than others. Some will need this time because they are struggling with the concept and need more reteaching and prompting. Some will need this time because they have quickly completed the task and need to be directed toward extension work. If you recognize in advance that you will need to spend a large amount of time with a particular group, plan activities for other groups in which minimal direction is needed.

The fifth area of effective grouping is, in part, an outgrowth of the third area: construct tasks so that students will be able to complete them independently after you explain the directions. Provide students with step-by-step written directions and clear criteria for assessment, such as rubrics or criteria sheets. If possible, share exemplars of student work that successfully meets the criteria.

Provide students with step-by-step written directions and clear criteria for assessment, such as rubrics or criteria sheets.

The sixth area of effective grouping is to set clear expectations with regards to appropriate and productive behavior. It may be helpful to post your expectations for group work. Teach these expectations as described in the section on routines that appears earlier in this chapter. Individual member expectations can include:

1. I shared my ideas and offered suggestions.
2. I spoke clearly and slowly enough for others to understand me.
3. I answered others' questions.
4. I remained on topic.
5. I remained on task.
6. I helped other members of the group stay on topic and on task.
7. I encouraged others to participate.
8. When I disagreed with someone I did so without hurting feelings.
9. I listened courteously and effectively.
10. I gave reasons for my opinions.
11. I was not critical of the ideas expressed by others.
12. My voice volume was such that other groups in the room could not hear me.

The seventh area of effective grouping is to establish a system of how students may get assistance from the teacher or their peers when needed. Some teachers use a designated spot on the white board in which students write their names when they need help. When the teacher is available, they know the teacher will either call them to his or her desk or will come to visit with them. Students also understand that they are to continue working (on an alternative activity if necessary) until the teacher is able to meet with them. Another strategy is to give the students three colored plastic twelve-ounce cups (preferably red, green, and yellow). The students begin the independent work time with the cups stacked on the corners of their desks, so only the green one is showing. The green signals to the teacher that the student or group is working well and does not need any help. When the student or group needs the teacher but has an alternative activity on which to work, the student puts the yellow cup on top. When the student or group is completely stuck and has no alternative work, the red cup is placed on top of the stack. The teacher attends to the students with red cups showing before going to the students with the yellow cups on top. Some teachers use a variation of this activity. When the yellow cup is on top, a student with a green cup may go and assist the student(s) with the yellow cup. A red cup on top indicates that the student has already received peer help but still needs the teacher's assistance.

The eighth area of effective grouping is to create a system in which students are held individually accountable for the progress made during each class period. Below is a description of how some teachers audiotape groups as a method of assessing the group's adherence to the areas of effective group work. Some group work is such that all the students produce a product, and the teacher has the students place their work in a work-in-progress folder that the teacher may view at any time. At other times, students turn in the work they completed during the class period so the teacher is able to make comments and return their work the following day.

> *Create a system in which students are held individually accountable for the progress made during each class period.*

The ninth area of effective grouping is to establish procedures for what students should do when they have completed the assigned task. Should they turn in their finished work? If so, where? What should they do when they are done? When this important step is missing, student misbehavior usually increases.

The tenth area of effective grouping is to provide a time for summary reports from the groups. Make time either at the beginning or at the end of the class session for students to share their work. Doing so sends the message to students that everyone's work is valuable. If one student is designated as the reporter, he/she should understand that the report is to be on the group's work, not his or her individual ideas and contributions.

The eleventh area of effective group work is assessment. This should include assessment of the task and assessment of the group's work as a group. There should be both teacher assessment and student self-assessment. Later in this chapter, you can find samples of teacher assessment and student self-assessment scoring guides that can be used for this purpose. As with assessment of academic growth, assessment of behavior should follow the gradual release or responsibility from teacher-implemented assessment to student self-assessment.

Using an Audiotape[11] as a Management Technique for Group Work

One technique we have found to be particularly helpful in teaching and managing expectations of group work is the use of an audiotape. (An audio recording is also useful for observing and analyzing student learning and for student self-reflection.)

Implementing This Tool

First, begin by introducing the audiotape and explaining to the students that this tool will be used to help you better understand where they are in their learning, to monitor their progress, and to listen to their conversations that you were unable to hear when you were working with another group. Explain to them that they will also have an opportunity to listen to their conversations.

Before actually using the audiotape to record conversations, have a discussion with the students about how the recording device works and how students might feel the first couple of times they are being recorded. Give students time to "play around" with the audiotape for a few minutes and allow them to practice using it. We found that this practice eliminates some of the silliness and uneasiness that sometimes goes along with being recorded.

Next, select a group to record for a collaborative activity. (We usually record only one group at a time.) Make sure the students understand that they need to speak clearly and into the microphone (if there is one). Be present until they get situated. Once they begin the activity, you will have more time to spend with the other groups, as you will be able to go back to the taped group and analyze their work at a later time.

Analyzing the Conversations

Try to listen to the audiotape as soon as possible. In this way, you may quickly address any learning misunderstandings or inappropriate group work behaviors immediately. For example, one teacher was able to uncover and consequently address an ongoing problem one literature circle group was experiencing. The audiotape allowed her to listen to this group's entire conversation and analyze what was happening with

---

11 The cost of the current technology has thus far made it difficult for teachers to use video. Doing so would require a camera or tablet with a wide lens. It also requires having a separate microphone in the middle of the group to pick up all the students' comments. We don't discourage the use of videotaping if the equipment is readily available and easy to use. However, the most important data can obtained through audiotaping. Video is just an added benefit.

regard to group dynamics. Without being able to do so, it is unlikely she would have uncovered what was happening in this particular group. In this case, one student dominated the conversation, and because he was so outspoken, all group members listened to him, agreed with him, and even changed their views. Because the teacher only listened to small pieces of the group's conversation during the class, she assumed that the vocal student understood the text and was able to clarify any confusion his group members had. Unfortunately, this student communicated his *misunderstandings* of the text to the other students. Because the teacher was able to take a deeper look at this group via the audiotape, she was able to address these issues the following day.

The teacher also had these students listen to their conversation and asked them to reflect on the dynamics of their group. The outspoken student immediately realized he had dominated the conversation and commented, "I never realized how much I talked. I guess I should work on giving other people a chance to talk, too." This group came up with a plan to help one another take turns talking and, consequently, had much more interactive, effective discussions in the future.

Unexpected Outcome

The students also remarked that the audiotape had the effect of keeping them on task, as they knew the teacher was going to be listening to their entire conversation at some point. The teacher found that she had to spend less time dealing with discipline issues with the group that was using the audiotape. The students seemed to like using the audiotape, as they felt that it helped them to stay more focused and eliminated some of the off-task behaviors groups experienced when a teacher wasn't working with them.

Homework Routines

Homework is one routine that seems to be an issue with which teachers and students at all grade levels struggle from time to time. When students do not complete homework assignments, they are often not adequately prepared for class. Homework is perhaps the most difficult routine to establish well in a classroom, because the teacher does not have full control over the environment surrounding the completion of the homework. The teacher cannot follow the student home and sit with the student to ensure the homework is adequately completed. There is much teachers can do proactively at the beginning of the year, however,

to increase students' success with homework. Teaching students during the first three weeks of school the routine of effectively completing homework will help make the homework experience a positive one for both parents and children.

The amount of time needed to teach the homework routine may vary, depending on grade level and the school population. In private schools and affluent suburban schools with highly educated parent (or guardian) populations, the level of support at home can be greater than it is in some urban or low socioeconomic communities. The time the teacher needs to get these students into a successful homework routine may be less because the teacher can depend on a higher level of parental involvement. Of course, this can be a double-edged sword. Teachers with students from homes with highly involved parents often need to devote considerable time to helping the students and the parents understand what an "appropriate" (but not too much) level of parent involvement is in homework assignments.

> *The amount of time needed to teach the homework routine may vary, depending on grade level and the school population.*

Teachers working with students from poverty face some different challenges. In many of these homes, no one is home to monitor or assist with homework. In one school in which we worked, 20 percent of the students lived in homeless shelters, with few opportunities to get homework assistance. Even in cases when a parent or guardian is home, there is a high number of parents unable to assist due to language barriers or their own lack of formal education. As one urban teacher told us, "You need to teach your homework routine with the assumption that no one is at home to help. If you have a class in which one or some parents are home and able to assist, you should consider that a bonus." Deborah Meier, in her work with students in New York City public schools, found that "a sizable number of students didn't really know how to do the homework, or at least how to do it well enough to get any satisfaction from it. [Another] group just couldn't or didn't plan" (2006, pp. 8–9). To deal with this problem, the staff ensured that students knew how to do the homework before the end of each class. The staff also provided direct instruction to students at the outset and during the year on how to do homework well.

It is important to note that overly involved and uninvolved (or less involved) parents can be found at every socioeconomic level. Therefore, it is important that teachers develop a routine and a plan for teaching the routine that will address all types of home situations.

Before establishing a homework routine, it is necessary for the teacher to think about his or her own beliefs about homework. The teacher must also consider the students' ages. High school and some middle school students are more sophisticated than younger students and may be more likely to challenge and ask questions about a homework policy. If the teacher hasn't given careful thought to the policy, it will be more difficult to explain and help students understand the importance of the policy and related routine. Unclear expectations at any level will lead to chronic issues related to homework completion.

Questions for the teacher to consider when establishing a homework policy and routine include the following:

- What is the purpose of homework? Some teachers use homework to extend the learning from the class and to try new concepts in preparation for the next day's lesson. Homework can also be used as a review of the day's lesson and as an opportunity to practice what is presented in class.

- What is the definition of homework for this classroom? Is homework a written assignment, a reading assignment,[12] a long-term project, or a combination of two or more of these? Explaining at the beginning of the year what constitutes homework gives students a more concrete idea of what will be expected of them.

- How often will you assign homework? Some teachers assign homework every night. Others choose to assign homework four nights per week, opting to give students a reprieve on the weekend. Regardless of the frequency, teachers should inform students of this, so that they know what to expect and can plan accordingly.

- How much does homework count? Consider how much weight homework should carry. Depending on the class and teacher, homework might count for a significant part of the term grade or a small portion of the grade.

> *Some teachers use homework to extend the learning from the class and to try new concepts in preparation for the next day's lesson. Homework can also be used as a review of the day's lesson and as an opportunity to practice what is presented in class.*

practice to show students what passes as acceptable for a homework assignment.

- What do you expect when a student does not understand a portion of the homework? Because homework is an opportunity for students to practice what they have learned in class, they may have occasional difficulty in completing the assignment at home without help. Have an idea of what is expected of students who are unable to complete the homework assignment.

- What kind of help is appropriate? How much help is too much?

- What is the routine for collecting homework? Some teachers prefer to collect homework at the beginning of the class to ensure that students aren't scurrying to complete it during class time. Others prefer to give students an opportunity to modify their homework as it is reviewed in class.

- What happens when a student does not complete homework? High school students have many competing interests, such as work, extracurricular activities, schoolwork, etc. Inevitably, there will be students who do not complete homework. Teachers need to have a plan in place to work with such students. Phone calls or emails home and after-school sessions are two ways by which teachers address this problem. How does it impact the student's grade? Keep in mind that even the best plan is ineffective unless there is *consistency* and *follow-through* in the plan's implementation.

- What does an "acceptable" homework assignment look like? Just as it is good practice to share model essays with students so that they know what is acceptable and what is not, it is also good

According to Nancy Frey and Douglas Fisher (2011), homework should serve as practice with skills/content that students already know how to do rather than a time to introduce new material. When students are not prepared to work on new material or material that they have not yet mastered, their responses may fall into four categories:

---

12 Assigning content area reading is one of the more difficult areas for teachers to monitor. At the end of this chapter, we have included a brief article titled "Reading for Understanding." The article provides teachers with guidelines for assigning and assessing content area reading for homework.

- **Completers** are those who get the work done with the assistance of an adult, leading the teacher to believe that mastery has occurred.

- **Neglecters** are those who don't attempt the assignment because either they don't understand or don't make time to complete it. The neglecters leave the teachers with little or no information about their level of true mastery.

- **Error-makers** are the students who try to complete the assignment, but, because of their lack of understanding, usually fail to get much of it correct, leaving the teacher to make choices about remediation or reteaching.

- **Cheaters** are the students who copy from another student, again, leaving the teacher with a false sense of mastery.

In each of these cases, the teacher is left with little accurate information about the work that students could complete independently or about students' levels of mastery. Frey and Fisher sum up their findings this way:

In reality, schools and classrooms are filled with a mix of all of these types of students, which likely contributes to the lack of consistent evidence of the effect of homework on student learning. … [W]hat educators need to figure out is how to ensure that students understand the homework that they are assigned so they actually complete it. To change a maxim, only perfect practice makes perfect.

Homework can be one of the most difficult routines to establish effectively in a classroom. Therefore, it is important that we devote adequate time at the start of the year to establish our homework routines.

We also must be ready to reteach the routine when we find the quality and quantity of the homework we are receiving begins to diminish.

The **flipped classroom** is seen by some as a comprehensive change in teaching. Others see it as a new way to think about what teachers do in class and what teachers assign for homework. We believe that, whatever position you take on the flipped classroom, it certainly does impact how we address homework.

In the flipped classroom, teachers record lectures, have students watch videos, or use other avenues in which the students learn knowledge-level content at home. When they come to school, class time is used to delve into the knowledge with greater depth. Sams and Bergman (2013, pp. 16–20), who are experts in "flipping," tell us that flipping is not for every classroom or every topic. Teachers must be sure that the media used is available to all students since some students lack adequate technology at home. Most of the homework issues we discussed above still exist with flipping. These must be resolved with careful planning and teaching such as that discussed above and in the following.

> *In the flipped classroom teachers record lectures, have students watch videos, or use other avenues in which the students learn knowledge level content at home. When they come to school class time is used to delve into the knowledge with greater depth.*

Lesson Plans for Teaching Routines

In this section of the chapter, we have provided sample lesson plans for teaching routines. As noted earlier, routines must be "taught," not "told." Effective teaching of classroom management expectations requires no less planning than the effective teaching of the curriculum information and skills. The first two lessons are sample plans for teaching the homework routine. These are followed by two more lesson plans for teaching other classroom routines. As stated above, homework can be the most difficult routine to teach; therefore, we have included plans for teaching the homework routine both to elementary and high school students.

Sample Plan for Teaching Homework Routines to Upper Elementary Students

What do I want students to know and be able to do by the end of the lesson?[13]

By the end of the lesson, the students will be able to

1. Complete 100 percent of the homework by the start of the next day's class.[14] Any student with extenuating circumstances that caused the homework not to be finished will have a note from his or her parent explaining the situation.
2. Set up papers as noted in the criteria posted in the classroom by the teacher.
3. Complete homework independently and only use parents or guardians (older siblings, etc.) to assist as a last resort. Students will solicit parent support only upon the following conditions:
    a. The student attempted the assignment independently without success.
    b. The student reviewed the classroom notes and/or textbook pages explaining the concepts required in the homework.
    c. The student attempted the assignment independently at least one additional time without success.
4. Complete the homework to the best of his/her ability. The homework will demonstrate a level of quality similar to that completed in class and accepted by the teacher as the student's best work.
5. Copy the assignment each day, exactly as written on the board, in their homework notebook.
6. Bring their homework notebook and all necessary materials home each night.

How will I formatively and summatively assess students' level of mastery?

1. I will review the homework completed in class during the instruction phase of teaching the students how to do homework.
2. I will keep the homework examples completed in class as a benchmark for the quality of homework completed at home.
3. I will record the quality and quantity of the homework completed by each student during the Do Now.

What are the activities and the sequence of the activities?

1. The expectations noted above in the criteria for success section will be taught during the first week of school.
2. The students will be given copies of exemplars saved from previous years.
3. The homework expectations will be posted on the wall. (See the sample below.)
4. Students will complete all homework assignments in class during the first three weeks of school. The teacher will closely monitor students' adherence to the expectations to ensure that all students understand and successfully follow the expectations.
5. A homework packet containing a letter describing the homework procedures, homework expectations, and ideas for setting up an area conducive for doing homework will be sent to parents during the first week of school. (See the sample below.)
6. The homework expectations (particularly the one about help from parents as a "last resort") will be explained on parents' night.
7. Students' homework during the first three weeks of school will be to bring home the homework assignments they completed in school for parent review and signature. Parents should be encouraged to write back with any questions they have about the homework procedure. Homework is the one routine that requires training the parents and the students!

---

13 You will note that these lesson plans do not have the question that asks for the district standard as the plans we saw in Chapter 1. This is the case because districts seldom have a set of behavior standards similar to the curriculum standards. However, if a district did have such standards, then that information would be included as well.

14 If you are implementing this plan after the year has begun with a class in which a low percentage of homework is returned, you will want to set for yourself incremental target percentages. As each incremental percentage is reached, you will move the target closer to the 100 percent mark. It is important to note that, with some student populations, the home demographics may make it impossible to get 100 percent of the assignments 100 percent of the time. However, a well-structured homework plan will lead to increasing percentages of homework assignments being completed.

The following pages contain sample letters and checklists that might be sent home to parents. It includes a specific list of the homework expectations referred to previously.

Sample Letter Explaining Homework for the First Two Weeks of School

September 4, 2017

Dear Parents and/or Guardians,

As we work to become more responsive to the needs of our students, I have developed the following approach to "teaching" homework. For the first three weeks of school, time will be devoted each day to clearly defining my expectations of good work and to teaching students how to successfully complete homework. Among many other things, we will discuss the following: how to become an organized student, how to prioritize assignments, how to get started on homework assignments, what to do when an assignment is difficult, and how to set up a space at home conducive to fostering good study habits. All written work will be completed in class for the first three weeks of school.

During this time, your child's homework will be to bring home and share and explain these assignments to you. This task will reinforce the learning that took place during the school day. In addition, all students are expected to read for at least fifteen minutes each night. I will give specific directions in class regarding at-home reading assignments.

In a couple of weeks, I will be sending home another letter that clearly outlines my policy on homework and identifies my classroom website where I will post homework assignments daily. If you have any questions, please contact me by email or by phone.

Please sign this letter below and have your child return it to me.

Sincerely,
Mrs. Deane
mdeane@bestschool.k12.school.us
(617)-987-1234
Parent/Guardian Signature: _____

Sample Letter Explaining Homework Policies and Procedures

Dear Parents and/or Guardians,

I believe homework is important because it is a valuable aid in helping students make the most of their experience in school. Homework is given because it is useful in reinforcing what has been learned in class, prepares students for upcoming lessons, extends and generalizes concepts, teaches responsibility, and helps students develop positive study habits.

Fifth graders will be given homework Monday through Thursday nights. Homework should take students no longer than 45–60 minutes each night, not including studying for tests and working on long-term projects. A mathematical problem of the week will be given each Monday, and students are expected to turn this assignment in on Friday. Spelling units will also be given each Monday and will be due on Thursday. A spelling test will be given each Friday. Students will be given at least one week's notice to study for most tests.

Students are expected to do their best on homework. Since homework reflects what one has learned, it should be done independently. If your child has difficulty with an assignment, s/he should ask for help only after giving his or her best effort. Please contact me if your child consistently needs help with homework. All homework will be posted on the class website at www.BESTSCHOOL.K12.school.us.

All homework assignments will be checked, and sometimes they will be graded. I will not always announce when I will be grading homework. Therefore, it is important for each child to be well prepared.

If students consistently choose not to complete their homework, I will ask that parents begin checking and signing their child's assignment notebook each night. If students still choose not to complete their work, they also choose to lose certain privileges, such as recess. If students choose to make up their homework the next day, their homework will be accepted. If they choose not to make up missed assignments, students will receive a grade of 60 for those assignments.

Please be assured that if there is a legitimate reason a student is not able to finish homework, I will make exceptions. Please send a note to me on the day the assignment is due.

I feel that parents and guardians play an important role in making homework a positive experience for children. Therefore, I ask parents to make homework a priority. You can do this by providing necessary supplies and a quiet work environment, setting a daily homework time, providing support and encouragement, and not allowing children to avoid homework. I encourage you to contact me if there is a problem or concern.

Please read and discuss this policy with your child and sign and return the bottom portion of this letter to me. Thank you for your cooperation. I look forward to working with you and your child.

Sincerely,
Mrs. Deane
mdeane@bestschool.k12.ma.us
I have read the homework policy and discussed it with my child, _____.
Comments:_____

_____
Parent Signature:_____

Homework Expectations

- All homework should have your name, the date, and the subject on the top of the page.
- All math homework should be completed in pencil.
- All other written homework should be completed in one color of pen or on the tablet.
- All work should be done in your neatest handwriting or word-processed if appropriate.
- All work should be carefully proofread and edited.
- No cross-outs.
- Paper should not be torn from a spiral notebook and should not have jagged edges.
- Homework should be clean and unwrinkled.
- Homework should be turned in on time.
- Remember always to do your best.

Helpful Homework Hints

Work Area
- clean
- quiet
- all supplies available

Time—Make a Plan For
- homework time
- break/snack time

Supplies
- pens, pencils
- erasers
- crayons, markers
- glue
- lined paper
- scissors
- ruler
- dictionary
- thesaurus

Prioritize your assignments. Assignments that are due the next day should be completed first. Map out a schedule for long-term assignments so that they are not left until the last minute.

When implementing this homework policy, teachers found this strategy to be well received by the parents and students alike. Parents and guardians commented that it really taught the students good study habits and gave them an opportunity to practice them with guidance. It also concretized what good study habits look like and how to develop them. Teachers found that it reduced the number of missing and incomplete homework assignments, as the expectations were laid out and practiced at the beginning of the year before bad habits were established. Although this strategy does take time during the first few weeks of school, we feel it is an invaluable process and ultimately saves time over the course of the year.

Sample Plan for Teaching Homework Routines to Middle School[15] and High School Students

Dear Student,

Welcome to Grade 9 English. I am looking forward to working with you this year and helping you to meet your full potential as a student. While we will complete much of our work together in class, it is necessary that you work independently at home to extend your learning and practice the skills presented in class. In order to assist you, all homework assignments will be posted on the classroom website.

To help you understand what I expect from you in terms of homework, I have addressed a number of common questions.

Frequently Asked Questions about Homework

- **What is the purpose of homework?** In this class, homework will be an opportunity to practice and apply what we have learned in the day's class. Homework can take the form of reading a selection from a novel, a written assignment, or a long-term project.

- **How often will homework be assigned and how long will it take to complete?** Expect to receive homework assignments Monday through Friday. It should take you about 30–45 minutes each night

15 Teachers of sixth- and seventh-grade students may find the elementary plan preferable for their grade level.

to complete your homework assignments. Keep in mind that studying for a test will require more time (and should be spread over several nights).

- **How much does homework count?** Homework will count for 15% of your term grade. Most homework assignments will be checked off if they are complete. More formal writing assignments may be subject to counting as a quiz or test grade. In cases in which homework counts as a quiz or test grade, I will let you know that ahead of time.

- **What does an "acceptable" homework assignment look like?** I will show you examples of acceptable homework assignments so that you have a clear idea of what your homework should look like. If you still have questions about expectations for the assignment, please ask me after class, and I will be happy to go over the assignment with you.

- **What if I get home, look at the assignment, and have trouble understanding it?** While you may not understand the whole assignment, you are expected to do as much as possible of the assignment. For example, if I assign a set of questions and you understand only three of the five, I expect that you answer the three that you know and make an attempt at those you don't. In cases in which you don't know where to begin, you need to explain in complete sentences exactly what is causing the confusion (e.g., vocabulary, comprehension of the reading passage, etc.) and what I can do to help you.

- **What is the routine for collecting homework?** I will collect homework at the beginning of the class. Homework that is not turned in at that time will be considered late and will receive half credit.

- **What if I am absent?** We will choose homework buddies during our first week of class. Students who are absent are expected to call their buddies to find out what the assignment is and make an attempt at completing the homework. Students who are out sick have one additional day to catch up on the homework they have missed.

- **What happens if I don't complete homework?** Late homework will receive no more than 50% credit. I will call your parent(s) if you have a chronic habit of not completing homework. Together with your parent(s), we will work on a plan to remedy the situation.

Additional Homework Expectations

- All homework should have your name, date, class, and assignment written at the top of the page.
- Homework should be written legibly or word-processed. Please skip a line between questions.
- Homework should be turned in on time.

If you have any problems associated with the completion of homework, you are expected to advocate for yourself and let me know about the issue.

I have read the above information related to homework expectations, and I understand what is expected of me.

Student name _____ Signature _____ Date _____

Parent/guardian signature _____ Daytime phone number _____

Comments or questions related to homework

_____

_____

_____

_____

Note: Teachers, students, and parents/guardians should all have a copy of the above letter. Students' copies should be kept in their binders. A copy of the policy should be posted in the classroom next to other important information, such as the class grading policy.

Plan for Teaching Homework Routine to High School Students

What Will Students Know and Be Able to Do by the End of the Lesson?

By the end of the lesson, students will be able to

1. Describe what to do if absent from class.
2. Describe what an acceptable homework assignment looks like.
3. Describe the consequences of not completing homework.
4. Have homework complete at the beginning of the class when it is collected.
5. Complete homework that follows the format outlined in the policy.
6. When having difficulty with a portion of the homework, complete the portion they understand and articulate in complete sentences what they do and do not understand about the rest of the assignment; they will also outline what type of help they need in order to complete the assignment.
7. Complete homework on a nightly basis.

How Will I Formatively and Summatively Assess Students' Level of Mastery?

1. Oral question-and-answer sessions
2. Ungraded quiz at the end of the presentation
3. Observations made during the first few weeks of class
4. Record in my grade book the quality and quantity of the homework completed the previous night during the Do Now in the subsequent class

What Are the Activities and Sequence of the Activities?

1. The teacher will take time during the first week of school to review homework expectations with the class.
2. The teacher will provide several examples of homework assignments to students.
3. Students will examine the samples and then determine which samples meet the criteria of an acceptable homework assignment. For examples that do not meet the criteria, students will identify the problem areas. Examples presented during this activity will include an incomplete assignment, an assignment with which a student had difficulty, an exemplary assignment, an assignment without the proper setup, and a late assignment.
4. The teacher will ensure that each student has a copy of the policy in his/her binder. In addition, the teacher will provide a copy for the parent and post a copy in a prominent place in the classroom.
5. The teacher will allow students to begin homework in class for the first two weeks of school. During this time, in addition to grading the content of the assignment, the teacher will comment on the setup of the assignment and adherence to the expectations.
6. During the first two weeks of teaching the routine, the teacher will contact parents of students who are experiencing difficulty with following the routine.
7. The students will self-assess their level of mastery for completing the homework routine.

Sample Plan for Teaching Classroom Routines to Middle School Students

Below is a plan created to teach middle school science students the routine for cleaning up after a lab.

What Will Students Know and Be Able to Do by the End of the Lesson?

By the end of this lesson, the students will be able to

1. Clean up their lab areas so areas are ready for the next class.
2. Have all equipment returned to its proper location and have their lab areas ready for the next class within five minutes of being given the direction to clean up.
3. Wipe all fluids from the microscope, dry the microscope thoroughly, and place the microscope on the shelf that corresponds with the number on the microscope (Partner 1).
4. Return the specimens to their containers and to the appropriate shelf and then wipe down the lab area and discard all disposable materials (Partner 2).
5. Check his/her partner's work to ensure it meets the criteria.
6. Leave the lab area with no sign that there was a lab.

How Will I Formatively and Summatively Assess Students' Level of Mastery?

1. During the instruction phase of teaching the routine, I will time each attempt at lab cleanup.
2. Throughout the year, I will begin the clean-up time by placing the timer on the SmartBoard counting down from the number of minutes allotted for cleanup.

What Are the Activities and the Sequence of the Activities?

1. I will explain this routine and explain why it is important at the end of the next science class, prior to the next lab.
2. At the start of the next class, I will explain the steps for correctly cleaning up and post the steps on a chart paper.
3. I will set up a lab area and have a pair of students demonstrate the procedure.
4. At the end of the next lab period, I will have the group that finishes first walk through the steps while I describe them to the class.
5. I will structure the lesson so there is more than the typical amount of time at the end for cleanup. I will plan my time so I am free to monitor and coach the groups during the cleanup.
6. Guided Practice: In the next lab period, I will review the steps and keep myself free to coach, but I will require the independent completion of the cleanup in ten minutes.
7. In each subsequent lab, I will slightly decrease the cleanup time until the targeted time is achieved.

Sample Plan for Teaching Classroom Routines to High School Students

Below is a plan created to teach high school students in an English class the routine for peer-editing drafts of each other's essays.

What Will Students Know and Be Able to Do by the End of the Lesson?

By the end of the lesson, the students will be able to utilize already created rubrics to peer edit the rough drafts of four to five other students in the class.

Expectations:

a) Students must place their own rough drafts on their desks along with a blank rubric.

b) Students will all stand up and find new seats where they will read and edit the rough draft of another student in the class.

c) Students will offer detailed comments on the blank rubric form.

d) Upon completing this task, students will go to the front of the classroom to pick up a second blank rubric form.

e) Students will then choose a second peer's rough draft to edit and peer review, using the blank rubric.

f) Students will repeat this process until they have read and edited the drafts of four to five of their peers.

How Will I Formatively and Summatively Assess Students' Level of Mastery?

1. I will circulate around the room and observe students' work.

2. I will randomly select one third of the student papers at the end of the class and check the comments written on the papers.

What Are the Activities and Sequence of the Activities?

1. I will first explain this routine in general terms when initially discussing the due date of students' rough drafts in order to emphasize the importance of having one's draft in school on the day on which feedback will be solicited from peers.

2. I will explain that the purpose is to support each other in producing high-quality final drafts and to practice catching spelling and grammatical errors.

3. I will explain the steps of this routine in detail at the beginning of the class period in which students bring their drafts to be peer edited.

4. I will ask the students to read and edit four to five of their peers' rough drafts by doing the following:
   - I will first ask students to clear their desks of all materials except for their rough drafts and rubrics.
   - Next, I will ask students to stand up and find new seats within the classroom.
   - Next, I will read through the various components of the rubric with my students.
   - Next, I will describe to students the procedure for acquiring a new rubric and finding a new rough draft to edit upon completing their edits of the rough draft currently in front of them.
   - Finally, I will remind students of the expectation that they edit four to five of their peers' rough drafts within the specified time.

5. I will float around the classroom, guiding students on the next steps to take as they complete their edits of the first manuscript: namely, acquiring a new rubric and finding a new peer's rough draft to edit and review.

6. Guided Practice: The second time that students bring in their rough drafts to be read and edited by peers, I will have them complete the peer edit routine independently. I will keep myself available to reinforce and re-explain the routine as needed.

Factor 5: Obtaining, Maintaining, and Regaining Student Attention Strategies

Teachers use a wide variety of strategies for signaling to students that it is time to be quiet. An article in the *Responsive Classroom Newsletter* (Farnsworth and McErlane 2002) categorizes these as visual attention strategies and auditory attention strategies. Visual strategies include hand signals, specific teacher posture (e.g., hands on hips), closing our eyes, and other teacher behaviors the students know mean it is time to be quiet. The second category of signals discussed in the article is auditory strategies. Auditory strategies include chimes, a bell, playing notes on a musical instrument, and other sounds that signal to the students that it is time to be quiet. It is important for teachers to have a large repertoire of strategies to gain student attention. If our voices are the only strategy we use to gain student attention, students soon learn to tune it out.

The following steps for establishing the effective use of signals for getting students to be quiet are based on the steps identified in the *Responsive Classroom Newsletter* (2002) by Mark Farnsworth, a high school physical education teacher.

1. Choose signals that are easily noticed.
2. Teach and practice the signals with the students before expecting students to use them.
3. Always use the designated signals to achieve quiet.
4. Expect everyone, even adults who enter your room, to adhere to the signal.
5. Don't begin talking until you have everyone's attention.
6. If some children aren't paying attention, stop and practice the signal again.
7. Use frequent and specific positive praise with the class and with individuals who demonstrate timely adherence to the signal.
8. Have clearly defined warnings and consequences for those students who do not respond.
9. Remember that the goal of the signal is to gain the children's attention. If everyone is paying attention, it is okay to start talking.

Auditory Strategies for Gaining Attention

- bell
- whistle (Often used by coaches and by teachers in large group situations. Mr. Farnsworth uses different numbers of whistles to indicate different behaviors in his physical education classes. For example, a single loud whistle can mean *everyone freeze and be quiet*. Two short whistles can mean *continue with the activity but stop talking and listen for instructions.*)
- speaking softly (Teachers who do this will give a direction in a voice volume that would allow all the students to hear the direction if no one was talking. The teacher gives the first two or three sentences of the direction knowing full well that few, if any, students are actually hearing the direction. He or she then repeats those sentences in the same soft voice as often as needed until all the students are listening. When the teacher starts talking, some students notice the teacher is talking and try to listen. When they cannot hear, they quiet down the other students so they can hear what the teacher is saying. When we speak softly, the student noise typically stops because students are curious to hear what the teacher is saying.)
- piano notes (or other instrument notes)
- chime
- alarm or buzzer from a timer when it reaches the set end time of a group or partner discussion activity
- humorous comment (Please note that educators make a distinction between humor and sarcasm. Humor is something that is funny—appropriately so—that does not make one of the students the target of the humor. Sarcasm, though at times seen as funny by many in the room, may have a derogatory impact on the self-image of the target student and/or generate fear among other students that they may be the next targeted student.)
- clapping hands to a familiar rhythm
- humming or singing a specific tune
- asking students to stop talking
- playing music as a signal that it is time to stop talking
- counting down (5, 4, 3, 2...) or counting up (1, 2, 3, 4...)
- telling students they may have or do something they all would like only when everyone is listening (This strategy places peer pressure on those still not listening.)
- saying "Excuse me" in a firm but calm voice and repeating "Excuse me" in a softer and softer voice until room is silent
- saying "Excuse me, Mark" to a particular student who is speaking
- making instructional statements that raise the students' curiosity (For example, one high school social studies teacher starts his classes by singing a humorous song that was popular with adolescents during the period they are studying.)

Visual Strategies for Gaining Attention

- flash the lights (This strategy may cause problems for some autistic students.)
- hand signal
  a. hands on head
  b. hand in the air (A variation of this used by some teachers when students are working in pairs or groups is to allow the students to put up one finger to request an additional minute to finish their conversation.)
  c. hold up two fingers as a peace sign
- close eyes
- point to or hold up a *Quiet, Please* sign
- place a single finger over lips
- humorous activity
- wave arms dramatically and humorously to signal for attention
- stand quietly in the front of the room until all students are quiet
- use a "Yacker Tracker" (This is a device that looks like a stoplight with green, yellow, and red lights and is sensitive to noise levels in the room. When the noise is at an appropriate level, the green light is on. If the noise nears the maximum appropriate level, the yellow light goes on. If the noise exceeds the appropriate level, the red light goes on.)
- signal for quiet and then hold up a stopwatch to gauge how many seconds it takes for the room to fall completely silent (Compliment students on a job well done or note the need for improvement if a quiet classroom took too much time to achieve. Some teachers make this a game by providing a point each time the class quiets down in a predetermined amount of time. The points can then be redeemed for incentives.)
- marble jar (Each time the class quiets down in the pre-determined time, a marble goes into the jar. Once the jar is filled, the class receives a reward.) In both of these examples, keeping the jar or score visible helps serve as a visual reminder to students.
- dramatize (For example, one middle school social studies teacher frequently greets students in an outfit from the period they are studying.)

Some high school and middle school teachers who use inanimate objects, such as the chime, music, and/or flashing lights, report that students who are displeased with the need to be quiet associate their

Some high school and middle school teachers who use inanimate objects, such as the chime, music, and/or flashing lights, report that students who are displeased with the need to be quiet associate their displeasure with the object rather than the teacher.

displeasure with the object rather than the teacher. They report statements from students such as "that darn chime," rather than indicating displeasure with the teacher. Although we can find no research that supports or refutes this, these teachers report that it helps them maintain their positive relationships with the students.

Strategies for Getting the Attention of Those Students Who Don't Respond to the Group Signal

- using the *hairy eyeball* (This is a stern look and stare teachers give to those students who are not yet adhering to the signal for quiet.)
- turning squarely to face the student, making eye contact, and saying that student's name in a calm but firm voice
- moving next to the student or students who are still talking
- praising those students who are quiet
- rewarding the students who are quiet (For example, you may allow these students to present their ideas first or leave for lunch first, etc.)
- asking those students who are talking to stop
- putting the name of the student who is talking on the board as a warning that there will be a consequence as the next step
- giving the student a *warning card* (The warning card indicates to the student that if the talking does not stop immediately, s/he will get a consequence.)
- giving the student a *consequence card*
- startling the students with a loud noise or surprise behavior

Deciding to Use Negative or Positive Strategies

The strategies above may also be categorized on a continuum of negative, neutral, and positive reinforcers. Those that directly identify a student who is not giving attention or provide a consequence for students not exhibiting the desired behavior are negative reinforcers. Those that affirm or reward appropriate behavior are positive reinforcers. Still others, such as a chime, are *neutral*. We identify attention strategies in this way to highlight the impact of relationships on classroom management. A consideration every teacher must include in his or her decision to choose a specific strategy to gain student attention is the impact it has on the self-image of individual students, the relationship between the teacher and the students, and the relationship among the students. As discussed above, sarcasm may effectively obtain student attention; however, most educators believe the negative impact on student self-image outweighs its value in gaining attention. Another example of an impact on students' self-image is the constant use of peer pressure after the teacher finds that certain students are always the ones who cause the class to miss some opportunity (e.g., go to recess late in elementary school or go to the pep rally late in high school). The impact this may have of undermining the classroom community or making the student angry with the teacher, thereby motivating additional acting-out behavior, might lead the teacher to use this strategy less often than some of the more positive strategies (e.g., rewarding those who are ready to go first or complimenting those who are ready). Later in this chapter, we will talk more about the impact of the student-teacher relationship on classroom management and appropriate ways to use peer pressure during classroom management.

Sarcasm may effectively obtain student attention; however, most educators believe the negative impact on student self-image outweighs its value in gaining attention.

Transitions

The easiest way to regain students' attention is never to lose it. As mentioned earlier, transitions between activities are a time when many teachers lose students' attention. Well-planned transitions help maintain student attention as we shift from one activity to the next. One technique for ensuring quick transitions from teacher-directed work to student group work is the cooperative learning jobs grid. Earlier in this chapter, we explained how to use the cooperative learning jobs grid strategy. Figures 3.5 and 3.6 are examples of cooperative learning jobs grids for working in groups of four or five students. Another technique is processing partners. In Chapter 5, we explain how this strategy works.

Almost all strategies discussed previously may be appropriate in certain situations. It is important to be aware, however, that disproportionate use of negative strategies or peer pressure as opposed to positive strategies may undermine some of the teacher's long-term goals, such as raising students' self-image, building a supportive classroom community among the students, and building trusting and supportive relationships between the teacher and the students.

Factor 6: Student Self-Assessment of the Expectations for Routines Using Rubrics and Criteria Sheets

Research is well established with regard to student performance and feedback (Andrade 2011). Student performance increases when students receive feedback on their work.

In the academic disciplines, we have learned that rubrics and criteria sheets are an excellent means of assessing student performance on various skills. We are increasingly asking students to use rubrics and criteria sheets as means of self-assessing their progress throughout the period of time they are learning new tasks. We do this so students may objectively measure their progress with the goal of determining how far they have come and how far they have left to go to be successful. It also serves as a concrete reminder of the expectations for successful completion of the task.

As Andrade notes, students can be taught to formatively and summatively assess their own performance from an early age. In order to do so, students must be taught the value of looking at their own work, using clear criteria sheets and rubrics, and be allotted time to act on their self-assessment to revise their work. Additionally, students must have direct instruction and modeling on how to self-assess, as well as practice to do so.

The same is true for student behavior. Once we have determined observable expectations for a routine and have taught those expectations to the class, we are in a position to have the students periodically self-assess their performance. The following are two samples of student self-assessments used by a high school teacher and a middle school teacher, respectively.

The sheet in the first sample is given to students at the start of each week. At the end of the class, students are given a minute to assess their performance on each of the areas. They put a check in the box for each criterion they successfully met. The comments section is for writing any information they want to tell the teacher or for the teacher to give comments to the student. For example, a student may wish to tell the teacher that s/he was late as a result of being called to the office at the end of the previous class. At the end of the week, the students count up the number of checks and place the number (1 to 20) in the box at the bottom of the last column. The sheets are passed in to the teacher on Fridays. The teacher records the students' "grades" for the week. If the teacher believes a student has not accurately filled out the form, he will change the final grade on the form to match his observation. At the start of the year, there are usually a couple of students who test the teacher by rating themselves higher than their actual achievement. Correcting the form and speaking to those students eliminates the behavior in the first two weeks.

Some teachers incorporate the student's performance on these sheets into the grade. For example, the teacher will add up the points every five weeks and use that total as a quiz grade. Other teachers don't incorporate it into grades but do provide other incentives.

Some teachers choose to be more specific with the expectations for the categories. For example, the category *Do not make any disruptions* might include the following criteria:

- Show respect for others by including no back talk.
- Use only appropriate language.
- Speak respectfully to others, no put-downs.
- Sharpen pencils only when others are not speaking.
- Keep hands and feet in your own space.

Name: _____ Period: _____

CHECKLIST FOR SUCCESS IN A HIGH SCHOOL CLASSROOM

Did I…	come to class on time?	come to class prepared? (This includes binder, writing utensil, & HW)	finish my class work?	participate positively at least once?	not make any disruptions?	Comments*
Monday						
Tuesday						
Wednesday						
Thursday						
Friday						
Total =						

*The teacher or the student may make comments.
Reprinted with permission from Richard Higgins, a teacher in the Weymouth, MA public schools.

Getting Started with Student Self-Assessment

If your students have no experience with self-assessment, then you will want to start small. A self-assessment form with just two or three areas should be used. The teacher should give more frequent feedback to help the students more accurately assess themselves. It is common for students to inflate or deflate their assessments when first beginning to self-assess. Frequent monitoring and feedback will help students to more accurately determine their level of success. It will also send a clear message that self-assessment must be accurate and that the teacher will change inaccurate assessments. Below is a modified version of the self-assessment from the previous page that can be used with students who are unfamiliar with self-assessment. As the year progresses and students' self-assessment competency increases, columns can be added.

Name: _____   Period: _____

CHECKLIST FOR SUCCESS IN A HIGH SCHOOL CLASSROOM

Did I...	come to class on time?	come to class prepared? (This includes binder, writing utensil, and homework)	Student comment	Teacher comment
Monday				
Tuesday				
Wednesday				
Thursday				
Friday				
Student's Total =				
Teacher's Total =				

The following self-assessment is one that would only be used with students who have a previous history of self-assessing. Teachers need to work with students with less comprehensive self-assessments before the students will be able to accurately complete the one below.

Mid-Quarter 1: Self-Assessment

Middle School Science

Now that you have had a chance to review your progress report, here is an opportunity to think about your actions, increase self-understanding, and take responsibility for your choices. The following worksheet includes questions on academic performance, class behavior, organizational skills, use of your agenda book, preparation for class, responsibility with homework, and ability to work in groups. After answering these questions, you will then design a plan to address your deficiencies and define steps you need to take to be successful in science class. This information will be the center of our discussion during student-teacher conferences, which will take place in the coming weeks.

Rate yourself according to the scale below. Be honest. This self-assessment does not factor into your final grade for the quarter; it is only a tool to help you succeed.

		1 Needs a Lot of Work	2 Needs Some Work	3 Achieved Near-Mastery	4 Achieved Mastery
HOMEWORK	My homework assignments are completed on time.				
	I check my work before I decide my homework is done.				
	If I'm absent, I go directly to the absent homework folder for my block.				
	I always have my agenda book for every class.				
	I have my HW assignments written down before the teacher reminds the class to do so.				
CLASS BEHAVIOR	I understand what I wrote in my agenda book when I get home.				
	The first thing I do when I come into class is look at the whiteboard.				
	I always come to class with a pencil and pen/marker.				
	My Science Journal (binder) is organized. I am not missing anything that I should have.				
	I am always ready to start class when the teacher is.				
	I do my best in every task.				

		1 Needs a Lot of Work	2 Needs Some Work	3 Achieved Near- Mastery	4 Achieved Mastery
CLASS BEHAVIOR (*continued*)	I always raise my hand when I would like to speak.				
	I actively listen to what my classmates say during class discussion.				
	I don't talk out of turn.				
	When the teacher makes transitions between class activities, I don't take that opportunity to talk.				
	When other students try to distract me, I ignore them or tell them to stop.				
	I don't distract other students from being successful in class.				
	I effectively communicate my ideas during class discussion.				
GROUP WORK	When working in a lab team, I respect the ideas of my classmates.				
	During lab activities, I am on task.				
	During lab activities, I follow directions correctly.				
	During lab activities, I communicate effectively with my partners.				
	During lab activities, I share tasks equitably.				
	During lab activities, I handle equipment safely and appropriately.				
	I check my work before handing in a lab.				
ACADEMIC PERFORMANCE	I actively seek help from the teacher when I need it.				
	I check my work before handing in a quiz/test.				
	For TTEs, I write for the entire time and use all the lines I'm supposed to use.				
	I feel prepared for quizzes/tests because I know what to study.				
	I do my best on quizzes/tests.				

Do lab activities help you better understand what is written in your textbook and talked about in class? Why or why not?

Does your lab grade correctly reflect your effort? Why?

What is your best work so far in this class? Why do you take pride in it?

Does your homework grade correctly reflect your effort? Why?

Does your quiz/test grade correctly reflect your understanding of the material? Why?

At this point, what areas do you feel are your deficiencies? (What areas do you need to work on?)

List three things you can do to improve upon your deficiencies.
1.
2.
3.

What do you need to be successful in science class?

What can the teacher do to help in executing your plan for success?

Reprinted with the permission of Mitzi Sales, a teacher in Rye, New York.

Factor 7: Reinforcement of Appropriate Behavior and Consequences for Inappropriate Behavior

The best way to maximize the effectiveness of our classroom management plan is to maximize the use of positive reinforcement when students are carrying out our expectations. A psychologist named Herrnstein (1961; 1974) wrote about his research related to what is known as "the matching law." Walker, Ramsey, and Gresham (2004, p. 2) describe the **matching law** as follows:

> The rate of any given behavior matches the rate of reinforcement for that behavior. For example, if aggressive behavior is reinforced once every three times it occurs (e.g., by a parent giving in to a temper tantrum) and pro-social behavior is

reinforced once every fifteen times it occurs (e.g., by praising a polite request), then the Matching Law would predict that, on average, aggressive behavior will be chosen five times more frequently than pro-social behavior.

Subsequent research (Snyder 2002) has shown that behavior does, in fact, closely follow the matching law.

Walker, Ramsey, and Gresham (2004, p. 4) describe effective praise as being genuine, immediate, frequent, enthusiastic, descriptive, varied, and involving eye contact. They suggest that teachers use praise at least four times as often as criticism and more often, if possible. They also found that teachers do tend to praise those students who regularly exhibit good behavior, but they tend not to seize opportunities to praise the more disruptive students when they are behaving well. This may create a cycle of behavior in which "the rich get richer, and the poor get poorer."

In addition to praise, teachers often use other **rewards** to reinforce appropriate behavior. In some instances, these are individual rewards and, in others, they are **group rewards**. An example of an individual reward in an elementary school is to provide those students who exhibit appropriate behavior over a period of time with the opportunity to enjoy extra computer time or an opportunity to help in another classroom with younger students. In middle and high schools, an individual reward might be the privilege to go to the library during study hall or to leave class first for the bus, so the student may acquire that coveted back seat. A note home or phone call to a parent commending the student's good behavior has been found to be an effective reward for students on all levels.

A classroom management plan with clearly taught and consistently enforced expectations coupled with ample positive reinforcement and a system of rewards will eliminate most disruptive behavior; however, there will be times when we need to give students consequences for not following our expectations.

Robert Marzano, in his book *Classroom Manage-*

> *Teachers do tend to praise those students who regularly exhibit good behavior, but they tend not to seize opportunities to praise the more disruptive students when they are behaving well.*

ment That Works (2003, pp. 28–32), tells us that the most effective plan for classroom management contains consequences as well as rewards. Consequences are not the same as punishment. In their book *Rules in School* (2003, p. 89), Brady, Forton, Porter, and Wood draw a clear distinction between consequences and punishments. Some of the characteristics of **punishment** are that it has an angry tone, is not related to the behavior, leaves the child feeling s/he is the problem rather than his or her behavior, uses fear as an external motivator for stopping the behavior, and leaves the child feeling shamed. **Consequences**, on the other hand, are assigned using a calm and matter-of-fact voice, are a logical outcome of the behavior, help the child understand the negative impact of the behavior on himself/herself and others, leave the child believing the behavior is the problem (not him or her), and build an intrinsic desire to use more appropriate behaviors. In their book *Engaging Troubled Students* (2005, p. 116), Scott Danforth and Terry Jo Smith tell us that "even when the teacher is confronting a student about a specific behavior or incident, the message within and throughout should be that even this incident does not diminish the student in the teacher's eyes."

Figure 3.7

Punishments...	Consequences...
use an angry tone.	use a calm and matter-of-fact tone.
are not related to the behavior.	are logical outcomes of the behavior.
leave child believing he/she is the problem.	leave child believing the behavior is the problem.
use fear as an external motivator of change.	help child understand the negative impact on self and others, thereby intrinsically motivating change.

Group Rewards and Consequences

Walker, Ramsey, and Gresham (2004, pp. 9–10) explain the appropriate and inappropriate use of group rewards and consequences for classroom management. Group reinforcement (the authors actually refer to it as *group reinforcement contingencies*) involves the group receiving a reward as the result of meeting a measurable behavior goal. It is important that the group reward we choose is one that we, our teammates, and the building administration feel is appro-

priate. For example, if a lab group completes science lab cleanup in the time allotted, it can earn a point toward leaving for lunch five minutes early one day. In elementary school, students can earn points toward extra recess time. Some teachers and/or administrators disagree with "free time" incentives. In those cases, reward points may be used toward time when the class will play an educational game like Jeopardy or for an extra point on a quiz. Group reinforcements have been found to be quite successful when used as part of the overall behavior plan; however, it is important to note that Walker, Ramsey, and Gresham warn that the group contingency should never be a group consequence. The distinction here is that the failure to obtain an additional benefit (such as extra recess) is appropriate; however, a group consequence, such as the class losing five minutes of recess should never be applied to the group because of the behavior of some or even most of the students. Consequences should be applied only to those individuals who fail to meet the behavior requirements.

Individual contingencies are most effective when the student, teacher, parent, and a third party in the school (assistant principal, special education teacher, etc.) are in agreement about the plan.

Reinforcements and Consequences for Students Who Do Not Respond to Our Classroom Management Plan

Up to this point, we have looked at the various components that make up a successful classroom management plan. Even the best classroom management plan may fail to cause some students to conform to our rules and routines. These students typically have antisocial behaviors that are the result of influences beyond the school. We may have students in our class who have experienced the trauma of a parent's death or who are the victims of verbal, physical, or sexual abuse. We may have students in our class who have been the victims of repression in their native countries, are experiencing the contentious divorce of their parents, or use drugs or alcohol. We have students who have chemical or brain abnormalities that are unrelated to their environment but do cause antisocial behavior. According to Walker, Ramsey, and Gresham (2004, p. 4), research indicates that troubled students may actually be between 2 percent and 16 percent of the general population, yet only about 1 percent of the school population has been identified with emotional disorders through the special education process.

Most troubled students can be accommodated by a well-constructed classroom management plan; however, for 1 to 5 percent of the classroom population, our classroom management plan will not be sufficient to make these students conform to classroom rules and expectations. For these students, we will need to have **individual contingencies** within our classroom management plan. The goal of these individual contingencies is to decrease the negative behaviors and limit their impact on the learning environment. It is hoped that the individual contingencies will bridge the gap between what these students need to be produc-

tive members of the class and the routines and expectations in our classroom management plans.

Individual contingencies are most effective when the student, teacher, parent, and a third party in the school (assistant principal, special education teacher, etc.) are in agreement about the plan. Individual contingencies should include both incentives and consequences. Effective incentives may vary from student to student, so it is important that you choose incentives that truly are valued by the students. They may be incentives given by the school or incentives given by the parent(s) [provided the parent(s) will follow through consistently with the incentives]. Some school-given incentives include:

a. a note home to the parent
b. a phone call home to the parent
c. lunch with the teacher, principal, or group of friends
d. a gift certificate to a favorite ice cream shop or fast food restaurant (our apologies to the Department of Education and their efforts to limit obesity)
e. a pass to a school dance or sporting event
f. homework passes
g. the privilege of a preferred activity (e.g., listening to music, drawing, computer, reading)
h. a magazine on a topic of interest to the student (cars, sports, wrestling, fashion)
i. stickers, pencils, or candy/food if appropriate
j. baseball cards or other collectibles
k. the privilege of borrowing a CD or DVD
l. time with a favorite/previous teacher
m. time assisting a teacher with a class of younger students

Some parent-given incentives include:

a. additional TV time
b. staying up an extra half hour
c. a play date or sleepover with a special friend
d. extra phone or computer privileges
e. a trip to a sporting or other enjoyable event
f. extra computer time or other technology opportunities
g. a pass from needing to complete a home chore
h. extra time with a preferred activity (e.g., play the guitar)
i. a trip to the mall
j. special time alone with a parent

Some teachers have asked the following logical questions related to school incentives: "Is it fair to the other students that these students get a reward for doing the same thing the other students must do without a reward?" or "Won't it be upsetting to the other students that they don't get a reward when they show the same behavior?" I would note here that students are often relieved if a system is implemented that reduces the disturbance a disruptive student causes within the classroom.

In response to these questions, we suggest that teachers respond by defining the concept of fairness in their classrooms as meaning that people get what they need. Fairness should *not* mean that everyone gets the same things. Most students understand this concept; however, some students may still raise questions. Typically, those students understand that fairness is getting what you need as it relates to academics. In those cases, we suggest pointing out privately to any student complaining of unfairness how fairness works with academics. For example, people get to ask all the questions they need to ask or get all the help they need to succeed with academics. This shows them that the definition for *fairness* is consistently applied, as it relates to behavior.

Many teachers find they have the ability to keep individual contingency reward plans a private matter between the adults in the students' lives and the particular students involved. The students involved often prefer this arrangement.

Rewards can be a very powerful motivator of appropriate behavior; however, they do not always achieve the desired results. In these cases, consequences (as defined earlier) will be needed. Some logical consequences in school are

a. losing recess to make up the time a student did not pay attention in class.
b. notifying parents/guardians of the misbehavior (for some this may by prior agreement be accompanied by a consequence at home).
c. losing points that are accumulating toward an incentive.
d. spending time after class or after school to make up the time a student did not pay attention.
e. moving a student's seat away from a student he/she frequently talks with.
f. sending a student from the class to a prearranged time-out area (office, in-school suspension room,

etc.)[16] in extreme cases when the previous interventions do not work.
g. keeping a student after class to discuss the disruptive behavior.
h. asking a student to take a walk for five minutes and to come back when s/he is ready to work.
i. sending a student into another teacher's classroom with work to complete silently.
j. not allowing a student to attend an extracurricular practice, game, or event.
k. calling in parents for a conference to discuss the disruptive behavior.

Factor 8: Engaging Teaching

Frustrated students either shut down or act out. Students who are not challenged either shut down or act out. Bored students either shut down or act out. In her book *Causes and Cures in the Classroom: Getting to the Root of Academic and Behavioral Problems* (2013, p. 129), Margaret Searle tells us, "When students feel discouraged, bored, left out, or mistreated, they are likely to learn less and misbehave more."

Frustrated students either shut down or act out. Students who are not challenged either shut down or act out. Bored students either shut down or act out.

Engaging teaching is an important part of preventing acting-out behavior. Teaching that engages students eliminates the following three reactions:

1. The frustrated student. This is the student for whom the teaching has not been sufficiently differentiated to enable him or her to successfully master the concepts. A student who does not feel successful in learning the content of the course often feels "stupid." The student who feels stupid will typically respond by either shutting down or acting out. Students who shut down may doodle, put their heads down, day dream, or ask to go the bathroom. These students are not disruptive to the class, but they are also not learning. Students who act out are often doing so to hide their embarrassment at not being able to do the work. They are sending the message: *This is not important so I don't need to learn it.* They are also looking to mask their failure by shifting the way people see them from being seen as "stupid" to being seen as "funny" or "bad." When frustration makes a student choose between being perceived by his/her peers as either "bad"

16 It is important to note that students should not be sent without supervision unless the teacher is absolutely certain that the student will report to the designated area. The designated area should be supervised. This consequence is most productive if students can be sent with class work or another productive activity; however, this may not be possible, given the students' emotional state at the time they are sent from class.

or "stupid," the student will almost always choose to be seen as bad.

2. The bored student. Students who master the information and skills in the lesson quickly and are not further challenged often behave in a similar way to those who are frustrated. They will either shut down or act out. Boredom causes these students to look for ways to entertain themselves. Some students entertain themselves in ways that are not disruptive, such as reading, drawing, daydreaming, going to the bathroom, etc. Others entertain themselves with disruptive behaviors such as talking to their classmates or inappropriately performing for their classmates.

3. For some students, the information is at the correct level of challenge, but the instruction is not engaging. Teachers who differentiate their instruction to appropriate levels provide opportunities for group and partner work, provide opportunities for student movement, and use engaging materials and media to keep students interested and focused. Boredom can come from lack of challenge or boring teaching. The teacher's modeling of enthusiasm for the information and skills being taught in the lesson is also important. In her book, *Increasing Student Motivation: Strategies for Middle and High School Teachers* (2006, 26), Margaret Theobald writes, "Students watch their teachers. If we cannot be excited about teaching and learning, then we cannot expect the students to be excited." Bored students, like frustrated students or students who are not challenged, either act out or shut down.

*T*he effectiveness of the preceding eight factors of classroom management is significantly enhanced when the teacher carries them out consistently.

Student engagement is meaningful student involvement throughout the learning process. Listed below are observable behaviors that may be seen in a walkthrough to identify student engagement or lack thereof.

Observable behaviors that show engagement include:
- eyes on teacher or activity
- working on task
- raising hand to ask or answer questions
- contributing to class discussion
- completing work
- responding to teacher questions/prompts
- taking notes
- answering questions
- completing assigned roles
- being prepared for class
- asking questions
- following directions
- having homework
- providing feedback to peers
- using materials appropriate to the lesson
- participating in the activity or work
- demonstrating knowledge or skill

Observable behaviors of *lack* of engagement include the absence of those above *plus*:
- head down
- talking to another student
- texting
- not facing teacher or other speaker
- drawing pictures
- playing video games
- looking out the window

Planning and teaching in ways that avoid boredom and frustration is often referred to as **pacing**. A lesson that is well paced moves through the content fast enough to keep students engaged but not so fast that students are lost or overwhelmed. Some of the factors that contribute to correct pacing are developing the cognitive context for learning well, giving clear and concise directions, frequent classroom assessment, using wait time and other effective questioning techniques, differentiating instruction, having effective and well-taught classroom routines, using effective attention signals, and sufficiently provisioning materials.

Factor 9: Teacher Consistency in Classroom Management

Children and adolescents are creatures of habit. They respond best when the classroom has predictable routines and expectations. Real estate professionals tell us that the three most important things in selling a house are location, location, and location. The three most important things in classroom management are consistency, consistency, and consistency. The effectiveness of the preceding eight factors of classroom management is significantly enhanced when the teacher carries them out consistently.

Being consistent may seem any easy goal at first glance. However, there are factors we need to be aware of that take us away from our consistency. The first is how we feel (emotionally or physically) on a given day. There are days when we have more or less energy and patience than on other days. It is important that on days we are feeling particularly well and certain behaviors feel less of an annoyance that we don't "let things go" that we would normally address. Conversely, when we are tired or our patience is at a lower level, we want to be careful to respond to student behavior in a manner consistent with the way we do so on other days.

Another issue that takes us away from our consistency is unusual school circumstances. Field trips, guest speakers, and assemblies are just a few of these situations. It is important that, prior to these events, we clearly state the routines and expectations. We should also maintain rewards and consequences that are consistent with our regular classroom management plan.

The level to which we are consistent with other staff members who also teach our students will impact student behavior. We recommend that teaching teams work to create the highest level of consistency possible. This does not mean everyone must be exactly the same and give up all their individuality. However, it does require some sacrifice of individual preference in the interest of the greater good. Consistent routines and expectations from class to class make it easier for each individual teacher to get students to respond appropriately and productively. Marzano (2007, p. 158) tells us

> Establishing clear learning goals, rules, and procedures [Author's note: We refer to these as routines] and positive and negative consequences can go a long way toward creating an atmosphere of guidance and control with students. ... However, these behaviors are not sufficient. If consequences are not executed consistently and fairly, their impact is negated.

Getting Started With Developing Your Classroom Management Plan

The following questions may be used as a guide to get teachers started on setting up a classroom management plan:

1. Can I clearly articulate to another adult in observable language all of the routines noted earlier in this chapter? If not, what do I need to do or with whom do I need to talk to reach this goal?
   a. Can I clearly articulate and teach these routines to my students?
   b. Do I have rubrics and criteria sheets that I can use to assess students' behavior on the routines and that they can use to self-assess their own behavior?
   c. When and how will I teach the routines to my students, using the steps noted earlier in this chapter?

2. Have I decided on group rewards that will be an incentive to the class but do not violate my beliefs, those of my team, and/or those of the school culture?
   a. Have I developed a consistent system (e.g., a point system) by which the students may earn the rewards?
   b. Do I have individual consequences set for those students who do not follow the routines, but are not on an individual contingency plan?

3. Have I decided on the strategies I will use to obtain and maintain student attention?
   a. Have I taught these to the students?
   b. Do I have group reinforcements set that are consistent with question No. 1?
   c. Do I have individual consequences set that are consistent with question No. 1?

4. Do I have a plan for building relationships that will result in my students feeling liked and respected by me (teacher to student)? Do I have a plan for building community among the students (student to student)?

5. How should I arrange the classroom furniture to maximize learning, teacher-to-student relationships, and student-to-student relationships?

6. Do I know which students need an individual contingency plan?
   a. Who, besides the student and me, should be a party to the plan?
   b. Do I have a reward for the student that will act as an incentive and that does not violate my beliefs, those of my team, and/or those of the school culture?
   c. Have I set a system in place to ensure I notice and reinforce this student whenever s/he is exhibiting the appropriate behavior?

Sample Elementary Classroom Management Plan

I. Opening Days

A. I will spend a good part of the first two weeks of school teaching my students the rules, norms, and expectations in my classroom, as well as establishing a community of trust and concern for others.

1. Creating classroom rules (Note: This process may take several sessions to complete.)
    a. Have the class brainstorm a list of ideas that students feel are important to helping them learn best, as well as achieve their desired goals.
    b. Have the class create approximately five general categories based upon the list of ideas. (Categories may include rules about how we treat one another, rules about how we take care of things, rules about how we do our work, and rules about safety issues.)
    c. From these general categories, create four to five rules to be posted in the classroom.
    d. Discuss, model, and role-play (where appropriate) what adherence to each of these rules looks like.
    e. Have students sign the poster with the list of rules.
2. Over the next two weeks, I will discuss, model, and practice classroom routines. For example, we will practice morning routines, beginning with unpacking book bags, placing book bags and coats in lockers, making lunch choices, reading the morning message and following the directions given in the morning message. We will also practice quietly lining up and walking down the halls, transitioning from one subject to another, and effectively completing homework, as well as many other routines (*learning class norms*).
3. Students will sit in clusters of four students, assigned by me. Name tags will inform students of their seats (*setting classroom norms, working in teams*).
4. Students will complete several Getting to Know You activities and projects. Activities will be completed independently and shared with the class at a later time, completed in pairs, completed in teams, or completed as a class. I will also participate in many of these activities. These activities will be incorporated into different subject areas and will provide some review of the curriculum for students.
5. Before students share their completed work, I will teach them how to share work, as well as how to respond when others share work. I will ask for student volunteers to model this process for the class.
6. The first night's homework assignment will include a questionnaire asking parents to answer a variety of questions about their children (*acknowledging importance of parental involvement and communication*). Students will also be asked to complete a reflection sheet about their first day of school that will provide me with more information about each student.
7. I will explain how I would like students to organize their desks, notebooks, and binders. This process will be completed as a class, and input from the students will be encouraged (*learning class norms*).
8. I will introduce and explain each of the centers for reading, math, and writing in my classroom. We will talk about how to use each center appropriately. Students will be given opportunities to practice using each of these centers.
9. I will explain the portfolio system that students will use throughout the year. As a class, we will decide what types of things should be placed in a portfolio.

II. Building Relationships

A. Effective behavior management is dependent upon positive teacher-student relationships and a classroom in which students care about one another.

1. I will write a morning message specific to the class every day to acknowledge successes of the class, offer encouragement when it is needed, and ask students to complete a task relevant to the curriculum.
2. We will begin each morning with a meeting, which we will begin with a greeting. In this way, everyone is greeted first thing each day. Our meeting will also include going over the message together, reviewing the academic task, and asking a few students to share something important to them. We will end our meeting with a brief team-building activity. (Note: This process will be discussed, modeled, and

practiced by the students.) Each component of the meeting, including the greeting, academic task, sharing, and team-building activity, will be introduced and practiced separately.

3. I will greet students as they come into the classroom each morning as well as in hallways and in the lunchroom.
4. I will make an effort to learn about each child's interests and ask questions regarding these interests.
5. I will make myself available to work with struggling students both before and after school.
6. I will attend my students' sporting events and performances when appropriate.
7. I will maintain consistent contact with parents through weekly newsletters, phone calls, in-class volunteers, and monthly breakfasts to share projects students have completed in class.
8. I will use community builders to increase the sense of community among the students.

III. Consistent Expectations

A. I will consistently enforce all rules and expectations with clear and logical consequences. The consequences of breaking rules will be known and discussed in advance.
   1. Consequences related to the infraction (a.k.a. logical consequences). For example:
      a. If a student hurts another child's feelings, he/she may "fix" this by writing an apology letter or asking that child to play a special game at recess.
      b. If a student repeatedly chooses not to complete homework, he/she also chooses to lose recess in order to complete the assigned homework.
      c. If a student has become particularly disruptive during group work, a time-out may be necessary. In this situation, I would ask the student to remove himself/herself from the group and work independently on the task at hand.
   2. Time-Out
      If the student previously discussed in 1.c. continues to be disruptive, I may ask him or her to work in the back of my colleague's classroom. *(Author's Note: This arrangement needs to be discussed in advance. We have found this change of scenery to be helpful for some students.)* As a last resort, I would send the student to the resource/behavioral room. In schools where no such room exists, this may be the point at which the student is sent to the office. Again, this arrangement needs to be worked out in advance. If the student appears to be out of control, it may be necessary to escort him or her or to call the resource teacher for additional assistance.
   3. Loss of Privilege
      In this instance, the student loses an opportunity that he/she might otherwise have had. For example, a student who is consistently talking to a neighbor in class may lose a part of his/her recess time. *(Author's Note: This consequence differs from the loss of recess for the purpose of completing homework, noted above, because the talking behavior and the consequence are not directly related. We use loss of privilege in those circumstances in which there is not a readily usable related consequence.)*

Sample Individual Contingency Plan

For the student who may have difficulty following the norms of the classroom, it may be necessary to develop an individual contingency plan. The following steps may be used to create a plan for a student experiencing difficulty in meeting expectations.
   a. Identify areas of weakness[17]
      i.   Is the student disruptive during whole-class instruction?
      ii. Is the student disruptive during independent work?
      iii. Does the student have difficulty working collaboratively?
      iv. Does the student have difficulty completing class and/or home assignments?
      v.   Does the student have difficulty during lunch and/or recess?
      vi. Is the student disrespectful to other students and/or adults?

---

17 These questions are often best answered when a colleague observes in our classroom to gather specific, objective data about a student's behavior.

Once the areas of weakness have been identified, I will set up a chart in which each weakness is stated positively. When a student is able to meet each expectation, he/she will earn a point. See the table below as an example.

	Monday	Tuesday	Wednesday	Thursday	Friday
I worked well independently.	AM: PM:	AM: PM:	AM: PM:	AM: PM:	AM: PM:
I worked well during group work.	AM: PM:	AM: PM:	AM: PM:	AM: PM:	AM: PM:
I completed my class assignments.	AM: PM:	AM: PM:	AM: PM:	AM: PM:	AM: PM:
I completed home assignments.					
Total Points:					

   b. Determine and explain to the student how points will be earned. We have found it to be extremely important to separate the school day into a morning session and an afternoon session. In this way, the student who is having a difficult morning has an opportunity to start over in the afternoon.

   c. Determine with the student what will happen when the student earns a certain number of points. It is important that the incentive is something that is meaningful for the student.

   d. Be sure to involve the parents, as well as any other adult who will be working closely with this student.

   e. Contact previous teachers to get information regarding which techniques worked well and which were not particularly helpful for this student.

   f. Determine a specific time at which you and the student will go over the chart together.

IV. Group Incentive System

A. I will utilize a group incentive system to reward my students for good work and behavior. As a class, students need to earn a total of fifteen points to earn the chosen incentive.

  1. The incentive will be decided upon by both the students and me. In the past, the following incentives have been chosen:

   a. Fifteen minutes of extra recess at the end of the day

   b. Fifteen minutes of a team-building activity

   c. Fifteen minutes of an educational game

   d. A special snack

   e. A pizza party during lunch time

  2. We will brainstorm and discuss how the class may earn points. In the past, the following behaviors were awarded points:

   a. Doing something extra to help another class or student

   b. Reducing lost class time through efficient transitions from one subject to another

   c. Achieving a class goal

   d. Doing exemplary collaborative work during literature circles or problem solving

   e. Working exceptionally well for another teacher or specialist

    (Note: We also discuss that there are certain behaviors and rules students are expected to follow at all times. The class cannot earn points for such expectations.)

  3. I will keep track of the point total in a corner on the whiteboard. In addition, it is not possible for the class to lose points.

Sample High School Classroom Management Plan

I. Opening Days

A. I will spend the bulk of the first few days of class teaching my students the rules, norms, and expectations in my classroom.
  1. Three to four clear and specific rules will be clearly posted on a classroom wall.
     a. Use professional language at all times.
     b. One person speaks at a time.
     c. Ask permission before leaving your seat.
     d. Treat everyone in the classroom with respect (*setting classroom expectations*).
  2. Students will sit in assigned seats (alphabetically) to enable me to learn their names more quickly (*setting classroom norms*).
  3. Students will fill out index cards with information about themselves and their parents for my records (*sending message about my willingness to communicate with parents*).
  4. I will not only tell my students about classroom procedures, but we will also practice them. For example, we will practice coming into the classroom, immediately sitting down, and getting started on the Do Now activity on the blackboard (*learning class norms*).
  5. The first night's homework assignment will include students setting up their binders and notebooks in the specified manner (*learning class norms*).
  6. I will ask my students to sign a contract signifying their understanding of the classroom expectations. I will photocopy these contracts and keep them on file. Students will be expected to keep their original copies in the front of their binders (*learning class norms*).
  7. I will explain the Choose Your Own Activity incentive system that we will use throughout the year (explained below).
  8. I will ask students to tell me a bit about themselves and their likes and dislikes, either orally or in writing. I will share a bit about myself and why I decided to become a teacher (*relationship building*).

II. Building Relationships

A. Effective behavior management is dependent upon positive teacher-student relationships.
  1. I will always make it clear, both orally and in writing, that I am committed to my students' success.
  2. I will greet students in hallways and in the lunchroom.
  3. I will always make positive comments (and not only constructive criticism) on students' graded work.
  4. I will make myself available to work with struggling students.
  5. I will try to attend my students' sporting events and performances.
  6. I will make phone calls or send emails home to parents for positive results (and not only negative results).

III. Consistent Expectations

A. From day 1, I will consistently praise behavior that supports the rules and immediately cease instruction to deal with any violation of the classroom rules listed above (*learning class norms*).
  1. If a student is disruptive in any way, I will immediately cease instruction, turn squarely to face that student, and say that student's name in a calm but firm voice. If the student returns to work, I will say "Thank you" in a pleasant voice and return to my instruction.
  2. If the student continues to be disruptive, I will calmly approach that student's desk and repeat the procedure above (but from a closer proximity).
  3. If the student continues to be disruptive, I have several options:
     a. I might ask to speak to that student out in the hallway.
     b. I might return to my instruction, but find a moment to move to my desk, find the index card filled out by that student at the beginning of the school year, and *subtly* place the card on the student's desk (with a *whispered* warning that I am considering making a phone call home).

      c. I might ask the student to take a brief walk around the school with the paraprofessional and return when he/she is ready to learn again.

      d. I might send the student on an invented errand: for example, to go to the library to find some materials. The student and I know from an earlier private conversation that he/she is to return at the end of the period to speak to me in private. It is important in such arrangements that the librarian know about the plan.

4. If (as happens in rare cases) the student refuses to leave, I have several options:

      a. I might call the school security guard or police officer (if they exist) to take the student away.

      b. I might tell the student, "Well, if you won't leave, please just sit quietly while I teach the rest of the class, and we'll talk about this at the end of class."

      c. If I know of an empty classroom nearby, I might actually instruct the rest of my class to come with me to another classroom and continue my instruction from there. (Note: This option is dependent upon having a strong relationship with the majority of the students.)

IV. Group Incentive System

A. I will use a group incentive system to reward my students for good work and behavior.

1. The incentive will be an educational game (of my students' choosing) to be played on Fridays.

      a. The length of time that the game is played is dependent upon my students' behavior during the week.

      b. For each day that every student (present in school) is in his or her seat when the bell signifying the start of class rings, I will give the class two minutes toward a game on Friday.

      c. For each day that every student (present in school) has his or her binder, notebook, and a pen or pencil with him or her at the start of class, I will give the class two minutes toward a game on Friday.

      d. I will also offer the opportunity to gain minutes through efficient, successful completion of various in-class assignments and group work.

      e. I will keep track of my students' accumulated minutes on a corner of the blackboard.

      f. If the students can accumulate some particular number of minutes (say, 15 minutes), they will receive an age-appropriate incentive on Friday.

V. Individual Contingency Plan

There are often students in our class for whom the group incentive system does not serve as a successful motivator. Typically, this student will negatively affect the impact of the group incentive system on the rest of the class. These students often can disrupt even when we have an effective classroom management plan. These students often have issues with impulse control and or weak self-monitoring skills. We recommend looking more deeply at the root causes of the behavior. The causes can be due to emotional disabilities, chemical imbalances, academic frustration from executive functioning, or other learning disabilities.

A student like this needs an individual contingency plan. At the high school level, most individual contingency plans are developed by counselors, special education teachers, or assistant principals, with input from the classroom teachers. A meeting with the counselor, teacher, student, and parent(s) may be helpful, so that all parties are aware of the plan and the efforts being made to help the student succeed. Searle (2013, pp. 130–131) and Caltha Crowe (2011, p. 2) discuss the importance of understanding triggers to counterproductive behavior for these students when beginning to construct an individual contingency plan. By doing so, we can be more proactive than reactive in our interactions with this student. We can limit the times the behavior is triggered. Green (2011, p. 27) tells us, "All too often, intervention for behaviorally challenged students occurs in the heat of the moment or immediately thereafter. ... Solving problems before they occur is far preferable and more productive." We are not suggesting that understanding all the triggers and avoiding them will eliminate all the inappropriate behaviors. Therefore, it is still important to have a plan specific to these students when proactive responses are either not feasible or do not have the desired result.

To start, we disassociate this student from the group incentive system. This student's behavior will not inhibit the class's ability to earn the incentive. Instead, we meet with the student to determine an individual incentive system for that student. Perhaps he/she would be motivated by getting time on Friday to read a sports, car, or fashion magazine of his or her choosing. Whenever possible, we recommend conferencing with that student and his or her parents/guardians to determine an incentive for successful behavior that the parents would then provide at home (extra time on the computer, more phone time, or more frequent opportunities to borrow the car). The ultimate goal is for the teacher to develop a relationship with this student that ultimately results in a joint decision by the teacher and the student to rejoin the group incentive system. Below is a sample of an individual contingency plan for a high school senior.

Robert Condon Individual Contingency Plan

Robert has difficulty staying seated, remaining still, and paying attention. He also has a tendency to distract other students. In order to keep Robert on track for a successful senior year, the following behavior plan has been agreed to by Robert, his mother, and all of his teachers.

The Expectations

- Robert should not ask to leave class, short of a medical emergency.
- Robert is required to have a pass if he is scheduled to see the school psychologist, nurse, guidance counselor, or another teacher (for extra help). He should not wander the hallways.
- He should use the nurse's bathroom before homeroom, between classes (specifically during the 9:22–9:28 AM break), and during his lunchtime.
- He should not be in the cafeteria (except for his lunch).
- If Robert does need to leave class, his pass will include a five-minute time limit to get to where he is going and back to class. (Robert may be allowed to leave his study hall only once per period and only for five minutes, unless scheduled to be somewhere else and holding a pass to that location.)
- Robert will not touch anyone (hugging, patting, hitting, etc.). If he does, the staff member who observes him doing so will warn him about this behavior. (Please document this, as Mr. Sanchez will be checking in regularly to determine the number of warnings Robert has received. Further action may be necessary.)

If Robert is disruptive in a class (e.g., makes inappropriate comments, interrupts lesson, gets up without asking, etc.), the teacher should use the following language with him:

First warning: "Robert, you are interfering with my teaching."

Second warning: "Robert, this is the second time today that I've told you that you're interfering with my teaching."

Third time: "Please go to Mr. Sanchez's office." He will then receive a detention, which he will serve on that same day.

If Robert is demonstrating a need to go to the nurse or psychologist, and a teacher gives him permission to go, the teacher should call the nurse or psychologist to let him or her know Robert is on his way.

Some Suggestions for Success

1. Robert may be helpful with classroom chores that involve movement (writing on the board, collecting papers, etc.); however, these are privileges that may be revoked if not successful or distracting to other students.
2. Help Robert to reflect about why he made a bad decision and what to do for the next time. Use calm, clear, and consistent language to communicate desirable and undesirable behaviors.
3. Be positive and compliment appropriate and on-task behaviors.
4. Make consequences clear and consistent. Good communication among staff is important. Please see Mr. Sanchez immediately with any problems or concerns.

Incentive: Robert will receive one point for each class in which he is able to remain in the room for the entire period. He will receive two points for any class in which he does not receive any warnings. Mr. Sanchez will email Mrs. Condon each Friday with a report on the number of points Robert earned during that week. Robert may use his points to "purchase" time using Mrs. Condon's car. Robert will be permitted to use the car for one hour for every ten points he earns.

We agree to the following behavior plan.

_____   _____
            Robert Condon   Mr. Sanchez

_____
            Mrs. Condon

Conclusion

Developing good relationships with students, strategically arranging the classroom, engaging students in teaching, carefully teaching students routines and expectations, and developing students' self-monitoring skills will significantly assist with classroom management. Coupling these factors with a plan that includes group incentives and individual consequences will result in a plan that will ensure that the time in your class devoted to student learning is maximized. The most important component for success in classroom management, however, is our consistent follow-through in carrying out the previously described components.

Additional Information about Reading for Understanding

This section provides additional information about reading for understanding, a vital skill to consider when assigning homework, as well as sample group work activities. You will also find information about teaching students with special needs and teaching students for whom English is a second or third language.

Reading for Understanding, a.k.a. Strategic Reading

Reading for understanding (a.k.a. strategic reading or content reading instruction) is the act of reading more than just the words. When students are asked to read for understanding, they are asked to absorb the information in the text.

Teachers often ask students to demonstrate they have read for understanding by

1. Requiring students to note in the reading selection (consumable books and articles) or on sticky

notes (non-consumable books) the important points. Students are also required to state in the notes why they believe those points are important. Alternately, students are asked to highlight important points and note why they are important.
2. Students are also asked to note questions they have about the text itself or higher-order questions prompted by the concepts and ideas conveyed in the text. Students are sometimes asked to graphically organize concepts in a passage.

Teachers assess strategic reading using one or a combination of two or more of the following:

1. They give students comprehension and/or higher order thinking questions (see Chapter 5) prior to the reading. Students must look for and note the information that helps answer those questions. Newer textbooks are providing pre-reading questions at the outset of the chapter. However, if your textbook does not do this, it can be helpful to have the students read the comprehension questions at the end of the chapter prior to reading the chapter.
2. They ask students to answer comprehension questions (orally or in writing) after they have read to test student understanding.
3. They circulate around the room and check student highlights, notes, and questions on the reading. Students are told that the teacher reserves the right to ask individual students questions about their highlights and notes to "test" their comprehension of the content that is noted. The teacher also has the expectation that the student understands any information for which there is not a question noted. Students who correctly explain their highlights and/or correctly answer the teacher's question receive a check plus. Students unable to explain their note or answer one of the

teacher's questions receive a minus. These grades are incorporated into the students' overall grades in the same way as written homework.

One of the authors of this book tells this story about his 14-year-old daughter who came home with the assignment to read a chapter in her social studies textbook:

> At homework time my daughter went off to her room to read the assignment. Twenty minutes later, she came out of her room reporting that she had finished reading the assigned chapter.
>
> Since she is a typical teenager (and I the typical suspicious father of a teenager), I took the book and began asking her questions. She was able to answer two of the four recall questions about the information in the text. However, when asked two comprehension questions, she was unable to answer any of the questions. It was clear to me that she had "read" the words in the chapter but had not read *for understanding*.
>
> She had probably read each and every word. However, lack of concentration on the content, distractions from the dog and her younger brother, and perhaps some surreptitious music listening with headphones had resulted in little or no understanding. I proceeded to write down three comprehension questions and one higher-order-thinking question and sent her back to her room (with a pouting face and grumbling about how annoying it is to have a father who is a teacher) to read the chapter again, this time for understanding.

For more information on reading for understanding or strategic reading, see

Beers, K. *When Kids Can't Read: What Teachers Can Do*. Portsmouth, NH: Heineman, 2003.

Goudvis, A. and Harvey, S. *Teaching Comprehension to Enhance Understanding*. York, ME: Stenhouse, 2000.

Ivey, G. and Fisher, D. "When Thinking Skills Trump Reading Skills." *Educational Leadership* (October 2006): 16.

McConachie, S., Hall, M., Resnik, L., Ravi, A., Bill, V., Bintz, J., and Taylor, J. "Task, Text, and Talk: Literacy for All Subjects." *Educational Leadership* (October 2006): 8.

Wilhelm, J., Baker, T., and Dube, J. *Strategic Reading: Guiding Students to Lifelong Literacy, 6–12*. Portsmouth, NH: Boynton/Cook Publishers, Inc., 2001.

Sample Group Work Activities

Jigsaw

The jigsaw (Aronsen 1978) is an excellent strategy for helping students to learn a large volume of information in an efficient and effective manner. The steps to the jigsaw can be as follows:

1. The teacher divides the information to be learned into equitable chunks. The number of chucks depends on the number of students in class. For example, if there are 25 to 28 students in the class then, five chunks is a good number. If there are 30 to 35 students, then the teacher may wish to break the information into six chunks.
2. The teacher creates a number of groups that is equal to the number of chunks. For example, if there are five chunks of information and 28 students, then the teacher would make five groups with five or six students in each group.
3. Each group is assigned one chunk of information about which they must become "expert" enough to explain to the others.
4. The teacher provides a sufficient amount of time for the individuals in each group to learn the information and for the group to develop a presentation that is given to the other groups. It is recommended that the teacher give a time range for the length of the presentation. For example, each group may need to keep their presentation to between two and three minutes. The teacher should also give the groups a fixed amount of time to learn the information and prepare their presentation.
5. The leader ensures the task is completed. The gopher keeps track of the preparation time to ensure the group finishes the task on time. As the presentation is created, the scribe writes presentation notes that can be used for the presentation of the information to the other groups. When the presentation is complete, the reporter gives it to his/her own group as a "practice run." During the practice run, each of the group members writes his/her own set of presentation notes, so every member of the group has a set of notes to use in the presentation. The scribe's notes can be used as a guide for the other group members when writing their presentation notes.
6. Once each group has its presentation completed and all members have their notes, the teacher regroups the class. Every student in each group is assigned a number. For example, if there are five people in the group and five groups, each student in the group is assigned a number 1 to 5. Once all the numbers are assigned to all the groups, the class is regrouped. All the 1s make a new group, all the 2s make a new group, etc.

For those groups that have six members (when there will only be five new groups), two students are assigned the same number. Those two students jointly present to the new group.

7. Once the new groups are made, the teacher indicates the person who is to give the first presentation. The teacher instructs the group that once the first person finishes, then the next person to present is the person to the left of the first person. This continues until all the students have presented. Thirty seconds before each presentation time is up, the teacher should give a 30-second warning so students know it is time to finish up the presentation.

Carousel a.k.a. Museum Walk (inventor unknown)

The carousel is an efficient and effective technique for brainstorming ideas or answers to questions. One science teacher used this at the outset of a unit on energy.

1. She broke her class of 29 into four groups of six students and one group of five students. On the whiteboard was the statement "List everything in the universe that has (or gives off) energy."
2. Each group made a list with a marker on a large sheet of chart paper. The leader led the work, the scribe wrote on the chart paper, and the gopher watched the time.
3. The teacher gave the groups five minutes to brainstorm.
4. The lists were then placed on top of each group's table (or grouped desks).
5. The teacher then instructed the groups to stand up together, rotate one group, and read the list of the group next to them. At the signal, the groups then moved on to read the next list, until all the groups had a chance to read all the lists.
6. During the "carousel," the scribe noted any questions the group had about any of the lists.
7. After the groups returned to their own tables, the reporter asked the groups questions.

Take a Sip

This protocol is a slight adaptation of the Take a Sip protocol developed by Jennifer Fischer-Mueller and named by Carol Daddazio.

Purpose

To explore the general idea of a text and to commit to an action based on new learning

The Protocol

1. If possible, participants receive the text before the meeting and are asked to read the text in preparation for the meeting.
2. The What: Each participant reviews the text for five minutes to identify a piece (word, phrase, sentence, or group of sentences) of the text that resonates with her or him. They highlight or circle this piece in the text. This is *The What*.
3. The So What: Each participant takes two minutes to write why that piece resonates with her or him. They answer the question, What does it mean to you? This is the *So What*.
4. The Now What: Each participant takes two minutes to write what she or he will commit to as a result of this new learning. This is the *Now What*.
5. In small groups, each participant has two minutes to share her or his responses to Steps 2–4 with the group members.

Debriefing the Protocol

Possible debriefing questions include
- What was it like to explore the general idea of a text in this way?
- Was this a useful way to explore the general idea of a text? If so, why? If not, why not?
- How did looking at the text this way expand your understanding of the topic?

Literature Circles in a Socratic Seminar Format

Protocol: This protocol fosters a deeper understanding of text through a close reading and analysis of a piece of writing. Through questioning and discussion participants analyze, interpret, and discuss the specific piece of text they have read.

1. Students face one another in their group.
2. Students should read the text prior to meeting. (The text itself must contain some ambiguity and be challenging, yet not beyond the students.)
3. Both teacher and students should prepare open-ended questions regarding the text to pose during the session.
4. Teacher sets norms for the class (or group), or teacher and students together set norms.
5. Students (or teacher) may begin the process by posing a question.
6. Students take charge of the discussion and questioning. The teacher serves as a facilitator to guide the process if necessary.
7. Teacher may pose the final question, whereby students may draw from their own experience and connect to the text or opinions voiced in the seminar.

References

Andrade, H. "Promoting Learning and Achievement through Self-Assessment." *Evidence-Based Education* (March 2011): 12–13.

Aronsen, E., Baney, N., Stephin, C. Sikes, J., and Snapp, M. *The Jigsaw Classroom.* Beverly Hills, CA: Sage Publishing Company, 1978.

Boyd, L. "Five Myths about Student Discipline." *Educational Leadership* 70, no. 2 (October 2012): 62–67.

Brady, K., Forton, M., Porter, D., and Wood, C. *Rules in School.* Greenfield, MA: Northeast Foundation for Children, 2003.

Brophy, J. and Good, T. *Looking in Classrooms* 8th ed. Boston, MA: Allyn & Bacon, 2000.

Crowe, C. "When Students Get Stuck: Using Behavior Agreements." *Educational Leadership* 68 (June 2011).

Danforth, S. and Smith, T. *Engaging Troubling Students.* Thousand Oaks, CA: Corwin Press, 2005.

Davis, D., Eshelman, E., and McKay, M. *The Relaxation Response and Stress Reduction Workbook*, 6th ed. Oakland, CA: New Harbinger Publications, 2008.

Dean, C, Hubbell, E., Pitler, H., and Stone, B. *Classroom Instruction That Works: Research Based Strategies for Increasing Student Achievement* Alexandria, VA: Association for Supervision and Curriculum Development, 2012.

Denton, P., and Kriete. R. *The First Six Weeks of School.* Greenfield, MA: Northeast Foundation for Children, 2000.

Ferlazzo, L. "Eight Things Skilled Teachers Think, Say, and Do." *Educational Leadership* 70, no. 2 (October 2012).

Farnsworth, M. and McErlane, J. "Signals for Quiet." *The Responsive Classroom Newsletter* 14, no. 3 (Summer 2002): 1–4.

Frey, N. and Fisher, D. "High-Quality Homework." *Principal Leadership* 12, no. 2 (2011): 56–58.

Greene, R.W. "Collaborative Problem Solving Can Transform School Discipline." *Phi Delta Kappan* 93, no. 2 (October 2011): 25–28.

Greene, R., 2011. "Collaborative Problem Solving Can Transform School Discipline." *Phi Delta Kappan* 93, no. 2 (2011): 25–29.

Hallowell, E. and Ratey, J. *Driven to Distraction: Recognizing and Coping with Attention Deficit Disorder from Childhood through Adulthood.* New York: First Anchor Books, 2011.

Hernstein, R. "Formal Properties of the Matching Laws." *Journal of the Experimental Analysis of Behavior* 21 (1974): 486–495.

Hernstein, R. "Relative and Absolute Strength of Response as a Function of Frequency of Reinforcement." *Journal of the Experimental Analysis of Behavior* 4 (1961): 267–272.

Jones, F. *Tools for Teaching*, 2nd ed. Santa Cruz, CA: Frederick H. Jones and Associates, Inc., 2007.

Jones, F. *Tools for Teaching.* 3rd ed. Santa Cruz, CA: Frederick H. Jones and Associates, Inc., 2013. Kindle version.

Kidron, Y. and Fleishman, S. "Promoting Adolescents' Prosocial Behavior." *Educational Leadership* 63, no. 7 (April 2006): 90–91.

Landrum, T., Lingo, A., and Scott, T. "Classroom Misbehavior is Predictable and Preventable." *Phi Delta Kappan* 93, no. 2 (2011): 30–34.

Lovoie, R. *Understanding Learning Difficulties: How Difficult Can This Be?* Washington DC: F.A.T. City Workshop, PBS Video, 1989.

Marzano, R. *The Art and Science of Teaching: A Comprehensive Framework for Effective Instruction.* Alexandria, VA: Association for Supervision and Curriculum Development, 2007.

Marzano, R. *Classroom Management That Works.* Alexandria, VA: ASCD, 2003.

Marzano, R. "Classroom Management: Whose Job Is It?" *Educational Leadership* 69, no. 2 (2011): 85–86.

Marzano, R. and Marzano, J. "The Key to Classroom Management." *Educational Leadership* 61, no. 1 (Sept. 2003): 6–13.

McLeod, J., Fisher, J., and Hoover, G. *The Key Elements of Classroom Management: Managing Time and Space, Student Behavior, and Instructional Strategies*, Alexandria, VA: ASCD, 2003.

Meier, D. "If They'd Only Do Their Work!" *Educational Leadership* 63, no. 5 (Feb. 2006): 9-10.

Mendler, A. *As Tough as Necessary: Countering Violence, Aggression, and Hostility in Our Schools.* Alexandria, VA: ASCD, 1997.

Mendler, A. *Connecting with Students.* Alexandria, VA: ASCD, 2001.

Mendler, A. and Curwin, R. *Discipline with Dignity.* Alexandria, VA: ASCD, 1999.

Mendler, A. *When Teaching Gets Tough.* Alexandria, VA: ASCD, 2012.

NEA Classroom Management E-Book. http://www.nea.org/assets/docs/110527_NEA_E-Book_Classroom_MgmtFINAL.pdf.

"Punishment vs. Logical Consequences: What's the Difference?" *Responsive Classroom Newsletter* 10, no. 3 (1998).

Quinn, T. "G-R-O-U-P W-O-R-K Doesn't Spell Collaboration." *Phi Delta Kappan* 94, no. 4 (December 2012): 46–48.

Reichert, M. and Hawley, R. "Relationships Play Primary Role in Boys' Learning." *Phi Delta Kappan* 94, no. 8 (May 2013): 49–53.

Sams, A. and Bergmann, J. "Flip Your Students' Learning." *Educational Leadership* 70, no. 6 (March 2013): 16–20.

Searle, M. *Causes and Cures in the Classroom: Getting to the Root of Academic and Behavioral Problems* Alexandria, VA: ASCD, 2013.

Snyder, J. "Reinforcement and Coercive Mechanisms in the Development of Antisocial Behavior: Peer Relationships. In *Antisocial Behavior in Children and Adolescents: A Developmental Analysis and Model for Intervention*, eds. Reid, J., Patterson, G., and Snyder, L., pp. 101–122. Washington, DC: American Psychological Association, 2002.

Theobald, M. *Increasing Student Motivation: Strategies for Middle and High School Teachers*. Thousand Oaks, CA: Corwin Press, 2006.

Vitto, J. *Relationship-Driven Classroom Management*. Thousand Oaks, CA: Corwin Press. 2003.

Walker, H., Ramsey, E. and Gresham, F. "Heading Off Disruptive Behavior." *The American Educator* (Winter 2003–2004): 1–15.

Bibliography of Related Readings

Anderson, M. "The Early and Elementary Years/The Leap into 4th Grade." *Educational Leadership* 68, no. 7 (April 2011): 32–36.

Brown, D. "Now That I Know What I Know." *Educational Leadership* 69, no. 8 (May 2012): 24–28.

Crowe, C. "Teaching Children with Challenging Behavior." *Educational Leadership* 67, no. 5 (February 2010): 65–67.

Curwin, R.L. *Affirmative Classroom Management: How Do I Develop Effective Rules and Consequences in My School?* Alexandria, VA: ASCD, 2013.

"Eight Classroom Disrupters: Getting Them Back on Track." *NEA Today Professional* (Fall 2011). http://www.nea.org/assets/docs/110527_NEA_E-Book_Classroom_MgmtFINAL.pdf.

Frey, N. and Fisher, D. "Making Group Work Productive." *Educational Leadership* 68, no. 1 (September 2010).

Garrett, T. "Classroom Management: It's More Than a Bag of Tricks." *NJEA Review* 86 (October 2012): 17–19.

Goodwin, B. "Research Says/New Teachers Face Three Common Challenges." *Educational Leadership* 69, no. 8 (May 2012): 84–85.

Goodwin, B. and Miller, K. "Research Says/For Positive Behavior, Involve Peers." *Educational Leadership* 70, no. 2 (October 2012): 82–83.

Greene, R.W. "Calling All Frequent Flyers." *Educational Leadership* 68, no. 2 (October 2012): 28–34.

Hansen, J. "Teaching Without Talking." *Phi Delta Kappan* 92, no. 1 (September 2010): 35–40.

Jensen, E. *Engaging Students with Poverty in Mind: Practical Strategies for Raising Achievement*. Alexandria, VA: ASCD, 2013.

Jensen, E. "How Poverty Affects Classroom Engagement." *Educational Leadership* 70, no. 8 (May 2013): 24–30.

Kraft, M.A. "From Ringmaster to Conductor: 10 Simple Techniques Can Turn an Unruly Class into a Productive One." *Phi Delta Kappan* 91, no. 7 (April 2010): 44–47.

Landrum, T.J., Scott, T.M., and Lingo, A.S. "Classroom Misbehavior Is Predictable and Preventable." *Phi Delta Kappan* 93, no. 2 (October 2012): 30–34.

Marzano, R.J. "Art and Science of Teaching/Ask Yourself: Are Students Engaged?" *Educational Leadership* 70, no. 6 (March 2013): 81–82.

Marzano, R.J. "Art and Science of Teaching/Classroom Management: Whose Job Is It?" *Educational Leadership* 69, no. 2 (October 2011): 85–86.

Marzano, R.J. "Art and Science of Teaching/The Inner World of Teaching." *Educational Leadership* 68, no. 7 (April 2011): 90–91.

Mirsky, L. "Building Safer, Saner Schools." *Educational Leadership* 69, no. 1 (September 2011): 45–49.

Poplin, M., et al. "She's Strict for a Good Reason: Highly Effective Teachers in Low-Performing Urban Schools." *Phi Delta Kappan* 92, no. 5 (February 2011): 39–43.

Poplawski, K. "A Principal's Job Is Also to Teach." *Responsive Classroom Newsletter* (Fall 2013). https://www.responsiveclassroom.org/article/principals-job-also-teach.

Pudelski, S. "The Option of Seclusion and Restraint." *School Administrator* 70, no. 2 (February 2013): 34–37.

Rappaport, N. "Why ADHD Medication Is Not Reform: Understanding Behavior Is Critical." *Education Week* 32, no. 22 (February 2013): 23, 25.

Rappaport, N. and Minahan, J. "Cracking the Behavior Code." *Educational Leadership* 70, no. 2 (October 2012): 18–25.

Thompson, M.D. "Rethinking Our Approach to School Discipline." *School Administrator* 70, no. 7 (August 2013): 45–47.

Vatterott, C. "Five Hallmarks of Good Homework." *Educational Leadership* 68, no. 1 (September 2010): 10–15.

Wong, H. and Wong, R. *The First Days of School: How to Be an Effective Teacher*. Mountain View, CA: Harry K. Wong Publications, 1991.

Students with Disabilities: Classroom Management

Reflecting on the concepts and strategies shared in Chapter 3 reminded me of my first year of teaching. I was excited to finally have my own group of students in my own classroom. Little did I know how much it would take to learn to organize my classroom and develop structures for my students in order to teach them.

The complexity of students' needs have increased since that time. Students are entering school with diagnosed and undiagnosed disabilities, such as sensory processing disorders, learning disabilities, anxiety, and trauma needs that affect their ability to be regulated and fully access the curriculum successfully.

During this time of Common Core in the United States, and national curricula in other countries, teachers are worried about how to help students meet the demands of the standards while also helping struggling students keep up. In addition to curricular concerns, teachers are also concerned about the climate and structure of their classrooms, given the complex makeup of their students. There are many areas of disability that often leave teachers believing that students are intentionally disruptive and have behavior problems. In fact, these behaviors are a result of the impact of the student's disability.

According to a 2006 report from the Spiral Foundation, it is estimated that five to thirteen percent of children entering school have a sensory processing disorder (SPD) and that boys are affected more than girls. Three out of four children identified are boys. Sensory processing disorder leads children to experience challenges with how they use sensory information for self-regulation and skill development. There are various types of sensory-processing problems, such as sensory modulation disorder, sensory discrimination disorder, postural-ocular disorder, and dyspraxia. Children with SPD may often have challenges with attention and behavior, social skills, play skills, gross and fine motor skills, daily living skills, sleeping, and eating. SPD is most often associated with other disability areas, such as learning disabilities, attention deficit disorder, autism spectrum disorder, language disorders, anxiety disorders, and behavioral disorders. The chart on the next page compares the types of sensory processing disorders and the common characteristics of each (May-Benson, et al. 2006).

According to the Center for Educational Statistics (2013), students with learning disabilities make up the largest group of individuals with disabilities: 42 percent. Students with learning disabilities often suffer from low self-esteem, low expectations for themselves, underachievement, and underemployment as adults. Students with learning disabilities will often act up and act out to hide their embarrassment. Teachers sometimes view this group of students as oppositional and defiant. Teachers who understand the cycle of fear, avoidance, stress, and escape (FASE) understand what "saving FASE" means. Teachers learn not to react to the behavior but to the underlying cause of the behavior. Teachers who understand FASE, and that all human behavior sends a message, see the oppositional behaviors, frequent trips to the nurse, being unprepared for class, and frequent absences as attempts to avoid the shame of underperforming in the classroom (Schultz 2011, pp. 137–142). In order for teachers to have success with managing their classrooms, it is imperative for them to understand that the students are not unmotivated or oppositional, but are sending a message regarding their need for help.

Anxiety and trauma are among the leading causes of disruptive classrooms in urban public schools across the nation. Unfortunately, children that live in poor, urban communities experience more incidences of violence, whether as a victim or a witness. These children are in a perpetual cycle of disruption and dysregulation. This disruption and dysregulation causes them to be more susceptible to maladaptive coping strategies when faced with the demands of the classroom. In urban school settings, many of the students have experienced some form of trauma; in some instances, it creates more aggressive, explosive, and oppositional situations in classrooms (Rawles 2010). Trauma-informed intervention is an evidenced-based approach to addressing the needs of these students in the classroom. The approach consists of skill development, exploring values, relationship building, and rewards for positive behavior. Creating a trauma-informed approach to prevention and intervention of school violence and behavior outbursts requires exploring the role of trauma in the development of school aggression and how it influences every aspect of the student and the systems they engage (Rawles 2010). Teachers and other students in the classroom are often the recipients of unwarranted aggression and disruptive behavior. However, teachers have the ability to design classroom systems for prevention and

Students with Disabilities: Common Disorders That Contribute to Challenging Behaviors

Disorder	Definition	Common Signs
Sensory modulation disorder	Problems regulating responses to taking in sensory information from our bodies and environment and organizing it in an effective, functional manner.	• easily distracted by noises • overly sensitive to sounds • dislikes nail/hair cutting • dislikes clothing of certain textures/fits • upset about seams in socks • difficult time falling/staying asleep • reacts defensively to tastes/textures of food • easily distracted by visual stimuli
Sensory discrimination disorder	Problems processing body sensations from touch, muscles, joints, and head movements.	• jumps a lot (beds, sofas, chairs) • bumps or pushes others • grasps objects too tightly or uses too much force • frequently drops things or knocks things over • mouths, licks, chews, or sucks non-food items • craves movement, likes to spin around • afraid of heights/swings or slides • has poor balance
Postural-ocular disorder	Problems controlling posture, quality of movement.	• seems weaker than other children • fatigues easily • frequently moves in and out of seat • slumps while sitting • difficulty making eye contact/tracking with the eyes, reading • falls and tumbles frequently
Dyspraxia	Problems planning, sequencing, and executing unfamiliar actions, resulting in awkward and poorly coordinated motor skills.	• problems with daily life tasks like dressing or using utensils • eats in a sloppy manner • difficulty following multistep directions • strong desire for sameness or routines • has an awkward pencil grasp • has poor handwriting • dislikes or reluctant to participate in sports

intervene successfully by fully understanding the approaches that can be used in creating more trauma-informed classrooms.

Anxiety in children is often a direct result of some level of trauma that the student has experienced. While a level of anxiety is a natural part of a child's development, the number of children entering school who have experienced some level of trauma is resulting in an increase in the number of students suffering from anxiety. Through maturation and the development of coping skills, most children learn to manage their anxiety; however, approximately three to twenty-four percent of children under the age of 12 experience significant anxiety problems that interfere with their daily functioning. The level of anxiety that students are experiencing has affected their ability to learn, which has resulted in lower academic performance than those not suffering from anxiety. Anxiety in children can present in many ways. These students are often misunderstood and labeled as lazy, oppositional, rigid, or aggressive. Students who suffer from an anxiety disorder often struggle with peer and adult interactions and relationships, poor parental relationships, and poor self-esteem (Headley and Campbell

2011). The following are simple strategies that can be embedded into daily classroom practices to support a well-managed classroom environment:

1. Embed classroom community-building into the classroom structure as a daily practice for students to engage with their peers and the teacher.
2. Implement a strong social-skills curriculum that focuses on skill development around coping and self-regulations skills.
3. Create safety zones in the classroom for students to access as part of developing coping and self-regulation strategies.
4. Develop visual cues for students to be redirected. This can be extremely helpful when students are experiencing times of heightened anxiety (Headley and Campbell 2011).

Although the instances of trauma and anxiety are increasing for children entering our schools and classrooms, teachers should be aware that recognizing early warning signs for students with a trauma background or anxiety disorder, and implementing preventative measures, ensures a well-managed classroom. If a student goes into the acting-out cycle, supporting students before they reach the peak phase of the cycle ensures students' success and classroom order. As teachers, we are not able to control what has happened to our students that can affect their success.

However, we are able to be thoughtful and responsive to their needs in a way that minimizes disruption but still builds strong classroom communities (IRIS Modules 2015).

References

"Addressing Disruptive and Noncompliant Behaviors (Part 1): Understanding the Acting-Out Cycle." *IRIS*. http://iris.peabody.vanderbilt.edu/module/bi1/.

"Fast Facts: Students with Disabilities." *National Center for Educational Statistics*. https://nces.ed.gov/fastfacts/display.asp?id=64.

Headley, C.J. and Campbell, M.A. "Teachers' Recognition and Referral of Anxiety Disorders in Primary School Children." *Australian Journal of Educational and Developmental Psychology* 11 (2011): 78–90.

May-Benson, T. "Parent Fact Sheet Signs and Symptoms of Sensory Processing Disorder." *The Spiral Foundation*. 2006. http://www.thespiralfoundation.org/toolkit_parents.html

Rawles, P. "The Link between Poverty, the Proliferation of Violence, and the Development of Traumatic Stress among Urban Youth in the United States to School Violence: A Trauma Informed, Social Justice Approach to School Violence." *Forum on Public Policy Online* no. 4 (2010).

Schultz, J.J. *Nowhere to Hide: Why Kids with ADHD and LD Hate School and What We Can Do about It*. San Francisco, CA: Jossey-Bass, 2011.

English Language Learners and Classroom Management

In order to fully understand expectations, behavioral norms, rewards, and potential consequences for conflicts or rule breaking, English learners require an environment that is both supportive and tolerant. Before they are expected to start decoding messages and navigating sociocultural contexts, ELLs must feel safe and respected.

One way to welcome linguistically diverse students is by showing interest in home cultures and encouraging the use of students' home languages as support when needed (Lems, Miller, and Soro, p. 17). Recognizing that ELLs arrive with rich life experiences and offer a variety of skills, knowledge, and proficiency in their own culture validates the individual as a learner and his or her expertise. Teachers can use more subtle approaches to put ELLs at ease, such as gestures to demonstrate friendliness and a positive tone when attempting to communicate the message that school is

a safe, comfortable place to learn. Many schools now have mentoring programs in which groups of peers are trained as "ambassadors" or "buddies" to welcome new students. Partnering with an empathetic, friendly peer will facilitate the transition of the ELL into school routines, rules, and schedules.

The first few weeks in an American school will be shockingly different from English learners' previous school experiences. They do not just feel "first day jitters." Most have recently had a sequence of anxiety-causing experiences, such as saying goodbye to family and friends and leaving the familiarity of their home setting. They then arrive to a new place with cultural and academic factors and rules that may conflict with their understood norms. ELLs in grades six through eight generated the following list when asked what was new for them during their first month in the US:

- not understanding any people or street signs
- American paper money and coins
- unusual fashion and food
- malls, stores, and too many choices of products
- snow and winter weather
- drivers on the left and driving on the right
- not knowing anyone in the neighborhood and not knowing what to say
- riding a school bus
- school start/end times, schedules, and changing classes
- desks set up in pairs or groups
- having a locker and a combination
- bell tones to change class
- snack time and buying/eating lunch at school
- noise in the cafeteria
- recess
- the Pledge of Allegiance and "moment of silence"
- student voices on the public announcement system
- fire drills and alarms
- time needed to complete homework
- being swarmed by peers the first week and left alone after that
- feeling isolated, lonely, and homesick
- feeling stupid and being unable to read
- hating school

Students with limited or interrupted formal education will have faced additional factors that may cause a higher level of anxiety. This includes trauma, such as leaving or losing a family member, witnessing violence, or experiencing poverty and/or neglect. Insightful teachers will be mindful of students' varying ability to cope with change. These educators predict and plan in advance for what may lead an ELL to withdraw, act out, or break down in social and/or academic environments.

Once a student has been given a warm welcome, and perhaps partnered with a student or students designated as peer mentors, messages must be comprehensible. For ELLs who are developing oral-language proficiency and initial literacy skills in English, visual support such as modeling, pictures, graphs, symbols, and signs facilitate the demonstration of expectations and routines. Explicit instruction may also include scripted teacher cues with student choral responses or mantras and consistent demonstrations of praise to reinforce desired behaviors. ELLs with advanced oral proficiency and literacy will continue to need language support in the form of slower speech rates, modeling, and regular references to posted classroom standards and resources.

Regardless of proficiency level, and recognizing the fact that the majority of English language learners have been born in the United States, the behavioral norms of a student's home culture may differ from what is expected in American schools. As teachers develop rules for classroom etiquette, task standards, and homework routines, it is important to investigate social and cultural factors that might influence classroom behavior. Respecting students' experiences and home cultures is essential to creating a nurturing learning environment for culturally diverse students. Investigating multicultural literature and bringing students' home cultures into curricula and lesson activities will peak student interest, promote students' self-esteem, and lower anxiety. Cloud, Genesee, and Hamayan (2009, p. 28) refer to Luis Moll's research (2005) when they encourage teachers to investigate students' funds of knowledge to provide a learning environment that provides continuity with ELLs' pasts and supports them as they learn new skills and subject matter.

Direct and effective communication with parents and families will further support and reinforce the students' understanding of expectations and norms. In order to provide information in a language parents understand, schools are obliged to locate interpreters and translation services when necessary. Parent handbooks and discipline policies and procedures are included in the list of required information schools must communicate with parents (US Department of Education Office for Civil Rights and US Department of Justice 2015).

ELLs who have school experience in their home countries may be at an advantage when they acculturate to American schools, because they have participated in a system of rules and consequences. However, what may put some of these students at a disadvantage is having to learn an entirely new set of rules. ELLs are unique from other new students in that they will have to learn these new rules while they acquire English. Teachers gain valuable insight by examining students' life experiences, including home cultures, skills learned at home and in prior schoolings, and hobbies. This can be done through informal dialogue with the student, interviewing or surveying parents, or by researching school culture of the country of origin. The following questions serve as launching points for understanding the school culture in a student's home country.

English Language Leaners: Launching Points for Teachers to Understand the Students' Home Country School Culture

- Did students raise hands to speak?
- Did students stand to speak in class or address adults?
- Were students expected to stay seated during class?
- Were there certain phrases or titles students used to address adults?
- Were students separated by gender, age, or skill level?
- Were meals served at school?
- Was there a mid-day break or recess?
- What was the expectation regarding attendance?
- Were students expected to take turns speaking?
- Were students permitted to talk at the same time?
- Were desks or chairs in rows or groups?
- How did the teacher handle discipline?
- Was good behavior rewarded?
- How often did teachers communicate with parents?
- What was the nature of parent-teacher communication?
- How often did teachers assign homework?
- How many hours of homework were assigned?
- Were parents expected to assist their children with homework?

The teacher who considers other belief systems and cultures will certainly be at an advantage for creating a supportive atmosphere for successful learning. For some ELLs, particularly those who come from unstable political or struggling economic communities, formal schooling may be a new experience. Students may not be accustomed to being at school for more than three or four hours at a time. Other ELLs may never have attended school with the opposite gender or have only attended religiously affiliated schools in which the behavioral norms were directed by faith and explicitly taught with a focus on doctrine. Students often report that changing classrooms for various content learning is new to them. Various learning environments may not have been a practice in their home country schools or teachers may have moved from class to class while students remained in the same room for all or most of the day. Other typical American school experiences such as field trips, use of technology, cafeteria culture, electronic communication, project-based learning, borrowing library books, health topics, or physical-education class may need prior consideration and preparation to facilitate success for students who come from non-US schools.

When learning about ELLs' experiences in school culture, it is crucial that teachers not make generalizations and assumptions about students who come from the same country, community, religious faith, or language group. Each student has a unique set of circumstances and his or her own personal story to tell if or when they choose to do so. Even though some students may have common experiences, assumptions about cultural or ethnic groups may lead to stereotyping, generalizations, and misunderstandings. In examining home cultures, the acculturation process and life experiences of culturally and linguistically diverse learners, teachers can anticipate obstacles, predict confusing elements, and consciously prepare students and students' parents for new rules and standards.

References

Cloud, N., Genesee, N.F., and Hamayan, E. *Literacy Instruction for English Language Learners: A Teacher's Guide to Research-Based Practices*. Portsmouth, NH: Heinemann, 2009.

Gonzalez, N., Moll, L.C., and Amanti, C. *Funds of Knowledge: Theorizing Practices in Households, Communities and Classrooms*. Mahway, NJ: Lawrence Erbaum, 2005.

Lems, K., Miller, L.D., and Soro, T.M. *Teaching Reading to English Language Learners: Insights from Linguistics*. New York: The Guilford Press, 2010.

US Department of Education Office for Civil Rights and US Department of Justice. "Information for Limited English Proficient (LEP) Parents and Guardians and for Schools and School Districts that Communicate with Them." 2015. http://www2.ed.gov/about/offices/list/ocr/docs/dcl-factsheet-le-parents-201501.pdf.

Using Teacher-Made, Local, State/Provincial, and National Assessments to Inform Instruction

Definition and Purpose of Assessment

How can assessment support teaching and learning? What is it that we want to know about our students? What tools will help us gather and analyze this information? What will we do with this information once we have interpreted the results? This chapter will answer all of these questions.

How do we assess understanding or growth? How do we measure learning? Grant Wiggins (1993) differentiates between learning and measurement. He believes the essential purpose of teaching is to support our students as they understand new ideas and concepts. Wiggins believes that "we cannot be said to *understand* something unless we employ our knowledge wisely, fluently, and aptly in particular and diverse contexts" (p. 200). Thus, to assess understanding, a teacher needs to assess if a student is using his or her newly acquired knowledge "wisely, fluently, and aptly" in a new or different context.

Assessment is a dynamic, interactive process that encompasses observing, teaching, describing, collecting, recording, scoring, and interpreting information about a student's learning. Assessment is interwoven into the teaching and learning processes. It requires two-way communication between the teacher and the student, and provides accurate and meaningful information that the teacher and the student can use to improve student learning, instructional practices, and educational options in the classroom—the three major purposes of assessment (Stuart 2003).

The primary purpose of assessment is to determine where students are in attaining learning goals; to develop activities, lessons, and scaffolds through this assessment to support student learning; and to get students to achieve mastery of their learning goals.

As teachers document students' learning, they can make appropriate adjustments in their instruction and achieve the second goal of assessment—to improve their teaching and assessment techniques—in order to meet the needs of individual students.

Finally, assessments may also be used to improve schools, as their use connects all members of the school community in striving toward continual improvement. A school-wide assessment system encourages the participation of the whole school community. "As community support for assessment expands through greater understanding of the school's goals and achievements, the ongoing school improvement needs are also recognized and addressed" (Stuart 2003, p. 35).

In Hattie's 2012 meta-analysis of what works in schools, he found that formative assessments are by far the most influential practices that improve student outcomes" (Duckor 2014, pp. 28–32).

Assessment for Learning

Assessment for learning is student-centered assessment, when testing results are used to determine (1) where learners are in their learning, (2) where they

One of the most powerful ways of improving learning and raising standards is through assessment for learning, which is more recently referred to as formative assessment.

need to go, and (3) how to get there. "Assessment for learning begins when teachers share targets with students, presenting those expectations in student-friendly language, accompanied by examples of exemplary student work. Then, frequent self-assessments provide students (and teachers) with continual access to descriptive feedback in amounts they can manage effectively without being overwhelmed" (Stiggins 2007, p. 22). Meanwhile, the feedback provides the guidance and support needed for students to achieve the shared targets. Assessment for learning maximizes student learning.

Assessment *for* learning is not assessment *of* learning. Assessment of learning's purpose is accountability, grading, and reporting (ARG 1999).

Research has shown (Black and Wiliam 1998, 2003; Wiliam 2011) that one of the most powerful ways of improving learning and raising standards is through assessment for learning, which is more recently referred to as *formative assessment*. Assessment for learning is different from traditional modes of assessment in many ways. Figure 4.1 outlines the differences between the characteristics of *assessment for learning* and those of *assessment of learning*. Generally, assessment for learning is a process embedded in teaching and learning whose focus is understanding. Assessment of learning focuses on assessments as grades and accountability—that is, as singular events or snapshots, but not as ongoing processes.

The following 12 characteristics of assessment for learning are based in part on the 10 research-based principles created by the Assessment Reform Group

Figure 4.1

Assessment for Learning	Assessment of Learning
Embedded in the teaching and learning process, and is ongoing.	Typically occurs at the end of a unit of study.
Focuses on how and what students learn.	Focuses solely on what students have learned.
Teachers work in teams to construct assessments.	Teachers use commercially produced tests.
Focuses on constructive feedback.	Focuses on grade or mark.
At the outset of the learning, students understand the learning goals and criteria that will be used for assessment.	Learning goals and criteria used to assess are unknown to students.
Fosters motivation for learning.	Fosters motivation for grades.
Main goal is improving understanding.	Main goal is acquiring data to give grades.
Self-assessment is key ingredient.	Self-assessment is not used.
All educational achievement is recognized.	High marks/grades are celebrated.

(2002) and on the Joint Task Force on Assessment of the International Reading Association and the National Council of Teachers of English. (2010).

1. Assessment for learning is part of effective planning of teaching and learning. A teacher's plans should include opportunities for both the students and the teacher to acquire and use information about the progress students have made toward the stated learning goal(s). Learners need to understand the goals they are pursuing as well as the criteria that will be used to assess their work. In addition, a teacher needs to clearly state how the students will receive data about their performance, how students will participate in assessing their own learning, and how they will be helped to make further progress toward the stated goal(s). In Chapter 1, we discussed planning our teaching in ways that facilitate this type of assessment.

> *If a rubric is going to be used, it should be shared with the students beforehand.*

2. Assessment for learning should focus on how students learn. Both teachers and students should be concerned with the process of learning when the assessment is planned and carried out. It is essential that learners be as aware of *how* they learn as they are of *what* they learn, in order to promote growth and understanding of the content. Students should be aware of how they are going to be assessed—that is, what tools or techniques will be used by the teacher. For example, if a rubric is going to be used, it should be shared with the students beforehand. Later in this chapter, we provide a comprehensive explanation of rubrics and their use.

3. Teachers need to inform students about why they are being assessed and how the results are going to be used. Too often, teachers neglect to tell students the purpose of a particular assessment. As students better understand the purposes of assessment, they will be able to use the results and feedback more effectively to improve their learning.

4. Assessment for learning is central to classroom practice. Much of what teachers and students do in the classroom may be described as assessment. Effective assessment practices will mirror instructional activities. The lines between instructional practices, lesson activities, and assessment tasks should be blurred. The tasks and questions teachers ask of students encourage the students to show their knowledge, understanding, and skills. As a teacher observes

and interprets what learners say and do, he or she is able to plan instruction so as to meet the needs of all students. Such formative assessment processes are critical to maximizing learning, and they include teachers and learners in reflection, dialogue, and decision-making.

5. Assessment for learning is a key professional skill. Teachers must clearly understand how to plan assessments, observe learning, analyze and interpret evidence of learning, give data about performance to students in a constructive manner, and support students in self-assessment. Later in this chapter, we discuss the use of students' self-assessment skills and effective feedback. Teachers must be given opportunities to develop and maintain these critical skills through initial and ongoing professional development. Chapters 10 and 11 describe examples of high-quality professional development that helps teachers to develop these skills.

6. Assessment for learning is sensitive and constructive. Teachers' comments and grades may greatly influence a learner's confidence and motivation. Teacher comments should focus on the quality of the work, rather than on the student. When teacher feedback is clear and focused on learning goals, student performance improves.

7. Assessment for learning fosters motivation. In order to encourage students' learning and motivation, the emphasis should be on progress toward goals and effective practice, rather than mistakes or failure. Comparison to other students should be avoided because it has a negative impact on the learning environment. Assessments should

- protect the student's autonomy by comparing his or her work to the standard, rather than to that of other students
- provide students some choice as to the method by which they demonstrate their learning
- offer constructive comments
- create opportunities for self-assessment

8. Assessment for learning promotes understanding of goals and criteria. Learners need to understand both their learning goals and desire to achieve them in order for effective learning to occur. When students participate in the decision-making process—for example, by deciding the criteria for assessing their progress and using the information from the assessment to set their individual learning goals—they will better understand what is expected of them and consequently be more committed to the learning process. Teachers should discuss assessment criteria with their students in terms the students understand and provide specific examples of how students may meet the established criteria. Students and parents[1] need to understand the process by which the students will be assessed. They must be informed about what students need to know and how they are expected to further their knowledge. Learners should also be engaged in both peer- and self-assessment.

9. Assessment for learning helps learners know how to improve. Teachers are responsible for guiding students in their learning. Teachers should highlight the students' strengths and offer guidance for further developing them. Weaknesses should be clearly addressed in a manner that is constructive to the student so that the student understands how learning may be further developed. Finally, teachers must provide students with opportunities to improve their work and demonstrate any new understandings.

10. Assessment for learning develops capacity for self-assessment. Students need to learn how to gain new skills, information, and understanding. It is essential that they are able to self-reflect and identify the next steps in furthering their learning. Teachers may help students acquire these lifelong skills by helping them understand how to self-assess or reflect on what they are learning and how well they are doing. Later in this chapter, we take an in-depth look at student self-assessment.

11. Assessment for learning recognizes all educational achievement. Assessment for learning should be used to help all learners achieve their maximum potential in all areas of the curriculum.

12. Assessment for learning minimizes the following factors, which have been found to be inhibitors of assessment for learning (Assessment Reform Group 2002).

Assessment for learning recognizes all educational achievement. It should be used to help all learners achieve their maximum potential in all areas of the curriculum.

Figure 4.2
Assessment Factors That Inhibit Learning

The following assessment factors inhibit learning when the assessor focuses on
- the task, not the learning
- the grade, not the feedback to support learning
- ranking students, which puts lower-performing students at a disadvantage
- content or pacing needs, not the needs of the learner

Many of the factors that inhibit learning are a function of a more traditional grading system in which behaviors other than performance or the level of learning are included in a student's grade. An example of this is when homework and class participation are incorporated into the grade in a traditional grading system. This chapter will provide examples of a system that supports student growth and avoids using grades to rank students, and instead uses grading to support the next step in a student's growth. See below for a summary of standards-based grading, which is essentially assessment for learning. "Rather than sorting students into winners and losers, assessment for learning can put all students on a winning streak"(Stiggins 2007, p. 22).

A Review of the Research on Classroom Assessment

After extensively reviewing the research on the use of assessment in the classroom, Robert Marzano (2006) has identified four ideas that should be considered when designing and implementing effective in-class assessments. These four principles support the assessment for learning and classroom assessments that

1. Clearly define progress in attaining learning goals
2. Encourage students to improve
3. Consist primarily of formative assessments
4. Use frequent formative assessments

1. **Classroom assessments that clearly define each student's progress**
   Classroom assessments should provide students with feedback that gives them a clear idea of their progress in relation to their learning goals, as well as how to improve. Grades and scores do not typically further a student's thinking. Marzano suggests that feedback and comments specifically

---

1   Chapter 9 takes a detailed look at techniques for effectively communicating with parents.

address how a student can improve. A rubric can provide this kind of feedback effectively and clearly (Leahy, Lyon, Thompson, and Wiliam 2007).

Some forms of feedback may negatively affect learning. Thus, it is important to understand how to provide feedback to students to improve student achievement (Marzano 2006). For example, feedback in which students are told only whether their answers are right or wrong has a negative impact on learning. Also, feedback that focuses on the student rather than the task may also cause a decline in performance (Clymer and Wiliam 2007). In order to have a positive impact on student learning, educators need to provide students with the correct response and, when necessary, the reasoning behind arriving at the correct answer. When students understand the criteria being used to judge their work and when a teacher provides an explanation as to why the responses were right or wrong, the impact of feedback is increased further (Marzano 2006).

2. Classroom assessments that encourage students to improve

Classroom assessments should provide students with feedback that encourages them to improve. Richard Stiggins (2006) asserts that many students give up for fear of failure. Stiggins says that we must give students a way to believe in their own academic success. "[I]f assessments are to support improvements in student learning, their results must inform students how to do better next time. This requires communicating results that transmit sufficient, understandable detail to guide the learner's actions" (Stiggins 2006). Marzano suggests using motivation theory to assess how teacher's responses will affect student achievement. Marzano (2006) suggests we specifically consider both drive and attribution theories to evaluate the potential for encouraging students in their classroom work.

Drive theory suggests that humans are motivated by two forces: "(1) striving for success and (2) fear of failure" (p.7). People generally favor one force or the other. Students who tend to be driven by success are motivated by challenges, as they associate positive feelings with success. Failure-avoidant students tend to be discouraged by challenges, as they associate negative feelings

> *When teachers phrase compliments so that students understand their own roles in the accomplishment, they will begin to see that their efforts allow them to meet their goals.*

with anticipated failure. To avoid these fears of failure, Marzano suggests that teachers give students a way to interpret low scores that does not lead students to believe that they have failed permanently or that being a failure is an attribute of this student (Marzano 2006).

Attribution theory provides insight into encouraging and discouraging feedback. Individuals attribute their success to one of four forces: ability, effort, luck, or task difficulty. Students who attribute achievement to effort tend to remain most optimistic about achieving success (Covington 1992, in Marzano 2006). The relationship between drive theory and attribution theory is that "students who tend to be success-oriented also tend to believe in the effort attribution" (p. 8). These students believe that, through hard work, they will achieve success. It is important to note that students can learn over time that effort does produce success if they do not initially believe this to be the case (Marzano 2006).

Douglas Fisher and Nancy Frey (2012) maintain that teachers need to shift students' mindset from being a fixed one based upon the belief that ability determines success or failure to a growth mindset, in which students believe that their effective efforts result in success. They maintain that if teachers recognize students' accomplishments and agency with statements connected clearly to students' work—and the connection between the quality of their work and choices—students will begin to believe that hard work results in quality work, and they will, over time, develop a growth mindset. Statements such as, "You wrote a clear introduction; tell me why you decided to use this quote" or, "Tell me what you think worked well and didn't work" emphasize the student's agency—that is, deliberate actions.

> When teachers phrase compliments so that students understand their own roles in the accomplishment, they will begin to see that their efforts allow them to meet their goals. In doing so, teachers can guide students to "attend to their internal feelings of pride" (Johnston 2004), which will build students' internal motivation and reduce their need for external praise (Fisher and Frey 2012, p. 58).

Chapter 7 explains the attribution theory in greater detail.

3. Formative classroom assessments promote student learning

The majority of classroom assessments should be formative, according to Marzano's research. *Formative assessments*, from which feedback and further teaching evolves, yield higher achievement and have a greater impact on learning (Crooks 1988, in Marzano 2006). Black and Wiliam (2010) define formative assessments "all those activities undertaken by teachers and/or by students which provide information to be used as feedback to modify the teaching and learning activities in which they engage" (Marzano 2006, pp. 7–8). Given this definition, formative assessments may begin at the start of a lesson, last throughout its entirety, and come in a variety of forms (Marzano 2006). Later in this chapter, formative assessment is discussed in greater detail.

4. Frequent formative classroom assessments.

Researchers have found that student achievement is associated with frequency of assessment. Students who are assessed more frequently tend to achieve greater success. In addition, frequent formative assessment allows educators and students to determine patterns of student learning. "In this way, both the learner and the teacher will be able to discern not only the student's current level of achievement, but also how much the student's capabilities have improved, which is a powerful booster for confidence and motivation" (Stiggins 2006). Marzano (2006) asserts that there is no magic number of assessments that teachers should use with students throughout a unit of study or grading period; however, "the message from the research is clear: systematic use of classroom assessments...can have a strong positive effect on student achievement" (p. 10).

John Hattie describes a turnaround school in which a shift in teachers' perception of students resulted in great achievement gains. As teachers shifted to looking at student results and at improving their own practice, and away from looking for compliance in homework, the results were good behavior and work, and students' attitudes toward themselves and their learning changed. Students began to focus on their learning, not grades, and began to see themselves as agents of their own success. Students gained an average two years of growth for each year of work (Hattie 2015, pp. 36–40).

In addition to understanding why some stu-

dents interpret feedback in a positive way while others interpret it negatively, Marzano (2006) and Heflebower (2011) suggest two techniques teachers can use to encourage learning through the assessment process. These strategies include tracking students' progress and encouraging self-reflection. Both of these techniques are discussed in following sections.

Pre-Assessments, Formative, Interim, Benchmark, Common, and Summative Assessments

Pre-assessments, formative assessments, and summative assessments are defined by their use by the classroom teacher. Pre-assessments are generally used for diagnosis. Formative assessments, which include interim and benchmark assessments, are used during the teaching and learning. They are used to assess the progress that students are making toward mastery or the learning target. Summative assessments are given at the end of a unit or year to determine the level of mastery that a student has achieved.

Diagnostic pre-assessments typically are given at the beginning of a unit of instruction and usually precede teaching. These assessments are used to determine a student's prior knowledge, level of skills, any misconceptions in relation to the particular unit of study, learning style preferences, and interests. These assessments are critical to educators for effectively designing and guiding differentiated instruction. Some examples of pre-assessments include skill and knowledge checks, K-W-L charts, concept maps, drawings, and interest and learning style profiles. Typically, pre-assessments are not used for grading because their purpose is diagnostic (McTighe and O'Connor 2005).

At the beginning of any unit of study, it is likely that some students may have already mastered some of the skills and concepts, and some students will have misconceptions about the skills and concepts. Understanding the varying levels of mastery of students gives a teacher "greater insight into *what to teach*, by knowing what skill gaps to address or by skipping material previously mastered; into *how to teach*, by using grouping options and initiating activities based on preferred learning styles and interests; and into *how to connect* the content to students' interests and talents" (McTighe and O'Connor 2005, p. 14).

Pre-tests are also used to determine student growth. At the end of a unit of study, a term, or a year, a post-test is given. The difference between the end result and the pre-test is used to understand the amount of learning over time that a student has made.

Formative assessments are assessments that are embedded in the teaching. They provide the teacher and students with information about the students' levels of mastery during instruction. The teacher uses this information to modify the teaching to meet the needs of the students. The students use the information to determine what they know and do not know, so they may ask questions or seek information in other ways to fill in the gaps in their learning. Formative assessments are powerful instructional tools for educators because they provide timely, pertinent information that can be used to effectively plan and implement differentiated activities that meet the specific needs of all learners.

Interim, benchmark, and common assessments are formal tests administered by a district, school, or department. All are formative assessments when they are used to adjust the instruction based upon the results of the assessment. Each is defined below.

Interim assessments are given at times determined locally; for example, interim assessments could be given every month, six weeks, term, or year. Their purpose is to see if the students are on track to achieve their mastery objectives or master specific skills or standards.

Benchmark assessments are similar because they are used to see if students are "on track" to proficiency or the learning target. The precise benchmark of, for example, reading at a specific reading level, is often based upon the history of students in the district. Students who are "above benchmark" are then offered challenge or enrichment work; those "at benchmark" are progressing adequately and continue; and those "below benchmark" may be provided additional interventions.

Common exams are exams developed by teams or departments of teachers, and are administered to all students at the same time. When they are final exams, their results aren't used to adjust instruction, so they are summative exams. When these common exams are given at pre-determined intervals, they could also be labeled *interim*.

Informal formative assessment is as important as the more formalized common, interim, and bench-

> *Informal formative assessment is as important as the more formalized common, interim, and benchmark exams.*

mark exams. These less-formalized assessments, from questioning to quizzes, provide on-the-spot data to the teacher and students to help them achieve their goals. These may include classwork, homework, exit slips, as well as questioning of all types.

The following are some examples of informal, classroom formative assessment:

- The teacher asks a recall question about some specific information that has been presented thus far during the lesson.[2]
- The teacher asks a comprehension question that requires students to apply the information that has been presented thus far in the lesson.
- The teacher projects a math problem on the white board at the front of the class that reflects the concept that has been taught thus far in the lesson. Students solve the problem on their individual white boards. The students all hold their boards up together so the teacher can scan the room and see who has solved the problem correctly, who has not, and where students have difficulty in solving it.[3]
- Each student uses a classroom response system using a handheld transmitter (called a *clicker*) to respond to the teacher's questions displayed on the white board about his or her understanding of meiosis and mitosis. Software on the teacher's computer collects and analyzes the responses, and produces a series of bar charts based on the number of students' responses to each question. Based on the responses, the teacher then makes decisions about whether to move on, reteach, or more deeply discuss the concepts.
- Students self-assess their progress against a criteria sheet, a rubric, and/or an exemplar.
- Students peer-assess each other's work based on a criteria sheet, a rubric, and/or an exemplar.
- The teacher observes students working independently or in groups and takes anecdotal notes. See the *Charlotte's Web* example later in this chapter.
- For the purpose of deciding whether to move the class on to new concepts or reteach, remediate, and/or extend the previously taught concepts, teachers use quizzes at the end of unit sections to assess each student's and the class's levels of

---

2 More information on questioning techniques that check student understanding can be found in Chapter 5.

3 Strategies for checking the understanding of all the students at one time are known by a term coined by Madeline Hunter, *dipsticking*. More information on dipsticking can be found in Chapter 5.

mastery on the information and skills taught in each section.

- For the purpose of deciding whether to move the class on to a new unit or to reteach, remediate, and/or extend the previously taught concepts, teachers use tests at the end of units to check each student's and the class's levels of mastery on the information and skills taught in each unit.
- Teachers use in-class assignments to check students' ability to apply the learning independently. The teacher checks these assignments and uses the information gathered to plan instruction for the next day of class.
- Teachers use homework assignments to check the students' ability to apply the learning independently at home.

Summative assessments are assessments that take place after the unit's teaching ends. They provide a grade, a score, or a local or national norm score for the student. Such assessments are often used by teachers at the culmination of a unit to determine the degree of learning that has occurred in a particular area of study. The purpose for which a teacher is assessing in large part determines which type of assessment will be given to students.

The following are some of the purposes for summative assessment:

- States and provinces use summative assessment data from competency tests to certify that the student acquired the requisite skills and knowledge for a particular grade.
- States and provinces use summative assessment data from competency tests to determine the level of success or failure in a particular district.
- Districts use summative assessment data to evaluate whether the curriculum is teaching the desired skills and knowledge in a particular subject area and/or at a particular grade level.
- Districts use summative assessment data to sort students for participation in certain courses and to determine which level of a specific course (e.g., standard, honors, or advanced placement) in which the student should enroll.
- Summative assessment data is used to norm students or groups of students in comparing their achievement relative to national groups or other populations.
- The Scholastic Aptitude Test (SAT) uses summative assessment data to predict students' potential for success in their first year of college.
- Employers and the military use summative assess-

ment data to predict their staff's potential for success in certain jobs.

- For the purpose of giving a grade, teachers use quizzes at the end-of-unit sections to assess each student's and the class's levels of mastery of the information and skills taught in each section of the unit.
- Teachers use summative assessment data to assess the level of mastery at the conclusion of a lesson.

Assessments can provide data that can be used to support students' learning by diagnosing their progress and determining their needs to gain mastery of skills or content. Assessment can be a powerful method for promoting and supporting student success—not simply measuring it. According to Paul Black and Dylan Wiliam (1998), students achieved unprecedented score gains on standardized tests when teachers applied the principles of assessment for learning. With appropriate training and understanding of the process, teachers may improve their daily assessments, make their comments to students more constructive, and more actively involve students in the assessment process. "In this way, classroom assessment for learning becomes a school improvement tool that helps create responsible, engaged, and self-directed learners" (Chappuis and Stiggins 2002, p. 43).

Assessments May Serve Multiple Purposes: Diagnosis/Pre-Assessment, Evaluation, and Feedback

If an assessment serves multiple purposes—for example, when a final exam on literary analysis of short stories (summative assessment) is used to plan the next unit—it can be considered both formative and summative. Thus, because of the timing (at the end of the unit) and because students' future learning is planned based upon the results of the exam, this assessment is both formative and summative.

> Formative and summative assessments can perform double duty; it's all in how we use them. If we use assessments only to assign a grade, they're summative, but if that information is recycled into the classroom and used to improve instruction, reteach, or refine student learning, it becomes a formative assessment (Dirksen 2014, pp. 26–31).

Beyond formal tests, quizzes, research, and presentations, formative assessments can take a variety of forms, as long as the information gathered by the teacher is used to adjust instruction. As Debra

Dirksen describes, formative assessment can function as a "reset button":

> Other tools that you're already using in your classroom, such as collaborative learning, writing activities, and graphic organizers, can also be used to identify areas in which students need to go back and relearn information or skills. We need to teach students by using the concept that gamers have used so well: Failure is OK as long as it leads to learning. There is a reset button in education. It's called formative assessment (Dirksen 2014, pp. 26–31).

Other common assessment terms include *interim assessments* and *benchmarks*, whose purpose is to determine if students are on their way to getting proficient scores on high-stakes tests and, at the same time, to provide support to students at risk (Chappuis and Chappuis 2007/2008, p. 14). Although these assessments are a summation of what a student has learned over a period of time—that is, a summative assessment—such assessments may also be considered formative in nature. Teachers then can use results from the assessments to make changes in their instruction in order to address the possible gaps in their students' learning, such as a benchmark test given in January to track the progress a student has made over the course of the last three months. Students who have not mastered the target skills and concepts are grouped together, and the teacher reteaches the necessary skills and concepts. The teacher provides the students who are ready to extend or deepen their learning with more challenging work.

The timing of benchmark and interim assessments is critical. They need to provide data that is actionable. Bambrick-Santoyo, in "Coaching and Teaching for Results," recommends the following timetable and considerations so that interim assessments can be used effectively (Bambrick-Santoyo 2013, p. 70–71):

- Have a six- to eight-week administration cycle.
- Re-assess previously learned skills.
- Analyze assessments to the level of specific errors.
- Have a defined follow-up in each classroom.

Figure 4.3 provides an overview of the different reasons for assessing students' work. It is imperative that we clearly understand the purpose of the assessment, as it relates directly to the type of assessment we use with our students. In the chart, note that summative assessments include only one square in the flowchart. In contrast, formative instruction leads to many other reasons for assessing student work, from reteaching to differentiating instruction to extended learning opportunities.

Figure 4.3

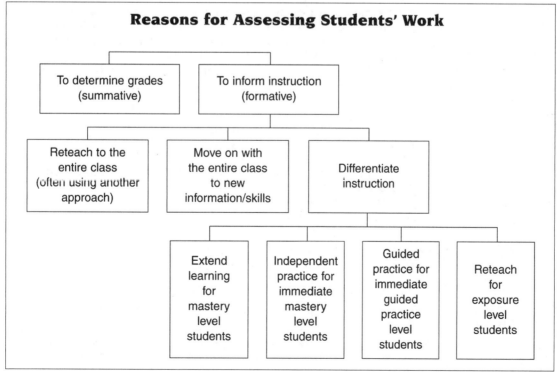

Reasons for Assessing Students' Work

Local Assessment Validity and Reliability

A good assessment task is one that is meaningful, purposeful, and connected to everyday life and aligned to local, state or province, or national standards. Figure 4.4 highlights the essential criteria for assessment tasks that foster higher-level learning.

Determining Which Formative Assessments Provide Useful, Actionable Data

Not all formative assessments provide useful information. As Jan Chappuis says in her article, "Thoughtful Assessment with the Learner in Mind," not all formative assessments provide diagnostic information (Chappuis 2014, p. 22).

Figure 4.4

Authenticity	• Does the task reflect real-life situations? • Does it require multiple levels of understanding?
Credibility	• Is the task purposeful, in that it helps students achieve the learning goals established for the unit? • Is the task aligned with other standards set at the district, state, provincial, and/or national level? • Is the task connected to an overarching question?
Validity	• Does the task assess what it claims to assess? • Does the task provide sufficient evidence of learning? • Does the task require multiple forms of written and oral evidence of learning? • Does the evidence allow us to make accurate inferences about student understanding? • Content validity: Does the content of the local assessment align with the district curriculum at the expected level of rigor? • Relative to other assessments: Do the scores agree with or predict other tests and/or criterion?
Reliability	• Does the evidence accurately reflect a student's abilities? • Can the task be used over time to show a student's progress in a particular area? • Twenty or more multiple-choice items provide high internal consistency. • Written or constructed response items are lower in reliability than multiple choice items because of scorer differences and fewer items. • Portfolio reliability is lower because of scorer differences and fewer responses. • Inter-rater reliability: How consistent are the scores between two or more raters (scorers)?
Feasibility	• Can the task be completed in a timely manner? • Is the task feasible in terms of logistics and resources?
User-Friendliness	• Is the task appropriate, engaging, and beneficial to the teacher and student? • Does the task challenge the students? • Does the task make sense to the students? • Are there clear instructions, guidelines, and criteria for the task?
Fairness	• Is the assessment equitable for all students? • Are the standards and criteria clearly established?
Rigor	• How aligned with the standards is the local assessment? Bloom's Taxonomy and Webb's Depth of Knowledge can be used to assess the rigor of a local assessment.

Adapted from "Technical Guide A: Considerations Regarding District-Determined Measures," Massachusetts Department of Elementary and Secondary Education (2013); Stuart (2003), Wiggins, and McTighe (1998); Herman, Aschbacher and Winters (1992); and Mitchell, Wills, and the Chicago Teachers Union Quest Center (1995).

If we examine students' responses, the questions asked or the student work needs to provide "instructionally tractable" information—that is, data that can inform a teacher's next steps. For example, it is essential that before we use data from assessments that we check it for accuracy and for the possible reasons that a student may not have provided an adequate answer. Also, assessments should provide helpful information to the teacher about what the next step in teaching should be.

Teachers can determine whether students are ready for a summative assessment of their mastery after students have been given ample time to learn.

Thus, educational decisions need to be based on assessment information that helps a teacher determine the next step. Formative assessments can range from informal teacher questions to formal quizzes, tests, or performances. As Dirksen says,

> Formative assessments don't necessarily need to be out-of-the-ordinary activities. You can employ the same tools you already use daily as formative assessment tools. Use rubrics to grade assignments, and use the data to improve instruction and student achievement. Use your summative evaluations formatively by taking the results and using that information to develop instruction designed to improve student outcomes, either through reteaching information on which students performed poorly or by changing how the information will be delivered in future [classes] (Dirksen 2014, p. 38).

The key, according to Chappuis, is the usefulness of the data, not the type of assessment administered. The data is useful when it can be used to diagnose or assess students' needs, that is, if it has "instructional traction" (in other words, actionable information) for the teacher (Chappuis 2014, p. 24).

Key to determining the usefulness of the data is whether it connects clearly to the mastery objective of the exercise, activity, lesson, or unit. In the example about the author's craft in *Charlotte's Web*, which follows this section, the diagnoses were all based on students' varied levels of understanding about the author's craft. In this example, the next steps for continuing to teach authors' craft in poetry were based upon data (from the teacher's analysis of student work and from discussions and observations of students) that indicated most students had not reached mastery of the skill of determining why and how authors accomplish tasks such as developing a character. If the teacher had been using a locally developed common exam or benchmark exam, the teacher would need to know exactly how specific test items connected to mastery objectives or local or state/provincial standards. Jan Chappuis says that to use items effectively, teachers first need to be sure that the content or skills were taught. Then, teachers need to work on clarifying learning targets (Chappuis 2014, p. 26). See Chapter 1 for further clarification of mastery objectives.

In Figure 4.5, the Sample Mastery Objective chart provides a place for the mastery objective. In this case, the objective of the fourth-grade lesson on *Charlotte's Web* by E.B. White is to explain the author's craft in an essay that explains developing the characters of Homer and Charlotte using evidence from the text. The example covers one day of instruction.

Figure 4.5 Sample Mastery Objective

| Mastery Objective (Tuesday):

Show how what the character says and does is part of the author's craft. | Using the graphic organizer, list an example of what your chosen character says (a quotation or two), does (an action), and looks like (list at least three adjectives). Draw your character and put what you think is the best quotation in a quotation bubble.

Beneath your character, tell the reader about the character as if you were the author. |

See the sample from *Charlotte's Web* below in Figure 4.6 for a model for this assignment.

Formative assessments are given throughout the learning process as a teacher is guiding all of her students toward mastery. In the *Charlotte's Web* example, as students found quotations and examples of actions, the teacher would work with individual and groups of students to support their mastery objective.

Teachers can determine whether students are ready for a summative assessment of their mastery after students have been given ample time to learn.

> During the learning, students' work will reveal some combination of incomplete understanding, flaws in reasoning, or misconceptions. Our job as teachers is to examine student work and offer sufficient penalty-free practice time, reteach and redirect students when needed, and provide both success and intervention feedback as called for (Chappuis 2014, p. 26).

Figure 4.6 Example of Performance Assessment

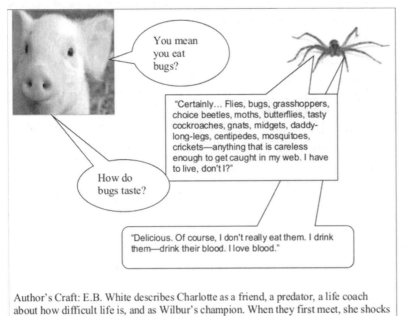

You mean you eat bugs?

How do bugs taste?

"Certainly... Flies, bugs, grasshoppers, choice beetles, moths, butterflies, tasty cockroaches, gnats, midgets, daddy-long-legs, centipedes, mosquitoes, crickets—anything that is careless enough to get caught in my web. I have to live, don't I?"

"Delicious. Of course, I don't really eat them. I drink them—drink their blood. I love blood."

Author's Craft: E.B. White describes Charlotte as a friend, a predator, a life coach about how difficult life is, and as Wilbur's champion. When they first meet, she shocks Wilbur by saying she eats bugs and she drinks their blood. Even though Charlotte is a friend, she does shock him, and later she will tell Wilbur about how difficult life is.

Pre-Testing Can Provide Valuable Data to Both the Teacher and the Student

Pre-assessing students gives a teacher a picture of his or her students' strengths and needs. A simple chart that asks what you know and what you want to know can provide the teacher with data, and it provides each student time to begin to think about the content and skills that will follow in the lesson or unit. A more formal test can also be used, as is often the case at the beginning of the year in elementary mathematics or literacy classrooms.

This data can provide a road map for the entire year for the teacher, and, according to recent research (Casey 2014), taking a pre-assessment, even if a student misses many of the questions, provides a student with a schema of the expectations for the course.

For example, if, as a pre-assessment in a high school history course, students are given two primary-source texts they are asked to read and from which to write an analysis of the relative strengths of the two arguments, they may struggle with the complexity of the question. However, by struggling to answer this kind of question at the beginning of the year, the student will begin to understand that readings are not simply for content to be memorized. Rather, he or she will see that readings, whether they are primary sources in history or poetry in literature, will be analyzed for their effectiveness in their messages. In his 2014 *New*

York Times Magazine article, Benedict Carey lists the positive impacts of pre-assessing on students.

- First, students get a glimpse of what the teacher intends to teach, which helps them see where instruction is headed and how the information fits into the course narrative. Students who get the pretest preview are more confident in judging what's important and what isn't.
- Second, wrong guesses puncture students' overconfidence about what they know.
- Third, retrieving is a different mental process than straight studying. The brain is digging out information, along with a network of associations, and that alters and enriches how the network is re-stored.

Thus, both students and teachers gain from pretesting. Carey cautions that the results of giving pretests are mainly positive in areas in which students have some knowledge, but they are not helpful if it is clear that students have no knowledge, such as in learning a new language.

Using Data to Support Learning: Tracking Students' Progress

Marzano's meta-analysis (2006) of research on assessment suggests that tracking students' progress or having students track their own progress over time is an effective assessment technique to encourage learning. In addition to improving students' learning as they become more aware of their progress, monitoring student progress allows teachers to make better instructional decisions (Safer and Fleischman 2005).

Students and teachers gain from pretesting.

Marzano developed the following form to track progress. Figure 4.7 illustrates how this form was used by a student in a math class to track her own progress over the course of a geometry unit. The student recorded the score she received on the pre-assessment for this unit and then set a goal of earning a score of 95 percent by the end of the unit. She also wrote down additional things she felt she might need to do in order to maximize her learning. For each assessment she took during this unit, she recorded the date on the lines provided and then plotted her scores on the line plot. Using this form during a unit of study enables students to visually track the progress they make over time. In this example, the teacher used percentages to score student work. A four- or six-point rubric or criterion-referenced rubric could also be used to track progress through the year.

Figure 4.7

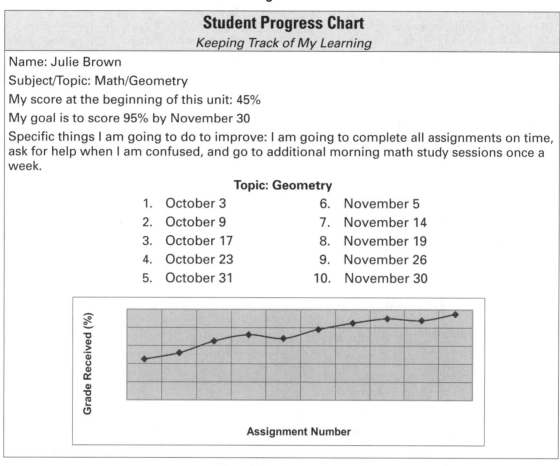

Student Progress Chart
Keeping Track of My Learning

Name: Julie Brown

Subject/Topic: Math/Geometry

My score at the beginning of this unit: 45%

My goal is to score 95% by November 30

Specific things I am going to do to improve: I am going to complete all assignments on time, ask for help when I am confused, and go to additional morning math study sessions once a week.

Topic: Geometry

1.	October 3	6.	November 5
2.	October 9	7.	November 14
3.	October 17	8.	November 19
4.	October 23	9.	November 26
5.	October 31	10.	November 30

Adapted from Marzano (2006).

The student progress chart in Figure 4.8 has not yet been filled in and can easily be adapted to use in one's classroom. This form "also provides a vehicle for students to establish their own learning goals and to define success in terms of their learning as opposed to their standing relative to other students in the class" (Marzano 2006). As students watch themselves grow as learners over time, they are more likely to believe that success is possible when they work toward their goal.

Classroom Assessment That Encourages Student Self-Reflection

One way in which teachers can encourage student reflection is by asking them to assign themselves a score using a rubric or a specific set of criteria. After both the teacher and the student have assigned a score to a particular assessment, these scores can be compared.

Discrepancies between the teacher's and the student's scores provide powerful opportunities for a teacher and student to converse. "If a student scored himself higher than the teacher, the teacher would point out areas that need improvement before the student actually attained the score representing his perceived status. If the student scored himself lower than the teacher, the teacher would point out areas of strength the student might not be aware of" (Marzano 2006, p. 92).

Cross (1998, in Marzano 2006) recommends using a "diagnostic learning log," in which students are asked to respond to four different questions to encourage student learning. These questions are as follows:

1. Briefly describe the assignment you just completed. What do you think was the purpose of this assignment?

2. Give an example of one or two of your most successful responses. Explain what you did that made them successful.
3. Provide an example of where you made an error or where your responses were less complete. Why were these items incorrect or less successful?
4. What can you do differently when preparing next week's assignment?

In addition, Cross suggests that teachers compile the responses to these questions and look for patterns in students' learning. In this way, such self-reflection can be used to inform future instruction for the whole class, small groups, or individuals (Marzano 2006).

Using the Data from External, Standardized Assessments

Standardized testing was developed about a hundred years ago to address concerns of unfairness and bias in grading procedures. Standardized tests provide educators, administrators, and policy makers with a snapshot of what students know in relation to what they are being tested on and how other groups of students perform on the test. Standardized test results yield comparisons across years, grade levels, and student populations both locally and nationally, and they may be used as one piece of data. "A data review of the test performance of a class, grade, or school can point out

Figure 4.8

Student Progress Chart — Keeping Track of My Learning

Name: _____

Subject/Topic: _____

My score at the beginning of this unit: _____

My goal is to score _____ by _____

Specific things I am going to do to improve: _____

_____

Topic: _____

1. _____   6. _____
2. _____   7. _____
3. _____   8. _____
4. _____   9. _____
5. _____   10. _____

1	2	3	4	5	6	7	8	9	10

Assignment Number

Adapted from Marzano (2006).

content that might not have been taught, aspects of test taking that are difficult for individual students or groups, and students' abilities to read and follow directions" (Stuart 2003, p. 217). See later in this chapter for an example of how standardized assessments were used by a teacher both on the high school and elementary levels.

> *Standardized test results yield comparisons across years, grade levels, and student populations locally and nationally.*

and credible feedback. However, a letter or number grade does nothing to help a learner improve because it does not provide feedback to the learner about how to improve performance.

The Confusion about Objectivity and Subjectivity

Often people describe assessments as "too subjective." Ironically, all assessments are subjective in that a person created them. Multiple-choice exam questions and choices for each question were developed by psychometricians or teachers. Yet, educators often call multiple-choice exams "objective," meaning that a person's attitude toward that learner does not have an impact on the score. Yet each question's topic, choices, and difficulty are all "subjectively" developed.

The idea of subjectivity is also often misinterpreted as something negative in assessment and grading. If subjectivity means that a teacher's bias for or against a student might lower or raise the grade, then subjectivity could be considered a negative term. Yet, professional judgment is an essential component in teaching, developing, and using assessments, and in judging how to use data. It is an essential component in creating multiple-choice (sometimes, unfortunately, called *objective tests*). Thus, all assessments are created by people and are, in a sense, subjective.

As Grant Wiggins said in an online chat,

All scoring by human judges, including assigning points and taking them off math homework is subjective. The question is not whether it is subjective, but whether it is defensible and credible. The AP and IB programs (are) credible and defensible, yet subjective. I wish we could stop using that word as a pejorative! So-called objective scoring is still subjective test writing (Wiggins 2000).

Thus, the term *subjective* does not mean biased. **To be clear, the only thing that is objective in a multiple-choice test is the scoring. Each question is developed by a person, and the fairness and credibility of each question should be addressed.** The key to professional judgment is to focus on what is fair or credible to say about the student's performance. When a teacher grades a set of papers, the feedback is a critical component and should be fair

Standards-Based Grading and Reporting

This chapter has addressed assessment that informs instruction. Data and the results of assessments are also used for grading and accountability. Grades are an important form of communication to parents and students. Many systems have shifted to standards-based or performance-based grading. To make that change effectively, the difference between the two systems, traditional and standards-based, needs to be understood.

Thomas R. Guskey, in *On Your Mark*, provides the six possible purposes for grades (Guskey 2015):

1. Communicating student achievement to family
2. Communicating to students for their self-evaluation
3. Selecting, grouping, or identifying specific students for educational programs, such as for honors, reading programs, or special education
4. Providing incentives for students to learn
5. Evaluating the effectiveness of an educational program
6. Documenting specific student behaviors, such as absences, suspensions, or high achievement

Education reformers have often recommended shifting to a standards-based grading system to de-emphasize ranking (see No. 3 in the list above) and to emphasize the importance of describing student growth in terms of the system's expectations for each grade. In addition, research points to the effectiveness of standards-based grading:

Decades of research point to indisputable evidence that grading penalties are far less effective than feedback and personalized learning. Responsive teaching has always reacted to the needs of learners over the agendas of teachers: it is less about delivering a grade than about delivering timely, accurate, and specific feedback (Reeves 2010).

In standards-based grading, instead of a single percentage or letter grade, report cards provide descriptors and the level of performance in that skill. So instead of receiving an A in English, a student would receive rankings, such as *advanced*, *proficient*, *needs improvement*, or *at risk*. Those rankings would address a variety of descriptors or behaviors connected to mastery objectives. For example, a content teacher would rank the quality of a student's ability to read complex text or to work independently as shown below:

Content Areas

- Reads complex text.
- Writes arguments with clear claims and evidence.
- Reasons precisely (in mathematics).
- Analyzes primary sources (in history).

Behaviors or Habits of Mind

- Works independently with little prompting.
- Collaborates with peers in group work.
- Finishes work in a timely manner.

In the traditional system, all of these discrete areas would be merged into a single grade.

Chappuis warns of "grading too soon," meaning that students receive a summative grade too early in the learning process. Thus, she recognizes that grading is a part of teaching and learning, but recommends that assessments remain formative until the student has had sufficient time to learn. Some teachers return student work with *A*, *B*, and *Not Yet* as grades, with an explanation that whatever the grade, students can continue to improve their work and also improve their grade. Traditionally, teachers would not provide the opportunity to redo an assignment or exam, but would instead give students a summative grade (Chappuis 2014, p. 26).

Heather Deddeh, a middle school teacher, compares traditional and standards-based grading and says that because traditional grading combined test and quiz grades, neatness, homework, and participation, they cause confusion or what she calls *grade fog*:

A key difference between traditional grading practices and standards-based grading practices is that standards-based grading communicates only content mastery. Traditional grading practices often lead to "grade fog," in which the level of content

> *Traditional grading practices often lead to "grade fog," in which the level of content mastery is distorted by such non-standards-based criteria as practice, neatness, organization, attendance, and behavior.*

mastery is distorted by such non-standards-based criteria as practice, neatness, organization, attendance, and behavior. Megan, a seventh grader, said, "I have an 'A' in my science class this year, and it is not because of extra credit, participation, and homework. It is because of my understanding of science." Grades earned in traditional grading systems are usually based on a combination of formative and summative assessments. With standards-based grading, grades are based solely on summative assessments designed to measure content mastery (Deddeh, et al. 2010, p. 54).

In this standards-based grading system, formative grades serve only as feedback to students, and summative grades are used only for evaluation. It is based on the idea that during the learning process, students' work reflects errors and misconceptions that are addressed during the learning process, and the student's work is at its best during the summative assessment. Those summative grades are focused on specific skills; skills and habits of mind or behavior are separated. Caution must be used here if the summative assessment does not accurately reflect the students' learning in the formative assessments. For example, some students have test anxiety and do not perform well under testing conditions.

Although teachers track formative assessments carefully, Deddeh recommends that formative assessments and homework do not "count" in the final grade:

Once you identify formative assessments, create a category in your grade book to record those results. Ideally, your category would be called *Formative Assessments*, but if your grading program doesn't allow for this, you can use *Homework*, *Classwork*, or *Practice*. A crucial element in standards-based grading is that formative assessments are weighted at zero percent: practice without penalties.... Homework is practice, and students should not be penalized if they didn't master the content of the homework each night. Their understanding is a work in progress, and homework is part of helping students form knowledge, not a time for them to be formally assessed" (Deddeh, et al. 2010, p. 57).

Deddeh found that since changing to standards-based grading, students' grades reflect other external measures and their grades are more consistent across the system.

We have never considered returning to our outdated grading practices. To be certain that making this switch was actually an improvement, we compared grades with test scores. We learned that, when traditional grading was used, students earning a C in class had standardized unit test scores ranging from 47 percent to 94 percent. After switching to standards-based grading, students earning a C in class have standardized unit test scores ranging only from 63 percent to 78 percent. This supports our belief that our grades now clearly communicate to parents and students exactly what the student has learned (Deddeh 2012, p. 64).

> *A crucial element in standards-based grading is that formative assessments are weighted at zero percent: practice without penalties.*

Ken O'Connor's work focuses on "fixing" the problems with a grading system that is sometimes punitive and unfair. He recommends 15 remedies for making sure that assessment feedback and grades are both supportive and fair. Please note that he is saying that students should be graded on the quality of their work. This does not mean that a separate grade on habits of mind or habits of work or effort should be eliminated, but that the quality of the work and the quality of behavior should be separated. An underlying perception of O'Connor is that late work may not be something over which students have control because their home life (they have to babysit, for example) may interfere with their ability to get their work done.

Below are some tips to assure that grades are based on student work and that student work and behaviors are separated:

1. Include only the level of achievement of the work; exclude attitude, behavior, that "he tried hard," and attendance. Behaviors and attitudes are important, but should be graded separately in a category called *study habits* or *habits of work*.

2. Late work is assessed only for the quality of the work; penalties for lateness are kept separate from the assessment of performance.

3. Extra work counts only if the work reflects a higher level of the skill; no bonus points are given for just doing more work without improvement.

4. Cheating or plagiarism may have disciplinary consequences, but should not affect grades.

5. Absences are not part of a student's grade on his work.

6. Group scores should not be included as part of an individual student's score. His or her work should be evaluated. Group participation can be graded for individuals, however.

7. Grade on specific standards separately; don't compile them into one grade.

8. Performance standards should be clear and provided to the student when the unit begins.

9. Grades should be based on the student's work, not his or her work compared to other students' work.

10. Use only quality assessments to assess students' performance.

11. Don't average work from the beginning of the unit to the end. Instead, the later performances should have more weight. Use your professional judgment to assess progress.

12. Avoid using zeros as part of an average; missing work does not mean that a student has no skill. Consider using incompletes or reassessing to find out the student's level of performance.

13. Generally, use the final product or final level of achievement as the grade; if a student has low scores on formative work but eventually becomes proficient, the student should be considered proficient and the other lower scores should be excluded. If, however, a student has test anxiety, accommodations and modifications can be made to ensure that the level of performance is given as the grade.

14. If a student is learning, emphasize the last performances as indicators of the student's level of achievement. Averaging would lower the grade and not indicate how well the student is performing.

15. Include students in the grading process so that they self-assess their work and their progress.

Adapted from O'Connor's *A Repair Kit for Grading: 15 Fixes for Broken Grades* (2010).

These 15 grading/report-card reforms bring into question many assumptions made by the traditional system that is sometimes called punitive and focuses primarily on ranking students—rewarding only those who comply with the rules. O'Connor would say that these changes are focused on learning and eliminate areas in which students were punished for conditions over which they may not have had control. Examples of those conditions include illness, home conditions, and the ability of the child to do homework and make-up work. Instead, the information that a student and parents would receive would be information that would support that student's success.

Separating the Student's Level of Proficiency from a Student's Habits of Work

Students' habits of mind—their attitudes, behaviors, and study habits—are recognized as essential skills, but they are reported as separate from a student's proficiency in a subject. In the following statement, Casco High School, in Casco Bay, Maine, describes the importance of attitudes, behaviors, and habits in its "Habits of Work" (HOW) description. HOW results determine whether a student can have additional time to complete work.

Habits of Work (HOW)

Quality habits of work are an essential part of students' Pathways to Success. Students receive a separate HOW grade in each course. There is a clear correlation between quality Habits of Work, academic achievement, and learning. The better one's Habits of Work, the more s/he will achieve and learn....

Habits of Work are regularly assessed in each course and each marking period, using the same grading scale (1–4). There is a HOW Honor Roll for all students who earn a 3 or higher for a HOW grade in every class. "HOW Students of the Week" are also recognized at School Meeting.

To Earn a HOW of 3, Do the Big 3

Students must consistently (about 80 percent of the time):
Complete homework
Meet deadlines
Participate effectively in class activities (includes regular, on-time attendance)

How Do You Earn a 4 in HOW?

Do the Big 3 all of the time.

A student with a HOW of 3 cannot receive a trimester grade of 1 or 2. At the end of the trimester, a student with a HOW of 3 or higher who has not met standards will receive an *Incomplete*. This means that the student will be granted additional support and time, two weeks, to meet remaining standards.

If a student has a HOW grade lower than 3 and is not meeting academic standards, the student will receive a 1 or 2 on the report card and may not have the opportunity to make up standards for the course until summer school.

Casco Bay Charter School Family Grading Guide, http://cbhs.portlandschools.org/UserFiles/Servers/Server_1098483/File/Migration/Casco-Bay-Family-Grading-Guide.pdf.

This school district recognizes the importance of a student's habits and even provides an honor roll for these behaviors, Also, a student earns—through positive behaviors—the ability to make up work.

Performance Assessment and Product Assessment

Performance assessment is an assessment in which students actively demonstrate the knowledge they have acquired by, for example, presenting, acting in a skit, writing, or debating. The *Charlotte's Web* assignment was a performance assessment in which the student had choices, drew, selected evidence, and explained his or her learning in his or her own words.

Authentic performance assessments take performance a step further into real-life applications. They provide students with tasks that are realistic and that measure skills and outcomes that students may use in their daily lives, such as presenting a proposal to a local board for improving the environment or writing a review for *Rotten Tomatoes* or *Amazon.com*. Wiggins and McTighe (1998) describe performance tasks and projects "as complex challenges that are realistic and authentic. They may range in length from short term to long term, and require a final product or performance." In addition, these types of tasks:

- usually require a student to address a particular audience (a school board)
- are based on a specific purpose related to the audience (new snow day make-up rules)
- allow the student an opportunity to personalize the task
- have a task, criteria, and standards to help guide the student throughout the process

McTighe and O'Connor (2005) suggest using project-based learning as "summative assessments to frame meaningful performance goals" (p. 12) that are aligned with state and local standards and benchmarks. These tasks should be presented at the beginning of a unit of study so that students know and understand how they are going to be assessed. The early introduction of the assessments, sometimes called *front-loading*, makes students "better able to focus on what teachers expect them to learn and what they will be expected to do with that knowledge" (p. 12). By asking students to complete a realistic and authentic task, rather than simply recalling facts, performance assessments enable "students to apply their learning thoughtfully and flexibly, thereby demonstrating their understanding of the content standards" (p. 12).

An example of a summative performance assessment developed for use with the book *Night of the Twisters* by Ivy Ruckman can be found later in this chapter.

Product assessments are the results of a performance assessment being completed, and they, in addition to a possible performance or debate, are what the teacher examines to determine what students have learned. Performance and product assessments may take on a variety of forms. Performance assessments may appear on standardized tests as well as in the classroom; however, these assessments often require a written response or a solution to a complex mathematical problem.

> *By asking students to complete a realistic and authentic task, rather than simply recalling facts, performance assessments enable "students to apply their learning thoughtfully and flexibly, thereby demonstrating their understanding of the content standards."*

Performance Assessments: Guidelines for Success

Performance tasks can contribute to the authenticity and richness of a curriculum. These complex tasks require that students use multiple skills and they demonstrate the knowledge they have gained in a meaningful way. These tasks require careful planning and ongoing feedback. Figure 4.9 highlights the guidelines to ensure a successful experience for students.

Figure 4.9

Creating an Effective Performance Assessment

- Performance tasks must take into account both process and product. At every stage of the process, feedback should be provided.
- Performance tasks should be manageable for both students and teachers.
- Performance tasks should be purposeful and should include clearly defined criteria and standards. Well-defined steps should help guide the students through this process.
- Performance tasks should be developmentally appropriate. Teachers must scaffold and differentiate tasks in order for all students to achieve success. Students should be encouraged to take risks. Teachers need to provide encouragement and direction.
- Performance tasks are more successful when developed by a team of teachers, as they are complex and take time to construct.
- Performance assessment tasks may require an authentic performance.
- Performance tasks should encourage students to think in new ways, develop a deeper understanding, and demonstrate greater complexity in their thinking.

Adapted from Stuart (2003).

Figure 4.10 illustrates a performance assessment task that was given to fifth-grade students after completing a literature unit based on the book *Night of the Twisters* by Ivy Ruckman. This book was used to teach students about point of view because the narrator in this disaster story is a 12-year-old boy who learns many lessons. In addition, a variety of comprehension strategies, as well as character, plot (using a story map), and setting, were included. Aside from demonstrating their understanding of this particular story, students were also asked to show their knowledge of how they used comprehension strategies and elements of a story on this assessment, and how the author made them think as they read the story. Students were given a week to complete this task in class. The teacher observed students throughout the week, and offered written and oral feedback to support each student's progress. In some cases, students needed suggestions as to how to include all of the expected elements to meet the criteria. Other students needed redirection to correctly sequence the events of the story. In some cases, students needed assistance in getting started— that is, coming up with a workable plan. The rubric used to assess their work was shared and discussed with the students before they began working, and the teacher consistently reminded students to refer to the rubric to ensure they successfully met the required criteria.

Figure 4.10 *Night of the Twisters* Assessment

Mastery Objective: Show what you understand about how a novel works by creating your own short story, creating a children's book, or using the exciting descriptions of twisters to tell a story on *The Weather Channel.*

Author's Craft

Demonstrate your understanding of point of view and of fiction based on true events. Why did the author tell the story with a first-person narrator? Why did he change the timing of the tornadoes? What did it add to this disaster story? Include point of view in your project.

1. **Comprehension Strategies**
   Show your understanding of the text through visualizing one scene.
   Visualizing/sensory images: Cite an exciting paragraph and discuss it, for example.

2. **Writing and Proofreading**
   Please be sure you and a partner have used the writing rubric to check the quality of your writing. (Get his or her signature on your draft.)
   After you have finished writing your project, proofread your project with a partner. (Get his or her initials on your draft.)

Projects — *Select only one from the five projects listed below.*

1. **In paragraph form, change the narrator (the point of view) and retell the story of how the *Night of the Twisters* traveled through Grand Island, Nebraska, and how it changed the lives of the characters.** Organize your story in sequential order. Use the story map graphic organizer to help you organize your thoughts and ideas. Make sure you retell at least one exciting scene that you visualized when you were reading.

2. **Create a picture book.** Draw pictures illustrating the main events and use both your own words and words from the novel to describe each main scene.

3. **TV weather forecaster.** Using vocabulary words and illustrations that you draw or find online, write a weather broadcast including the events before, during, and after the tornadoes swept through Grand Island, Nebraska, on June 4, 1980.

4. **Interview the main character on a TV broadcast.**

5. **Create a PowerPoint presentation. Base it on the real events that the book was based on.** Imagine that you are making a documentary video about the Nebraska tornadoes. Plan how you would present the story of the tornadoes in a documentary, and make a list of the important scenes and characters you would cover. Based on your plan, create a PowerPoint presentation for the documentary. Include as many vocabulary words as you can. (Refer to your reading journal for ideas.)

Figure 4.11 *Night of the Twisters* Assessment Rubric

Wow!	Solid Work!	Needs Some More Work	Not Yet	Student Score and Comments	Teacher Score and Comments
You show how clearly you understand how the author crafted an exciting novel with your many vivid details and drawings or pictures.	You show how you understand how the author crafted an exciting novel with your details and drawings or pictures.	To a degree, you begin to show how you understand how the author crafted an exciting novel with your details and drawings or pictures. See me. We'll work on this!	You don't yet show how clearly you understand how the author crafted an exciting novel with your details and drawings or pictures. See me. We'll work on this!		
You show your understanding of visualization by showing us what the words in the novel say, either in detailed pictures or through your own precise words.	You show your understanding of visualization by showing us what the words in the novel say, either in pictures or through your own words.	To a degree, you begin to show your understanding of visualization by showing us what the words in the novel say, either in pictures or through your own words. See me. We'll work on this!	You don't yet show your understanding of visualization by showing us what the words in the novel say, either in pictures or through your own words. See me. We'll work on this!		
The writing ideas, organization, voice style, and mechanics are carefully constructed. Proofreading was well done.	The writing ideas, organization, voice style, and mechanics are constructed. Proofreading was fairly well done.	The writing ideas, organization, voice style, and mechanics need some more work. Proofreading was not completely done. See me. We'll work on this!	The writing ideas, organization, voice style, and mechanics need some work. Proofreading needs some further work. See me. We'll work on this!		

Gathering Information about Learning (Data Collection)

Teaching and learning are interconnected, occur simultaneously, and must be interwoven to function effectively. Teachers must clearly understand their students' strengths and weaknesses in learning in order to adapt their teaching to best meet the needs of their learners (Black and Wiliam 1998). Fortunately, teachers have a variety of tools and techniques they can use to gather information about their students to assess their progress. General sources of assessment evidence that may be collected in the classroom may be categorized as follows: *observations* of learning, *products* students create, and *conversations* discussing learning with students as well as group work. It is important for teachers to collect evidence from different sources over time in order to increase the reliability and validity of classroom evidence (Davies 2000).

> *Teaching and learning are interconnected, occur simultaneously, and must be interwoven to function effectively.*

Observations of Learning

Observations are powerful sources of information. They include a teacher's observance of either anything a student is doing or the performance of a task he or she has asked a student to do. Observations are critical to ensuring the validity and reliability of classroom assessment, as some learning may only be observed. Some students, particularly younger children, have difficulty writing about what they know and need opportunities to present their knowledge in action. **Observation may also be effectively used with projects "under construction," as a teacher may observe and offer feedback to students as they are engaged in the learning process** (Davies 2000).

The purpose of the activity will determine the focus of your observations. The following questions may be useful when designing focused observations and will be helpful in designing subsequent learning activities (Davies 2000).

- What is the mastery objective or standard that is the focus of the unit or lesson?
- What part of that objective or standard is the purpose of this specific learning activity?
- Does this student have specific areas on which I need to focus?
- How will I record and organize my observations so they are useful?

Figure 4.12 outlines some possible activities that teachers might observe.

Tools and Techniques for Observing and Documenting Student Learning

Teachers may keep track of their observations in a variety of ways. It is essential that, as teachers observe their students, the teachers are recording information that is pertinent to the established learning goals. This section highlights methods that teachers have found particularly helpful when keeping track of students' learning.

- *Clipboard with class list, checklist, or observation guide.* For example, if you are observing students engaged in literature circles, it is not enough to observe that a student has come prepared to the discussion. Rather, you might choose to observe that the student whose role is Summarizer has properly summarized the main points of the chapter, or that the Vocabulary Enricher has correctly defined identified terms as well as used these words appropriately in sentences. Students may also be given a series of questions that they have to write about after the literacy circle. The teacher might then use information from these observations to address the group's problem areas when teaching a mini-lesson, determining how to group students, or providing students with additional practice activities. These observations will also provide evidence of progress for students.

- *Spiral notebook with tabs for each student to be used in recording observations.* This tool may be helpful for looking at student growth over time, and the information gathered may be particularly useful during parent-teacher conferences and when writing progress reports.

- *White board to record comments and observations*

- *Tablet or iPad for students or teachers to use in making conference notes*

- *A spreadsheet to track data over time*

- *Video or tape recorder to record group presentations, literature circles, collaborative mathematical activities, writing conferences, etc.* (You can learn more about how to do this in Chapters 3 and 10.)

- *Journals or notebooks to use in documenting student work.* Interactive observational assessment is a technique in which students write in journals about their thinking and/or the processes they use to com-

Figure 4.12 Observing Learning

Oral/Kinesthetic Presentations	Labs/Project-Based Work
• formal and informal presentations • drama presentations • music-related activities • reading aloud • talking about one's work • persuading • giving opinions • debating • charades • dances • demonstrations • giving instructions • reader's theater	• scientific method being applied • planning and designing a Web page • planning and designing a PowerPoint presentation • measuring objects • cartooning • simulations
Written Reports	**Group Work**
• writing a narrative, an informational essay, or an opinion/argument • doing mini-research • creating a presentation • journal entries • reflections	• group or partner activities • debating • communicating ideas to others • conflict resolution • discussions • giving and receiving descriptive feedback • peer critiquing a fellow student's writing

plete a task. The teacher responds in writing by asking questions or making comments to promote further thinking. Such interaction helps the student to move to deeper levels of understanding of the content. This strategy can be used as an ongoing assessment piece, serving as a record that can be revisited in the future (Albert, Mayotte, and Sohn 2002). Chapter 1 contains an example of a criteria sheet used to assess a science journal.

The strategy of interactive observation can be a manageable and effective strategy if used in situations that are conducive to circulating around the classroom to interact with individual students and in which specific comments may be necessary to further students' thinking. Writer's and Reader's Workshops, for example, provide time for students to work and for individual conferences. In addition, it may be helpful to tentatively determine ahead of time when you are going to interact with each of your students. It is not feasible to write in more than five to eight journals during one class period.

One teacher who uses the interactive observational strategy in her mathematics class finds it works well with activities that involve algorithms and open-ended problems on which students work independently. As students work on problem-solving activities, they are asked to record, step by step, in their math journals the processes they use to solve each particular problem. As the students record their thinking, the teacher circu-

lates around the classroom and reads their developing thoughts. She responds to the students' work in their notebooks by posing a question or commenting in a way that promotes further thinking (see Figure 4.13 for an excerpt from a journal during an interactive session). "Writing descriptions of mathematical reasoning allows students to reflect on their own work, explain their thoughts, and gain insight into their own thinking" (Albert 2000).

Figure 4.13

Paragraph on Probability

Student response: I think that the coin lands on heads 50% of the time because there are 2 sides of the coin. If there were 6 sides of a die, you would have a 1/6 chance of it landing on your number.

Teacher response: If you rolled again ... (a 6-sided die), would it still be a 1/6 chance that you would get a particular number?

Student response: Yes, it would, because there are 6 sides and the chances of it landing on that particular number will still be the same. (Some people would say that it would be less of a chance, but I think that is a superstition.)

Teacher response: Good logic ... we'll learn about 6-sided die rolling a little later. I think you will be surprised at the results.

From Sheila Cutler Sohn's classroom (2002).

This particular teacher uses this strategy once or twice per week and occasionally collects her students' journals to allow for additional time to assess student work. For students who have difficulty with writing or are not native speakers of English, special arrangements should be made with the special educator or an assistant when this form of assessment is being implemented. Students with fine motor difficulties may need to type their work on a computer (Albert, Mayotte, and Sohn 2002).

Figure 4.14 offers suggestions for teachers implementing an interactive observational assessment during mathematics instruction.

Figure 4.14

- **Maximize classroom space for easy movement.** Seating students in groups allows a teacher to access students more easily. In addition, you may decide to target a cluster of students seated together to write in their journals. In this way, it may be easier to keep track of students with whom you have interacted. Chapter 3 contains some samples of seating arrangements.

- **Use a variety of problem-solving and critical-thinking activities.** A variety of written questions and comments helps teachers better assess students' mathematical thinking and, consequently, scaffold their learning. Comments should be as specific as possible.

- **Write in every student's notebook.** Interacting with all students over the course of several sessions is important. In order for students to value this process, they need to know that the teacher might write in their journals during any of the interactive sessions. A special educator or assistant might also write in the journals if assisting in the classroom at the time.

- **Revisit students a second or even third time to write in their journals.** Teachers should let students know that they may revisit their work more than once during an interactive session to encourage new and deeper ways of thinking. Revisiting journals sends the message to students that they are accountable for responding to your comments.

- **Write brief, clear, and direct questions and comments.** Write something to which the student can respond immediately. Keeping questions brief will help students to write more precisely with regard to their mathematical reasoning.

- **Use this strategy with other assessment techniques.** After using this strategy, the teacher should follow up with whole class discussions, as both oral and written communication are important in mathematics.

Adapted from Albert, Mayotte, and Sohn (2002).

Collecting Products or Looking at Student Work (LASW)

Teachers collect a variety of products including graphic organizers, quizzes, Do Nows, or journals to use as evidence to show what knowledge students demonstrate. **Providing choices for how to demonstrate their learning supports students' learning preferences and can provide motivation.** Figure 4.15 is a list of possible products students might create.

Figure 4.15 Ideas for Student Products

Oral/Written Reports	Technology Projects	Creative Projects
• Write a story. • Make an oral presentation. • Write a poem. • Write a report. • Write a song/rap. • Write a play. • Write a journal entry. • Research an area of interest from the unit. • Create a class "museum" or "zoo," with each student presenting and researching one area.	• Design a Web page. • Create a PowerPoint presentation. • Make a video. • Make an audiotape. • Create a public service announcement.	• Draw a diagram. • Make a timeline. • Make a poster. • Build a model. • Create a puzzle. • Design a T-shirt. • Create a collage. • Build a diorama/model. • Write a children's book.

Adapted from Davies (2000).

It is important to clearly outline the criteria and expectations for students for any given product. Creating and using rubrics with students will be discussed later in this chapter. **Providing learners with guidance and support in the form of feedback and constructive comments throughout the process is necessary to ensure that optimal learning occurs.**

Conversations Centered on Learning

Conversations about learning allow teachers to acquire information about students' thoughts, understandings, and feelings about their learning in a given subject area and serve as part of assessment. More important, conversations support deeper learning.

Perhaps too often, the quiet classroom continues to serve as a model of appropriate behavior when all of the research points to the need for talk. Discussion, both with a teacher and with peers, supports student learning. As Joseph Mayo said:

> In the social constructivist tradition, Lev Vygotsky (1962/1986) argued that social interaction is crucial to active construction of negotiated meaning—yet he did not preclude the eventual importance of an internalized knowledge base for each individual. In short, Vygotsky posited that what learners can accomplish on their own is less indicative of their intellectual development than what they can do with others' assistance in a social context (Mayo 2013).

Thus, discussing with a peer or group or interacting with a teacher can help students understand more deeply and accomplish more than they could have performed on their own. Mayo goes on to explain how the social construction of knowledge works:

> This form of learning "provides opportunities for students to talk and listen, read, write, and reflect as they approach course content through problem-solving exercises, informal small groups, simulations, case studies, role playing, and other [applied learning] activities" (Myers and Jones 1993, p. xi;. Mayo 2014, pp. 52–64).

Thus, conversations and group work deepen students' learning and may even help to move it further along.

In the article "Academic Conversations: Classroom

Discussing with a peer or group or interacting with a teacher can help students understand more deeply and accomplish more than they could have on their own.

Most classrooms are dominated by teacher, not student, talk.

Talk That Fosters Critical Thinking and Content Understanding," Zwiers provides research-based reasons for discussion. He says that conversation builds, promotes, or cultivates

- academic language
- vocabulary
- literacy skills
- oral language and communication skills
- critical-thinking skills
- different perspectives and empathy
- creativity
- skills for negotiating meaning and focusing on a topic
- content understanding
- connections
- engagement and motivation
- ways for teachers and students to assess learning

And yet, Zwiers says most classrooms are dominated by teacher, not student, talk. Often at-risk students and English learners have less opportunity to develop language than average students, averaging from no time devoted to dialogue to 4 percent, according to recent studies (Zwiers and Ford 2011, pp. 27–45).

We encourage students to think about their learning when we engage in conversations with them in these ways. We gather evidence about students' knowledge and understanding as we listen to them think and explain. Through such dialogue, it becomes apparent what was difficult or easy for students, what risks they took, and what they might do differently next time (Davies 2000). With this knowledge, teachers are better able to support students in the most effective manner. When teachers take the time to engage students in self-assessment, learning is maximized (Black and Wiliam 1998; Young 2000).

Teachers may use the questions below to obtain information about their students. These questions may be used either in an oral conversation or through a written activity. It is important to prepare a list of questions ahead of time; however, student responses may necessitate asking different questions from those originally planned.

When students solve open-ended mathematical problems, they often misinterpret what the question is asking them to do. The following questions may be used to determine whether the student is properly interpreting a problem-solving activity (Stenmark 1991):

- What is the task about?
- How would you interpret that?
- What can you tell me about it?
- Would you explain that in your own words?
- Can any information be eliminated or is there any missing information?

In addition, it is important to help students formulate a plan. Students need an organized approach to the task. The following questions may be used to assess whether students have chosen an appropriate plan and strategy (Stenmark 1991):

- Where might you find the needed information?
- What have you tried? What steps did you take?
- How did you organize the information? Do you have a system or strategy to solve this problem?
- Can you explain your strategy or plan to me?

The following example illustrates how this questioning technique was used during a problem-solving task.

Problem: Derrick is planning his tenth birthday party. He invited 10 classmates and plans to order three eight-slice pizzas. If Derrick and his friends (who happen to really love pizza!) eat three pieces each, will he run out of food at this birthday pizza party? Explain and show how you determined your answer.

Teacher: In your own words, tell me what this problem is asking you to do.

Student: I need to find out if Derrick will have enough pizza for his friends at his birthday party.

Teacher: How many people will be eating pizza?

Student: Ten.

Teacher: Let's go back to the problem and carefully reread the highlighted information. (*Teacher gives the student time to reread the problem.*)

Student: Oh, we need to include Derrick in our count for pizza, too. So there will be 11 people eating pizza.

Teacher: What other information will you use to help you figure out this problem?

Student: We need to know how many pizzas they are ordering, and in the problem it says three eight-slice pizzas.

Teacher: What strategy or strategies will you use?

Student: I might draw a visual.

Student: Guess, check, and revise.

Teacher: Can you explain how you would use that strategy?

In this example, the conversation that occurred between the teacher and student allowed the teacher to understand where the student was experiencing confusion. It became clear to the teacher that the student was not correctly identifying what the problem was asking him to do, and he was not using all the important information that was given in the problem. Fortunately, by prompting the student with guiding questions, the teacher was able to help the student clearly understand the problem. In this case, the student was able to find an accurate solution to the problem.

In addition to questioning the student who appears to be experiencing confusion, it is equally important and effective to question the student who has correctly responded to a question. Marilyn Burns (2005) discusses the problematic nature of assuming that the students who correctly respond also understand the mathematics embedded in the problem at hand: "The problem was that when a student gave a correct response, I assumed that both the students who had answered correctly and his or her classmates understood the mathematics behind the problem. I never probed students' level of understanding behind their responses; I just happily continued on my teaching trajectory. As a result, I never really knew what students were thinking or whether their correct answers masked incorrect ideas. I only knew that they had given the answer I sought" (p. 27). Asking students to communicate their reasoning, whether they respond correctly or incorrectly, is critical to effective classroom assessment.

> *In addition to questioning the student who appears to be experiencing confusion, it is equally important and effective to question the student who has correctly responded to a question.*

Student Self-Assessment: A Key Ingredient in the Assessment Process

Involving learners in the process of assessment—that is, providing them with opportunities to assess their own work—helps students deepen their understanding of the learning process. Students are able to learn more effectively when they are provided with opportunities to play an active role. "The most effective learners set personal learning goals, employ proven strategies, and self-assess their work" (McTighe and O'Connor 2005, p. 16). Some of the strategies we use to promote self-assessment include the following:

- sharing the learning objectives to facilitate self-assessment as students better understand the learning goals for which they are striving
- providing students with recommendations, commendations, and feedback that helps them determine what steps they need to take next to further their learning
- creating an environment that promotes risk-taking, since students must feel supported and confident in their environment in order to take risks
- using rubrics, criteria sheets, exemplars, anchor papers, and other items that enable students to assess their performance against clearly evident standards
- planning time for student self-assessment into the lesson

Benefits of Self-Assessment for the Teacher and Student

Self-assessment is an essential component in assessment for learning, and, as such, it must be embedded in the learning and teaching that occurs in the classroom. Students take responsibility for their learning and become active in this process when they self-assess (Gator, Jones, et al. 2000). Figure 4.16 illustrates the benefits for both students and teachers when self-assessment is implemented.

Teachers should encourage students to think about the following questions in order to help facilitate self-reflection:

- Am I learning in the best way for me?
- What strategies help me learn best?
- What can I remember and understand?
- What questions do I still have?

- Where do I have to focus my revision?
- What are my learning goals?
- What are my strengths and weaknesses?
- How am I doing?
- What is really making me think?
- How will I know if my work is good?
- What do I need to do in order to improve?
- How am I going to make this improvement?

When students consistently self-assess, they take more responsibility for their learning.

These questions can be posted in "anchor" charts in the classroom or laminated in checklists in notebooks or journals to consider when they are working on reflecting.

When students consistently self-assess, they take more responsibility for their learning (Shephard 2001, in Chappuis and Stiggins 2002). It provides students with a means of monitoring and communicating to others the progress they have made in their learning.

Self-Assessment Forms

To help children reflect upon their own work, it is important for teachers to provide them with tools to help guide their thinking. This section provides a variety of self-assessment forms that are appropriate for different situations. Figure 4.17 includes a general assessment form that may be used at the beginning, middle, and end of the year to help children think about where they are and where they are going in terms of their learning. It also encourages them to think about how they learn. It asks them to write about both their strengths and weaknesses as well as set goals for the remainder of the year. In addition, the teacher should follow up with the student either in writing or by conferencing with him or her.

Figure 4.16 Benefits of Self-Assessment

Students...	Teachers...
• become more responsible for own learning	• shift more responsibility to students
• are able to recognize next steps in learning	• are able to plan smoother, more efficient, and challenging lessons, as students are independent and motivated
• feel secure about not always being right	• benefit from feedback, as it helps them identify students' progress
• raise self-esteem	• are better able to identify next steps for a group and/or individual
• become more independent and motivated	• are able to identify thinking process, as students explain their strategies

Adapted from Gator, C., et al. (April 15, 2000).

Figure 4.17

All About My Learning

On a scale of 1–10 (1 being *never*, 10 being *always*), how well do I...

- follow directions? _____
- manage my time? _____
- cooperate with others? _____
- participate in class discussions? _____
- work independently? _____
- work in groups? _____
- complete my work? _____
- bring in my homework? _____

1. These are some things that are easy for me in class and why:

2. These are some things that are difficult for me in class and why:

3. These are some things I like in class and why:

4. This is something on which I should be working harder and an explanation of my choice:

5. This is the person with whom I work best and an explanation of why:

6. Reflections about subject areas:

   a. Math

   b. Reading

   c. Writing

   d. Spelling

   e. Science

   f. Social Studies

7. Two goals I have for the rest of the year are...

8. My plan for achieving each of these goals is...

Adapted with permission from Joyce Silberman, fifth-grade teacher, Newman Elementary School, Needham, MA.

The next student self-assessment form may be used in most subject areas. The first section is an activator that should be completed at the beginning of a lesson. The teacher might use this information as a pre-assessment to assess prior knowledge of a particular concept. The second section might be used at the midpoint of a lesson to gather information about a student's progress toward a specific learning goal. The third section is a summarizer that should be used at the end of a lesson to help both the student and teacher clarify what was learned, to ascertain whether a learning goal has been achieved, and to adjust instruction so that any points of confusion are clarified. Lessons may range in length from one class period to many class sessions.

Figure 4.18

Student Self-Assessment

Section 1

1. What do I know about this topic?
2. What would I like to know about this topic?
3. How might I learn more about this topic?

Section 2

1. What do I know now about this topic?
2. What questions do I still have?
3. Why am I learning about this topic?
4. How does this new information help me?

Section 3

1. What have I learned about this topic?
2. What were the main points of this topic of study?
3. What confusion/questions do I still have?

The next self-assessment form is specific to reading. This form may be adapted to be used at the beginning, middle, or end of the year. The questions help children to think about themselves as readers, as well as to better understand their strengths and weaknesses in this area. The teacher is provided with information that may be used to inform instruction so that individual needs are more appropriately addressed. Again, a teacher should either comment in writing or orally after this form is completed by the students.

Figure 4.19

Self-Assessment: Reading

1. How many books did you read this year?
2. What are the different kinds of books you read? (Genres: realistic fiction, fantasy, biography and autobiography, historical fiction, informational books, articles, etc.)
3. What are your favorite genres to read? Why?
4. Which were the best books you read this year? What made these books so good?
5. What are two of your favorite authors, and why do you like them?
6. What is your favorite poem? Why do you like it?
7. What do you know how to do well as a reader?
8. What did you learn this year as a reader that you are proud of?
9. What did you learn about reading fiction this year?
10. What did you learn about reading nonfiction this year?
11. What is one skill you would like to improve in your reading? What is your plan for improving?

Teacher comments:

The following form might be used after a student has completed a problem-solving activity and the student work has been evaluated by the teacher. Providing students with such a form encourages them to use teacher feedback to improve their performance. Too many times, students are more concerned with their scores and do not take the necessary time to read and think about the comments and questions the teacher has posed.

Figure 4.20

Evaluating My Problem-Solving Skills

Carefully look over your corrected work and answer the questions below.

1. I used a strategy that made sense. Yes   No
2. I found a correct solution.   Yes   No
3. I explained my strategy clearly and step by step.   Yes   No
4. My score was _____.
5. Explain what you feel you did well on this task.
6. Explain how you will improve your work in the future.

The next form is an example of how one teacher incorporates self-assessment into her homework assignments. By providing students with a checklist of all of the things they need do in order to successfully complete the assignment, the teacher encourages students to review their homework before turning it in. Students are also required to reflect and write a statement about their work for each question. Such a self-regulating activity improves the quality of the students' assignments as well as their work habits.

Figure 4.21

Number the Stars: Homework Self-Assessment			
Homework	Yes	No	Comments
Chapters 1 and 2			
1. Did I complete the vocabulary carefully?	_____	_____	
2. Does the summary sentence effectively reflect the chapter?	_____	_____	
3. Have I answered the questions thoroughly?	_____	_____	
4. Have I used specific examples from the book to support my answer?	_____	_____	
5. Have I used complete sentences, and is this homework museum quality?	_____	_____	

Adapted with permission from Rita MacDonald, fourth-grade teacher, Eliot Elementary School, Needham, MA.

These questions might be used in most content areas to help children think more deeply about how they are learning, as well as how they are making progress toward a specific learning goal. The teacher is provided information about how students view themselves as learners.

A high school special-education department uses weekly "exit slips" for students to assess their progress on their selected goals. They conference quarterly unless it's clear that a goal is not working. At the end of the quarter, the teacher and the student discuss what their performance demonstrates. An *A* means mostly four and five stars, a *B* is mostly four stars, and a *C* is mostly three stars.

Figure 4.22

Name	Monday	Tuesday	Wednesday	Thursday	Friday
Goal 1: Advocate for myself					
Goal 2: Do writing homework					
Goal 3: Stay Organized					

Goal Setting: Goal 1: I will ask for help when I need it from my teachers and from my coaches.
Goal Setting Goal 2: I will do my writing homework first because it's what I like to procrastinate.
Goal 3: I will stay organized and put things where they belong. I'll check my backpack, my bag, and my notebooks to make sure I'm keeping things together.

Note: Self-assess your two goals and give yourself…
Five stars: I did things that are challenging for me.
Four stars: I did OK, but put off my writing.
Three stars: I need to focus on my goals more.

Reflection: This week I did my argument for Lit. Class and worked on it until it was up to my standards. I didn't have to do much advocating, though I asked Mr. L. to explain the assignment again during class. My organization is OK, but I need to dump everything out of my backpack.
I give myself a 4.

Figure 4.23

Reflection Questions

1. List three strategies (and provide possible examples) you used in … that helped you.
2. List three important things your teacher did to help you better understand…
3. Compare your work now to the work you were doing at the beginning of the year. Compare the amount of effort you are putting forth now to the amount you were giving at the beginning of the year.
4. Describe the quality of your work.
5. Describe your focus during class.
6. Write a letter to yourself. Be sure to congratulate yourself on specific successes. Encourage yourself to improve those skills, strategies, ideas, and understandings that you need to continue working on during the next few weeks. Include specifics that explain what works best for you.
7. I am confused about…
8. Now I understand…
9. The most important thing I learned today is…
10. I can use what I learned today when I…
11. When I don't know what to do, I…
12. When I work with a partner, I feel…
13. When I work with a group, I feel…
14. I need help on…
15. I get frustrated when…
16. If I could hear one lesson over again, it would be…

The next three assessment forms might be used in conjunction with discussion groups. The first form is to be used by the students, and it is important to share this form with students before they begin group work so that they are aware of group behaviors for which they should be striving. This form assists students by helping them to think about group dynamics, what actions benefit the group, what behaviors are detrimental to the learning process, and how they might improve their performance next time they meet. The second and third form might be used by the teacher to monitor each student's or each group's collaborative work skills while students are engaged in group work.

Figure 4.24

Assessment Form for Discussion Groups

Names: _____

Date: _____

Group's discussion topic: _____

Circle the appropriate responses. Provide evidence where possible.

1. Everyone participated and shared in the discussion process.
    Yes   No   Sometimes
    Evidence:

2. The group is supportive of its individual members.
    Yes   No   Sometimes
    Evidence:

3. Group members often ask questions for clarification and elaboration.
    Yes   No   Sometimes
    Evidence:

4. The group discussion stays on topic.
    Yes   No   Sometimes
    Evidence:

5. The group is energetic and enthusiastic.
    Yes   No   Sometimes
    Evidence:

6. What was the best thing about the way this group worked together?

7. What was one problem this group had? Did we violate any norms?

8. How did you solve it?

9. What else might you have done?

10. What specific plans do have for improving your group's performance the next time you meet?

Adapted from Saskatchewan Education (1996).

Figure 4.25

Teacher Assessment Form for Collaborative Work Skills

CATEGORY	4	3	2	1
Participation	Consistently provides useful ideas when participating in the group. A definite leader who contributes a lot of effort.	Generally provides useful ideas when participating in the group. A strong group member who tries hard!	Sometimes provides useful ideas when participating in the group. A satisfactory group member who does what is required.	Rarely provides useful ideas when participating in the group. May refuse to participate.
Support for group members	Is supportive of group members by listening and helping the discussion when needed.	Is generally supportive of group members.	Occasionally is publicly critical of the project or the work of other members of the group. Does not always support group members.	Often is publicly critical of the project or the work of other members of the group. Does not usually support group members.
Communication	Consistently asks questions for clarification and/or elaboration when appropriate. Is able to clarify confusion other group members have through answering questions and through elaboration.	Generally asks questions or asks for clarification and/or elaboration when appropriate. Can usually clarify confusion other group members have through answering questions and through elaboration.	Sometimes asks questions or asks for clarification and/or elaboration. Sometimes can clarify confusion other group members have through answering questions and through elaboration.	Rarely asks questions or asks for clarification and/or elaboration. Is unable to clarify confusion other group members have through answering questions and through elaboration.
Focus on the task	Consistently stays focused on the task and what needs to be done. Very self-directed.	Focuses on the task and what needs to be done most of the time. Other group members can count on this person.	Focuses on the task and what needs to be done some of the time. Other group members must sometimes nag, prod, and remind to keep this person on-task.	Rarely focuses on the task and what needs to be done. Lets others do the work.
Group dynamics	Consistently has a positive attitude, and is energetic and enthusiastic throughout the process.	Generally maintains a positive attitude, and is energetic and enthusiastic throughout most of the process.	Sometimes maintains a positive attitude about the task(s), and is energetic and enthusiastic throughout some of the process.	Often maintains a negative attitude about the task(s), and is not energetic and enthusiastic throughout the process.

Adapted from Rubistar.4teachers.org, rubric ID 1004399 (September 18, 2003). Copyright ALTEC at the University of Kansas (2008).

Figure 4.26

Teacher Assessment Form for Collaborative Work Skills

CATEGORY	4	3	2	1
Participation	All group members routinely provide useful ideas when participating in the group.	Most group members provide useful ideas when participating in the group.	Some group members provide useful ideas when participating in the group. One group member may refuse to participate.	Most group members do not provide useful ideas when participating in the group. One or more group members may refuse to participate.
Support for group members	Group members are never publicly critical of the project or the work of others. Group members are supportive of other group members.	Group members are rarely publicly critical of the project or the work of others. Group members are usually supportive of other group members.	Group members are occasionally publicly critical of the project or the work of other members of the group. Group members do not always support other group members.	Group members are often publicly critical of the project or the work of other members of the group. Group members do not usually support other group members.
Communication	Group members routinely ask questions for clarification and/or elaboration when appropriate. Group members are able to clarify confusion others have through clearly answering questions.	Group members usually ask questions or ask for clarification and/or elaboration when appropriate. Group members can usually clarify confusion others have through answering questions.	Group members sometimes ask questions or ask for clarification and/or elaboration. Group members sometimes can clarify confusion others have through answering questions.	Group members rarely ask questions or ask for clarification and/or elaboration. Group members are unable to clarify confusion others have.
Focus on the task	All group members consistently stay focused on the task and what needs to be done.	Group members focus on the task and what needs to be done most of the time.	Group members focus on the task and what needs to be done some of the time. At times, group members must sometimes nag, prod, and remind one or more group members to keep them on-task.	Group members rarely focus on the task and what needs to be done. One or two group members may end up doing all of the work in order to complete the task(s).
Group dynamics	All group members consistently have a positive attitude about the task(s), and are energetic and enthusiastic throughout the process.	Group members usually maintain a positive attitude about the task(s), and are energetic and enthusiastic throughout most of the process.	Group members sometimes maintain a positive attitude about the task(s), and are energetic and enthusiastic throughout some of the process.	Group members maintain a negative attitude about the task(s), and are not energetic and enthusiastic throughout the process.

Adapted from Rubistar.4teachers.org, rubric ID 1004399 (September 18, 2003). Copyright ALTEC at the University of Kansas (2008).

The next self-assessment form should be completed by individual students after engaging in group work to help them reflect on their own interactions. Again, this form should be shared and discussed with students before they begin their collaborative work so as to help them better understand appropriate behaviors during group work.

Figure 4.27

My Contribution to Group Work

My group was discussing/solving…
Rate each entry as:
1-Needs Improving   2-Satisfactory   3-Excellent

Please also provide an example for each of the following questions.

1. I shared my ideas and offered suggestions.   1   2   3
Example:

2. I spoke clearly and slowly enough.   1   2   3
Example:

3. I answered others' questions.   1   2   3
Example:

4. I remained on topic and helped the group stay focused.   1   2   3
Example:

5. I encouraged others to participate.   1   2   3
Example:

6. I disagreed without hurting others' feelings.   1   2   3
Example:

7. I summarized or repeated my ideas when necessary.   1   2   3
Example:

8. I gave reasons for my opinions.   1   2   3
Example:

9. I listened courteously and effectively.   1   2   3
Example:

10. I tried to understand and extend the suggestions of others.   1   2   3
Example:

11. My most important contribution to the discussion was

12. I would like to improve _____ the next time we meet.

13. My plan for improvement is

The next form is specific to students working on solving mathematical problems in collaborative groups. This form asks students to think about both the process used to complete the task and group inter-actions. This form should be completed by the group as a whole, and should be shared and discussed before beginning the task. Again, sharing the form before-hand helps the students to focus on important parts of the problem-solving process and the behaviors that support a collaborative activity.

Figure 4.28

Assessment Form for Problem-Solving Groups

Names:
Title of Problem:

Circle the appropriate response. Provide evidence where possible.

1. The group understood what the problem was asking.
Yes   No   Sometimes
Evidence:

2. The group formulated a plan and selected appropriate strategies.
Yes   No   Sometimes
Evidence:

3. The group solved the problem, labeled work, and used visuals.
Yes   No   Sometimes
Evidence:

4. The group clearly explained how the problem was solved, step by step.
Yes   No   Sometimes
Evidence:

5. Everyone participated in the problem-solving process.
Yes   No   Sometimes
Evidence:

6. The group was supportive of its members.
Yes   No   Sometimes
Evidence:

7. Group members asked questions for clarification.
Yes   No   Sometimes
Evidence:

8. The group discussion stayed on topic.
Yes   No   Sometimes
Evidence:

9. The group was enthusiastic.
Yes   No   Sometimes
Evidence:

One problem we had was…

We will improve our work next time by…

Checklists are another tool that students may use to help them assess their own work. Such lists should highlight what students must do in order to successfully complete a task. Providing children with such lists gives them a means to monitor their progress toward a particular task. Checklists also encourage students to review and revise their work before turning it in to be assessed by their teacher. The following two checklists are specific to solving open-response mathematical problems and writing activities, respectively.

Figure 4.29

Checklist for Assessing Open-Response Questions		
Are all parts of the question answered?	___Yes	___No
Are all directions followed?	___Yes	___No
Are all parts and answers labeled?	___Yes	___No
Is the explanation clear for the reader?	___Yes	___No
Does the explanation include a combination of pictures, numbers, and/or words?	___Yes	___No
Are appropriate math vocabulary and symbols included in the response?	___Yes	___No
Is the work neat, organized, and spelled correctly?	___Yes	___No

Figure 4.30

Editing Checklist

Topic/Organization/Language
___ My first paragraph begins with a topic sentence that restates the question.
___ Every paragraph begins with a topic sentence.
___ The sentences provide evidence or examples for the topic sentence.
___ I have introductory, supporting, and concluding paragraphs.
___ My sentences begin in many different ways.
___ I remembered to indent each new paragraph.
___ I made an effort to use interesting vocabulary words by consulting a thesaurus.

Mechanics
___ I capitalized the first word in each sentence and all proper nouns.
___ I punctuated the end of each sentence.
___ I used commas and apostrophes appropriately.
___ My handwriting is legible.

Spelling

Dictionary:
The following is a list of some words I needed to fix because of the spelling.

Thesaurus:
The following is a list of some words I learned in the thesaurus to expand my written vocabulary. (Include the word you looked up and the word you found.)

Student Portfolios as a Means of Student Self-Assessment

Purposes of Portfolio Assessment

A portfolio serves many purposes. It displays and documents students' actual work and progress over time. Teachers use portfolios to determine students' strengths and weaknesses, and, in this way, portfolios may inform instruction as teachers become more aware of students' needs. Portfolios also help students determine their own strengths and weaknesses. Once students clearly understand the areas they need to improve, they may set realistic and effective goals for themselves. In this way, a portfolio is a tool that may be used to help children think about their learning.

Sharing a student's portfolio with parents during conferences is an effective way to show parents the progress their child has made over time. Parents may celebrate their child's successes and growth. As parents look at their child's work and are able to more clearly understand areas of weakness, they will better be able to support their child's learning at home.

Implementing Portfolios in the Elementary Classroom

The way in which one teacher implemented a classroom portfolio system in her elementary classroom evolved over the years. Although she felt her first few attempts were not very successful, she learned from these experiences and, consequently, was able to eventually construct the following system, which works well for both her students and herself.

First, she begins by asking students what they know about portfolios. If necessary, she prompts them with questions such as, "What do they look like?" "What are they used for?" and "What goes in them?" After brainstorming as a class, they define *portfolio* in their own words.

Next, they discuss what types of things go into a portfolio and why. The teacher explains that work from all academic disciplines, such as math, reading, writing, science, and social studies, should be included and will have a special section. There will also be a section for students to place work that may not fall under one of the specified categories. Most of the pieces will be selected by the students; however, the teacher explains to the class that she will, at times, ask them to include particular pieces.

Students typically think that only exemplary pieces

should be placed in a portfolio. Therefore, it is important to help students understand why it is important to include work of which they are not so proud or that on which they did not perform well. The teacher talks about how "Not Yet" work may be used to help set goals and determine areas in which they need more support. She also emphasizes that it takes time, practice, and effort to become proficient in many things in school, and that **it is a rewarding experience to see firsthand how much progress they have made over time as students look through their portfolios.** An example of items to include in a portfolio is as follows:

- tests and quizzes
- journal entries
- self-reflections
- homework
- group work assessment forms from literature circles or problem-solving groups
- problem of the week
- pictures taken of oral presentations or projects
- reports
- technology projects
- science lab reports
- artwork
- work the student did really well on
- work the student didn't do very well on

Next, the teacher gives each student a white binder that has been divided into six sections with tabs: *math, reading, writing, social studies, science,* and *miscellaneous.*

After students understand the various pieces that are appropriate for a portfolio, the teacher explains the process they will use to place such items in the portfolio. For the pieces included, students are to use index cards to record the following:

- date and subject
- what they learned
- why they included these pieces

Once they have finished writing the required information on the index cards, they are to staple them to the pieces of work and place them in the appropriate sections in their portfolio binders. The teacher also explains to the students that it is not necessary to fill out index cards for the few pieces that she asks them to place in their portfolios. During the first year she implemented portfolios, she selected most pieces for students to place in their binders; however, she made the mistake of asking students to fill out index cards, including an explanation of why they included these pieces. She found many students

> *Sharing a student's portfolio with parents during conferences is an effective way to show parents the progress their child has made over time.*

wrote that they "included the piece because my teacher made me," a comment that was not very effective in terms of self-reflection. Figure 4.31 shows actual pieces that students in this teacher's fifth-grade class chose to include in their portfolios. The first is from science, and second is from mathematics.

Next, the teacher explains that students' work will be kept in file folders until Friday morning. Before school, she will pass out all student work from the week. She often asks for student volunteers to come in early to help save time by passing out papers; however, she makes sure she passes out any tests, quizzes, or other items students may not want others to see. When students come into school on Friday, their morning work is to choose at least three items to place in their portfolios. They need to create index cards for each of these items and then place them in the portfolios. It is important to remind students they need to take home all other work and share it with their parents. It may also be helpful to explain this system to parents at "Back to School" night and tell them that they are welcome to browse through their children's portfolios at any time (in addition to conference time) to better understand what their children are learning at school.

The students seem to take great pride in their portfolios and enjoy sharing them with their parents. This teacher also has students look through their work periodically to come up with particular goals for each academic area that they would like to achieve over the next couple of weeks or even months. It is important to have students determine successes and ask them to show evidence of their growth. Such concrete evidence really helps students understand their learning, in terms of both areas of strengths and areas of weaknesses.

Figure 4.31

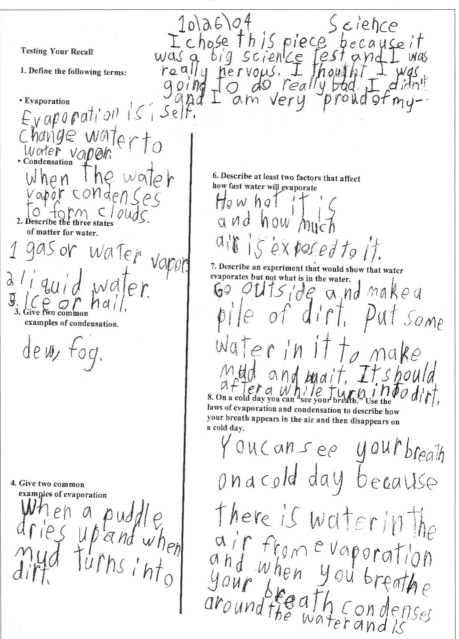

Implementing Portfolios in the Secondary Classroom

While portfolios are used at the high school level in much the same way as described for the elementary school level, there are a few distinctions. Rather than having students create a single large portfolio that includes material from each of their different subjects, high school students are typically asked to create a portfolio for each of their core academic subjects (a portfolio for English, a portfolio for science, etc.). These portfolios tend to consist of the same types of student work described at the elementary school level,

Figure 4.31 *(continued)*

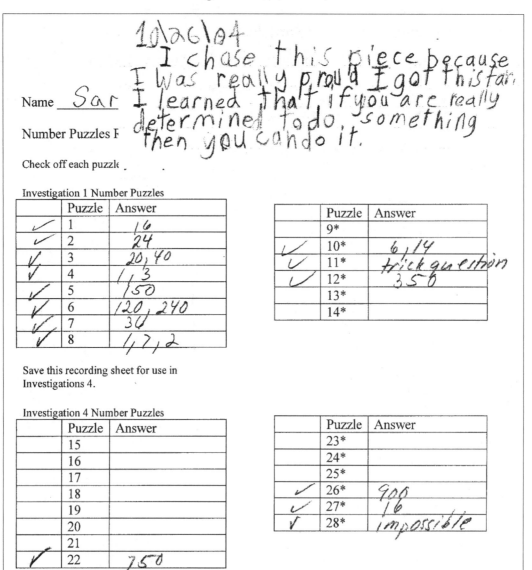

but, especially in the case of term papers and other types of writing assignments, students are generally expected to include the various brainstorming activities and drafts that helped them to ultimately put together a final product.

The last item that high school students typically place into their portfolios is a piece of reflective writing about the various pieces of work that they have included in their portfolios. Generally, such a reflec-tion activity asks students to page through their own portfolios, looking for areas in which they see their own progress as learners, as well as areas for which they recognize a need for continued improvement. Though this assignment is generally the last piece of student work added to the portfolio, it is placed at the very front of the portfolio in order to provide the portfolio's reader with an overview of the work contained therein.

Figure 4.32

Sample High School Portfolio for English or for History
11th Grade American Studies Course
11th Grade Honors American Studies

Final Portfolio Requirements

Your Honors American Studies portfolio is meant to highlight your growth as a student. To prepare your portfolio, you will need to select SIX pieces of your work that best demonstrate the skills that you have developed over the course of the year. For each skill, you will include a work sample, as well as a thoughtful reflection that analyzes your growth and considers the questions below.

PART I

1. Collaboration

How well do I work with others? What role did I play in the group? How did I help my group achieve my goal? How do I respond to feedback from my peers and/or how did I give feedback to them?

2. Critical thinking

How did I gather my evidence? How did I demonstrate my analytical skills? How did I solve problems and what steps did I take to solve problems?

3. Creativity

How did I express my ideas in a creative way? How did I implement my own original ideas? How did I use my imagination to create this of work?

4. Making connections

What connections did I make from this piece to other areas of my learning? How does this relate to life outside the classroom? What connections can I make about myself?

5. Communication

How effectively did I communicate through this piece? Through which ways did I express my ideas? How did I communicate any problems throughout the process?

6. Initiative

Describe a situation related to this project when I persevered, despite personal obstacles. How did I set my own goals for completion of this project, and then achieve them? How did I take initiative to go above and beyond the basic expectations of this project?

PART II: Letter to Next Year's Teacher

Next, you will write a letter to the English teacher you will have next year. This should describe your learning journey thus far. Focus on both personal and academic characteristics, describing the things that you love and are passionate about and also what makes you stumble. Describe your strengths and weaknesses, and where you grew the most, giving examples from the year's work. The letter should conclude by identifying an academic action plan for the following year.

PART III: Final Reflection

Finally, you will write a final reflection in class during your final exam block. Be prepared to reflect on your overall progress and experience in HAS.

Hudson Public Schools, Hudson, MA. Work collected by the Massachusetts Department of Education.

Students in the American Studies course include work that they have done and describe situations in which they have demonstrated a specific task, such as when they persevered. They are documenting their own learning in this project, and they also are required to reflect on the process and experience in the class.

Rubrics

Developing Rubrics That Support Teaching and Learning

Rubrics are essentially scoring guides in which specific criteria—descriptors of the quality of student work—are used to differentiate among different levels of student proficiency. According to Susan Brookhart,

> *Rubrics help keep teachers focused on criteria, not tasks.*

Really good rubrics help teachers avoid confusing the task or activity with the learning goal, and therefore confusing completion of the task with learning. Rubrics help keep teachers focused on criteria, not tasks (Brookhart 2013, p. 6).

The critical elements of the learning goal are specified as criteria. Often, rubrics are accompanied by examples of student work to illustrate each level of quality. We talk more about anchor papers, projects, and exemplars as examples of student work later in this chapter. A rubric may be used in conjunction with a variety of assessments and may help improve learning and instruction. An effective rubric will define the quality of the performance and will clearly delineate the levels of performance.

Rubrics help teachers focus their instruction on expected outcomes about learning for their students, not on the various tasks that will be worked on to accomplish these expected outcomes. As Brookhart says, "Without clarity on outcomes, it's hard to know how much of various aspects of the content to teach. Rubrics help with clarity of both content and outcomes" (Brookhart 2013, p. 9). To make this distinction clearer, see Figure 4.33 below with a student-centered, outcomes-based rubric and a task-based rubric.

Figure 4.33 Comparison of an Effective and Flawed Rubric

Effective Rubric Student-Centered Outcomes-Based (Using *Charlotte's Web* Unit)	Flawed Rubric Task-Centered (Using *Charlotte's Web* Unit)	Commentary
• You show that you understand why authors write novels, and use techniques such as point of view and imagery. • You demonstrate understanding of character development by using what one character says, does, or thinks and explain the author's craft.	1. Take notes on the novel and find at least two quotations. 2. Make sure your work is turned in on time and neat. 3. Include at least three quotations. 4. Make sure your quotation is accurate and correctly punctuated. 5. Make sure your drawing is neat, attractive, and clear.	The descriptors in the first column describe what the student will know and be able to do as a result of the unit. The descriptors in the flawed column focus on only what will be done.

Brookhart cites five major flaws in rubrics. Each is illustrated by the corresponding number in the "Flawed Rubric" column:
1. Confounding the outcomes being measured (scoring more than one content-area skill at a time, without recognizing them as separate skills)
2. Scoring for extraneous features (e.g., neatness, color, etc.)
3. Scoring by counting up parts or components, rather than by looking for evidence of proficiency in the outcome(s) being measured
4. Scoring for things students have not been cued to do
5. Scoring products rather than outcomes (Brookhart 2013, p. 7)

Steps that a student needs to take to finish a task are more appropriately covered in a checklist, which is far less time-consuming than a rubric. Both checklists and rubrics support students as they are working in class.

Using Rubrics as a Teaching Tool

Teachers often have two or three rubrics that they use all year, such as a rubric on an important and frequent activity like writing, solving math problems, or group participation. Sometimes rubrics are generated with the help of the class, which engenders more engagement with the goals for the project. As a class learns, the expectations may be changed and made more explicit in the rubric.

Because the rubric defines the learning target or mastery objective, it should be distributed at the beginning of the unit or the year. In this way, the rubric supports students as they see the qualities of higher levels of performance and they work to attain them.

The criteria and performance-level descriptions in rubrics help students understand what the desired performance is and what it looks like. Effective rubrics show students how they will know to what extent their performance passes muster on each criterion of importance, and, if used formatively, can also show students what their next steps should be to enhance the quality of their performance (Brookhart 2013, p. 12).

Research has demonstrated that rubrics, including those that are generated by the students themselves, as well as those used by peers to critique another peer's work, are effective teaching techniques and resources for helping students improve their work. They also help students themselves as learners from kindergarten through grade 12. In research studies, in all grades and in different content areas, students using rubrics outscored those who worked without them (Brookhart 2013, p. 14).

The following chart shows three types of scoring guides, beginning with the most complex (Stage 3) and descending to the least complex (Stage 1). We will discuss each of these types of scoring guides in the next sections.

In research studies, in all grades and in different content areas, students using rubrics outscored those who worked without them.

Holistic and Analytical Rubrics

A rubric may be used either holistically or analytically in assessing student work. After the criteria for the task have been established, the teacher may look at the criteria as a whole, or list all the criteria separately but give one score for the rubric, which would be considered a holistic assessment. Generally, holistic rubrics are used summatively, since they take less time and provide less diagnostic feedback about each criterion. On the other hand, a teacher might also use an analytical rubric, in which the criteria are divided into essential dimensions so that they are judged separately. A separate score is assigned to each of the defined criteria. In this way, the rubric is descriptive and can be used by teachers and students to determine relative strengths in each area. Figures 4.35, 4.36, and 4.37 illustrate examples of a holistic rubric and two analytical rubrics, respectively. Figures 4.35 and 4.36 might be used together to assess both the student giving an oral presentation and the students in the audience. In this way, students listening to an oral presentation are held accountable.

Figure 4.34

Scoring Guides for Students

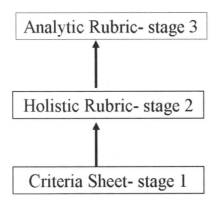

Figure 4.35

Holistic Problem-Solving Rubric

1
- didn't think through the problem
- didn't come up with an appropriate strategy and plan to solve the problem
- didn't answer all parts of the problem
- made basic mistakes in methods and calculations
- didn't explain the work in an organized, step-by-step manner
- didn't label the work and visuals

2
- gave some thought to the problem
- used a good strategy and plan to solve the problem
- answered most parts of the problem
- made some calculation errors
- explained the work in a semi-organized manner
- labeled some of the work and visuals

3
- thought carefully about the problem
- used a clear strategy and plan to solve the problem
- answered all parts of the problem
- made only a few calculation errors
- explained the work in an organized, step-by-step manner
- labeled all work and visuals clearly

4
- thought carefully about the problem
- used an excellent strategy and plan to solve the problem
- answered all parts of the problem

- made no calculation errors
- explained the work in an organized, step-by-step manner
- labeled all work and visuals clearly
- solved the problem in more than one way

Figure 4.36 Analytical Oral Presentation Rubric

Criteria	Excellent 4	Proficient 3	Competent 2	Limited 1	Score
Content	Student shows a full understanding of the topic.	Student shows a good understanding of the topic.	Student shows a good understanding of parts of the topic.	Student does not seem to understand the topic very well.	
Organization	Presentation includes a strong introduction that gains audience attention, followed by organized progression of ideas.	Presentation includes a good introduction, followed by an organized progression of ideas.	Presentation includes an introduction, followed by a relatively organized progression of ideas.	Presentation has a weak introduction and ideas are difficult to follow.	
Posture and Eye Contact	Student stands up straight and looks relaxed and confident. Student establishes eye contact with everyone in the room during the presentation.	Student stands up straight and establishes eye contact with everyone in the room during the presentation.	Student sometimes stands up straight and establishes eye contact.	Student slouches and/or does not establish eye contact during the presentation.	
Speaks Clearly	Student speaks clearly and distinctly all the time and does not mispronounce any words.	Student speaks clearly and distinctly all the time, but mispronounces one word.	Student speaks clearly and distinctly most of the time, and mispronounces no more than two words.	Student often mumbles and cannot be understood, or mispronounces more than two words.	
Enthusiasm	Facial expressions and body language generate strong interest and enthusiasm about the topic in others.	Facial expressions and body language sometimes generate strong interest and enthusiasm about the topic in others.	Facial expressions and body language are used to try to generate enthusiasm but seem somewhat faked.	Facial expressions and body language are used very little and did not generate much interest in topic being presented.	
Comprehension	Student is able to answer accurately almost all questions posed by classmates about the topic.	Student is able to answer accurately most questions posed by classmates about the topic.	Student is able to answer accurately a few questions posed by classmates about the topic.	Student is unable to answer accurately any questions posed by classmates about the topic.	

Figure 4.37 Analytical Rubric for Audience Responsibilities

CATEGORY	4	3	2	1	Comments
Attentive Listening	Student gave full attentive listening to each speaker with his/her eyes, ears, and heart.	Student showed attentive listening most of the time.	Student showed attentive listening some of the time.	Student didn't show attentive listening.	
Comments and Opinions	Student withheld his/her comments and opinions during the presentations, but asked appropriate questions after many presentations.	Student withheld his/her comments and opinions during the presentations, but asked appropriate questions after some presentations.	Student withheld his/her comments and opinions during the presentations.	Student didn't withhold his/her comments and opinions during the presentations, and/or didn't ask questions after any presentation.	
Body Language	Listener responds appropriately all of the time to comedic and/or dramatic moments of the presentations. Demonstrated by body language, laughter, and/or silence.	Listener responds appropriately most of the time to comedic and/or dramatic moments of the presentations. Demonstrated by body language, laughter, and/or silence.	Listener responds appropriately some of the time to comedic and/or dramatic moments of the presentations. Demonstrated by body language, laughter, and/or silence.	Listener rarely responds appropriately to comedic and/or dramatic moments of the presentations. Demonstrated by body language, laughter, and/or silence.	
Curiosity and Respect	Student shows curiosity and respect all of the time through body language and questions.	Student shows curiosity and respect most of the time through body language and questions.	Student shows curiosity and respect some of the time through body language and questions.	Student doesn't show curiosity and respect through body language and questions.	

Adapted from Rubistar.4teachers.org, rubric ID 1153873 (May 9, 2005). Copyright ALTEC at the University of Kansas (2000–2008).

Deciding which type of rubric to use, holistic or analytical, depends upon the purpose of the assessment. Each type of rubric has advantages and disadvantages. **Arter and McTighe (2001) recommend using an analytical rubric for daily classroom use, in which an ongoing assessment is embedded in instruction and specific feedback is necessary for improving teaching and learning.** Rubrics allow teachers to provide specific comments in an efficient manner and provide students with a clear description of the performance expected so that they can improve their work.

Holistic scoring is more appropriate for a summative assessment, which takes less time to score and requires a single overall score, rather than detailed feedback. It takes less time to assess holistically, but all of the criteria are included in the rubric.

Instructional Writing Rubrics

Writing rubrics can support students' growth. Instructional rubrics are often created with student input and written in student-friendly language. When rubrics are presented to students before they begin a writing assignment, it supports their learning so that they clearly understand the goals of the task and so that the rubric is used "to guide them in self-directed planning and goal setting, revising, and editing" (Saddler and Andrade 2004, p. 49).

Planning and Goal-Setting Stage Using a Rubric

An instructional rubric is a tool that describes high-quality work as precisely as possible. The first three criteria of the "6+1 Traits for Ideas" rubric for grades 3–12 are provided below in Figure 4.38. The rubric has six levels from *Beginning* to *Exceptional*. The descriptors for *Main Idea, Details and Support* and *Reasoning and Thinking* are provided with descriptions of what the writing looks like if a student is, for example, "exceptional" at providing reasoning and thinking. The student's writing at that level:

> Develops the main idea with convincing, supportive information, and/or concrete details that go beyond the obvious In Argument or Opinion writing at grade 7 and beyond, [and] the writing thoroughly examines counterclaims and addresses them in original ways that enrich the author's claim (Education Northwest 2004).

Brookhart suggests a simple method to introduce students to a rubric. She says, "If rubrics are well constructed, and if students understand the performance criteria and quality levels encoded into them, then the *Proficient* level of the rubrics describes what learning looks like." In this case, the rubric for the criterion *Ideas* describes the writing outcome: "Produces a clear, focused, accurate, and complex main idea with convincing development and/or support."

Brookhart then recommends a simple exercise:

1. Give students copies of the rubrics. Ask them, in pairs, to discuss what the rubrics mean, proceeding one criterion at a time.

2. As they talk, have them write down questions. These should be questions the pairs are not able to resolve themselves.

3. Try to resolve the questions with peers. Put two or three pairs together for groups of four or six. Again, students write down any questions they still can't resolve.

4. Collect the final list of questions and discuss them as a whole group. Sometimes these questions will illuminate unfamiliar terms or concepts, or unfamiliar attributes of work. Sometimes the questions will illuminate a lack of clarity in the rubrics and result in editing the rubrics.

At this point, the class's suggested language can be substituted or added for clarification of any of the criteria. In this case, *Main Idea, Details and Support*, and *Reasoning and Thinking* outcomes have been discussed by all students.

Figure 4.38 Education Northwest 6+1 Traits Rubric

Traits Rubric for Ideas: Grades 3–12

Key question: Does the writer engage the reader with fresh information or perspective on a focused topic?

	Not proficient			Proficient		
	1 Beginning	**2 Emerging**	**3 Developing**	**4 Capable**	**5 Experienced**	**6 Exceptional**
	Does not reflect a main idea or purpose; includes content that is off topic.	Has a main idea that begins to emerge, but author's direction is unclear.	States or implies a main idea, but is unclear, unfocused, inaccurate, and/or underdeveloped.	Conveys a clear, focused, and accurate main idea with adequate development and/or support.	Produces a clear, focused, accurate, and complex main idea with convincing development and/or support.	Conveys a clear, focused, accurate, and significant main idea and includes unique, substantial insights that are fully developed and supported.
Main Idea	Does not convey a main idea or topic.	Focuses on a general topic but does not suggest a main idea.	Suggests a main idea, but the direction of the piece is still unclear.	Has a clear, focused main idea.	Conveys a clear, focused, and substantive main idea.	Conveys a clear, focused, substantive, and original main idea that drives the piece.
Details and Support	Does not develop or support a main idea.	Attempts to develop or support the main idea with limited, repetitious, faulty, and/or unclear information and/or details.	Provides incidental support of the main idea with information that lacks specificity and relevance, and may be inaccurate; may include some generic details. In A/O writing at grade 7+, includes one or more counterclaims that are acknowledged but not addressed.	Develops the main idea with generally accurate and relevant supportive information and/or details. In A/O writing at grade 7+, addresses one or more counterclaims.	Develops the main idea with specific, relevant, accurate information and/or some vivid details. In A/O writing at grade 7+, addresses and thoroughly examines counterclaims.	Develops the main idea with convincing, supportive information and/or concrete details that go beyond the obvious. In A/O writing at grade 7+, thoroughly examines counterclaims, and addresses them in original ways that enrich the author's claim.
Reasoning and Thinking	Does not show author's thinking in developing or connecting ideas.	Generalizes about the topic without providing logical connections among ideas, or uses connections that are faulty.	Begins to develop supporting ideas, some of which lack clarity or obvious logical connection.	Presents useful information that helps the reader understand the author's reasoning, logic, or perspective.	Presents useful, fresh information or perspective with logical reasoning that clarifies complex ideas.	Conveys fresh, useful information using higher-order thinking skills and convincing reasoning to provide unique insights into complex ideas.

Education Northwest (copyright 2004).

The next steps include those of the writing process. In this assignment, American history students will be comparing two primary sources and determining what part idealism played in America's deciding to fight in World War I. The process could be covered not by a rubric, but by a checklist to support students' writing process. In addition, samples of other primary source analyses at different levels of performance would also be provided.

Revising Writing

Often, students substitute editing for revision. Editing is done after all of the major thinking is completed. Before that, the focus needs to be on the ideas and their relationships—not on the "surface errors" of spelling and punctuation, which can be easily fixed. The revision process, described as part of the checklist above, is an integral part of writing. Its focus is on ideas and organization of ideas. Good writers spend much of their time revising. Instructional rubrics can assist writers during this phase by helping students to identify their strengths and weaknesses, and offering suggestions for improvement. If the student discovers through self-assessment and peer assessment that the quality of any of the criteria is low, the rubric provides the criteria for improvement, such as by clarifying examples or including vivid examples. "By identifying problems and their possible solutions, rubrics provide important information for students to use in revision" (Saddler and Andrade 2004).

Editing Writing

Editing should be a process that is separate from revision. Editing is about grammar, spelling, and punctuation. It is recommended that students keep a list of their most frequent editing concerns because most students have a consistent pattern of mechanical problems. Rubrics can help students at this stage of the writing process by reminding them to check their work for a variety of errors—punctuation, capitalization, spelling, grammar, paragraphing, etc. Again, a teacher might refer a student to the *Conventions Criterion* to ensure that he or she has checked and edited

Figure 4.39 Checklist for Writing an Analysis of Primary Sources

(Remember, writing is a recursive process, so you may return to a step more than once.)

__ Read the primary source documents on your own or with a partner. Annotate the documents with notations that connect to the idea of idealism.

__ Underline quotations that you might want to incorporate into your paper.

__ Begin to develop your "working thesis" or main idea. Remember, this is a hypothesis, and your thesis or claim may have counterclaims from other primary sources. Your claim needs to answer the question about idealism.

__ Develop "bins" for your evidence. Label those bins with, for example, Wilson's speech to the Congress. And write your analysis of this idea, such as how Wilson used idealism to convince Congress to vote for the war. You'll need at least three or four main ideas. You may also want to include counterclaims that you will discuss (and refute).

__ Write a draft of your paper with an introduction, a paragraph for each claim and counterclaim, and a conclusion.

__ With your partner, review the rubric for the three criteria described. Discuss your idea, your evidence, and your explanation of the evidence (your analysis).

__ Schedule a conference with me.

__ Find two other classmates and discuss your ideas. After you have time to revise, if necessary, exchange papers and rank the other three papers using the writing rubric.

__ Bring this revised draft to class Friday, and we will have a Socratic seminar, in which we discuss the claims of all students, their evidence, and their reasoning.

__ The draft can be written or typed.

__ After the class discussion, return to your paper to revise it based on new information and insights gained from the seminar.

__ Again, find a partner to exchange your paper with for a final edit.

__ Submit your paper for a grade.

thoroughly, and to a uniquely developed list of areas on which they have worked in earlier papers.

How Peer Review and Self-Reflection Can Improve Student Writing

When students review their own work as well as that of their peers, they become better writers. Self-reflection, self-assessment, and applying the standards for writing as a student works with a peer all improve student writing. The process must be gradual and supported by checklists, rubrics, anchor charts, and possibly peer-to-peer simulations, but the process both improves individual student writing and increases self-efficacy and independence over time.

"**Student assessment has the additional advantage of promoting self-regulation because it gives students some of the responsibility for judging written work instead of placing that responsibility solely on the teacher**" (Saddler and Andrade 2004, p. 51). It also provides a wider audience beyond that of the teacher.

"Informing Writing" is the title of a research paper based on a meta-analysis of the impact of formative assessment on improving writing. The researchers from Vanderbilt University found teacher feedback and student self-assessment of their own writing had a strong positive impact on writing (Graham, Harris, and Hebert 2011).

According to Laura Varlas in *Educational Leadership*, students' writing improved when students were provided with three essential components:
1. Students had a model for comparing to their writing.
2. They received feedback that described their strengths and weaknesses. This feedback could come from either peers or their teacher.
3. Their teacher provided the next steps that students needed to take to improve their writing (Varlas 2012).

All of this kind of information described the quality of the work, not the student, as Sue Brookhart also advises in "Feedback That Fits" (Brookhart 2007, p. 4).

Graham recommends that feedback should be limited and focused on the next steps that a student needs to improve his or her writing. "Too much feedback can actually crush a student's motivation to become a better writer," says Graham. A paper covered with red notations and circled words can seem overwhelming. Alternatively, a teacher can say, "Amy, I want you to

Too much feedback can actually crush a student's motivation to become a better writer.

read your first sentences and make sure that every sentence in that paragraph that follows it is directly related to that thesis or claim. You've done a good job in developing claims, now just make sure each claim has evidence and that you explain that evidence." With this targeted advice, Amy is looking at the flow of her ideas paragraph by paragraph.

Also, it is important that teachers spend time demonstrating how students can give appropriate feedback to their peers. This kind of feedback should start small. For example, initially, a teacher may suggest that only one positive comment and one question can be provided as feedback while the class is beginning to learn how to critique one another in a way that encourages growth. Protocols or samples of questions—such as "Can you tell me more about this idea? Can you explain who this person is?"—can be posted in anchor charts that remind students to stay positive, find something that works, comment on a strength in the writing, and ask a question that helps the writer elaborate or clarify his or her writing. Taylor suggests two protocols that can support peer responses to others' writing:

PQP: Praise, Question, Polish. First, in small groups of two or three, students read one another's papers aloud. Taylor says, "This oral reading helps writers hear how well the paper flows and independently identify possible changes." Students then fill out the form with (1) *praise*: what is good about the writing and why it's good; (2) *question*: a question or a request for clarification or for more details; and finally, (3) *polish*: peers make specific suggestions for improvement. These suggestions might be directly linked to descriptors on the rubric.

Drafting. In small groups of two or three, students read and comment on one another's papers in the margins and return the essays with comments. During the next day, as they revise, they discuss their work with their group (Taylor 2014).

As with other units of study, tracking progress toward the goal is essential. Graham suggests using a rubric like the "6 + 1 Trait" rubric (see Figure 4.38), and then tracking student progress data and using that information to adjust instruction. This practice can have a school-wide impact if teachers collaborate to assess student writing. See Chapter 10 for protocols for establishing inter-rater reliability, collaboratively looking at student work, and collaboratively developing action plans based on different levels of student writing.

Initially, quality rubrics take a great deal of time. Often, districts work collaboratively to develop school-wide or district-wide rubrics. Chapter 10 provides a collaborative process for developing a rubric from student work.

Avoid converting rubrics into percentages or grades.

Brookhart (2013), Goodrich (1996–1997), and Strickland and Strickland (2000) have developed several suggestions that are useful in writing rubrics. These recommendations are listed and explained in the following section.

Teachers Working Together to Assess Student Work

The strategy for examining student work is best done in groups of three or four teachers. The assignments chosen for this activity should be ones that require a rubric to assess the assignment. Writing pieces, multi-step math problems, science lab reports, history position papers, etc., will work well because students are dependent on the rubric to self-assess and guide them as they complete the work. The four teachers working together each choose an assignment. After students have completed the selected assignments, the teachers make four sets of the assignments prior to evaluating. Each teacher brings the four sets of uncorrected assignments and the four copies of the scoring guides to the meeting.

Teacher 1 gives each of the other three teachers a copy of the rubric and an uncorrected set of the assignments. He or she then gives a brief overview of the lesson(s) that led up to the completion of the assignment. The three teachers review and discuss each assignment and eventually assess the assignment based only on the information contained in the scoring guide. Teacher 1 listens to determine ways in which he or she could modify the assignment or rubric to make it clearer to students. After Teachers 2, 3, and 4 finish assessing the papers, their assessments are compared to the assessment done by Teacher 1. Together, the four teachers discuss the lesson and rubric, and answer the following questions:

1. How could the rubric be improved so it is a more effective guide for students?
2. How could the lesson be modified to provide higher levels of student success on the assignment?

The group then repeats the process with Teacher 2 and so on, until all four of the teachers' assignments and student work have been analyzed. Chapters 10 and 11 provide protocols for collaboratively evaluating student work and for generating local rubrics and action plans for supporting students in their next steps based upon their achievement on this assignment. The website www.nsrfharmony.org is an excellent resource for teachers who want to collaboratively evaluate and share student work.

List Criteria of the Student Work

Start by listing the specific criteria that describe goals of the learning (not the task; that is for a checklist). The challenge is to say exactly what is expected. Sometimes this process takes a few iterations and a try-out with students. For example, if creating a rubric for problem-solving activities, possible criteria may include mathematical strategies, mathematical reasoning, explanation, and providing more than one way to answer the question.

Articulate Gradations of Quality

Typically, three to six gradations seem to be most appropriate for all levels. There is an ongoing debate with regard to using either an odd or even number of gradations. Some feel that when an odd number of gradations are used, people tend to choose a middle score which falls between proficient and not proficient work, and does not clearly communicate if the work needs improvement or is proficient.

Avoid Converting Rubrics into Percentages or Grades

Develop a rubric to assess what you want to assess, not to match an ABC grading system. Focus on articulating the quality of the work. The gradations should appropriately match the purposes of using a rubric. If you are required to grade, as most teachers in upper elementary and secondary schools are, you may convert the information from the rubric into grades at a later point. A website, www.roobrix.com, converts rubrics to percentages without distorting the grading.

Allow Class Time for the Development and Use of Assessment Tools, Such as Rubrics

Creating a rubric is a time-consuming process and should be spent on major learning goals that recur throughout the year or course. Assessment is part of the learning process, and it is a valuable process for both the students and the teacher. Keep in mind that it usually takes several revisions before the rubric works in the way that you want it to work. In the beginning, it is important to get your ideas on paper and come up with a framework for your rubric, but it doesn't have to be perfect. A protocol for developing a rubric collaboratively by using the work of students in your school or district is discussed in Chapter 10.

Have Trial Runs with the Rubric

After you get your ideas down on paper, use the rubric with your students. Make adjustments based on student work. Both teachers and students may practice using the rubric with student samples.

Be Willing to Revise the Rubric

The rubric should be designed to help students revise their work; however, the rubric will also need to be revised as part of the rubric-development process. As revisions are made to the rubric, it is important that students understand the changes that were made and why they were made.

Use the Rubric for Self- and Peer Assessment

The rubric should be used as often as possible for both self- and peer assessment, which will further students' understanding of how to improve their performance. For example, one school's faculty uses a problem-solving rubric (see Figure 4.35) with students for the evaluation of their work, self-assessment, and peer assessment. After students complete a problem-solving task, they are asked to assess their work and determine a score for it. They must provide a rationale for the particular score they give themselves. Doing this encourages students to review and reflect upon their work and make any changes or additions that are necessary. After the students turn in their work, we use the same rubric to evaluate it ourselves. In addition, from time to time, students are given samples of other students' work (from previous years) and asked to use the rubric to score the student work.

On the following page is an example of a rubric used district-wide that went through the development steps noted above. The rubric is used by teachers to assess district-wide writing samples that evaluate student performance. It is an adaptation of the "6 + 1 Traits" rubric with its six criteria (topic, ideas, organization, voice, language, and mechanics) and many of its descriptors. The faculty made the rubric "theirs" through discussions and using the rubric to assess their students' work.

Figure 4.40

Needham Elementary School: Writing Rubric for Grade Five

(Levels three and four are acceptable ranges of grade-five performance, mid-year; level 4 is the standard expectation for grade-five students by the end of the year.)

1	2	3	4	5
The writer is able to convey the basic theme using a few details. Organization is random, but shows beginning understanding of paragraphing. Many ideas are repeated. Mechanical errors may interfere significantly with meaning. Writer demonstrates an inconsistent use of punctuation. There may be some sentence fragments and run-on sentences. Common high-frequency words may be misspelled. Word agreement errors may appear.	The writer is able to focus the topic through two or three loosely connected paragraphs. Details usually support the theme, but with few if any elaborations. Introduction and conclusion are brief and simply stated. Minimal sentence variety and limited word choice, as well as occasional lapses in clarity of expression, are present. Mechanical errors may interfere with meaning. Difficulty is noted with punctuation of complex sentence structures and some spelling conventions. Word agreement (pronoun/subject/verb tense) errors may occur frequently.	The writer is able to maintain the topic through several paragraphs. Ideas are supported with details. Some elaboration of details is evident. Organization utilizes the basic three-phase paragraph structure. There is evidence of varied sentence structure. Generally correct basic punctuation is used. Use of internal punctuation is emerging. Few agreement (pronoun/subject/verb tense) errors. Conventional spelling is generally accurate.	The writer is able to develop and maintain focus throughout multiple paragraphs. Organization of paragraphs and sequence of ideas follow logical patterns. Theme is supported by relevant details, with several elaborations of details. Sentence structure shows developing variety and complexity. Transitions and connecting paragraphs are usually evident. There are only minor errors in mechanics, usage, and grammar.	The writer creatively approaches the topic with a strong voice and clear sense of audience and purpose. Organization and development are thorough and enhanced by effective elaboration of details and connections, as well as richness of language. Transitions are accomplished with ease. Very few, if any, mechanical or grammatical errors.
Topic	**Topic**	**Topic**	**Topic**	**Topic**
• Purpose may not be clear. • Minimal awareness of audience and task • Basic topic may be conveyed or recognizable. • Details support topic but with little or no elaboration.	• Attempts to establish and maintain purpose. • Demonstrates some awareness of audience and task. • Topic focus maintained but may be simplistically stated. • Topic supported with many details. • Few details are elaborated.	• Establishes and maintains clear purpose. • Demonstrates awareness of audience and task. • Three-phase paragraph structure used where appropriate. • Introductory sentence/paragraph focuses reader. • Conclusion sentence/paragraph pulls ideas together.	• Establishes and maintains clear purpose. • Demonstrates awareness of audience and task. • Strong introduction and conclusion paragraphs • Topic and sub-topics supported with relevant details and elaboration.	• Clearly demonstrates awareness of audience, purpose, and task. • Creative, unique approach • Multiple use of well-developed, clearly focused paragraphs • Topic and sub-topics supported with many elaborate details.
Organization	**Organization**	**Organization**	**Organization**	**Organization**
• Minimal sequencing • One-, two-, or three-sentence paragraphs • May attempt to use three-phase paragraph structure, but shows little evidence of	• Some inconsistent sequencing	• Some body paragraphs are well developed and expanded, but others are brief with one or two details.	• Sequencing of ideas moves reader smoothly along. • Logical organization of paragraphs • Multiple paragraphs within body where appropriate • Most ideas/paragraphs are organized.	• Compelling presentation; flows smoothly • Good organization and sequencing of ideas • Maintains clarity of expression and word choice throughout. • Each paragraph is developed with topic and conclusion sentences. • Transition words/phrases

Needham Elementary School: Writing Rubric for Grade Five (continued)

(Levels three and four are acceptable ranges of grade-five performance, mid-year; level 4 is the standard expectation for grade-five students by the end of the year.)

- understanding of paragraph development.
- May lack clarity and cohesiveness.
- Some random and/or repeated ideas

Language
- Basic vocabulary
- Some variety in sentence types

Voice
- Personal voice may be emerging.

Mechanics/Usage/Grammar
- May have end-punctuation errors.
- Some sentence fragments and run-ons
- Message confused because of spelling and/or punctuation errors.
- Pronoun/subject/verb tense disagreements
- Errors in spelling of some common sight words

- May have some lapses in clarity of ideas
- Evidence of paragraphing
- Body paragraphs are short and not fully developed around sub-topic.
- Occasional loose connection of details
- Weak or absent transitions

Language
- Common vocabulary
- Little variety of sentence beginnings
- Standard and predictable sentence structure for the most part

Voice
- Personal voice may be emerging.

Mechanics/Usage/Grammar
- Accurate punctuation for simple sentences
- May show little understanding of correct punctuation when more complex sentence structure is used.
- Lack of understanding of internal punctuation
- Conventional spelling of high-frequency and phonetic words
- Minor lapses in syntax

- Most details are grouped and sequenced.
- Some topic sentences guide paragraphs
- Emerging use of transition words and phrases

Language
- Deliberate word choice enhances meaning.
- Some variation in sentence structure and beginnings
- May have occasional sentence run-ons/fragments in more complex structures.

Voice
- Personal voice is emerging.

Mechanics/Usage/Grammar
- Capitals and punctuation used correctly.
- May have some errors in punctuation in complex sentence structures.
- Emerging use of correct internal punctuation
- Indents for new paragraphs
- Spelling demonstrates knowledge of spelling conventions and high-frequency words.
- Pronoun/subject/verb tense agreement

- Topic sentences focus paragraphs.
- Transition words/phrases connect ideas and/or paragraphs.

Language
- Most ideas expressed with deliberate, appropriate word choice.
- Expanded vocabulary and imagery
- Sentence beginnings show further development (e.g., prepositional/adverbial phrases, etc.).
- Variety of sentence types
- Use of transition words and phrases to connect paragraphs

Voice
- Personal voice heard

Mechanics/Usage/Grammar
- Capitals and end punctuation used correctly
- Internal punctuation correct, with some minor errors
- Indents used properly
- Pronoun/subject/verb tense agreement
- Accurate spelling appropriate to grade level

- connect ideas and paragraphs.

Language
- Creative, unique, original approach
- Precise/powerful use of vocabulary; imagery is relevant, with vivid details that enrich central theme
- Rich variety and complexity of sentence structure
- Transition words/phrases connect ideas and paragraphs.

Voice
- Distinctive voice throughout

Mechanics/Usage/Grammar
- Few mechanical errors, if any, relative to length and complexity
- Consistent use of correct, internal punctuation
- Proper indentation
- Conventional spelling
- Correct grammar and usage, for the most part

NS = nonscorable—illegible, incoherent, or blank paper; OP = off prompt—does not answer prompt.

Anchor Papers, Exemplars, and Models

Rubrics are beneficial to teachers in that they serve as guides in assessing student work. However, since rubrics are a collection of individual criteria, both teachers and students profit from examples of a specific level of work. Models or exemplars can be posted as anchor papers to increase students' understanding of how the criteria in the rubric are integrated into the final product, as well as to help students understand the expectations of the assignment. Exemplars help teachers consistently assess the students' final products with inter-rater reliability.

Anchor-paper samples of actual student work that correspond to the different levels of proficiency within the rubric also help students understand how the quality of work translates into a particular score for an assignment. The examples of anchor papers (and accompanying rubric and writing task) provided in Figure 4.41 are taken from a ninth-grade English classroom. The teacher began by presenting a writing task on *Romeo and Juliet* and sharing with students the rubric that would be used to assess this task. The teacher then distributed four anchor papers from the previous year (with the names concealed). Students read through each of these four anchor papers and used the assignment's rubric to assess each one. A discussion followed on the strengths and weaknesses of each of the four anchor papers, and, through this discussion, students were able to come to a deeper understanding of the teacher's expectations for the present writing assignment.

Figure 4.41

English 9   Seider
Romeo and Juliet Writing Assignment, Act V, Scene i

In Act V, Scene i, of *Romeo and Juliet*, Romeo buys poison from an apothecary in order to kill himself because he believes that Juliet is dead. The apothecary is initially reluctant to sell Romeo the poison but ultimately agrees to do so explaining, "My poverty but not my will consents" (V, i). Was the apothecary wrong to sell Romeo the poison? Is he partly to blame for Romeo's and Juliet's deaths?

   As a means of exploring these questions, imagine that you have recently graduated from college with a degree in accounting. A prominent cigarette manufacturer offers you a six-figure salary to work as the company's accountant. Would you take the job? Why or why not?

English 9   Seider
Romeo and Juliet Writing Assignment, Act V, Scene i
Rubric for Writing Assignment

Organization of the Essay

Criteria	Not Yet	Needs Improvement	Proficient	Advanced
Topic Sentence	No topic sentence	Topic sentence exists, but does not describe content of paragraph.	Topic sentence to a limited degree conveys somewhat the content of the paragraph.	Topic sentence successfully conveys content of paragraph.
Provides Evidence	No evidence provided	Evidence provided, but does not support claim.	Evidence somewhat supports claim.	Evidence strongly supports claim.
Concluding Sentence	No concluding sentence	Concluding sentence exists, but does not wrap up content of paragraph.	Concluding sentence successfully wraps up content of paragraph.	Concluding sentence successfully wraps up *and* *extends* content of paragraph.

Mechanics: Punctuation and Grammar

Criteria	Not Yet	Needs Improvement	Proficient	Advanced
Grammar and Usage	Many grammar and usage errors are present.	Several grammar or usage errors are present.	Few grammar or usage errors are present.	No grammar or usage errors are present.

Argument: Claims and Evidence

Criteria	Not Yet	Needs Improvement	Proficient	Advanced
Claim	No claim stated in topic sentence.	Claim in topic sentence is unrelated to assignment.	Claim is stated with some ambiguity in topic sentence.	Claim is clearly stated in topic sentence.
Quality of Evidence Provided	No evidence to support claim made in topic sentence.	Evidence presented to support claim is confusing and unclear.	Evidence presented to support claim is clear.	Several clear, compelling pieces of evidence support the claim made in topic sentence.

Student 1: Needs Improvement

I would take the job if I could. People know exactly what they are doing when they start smoking. Everyone knows they're addictive and that you can die from smoking. I would feel kind of guilty going to work every day, but people are responsible for themselves, not me for them. People make the decision to smoke on their own, no one forces them. People also don't buy cigarettes because their trying to kill themselves, they buy them for the enjoyment of smoking. In the book *Romeo and Juliet,* I don't think the apothecary should have sold Romeo the poison because the apothecary knows Romeo is going to kill himself immediately, that's why he wanted the poison. People aren't looking to kill themselves when they buy a pack of cigarettes but it is 100% their own decision to smoke, they know what they are getting into before they start. In conclusion, I would definitely take the job because I wouldn't be the one actually making or selling them, I would just be figuring out the company's taxes.

over human beings. Working as an accountant for one of these companies would make me part of their business and as guilty as anyone else working there. Finally, I wouldn't work as an accountant for a cigarette company because cigarettes are so addictive. Cigarette companies make money off people's addictions. Smokers have no choice but to keep buying more cigarettes. Making money off people's addiction is practically evil. It is bad enough that cigarettes cause so much misery, but the fact that smokers can know what they're doing to their bodies and want to save themselves but can't, that is even worse. An addiction is like a disease. The tobacco companies take advantage of smoker's disease. If you saw a sick man lying in a hospital bed, would you run up and steal his wallet? Cigarette companies do this every day, but it is even worse because it is not only a man's money they are taking, it is a man's life. I could not look at myself in the mirror if I helped do the accounting for companies that sell cigarettes. I would be as guilty as a CEO. I just couldn't do it.

Student 2: Proficient

If given a fancy job at a tobacco company, I would absolutely turn it down. There are several reasons behind my decision. First, I don't want to do work that is selling a harmful substance. Cigarettes are harmful in many ways. They poison our air, they cause cancer in the people that smoke them, and their second hand smoke can cause cancer in millions of other innocent bystanders. It is amazing to think about how much damage cigarettes cause. Second, cigarettes bring no positive effects to the world, the only point of cigarette companies is to earn money. Cigarette companies value money

Student 3: Advanced

If I were offered a high-paying job as an accountant for a cigarette company, I would definitely accept the position. My decision to accept the position is not because I believe that marketing and selling of cigarettes is okay, but because I believe that people make their own choices in life. Each person is capable of making his or her own decision about whether or not to smoke. With all of the anti-smoking advertisements today, it is hard to believe adults and even children do not know the risks they are taking when they start smoking. As long as cigarette companies do not lie to their customers about the risks and health hazards associated with smoking, these companies are doing nothing wrong. Rather, these companies are simply providing an option for people to take or not as they wish. Are automobile companies responsible for the people who die in automobile accidents? Of course not. People who purchase cars know that there are some risks associated with driving, and they make the decision to take their chances. The same is true with cigarette companies and these companies' clients. The men and women who purchase cigarettes do so knowing full well that there are risks associated with this habit. As a result of this belief—that men and women who purchase cigarettes understand the pro's and con's of smoking cigarettes—I feel certain that I *would* accept a position as an accountant for a cigarette company. In fact, the job sounds like a great opportunity. In exchange for doing the company's finances, I would receive a good paycheck and a nice home. And should the company ever go out of business or I need to move to another part of the country, I would have excellent accounting experience on my resume to help me find a new job. In closing, I don't see why anyone would hesitate to take this position, and I know that my belief that people are free to make their own decisions would lead me to accept the job if it were offered to me.

Criteria Sheets

A criteria sheet is a scoring guide that specifically explains the criteria the students and the teacher will use to assess an assignment. A criteria sheet is not a rubric, and it resembles a checklist in that it describes the task and not the mastery objective for the student. Criteria sheets and checklists (see Figures 4.27, 4.28, and 4.39) take less of a teacher's time, but they do not define the goal of the task; rather, they define the steps in the process.

Honors Chemistry

Laboratory Report Format

Laboratory reports are written to communicate to others the work that you have done. When preparing your report, you should always write with the idea that the reader will be using your report and no other instructions to repeat the experiment. Therefore, you should be complete in all of your descriptions and calculations. The format given below is a typical format for a published research paper. Unless you are told otherwise, all of the laboratory reports that are turned in this year should follow this format.

Don't use the active voice. Only use the passive voice. You should refrain from using pronouns such as *I, me, you,* or *we.* For example, instead of writing, "I added 30.0 ml of water to the reaction flask," you should write, "Thirty milliliters of water were added to the reaction flask."

Standard Report Format

I.   **Title** (5 pts.)—A report of any kind should have a title that gives the reader an idea of what was accomplished by the investigation. The title should be brief.

II. **Objective** (5 pts.)—This section should give a clear description of the problem being investigated and what you were attempting to accomplish in the investigation.

III. **Background** (15 pts.)—The background section should summarize all of the relevant information that the reader would need to carry out the experiment. This includes the definitions of the quantities being investigated and equations that are needed to calculate the quantities. The equations should be correctly written and clearly presented. Remember that your laboratory report should be written so that any reasonably knowledgeable reader should be able to use your report and no other directions to repeat the experiment.

IV. **Materials** (10 pts.)—Include any materials that were used to carry out the experiment that you are reporting. This includes the type of glassware used, whether you used a Bunsen burner, the types of substances, etc.

V.   **Safety Issues** (5 pts.)—Include any areas in the investigation where safety was a concern. In most cases, the use of the proper eyewear is a minimum safety requirement, but there will be others, depending on the activity.

VI. **Procedure** (25 pts.)—This section will include the step-by-step procedure required to correctly carry out the experiment. It should include diagrams of the experimental setup. If a procedure that you used has been published in a textbook or other readily available source, you may reference the source with a complete MLA bibliographic reference in a reference section at the end of the report. Otherwise, you must write the complete procedure.

VII. **Results** (25 pts.)—Include all of the data (numerical and otherwise) collected in the experiment, as well as all tables, graphs, and calculations. All numbers should be justified, meaning that you should indicate where you obtained all of the numbers that are used in your calculations. The source of any known values that are used should be referenced in a reference section at the end of the report.

VIII. **Conclusion** (10 pts.)—Summarize the investigation and what you accomplished. You should also discuss any possible sources of error in your experiment that may have affected the accuracy and precision of your results and ways that these errors might be avoided in the future.

References (If this section is needed, points for it will be included in the point values for sections VI and VII.)

In contrast to a checklist, a rubric for this assignment would define the goal of the activity—that is, to write a quality lab report—and would describe what quality looks like with incremental levels from highest to lowest. Instead of, for example, the 25 points allocated to "Results," the levels of performance would be described. In the table below, a checklist is compared to a rubric. The checklist gives instructions; the rubric provides descriptions of the degrees of quality of the work. All of the data and their relationships to one another are compared and evaluated with clearly reasoned analyses.

By describing the task and not the outcomes in learning, the focus of a student's energy is on finishing the tasks, but it is not connected to his or her progress as a novice scientist or someone still learning how to follow the scientific method and provide evidence in a form that authentic scientists use and publish.

Without gradations of quality, if a student has seven points taken from this Results section, he or she does not know what he or she should do the next time unless the teacher has written the rationale for deleting those points.

A scoring guide or checklist (below) serves students well when the focus is finishing the task. Rubrics support students' learning. Because they are time-consuming, rubrics need to be generated for the major learning goals of the course.

District, State (Province), and National Assessments

Provincial and State Testing

The educational reform movement in the 1970s and 1980s brought about accountability changes such as graduation requirements, curriculum testing, and minimum competency tests. Recently, however, standards-based education has become more prevalent, and many states have developed assessments that are aligned with their state or province's curriculum standards. "Accountability in these states focuses on output evidence: How well do students perform on the state test?" (Stuart 2003, p. 218).

At times districts, schools, and, more recently, individual teachers have been evaluated based upon the performance of their students on these assessments. These "high-stakes" assessments often have an impact on teaching and learning.

Rick Stiggins, in his 2014 article about assessment literacy in *Phi Delta Kappan*, says that national, standardized results have become relied upon too much and have been detrimental to local and classroom exams. He does not oppose these assessments,

Checklist Example (Teacher's Instructions)	Rubric Example (Levels of Quality)	
	Advanced	**Proficient**
Include all of the data (numerical and otherwise) collected in the experiment, as well as all tables, graphs, and calculations. All numbers should be justified, meaning that you should indicate where you obtained all of the numbers.	The lab provides a precise and comprehensive description of the lab and includes all calculations, and clearly displays all data and their significance in the experiment.	The lab report provides an adequate description of the lab. It includes all calculations and data is effectively displayed in tables or graphs.

but sees some negative impacts on teaching and learning. He says,

To be clear, I support using these tests in a certain limited array of instructional decision-making contexts. But a societal blind spot has been created by the common belief that standardized test results are the only truly acceptable evidence of student achievement.

If the evidence comes from the teacher and the classroom, applies to just one group of students, and doesn't yield comparable results beyond that context, then it's deemed untrustworthy. Our collective faith in the power of standardized tests has become a light so brilliant in our collective eyes that we're unable to see the severe limitations of the tests or that more powerful classroom applications of assessment can promote far greater student learning success (Stiggins 2014, pp. 67–72).

The richness of a teacher's understanding about her individual students and her ability to help her students improve is not a part of most standardized state/provincial exams. Most of these state and provincial assessments provide feedback on the curriculum and the degree to which students in different grades have mastered the state, province, or national curriculum. Thus, a student or district or school may receive a low score in, for example, measurement for its grade-four students, but the assessment does not provide any indication of how to remedy this concern, nor is it necessarily clear whether the low score was because the measurement concepts were not taught, were not effectively taught, or had not been taught before the time the assessment was given. Nor does it indicate if the complexity of the question or the familiarity of the vocabulary or students' reading capacity were involved in their ability to answer a questions.

State, national, and provincial exams generally assess the curriculum (poetry or geometry), but do not indicate the reason for the student's achievement (reading fluency or ability to work with multi-step problems). They do not provide feedback on the possible cause of errors in the curriculum, such as the complexity of the problem, not understanding specific vocabulary, or a student's reading ability. In an analysis of the ACT exam, researchers found that although the assessment indicated that students struggled with the main idea, the real struggle was with the complexity of the text. Students could

> *S*tate, national, and provincial exams generally assess the curriculum (poetry or geometry), but do not indicate the reason for the student's achievement (reading fluency or ability to work with multi-step problems).

identify the main idea in easier texts, but when the complexity of the reading was beyond their reading ability, they could not. Thus, the problem was the ability to read complex texts, not the ability to determine the main idea. (ACT 2006)

Grant Wiggins says that state tests are valuable:

Standardized tests can give us surprisingly valuable and counterintuitive insights into what our students are *not* learning. The myth is that the tests demand and reward low-level "coverage." The results say otherwise (Wiggins 2010, pp. 48–52).

Based upon the results, Wiggins sees a problem with making inferences across the states' results. In, "Why We Should Stop Bashing State Tests," he says

Over and over, in looking at fully disclosed tests and results where they are available—especially in Massachusetts, Florida, and Ohio, where the data are rich and revealing—I have found that far too many of our students at all grade levels do poorly on questions requiring inferences. Students are especially weak at drawing conclusions from nonfiction pieces of writing. On average, across all three states, only about 60 percent can identify the main idea or the author's purpose related to reading passages (Wiggins 2010, p. 48).

Researchers at ACT went further in their analysis of the reading needs of some high school graduates. Based upon the 2005 ACT results, researchers found the following.

State standards do not address text complexity. Although 10 of the 49 states with standards provide names of works or authors that could be used as indices of the complexity of recommended high school reading material, none of the state standards attempts to define explicitly the degree of complexity a specific grade-level text should have. Relationships, Richness, Structure, Style, Vocabulary, Purpose—none of these "RSVP" aspects is described in detail anywhere in any state's reading standards (ACT 2006, p. 7).

Just as the grades 3–12 results of many national and state tests indicate a problem with reading comprehension, the ACT researchers concluded in their last analysis of this data that "only 51 percent of 2005 ACT-tested high school graduates are ready for college-level reading—and, what's worse, more students are on track to being ready for college-level reading in eighth and tenth grade than are actually ready by the time they reach twelfth grade (ACT 2006, p. 7).

Shanahan, a reading researcher, provides some techniques that all teachers can use to help students both improve their scores on large-scale texts and to comprehend more and more complex texts. He says that there is a substantial research base for the following:

- sentence-level revision that includes combining simple sentences into more complex sentences, and, conversely, making complicated sentences more concise
- developing the stamina over time for reading more and more lengthy passages independently, beginning with one sentence and gradually expanding
- vocabulary development using many modalities: seeing, word walls, spelling, drawing, seeing images, creating skits using the words, to connect words to students' experience, and multiple opportunities to practice using the word

Shanahan believes if we teach these three things well, students' reading comprehension will improve, their large-scale test performance will improve and students will be better readers.

In the United States, two new assessments have been developed to assess a curriculum developed collaboratively by the states. These tests shift their focus from curriculum mastery to literacy and mathematical skills. When the Common Core State Standards (CCSS) were being developed, researchers found a three- to four-year gap between high school students and college expectations in the United States. Their literacy skills include the following:

- *Reading:* Students can independently read and closely analyze a range of increasingly complex texts.
- *Writing:* Students can produce well-grounded and effective writing for a variety of purposes and audiences.
- *Research:* Students can build and present knowledge through research and the integration, comparison, and synthesis of ideas.

In mathematics, the skills include the following (Herman and Linn 2014):

- *Concepts and procedures*: Students can explain and apply mathematical concepts and procedures, and carry out mathematical procedures with precision and fluency.
- *Problem solving*: Students can solve a range of complex, well-posed prolems in pure and applied mathematics.
- *Communicating/reasoning*: Student can clearly and precisely construct viable arguments.
- *Modeling and data analysis*: Students can analyze complex, real-world scenarios, and construct and use mathematical models to interpret and solve problems.

> *Modeling and data analysis: Students can analyze complex, real-world scenarios, and construct and use mathematical models to interpret and solve problems.*

Below is a sample series of Partnership for Assessment of Readiness for College and Careers (PARCC) questions. Students have the opportunity to demonstrate their ability to read and comprehend complex informational and literary texts. Figure 4.42 below demonstrates the last question of the year-end assessment. The question is on the left; on the right are the rationale for the question, its alignment to the CCSS, the specific standards, and the method for scoring. The chart documents the complexity of the question (compare the strength of three arguments); the expectation of synthesis (an essay/argument); the use of multiple texts (a biography, an article, and a video); the argument claims and evidence from two of the sources that assess both the accuracy of comprehension; and the ability to write an essay that compares and synthesizes.

Figure 4.42 Sample Grade 7 ELA End-of-Year Assessment

Sample Items for Grade 7: "Amelia Earhart: Life and Disappearance"	
Sample Item 10: Questions and Standards	**Sample Item 11: Advances and Answers**
Question: You have read a website entry and an article, and watched a video describing Amelia Earhart. All three include information that supports the claim that Earhart was a brave, courageous person. The three texts are: "The Biography of Amelia Earhart" "Earhart's Final Resting Place Believed Found" "Amelia Earhart's Life and Disappearance" (video) Consider the argument each author uses to demonstrate Earhart's bravery. **Write an essay that analyzes the strength of the arguments related to Earhart's bravery in at least two of the three supporting materials.** Remember to use textual evidence to support your ideas.	**Item Advances:** The ability to compare and synthesize ideas across multiple texts is a critical skill for college and careers, as is the ability to analyze the strength of various arguments. Traditionally, writing prompts have not called for the use of textual evidence in a student's response. This Prose Constructed Response prompt allows students to delve deeply into multiple texts to gather evidence to analyze a given claim, simulating the research process. This prompt also demonstrates clearly what PARCC means by "writing using and analyzing sources"—students must draw evidence from multiple texts and cite this evidence clearly to demonstrate the reading and writing claims measured. Students are also required to demonstrate that they can apply the knowledge of language and conventions when writing (an expectation for both college and careers).

Can High-Quality Local Assessments Replace Standardized Assessments?

As assessment literacy increases, some teachers have begun to feel (or perhaps wish, since some contend that students are subjected to too much assessment) that local assessments could replace standardized tests. Greg Jouriles, a veteran California teacher, maintains in an *Education Week* article, "Standardized tests are unnecessary because they rarely show what we don't already know. So trust the teacher. Publish grade distributions."

His district has worked its way through a collaborative process of looking at their students' work and they have calibrated their standards so that an A essay in one course would rate an A in another teacher's course.

Quality Local Assessments

David Conley and Linda Darling-Hammond recognize the increasing assessment literacy of teachers as described by Jouriles, but see a place for state assessments along with classroom assessments as part of a system of assessments. They recommend in their article, "Creating Systems of Assessment for Deeper Learning," that, in most states, local assessments need to expand to ensure the complete assessment of the CCSS. PARCC and Smarter Balance could not assess the following standards because of the limitations of

large-scale testing, but the following could be assessed locally:

- conducting extended research using multiple forms of evidence
- communicating ideas—discussing or presenting orally or in multimedia formats
- collaborating with others to define or solve a problem
- planning, evaluating, and refining solution strategies
- using mathematical tools and models in science, technology, and engineering contexts (Conley and Darling-Hammond 2013, p. 7)

Darling-Hammond sees the new Common Core standards as an "opportunity to pivot toward a richer and more rigorous system of assessment." Yet she sees the need to go beyond state testing and provide other kinds of assessment that large-scale assessment cannot. She includes many of the examples mentioned in this chapter, including performance tasks, portfolios, and presentations. Specifically, she includes the following as important kinds of assessment that only local assessment can provide (Darling-Hammond 2014, pp. 8–12):

- performance tasks, including research in the content areas, mathematical solutions, engineering designs, and performance art

- portfolios of student work, including writing samples, artwork, and projects
- oral presentations and scored discussions
- assessments of note-taking skills, collaboration, persistence with challenging tasks, and other evidence of skills described in the CCSS

Conley and Darling-Hammond recommend a continuum of assessments or a system of assessments (Conley and Darling-Hammond 2013, p. 7):

> One of the key characteristics of a system of assessments is a continuum of options and methods for determining what students know and can do. A benefit of this approach is that different types of information can be used for different purposes, instead of trying to have one assessment address all needs. Performance assessments can be designed to gauge student growth on learning progressions, can be incorporated into proficiency determinations or end-of-course exams, or can be combined in a culminating fashion, as in the case of a graduation portfolio.

They suggest a shifting of the types of assessments given, as shown in Figure 4.43. In the new configuration, Conley and Darling-Hammond recommend that more formative and interim assessments take place. In the old system, formative and interim assessments make up about 25 percent of the assessments, and summative (both large-scale and local) make up about 30 percent. In the new system that Conley recommends, formative and interim would make up 75 percent of the assessments in a classroom, and summative would make up about 10 percent.

Figure 4.43

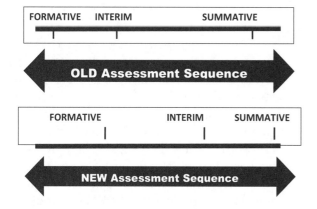

Source: Paul Leather, personal communication, Sept. 3, 2013

In the new configuration, Conley and Darling-Hammond recommend that more formative and interim assessments take place.

In a new system of assessment, we should be able to move from an over-emphasis on entirely external summative tests to a greater emphasis on assessment that can shape and inform learning (p. 18).

As educators become more assessment-literate, their teaching can become part of a system of assessments that ensures students are college-ready by the time they have left high school.

District-Based Assessments

District-based assessments provide school systems with measures of how the students are doing in particular content areas. Using this information, districts determine the students' overall strengths and weaknesses, and make decisions about how to improve instruction in the weaker areas. Teachers and administrators use this information as a guide for where to add more supports, professional development, etc. The following strategies have been used effectively by one school system to assess student learning:

- District-wide mathematical assessments developed by the district are administered at selected grade levels.
- A classroom-based, district-wide writing assessment is scored using a district-developed rubric by classroom teachers and placed in students' permanent portfolios to document growth over time.
- Permanent portfolios are maintained by teachers in which they are required to place certain items that demonstrate students' mastery of specifically designated performance competencies.
- Classroom-based portfolios (more student-centered than the permanent portfolios) demonstrate students' progress toward meeting the grade-level competencies over the course of the school year.

Using the above district-wide classroom-based strategies may benefit practice at the classroom, school, and district levels in many ways. For example, in one school system, when a mathematics end-of-the-year assessment was administered in the first year, it was recognized that students with special needs did particularly poorly. After further analysis, it was determined that when the test was given, the teachers were unclear about what types of modifications were acceptable. As a result, classroom teachers made few necessary modifications for these students. In addition, teachers determined that the students were not reaching the level of mastery needed for many of the skills. To address these issues, teachers decided to use additional instructional strategies when teaching skills, to use more frequent formative assessments, and to make the appropriate modifications for both the final assessment and daily classroom use. Incorporating such changes to one's teaching practices is likely to improve students' understanding and students' test scores.

In another example in which a district-wide mathematics end-of-year assessment was beneficial, the results of the assessment were analyzed, and it was determined that, across the board, students did poorly in the area of measurement. After examining the reasons for the lack of success in this particular area, it was discovered that the program teachers had used did not adequately provide materials, activities, lessons, and information on this topic. In addition, many teachers ran out of time before teaching this unit of study. Consequently, recommendations were made for prioritizing mathematical content to be taught throughout the year—that is, curriculum mapping—so that all mathematical strands were addressed in some capacity. Supplementary materials were also developed and given to teachers to support their instruction in this area.

Both district and state/provincial assessments should be used in conjunction with other sources of information, such as classroom quiz and test scores, performance assessments, lab reports, homework, observations, and journals to make effective decisions that support student learning.

Analyzing Test Results

Data plays a crucial role in assessment and accountability. It is important to understand what the results tell us and how they may be used to make improvements in the education system. Both district and state/provincial assessments should be used in conjunction with other sources of information, such as classroom quiz and test scores, performance assessments, lab reports, homework, observations, and journals to make effective decisions that support student learning.

To fully understand and identify a student learning problem, "it is critical to look not just at the end product of the work, but at the path a student took to get there" (Mintz, Fiarman, and Buffett 2006, p. 86). Fully understanding a student's thinking and approach to different problems and activities enables us to understand more precisely what that student needs as a learner and how we can help him or her. Mintz, Fiarman, and Buffett suggest trying to answer questions such as the following in an attempt to un-

derstand student thinking and to identify a student-centered problem:

- Do students have the necessary background skills and knowledge required for understanding a particular skill or concept?
- Do the students need to be retaught the skill or concept?
- Do the students lack the necessary skills and concepts, or is the design of the assessment faulty?

How One School System Used District-Wide Assessments

In one particular school system, a district-wide mathematics assessment was administered to all elementary grades—kindergarten through fifth—at the end of each year. The construction of these assessments was based on the district's "Mathematics Scope and Sequence," which encompasses both state and national standards. The results of this comprehensive mathematics assessment were entered into a spreadsheet and were analyzed in a variety of ways. Individual students' results were entered into the program, and data was collected for each test item number. A composite score was used to summarize each student's test results according to each of the five mathematical strands: *number and operations*, *algebra*, *geometry*, *measurement*, and *data, statistics, and probability*. The data was organized by school, grade, and teacher, thus providing each teacher with a mean class percentage score for every item number and mathematical strand.

The test questions were then analyzed to document general strengths and weaknesses in specific schools. The strengths for both individual schools and the district were recognized by noting those strands in which average student performance exceeded 75 percent. Scores between 65 percent and 75 percent were considered average performance. The weaknesses were determined by examining each item and noting those questions for which the class average was below 65 percent. District weaknesses were determined by recording item numbers for which more than two schools averaged below 65 percent. These items in which students had more difficulty were categorized by mathematical strand. Each problematic question was studied to determine possible reasons for error. The possibilities included students' inability to follow directions, minimal exposure to a particular concept, and poor test design.

Data was also organized by school and grade to determine the number of students who scored in each of the following intervals for each mathematical strand.

90–100%   Advanced
80–89%   Proficient
70–79%   Proficient
60–69%   Needs Improvement
50–59%   Needs Improvement

Tables and bar graphs for each grade level were constructed to clearly show these results. See Figure 4.44 for an example of grade four.

Figure 4.44 Grade 4—334 Students

	Number and Operations	Algebra	Geometry	Measurement	Data
90–100%	23%	36%	24%	14%	55%
80–89%	19%	35%	22%	17%	21%
70–79%	18%	0%	22%	10%	12%
60–69%	16%	18%	13%	18%	7%
0–59%	25%	11%	20%	40%	6%

Figure 4.45 Points per Strand

Strand	Points
Number and Operations	12
Algebra	5
Geometry	4
Measurement	4
Data	5
Total	30 points

In addition, findings were summarized, trends were noted, and recommendations were made for each grade level after the analysis was completed. The following paragraph was part of the final report, and it highlights the findings and recommendations at the fourth-grade level (Levin and Deane 2003).

The data indicates that measurement is a weakness in fourth grade. It has been recognized that the grade-four mathematics program does not provide adequate experiences for conceptual understanding in measurement. Therefore, supplementary materials have been prepared to provide both students and teachers with the necessary experiences to meet the requirements of the Scope and Sequence for this strand. Similar to

Teachers were able to strategize and plan how the noted weaknesses would be addressed in the classroom.

second and third graders, students in fourth grade also experienced difficulty completing in-out function machines and describing the rule. It is also evident students need consistent opportunities to answer open-response questions. Teachers need to both model appropriate responses and clearly state expectations for adequate responses. It is recommended that teachers use word walls or vocabulary charts or journals that include a visual and explanation to reinforce mathematical language. Students at this grade level performed well on questions involving data analysis. Fourth graders were also able to successfully complete most algebra-related questions.

Teachers at each grade level met as a group,[4] and these results were shared and discussed. As a group, these teachers were able to strategize and plan how the noted weaknesses would be addressed in the classroom. **Students who did particularly poorly were noted and their progress was documented by their teacher in the following year.** Students and teachers who needed additional support were provided assistance by special educators, the mathematics instructional leader, and the math coach. Supplementary materials were organized and given to classroom

---

4   See Chapter 11 for more specific information about data teams.

teachers for units of study in which resources were inadequate.

Questions that individual teachers might ask themselves as a result of the dissemination of such test results include:

- Why are so many students performing poorly in the area of measurement?
- Do I teach this topic for mastery? Do I spend enough time on this topic?
- Do I use/have appropriate curriculum materials needed to successfully teach this topic?
- Why was there a cluster of students who performed poorly in algebra?
- What types of questions were difficult for them?
- What types of problems were problematic for students in numbers and operations?
- Did students understand the language embedded in the problems? Am I checking for understanding with regards to students understanding mathematical vocabulary?

This local use of a statewide assessment also demonstrates an assessment of curriculum that sends the teachers in this district back to looking at the local curriculum standards and pacing guides. Again, this assessment does not diagnose individual students' needs; quality classroom assessments, as discussed earlier in this chapter, address how teachers can move from the standards (the mastery objectives, learning goals or learning targets) to support each student's progress through classroom formative assessment.

How a Secondary School Used State-Wide Assessments

Secondary school teachers use standardized test data in much the same way as elementary school teachers. As you can see in the chart below, at one high school, the percentage of tenth-grade students who fell into each scoring category on the state math test was first compared to similar data from the previous two years.

Figure 4.46   Percentage of Glenbrook Students Scoring in Each Category

	2005–06	2006–07	2007–08
Advanced	3%	0%	4%
Proficient	21%	7%	26%
Needs Imp.	52%	60%	50%
Failing	24%	33%	20%

The information gleaned from this data was generally good news. More students moved out of the *Failing* and *Needs Improvement* categories and into the *Proficient* category.

Next, this data was broken down by the school's various demographics: race/ethnicity, gender, students eligible for free/reduced lunch, etc., and relevant observations were noted, as follows:

Figure 4.47

87% of the students eligible for F/RP lunch passed the math assessment.
74% of the students not eligible for F/RP lunch passed the math assessment.
89% of Glenbrook's African American students passed the math assessment.
77% of Glenbrook's mixed/other students passed the math assessment.
81% of Glenbrook's white students passed the math assessment.
83% of Glenbrook's female students passed the math assessment.
79% of Glenbrook's male students passed the math assessment.

Next, the success of the tenth graders on the different types of questions that made up the math exam was examined in comparison to the results of their peers within the school district.

Figure 4.48 Average Percentage of Questions Answered Correctly, By Category

	Number Sense	Patterns, Relations, Algebra	Geometry	Measurement	Statistics, Probability, Data Analysis
Glenbrook HS	42% correct	45% correct	31% Correct	38% correct	47% correct
District HS	45% correct	44% correct	40% correct	42% correct	51% correct

The data revealed that, in virtually all of the categories, a smaller percentage of Glenbrook's tenth graders correctly answered these questions when compared to the district's tenth graders as a whole. This data was cause for concern. Why did the Glenbrook tenth graders score worse than those in the district as a whole? To answer this question, the administrators and teachers turned to an item analysis in which they examined each question on which the school's tenth graders fared worse than the district's tenth graders. They collected the following information:

5. What is the simplified form of the expression $\sqrt{450}$?
   A. $15\sqrt{2}$
   B. $45\sqrt{2}$
   C. $75\sqrt{2}$
   D. $225\sqrt{2}$

#5 Square Root Question (Multiple Choice, Number Sense)

- 17 percent of Glenbrook students answered correctly (A).
- 35 percent of District students answered correctly.
- 63 percent of Glenbrook students answered D.

It's interesting that so many students thought the answer was D. Perhaps they saw the square root sign as indicating multiplication?

By noting not only how many of the students answered the question correctly but also whether there was another (incorrect) answer that students were drawn to, Glenbrook could start to understand how it should adjust its curriculum to meet the needs of its students. Upon completing an item analysis like this one for each question on the exam, for which the students fared worse than the district as a whole,

Glenbrook could then lay out recommendations for the math department to consider in adjusting its curriculum to support student success. For example, teachers might need to reteach mastered prerequisite skills needed to successfully find the square root of a given number in this particular case.

Achievement versus Growth on Local Assessments

Measuring growth, as opposed to achievement, is a new practice for some teachers. Benchmark tests set goals for specific levels of achievement at different points during the year. For example, some districts want all students to be reading grade-three-level materials by end of the third grade. If a student is above the benchmark, then he or she has achieved more than expected; if another student is below the benchmark, then he or she is at risk for having to struggle with classroom work. In some districts, students below the benchmark are provided targeted instruction to help them meet the benchmark for reading achievement.

In contrast, to measure growth often districts pre-test students at the beginning of the year with the same assessment (or similar in rigor) that they will receive at the end of a unit or course. Unlike being measured for achievement, students who are assessed for growth are not measured against a standard or scale that they must achieve at a specific time. Instead, their change over time is measured, and they are compared only to themselves. The student who was below benchmark might show high growth in third grade because he has worked hard, but may still be below a benchmark. Similarly, a high-achieving student may be above the benchmark, but if at the beginning of the year he or she was above the benchmark, he or she may not demonstrate a high rate of growth.

Measuring the growth individual students make from year to year allows educators to determine the impact schools are having on student learning.

However, some argue that a growth model poses many problems—including deciding how much growth is low growth or high growth, and ensuring that growth expectations calibrated across grades are accurate measures (Olson 2004).

A local assessment of student growth scores is displayed in Figure 4.49 on the next page. The figure shows the results of three classrooms—that of teachers A, B, and C—on a kindergarten writing assessment that used a six-level rubric. Students' scores at the beginning and end of the year were assessed with a local rubric, and the differences between those scores were calculated for each of the students. The median point (middle grade) for these scores was three. It is displayed in black for each class. The low and high scores were locally determined, based on beginning with the lowest 10 percent, and then looking at the individual students' progress during that year based upon other writing assessments and on teacher and specialist discussion. Low improvement was determined to be a movement up two levels. Those scores were for eight students altogether (two, four, and two students in class A, B, and C, respectively). The high scores were determined to be a change of four levels on their six-point rubric. Eleven students were seen as having high growth. When the grade-level team looked at who had made low and high growth, they found that both high- and low-achieving students were in both categories. In other words, a few high-achieving students showed little growth, a few showed average growth, and a few at-risk students also showed little growth. The same held true at the high-growth end of the scale; high growth was seen in high, average, and at-risk students. This check of the achievement levels in both the high and low groups is an important check that all students, high and at risks, had opportunity to demonstrate growth. This assessment provided equal opportunity for all students to show growth.

In its analysis of the growth of its students, one district discovered that those students who began the year scoring well often made little progress. The district decided to look more carefully to see if sufficiently challenging work was provided to the students, if the assessment itself put a "ceiling" on the students' opportunity to demonstrate growth, or if the assessment itself was flawed.

> *Teachers' assessment literacy is beginning to increase as teachers become more fluent in using results of standardized, state or province, district, and teacher-developed formal and informal assessments.*

Conclusion

Effective assessment and learning are interwoven within the teaching and learning process. Because of many years of accountability testing, teachers' assessment literacy is beginning to increase as teachers become more fluent in using the results of standardized, state or province, district, and teacher-developed formal and informal assessments. In addition, many teams of educators work to align their grades with one another in order to calibrate their scoring and ensure inter-rater reliability within their school or district. In addition, in many classrooms, assessment has progressed beyond textbook quizzes and tests and often encompasses observation, conferencing, providing feedback, data collecting, recording, standards-based grading, and analysis.

Formative assessment's power to support students' learning has been recognized and documented by research. Teachers now know that to be effective, both the teacher and the student must play an active role in setting and achieving educational goals using the assessment process as a powerful tool. Effective formative assessment requires that teachers and students communicate frequently throughout the learning process. Instead of having a test locked away in a closet, as in years past, assessment in the classroom has become a transparent and ongoing process—not simply a test at the end of a unit, but an open process in which the learning goals are shared at the beginning of the unit, and students practice without fear of grades until they are prepared for a summative assessment.

As educators, it is our responsibility to use a variety of assessments effectively in order to maximize success for each and every one of our students.

References

ACT. *Reading between the Lines: What the ACT Reveals About College Readiness in Reading.* Iowa City, IA: ACT, Inc., 2006.

Albert, L.R. "Outside-In—Inside-Out: Seventh Grade Students' Mathematical Thought Processes." *Educational Studies in Mathematics* 41, no. 2 (2000): 109–142.

Albert, L., Mayotte, G., and Sohn, S, Cutler, S. "Making Observations Interactive." *Mathematics Teaching in the Middle School* 7, no. 7 (2002): 396–401. Reprinted with permission. All rights reserved.

References continue on page 206

Figure 4.49   Kindergarten Writing Assessment

Teach. A		Beginning	End	Growth	Teach. B		Beginning	End	Growth	Teach. C		Beginning	End	Growth
Teach. A	student	0	2	2	Teach. B	student	0	0	0	Teach. C	student	0	2	2
Teach. A	student	0	2	2	Teach. B	student	0	2	2	Teach. C	student	0	2	2
Teach. A	student	0	3	3	Teach. B	student	0	2	2	Teach. C	student	0	3	3
Teach. A	student	0	3	3	Teach. B	student	0	2	2	Teach. C	student	0	3	3
Teach. A	student	0	3	3	Teach. B	student	0	3	3	Teach. C	student	0	3	3
Teach. A	student	0	3	3	Teach. B	student	0	3	3	Teach. C	student	0	3	3
Teach. A	student	1	4	3	Teach. B	student	0	3	3	Teach. C	student	0	3	3
Teach. A	student	0	3	3	Teach. B	student	0	3	3	Teach. C	student	0	3	3
Teach. A	student	0	3	**3**	Teach. B	student	0	3	**3**	Teach. C	student	0	3	3
Teach. A	student	0	3	3	Teach. B	student	0	3	3	Teach. C	student	0	3	**3**
Teach. A	student	0	3	3	Teach. B	student	0	3	3	Teach. C	student	0	3	3
Teach. A	student	0	3	3	Teach. B	student	0	3	3	Teach. C	student	0	3	3
Teach. A	student	0	3	3	Teach. B	student	0	3	3	Teach. C	student	0	3	3
Teach. A	student	0	3	3	Teach. B	student	0	3	3	Teach. C	student	0	3	3
Teach. A	student	0	3	3	Teach. B	student	0	3	3	Teach. C	student	0		3
Teach. A	student	0	3	3	Teach. B	student	0	3	3	Teach. C	student	0	3	3
Teach. A	student	0	4	4	Teach. B	student	0	3	3	Teach. C	student	0	3	3
Teach. A	student	0	4	4	Teach. B	student	0	3	3	Teach. C	student	0	3	3
					Teach. B	student	0	4	4	Teach. C	student	0	4	4
					Teach. B	student	0	4	4	Teach. C	student	0	4	4
					Teach. B	student	0	4	4	Teach. C	student	0	4	4
					Teach. B	student	0	4	4	Teach. C	student	0	4	4

median		
	2	Class median
	2	Low Growth
	4	High Growth

Arter, J.A. and Busick, K.U. *Practice with Student Involved Classroom Assessment.* Portland, OR: Assessment Training Institute, 2001.

Arter, J. and McTighe, J. *Scoring Rubrics in the Classroom: Using Performance Criteria for Assessing and Improving Student Performance.* Thousand Oaks, CA: Corwin Press, Inc., 2001.

Assessment Reform Group. "Assessment for Learning: 10 Principles." London: School of Curriculum, Pedagogy and Assessment, Institute of Education, 2002.. http://www.assessment-reform-group.org.uk/publications.html.

Atkin, J.M., Black, P., and Coffey, J. *Classroom Assessment and the National Science Education Standards.* Washington, DC: National Academy Press, 2001.

Baldwin, D. "A Guide to Standardized Writing Assessment." *Educational Leadership* 62, no. 2 (October 2004): 72–75.

Bambrick-Santoyo, P. "Coaching—and Teaching—for Results." *Phi Delta Kappan* 94, no. 5 (2013): 70–71.

Black, P. and Wiliam, D. "Assessment and Classroom Learning." *Assessment in Education: Principles, Policy, and Practice* 5, no. 1 (1998): 7–74.

Black, P. and Wiliam, D. "Inside the Black Box: Raising Standards through Classroom Assessment." *Phi Delta Kappan* 80, no. 2 (October 1998): 139–148.

Bloom, B.S., Madaus, G.F., and Hastings, T.J. *Evaluation to Improve Learning.* New York: McGraw-Hill, 1981.

Brookhart, S.M. *How to Create and Use Rubrics for Formative Assessment and Grading.* Alexandria, VA: Association for Supervision and Curriculum Development, 2013.

Burns, M. "Looking at How Students Reason." *Educational Leadership* 63, no. 3 (November 2005): 26–31.

Carey, B., "Exams Measure What We Know, But They're Also One of the Best Ways to Learn," *New York Times Magazine,* September 7, 2014.

"Casco Bay Charter School Family Grading Guide." http://cbhs.portlandschools.org/UserFiles/Servers/Server_1098483/File/Migration/Casco-Bay-Family-Grading-Guide.pdf.

Chapman, C. *Authentic Writing Assessment.* ERIC Document Reproduction Service no. ED 328 606. Washington, DC: American Institutes for Research, 1990.

Chappuis, J. "Thoughtful Assessment with the Learner in Mind." *Educational Leadership* 71, no. 6 (2014): 20–26.

Chappuis, S. and Chappuis, J. "The Best Value in Formative Assessment." *Educational Leadership* 65, no. 4 (December 2007/January 2008): 14–19.

Chappuis, S. and Stiggens, R J. "Classroom Assessment for Learning." *Educational Leadership* 60, no. 1 (2002): 40–43.

Clarke, S. *Unlocking Formative Assessment.* London: Hodder and Stoughton, 2001.

Clymer, J. and Wiliam, D. "Improving the Way We Grade Science." *Educational Leadership* 64 (2006/2007): 36–42.

Conley, D.T. and Darling-Hammond, L. *Creating Systems of Assessment for Deeper Learning.* Stanford, CA: Stanford Center for Opportunity Policy in Education, 2013.

Darling-Hammond, L. "Testing To, and Beyond, the Common Core." *Principal* 93, no. 3 (January/February 2014): 8–12.

Davies, A. *Making Classroom Assessment Work.* Courtenay, BC: Classroom Connections International, Inc., 2000.

Deddeh, H., Main, E., and Ratzlaf Fulkerson, S. "Eight Steps to Meaningful Grading." *Phi Delta Kappan* 91, no. 7 (2010): 54–60.

Dirksen, D.J. "Hitting the Reset Button: Using Formative Assessment to Guide Instruction." *Phi Delta Kappan* 92, no. 7 (April 2011): 26–31.

Dueck, M. *Grading Smarter, Not Harder: Assessment Strategies that Motivate Kids and Help Them Learn.* Alexandria, VA: ASCD, 2014.

Duckor, B. "Using Assessments Thoughtfully: Formative Assessment in Seven Good Moves," *Educational Leadership* 71, no. 6 (2014): 28-32.

Education Week Research Center. "A Fresh Approach to Ranking States on Education." *Education Week* 34, no. 16 (January 2015): 32–33. http://www.edweek.org/ew/articles/2015/01/08/a-fresh-approach-to-ranking-states-on-education.html.

Fisher, D. and Frey, N. "Choice Words." *Principal Leadership* 13, no. 4 (2012): 57–59.

Gardner, H. *Frames of Mind: The Theory of Multiple Intelligences.* New York: Basic Books, 1984.

Gator, C., Jones, J., O'Brien, A., Patterson, S., Rooney, R., Good, E., et al. *Pupil Self-Assessment.* Retrieved April 15, 2004, http://www.aaia.org.uk/pdf/aaia format4.pdf.

Goodrich, H. "Understanding Rubrics." *Educational Leadership* 54, no. 4 (December 1996/January 1997): 14–17.

Graham, S., Harris, K., and Hebert, M. *Informing Writing.* New York: Carnegie Corporation, 2011.

Guskey, T.R. *On Your Mark: Challenging the Conventions of Grading and Reporting.* Bloomington, IN: Solution Tree Press, 2014.

Hattie, J. "High-Impact Leadership." *Educational Leadership* 72, no. 5 (February 2015): 36–40.

Herman, J., Aschbacher, P., and Winters, L. *A Practical Guide to Alternative Assessment.* Alexandria, VA: ASCD, 1992.

Herman, J. and Linn, R. "New Assessments, New Rigor." *Educational Leadership* 71, no. 6 (March 2014): 34–37.

Hess, K. *Cognitive Rigor Matrix.* Dover, NH: Center for Assessment, 2009. www.nciea.org.

Jouriles, G. "We Don't Need Standardized Tests. Here's Why." *Education Week* 33, no. 36 (July 2014).

Leahy, S., Lyon, C., Thompson, M., and Wiliam, D. "Classroom Assessment Minute by Minute, Day by Day." *Educational Leadership* 63, no. 3 (November 2005): 19-24.

Levin, L. and Deane, J. Report to the School Committee of the Needham, MA, Public Schools, October 2003.

Lincoln, Y. and Guba, E. *Naturalistic Inquiry.* Beverly Hills, CA: Sage Publications, 1984.

MacDonald, R. Unpublished list of questions acquired from Mike Costello, 2007.

MacDonald, R. "Number the Stars Homework Self-assessment." Unpublished self-assessment, 2007.

Marzano, R. *Classroom Assessment and Grading that Work.* Alexandria, VA: ASCD, 2007. Adapted with permission.

Mayo, J.A. "Socially Constructed Knowledge: Using Cooperative Learning in Assessment Instruction." *Pedagogy and the Human Sciences* 1, no. 3 (2013): 52–64.

McTighe, J. and O'Connor, K. "Seven Practices for Effective Learning." *Educational Leadership* 63, no. 3 (November 2005): 10-13.

Mintz, E., Fiarman, S., and Buffett, T. "Digging into Data," in *Data Wise,* eds. Boudett, K.P., City, E.A., and Murnane, R.J. Cambridge, MA: Harvard Education Press, 2006.

Mitchell, R., Willis, M., and Chicago Teachers Union Quest Center. *Learning in Overdrive: Designing Curriculum, Instruction, and Assessment from Standards.* Golden, CO: North American Press, 1995.

Joint Task Force on Assessment of the International Reading Association and the National Council of Teachers of English. *Standards for the Assessment of Reading and Writing,* revised ed., 2010.

O'Connor, K. *A Repair Kit for Grading: 15 Fixes for Broken Grades,* 2nd ed. New York: Pearson, 2010.

Olson, L. "'Value Added' Models Gain in Popularity." *Education Week* 21, no. 12 (November 2004): 1, 14–15.

Partnership for Assessment of Readiness for College and Careers (PARCC). www.parcconline.org/parcc-assessment.

Reeves, D.B. "High Performance in High Poverty Schools: 90/90/90 and Beyond." Center for Performance Assessment, 2003. http://www.lmsvsd.net/cms/lib2/CA01001633/Centricity/Domain/566/90%20Schools.pdf.

Reeves, D.B. *Standards, Assessment, and Accountability: Real Questions from Educators with Real Answers from Douglas B. Reeves, Ph.D.* Englewood, CA: The Leadership and Learning Center, 2010.

Rickards, D. and Cheek, E. *Designing Rubrics for K–6 Classroom Assessment.* Norwood, MA: Christopher-Gordon Publishers, Inc., 1999.

Rutherford, P. *Instruction for All Students.* Alexandria, VA: Just ASK Publications, 2002.

Sadler, D.R. "Formative Assessment and the Design of Instructional Systems." *Instructional Science* 18 (1989): 119–144.

Saddler, B. and Andrade, H. "The Writing Rubric." *Educational Leadership* 62, no. 2 (October 2004): 48–52. Used with permission.

Safer, N. and Fleischman, S. "How Student Progress Monitoring Improves Instruction." *Educational Leadership* 62, no. 5 (February 2005): 81–83.

Saphier, J. and Gower, R. *The Skillful Teacher.* Carlisle, MA: Research for Better Teaching, 1997.

Shanahan, T. "Let's Get Higher Scores on These New Assessments." *The Reading Teacher* 68, no. 6 (March 2015): 459–463.

Shepard, L.A. *Using Assessment to Help Students Think about Learning.* Keynote address at the Assessment Training Institute Summer Conference, Portland, OR, July 2001.

Silberman, J. "All about My Learning Self-Assessment." Unpublished self-assessment, 2003.

Stenmark, J.K. *Modern Assessment: Myths, Models, Good Questions, and Practical Suggestions.* Reston, VA: National Council of Teachers of Mathematics, 1991.

Sternberg, R. *Successful Intelligence: How Practical and Creative Intelligence Determines Success in Life.* New York: Simon and Schuster, 1996.

Stiggins, R. "Assessment for Learning: A Key to Motivation and Achievement." *EDge* 2, no. 2 (November/December 2006): 3–19.

Stiggins, R. "Assessment through the Student's Eyes." *Educational Leadership* 64, no. 8 (May 2007): 22–26.

Stiggins, R. "Improve Assessment Literacy Outside of Schools Too." *Phi Delta Kappan* 96, no. 2 (October 2014): 67–72.

Strickland, K. and Strickland, J. *Making Assessment Elementary.* Portsmouth, NH: Heinemann, 2000.

Stuart, L F. *Assessment in Practice: Creating a School Culture of Learning and Assessment.* Newton Lower Falls, MA: Teachers 21, 2003.

Taylor, S. "Can Peer Review Help Johnny Write Better?" *Education Digest* 80, no. 4 (October 2014): 4–10.

Tomlinson, C.A. "The Bridge between Today's Lesson and Tomorrow's." *Educational Leadership* 71, no. 6 (2014): 10–14.

Varlas, L. "Improving Student Writing through Formative Assessments." *Educational Update,* 54, no. 2 (2012),1.

Westley, J. *Puddle Questions: Assessing Mathematical Thinking: Grade 5.* Mountain View, CA: Creative Publications, 1994.

Wiggins, G. *Assessing Student Performance: Exploring the Purpose and Limits of Testing.* San Francisco, CA: Jossey-Bass Publishers, 1993.

Wiggins, G. *Educative Assessment: Designing Assessments to Inform and Improve Student Performance.* San Francisco, CA: Jossey-Bass, 1998.

Wiggins, G. and McTighe, J. *Understanding by Design.* Alexandria, VA: ASCD, 1998.

Wiggins, G. "Why We Should Stop Bashing State Tests." *Educational Leadership* 67, no. 6 (March 2010): 48-52.

Young, E. "Enhancing Student Writing by Teaching Self-Assessment Strategies That Incorporate the Criteria of Good Writers." Unpublished doctoral diss., Rutgers University, 2000.

Zwiers, J. and Ford, M. *Academic Conversations: Classroom Talk that Fosters Critical Thinking and Content Understanding.* Portland, ME: Stenhouse Publishing, 2011.

Students with Disabilities: Assessing Learning

Starting with No Child Left Behind (NCLB) and continuing with Common Core (CC), the purpose, use, feeling, meaning, and understanding of assessments in education varies depending on who is engaged in the discussion. One thing is certain: NCLB changed the playing field for students with disabilities, from how and where they are taught to their participation in various assessments. As the educational system continues to evolve, balancing the use of assessments and how they inform instruction, interventions, and accommodations for students with disabilities will continue to be part of the process.

The negative impact of 40 years of a separate curriculum for students with disabilities raises the question of whether we continue to use assessments to measure the status quo or use good assessments to ensure that students with disabilities have access to, and are successful in, a rigorous general education curriculum (Thurlow 2011). Much of the literature and guidance on the Common Core and other national curricula speaks of ensuring that there are rigorous grade-level expectations in math and English language arts (ELA), and that students with disabilities must be challenged to excel within the general curriculum and be prepared post-school, including college and careers. Assessments elucidate an important concern of teachers and families of students with disabilities, and that is *how* the high standards will be taught (Common Core State Standards Initiative 2015).

This chapter outlined the three major purposes of assessment: to improve student learning and performance, to improve teaching, and to improve schools. Those three purposes fall into one or both areas: *assessment for learning* or *assessment of learning*. For students with disabilities, assessment for learning makes the difference in how successful they are accessing the general education classroom and curriculum.

The impact of a student's disability often challenges his or her connectedness to the general education classroom. Using assessment for learning is very focused on the interaction between the teacher and the student; this could greatly support the goal of creating a sense of connectedness to the general education classroom that the student needs.

Ongoing and frequent progress monitoring guides teachers in adjusting their instruction or exploring different accommodations to meet student's individual needs, while giving the student feedback on his or her performance and skills. The feedback that a teacher gives is very descriptive, such as exploring the step(s) that a student may have missed while working a mathematical equation, and talking with the student about how to correct the problem. Progress monitoring is a process to assess students' academic performance to quantify a students' rate of improvement in response to the instruction that is given (Progress Monitoring 2015). Progress monitoring is a powerful way to use assessment for both the teacher and student.

Students with disabilities often struggle with maintaining their motivation. Using student progress-tracking charts with a student with a disability can serve as a motivator for the student by allowing them to not only see areas where they are doing well, but also areas that the student requires a different instructional strategy or support. Tracking student progress is becoming easier with technology. A number of websites and tablet applications have been developed for this purpose.

The academic challenges that students with disabilities face as they get older have unintentional consequences, such as interfering with the ability to understand the purpose of a task or activity. Other unintentional consequences are low self-esteem and fear of failure. Therefore, as teachers give attention to the characteristics of good assessment tasks by making assessments meaningful, purposeful, and connected to everyday life, they also support students with disabilities to overcome the unintentional consequences that are a result of their academic challenges.

Working with Students with Disabilities: Portfolios, Test Anxiety, Exemplars, Anchor Papers, and Rubrics

The use of student portfolios are very effective in working with students with disabilities. Since the spectrum of disabilities and their effects vary greatly depending on the individual, using portfolio assessments allows students with greater effects of their disability to participate in the general education classroom and have meaningful, purposeful tasks and experiences that are aligned with the general curriculum. For students whose disabilities have a lesser effect, portfolio assessments help them assess their own level of growth and progress over time. They also give families more insight into the level of growth and how they can support their student at home. It should be noted that portfolio assessments can be taxing on teachers to compile; therefore, instructing students and modeling the compilation of the portfolio allow students to take more responsibility and oversight of this part of their work. These actions also allow the teacher to act as the facilitator, rather than taking on another task. Students gain valuable skills while compiling their own portfolios, such as improved organization, analysis, and self-assessment—all needed to be successful in the general curriculum. Portfolios are also a great way to connect to the monitoring and development of the student's Individualized Education Plan (IEP) goals and objectives. For students with disabilities, any connections that can be made between general education curriculum and special education services ensure the success of closing the achievement gap for the student.

Test anxiety, for many learning-disabled students, is also a very real debilitation and may affect the outcome of the typical paper-and-pencil summative assessment. It is for these reasons that summative assessments should have options for demonstrating student knowledge, for example, presentations, podcasts, or projects. If the choices are carefully planned and designed based on the standards, then it should be easy for the teacher to determine the student's level of mastery.

For many learning-disabled students, it is difficult to read a set of directions for a project or paper and visualize exactly what the teacher is requesting. They need to see a **model or exemplar (or anchor papers)** of the finished product to fully understand the teacher's expectations. Providing a **rubric** up front will also help the learning-disabled student know what criteria will be factored into the grading and how the product will be evaluated.

Rubrics containing more than one criterion within a rubric 'box' are often difficult to score, as it is unlikely that a student will meet all the criteria within the 'box.' Therefore, it becomes necessary to highlight the conditions met as they are scattered throughout the numerical headings. A good example of this is the *Romeo and Juliet* Writing Assignment Rubric found in this chapter. With just one criteria within each 'box,' it is easier for the teacher to score and for students to know where they stand in meeting that skill.

For rubrics to be a truly valuable tool for students with learning disabilities to use as the standard of quality by which to assess their own work, they need to become a routine (see Chapter 3 for information on effectively teaching routines) that is taught and practiced in the classroom. To make a rubric an even more valuable writing tool, with each new writing assignment, students should be asked to refer to their previously scored rubrics and choose a criterion that they specifically want to address in the new assignment. This form of **self-assessment** allows students with learning disabilities to target a skill on which to focus, and because they chose it, they will be more invested in meeting their own goals.

References

"Application to Students with Disabilities." *Common Core State Standards Initiative*. http://www.corestandards.org/assets/application-to-students-with-disabilities.pdf.

Center on Response to Intervention. "Progress Monitoring." *American Institutes for Research*. http://www.rti4success.org/essential-components-rti/progress-monitoring.

Thurlow, M.L. "Common Core State Standards: Implications for Students with Disabilities." Lecture, regional meeting of National Association of State Boards of Education, Las Vegas, NV, August 12, 2011.

English Language Learners and Using Teacher-Made, Local and State Assessments to Inform Your Instruction

English Learner Identification

To identify potential English learners, districts and school boards have a registration process for all public school students that may be conducted at a central location or at the child's school. First, qualified staff will conduct an interview that includes a home-language survey or another instrument that assesses which language(s) is or are spoken at home, with whom the student communicates in those languages, and how frequently the child listens to and/or speaks languages other than English. It is important that family members and students feel welcomed and comfortable so that relevant information is discussed simply and accurately. Some parents may not be accustomed to school personnel asking questions that seem personal. It helps to reassure the family that their responses will only be used to place the child in the most appropriate academic program. When possible, the interview should be conducted in the family's home language or an interpreter should be present. The purpose of the initial interview is to discern whether a child should participate in an English proficiency assessment—the results of which will determine the student's need for English language development support.

The responses from the intake interview and on the home-language survey determine whether a child should participate in English proficiency testing. Some potential English learners, such as foster children or adoptees, may have English as their home language but also understand and speak a language other than English. For these children, other means of identifying language proficiency are recommended. In addition, if a classroom teacher observes that a linguistically diverse student is struggling because of language barriers, the teacher can recommend the student for further English language proficiency testing, even if the child was found to be a fluent English speaker upon registration and after initial testing.

When the home-language survey indicates a potential English learner, the child participates in an English language proficiency assessment. Districts and school boards may decide which assessment tool to use, but the assessments must be valid and reliable ones, such as the Individuals with Disabilities Education Act (IDEA) proficiency test (IPT), Language Assessment Survey Links, or the World Class Instructional Design and Assessment (WIDA) Access

Placement Test. The ESL teacher, bilingual educator, or other qualified designee administers ELP test items and interprets results in reading, writing, speaking, and listening. The student's English language proficiency levels are communicated with parents and guardians and used to determine in which class or classes the student will be placed. The ELP data can also serve as a baseline for evaluating students' future progress in acquiring English proficiency. ELP test scores, results of interviews, the home-language survey, and evidence of previous English language support are placed in each student's cumulative records folder. ESL and other support teachers may keep their own files that contain copies of ELL-related data, so that they may easily access and share for placement, planning, and assessment purposes.

English Language Learner Placement

Once the ELP assessment results determine a student is an English learner, he or she will be placed in a classroom that facilitates access to an English language support program. Districts with high incidence populations of English learners will have several teachers licensed in ESL and/or bilingual education. These educators collaborate with general education teachers and support staff on teams that are intentionally organized to address and meet the needs of English learners. The team collectively makes decisions regarding placement, additional support programs, assessment, and instruction. Schools with low-incidence populations of English learners may rely on the ESL, Title 1, or reading teacher to make educational recommendations and to provide direct individual or small-group instruction for English language development. States and provinces provide guidance on the amount of time students at each proficiency level should receive for support in English language development/ESL. The number of minutes may be increased or decreased according to progress made in learning English and in acquiring subject matter knowledge and skills.

Local Assessment

Upon placement or soon thereafter, English learners often participate in tests that aim to assess grade-level literacy and math skills. Since first-language literacy is a precursor to success in acquiring English (Goldenberg 2008), testing students in their home language is highly recommended. English learners will also participate in locally made grade-level or benchmark assessments, screening tools, or progress-monitoring tests meant for the general education population. Examples of these tests include the Developmental Reading Assessment (DRA or DRA2), Scholastic Phonics Inventory (SPI), and Dynamic Indicators of Basic Early Literacy Skills (DIBELS). Guidance is available on how these tools should consider English learners, and it is beneficial to use these instruments in conjunction with other literacy assessments that are specifically developed to assess the skills of English learners (e.g., Language Assessment Scales Links or WIDA MODEL). General literacy screening may suggest potential reading issues, and when this happens, English learners should receive additional academic support. This might be one-on-one or small-group instruction provided by a licensed reading teacher, Title 1 teacher, or literacy specialist. Some subpopulations of English learners require more intensive academic support and potentially a different learning environment. These students may include those who have limited or interrupted formal education, physical disabilities, or diagnosed learning disabilities.

Accountability: State and Provincial Assessments

Students with disabilities and English learners are often included in state, provincial, or national assessments of English language arts, math, social studies and science. English learners in their first year in US schools may be exempt from the English language arts test, but participate in all other testing. Accommodations for English learners can include a bilingual word-to-word dictionary, extended time, and sometimes, based on proficiency level, access to an interpreter.

Since districts, states, and provinces can be accountable for measurable progress in attainment of English fluency, English learners are required to participate annually in testing that measures progress in English language proficiency. Examples of these include the New York State ESL Achievement Test (NYSESLAT), the Texas English Language Proficiency Assessment System (TELPAS), or WIDA's Assessing Comprehension and Communication in English State-to-State (ACCESS). Similar to the baseline ELP screener assessment, the results of state, provincial, or national proficiency testing measures student progress in reading, writing, speaking, and listening. Results are sent home to parents and guardians in a language they can understand, and scores include explanations of measurable progress. For the districts, regions, or school systems that have a high incidence of English

language learners, there are three areas of ELL progress that are measured: learning English, attainment of English, and progress in assessment results on tests for all students.

Guidance for Teachers: Activities and Assessments of Skills and Knowledge

When English learners participate in lessons and assessments in the general-education or mainstream classroom, their tests, activities, and assignments can be analyzed for obstacles than might hinder English learners' performance. English learners struggle with unfamiliar cultural assumptions, de-contextualized vocabulary, and language that is dense or demanding (e.g., figurative language, challenging sentence structures, and colloquial speech). When creating assessments for English learners, thoughtful consideration should be given to these influential factors:

English Language Learners: Factors to Consider When Creating Assessments

- cultural background and educational experience
- oral fluency, pre-literacy, or literacy assessment results in English and the primary language (when possible)
- English language proficiency standards and general-education curriculum standards for student's age and grade level
- diagnosed learning disability and/or other disability or learning need(s)
- linguistic demand of content-area class, projects, and class discussion
- context needed for comprehension during text-rich or cognitively challenging lessons
- kind and amount of printed and oral language, specific vocabulary, and complexity of language necessary to demonstrate understanding and skills

Teachers can ask themselves, "Is this a language test, a science test, or both a language and science test? Am I asking my students to summarize what they have read, or am I expecting students to understand and apply language from the text/discussion? Will students understand and use expected vocabulary and phrases? What language does the text, discussion, or assessment include that might not be comprehensible to an English learner?" In order for teachers to fully understand what knowledge and skills an English learner possesses, the activity and assessment tools must rely on which language students at each proficiency level are capable of understanding and producing. When assessment items are not comprehensible, test results will demonstrate which language the student does not know but fails to measure what the student does know about literature, math, social studies, or science.

The following table provides ways for students at varying English proficiency levels to demonstrate what they know or have learned. These activities can rely solely on oral-language production and listening skills for students who are developing reading skills in English.

English Language Learners: Ways for Students at Varying English Proficiency Levels to Demonstrate What They Know or Have Learned

Student New to Learning English	Student with Intermediate English Proficiency	Student with Higher English Proficiency
• Responds physically to oral prompts for sequencing and identifying vocabulary. • Matches new vocabulary with visuals, charts, or graphs. • Sequences events using pictures. • Label maps, diagrams, and parts of a whole. • Manipulates and classifies real-life objects, countables, and tools. • Identifies, understands, and uses data collected on graphs. • Participates in activity, task, or dialogue that contextualizes language and employs new academic vocabulary. • Answers questions with simple language structures and vocabulary. • Identifies, understands, and uses sample solutions, phrases, sentence frames, or language structures.	• Understands and uses comprehensible language and text with familiar structures and vocabulary. • Uses sentence samples and sentences frames that require some technical vocabulary. • Answers objective questions with familiar structures and vocabulary. • Identifies solutions and answers when given multiple-choice (both oral and written) questions. • Responds to prompts with multiple sentences, appropriate register, and some technical vocabulary. • Locates and summarizes information. • Retells stories with details and logical order. • Connects topics, activities, and texts to personal experiences. • Analyzes and interprets data from graphs and charts.	• Makes inferences and conclusions on information presented with academic language and/or formal register. • Participates in extended discourse with academic language. • Identifies others' opinions and defends own opinion on topics. • Persuades using appropriate academic register. • Interprets information and reports out on findings/conclusions. • Synthesizes ideas and information. • Collects and uses information in inquiry-based assignments and projects.

References

2012 Amplification of the English Language Development Standards, Kindergarten–12th Grade. Madison, WI: Board of Regents of the University of Wisconsin System/WIDA, 2013.

Donnelly, W.B. and Roe, C.J. "Using Sentence Frames to Develop Academic Vocabulary for English Learners." *Reading Teacher* 64, no. 2 (2010): 131–136.

Goldenberg, C. "Teaching English Learners: What the Research Does—and Does Not—Say." *American Educator* 8, no. 44 (Summer 2008): 8–44.

Goldenberg, C. "Unlocking the Research on English Learners: What We Know—and Don't Yet Know—about Effective Instruction." *American Educator* 37, no. 2 (Summer 2013): 4–38.

Hellman, A. "Assessment with P–12 English Language Learners." http://www.academia.edu/466047/Assessment_with_P-12_English_language_learners, accessed May 18, 2015.

Kaminski, R. and Cummings, K.D. "DIBELS: Myths and Facts." Dynamic Measurement Group. 2007.

https://dibels.org/dmgaction.html. https://dibels.org/papers/Myths_0208.pdf.

Linquanti, R. and Bailey, A.L. "Reprising the Home Language Survey: A Summary of a National Working Session on Policies, Practices, and Tools for Identifying Potential English Learners." Washington, DC: The Council of Chief State School Officers, 2014.

"Supporting English Learners: A Practical Guide for Ontario Educators, Grades 1–8." Ontario, Canada: Queen's Printer for Ontario, 2008.

US Department of Education. "Tools and Resources for Identifying All English Learners," http://www2.ed.gov/about/offices/list/oela/english-learner-toolkit/chap1.pdf, 2015.

Wolf, M.K., Herman, J.L., and Dietel, R. "Improving the Validity of English Language Learner Assessment Systems." *CRESST Policy Brief 10* (Spring 2010). Los Angeles, CA: University of California, National Center for Research on Evaluation, Standards, and Student Testing (CRESST).

Questioning, Dipsticking, and In-the-Moment, "Short-Cycle" Formative Assessments That Target Mastery

Objectives for the Chapter

After reading the chapter, the reader will be able to

a. use questions effectively

b. use student responses to assess their students' progress toward mastery

c. provide students with effective, actionable feedback

d. use formative and in-the-moment assessment results to move all students toward mastery

e. use formative and in-the-moment assessments to modify instruction to meet students' needs

f. increase the number of students who ask and answer questions

g. elevate the level of responses to oral and written questions and to student responses

"Who has 17.3 as an answer?

"Thumbs halfway if you still have questions about developing a hook."

"Vote with your feet! Is Gatsby Great? Go to the back of the class if you agree; to the front if you disagree. Stand in the middle of the classroom if you're split between the two sides."

Questions make up a central part of the dialogue between teachers and their students. Research indicates that questioning is second only to lecturing in popularity as a teaching method and that classroom teachers spend anywhere from 35 to 50 percent of their instructional time conducting questioning sessions (Cotton 2012, p. 3).

Questions are a powerful tool that can support student learning when they are used to modify instruction. The three questions above serve as formative assessments if the way students respond determines the next step for the lesson or confirms that they should proceed as planned. For example, if 17.3 were an incorrect answer resulting from a specific misunderstanding, the teacher might reteach the concept to those who misunderstood instead of moving on. Or, if the thumbs indicated no general confusion about developing a hook, the teacher could move on to the next step in writing a paper as planned. Finally, if most of the class took one position when they voted with their feet, the teacher might invite some of the students to be "devil's advocates" and take the opposite side so that the class was more equally balanced as they began a debate.

213

Purposes of Questioning

Teachers ask students questions for five major purposes: (1) to assess student learning and inform instruction, (2) to probe more deeply about students' thinking and promote higher-order thinking, (3) to keep students engaged, and (4) to activate prior learning. In the first section on questioning in this chapter, we will examine each of the reasons for asking students questions, as well as the particular strategies and types of questions most effective for achieving the desired results. Figure 5.1 briefly summarizes the various purposes for questions.

Responses to a teacher's questions can also be considered data that teachers invite with their questions—that is, as formative assessments. The second half of this chapter focuses on how to use student in-the-moment answers to significantly improve student achievement.

The Questioning Process for Teachers

In *Highly Effective Questioning*, Ivan Hannel (2005) writes that a common and appropriate time for teachers to ask students questions is upon completing a "mini-lesson" of direct instruction. Such questioning "helps to indicate to the teacher whether or not a student has learned something that was assigned." Hannel also notes that an intense period of questioning following direct instruction enables the teacher to understand how the students understand the content to which they have been exposed. For example, upon completing a read-aloud of the final scene from *A Raisin in the Sun* in which different students have taken on the roles of various characters, we might follow this activity with several questions about the plot, themes, and literary elements that emerge during the scene, such as the following examples:

Figure 5.1 Purposes for Questioning

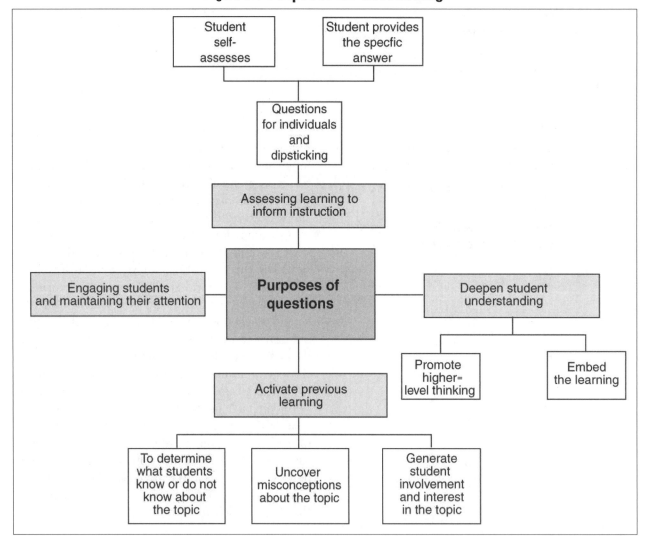

1. What is the final object that Mama takes with her as she leaves the apartment?
2. Why was that old plant so important to her?
3. What kind of look do the stage directions describe as coming over Mama's face as she takes one final look around her apartment?
4. What kind of challenges might the Younger family face in their new neighborhood?
5. How would you describe this play's resolution?

In different ways, each of these questions seeks to assess the degree to which students understand the play's conclusion. As you can see from these questions, the final scene in *A Raisin in the Sun* depends on a few small symbols and gestures to make significant points. For example, Mama carries her withered old houseplant as she leaves the apartment. The first two questions are checking if students remember that Mama had purchased this plant several decades previously when she and her husband first moved into the apartment and that, earlier in the play, Mama had spoken admiringly of the plant's ability to stay alive despite the scarcity of light the apartment receives. (A higher-order thinking question, described in subsequent pages of this chapter, might ask students to note the ways in which the plant's life is symbolic of Mama's life.) The third question—about Mama's facial expression described in the stage directions—seeks to determine if students noted this subtle but important descriptor and, more importantly, if they understand why Mama's face might betray a wide range of emotions as she leaves behind the apartment in which she has raised her family and experienced her husband's death.

Finally, questions four and five seek to find out if students understand the complexity of the play's resolution—that the African American Younger family is ready to leave behind their decrepit old apartment, but that uncertainty and danger may await them in their new, all-white neighborhood. Asking these questions allows the teacher to assess students' understanding of the play and also to gain a deeper understanding of how students are reacting to the play. The benefit of incorporating these questions into a class discussion is that students with varying levels of insight into the play's conclusion may learn from one other's comments and questions. Asking students to respond to these questions in writing in a "quick write," for example, would provide a clearer gauge of the depth of each student's understanding and could

Hannel also notes that an intense period of questioning following direct instruction enables the teacher to understand how the students understand the content to which they have been exposed.

be used as a formative assessment to shape future questions and activities. For example, if students did not notice the description of Mama's facial expression in the stage directions or are having difficulty deciphering its meaning, we might arrange for students to watch this final scene on video and pay close attention to the facial expression that the actress playing Mama conveys in the play's final moments. Or students might be asked to return to the stage directions to discover why her expression was important in the play. Watching a video might benefit the class's more visual learners; returning to the text might make the importance of stage directions clearer. Both activities would allow more students to gain a deeper understanding of the author's craft of the playwright, Lorraine Hansberry, in the final pages of *A Raisin in the Sun*.

In addition, some of these questions are closed, recall questions with one answer, and others are open-ended and higher-order questions with many appropriate ways of responding. The balance of higher-order and recall questions changes as students progress through the grades. After fourth grade, according to Jessica Fries-Gaither from the Science Foundation:

The use of a high frequency (50 percent or more) of higher-cognitive questions with older students is positively related to increases in on-task behavior, length of student responses, the number of relevant contributions, the number of student-to-student interactions, student use of complete sentences, thinking, and relevant questions posed by students (Fries-Gaither 2008).

Thus, questions five and six would support academic discourse and elevate the level of discussion in this high school class.

Questioning during a Mini-Lesson

Consider an elementary example of questioning about similes. Before presenting the lesson, the teacher asks the students what they know about similes. By pre-assessing his or her students, the teacher is able to gather data about what they already know about similes so that he or she can match the lesson with the needs of the students.

Next, the teacher defines the term *simile* and provides the students with several examples. Then he or she gives the students 10 sentences, some of which contain a simile and others do not. The teacher asks a student to read the first sentence, and students are asked to put their thumbs up if they think the sentence contains a simile and their thumbs down if they believe the sentence does not. In this way, the teacher quickly assesses his or her students formatively and now knows there is a need to provide more direct instruction or if the teacher should move the lesson forward.

In the next type of questioning, the teacher asks students to compare two different objects using a simile. He or she then asks the students to share their similes. Again, the teacher is formatively assessing students as he or she looks at their work and listens to their responses. When the teacher determines that students can successfully write similes, they are asked to begin incorporating them into a quick write about a humorous, wordless video by Pinkar, "For the Birds," or another quick story with vivid images that support creating comparisons.

Dipsticking to Decide Whether to Move On, Reteach, or Differentiate

Another quick form of assessment that can be used as the teacher is providing direct instruction or directing a learning activity is called **dipsticking**, a term coined by Madeline Hunter (1982). Just as one uses a dipstick to gauge a car's oil level, a teacher uses questions to gauge the level of understanding of his or her students. And just as the prudent car owner regularly checks his or her oil level in order to detect potential problems in their early stages, dipsticking provides clear evidence of miscommunications and misunderstandings as they occur so that reteaching or clarification can be added to the lesson. Depending on the level of misunderstanding, a teacher can make the decision to reteach a concept to the entire class, move on to the next activity if students demonstrate keen understanding of the lesson, or differentiate instruction to allow some students who "get it" to move on while simultaneously reteaching students still struggling for mastery of the particular skill or concept. More information on differentiating instruction can be found in Chapter 6.

While the term *dipsticking* may refer to teachers asking questions of individual students over the course of a lesson, it can also be used more deliberately as a system that allows a teacher to quickly "check in" with each student in the class simultaneously. For example, a middle school teacher we know purchased a large dry-erase board from a local hardware store and asked the

> *Just as one uses a dipstick to gauge a car's oil level, a teacher uses questions to gauge the level of understanding of his or her students.*

hardware store to cut up the board into individual, one-foot-by-one-foot squares. At the beginning of this teacher's class, each student would pick up a mini dry-erase board and a dry-erase marker from the back of the classroom and keep it on his or her desk for the entire class. At various points in a given lesson, the teacher poses a question to the entire class and then instructs students to write their responses on the dry-erase boards. After a minute or two has passed, the teacher asks students to hold up their responses, and she quickly assesses the level of understanding for the class.

Audience response systems—which use software and whiteboards sometimes called *clickers* that can collect student responses and display the results immediately in graphs—can be used for dipsticking. Websites like Edmodo and mobile apps like Socrative also provide free access to quizzes in mathematics and language arts questions with immediate results for each student, groups of students, and the whole class. Thumbs up, note cards with quick answers, exit slips, or multicolored slips of paper can also be used without using technology. These in-the-moment assessments for analyzing these quick sorts of student work will be more fully addressed later in this chapter.

According to Todd Finley in an article in *Edutopia*, dipsticking is a form of formative assessment. He writes of the power of assessing mid-class, saying that formative assessments are particularly effective when "students are given tactical feedback, immediately followed by time to practice the skill" (Findley 2015).

For dipsticking on the fly, a math teacher might put a problem on the board for students to solve and offer four possible solutions—Nos. 1, 2, 3, and 4—only one of which is correct. Students solve the problem at their seats and then, at the given prompt, hold up the number of fingers (or numbered pieces of paper) that correspond to the solution they believe is correct. Alternatively, this math teacher might take his or her cue from a professional sports announcer exhorting fans to guess the day's attendance at a sporting event. The teacher asks students to raise their hands or cheer for the solution they believe to be correct, and then, with great fanfare, reveals the answer: "If you guessed No. 2, you're … absolutely … right!"

In a video on the *Teaching Channel*, Leah Alcasia, a middle school math teacher, has devised her own alternative to clickers: the simple and available notecard. At the beginning of class, she asks all students to solve a problem. She then collects them into a correct pile and an incorrect pile. From the pile of incorrect answers, she selects her "favorite no." This is a solution that has many correct steps, but has an area that she has seen in her quick appraisal (formative assessment) of their work that the class could profit from reviewing. The class looks at the "favorite" partially incorrect problem, projected with a digital camera onto a whiteboard. First, students are asked to describe what procedures are "right" with the incorrect solution, such as the distributive function. They then explain what needs to be changed in the problem. This quick warm-up provides reinforcement for what has already been learned, and with the "favorite no" the teacher has provided both a classroom where mistakes are accepted as a normal part of learning and feedback about actionable next steps for the students who had made that mistake (Alcala 2015).

Questions To Activate Previous Learning

Marzano, in *Classroom Instruction That Works* (2012), explains that "teachers can use questions before a learning experience to establish a mental set with which students process the learning experience." He notes that **"educational researchers have shown that the activation of prior knowledge is critical to learning of all types**. Indeed, our background knowledge can even influence what we perceive." Even providing a pretest on knowledge not already covered in class can be a positive experience for students.

Pretesting Can Help Develop a Schema for Students

Taking a pretest prior to instruction can benefit students. The research indicates that if the assessment describes the expectations—for example, that students will need to explain in their own words how to correct mathematical problems in assessments or that they will be comparing the arguments of two primary sources—students begin to have a clearer concept of what the course will expect (Carey 2014). This benefit is discussed more fully in Chapter 4.

Prior to beginning the study of a new historical time period, often history teachers ask students what they know about this time period already. One way in which such an activity may be organized is by first giving students the opportunity to brainstorm independently at their desks and then transcribing the results of their brainstorming on the whiteboard with a chart sometimes called a *K/W/L chart*, which collects

what students know, want to know, and, in the third column, what they've learned.

For example, imagine that we are beginning a unit on the Salem witch trials. We might hand out paper for our students to use in jotting down anything and everything they know about the Salem witch trials before calling on students to share their thoughts with the class. Rather than seeking volunteers, a practice that might only draw in the most engaged students, an alternative would be to put the *K/W/L* chart on the white board. The teacher might provide each row or group with a marker, and ask the group to take turns adding examples of what they already know to the list.

Making Predictions

Another related method of activating student learning involves asking students to make predictions about an upcoming unit of study. For example, prior to starting a new literary work, we might ask our students to predict what they think the work is going to be about based on the title, the front cover, or the blurb on the back. This strategy of asking students to make predictions may be continued throughout our study of this literary work. For example, upon assigning a new chapter of *To Kill a Mockingbird* to read for homework, we might ask students to make predictions about what events they believe will occur in the upcoming chapter.

As explained by Marzano, Pickering, and Pollock (2001), this strategy activates students' thinking. As they complete their reading assignment that evening at home, they will be actively comparing the events they are reading in *To Kill a Mockingbird* to those they predicted several hours earlier in class. Such a mental comparison makes students sharper readers, more likely to focus on what they are reading, and more likely to remember it the next day in class or later that semester. Moreover, such an activity provides a natural lead-in to a literary discussion the next day in class comparing what students expected to occur in the plot in *To Kill a Mockingbird* with what actually happened. Of course, such a question ("How did the events in last night's chapter compare to what you expected?") may serve as a means of assessing students' knowledge and understanding of the chapters they read for homework and provide an opportunity for the teacher to determine the degree to which these chapters should be focused on during the current class period. For example, students often find the final chapter of *To Kill a Mockingbird* confusing. If our warm-up questioning reveals general confusion, a teacher might choose to postpone a more abstract, higher-level discussion of symbolism and theme in favor of taking the class period to clarify the plot sequence.

The strategy of making predictions also works well in an elementary mathematics classroom. Before beginning a unit on fractions, decimals, and percentages, a teacher might ask students to predict the relationships among fractions, decimals, and percentages. Throughout the unit of study, the teacher would refer to the list of students' ideas to determine the accuracy of their initial predictions. The value of such an activity is similar to that described above for ninth-grade students reading *To Kill a Mockingbird*. As students increase their knowledge about fractions, decimals, and percentages, they actively compare the information and skills they are acquiring to their initial predictions. Such comparisons sharpen their abilities to understand and remember the functions of these various mathematical representations. Prediction works similarly across the disciplines in the arts, music, or health. If a student predicts that he or she will shave a second from his time, or if a student predicts with his or her new exercise regimen then he or she will change her body mass index, the ideas are solidified as the student compares his or her progress against predictions.

The *Do Now*

A third way in which teachers activate students' previous learning is through an activity that Lorraine Monroe calls a *Do Now* (Checkley 2004). The Do Now, described in more detail in Chapter 2, is a routine that students begin immediately upon entering the classroom and taking their seats. Many teachers combine the practice of Do Nows with journals or reflection logs. For these teachers, the Do Now takes the form of a question or prompt related to the day's lesson. Students begin the class by answering a question in their logs that will activate their thinking about the learning they will embark upon for the rest of the period. A health or physical education teacher might expect students to monitor and record their heart rates daily before they begin to exercise, or to journal about their diet or exercise goals. The mathematical warm-up mentioned earlier, "My Favorite No," is a Do Now that connects to their prior learning and the lesson of the day. A graphics arts teacher beginning a unit on creating an effective ad campaign might use a Do Now to activate students' thinking about advertisements they have recently seen in magazines and

> *When we ask a question to embed the learning, we cause students to reflect again on the knowledge just taught so that it is established more solidly in their memories.*

on billboards. In this case, the Do Now may serve as a means of helping students to start thinking about the different components of effective campaigns. Such an activity provides an opportunity for students to make connections between what they are about to learn and their own experiences and, as Marzano, Pickering, and Pollock (2001, p. 114) explain, to "establish a mental set with which students process the learning experience."

Deepening Understanding—Looking at Student Responses to Questions

The deepening of understanding refers to two processes: embedding the learning and using higher-order thinking skills.

When we ask a question **to embed the learning**, we cause students to reflect again on the knowledge just taught so that it is established more solidly in their memories. For example, to teach the elements of fiction, the teacher may provide a word splash that includes the eight elements of plot, setting, character, theme, point of view, tone, symbol, and style and randomly splashes each of the eight definitions. As a first step, students are asked to match the element with the definition. To embed the learning, students may be asked to apply those terms to a story that they've read. Often when a new concept is introduced, it is beneficial to select an easily understood story, so, for example, *Where the Wild Things Are* or "Little Red Riding Hood" could become the model story. By applying the elements to a story, the learning becomes more embedded. If students are asked to illustrate the definitions using the story they've just read, again, the elements are further embedded or deepened. Students then might be challenged to apply these terms to a more complex story or novel to demonstrate their independent mastery.

The second way we deepen understanding is through questions that push students to think at high levels. Marzano, Pickering, and Pollock (2001) emphasize the importance of asking questions that push students to use the **higher-order thinking skills** of *analysis*, *synthesis*, and *evaluation*. Matching the elements of fiction are on a lower level of understanding, but independently applying them to a new story would require an analysis of the story to apply each term to the story.

In a class on the visual arts, the class might study a technique used by painters, such as the Impressionists' use of light, and then they might be asked to analyze a particular painting and its use of light or to attempt to duplicate an artist's technique.

A high school lesson on metaphysical poet John Donne's "A Valediction Forbidding Mourning" provides another example of using questioning practices strengthening students' higher-order thinking skills and deepening understanding is given below.

One of the images of the "Valediction" poem describes the closeness of two people in love, comparing them to the legs of a compass—the kind used to draw circles in geometry. Donne writes the following lines:

> Thy soul, the fix'd foot, makes no show
> To move, but doth, if th' other do.
> And though it in the centre sit,
> Yet, when the other far doth roam,
> It leans, and hearkens after it,
> And grows erect, as that comes home.

A question that engages students' lower-order thinking skills might be simply, "What kind of compass is Donne using for this extended metaphor?" However, asking students to interpret the meaning of Donne's conceit, or extended metaphor, which compares two people in love to the "legs" of a compass, extends students' thinking. It asks students to draw a comparison between the movements of this concrete object and love that exists between two people. A student might note that, because the two legs of a compass are attached to each other, one cannot move without affecting the other. If the teacher asked students to go back to the text and identify exactly how this is expressed, a student might cite: "Yet, when the other far doth roam, / It leans, and hearkens after it." And if the teacher asks what this means, both literally in the movement of the compass and figuratively in the love relationship, the student would have to synthesize his or her knowledge of a real compass with the literal meanings of "leans" and "hearkens." The student might say that the man or woman who waits yearns (leans) and hopes to hear of the arrival (hearkens) of the other. If the teacher asks about the author's craft as a metaphysical poet, the student might discuss how metaphysical poets used extended comparisons that showed off their knowledge, often of academics and science (the compass) and used lengthy and often somewhat strange metaphors to describe emotions, which is shown in this conceit.

Donne's poetry is unquestionably challenging, and using the higher-order thinking skills necessary to make sense of his metaphors requires hard work on the part of students (and teachers). Questions that move students to focus on the literal meaning and on restating the language in the text in everyday terms may greatly facilitate their ability to make sense of Donne's metaphors and abstractions. A follow-up formative assessment of the discussion could be a "quick write" in answer to any one of the following questions, through which the teacher could assess each student's understanding of the extended metaphor in the excerpt from the poem.

1. How could Donne's lines about how the legs of a compass move relate to the actions of two people in love?
2. When you draw a circle with a compass, what does the "center leg" do? How could this be similar to a lonely lover?
3. How could the way in which the two legs of a compass straighten when you push them towards each other be symbolic of the actions or emotions of two people in love who are brought together?

These questions offer some preliminary examples of the type of questions that promote higher-order thinking on the part of students. Later in this chapter, we will look in more detail at the difference between questions intended to recall information and questions such as those given above that promote higher levels of understanding and thinking. See also Chapter 6 for more information on higher-order thinking skills and differentiated instruction.

Asking Students Questions

The types of questions that teachers ask are generally divided into the following three categories: recall questions, comprehension questions, and higher-order thinking questions. It should be noted at the outset, however, that there is some overlap among these categories. A challenging recall question might legitimately be classified as a comprehension question; likewise, a more complex comprehension question could be regarded as a higher-order thinking question. **The questions can be distributed along a continuum, such as that shown in Figure 5.2**.

Recall Questions

- What is the name of the main character of the story?
- Who remembers the quadratic formula?
- In what year did the Civil War begin?

As may be seen in the three examples above, a **recall question** is for a factual response that a student either knows or does not know; there is nothing to calculate or analyze. Benjamin Bloom calls these *knowledge*

Figure 5.2

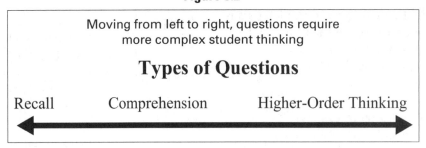

questions (a chart explaining Bloom's levels of questions can be found in Chapter 6). A teacher uses recall questions to activate students' previous learning and/or assess students' knowledge of a particular skill or concept that has already been learned. A challenging recall question could ask a student to name all of the bones in the human hand. Recall questions are not necessarily easy, but their information comes from previously learned material.

Recall Questions to Activate Previous Learning

In a social studies class focusing on the Boston Tea Party, we might begin the class with a series of questions that push students to recall the previously studied actions and laws imposed by the British government and that angered the colonists. "What was the Stamp Act?" "What law forced colonists to board British soldiers in their homes?" The purpose of such questions is to activate students' prior learning to allow them to connect previously held knowledge to the day's lesson. In *Accessing the General Curriculum*, Nolet and McLaughlin (2000, p. 360) explain what happens when a student's brain takes in new information:

> [This] information is held in working memory temporarily while it is compared with information already stored in long-term memory. If the new information is related to some prior knowledge, it is moved out of working memory and stored along with that related information in long-term memory.

In other words, **there is a physiological reason why students can remember information longer if this information is connected to their previous learning.**[1]

Comprehension Questions

- If an object's mass is 8 kilograms and it is accelerating at 9.8 m/s/s, what is its force?

- What does "No taxation without representation" mean?
- Why did Max decide to return home from the Land of the Wild Things?
- Explain what the biosphere contains.
- What is rhythm? How do you measure rhythm?

As can be seen in the three types of questions in Figure 5.2, **recall, comprehension, and higher-order thinking,** are those that assess whether students *understand* a particular concept, operation, or idea. A comprehension question, then, is more complex than a recall question. Because to answer a comprehension question correctly, a student must not only recall a previously learned piece of information, but also apply this information to something new. For example, a recall question given in the previous section was, "Who remembers the quadratic formula?" Correctly answering this question merely requires a student to *recall* the particular formula. In contrast, a comprehension question might be, "What is × in the equation 5 X 2 − × + 6?" To answer this question correctly, students must not only *recall* the quadratic formula, but also *comprehend* how to use this formula to solve for ×.

Higher-Order Thinking Questions

- What might the colonists involved in the Boston Tea Party have been thinking as they threw the tea overboard?
- What information is conveyed in this advertisement? How is this information misleading?
- How has mankind influenced the biosphere? Is this influence mainly negative or positive?
- What evidence supports the claim that Romeo and Juliet were not truly in love?
- How has American Jazz influenced present-day popular and classical music?

The most difficult type of question for students to answer is a question that asks students to analyze, synthesize, or apply their knowledge to a new situation. All students should be exposed and expected to respond to higher-order questions. Benjamin Bloom

---

1   Chapter 2 discusses in more detail the importance of connecting new information and skills to previous learning.

developed his taxonomy in 1956. He developed an instructional model that categorized thinking skills from the most concrete to the most abstract. In Bloom's model, a concrete form of thinking, such as memorization, is classified as an example of a *lower-order thinking skill*, whereas *higher-order thinking skills* constitute more abstract forms of thinking, such as analysis, synthesis, and evaluation. Teachers need to balance these questions; as students get into the fourth grade and higher, about half of the questions should be higher order. More information on Bloom's taxonomy of thinking skills can be found in Chapter 6.

There is a physiological reason why students can remember information longer if this information is connected to their previous learning.

In *Classroom Instruction That Works,* Marzano, Pickering, and Pollock (2001) describe four types of questioning that help students to hone their higher-order thinking skills: questions that push students to make inferences, analyze an error, construct support, and analyze perspectives. Each of these analytical skills and the questions that encourage students to use these skills will be examined briefly below.

Making Inferences

The *Merriam-Webster Dictionary* (1994, p. 598) defines making an *inference* as "the act of passing from one proposition, statement, or judgment considered as true to another whose truth is believed to follow from that of the former." In other words, making an inference involves drawing on something we already know to be true in order to make an educated guess about something we believe to be true. An example of a question that requires an inference might be "What were the colonists who participated in the Boston Tea Party thinking as they threw the tea overboard?" Of course, students don't actually know the thoughts that were running through the colonists' minds; however, learning about the actions and laws imposed on the colonists by the British in the months leading up to the Boston Tea Party would provide them with a factual base on which to draw a reasonable inference about the colonists' mindset on that fateful evening.

Analyzing Errors

In the "My Favorite No" example, students were asked to look at the solution of a problem and find both what was done correctly and the errors. When students evaluate their own writing or as peers provide feedback to another student, they are analyzing errors in, for example, organization, sentence structure, or logic.

Constructing Support

Perhaps the most important analytic skill for students to hone is the ability to construct support for a particular viewpoint. Virtually every academic discipline and profession requires its practitioners to state ideas or plans of action and then construct support for why such a plan should be implemented. For example, lawyers are expected to apply previous case law to a pattern of evidence to support their clients' claims. Accountants responding to an auditor's queries must be able to reference specific tax codes that support the manner in which they have managed their clients' finances. Business people proposing that their organizations develop new products will be expected to cite market research that demonstrates the wisdom of such a change.

In class, a teacher might ask students to construct support for various statements, such as the following two examples:

"Do you believe Odysseus acted heroically? Explain your reasoning with examples from *The Odyssey.*"

To answer this question, students will need not only to state their opinions, but also to offer textual evidence to support them. For example, a student claiming that Odysseus did act heroically might note that he devised a brilliant plan to save himself and members of his crew from being eaten by the Cyclops. A student arguing that Odysseus did not act heroically, however, might counter that it was Odysseus's lack of caution that led to his crew's imprisonment in the Cyclops's cave in the first place. Neither of these responses is necessarily more correct than the other. Rather, when students are asked to discuss Odysseus's heroism, they need to analyze the traits that they have described in their examples and to discuss which of these traits seem to be the most predominant.

"How can you prove to someone who doesn't know anything about math that $3/4$ is greater than $2/3$?"

This question, a variation of which was posed by Professor Eleanor Duckworth to a classroom of teachers, is more challenging than it initially appears. Were it not for the phrase "to someone who doesn't know anything about math," this question might simply be a comprehension question assessing whether students understand the process of finding the least common denominator of two fractions or, alternatively, the process of cross-multiplying. Asking students to prove that $3/4$ is greater than $2/3$ without using mathematical terms in their explanation, however, requires students to come up with different forms of evidence. How can a student prove that one fraction is greater than the other? One student might transpose two circles on top of each other, one of which has ¾ of its area shaded and the other ⅔ of its area. By transposing one on top of the other, the student could demonstrate that ¾ of a circle covers more area than ⅔. Other students might come up with entirely different strategies using a number line, physical objects, or people in the room. Again, the goal is to encourage students to find real-world evidence that will prove the statement instead of comparing the fractions as percentages.

How do researchers use qualitative and quantitative evidence? In a psychology class, after understanding the differences between qualitative and quantitative data, the students were asked to create an experimental question about a classroom and to observe and collect data. One of the questions was "Who answers more questions, boys or girls?" Another question was "Who says more words, boys or girls?" They were then asked, "What the type of data have you collected, and how have you used it to answer your questions?"

All three of these questions require that students construct support in the form of textual or real-world evidence, a skill that they will likely rely upon heavily throughout their academic and professional careers.

Analyzing Perspectives

History teachers often ask students to analyze the perspective of the author of a primary source when they ask them to explain the context in which a primary source was written. For example, when discussing "The Gettysburg Address," one teacher asks students to look at each paragraph and decide which group Lincoln was addressing in each one: Northerners, Southerners, or those who supported ending the war. This encourages students to be aware of the time when the address was delivered and to leave their own perspective in the twenty-first century.

Like the history teacher, a science teacher might ask students to read two essays about genetic engineering and ask them to explain the perspective of the essay that supported genetic engineering and the one that found it ethically unacceptable.

In the unit on the Boston Tea Party, a teacher might ask students how they would expect English citizens reading about the Boston Tea Party in their weekly newspapers to react to the actions of the colonists. What might have been their thoughts and feelings? How might the King of England have reacted to this news? What about the average colonist? By

pondering these questions, students strengthen their ability to examine a scenario or situation from multiple perspectives, an important higher-order thinking skill. Students could transform their ideas into dialogues or mock debates among the many colonists, or, in a more academic vein, they could construct an essay that argues for or against the rebellion against England.

Perspectives are major concept in the visual arts. As a first application of three-dimensional perspective, students are often asked to draw an object in their art class from different perspectives, and later they might be asked to draw their own home or their own street.

For elementary students, one way to help them understand others' perspectives during a unit on immigration might involve asking them to construct a diary written from the perspective of an immigrant child coming to America. In their journal entries, students would address their trip to America, how they feel about being from a different country and being in a new land, and about how others treat them. To provide context, the teacher can provide the students with several nonfiction or historically accurate fictional narratives about immigration to help students write more historically accurate and detailed journals.

Using Processing Partners to Raise the Level of Student Answers in Response to Higher-Order Thinking Questions

It is often helpful for students to discuss their responses to higher-order questions with a partner. Doing so enables them to build upon one another's thinking, thereby producing high-level answers. One strategy teachers use to get students to effectively process questions with a partner is **processing partners**.[2] In this strategy, students quickly discuss a higher-level (or any) question with a partner and then quickly return to their seats to join a general discussion. Teachers create a partner sheet using terms they want the students to learn through repetition. In the following example, the generals from the Civil War are used. The students then follow the instructions below to get one partner for each blank line.

The instructions given to the students are as follows:

1. When the teacher gives the direction, find one class partner for each of the generals noted below.
2. Be certain that, for any space in which you have the name of a classmate, your classmate has your

---

2   The use of processing partners is also an excellent strategy to use with recall and comprehension questions when teachers want to firmly embed a piece of information.

name in the same space. For example, if you have John Doe's name in your Stonewall Jackson space, then John Doe should have your name in his Stonewall Jackson space.

3. You may not have any partners who sit at your table (or sit at a contiguous desk).

4. You may not have a partner more than once.

5. Fill as many slots as you can in the five minutes given. Don't worry if you don't fill them all. We will help you to do so after the five minutes are up.

After the five minutes have passed, students are asked to return to their seats. At this time the teacher asks, "Who does not have a Robert E. Lee?" If an even number of students raise their hands, then the teacher has them take each other's names to fill that slot on their sheets. If some students still have blanks, it is fine to bend the rules at this point and let students partner with someone at their table or someone they already have had as a partner. If there are an odd number of students with a blank slot, the teacher pairs up as many as possible and assigns the one remaining

student the name "wild card." The teacher completes this process for all the spaces on the sheet. When it comes time to share, the "wild card" student partners with someone whose partner is absent or is assigned as a third person joining a pair of partners.

The teacher is now ready to ask a higher-order thinking question, and he or she tells the students to find their partners for a particular category. For example, the teacher might say, "Pair up with your Stonewall Jackson partner." Once the students are sitting with their partners, the teacher then asks the higher-order thinking question for the pairs to discuss. After the students finish discussing the higher-order thinking question in pairs, they return to their original seats and either share their answers orally or write them in their response journals.[3]

---

3 The following sample is for a high school history class. Teachers in other disciplines have used terms such as *the being verbs, poets of the nineteenth century, titles of Shakespeare plays, elements from the periodic table, the continents, words that are difficult to spell*, etc. A partner sheet can be made from any list of content-related terms a teacher wishes to have students frequently review.

Civil War General Processing Partners

Robert E. Lee _____

Ulysses S. Grant _____

Stonewall Jackson _____

George Meade _____

William T. Sherman _____

Joseph Johnston _____

Joseph Hooker _____

Pierre Beauregard _____

William Hayes _____

Alfred Sully _____

John Jones _____

James Longstreet _____

Using Teacher "Think Alouds" to Model Answering Higher-Order Thinking Questions

A strategy that teachers use to demonstrate the cognitive strategies students may employ to answer a higher-order thinking question is a Think Aloud, in which teachers model their own thinking as they try to answer a question. For example, a teacher might model solving a mathematical problem or how to decide what the tone of a poem is.

1. The teacher presents the class with a higher-order thinking question.
2. The teacher works out the answer to the question, verbalizing all of his or her thinking.
3. The students listen to the teacher and note what the teacher did in the process of thinking through the answer.
4. After the verbalization is completed, the class analyzes the teacher's thinking and identifies the strategies the teacher used to answer the question.

For example, when teaching students to solve the analogy *mason : stone*, the teacher might use the following script to model answering the question below.

Figure 5.3

A mason is to stone what a _____ is to _____.

  a. soldier : weapon
  b. lawyer : law
  c. blacksmith : forge
  d. teacher : pupil
  e. carpenter : wood

A mason is to stone what a soldier is to a weapon. That seems to work, because a mason uses stone and a soldier uses a weapon. Let me try the next answer to see whether it is a better fit. *A mason is to stone what a lawyer is to law.* That seems to work also because a lawyer works with the law; however, stone is something the worker physically moves around, while the law is something you work with more intellectually than physically. I think I still prefer answer *a*. Let me try the next one. *A mason is to stone what a blacksmith is to a forge.* That seems to fit the criteria I used for *a*. The blacksmith uses a forge, and he uses it with physical activity; however, stone is the actual substance from which the mason makes a product. The blacksmith uses the forge as tool rather than as the actual substance used to make a product. Using that definition, then, *soldier* and *weapon* don't appear to work anymore.

Certainly, the soldier physically uses the weapon, but he uses it as a tool. It is not a substance used to make a product. It appears *a* and *c* have some characteristics that match the mason : stone analogy, but they also have at least one part that does not seem to fit. *Teacher* and *pupil* work, in that the pupil is the raw material the teacher develops into a final product; however, the teacher does not physically handle the pupil to make the product. Finally, let me try *carpenter* and *wood*. A carpenter uses the wood to make a product. The carpenter physically manipulates the wood to make the product. The carpenter uses tools on the wood to make the final product. I think carpenter : wood is the analogy that is most similar to mason : stone.

An alternative method that the teacher might use is the sentence method. The original analogy becomes: A mason *works* with stone. Then try out *works* with each choice. They all seem to work. A mason *shapes* stone into *something*. In this case, both the teacher and the carpenter seem to work, but the student is only figuratively shaped. So a mason *shapes* stone *into a useful object* works only for the last choice.

The students analyze the strategies that the teacher used to solve the analogy. For example, the teacher took the options in sequential order. While working with each option, the teacher found those characteristics about the option that were the same as the original analogy. Even though an early option appeared to work, the teacher continued to assess the other options in order to find the option that worked best. As the teacher progressed through the options, he or she noted those options that had more similar characteristics than the others and began to eliminate some of the options.

Using Questions to Engage Students and Maintain Their Attention

Questioning can also be used to keep students engaged in the class's work. As Hannel (2003, p. 1) writes, "Questioning reduces the stream of information coming at the student to bite-size pieces and better attends to active listening." In Larry Ferlazzo's "Ways to Cultivate 'Whole-Class Engagement,'" educator and behavioral therapist Jim Peterson describes how to motivate students to answer questions by contrasting two types of pre-reading prompts. The first prompt gives only the assignment and explains the task: "Read these pages and answer the questions at the end of the text." The second gives students less than two minutes to read and highlight the main idea.

The students are told that when they finish they will share their responses with a peer (Finley 2014).

Peterson says the second questioning option is more motivating because it asks students to do the five most motivating activities that the time, amount, public, and novelty (TAPN) method for effective questioning recommends that teachers can use to build engagement (Finley 2014).

Time: By limiting time, students focus on the task more intensely.

Amount (of work) to answer the question should be challenging, but possible.

Public: When students will share their answers with their peers, they are more engaged.

Novelty: Ask them to do something slightly different—for example, highlight specific words, illustrate their answer, write on the white board—to motivate students.

The following task has all of the four characteristics described by Peterson: read the paragraph (the **amount** of reading is reasonable, but challenging given the time) with a partner (**public**), and after five minutes (**time**), summarize the main ideas (**amount** of writing is reasonable, but challenging) in a sentence of 10 words or less (**novelty**), and post it on the white board (**novelty**).

Calling on Students Who Have Not Volunteered

Walsh and Sattes (2005) report that a study of fourth-through eighth-grade students revealed that 25 percent of students never participate in class. Another study of high school science classes found that approximately 29 percent of students were completely silent during each class period, while a small number of students (15 percent of the class) volunteered more than 16 times apiece. When researchers examine the demographics of who participates in class, they find that white males participate significantly more than females and students of color.

Fisher and Frey, in their text *Checking for Understanding*, summarize the challenging conditions for many at-risk students. In classrooms with high-achieving students, teachers talk half of the time, while in classrooms with low-achieving students, teachers talk at least 80 percent of the time.

In other words, the amount of teacher versus student talk in a classroom varies by the demographics of the students. In addition, students who live in poverty or are English language learners, have disabilities, or are otherwise at risk in school spend more of their time on basic skills and less time engaged in activities, lessons, or inquiry that requires language and fosters creative and critical thinking (Fisher and Frey 2014, p. 37).

Thus, inviting all students into the conversation is essential. Small-group work and dyad work provide opportunities for quieter students to talk. These alternatives to whole-class work are addressed later in this chapter.

Each of these findings is troubling and leads educators such as Walsh and Sattes (p. 13) to argue that "teachers, not students, should usually decide who will answer questions." And yet, many teachers feel understandably uneasy about "cold calling" students to answer questions rather than asking for volunteers.

"I Don't Know"

In *Highly Effective Questioning*, Hannel (2003) suggests that teachers should not accept "I don't know" as a satisfactory response to a query. If a student does respond with "I don't know," Hannel (p. 82) advises teachers either (1) to change the phrasing of the original question or (2) to narrow the scope of the question. In this way, students who answer with "I don't know" to avoid doing the thinking necessary to answer the question will quickly learn that a response of "I don't know" only leads to additional questioning.

The following two scenarios stand as examples of this questioning strategy in action.

Teacher: Bobby, what do you remember from our unit on civil rights?

Bobby: I don't know.

Teacher (rephrasing): Bobby, tell me something that interested you from the unit we finished yesterday on civil rights.

Bobby: I thought the stuff about the Black Panther Party was interesting.

Teacher: What interested you about the Black Panthers?

Here, the teacher responds to Bobby's initial "I don't know" response by simply rephrasing the question. Then the teacher asks Bobby to expand upon his response that he had found their study of the Black Panther Party to be particularly engaging. By asking an additional two questions, rather than simply calling on someone other than Bobby, the teacher successfully encourages Bobby to make a genuine contribution to the class's review of the previous unit. The Black Panther Party may well have been an aspect of the unit on which the teacher had placed little emphasis. This exchange could potentially lead to Bobby's preparing a report or presentation on the Black Panthers for extra credit.

In the first scenario above, the teacher chose to simply rephrase the question for Bobby's benefit. Had the teacher believed Bobby to be genuinely stymied by the initial question, however, he or she might have chosen to narrow the question's scope, as in the example below.

Teacher: Bobby, what do you remember from our unit on civil rights?

Bobby: I don't know.

Teacher (narrowing the question's scope): Bobby, name one person from our unit on civil rights who interested you.

Bobby: John Lewis.

Teacher: Really? Why Congressman Lewis?

In this scenario as well, the teacher chose to stay with Bobby and narrow the scope of the question instead of moving on to another student. Here, again, Bobby's response may well lead to an unanticipated but productive class discussion about civil rights activist and Congressman John Lewis or perhaps to Bobby's carrying out some additional research on his own. In short, then, we encourage educators to regard the ability to answer questions and contribute to class discussions as an essential academic skill. As Hannel (2003, p. 54) reminds us, "This is not to say that every student must answer each question correctly or perfectly, but to say that students may not opt out of participating in the questioning process."

Some students may give incomplete responses. Imagine, for example, a teacher who asks his or her students to name their favorite explorer and explain their reasoning for this choice. A student who responds "Magellan" has not thoroughly responded to his or her teacher's question. According to Walsh and Sattes (2005, p. 15), several different studies have found that when students answer a question incompletely, "teachers generally accept these answers as sufficient without probing or prompting correct responses." This tendency on the part of teachers likely stems from a fear of embarrassing a student in front of his or her classmates, and yet this tendency is concerning for several reasons. First, studies have demonstrated that probing students to explain their thoughts more thoroughly is positively associated with student achievement. In other words, students learn more in classrooms where their teachers push them to explain their answers thoroughly and justify their thoughts. Second, when a teacher accepts a half-answer to a

> *The most effective questions are expressed precisely and succinctly.*

question as sufficient, he or she is sending the message to the entire class about the quality of response that will be acceptable in that classroom. To accept a single student's half-formed response, then, is to convey to the entire class that the teacher either has low standards or expects little of his or her students.

Clarity of Questions

Clarity and precision of questions is essential so that students remain focused. The most effective questions are those that are expressed precisely and succinctly. Teachers who surround their questions with superfluous commentary only serve to confuse students. In *Accessing the General Curriculum*, Nolet and McLaughlin (2000, p. 34) make the following observation:

> To allocate attention to something, a student must select it from among many sensory inputs that occur simultaneously. Teachers can assist students in this process by limiting the amount of information to which they ask students to attend at any one time. For example, teachers who use clear, concise wording in their presentations often are better able to maintain and focus student attention than those who require their students to pick the most important information out of an endless stream of superfluous "happy talk."

Note the first wordy example and the second more succinct and focused example.

Teacher 1: Romeo and Juliet are probably the most famous couple in the history of literature. Their story is known all over the world. But were they really in love? When you think back over the course of the play, do their actions and thoughts, their innermost feelings, reveal them to be two people deeply, truly in love with each other, or is this just a case of childish flirtation or perhaps even adolescent lust?

Teacher 2: Do you think Romeo and Juliet were truly in love with each other? Why or why not?

Clearly, teacher No. 2 expresses his or her question in a more succinct manner than teacher No. 1. The students of teacher No. 2 may immediately begin to consider the question at hand, whereas the students of teacher No. 1 must first sift through all of the superfluous "happy talk" to determine precisely what they are being asked. On paper, the question asked by teacher No. 1 may strike us as so exaggerated an example as to constitute caricature; however, when we consciously focus on and listen to our own questioning practices or those of our colleagues, we often find ourselves to be perilously close to the level of happy talk achieved by teacher No. 1.

Avoiding Multiple Questions in Quick Succession

Related to the concept of happy talk is the tendency on the part of many of us to pose several questions in a row before giving our students the opportunity to respond. Take, for example, the questioning pattern of teacher No. 3.

> **Teacher 3**: Should President Harry Truman have made the decision to drop the atomic bomb on Hiroshima and Nagasaki? Do you think racism against Asians played a role in this decision? Would Truman have been willing to drop an atomic bomb on Berlin or Rome? What decision would you have made?

All of these questions posed by teacher No. 3 have the potential to form the basis of a powerful class discussion; however, firing all four questions at the class in quick succession only serves to confuse students. Some students will simply forget the first two or three questions posed and focus only on the final question they hear. Other students will be uncertain about which question they are expected to answer. Still, other students will be reflecting on the potential racism behind the decision to drop the atomic bomb on Hiroshima and Nagasaki, while other students are volunteering their thoughts on what they would have done in Truman's place. As a result, teacher No. 3 will have difficulty leading a coherent, focused discussion. He or she has simply floated too many different ideas for students to consider at one time. Instead, teacher No. 3 needs to focus on one of these questions and solicit student responses before moving on to the next question.

Why do we as educators sometimes fall into the trap of posing multiple questions in quick succession to our students? One reason seems to be that we have seen this technique used with great success in speeches by politicians and graduation speakers, as well as TV lawyers making closing statements. We must remind ourselves, however, that an effective oratory technique in front of a passive audience does not meet with the same success in a student-centered classroom. Another reason is the discomfort some of us feel when silence ensues after we ask a question. Teachers unfamiliar with the use of wait time after asking a question often assume that students don't

know the answer, rather than that they are thinking about the answer. In these instances, we often fill the silence with additional questions. The role of silence and wait time in classrooms will be examined in detail in the next section, but we wish to note here that students benefit deeply when we resist the urge to follow a question we have just posed with an additional question or comment. We must give students the opportunity to reflect and formulate a response to our first question before posing another.

Avoiding "Double-Barreled" Questions

Related to asking multiple questions in quick succession is what Walsh and Sattes (2005) refer to as *double-barreled* questions. A double-barreled question is one that actually asks students two different questions at once and thus requires two distinct answers. An example of a double-barreled question would be the following: "Who broke Babe Ruth's homerun record, and what is another important record that baseball player holds?" This question has two different answers. There is nothing intrinsically wrong with a double-barreled question, but for the reasons described above, it is easier on students if this teacher divides this question into two separate questions—first asking one and, after getting a correct response, then posing the second.

Avoiding Overly Vague Questions

Also related to the issue of our clarity when posing questions to students is avoiding overly vague questions. An example of an overly vague question might be the following:

Teacher 4: What do you think about World War I?

Such a question provides no clue to students about the type of response the teacher expects. These questions typically occur when the teacher has not thoroughly considered the type of answers he or she wishes to get from the students. You'll recall that in our discussion earlier in this chapter of the types of questions that teachers pose to students—recall questions, comprehension questions, higher-order thinking questions—there was no category of questions that involved students simply offering guesses. Questions that lead to wild guessing are likely too vague and result in students feeling unclear about the purpose of such questions or the responses the teacher expects.

Avoiding "Yes or No" Questions

Of course, it is impossible *never* to ask students a question that can be answered with a simple "yes" or "no." However, according to Caram and Davis (2005,

p. 21), "Yes or no questions encourage students to respond without fully understanding or thinking through the issue." As is described in more detail in Chapter 8, students are more likely to retain information and understand material when they have to put this content into their own words. Whenever possible, pose questions to students that require them to answer with more elaborate responses than a simple "yes" or "no."

The Importance of Strong Preparation

The best defense against the pitfalls of happy talk, questions in a series, and overly vague questions is strong preparation. According to Caram and Davis (2005, p. 20), preplanned questions "are those prepared by the teacher to introduce new concepts, focus the discussion on certain items, steer the discussion in specific directions, or identify the level of student knowledge on the topic." As young educators (and even now as veteran educators) teaching a new unit or concept, we found it crucial to write into our lesson plans the specific questions that we intended to pose to our class. Having these questions written on paper to glance down at as we taught a particular lesson meant that we weren't struggling in front of our students to find the right wording or phrasing for a particular query; that work had already been done.

A novice teacher initially resisted the idea of planning questions to pose to the class ahead of time. His contention was that he wanted to pose questions to his students that sprung naturally from the class's own comments and that he could think quickly enough "on the fly" to form these questions as the lesson occurred. While this young teacher was unquestionably a bright young man, his on-the-fly strategy led him to practice many bad habits, such as the happy talk described in this section. Additionally, we have found that, rather than negatively affecting the spontaneity of a classroom discussion, a teacher who spends time anticipating the direction that an upcoming classroom discussion might take—and developing questions relevant to such a discussion—is a more effective discussion leader, even when the discussion does not unfold precisely as anticipated. The time the educator has spent reflecting and planning for this lesson enables him or her to be *more*—not less—flexible if students raise unanticipated ideas or points.[4] Clearly, with the tremendous demands competing

Striving to pose a balanced mix of recall, comprehension, and higher-order thinking questions "on the fly" is a challenge we find nearly impossible.

for a classroom teacher's attention, none of us can enter every single class every day with thoroughly prepared questions. Walsh and Sattes (2005, p. 49) note that "a few pivotal questions, carefully crafted, can move a class into the heart of a lesson—and move student thinking to higher levels." Even just three or four questions prepared in advance can play a significant role in pushing students' learning forward.

Using a Range of Questioning Levels

Finally, in *Accessing the General Curriculum*, Nolet and McLaughlin (2000, p. 35) suggest that teachers "ask a variety of related questions that require students to recall declarative information, make inferences, form opinions, and make evaluations." This practice reinforces the students' need to know the details, understand the concepts, and then use their knowledge to analyze the ideas. For example, a teacher leading a review of the Cold War might ask the following questions over the course of the lesson:

1. In what year was the Berlin Wall erected?
    This is a **recall question***. Students simply do or do not remember the year the wall was erected.*
2. How did the theory of Mutually Assured Destruction (MAD) affect America's nuclear arms policies during the Cold War?
    This is a comprehension question. *Students must not only recall the definition of* **Mutually Assured Destruction***, but also understand how this theory played out in American nuclear policy during the Cold War.*
3. What would you say represented the start of the Cold War, and what evidence can you give to support this view?
    This is a **higher-order thinking question***. Students must develop their own opinions about the particular event that set off the Cold War and then construct support in the form of historical facts to support this viewpoint.*

Asking different types of questions, such as those listed above, encourages students to engage in different kinds of thinking, encourages a variety of students to volunteer responses, and keeps students more engaged in the lesson. Preparation for the lesson, including diligent lesson planning and developing the questions, provides an opportunity to monitor the diversity of the questions that will be asked. In contrast, striving to pose a balanced mix of recall, comprehen-

---

4   In Chapter 1, we discuss mastery-based planning. Teachers who use that model find that their questions become more succinct and better enhance student learning.

sion, and higher-order thinking questions "on the fly" is a challenge we find nearly impossible.

Sequencing Questions

In addition to simply diversifying the types of questions asked, Vogler (2005) encourages educators to consider the *sequencing* of their questions. Specifically, he recommends five different patterns of questioning, all of which can be effective for different types of lessons. **Extending questioning** involves asking a series of questions "all at the same cognitive level," while **extending and lifting** questioning involves "asking a number of questions at the same cognitive level, or *extending*, before lifting the level of questions to the next higher level" (p. 99). The **circular path questioning** involves "asking a series of questions that eventually lead back to the initial position or question" (p. 100). **Narrow to broad questioning** involves "asking lower-level, specific questions followed by higher-level, general questions," while **broad to narrow questioning**, or *funneling*, follows the opposite pattern; the teacher "begins with low-level, general questions followed by higher-level, specific questions" (p. 100). None of these sequencing patterns is intrinsically better or worse than any other. The key, like any form of lesson planning, is to consider the goal of the lesson in terms of student learning and then choose the sequencing pattern that can best support students in meeting that goal.

Between Asking and Answering

Wait Time

Educator Mary Budd Rowe conducted the pioneering research on wait time in the late 1960s. In her article "Wait Time: Slowing Down May Be a Way of Speeding Up!" Rowe (1987, p. 38) identifies two types of "wait time" that teachers may use to have a significant impact on students' learning. As she explains, "If teachers can increase the average length of the pauses at both points, namely, after a question and, even more important, after a student response, there are pronounced changes in student use of language and logic as well as in student and teacher attitudes and expectations." In this section, we will examine the mechanics of both types of wait time in more detail.

Rowe (1987) describes **Wait Time I** as the length of time that passes between a teacher asking a question of his or her class and a student's starting to respond. Rowe defines **Wait Time II** as the length of

time that passes before a teacher responds to a student's comment or question. In a study of wait time in both elementary and high school classrooms, Rowe found that the average wait time for both situations is less than one second. Having made this observation, Rowe then embarked on a series of experiments that sought to observe the impact of increasing Wait Time I and Wait Time II from an average of less than one second to an average of three seconds. Her study uncovered the results that follow.

Impact of Increased Wait Time on Student Learning

1. **When wait time is increased, the length of students' responses increases between 300 percent and 700 percent.** Students are less likely to answer in short phrases and more likely to give explanations of their responses. The reasoning for this increase is likely twofold. First, increased wait time means that students who are more deliberative and methodical thinkers are less likely to have their thinking time cut off prematurely by the teacher or another student. Rather, their teacher will wait patiently until students attempt thoughtful responses.

2. **When wait time is increased, students are more likely to offer evidence to support their points.** Given more time to reflect upon questions, students have time to return to the text.

3. **When wait time is increased, students ask more questions of the teacher.** Slowing down the pace of the exchange between a teacher and his or her students allows students the opportunity to form questions and then to put those questions into words.

4. **When wait time is increased, students are more likely to interact with each other, answering and responding to each other's questions.** This finding by Rowe suggests that increasing wait time not only benefits the specific student who has been called upon by the teacher, but also allows other students in the class to take advantage of this slower pace to form questions and thoughts as well. Given the time to formulate these thoughts and questions, students may then begin to speak and question each other, rather than interacting solely with the teacher.

5. **When wait time is increased, students are less likely to answer with "I don't know."** Here again, it would seem that increasing wait time sends the dual message to students that, when called on, they will be given an adequate amount of time to formulate an answer and, additionally, that they will not simply be

"let off the hook" with a hasty or inadequate response. In a previous section of this chapter, we discussed the importance of rephrasing the question or narrowing the scope of the question when a student responds with "I don't know." Both of these strategies remain sound ones, but Rowe's research suggests that an effective initial strategy to this type of response is simply to increase wait time.

6. **When wait time is increased, disciplinary problems within the class decrease.** This finding by Rowe initially strikes teachers as counterintuitive. We assume that increasing the amount of time in which the class is sitting silently will lead to an increase in opportunities for mischief. It would seem that the reverse is true, however, most likely because increasing wait time provides students with more opportunities to think about the content they are learning, to ask questions, and to express their own ideas about this content. As a result, students are less likely to become frustrated and confused during the course of a lesson, and these are the emotions that often lead students to act out.

7. **When wait time increases, a broader scope of students' voluntary responses to questions increase.** It is unquestionably the case that different students process information at varying speeds. Thus, a teacher who fires questions at his or her class and then immediately calls upon the first student to volunteer could be favoring those students who can most quickly process the teacher's question. In contrast, a teacher who poses a question and then waits for several seconds before calling on a student to respond will provide those students who process information more slowly (but perhaps more deeply) with an opportunity to participate in the class's discussion.

Obstacles to Increasing Wait Time

In short, Rowe (1987) uncovered a number of dramatic improvements in student performance that come with increasing Wait Time I and Wait Time II from the typical one second to approximately three seconds. Unfortunately, learning to slow down and increase wait time between asking a question and eliciting a response (Wait Time I) and responding to a student's question or comment (Wait Time II) may be challenging for teachers.

Rowe (1987) has observed that increasing the length of Wait Time II may be particularly challenging for teachers because many of us have gotten into the habit of repeating our students' responses to a given question to avoid the discomfort with silence. We seem

to live in a society that regards silence as negative and something to be eliminated as quickly as possible. Rowe's work suggests that teachers' discomfort with silence can have a negative impact on teaching and learning.

Also, if a teacher's question is met with total silence, the teacher may conclude that his or her lesson did not successfully teach the material to the students. Imagine now that we ask our question about the final step of the scientific method, and one student's hand shoots up in the air. We immediately call upon this student to answer, relieved by this validation that our students "get it." Of course, such validation is not necessarily warranted. What has really been proven is that one student—not the entire class—gets it. Too often, however, we accept this single response as representative of the entire class's level of comprehension and make the decision to move on to the next concept to be studied. An opportunity to quickly formatively assess students has been missed. It would be more effective to use a technique that assesses the entire class's understanding of the particular skill, such as a quick write on the final step in a science experiment which the teacher checks by walking around the room, or a processing partner pause asking students to discuss their understanding.

Finally, a teacher's efforts to increase wait time may be derailed by students in the class who simply blurt out answers without waiting to be called on. Waiting to be called on without shouting out is an important skill for students—elementary through high school—to develop and practice. The most important defense against students' shouting out is defining clear expectations for class behavior during the first days of school when class norms are established. When this norm is broken, the classroom expectations would define the results—a chat with the teacher—and, if this is a consistent problem, a behavior plan could be developed.

Techniques to Increase Wait Time

Rowe (1987) and other researchers have found that the most effective technique for helping teachers to lengthen their wait times is for a teacher to make a recording of a typical lesson and then listen to the recording with a stopwatch in order to monitor his or her wait times. This technique must be repeated regularly, however, to prevent a teacher from slipping back into his or her previous patterns. Another technique that may be effective is inviting a colleague to observe one's teaching and then offer information on the average length of wait times observed. Finally, some teachers have had success actually using their own students to help them to monitor wait time. By explaining to students what they would like to accomplish in terms of increasing Wait Time I and Wait Time II, students may play a role in ensuring that both they and the teacher are leaving adequate pauses after both teacher and student responses.

Since Rowe's pioneering work on wait time, other researchers and educators have added to this area of research. In fact, other opportunities for wait time in a typical classroom have been identified, such as the amount of time a student pauses in the process of answering a teacher's question. Robert Stahl (1994) writes that a teacher typically cuts a student off if a pause extends beyond one-half second. Stahl also comments on the value of teachers creating wait time in the midst of their own presentations. He writes, "Within-teacher presentation pause-time occurs when teachers deliberately stop the flow of information and give students three or more seconds of uninterrupted silence to process the just-presented information. This period of silence provides students uninterrupted time to consider the information of the teacher's presentation in smaller, bite-sized chunks" (p. 2).

Avoid Designating a Respondent

Craig and Cairo (2005) report that many educators will name a student to answer a question before they actually pose the question. For example, an educator might say, "Franklin, I have a question for you to answer" or, "Elsie, why don't you take this one?" However, these researchers report that students in a class are more likely to pay attention to the question being asked and to mentally prepare a response if their teacher *first* poses a question and *then* calls upon a particular student to answer it. Caram and Davis (2005) concur. They suggest: "Pose the question to the entire group and wait before identifying a student to respond" (p. 21).

Gaze Aversion

Educators and researchers have long observed a tendency in some individuals to look away from the person they are talking to while preparing to answer a question. Research by psychologists Phelps, Doherty-Sneddon, and Warnock (2006) has found that there are benefits to such "gaze aversion." Specifically, these researchers have found that "when questions prove challenging yet solvable, looking away from

Within-teacher presentation pause-time occurs when teachers deliberately stop the flow of information and give students three or more seconds of uninterrupted silence to process the just-presented information.

an interlocutor's face can benefit performance" (p. 578). It would seem that looking away from the visual stimuli of another person's face can increase one's concentration and problem-solving ability. Thus, educators should never discourage children and adolescents from practicing gaze aversion while reflecting upon the answer to a problem or question. As Phelps, Doherty-Sneddon, and Warnock conclude, such children are unconsciously drawing on a strategy through which they "can more effectively exert control over their own cognitive processing, potentially offering a means to more effective learning" (p. 587).

Responding to Students' Answers

Responding to Students' Correct Answers: Diversify the Praise to Match the Student or the Student's Response

On the surface, responding to students who have answered a question correctly seems significantly easier than responding to students who have answered incorrectly; however, this is not always the case. A college professor of ours had the habit of responding "Well done!" in a bright, enthusiastic tone to virtually every comment a student made. Initially, students in the class beamed at this enthusiastic praise, but after a few weeks, it became apparent that virtually every correct response received a "Well done!" in that same enthusiastic tone. In short, the praise lost its luster through overuse.

There was much that this college professor was doing correctly when it came to responding to our correct answers. Perhaps most importantly, his tone conveyed warmth and enthusiasm. This educator's method also serves as a cautionary tale, however, in that he came to rely too heavily on one particular phrase. Whether we realize it or not, students are paying close attention to our every move, and that includes the ways in which we offer praise. Thus, we must consciously work to diversify the ways in which we praise student responses.

Tone

A teacher's tone of voice and body language also lend meaning to his or her words.

A tone of sarcasm can contradict positive words.

Be Specific about What Is Praiseworthy

Teacher: What do you consider to be the start of the Cold War?

Student: I think the Cold War was getting started even before World War II ended. I think that President Truman began to see Russia as a future competitor, and some historians say that Truman dropped the atomic bomb on Hiroshima to intimidate Stalin.

Teacher: Your answer brings up an interesting proposition, that the US's act in Japan had a motivation that included sending a message to Stalin.

As may be seen in this dialogue, the teacher's acknowledgement goes beyond simply: "That's a great contribution." Rather, the teacher explicitly notes what the student contributed to the class's discussion. Such praise is more likely to strike the student as authentic.

Body Language

Facing a student, nodding or smiling as he is speaking, remaining focused on his words rather than taking attendance, reading your email on your cell phone, or turning away speak volumes to students and communicate either respectful listening or its opposite.

Direct and Non-Attributive Praise

In *How the Way We Talk Can Change the Way We Work*, Robert Kegan and Lisa Lahey (2000) argue that praise is most powerful when it is direct and non-attributive. By direct, Kegan and Lahey suggest that praise should be directed *toward* the work and not the recipient of the praise. For example, if Albert answered a question correctly, we would say, "Albert, that is a compelling argument." This non-attributive praise is more effective than stating more generally to the entire class: "Albert is absolutely right."

Kegan and Lahey (2000) suggest that praise is most effective when, in addition to focusing on the work, it does not describe that student's intellect, personality, or skill set. For example, rather than saying, "Alex, you are an excellent writer," we might choose to say, "Alex, I enjoy reading your papers because I find the writing so clear." In the second example, we are describing Alex's writing, his work.

Non-Repetitive

Craig and Cairo (2006) observe that, after asking students a question and then listening to a particular student's response, many teachers instinctively repeat that response for the benefit of the rest of the class. However, Craig and Cairo report that when teachers refrain from repeating their students' responses, studies have found that "students pay greater attention to and show increased respect for their classmates' responses" (p. 2). In other words, when students know that their teacher is not going to repeat a classmate's words, they pay more attention to what their classmate is saying in the first place.

Sincere Responses

Cognitive scientist Daniel Willingham explained in a 2006 article that another key to effective praise is sincerity. According to Willingham (2006, p. 2), "To motivate students—especially older students who are more discerning and better able to appreciate the differences between what is said and what is meant—teachers need to avoid praise that is not truthful, is designed to control behavior, or has not been earned." Interestingly, he found that students react particularly negatively to praise that is meant to control behavior. For example, imagine a teacher who offers the following "praise" to a student: "Good job answering that question; you should do your homework every night!" While the teacher who offers this statement is simply trying to make the point that doing one's homework yields good results in class, students tend to hear such a statement not as praise, but as a reprimand. In other words, the students focus less on the "good job" and more on the "you *should* do your homework every night." For this reason, it is important to offer sincere, simple praise and resist the urge to add in a directive about future behavior.

Figure 5.4

Summary of Characteristics of Effective Praise

- diverse phrases
- warm tone
- attentive body language
- specific praise
- direct praise
- non-attributive
- non-repetitive
- sincere

Responding to Incorrect Answers or Partially Incorrect Answers

The important principle to remember when responding to a student's incorrect answer is to respond in such a way that the student won't be put off from volunteering again later in the class period or in future class periods. Determining which responses will accomplish this goal for particular students requires us to know our students well and to use this knowledge in formulating a response. Perhaps the most effective measure is to create a class in which making mistakes is a normal part of learning, as the middle school teacher did in "My Favorite No" because she, along with her students, explicitly described all of the procedures that were correct; and after going through all of the right moves, they discussed the one mistake.

1. **Try to hear something in the student's response with which you can agree.** This strategy was used in the case of a student who had given a response that was partly right and partly wrong. In pointing out that the second part of her response was incorrect, the teacher made sure to observe that the first half of Selma's answer was correct. When possible, start with praise and move on to constructive criticism. By starting with the positive, a teacher's ensuing constructive criticism is more likely to be heard and processed by the student.

2. **Don't pretend an incorrect answer is correct.** While our goal is to respond to students' answers in a way that won't inhibit them from volunteering in the future, this goal does not mean that we should avoid telling a student he or she is incorrect. Such a move will only serve to confuse or provide inaccurate information to the entire class. Often, this aversion to telling a student that his or her response is incorrect results in the teacher speaking ambiguously. Take the following example:

Ellen: I think the assassination of Ferdinand was an underlying cause of World War I.
Teacher: That's an interesting point, Ellen. Does anyone else have an alternative theory?

While the assassination of Francis Ferdinand certainly played a role in the start of World War I, we would be hard pressed to find historians who consider it one of the *underlying* causes of the war. Unfortunately, in her response to Ellen, the teacher's desire to encourage Ellen's participation led her to avoid explicitly stating that Ellen's response was incorrect. The danger is that Ellen and her classmates now likely regard Ellen's statement to be an accurate one. A more appropriate response to Ellen might have been the following:

Teacher: Ellen, you're right that Ferdinand's assassination played a role in the start of World War I; however, the assassination of Ferdinand is not considered an *underlying cause* of the war. Do you

remember how his assassination contributed to the start of the war?
Ellen: His assassination set off a conflict between Austro-Hungary and Serbia that escalated into World War I.
Teacher: If that's the specific event that started the fighting, can you name one of the forces that may have led that one assassination to turn into a worldwide war?

As you can see here, the teacher explicitly notes that Ellen's response is incorrect; however, the teacher also finds something to praise in Ellen's response and then follows up this praise with additional questions that will draw out Ellen's knowledge. In this way, the teacher allows Ellen to demonstrate that she knows quite a bit about the start of World War I. In contrast, a teacher who responded, "No, that's not right," and then asked another student to supply the correct answer might be hard pressed to convince Ellen to volunteer in the future.

3. **Question to make sure you understand the student's response.** There are two components of answering a teacher's question correctly. A student must not only possess the knowledge to supply the answer, but the student must also express that knowledge in an articulate way. Sometimes, the source of a student's incorrect response lies more with the second component, articulateness, than with the first, lack of knowledge. For this reason, a teacher is often well served by asking additional questions that might help a student reshape his or her knowledge into an answer that makes sense. Take the following conversation, for example:

Teacher: Allan, why did Mercutio say on his deathbed, "A curse on both your houses"?
Allan: I think he felt mad that he was dying alone.
Teacher: Why do you say that?
Allan: Because the reason Tybalt was looking to fight someone in the first place was because of the feud between the Montagues and the Capulets, and then Mercutio sort of got caught up in the middle of it.
Teacher: So why do you think he cursed both families?
Allan: I bet he wanted them to be cursed since he was dying because of their feud with each other.

In this scenario, the teacher could have declared Allan's initial response—that Mercutio was angry to be dying alone—incorrect and then moved on to another student. Instead, the teacher asked several probing questions to better understand Allan's thinking, and it turned out that Allan did understand the motivation behind Mercutio's final words; his initial response hadn't revealed all that he knew. Moreover, it is notable that the teacher's initial probing question to Allan was, "Why do you say that?" In this instance, the teacher's follow-up question unearthed a motherlode of additional information that the student possessed. The right answer was in there, but the student needed help digging it out.

4. **Don't answer the question yourself. Redirect it.** Many teachers, after a student has answered a question incorrectly, will follow up by providing the correct answer themselves. A better strategy, however, is to redirect the same question to another student. Craig and Cairo (2006) report that when teachers use such a strategy of redirection, "Students are held more accountable for answering all questions" and "the interaction among and between students increases" (p. 2).

5. **Cue, Clue, or Probe.** Walsh and Sattes (2005) argue that a teacher should respond to an incorrect response by either cueing, clueing, or probing. **Cueing** involves offering students a word or words that might trigger their memory of previous learning. For a student who has forgotten how to multiply two binomials, a teacher might cue this student by simply saying the word *foil*. This reminder of the "foil method" may trigger the student's memory of the previous day's lesson when the entire class learned how to multiply binomials. **Clueing** involves an even more substantial hint about how to answer the question. To return to the student confused about multiplying binomials, a teacher who uses a clueing strategy might suggest that the student start by multiplying the outside term in each set of parentheses. Finally, **probing** involves pushing a student to revise his or her answer. In the case of a student who multiplies two binomials together but comes up with an incorrect answer, his or her teacher might offer a probe by suggesting that he or she recheck her work on the two "inside" terms. Of course, probing does not have to occur only in cases where the student has answered incorrectly. If the teacher simply does not understand the student's response, the teacher might probe for clarification.

Jan Chappuis describes three key errors that students make and says that teachers need to go beyond thinking of them as errors. Instead, she contends, teachers need to look for the cause of the errors and, when there is time to work with students privately, to help them to understand. Below are some examples of these types of errors:

1. **Errors due to incomplete understanding, which should not be marked wrong; instead students should be retaught.** For example, if a kindergartener puts a period between each word in a sentence, the teacher should spend time explaining where the period is needed and how it works.

2. **Errors due to flaws in reasoning.** If a student summarizes, but includes too many details or unimportant details or cannot find the textural examples, the teacher needs to address these errors by providing the student with examples and non-examples.

3. **Errors due to misconceptions.** A student may use the possessive ('s) instead of a plural or is unable to explain how the distance from the sun causes the seasons. These errors may take more time for the teacher because people tend to hang onto their misconceptions despite specifics that conflict with them (Chappuis 2014).

Monitoring the Responses of Other Students to Incorrect Answers

It is important that teachers explicitly set out expectations on the first day of class regarding appropriate student behavior. One high school expects all students, faculty, and visitors to follow its safety rule of "No Shame, Blame, or Attack." This safety rule is taught to all incoming ninth graders on the first day of school and is posted in every classroom and corridor. Moreover, in teaching this safety rule to their students, teachers emphasize the importance of responding respectfully to other students' ideas, comments, questions, and opinions. It may be appropriate to issue a stern warning for a first offense, but a student who repeatedly makes fun of other students' responses is not acting as a positive member of the classroom community and should not be allowed to remain in the classroom. Later, this chapter addresses "accountable talk" in greater depth and how not to only maintain the norm of respect, but also how to elevate the vocabulary and language of the exchange among members of the class. In addition, Chapter 3 provides explanation of how to establish effective classroom routines.[5]

5   More information can be found in Chapter 3 about an important classroom routine for how students respond to an incorrect answer given by another student.

Supporting Shy, Anxious, and Introverted Students in the Classroom

The focus in this section is on whole-class lecture as well as questions and responses, the most common forms of teaching found in our classrooms. Since the publication of Susan Cain's *Quiet: The Power of Introverts in a World That Can't Stop Talking*, educators have begun to recognize that about a third to half of each class is made up of introverts who are not comfortable with public processing of their thinking, nor are they good at demonstrating their knowledge. Some writers have argued that class participation is an essential twenty-first-century skill. Cain argues that American culture has privileged extroverts and discounted the contributions of introverts, who are not necessarily shy but need time to process ideas internally, as opposed to extroverts, who process their thinking with others. According to research, introverts—many of whom are successful leaders—think more, are less spontaneous, and focus on internal values. In contrast, extroverts gain energy from social situations and tend to be assertive risk-takers who process their thinking in public and comfortably think on their feet. Katherine Schultz says that the contribution of introverts needs to be valued equally with that of extroverts. Not all students who do not volunteer are shy or introverts.

> There are many reasons students may choose not to verbally participate in school. Some students *are* painfully shy and perhaps even introverts. Other students choose their moments to speak carefully, participating in silence for long periods before they decide to speak aloud. Some are quiet in school and loud in other contexts. Sometimes a student's silence protects him or her from ridicule or bullying. In many cultures, silence is a sign of deep respect and more highly valued than talk (2013).

Schultz, author of *Rethinking Classroom Participation: Listening to Silent Voices*, contends that other methods of class participation can be considered, including those "thumbs-up-or-down" silent responses to dipsticking or the "less public" participation of pair work, group work, and multimedia projects in which students speak through prerecorded video presentations, podcasts, and other multimedia alternatives (Schultz 2013).

Schultz describes classrooms where those who

> *When the time comes to solicit responses, students who may be hesitant to speak off the cuff often feel more confident speaking out with a written response in front of them.*

answer questions quickly are seen as the most capable students.

Rapid-paced classrooms favor students who can respond quickly and accurately; other students may need time to reflect and the opportunity to try out ideas in small groups or through writing. Teachers may need to learn to read students' nods and facial expressions to understand silence as a form of participation and to understand that students who are silent may be as engaged in learning as the student who speaks frequently, dominating the conversation (Schultz 2013, p. 23).

Below are some strategies to provide students with time to think, small groups with time to practice, and balanced ways of encouraging student engagement.

The Ball of Knowledge

Teachers may encourage participation with "gimmicks." One teacher with a class of particularly chatty students brought a foam ball into class and made a rule that only the student holding the ball could speak. While the intended purpose of this strategy was to encourage only one student to speak at a time, this teacher discovered another unintended benefit: students were intrigued by the prospect of having the ball thrown to them and then getting to throw the ball back to the teacher following their comments. As a result, the number of student volunteers to respond to the teacher's questions increased dramatically. This method also provides a safer method for participation, since the student can pass and signal to the teacher that he or she wants to contribute. On a side note, this exercise with the ball had a second unintended benefit related to questioning. Such an activity created a concrete tool for the teacher to observe the number of times within a class period that students responded directly to each other, instead of communicating solely with the teacher. The teacher could count the number of times within the period that a student threw the ball to another student, as opposed to throwing it straight back to the teacher.

Processing in Writing Prior to Answering

Another technique that can be used to provide time for students to process and to increase the number of student participants in class discussion is posing a question to students, then asking them to write out an answer to the question prior to when the teacher asks for volunteers. When the time comes to solicit responses, students who may be hesitant to speak off the cuff often feel more confident speaking out with a written response in front of them. This is particularly helpful to those students who use writing as a form of processing. Many adults have learned that they can best think through a problem by writing about the problem. Many students also think best through writing.

Processing Partners

In a similar vein, providing students with two minutes to talk with a partner can provide time to practice, think, and perhaps encourage participation. Using a stopwatch, ask one student to share his or her thoughts for 60 seconds, and then ask the second student to share his or her thoughts for 60 seconds. At the conclusion of this "pair-share" activity, we might ask for volunteers to explain their partners' perspectives. Some students who are hesitant to share their own opinions are less inhibited about sharing someone else's. Sharing the perspective of the other also helps students learn to be better listeners. Earlier in this chapter, we describe a management technique known as *processing partners* for getting students quickly into and out of partner pairs.

If students are particularly shy, we might sit down with them to look over the next day's lesson plan and plan ahead of time the question we will ask and how the student will answer.

Pair-Square

This activity is an extension of pair-share and asks the processing partners to find another pair and continue processing. This is a way of increasing group size gradually.

Calling Sticks

For teachers reluctant to "cold call" students, another perhaps more agreeable technique is writing the name of each student in the class on a popsicle stick and placing all of the sticks in a hat. When the time comes for a student response, the teacher simply reaches into the bag and pulls out a popsicle stick with a student's name on it. That student is then responsible for answering the question.[6] Students often respond better to this type of randomization than they do to the teacher's choosing a person who does not have his or her hand raised. Students tend to feel this is a fairer method. In some cases, the teacher will remove the stick once a student is called. This helps the teacher keep track of who has been called and who has not been called. When using this strategy, it is important

to occasionally go back to the "already-called pile" to ensure that students don't tune out once they have answered a question. Other teachers put the stick back into the container after a student answers, thereby giving that student an equal opportunity to be randomly chosen later in the class period.

Providing the Question to the Student Prior to the Class

If a student is particularly shy, we might even sit down with the student to look over the next day's lesson plan and plan out ahead of time the question that we will ask and how the student will answer. Actually giving the student a question ahead of time may go a long way toward calming his or her nerves. If necessary, we might meet with this student for the first several days after the deal has gone into effect, choosing the question ahead of time that the student will answer. We might even work out a secret signal to alert the student when we are on the verge of posing the previously determined question. For example, we might agree to casually approach the student's desk a moment or two before posing the question. Even after such planning is no longer necessary, we would keep this student's reluctance to volunteer in mind and immediately call on this student to answer whenever he or she raises a hand. In this way, we try to positively reinforce the student's attempts to contribute to the class's discussion.

Alerting the Student That He or She Will Be Asked the Next Question and Providing the Question in Advance

Some students reluctant to answer questions in class feel this way not because they are shy but because they find it difficult to collect their thoughts quickly enough to offer a coherent answer. Increasing wait time is one response to this situation. Students who fit this description might also benefit from the teacher giving them a question ahead of time and telling them that they will soon be called upon to answer it. For example, imagine the following scenario:

Teacher: In *Of Mice and Men*, was Lenny really a good friend to George?

Teacher allows a full three seconds of wait time.

Teacher: I'm going to call on Michelle to answer this question, but, Allison, would you think about specific examples of ways in which Lenny *was* a good

---

6   Some teachers prefer to use index cards (referred to as *calling cards*).

friend to George? And, Peter, would you think about specific examples of ways in which Lenny *was not* a good friend to George? I'm going to call on you both after we hear Michelle's answer.

In this way, the teacher has given both Allison and Peter a few moments to think about the question each will be asked and to formulate a response.

Pygmalion Effect

The way a teacher responds to students' comments or ideas has a dramatic impact on the willingness of students in that class to become regular volunteers and contributors. In asking students questions and then responding to students' answers, teachers need to convey through their tone of voice, body language, and responses that they deeply value their students' contributions to class discussion and instruction. Conveying these beliefs to students has a dramatic impact on their performance. In the classic 1968 work, *Pygmalion in the Classroom,* Rosenthal and Jacobson describe an experiment in which they measured the IQs of the elementary school students in a particular school, chose 20 percent of these students at random, and informed these students' teachers that these particular students were extremely bright and could be expected to make great gains academically over the course of the year. At the end of the school year, Rosenthal and Jacobson measured the IQs of all of these elementary school students once again and discovered that the students they had chosen at random and described to the teachers as extremely bright had increased their IQ scores significantly more than their peers had. The implications of this experiment suggest that a teacher's expectations for his or her students, and the way in which these expectations are conveyed through tone of voice, body language, etc., have a significant impact on these students' achievement.

Group Questions

Providing a small group can create a safer environment for students in which they may answer questions about something that has just been taught. The students are placed in small groups usually composed of three or four students. The group is presented with one or more comprehension questions related to the information or skills that were just taught. Students discuss the question together until they reach consensus on the correct answer. Any questions for which they cannot find consensus answers are listed by the group scribe. Also added to the list are any additional questions raised by members of the group that were not sufficiently answered. The questions on the list are then read to the class by the scribe, without attributing them to any one member of the group. In this activity, reticent students are more willing to ask questions when it will not be known by the class that they originated the questions.

In another variation of this strategy, students are asked to individually complete a reading and to write down any question they have about the reading. Once all the students have written their individual questions, each group leader facilitates a "Q&A" of the group members' questions. Any questions for which the group cannot find a consensus answer are written down by the scribe. These unanswered questions are later read to the entire class by the reporter, without attributing them to any single member of the group. By having the reporter read the questions, the scribe is forced to write legibly. This enables the teacher to collect the questions at the end of the class for the purpose of checking each group's work.

Improving Patterns for Calling on Students

In recent years, much research has been done on the topic of teachers' patterns for calling on students. In racially diverse classrooms, are teachers more likely to call upon students of one race than another? Are teachers more likely to call on boys than girls? Are teachers more likely to call on regular education students than special education students, or students who sit in the front of the classroom versus students who sit in the back? Do right-handed teachers favor students seated on the right side of the room and vice versa for left-handed teachers? To some degree, despite our best intentions, it seems likely that virtually all of us end up favoring one group of students or another in our solicitation of student responses, if only because the student sitting in the front row is more likely to catch our attention, or the young man who waves his arms so frantically that he practically falls out of his seat distracts us from the young lady quietly raising her hand behind him.

Determining our own selection patterns for calling on students, like anything else, requires some action research. Probably the easiest way to conduct this research is to ask a colleague or department head to observe your teaching and to keep track of the students whom you call upon to answer questions. Providing this observer with a seating chart will enable the two of you, afterward during a debriefing session, to note whether students on one side of the room answered a disproportionately higher or lower number of questions than the rest of the class. You may also break your data down by race, gender, special education, and so forth. A teacher could ask your department head or administrator to focus on your questioning patterns during his or her annual observation. This focus is far more likely to be of benefit to you when added to the observation standards that these administrators are using to supervise younger, novice teachers.

If you want to take the issue of questioning and patterns one step further, you might ask a colleague to keep track of the number of times that students respond to each other rather than to you directly. As was mentioned in the section of this chapter discussing wait time, even the most skilled teachers are sometimes surprised by the rarity with which students in a given classroom are actually questioning and responding to each other. Yet, for many of us, our most exciting moments as teachers are those times when students become so engaged in a discussion or activity that we feel confident we could leave the room without the discussion faltering or perhaps even without anyone noticing. For most of us, such an occurrence is not an everyday affair, and yet, paying attention to the volunteering patterns in our classrooms and enlisting the aid of colleagues or supervisors in this endeavor may lead to significant gains in both the quantity and quality of student responses to our questioning practices.

Child Development and Asking Questions

In this chapter, we have divided questions into the categories of recall, comprehension, and higher-order thinking, three ways of classifying thinking that are generally linked to Bloom's taxonomy. Elder and Paul (1997) categorize different types of questions in terms of the cognitive complexity required to answer them. Specifically, they refer to *one-system* questions, which call for clear, concrete answers, and *multi-system* questions, which call for more complex, higher-order responses. Thus, a recall question might be described as a one-system question, while a higher-order thinking question can be categorized as requiring a multi-system response. Comprehension questions typically fall somewhere in between. Professor of education Lesley Farmer (2006) argues that as children mature cognitively, they are able to ask and answer more complex questions. Thus, Farmer recommends that as children approach adolescence, educators begin to pose more abstract questions to their students, as well as ask students a series of questions that build

Those who ask questions—teachers—are not seeking knowledge; those who seek knowledge—students—do not ask questions.

systematically upon each other. In turn, educators can expect their students, with increased age, to use more inferential reasoning in their responses.

In this chapter, we have focused on the purposes and techniques with which teachers pose questions to students. However, an important pitfall to avoid is creating a classroom environment in which "those who ask questions—teachers—are not seeking knowledge; those who seek knowledge—students—do not ask questions" (Dillon 1988, p. 197). On the contrary, significant research exists about the value of student-generated questions.

Shira Lubliner (2001, p. 3) notes that "to form a question, the student must [first] make sense of the text." In "Inviting Student Engagement with Questioning," Caram and Davis (2005, p. 23) describe student-generated questions as a "powerful force for encouraging creative dialogue." According to these educators, student-generated questions lead students to consider multiple perspectives, clarify their own thinking, and strive to influence the opinions of others. Caram and Davis also report that student-generated questions can lead to increased cooperation and decreased competition within a classroom. Finally, Pedrosa de Jesus, Almeida, and Watts (2004) report that classrooms that encourage students to ask questions are more likely to (1) create a culture of inquiry, (2) heighten students' conceptual understanding of the material they are studying, (3) foster engaging discussion and debate, and (4) promote student autonomy in learning.

Recall, however, from earlier in this chapter that researchers have found that students become *less* likely to ask questions as they advance to higher grade levels. Struggling students are reluctant to call attention to their confusion and invite ridicule from their classmates and their teacher. It is crucial, then, that educators take conscious steps to create a safe, respectful classroom atmosphere in which student-generated questions are not just accepted, but also strongly encouraged.

Demand and Cognitive Complexity

The cognitive demand—that is, the specific level of thinking—of the Common Core was based upon Webb's rubric for cognitive complexity, called *depth of knowledge* (DOK). It includes Bloom's taxonomy as part of the model, and adds even more specificity to the rubric and describes tasks for specific content areas, such as reading, writing, science, math, and the arts. A small section for writing is illustrated in Figure 5.5. Hess's categories are listed horizontally; Bloom's categories are listed vertically. For Hess, the categories include four levels: (level 1) recall and reproduction, (level 2) skills and concepts, (level 3) strategic thinking and reasoning, and (level 4) extended thinking. Although Bloom and Hess have similarities, Hess's model goes beyond the verbs used in questions (*apply*, for example) and describes what students need to do. For example, "Use reasoning, planning, and evidence to support inferences" or "Justify or critique conclusions." A complete example is provided in a ninth-grade writing assignment later in this chapter, based on the Common Core standard: "Write arguments to support claims in an analysis of substantive topics or texts, using valid reasoning and relevant and sufficient evidence." This standard comes from the Common Core and falls, as indicated in Figure 5.5 below, in level 3 of Webb's category of **strategic thinking** and within the higher-order thinking skills of **analysis** and **evaluation** from Bloom's taxonomy.

Figure 5.5 Webb's Depth of Knowledge and Bloom's Taxonomy

Bloom	Webb: Level 3 Strategic Thinking
Analysis	• Analyze interrelationships among concepts, issues, and problems. • Apply tools of author's craft (literary devices, viewpoint, or potential dialogue) with intent. • Use reasoning, planning, and evidence to support inferences made.
Evaluation	• Cite evidence and develop a logical argument for conjectures. • Describe, compare, and contrast solution methods. • Verify reasonableness of results. • Justify or critique conclusions.

The descriptors above are modified for each grade level in the Common Core curriculum. Below are the writing standards for argument and opinion for grades one, four, nine, and eleven in the Massachusetts version of the Common Core for English language arts and literacy in history/social studies, science, and technical subjects (Massachusetts Department of Elementary and Secondary Education 2011).

At grade 1: Write opinion pieces in which they introduce the topic or name the book they are writing about, state an opinion, supply a reason for the opinion, and provide some sense of closure.

At grade 4: Write opinion pieces on topics or texts, supporting a point of view with reasons and information.

At grade 9: Write arguments to support claims in an analysis of substantive topics or texts, using valid reasoning and relevant, ufficient evidence.

At grade 11–12: Write precise, knowledgeable claim(s), establish the significance of the claim(s), distinguish the claim(s) from alternate or opposing claims, and create an organization that logically sequences claim(s), counterclaims, reasons, and evidence.

From the four examples above, it can be seen that learning targets in writing have a clear progression in the complexity of the thinking, from stating an opinion about a book or idea in grade one, to adding supporting reasons and information for opinion, analysis of "substantive" topics, and using "valid" reasoning with "relevant" and "sufficient" evidence. And, finally, in grades 11–12, the student must establish the significance of his or her opinion, discuss other opinions, and organize the claims, counterclaims, evidence, and reasons logically. The progression of the Common Core standards, based on Hess's rubric, provide teachers developmental guides for thinking in all areas of the curriculum.

While children increase their ability to answer complex questions as they grow older, their likelihood of *asking* questions may actually diminish with age. Specifically, studies have shown that low-achieving kindergartners ask more questions than their high-achieving classmates because they want to understand the content that is confusing them. Unfortunately, as students progress through primary and secondary schools, low-achieving students begin to ask fewer and fewer questions in comparison to their high-achieving classmates. They are fearful of looking silly and being teased by classmates. In fact, Dillon (1988) reports that struggling high school students are more likely to ask a classmate a question than they are their teacher. It is crucial that educators in the upper grades be aware of this tendency in order to do everything in their power to create a classroom environment that encourages struggling students to ask questions and clear up confusion. Pedrosa De Jesus, Almeida, and Watts (2004, p. 533) report that "learners will ask questions when they have high levels of self-confidence and self-esteem within the learning context, when their questions are seen to be valued, and when the class environment leads to the disequilibrium needed for the generation of questions." Thus, the educational environment needs to be safe and, at the same time, lead to "disequilibrium," which refers to the cognitive dissonance or disruption caused by inquiry and by asking good questions that engage and involve students in the pursuit of answers. These are all-important steps that educators can take to ensure that their classrooms are "safe spaces" for asking as well as answering questions. These safe classrooms support the notion that misunderstandings are part of learning and that mistakes are understood as part of everyone's process of learning.

Increased Cognitive Complexity's Impact on Questioning and the Classroom

The increase of cognitive complexity, as illustrated with writing in the "Cognitive Demand and Cognitive Complexity" section in this chapter, reinforces the need for higher-order questioning in the classroom. In addition, the higher expectations for literacy and numeracy make it even more necessary that teachers deliberately collect, analyze, and provide effective feedback to student responses to these questions.

The Need for Increasing the Use of Formative Assessments and Deepening Practice

In *Education Week*, Liana Heiltin says teachers need to consciously use data (Heiltin 2015):

> As the majority of teachers around the country transition to the Common Core State Standards—which are designed to emphasize complexity, critical thinking, and skills like collaboration and reasoning—some experts say more teachers need to deepen their assessment practices. In other words, they need to begin seeing themselves … as teacher researchers.

Margaret Heritage, the assistant director for professional development at the National Center for Research on Evaluation, Standards, and Student Testing at the University of California, Los Angeles, says,

> To get a full picture of student understanding, teachers need to ask open-ended questions and push students to explore ideas aloud. We need to know if [students are] grappling with complex ideas. … Where are they? Is the idea beginning to consolidate? What do I need to do to go deeper and really help them get this? (Heiltin 2015)

The questioning techniques addressed in the first half of this chapter provide the first step in asking more from students. In addition, Heritage says, "We'll need a lot more talking, more focus, more discourse, more depth." Teachers will need to ask guiding questions and to get students talking about their thinking and how they learn in all content areas.

The Potential Impact of Formative Assessment

The impact of effective, systematic formative assessment at its best can increase a student's learning by an additional half year. According to a meta-analysis of the many variables that affect student learning, John Hattie (2009, 2011) found that formative assessment had an effect size of 0.71 in 2009, updating that number to 0.9 in 2011. To understand how great this impact is, an effect size of 1.0 is equivalent to increasing one standard deviation. To relate the number to one year's learning, an effect size of 1.0 means that the defined instructional strategy improved the rate of learning by 50 percent of one year's worth of growth. The typical effect size of teachers' impact on students is 0.4. Hattie uses 0.4 as the "hinge point," the place to begin his study of high-impact teacher moves, to determine the techniques that improve or have little impact on student achievement (Hattie 2009).

Thus, students learn far more when both long-term interim assessments and in-the-moment assessments are used to verify that students understand a concept sufficiently to move on, or that the lesson needs to slow down and that the teacher needs to modify the planned lesson to make sure that students understand.

Consistent use of formative assessment is a change in practice for many teachers who have not used "in-the-moment" assessment as a tool for deciding whether to move on, re-teach, or differentiate instruction. Research (Black and Wiliam 2003; Hattie 2009; Hattie 2012; Wiliam 2011), with Hattie (2007, p. 102) has found that this single change in teaching by checking student's progress throughout the teaching process, as described below, can result in a profound increase in student achievement in the entire class.

The techniques for in-the-moment formative assessment are provided in detail below.

Assessing Student Learning to Inform and Target Instruction

Many international experts consider formative assessment to be one of the most important elements of assessment for learning (Black and Wiliam 2003; Hattie 2009; Hattie 2012; Wiliam 2011), with Hattie (2007, p. 102) calling it "among the most critical influences on student learning." In his 2012 meta-analysis of what works in schools, Hattie found that formative assessments are by far the most influential practice that improves student outcomes" (Duckor 2014, pp. 28–32).

Beyond improving student achievement, formative assessments and effective feedback can increase learner satisfaction and persistence (Kluger and DeNisi 1996), and contribute to students adopting more productive learning strategies (Vollmeyer and Rheinberg 2005). However, what counts as "good feedback" needs to be clarified, as feedback is considered the element of formative assessment "most laden with a legacy of bad practice and misguided views" (Brown, Harris, and Harnett 2012).

Teachers also recognize the importance of formative assessment and feedback within an assessment for learning environment, and they believe that they can increase student achievement when it is focused on learning targets and is part of an interactive process between teacher and students (Fisher and Frey 2014). **Educational researcher Robert J. Marzano states that it is formative assessment, not summative, that has a strong research base supporting its impact on learning** (Marzano 2006).

According to Dylan Wiliam, "The strongest evidence of improved gains comes from short-cycle formative assessment (over seconds or minutes within a single lesson), rather than medium to long-term assessment where assessment is used to change the teacher's regular classroom practice" (Wiliam 2006).

Interim and common assessments do not have as strong of an effect on student achievement. These "medium-cycle" assessments are formal exams given periodically to assess students' progress toward goals. They are often used to identify individual student needs, the strategies needed to achieve mastery, and the areas of the curriculum that provide the greatest challenges (Dufour, Eaker, et al 2005). While such assessments clearly have a valuable role to play in aligning instruction with standards, providing a focus for professional dialogue, and for supporting good management and supervision, the evidence on the impact of such "medium-cycle" formative assessments, common exams, and interim assessments[7] on

> *Medium-cycle formative assessments, common exams, and interim assessments on student achievement is weak, especially when compared to "short-cycle" formative assessments that take place daily in classrooms.*

student achievement is weak, especially when compared to "short-cycle" formative assessments that take place daily in classrooms.

Teachers also see formative assessment as a powerful tool for supporting student achievement, as reported by the Scholastic and Gates Foundation survey of 40,000 American public school teachers:

Ninety-two percent of teachers say ongoing in-classroom assessment is either very important or absolutely essential in measuring student performance. Teachers indicate that formative, ongoing assessments during class, along with class participation and performance on class assignments, are the most important measures of student achievement" (Scholastic and Gates Foundation 2010).

Most importantly, effective formative assessment provides major gains for all students:

The research evidence suggests that **when formative assessment practices are integrated into the minute-to-minute and day-by-day classroom activities of teachers, substantial increases in student achievement—of the order of a 70 to 80 percent increase in the speed of learning—are possible**, even when outcomes are measured with externally mandated standardized tests. Indeed, the currently available evidence suggests that there is nothing else that is remotely affordable that is likely to have such a large effect (Leahy and Wiliam 2012, p. 18).

The last half of this chapter is focused on the data that surrounds teachers every day. After teachers ask questions, next they have to analyze the results of the questions and provide feedback that provides students with clear next steps.

Using Student Responses Effectively

To use formative assessment effectively, the teacher first needs to be clear about the destination for every member of the class. He or she needs to define the destination—that is, the goal—of the class, unit, or course through a clearly stated mastery objective. In addition, to engage in sound formative-assessment practice, teachers need to keep five things in mind.

1. **Setting clear mastery objectives.** Clearly laying out what they want students to learn in mastery objectives or learning targets.

---

7   See Chapter 4 for a full discussion of interim and common assessments.

2. **Gathering and analyzing evidence of learning.** Eliciting evidence of that learning through questioning, in-the-moment assessments, Do Nows, student work, group work, exit slips, quizzes, and tests.

3. **Interpreting evidence in relationship to the students' progress** toward the learning goal. Rubrics and checklists may serve as guides.

4. **Providing actionable feedback** is the next step that students need to continue their trajectory toward independent mastery.

5. **Adjusting teaching in response to students' needs.** Acting on the evidence to adjust teaching if necessary, which may include reteaching, differentiating instruction, conferencing, peer conferencing, group work, and individual conferences.

According to Ruth McKenna, a facilitator for WestEd, "Without the clear articulation of what students must do to show mastery, teachers can't give students solid 'actionable feedback' so they know how to move forward" (Gewertz 2015).

The Necessity of a Feedback Loop with "Actionable Feedback"

The two key elements in the effective use of formative assessment are analyzing the data and providing quality feedback. That feedback needs to be focused on the appropriate next step toward the mastery objective for either the class, specific groups of students, or specific students. The next step may be what has been planned for the day or a change in direction for the lesson. Formative assessments provide essential, often in-the-moment data that helps teachers decide on the appropriate next step for the class, groups of students, or individual students as they move toward application mastery[8] of their learning targets.

Some researchers describe the formative assessment process as a *feedback loop* both for teachers and for students. Teachers gain a clear picture of how each student is learning, and students have time to reflect on their learning so far and to take actionable steps to improve their work. It is essential that students are engaged in every step of this feedback loop. They must take action to gain mastery. In the next section, you will see how this feedback loop works in a three-day unit on writing.

As seen in Figure 5.6, both teachers and students receive feedback throughout the entire unit as all students and the teacher work together to achieve ap-

Figure 5.6
Formative Assessment Feedback Loop

plication mastery of the learning target. The teacher is responsible for providing actionable feedback, and the students are responsible for acting on this feedback as well as on reflecting meta-cognitively on their progress. Peers can also be involved in this loop as they work as processing partners and perhaps conference with others in the class.

Limitations for Implementation of an Ongoing System of Formative Assessment

In classrooms in which the pacing chart, the textbook, or the lesson plan drives the timing of a lesson, and the teacher does not collect or act on how students are learning, the lesson might proceed without the teacher's knowing or acting on the knowledge that some or all students are confused. In traditional classrooms, the summative assessment occurred when a teacher discovered the degree of understanding of his or her students. The traditional model is often described as teach, test, move on. In traditional classrooms, teachers taught to "the middle," or to average students, and followed a predetermined pace for coverage of the content, not for the students' learning.

Thus, taking the time for ongoing assessment and analysis of this information is a challenge when implementing formative assessment in every classroom. The remaining half of this chapter will provide examples of how to assess, track, analyze, and give effective feedback and how to do all of these things efficiently.

The need for making formative assessment a daily,

---

8   See Chapter 1 for a full explanation of mastery learning and mastery objectives.

ongoing process is essential if a teacher wants to improve the achievement of all students. Fisher and Frey describe the unique nature of formative assessment:

> Only formative assessment practices can deliver timely data about what students understand. Without formative assessment data, teaching is aimed at the middle. We'll never know which students were ready for a stretch, and which needed reteaching. Unfortunately, too often formative assessment has been reduced to two or three district benchmark tests, with little attention given to the data that surround us every day (Fisher and Frey 2014, p. vii).

Formative Assessments: From Introduction to Mastery

The process of learning begins with the introductory stage of mastery and ends with application mastery. The "target" in targeted instruction is application mastery, which occurs when a student can independently demonstrate his or her knowledge in a new context. See Chapter 1 for a complete description of mastery learning, as illustrated in the table below.

Figure 5.7   Mastery Learning

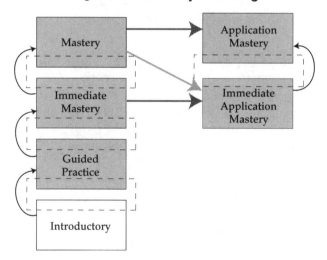

In-the-Moment Formative Assessments

Researchers would call the responses that students give *data*, regardless of whether those responses come from the whole-class or a small group, whether they're written or oral, or whether they occur "on the spot" or are planned by the district. Teachers need to use this information, or data, to make decisions about whether to modify their instruction by, for example, reteaching, differentiating their instruction, or moving on to the next unit. Because the data collected may

confirm that students are ready to move on and that the lesson, as planned, is the best course for all learners, formative assessments do not necessarily need to result in changes in the direction of the lesson (Leahy and Wiliam 2012).

This data from classroom-based formative assessments provides information *both* to teachers and to students because learners need to assess the progress of their learning, too. Monique Boekaerts, in the *Handbook of Child Psychology*, contends that learners *first* need to decide *that* they will learn. For without that willful choice by the learner, limited learning takes place for that student (Boekaerts 2006, p. 367). In addition, Wiliam again affirms that student involvement in the entire formative cycle is essential, for they must respond to the actionable feedback from the teacher.

Black provides a comprehensive definition of classroom formative assessment:

> **Practice in a classroom is formative to the extent that evidence about student achievement is elicited, interpreted, and used by teachers, learners, or their peers to make decisions about the next steps in instruction that are likely to be better, or better founded, than the decisions they would have taken in the absence of the evidence that was elicited** (Black and Wiliam 2009, p. 9).

Based on Black's definition, Leahy and Wiliam clearly defined the learning roles and responsibilities of both students and teachers in their research. Their schema, summarized in Figure 5.8, includes the following perspectives:

* the teacher who designs the tasks, the learning targets, the measurement, and who also provides feedback
* the student-as-learner whose role is to actively seek his own growth
* the student-as-peer-teacher who would need ongoing training in providing feedback, but who would also play an active role in providing resources for other students' learning

According to Fisher and Frey in *Formative Assessment*, "Intentional and targeted instruction is based on the gradual release of responsibility (GRR) framework" (2014). This chapter will follow Vygotsky's recommended sequence for teaching and learning—that is, a gradual increase of independence for the student as the teacher modifies his or her role from direct teacher to guide or coach. This four-step

Figure 5.8 Teacher and Student Roles in Mastery Learning

Introductory	Guided Practice	Immediate Application Mastery	Independent Application Mastery
Teacher • Develops and presents the target goal. • Models. • Asks questions. • Demonstrates. • Describes expectations with rubrics and checklists.	**Teacher** • Guides. • Provides graphic organizers and examples. • Gives feedback. • Provides mini-lessons.	**Teacher** • Coaches. • Gives feedback. • Conferences.	**Teacher** • Conferences. • Guides. • Gives feedback.
Students Learn from teacher. Meta-cognitive phase: need to decide to learn.	**Students** *Gradually* assimilate the skill or concept and gradually try out ideas. Meta-cognitive phase: need to self-assess progress and decide on next steps.	**Students** *Begin to* put the target goal's ideas into their own words, or begin to apply the skill or concept. Meta-cognitive phase: need to self-assess progress and decide on next steps.	**Students** Can *independently* use the skill or concept in a new context. May refer to "guardrails," such as rubrics, anchor charts, and checklists. May ask questions of teacher or peers. Meta-cognitive phase: need to self-assess progress and decide on next steps. Need to assess the whole process of his or her learning.
Peers May work with others, such as taking cooperative notes. Role: co-learner Learns about collaborative work.	**Peers** May work with others, such as annotating a text. May work in groups with specific role. Role: co-learner Learns about collaborative work.	**Peers** May work in groups, such as a Socratic seminar. May conference with peer. Role: student-as-teacher possibly May evaluate peers' work. Learns about academic conversations and elevating responses.	**Peers** May work in groups, such as a group presentation or skit. May conference with peer using a rubric or checklist Role: student-as-teacher possibly May evaluate peers' work.

process parallels the four-step process of attaining mastery. Figure 5.8 illustrates the changing roles of both teacher and student through the four-stages of attaining mastery or, in Vygotsky's words, independence. The next sections will provide several examples of formative assessments for each of the four phases of mastery learning: (1) introductory, (2) guided practice, (3) immediate application mastery, and (4) application mastery. Students play an essential role as they gain independence and mastery, and they have a second—and equally important—role as a peer to other students as they learn collaboratively with their peers and provide feedback to them when they assess

one another's work using classroom guides. This also happens as they take on roles that can improve the academic conversations in the class. This process is illustrated for the teacher, the student, and peers in Figure 5.8.

It is important to note that this model for formative assessment illustrated in Figure 5.8 describes a *collaborative* classroom in which peers play a major role as they work in groups and in peer-to-peer conferences. The individual learner, too, has a major role for formative assessment's power to be effective.

Working Smart with Actionable Feedback

To make efficient use of student responses, Fisher and Frey have four recommendations for teachers:

1. Focus on the most important error that needs to improve the quality of the work. If most students are having difficulty in writing a conclusion in a science lab, focus on improving conclusions.
2. Look for patterns of errors in individual students' work and in the work of the class as a whole. In a science lab report, do you see pervasive problems in conclusions? Or do you see unique problems, such as displaying data in a graph for one or two students?
3. Distinguish between errors that apply to most of the class and unique errors; address the class's concerns as a class, and unique errors with individual or small-group feedback.
4. Use prompts and cues, rubrics, checklists, anchor charts, and examples to support students (Adapted from Fisher and Frey 2012, pp 42–47).

Just as important as the involvement of teachers is the engagement of students as learners and as collaborators. Wiliam cites Kluger and Denisi's 1996 study on the results of 90 years of research. They found that in 38 percent of the studies, feedback made performance worse (Wiliam 2015). These findings indicate that in order to be successful in moving all students to their target performance, the quality of the feedback must be high and that it is clearly a next step. In addition, students need to respond to this feedback.

A clear example of an efficient formative assessment that follows the first three principles for the teacher is one described in "My Favorite No." The middle school math teacher collected student responses from their warm-ups on note cards and focused on a pattern of errors that applied to most of the class (principles one, two, and three).

Another method for making efficient choices is to use the rubric for the mastery objective on a clipboard to record the level of students' work both as individuals (Amy, Cathy, Emily, etc.) and as a flexible group with a shared need. In addition, the chart notes the level of work (Mastered, Proficient, Needs Improvement, and Basic). The teacher has sorted their work on their first paragraph of a research paper into levels of mastery and has described the next step for each category. This rubric could be used for research in all content areas. The level of mastery would vary by grade level.

Thus, all four recommendations were followed in Figure 5.9 on the next page. The teacher in a fifth-grade social studies class had this form on a clipboard, and as students were working, she looked at each student's work. As she looked at the collected paragraphs, she determined the level of the work and the next actionable steps for each group. As she made these decisions, she also decided that she would teach a mini-lesson to all students about the next step in peer conferencing to support all students and provide herself time to have focused conferences with the *basic* and *needs improvement* groups. She would, of course, visit every group to check on their progress.

Using a rubric to give feedback is efficient for the teacher and provides supportive feedback about the student's learning in terms that the class has already discussed. By using a rubric, which may even have been developed by the class, the work stays focused on the destination—the final essay—and through the descriptors in the rubric, the work is carefully described by each level of proficiency.

In addition, in this example, the teacher also provided other scaffolds, including a template for writing a first paragraph, as well as an opportunity to receive structured feedback from a peer.

Deal-Breaker Question

In addition, the teacher looked for the answer to her "deal-breaker" question that she had prepared in advance: *Do you have a draft of a paragraph with at least a claim and one piece of evidence?* After a day of work, most students were still struggling with the claims, so she had provided samples from students from the year before for small groups of students to identify by highlighting claims and evidence. The assessment in Figure 5.9 is from the following day, when it is clear that many students had both claims and evidence.

Skip Fennel suggests planning quick formative assessments in advance. If students cannot answer them, the teacher will plan to reteach or revisit the concept until students can move along (Fennell, et al. 2015, pp. 325–327). Students in the *basic* level were struggling with writing a claim and needed more scaffolds, including a template, examples, and a conference in order to make progress.

The Quick Sort

The chart in Figure 5.9 can be used to gather information and analyze the results quickly. If a teacher collects student work and does a quick sort based on a rubric or on the major problems that influence the mastery objective, then the teacher has a clear focus that will allow him or her to sort students' work quickly and efficiently in order to plan actionable next steps for students. It needs to be noted that when

Figure 5.9 Tracking Student Mastery

Description: Introductory Paragraph: Hook, Claims, Evidence			
Quality: See rubric			
Level of Mastery	Mastered	Proficient (Immediate Application Mastery)	Needs Improvement (Guided Practice)	Basic (Introductory)
Student	Amy	Cathy	Emily Hook	Heidi Use template
Student	Bob	Dave	Frank Hook	Jim Use template
Student			Kim Details	
Student			Leon Details	
Next Step	Peer conference using checklist and rubric	Peer conference using checklist and rubric	Peer conference focusing on area of need: hook or details (handout)	Use template and conference first with me, then work together
Whole Class	Mini-lesson on peer conferencing using the template, a checklist, and the rubric. Create handout for conferencing: 1. Trade papers. 2. Be positive; ask questions; go over the checklist, rubric, and template and what you did with each. 3. Exchange papers and select 2 areas for comments. a. One positive b. One question 4. Work on your own paragraph and discuss what you did with partner if you have time.			

evidence is collected, at times it will indicate that all but a few students are ready to go on. In this case, the teacher might develop work for a few students, and perhaps they can do this when they conference with the teacher or as homework, but he or she may decide to continue with the lesson or unit as planned for the rest of the class.

Exit Tickets: Quick Assessments of Mastery

Marzano suggests using exit slips for a variety of purposes in addition to assessing students' progress toward mastery. These exit slips could prompt reflection on the student's or group's progress, or even address the activities that have worked for students or that have not worked for a specific student (Marzano 2012, pp. 80–81).

For example, in a programming class, the teacher had red, yellow, and green circles near the exit. Students were asked to use sticky notes on the green circle to indicate what was going well, what they had some questions about on the yellow circle, and what, if anything, was stopping their progress. Their assignment was to create an infographic based on their research on projected employment in an industry of their chosen field, including information technology, culinary arts, mechanical engineering, and construction.

Accountable Talk: Improving the Quality of Student Responses

In their book, *Academic Conversations: Classroom Talk That Fosters Critical Thinking and Content Understandings*, Zwiers and Crawford found that classroom discussions were essential for student growth. The intense discussions that probe deeply into understanding concepts enhance academic achievement. In addition to responding to higher-order questions from their teachers and their peers, students are learning the language both of academia in general and of literacy as it works within the academic disciplines.

Robert Gallimore, in *Teachers College Record*, describes the essential element of discussions that improve student achievement, slowing down and emphasizing. Gallimore found that what distinguished higher-achieving countries from the US was the nature of learning opportunities provided to students. He states:

> With varying degrees of frequency, all higher-achieving countries slowed down instruction at some point in some lessons to ensure that students had *rich opportunities to learn*—time to grapple with the key… ideas and connect them (Gallimore, Hiebert, and Ermeling, October 2014, pp. 1–3).

In these moments of "slowed-down instruction," teachers led discussions that focused on major, and sometimes difficult to understand, key ideas. For example, a fifth-grade teacher did a lesson on the Colonists and taxation. Some students realized that their original pile of 20 candies were gone to the tax collector and King George because they were taxed for having a house, a horse, a pet, and four children in their role-playing, but that others still had all of their candies. The teacher saw an opportunity to help students understand why the "rebels" wanted independence and how taxation worked. They were going to have a debate the next day, and this discussion about how wars started and why taxes made a difference was a perfect opportunity for deep thinking and a "rich opportunity to learn" from this simulation.

Although the intention for some groups is to provide opportunities for grappling with important ideas, Deanna Kuhn has described the flaws in the group work that she observed during her research.

> When students work in groups, the most-competent members sometimes do the heavy lifting, coming up with the answer (or solving the problem) without transmitting their skills and knowledge to their peers. Group members sometimes engage in parallel work without truly engaging with each other's thinking. And some students work better alone than in a group (Kuhn 2015, pp. 46–7).

Teachers need to set expectations for roles and responsibilities as well as provide specific practice in accountable talk and deep conversations. See Chapter 3 for a complete discussion of the essential components of effective group work. When Kuhn observed students working in groups, she found that the key ingredient for learning was not group work or collaboration. Instead, it was "grappling with a challenging problem with knowledge insufficient to solve it, which required students to extend and apply existing knowledge and understanding to generating a solution" (Kuhn 2015, p. 48). If students were grappling with a problem, she found that working alone was as effective as working collaboratively.

However, Kuhn found that collaboration did have a positive impact when the problem that they were grappling with had two opposing views. So, when students were working on developing an argument and dealing with two opposing views, working collaboratively improved student performance, because to write an effective argument, they had to deal with how they thought as individuals about the differing perspectives. She found that working alone or sharing written responses was not nearly as productive as collaboration had been for writing arguments.

> Intellectual collaboration is a[n academic conversational] skill, learned through engagement and practice and much trial and error. Without sufficient skill development, children may fail to benefit from it (Kuhn 2015, p. 50).

Gallimore found, too, that quality discussions were essential for student learning, and their quality and depth seemed to be the "critical and significant distinction between the US and higher-achieving countries." He emphasizes that discussions may have been spontaneous or unplanned in those other countries, but what distinguishes them is that the teaching "slows down" and provides "time to grapple with the key ideas." When he observed American classrooms, he saw more group work in which students were discussing, but he did not necessarily see the intentionality and deliberate focus on grappling with key ideas and connecting them that he had observed in deep discussions in other countries (Gallimore, Hiebert, and Ermeling 2014).

Many of the teaching techniques described in the first half of this chapter can provide opportunities for rich discussions. Evelyn Ford-Connors and Jeanne Paratore, describe the teacher "moves" that raise the level of student discourse:

> Variety in teachers' questioning techniques extends and challenges students' thinking while encouraging the exploratory talk that supports critical analysis of content. A broad repertoire of teacher talk moves, including, for example, questioning,

elaborating, or speculating, scaffolds students' participation and offers students models for engaging in academic inquiry (Ford-Connors and Paratore 2015, p. 85).

Zwiers and Crawford cite four essential areas that students need to become more competent in academic discussions throughout their school years:

1. The **vocabulary** of a specific discipline must be used in academic discussions. For example, in history, vocabulary may include primary sources, historical context, or point of view; in science, the language of the scientific experiment, such as hypothesis, data, and conclusions, or the specific steps in design engineering; in the arts, portfolio development to demonstrate learning; in language arts, the genres of literature and the types of writing as well as their forms and uses; in mathematics, the language of algebra, geometry, and the higher mathematics areas.

2. **Critical thinking skills** of each discipline, such as how to write a scientific conclusion or how to analyze data; how to put a primary source into its appropriate historical context; how to critique a work of art, a concert, or a dance; how to write a literary analysis and include multiple perspectives; in mathematics, finding the most economical and clear solution; or in research, how to analyze, summarize, paraphrase, and synthesize ideas.

3. **Literacy skills** of reading and writing in each discipline: reading and interpreting scientific research and experiments; reading and writing like a historian; reading and interpreting a graph or data; reading and interpreting literature.

4. **The tone and quality of academic discussions**: How to listen closely, give others credit for their ideas, disagree respectfully, invite all into the conversation, and work collaboratively (adapted from Zwiers and Crawford 2011).

Kyleen Beers, in *Notice and Note: Strategies for Close Reading*, has developed a helpful Rigor and Talk checklist listing all of the social and academic areas that need to be considered as students acquire the literacies of science, history, mathematics, language arts, and all other disciplines. She describes the following categories:

1. **Dispositions**. Students need to have certain attitudes to have effective discourse, such as curiosity, patience, courtesy, and acknowledging the work of others.

2. **Use of text**. Students need to return to the text to find evidence and to connect the themes, format, or ideas from one text to another.

3. **Ideas**. Students need to be able to use ideas in a variety of ways, including hypothesizing, seeing alternative perspectives, and building on others' ideas.

4. **Reasoning**. Students need to use evidence to prove their claims and need to understand the art of persuasion, including using emotional appeals and logic.

5. **Academic language**. Students need to understand the vocabulary of different disciplines—such as hypotheses, primary sources, literary devices—and to understand the conventions of different disciplines, such as taking an objective stance in science, considering the context in history, or understanding the author's attitude or tone in literature (adapted from Beers and Probst 2013, p. 202).

It is important to note that both the social-emotional attitudes, such as curiosity and patience, as well as academic skills, such as the use of evidence and seeing alternative perspectives, are included in Beers' list for essential classroom discussions.

Changing the Quality of Classroom Discussions

The research indicates that engaging students in the higher-order thinking required in academic conversations requires good questioning from teachers; the setting of classroom expectations for engaging in conversations with the whole class and small groups; and a shift from the language of the corridors and schoolyard to that of a classroom. The University of Pittsburgh has developed a program to accomplish this goal called "Accountable Talk." The shift is significant both in the language that is used and in the social norms that are followed.

When classroom talk is accountable to the learning community, students listen to one another, not just obediently keeping quiet until it is their turn to take the floor, but attending carefully so that they can use and build on one another's ideas. Students and teachers paraphrase and expand upon one another's contributions. If speakers aren't sure they understood what someone else said, they make an effort to clarify. They disagree respectfully, challenging a claim, not the person who made it. Students move the argument forward, sometimes with the teacher's help, sometimes on their own (Michaels, O'Connor, and Resnick 2010, pp. 2–3).

Students are taught and supported to be accountable to

- their community, that is, they respectfully listen and contribute
- accurate knowledge
- rigorous thinking

Through protocols, specific expectations for participation when discussing, and well-defined discussion activities such as partner talk, whole-group discussion, and small-group talk, students learn to engage in purposeful academic conversations. Accountable Talk provides clear standards for K–12 classrooms.

There are five academic and conversational principles for Accountable Talk (Michaels, O'Connor, and Resnick 2010, pp. 2–3):

1. Press for clarification and explanation.
2. Require justification of proposals and challenges.
3. Recognize and challenge misconceptions.
4. Demand evidence for claims and arguments.
5. Interpret and use each other's statements.

Lisa Arter has developed an activity that scaffolds academic discourse, which she calls the five R's: respond, repeat, restate, rebut, and reinforce. She describes the process in which she uses a Koosh ball as what is sometimes called a *conversation stick* to provide focus on the speaker. She describes the four-step sequence (Arter 2015, p. 8):

1. When a student finishes responding to a question, the teacher tosses a Koosh ball to another student and says, "**Repeat**," and the student tries to reiterate what the first student said.
2. The Koosh ball then returns to the first student, who is asked to **restate** if the previous student didn't capture his or her meaning.
3. The Koosh ball then comes back to the teacher, who tosses it to another student and says, "**Rebut**," and that student has to disagree or agree with the original response and give a reason.
4. The Koosh ball then goes to another randomly selected student to "**reinforce**." This student has the option to support either the original response or the rebuttal with additional supporting evidence.

In one elementary school, teachers who had been successful in developing the norms for academic talk for fifth graders worked with third-grade teachers to develop norms, to read a book in both fifth and third grades, and then to pair up fifth graders with third

When classroom talk is accountable to the learning community, students listen to one another, not just obediently keeping quiet until it is their turn to take the floor, but attending carefully so that they can use and build on one another's ideas.

graders to discuss the book using the protocols. The classrooms met several times and the teachers videotaped the conversations. They found that the third graders became more and more comfortable with the norms on their anchor charts and would say, "I agree with what Susan said, and I'd like to add," and invited students into the conversation with questions like, "Ian, is there anything you want to add?" The video recordings also showed that students' responses became longer, more elaborate, and stayed focused on author's craft and the notes that they had developed before they began the conversation. When they tried the same experiment with the two grades in mathematics, they were initially disappointed because the students did not talk as fluently or as easily as they had about the shared novel. After some deliberation, the teachers found that students needed manipulatives or something to write on in order to have conversations about mathematics. Once they were provided with small white boards and erasable markers, they had sustained conversations and "grappled with" the mathematical questions as effectively as they had worked with literature (Action Research on Accountable Talk 2015).

Figure 5.10

Accountable Talk...

"As Jim said before..."
　　to give credit to someone else's ideas

"I respectfully disagree..."
　　to dispute someone's ideas

"Have you had a chance to talk?"
　　to make sure everyone talks

"Thank you..."
　　to end the discussion

We will listen closely.
We will bring the notes we have on the topic.

Accountable Talk needs to become a part of the classroom norms for the secondary classroom as well. In an international baccalaureate theory of knowledge class, students developed the norms for discussion together and then posted their rules (see Figure 5.11).

Figure 5.11

In Our Discussions, We Will

- listen to one another (not just wait until the other person stops talking)
- respond to other people's ideas by giving them respect and credit
- give credit to others in the class and to other writers we've read
- accurately characterize ideas (both those that we agree with and those that we don't)
- not take someone's disagreement with our ideas personally
- prepare so that we can contribute
- appreciate others
- add to this list as we go along

A Classroom Example of the Complete Formative Assessment Process—One-Week Unit in Developing an Introductory Paragraph for Ninth Graders

What follows is a step-by-step description of the four-stage process of moving students to mastery in this case in writing an argument. With the Common Core, students are expected to demonstrate literacy in each content area. They are expected to write arguments in social studies, history, science, the technical subjects, literature, and English language arts, although these arguments may be called primary-source analysis, scientific journal articles, art or music critiques, or proposals or business plans in the world of manufacturing, construction, and marketing. Literacy standards apply to all of these content areas. In mathematics, too, the Common Core frameworks state that mathematically proficient students

> justify their conclusions, communicate them to others, and respond to the arguments of others. They reason inductively about data, making plausible arguments that take into account the context from which the data arose. Mathematically proficient students are also able to compare the effectiveness of two plausible arguments, distinguish correct logic or reasoning from that which is flawed, and—if there is a flaw in an argument—explain what it is (Massachusetts Curriculum Frameworks for Mathematics 2011, pp. 15–16).

Figure 5.12 on the next page provides a step-by-step narrative about how to use rubrics, templates, quick sorts, peer feedback, conferences, and many formative assessments to group students flexibly for actionable feedback so that they can reach their goal of writing a good introductory paragraph. The process moves all of the students from the introductory stage to mastery, though the quality of students' work will vary based upon many factors.

The table below provides the four-step sequence from introduction to application mastery. The chart describes the teacher's responsibilities alongside the student's progress in his journey from novice to application mastery. It also includes peer activities as the weight responsibility shifts from the teacher in the introductory phase to the student in the final application mastery phase. As a reminder, students have two roles: learner and peer to other learners in the class.

Day 1: Introductory Phase

The teacher provides the learning target or destination of the lesson or unit. Students are novices at this time, though they all have written research in world history before. In this example, we follow three students working on a ninth-grade unit for developing a strong introductory paragraph. In the introductory phase, the teacher provides students with a complete description of the mastery objective for the entire research paper, a sample rubric that describes what the first paragraph will look like, and examples of strong and weak introductory paragraphs. The class works through these documents as the teacher takes the lead and as students work with peers and ask clarifying questions.

Figure 5.12 **Teacher and Student Activities in the Stages of Mastery**

Stage of Attaining Mastery	Classroom Activities	
	Teacher	**Students**
1. Introductory	**Direct Teaching** Introduces the mastery goal. Leads the instruction and asks most of the questions. Provides the assignment, examples, rubrics, and checklists. Assesses progress formatively. Provides feedback. May teach mini-lessons, lecture, and have question-and-response and discussions.	Begin to develop an understanding of the mastery learning target. May work collaboratively to develop a description of a good introductory paragraph.
2. Guided Practice	**Guides Students Closely** Provides graphic organizers, templates, and organizes activities. Assesses progress formatively. Provides feedback. May teach mini-lessons. May have discussions.	**Gain comprehension** in group and individual work in the moment, using goals of mastery to assess progress. May work collaboratively.
3. Immediate Application Mastery	**Organizes, Coaches Activities** Coaches. Conferences with individuals. Conferences with groups. Assesses progress formatively. Provides feedback. May teach mini-lessons. May have discussions.	**Moving toward Owning the Ideas Independently** Begin to gain independence with the mastery objective. Practice in seminars, discussions, on-demand writing, and individual problem solving. Differentiated feedback using mastery goals/rubrics. Work collaboratively much of the time.
4. Application Mastery	**Guide on the Side** May teach mini-lessons. May have discussions. Conferences with groups. Conferences with individuals.	**Independent Mastery** Demonstrate competence in projects, presentations, and tests. Using rubrics, checklists, self-evaluation, and common exams. Work independently and collaboratively. Work in peer conferencing.

Figure 5.13 Introductory Phase

Stage of Attaining Mastery	Classroom Activity	
1. Introductory	**Teacher Direct Teaching** Provides examples of first paragraphs. Provides a labeled first paragraph for "Little Red Riding Hood." Provides steps for creating a thesis with sentence frames.	**Students** Begin to develop an Understanding Students work collaboratively, and read and analyze paragraph examples.
Formative Assessment: The teacher judges student understandings based on their questions as they discuss the assignment and the goals.		

The Mastery Objective: Write an effective introduction for an argument.

The Common Core Standard: 9.1. Write arguments to support claims in an analysis of substantive topics or texts, using valid reasoning and relevant and sufficient evidence.

The Assignment: Write a strong introductory paragraph with a clear thesis using *Where the Wild Things Are* (*WTWTA*), the children's book.

First, you need to determine one of the themes of the story and the eight elements of fiction.

Then, you will develop your thesis from the answer to the question: How does Sendak develop the theme, with your choice of any single element of fiction: plot, setting, character, tone, symbol/motif/image, style, and point of view?

Figure 5.14 Student Handout on Introductory Paragraph: Developing the Theme

1.   What is the lesson learned by the main character?
Max learns that _____.

2.   Now, take Max's lesson and apply it to everyone. That's the beginning of your statement of the theme.

For example (from "Little Red Riding Hood"), LRRH learns that you need to listen to your mother, stay on the path, and not talk to strangers.

Theme: You need to be careful and listen to the advice of your elders and not be fooled by false words and false appearances.

Detail (plot): LRRH leaves the path, and her mother told her not to.

Detail (plot): She tells the wolf she's going to her grandmother's. She talks to a stranger.

Detail (plot): LRRH listens to the wolf dressed as her grandmother as he lies to her about being her grandmother.

Sample Paragraph with Hook, Thesis, and Author's Craft

Hook: "What big teeth you have, Grandma!"

Thesis: The author crafts a story for children who sometimes don't listen to their parents by using the character of Little Red Riding Hood. **Detail 1, Character**: He creates a naïve little girl who doesn't follow her mother's advice and leaves the path and talks to a stranger. **Detail 2, Character**: Red senses something is wrong with her grandmother: her eyes, her deep voice, and her big teeth. Red gets closer and closer, asking questions and trusting the Wolf in Grandma's clothing. Finally, when the Big Bad Wolf admits his teeth are big, "The better to eat you with, my dear," and jumps out of bed to eat Red. **Detail 3, Character**: She screams in fear. If it weren't for the woodsman, the ending would have been tragic. Red learns a lesson and the adults rescue her Grandmother from the Wolf's stomach. **Theme**: The author wrote this story to teach children to listen to the advice of adults if they want to be safe.

Figure 5.15 Sentence Frames for Thesis Statement

Thesis Sentence Frames

(Symbols): Sendak crafts the symbols _____, _____, and _____ in *Where the Wild Things Are* to develop the theme of _____ _____.

(Plot): Sendak uses the incidents_____, _____, and _____ to develop the theme of _____.

Day 2: Guided Practice

The students work in pairs and describe what they see as components of a strong introductory paragraph, based on examples provided by their teacher. All of the students share their sticky notes on the whiteboard, and then in a silent exercise, they group similar notes together, draw a circle around like categories, and describe the category. From the work, they develop their class's checklist for a proficient introductory paragraph.

Stage of Attaining Mastery	Classroom Activity	
2. Guided Practice	**Teacher Guides Students Closely**	**Students Gain Comprehension**
	Provides model paragraphs for students to label and to develop a checklist for a good first paragraph.	Develop a checklist for a good introductory paragraph.
Formative Assessment: The teacher checks as students develop their checklist from the examples she has provided. She checks their work developing checklists to see if students understand the components of an introductory paragraph, and she conferences with students who have questions or who are not progressing well.		

Checklist for Introduction Paragraph

☐ Hook that is interesting and maybe even funny. It can be a quote.

☐ Theme: what the main character learns

☐ Thesis: how the author uses one element of fiction to craft the theme

☐ Good details from the story

☐ Good explanations

The teacher expands the checklist into a rubric and provides this rubric to all students the next day as they begin their own paragraphs. See Figure 5.16 for the rubric.

Figure 5.16 Rubric for First Paragraph

Criteria	Advanced	Proficient	Needs Improvement	Basic
Introductory Paragraph	• Uniquely, completely finishes all aspects of the assignment. • Begins with engaging hook. • Insightfully addresses all aspects of the prompt. • Introduces at least three artful and precise claim(s) in a sophisticated thesis statement focused on the author's craft.	• Competently addresses all parts of the assignment (the hook, the theme, the author's craft, the elements of fiction, and the thesis). • Begins with a good hook to interest the reader. • Introduces claims in a thesis statement that includes the theme and the author's craft in creating the theme.	• Partially addresses the aspects of the assignment. • Begins with hook that connects to the thesis. • Introduces superficial or flawed claim(s) in a weak thesis statement.	• Minimally addresses some aspects of the assignment. • The hook may not connect to the prompt. • Lacks relevant claims and/or lacks a thesis statement.

Day 3: Collaborative Note-Taking

Guided practice (day 3): The students are paired by the teacher and watch a video of *Where the Wild Things Are* with the images and exact language of the story. They take notes collaboratively. They are given time to note the eight elements of fiction. They all have copies of the book and sticky notes, which they use to annotate the text for the theme and the elements of fiction.

Students are provided a checklist of the process of creating a good introductory paragraph. We have labeled it with the phases of the mastery process for this textbook, but it wouldn't be provided for the students.

Figure 5.17 Immediate Application Mastery

Stage of Attaining Mastery	Classroom Activity	
3. Immediate Mastery/ Immediate Application Mastery	**Teacher** Organizes, Coaches Activities Provides video and expectations for taking notes on the elements of fiction.	**Students** Moving toward Owning the Ideas Independently Students work in pairs and identify the eight elements of fiction in *WTWTA*.
Formative Assessment: The teacher assesses student progress in their paired work on the elements of fiction as she talks to each pair of students.		

Checklist for Writing First Paragraph

☐ [Guided Practice[9]] Work with your partner to analyze the eight elements of fiction for *WTWTA*. Make sure you included at least two themes or motifs in your elements.

☐ [Immediate Application Mastery] Participate in a Socratic seminar that discusses Sendak's craft in using the elements of fiction to support its themes.

☐ [Immediate Mastery] As a summary activity for the seminar, work with your partner to craft at least three thesis statements that focus on how the author crafted his story. Each thesis statement should focus on one of the elements of fiction. For example, to show children that many people have wild things inside of them, but that they need to control them [a theme], Sendak used the point of view [element of fiction] of a child who acted out. Through his vivid imagination he became King of the Wild Things, and returned home to where someone loved him best of all.

☐ [Application Mastery] Share your work in a carousel and provide feedback to two other students' three thesis sentences. (Put five stars next to those that you like. Explain what you like about them in a few bullets or sentences.)

☐ [Application Mastery] Read the sample introductory paragraphs with your partner on the handout. Label the hook, theme, element of fiction, and thesis.

☐ [Application Mastery] Draft your own paragraph independently. Schedule a conference with your teacher after you have received feedback based on the rubric and checklist from at least one peer.

Day 4: Socratic Seminar on Thesis Development for *Where the Wild Things Are*

In the **approaching immediate application mastery phase**, students participate in a structured Socratic seminar. Half the class (one of the members of the pairs) sit inside the circle, and present and discuss one of the two themes that they have identified with their partner. They discuss how their selected element of fiction supports the theme in the story. After 30 minutes, the inside and outside of the circle switch, and again they discuss the themes and how they are accomplished.

---

9 The stages of mastery, such as *guided practice*, are included for the reader. They would not be provided to the student.

Figure 5.18 **Immediate Application Mastery**

Stage of Attaining Mastery	Classroom Activity	
3. Immediate Application Mastery	**Guide on the Side** Provides the expectations for the Socratic seminar participation.	**Immediate Application Mastery** Students discuss the elements of fiction, the theme, and their thesis.
Formative Assessment: The teacher observes the students as they share their themes, connections to an element of fiction, and their theses. Halfway through the class, the other half of the class discusses their work. She notes the students who need to have follow-up in individual or pair conferences the next day.		

Days 5 and 6

Students are beginning the independent **application mastery phase**. The students write drafts of their own first paragraphs and exchange their papers with peers. They apply the rubric for a strong introductory paragraph to their writing and to their peer's writing. Students are gaining deeper understanding about thesis statements.

Figure 5.19 **Independent Application Mastery**

Stage of Attaining Mastery	Classroom Activity	
4. Independent Application Mastery	**Guide on the Side** Conferences with students.	**Independent Mastery** Students write and revise their first paragraphs. Students conference with two peers and the teacher.
Formative Assessment: Peer conferences and teacher-student conferences provide information. The teacher and the peers use the checklist and rubric to assess the first paragraph, and discuss the specific next steps for each student.		

The teacher will give students feedback on their actionable next steps, and students will revise their introductory paragraphs accordingly. Then the cycle begins again as students develop their body paragraphs and their concluding paragraphs.

Elevating the Level of Student Responses

The quality of student answers has been recognized by the importance of wait time, which increases student responses from a single word or phrase to one or more sentences. Fisher and Frey address purposeful student talk in their text, *Content-Area Conversations: How to Plan Discussion-based Lessons for Diverse Language Learner* (2008).

The kinds of responses become gradually more elaborate during the gradual release of responsibil-ity evoked by the four phases of introduction, guided practice, immediate application mastery, and independent application mastery.

Students become more capable of elaborating their thinking as the responsibility for the knowledge transfers from the teacher to the student.

The following Figure 5.20 provides some examples of the kinds of activities and student responses that are typical in each phase. These activities can take place over a single class, a unit, or a full year.

Figure 5.20 Activities during Mastery Learning

Phase	Quality of Student Response	Possible Activities
Introduction	Mainly consists of responses to the teacher's questions. May ask clarifying questions.	They are novices in the concept. Interactive lecture Question-response with the entire class Collaborative note-taking with partner Turn-and-talk
Guided Practice	Students begin to assimilate the concept. They begin to understand. They may have misconceptions or struggle with understanding.	Graphic organizer (individual work or in dyad) Processing partners Collaborative note-taking
Immediate Application Mastery (Teacher is coaching)	Students take on more responsibility for understanding. They try to use the new idea or concept. Students begin to be able to explain the concept.	Group work with specific learning goals Socratic seminar Debate Writing draft Conferences with peers and teacher
Independent Application Mastery	Students take full responsibility for using the concept. They may have "guardrails," such as rubrics, anchor charts, and checklists to support their independent application.	Conferences with peers and teacher Presentations Drafts and final papers

To encourage higher-level responses and elevate students' language to a higher academic levels, teachers can

- use Wait Time I to allow students time to process their responses
- use Wait Time II to encourage further elaboration
- provide anchor charts that model academic "moves"
- provide group work in which higher-level thinking and academic language are required and recognized

Each phase has interactive or group work examples that support elevated language for the students. For example, in the introduction phase, Wait Time I and Wait Time II provide time for students to think more deeply (Wait Time I) and to elaborate on their answers (Wait Time II). In guided practice, both processing partners and turn-and-talk provide time for students to put the new ideas of the lesson into their own language. In immediate application, the groups may be larger and the tasks more elaborate, such as Socratic seminars or debates. Finally, in presentations and in the fourth phase, students use their own words to demonstrate their mastery.

Below are more detailed examples of how these student-to-student and group talk activities foster higher-order thinking and result in more academic talk.

Formative Assessments of Three Students

All students in the class are working to attain proficiency (or to go beyond proficiency) of their application mastery objective target. In the sequence just described, the ninth graders are writing their first literary analysis. This process is carefully structured and scaffolded by beginning their writing with an easy children's book, *Where the Wild Things Are*. They have studied themes in literature, but this is their first attempt to write a thesis about a theme.

Sort students' work using the rubric to differentiate instruction and give actionable feedback. The students' theme and thesis sentences are the focus of the analysis and actionable feedback. The final mastery objective is based on the standard: Write arguments to support claims in an analysis of substantive topics or texts, using valid reasoning and relevant and sufficient evidence.

The thesis is the first scaffold. The checklist indicates that students should first identify a theme, and then write a thesis that tells the reader how the author crafts this story, using at least three examples from the text.

The themes and theses have been sorted into three levels of the rubric: *advanced, proficient,* and *needs improvement.* The level of the work is part of the feedback. The actionable feedback is provided for the advanced level in Figure 5.21 below.

Figure 5.21 Rubric for Theme and Thesis

Criteria	Advanced	Proficient	Needs Improvement (Not yet)	Basic (Not Yet)
Theme Thesis	Introduces at least three artful and precise claims in a sophisticated thesis statement that includes a theme and the author's artistry in creating the theme.	Introduces at least three accurate claims in a thesis statement that includes the theme and how the author crafted the theme using one element of fiction.	Introduces superficial and/ or flawed claim(s) in a weak thesis statement.	Lacks relevant claims and/or lacks a thesis statement.

Figure 5.22 Actionable Feedback

Criteria	Advanced	Proficient	Needs Improvement
Theme	**Theme:** The theme of *WTWTA* is that, as parents, we need to understand that a child's being angry is normal; we all have "wild things" in our nature, but we need to help our children gain control of their anger.		
Thesis and	**Thesis:** The style of *WTWTA* develops the theme by changing the idea and image of "wild things" from scary to humorous to disarmed.		
Three Examples	**Example 1:** Max in his wolf suit is aggressive and out of control.		
	Example 2: In the land of wild things, the creatures have a wild rumpus and become less frightening.		
	Example 3: Max then sees he doesn't want to continue being a wild thing or its king, and he takes off his wolf suit and returns home, no longer a wild thing, but is glad to be home.		
Teacher Feedback Actionable	**Next Steps** 1. *Your theme and thesis are on the advanced level. They're in good shape.* 2. *Now put these sentences together and add a "hook" to capture others' attention. The hook needs to connect to your thesis.* 3. *Share this paragraph with a peer for feedback. Use the rubric and checklist with your peer.* 4. *Schedule a brief conference with me.*		

Purposeful Group Work

Learning how to discuss academically is an ongoing learning process, and it takes time for students to develop the social skills necessary to have a thoughtful discussion that allows for disagreement appropriately. Below are listed a variety of activities that can support and scaffold improving student responses, discussion, and talk. Below each activity, in parentheses, the possible area that might be used to improve academic

discourse is provided. For example, a fishbowl is an activity that supports discussion in all content areas.

Fishbowl or Inside-and-Outside Circle (How to Discuss)

Half of the students sit within a circle in a smaller circle, the other half of the students sit around the central group. The students in the inner circle discuss, while those in the outer circle observe and may take notes or evaluate. Then, the two groups switch roles and the inner circle discusses while the outer circle observes.

The fishbowl activity allows you to explicitly teach academic conversation skills. Before the discussion, provide students with the norms for academic discussions, which may include models of how to agree, disagree, or give someone else credit.

Scaffolding and practice can take place before the entire class is divided into an inner and outer circle. Students can practice in smaller groups with the topic that is assigned. Accountability can be supported by asking the outer circle to rate participation on a rubric.

Timing: Allow half of the time for each half of the class. Provide verbal feedback immediately after the discussion, and provide peer assessments on the following day.

Twosomes or Dyads: Turn and Talk, Processing Partners, Paired Verbal Fluency, and Think-Pair-Share

The following two-person activities can be short (less than a minute) or can be a longer-termed partnership.

Turn and talk or elbow partners: Two students sitting near one another turn (to the left or right) and discuss. This twosome strategy requires no movement, but gives students time to process the ideas just introduced. Teachers can formatively assess students' progress by listening in to some of the conversations.

Paired verbal fluency: This strategy can be used to activate thinking about a topic or provide an opportunity for review. (1) Establish partners. Have each dyad decide who will be partner No. 1 and partner No. 2. (2) Assign the topic each partner will discuss in turn. Partners listen carefully to each other. During their turn, they try not to repeat anything said by the other person. (3) When you say "go," partner No. 1 begins. After the designated amount of time elapses, you say "switch" and partner No. 2 takes over. The turn-taking can be done more than once if necessary.

Processing partners (clock buddies): This strategy begins with a handout for each student containing a series of six to ten terms that will be used during a unit with a line for a signature following it. Students trade their signatures with a different partner for each term. When the teacher asks students to discuss a topic for a limited time, he or she asks students to process the idea with their processing partners. This is a helpful way to get students to work with others for a limited time. This strategy requires movement.

Dyads: Think-Pair-Square and Snowballing

Think-pair-share: Students may have a partner based upon a protocol such as using a clock as with clock buddies, or they may be asked to turn to a neighbor, as with elbow partners. This process provides an opportunity to process the recently presented information immediately and briefly with a peer. This group can last from a minute or two to five minutes.

Think-pair-square: In this pairing, two pairs who have already shared become a foursome (a square) and they share. This addition of another twosome allows further sharing and deepening of the ideas. This gives shyer students an opportunity to share their ideas twice before they may be asked to give whole-class feedback. Once more, it is about adding depth to ideas, stimulating debate, and collaborative thinking.

Snowballing: In this case, the groups of four (square) could become a group of eight. Similar to the 'square' approach mentioned in think-pair-square, the snowballing activity is another simple but very effective way of building on ideas by starting with small groups and expanding the groups in a structured way. As the metaphor of the snowball suggests, you can begin with an individual response to a question, followed by pairing up students, then creating groups of four, and so on.

Peer-Assisted Learning Strategies (Each Partner Is Responsible; Research-Based Method)

Students work together as a class to describe, step by step, how to solve an algebra problem, for example. The whole class rehearses the protocol of how to solve the problem; the protocol might be the mathematical order of operations. Then, students alternate as coach and learner, using the protocol to solve a series of problems until the process is mastered—in this case, until both students follow the order of operations effectively. The peer-assisted learning strategy enables teachers to circulate around the classroom and observe students, providing feedback where necessary. The coaches do not "correct," but read the procedure that the student did not follow.

Pairs of students are changed regularly, and all students participate as both "coaches" and "players."

A variation of PALS is partner reading, which is a cooperative learning strategy in which two students work together to read an assigned text in any content area. This strategy is often used as part of PALS. This activity is a class-wide peer-tutoring program in which teachers carefully partner a student with a classmate. The teacher develops the protocol, and the two students follow it carefully. For example, they may each read aloud for five minutes. The partner reading strategy allows students to take turns reading and provide each other with feedback as a way to monitor comprehension. Partner reading does not require special reading materials and consequently enables teachers to use the reading material of their choice. This offers teachers flexibility for incorporating the strategy into various content areas. Partner reading provides direct opportunities for a teacher to circulate in the class, observe students, and offer individual remediation.

Each member of the teacher-assigned pair takes turns being "coach" and "player." The coach and the player check their understanding as they read together, alternating every five minutes. The coach reads along and helps the player with any problem words, and then the coach reads while the player reads along. These pairs are changed regularly and over a period of time as students work. Thus, all students have the opportunity to be coaches and players.

Interactive Annotation/Interactive Reading/Interactive Note-Taking (Collaboration, Comprehension, and Deep Reading)

Reading and constructing meaning from a text is a complex and active process. One way to help students slow down and develop their critical analysis skills is to teach them to annotate the text as they read. Suggestions for annotating text can include labeling and interpreting literary devices; labeling and explaining the writer's rhetorical devices and elements of style; or labeling the main ideas, supportive details, and/or evidence that leads the reader to a conclusion about the text. To differentiate, teachers can annotate some of the more difficult parts of a text to aid the students, begin the annotation with the entire class to get them started, or form heterogeneous or homogeneous groups based on skill levels and the teacher's discretion for the best way to proceed.

Jigsaw (Individual Accountability, Comprehension, Deeper Reading, and Discussion)

Students read a section of text assigned to them. When the reading has been completed, the students meet for approximately 20 minutes with others assigned to the same topic. They discuss the material, identify the most important learning points, and return to their "home groups" to instruct the others about information in which they have become an "expert." Each student takes turns teaching what he or she has learned to the other home group members.

Get the Gist (Improves Comprehension, Collaboration, and Literacy)

Get the Gist (GtG) is a comprehension strategy that is used both during reading and after. In pairs of two, students are assigned a part of a text to summarize with a specified number of words. Its effectiveness has been verified by research. When using GtG, students create summaries that are 20 words or less for increasingly large amounts of text.

Socratic Seminars, Scaffolded Socratic Seminars, Pinwheels, and Individual/Partner/Small-Group Seminars (Academic Discussion and Deep Reading)

Socratic seminars: These whole-class dialogues explore ideas, values, and issues drawn from readings or works of art chosen for their richness. Leaders help participants to make sense of a text and of their own thinking by asking questions about reasoning, evidence, connections, examples, and other aspects of sound thinking. A good seminar is more devoted to making meaning than to mastering information. Participants are actively engaged in rigorous critical thought. They must involve a relatively short text, piece of art, etc., and after the seminar are often followed by periods of reflection that may be written or spoken. In its simplest form, students are given an unknown work of art and are asked to determine its name based upon the qualities and objects that they see in it.

Scaffolded Socratic seminars provide more structure to support students' active participation. For example, the class may be divided into four teams that initially study and prepare for the Socratic seminar with their assigned aspect of the topic. One member of each team participates at a time and the team members provide information and feedback, and reflect on their topic after the meeting. The focus could originate in any content area, but, for example, students could research and then take positions on the ethics of genetic research or the data for global warming. In an American history class, students could debate whether the United States should have dropped atomic bombs on Japan during World War II.

Partner/small-group seminars: These seminars are more formal and focused than large-group seminars. A text, graphic, or artwork is selected, and the students analyze the text based on the models and guided practice from class. The students then create a thesis that needs to be supported by evidence and set up the seminar in an outline form. Partners and group members discuss the materials, but each of the individuals is responsible for submitting and presenting their own position. For example, students could receive three scientific data collections about the proliferation of the bubonic plague: one that said it was caused by the rise of the city and its lack of cleanliness, another that it was caused by a mutation of the virus, and a third that said it was a "perfect storm" caused by both a mutation and people living so closely together.

Carousel/Carousel Brainstorming/Scavenger Hunt (Sharing Information and Providing Feedback)

Carousel brainstorming provides scaffolding for new information to be learned or existing information to be reviewed through movement, conversation, and reflection. While taking part in carousel brainstorming, small groups of students rotate around the classroom, stopping at various "stations" for a designated period of time (usually one to two minutes). At each station, students activate their prior knowledge of a topic or concept and share their ideas with their small group. Each group posts their ideas at each station for all groups to read. This can work as a "museum" or a science or art fair. Each station of the carousel could have a "docent," a scientist presenting his or her scientific experiment or research, or an artist presenting his or her artwork. Half of the class can become the audience and walk through the stations while the other half presents. Then, the museum, science fair, or art fair has a different set of displays described by different students. This provides shyer students a small group with whom to share their ideas.

Variation: The students can be assigned specific topics to present as steps in the carousel.

Numbered Heads Together (Individual Accountability to the Group and Participation)

In this activity, students are divided into groups of four, and each one is assigned a letter—A, B, C, or D. The teacher then poses a question or problem for each group to solve. They may work together, but they must make sure that every member of their group will be capable of answering the question. After a sufficient amount of time has passed, the teacher says something to the effect of, "All right, I will take the answer from anyone who is a B." Only the student assigned the letter B in each group may answer. The teacher then repeats the process with a new problem, but this time calls on students assigned the letter D to answer. This activity creates an opportunity for shyer students to get into the action. If their letter is called, they will likely also receive some positive peer pressure from other members of their group to raise their hands and share the group's response.

Agree/Disagree, Vote with Your Feet, and Living Likert Scale Activator (Quick Formative Assessment, Active Participation, and Varying Perspectives)

In Chapter 2, one of the examples we offer of an activator is an agree/disagree questionnaire about illegal immigration. The activator contained a series of statements about illegal immigration, and students were asked to indicate their level of agreement or disagreement with each statement. One way in which this activator can be used to encourage wider class participation is by asking students to imagine a line cutting across the center of the classroom. Designate one side of the room as the "strongly agree" side and the other side of the room as the "strongly disagree" side. Then, read one of the statements on the activator and ask students to stand up and physically move to the spot along the invisible line that represents the strength of their opinion on the particular statement. Once students have assumed their various positions in the classroom, we can ask students why they feel the way they do (i.e., why did they choose to stand in that particular spot in the classroom?). We have found that this activity can be an effective way of both generating a lively discussion and pulling in some of our shyer students.

Say-It-in-a-Word and Whip (Quick Formative Assessment and Participation)

An activity offered by Walsh and Sattes (2005, p. 71) is called say-it-in-a-word. In this activity, the teacher poses a question to the class and asks each student in the class to come up with a single word that best expresses his or her reaction to the question. For example, the music teacher could play a portion of a piece of music, and each student could describe his or her reaction. The teacher could play another and ask for words from each. The students might then be asked if this was probably created by the same composer. We have found that this strategy, as well, can be a powerful tool for drawing in our more reluctant students, and that once they have taken a stand on an idea they are then drawn into a conversation.

Generating Test Questions (Collaborative Work)

One activity that we have used to encourage students to develop meaningful questions takes place on the day prior to a test or quiz. We divide the students into groups and ask them to develop questions that they believe would be appropriate for the following day's exam. We give students specific instructions for the types of questions they should create (e.g., ten multiple-choice, five short-answer, two open-response questions, etc.). At the end of the period, we collect the questions that students have produced and create a test or quiz using the best of the submitted questions.

Writing Their Own Test (Collaboration)

Another teacher we know uses a similar activity. On the day before a test, she divides the class into groups, gives directions for the type of test she wants them to create, and collects one test from each group at the end of the period. She then chooses the best of these tests to give to the entire class. The students in the group that created the test automatically receive As and don't have to take the test at all (though they do have to write an answer sheet while the rest of the class is taking the test). The catch is that the winner of the test-writing contest isn't announced until the next day, when students come in to take the test, so all students must study for the test without knowing whether their test has been selected as the winner. The benefit to such an activity, of course, is that all students get off to a strong start in their studying through the process of devising the test questions that they believe should appear on the next day's exam. More than just serving as a means of reviewing content, asking students to devise the questions that they believe to be most relevant to the unit of study pushes them to choose the most important and fundamental concepts within the just-completed unit of study. Simultaneously, this activity pushes students to see their input as "real." Their teacher is not simply questioning them to determine what they do and do not know (as if in a game of "gotcha"), but rather has suggested through her actions that their questions and insights are important enough to form the content of the test that will be used to assess the class's learning. Such an explicit vote of confidence in students' abilities conveys a powerful message about their learning and knowledge.

Hot Seat and 20 Questions (Encourages Student Questioning)

There are many other activities that can help students to strengthen their questioning skills. One such game, "Hot Seat," involves placing a chair in the front of the classroom facing the rest of the class. We invite one student to come sit in the hot seat and then ask that student to think of a term relevant to our current unit. That term could be a vocabulary word in a foreign language class, a math equation in an algebra class, a grammar term in an English/language arts class, or a historical figure in a social studies class. When the student in the hot seat has come up with a term (and whispered it in the teacher's ear), the rest of the class may begin asking yes-or-no questions to the student in the hot seat in order to figure out what the term is. This game can take many different forms. The teacher can divide the class into two teams and turn the questioning into a competition. Alternatively, the teacher can limit the entire class to a total of 20 questions in order to encourage students to work together and listen carefully to each other's questions (and the hot seat student's answers). As the game proceeds, another student can be assigned to write the questions on the blackboard. This way, at the game's conclusion, the class can examine the various questions asked and discuss which questions proved useful and which proved extraneous. Such a reflection encourages students to think deeply about what makes for a good question.

Conclusion

This chapter has addressed the many ways in which teachers engage students with questions and assess their progress toward a specific learning goal. The teacher maintains the stance of an assessor as students move toward mastery. In a variety of in-the-moment activities, from lecturing to question-and-answer discussions to group work to the development of the final product, the teacher actively considers the progress of students on a consistent basis as he or she assesses students formatively.

The student must be an active participant in this learning process in order to progress to independent mastery. In addition to their individual progress, students can work with a peer or in groups to gain deeper understanding. Peer feedback benefits both the peer and the student who is provided with feedback.

Elevating the level of student work is achieved through a clear understanding of questioning and higher to order thinking skills. Also, students need to have opportunities to practice accountable talk that includes both the manner in which students agree, disagree, and give one another credit for ideas, as well as the level of thinking of the discussion.

The quality of the feedback is the pivotal component of moving students along. Students need to know clearly what their next step is to improve their performance. Actionable feedback provides clear and attainable next steps.

References

Alcala, L. "My Favorite No: Learning from Mistakes, Grades 6-9, Math, Warm-Up." *TeachingChannel* video, 2015. https://www.teachingchannel.org/videos/class-warm-up-routine.

Arter, L. 2015. "Calling Mulligan! Two Rules for Dynamic Discourse." *Education Update* 57, no. 2 (2015): 8.

Black, P. and Wiliam, D. "Developing the Theory of Formative Assessment." *Educational Assessment, Evaluation, and Accountability* 21, no. 1 (2009): 5–31.

Black, P. and Wiliam, D. "'In Praise of Educational Research': Formative Assessment." *British Educational Research Journal* 29, no. 5 (2003): 623–637.

Boekaerts, M. "Self-Regulation and Effort Investment," in *Handbook of Child Psychology, Volume 4: Child Psychology in Practice*, 6th ed, eds. Renninger, K.A. and Sigel, I.E. New York: Wiley, 2006.

Brown, G., Harris, L., and Harnett, J. "Teacher beliefs about feedback within an Assessment for Learning environment: Endorsement of improved learning over student well-being." *Teaching and Teacher Education* 7, no. 28 (October 2012): 968–978.

Carey, B. "Exams Measure What We Know, But They're Also One of the Best Ways to Learn." *New York Times Magazine*, September 7, 2014.

Chappuis, J. "Thoughtful Assessment with the Learner in Mind." *Educational Leadership* 71, no. 6 (March 2014): 20–26.

Caram, C. and Davis. P. "Inviting Student Engagement with Questioning." *Kappa Delta Pi Record* 42, no. 1 (Fall 2005): 19–23.

Checkley, K. "A is for Audacity: Lessons in Leadership from Lorraine Monroe." *Educational Leadership* 61, no. 7 (April 2004): 70–72.

Cotton, K. "Classroom Questioning." *School Improvement Research Series. Close-Up* no. 5 (2012): 1–16.

Craig, J. and Cairo, L. "Assessing the Relationship between Questioning and Understanding to Improve Learning and Thinking (QUILT) and Student Achievement in Mathematics: A Pilot Study." Charlestown, WV: Evantia Inc., 2005: 1–20.

Dillon, J.T. "The Remedial Status of Student Questioning." *Journal of Curriculum Studies* 20, no. 3 (1988): 197–210.

Donne, J. "A Valediction Forbidding Mourning," in *The Broadview Anthology of Poetry*, eds. Rosengarten, H. and Goldrick-Jones, A. Peterborough, ON: The Broadview Press, 1994.

Duckor, B. Formative Assessment in Seven Good Moves. *Educational Leadership* 71, no. 6 (March 2014), 24–26.

DuFour, R., Eaker, R., DuFour, R.. Closing the Knowing-Doing Gap. On Common Ground: The Power of Professional Learning Communities. Bloomington,IN: The National Education Service, 2005.

Elder, L. and Paul, R. "Critical Thinking: Crucial Distinctions for Questioning." *Journal of Developmental Education* 21, no. 2 (1997): 34–25.

Farmer, L. "What is the Question?" Paper presented at World Library and Information Congress. Seoul, Korea: August 2006.

Fennell, F., Swartz, B.A., McCord Kobett, B., and Wray, J. "Classroom-Based Formative Assessments—Guiding Teaching and Learning." *Teaching Children Mathematics* 21, no. 6 (2015): 325–327.

Finley, T. "Dipsticks: Efficient Ways to Check for Understanding." *Edutopia* July 30, 2014. http://www.edutopia.org/blog/dipsticks-to-check-for-understanding-todd-finleynding.

Fisher, D. and Frey, N. *Checking for Understanding: Formative Assessment Techniques for Your Classroom.* 2nd ed. Alexandria, VA: ASCD, 2014.

Fisher, D. and Frey, N. "Making Time for Feedback." *Educational Leadership* 70, no. 1 (September 2012): 42–47.

Ford-Connors, E. and Paratore, J. "Vocabulary Instruction in Fifth Grade and Beyond: Sources of Word Learning and Productive Contexts for Development." *Review of Educational Research* 85, no. 1 (2015): 50–91.

Fries-Gaither, J. Ohio State University National Science Foundation Grant, 2008.

Gallimore, R., Hiebert, J., and Ermeling, B. "Rich Classroom Discussion: One Way to Get Rich Learning." *Teachers College Record* (October 2014): 1–3.

Gewertz, C. "Teachers Learn to Judge Utility of Formative-Testing Tools." *Education Week* 33, no. 24 (March 2014): 8.

Hannel, G. *Highly Effective Questioning: Developing the Seven Steps of Critical Thinking*, 2nd ed. Phoenix, AZ: Hannel Publications, 2005.

Hannel, I. "Insufficient Questioning." *Phi Delta Kappan* 91, no. 3 (November 2009): 65–69.

Hattie, J. *Visible Learning: A Synthesis of Over 800 Meta-Analyses Relating to Achievement*. New York. Routledge Press, 2008.

Heiltin, L. "Teachers May Need to Deepen Assessment Practices for Common Core." *Education Week* (2015). http://www.edweek.org/tm/articles/2014/03/05/ndia_formativeassessment.html

Hunter, R, *Mastery Teaching*. El Segundo, CA: TIP Publications, 1982.

Kegan, R. and Lahey, L. *How the Way We Talk Can Change the Way We Work*. San Francisco, CA: Jossey-Bass, 2002

Kluger, A. and DeNisi, A. "The Effects of Feedback Intervention on Performance: A Historical Review, a Meta-Analysis, and a Preliminary Feedback Intervention Theory." *Psychological Bulletin* 119, no. 2 (1996): 254-284.

Kuhn, D. "Thinking Together and Alone." *Educational Researcher* 44, no. 1 (2015): 46–53.

Leahy, S. and Wiliam, D. "From Teachers to Schools: Scaling up Professional Development for Formative Assessment" in *Assessment and Learning*, 2nd ed., ed. Gardner, J. Thousand Oaks, CA: Sage Publishers, 2005.

Lubliner, S. "Reciprocal Teaching: An Alternative to Gatekeeping Practices." *Classroom Leadership* 5, no. 3 (November 2001): 1–5.

Marzano, R. *Classroom Assessments and Grading That Work*. Alexandria, VA: ASCD, 2006.

Marzano, R. "The Many Uses of Exit Slips." *Educational Leadership* 70, no. 2 (2012): 80–81.

Marzano, R., and Heflebower, T. *Teaching and Assessing 21st Century Skills: The Classroom Strategies Series*. Bloomington, IN: Marzano Research Laboratory, 2012.

Marzano, R., Pickering, D., and Pollock, J. 2001. *Classroom Instruction That Works: Research-Based Strategies for Increasing Student Achievement*. Alexandria, VA: ASCD.

Massachusetts Curriculum Framework for English Language Arts and Literacy: Grades Pre-Kindergarten to 12. Malden, MA: Massachusetts Department of Elementary and Secondary Education, March 2011.

Merriam-Webster's Collegiate Dictionary. 10th ed. Springfield, MA: Merriam-Webster, 1994.

Michaels, S., O'Connor, M.C., and Resnick, L. *Accountable Talk Sourcebook: For Classroom Conversation That Works*, version 3.1. Institute of Learning. Pittsburgh: University of Pittsburgh, 2010.

Monroe, L. *The Monroe Doctrine: An ABC Guide to What Great Bosses Do*. New York: Public Affairs Inc., 2003.

Morgan, N. and Saxton, J. *Asking Better Questions*. Markham, ON: Pembroke Publishers Limited, 2006.

Nolet, V. and McLaughlin, M. *Accessing the General Curriculum: Including Students with Disabilities in Standards-Based Reform*. Thousand Oaks, CA: Corwin Press Inc., 2000.

Pedrosa de Jesus, H., Almeida, P., and Watts, M. "Questioning Styles and Students' Learning: Four Case Studies." *Educational Psychology* 24, no. 4 (2004): 531–548.

Phelps, F.G., Doherty-Sneddon, G., and Warnock, H. "Helping Children Think: Gaze Aversion and Teaching." *British Journal of Developmental Psychology* 24, no. 3 (2006): 577–588.

"Primary Sources: American Teachers on American Schools." Scholastic and the Bill and Melinda Gates Foundation, 2010. http://www.scholastic.com/primary-sources/pdfs/100646_ScholasticGates.pdf.

Rosenthal, R. and Jacobson, L. *Pygmalion in the Classroom: Teacher Expectations and Pupils' Intellectual Ability*. New York: Holt, Rinehart, and Winston Inc., 1968.

Rowe, M. B. "Wait Time: Slowing Down May Be a Way of Speaking Up." *American Educator* 11, no. 1 (Spring 1987): 38-43, 47.

Schultz, K. "The Role of Silence in Teaching and Learning." *Educational Horizons* 91 (December 2012/January 2013): 22–25. http://pilambda.org/horizons/the-role-of-silence-in-teaching-and-learning/.

Schultz, K. "Why Introverts Shouldn't Be Forced to Talk in Class." *Washington Post*, Answer Sheet blog, February 12, 2013. https://www.washingtonpost.com/news/answer-sheet/wp/2013/02/12/why-introverts-shouldnt-be-forced-to-talk-in-class/.

Stahl, R. "Using 'Think-Time' and 'Wait-Time' Skillfully in the Classroom." *ERIC Clearinghouse for Social Studies/Social Science Education* (May 1994): 1–4.

Vogler, K. "Improve Your Verbal Questioning." *The Clearing House* 79, no. 2 (2005): 98–103.

Vollmeyer, R. and Rheinberg, F. "A Surprising Effecty on Feedback and Learning." *Learning and Instruction*, 15, no. 6 (December 2005): 589-602.

Walsh, J. and Sattes, B. *Quality Questioning: Research-Based Practice to Engage Every Learner*. Thousand Oaks, CA: Corwin Press, 2005.

Wiliam, D. and Leahy, S. *Embedding Formative Assessment*. Bloomington, IN: Solution Tree Press, 2015.

Wiliam, D. "Formative Assessment: Getting the Focus Right." *Educational Assessment* 11 (2006): 283–289.

Willingham, D. "Ask the Cognitive Scientist: How Praise Can Motivate—or Stifle." *American Educator* (Winter 2005/2006): 1–7.

Zwiers, J. and Crawford, M. *Academic Conversations: Classroom Talk That Fosters Critical Thinking and Content Understandings*. Portland, ME: Stenhouse Publishing, 2011.

Students with Disabilities: Effective Questioning Practices

Questioning is a frequently used strategy that teachers rely on in general education classrooms. Chapter 5 has a detailed flowchart that points out the purpose of questions. Questioning is designed to activate previous learning, deepen student understanding, engage students, maintain their attention, and assess learning to inform instruction. The purpose and importance of questions is the same for both students with and without disabilities. However, the impact of questioning can be different for students with disabilities, especially if they struggle with slow processing speed or some level of anxiety. Round robin question-and-answer sessions in the classroom can be very unproductive and anxiety-producing for this group of students.

In reality, many students with disabilities begin to hide in the classroom, rarely answering questions (Clowes 2011). Therefore, the **goal** behind asking questions is not achieved. The use of strategies that allow students more time to process and reduce anxiety ensures that students reap the benefits of questioning by their teachers.

Anxiety and Memory

Anxiety is a characteristic of students across the disability spectrum. There are varying levels of anxiety depending on the individual student. A common impact for every person who becomes anxious is that as the anxiety intensifies, working memory drops (working memory will be explored more in Chapter 8 of this book). For students with disabilities, this relationship between anxiety and working memory complicates the teaching and learning process even more. Students are not able to form an initial thought that could lead to answering the question. Using scripts or teacher think aloud will help students begin to form their thoughts in order to respond to the questions.

The questioning techniques that teachers use can ease student anxiety and improve classroom performance and overall outcomes. Using individual dry-erase boards allows students to answer without the fear of being embarrassed about other students seeing their answers. Any dipstick method that allows the student some level of anonymity with their peers helps to lessen their anxiety.

As explained in this chapter, questioning is often used to activate previous learning. The more a teacher knows how anxiety affects their students, the better able they are to determine which questioning tech-

nique to use throughout the lesson. If a teacher chooses to use brainstorming as a questioning technique to activate previous learning, using previewing strategies as outlined in Chapter 2 will better support students with disabilities who suffer from anxiety.

Students who suffer from slow processing speed tend to struggle with fluently and automatically performing cognitive tasks. The ability to do those tasks is often referred to as *mental quickness* (Learning Disabilities Association of America 2015). These are the students in your class who often perform exceptionally well on independent work tasks such as homework or projects but are not able to respond to questions during instruction. For these students, avoiding quick-succession questions and increasing the wait time is extremely beneficial. When there is either no wait or a short wait time, these students are not allowed to process the question fully before the answer is given and the teacher has moved on. Increasing the amount of time between asking and allowing a response to questions gives these students the opportunity to process the questions in their brains, determine a response, and then respond in a way that aligns with their peers.

Students with disabilities who suffer from some level of anxiety disorder or slow processing speed require additional supports and consideration when using questions as part of the teaching and learning process. Anxiety and slow processing speed impact students in a way that is often hidden and not readily thought of when students are underperforming in the classroom. Implementing thoughtful questioning techniques can support students with disabilities in performing at levels that are more in line with their peers and potential.

References

Clowes, G. "The Essential 5: A Starting Point for Kagan Cooperative Learning." *Kagan Online Magazine*. http://www.kaganonline.com/free_articles/research_and_rationale/330/The-Essential-5-A-Starting-Point-for-Kagan-Cooperative-Learning

Schultz, E. "SLD Evaluation: Linking Cognitive Assessment Data to Learning Strategies." *Learning Disabilities Association of America*. http://ldaamerica.org/sld-evaluation-linking-cognitive-assessment-data-to-learning-strategies/.

English Language Learners: Four Language Domains

Questioning Practices That Improve Student Performance and Promote Higher-Order Thinking

Learning what language English learners can comprehend and produce can be a precursor to developing appropriate questions, prompts, and inquiry-based projects. Results from students' initial and yearly English-language proficiency assessment will offer scores in four domains of language: reading, writing, speaking, and listening. Most ESL curriculum documents separate learning standards into the four domains. Sometimes speaking and listening are grouped together for oral-language comprehension objectives, while literacy skills will include objectives in reading and writing. Learning standards can also be grouped into *receptive language skills* (listening, reading, and watching) and *productive language skills* (speaking, writing, and gesturing/signing). Students new to learning English will require questions accompanied by other sensory/language stimuli, such as visuals or actions. Questions and prompts for students with less proficiency will also have simple structures and can be answered with a gesture, yes, no, or one- to two-word phrases. As students' English proficiency increases, scaffolding supports will decrease, and questions and prompts will look more like what teachers offer the general education population of students. It is impor-

tant to note that increasing and decreasing the amount of scaffolding for English learners is directly linked to a student's proficiency level and progress in English language development. English learners may have other learning issues, such as diagnosed learning disabilities, which will call for additional strategies and support.

Language Demand of Content Areas

Echevarria, Vogt, and Short (2013) encourage general education teachers to "know how language is used in the content area in order to convey information (orally or in text) and to use and apply that information (through class reading, writing, and discussion activities)" (p. 29). When teachers think about the language demands of their particular curriculum content and grade level, they can better plan for varying proficiency levels of English learners. However, a linguistic analysis of subject-matter knowledge and skills may be a new practice for general education or content teachers. The following table offers an example of a brief look at vocabulary and sentence formation for a lesson in which English learners will participate. For students who are still developing English literacy, "language" will be mostly thought of as language heard and produced orally.

Language Analysis Sample Unit: Second Grade, *Life Cycle of a Butterfly*

Vocabulary		
What words are necessary for all students to understand, ask questions, and demonstrate what they know about *butterflies?*		
Everyday words; able to be represented by visuals or acted out; easy for English learners to understand and remember	*More technical words; necessary for discussions and texts; may be challenging for English learners*	*Content-specific words; necessary for grade-level subject matter texts; challenging for all students*
egg, caterpillar, legs, body, bug, fly, home, make, round, scientist, change, watch, first, second, next, finally	insect, habitat, lay, j-shaped, nectar, molt, abdomen, antennae, observe, stage, life cycle, mate, stages, hand lens	larva, pupa, chrysalis, barb, spinneret, entomologist, metamorphosis, proboscis, thorax

Phrases/Sentences

What sentences do I expect my students to understand and produce *when making observations about butterflies?*

Language Skill	Receptive Language	Productive Language
To describe	The caterpillar/butterfly (hatches/hatched), (climbs/climbed), (eats/ate/has eaten), (grows/grew/has grown), (makes/made), (sheds/shed), (lays/laid).	• *"The caterpillar is ____."* • *"I see/saw, observe/observed ___,"* • *"The larva/pupa changed by/when ____,"*
To explain	The chrysalis hangs (by/from/for ___), for (6-10 days). The butterfly uses (its proboscis) to (drink nectar).	• *"Caterpillars ____ when ____."* • *"Caterpillars can ____ by ____."* • *"The butterfly uses ____ to ____."* • *"The caterpillar grew the most on day____. I know this because ____."*
To summarize	The butterfly (was upside down), (emerged/came out of its chrysalis), (hung from the chrysalis), (dried its wings), (flew away).	• *On day one _____, then _____.* • *On day _____, the caterpillar _____.* • *First, _____. Then _____. Finally, _____.*
To analyze	The ____ is (long/longer/the longest), (more/the most active). The butterfly ____ so it can ____.	• *"I agree/disagree with ____ because ___."* • *"The caterpillar is in the ___ stage because ___."* • *"The cause of ____ was ____."* • *"I think that ___ is due to ___"*

Generating Questions for English Learners at Varying Proficiency Levels

Anticipating possible student responses will assist teachers in choosing strategies and word choice for questions or prompts. In order to do this, teachers will need to understand how much and what kind of language English learners at each proficiency level are capable of understanding and producing. Thinking about how English learners might respond will also aid teachers in preparing resources, supports, and questions. Figure 5.23 on the next page offers appropriate materials, questions and prompts, expected responses, and response goals for English learners based on proficiency level.

Teaching Students to Create, Evaluate, and Generate Questions for Inquiry

English learners at early proficiency levels will benefit from explicit language instruction for the structure and word order of questions and for "turning the question around" to write a formalized answer. The ESL teacher can address these skills at the elementary level in a pull-out lesson or in the scheduled ESL class/block for middle and secondary levels. When the ESL

and content teachers plan together, the pull-out ESL lesson can connect meaningfully to content themes and skills. English learners will not miss out on what is being taught in the general education classroom, and the language skills they learn become contextualized with meaningful content.

Students with speech emergence can begin to evaluate and generate questions as early as second grade. By providing time for oral interaction between English learners and English-fluent peers, all students can talk about, discuss, and arrange questions from easiest-to-answer to hardest-to-answer. Students might discuss the vocabulary of questions with a one- to five-minute turn-and-talk, brainstorm, task, or opinion share. English learners can collect and record a bank of tiered question words, phrases, and inquiry starters. This will assist English learners when they generate their own tasks, projects, and responses. In highlighting vocabulary strategies, Calderón (2011) states, "Using students' ideas … allows the students to contribute to the process and enhances their self-esteem when their ideas are accepted" (p. 78).

It should be acceptable for English learners to evaluate words and phrases on assignments and tests and ask the teacher for clarity. This helps both the student and teacher to understand whether English

Figure 5.23

English Language Learners: Resources, Supports, and Questions by Proficiency Level

Proficiency Levels (Stage)	Multisensory Materials*	Receptive Language Comprehension Expected*	Productive Language Expected*
Pre-Production–Early Production	First-language oral and/or written support; word-to-word translation dictionary; translation application (app for tablet); pictures; photos; diagrams; charts; real-life objects; props; musical/ voice queues; peer-to-peer and peer-to-teacher dialogue; simplified texts; word banks accompanied by visual/audio support (prompts may need explicit modeling, repetition, or rephrasing)	*Oral prompts:* touch; point to; click on; get; gather; open/close; cut; match; put; take; listen; go; turn; put on/up/down; take off; follow; repeat; say; tell; ask; *Questions* have familiar words *Writing prompts:* label; draw; fill in; match; choose/select; write; identify; show; cover; circle; underline; highlight; copy; sequence	*Non-verbal responses:* head nod; gesture; action; hand signal; pointing; counting; solve with manipulatives; follow a model; other appropriate physical response *Oral/writing responses:* yes/no; first-language response; one- to two-word responses; simple/familiar phrases; some academic vocabulary
Speech Emergence–Intermediate Fluency	Word-to-word translation dictionary; translation application; thesaurus; intermediate text accompanied by visuals/ audio stimuli; use of manipulatives; word/phrase banks; sentence frames; sample responses (prompts may need to be repeated or clarified)	*Oral/writing prompts:* discuss; explain; retell; rephrase; summarize; sequence; *Questions* have simple phrases and require yes/no; short phrases or one- to two-sentence answers	*Oral/writing responses:* phrases; accurate simple sentences; simple verb tenses; some irregular verbs; familiar phrasal structures; accurate pronouns; some academic vocabulary; pauses to translate or recall vocabulary; errors that do not usually impede message; attempts at rephrasing/editing
Intermediate–Advanced Fluency	Word-to-word translation dictionary; thesaurus; translation application; intermediate-grade level text read aloud; use of manipulatives; word/phrase banks; sentence frames; sample responses (prompts rarely need to be repeated or clarified).	*Oral/writing prompts:* synthesize; apply; express; evaluate; persuade; argue; defend; critique *Questions* may have more than one part or multiple steps	*Oral/writing responses:* extended discourse; multiple sentences and/or paragraphs; examples; details; compound/complex sentences; attempts at rephrasing ideas; editing; proofreading; using feedback to clarify; errors sometimes typical of native English speakers

* Dependent on age, grade, and literacy level.

language or content knowledge (or both) is being assessed. Encouraging learners to "question the questions" will make educators more aware of language demands and how to minimize obstacles that could prevent English learners from demonstrating what they know and can do. Teaching English learners to be aware of and advocate for their own learning allows them to identify, own, and control the process of developing academic language and acquiring subject-matter knowledge.

References

2012 Amplification of The English Language Development Standards, Kindergarten-12th Grade. (2013). Madison, WI: Board of Regents of the University of Wisconsin System/WIDA. 2013.

Beck, I.L., McKeown, M.G., and Kucan, L. *Creating Robust Vocabulary: Frequently Asked Questions and Extended Examples*. New York: Guilford, 2008.

Calderón, M. *Teaching Reading and Comprehension to English Learners*. Bloomington, IN: Solution Tree Press, 2011.

Echevarria, J., Vogt, M., and Short, D. *Making Content Comprehensible for English Learners: The SIOP Model.* Boston: Pearson, 2013.

Hill, J.D. and Miller, K.B. *Classroom Instruction That Works with English Language Learners.* 2nd ed. Alexandria, VA: ASCD, 2012.

6

Differentiating Instruction with a Connection to Universal Design for Learning

Objectives for the Chapter

After reading the chapter, the reader will be able to

a. define the key components of differentiated instruction to a colleague

b. plan lessons that flexibly provide reteaching, practice, and extension as needed

c. manage differentiated activities in a single lesson

d. explain the connections between differentiated instruction and universal design for learning

e. explain how Response to Intervention (RtI) and Universal Design for Learning support differentiated instruction

f. use graphic organizers and other strategies that attend to various learning styles

g. use a variety of instructional strategies to differentiate instruction by content, process, and product

What Is Differentiated Instruction?

The aim is clear. Each child—each of the young—should be able to advance to full capacity in accordance with general and special ability and aptitude.
— Paul Brandwein, Memorandum: On Renewing Schooling and Education

Differentiating instruction is adapting curriculum (what is taught, or content), instruction (how it is taught, or process), and assessment (how it is assessed, or product), based on the different levels of readiness, learning styles, and interests of the students (Tomlinson 1995). Today's classrooms are very different from those of the past. Teachers today must contend with learners possessing a wide range of abilities and talents. The standards to which both teachers and students are held have become more rigorous and comprehensive, as students must be prepared to face and succeed in an ever-changing, technologically advanced world.

It is highly unlikely that a teacher will be able to help all students master the required standards as well as maximize the learning potential of each student unless differentiated instruction is provided. Fortunately, we understand much more about the teaching and learning dyad than we did even a decade ago.

269

Table 6.1

Differentiated instruction is...	Differentiated instruction is not...
multiple approaches to content, process, and product	individualized instruction
student-centered	teacher-centered
a variety of groupings that are in a constant state of change, or flexible grouping	homogeneous, static groupings
organized with purposeful movement and student discussions	chaotic
concept-focused	focused on memorization of discrete facts or skills
ongoing assessment to inform instruction to better meet the needs of each student	only summative assessments given at the end of the lesson or unit
proactively planning instruction to meet the range of learner needs	assignments that are the same for all the students, and teachers reactively adjusting lessons when they don't work
expectations that are the same for all students	grading some students harder than others
providing new and different challenges	asking students to do more of what they already know

Differentiated instruction emerged as a developed model in 1995 (Tomlinson 1995). Tomlinson, who first wrote about differentiated instruction in the 1990s, argues that differentiation is not an approach, but rather highly effective teaching whereby the teacher presents lessons and assignments in ways that meet students' interests and needs. This type of instruction was conceptualized as a teacher's response to the diverse learning needs of students. Parts of Tomlinson's work at this time were based on Howard Gardner's theory of **multiple intelligences**.

Gardner (1991, 1993, 1997, and 2011) describes eight intelligences that humans possess in varying degrees: verbal-linguistic, logical-mathematical, visual-spatial, bodily-kinesthetic, musical-rhythmic, interpersonal, intrapersonal, and naturalistic. As a result, students arrive at each task with a different intelligence level related to that task. Tomlinson refers to these intelligences as various abilities that diverse learners bring to the classroom. Thus, teachers must seek to understand how each student learns and thinks, and incorporate a variety of instructional tasks that focus on the different intelligences throughout any given unit of study. We may then use teaching processes and require student products that maximize the likelihood that each student will learn the information and skills being taught. In Chapter 7, we look in depth at ways teachers can use the knowledge about human intelligence to increase the level of student success. It is critical that teachers provide students with a variety of learning experiences in order to help all students achieve their learning potential.

Differentiated instruction is good instruction for many reasons. Recent research suggests that classrooms that cultivate individuality are most effective. Use the inventory in Figure 6.1 to determine what differentiated practices you are already using in your classroom. Place an X on the line to illustrate where your teaching practices currently are on the continuum. It is important for you to understand all that you are doing to differentiate instruction for your students.

A deeper understanding of teaching and learning has resulted in multiple shifts in education. Such research has also affected how differentiated instruction teaching practices are carried out in classrooms today. The Universal Design for Learning framework has great implications for how teachers respond to diverse learning needs and should be considered when differentiating instruction in order to ensure all students are able to access the curriculum. Other factors influencing teachers' ability to deliver highly targeted instructional supports include recent research on brain-compatible learning, advances in technology, and Response to Intervention (RtI) (Bender 2012).

Universal Design for Learning

The basis for Universal Design for Learning (UDL) is in neuroscience and assumes that "individual learners differ in the way in which they are motivated (affective

Figure 6.1

Differentiated Classroom	Traditional Classroom
I base my teaching on students' learning needs *and* on the curriculum.	Covering the curriculum is my first priority and directs my teaching.
Learning goals are adjusted for students, based on their needs.	Learning goals remain the same for all students.
I emphasize critical and creative thinking, as well as the applications of learning.	I emphasize mastery of content and skills.
I match students to specific informational resources, based on their learning needs and abilities.	Students use the same informational resources (books, articles, and websites).
I use several instructional formats (for example, whole-class, small groups, partners, individuals).	I primarily use whole-class instruction.
As appropriate, I group students for instruction based on their learning needs.	I tend to group students heterogeneously.
The pace of instruction may vary, based on students' learning needs.	All students move through the curriculum together and at the same pace.
As appropriate, I give students opportunities to choose activities based on their interests.	All students complete the same activities.
I use a variety of instructional strategies (for example, lectures, manipulatives, role-plays, simulations, and readings).	I tend to use similar instructional strategies day to day.
Students complete different activities based on their needs or learning preferences.	All students complete all activities.
I use methods for testing out of work and for compacting (speeding up, eliminating, and replacing) work, as appropriate.	All students are involved in all instructional activities.
My enrichment work demands critical and/or creative thinking and the production of new ideas, thoughts, and perspectives.	My enrichment work provides more content application of skills.
In reteaching, I use a different instructional method than the one I used to teach the material the first time.	In reteaching, I provide more practice using a similar instructional method.
My reteaching activities demand higher-level thinking while reinforcing basic skills and content.	My reteaching activities typically involve lower-level thinking—knowledge and comprehension—to reinforce basic skills and content.
Before beginning a unit, I use pre-assessment strategies to determine what students already know.	I assume that students have limited or no knowledge of curriculum content.
I use ongoing assessment to check students' learning throughout an instructional sequence.	I usually assess students' learning at the end of an instructional sequence.
I allow for learner differences by providing a variety of ways to show learning.	I typically use the same assessment tool, product, or project for all students.

Excerpted from *Differentiating Instruction in the Regular Classroom: How to Reach and Teach All Learners, Grades 3–12* by Diane Heacox, 2012. Used with permission of Free Spirit Publishing Inc., Minneapolis, MN; 800-735-7323; www.freespirit.com. All rights reserved.

network), how they comprehend information (recognition network), and how they express what they know (strategic network)" (National Center on Accessing the General Curriculum 2014, p. 8). UDL provides a framework for designing learning goals, tasks and lessons, and assessments to support a broad range of students at the onset of a lesson. **The tenets of UDL encourage teachers to design curriculum so that all students have opportunities to become expert learners in any context by providing multiple means of engagement, representation, and action and expression.** Expert learners are resourceful, strategic, and purposeful in their learning (CAST 2013).

Table 6.2 outlines the guidelines for Universal Design for Learning. These guidelines are organized around the three main principles of UDL previously mentioned: provide multiple means of engagement; provide multiple means of representation; and provide multiple means of action and expression. These guidelines represent areas of learner variation and provide opportunities to maximize student engagement with learning (Meyer, Rose, and Gorden 2014). In the next section, specific examples for differentiating instruction based on each of these principles are highlighted.

Table 6.2 Universal Design for Learning Guidelines

Provide Multiple Means of **ENGAGEMENT** *Purposeful, motivated learners*	Provide Multiple Means of **REPRESENTATION** *Resourceful, knowledgeable learners*	Provide Multiple Means of **ACTION & EXPRESSION** *Strategic, goal-directed learners*
Provide options for self-regulation • Promote expectations and beliefs that optimize motivation. • Facilitate personal coping skills and strategies. • Develop self-assessment and reflection.	Provide options for comprehension • Activate or supply background knowledge. • Highlight patterns, critical features, big ideas, and relationships. • Guide information processing, visualization, and manipulation. • Maximize transfer and generalization.	Provide options for executive functions • Guide appropriate goal setting. • Support planning and strategy development. • Enhance capacity for monitoring progress.
Provide options for sustaining effort and persistence • Heighten salience of goals and objectives. • Vary demands and resources to optimize challenge. • Foster collaboration and community. • Increase mastery-oriented feedback.	Provide options for language, mathematical expressions, and symbols • Clarify vocabulary and symbols. • Clarify syntax and structure. • Support decoding of text, mathematical notation, and symbols. • Promote understanding across languages. • Illustrate through multiple media.	Provide options for expression and communication • Use multiple media for communication. • Use multiple tools for construction and composition. • Build fluencies with graduated levels of support for practice and performance.
Provide options for recruiting interest • Optimize individual choice and autonomy. • Optimize relevance, value, and authenticity. • Minimize threats and distractions.	Provide options for perception • Offer ways of customizing the display of information. • Offer alternatives for auditory information. • Offer alternatives for visual information.	Provide options for physical action • Vary the methods for response and navigation. • Optimize access to tools and assistive technologies.

The UDL Guidelines, 2013, CAST, Inc., in *Universal Design for Learning*. Meyer, A., Rose, D.H., and Gordon, D.: p. 111. Copyright 2014 by CAST, Inc.

Susan Trostle Brand (University of Rhode Island), Antoinette Favazza (University of Rhode Island), and Elizabeth Dalton (Tech ACCESS) offer several suggestions for how teachers can make lessons accessible to a variety of learners (2012):

- **Multiple means of representation**
  - Present information and lessons in different formats, such as interactive whiteboards, flip charts, videos, graphic organizers, and using manipulatives.
  - Use body language, connections, visuals, and graphics.
  - Activate students' prior knowledge (several examples of activators can be found in Chapter 2).

- **Multiple means for engagement**
  - Tap into students' interests by making the curriculum relevant.
  - Clearly communicate learning goals and objectives, vary the level of challenge and support, and encourage student collaboration.
  - Have students set personal goals and scaffold with rubrics, checklists, and notes.

- **Multiple means for action and expression**
  - Have students use their bodies to explore materials.
  - Allow students to use the computer rather than pencil and paper.
  - Allow students to use manipulatives and/or a calculator during math.
  - Provide a variety of tools for composition and problem-solving, offering different levels of scaffolding.
  - Provide multiple supports for goal setting, planning, and learning strategies, such as checklists, outlines, color-coded pages, software tools, etc.

When planning a lesson or unit of study, Meyer, Rose, and Gordon (2014) suggest that teachers think about the following key questions:

Figure 6.2

Think about how learners will engage with the lesson:

- Does the lesson provide options that can help all learners regulate their own learning?
- Does the lesson provide options that help all learners sustain effort and motivation?
- Does the lesson provide options that engage and interest all learners?

Think about how information is presented to learners:

- Does the information provide options that help all learners reach higher levels of comprehension and understanding?
- Does the information provide options that help all learners understand the symbols and expressions?
- Does the information provide options that help all learners perceive what needs to be learned?

Think about how learners are expected to act strategically and express themselves:

- Does the activity provide options that help all students act strategically?
- Does the activity provide options that help all learners express themselves fluently?
- Does the activity provide options that help all learners physically respond?

Meyer, A., Rose, D.H., and Gordon, D. "Key Questions to Use to Consider the UDL Guidelines." CAST, Inc. *Universal Design for Learning,* copyright 2014: p. 112.

Although UDL emphasizes proactively addressing students' needs by designing for variability, and while differentiated instruction emphasizes responding to individual needs, these two frameworks intersect and overlap in multiple ways. Figure 6.3 (on next page) demonstrates how the principles of UDL and differentiated instruction converge and overlap. Both recognize the natural variability and emphasize learning environments that support high expectations and meet the needs of all students.

Brain-Compatible Learning

The research on **brain-compatible learning** provides solid evidence for differentiated instruction. Caine and Caine (2006), two leading researchers in the field of brain-compatible learning, have found that high-impact activities result in increased understanding and enhanced memory. These findings suggest that the brain learns best in the following conditions:

- Students are able to tie sensory and emotional experiences to the content, because sensory and emotional tags associated with content learning enhance memory.
- Students are able to connect new information and understandings to existing knowledge and their own experiences—that is, their schemas.
- Students are presented with tasks that are slightly more challenging than tasks the students can perform independently.
- Students are actively engaged with content through movement or action related to understanding the content (Bender 2012).

An example of a movement technique in a mathematics class entails learning about different angles. The teacher asks the students to stand and form a right angle with both arms. Students are then directed to move their arms to form an acute angle, and then an obtuse angle. Students may even be asked to approximate angles based on a given measure of degrees. Students are more likely to retain an understanding of angles because, as research has shown, when motor skills are used, a deeper form of learning takes place.

It is important for educators to understand all of these principles as they plan lessons for their students. What may be challenging for one student may be too simplistic for another. For this reason, as well as many others, it is important for teachers to provide differentiated learning experiences for their students. In this way, all students will be able to achieve their learning potential.

Chapter 2 describes the ways in which teachers make learning connected, meaningful, and relevant to students. Chapter 8 describes in detail the way in which teachers best use their knowledge of the brain

Figure 6.3

Three Principles of UDL

("With UDL, we start with high standards for all and apply flexible means so that each learner finds appropriate learning challenges and supports."
Meyer, Rose, and Gordon 2014, p. 89.)

Multiple means of engagement	Multiple means of representation	Multiple means of action and expression
Stimulate interest and motivation for learning.	*Present information and content in different ways.*	*Allow students to express what they know in various ways.*

Converge with Differentiated Instruction

• Use effective classroom management to foster engagement. • Offer choices based on student readiness, interests, and learning profile. • Use flexible instruction to increase motivation.	• Use a variety of materials to support instructional content. • Use varying levels of difficulty to present information and skills. • Use multiple examples. • Use concept focused lessons to avoid learning discrete facts.	• Use a variety of instructional strategies to reach all learners • Use scaffolding to build support, fluency and eventual independency. • Use flexible, multiple options for students to express what they know and understand, including degree of difficulty and way in which student understanding is evaluated.

Lead to...

...flexibility in all parts of the curriculum, including goals, methods, materials and assessment.

...all students being supported in access, participation, engagement, and ongoing progress monitoring.

...learning goals that separate means from the end.

to facilitate the highest levels of student learning. As you read this chapter, you will learn how to manage providing differentiated experiences in classrooms in which there are many students and only one of you.

Advances in Technology

Technology advances have directly enhanced teachers' abilities to differentiate instruction and implement principles of UDL. "While differentiated instruction has always emphasized consideration of students' learning styles, strengths, and the formation of instruction groups based on those, the increased availability of technology, social networking, and computerized curricula in the classroom today allows for a totally differentiated instructional program" (Bender 2012, p. 10). Teachers using digital media have the ability to present the same material in multiple ways as well as to provide various entry points through which students can access the material.

In order to best prepare our students for the 21st century, modern technology should be integrated throughout the curriculum. Students today have much experience with several different types of technology, and by incorporating such tools, educators are more likely to sustain the interest of their students. By capitalizing on the interests of students, teachers will better be able to maintain student engagement and will maximize student learning for all learners.

The following list includes some general ways in which technology can be utilized to differentiate instruction:

- educational software programs that provide instruction geared toward students' specific learning needs and are responsive in nature
- educational gaming options and simulations
- WebQuest (a structured, teacher-designed research project completed using Internet resources; many WebQuests can be found online)
- blogging (an online journal which both students and teacher can create and share written work)
- wiki (a website that can be edited by various users)
- Google Docs, which allow for creating, editing, and sharing written work online and are free (Bender 2012)

The following list provides specific examples of innovative digital media teachers can use to effectively differentiate instruction using the principles of UDL:

- multimedia composition tools, such as HyperStudio 5, Kid Pix Deluxe 3X, and PowerPoint
- graphic organizer software, such as Inspiration Software and Kidspiration
- text-to-speech and text-to-image programs, such as Texthelp Read and Write GOLD, Kurzweil firefly, JAWS, and Intellitools Classroom Suite
- digital books tools, such as StoryJumper and CAST UDL Book Builder (http://bookbuilder.cast.org/)
- learning software, such as Funbrain.com, Sebran's ABC, and Edmark's various learning games (National Center on Accessing the General Curriculum 2014, p.15).

Teachers using digital media have the ability to present the same material in multiple ways as well as to provide various entry points through which students can access the material.

One of the newer models of differentiated instruction in which technology is used is the "flipped" classroom. Teachers that use this strategy flip the order of instructional activities. The direct instruction component is shifted to outside the classroom via a teacher-created video or online viewing of new content. In this way, the teacher can more effectively facilitate student learning to apply what they have learned. This targeted instruction provides struggling students with the scaffolding they need, and it challenges those students who have mastered the material (Bender 2012).

Salman Khan, founder and original faculty of Khan Academy, supports this model because students move through the curriculum at a pace that is appropriate for them. Students must master certain key building blocks before moving on. "The most important skill that anyone can learn is how to learn. Students tend not to learn when they are force-marched through a curriculum and focus only on what they are told to do next" (Pinkus 2015, p. 44).

Response to Intervention

Response to Intervention (RtI) identifies struggling students early and provides increasingly intensive levels (or tiers) of support depending on how students respond (National Center on Response to Intervention, n.d.). **The RtI process and differentiation are complementary in that both approaches are built on the concept that education is most effective when learner variability—with respect to different levels of readiness, learning profiles, and interests—has been considered.** "If students are grouped by readiness level, some groups may have more structure in their work or more time to complete their assignment; others may have more complex problems to address. If the students are grouped by learning style, some student groups may be writing, some acting out concepts, some designing a computer presentation, and some working on an oral presentation" (Allan, S.D. and Goddard, Y.L. 2010, p. 1).

Throughout a lesson, effective teachers constantly assess students' responses. Teachers then use this information to differentiate instruction, materials, or group size so that all learners achieve success. Through prevention, intervention, and identification, the RtI model provides students with multiple layers of differentiated support. In addition, individual responses to support are carefully documented. "This intense monitoring and documentation facilitates differentiation as well, because it enables teachers to keep a continuous finger on the pulse of students' progress and thus design differentiated lessons more accurately" (Allan and Goddard 2010, p. 2).

The Role of the Teacher

Knowing one's students is paramount to effectively differentiating instruction for students. Fortunately, educators have a wide variety of tools to use in gathering information about their students. The following list provides some ways in which teachers learn about their students:

- pre-assessments
- interest inventories
- informal conversations
- questions (recall, comprehension, and higher-order thinking)
- observations
- tests and quizzes
- performance assessments
- self-assessments
- student portfolios
- academic histories
- parent questionnaires
- student questionnaires
- K-W-L charts

In a classroom in which differentiated instruction is being used, the primary role of the teacher is that of a facilitator. It is the responsibility of the teacher to provide a variety of different learning opportunities for students. The teacher will choose some of the activities for students to complete while, at other times, the students will choose what activities they will do.

The teacher must also appropriately organize students for learning. Will the students work individually, in pairs, in flexible groups, or as a whole class? In addition, the teacher must decide if students will be differentiated based on readiness, interest, or learning profile.

Teachers using differentiated instruction must be flexible in terms of how they use their time. Students who need more explanation, review, or practice must be provided with such opportunities. Students who have already mastered skills and concepts being taught must be given opportunities to expand their thinking (Heacox 2002, 2012).

Differentiating instruction in the classroom requires much time and effort, particularly when you are first getting started. For this reason, it is important to work collaboratively with colleagues. The following are ideas for working with others:

- Work with teachers at your grade level or in your department. Divide up the task of creating remediation and extension activities for each of the concepts in the curriculum. Sharing the resources and working with colleagues decreases the burden on any one teacher.

- Designate blocks of professional development time for differentiating curriculum. Activities such as lesson study may be extremely valuable in modifying lessons to meet the differentiated needs of students. Chapters 10 and 11 describe ways in which teachers may conduct this type of professional development.

- Work with the media or technology specialist in your school. They can help with finding websites and other valuable sources of information that students may readily access independently or with minimal teacher prompting.

- Work with other specialists, such as the reading or math specialists (in elementary and middle schools), special educators, English as a second language teachers, etc. These teachers have significant experience and a substantial knowledge base related to working with students who may need more reteaching than the majority of the students, and/or extensions for students who master concepts more quickly than the majority of the students.[1]

Tomlinson (2001) outlines several general guidelines that teachers should attend to in order to make differentiating instruction possible.

- **The key concepts and generalizations that give meaning to the topic of study should be clear.** Focusing on key concepts within a unit helps all learners gain a better understanding that will serve as a build-

---

1   Chapters 10 and 11 provide a range of protocols and other tools designed to assist teachers with collaborative work.

ing block for future learning. When planning a unit of study, we start with determining the most important information and skills we would like our students to have mastered at the end of the unit. Chapter 1 describes this process in more depth.

- **All lessons for students should encourage higher-order thinking skills**. All students, regardless of their abilities, should be required to engage in tasks that require students to think at higher levels. While some students may need more support and scaffolding with this process, others may benefit from being challenged with more advanced materials and/or activities. However, it is important that all students are provided with activities that push them to a higher level of understanding. Chapter 5 describes ways in which questioning practices promote higher-order thinking skills. Later in this chapter, we will look at graphic organizers as another means of developing higher-order thinking skills.

- **All lessons for students should be engaging.** Although all students may need to engage in drills and practice to master required skills, it is important that *all* students are provided with opportunities to use this information in more meaningful ways. Although some students will need more time to grasp basic skills, these students need opportunities to apply the concepts and/or skills in more complex ways that are meaningful to their own lives.

- **A balance of student-selected and teacher-assigned tasks should exist in a differentiated classroom.** This balance will vary from student to student, based on individual needs; however, it is critical that all students have choices as well as curricula that are appropriate to their levels of readiness and interests, and their learning profiles. Although the choices the teacher presents to students will vary from student to student, based on specific needs, it is important that all students have choices in some part of their curricula. In this way, students feel as though they have more ownership of their learning.

- **Assessment should serve as a guide to our thinking and planning.** We should use assessments as a way of learning about our students. Observing students, homework, collaborative work, projects, tests, quizzes, and oral presentations are just some of many ways to assess or better understand where our students are in terms of their learning and understanding. Chapter 4 explains the ways in which teachers may use assessments of student learning to inform instruction.

- **Fairness is redefined.** In a differentiated classroom, fairness means every student gets what he or she needs in order to maximize his or her learning. This means that students will be working on different tasks at times. It may be helpful to have a discussion on fairness with students so that they understand what fairness looks like in a classroom. Students need to understand that fairness means all students get what they need in order to maximize their learning. This means that there will be times when different students will be working on different tasks, and different supports will be provided for students.

Grading and the Differentiated Classroom

Grading should reflect student mastery as well as a student's growth over time. In some classrooms today, grades do not accurately portray a student's mastery of the subject matter. Instead, we put too much emphasis on other things, such as attendance, participation, and behavior. Doing so can distort what grades are intended to do: that is, "document mastery, provide feedback, and guide instructional decisions" (Wormeli 2006, pp. 103–104). Rick Wormeli (p. 103) suggests the following working premise with regard to grades: "A grade represents a clear and accurate indicator of what a student knows and is able to do—mastery. With grades, we document the progress of students and our teaching, we provide feedback to students and their parents, and we make instructional decisions regarding the students." In addition, Wormeli also suggests several practices for teachers when grading in a differentiated classroom:

- Incorporate only (or primarily) academic factors in students' final grades. Things such as behavior, participation, effort, and attendance do not accurately reflect students' learning of a particular concept or skill and should not have a significant impact on the grade. Although these work behaviors (effort, behavior, participation, and attendance) are important for life-long learning, they are "not demonstrations of mastery themselves; they are routes to that mastery" (p. 110). Some schools are now providing separate grades that addresses these behaviors. Further, Rick Stiggins, an educator assessment expert, believes that if we use grades to help motivate our students, we discourage risk-taking and creativity, and grades lose their intended value (2006, p. 102).

- Allow students multiple attempts at achieving mastery. Students should not be punished for needing more time to master a particular concept. We should respect each individual student's development, and understand that students learn at different paces and through different means. Allowing students to use feedback from a teacher on an initial assessment to revise or redo a second assessment encourages students to master the material. According to Nolen and Taylor in *Classroom Assessment*, "Feedback that is given on an assignment that can't be revised or that is not clearly or specifically related to future work is unlikely to be seen as useful to the student. Policies that give only partial credit for revisions are little better than no-revision policies—why should the student spend time and effort revising something if the best he can hope for is a slight improvement in the grade, despite the fact that he now understands how to do the work?" (2005, p. 60, in Wormeli 2006, p. 115). However, it is important for teachers to establish guidelines and conditions for redoing work so that students do not take advantage of the "redo" option.

> *Allowing students to use feedback from a teacher on an initial assessment to revise or redo a second assessment encourages students to master the material.*

• Homework should be assigned to students only after they have a good understanding of the material or have mastered the material. One exception to this rule is the "flipped" classroom, which was discussed earlier in this chapter. In a differentiated classroom, different homework assignments may be assigned to different students on any given day. **The purpose of homework is to practice, reinforce, or extend learning.** Asking students to complete homework in areas that have not been mastered is doing students a disservice, as students may learn and practice the material incorrectly. Although homework should not be used to demonstrate mastery or be graded, it is important to provide students with specific feedback on given assignments. Finally, if teachers feel compelled to incorporate homework into their students' grades Wormeli recommends having homework count for no more than 10 percent of the final grade.

• Assess students in ways that accurately reflect their level of learning. Provide appropriate supports and scaffolding for learning to students when clearly needed. For example, if a student needs a graphic organizer to help him or her demonstrate mastery of a particular concept or skill, we teachers need to provide it. If a testing format is inappropriate for a student, we need to create a more appropriate one in order to accurately assess that student's level of mastery. As teachers, we need to be flexible in our teaching and provide our students with the necessary tools to enable them to successfully demonstrate mastery of their learning. Different students will require different supports and

scaffolding. It is our responsibility to know and understand our students well enough to provide each and every student with the appropriate assistance.

• When assessing cooperative group work,[2] exercise caution. Students' grades should be representative of their individual levels of mastery. Students should not be penalized for another student's lack of achievement. However, group work should include an assessment component that reflects how well the group worked together. You can find more information about how to effectively incorporate, manage, and assess group work in Chapter 3.

• If a student consistently turns work in late, consider giving partial credit rather than automatically assigning a zero. Some teachers turn the zero into a 60 so that the grade can still accurately reflect the level of mastery the student achieved. Mathematically, assigning zeros to late work can skew the grade so that it is no longer useful to the student, parent, or teacher. "Adjusting zeros to sixty is not giving students something for having done nothing. It's adjusting the grading scale so that it is ethically justifiable, so that each grade has an appropriate amount of influence on the student's summative evaluation and the grade can be used in decision making" (p. 140).

• Use criterion referenced attributes to report what students know and are able to do. Standards-based grades should report what an individual student has mastered, not what he or she has learned in comparison to other students in the classroom.

Establishing Routines in the Differentiated Classroom

In any classroom, it is important to establish routines for students. In Chapter 3, we discuss in detail how to establish effective routines for students. Routines help students know what to expect, the teacher has more time for individualizing instruction, and students are able to assume more responsibility for themselves, regardless of their grade level. If a teacher is going to successfully differentiate instruction, it is imperative that routines are established, practiced, and mastered by students. In particular, routines and procedures should be established that facilitate small group management and efficient transitions. The following exam-

---

2   See Chapter 3 for information on how to establish effective work groups in your classroom.

ple illustrates how one teacher uses several routines to support small-group differentiated instruction. A typical lesson begins with a whole-group mini-lesson that accesses prior knowledge and then builds on that existing foundation. After the mini-lesson, the teacher refers to her rotation chart that outlines group membership for each student and the specific activities students are expected to complete. Routines and procedures have been established so that students know where to go and what they need to do to successfully complete the given task. Students who are working with the teacher meet at a round table at the back of the classroom, those working on independent work remain at their seats, and students working on partner work find a quiet spot with their assigned partner on the floor using a clipboard. Students spend approximately 20 minutes working in each rotation. Three minutes before a transition is to occur, the teacher rings a chime. This signal is used to alert students that they need to clean up their workspaces, place completed work in the designated location, and get ready for their next rotation. Again, the teacher refers to her rotation chart that clearly delineates the activity and location for which each student should be working.

As teachers, it is our responsibility to provide struggling students with more basic instruction while providing advanced learners with more challenging tasks.

Prior to students working in these rotations, the teacher sets up a system for students working independently or in pairs who have questions about an assignment. Students working in pairs should first try to figure out the question with their partner. If unable to do so, the pair should ask another pair of students working on a similar task. Students working independently should ask another student who is also working independently for help. When students are unable to find a peer to clarify their questions, they should place their name in the "Emergency Red Cross Can." The teacher puts this system in place at the beginning of the year. Every student has a tongue depressor with his or her name that is stored in a green can. When students are unable to find peers to help clarify confusion, they put their depressor in the "Emergency Red Cross Can." In this way, the teacher can quickly determine who needs help, and can provide assistance when he or she is finished working with her small group.

The classroom routines discussed above—including a rotation chart, an "Emergency Red Cross Can" system in place for seeking help, a chime to signal transitions, and a designated spot for each rotation as well as completed work—all support differentiated instruction. These routines should be modeled for students, practiced by students, and reviewed periodically in order to maximize successful differentiation.

Differentiating by Readiness

As teachers, it is our responsibility to provide struggling students with more basic, foundation-building instruction while providing advanced learners with more complex, challenging tasks. Vygotsky, a developmental theorist and researcher of the 1920s and 1930s, felt that children's learning was maximized when instruction was appropriate to each child's cognitive development. To ask students to complete a complex task in which a more capable "other" is needed to guide them through unfamiliar territory—without providing the necessary support—will lead to frustration and inhibit student learning and growth. At the same time, asking students to complete tasks that are too simplistic will result in boredom, and students may become less motivated to learn. It is imperative that educators provide students with appropriate assistance as well as develop instruction geared to a child's "zone of proximal development," which is defined by Vygotsky (1978) as

> [The] distance between the child's actual development, as determined by independent problem solving, and the level of potential development, as determined through problem solving under adult guidance or in collaboration with more capable peers (p. 88).

In other words, the **zone of proximal development** is the distance between what a student knows and what he or she may learn without being over-challenged (or frustrated) or under-challenged (or bored).

Teachers who use students' readiness levels to differentiate content, process, or product, design tasks that will push students beyond their current levels of understanding. A task that is designed to meet a student at his or her appropriate level of learning will extend that student's level of understanding and knowledge to a level beyond his or her independent level. It is important to remember that readiness is always changing, and students should move in and out of groups as they meet the stated learning goals. Later in this chapter, we will discuss the importance of flexible grouping, as well as how to manage such groups.

According to (Tomlinson 1995a, 2001, 2014), teachers may create "readiness-based adjustments" by offering students a range of learning tasks developed along one or more of the following continua:

1. Concrete to abstract
2. Simple to complex
3. Fewer steps to multi-steps
4. Smaller leaps to greater leaps
5. More structured to more open
6. Less independence to greater independence
7. Slower to quicker

As you read on, you will see that differentiating instruction in these ways is not as daunting as it may initially appear when looking at this list. A single teaching activity often incorporates several of the items on this list, as noted in the sample lesson later in this chapter. Differentiating instruction in several of these areas may be as simple as carefully wording a higher-order thinking skills question and asking the students to address the question using the group questions strategy.

After you read a brief explanation and example of each of the above ways in which to differentiate instruction, you will find a differentiating lesson plan exemplar for an elementary mathematics class that uses Investigations as its math program. As you read through it, you will find that the activities move from a more concrete level, in which manipulatives are used (in this case, pennies), to a more abstract level. The problems that students are asked to complete at the beginning of the lesson are simple and become more complex as students become more proficient. In addition, as students become more competent, they will be asked to solve problems in which more steps are required and less structure is provided. Finally, when students are at the application-mastery level, they are asked to solve a problem of the day that requires them to carefully read the problem, determine the important and relevant information, choose an appropriate strategy, carry out their plan, find a correct solution, and write about the steps they took to solve this problem. This problem is more abstract and open in nature, and requires more complex thinking. In addition, this multi-step problem requires students to take greater leaps in transferring their knowledge of multiplication. Finally, you will notice this lesson allows all students to move at a pace that is appropriate for them.

Concrete to abstract. Information, ideas, and concepts are **concrete** if they can be physically manipulated, demonstrated, or explained, or are literal and/or tangible. They are **abstract** if they focus more on meanings, implications, or principles; are symbolic or metaphorical; or cannot be demonstrated or explained. When students are first introduced to a concept or skill, they often need to become familiar with the new information in a more basic, hands-on manner. Once this new information has become part of their schemas, students will benefit from tasks that involve more abstract materials, representations, ideas, or applications than would peers who are less advanced in their mastery. For example, students may need to work with concrete arrays or other models when first introduced to multiplication. Once a basic understanding of multiplication has been mastered, students may be able to move on to applying multiplication in a problem-solving activity. The pace at which students move from concrete to abstract will vary from student to student.

Simple to complex. Information and resources that are presented in **simple** form only use the idea or skill that is being taught, work with few abstractions, and are more basic in terms of vocabulary and readability. Events are also presented in simple form when the student is given the general overview at the outset. If the idea or skill being presented is combined to previously learned material, many meanings may be ascertained, multiple events are presented, or the vocabulary and readability is more advanced, then the material is considered **complex**. Further, more complex tasks may require more originality.

Many students need to see the big picture of a topic when it is first introduced; however, once learners understand the big picture, they will benefit from and are better able to complete classroom activities that

- require more complex resources
- have more complex research requirements
- contain more complex issues
- address more complex problems
- require more complex skills
- contain more complex goals

For example, a teacher introducing a unit of study on simple machines first presents students with the general concept that simple machines help people to do work more easily. Once this general concept is understood by students, it is appropriate for the teacher to begin describing the complexities of how each of the six simple machines helps people to do work more easily. Students may be asked to compare and contrast the different types of simple machines, or they may be asked to create their own simple machines and describe how they use mechanical advantage to multiply force. After the whole-class introduction, the rate at which students will move from simple to more complex resources, research, issues, problems, skills, and goals will vary from student to student.

Fewer steps to multi-steps.[3] Some projects, problems, and activities require students to take **fewer steps**, while others involve **more steps and applications**. Some students may need to work on projects, activities, or problems in which only a few steps are involved. Learners who are more advanced in a subject benefit from tasks that have more complex directions, more connections within or across subjects, or from tasks that require more complex planning and execution. The following two problems represent how to differentiate a mathematical problem-solving situation to better meet the needs of different learners. In the first problem, students need only work through a few steps in order to find the correct solution; they need to find the percent of each number. However, in the second example, students are asked to think in more complex ways, and they will need to go through several steps to effectively solve the problem.

> *All learners must make leaps in their learning for it to be meaningful. When memorization of facts is the goal, learning is of little long-term benefit until the memorized information is used to make leaps to higher-order thinking.*

Problem 1: You are the owner of a running store who sold 400 pairs of running shoes in the previous quarter. Fifty percent of those pairs of shoes were Nike, 15 percent were Reebok, 15 percent were New Balance, and 20 percent were Adidas. How many pairs of each brand of shoe did you sell?

Problem 2: You are the owner of a running store. The following table shows data about your sneaker sales in a recent week.

TYPE OF SNEAKER	NUMBER SOLD
Adidas	124
Nike	64
Reebok	49
New Balance	42
Asics	21

Next week, you plan to order 36 dozen sneakers. Explain how you would use the data to decide how many dozen of each type to order, and state how many dozen of each you plan to order.

Smaller leaps to greater leaps. When students apply ideas in ways that are familiar to them or make connections to familiar ideas, they are considered to be making **smaller leaps** of transferring information. If students are asked to use ideas in new and unfamiliar ways or to make connections between previously unrelated ideas, they will need to make **greater leaps** of transferring information. All learners must make leaps in their learning for it to be meaningful. When memorization of facts is the goal, learning is of little long-term benefit until the memorized information is used to make leaps to higher-order thinking. For example, among students learning about perimeter, some may be able to determine how much fencing would be needed to enclose a 36-square-foot pen for their dog. Other students may be able to find the solution in which the least amount of fencing is needed and approximate the cost. In addition, these students might be asked to find the additional costs if the pen is enlarged by varying amounts, and then to provide a written rationale and recommendation of a size for the pen. Learners advanced in a subject often benefit from tasks that require greater mental leaps in insight, application, or transfer than less-advanced peers.

More structured to more open. Some students need to complete tasks that are direct and require them to follow a specific format with clear directions. As students become more proficient in a particular area of study, however, they will benefit from tasks that are more open with regard to solutions, decisions, and approaches. For example, some students may need more structure in the area of problem-solving. For these students, it might be necessary to help them set up an organized table (assuming that this is the appropriate strategy to use with the specific mathematics problem) before they solve the problem independently. More advanced learners would be expected to choose an appropriate strategy and implement this strategy on their own. They may even be asked to solve the problem using two or more different strategies.

---

3   Fewer steps to multi-steps and smaller leaps to greater leaps are two differentiating instruction structures that special education teachers say are particularly important for students with learning disabilities.

The Lemonade Stand

The following problem illustrates how one teacher provided more support for those students who needed it to solve a mathematical problem. In this instance, the additional support some of the students were given was a table constructed by the teacher.

Jack and Susan found they were collecting more and more money from their lemonade stand each day. On the first day, they collected $5.35; then, on the second day, they collected $6.45. They collected $8.70 on the third day, $9.80 on the fourth day, and $12.05 on the fifth day. On what day did they collect $22.10?

Day	Money Collected
Day 1	$5.35
Day 2	$6.45
Day 3	
Day 4	
Day 5	
Day 6	
Day 7	
Day 8	
Day 9	
Day 10	
Day 11	
Day 12	

Providing a table for students at lower levels of mastery enabled them to organize the information so that they were able to solve the problem successfully. By providing students with the support they need, these students will develop the ability to solve similar problems with less scaffolding over time.

For more capable students, the teacher gave the same problem without the table. These students were expected to organize the information and select a strategy that made most sense for them.

Answer to the Lemonade Stand Problem

Day	Money Collected
Day 1	$5.35
Day 2	$6.45
Day 3	$8.70
Day 4	$9.80
Day 5	$12.05
Day 6	$13.15
Day 7	$15.40
Day 8	$16.50
Day 9	$18.75
Day 10	$19.85
Day 11	$22.10
Day 12	

Less independence (more teacher-guided) to greater independence (less teacher-guided). Less independent tasks are those that are primarily designed and modeled by the teacher. As students become more independent, they become more responsible for the planning, designing, and execution of the particular task at hand. **A goal for *all* students is to become independent learners; however, learners reach varying levels of independence at different rates.** More advanced learners in a subject will be able to be more independent in terms of planning, designing, and self-monitoring than their less-advanced peers. For example, when first introducing literature circles to students, it is important to model the process for them as well as provide them with a structured format. Each student is assigned a specific role and given directions for fulfilling the role. As the teacher scaffolds the students' learning, students become more competent, responsibility is gradually released to the students, and they may modify the structure presented to them to better fit their group. Some groups may even create new roles. It is important to note that each group will reach varying levels of independence at different rates.

Slower to quicker. In Chapter 1, we looked at the various levels of mastery that students progress through when learning new information and skills. **Students require differing amounts of time to reach each of the mastery levels when they are taught information and skills.** Some students will grasp the new information and skills immediately, while other learners will require more modeling and practice before moving to the next level of mastering the same information and skills. Sometimes, learners who are advanced in their grasp of the information or skill will benefit from moving quickly through prescribed materials and tasks. At other times, they may need a greater amount of time with a particular area of study than less-advanced peers in order to explore the topic in greater depth and/or breadth. By differentiating the pace for learners, the more advanced students are able to move forward, and the struggling learners are provided the time and reteaching they need.

Figure 6.4 illustrates an example of a differentiated instruction mathematics lesson. We have inserted *author's note* in places where we point out to the reader the type of differentiation demonstrated by that part of the lesson.

Figure 6.4 Differentiating Instruction Exemplar: Elementary Mathematics

1. **What are the district's curriculum standard and/or benchmark from which these concepts are derived?**
   Multiply two two-digit numbers using strategies based on place value and properties of operations.

2. **What do I want the students to know and be able to do by the end of the lesson (my mastery objectives)?**
   By the end of the lesson, students will be able to correctly complete a two-digit by two-digit multiplication problem using cluster problems up to $49 * 49$.

3. **How will I formatively and summatively assess the students' level of mastery?**
   a. **How will I pre-assess the students' level of knowledge?** (*If you are not planning to do a mini-lesson, go directly to differentiating, which is question 3b after this pre-assessment.*)
   I will put the example $12 * 12$ on the whiteboard. All students will be asked to complete the problem by using smaller cluster problems on their whiteboards. Those students who do not know how to complete the problem using this strategy will write the problem on their whiteboards and stop when they are stuck. I will then put up the example $24 * 25$ and have the students follow the same procedure on their whiteboards.
   b. **How will I formatively assess after the mini-lesson to determine each student's level of mastery?**
   - The colored cups will enable me to constantly dipstick.
   - I will have some idea of the rate at which students are moving to mastery based on their whiteboard work.

This allows the teacher to monitor the level of each student's success and provide higher levels of independence (or teacher direction) based on the needs of individual students.

The students' pace will be determined by their level of mastery, as demonstrated by the process each student follows in solving the problem and each student's answer. Students who demonstrate mastery will be able to move more quickly to more complex tasks.

Figure 6.4 *(continued)*

This gives the teacher a summative record of each student's level of mastery for use in flexibly grouping the students. It may be determined that some students are capable of greater leaps and, therefore, would be better challenged by skipping altogether some of the activities noted below. Other students may need to be given smaller leaps by using activities with a smaller gradation than those noted below.

This is a concrete experience.

This is moving toward abstract.

This problem is becoming more complex as the numbers become greater.

In steps b–d, students move at their own pace. This allows for slower to quicker and less independence to greater independence.

Students are moving from simple to complex.

Students are moving from structured to more open, and the problems are requiring a greater number of steps.

- During the independent work, I will circulate around the room with the class list on a clipboard and observe the students working. I will record an *i* (introductory), *g* (guided practice), *im* (immediate mastery), or *iam* (immediate application mastery) for each student.

4. **Describe the sequence of events.**
   a. **What information and skills will I teach during the whole-class mini-lesson?**
      - I will explain to students that cluster problems are smaller multiplication problems that you solve in your head (without paper and pencil) and may be combined to solve more complicated multiplication problems.
      - I will take the penny jar and make 11 piles of 11.
        I will have the students come up to the table to see what they look like. I will also tell students that multiplying a two-digit number by a two-digit number is very similar to the multiplication problems they have solved previously (e.g., multiplying a two-digit number by a one-digit number).
      - I will write the addition algorithm with 11 added 11 times on the board and have the students add it on their whiteboards. I will direct teach two-digit multiplication using cluster problems to solve 11 * 11.
      - I will then direct teach 12 * 12 using cluster problems. I will have the students complete the problem on their whiteboards while I teach it on the front board.
      - I will then direct teach 24 * 25.
      - I will again have the students complete the problem on their whiteboards while I teach it on the front board.
      - I will show the students the chart paper with a diagram of the steps taken to complete the problem 12 * 12, which will serve as an anchor chart.
      - I will give the students four similar problems to solve on a worksheet. Students will work on the problems using their yellow cups to signal if and when they need help from a peer. Only those students who have finished all three problems may give help. No student may help more than two students. If they are still stuck after peer support, they will put up their red cups. Students who finish early will be asked to write situations for each of the problems they solved on the worksheet. Such an activity will help me to determine if students are able to apply multiplication in appropriate situations.
   b. **What activity will I use with the students who are at introductory level?**
      These students will come to the table area with the guided practice students for more direct teaching of double-digit multiplication using cluster problems.
   c. **What activity will I use with the students who are at guided practice level?**
      These students will come to the table area with the introductory students for more direct teaching of double-digit multiplication using cluster problems. I will use the guided practice students to guide me through some examples.
   d. **What activity will I use with the students who are at immediate mastery level?**
      These students will complete four additional, more complex examples to embed their learning. In three of these problems, students will be provided with samples of cluster problems to use. In the last problem, students will be asked to create their own clusters to solve each of the original problems.

Figure 6.4 *(continued)*

In addition, students will be asked to choose one of the problems and show how it may be solved in two different ways. They will then check their work with another student at this level. If the students have different answers, they will do the problem together to determine the error(s) and find a solution with which they both agree. If both have the same answer and agree, they will move on to the problem of the day.

This allows for a high level of independence (non-teacher-directed) where appropriate.

The problem of the day will be completed individually, using the problem-solving format sheet that can be found in Chapter 7. When a student finishes, he or she will check the work with another student who has completed the problem of the day. If they have different answers, they will do the problem together to determine where they differ and find a solution with which they both agree. When both agree on a solution, they will move on to the website http://www.coolmath4kids.com.

e. **What activity will I use with the students who are at the immediate application mastery level?**

These students will move on to the problem of the day. The problem of the day will be completed individually using the problem-solving format sheet. When a student finishes the problem, he or she will check the work with another student at this level. If they have different answers, they will do the problem together to determine where they differ and find a solution with which they both agree. When both agree on a solution, they will work with their partners on one of the problems found on http://www.coolmath4kids.com. The problem(s) they complete will be printed out and placed in their math problem-solving folder.

5. **What other person can assist me with planning this lesson?**
I will ask the other fourth-grade teacher to make and copy one of the worksheets, and I will make and copy the other.

6. **What materials do I need?**
I need dipsticking cups, two worksheets, a class list and clipboard, whiteboards and dry erase markers, chart-sized sheet for the problem of the day, and problem-solving format sheets.

Differentiated Instruction Planning Template

1. What are the district's curriculum standards and/or benchmarks from which these concepts are derived?
2. What do I want the students to know and be able to do by the end of the lesson (my mastery objectives)?
3. How will I formatively and summatively assess the students' level of mastery?
   - How will I pre-assess the students' level of knowledge? (If you are not planning to do a mini-lesson, go directly to differentiating, which is question 3b after this pre-assessment.)
   - How will I formatively assess after the mini-lesson to determine each student's level of mastery?
4. Describe the sequence of events.
   - What information and skills will I teach during the whole-class mini-lesson?
   - What activity will I use with the students who are at introductory level?
   - What activity will I use with the students who are at guided practice level?
   - What activity will I use with the students who are at immediate mastery level?
   - What activity will I use with the students who are at the immediate application mastery level?
5. What other person can assist me with planning this lesson?
6. What materials do I need?

This page and the next show chart-sized sheets noted in the materials section above. Some teachers make these charts on easel papers. Others make the charts on the computer on standard-size paper. The charts are then printed out, taken to a copy center, and enlarged to four-foot-by-three-foot charts. After they are used, the charts can be folded up and stored in a file cabinet until the next time the concept is taught (during review or in a subsequent year). As noted earlier, planning a differentiated instruction lesson is time-consuming during the initial planning; however, if we save the lesson and charts, the planning time is significantly reduced during the subsequent teaching of the lessons.

Figure 6.5

Using Cluster Problems to Solve 12 × 12

$$12 \times 12 =$$

Step 1
$12 \times 10 = 120$

Step 2
$12 \times 10 = 120$
$12 \times 2 = 24$

Step 3
$$12 \times 10 = 120$$
$$12 \times 2 = + 24$$
$$\overline{ 144}$$

Using Cluster Problems to Solve 24 × 25

$$24 \times 25 =$$

Step 1
$25 \times 20 = 500$

Step 2
$25 \times 20 = 500$
$25 \times 4 = 100$

Step 3
$25 \times 20 = 500$
$25 \times 4 = + 100$
$ 600$

Problem of the day: Two-digit multiplication

Each soccer team puts 11 players on the field at one time. Ninety-seven teams will enter this year's soccer tournament. Each team has enough players on its roster to make three 11-man teams. Each team has three coaches and three water carriers who are not players. What is the total number of players who will come to the tournament?

Bonus: Forty-eight teams will be eliminated in the first round. How many players will play in the second round?

Answer: 3201
Answer for bonus: 1617

Worksheet for Students

1. Solve the cluster problems below.

$$25 \times 45 =$$

25×10	25×5
25×40	25×50

$$15 \times 15 =$$

15×1	15×2
15×10	15×20
15×5	

$$75 \times 25 =$$

25×7	25×8
25×70	25×80
25×5	

$$85 \times 40 =$$

2. Choose one of the problems above and solve it using a different set of clusters.
3. When you have finished Steps 1 and 2, check your work with another student who has also finished Steps 1 and 2, and compare your answers. If you have different answers to a problem, do the problem together to determine the error(s), and find a solution on which you both agree. Once you both have the same answers and agree, move on to the problem of the day.

Differentiating Instruction for Varied Learning Profiles, Gender, and Culture

In Chapter 7, we take a comprehensive look at intelligence and how this affects instruction. In Chapter 8, we look in depth at the brain and its impact on differentiating our instruction. In the next section, we will focus on three student characteristics that generate a need for varying instruction to meet students' various learning needs. These three characteristics are learning style, gender, and cultural influences. Gaps in achievement will then be addressed, and recommendations for closing these gaps will be suggested.

Learning Profiles

Learning profiles encompass how an individual learns. Students' profiles can reflect preferences in the learning environment, learning modalities, and mental processing styles, including the multiple intelligences.

Environmental Preferences

One aspect of a student's learning profile has to do with one's environment and personal likes and dislikes. Some students prefer working in a quiet environment, while others prefer to have noise or music in the background. Some students prefer a bright, colorful room, while others prefer a darker, more subdued room. Some students prefer to work on one task at a time, while others prefer to work on multiple tasks simultaneously (Sousa and Tomlinson 2011). Further, students have different preferences with regard to the social organization, in that some prefer to work alone, some prefer to work in pairs, and some prefer to work in small groups. Although it is impossible for a teacher to incorporate all of these preferences at the same time, it is important to use a variety of teaching methods when presenting a new skill, concept, or strategy in order to maximize learning for all students. A teacher might also set up the classroom so that some of these different learning preferences might be addressed at the same time.

One teacher found some of her students who preferred working in a quiet environment had a very difficult time with collaborative activities due to a higher noise level. To accommodate this aspect of their learning style, she had these students work with their group at a table in the hallway when possible.

In another case, a teacher had students who preferred working alone to working in a group. Because it is critical that students develop the skills needed to work collaboratively, these students were still required to participate in group work. At times, however, these students were permitted to work independently on their tasks. Their independent work would later become part of the group project or activity. As tasks were divided among the group members, this student would be assigned to do the library research or go on the computer and search the Internet for new resources.

Learning Modalities

Students vary in their preference of learning modality, that is, hearing, sight, and touch. Some students are oral rather than visual learners. They need to talk through their ideas before they begin writing. In these situations, students may record their ideas as the first step in the writing process. These students are able to then listen to their ideas through earphones before making a decision about which idea to use in their writing piece.

Students who are visual learners particularly benefit when they can see what they are learning through reading, writing, and observing (Heacox 2012). **Graphic organizers** are tools that can be helpful in writing activities in which students need to organize their ideas and thoughts. Graphic organizers can also help students develop a deeper understanding of story structure by having students highlight the important story elements.

Another time you may want to use graphic orga-

nizers is when introducing major concepts. For example, one teacher presents the concept of the water cycle using a cyclical graphic organizer. It is interesting to note that when students were asked to explain the water cycle in their own words, the visual learners represented this information in a graphic organizer, while many of the other learners wrote out the steps and/or drew pictures. You will read more about graphic organizers later in this chapter.

Some students learn best by moving, doing, and touching. These students prefer to manipulate objects. Although many students benefit from having concrete experiences with mathematical concepts before moving to a more abstract understanding, tactile learners prefer to work with **manipulatives** even after they have developed a deeper understanding of the concept. For example, many teachers use fraction bars to introduce adding fractions with unlike denominators to students. Through manipulation of these bars, students are able to see and understand how to add such fractions. Some students, as a result of their particular learning styles, need to use these fraction bars for a longer period of time in order to conceptualize how and why fractions need to have a common denominator before they can be added. For those students who need this concrete support to work independently, teachers may want to keep several bins of fraction bars easily accessible to students so that they may bring them to their desks during group and individual work.

Some teachers find the following inventory useful in determining how their students learn best—visually, aurally, or through tactile experiences. A scoring guide is included, as well as suggestions for maximizing learning for each particular learning style.

Figure 6.6

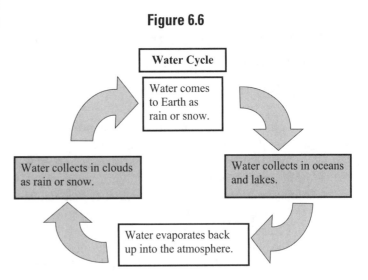

Learning Style Inventory

Use this inventory to better understand how you prefer to learn and process information. Place a check in the appropriate space after each statement below. Use the scoring directions below the figure to evaluate your responses. Use what you learn from your scores to better develop learning strategies that are best suited to your particular learning style. This 24-item survey is not timed. Respond to each statement as honestly as you can.

Figure 6.7

	Often	Some-times	Seldom
1. I can remember best about a subject by listening to a lecture that includes information, explanations, and discussion.			
2. I prefer to see information written on a whiteboard and supplemented by visual aids and assigned readings.			
3. I like to write things down or to take notes for visual review.			
4. I prefer to use posters, models, or actual practice and other activities in class.			
5. I require explanations of diagrams, graphs, or visual directions.			
6. I enjoy working with my hands or making things.			
7. I am skillful with and enjoy developing and making graphs and charts.			
8. I can tell if sounds match when presented with pairs of sounds.			
9. I can remember best by writing things down several times.			
10. I can easily understand and follow directions on a map.			
11. I do best in academic subjects by listening to lectures, etc.			
12. I play with coins or keys in my pocket.			
13. I learn to spell better by repeating words out loud than by writing the words on paper.			
14. I can understand a news story better by reading about it in the newspaper than by listening to a report about it on the radio.			
15. I chew gum or snack while studying.			
16. I think the best way to remember something is to picture it in your head.			
17. I learn the spelling of words by "finger spelling" them.			
18. I would rather listen to a good lecture or speech than read about the same material in a textbook.			
19. I am good at working and solving jigsaw puzzles and mazes.			
20. I grip objects in my hands during learning periods.			
21. I prefer listening to the news rather than reading about it.			
22. I prefer obtaining information about an interesting subject by reading about it.			
23. I feel very comfortable touching others, hugging, handshaking, etc.			
24. I follow oral directions better than written ones.			

Adapted from *Psychology at Red Rocks Community College*, July 28, 2007.

Scoring Procedures

DIRECTIONS: Place the point value on the line next to the corresponding item below. Add the points in each column to obtain the preference score under each heading.

OFTEN = 5 points   SOMETIMES = 3 points   SELDOM = 1 point

VISUAL	AUDITORY	TACTILE
NO. PTS.	NO. PTS.	NO. PTS.
2 ___	1 ___	4 ___
3 ___	5 ___	6 ___
7 ___	8 ___	9 ___
10 ___	11 ___	12 ___
14 ___	13 ___	15 ___
16 ___	18 ___	17 ___
19 ___	21 ___	20 ___
22 ___	24 ___	23 ___
VPS = ___	APS = ___	TPS = ___

VPS = Visual Preference Score   APS = Auditory Preference Score   TPS = Tactile Preference Score

If you are a VISUAL learner, by all means be sure that you look at all study materials. Use charts, maps, filmstrips, notes, videos, and flash cards. Practice visualizing or picturing words and concepts in your head. Write out everything for frequent and quick visual review.

If you are an AUDITORY learner, you may wish to use recordings. Record lectures to help fill in gaps in your notes. However, do listen and take notes, and review your notes frequently. Sit in the lecture hall or classroom where you can hear well. After you have read something, summarize it and recite it aloud. Talk to other students about class material.

If you are a TACTILE learner, trace words as you are saying them. Facts that must be learned should be written several times. Keep a supply of scratch paper on hand for this purpose. Taking and keeping lecture notes is very important. Make study sheets. Associate class material with real-world things or occurrences. When appropriate, practice role-playing (Psychology at Red Rocks Community College 2007).

Mental Processing Styles

In addition to Gardner's work, which focuses on cognitive preferences and was discussed earlier in this chapter, another alternative for conceptualizing students' mental processing styles has emerged. Bender (2012) suggests using the work of Silver, Strong, and Perini (2000) as another way to look at how learners prefer to process information. Once a specific processing style has been determined, a teacher can then create specific instructional tasks and strategies that complement the processing style. Figure 6.8 outlines each of these four styles and suggests specific instructional tasks that might work best with the various learners.

Figure 6.8

Silver, Strong, and Perini's Learning Styles

Mastery style: Students with this learning style proceed in a step-by-step fashion, focusing on practical implications of the content. These students are highly motivated by success, take pride in developing new understandings, and respond well to competitive and challenging learning tasks.

Understanding style: Students with this style question the content, analyzing the implications of it and fitting the pieces of a construct together. These students want to make sense of the academic content and respond well to puzzles, games, or discussions of controversy.

Self-expressive style: Students with this learning style demonstrate innovative thinking and imagination when undertaking a learning task. They long to be unique in their thinking and original in their approach to any task, seeking understanding that only they have reached. These students respond well to choices in their work and creative assignments.

Interpersonal style: Students with this learning style learn best in the social context, exploring their own feelings or the feelings and understandings of others. These students thrive in cooperative learning situations and are highly emotive in sharing their feelings.

Source: *Differentiating Instruction for Students With Learning Disabilities: New and Best Practices for General and Special Educators.* Thousand Oaks, CA: Corwin: p. 8.

Most educators today are in agreement that students learn in a variety of ways and that attending to these differences positively affects student learning. Understanding your students' learning profiles can effectively inform your instruction. That being said, "[the goal ought not to be to label or pigeonhole students as particular 'kinds' of learners, but rather to offer varied ways of approaching learning and then helping students determine which of those ways—or others they may propose—seem most effective in supporting their learning at a given time" (Tomlinson 2014, p.19).

Gender Differences

There has been considerable debate about the real significance of gender differences in terms of our students' learning. Recent and ongoing research confirms that structural differences exist between the male and female brains. These differences account for the variation in the ways in which boys and girls process information and learn. However, the extent to which these differences influence learning is modest to moderate. In fact, a very small gap exists between what boys and girls can learn, and these differences are most pro-

nounced in young children. In Chapter 8, we discuss this perspective in greater detail. In this chapter, we present the perspective that we may want to keep the differences between boys and girls in mind when planning lessons for our students and when we are teaching our students, as it has been determined that the learning environment has a significant impact on "the way we learn and what we learn" (Gross 2014).

According to Poe (2004) and Gurian (2015), the following statistics illustrate cause for concern:

- Boys account for up to 70 percent of failing grades.
- Boys receive up to 90 percent of disciplinary referrals.
- Of the children diagnosed with ADHD, 80 percent are boys.
- Special education classes consist of a disproportionate number of boys.
- Girls generally get higher grades than boys.
- Girls outperform boys across the board in verbal skills, but often when they hit middle school their math performance plummets.
- Fewer boys pursue higher education than girls.
- More boys drop out of school than girls.
- The percentage of boys completing high school (70 percent), going to college (40 percent), and going on to graduate school (8 percent), has stagnated over the last 10 years, while girls have continued to advance in all of these areas.

Gender plays a role in how we learn. Positron emission tomography (PET) and MRI technologies have given us the ability to more closely examine the brains of girls and boys. This recent research in neuroscience has revealed differences between the brains of boys and girls throughout the world and across cultures. In addition, there seems to be a mismatch between how each gender learns best and how our educational system currently functions (Gurian and Stevens 2004; Gurian and Stevens 2010). The general characteristics of both girls' and boys' cognitive functioning will be discussed so as to shed some insight on best teaching practices to maximize learning for both genders.

A Look inside Girls' Minds

Gurian and Stevens (2004, 2010) found several characteristics of girls' minds that affect student learning:

- The corpus callosum of a girl's brain tends to be larger than that of a boy's, thus allowing more "cross-talk" between the two different hemispheres in the girl's brain.
- Girls tend to have stronger neural connectors in

their temporal lobes than boys do. As a result, these connectors allow girls to have more sensually detailed memory, better listening skills, and the ability to more easily distinguish between different voice tones. In addition, this particular difference between boys and girls allows girls to use greater detail in writing assignments.

- Girls tend to have a larger hippocampus (a memory storage area in the brain) than boys, which gives girls a learning advantage, particularly in the language arts.
- The prefrontal cortex of girls is more active than that of boys, and it develops at an earlier age, thus allowing girls to have better impulse control than boys. In addition, girls tend to have more serotonin in their bloodstreams, which also makes them less impulsive.
- Girls tend to use more cortical areas of their brains for verbal and emotive functions, whereas boys tend to use more cortical areas of their brains for spatial and mechanical functions.

Although these are just some of the characteristics that define a girl's mind, understanding these factors helps us better understand why girls generally do better than boys in reading and writing (Conlin 2003 in Gurian and Stevens 2004, 2010). In contrast, because the girl's brain devotes more of the cortical area to verbal and emotive functioning, it does not use as many of its cortical areas for abstract and physical-spatial functions as does a boy's brain. This difference may in part explain why fewer girls are interested in physics, industrial engineering, and architecture. Children are drawn to activities that their brains find pleasurable. By *pleasurable*, we mean, "in neural terms, the richest personal stimulation. Girls and boys, within each neural web, tend to experience the richest personal stimulation differently" (Gurian and Stevens, p. 22).

A Look inside Boys' Minds

Gurian and Stevens (2004, 2010) have also uncovered several characteristics with regards to boys' brains:

- Boys generally use half as much brain space for verbal-emotive functions as girls do because more of their cortical areas are dedicated to spatial-mechanical functioning. For this reason, many boys gravitate toward moving objects such as balls, model airplanes, or their bodies.
- Boys have less serotonin and oxytocin (the primary human bonding chemical) than girls do, which makes boys more physically impulsive. In addition, it is more difficult for boys to sit and listen

empathetically to a friend (Moir and Jessel 1989; Taylor 2002, in Gurian and Stevens).

- Boys' brains operate with less blood flow than those of girls and also tend to compartmentalize learning. As a result, girls are better at multitasking, have longer attention spans, and are able to transition between lessons and classes more easily (Havers 1995, in Gurian and Stevens).
- Boys' brains renew and recharge themselves by entering a rest state, whereas girls' brains are able to reorient neural focus without ever entering this rest state. This is why teachers more often find boys fidgeting or tapping pencils in an attempt to stay awake. Boys, more so than girls, tend to nod off before completing their work or in the middle of a lecture. Boys generally stay more engaged in a lesson if the teacher uses fewer words and more diagrams, pictures, and movement.

The qualities that characterize a male's brain explain why boys generally perform better in higher-level mathematics and physics than girls when these subjects are taught abstractly; why more boys than girls prefer to play combat-centric video games; and why boys tend to get in trouble more than girls for impulsivity, fidgeting, and boredom, as well as for their "inability to listen, fulfill assignments, and learn in the verbal-emotive world of the contemporary classroom" (Gurian and Stevens 2004, p. 23).

Gurian and Stevens (2004, 2010) recommend the following specific strategies to elementary teachers in order to help both girls and boys reach their maximum learning potential.

Teaching Boys

- Use manipulatives to help boys develop fine motor skills, as they tend to lag behind girls in the early schooling years.
- Place books in several areas of the classroom so boys get used to the idea that books are everywhere.
- Teach students in ways that that are kinesthetic and experiential.
- Verbal directions should be limited to one minute or less.
- To help boys feel more emotionally attached, label their desks, coat racks, cubbies, etc., with their names.
- Male role models or mentors, such as fathers, grandfathers, or volunteers, should be utilized when possible.
- Allow boys to nurture one another through direct empathy or appropriate aggression.

Teaching Girls

- Play physical games to help girls develop gross motor skills, as they tend to lag behind boys in the early schooling years.
- Take pictures of girls succeeding at different tasks.
- Have students use water and sand tables to illustrate science in a spatial manner.
- Use puzzles to stimulate perceptual learning.
- Have students work in cooperative groups to help girls develop necessary negotiation skills and leadership abilities.
- Use manipulatives when teaching mathematical concepts.
- Use verbal language to encourage the quieter girls to express their ideas.

It is important to note that the generalizations discussed above are not always the case; however, being aware of the possibility of these gender differences helps educators address these issues and create more equitable classrooms. Recognizing these differences between the minds of boys and girls does not mean that we only teach certain subjects to girls and certain subjects to boys, nor does it mean that we encourage girls and boys to pursue only certain professions. Instead, "We raise these issues to call on our civilization to realize the differing natures of girls and boys, and to teach each subject according to how the child's brain needs to learn it" (Gurian and Stevens 2004, p. 23).

Cultural Influences

Culture influences how students participate in our education system. Culture influences beliefs about education, the value of education, and the way in which students interact with others. "To truly engage students, we must reach out to them in ways that are culturally and linguistically responsive and appropriate, and we must examine the cultural assumptions and stereotypes we bring into the classroom that may hinder interconnectedness" (Teaching Tolerance 2015). Teachers must not rely on racial or ethnic stereotypes or previous experiences with students of similar backgrounds; instead, they must know their students and their academic abilities individually. "Many teachers, for example, admire the perceived academic prowess and motivation of Asian American students and fail to recognize how even a 'positive' stereotype isn't positive if it presses students into molds not built for them individually" (Teaching Tolerance 2015). Geneva Gay (2000), a professor of education at the University of Washington-Seattle, suggests that children begin school with a learning style that has been internalized through the experiences that are part of his or her culture. Figure 6.9 illustrates cultural differences that may affect learning and should be considered when planning learning experiences for children.

Figure 6.9 Examples of Cultural Differences

• reserved, quiet	• outspoken, engaged in discussions
• whole to part	• part to whole
• discrete, impersonal material	• contextual, personal material
• individual orientation	• group orientation
• conformity	• creativity
• parents yield to teacher expertise	• active parental involvement

Unlike those in more homogeneous societies found in countries like Japan, schools in the United States, Canada, and many European countries often have students from a wide variety of cultures with varying learning styles. In recent years, we have become very aware of the achievement gap that exists among Asian American, white, African American and Latino/Hispanic students. In addition to the 14 factors that affect student achievement described later in this chapter, this gap is also due in part to differing learning styles, based on culture and, in part, to the lack of training that teachers have received to better enable them to meet these varied styles.

The following example illustrates the importance of understanding different cultural values in relation to how children learn. The information on Latino students noted in this section comes primarily from a long-term project that studied the learning styles of Latino/Hispanic students in the Los Angeles public schools. This study found that, because Latino/Hispanic children are often raised in families that emphasize collectivism, it is important that educators understand how such values will influence learning in the classroom. "**Collectivism**" is a cluster of interrelated values that emphasize the interdependence of family members. Within this value system, children are taught to be helpful to others and to contribute to the success of any group they belong to—beginning with the family" (Rothstein-Fisch, Greenfield, and Trumbell 1999, p. 64).

Further, collectivism emphasizes scientific information as part of social experiences. In contrast, individualism focuses on scientific information as being separate from social contexts (Rothstein-Fisch, Greenfield, and Trumbell 1999). In order to most effectively teach Latino students about scientific concepts, it is important that teachers understand that these students first need to explore scientific concepts in the context of shared family experiences. One teacher who was teaching her students about birds first asked students to share their family stories about birds. This teacher wrote the highlights of each story on one side of the chalkboard and the corresponding scientific aspects of these experiences on the other side. By doing so, the teacher demonstrated that both the children's stories and the scientific information were equally valued in the classroom (Rothstein-Fisch, Greenfield, and Trumbell 1999).

Although generalizations may be made for particular cultures, students will vary in their preferences, and it is important that a teacher discovers the ways in which individual students are able to work most productively.

Gaps in Achievement
The Gaps

Achievement gaps "are broadly defined as the differences in academic performance between groups of students of different backgrounds and have been documented with respect to students' ethnic, racial, gender, English language learner (ELL), disability, and income status" (National Education Association 2015, p. 1). The National Assessment of Educational Progress (NAEP) has been recording results of academic tests since the 1970s. Although overall increases have been documented in student achievement in both mathematics and literacy for all groups of students, gaps in achievement continue to persist for many groups, including low-income students, English language learners, students with disabilities, and students from various racial and ethnic backgrounds. Changing demographics in the United States related to race and ethnicity, ELL status, and income level indicate that the public school system is going to be responsible for educating an increasingly diverse population of students from groups that currently experience the largest achievement gaps. "By as early as 2044, the majority of the US population will be comprised of people currently considered to be racial or ethnic minorities" (Teixeira, Frey, and Griffin 2015).

There is a significant, well-documented gap between the achievement of Asian American and white students, compared to that of the African American and Latino/Hispanic students. The research (Ferguson 2008) indicates that part of that achievement gap may be explained by the parents' education levels and the

The gap lessens, but continues to exist, even when students from the same parent education and socio-economic levels are compared.

families' socioeconomic levels. However, the gap lessens, but continues to exist, even when students from the same parent education and socioeconomic levels are compared.

The gap in academic achievement between students with learning disabilities and their peers does not typically receive the same attention as does the racial achievement gap. The 2013 NAEP scores and graduation rates indicate that a large gap exists between students with learning disabilities and their peers. "In 2013, students with disabilities demonstrated proficiency levels in reading and math that were 20–27 percentage points below their nondisabled peers, with few fourth- and eighth-grade students with disabilities demonstrating proficiency in math or reading" (National Center for Education Statistics 2015). In addition, the graduation rate for students with learning disabilities is 20 percentage points lower than that of the national graduation rate of 81.4 percent. Many of these students identified with a learning disability are not cognitively impaired, but learn differently and may need a more specialized approach to learning. This does not mean that they cannot learn or that their learning should not be measured. At the end of each chapter in this book, you will find a section designed to assist classroom teachers in their work with students with learning disabilities.

Below are tables that compare fourth-grade and eighth-grade achievement nationally in both mathematics and reading. The data from the scaled scores are from the NAEP.[4] The NAEP is the test data reporting required by the federal No Child Left Behind Act (NCLB). These tables compare white, black, Hispanic, Asian/Pacific Islander, and American Indian/Alaska Native students. Within these different groups, the data is then broken into non-ELL students with no learning disability, ELL students who have a learning disability, students with a learning disability only, and ELL students only. Of all of the groups reported, Asian Pacific Islanders and whites score at a higher level in all categories.

---

4   Scaled scores are used when comparing results from different tests that report results in unlike forms. Since the scores from unlike tests are not readily comparable, the scores are converted to scaled scores that are based on a numeric scale with intervals of equal size. This allows the varying measures to be joined together for an accurate comparison. The raw scores from the various state tests were converted to scaled scores to aid in interpretation by providing a quantitative measure of each student's performance relative to a comparison group across the states. A scale has been applied to these state tests so that direct comparisons among students, between individual scores and groups, or among the scores within a specific subject area across grades, can be made in a way that is statistically valid. This comparison cannot be done with the percentile or grade equivalent scores that these tests typically produce.

Table 6.3

Fourth-Grade Math: National Average Scale Scores, 2013 (Student with Disability-SD, English Language Learner-ELL)					
	White	Black	Hispanic	Asian/Pacific Islander	American Indian/ Alaska Native
Neither SD or ELL	253	228	240	264	234
Both SD and ELL	206	199	199	219	180
Student with Disability (SD)	228	203	214	232	207
English Language Learner (ELL)	231	216	221	235	207

Source: US Department of Education, Institute of Education Sciences, National Center for Education Statistics, National Assessment of Educational Progress (NAEP), 2013 Mathematics Assessment.

Table 6.4

Fourth-Grade Reading: National Average Scale Scores, 2013 (Student with Disability-SD, English Language Learner-ELL)					
	White	Black	Hispanic	Asian/Pacific Islander	American Indian/ Alaska Native
Neither SD or ELL	237	212	221	245	215
Both SD and ELL	167	167	147	166	NA
Student with Disability (SD)	196	168	180	203	171
English Language Learner (ELL)	202	167	190	202	167

Source: US Department of Education, Institute of Education Sciences, National Center for Education Statistics, National Assessment of Educational Progress (NAEP), 2013 Reading Assessment.

Table 6.5

Eighth-Grade Math: National Average Scale Scores, 2013 (Student with Disability-SD, English Language Learner-ELL)					
	White	Black	Hispanic	Asian/Pacific Islander	American Indian/ Alaska Native
Neither SD or ELL	298	269	281	313	277
Both SD and ELL	234	220	222	244	224
Student with Disability (SD)	260	232	245	259	242
English Language Learner (ELL)	258	238	248	270	241

Source: US Department of Education, Institute of Education Sciences, National Center for Education Statistics, National Assessment of Educational Progress (NAEP), 2013 Mathematics Assessment.

Table 6.6

Eighth-Grade Reading: National Average Scale Scores, 2013 (Student with Disability-SD, English Language Learner-ELL)					
	White	Black	Hispanic	Asian/Pacific Islander	American Indian/ Alaska Native
Neither SD or ELL	280	256	265	287	258
Both SD and ELL	212	NA	201	210	193
Student with Disability (SD)	242	218	230	246	221
English Language Learner (ELL)	238	223	229	235	224

Source: US Department of Education, Institute of Education Sciences, National Center for Education Statistics, National Assessment of Educational Progress (NAEP), 2013 Reading Assessment.

Factors That Affect the Gap

The achievement gap is often viewed as a failure of our educational system today. However, both school and non-school factors influence student achievement. Researchers have uncovered 14 factors that affect student achievement. Low-income and minority children are at risk in most of these areas. Barton (2004) outlines the factors associated with student achievement into two different categories—"before and beyond school" and "in school." It is important to keep in mind, however, that "the conditions that improve learning in school and out of school are intertwined" (Barton, p. 11). These factors are as follows:

Before- and Beyond-School Factors

- Birth weight: Children who are born with low birth weight often present with delayed motor skills as well as social development. Such students are more likely to perform poorly in school.
- Lead poisoning: Lead poisoning is a serious problem and primarily found in children living in older homes.
- Hunger and nutrition: Children who are malnourished and often hungry are negatively affected with regard to their cognitive abilities.
- Reading to young children: Children who are read to frequently are at a much greater advantage for language acquisition, literacy development, and becoming successful students.
- Television watching: Watching television excessively is associated with lower achievement and attention problems.
- Parent availability: The number of families in which two parents are available to spend time with children is declining.
- Student mobility: Student mobility is often affected by job availability and affordable housing. It is difficult for students to change schools, particularly in the middle of a school year. When students enroll in new schools partway through the year, the curriculum tends to be disjointed, and students have to quickly adjust to new rules, routines, and expectations.
- Parent participation: The importance of a strong home-school connection should not be underestimated. The online Child Trends Data Bank reports that "students with parents who are involved in their school tend to have fewer behavioral problems and better academic performance, and they are more likely to complete secondary school" (2003).

In-School Factors

- Rigor of curriculum: Although many low-income and minority students are taking more advanced courses today than they have in the past, they still lag behind in advanced placement courses. Barriers to more advanced courses must be removed, and these students should be strongly encouraged to pursue academic challenges.
- Teacher expectations: Teacher expectations affect how well a student performs in class. Lower teacher expectations prevent students from taking more advanced courses, due to lack of prior preparation. The importance of consistently higher yet realistic teacher expectations for all students, regardless of previous performances, cannot be overemphasized. More information on how teacher expectations affect student motivation and performance can be found in Chapter 7.
- Teacher experience and attendance: Teachers with at least five years of experience are more effective than those with fewer years in the classroom. Minority and lower-income students typically have less-experienced teachers and tend to be in schools with higher teacher-turnover rates. Teacher assignments should be based on best meeting the needs of the students. Principals should carefully place teachers so that their abilities and backgrounds are best matched to the needs of their students. Moreover, teacher absenteeism is more prevalent in minority schools, and substitute teachers tend to have less experience than regular classroom teachers. The rate of absent teachers on a given day for minority students is more than double the rate for white students.
- Teacher preparation: Teacher preparation directly affects the quality of teaching, and minority and low-income students tend to have more unqualified teachers who are unable to prepare and deliver effective instruction. Schools need to offer newer teachers support in the areas of curriculum and instruction.
- Class size: Overall, minority students typically have larger class sizes than white students. Barton (2004) reports that "classes with a high percentage of minority students are more likely to have 25 or more students" (p. 12). Administrators need to adjust the sizes of classes to afford struggling students more individualized attention, while more capable students are in classrooms with a larger student-teacher ratio.
- Technology-assisted instruction: Low-income students have less access to computers in the classroom than middle-class students. "This gap widens in terms

of Internet availability in the classroom, and it widens further in the case of more advanced uses, such as using the Internet to conduct research" (Barton, p. 12).

• School safety: Clearly, fear is not a favorable condition for effective learning. If students fear for their safety, they certainly are not going to be mentally and emotionally present for learning.[5]

Although many of these factors are not in the control of the teacher or school, it is important for educators to understand the different variables that continue to affect student achievement. Richard Rothstein, a research associate at the Economic Policy Institute and a visiting professor at Columbia University's Teachers College, makes several recommendations that address both in- and out-of-school factors for closing the achievement gap. He believes that improving the quality of our schools will most certainly narrow the gap. However, school reform alone is not enough to close this gap. He also suggests that we attempt to provide additional resources for these children during out-of-school hours, including summer programs. Early childhood programs should be developed to give these children the same types of experiences that their middle-class peers have before formal schooling begins. Lastly, he proposes more state and federal government intervention should be aimed at social and economic reform policies to give children more support so that they are ready to learn once formal schooling starts (Rothstein 2004).

Closing the Gap: Other Recommendations

As discussed previously, some of the recommendations for closing this gap are out of the control of a classroom teacher. For example, the class size is determined by the school district. It is more difficult for teachers to adequately meet the needs of all learners with a greater number of students. The socioeconomic status of students, as well as the amount of support received at home and learning resources in the home, are, for the most part,[6] also out of the control of the teacher. There are, however, a number of things we as teachers may do to improve the achievement of African American and Latino/Hispanic students.

Ferguson (2002, 2008), Reeves (2007), and Chenoweth (2007) list several recommendations for schools and communities, based on their research of the achievement gap:

1. **Assume no motivational differences.** Teachers should assume there are no differences in effort or motivation to succeed based on a particular race, although observable differences in behavior and academic performance may be seen.

2. **Address specific skill deficits.** Schools need to identify and address any gaps in knowledge and/or skills that certain groups of students may have that result from influences such as living in a home that isn't conducive to developing academic skills (e.g., watching more TV and reading less), second language issues, or previous school experiences. These students will typically need an infusion of skills-teaching to catch up to the others. African American and Latino/Hispanic students report less understanding of teacher lessons related to the material they read for school. Teachers may address this issue by employing more responsive instructional strategies to meet these students' learning needs. These students may also need to be retaught certain skills and concepts. In addition, teachers should require *all* students to read and write in complete sentences on a daily basis in order to improve writing skills (Bell 2003).

3. **Higher-order thinking skills should be taught to all students, as all children need to possess such skills to succeed in today's world.** Many Latino/Hispanic students have not yet fully mastered English. As a result, they master curriculum more slowly because of the need to translate concepts from English to Spanish and vice versa. This need to translate may cause these students to be placed in groups in which concepts are taught at a slower pace. Many of these groups are not exposed to the same level of thinking-skills tasks as the other groups. These students fall further and further behind the others in their ability to successfully complete higher-order thinking tasks. This gap in their knowledge is then reflected in state (or province) and national test scores. It is important that we remember that such gaps are due to the students' experiences and not to their innate intelligence.

4. **Time is reallocated.** In elementary schools, students should spend three hours a day on literacy: two hours of reading and one hour of writing.

---

5   It is important to remember that the proportion of black and Hispanic students in society who live in poverty exceeds the overall percentage of black and Hispanic students in the total population. Therefore, they are disproportionately affected by the factors that inhibit student achievement.

6   Chapter 9 gives descriptions of ways in which districts and individual teachers have successfully worked with parents to improve the parents' ability to support their children's learning at home.

In secondary schools, students should have double periods of mathematics and English. Longer, uninterrupted instructional periods should be the norm rather than the exception.

5. **Supply ample encouragement routinely.** Teachers need to provide effective encouragement for students routinely. Teacher encouragement has been found to be particularly important for students of color as a source of achievement motivation. Chapters 5 and 7 both contain descriptions of the types of praise that have the greatest impact on furthering student achievement. It is also extremely important for teachers to establish a trusting, caring relationship with all students at the beginning of the year. However, research indicates that doing so will have a greater impact on both African American and Latino/Hispanic students (Ferguson 2002) than on whites or Asian Americans. Research also indicates that the explicit and implicit messages teachers send these students about their ability to achieve at high levels have a greater influence on African American and Latino/Hispanic students' perceptions of their abilities than they do on that of white and Asian American students.

6. **Teachers provide students with frequent feedback.** Chapter 4 describes ways in which teachers can effectively provide students with specific feedback in order to improve student achievement.

7. **Common assessments are frequently administered to track student progress.** The data gleaned from these assessments should be transparent, since all teachers should have access to each student's assessments. Teachers should also focus on student data from multiple sources, and these students should be compared to themselves rather than to other groups of students. In this way, teachers can focus on instructional strategies that best meet the needs of the individual students.

8. **Provide access to resources and learning experiences.** Due to the differences in learning resources in the home, schools should provide more books, computers, and extracurricular activities to those families that are in need of such supports.

9. **Parents are given packets of information that clearly outline and explain how they can best help their children master the necessary skills and concepts.** Often, these parents do not have all of the skills needed to help their children, as their educational experiences may have been limited. It is thus critical that we equip these parents with the tools that they need in order to help their children become successful students.

10. **All adults in the school system are used as resources to help improve student achievement.** Specifically, community volunteers, including retirees, should be trained to help students in the areas of literacy and mathematics.

11. **Teachers collaborate to examine student work and determine the meaning of "proficiency."** Teachers should also engage in action research. Chapter 11 describes ways in which teachers can use action research to improve student achievement.

The Tripod Project

Ferguson (2002, 2013) has also developed a project, dubbed the Tripod Project, which is based on his research with regard to the achievement gap. Content, pedagogy, and relationships are the three legs of what he calls the "**instructional tripod.**" Professional development opportunities should equip teachers to attend to all three of these legs.

Recent research has shown that Tripod's seven "C's" help to predict both student engagement and yearly gains in student achievement on standardized tests

1. CARE: "Your success and well-being really matter to me. I will support you."
2. CHALLENGE: "I insist upon rigor and understanding, not just memorization. I expect your best effort always."
3. CONTROL: "Our class is orderly, in-control, and respectful, with learning being our first priority."
4. CLARIFY: "I have multiple explanations for skills and concepts that seem difficult. Let me know when you are confused and I will help you better understand."
5. CAPTIVATE: "I make lessons intellectually relevant and stimulating because they are important."
6. CONFER: "Your ideas are important, and I will give you time to explain your ideas."
7. CONSOLIDATE: "I summarize lessons and check for understanding to make learning coherent and connected" (The Tripod Project and Cambridge Education LLC 2013).

In addition, Ferguson (2002) outlines five tasks that are part of the Tripod Project. He indicates that students will be more likely to succeed if the following conditions are met:

1. Students begin the semester feeling trustful of the

teacher and interested, instead of feeling mistrustful and uninterested.

2. Students experience a good balance between teacher control and student autonomy, instead of too little or too much of either.
3. Students are goal-oriented in their learning, rather than feeling ambivalent.
4. Students work industriously in pursuing their goals for learning, instead of becoming discouraged in the face of difficulty or disengaged due to boredom.
5. Teachers help students consolidate their new knowledge and, thus equipped, students are well prepared for future classes and life experiences."

Chapter 7 explains in depth how a teacher may help students with items 1, 3, and 4. We strongly recommend that establishing a project, such as the one described below, in your school includes professional development in the concepts explained in Chapter 7.

The Tripod Project is centered on five school-wide faculty workshops. At each meeting, one of the five stages listed above is explored, and teachers work in small groups, sharing their ideas with regard to each task and stage. As teachers share their best practices with others, they will find themselves strengthening each leg of the tripod within their own classrooms.

Teachers should be encouraged to test the strategies described by their colleagues in their own classrooms. After teachers try these strategies, it is important that they have opportunities to come together with their colleagues to discuss the following:

- what worked and why it worked
- what did not work, why it did not work, and how they might try it again differently

Another Successful Model

The Lexington Public Schools in Massachusetts represent another model of effectively addressing the achievement gap between white and Asian students, and black and Latino students. Between 2008 and 2015, this school system carried out a plan that targeted instruction, professional development, and METCO support programs (METCO is a program that brings students of color from the city of Boston to study in Lexington and other high-performing districts, from kindergarten through high school). Those who closely followed this study believe that the following directives contributed to the success this school system experienced:

- "Support teacher collaboration and professional development from the highest level of official authority in the district.
- Expand and protect integrated, whole-district professional learning for all adults, not only teachers.
- Protect extended learning time in elementary schools.
- Design and implement an expanded array of supplemental supports for middle and high school students, offering an array of intervention strategies before, during, and after the school day, serving whatever students may need them.
- Use school data teams to monitor performance and identify students not meeting learning expectations. Stay committed to the design and delivery of classroom interventions for students who need them.
- Build capacity for culturally competent communication among administrators, teachers, students, and parents" (Ferguson, Ballantine, Bradshaw, and Krontiris 2015, p. 51).

Chapters 10 and 11 describe structures that enable teachers to examine their own practices independently and/or with their colleagues.

English Language Learners

It is imperative that English language learners acquire the language skills necessary for everyday communication and specific subject-matter learning. It is unrealistic to assume children will learn these skills on their own.

Knowing and understanding at which stage a child is (see Figure I-3 in the Introduction) will allow the educator to meet that student's needs within his or her **zone of proximal development (ZPD)**. Vygotsky suggests that when a teacher understands and works within a student's ZPD by providing the appropriate supports, language development will be furthered and a higher level of learning achieved. Some ways in which a teacher can provide scaffolds are through modeling correct language and articulation, by direct instruction, or by asking challenging questions. "When you are familiar with the stages of second-language acquisition, you will be more attuned to the types of questions and prompts to use to engage and motivate your ELLs. By understanding your students' levels of linguistic proficiency, you will become more competent at differentiating instruction to promote linguistic and academic achievement" (Hill and Flynn 2006, p. 20). At the end of each chapter, you will find a section designed to assist classroom teachers in their work with the English language learners in their classrooms.

It is imperative that English language learners acquire the language skills necessary for both everyday communication and specific subject-matter learning. It is unrealistic to assume that these children will learn these language skills on their own. Instead, educators must provide instructional activities that help children develop language in the context of learning. Subject-matter educators also need to integrate "modified language" into their lessons. "Modified language" is discipline-specific vocabulary made more readily understandable for English language learners. For example, a history teacher can create a glossary of important terms for the unit of study, a science teacher can use simplified definitions and drawings to help students better understand concepts, and a reading teacher can use pictures and simplified definitions of key vocabulary words for a particular story (Bielenberg and Fillmore 2004–2005).

In addition to teaching discipline-specific language to English language learners, teachers should also focus on how language is used in the classroom and in classroom discussions. Classroom language often is used for "checking for understanding (as in, 'Do you follow?'), summarizing (as in, 'The main point here is …'), and defining (as in, 'What does this mean?')" (Dong 2004–2005, p. 15). An English language learner who is unfamiliar with the functional uses of language will have difficulty understanding what is being asked and consequently will be unable to participate in class discussions. Such uses of language must be explicitly taught to these students.

Unfortunately, many schools find it difficult to provide adequate instruction and resources for English language learners. This is due in part to a lack of available funding; however, it is also due in part to misconceptions about how these students learn. According to the research, reading, speaking, listening, and writing are highly interdependent and interrelated processes in which both first and second language learners should be engaged (in Gebhard 2002–2003). Given this understanding, it is important that educators provide English language learners with opportunities that enable them to use these processes simultaneously, rather than presenting these learners with a step-by-step curriculum in which students practice these as discrete entities. More information about how English language learners learn best and instructional strategies that have proven to be beneficial with these learners is provided at the end of this chapter.

The Advanced Learner (a.k.a. the Gifted and Talented Learner)

Advanced learners or gifted and talented children are those who demonstrate the ability to perform at significantly higher levels of achievement than others of the same age, experience, and environment. While many of these children tend to have IQ scores above the 140 range, others may demonstrate an exceptional level of accomplishment in one or more specific academic areas. These students tend to experience the world differently than most children, due to their high cognitive abilities and high intensities, and their unique abilities cause these children to be particularly vulnerable (Hollingworth Center for Highly Gifted Children, n.d.). The following list includes characteristics that gifted children may exhibit (A Different Place, n.d.).

- has outstanding memory and has broader knowledge base than peers
- reads earlier than peers
- possesses advanced vocabulary
- learns quickly and easily
- enjoys learning
- enjoys complex learning
- has the ability to concentrate for longer periods of time
- tends to be impatient and intolerant
- initiates own learning
- asks insightful and higher-level questions
- tends to be curious about many different things
- has a variety of interests
- may be intense and gets highly absorbed in activities and thinking
- is able to think abstractly
- tends to be analytical
- has strong ideas, opinions, and feelings
- may care about ethical issues at an early age
- has high expectations for self and others
- tends to be persistent and motivated
- has a sophisticated sense of humor
- is able to transfer learning to new situations
- is able to connect different activities and ideas
- may prefer to spend time with older children and adults
- works well independently
- possesses leadership qualities
- has original ideas

- has flexibility with regard to problem-solving
- is able to see multiple possibilities for situations and uses of objects

It is important to provide these learners with a curriculum that appropriately challenges them. Figure 6.10 provides educators with a set of questions adapted from Robert Eberle's creative thinking checklist that may help you think about how to most effectively differentiate for these learners.

Figure 6.10
Differentiation "SCAMPER": For Gifted and Talented Students

Substitute: What basic content could I replace with more abstract, advanced, or sophisticated content?

Combine: How can I combine learning with creative thinking to encourage originality and innovation?

Adapt: How can I adapt curriculum to accelerate the pace of instruction? How can I adapt activities to elicit high levels of performance?

Modify: How can I modify learning to provide greater depth and complexity?

Put to other use: How can I accelerate the pace of instruction so class time can be used for in-depth or advanced learning reflecting students' specific interests and talents?

Eliminate: What mastered content or skills can I eliminate so students can focus on more advanced learning?

Reverse/Rearrange: How can I rearrange or reorganize curriculum to give students time to develop original ideas and products?

Adapted from *Scamper* by Robert Eberle. Waco, TX: Prufrock Press, 1971. Excerpted from *Differentiating Instruction in the Regular Classroom* by Diane Heacox. Minneapolis, MN: Free Spirit Publishing, 2012. Used with permission.

"Giftedness either progresses or regresses and can be stifled in an educational environment that does not enhance individual growth. Talents develop when the environment challenges and stimulates the innate ability of the person" (2000 Kansas Special Education Regulations, 91-40-1, at A Different Place, n.d.). It is imperative that educators provide such learners with the challenges they need to help them reach their maximum potential.

Community Mentors

Classroom teachers can also address the unique needs of the gifted and very high-achieving students through the use of community mentors. Sometimes these students' intellectual needs extend beyond available differentiated challenges and extensions within the classroom. These students who have extraordinary abilities and academic appetites in a particular area, such as math or science, may benefit tremendously from mentors. Possible mentors include an older student in the school with expertise in the area of strength as well as collaborative ability, an older student in another school, a parent volunteer, a college student, or a community mentor, such as a retired physicist or mathematician. A mentor may teach the gifted student new and unfamiliar aspects of his or her favored subjects. The mentor-student relationship may provide a positive and powerful social experience as well. Lastly, a mentor may provide resources that meet the gifted student's needs within the school community.

First Steps to Differentiating Your Instruction Based on Learning Profile

Tomlinson (2001, 2014) offers the following guidelines for implementing learning-profile-based differentiated instruction:

Step 1: Keep in mind that not all students share your learning preferences. It is important to remember that you are teaching to diverse learners and that a variety of learning preferences should be addressed. If you are an auditory learner and teacher, you may be more inclined to present your lessons aurally. However, it is important to use a variety of teaching methods in order to reach all of your students.

Step 2: Help students recognize their learning preferences. It is important to help students understand how they learn best. In addition, let students know what type of learning they will be doing in a particular activity. For example, if you are presenting a lesson in which students will participate in visual, oral, and kinesthetic activities, let the students know what type of activity they are doing as they are doing it. Afterwards, ask students which mode of learning was most effective for them and which was most difficult.

The following form is one that students complete at the beginning of the year to help both students and the classroom teacher better understand each student's learning profile with regard to learning mathematics. Such a form can be adapted and used with other academic subjects as well.

Figure 6.11 Personal Mathematics Learning Profile

Please check the learning preferences that apply to you.

In math, I generally

_____ demand attention   _____ am well organized
_____ want to please   _____ keep working on a task until I finish
_____ am slow to get started   _____ like teacher encouragement
_____ ask questions   _____ like to work alone
_____ am unhappy   _____ am comfortable/happy

I am most successful in math when I

_____ get enough practice on the skills/concepts we are working on
_____ am not absent or I make up my work (with teacher help, if needed) when I am absent
_____ put forth extra effort to really pay attention in class
_____ do all of my homework
_____ get extra help outside of class
_____ ask questions in class

I am least successful in math when

_____ students around me are distracting
_____ the teacher goes too quickly, and I do not ask him or her to slow down
_____ I let other things on my mind interfere with my listening in class
_____ I do not complete my homework
_____ I am absent a lot
_____ I do not ask for extra help when I need it

My teacher helps me achieve success in math class when he or she

_____ provides lots of practice before a test
_____ works with me one on one
_____ allows me to correct the wrong answers on a test
_____ keeps the class quiet so I can concentrate
_____ makes sure I am not sitting next to someone who may distract me
_____ provides lots of concrete examples of what we are learning
_____ uses manipulatives when we are learning new concepts
_____ makes it clear exactly what we are supposed to do
_____ has us work alone
_____ has us work in pairs
_____ has us work in groups
_____ enforces the classroom rules

I prefer to be assessed by

_____ teacher observation
_____ paper and pencil tests/quizzes
_____ performance assessments (project-based assessments)
_____ take-home/open-book tests
_____ writing a report
_____ oral presentations

My biggest success in math last year was _____.
In math class, it is difficult for me to _____.
These are my recommendations to my teacher this year to help me be a successful learner:

_____
_____
_____

Step 3: Start small as you begin. When you first begin to differentiate instruction by learning profiles, select only one or two differences. Differentiating lessons based on learning profiles may be a daunting task, as there are multiple ways to look at learning differences in students. Once you feel confident in using one or two strategies for differentiating instruction, branch out and try new ones. For example, you may want to begin by differentiating instruction according to intelligence style preference. You might present a lesson in which students are expected to learn the same content but are able to choose to complete verbal, visual, or kinesthetic activities to demonstrate their understanding.

Figure 6.12 illustrates how one of our colleagues differentiated instruction according to learning styles for a fifth-grade unit of study in science. The class was studying endangered animals: specifically, the causes of endangerment of specific animals and what can be done to preserve the particular species being studied. In order to help students decide how to present their findings, the teacher brainstormed with the class about different ways to complete this project. The list included ideas such as creating a PowerPoint presentation, making a poster, writing a report, making up a song, constructing a diorama, role-playing, creating a video, etc.

The visual learners drew pictures illustrating the required information. The auditory learners prepared an oral presentation based on the information they found. The kinesthetic learners role-played the causes of endangerment as well as what might be done to help these animals. The following figure outlines this particular project.

Figure 6.12 **Endangered Animal Project**

You are about to embark upon an exciting journey into the wild world of endangered animals. You will have the opportunity to choose an endangered animal and will be responsible for representing your findings to the class. There are several components that must be included in your representation. These components are as follows:

1. Description of your animal (including a picture)
2. Description of animal's habitat (including a map showing where the animal lives)
3. Explanation of why this animal is endangered
4. Explanation of things people can do to help save this animal
5. At least three resources must be used
6. Bibliography must be included

The following steps should be followed to help you organize your time:
1. Choose an endangered animal
Due Date:_____
2. Collect at least three resources
Due Date:_____
3. Read and take notes using note-taking organizer
Due Date:_____
4. Decide how information will be represented
Due Date:_____
5. Draft of project
Due Date:_____
6. Final project
Due Date:_____

In this example, the content learned was the same for all students; however, the manner in which the students processed the information, as well as the way students represented their findings, varied according to their learning profiles.

Differentiating by Interest through Project-Based Work

Teachers may also use students' interests as a way in which to differentiate information and skills, process, and product. Students are more inclined to be motivated when they are pursuing an interest and have a choice in their learning.

Tomlinson (2001, 2014) offers the following guidelines to follow when implementing interest-based differentiation:

1. Link interest-based exploration with key areas of the curriculum.
2. Provide students with structures to help them succeed.
3. Create efficient ways for students to share their work.
4. Encourage students to discover new ways of learning.
5. Combine interest-based differentiation with other forms of differentiation.

Interest-based exploration should be linked with key areas of the curriculum. It is important for teachers to connect students' interests with information and/or skills that are integral to the curriculum. In this way, the goals of both the student and the curriculum can be met at the same time. For example, if part of the reading curriculum specifies that students should develop strategies for reading nonfiction, a student who is passionate about frogs might develop these reading strategies by reading nonfiction articles or books about frogs.

Provide students with structures to help them succeed. When students are working on interest-based projects, there will be an element of independence, as students will be working on different things. Some students are capable of greater independence, while others need more scaffolding in order to succeed. The teacher will need to provide the appropriate level of scaffolding to ensure success for each student. One technique that benefits all students is clearly outlining for students the criteria they are expected to meet to be successful.[7] Students perform at high levels when they know ahead of time how they are going to be assessed. For example, if a rubric or criteria sheet is going to be used to assess student success, the teacher should share it with the students before they begin working on their tasks. The following list provides more ideas for helping students in this process:

- checklists
- timelines
- check-ins with the teacher
- rubrics
- criteria sheets
- exemplars
- step-by-step directions
- mini-lessons related to skills and/or strategies needed to complete the task

Create efficient ways for students to share their work about their areas of interest. Having 25 students present their work to the class can be a time-consuming process. Instead, you may want to ask students to share their work in small groups or pairs, or you may have students share one aspect of their projects with the class. It is important that students are taught both how to appropriately share their work and how to be a good listener while others are presenting. As a class, you may want to create and post a list of what a good listener looks like. Student responses may include things such as maintaining eye

One technique that benefits all students is clearly outlining for students the criteria they are expected to meet to be successful.

contact, not doodling or playing with objects, asking appropriate and related questions, and giving specific feedback to the presenter. These behaviors should be modeled for students. It may also be beneficial to have students role-play being both a good listener and a poor listener. Finally, teachers may want to ask students to reflect on themselves as listeners after role-playing and after students present their work.

Encourage students to discover new ways of learning. Invite students to propose new ideas for tasks and projects, and let them know you will help them in their endeavors. Doing so instills a greater sense of shared ownership in learners and ignites creativity and greater enthusiasm for learning.

The following teaching experience took place in one fifth-grade classroom.

This particular teacher had divided her class into four different groups for an author study of Avi. Each group read a different book written by Avi, according to the students' instructional reading levels. At one point, one of the groups approached the teacher and asked if each group could present a Reader's Theater to the class, based on the particular book they were reading. In this way, the students would have an opportunity to compare and contrast different books written by Avi. After giving it some thought, the teacher agreed to this idea.

As a class, they established guidelines. Some of the guidelines included that students needed to present a summary of their stories with a clear problem and solution, character development, and an overriding theme. Students were enthusiastic and worked diligently to create and perform a well-organized Reader's Theater.

Each group presented the story in an innovative way, and all groups met the criteria that had been outlined. After the groups made their presentations, the class had a rich discussion regarding the differences and similarities found among these books. The students discovered a surprising similarity that appeared to be present in each of these particular books written by Avi. Contrary to the previous reading experiences of many of the students, these books all had resolutions that encompassed tragedy. Students talked about how this made Avi's stories more realistic and unpredictable. Some students preferred knowing a story was going to end happily, while others preferred the element of surprise that was sometimes accompanied by disappointment.

Although this project did take time to complete, according to the teacher, it was an invaluable learn-

---

7   See Chapter 1 for an explanation of how to create mastery objectives that clearly describe for students what they will know and be able to do at the end of the learning time. Chapter 4 contains examples of rubrics and criteria sheets that also may be used to clearly outline for students the criteria for success.

ing process, as students developed a new and more sophisticated understanding of story structure.

Interest-based differentiation may be combined with other forms of differentiation. It is possible to design a task that is differentiated by readiness, interest, and learning profile. In the inventor example presented below, the project was differentiated by readiness, in that students were provided with research materials appropriate to their reading levels and understanding. The task was differentiated by interest, in that students were given the opportunity to choose the inventor they wished to further explore. This project was also differentiated according to learning profile, as students were able to create a final product that most closely matched their learning profile.

Part of the science curriculum that fifth-grade teachers were expected to teach each year involved learning about different inventors and how their work affected society. In order to generate greater enthusiasm for this unit of study, the fifth-grade teachers differentiated the information and skills by having students select inventors who were of interest to them.

The process was also differentiated as the teachers helped guide the students in selecting appropriate research materials. Some students were capable of using multiple sources that were more complex in nature, while others needed to read more basic sources (e.g., lower reading levels, fewer primary-source materials) in order to understand the information. Additionally, some students needed a more structured format to follow, while other students were able to conduct their research using their own ideas for organizing information. The final product was also differentiated, in that students had available to them a wide range of choices of ways to present their information. These choices were generated by the students as they brainstormed different ways of representing the information they had acquired. Some students created a PowerPoint presentation, while others created a visual poster and oral report. Some students created a game show, and others wrote a standard research report. This project was one of the students' favorite projects of the year, as they were able to pursue their genuine interests as well as choose how to present their work. The actual project is provided in the following boxes.

Figure 6.13

Welcome to the World of Inventors and Inventions

Why do people invent? People invent for a variety of reasons. They are curious about that which is new, untried, and unknown. They are stimulated by a natural desire to learn. Because of past inventions, they have a certain amount of leisure time in which to dream and experiment with new ideas. They want to solve a problem, improve a product, achieve fame, or help humanity.

Now, with this activity, you will take an exciting journey into the mind of a famous inventor. You will need to follow several guidelines; however, you will have an opportunity to make several decisions along the way.

Guidelines

1. Choose an inventor about whom you would like to learn more. If you need help with selecting an inventor, see the attached list for some ideas.

2. Fill out the planning sheet I have provided for you. You will need to decide
   - how you would like to represent the knowledge you gain from your research
   - what materials you will need
   - if you would like to work alone or with another person

3. Turn in your planning sheet for my approval.

4. Gather information about your inventor and his or her invention. You need to use at least three resources. You will be given time at the library and the computer lab to look for your resources. I also have several books on inventors in the classroom.

5. Take notes using the note-taking sheet I have provided for you.

6. Execute the plan you chose on your planning sheet.

Note: You will have class time to work on this project. However, you may need to work on parts of this project at home in order to meet the agreed-upon deadline.

Figure 6.14

My Planning Sheet for Inventors and Inventions

Name(s):_____ Date:_____

I am going to research_____who invented_____.

I plan to work (check one): _____alone _____with_____.

I need to demonstrate my knowledge about my chosen inventor in the following areas:

1. A description of the inventor, including how he or she came up with his or her ideas
2. A description of the invention created by the inventor
3. How the invention changed the lives of people at the time the it was invented
4. Why this invention is important to us today

I/we plan to demonstrate our knowledge by

_____

Materials I/we will need to complete this project are

_____

_____

Resources (at least 3) I/we will use are

_____

_____

_____

Deadline:_____ Teacher Approval:_____

Figure 6.15

Note-Taking Sheet

Inventor: _____

Invention: _____

Description of inventor: _____

_____

_____

Description of invention: _____

_____

_____

How this invention changed the lives of people at the time the invention was created:

_____

_____

_____

Resources used:

1. _____

2. _____

3. _____

Figure 6.16
Inventor Project Timeline

1. Select inventor to research
Due Date: _____

2. Planning sheet completed
Due Date: _____

3. Gather resources (at least 3)
Due Date: _____

4. Notes completed
Due Date: _____

5. Draft of project
Due Date: _____

6. Project completed
Due Date _____

7. Project presentation
Due Date: _____

Differentiating Content (Information and Skills), Process, and Product

This section discusses differentiating instruction by content (information and skills), process, and product as separate components. It is important to note, however, that these elements are interrelated, and often the lines are blurred between how and what is being differentiated. These curricular elements will be discussed separately for purposes of more clearly defining how to differentiate instruction in each of these ways.[8]

Differentiating Content

Content refers to information and skills being taught and is often mandated by the state or district. In other words, the prescribed content is often found in state curriculum standards.

Content may be differentiated by emphasizing the highest-priority information and skills or by making the learning more complex.

Some students may need more practice and direct

---

8   Earlier in this chapter, we discuss the convergence and overlap of UDL and differentiated instruction. In addition, the RtI process, differentiation, and UDL are complementary in that they are built on the concept that education is most effective when learner variability with respect to different levels of readiness, learning profiles, and interests have been considered.

When a student is struggling with an aspect of the curriculum, RtI is often implemented. In this model, a student's progress is carefully monitored and documented so that a teacher is able to design differentiated lessons that most effectively meet that student's needs.

instruction in order to master information or a skill, while other students are able to quickly master the same content and need a greater challenge (Heacox 2002).

Content may be differentiated in a variety of ways according to readiness, interests, or learning profile. Tomlinson (2001, 2014) outlines the following strategies that may be used to differentiate content.

- **Curriculum compacting**: more information about using this strategy can be found later in this chapter.
- **Using varied text and resource materials**
- **Learning contracts**: more information about using this strategy can be found later in this chapter.
- **Mini-lessons**: mini-lessons are brief lessons that a teacher can use to reteach a lesson, present a lesson in a different manner, or extend a lesson. These lessons may be used with a whole class or with smaller groups of students.
- Varied support systems
  - audio-video recorders
  - note-taking organizers
  - highlighted print materials
  - digests of key ideas: a **digest of key ideas** is a one- to two-page graphic organizer, list, or summary of key ideas within a unit of study. It may also include important vocabulary words as well as essential questions.
  - peer and adult mentors

The following example illustrates how one seventh-grade teacher differentiated content for a weather disaster reading unit. Students were required to read one of several books based on a weather disaster. The selection of books reflected a variety of reading levels, and students were matched to books that were appropriate to their instructional reading levels. All students were asked to describe both the causes and effects of the weather disaster. As a culminating activity, the class as a whole created a chart of causes and effects of the different weather disasters studied. In addition, those students who needed more challenging work or had a strong interest in weather events were encouraged to conduct further research using more technical and more sophisticated materials.

In this example, although students read different texts of varying difficulty, they were all required to master the skill of cause and effect, and were able to do so using text that was at a reading level appropriate to their levels of understanding. Furthermore, those students who were ready to explore more sophisticated information were provided the opportunity.

These students were then able to share their findings in science class.

Early in this chapter, we talked about the importance of sharing the work of differentiating by planning with other teachers. Both of the previous two projects would be much more *doable* if the work were divided among several teachers teaching the same curriculum. For example, for the inventor project, assuming there were four fifth-grade teachers in the school, the teachers might divide the list of inventors and each locate resources for their assigned inventors. The building literacy teacher might give the teachers advice on the reading level of each resource so the resources might be assigned to students with appropriate reading levels. The teachers might even divide the students based on the inventors they chose so that each teacher was responsible for being knowledgeable about only one fourth of the inventors.

Differentiating Process

Instruction may be differentiated by varying the process or the means by which the content is being taught. Your teaching, when feasible, should reflect the styles and preferences of your learners. You may differentiate the process in response to student readiness, learning profile, and/or student interest.

The following strategies may be used to differentiate process:

- journals
- graphic organizers
- literature circles
- interactive journals
- creative problem-solving
- think-pair-share
- mind-mapping

Students may be provided the opportunity to learn the information and skills using the strategy that is best matched to their learning profiles. For example, some students working on the previous weather disaster unit might be given the opportunity to describe the disaster and note the cause and effect by writing a journal about the events from the point of view of a meteorologist reporting on the event. Other students may choose to describe the same information by creating both a sequence of events and a cause-and-effect graphic organizer. A group of students reading the same book may choose to conduct a literature circle (with or without the teacher) in a small circle, while the remainder of the class sits around them in a larger circle, listening to the discussion.

In addition to offering a variety of strategies, teachers may also structure each of the strategies in this example to vary the level of complexity to match student readiness and/or to require differing levels of creativity and critical thinking.

Differentiating Product

The manner in which students are assessed may also be varied as a means of differentiating instruction. Students' products demonstrate their understanding at the end of a unit of study. Many of the items listed as processes in the previous bulleted list may also result in differentiated products. Products may be differentiated by providing students with choices of the way in which they demonstrate their mastery of the information and skills and/or by providing greater levels of challenge. Units of study in which learning may be represented in a variety of ways are examples of lessons planned to allow for differentiating products (Heacox 2002).

The following strategies may be utilized for differentiating products.

- Build assignments around a theme, concept, or issue that is central to the topic being studied.
- Use variations on a theme to address individual interests and readiness.
- Design assignments to help children connect key ideas to their own world.
- Support students' use of varied modes of expression and materials.
- Give clear criteria for success—more information about creating and using rubrics can be found in Chapter 4.

The following example represents a way in which one of our colleagues differentiated the product at the culmination of a mathematics unit on decimals, fractions, and percentages. The *concept* students were required to demonstrate was the relationship among decimals, fractions, and percentages. All students were required to demonstrate that decimals, fractions, and percentages are different ways to express numbers that are less than one whole. To demonstrate knowledge or *variations of the theme* and *connect to their own world*, students were required to describe the importance of having different ways of expressing the same number (for example, when dealing with money, we use a decimal, and when we talk about the chance of rain, we use a percentage, etc.). Students were asked to provide an example showing when each mode of expression would be most appropriately used. Students were also asked to choose a fraction and express it as both a decimal and percentage.

The description of the activity piqued students' *interests* and they were given *the option to use varied modes of expression and materials.* Some students wrote a song to demonstrate the connection among the three concepts. Some students created a game in which players had to use their knowledge of the relationship among these three concepts to play. Other students created a poster that visually showed the relationships, and others wrote a picture book both explaining and illustrating how decimals, fractions, and percentages are connected. Each option was accompanied by a rubric that *clearly stated the criteria* for successfully completing the assessment.[9]

> *Flexible grouping is a central practice of differentiated instruction, and it is accomplished by assigning students to a variety of instructional groups based on levels of readiness, learning styles, and interests.*

Using Instructional Strategies to Differentiate Instruction

A number of instructional strategies may be used to differentiate instruction by content, process, and product according to learners' readiness, interests, and learning styles. Often, you will use a variety of instructional strategies to differentiate instruction in more than one way simultaneously. This section highlights instructional strategies that teachers have found to be particularly effective for differentiating instruction.

Flexible Grouping

Flexible grouping is a central practice of differentiated instruction, and it is accomplished by assigning students to a variety of instructional groups based on levels of readiness, learning styles, and interests. The composition of the groups varies. Sometimes these groups are homogeneous, sometimes heterogeneous, sometimes random, and sometimes composed of the whole class, depending on learning goals and students' needs and interests. Flexible grouping is not typically used on a daily basis, but instead used as needed. This type of grouping allows the teacher to more effectively match students with their instructional needs.

One of our colleagues used flexible grouping in her reading program in the following manner. When doing an author study with students, the teacher selected a variety of books of varying levels and themes but written by the same author. Although students needed to choose a book that was at their instructional reading levels, they did have some choice in determining which book they would read, as there were a few books at each reading level. By using different books by the same author, the teacher was able to capitalize on students' interests while, at the same time, grouping students according to their levels of readiness. Moreover, throughout this unit, the teacher often met at the same time with students reading different books when they needed more direct teaching and/or practice with one of the comprehension strategies they were learning. Chapter 3 provides more information on how to use flexible grouping in the classroom.

Anchor Activities

Anchor activities are familiar activities that are engaging and self-sustaining. They are assigned to students so that the teacher can work with individuals or small groups of students on other differentiated tasks. Some teachers present students with a list of activities they may do when they have completed assigned work. These activities must be appropriate to the needs of the students and relevant to the curriculum. Students should be able to access the activities and complete them independently.

The following examples illustrate how one of our colleagues uses anchor activities in her classroom.

Reading

When students finish their assigned reading work for the day, they know they need to read their independent reading books. In order to establish more accountability for students, the teacher provides them with focus questions, which they are to answer after reading an assigned number of pages in their independent reading books. These questions usually relate to the particular skill or strategy the class is focusing on at the time. For example, when students are working on making connections to the texts they are reading, their anchor activity is to explain three different connections (e.g., text to text, text to self, and text to world) they make while reading their independent reading books.

The teacher collects journals weekly to read student responses. Often, she responds in writing; however, at times, she only reads over student work to check for understanding and completion. Then she asks for student volunteers to share their responses in

---

9   More information about assessing student learning can be found in Chapter 4.

class or in small groups. It is important for students to listen to how other students respond in their reading journals, and the teacher has found that it gives other students different ideas about responding to texts.

Mathematics

An example of using mathematics anchor activities is setting up a problem-solving center at which students select different problems to solve. If the current unit of study were fractions, the problem-solving center might include different activities of varying complexity for which students need to use their knowledge of fractions or related concepts. In addition, students would be required to follow a particular format when they solved these problems. They would also be asked to turn in their work (finished or unfinished) at the end of each class period, so the classroom teacher can check it, make comments, and clarify any misunderstandings. Because students would be able to choose which activities to complete, they would enjoy working on these activities and would not view them as "extra work."

A variation of this strategy that is often used in upper elementary, middle school, and high school is featuring a problem of the day or of the week. The teacher posts a mathematics problem on a bulletin board or writes it on a whiteboard. Students complete the assigned task before they work on the more challenging problem. Typically, a multi-step problem is used. The problems that teachers find work best are those that interest students. For example, a class with a high number of students interested in sports may solve problems that use the batting averages of the local major league baseball team.

One teacher uses this technique in a very time-efficient manner. She downloads problems from mathematics websites and collects them from other teachers. She has the problems enlarged to three-by-four-foot charts. Her collection of problems is kept folded up in a drawer. She need only take out the problem that best matches the group, topic being taught, and/or time of year, and thumbtack it to a bulletin board. In doing this, she has successfully differentiated her lesson for the day or week in less than three minutes!

Co-Teaching

Having more than one adult in the classroom enables a teacher to provide more individualized support to students while simultaneously allowing students to learn from one another through collaborative work. This is an invaluable process. An elementary teacher describes one of her most valuable experiences as a teacher as one in which the literacy specialist and she worked closely together and co-taught two reading lessons weekly in the classroom. They chose to co-teach rather than have the reading specialist work with students outside of the class. By doing so, the teachers found that they were able to more effectively support those students who needed it as well as provide more challenging activities for those students who were ready to move forward. When teaching students the comprehension strategy of summarizing, the teachers found that some students quickly grasped the concepts and were able to identify key points in a chapter and succinctly explain these ideas in a well-written, organized summary. At the same time, many students were unable to identify the main points, and, consequently, retold the entire chapter, including all minor points in addition to the major points. These students needed more direct instruction and practice to master summarizing, while other students were ready to apply the strategy on their own. Because there were two teachers in the classroom, they were able to meet students at their current levels of understanding.

Many special education teachers identify co-teaching as an effective means for meeting the needs of special education students for the following reasons:

1. The classroom teacher and the special education teacher may alternate between teaching the students who master concepts quickly and teaching those who need additional guided practice. Special education teachers report that this alternating decreases some of the stigma students with special needs may feel when they are removed from class.
2. The special education teacher is always fully aware of what is being taught in the classroom, enabling him or her to ensure classroom success for the special needs students.
3. The special education teacher gets firsthand information about the ways in which the special needs students interact with the teacher and the other students in the regular classroom.

In Chapter 10, we discuss in depth several different models of co-teaching. Some of these models include the classroom teacher working with an ELL teacher, a literacy specialist, a technology specialist, a speech and language pathologist, etc.

At Least

At Least is a very simple strategy that provides some differentiation with relatively little effort on the part of teachers. When asking students independently, or with a partner or group, to make a list of items, we insert the words at least into the explanation. Below are some examples:

"With your partner, name four presidents who served during a time of war."

becomes

"With your partner, name *at least* four presidents who served during a time of war."

"In your group, list three causes for the Civil War."

becomes

"In your group, list *at least* three causes for the Civil War."

By inserting the words *at least*, we require those students who think of three causes of the Civil War quickly to push their thinking to include other causes. It also generates a discussion using higher-order thinking skills, as the students look at the more subtle and more complex causes. For example, some students may expand their discussion to talk about the impact that England had in encouraging secession because of its trade with the Southern cotton industry.

Tiered Assignment

A **tiered assignment** is one in which a teacher provides a series of related tasks at levels of varying complexity. These assignments are usually presented at three levels. Some teachers use a pre-assessment to determine which tasks are most appropriate for which students. Students complete tasks most suitable to their academic readiness. All activities should focus on the key concepts that students are expected to master.

Heacox (2001, 2012) suggests six different ways to structure tiered assignments: by challenge, complexity, resources, outcome, process, and product. The following section will identify and briefly describe each of these approaches.

1. **Tier by challenge level.** Bloom's taxonomy, found in Table 6.8 later in this chapter, is helpful in creating tiered activities, ranging from basic to more challenging. This method of tiered assignments works well when some students are at introductory (or exposure) levels of learning, while others are at more advanced levels. This type of tiered activity is also effective when some students need more time to work on skills, strategies, or content, while others are ready to work with more advanced skills, strategies, or content. The activities listed in Table 6.8, Bloom's Taxonomy, provide an example of how to tier assignments by challenge level. One middle school teacher tiers vocabulary studies by

challenge level. All students have words that contain the same Greek and Latin roots; however, students who are at more advanced reading and writing levels are responsible for more difficult words.

2. **Tier by complexity.** When some students are at introductory levels of learning while others are ready for more abstract, analytical work, tiering by complexity allows you to differentiate the learning by giving more advanced tasks, not just more work. The following example illustrates how one teacher tiered by complexity.

Least complex: Create a presentation that will inform your classmates about greenhouse warming.

More complex: Create a presentation that will inform your classmates of different points of view about greenhouse warming.

Most complex: Create a presentation that provides various positions on greenhouse warming. Determine your position on this issue and present a convincing argument for it.

3. **Tier by resources.** Tiering activities by resources takes into account the differences in students' reading abilities as well as their knowledge of the topic. When you tier by resources, you choose reading materials of varying degrees of difficulty with regard to content. This type of tiered task works well when varied levels of resources can be used to match students' levels of readiness with appropriate materials. For example, you would like all students to learn about endangered species and write a research report based on their findings. To best meet the needs of all learners, you provide varied reading materials and match students with the resources most suitable for them.

4. **Tier by outcome.** At times, you will want all students to have experiences with the same content and material. However, some students may be more ready than others to work on advanced applications of their learning. Differentiating in this way requires you to possess a deep understanding of each of your students' readiness levels. This type of tiered task works well when students can use the same materials to work on both basic and more advanced outcomes. The example described in figure 6.12, in which students were required to demonstrate their understanding of endangered species, represents a project tiered by outcome. Students had experiences with the same content; however, some students were able to express their knowledge in more sophisticated and complex ways than others.

5. **Tier by process.** Sometimes you will want students to have the same outcomes, but different students may need to get there through different means—that is, by using a different process. For example, a class has just finished a unit of study based on weather disasters. A question for this unit might be, "What are the effects of two different weather disasters we have studied?" The following two assignments that are tiered by process address this question.

> **Basic level**–Choose two different weather disasters we have studied. Using the resources we have used throughout this unit of study, compare and contrast the effects of these two disasters.

> **Advanced level**–Choose two different weather disasters we have studied. Interview at least two survivors of each disaster. Using the information received from these persons, compare and contrast the effects of these two disasters.

6. **Tier by product.** Tiering by product can be used when there is more than one way for students to demonstrate what they have learned. Such assignments can be differentiated by product using Howard Gardner's theory of multiple intelligences.

Curriculum Compacting

To **compact the curriculum**, a teacher assesses students' information and skills at the beginning of a unit of study and moves students who demonstrate that they have mastered the information and skills to alternative activities. Compacting works well in classrooms in which there are both high-achieving and gifted and talented students whose content knowledge and skills are far more advanced than their peers. The regular classwork is replaced with an advanced, interest-based project that these students can work on during class time. For example, in a math class, a teacher may pre-assess students for mastery on coordinate graphing. After determining the high-achieving[10] students who already understand this concept, the teacher might have these students work on a project in which students are required to apply their knowledge of coordinate graphing in real-world context.

If you decide to use compacting, be careful that more advanced learners do not feel as though they are being given more work. This strategy may work well for short periods of time when students are given specific choices of additional activities. Many teachers who use this pedagogy send letters home to parents,

explaining the rationale and expectations of using such a strategy (Benjamin 2003).

Stations

Using **stations** is another effective way in which to differentiate information. Stations can be used with any subject and at every grade. Stations allow different students to work on different tasks at the same time. The following characteristics are representative of stations:

- Students simultaneously work on varied tasks in different parts of the classroom.
- Teachers can assign students to different stations.
- Conducive to flexible grouping.
- Time students spend at each station is based upon students' needs.
- Students may or may not visit every station.
- The assignments at each station may vary each day based upon students' needs.
- Both teachers and students have choice.

The following vignette comes from a fifth-grade teacher who has had much success implementing math stations. This master teacher discusses how she sets stations up in her classroom, touching on classroom management, a description of each of the stations, and how she is able to incorporate differentiation into each of these in order to meet the individual needs of all students.

Using Math Stations in a Fifth-Grade Classroom to Differentiate

The key to effectively implementing math stations is classroom management. At the beginning of the year, I set up a *Math Center Board* at the front of my room. The board is broken up into four centers: *Math Mania*, math review problems; *At Your Seat*, independent math work; *Hands-On*, math games and manipulatives; and *Teacher's Choice*, teacher-led small group work. I begin the year by teaching the students how to read the board and how to rotate to each station. Students then practice how to do so. It is critical that behavioral expectations and noise levels are very clear to the students. I created a sign that reads **N O I S E**. If the students are too loud, I ring the bell and silently remove the last letter (**E**). If I ring the bell three times, then the only two letters left spell the word **NO**. At that point, no talking is allowed for the rest of that class period. This logical consequence is extremely effective as students truly enjoy collaborating with their peers and learning from them.

---

10 We make a distinction between high-achieving students and gifted students. We consider gifted students only those who are achieving in the top 1 percent of all students in their age group.

When it is time for students to rotate to the next station, I ring the bell two times in a row to signal to students that it is time to start the cleanup process. Finally, when all the students are silently standing and looking at me, I ring the bell three times to signal that it is time to rotate to the next station. It is imperative to take the time at the beginning of the year to establish and practice clear expectations and procedures.

Math Mania

I use this station to practice math skills that have already been taught. Sometimes I even use math games from earlier in the year to review concepts. Two or three different colored folders are used at this station, depending on the various learning needs of my students. For example, my green group might be working on math problems that focus on fifth-grade standards. My yellow group might be working on a review sheet that focuses on fourth-grade math standards that they have not yet mastered.

Although students are working on problems that are appropriate for their level, at times some students still need additional assistance. For these students, I provide scaffolds in which they can access independently when necessary. For instance, I have found that many of my students struggle with exponents. Early in the year, I include a reference sheet that includes step-by-step instructions. I also provide one or two examples to which these students can refer. As the year progresses and the students move toward mastery, I gradually remove the aides.

If students finish their review problems before it is time to rotate to the next section, they work on the challenge packet, which is kept in their math folders. These challenging problems are also differentiated, and all students have opportunities to solve higher-level thinking problems throughout the year. Some of the materials I use for these packets are Problem Solvers, Extra Math Review, Balance Math and More Levels 1 and 2, Ken-Ken Puzzles, Perplexors, and real-world word problems.

At Your Seat

This station provides students with an opportunity to try a skill or concept on their own. If a child is stuck, he or she is encouraged to quietly ask another student for help in order to get started. Then, the student attempts to complete the work independently. This station also has green and yellow folders based on the level of support a child needs. The yellow group may complete the even numbers only, or I may include a model for the students to follow based on the lesson. The yellow folder may also include a multiplication grid or math manipulatives to help work through the problems. If I do not collect the sheets that day, each colored folder will have an answer sheet so that students can self-correct their work.

Hands-On

This station is the one that everyone loves! This station usually includes a game and/or an activity in which math manipulatives are used. I have found that most students enjoy math games when they are partnered with another student that is at a similar math level. Although the larger group at that station may be a heterogeneous group, I typically create homogeneous pairings for games. However, a benefit to having the larger, heterogeneous group is that my higher-level students can help explain the game to students that may be confused.

Some of my games include different levels: an easy side and a more challenging side. I have to modify most of my games so that all my students will be successful. For example, I have a few matching games that have too many cards for my lower-level students. In one, the students have to find equivalent fractions. My higher-level students are able to use 50 cards, while my struggling students need to use 25 in order to have a successful learning experience. Another way I differentiate this game is to have my higher-level students play with the cards facedown, like a memory game, while the lower-level students have the cards facing up so that they are able to fully focus on finding equivalent fraction matches. I might also give my lower group a colored fraction reference sheet that clearly shows which fractions are equivalent. However, I encourage my students to challenge themselves and to only use the "help sheet" if necessary.

Another example of a differentiated game is a volume board game that requires every player to solve the volume problem. The players who solve the problem correctly on the first try get to roll the die and move on. I differentiate this game by allowing my struggling learners two tries to get the correct answer. A "help card" with the formula for volume is also provided. Some of my students will need a multiplication grid for this activity as well.

As mentioned earlier, manipulatives are often used at this station. After students work with manipulatives at the *Teacher's Choice* station and understand how to effectively use them, they will then be able to access them at the *Hands-On* station. Students can independently use the manipulatives to solve problems.

Teacher's Choice

This station is my teacher-led station. I use both heterogeneous and homogenous groupings at this math center. The following example illustrates an effective use of using a heterogeneous group while simultaneously differentiating. When I teach rounding decimals, I create manipulatives to help guide my students through the rounding process. I use number cards to concretely show a number like 134.45. I then explain to the students that we are going to round to the tenths place and put a laminated line under the number 4 to emphasize that this number is in the tenths place. Next, I put a laminated circle (with a cutout in the middle so you can see the number) around the number in the hundredths place. After students figure out that rounding this number to the tenths place results in 134.5, I ask a student to explain the process. At this point, the higher-level students are able to model their thinking out loud, and my struggling students are able to have the process reiterated by a peer who may be able to explain it in a way that makes more sense.

My higher-level students typically understand the concepts before my struggling students. If I have a heterogeneous grouping of seven students, four or five may be ready to work on their own more quickly, and I can reteach and/or provide more guided practice for the other two or three students. Students who finish early will practice the skill using a real-world word problem. As always, my students are encouraged to share answers and to help each other.

If a student has already mastered a particular concept before it is taught, then he or she will be given an alternative assignment. For example, a student may use the Explain Everything app to narrate a lesson or create a presentation for his or her peers. I may choose to show the whole class the presentation or just share it with a small group of struggling learners. At times, two students may work together to create a game that can be included in our *Hands-On* station. In the past, some students created a "scoot game" for adding fractions, while others have made a fraction board game with game cards and rules. These activities keep children engaged, push the boundaries of their understanding of mathematical concepts, and improve their critical thinking. Watching my students have fun in math class is so rewarding!

Learning Centers

Learning centers differ from stations in that centers are distinct and stations work in concert, meaning all students are working at different stations simultaneously. According to Tomlinson (2014), "A learning center is a classroom area that contains a collection of activities or materials designed to teach, provide practice on, or extend a student's knowledge, skill, or understanding. An interest center is designed to motivate students' exploration of topics in which they have a particular interest. In general, centers should

- focus on important, clearly identified goals
- contain materials that promote individual students' growth toward those goals
- use materials and activities addressing a wide range of reading levels, learning profiles, and student interests
- include activities that vary from simple to complex, concrete to abstract, and structured to open-ended
- provide clear directions for students
- offer instructions about what students should do if they need help
- include instructions about what students should do when they complete a center assignment

- use a record-keeping system to monitor what students do at the center and the quality level of their work
- use formative assessment to guide development of center tasks and assignment of students to appropriate tasks" (2014, pp. 123–124). You can read more about formative assessments in Chapter 4.

One teacher used learning centers in her classroom when she wanted students to have different experiences during a science unit on simple machines. She set up a learning center in the classroom that included a variety of tasks based on different simple machines. Some of the tasks required students to build, some to manipulate objects, and others to draw, conduct an experiment, or identify the particular simple machine. Students were encouraged to engage in particular tasks based on their readiness, interests, and learning styles. All students were expected to have at least one experience with each of the six simple machines in order to develop a basic understanding of how each machine works and how to apply its use in everyday life. However, students explored these centers at different times. This flexibility also provided meaningful activities for students who finished their work early.

Learning Contracts

A **learning contract** is an agreement between the teacher and student in which students work independently to complete tasks that are designed to match skills and/or content to their readiness, interests, and/or learning profiles. The contract should state the particular task the student is expected to complete, as well as establish a deadline. Such contracts help students set daily or weekly work goals and manage their time.

The learning contract shown in Figure 6.17 is used by one of our colleagues in an eighth-grade mathematics class throughout a unit of study on functions. Students choose three of the nine activities to complete, and class time is set aside each week to complete them. Students are encouraged to consult with the teacher on their progress during class time, and as assignments are completed, students place their work in a spot designated by the teacher.

Figure 6.17

Function Portfolio	Computer Game	Write Your Own Fairy Tale
Using graphing software, or pencil and paper, create a function portfolio. The portfolio should contain functions that are grouped by the following characteristics: linear vs. non-linear, linear and proportional vs. linear and non-proportional, increasing linear and decreasing linear.	Create a game on the computer in which a classmate can be quizzed on whether a graph, table, or set of ordered pairs is a relation or a function. The person playing the game should receive feedback from the game about whether they are correct.	Create a fairy tale with a plot that can be graphed (e.g., distance vs. time, displacement vs. time, pounds of candy eaten vs. time, trolls under the bridge vs. days, etc.). The fairy tale and the graphs will be displayed in a "book."
Compare Functions	**Interpret Functions**	**Matching Game**
Create eight different functions. Two should be represented by equations, two by tables, two with words, and two with graphs. Write five questions about the functions that allow a classmate to compare the functions and their rates of change.	Find three representations of different functions used in current events (e.g., election results, oil prices, interest rates, etc.). Describe what the function is conveying to the reader. Be sure to attach the function to your analysis of it.	Create a game that has multiple modes of representations for functions. Functions are represented in words, graphs, tables, and equations. At least five different functions will be represented, with all four modes of representation for each.
Sales Pitch	**Research Functions**	**Interview Your Classmates**
For a product of your design, create a sales pitch that has a starting value and a constant rate of change. To convince people to buy your product, represent the linear function with a graph, table, words, equation, and an illustration.	How are functions used and analyzed in the business world? In science and engineering? What are the contexts in which they are used, and what can be learned by analyzing them?	What is something relevant to your world as eighth graders that has a functional relationship? Interview your classmates to acquire data and represent the data using your multiple modes of representation sheet (words, table, graph, and equation).
Student Choice #1	**Student Choice #2**	**Student Choice #3**

Another example of a learning contract is shown in Figure 6.18. This differentiated activity illustrates a variation of a learning contract that one of our colleagues uses in her seventh-grade mathematics class during an algebraic expressions unit of study. Students must choose a role from whose perspective they will write, an audience to whom they are writing, the format they will use, and the purpose of their writing. In addition, students are required to use specific mathematical vocabulary and must include *at least* three examples of algebraic expressions. Students are given a rubric that outlines how they will be assessed. As students finish an activity, they submit their work through Google Classroom.

Figure 6.18

ROLE	AUDIENCE	FORMAT	TOPIC
Write as though you are . . .	Writing something to be read or heard by . . .	The writing will take the form of . . .	The purpose of your writing will be to . . .
a friend	absent student	a letter	tell the student what we learned in math and how to do it
a journalist	students in the 7th grade	an article	share the latest topic being taught in math
an investigative reporter	the viewers of the 6 o'clock news	a 3-minute speech	report the good and bad about algebraic expressions
a writer	a publisher	a poem	explain algebraic expressions
a teacher	a class of adults who are planning on going to college and need to review pre-algebra before they can take a college math class	notes for a step-by-step demonstration	introduce algebraic expressions
a math professor	future math teachers	a 30-second speech	inspire your audience to teach algebraic expressions
a scientist	space aliens	a how-to manual	explain how to read and write algebraic expressions

Your writing <u>must</u> include the words variable, coefficient, constant, and the phrase 'algebraic expression.' Your writing <u>must</u> include at least 3 examples of algebraic expressions in words and symbols.

<u>Optional</u>: Feel free to include the following ideas in your RAFT: no multiplication signs between the variable and coefficient, the coefficient always comes before the variable, and interpreting English.

Submit your RAFT through Google Classroom. In addition, you will be required to fill out a document that indicates the role, audience, and format you chose.

Rubric for your RAFT:

- used required words (8 points, 2 points each)
- provided examples (6 points, 2 points each)
- demonstrated/explained algebraic expressions correctly (7 points)
- RAFT is creative (2 points)
- used correct form and style (2 points)

Total: 30 points

Adjusting Questions

In whole-class discussions, tests, quizzes, and homework, a teacher may adjust questions to better meet the needs of students based on their readiness, interests, and learning profiles. **However, all students should be expected to answer important questions that require them to think.** Some teachers keep a list of Bloom's verbs (see Table 6.8, Bloom's taxonomy) readily accessible to assist them in differentiating questions. More information about questioning techniques can be found in Chapter 5.

Independent Study

An independent study is a research project in which students develop skills for independent learning through research. The student and teacher identify problems or topics of interest to the student, decide how to investigate the problems or topic, and determine the product the student will create to demonstrate his or her learning. This strategy works well with older, more independent students. Specialists in gifted and talented education highly recommend this technique, provided that students have adequate levels of teacher contact.

Reading Buddies

In using the reading buddies strategy, students are paired and gain additional reading practice away from the teacher. This strategy is most appropriate for elementary students. It is important that students read for a specific purpose set forth by the teacher and are given an opportunity to discuss what was read. For example, a teacher may want students to focus on making predictions. Before reading the assigned text, students would be asked to make predictions based on prior readings, the chapter title, or book title. After reading the assigned text, they would be asked to confirm their predictions and reflect on the accuracy of them. Finally, students may be asked to make new predictions using what they learned from their reading that day. Reading buddies may be reading at different or similar levels; however, the follow-up tasks and/or questions should be assigned based on readiness levels. Some teachers use this strategy across grade levels.

Graphic Organizers

A **graphic organizer** is any kind of diagram or outline that assists children in visually arranging information in such a way that the information is made more accessible. Graphic organizers have many names, including *visual maps, mind maps, visual organizers, concept maps,* or *webs.* Graphic organizers may be created by teachers and/or students using pencil and paper or technology tools. They may be used during all phases of learning, from brainstorming to presentation of findings. In addition, teachers may use these organizers with the whole class or with individual students.

Graphic organizers may be used to help students of all ages in

- clarifying concepts
- organizing and remembering information
- explaining complex relationships in a more simplistic manner
- speeding up communication of information
- focusing on essential information

There are many instructional uses for graphic organizers:

- teaching students to think about information in new ways
- reviewing and summarizing concepts
- representing large chunks of information in a concise manner or in the big picture
- editing and revising easily

(The two lists above were adapted and reprinted with the permission of Jeanette Bastien, a middle school teacher in Westfield, MA.)

Graphic organizers are categorized as *hierarchical, sequential, conceptual,* or *cyclical.* The following table highlights some of the uses of each of these organizers.

Table 6.7

Hierarchical	• main concept with ranks, levels, or sub-concepts • generalizations • classifications • main idea
Sequential	• chronological order • cause and effect • events in a story • explanation of a process • problem/solution
Conceptual	• central idea, category, and class, with supporting ideas • description • compare/contrast • charts, tables, or matrices
Cyclical	• series of events in a circular formation • continuous sequence of events having no beginning or end

Source: Unknown.

Figure 6.19

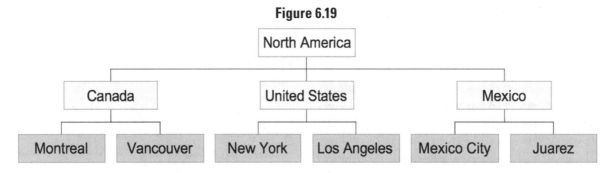

Hierarchical

The most common type of hierarchical graphic organizer we see is the flowchart for the hierarchy of positions in an organization. The graphic organizer in Figure 6.19 shows the relationship among continents, countries, and cities.

Sequential Graphic Organizer

A sequential graphic organizer is used to show when one thing follows another; however, the events do not have a cyclical nature that leads back to the beginning, as we saw in the cyclical graphic organizer earlier. The story map and cause and effect graphic organizers that follow are examples of sequential graphic organizers.

Figure 6.20

Beginning _____
_____
_____
_____

Middle _____
_____
_____

End _____
_____
_____
_____

Figure 6.21 **Cause and Effect Organizer**

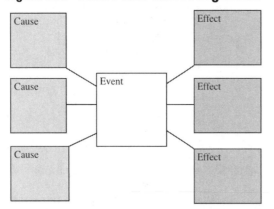

Conceptual Graphic Organizer

The conceptual graphic organizers that are most well known are those that compare and contrast two concepts. Figure 6.22 is an example of a compare and contrast graphic organizer used to compare the economy of the North with that of the South during the Civil War. The box on the left has characteristics that are unique to the South. The box on the right has characteristics that are unique to the North. The box in the middle contains those items that are true for both the North and the South.

Source: Educational Performance Systems, Inc. Reprinted with permission. For more information on how graphic organizers can be used to promote metacognition, visit EPSI's website at www.epsi-usa.com.

Figure 6.22
Compare and Contrast Graphic Organizer

The South	Both Regions	The North

The above compare and contrast can also be done with the interlocking circles commonly referred to as a *Venn diagram*.

The following websites provide blank graphic organizers that you may print out to use with your students.

- www.teachervision.com
- www.graphic.org
- www.eduplace.com/kids
- http://www.studenthandouts.com/graphic-organizers/
- www.teacherprintables.net/free-printable-organizers.html

The website www.teach-nology.com will allow you to customize a graphic organizer to meet the needs of your students.

Inspiration (or Kidspiration for younger students) is a software program made for creating graphic organizers. It allows students and/or teachers to create a variety of graphic organizers. We have found this program to be very kid-friendly and easy to navigate. Students with fine-motor issues have found this to be an invaluable program for helping them to organize their thoughts and ideas. Words, clip art, and actual photographs can be used with this program. The Inspiration website (www.inspiration.com) has many ideas for classroom applications and also allows you to download a free trial version.

Strategies Discussed in Other Chapters

Many of the strategies discussed in Chapters 2, 7, and 8 enable us to differentiate by learning profile. For example, **giving the mastery objectives at the start of the lesson** particularly helps those students who learn from whole to part. **Posting and reviewing the**

Keep in mind that all students need to use higher-order thinking skills and that the higher level of learning can be used to reteach and reinforce basic content.

agenda helps those students who need to know at the outset what will happen at each stage of the lesson before they are able to focus on the content. **Group activators** of the students' previous learning on the topic helps those students who were only at the introductory, guided practice, or immediate mastery level the last time the topic was addressed. **Connecting to the students' own world** is important for students with particular learning styles to move the information and skills into their long-term memories. **Summarizers** are particularly important for students with learning styles that need the information pulled together at the end of the learning period before they move it into their long-term memory. **Learnable intelligence** strategies are particularly important for students who have low confidence as learners.

Bloom's Taxonomy

Another effective way in which to differentiate instruction is to use Bloom's taxonomy as a guide. Bloom's different levels of learning help you determine the level of complexity of a particular task. Keep in mind that all students need to use higher-order thinking skills and that the higher level of learning can be used to reteach and reinforce basic content (Heacox 2001). Table 6.8 on the next page outlines Bloom's six varying levels of learning, from most basic to most complex.

Some teachers may use these different levels of learning in planning a differentiated instruction lesson. You can also use the verbs listed to assign levels to the mastery objectives for the tasks.[11] The following activities are examples of different levels of objectives for students' learning in a unit on immigration. They are arranged so that Level 1 requires the lowest level of thinking and Level 6 requires the highest level of thinking.

By the end of the class you will be able to
(Level 1) *List* four different immigrant groups that came to America during the 1800s, and *tell* why they wanted to come to America.
(Level 2) *Pretend* you are an immigrant in steerage class in the late 1800s and *describe* your life when coming to America on a ship.

---

11 Chapter 1 explains the writing of mastery objectives for planning lessons and units. It includes a list of verbs teachers can use to develop mastery objectives that require higher-order thinking skills.

Table 6.8 Bloom's Taxonomy Action Verbs

Definitions	I. Remembering	II. Understanding	III. Applying	IV. Analyzing	V. Evaluating	VI. Creating
Bloom's Definition	Exhibit memory of previously learned material by recalling facts, terms, concepts, and answers.	Demonstrate understanding of facts and ideas by organizing, comparing, translating, interpreting, giving descriptions, and stating main ideas.	Solve problems to new situations by applying acquired knowledge, facts, techniques, and rules in a different way.	Examine and break information into parts by identifying motives or causes. Make inferences and find evidence to support generalizations.	Present and defend opinions by making judgments about information, validity of ideas, or quality of work, based on a set of criteria.	Compile information together in a different way by combining elements in a new pattern or proposing alternative solutions.
Verbs	choose define find how label list match name omit recall relate select show spell tell what when where which who why	classify compare contrast demonstrate explain extend illustrate infer interpret outline relate rephrase show summarize translate	apply build choose construct develop experiment with identify interview make use of model organize plan select solve utilize	analyze assume categorize classify compare conclusion contrast discover dissect distinguish divide examine function inference inspect list motive relationships simplify survey take part in test for theme	agree appraise assess award choose compare conclude criteria criticize decide deduct defend determine disprove estimate evaluate explain importance influence interpret judge justify mark measure opinion perceive prioritize prove rate recommend rule on select support value	adapt build change choose combine compile compose construct create delete design develop discuss elaborate estimate formulate happen imagine improve invent make up maximize minimize modify original originate plan predict propose solution solve suppose test theory

Source: ANDERSON\ KRATHWOHL\AIRASIAN\CRUIKSHANK\MAYER\PINTRICH\RATHS\WITTROCK, A TAXONOMY FOR LEARNING, TEACHING, AND ASSESSING: A REVISION OF BLOOM'S TAXONOMY OF EDUCATIONAL OBJECTIVES, ABRIDGED EDITION, 1st Ed., ©2001. Reprinted by permission of Pearson Education, Inc., New York, New York.

(Level 3) *Research* the procedures that immigrants had to endure once they arrived at Ellis Island during the late 1800s, and demonstrate the knowledge acquired in your research by *dramatizing* an immigrant arriving at Ellis Island during this period.

(Level 4) *Compare and contrast* the reasons two different immigrant groups came to America.

(Level 5) *Predict* specific ways (e.g., food, language, holidays, economy, etc.) in which our country would be different today if immigration was outlawed during the 1800s.

(Level 6) It is 1895 and you are a quality-control expert hired to improve the procedures for processing immigrants on Ellis Island. You are given three charges. First, you must increase the thoroughness with which immigrants are screened. Second, you must increase the speed with which immigrants are processed. Third, you must improve the conditions for the immigrants while they are on the island. Your report should describe the present procedures and your recommendation for improving those procedures.

Assessing and Improving Your Lessons by Increasing Differentiation

Effective differentiated instruction begins with lesson planning, such as that described in Chapter 1. It is then followed by teaching the lesson and assessing its success. It is important when you first start differentiating your lessons that you don't try to plan the perfectly differentiated lesson the first time. This will only lead to frustration and disappointment. We recommend that you initially take a few manageable steps toward differentiating your lesson based on the concepts in this chapter. You should then assess the success of the lesson and make additional modifications. You will probably need to repeat this process several times before you feel as though the lesson has sufficient differentiation. The following template may be used to assess your lesson when you have determined that the current lesson is not differentiated sufficiently to meet the varied needs of students in your classroom.[12]

Figure 6.23

Using Differentiated Instruction to Modify a Lesson That Is a Mismatch for Some Students

What are the mastery objectives for the lesson? Do they address higher-order thinking skills? If not, what high-level objectives do I want to add?

Which students do not receive sufficient challenge from the lesson as planned?

Which students are frustrated because activities do not provide sufficient scaffolding for them to master the concepts?

Are there other factors in the lesson that are not working?

How can I modify or change the lesson to better extend or scaffold the learning? Do I need to differentiate content, process, or product?

Which differentiated instructional strategy would be most effective?

Are there other modifications that would make the lesson more successful?

What resources do I need to make these modifications?

What will the differentiated lesson look like? How will it be different from the lesson as presently planned?

Conclusion

Successful differentiation takes time to plan and prepare. The steps in this chapter are designed to give you a road map for increasing the level of differentiated instruction that you provide for students. **Differentiated instruction becomes more manageable when we undertake it in doable steps and share the work with our colleagues.**

The result of differentiating our teaching is higher student achievement, increased student interest, and better student behavior.

---

12 The question, "How can I differentiate this lesson to better meet the needs of all my students?" is an excellent research question for a lesson-study project. In Chapter 11, we explain the process of professional development through lesson study.

Differentiating Instruction Exemplar
High School English – *Julius Caesar*

1. What is the district's curriculum standard and/or benchmark from which these concepts are derived?

General STANDARD 2: Questioning, Listening, and Contributing

Students will pose questions, listen to the ideas of others, and contribute their own information or ideas in group discussions or interviews in order to acquire new knowledge.
2.5: Summarize in a coherent and organized way information and ideas learned from a focused discussion.

GENERAL STANDARD 4: Vocabulary and Concept Development

Students will understand and acquire new vocabulary and use it correctly in reading and writing.
4.24: Use knowledge of Greek, Latin, and Norse mythology, the Bible, and other works often alluded to in British and American literature to understand the meanings of new words.

GENERAL STANDARD 8: Understanding a Text

Students will identify the basic facts and main ideas in a text and use them as the basis for interpretation.
8.29: Identify and analyze patterns of imagery or symbolism.
8.30: Identify and interpret themes and give supporting evidence from a text.

2. What do I want the students to know and be able to do by the end of the lesson (my mastery objectives)?

By the end of the lesson, students will be able to analyze a selection from Shakespeare's *Julius Caesar* (act I, scene ii, exchange between Brutus and Cassius), identify elements of persuasive speech—ethos, pathos, and logos—and analyze these elements for their effectiveness. Because of the complexity of the text and the diversity of the learners in terms of reading level, this lesson must address learners' needs on multiple levels. To reach the mastery objective, it will first be necessary to work with students who have difficulty comprehending the text itself. Only when these students comprehend the text will they be able to analyze it.

3. How will I formatively and summatively assess the students' level of mastery?
    a. How will I pre-assess the students' level of knowledge?

By the time students reach this portion of the play, I will have had several opportunities to pre-assess their knowledge. First, I will have dipsticked with questions during class discussion. In addition, I will have had a brief written assignment that will help me to gauge students' level of understanding. Finally, a prior quiz, class discussion, students' self-assessment, activators, and summarizers will also provide insight.

Prior to the lesson, I will have a class list and will write my impressions of where students fall in the mastery spectrum, indicating their current level of mastery. During a portion of this lesson (described below), I will circulate among the students to view their work and will either confirm or modify my comments as necessary. My notes will determine to which group students are assigned.

    b. How will I formatively assess after the mini-lesson to determine each student's level of mastery?
As students work independently, I will circulate among them, observing students' progress and offering support when needed. I will make notes on my class list to either confirm the content of my notes or prompt me to modify them. My notes about students' levels (introductory, guided practice, immediate mastery, or immediate application mastery) will determine to which group I assign them.

The work students complete in class today will become the foundation for a five-paragraph essay that will be introduced in a subsequent class. This essay will allow students to demonstrate the depth of their understanding.

4. Describe the sequence of events.
    a. What information and skills will I teach during the whole-class mini-lesson?
I will use an activator that provides students with a real-life scenario in which they will be required to use their persuasive speaking skills. For example, I will ask them to describe the techniques (words or actions)

they would use to convince their parents to let them stay out overnight on an unchaperoned trip. I will ask students to write their suggestions individually first, then have them share their suggestions as I or a student acts as a recorder for the class. I expect they will come up with suggestions such as

- behaving exceptionally well at home to convince parents that they are responsible
- planting a seed/getting "a foot in the door"—mentioning the event repeatedly and then casually asking permission once the parent is "used to the idea"
- using guilt—"I am the only one not going"
- repetition—"wearing them down" by repeated requests

I will then provide an explanation of ethos, pathos, and logos, noting that the strategies they suggested have been used throughout time. Together, we will categorize the students' examples, identifying the technique evident in each example. I will ask students to discuss what elements a truly persuasive speech would employ—ethos, pathos, logos, or a combination of the three and why. *Providing this real-life example allows students to move from what they know into an area that is unfamiliar to them.*

We will then listen to a recording of this section of the play. Students will read along at their seats. This way of presenting the text will address differentiating a lesson on another level, appealing to both visual and auditory learners.

Because students will need to comprehend the scene before they can analyze it for elements of persuasive speech, I will ask students to paraphrase the selection and explain the connection between our opening activity and the reading. Engaging in this activity will help me determine if students (a) understand the text and (b) can apply what they know from their own experience to a piece of unfamiliar literature.

As students work, I will circulate with my initial notes on levels of mastery, adjusting the notes if students demonstrate a change in their level of understanding. I will note the level of students' understanding (introductory, guided practice, immediate mastery, and immediate application mastery level). Students will then be divided into groups based upon their mastery level.

   b. What activity will I use with the students who are at the introductory level? *[Author's note: In steps b–d, students are to move at their own pace. This allows for slower to quicker and less independence to grater independence.]*

Students at the introductory level will have difficulty understanding the text and will need guidance in this area before moving to the assignment that will ask them to analyze the speech. With this group, I will distribute copies of the selection (so that students aren't overwhelmed by the quantity of the material and can mark up the text with their notes). At this table, students will receive more direct teaching. I will provide them with some guiding questions that will help them comprehend the content. Next, I will review with them ethos, pathos, and logos, and then move into the next portion of the lesson: helping them identify these elements in the text. To do this, I will have a sheet of examples of ethos, pathos, and logos that I will have previously selected. I will read each example with the students. I will then ask them to identify which device is being used and its effect on the character of Brutus. I will refer to the activator activity if students become confused and need to review some concrete, relevant examples before moving into the text.

   c. What activity will I use with students who are at the guided practice level?

Students at the guided practice level will join the introductory level students as described above. As students begin to demonstrate a mastery of the content—by correctly identifying examples of ethos, pathos, and logos, and correctly explaining their contribution to the selection (i.e., How do the words affect Brutus? How does Cassius appeal to Brutus?)—I will have them move into the immediate mastery group.

   d. What activity will I use with the students who are at immediate mastery level?

Students at this level will work in pairs to complete a worksheet of items that will isolate specific areas of text and require students to identify examples of ethos, pathos, and logos, and write about how these elements affect the passage. I will provide them with four examples of this nature. Once they have completed their work with these four examples, they will work independently to read through the text and select three examples of their own, identifying the portion of the text and analyzing each technique's effect on Brutus. Once they have completed this portion of the task, they will pair up to share and modify their answers.

(continued on next page)

e. What activity will I use with the students who are at the immediate application mastery level? Students at this level will receive instructions to read the text independently (without cues) and select a total of six examples that illustrate Cassius' use of ethos, pathos, and logos. They will also be asked to explain in writing each technique's effect on the passage and/or on the characters in the passage. Once they have completed their independent work, students will then share their findings with another student from the group, adding to or modifying their examples.

For students who complete this portion of the assignment, I will have an example of a modern-day persuasive speech for use as enrichment. Students may work together to read the modern speech, identify examples of ethos, pathos, and logos, and discuss their impact on the audience. Providing this activity will allow students to move from the concrete examples in the opener into the unfamiliar text, then apply what they have learned to a real-life, modern example.

The follow-up to this lesson will be to write a five-paragraph essay that requires students to analyze this selection from Shakespeare, noting how the elements of ethos, pathos, and logos affect the scene and its characters.

5. **What other person can assist me with planning this lesson?**
I will ask a colleague from the special education department to offer suggestions for ways to accommodate the special education students in my class. The special education teacher may offer suggestions like arranging the text so that students are not overwhelmed by the quantity and/or layout of the page.

6. **What materials do I need?**
- textbook
- list of students with preliminary notes related to students' level of mastery
- photocopies of the selection of the text that students may mark up
- teacher-created sheets for introductory/guided practice/immediate mastery groups that will isolate specific examples of ethos, pathos, logos
- guiding questions that will help introductory groups to comprehend the selected text
- enrichment material (modern speech) that students in the application mastery group will analyze upon completion of their primary task

Differentiating Instruction Exemplar
High School Mathematics — Algebra

1. **What are the district's curriculum standard and/or benchmark from which these concepts are derived?**

Learning Standards for Grades 10 and 11:
Patterns, Relations, and Algebra

10.P.1 Describe, complete, extend, analyze, generalize, and create a wide variety of patterns, including iterative, recursive (e.g., Fibonacci numbers), linear, quadratic, and exponential functional relationships.

10.P.2 Demonstrate an understanding of the relationship between various representations of a line. Determine a line's slope and x- and y-intercepts from its graph or from a linear equation that represents the line. Find a linear equation describing a line from a graph or a geometric description of the line, e.g., by using the "point-slope" or "slope y-intercept" formulas. Explain the significance of a positive, negative, zero, or undefined slope.

2. **What do I want students to know and be able to do by the end of the lesson (my mastery objectives)?**
By the end of the lesson, students will be able to graph linear equations using the slope and y-intercept.

3. **How will I formatively and summatively assess the students' level of mastery?**
a. **How will I pre-assess the students' level of knowledge?** (If you are not planning to do a mini-lesson, go directly to differentiating, which is question 3b after this pre-assessment.)

As a "Do Now" activity, I will write the equation on the board. Upon entering the class, students will receive a slip of paper asking them to identify the slope, define slope, identify the y-intercept, and define y-intercept. I will circulate around the room to gauge each student's level of success.

b. How will I formatively assess after the mini-lesson to determine each student's level of mastery?
During the independent work, I will circulate through the room and observe students working. As I do so, I will put a red sticker dot on the top of students' papers if they show introductory level work, a yellow dot if the work shows guided practice level, a green dot if they show immediate mastery, and a blue dot if they show immediate application mastery. I will put the same color dot on my student worksheet inventory (has student names down left side column and names of worksheets across the top) for record-keeping.

4. **Describe the sequence of events.**
   a. **What information and skills will I teach during the whole-class mini-lesson?**
   - I will explain to students that once the slope and y-intercept of a linear function have been identified, we can graph the function and use the graph to determine other function values.
   - We will discuss real-world uses for linear functions, including direct variation, such as depreciating and appreciating values of consumer goods (cars, electronic equipment, and real estate).
   - I will explain to students that when a linear equation is written in the form y = 2x – 5, the slope = m and the y – intercept = b.
   - I will call on students to give their answers to the warm-up prompts.
   - As students provide definitions for slope and y-intercept, I will help them refine the terminology and help them visualize the definitions using the graph board. Students will record the definitions on their note page.
   - As we discuss slope, I will remind students of the "rise over run" definition discussed in a previous lesson. This will help students identify the slope as "2/1," as opposed to "2."
   - I will then use the slope and y-intercept to graph the equation y = 1/2x + 3 as students graph it on their note page.
   - Next, I will put the equation y = –2/3x + 8/3 on the board and talk students through the process of identifying the slope, identifying the y-intercept, and graphing the equation. Students will record the work on their note page.
   - Finally, I will give students the class worksheet requiring them to graph four linear equations that have combinations of positive integers, negative integers, and fractional slopes and y-intercept values. The last problem will be in standard form rather than slope-intercept form, requiring students to manipulate the equation before graphing. (Students have mastered manipulating equations in the past.) As students complete the problems, I will circulate and again mark their papers and my student worksheet inventory with the colored dots as described above.

   b. **What activity will I use with the students who are at introductory level?** *[Author's note: In steps b–d, students are to move at their own place. This allows for slower to quicker and less independence to more independence.]*
I will form a group with these students and the guided practice students. We will complete the graphs of the first two equations on the class worksheet as follows: for each equation, we will select consecutive integer values for x, including zero, and find the functional values associated with the selected x-values. We will graph these points (students have already mastered this process for graphing linear equations) so that students can see that the graph crosses the y-axis at the value b, and that "rise over run" from one value to the next is always equal to m. Students will try No. 3 independently as I watch. I will guide individuals when necessary. We will then discuss the need to manipulate the equation in No. 4, and students will try to manipulate and graph on their own. Again, I will guide individuals when necessary.

   c. **What activity will I use with the students who are at guided practice level?**
These students will join the group with the introductory level students as described above. After each problem, these students will be allowed to leave the group if they demonstrate sufficient progress. They will need to

(continued on next page)

express the ability to complete No. 4 before leaving the group. I will ensure multiple opportunities for them to do so as students are working on the problems.

d. What activity will I use with the students who are at immediate mastery level?

These students will work in pairs to complete a worksheet that requires them to provide the graphs of three additional equations that are given, in forms other than slope-intercept. Thus, they will have to first change the equations to slope-intercept form before graphing. When each pair has completed the three graphs, they will compare with another pair of students at this level to ensure they have the correct answers. This will connect past lessons to the current lesson while embedding the concept of graphing using slope and intercept.

Once students have completed the three-equation worksheet, they will work independently to complete a word problem for which they will have to find the equation, put it in slope-intercept form, graph the equation, predict a value using their graph, and check that value using their equation. They will check their answers with another student at this level. If their answers differ, they will discuss the problem until they come to consensus.

e. What activity will I use with the students who are at the immediate application mastery level?

These students will move directly to independently completing the word problem described above. They will check their answers with another student at this level. If their answers differ, they will discuss the problem until they come to a consensus. When they both agree on the correct answer, they will move to the extension worksheet on which they have to describe a real-world scenario that can be modeled using a linear equation with a given slope and y-intercept. They will have to describe the scenario in detail, provide an equation for the scenario, and illustrate the scenario using a graph.

5.   What other person can assist me with planning this lesson?

I can talk to the other algebra teachers to see if they are interested in preparing materials that we can all share. I can also talk to the math coach in my building to see if he has any ideas.

6.   What materials do I need?

- slips of paper with the warm-up questions on it
- class note sheets
- a worksheet with four linear equations and graphing grids; first three equations in slope-intercept form and the last equation in standard form.
- worksheet with three linear equations that are not in slope-intercept form and graphing grids for each equation
- a worksheet with a word problem that can be modeled by a linear equation; this worksheet needs a graphing grid.
- worksheets with slope and y-intercept for which students describe a real-world scenario in detail; this worksheet needs a graphing grid and writing space.
- red, yellow, green, and blue sticker dots (4 x number of students)
- student worksheet inventory
- rulers

Differentiating Instruction Exemplar
Grade 7 Mathematics— Equations and Expressions

1. **What are the district's curriculum standard and/or benchmark from which these concepts are derived?**

7.EE.4—Students will write an equation or inequality to model a given situation. Students will explain how they determined whether to write an equation or inequality and the properties of the real number system that they used to find a solution. In contextual problems, students will define the variable and use appropriate units.

7.EE.4a—Students will solve multi-step equations derived from word problems. Students will use the arithmetic from the problem to generalize an algebraic solution.

2. **What do I want the students to know and be able to do by the end of the lesson (my mastery objective)?**

Main mastery objective: By the end of the lesson, the students will be able to write a multi-step equation to represent a problem-solving task that involves perimeter and solve for the missing variable.

Whole-class mini-lesson mastery objective (introductory level): Students will be able to explain, both orally and in writing, the steps necessary to do the following:
- combine like terms on both sides of an equation
- use the distributive property with variables
- find a missing variable
- distribute a term throughout an expression in a problem-solving context

Small-group behavioral mastery objectives: Students will be able to work constructively in cooperative learning groups and/or pairs by demonstrating the following:
- use 12-inch voice
- distribute work equitably
- respect all group members and their ideas
- remain focused on the task

Guided practice level mastery objective: Students will be able to solve problems that involve combining like terms, using the distributive property, and solving for missing variables when the perimeter is given with teacher scaffolding. Students will then accurately record the steps used to solve these problems for future reference.

Immediate mastery level mastery objective: Students will be able to critique and correct errors in student work involving combining like terms, using the distributive property, and solving for missing variables when the perimeter is given.

Immediate application mastery level objective: Students will be able to demonstrate how to identify and use important information from a problem-solving task. Students will be able to create and solve multi-step, real-life mathematical problems using numerical and algebraic expressions and equations for problems that involve perimeter and for problems that include a different context.

Example: The youth group is going on a trip to the state fair. The trip costs $52. Included in that price is $11 for a concert ticket and the cost of two passes, one for the rides and one for the game booths. Both of the passes cost the same price. Write an equation and draw a model representing the cost of the trip and determine the price of one pass.

3. **How will I formatively and summatively assess the students' level of mastery of these concepts?**
    a. **How will I pre-assess the students' level of knowledge?**
    I will use the exit ticket that students completed the day before to pre-assess their knowledge. In

(continued on next page)

addition, class discussions, observations, and performance on prior quizzes and assessments will also provide me with information, specifically with regards to whether or not students have the prerequisite skills needed to access the content in the lesson I will be teaching. Prior to the lesson, I will have a list with students' names and where I think they are on the mastery level spectrum. During the Do Now, I will circulate among the students to view their work and modify my comments regarding students' current level of mastery as necessary.

b. How will I formatively and assess students' level of knowledge?

As students work with me in a guided math group and independently, I will observe students' progress and scaffold learning when needed. I will record anecdotal notes on students' understanding. All students will be required to turn in completed work. My evaluation of this work will inform future instruction. At the end of the week, students will take a quiz that will assess student understanding on the skills and concepts that were part of the lesson. I will use this information to inform my instruction and to form small groups for remediation, practice, and extensions.

c. How will I summatively assess students' level of knowledge?

At the end of this unit, students will write and solve a multi-step perimeter problem. Students will need to write an equation and draw a model to represent the problem. They will also need to solve for the missing variable and clearly show each step that was used to solve the problem. Students will be given a rubric and will be asked to self-assess their work once it is completed.

4. Describe the sequence of events.

a. Do Now (5–10 minutes):

Students will enter the room and begin the Do Now. The Do Now will ask students to solve a perimeter problem for x by applying properties of operations as strategies to add, subtract, factor, and expand linear expressions to activate prior knowledge. After students complete the problem, they will work with a partner for one minute to discuss the Do Now. If students disagree on the solution, they need to determine the error. As students work and discuss, I will circulate and take notes on students' levels of understanding. After about a minute, we will have a whole class discussion and I will ask questions to clarify misconceptions, scaffold thinking, and /or extend thinking. I will collect each student's Do Now for further analysis.

b. What information and skills will I teach during the whole-class mini-lesson? (about 15 minutes):

Students will record the steps used to solve the following problem: Solve: $\frac{2}{3}x - 4 - 7x = -16$

As I solve this problem, I will model my thinking. The equation presented requires combining like terms on both sides. I will ask for student input as we solve the additional problems together as a class. These problems will increase in complexity and will require students to use the distributive property. The final problem will also include perimeter.

c. What activity will I use with the students who are at the introductory level?

I will ask students to solve for x in the given problem: $3(x + 5) - 2 = 15x$. Students will need to use the distributive property and combine like terms. I will ask them to solve similar problems while providing scaffolding. Students will then be asked to apply the skills to problems involving perimeter. Next, I will use the Think-Pair-Share strategy and ask students how to solve for x if only given expressions for each side of a figure and the perimeter. Possible questions to be used include:

- What operations are we using to combine each of the expressions together? What would happen if we subtracted?
- Why are we only using one variable? What would happen if we used two or more?
- How would you solve this problem if you needed to find the value of the variable and the perimeter was an expression and one of the sides was a given number?

d. What activity will I use with the students who are at the guided practice level?

In this group, students will have to find the value of a variable if given the perimeter as an expression and one of the sides as a given number (a deviation from the given expression as the sides and the total perimeter). I will have each student solve the problem on an index card. When students finish I will collect them and group them according to the level of understanding demonstrated in solving this problem. We will end this small group session with "My Favorite 'No'" in which I will choose a problem that includes a common student error. We will work together to critique the mistake and clarify any misconceptions.

e. What activity will I use with the students who are at immediate mastery level?

Students will find the errors and make corrections in problems that have been solved incorrectly. Students will initially work independently. Next, they will work in pairs to ensure all errors were identified and the all corrections were made.

f. What activity will I use with the students who are at the immediate application mastery level?

Students will solve a problem based on real-life context. Students will be required to identify the important information and to solve a problem that includes drawing a model, writing an expression to represent the contextual situation, and finding the value of the variable. Next, students will be asked to create their own word problem and solve it by drawing a model, writing an expression to represent the contextual situation, and finding the value of the variable

g. Summarizer (10 minutes):

Students will answer an exit-ticket question based on perimeter that requires students to combine like terms, use the distributive property and find the missing variable. I will collect these to use as a quick assessment tool to inform instruction.

5. What other person can assist me with planning this lesson?

Team members can assist me by sharing ideas regarding different strategies that can be used to help students conceptualize the skills and concepts embedded in the lesson.

Educational consultants can help me to plan effective lessons that are differentiated to meet the needs of the range of learners in my classroom.

6. What materials do I need?
- list of students with preliminary notes related to students' level of mastery
- photocopies of Do Now, exit ticket, and problem-solving tasks
- teacher-created sheets with problems for introductory/guided practice/immediate mastery groups
- guiding questions that will help introductory groups
- index cards

References

A Different Place. "Characteristics of Giftedness." Retrieved June 15, 2007. http://adifferentplace.org/characteristics.htm.

A Different Place. "Giftedness Defined." Retrieved June 23, 2007. http://adifferentplace.org/characteristics.htm.

"Achievement Gap." *Wikipedia*. Retrieved July 22, 2007. http://en.wikipedia.org/wiki/Achievement_gap

Allan, S.D. and Goddard, Y.L. "Differentiated Instruction and RTI: A Natural Fit." *Educational Leadership* 68, no. 2 (October 2010).

Anderson, L.W. and Krathwohl, D.R. *A Taxonomy for Learning, Teaching, and Assessing*, abridged edition. Boston: Allyn and Bacon, 2001.

Anonymous. *Graphic Organizers*. Woburn, MA: Educational Performance Systems.

Asperger Syndrome Coalition of the United States. Retrieved May 12, 2008. www.aspergersyndrome.org.

Association for Supervision and Curriculum. *The Common Sense of Differentiation: Meeting Specific Learner Needs in the Regular Classroom*. Alexandria, VA: Association for Supervision and Curriculum, 2005.

Attwood, T. "Asperger's Syndrome." www.tonyattwood.com.au.

"Autism: What Is It?" *National Autistic Society*. http://www.autism.org.uk/autism.

Barton, P.E. "Why Does the Gap Persist?" *Educational Leadership* 6, no. 3 (November 2004): 8–13.

Bastien, J. Unpublished paper used with teachers and students in the Westfield Public School District, 2003.

Bell, L. "Strategies That Close the Gap." *Educational Leadership* 60, no. 4 (December 2002/January 2003): 32–34.

Bender, W. *Differentiating Instruction for Students with Learning Disabilities: New Best Practices for General and Special Educators*, 3rd ed. Thousand Oaks, CA: Corwin, 2012.

Benjamin, A. *Differentiated Instruction: A Guide for Elementary School Teachers*. Larchmont, NY: Eye on Education, 2003.

Bielenberg, B. and Fillmore, L.W. "The English They Need for the Test." *Educational Leadership* 62, no. 4 (December 2004/January 2005): 45–49.

Bloom, B.S. *Taxonomy of Educational Objectives, Book 1: Cognitive Domain*. Reading, MA: Addison Wesley, 1984.

Brand, S.T., Favazza, A.E., and Dalton, E. "Universal Design for Learning: A Blueprint Success for All Learners." *Kappa Delta Pi Record* 48 (July–September 2012): 134–139.

Caine, R.N. and Caine, G. "The Way We Learn." *Educational Leadership* 64, no. 1 (2006): 50–54.

CAST. *UDL Intersections: Universal Design for Learning and Universal Design*. Wakefield, MA: CAST, Inc., 2012.

Chenoweth, K. *It's Being Done: Academic Success in Unexpected Schools*. Cambridge, MA: Harvard Education Press, 2007.

Child Trends Data Bank. "*Parent Involvement in Schools*." Retrieved June 25, 2007, from www.childtrendsdatabank.org/pdf/39.

Christian, J. "Pervasive Development Disorders Overview," in *The Autism and Related Disorders Handbook*, Spring 2002. Retrieved April 30, 2008. http://www.usd.edu/cd/autism/Autism%20Handbook.pdf.

Conlin, M. "The New Gender Gap." *Business Week*. May 26, 2003. http://www.bloomberg.com/news/articles/2003-05-25/the-new-gender-gap.

Diagnostic and Statistical Manual of Mental Disorders, fourth ed., text revision. Washington, DC: American Psychiatric Association, 2000.

Dong, Y.R. "Getting at the Content." *Educational Leadership* 62 (December 2004/January 2005).

Edelson, M.G. "Autism-Related Disorders in DSM-IV," 1995. Retrieved April 4, 2008. http://kildall.apana.org.au/autism/articles/dsm.html.

Ellis, C.R., Kulkarni, R., and Geffen, D. "Autism Overview." *Autism Causes, Symptoms, Diagnosis, and Treatment Information*. October 21, 2005. http://www.emedicinehealth.com/script/main/art.asp?articlekey=59039&pf=3&page=.

Ferguson, R. *Toward Excellence with Equity: An Emerging Vision for Closing the Achievement Gap*. Cambridge, MA: Harvard Education Press, 2008.

Ferguson, R. "The Tripod Project – Weebly," 2013. http://eesadmin.weebly.com/uploads/1/4/0/3/14039000/tri_samplereport_elem_teacher_2013-02-12.pdf.

Ferguson, R. *What Doesn't Meet the Eye: Understanding and Addressing Racial Disparities in High-Achieving Suburban Schools*. Naperville, IL: Learning Point Associates, 2002.

Ferguson, R., Ballantine, A., Bradshaw, R., and Krontiris, C. *Narrowing Achievement Gaps in Lexington Public Schools*. Cambridge, MA: Harvard Graduate School of Education and Harvard Kennedy School of Government, 2015.

Gay, G. *Culturally Responsive Teaching: Theory, Research, and Practice*. New York: Teachers College Press, 2000.

Gardner, H. *Frames of Mind: The Theory of Multiple Intelligences*, 10th anniversary ed. New York, NY: Basic Books, 2011.

Gebhard, M. "Getting Past 'See Spot Run.'" *Educational Leadership* 60, no. 4 (December 2002/January 2003): 35–39.

Gould, J. and Wing, L. "High-Functioning Autism and Asperger Syndrome: What's the Difference?" *The National Autistic Society.* Retrieved September 2008. http://www.autismhampshire.org.uk/about-autism/high-functioning-autism-and-asperger-syndrome-what-is-the-difference.html

Gross, G. "How Boys and Girls Learn Differently." *Huffington Post*, May 16, 2014. http://www.huffing tonpost.com/dr-gail-gross/how-boys-and-girls-learn-differently_b_5339567.html.

Gurian, M. *Boys and Girls Learn Differently!* New York: John Wiley and Sons, 2001.

Gurian, M. "Boys and Girls Learn Differently." *Gurian Institute.* 2015. http://gurianinstitute.com/boys-and-girls-learn-differently.

Gurian, M. and Stevens, K. *Boys and Girls Learn Differently! A Guide for Teachers and Parents,* revised 10th anniversary ed. San Francisco, CA: Jossey-Bass, 2010.

Gurian, M. and Stevens, K. "With Boys and Girls in Mind." *Educational Leadership* 61, no. 3 (November 2004): 21–26.

Heacox, D. *Differentiating Instruction in the Regular Classroom: How to Reach and Teach All Learners, Grades 3–12.* Minneapolis, MN: Free Spirit Publishing, Inc., 2002.

Heacox, D. *Differentiating Instruction in the Regular Classroom: How to Reach and Teach All Learners, Grades 3–12,* updated anniversary ed. Minneapolis, MN: Free Spirit Publishing, Inc., 2012.

Hill, J D. and Flynn, K.M. *Classroom Instruction That Works with English Language Learners.* Alexandria, VA: ASCD, 2006.

Holloway, J. "Closing the Minority Achievement Gap in Math." *Educational Leadership* 61, no. 5 (February 2004): 84–86.

Khan, S. *The One World Schoolhouse: Education Reimagined.* New York: Hachette Book Group, 2012.

Martin, E., Marshall L., and Sales, P. "A 3-Year Study of Middle. Junior High, and High School IEP Meetings." *Exceptional Children* 70, no. 3 (2004): 285–297.

Meyer, A., Rose, D.H., and Gordon, D. *Universal Design for Learning: Theory and Practice.* Wakefield, MA: CAST, Inc., 2014.

National Center on Accessing the General Curriculum. *Differentiated Instruction and Implications for UDL Implementation.* Wakefield, MA: CAST, Inc. and US Department of Education, Office of Special Education Programs, 2014.

National Center for Education Statistics. *National Assessment of Educational Progress: The Nation's Report Card.* Washington, DC: US Department of Education, 2000.

National Center for Education Statistics. National Assessment of Educational Progress: *The Nation's Report Card Mathematics and Reading, 2013.* Washington, DC: US Department of Education, 2014. http://www.nationsreportcard.gov/reading_math_2013/#/student-groups.

National Education Association. *Understanding the Gaps: Who Are We Leaving Behind—and How Far?* Washington, DC: Center for Great Public Schools, 2015.

Pinkus, A. "Toward a One-World Schoolhouse: Interview with Sal Khan." *Independent School* 74 (Winter 2015): 42–46.

Poe, M. "The Other Gender Gap." *The Atlantic* 293, no. 1 (January/February 2004): 137–139.

Reeves, D. "High Performance in High-Poverty School: 90/90/90 and Beyond." http://www.lmsvsd.net/cms/lib2/CA01001633/Centricity/Domain/566/90%20Schools.pdf.

Psychology at Red Rocks Community College. "Learning Style Inventory." Retrieved July 28, 2007. http://www.rrcc-online.com/~psych/LSInventory.html.

Psychology at Red Rocks Community College. "Scoring Procedures." Retrieved July 28, 2007. http://www.rrcc-online.com/~psych/LSscoring.htm.

Rogers, K. *Challenges of Promise.* Edina, MN: Edina Public Schools, 1990.

Rothstein, R. "The Achievement Gap: A Broader Picture." *Educational Leadership* 62, no. 3 (November 2004): 40–43.

Rothstein-Fisch, C., Greenfield, P., and Trumbell, E. "Bridging Cultures with Classroom Strategies." *Educational Leadership* 56, no. 7 (April 1999): 64–66.

Silver, H., Strong, R., and Perini, M. *So Each May Learn: Integrating Learning Styles and Multiple Intelligences.* Alexandria, VA: Association for Supervision and Curriculum, 2000.

Singham, M. "The Achievement Gap: Myths and Reality." *Phi Delta Kappan* 84, no. 8 (April 2003): 586–591.

Singham, M. *The Achievement Gap in US Education: Canaries in the Mine.* Lanham, MD: Rowman and Littlefield Education, 2005.

Smith Myles, B. and Adreon, D. *Asperger Syndrome and Adolescence: Practical Solutions for School Success.* Shawnee Mission, KS: Autism Asperger Company, 2001: 48–134

Sousa, D.A. and Tomlinson, C.A. *Differentiation and the Brain: How Neuroscience Supports the Learner-Friendly Classroom.* Bloomington, IN: Solution Tree Press, 2011.

Stokes, S. "Structured Teaching: Strategies for Supporting Students with Autism." *Autism Papers.* http://www.specialed.us/autism/structure/str10.htm.

Stowe, C.M. *Understanding Special Education: A Helpful Handbook for Classroom Teachers.* New York: Scholastic, Inc., 2005.

Teaching Tolerance. "Culture in the Classroom." http://www.tolerance.org/supplement/culture-classroom.

Teixeira, R., Frey, W.H., and Griffin, R. "States of Change: The Demographic Evolution of the American Electorate, 1974–2060." American Enterprise Institute, Brookings Institution and Center for American Progress, February 2015.

Tomlinson, C.A. "Deciding to Differentiate Instruction in Middle School: One School's Journey." *Gifted Child Quarterly* 39 (1995): 77–87.

Tomlinson, C.A. *The Differentiated Classroom: Responding to the Needs of All Learners*. Alexandria, VA: ASCD, 1999.

Tomlinson, C.A. *The Differentiated Classroom: Responding to the Needs of All Learners*, 2nd ed. Alexandria, VA: ASCD, 2014.

Tomlinson, C.A. "Differentiating Instruction for Academic Diversity." *In Classroom Teaching Skills*, 7th ed., ed. Cooper, J.M. Boston: Houghton Mifflin, 2003.

Tomlinson, C.A. *Fulfilling the Promise of the Differentiated Classroom: Strategies and Tools for Responsive Teaching*. Alexandria, VA: ASCD, 2003.

Tomlinson, C.A. *The Differentiated Classroom: Responding to the Needs of All Learners*, 2nd ed. Alexandria, VA: ASCD, 2014.

Tomlinson, C.A. *How to Differentiate Instruction in Mixed-Ability Classrooms*. Alexandria, VA: ASCD, 1995.

Tomlinson, C.A. *How to Differentiate Instruction in Mixed-Ability Classrooms*, 2nd ed. Alexandria, VA: ASCD, 2001.

Tomlinson, C.A. and Moon, T. *Assessment and Student Success in a Differentiated Classroom*. Alexandria, VA: ASCD, 2013.

Vygotsky, L.S. *Mind in Society*. Cambridge, MA: Harvard University Press, 1978.

"Who are the Highly Gifted?" *Hollingsworth Center for Highly Gifted Children*. http://www.hollingworth.org.

Willey, L.H. No title. Aspie.com. www.aspie.com

Wormeli, R. *Fair Isn't Always Equal: Assessing and Grading in the Differentiated Classroom*. Portland, ME: Stenhouse Publishers, 2006.

Students with Disabilities: Differentiating Instruction

The challenges of being a teacher in today's schools are increasing. One of the primary challenges for teachers is meeting the myriad needs of a diverse student group. Some other challenges include meeting the demands of the curriculum and the accountability that is tied to student achievement. Each decade, there is a shift in the diversity of the students who make up today's classrooms. Currently, 51 percent of the students enrolled in public schools in the United States are considered low-income students (Layton 2015). Approximately 13 percent of students in public schools in the United States are eligible for special education services and have a disability (Institute of Education Sciences 2012). The number of students from culturally and linguistically diverse backgrounds has risen steadily over the past decade to approximately 15 percent nationwide (Layton 2015). These trends are evidence that our classrooms have changed. This requires us to reevaluate our classroom practices to meet the needs of the students who enter every day.

As discussed in this chapter, differentiated instruction is a means to ensure that our strategies align with the needs of the students, it is a responsive approach to the teaching and learning process by which teach-ers use strategies to respond to the instructional needs of their students. As noted earlier, approximately 13 percent of the students in public schools receive special education services. The learning profile for students with disabilities is more complex than that of their peers without disabilities. Teachers are teaching students that have multiple challenges, such as a disability, a second language, and also the impacts of poverty. Therefore, using proactive approaches such as Universal Design for Learning (UDL) and responsive approaches such as differentiated instruction (DI) to meet the needs of our students ensures consistent and improved outcomes for students with disabilities. UDL is a set of principles for curriculum development that gives all individuals the opportunity to learn. It provides a blueprint for creating instructional goals, methods, materials, and assessments that work for everyone, while offering flexibility and the ability to customize based on individual needs (National Center on Universal Design for Learning 2014).

The intensity of various disabilities falls within a spectrum. There are many similarities among students who have a disability, but the where they fall in that spectrum, in terms of the intensity of a disability, can be very different. This is why pairing the principles of UDL with the strategies of DI creates a greater opportunity for students to be successful. One of the key areas outlined in this chapter focuses on the role of the teacher and how important it is to know one's student. Using pre-assessments and interest inventories are two ways to do this. However, in working with students with disabilities, it is important to develop the pre-assessments and inventories in a way that ensures students are able to benefit from taking the pre-assessment or the interest inventory. Pairing principle I of UDL—which calls for providing multiple means of representation—with this differentiated strategy helps ensure that the information is perceivable to the learner and that there are alternate modalities for the student to engage with the pre-assessment or interest inventory.

Learning is impossible if the information is not able to be perceived by the learner (National Center on Universal Design for Learning 2014). Prerecording the pre-assessment or interest inventory allows the student to engage with the same learning activity as the other students, but they do so using a varied modality to meet his or her need. Using recorded assessments is a great opportunity to collaborate with the special education teacher. The general education teacher would provide a copy of the pre-assessment or interest inventory to the special education teacher a few days prior to its being used in the classroom. The special education teacher would read the pre-assessment or inventory and record each item, along with prompts, so that the students are able to complete it. The prompts are to clarify or simplify vocabulary and meaning. Completing the interest inventory can be done by setting up centers in the classroom, giving all of the students choices throughout the class, and recording their level of interest in each activity. For example, free-choice centers would be set up around the room, and students would be instructed to visit each center and rank each center from their favorite to their least favorite. This creates an opportunity for increased engagement and an authentic understanding of the students' interest.

There were several general guidelines referenced in this chapter that have been proven to make it possible for teachers to differentiate their instruction. One guideline is focused on ensuring clarity about key concepts and generalization on the topic of study. For students with disabilities, pairing this guideline to ensure differentiation to UDL principle I ensures access to the unit of study from the planning stage of the unit. Preparing pictures, symbols, and images—versus using words for the students—can ensure clarity. In addition, pre-teaching vocabulary, or using simplified vocabulary and building up to more complex vocabulary over time, can also support students in accessing the unit of study.

Student readiness in a classroom of diverse learners is very important with regard to creating a differentiated classroom. Pairing "readiness-based adjustments" (readiness level is a student's current performance level or his or her level of skill and understanding) with UDL principle II (providing multiple means of action and expression) and principle III (providing multiple means of engagement) expands the opportunity for students with disabilities to access the learning more successfully in the general education classroom (National Center on Universal Design for Learning 2014). For example, using only textbooks or workbooks in print formats limits students whose disability affects them physically. Students with physical disabilities may not have full use of their limbs to turn the pages. Therefore, creating varied methods for response and navigation, such as expanded keyboards or voice-activated switches, are very helpful with students who have these needs. Students who have learning disabilities such as dyslexia, dysgraphia, or language processing disorders would benefit from having options for expression and communication. It is important to note that there is not any one medium of expression that is suited for all learners or for all kinds of communication. For example, a student with dyslexia may be a wonderful oral storyteller; however, when it comes to writing the same story, it will be more challenging or the story will be vastly different than the one that was told orally. The mode of expression should match the readiness and need level of the learner. Matching readiness-based adjustments creates the opportunity for teachers to plan for this based on the needs of their student groups. For teachers, it is helpful to use multiple-media communication when differentiating, such as text-to-speech/speech-to-text technology tools, drawings/illustrations, film/music, or physical manipulatives. For students who struggle academically, being engaged throughout an entire unit of study can often be challenging. For this group of students, starting with less independence and building to greater independence supports them in being engaged throughout the unit. For example, when a standard is first introduced, the teacher may do a lot of direct instruction with the student and work directly with the student on the task. Over time, as the student's level of skill increases, the teacher will give the student a certain amount of the task to complete independently until the student is able to complete the entire task independently. There is one caution, and that is to not take away the opportunity for the students to be challenged. Every student needs to be challenged, just not in the same way. Striking a balance between providing the right resources and building to greater independence gives the students what they need to be successful with the unit or task (National Center on Universal Design for Learning 2014).

Lastly, to create a classroom structure of differentiation that supports students with disabilities requires planning and preparation among teachers and specialists. Finding time to plan and prepare is always a challenge, and will take flexibility and creativity. There are a few creative approaches to secure planning time, such as using early release days and planning units of study instead of individual lessons. This also includes grade levels supporting one another vertically by planning for large group activities and releasing grade-level teachers to plan periodically throughout the year. The building principal can support teachers by provid-

ing substitute teachers at various points throughout the school year so teachers can plan together. Meeting the unique learning needs of students with disabilities in addition to all the other needs in today's classrooms can be a challenge. However, it is a challenge that can be overcome with strong collaboration between grade-level teachers, content-area teachers, and special education teachers and service providers to differentiate the instruction for the students. Chapter 10 will be helpful in better understanding the best practices of co-planning and collaboration.

References

Center for Applied Special Technology. "Universal Design for Learning Guidelines version 2.0." *National Center on Universal Design for Learning*. July 31, 2011. http://www.udlcenter.org/aboutudl/udlguidelines.

"Children and Youth with Disabilities." *Institute of Education Sciences*. January 1, 2014. https://nces.ed.gov/programs/coe/indicator_cgg.asp.

Layton, L. "Majority of US Public School Students Are in Poverty." *Washington Post*, January 16, 2015. http://www.highbeam.com/doc/1P2-37585044.html.

English Language Learners: Differentiating Instruction for Subgroups of ELLs

English learners enter school with rich life experiences during which they have developed the language and culture of their families and communities. They want to figure out how to fit in and immediately participate in school, but they need explicit modeling and teachers' facilitation to use what they know and can do to succeed in school. "They use whatever they know and have learned to make sense of new surroundings, to decipher new routines, to make a friend, to understand language, and to interpret conversations and stories" (Cloud, Genesee, and Hamayan, p. 9). The kind and amount of differentiation teachers provide will depend on an English learner's school experience and skills in his or her native language, reaction to a new environment, current English proficiency level, and rate of progress in attaining English proficiency. While instructional guidance can be offered in relation to general subgroups of English learners, some students may need more or less support because of individual factors (such as diagnosed disabilities, response to trauma, or physical health issues) that

impede or hinder language learning. To differentiate instruction for English learners at various language acquisition stages or proficiency levels, educators can first learn to recognize the characteristics of English learner subgroups. Learners who belong to the subgroups explained in the next section may be additionally affected by conditions related to socioeconomics, immigration, refugee status, and migrant-working conditions. They may have characteristics of more than one subgroup or have other less obvious factors that impede learning, such as home transitions, a new caretaker, a parent that travels for extended periods of time, or family that has recently returned to or has been detained in the home country. English learners will vary in their home-language experiences, educational backgrounds and socioeconomic statuses. Despite their varying characteristics, every English learner will require some differentiated, or sheltered, content instruction based on English proficiency level and academic experience.

Students with Strong Academic Backgrounds in Their Home Language

These English learners may have been born in an English-speaking country or in another country in which a language other than English is spoken. They often read on or above the level expected for their age and grade, and have demonstrated success in learning subject-matter skills and knowledge. Research shows that learners with strong first-language skills are more likely to succeed in acquiring additional languages because they will have what Cummins (1981) calls "common underlying proficiency." This feature of developing bilingualism allows learners to transfer and apply skills, knowledge, and awareness of linguistic patterns learned in the first language to another language. For example, if a student has learned to read in the home language, he or she will not have to relearn the processes of reading or the cognitive abilities to predict, infer, synthesize, or apply knowledge. Instead, when these learners are new to English, they will need rules for decoding words, using language structures, forming sentences (syntax), and learning about meanings in social contexts (pragmatics). When they apply what they already know to demonstrate understanding and skills, instructional scaffolding should decrease rapidly. This type of learner usually learns English quickly, becomes bilingual, and performs at or above native English-speaking peers on high-stakes assessments.

Recommended Support for Success in General Education Classrooms

Like all other students new to English, these learners at the beginning levels will still need to temporarily rely on multisensory support such as modeling, visuals, routines, simple language structures, and tasks. They will immediately make connections between their first language and English, and if the student has developed literacy skills, a word-to-word bilingual dictionary will be useful. When content teachers learn cognates, syntax patterns, word order, and structures used in students' first languages, they can make small adjustments to texts, prompts, and assessments. ESL teachers can also share information about home languages to assist content-area teachers in exploring language connections for core academic classes. For example, students with Latin-based home languages will find connections to scientific vocabulary when they learn to seek out common words or word parts (e.g., English: *education*; Spanish: *educación*; French: *éducation*; Portuguese: *educação*) As these students

rapidly develop English language skills, supports and scaffolding should be removed or changed for the next language proficiency level.

Long-Term English Learners

Long-term English learners are often born and raised in the US or Canada, but the native language is almost always spoken at home. They may code-switch, or insert home language words or phrases into discourse and conversations. It is common for these students to say that they respond in English when they are spoken to in the home language. While they are able to communicate socially in two languages, most long-term English learners have "not yet developed grade-level literacy skills or academic language proficiency in either language" (Echevarria, Short, and Vogt., p. 6). As the language demands in the primary grades increase and rely on literacy skills, the academic gap for long-term English learners begins to widen. By fourth or fifth grade, these students fall far behind their peers because they have not been supported with consistent, explicit modeling of complex language structures, use of academic vocabulary, or study skills. Long-term English learners are often referred for special education services due to a lack of progress in reading and math. By middle school, long-term English learners struggle with motivation and begin to have what Olsen describes as a "sense of failure" (Olsen, p. 7). They lose interest in school and drop out at a rate approximately four times greater than the average (Olsen, p. 7).

Recommended Support for Success in General Education Classrooms

Early identification of potential long-term English learners can activate intensive intervention to develop native language skills. These learners do well on tasks and activities that rely on social discourse, but they struggle with class work that applies literacy skills and academic language. The ESL teacher, reading specialist, and content teacher can meet to plan approaches for explicitly teaching vocabulary, complex language structures, decoding skills, and reading strategies. Long-term English learners will benefit from small-group work focused on intensive literacy and math support to catch up and keep up with their peers who are native English speakers. They will also need to be placed in content classes with native English-speaking peers to engage with challenging curriculum standards and assessments. These learners gain from experience and project-based lessons that provide multisensory ways to acquire information and skills. Likewise, they will need a variety of assessment activities to demonstrate what they have learned and can do. Also recommended are extended-day programs and tutoring that develop study skills and test-taking strategies. A strong home-school connection for homework assistance, independent reading time, and ways to support math-fact practice will help increase success for long-term English learners.

Students with Limited or Interrupted Formal Education (SLIFE)

Most often, these students have been born in a country or community that speaks a language other than English. They enter their new schools in second grade or later with academic skills far below the expected level of K–12 public schools. This English-learner population may have experienced limitations or interruptions in schooling due to war, poverty, lack of access to school, migration, political unrest, natural disaster, or shortage of educational resources and qualified teachers (DeCapua 2009, p. 2). Many students with limited or interrupted formal education (SLIFE) attend school while recovering from the effects of trauma. In addition, SLIFE may experience a period of what Marshall and DeCapua (2013) call "cultural dissonance" or feelings of isolation and bewilderment caused by unfamiliar routines, a new school culture, or unfamiliar approaches to learning. Many SLIFE come from school and community cultures that rely on a collectivist approach to teaching, learning, and living. They rely on others and are encouraged to solve problems through cooperation and teamwork. Relying on a schedule, opening a locker, moving from class to class, and eating at school may be strange and shocking experiences for SLIFE. Multimedia experiences, working with manipulatives, and taking and studying from notes may also be unique practices. Like long-term English learners, SLIFE often become frustrated and unmotivated as the achievement gap widens and they fail to make progress.

Recommended Support for Success in General Education Classrooms

Offering communication, orientation, and skills-building in the home language will ease SLIFE into their new learning environment. On the average, SLIFE will need additional time to acclimatize to routines, schedules, and school culture. They will benefit from all of the strategies used for long-term English learners, but they will also need explicit modeling and discussion of Westernized schooling and academic expectations. SLIFE will need structured and apparent introduction to new entities and activities. They will require intensive literacy and math instruction that considers cultural, emotional, and social factors that may impede learning and successful participation. Providing families with comprehensible information about school culture, academic expectations, community resources, and family support services will also assist SLIFE to be successful in school. Mental health workers, the school counselor, social worker, or psychologist can provide professional development on strategies for helping students feel safe. The ESL teacher or cultural advocate can advise school staff on culturally responsive learning environments and teaching approaches.

English Learners with Diagnosed Disabilities

Distinguishing English learners who struggle from English learners with disabilities can be challenging. Those who make little progress in learning content and language may be referred to a child-study team for interventional strategies. In order to decipher whether an English learner has a disability, several factors should be considered: access to school, educational experience, time spent developing skills in English, and progress made during and after intervention strategies are attempted. If adequate progress is not made with intervention strategies, the team may make a request for evaluation. Before any testing is done, parental consent is necessary, and communication must be done in a language comprehensible to parents and guardians. The results of a recent English-language proficiency assessment and first-language communication should be used to determine the most appropriate language or languages for assessment. Native language testing is appropriate if it is the child's dominant language, or, if the child is bilingual and has two dominant languages, both languages may be used for evaluation.

Once a child has qualified to receive special education services, then ESL, content and special education teachers can meet to discuss best practices and strategies for teaching academic language and content.

Obstacles All Learners Can Overcome

Social, emotional, or cultural factors may become obstacles for any school-age learner regardless of his or her cognitive capability, socioeconomic status, or subgroup. Students learn quicker when they feel confident, motivated, accepted, and happy. Likewise, when students feel isolated, ashamed, or resistant to acculturating to a community, they may lose their motivation and learning will be hindered. While some diverse students demonstrate positive excitement to be in their new environment, and are proud to be bilingual, others may be homesick or resentful due to moving away from familiar surroundings. It is important to keep in mind that children do not change their own environment; rather, adult family members or guardians make the decision to immigrate, work abroad, or move away from home. Families are sometimes unprepared for children's (and their own) reactions to changes in living conditions, home communities, or school cultures. By understanding linguistically diverse learners, schools can better prepare a strong home-school-community network with consistent, comprehensible communication and accessible support resources.

References

Cloud, N., Genesee, G., and Hamayan, E. *Literacy Instruction for English Language Learners: A Teacher's Guide to Research-Based Practices*. Portsmouth, NH: Heinemann, 2009.

Cummins, J. "The Role of Primary Language Development in Promoting Educational Success for Language Minority Students." *Schooling and Language Minority Students: A Theoretical Framework*. Los Angeles, CA: Evaluation, Dissemination, and Assessment Center, California State University, Los Angeles, 1981.

DeCapua, A. and Marshall, H.W. *Breaking New Ground: Teaching Students with Limited or Interrupted Formal Education in US Secondary Schools*. Ann Arbor, MI: University of Michigan Press, 2014.

DeCapua, A., Smathers, W., and Tang, L.F. *Meeting the Needs of Students with Limited or Interrupted Schooling: A Guide for Educators*. Ann Arbor, MI: University of Michigan Press, 2009.

Echevarria, J, Short, D.J., and Vogt, M. *Making Content Comprehensible for Elementary English Learners: The SIOP Model*. Boston: Pearson Education Inc., 2014.

Marshall, H.W. and DeCapua, A. *Making the Transition to Classroom Success: Culturally Responsive Teaching for Struggling Language Learners*. Ann Arbor, MI: University of Michigan Press, 2014.

Olsen, L. *Meeting the Unique Needs of Long-Term English Language Learners: A Guide for Educators*. Washington, DC: National Education Association, 2014.

7

Student Motivation and Succeeding with Students from Poverty

Objectives for the Chapter

After reading the chapter, the reader will be able to

a. increase student motivation of all students by
   i. making learning relevant to students by connecting the curriculum to students' own lives, the real world, and previous learning
   ii. demonstrating our (the teachers') enthusiasm for the knowledge and skills we are teaching
   iii. making learning engaging
   iv. differentiating instruction to make the knowledge and skills accessible to all students
   v. developing respectful teacher-to-student and student-to-student relationships
   vi. demonstrating and developing in students a growth mind-set related to life challenges

b. understand the challenges facing students from poverty and use strategies designed to help them overcome those challenges[1]

c. implement classroom strategies that move students toward the belief that success is due more to effort and acquired strategies than to innate ability and luck

d. explain the key aspects of the following theories of intelligence and their relationship to student motivation
   i. innate, single-entity intelligence (e.g., fixed mind-set)
   ii. growth mind-set (e.g., learnable intelligence)
   iii. multiple intelligences
   iv. attribution of intelligence
   v. deficit mind-set

e. increase student motivation by creating the belief in students that they control their ability to "be smart"

---

1 I use the terms *poverty* and *low-socioeconomic status* interchangeably in this chapter. Growing up next door to a public housing project and trailer park, nearly all of my friends could be classified in this way. Many take offense to the word poverty to describe their circumstances. I use it reluctantly because it has become the "accepted" term by educators, and we strive throughout this book to create and maintain a single common language for educators. I therefore make my apologies to all who take offense at this term.

Bob and Joe were brothers who were separated in age by four years. They lived in a housing project with their parents during the 1960s and early 1970s. Their mother supported the family with her job as a waitress in a diner. Their father was an unemployed alcoholic who would eventually die of cirrhosis of the liver when the boys were approximately 15 and 11 years of age.

Bob was the brother who appeared to have more potential for success (or more "intelligence," as some would say). He attended the local public high school from which the majority of the graduates went on to four-year colleges. He played on the basketball team and was in college preparatory courses.

Joe was a likable young man who made friends easily and was a cooperative student. He went to the regional vocational high school, rather than the high school attended by his brother. At that time in public education, the move to high school was a filtering process. Those who were "smart" enough for college went on to the local public high school. Those who were not went to the technical high school to acquire a trade.

Joe enjoyed his time at the technical high school and became a draftsman. He went to work for a local company. His boss noticed right away that Joe was a hard worker, was personable, and had the potential to advance in the company. He encouraged Joe to go to college. Joe thought about this idea for a long time, because he was unsure if he was "college material." After all, didn't his elementary and middle school teachers indicate he was not college material by recommending vocational high school, rather than the local college preparatory high school? Joe finally decided he would give college a try. Since he was now married and needed the income from his job, he decided he would start going to college at night. Joe eventually received a bachelor's degree in business administration. His degree and hard work earned him a promotion in the company. His confidence in his ability to succeed in the professional and academic worlds (as engendered by his boss and some of his college instructors) rose significantly. Joe enrolled in an MBA program at night while he continued at his job. He completed the MBA and achieved further success in the company. During his MBA work, he developed a particular interest in business law, since this area of study was most relevant to his current employment. He decided to enroll in a part-time law school program. He completed law school and passed the bar exam. Joe went on to become a successful attorney practicing business law.

What about Bob? During high school, Bob worked as a cook in the diner where his mother waited tables. After high school, he continued in that position. During and after high school, Bob also began drinking alcohol to excess. Bob continued to work as a cook in the diner until his untimely death at the age of 47 due to alcohol-related physical problems.

The previous story is a true story. We provide it as context for the following discussion about motivation and the nature of intelligence.

Effective Teaching and Intelligence Theory, and Their Connection to Motivation

There is nothing more exciting than teaching a motivated learner. Their innate enthusiasm for the subject leads to endless motivation to work hard and succeed.

Few things are more challenging for teachers than teaching a learner who lacks motivation.

As teachers, we lay before them the tools for learning (knowledge and skills), and they grasp these tools and proceed to fulfill their insatiable appetite to learn. We feel pride in the part we played in their continuing success.

Few things are more challenging for teachers than teaching a learner who lacks motivation. Bored looks, misbehavior, lack of attendance, lack of attention, and the complaining that accompanies the unmotivated student all serve to make teaching difficult and, at times, discouraging. It would make teaching so much easier if we were able to "cherry pick" our students to ensure that every student entered our class motivated to learn. Unfortunately, that is not the case. Every year, some percentage of the children in our classes lack motivation. Sometimes, this is due to the personal characteristics of the learner; in other instances, it is due to family circumstances; there are also cases where it is due to the previous teaching they received; and, in some cases, it is a combination of all three factors.

A few years ago, one of the authors of this book was training a group of inner-city teachers in the strategies of effective standards-based teaching. Eighty-three percent of the students in the district in which these teachers taught lived below the poverty level, and 93 percent of the students came from homes in which English was not the first language. In the course, the teachers learned new strategies then discussed in their groups how they would implement each strategy in their own classrooms. The instructor found that one group was dominated by a particularly negative teacher. Despite the instructor's and other participants' subtle efforts to move this teacher off of her complaining, she continued to drone on about how "fed up" she was with the students' lack of motivation. She talked about the futility of trying to teach when so many of the students came from homes in which the parents didn't "make them value education" and didn't "help students at home." One of the teachers in the group reached a point where she could no longer listen to the complaining. She turned to this teacher and stated in a loud and annoyed manner, "Ellen, these are the lives of the students who live in this city. These are the children we chose to teach when we decided to teach here. The parents aren't keeping the motivated ones at home!"

We all have times when we feel the same frustration as our complaining teacher. However, it is important that we move on from that frustration and take control of what we can control. It is certainly true that we don't have full control of student motivation.

However, there is much that we can do to increase the motivation of unmotivated students.

Eric Jensen (2013, e-book p. 159 of 3,396) citing studies by Hattie (2008) and Hanushek (2005), determined that, "Teaching matters more than any other factor in a student's school years. In fact, research tells us that quality teaching can completely offset the devastating effects poverty has on students' academic performance. ... If any teacher performs at one standard deviation in quality (as measured by student achievement) above the district's mean adequate yearly progress rate for five years in a row, the resulting improvement in student learning would entirely close the gap between the performance of a typical student from poverty and a higher-income student."

This is not to say that all low-motivation students are students living in poverty or that all students living in poverty have low motivation. However, students from poverty more often have factors in their lives that can inhibit motivation. For example, one motivation-inhibiting factor that is more prevalent with students from poverty is inadequate nutrition. In the case of students from poverty, good nutrition must be added as the seventh component for increasing student motivation. The following seven components are needed for all low-motivation students, regardless of their socioeconomic status.

Seven Components for Increasing Student Motivation

As we have learned more about the nature of intelligence and the components of effective teaching, we've become acutely aware of the connection between these two areas and student motivation. Most experts on student motivation agree that motivation must come from within an individual. True motivation is the result of intrinsic, not extrinsic, forces. External factors such as rewards and consequences can provide temporary motivation or simulate intrinsic motivation. They can also be used to diminish the negative impact a low-motivation student has on the learning of the other students in the class. However, the truly motivated person is driven by a force from within rather than one from the outside. It is a fact of life that people are better at things they like doing than things they don't like doing.

This is not to say that we shouldn't use external rewards and even consequences to get students to work and learn. However, we should only use these

It is true that we don't have full control of student motivation. However, there is much we can do to increase the motivation of unmotivated students.

in circumstances in which we have not yet discovered the "button" that starts a student's (or students') internal motivation.

In this chapter, we will look at the following seven components teachers must develop in their classrooms to maximize student motivation by developing an intrinsic desire to learn:

Component 1: Connecting the curriculum
Component 2: Teacher enthusiasm
Component 3: Engaging teaching
Component 4: Differentiating instruction
Component 5: Interpersonal relationships
Component 6: Teacher and student beliefs about the nature of intelligence and its connection to student motivation
Component 7: (Some students from poverty) Adequate nutrition

The specific strategies used in the implementation of motivation components one through five are discussed in depth in Chapters 1 through 6 of this book. As we discuss each of the first five ways we affect motivation in this chapter, we will refer you back to Chapters 1 through 6 so as not to be repetitive. The large part of this chapter will be spent looking at the sixth way we affect motivation. It examines the ways in which students and teachers view intelligence and how these views and the practices they engender affect student motivation.

It is important to keep in mind as you read this chapter that there isn't a one-size-fits-all solution to the issue of unmotivated learners. Each learner is motivated in his or her own way. Therefore, some strategies will work well with some learners and not work at all with others.

Changing a student's motivation is a process that can be slow in developing. The older the student, the longer it often takes to make the change. We should remember that when the student comes to us, he or she has lived for years within a negative cycle that has contributed to the current lack of motivation. In Figure 7.1 on the next page, we see that failure or the fear of failure has led to masking behaviors (avoidance and disruptive behavior). These masking behaviors have led to reactions from adults and peers that have reinforced the student's belief that he or she is not intelligent, which in turn leads to more avoidance behavior, and so on.

This chapter looks at the ways we can reverse this negative cycle and create a new cycle like the one in Figure 7.2. In this cycle, the teacher implements strategies that start the change. We must remember

Figure 7.1 Creates a Deficit Perspective

Lack of effort because of the belief that my failures are due to an innate lack of intelligence and so effort will not contribute to the same level of success others enjoy.

This reinforces my belief that intelligence is innate and that I was not one of the people with the good fortune to have been born intelligent.

Cycle of Low Internal Motivation

Disruptive and/or avoidance behaviors (e.g., not doing homework) that hide my perceived lack of intelligence behind a message to my teachers and my peers that my lack of success is due to my indifference about learning and my belief that school success is not important (or even to be reviled).

Teachers (and at times parents and peers) respond to my constant display of these behaviors with frustration that leads to a diminished relationship and sends me the message that they see me as "bad" or not intelligent.

that the change in the student's behavior will come slowly because there have been many previous years in which the old cycle has been nurtured, resulting in deep roots. In some cases, we may see only small changes during our year with this student. However, the new cycle we set in motion will move on with the student and benefit him or her in future years.

As educators, there are specific ways we can change this cycle in the classroom. We can also work with parents (see Chapter 9) to help them to understand the cycle and support the change at home. However, as is the case in many families from poverty, this may be more difficult because of the barriers to home communication and the difficult family situations that are more prevalent in those homes. As we saw above, Joe's cycle was changed by people in his life other than parents who provided him with the belief that he could acquire the skills to make himself intelligent. The dynamics in his home made it less likely (probably unlikely) that the parents would have been able to take an effective role in this process.

Component 1: Connecting the curriculum. In Chapter 2, we looked at the importance of creating a cognitive context for learning. One of the ways in which we discussed achieving this was to make learning relevant by helping students make connections.

These included connecting the curriculum to students' own lives, connecting the curriculum to the real world, and connecting new learning to prior knowledge. These connections are important to all students. However, they are particularly important to students with low motivation. For many of these students, "school" has no relevance to their lives. Connecting learning and making learning relevant create a sense of interest. In her book, *Increasing Student Motivation Strategies for Middle and High School Teachers*, Margaret Theobald (2006) tells us, "Students need to recognize and find the relevance to their own lives in what you are teaching. If students can make a connection to what they already know about in their lives and experiences, it is more likely they will be more interested in what you have to say" (pp. 6–7).

Component 2: Teacher enthusiasm. Demonstrating our (the teacher's) enthusiasm for the knowledge and skills we are teaching can infect students with enthusiasm. In Chapter 2, we talked about the impact of teachers conveying passion and enthusiasm for the content and for learning in general. Theobald (2006) says it well: "Students watch their teachers. If we cannot be excited about teaching and learning, then we cannot expect the students to be excited" (p. 26). This excitement helps generate students' focus on

Figure 7.2 Creates a Growth Mind-Set

Lack of effort because of the student's belief that failures are due to an innate lack of intelligence and that effort will not contribute to the same level of success others enjoy.

Teacher has more to praise, continues relationship-building, continues teaching effective effort strategies, continues to use teaching that engages the student and is matched to his/her learning style, and continues community-building.

Teacher uses relationship-building strategies that cause the student to feel liked and respected by the teacher. The teacher uses engaging and differentiated teaching that enables the student to have small successes. The teacher uses effective praise, strategies that teach the student that success is due to effective effort, and uses strategies that build class community.

Reversing the Cycle of Low Internal Motivation

Student expends more effort, acquires more strategies, and has more success.

Student begins to believe he/she can succeed with effective effort, and experiences the good feelings related to success. This results in a reduced need to use disruptive and/or avoidance behaviors to hide his/her lack of perceived intelligence behind a message to the teachers and peers that his/her lack of success is due to indifference about learning and the belief that school success is not important.

what is being taught. Focus is an important part of this component, as is making teaching engaging, which we discuss in the next component.

"We learn best with **focused attention**. As we focus on what we are learning, the brain maps that information on what we already know, making new neural connections" (Goleman 2013, e-book p. 15 of 258). As described in Chapter 2, these connections lead to deeper understanding and longer retention of the knowledge and skills.

Component 3: Engaging teaching. Chapters 1 through 6 of this book discuss myriad ways teachers make learning engaging. Chapter 1 talks about planning and teaching in ways that begin by clearly telling students what they will know and be able to do as a result of the teaching. Theobald (2006) tells about the "need to understand how several small tasks can lead to the accomplishment of a larger goal. Teachers need to communicate to students what the relationship is. Knowing that small successes will lead to a larger one will motivate students to continue to work" (p. 64). Using agendas (a.k.a. itineraries) and posting and stating mastery objectives are two of the ways we do this for students. Another way we do this is by providing students with scoring guides (criteria sheets, rubrics, exemplars, or anchor papers), as described in Chapter

4, which enable them to check their own incremental progress toward the larger goal. Chapters 4 and 5 also teach us to assess student progress in ways that will enable us to differentiate instruction so the knowledge and skills are at a level more closely matched to each student's **zone of proximal development**. In Chapter 3, we discussed that learning geared above or below a student's zone of proximal development can lead to frustration or boredom, respectively. Boredom leads to low motivation. Frustration leads to the feelings of being "dumb." As we will see later in this chapter, this leads to students either giving up or trying to hide the fact that they are "dumb" behind misbehavior or an attitude of indifference.

Jensen (2013, e-book p. 86 of 3,396) tells us that engagement is particularly important for students from poverty. He explains that home factors such as poor nutrition (e-book p. 198 of 3,396) and family relationship deficits (e-book p. 296 of 3396) can make engaging these students even more challenging. All the strategies discussed in this book become even more important for our students from poverty.

Brain development related to nutrition and other factors in poverty homes may also contribute to lower engagement. **A longitudinal study analyzing MRI scans of 389 typically developing children and** adolescents at six US (research) sites found that children from poor families showed systematic structural differences in brain development, specifically in the hippocampus and in the frontal and temporal lobes. In contrast, there were no statistically significant differences in the brain regions between children of near-poor families and those from higher socioeconomic-status groups.

Component 4: Differentiating instruction. Differentiating instruction, as taught in Chapter 6, will make the knowledge and skills accessible to all students. Many students experience frustration because the way in which the knowledge and skills are taught is incompatible with the way they learn. The content may be at a level that is well matched to the student. However, the process used to teach the knowledge and skills may keep the student from successfully acquiring the knowledge and skills. In other circumstances, the students have acquired the appropriate knowledge and skills; however, they are unable to demonstrate this because the assessment is structured in a way that does not allow the student to demonstrate his or her level of mastery.

Component 5: Interpersonal relationships. Developing teacher-to-student and student-to-student relationships plays a key role in student motivation. In recent years, we have seen a proliferation of information about the importance of these relationships in improving student motivation and achievement. In his book, *Activating the Desire to Learn*, Bob Sullo tells us, "Related to the universal need to connect, positive relationships improve the mental health of students. Connected, happier students are likely to do higher-quality work as well" (2007, p. 16). Sullo (2013, e-book, p. 307 of 2,332) also talks about how the relationship between teacher and student influences our ability to change behavior that gets in the way of the students' learning. "If we have negative feelings about someone, it significantly affects how we interpret information they offer. If you and I have a negative relationship and you try to help me see my behavior is causing me problems, I will perceive you as meddlesome even if you are well meaning." Jones, Boffard, and Weissbourd (2013, p. 62) cite numerous studies that indicate that "when students have high-quality relationships with teachers, they have better social adjustment and higher academic competence."

Relationships with other students are also important. In their article, "Promoting Student Resilience in School Contexts" (2007), Gale Morrison and Megan Redding Allen tell us, "If students have poor social skills, a lack of friends, and have poor relationships with teachers, they are at serious risk of failure" (p. 63).

In Chapter 3, we discussed the impact of positive teacher-to-student and student-to-student relationships in fostering appropriate student behavior. The strategies suggested in that chapter that resulted in students feeling connected to their peers and their teacher can also lead to increased motivation in many students. In their book, *Engaging Troubling Students,* Scot Danforth and Terry Jo Smith (2005) talk about the close interconnection between student behavior and student motivation and how poor interpersonal relationships negatively affect both of these areas.

> The most common teacher complaints about students considered troubling are that (a) they are frequently off task, not doing their assignments, and not sufficiently engaged in academic work; and (b) they don't get along well with their peers, interacting in negative or disrespectful ways. There are many emotional, human reasons why academic disengagement and socially disruptive behavior go together.… Some students fear being exposed as poor readers or unable mathematicians. The average classroom places academically struggling students in difficult emotional positions all day long by highlighting weaknesses. Frustration and feelings of inadequacy are daily events that confound attempts to build a positive concept of self. For these students, preserving the self and saving face in the context of a devaluing academic environment is often crucial. Taking on the role of "bad guy" or "tough guy" may be greatly preferred to seeming and feeling stupid (p. 111).

One of the traps we can fall into when working with low-motivation students is letting our well-deserved frustration with their lack of effort (and, in some cases, with their disruptive behavior) show in our interactions with them. In their article, "The Importance of Teacher-Student Relationships for Adolescents with High-Incidence Disabilities" (2007), Christopher Murray and Robert Pianta tell us that,

> historically, teachers have held more negative attitudes and directed more negative behaviors towards students with disabilities and low-achieving students than towards high-achieving students. This includes lower levels of emotional support, praise, and other positive behaviors and greater levels of criticism, ignoring, and negative behavior.

In our work with hundreds of teachers in the area

of classroom management, we have found that this behavior toward these students is often unconscious. This dynamic should not be surprising, given that the motivated student who behaves well is easy to praise and enjoyable to teach. The low-motivated students, particularly those who act out in class, generate frustration and even anger in us. Despite our best efforts not to show these feelings, they can sneak through in our tone of voice, facial expression, and even in our words. Oftentimes, we are not even aware of this. After all, we are only human! Unfortunately, the result is that some of the students who are most motivated by the need to be liked and respected by their teachers are the ones who least feel this connection with the teacher.

"Often, low-SES (socioeconomic status) students have no stable adult role models, so teachers need to embrace the 'parent' (matriarch or patriarch) role in school. Treating your class as a family can reduce discipline issues and improve learning. For example, social bonding and trust help mitigate the adverse effects of chronic stress by prompting the brain to release oxytocin, a neuropeptide that suppresses the 'classic' stress hormones, such as cortisol" (Kosfeld, Heinrichs, Zak, Fischbacher, and Fehr 2005).

Feeling frustrated by a student who exhibits a lack of effort and demonstrates disrespect and even disdain toward us is a natural human response. Telling teachers not to feel this way is not very helpful. Although we have some capacity to control these feelings, the reality is we feel what we feel. Just as there are adults we like and dislike in our lives, there are students we like more than others and some we may even dislike. The difference in a classroom situation is that we are in a captive relationship with one another for a full school year. The best way to approach these situations is to "fake it 'til we make it." Even though our emotions toward a certain low-motivated student may not be positive, we should work to ensure that our behavior does not betray these feelings. Searching for small successes to praise[2] in a sincere fashion is an

> *Often, low-SES (socioeconomic status) students have no stable adult role models, so teachers need to embrace the "parent" role in school. Treating your class as a family can reduce discipline issues and improve learning. For example, social bonding and trust help mitigate the adverse effects of chronic stress by prompting the brain to release oxytocin that suppresses the "classic" stress hormones.*

essential first step to getting this student to begin to reverse his or her low-motivation behavior.

We have all had students who produced high-quality schoolwork for us who would not produce similar quality work for other teachers. We have also known students who don't produce quality school work for us but do produce it for another teacher. We have seen this situation in a number of urban high schools in which we have worked with teachers. An example of this is the student athlete who shows no motivation or interest in any class except the one taught by his or her coach. Or the student who loves acting, participates in the school plays, and produces his or her best work for the English teacher who also happens to be the head of the drama club. Sometimes this is motivation by fear. However, more often, it is due to the relationship that has developed between the teacher and student, within and outside of the classroom.

For some low-motivation students, there is also a feeling of isolation from their peers. Their lack of connection with the teacher is compounded by a lack of connection with others in the class. In Chapter 3, we discussed how this lack of connection with peers and the teacher can lead to acting-out behavior on the part of these students. Above, we discussed how this lack of connection can also result in low motivation. Chapter 3 contains some specific strategies teachers can use to develop a sense of community in classrooms.

This connection is often more difficult to establish for elementary music, art, and P.E. teachers, and/or middle and high school teachers. In regular elementary school classrooms, students often spend the full day with the same teacher. This provides ample opportunity for the teacher to connect with students and for students to connect with one another. In middle schools, the students may or may not stay with the same classmates all day. However, they almost always have two, three, four, or more teachers in a given day. Connecting in high school can be even more difficult than in middle school. Students see few of the same students from class to class and have five, six, or more teachers in a week.

In elementary art, music, and P.E., students often attend these classes with the same classmates. However, the amount of time they are with this teacher is significantly less than the time they spend with their classroom teachers. From the teacher's perspective,

---

2   For these students, we will need to decide whether public praise or private praise is the best match for the student. Some of our low-motivation students have spent years criticizing school success, with their words and actions, in front of their peers as a defense against their feelings of inadequacy. Praising them in public for academic or behavioral success could negatively affect their behavior as they seek to prove to their peers that success in school is something to be shunned, not sought. For more information on the effective use of praise, please refer to Chapter 5.

it is not unusual for a teacher in these disciplines to see 200, 300, or more students in a week. High school classroom teachers have a similar dilemma. It is not unusual for these teachers to see 100, 120, or more students in a day. Under these circumstances, the opportunity to build relationships is restricted to short periods of time.

To counter this challenge, many middle and high schools are adopting advisor-advisee programs. These are programs in which each teacher is assigned a small group of students with whom he or she meets regularly. The activities in these group meetings can include academic counseling, social skills training, and other forms of community-building. The students have an opportunity to build strong connections to a small group of students and at least one member of the faculty.

We also saw the role of connections come into play in the case of Bob and Joe, whom we read about at the start of the chapter. Joe's ability to connect with and cooperate with classmates and work colleagues made it easier for him to avoid the tag of "problem student/worker" with his teachers and employers. The extra attention and encouragement given to him by one boss contributed significantly to changing the direction of his professional life.

Creating relationships that result in higher motivation with our students and among our students can feel overwhelming, given the demands of the curriculum. To avoid our own frustration and feelings of failure at not being able to do this as well as we would like, it is important that we start small and be realistic about the level of change that will occur. For example, try the following:

1. Choose one low-motivation student to work with and work to build the relationship with this one student.
2. Acknowledge to yourself any negative feelings you have toward this student, and then commit yourself to consciously ensuring that your facial expressions and tone of voice don't betray your frustration when interacting with this student.
3. Next, you can move toward looking for opportunities to praise the student and finding small pieces of time when you can have a private conversation with the student about something that is important to him or her.
4. Remember, it is important that you don't expect to see significant change in this student, as this

By age 3, children from professional, educated families have heard at least 30 million more words than children from less educated families who receive welfare.

will result in your feeling disappointed and perhaps feeling like a failure. Remember, this student has had many years of negative feelings related to school success building in him or her prior to coming to you. Any change will be slow in coming and will often be followed by periods of regression. Like so many things related to changing student behavior, this is a two-steps-forward, one-step-backward process.

Component 6: Teacher and student beliefs about the nature of intelligence and its connection to student motivation. Above, we have looked at five ways teachers can help engender intrinsic motivation in students. In the remainder of the chapter, we will look specifically at the sixth way we can influence student motivation. This section examines the way in which students and teachers view intelligence and how the practices and behaviors that result from these views affect student motivation.

Many unmotivated students have given up. They have come to believe they are "dumb" and that they have no power to make themselves smart. We will look at ways that teachers help students to believe that they control their ability to "be smart." We will identify specific classroom strategies used with students that move students toward the belief that success is due more to effort and implementation of acquired strategies than to innate ability and luck.

With children from poverty, this belief can be even more prevalent. Many arrive at school with learning deficits as compared to their counterparts from higher-socioeconomic status families. For example, by age three, children from professional, educated families have heard at least 30 million more words than children from less educated families who receive welfare. Their reduced ability to understand what the teacher is saying can lead to lower achievement and feeling stupid (Hart and Risley 2003).

The Nature-versus-Nurture Debate

For more than 130 years, educators, social scientists, and psychologists have debated the question of whether intelligence is innate or acquired. It is part of the age-old nature-versus-nurture argument that continues to this day. We begin this next section by looking at the two perspectives on the nature of intelligence and their impact on motivation. The first is the idea that all or most of *our intelligence is genetic and a single entity*. Theorists in this school of thought say that there is relatively little that schools can do to influence the intelligence of a student. The second idea is that *intelligence is learnable and multifaceted.* This school of thought's proponents believe that most of a person's school and career success (up to 75 percent, according to some theorists) is the result of environment (school, home, and others), effort, acquired strategies for thinking and learning, and the person's attitude toward success and failure.

Intelligence as a Single Entity and Primarily Due to Heredity

As early as 1869, British scientist Francis Galton wrote the book *Hereditary Genius: Its Laws and Consequences.* In it, he spoke about genetics as the primary determinant of intelligence. American psychologists extrapolated from this the concept of **intelligence quotient (IQ)**. This was a measurable intelligence that was native and stayed constant throughout a person's life (Devlin, Fienberg, Resnick, and Roeder 1997, p. 2).

In their book *Intelligence, Genes, and Success* (Devlin, Fienberg, Resnick, and Roeder 1997, p. 5), the authors describe Galton's work as follows:

> Galton was a central figure in the founding of the **eugenics** (a term he coined in 1883) movement and the study of the relationship of heredity to race and talent. From his analysis of biographical dictionaries and encyclopedias, he became convinced that talent in science, the professions, and the arts ran in families so that it would be 'quite practicable to produce a highly gifted race of men by judicious marriages during several consecutive generations' (Kelves 1985).

Interesting to note is that Galton was a cousin to Charles Darwin and was influenced by his cousin's work as it appeared in Darwin's famous book, *On the Origin of Species by Means of Natural Selection.*

Karl Pearsons, one of the founders of modern statistical methods, devised statistical methods for establishing the correlation between hereditary intelligence and success in society. Pearsons would later join the University of London and become the Galton Eugenics Professor. He went on to publish some 300 works dealing with the relationships between population traits and social behaviors, occupations, and diseases. In describing intelligence, he was quoted as stating,

> *Binet was not a proponent of the idea that intelligence was a fixed, single entity that was established at birth.*

"No training or education can create [it]. You must breed it" (Kelves 1985).

The person best known for developing a measurement for intelligence was Alfred Binet, a psychologist at the Sorbonne in France between 1894 and 1911. The first intelligence test described by Binet and a colleague in 1896 involved counting objects in pictures, noting similarities among familiar objects, filling in missing words in sentences, and describing how terms had different meanings (Devlin, Fienberg, Resnick, and Roeder 1997, p. 9). In 1904, Binet was asked to develop a way to determine which French schoolchildren needed extra help. He introduced his method for measuring a child's performance against the trends of other children in 1908. His system measured a child's mental age in relation to the child's physical age. This was the first step in developing the concept of *intelligence quotient* or *IQ* (Perkins 1995, pp. 23–26).

Binet, however, was not a proponent of the idea that intelligence was a fixed, single entity that was established at birth. Perkins (1995) describes Binet's reticence to reach this conclusion:

> He (Binet) did not jump from the fact that some people behave more intelligently than others to the presumption that there was one essence, a single mental resource, that some people had more of and some less. … He feared it would offer educators the excuse to ignore the plight of poorly performing students on the grounds that they lacked the intelligence to do better. It also might give educators grounds for dismissing under motivation and behavior problems as symptoms of low intelligence (p. 29).

Carol Dweck (2006) quotes Binet (1909) from his work, *Modern Ideas about Children*:

> A few modern philosophers … assert that an individual's intelligence is a fixed quantity, a quantity which cannot be increased. We must protest and react against this brutal pessimism. … With practice, training, and, above all, method, we manage to increase our attention, our memory, [and] our judgment, and literally to become more intelligent than we were before. (p. 6)

Henry Goddard authored the first American version of an IQ test in 1908 and administered it to 2,000 school children in Vineland, NJ. It was the Americans, between 1908 and 1925, who took Binet's individually administered intelligence tests and turned them into paper-and-pencil, group-administered tests. To do this, they created a single-entity IQ score to replace the mental age and chronological age scores developed by Binet that were difficult to interpret. Stanford psychologist Lewis Terman imported Binet's test to the United States and developed the Stanford-Binet IQ test (Gould 1995, in Fraser 1995, p. 11). Terman recognized that as long as IQ tests had to be administered one on one by a trained psychologist, they would be too expensive to use widely. He and graduate student William Otis developed the first Army Alpha test that was administered to 1.7 million army recruits between 1917 and 1919. That test would eventually be renamed the Armed Services Vocational Battery and was used during World War II. It continues to be used today by all branches of the military service (Devlin, Fienberg, Resnick, and Roeder 1997, pp. 9–10).

Terman believed that intelligence was hereditary, as documented in his 1922 article, "Were We Born That Way?" that appeared in the journal *World's Work*. In that article, he states:

> The common opinion that the child from a cultured home does better in tests by reason of his superior home advantages is an entirely gratuitous assumption.... The children of successful parents test higher than children from wretched and ignorant homes for the simple reason that their heredity is better.

The data derived from the Alpha tests began to drive the belief in American society that certain cultures were genetically more intelligent than others. Princeton psychology professor Carl C. Brigham wrote the book *A Study of American Intelligence* based on the findings from the Alpha tests. Brigham (1923) concluded that the immigration of southern and eastern Europeans to the United States would lower native American intelligence. One year later, Congress passed the Immigration Restriction Act of 1924, which enabled a disproportionate level of immigration by northern and western Europeans, who were thought to be more intelligent. In the United States Supreme Court case *Buck v. Bell* in 1927, the court supported sterilization laws passed in 16 states between 1907 and 1917. In that opinion, noted justice Oliver Wendell Holmes wrote, "Three generations of imbeciles are enough" (Hernstein and Murray 1994, p. 5).

In 1912, German psychologist W. Stern improved

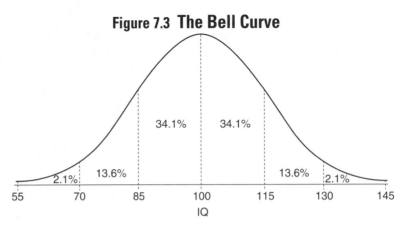

Figure 7.3 The Bell Curve

on Binet's format for determining IQ. Stern (Perkins 1995, pp. 26–28) developed a system in which a person's mental age was divided by his or her actual age. This number was then multiplied by 100. For example, a 10 year old who had a mental age of 10 would have an IQ of 100—that is, 10 divided by 10 equals one. One multiplied by 100 equals 100. A 10-year-old with a mental age of 11 would have an IQ of 110. Eleven divided by 10 equals 1.1, and 1.1 multiplied by 100 equals 110. A 10 year old with a mental age of nine would have an IQ of 90. This gave rise to the bell curve with which we are all so familiar (see Figure 7.3).

Stern's method worked well for children but became a problem when applied to adults. The mental-versus-chronological age comparison no longer worked when applied to people in their 40s and 50s. Another method was needed that might be applied to adults and children. Today, psychologists still use a bell-shaped curve such as the one in Figure 7.3. In today's model, IQ is no longer determined by dividing mental age by actual age. Instead, it is normed against the results of a large number of people who are tested to determine average scores and the various standard deviations from the average. The number 100 continued to be used for the average score solely to be consistent with Stern's model. The standard deviation of 15 was also used so as to continue with the familiar numbers from Stern's work. Stern found a standard deviation of approximately 15 or 16.

In the general population, more than 68.2 percent of the people have IQs between 85 and 115, while 13.6 percent of the population has an IQ between 115 and 130. Another 2.1 percent of the population has an IQ between 130 and 145. Only 0.2 percent of the population has an IQ above 145. The same is true for the left side of the distribution, with 13.6 percent of the population having an IQ between 85 and 70, 2.1 percent with an IQ between 70 and 55, and only 0.2 percent with an IQ lower than 55.

In the 1930s and 1940s, the United States' public was well on its way to believing that intelligence could be defined by a single score, was genetically inherited, and varied by race. Everyone in education has at some time come across the Wechsler Intelligence Scale for Children, commonly known as the WISC. Psychologist David Wechsler developed his first version of the test in the 1930s. This test, in its revised form, is still used in schools to determine student IQ.

In 1957, psychologist Ann Anastasi noted at meetings of the American Psychological Association that the nature-versus-nurture debate about intelligence had subsided because geneticists, psychologists, and social scientists had become convinced that nature and nurture were interactive and interrelated as they pertained to intelligence. In 1958, she indicated in an article in *Psychological Review* that the focus on the study of intelligence must be on the interaction of both nature and nurture (Anastasi, in Devlin, et al. 1994).

As the 1960s approached, most educators believed that some part of intelligence (or lack thereof) was developmental and not hereditary. Lyndon Johnson's Great Society program brought Head Start to schools in an effort to reverse the negative impact of the home environment in socioeconomically deprived homes. The belief was that early intervention would enable students to "catch up" intellectually with their peers from socioeconomically advantaged homes.

Nevertheless, educators were not ready to let go of the concept that intelligence was fixed at some point early in a child's life. Educators determined that tracking by ability in schools was required to ensure that the less intelligent were not frustrated and overwhelmed and the more intelligent were not held back by the slow pace of the others. Millions of Baby Boom children were placed in fixed-ability reading and math groups as early as first grade. Junior high and high schools were tracked by ability. Junior high students like Bob and Joe were even funneled to either academic college preparatory high schools or vocational high schools, depending on whether they were deemed intelligent enough to go to college.

One school district in southern Connecticut during the late '60s and early '70s went so far as to place eighth graders into fourteen[3] separate "divisions"

Millions of Baby Boom children were placed in fixed-ability reading and math groups as early as first grade.

based on ability. The elementary schools in the city were neighborhood schools from kindergarten to grade seven. All eighth-grade students in the district attended a single school before moving on to high school. Based on the students' grades, scores from the Iowa Tests of Basic Skills, teacher recommendations, and aptitude tests in mathematics and foreign language, each student was placed in one of the 14 levels. Each level had a distinct and public number designation from one to 14, which was used to identify the class for various school activities. For example, on school picture day, the secretary would periodically make an announcement when it was time for another class to come for their pictures. "Division 14, please report to the cafeteria for your pictures" would be announced in all classrooms.

These educators were not cruel or uncaring. Contemporary wisdom firmly believed that the needs of all the students were best met when grouped by ability. This belief was so strong in society that neither the public nor professional educators saw any problem with grouping students by ability and clearly identifying them, as in this example from the Connecticut school.

The late '70s through the '80s and '90s brought an increased belief in the malleability of intelligence based on home and school environment. This belief led to a reduction of tracking in our schools, typically occurring first in the lower grades. Fixed reading and math groups were reduced or eliminated first in the primary grades. This change slowly moved up the grades until heterogeneous and flexible grouping became the primary structure in most schools through fifth grade. Many districts changed to the middle school concept (with sixth, seventh, and eighth grades grouped together) and reduced the degree of tracking.

Myths about Families Living in Poverty

Those of us who work with children from low-socioeconomic (low-SES) or poverty families must be cautious that we do not fall into the trap of believing some of the myths about low-income families. In his article, "The Myth of the 'Culture of Poverty,'" Paul Gorski (2008) coined the phrase *deficit perspective*. **Deficit perspective is the tendency some of us have to consciously or unconsciously focus on what students from poverty lack rather than their strengths. For most of us, this comes from a heartfelt compassion for these children.** We recognize the gap between the opportunities they have and those available to

---

3   There were actually 18 separate ability-based divisions in the city. However, because the eighth-grade building was overcrowded, four of the divisions were housed in the high school at a different location. These four classes operated as their own school, with the classes labeled as Divisions 1, 2, 3, and 4. This left 14 divisions in the primary building.

middle- and upper-income children. This can lead to lower academic expectations for these children. These lower expectations can, in turn, lead to a self-fulfilling prophecy that results in lower academic achievement on the district standards. This is not to say that these students don't have more obstacles to overcome than middle- and upper-income students in order to reach the same level of achievement. However, the response to this reality is to create scaffolds that overcome these obstacles rather than to reduce expectations. Later in this chapter, we will talk about the ways in which school districts have dealt with the obstacles to reading more frequently faced by children from low-income families who have less access to reading material.

The deficit perspective sometimes results from mistaken beliefs about families living in poverty. Below are some examples of these mistaken beliefs and the reality of these families.

1. There is a "culture of poverty" that defines the values of most children and families who live in poverty. For example, some believe these families have less of a work ethic and lower motivation. The National Center for Children in Poverty (2004) found that 60 percent of these families have at least one parent who works full-time year round. In fact, the Economic Policy Institute (2002) found that poor working adults often work two and three low-wage jobs, spending more hours working each week than their wealthier counterparts.

2. Low-income parents attend few school events because they don't value education as much as higher-income parents. The National Center of Education Statistics found that these parents attend fewer school events because they have less access. Working multiple jobs, having jobs that lack paid leave to attend school events, lack of child care, and the lack of transportation were found to be significant impediments to these parents' ability to attend school events.

3. Poor people tend to abuse drugs and alcohol more readily than their wealthier counterparts. Diala, Muntaner, and Walrath (2004) and Galea, Ahern, Tracy, and Vlahov (2007) found that when alcohol use was grouped with illicit drug use, wealthy people were more likely than poor people to be substance abusers.

Expectations and modified beliefs alone will not equalize achievement among the students from all socioeconomic levels. However, targeted scaffolds accompanied by higher expectations and the avoid-

ance of inaccurate beliefs will go a long way toward equalizing these levels of achievement.

The Nature-versus-Nurture Debate Continues

Even with these changes occurring in schools, proponents of the concept of intelligence as a single, fixed entity and primarily determined by heredity continued to promote these concepts. In the books *The Bell Curve* (1994) and *Real Education* (2009), the authors reestablished the concept of inherited, fixed, single-entity intelligence as a viable theory of intelligence. The authors, Richard Hernstein and Charles Murray, used a comprehensive review of the research on intelligence over the previous 125 years to conclude that intelligence was primarily hereditary and that it varied by race and culture. The book reignited a fiery ideological debate in academia and among the general public between those who adhere to this theory and those who believe that intelligence has multiple components and may be enhanced by home and school environments.

An article in the November 11, 2007 *New York Times* warns that "nonscientists are already beginning to stitch together highly speculative conclusions about the historically charged subject of race and intelligence from the new biological data." It notes several occurrences of these nonscientists making the case for superior genetic intelligence based on a person's continent of origin or race. The article goes on to describe several recent studies by geneticists that have isolated specific genes to specific races or continents of origin as they relate to a predisposition to certain diseases or illnesses. However, these geneticists are quick to point out that there is no genetic evidence at this time that supports any genetic link to higher intelligence in people of one race or continent of origin over another.

Intelligence as Having Multiple Components That May Be Enhanced by Home and School Factors

The genesis of the idea that intelligence is actually a composite of multiple components came from Alfred Binet. David Perkins (1995) credits Binet with presenting us with the first suggestion that there may be multiple intelligences:

Binet looked at a great variety of kinds of human

behavior to gauge intelligence.... He tested children every which way, and the more ways the better. So long as the task did not depend much on unusual rote knowledge or reading and writing it was fine with Binet.... He took this approach because he believed that intelligence, far from being one thing, was a potpourri, a mix of this ability and that ability all jumbled together (p. 25).

For the next 50 years, Binet's thoughts about intelligence containing multiple components were largely ignored as psychologists, educators, and social scientists strove to find ways to establish a person's innate intelligence as a way of socially engineering aspects of society, including the military, education, and the workforce. As stated earlier, the largest body of work in this area at the turn of the twentieth century was for the purpose of efficiently determining job classifications for the military. Schools used the results to determine effective means of tracking students for efficient instruction. Bob (whom we spoke about at the beginning of this chapter) was sent from junior high school to a high school to prepare him for college. Joe went off to a vocational school to prepare him to enter the workforce with a trade after high school graduation.

In the 1970s, University of Pennsylvania psychologist Jonathan Baron examined the relationship between strategies and intelligence. Baron's studies looked at the memories of mildly retarded children versus those of children with average intelligence. In his 1978 article, "Intelligence and General Strategies," Baron showed that the significant gap in the achievement on memory tasks that existed between children with average intelligence and mildly retarded children might be closed by teaching the mildly retarded children strategies that enhanced their memory.

Lloyd Humphreys, a psychologist at the University of Illinois in Urbana, looked at the changes in the IQ test scores between soldiers tested in 1917 and those tested in 1942. Humphreys found a 15-point increase (one standard deviation) in the scores of those tested in 1942. Humphrey credits that increase to the expansion of public education during those years (Perkins 1995, pp. 77–79).

In the 1980s, University of Virginia psychologist Sandra Scarr examined the relationship between genetics and environment in a series of studies using identical twins. Identical twins were chosen because of their identical genetic makeup. Scarr identified groups of twins who were separated at birth and raised in different homes. Scarr's work, combined with that of others, established that IQ was 50 percent to 60 percent attributable to heredity, with the remaining 40 percent to 50 percent attributable to nurturing factors.

The research on the variability of IQ continues to uncover new evidence of the importance that both school and home environment play in increasing (or decreasing) IQ. Eric Turkeheimer, a psychologist at the University of Virginia in Charlottesville (Jacobson 2003), found the correlation between IQ and heredity is even lower for children from homes with low socioeconomic status than it is for children in socioeconomically advantaged homes. Turkeheimer's research, based on twin studies, indicates that the correlation for children from homes with low socioeconomic status is 0.1 on a scale with a maximum level of 1.0.[4] This would indicate that the environment, of which schools are an important part, is a significant component of the factors that shape the IQs of children from disadvantaged environments.

Perkins (1995) explains to us that a person's IQ is only 50 percent due to genetics. He further explains that the correlation between IQ and a person's success in school and in the workforce is approximately 0.5 (p. 61). That means that a person's genetic intelligence accounts for only 25 percent of his or her success in school and work. The remainder of a person's success is attributable to learned knowledge, strategies, and effort. **This appears to show that 75 percent of a person's school and work success may be shaped by parents, teachers, and other nurturing influences.**

To better understand this idea, let's look again at our brothers, Bob and Joe. Let's assume that the decision for Bob to attend the college preparatory high school was based on his having an estimated IQ of 110, along with school grades, Iowa tests, and teacher observations. Let's further assume that Joe's estimated

---

4 Correlations between two factors range on a scale of 1.0 to -1.0. A 1.0 correlation between two factors means there is a perfect match. A –1.0 correlation indicates that each factor has an opposite correlation. For example, the correlation between a person's height and his shoe size is a positive correlation. On the other hand, the correlation between days when the temperature is zero in a given region and the number of flowers that bloom on those days in that region is probably about –1.0.

IQ was 90 and that this score prompted the recommendation that he not attend the college preparatory high school. This would indicate a difference of more than one standard deviation between the brothers. If Perkins and others are correct, then 75 percent of what determined Bob's and Joe's ultimate academic and career achievements (or lack thereof) was attributable to family, school, and other nurturing factors (such as the encouragement of Joe's boss for him to attend college). To take this a step further, we may eliminate home as a factor in this example, because both boys grew up in the same home with the same parents. One might then conclude that Bob's and Joe's career achievements are due to nurturing factors outside of the home.

During the 25-year period between Joe's entering ninth grade and his becoming a successful attorney practicing business law, Joe acquired on his own, or with the guidance of others, the mental capacity to achieve at a high level. He acquired the following traits:

1. Confidence in his ability to succeed at academic tasks
2. The studying, writing, verbal, and problem-solving strategies needed to succeed in undergraduate, graduate, and law school
3. The motivation to maintain a full-time job and part-time college study for a span of more than 10 years
4. Confidence in his ability to work successfully in a professional environment
5. The verbal, writing, and problem-solving strategies needed to succeed in both the business and the legal professions
6. The motivation to succeed in the competitive environment of business law

Learnable Intelligence

David Perkins' theory of **learnable intelligence** looks at intelligence as comprising three components. The first is **neural intelligence**. This is the part of our intelligence that is primarily determined by heredity and only changes as a result of the physical maturation of the brain—i.e., the *nature* portion of our intelligence. In his book *Outsmarting IQ* (1995), Perkins defines neural intelligence as

> *It was their increased level of experience with the various configurations of pieces as they appeared in games that resulted in a greater ability to remember the location of the pieces during the experiment.*

the contribution of the efficiency and precision of the neurological system to intelligent behavior. This contribution may involve a single unified factor or some mix of several factors. In any case, it is influenced strongly by genetics and physical maturation (p. 102).

The second component of intelligence described by Perkins is **experiential intelligence**. He supports this component of the theory by citing the work of Dutch psychologist A.D. de Groot (Perkins 1995, pp. 80–81) and others. De Groot studied the similarities and differences between the cognitive abilities of amateur chess players and those of professional chess masters. He found that amateurs and professionals explored future moves with the same level of depth; however, the professionals easily beat the amateurs. To understand the reason for this, de Groot showed players a chessboard with a typical game situation and quickly removed the board from their sight and study. The amateurs could only remember the exact location of a fraction of the total number of the pieces on the chess board. The professionals, on the other hand, could remember *all the locations of all the chess pieces.* When he repeated the experiment with a random placement of the pieces that would not occur in a game situation, however, the amateurs and professionals had the same level of success in remembering the positions of the pieces. De Groot concluded that the professionals, who played much more frequently than the amateurs, had a much more highly developed memory based on the experience of studying chess pieces during game situations. It was their increased level of experience with the various configurations of pieces as they appeared in games that resulted in a greater ability to remember the location of the pieces during the experiment.

Perkins describes experiential intelligence as

> the contribution of context-specific knowledge to intelligent behavior. This contribution is learned, the result of extensive experience thinking and acting in particular situations over long periods of time. While there may be an initial ability to learn efficiently in a domain (for example, musical giftedness), the accumulated knowledge and know-how of thinking in that domain constitutes experiential intelligence (p. 14).

The third component of intelligence is **reflective intelligence**. Perkins (1995) describes this as

the contribution to intelligent behavior of strategies for various intellectually challenging tasks, attitudes conducive to persistence, systematicity, and imagination in the use of one's mind, habits of self-monitoring, and management. Reflective intelligence is in effect a control system for the resources afforded by neurological and experiential intelligence, bent on deploying them wisely (pp. 102–103).

In this model of intelligence, teachers, parents, and individuals have little or no control over neural intelligence; however, teachers, parents, and individuals have a great deal of control over the development of the experiential and reflective intelligences. Later in this chapter, we will look more at the role of teachers and parents in developing the motivation in students to maximize the growth of their experiential and reflective intelligences (see the following section on Carol Dweck's work on self-theory).

Let's place the three intelligences in the real-life context of Bob and Joe. Bob and Joe came from the same parents, so in all likelihood they had similar neural intelligence. One might even argue that, based on Bob's early school success, his neural intelligence may have even been higher than Joe's. At some point in time, during their adolescence and into adulthood, Bob and Joe took very different paths related to their experiential and reflective intelligences. If we track Bob's life after high school, we might argue that Bob experienced no increase in experiential or reflective intelligence.

Joe, on the other hand, acquired increased experiential intelligence as academic and career building blocks. Joe's acquired knowledge and skills at work and in high school led to a sufficient knowledge base to attend college and succeed in college. Joe's acquired learning in college and in his career led to his ability to succeed when attending graduate school. The learning acquired in the MBA program and at work led to his success when attending and successfully completing law school. The building blocks constructed to this point in academia and in his job ultimately led to a successful career as an attorney.

Reflective intelligence also plays an important role in this story. Joe's decision to attend college at night while working required a high level of self-sacrifice,

determination, and the delay of the gratification of free-time activities until some future time in his life (a.k.a. motivation). It is a decision almost anyone from any background might make. However, it is a decision that many people choose not to make. In this example, Joe increased his experiential intelligence and his reflective intelligence.

People who hear the story about Bob and Joe are often left asking themselves why Joe worked to increase his experiential intelligence, while Bob chose to take no action in that direction. Stanford University social psychologist Carol Dweck offers interesting reasons for Joe's and Bob's behavior. In her book *Self-Theories* (2000), Dweck indicates that some students respond to challenges with an "entity" belief in their intelligence (pp. 3–5). This is a belief that intelligence is a fixed entity and, therefore, if a task is difficult for me to do, it must be because I am not smart enough to do it. In her latest book, Dweck (2008, e-book p. 6 of 246) labels this the *fixed mind-set*. Other students—those who believe that intelligence is what Dweck calls *incremental intelligence*, or intelligence that may be increased with effort and new strategies— see challenges as interesting problems to be tackled step by step. Mistakes are seen as learning opportunities rather than failures. Dweck labels this mind-set *the growth mind-set*. In her research, Dweck found that, contrary to popular belief, some students with low confidence in their intelligence still threw themselves wholeheartedly into difficult tasks and stuck with them to fruition. These students had an incremental belief about intelligence. Other students with high confidence did not want their intelligence tested, and their high confidence was quickly shaken when confronted with a difficult task. These students had an entity belief in intelligence.

In another surprising finding, Dweck (2000, pp. 112–113) found that students who had high achievement during their elementary and middle school years were the most, rather than the least, vulnerable to entity thinking when faced with a difficult task (p. 53). They worried about failure, questioned their ability, and were likely to wilt when they hit obstacles. The other students, those with a history of lower achievement, had developed the capacity to stay with a task even when their initial attempts led to failure.

> *In another surprising finding, Dweck found that students who had high achievement during elementary and middle school were the most vulnerable to entity thinking when faced with a difficult task.*

Making Kids Smarter in Schools

David Perkins tells us that our intelligence is 40 percent to 50 percent learned and our success in school and life is at least 75 percent due to the strategies we learn, the effort we exert, and the people who guide the development of these two factors. Clinical psychologist Daniel Goleman, PhD, the author of numerous books and articles on emotional intelligence, estimates that IQ only accounts for between 10 percent and 20 percent of a person's success in school and career (1999). That means 80 percent to 90 percent of success in life is in the control of the individual and the people who affect their lives, such as teachers and parents. Social psychologist Carol Dweck has shown us that how we interact with children has a significant impact on how they react when confronting unfamiliar and challenging situations. What an exciting prospect for those of us who work in the education profession,

By retraining students to think of intelligence as something we acquire with hard work and strategies (growth mind-set), we develop in them the desire to work on challenging school assignments to completion.

which is primarily charged with preparing students for successful lives!

The next part of this chapter shares ideas that classroom teachers have used to help students "get smarter" and more motivated. By that, we mean developing students who

- willingly exert more effort
- use strategies to more efficiently learn new knowledge and skills
- use strategies to solve problems
- stick with problems until they are solved
- believe in their abilities to succeed in school and life by applying effort and strategies

Carol Dweck (2000) offers some techniques for assessing whether individual students have an entity or incremental approach to their intelligence. The following activity sheet may be used to assess students' beliefs about the nature of intelligence. This activity sheet is designed for use in upper elementary, middle, or high school; however, it may be simplified or given orally to younger students (pp. 53–63).

Name: _____

Teacher's Name: _____

Date: _____

Please answer the following questions. It is important that you answer them as honestly as you can and are not influenced by what you think others will answer. **There are no right or wrong answers.**

1. Write a definition for *intelligence*.

2. Think of a person whom you consider intelligent. It might be someone you know personally or know of from the news or another source. Describe what this person does that causes you to think of him or her as intelligent.

3. Are there times when you feel intelligent? If so, when?

4. Is there a time or are there times when you have felt dumb (unintelligent)? If so, when?

5. Fill in the equation below so the total equals 100%:

Intelligence = _____% effort + _____% innate ability

In her research with fifth graders, Dweck (2000) found that students with an entity (fixed) mind-set defined intelligence as:

"What your IQ is or how smart you are."

"Intelligence is how smart you are."

"Very smart, brilliant, or bright."

But the incremental (growth) mind-set students defined intelligence as

"I think it is what you know."

"How much you look at a problem and check it over to find stuff wrong."

"I think it is to try your best."

"Studying hard."

"Intelligence is how hard you work to do something" (pp. 61–62).

Entity theorists tended to answer Question 5 with a higher percentage, indicating ability. Incremental theorists assigned a higher percentage to effort.

Dweck speaks about the need to do "attribution retraining" (2000, p. 56) with all students and particularly with those who respond to challenges with the entity reaction of feeling dumb and giving up. By retraining students to think of intelligence as something we acquire with hard work and strategies (growth mind-set), we develop in them the desire to work on challenging school assignments to completion. We motivate students not to give up when something is difficult, but to learn from their mistakes and try again.

Strategies that teachers use to develop the belief that intelligence is incrementally achieved through effort and learning new strategies are discussed later in this chapter.

Component 7: Nutrition. Poor nutrition on a daily basis can occur with students of any socioeconomic level. As students, particularly as they get older, can fall susceptible to skipping breakfast or eating foods that are less likely to promote motivation. However, the long-term impact of substandard nutrition that can be prevalent in both prenatal and early childhood is more prevalent with students from poverty.

Children in the US are mostly safe from the severe hunger often seen in poor and developing countries. However, many children live in families who do not have a consistent and dependable supply of healthy food. Researchers refer to this as *food insecurity*. Food insecurity is not the same as hunger. Food-insecure families are often able to avoid hunger by choosing cheaper, more filling types of food over more costly nutritious foods. For young children, the result is often a diet that

provides inadequate nutrients for normal growth and development (Urban Child Institute 2011).

Students may not be hungry when they come to school. However, they may not have the nutrients needed for optimum learning. With students from poverty, this lack of appropriate nutrients for many years can lead to learning deficits.

Shortages of nutrients such as iron iodine can impair cognitive and motor development, and these effects are often irreversible. Similarly, there is growing evidence that DHA, an essential fatty acid, is a key component of the intensive production of synapses that makes the first years of life a critical period of learning and development. Many other nutrients—choline, folic acid, and zinc, to name just a few—have been linked specifically to early brain functioning (Urban Child Institute 2011).

As we saw above, the impact of nutrition can be both short-term, such as a lack of energy and engagement on a single day, or long-term, as noted in the impact on brain development. As educators, we can counteract these issues in four ways:

1. Provide opportunities for students to receive the nutrients they need by allowing for healthy snacks early in the day and at low-energy times.
2. Family education programs inform parents about the importance of nutrition from prenatal through high school graduation.
3. With upper elementary, middle, and high school students, teach them the link between good nutrition and school success.
4. Incorporate motivation components 1–6 discussed earlier in this chapter into your work with all students.

Strategies for Motivating Students by Developing an Incremental Belief about Intelligence (Growth Mind-Set)

In this section, we look at some of the strategies teachers use to build in the students the idea that they have control over their level of success. We then move into effective effort strategies teachers can teach students that enable them to be more successful. It is only when the student starts to believe he or she has control over how "smart" he or she can become that the acquisition of effective effort strategies to be successful becomes relevant and has some importance. Acquiring the effective effort strategies then leads to some academic success. These early successes increase the students' belief that they can control their level of success with effective effort strategies. This changes the negative cycle, shifting from a lack of internal motivation to higher levels of internal motivation.

"Yet" and "Already"

Carol Dweck introduced the importance of using the words *yet* and *already*. Teacher Julia Dermody (2012, p. 2) explains the power of these words best:

> The first word, *yet*, provides hope. Instead of telling a learner you haven't solved this equation, I now say, "You haven't solved this equation yet." This word has made a profound difference in the way my students view learning. They know that with more support, they understand the problem. It's their job to know they don't understand something and my job to help them understand it. When students ask me for help, I ask, "What do you already know about the problem?" By saying *already*, I recognize that they have some understanding of the problem in place, which is important.

Wait Time and Open-Ended Questions

We talk in-depth about the "how to" and "reasons for" wait time in Chapter 5. Mark Jacobson (2013, pp. 40–43) tells us the importance of coupling wait time with open-ended questions as a strategy for building student confidence.

Incremental Messages Posted on Classroom Walls

Many teachers from elementary school through college have begun to post quotations that promote the belief that success and intelligence are due to acquiring new knowledge by using strategies and hard work. Some that we have seen include the following:

"Ball players are not born great. They're not born great hitters or pitchers or managers, and luck isn't a big factor. No one has come up with a substitute for hard work. I've never met a ballplayer who didn't have to work harder at learning to play ball than anything else he ever did."—*Ted Williams, Boston Red Sox*

"You can have unbelievable intelligence, you can have connections, [and] you can have opportunities

fall out of the sky. But in the end, hard work is the true, enduring characteristic of successful people."—*Marsha Evans, rear admiral, US Navy*

"I'm a great believer in luck, and I find the harder I work, the more I have of it."—*Thomas Jefferson, US President*

"The dictionary is the only place that success comes before work. Hard work is the price we must pay for success. I think you can accomplish anything if you're willing to pay the price."—*Vince Lombardi, National Football League coach*

"Continuous effort—not strength or intelligence—is the key to unlocking our potential."—*Black Elk (1863–1950), Native American*

"Genius is 1 percent inspiration and 99 percent perspiration."—*Thomas Edison, inventor of the lightbulb*

"Satisfaction lies in the effort, not in the attainment. Full effort is full victory."—*Indira Gandhi (1917–1984)*

"Believe me, the reward is not so great without the struggle."—*Wilma Rudolph, Olympic track and field sprinter*

"Measure a person not by the heights they achieve but from the depths from which they've come."—*Frederick Douglass, slavery abolitionist*

"The journey of 1,000 miles begins with the first step."—*Chinese proverb*

"All mankind is divided into three classes: those that are immovable, those that are movable, and those that move."—*Benjamin Franklin, Founding Father of the United States*

"The three great essentials to achieve anything worthwhile are, first, hard work; second, stick-to-itiveness; [and] third, common sense."—*Thomas Edison, inventor of the lightbulb*

"Smart is not something you are. It is something you become."—*Unknown*

"Successful people work smart *and* work hard.—*Unknown*

Incremental Stories about Celebrities Familiar to Students

This strategy becomes more effective as students leave the primary grades and enter a point in their lives when they become aware of the achievements of people in the news. Once students can identify famous people and the attention those people receive, they are ready for stories of incremental success. For example, many high school students know Oprah Winfrey as a famous TV personality, wealthy philanthropist, and successful businesswoman. Most students only see Winfrey as the "finished product." They don't know that Winfrey was raised in very difficult circumstances. They don't know that she was born to an unwed mother who left her to be raised by her maternal grandparents, who were poor farmers in Mississippi. They don't know that, at age six, Winfrey went to live with her mother in poverty in a tenement, where she suffered sexual abuse. Over the next 10 years, she would be shuffled from her grandparents to her mother to her father to her mother and back to her father. They don't see the years of struggle and hard work Winfrey devoted to her career that eventually resulted in the success she has achieved. They don't equate the hard work and acquired skills she obtained as she incrementally worked her way up the ladder of success in the entertainment industry as the required prerequisite skills for being the successful woman she is today.

Another famous person many high school students have heard of is Michael Jordan. Jordan is considered by many to be the greatest basketball player of all time. Jordan is now a highly successful businessman often seen on TV commercials. Few know that he was cut from his high school basketball team. His reaction to being cut was to leave the house every morning at 6:00 AM to practice before he went to school. He continued to work like this year-round until the next season, when he made the team. Even with all this hard work, Michael was not offered a scholarship to his first-choice college, North Carolina State University. He went to North Carolina and was the hardest-working member of the team. One year, after the team lost the last game of the season, Michael went out after the game and practiced shooting for four hours. He continued to work like that throughout the off-season in preparation for the next season. In a time when as many as 50 percent of NBA players are broke within five years of the end their career, Jordan has become a highly successful businessman by refocusing his effort from basketball to business.

As with Oprah Winfrey and Michael Jordan, children often see famous people only as the finished product. They don't know the story of hard work, perseverance, and incremental success that preceded their present levels of success. Many teachers are helping students to see that the finished products they admire and aspire to emulate are the result of significant effort and incremental growth and achievement.

Keep in the Classroom the Biographies of People Who Have Achieved as a Result of Hard Work and Perseverance

In the past 20 years, there has been a proliferation of literature, including biographies, that has been written at age-appropriate reading levels for most students. Biographies of this type are an excellent source of information about the incremental growth to success of the famous people that students typically only know as finished products.

Biographies for Secondary School Students

Maya Angelou, *I Know Why the Caged Bird Sings*
Arthur Ashe, *Days of Grace: A Memoir*
Jack Canfield and Mark Victor Hansen, *Chicken Soup for the Teenage Soul: 101 Stories of Life, Love, and Learning*
Lorene Cary, *Black Ice*
Richard Feynman, *Surely You're Joking, Mr. Feynman: Adventures of a Curious Character*
Viktor Frankl, *Man's Search for Meaning*
Helen Garson, *Oprah Winfrey: A Biography*
Jacqueline Harris, *The Tuskegee Airmen: Black Heroes of World War II*
Ji-Li Jiang, *Red Scarf Girl: A Memoir of the Cultural Revolution*
Malcolm X, *The Autobiography of Malcolm X*
Chris Mead, *Joe Louis, Black Champion in White America*
James McBride, *The Color of Water: A Black Man's Tribute to his White Mother*
Frank McCourt, *Angela's Ashes: A Memoir*
Barack Obama, *Dreams from My Father: A Story of Race and Inheritance*
Michael Oher, *The Blind Side*
Libby Riddles, *Race across Alaska: First Woman to Win the Iditarod Tells Her Story*
Jeanne Wakatsuki, *Farewell to Manzanar*
Elie Wiesel, *Night*
Tobias Wolff, *This Boy's Life: A Memoir*
Richard Wright, *Black Boy*

Biographies for Elementary Students

Zlata Filipovic, *Zlata's Diary*
Anne Frank, *The Diary of a Young Girl*
Russell Freedman, *Lincoln: A Photobiography*
Rosa Parks, *I Am Rosa Parks*
J.L. Wilkerson, *A Doctor to Her People: Dr. Susan La Flesche Picotte* (the first female Native American doctor)

Growth Mind-set Stories about Ordinary People's Lives

Not all incremental success stories are about celebrities. Almost every adult has his or her own incremental story or stories. Tell students about times when you (their teacher) were faced with a difficult task and solved it through perseverance and by developing new strategies. As in the case of the celebrities discussed previously, students see you as a finished product also. They think you always read as well as you do now. They think you always solved math problems and spoke in front of the class as well. Bring in parent and community speakers to tell their incremental success stories.

Praise Student Effort

We often praise student achievement. It is a natural tendency to see success and then praise the accomplishment. We need to make praising *effort* a frequent phenomenon in our classrooms as well. We should praise effort and the use of effective strategies, and we should encourage students to praise one another when they witness effort and/or the use of effective strategies by their peers.

Help Students to Examine and Understand Strategies Used to Succeed

Students typically need help in examining and understanding the strategies they used to complete tasks. They will only be able to replicate a strategy if they know what strategy they used and how they used it. In Chapter 5, we looked at questioning techniques that help students to understand the thinking processes they use when solving a problem.

Respond to Students' Successes with Praises of Their Efforts and the Strategies They Used

Carol Dweck (2000) found in her research that students made no movement away from entity thinking and toward incremental thinking when they were praised, upon completing a task, with what she calls *person-oriented praise statements*, such as

"You're a good boy."
"I'm proud of you."
"You're smart."
"You're very good at this."

Students who were praised with statements that she termed *outcome-oriented* made some movement away from entity thinking and toward incremental

thinking. Outcome-oriented praise statements include the following examples:

"That's the right way to do it."
"You did an excellent job of …"

The students who made the greatest growth toward incremental thinking were those who were praised for their effort or strategies with statements or questions, such as the following:

"You really tried hard."
"You found a way to do it."
"You found more than one way to do it."
"You kept trying even when you didn't get it right the first time."
"You've tried it that way and it didn't work. What is another way you might try to solve this problem?"
"You really put the time in to make this work pay off."
"All of these drafts really made this an excellent piece of work."
"You were determined to turn this into a really excellent piece of work."
"I'm impressed by your dedication to this assignment."

In the home, these statements are frequently made by parents with a high education level because of their knowledge of child development. For students from poverty, that is often not the case. Parent education about this strategy will be important to extend this practice to the home.

Teach Your Students about the Difference between Entity Thinking and Growth Mind-set

In middle school, students are at the beginning stages of understanding the difference between attributing success to effort and strategies versus attributing it to innate ability. It is particularly powerful to explain these theories in relation to the areas students find difficult. High school students respond very well to the direct teaching of the two theories. We may teach students that learning new strategies, trying new approaches after an initial failure, and persevering will lead to more success. We may also teach them that getting down on themselves and giving up leads only to failure. A simple but effective method for doing this is to teach students to attribute success to effort and strategies using what has come to be known as "attribution theory" (Hunter 1987).

As noted in a *Kappan* article by one of the au-

Figure 7.4 Attribution Theory

Factor	Participant's Control over the Factor	Consistency or Variability from Participant to Participant
Effort	Completely within the participant's control	Variable from person to person, based on levels of interest and perseverance
Task Difficulty	Completely out of the participant's control	Remains constant for all participants
Ability	Partially innate and out of the participant's control, and partially determined by prior strategy development	Innate ability varies among participants, and level of strategy acquisition varies among individuals.
Luck or Opportunity	Partially determined by circumstances out of the participant's control and partially determined by preparation	Some of the circumstances (such as how the person is feeling that day) are variable. Others (such as the weather on the day of the game) are consistent for all participants.

thors of the second edition of this book (Seider 2013, p. 29), "A number of scholars have found that a key commonality in high-achieving artists, athletes, chess players, and mathematicians is an ability and willingness to put in long hours of time and effort" (Bloom 1985; Ericsson, Krampe, and Tesch-Romer 1993; Simon and Chase 1973). Most recently, Angela Duckworth and colleagues (2005, 2006, and 2007) found that an individual's grit and self-discipline are stronger predictors of success than IQ in populations ranging from middles school students to West Point Cadets.

Attribution theory tells us there are four forces that come into play when we confront a new task. These forces are: effort, our ability in the area of the task (see the discussion later in this chapter about multiple intelligences), the difficulty of the task, and luck or opportunity. When we first confront a task, the one area we have control over is our effort. Our ability is initially set at a certain level; however, we can increase our ability with preparation. The task difficulty is fixed. Running a mile or solving a two-digit multiplication problem or a quadratic equation is the same task no matter when we do it. Opportunity or luck[5] is fixed at the time we begin the task. Take, for example, a high school athlete who must run a mile in seven minutes to be eligible to play on the basketball team. Expending greater effort is going to lead to a better time than expending less effort; however, different athletes come with different abilities at the start of the task. The task is the same for all. Everyone has

Teaching students that luck is the interaction of preparation and opportunity, rather than a totally random and uncontrollable factor, is empowering and motivating.

to run a mile. No one gets to run a half-mile and no one has to run two miles. Luck or opportunity is variable by person and out of his or her control. The athlete who breaks an ankle will not be able to run the mile no matter how hard he or she tries at the outset.[6] A student who has run the mile as an event in the fall track season will report for basketball season better able to run the mile than most of the other athletes.

In this example, the effort and ability are in the control of the athlete. As mentioned previously, trying harder will lead to a better running time. The athlete can increase his or her ability with practice and the development of strategies. Setting up a training schedule during the weeks prior to the first basketball practice will result in higher ability at the first basketball practice. Learning to run with a steady gait, longer strides, and effective breathing are strategies that will also increase the athlete's ability. One might even argue that an athlete may influence opportunity or luck. A well-established preparation program prior to the season will limit the possibility of injury. Running on an even surface, such as a track or a road, will decrease the likelihood of twisting and injuring an ankle prior to the first day of practice. Luck is an interesting concept. Teaching students that luck is the interaction of preparation and opportunity, rather than a totally random

---

5   In her article, Hunter (1987) talks about ability as being innate and completely out of a student's control. Others see ability as a combination of innate ability and ability that is changeable with practice and the development of strategies.

6   Hunter (1987) talks about luck or opportunity as a circumstance completely out of the control of the student. Others see an ability to maximize a lucky event or opportunity with preparation. There is an old saying that refers to a person's "ship coming in" as a time when they get the opportunity to succeed. We would argue that people's ships come in quite frequently during life. The difference between getting on it and sailing away to success and getting on the ship and ramming it into a reef is the degree to which the person is prepared for the opportunity.

and uncontrollable factor, is empowering and motivating.

We are reminded of an interview with a professional golfer. The interviewer asked the golfer what part luck played in winning golf tournaments. The golfer replied, "Winning in golf is all luck. And I find the more I practice, the luckier I get."

Help Students Understand That There Are Multiple Intelligences

When students are frustrated by a task, remind them of the fact that everyone has strengths in different intelligences. Success with tasks in those intelligences that don't come easily to the student will require greater effort and the development of more strategies. Success with tasks in those intelligences in which the student has a more developed or innate ability at the

Students who have low ability in an area need to expend more effort than those who have high ability in the same area, but they can eventually have a similar result.

outset of the task will require less effort to achieve the same level of success.

Howard Gardner's (1985) **theory of multiple intelligences** tells us that different people have different levels of innate ability in eight specific areas. He supports this theory with brain research that ties different tasks and their related intelligences to different parts of the brain (see Chapter 8 for more information on how the brain functions). His theory has been drawn into question by some, but it still gives a framework for helping students understand that people have different "strengths" when it comes to mastering tasks. As teachers, it is important to help students understand their areas of strength and their areas that require more effort for success.

The Cambridge Handbook of Intelligence (pp. 485–504) briefly describes these eight intelligences as follows (Davis, Christodoulou, Seider, and Gardner 2011).

Linguistic Intelligence	an ability to analyze information and create products involving oral and written language, such as speeches, books, and memos
Logical-Mathematical Intelligence	an ability to develop equations and proofs, make calculations, and solve abstract problems
Spatial Intelligence	an ability to recognize and manipulate large-scale and fine-grained spatial images
Musical Intelligence	an ability to produce, remember, and make meaning of different patterns of sound
Naturalistic Intelligence	an ability to identify and distinguish among different types of plants, animals, and weather formations that are found in the natural world
Bodily-Kinesthetic Intelligence	an ability to use one's own body to create products or solve problems
Interpersonal Intelligence	an ability to recognize and understand other people's moods, desires, motivations, and intentions
Intrapersonal Intelligence	an ability to recognize and understand his or her own moods, desires, motivations, and intentions

Sample Activities That Require Each of the Intelligences

Students who have low ability in an area need to expend more effort than those who have high ability in the same area, but they can eventually have a similar result. Let's look for a minute at the example of learning to ride a two-wheeled bike. A child with high bodily-kinesthetic intelligence may learn to ride in a couple of hours with the assistance of an adult.

Another child may need several practice sessions with that adult over the course of several days. Ultimately, almost every child, regardless of his or her bodily-kinesthetic intelligence, learns to ride a bike.

Linguistic Intelligence

- writing an essay
- writing a short story
- writing from the perspective of an historical figure
- reciting a poem

- making an oral presentation
- explaining the solution of a math problem to the class
- writing a lab report

Logical Mathematics Intelligence

- solving a word problem
- solving a geometry proof
- deriving an equation

Spatial Intelligence

- interpreting a map
- interpreting various types of graphs
- drawing, painting, or working on other types of art projects
- interpreting a painting

Bodily-Kinesthetic Intelligence

- performing an interpretive dance
- presenting a tableau
- acting out a scene
- miming
- taking part in an athletic event

Musical Intelligence

- singing
- playing an instrument
- interpreting a song
- writing music
- composing a song

Interpersonal Intelligence

- interpreting the mood, feelings, and attitude of a literary character
- taking part in all types of group work
- role-playing
- taking part in simulations

Intrapersonal Intelligence

- reflecting activities
- working in groups
- taking part in simulations

Naturalistic Intelligence

- recognizing flora and fauna
- studying natural phenomena, such as mountains and clouds

Figure 7.5 shows the different levels of effort we need to assert, depending on the level of intelligence, similar previous experience, and personal interest we bring to the task. The greater our level of each of these three factors at the start of the task, the less effort we need to exert in order to succeed. Conversely, those tasks for which we have low intelligence, no similar previous experience, and low interest require a great deal of effort to succeed. Thus, it took much more effort for Joe to become a successful business attorney than it would take for a person who came from a family with a high parental education level, a high appreciation for education, and a high socioeconomic level and for a person who also attended high-performing schools in grades K–12 and beyond.

Remind Students about Previous Tasks That They Eventually Mastered

School days should be and are filled with situations in which students are confronting new learning. There is ample opportunity to become frustrated or feel dumb when a task is difficult. Reminding students of their previous successes and of how far they have come helps encourage and motivate their efforts. A high school student who starts out in calculus becomes discouraged and wants to drop the class when it becomes difficult. The student might be reminded that he or she felt the same way when first starting geometry

Figure 7.5

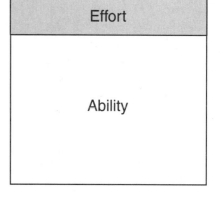

When Confronted With New Information and/or Skill

Effort

Ability

- Little or no previous experience with similar tasks and/or
- Area of lower aptitude (an area of weaker intelligence as defined by Gardner) and/or
- Area of low interest

Effort

Ability

- Many previous experiences with similar tasks and/or
- Area of high aptitude (a stronger intelligence as defined by Gardner) and/or
- Area of high interest

and that he or she went on to eventually learn geometry and pass the class. An elementary student who is having difficulty with two-digit multiplication might be reminded of when he or she was first learning to add or first learning single-digit multiplication. Pausing to see how far he or she has come with these skills is a powerful motivator for tackling problems in the future.

One of our colleagues had the following experience with one of his high school students:

"I can remember working with a high school student who was frustrated by the challenge of understanding Shakespeare's *Romeo and Juliet*. I reminded him that, at the beginning of the year, he had believed that Homer's *Odyssey* was equally impossible, and yet we had actually managed to get him through and completely understand that work. So there was no doubt in my mind that he was going to succeed with *Romeo and Juliet* as well."

Have Students Analyze How They Got Good at Things That They Do Well

We have seen this technique used effectively with athletes who struggle in school. In one circumstance, a high school basketball player was very frustrated with mathematics. He felt and verbalized that he was dumb in math. The teacher asked him how he got to be so good in basketball. His initial response was that he "just was." The teacher went on to ask him how many hours in a typical week he played basketball. He responded that it was about 15. She then said, "That means you play about 60 hours a month and 780 hours a year." At this point, he added that in the summer he played all day, every day, so it was probably more hours in the year than what the teacher had stated. The teacher then asked him how many hours a week he spent on mathematics during the school year. The answer was six or seven. She then asked how many hours a week he spent on mathematics during vacations. The student laughed and made the zero sign with his thumb and index finger. The teacher then summarized that he spent more than 1,000 hours a year on basketball and only about 220 hours a year on mathematics. She further pointed out that this had been something that had been going on in his life for 10 years. That meant he had spent almost 8,000 more hours on basketball than on math. "Of course you are better in basketball than math! Now, if you start to put more time into math, just as in basketball, you will get better and better."

Examples of Developing in Students Strategies That Will Make Them Smarter

Reading for Understanding (a.k.a. Strategic Reading): Helping Students Become Strategic Readers

Teachers may help their students become more active readers by teaching them a multitude of comprehension strategies. The following strategies are those that good readers use all the time as they read.

- visualizing
- predicting and confirming
- making connections
  - text to self
  - text to text
  - text to world
- analyzing vocabulary
- questioning what they have read and posing discussion questions
- summarizing
- highlighting important information
- noting questions

The following section illustrates how teachers might teach elementary and middle school students how to use visualization to help them better comprehend what they are reading.

Teaching the Comprehension Strategy of Visualizing

This particular comprehension strategy may be used with students as young as first graders and as old as fifth graders. Teachers should begin the lesson by modeling this strategy: that is, by thinking aloud about their own process of visualizing or evoking images while reading. Modeling should occur frequently, using short selections appropriate for the particular grade level. In addition, it is important that teachers use a variety of genres when modeling. Although modeling occurs primarily when this strategy is introduced, teachers should periodically model this strategy from time to time. Teachers should concentrate on visual images and on those that emanate from the other senses and should also focus on how they created those images. It is important for teachers to think aloud about how concentrating on visual images enhances comprehension. Gradually, teachers should ask the students to share their own images inspired by a variety of texts.

An example of how an elementary teacher might introduce this strategy by modeling visualization is as follows:

Teacher reads the following passages from *Through Grandpa's Eyes* by Patricia MacLachlan.

"In the morning, the sun pushes through the curtains into my eyes. I burrow down into the covers to get away, but the light follows. I give up, throw back the covers, and run into Grandpa's room."

As I read this passage, I immediately think of myself waking up on a bright summer morning. In my mind, I can see the yellowish-orange-like sun filtering through blue-and-white curtains, while John tries to escape the light by trying to hide underneath his covers. I imagine him struggling to find darkness so that he can sleep a bit longer. Having no luck, I picture him quickly jumping out of bed. I hear the floorboards creaking as he runs with a grin from ear to ear to see Grandpa.

As students become more familiar with visualizing, teachers of both lower and upper elementary students might ask students to draw what they visualized as they read a short passage. Older students might meet in small groups or pairs to compare images and to discuss the components of the text that inspired those images. All children should be encouraged to discuss the ways in which their comprehension is enhanced by mental images.

During literature circles or book clubs, students might be asked to focus on this particular strategy in their conversations. In reading conferences with students, conversations might focus on the children's images and the parts of the text that evoked these images. Small flexible groups might be created for those students who need more modeling and explicit instruction. The teacher might focus sharing time on images that individual children discovered in their independent reading for the day, how those images were evoked, and how thinking about important images enhanced their comprehension. As students read independently, they might use sticky notes to mark places in the text in which images were particularly vivid.

The following form may be used by students to encourage them to visualize as they read. Although this form is most appropriate for grades three through five, it may be adapted for younger grades.

Visualization

Good readers create pictures in their minds as they read. This strategy is known as visualization. Readers find their comprehension improves as these mental pictures help make the text more meaningful. Good readers practice this skill often as they read.

Directions: As you read the assigned pages, practice the skill of visualization. Place sticky notes over parts of the text where you find yourself "painting pictures in your mind." After reading the entire selection, go back and select one of your favorite and/or most meaningful visualizations. Recreate this scene in color, copy the section of the text underneath, and record the page number.

The following forms might also be used to help children read more actively by helping them focus on a particular strategy. Keep in mind that these forms should only be used after a strategy has been introduced, modeled, and practiced by the students. Again, these forms are most appropriate for students in grades three through five, but might certainly be adapted for younger children.

Predicting and Confirming

Good readers naturally make predictions as they read and like to think back to how close their predictions were to the actual story events.

Directions: Make a **minimum of two predictions** before you read the assigned chapter/pages. When you finish reading, make another prediction about what you think will happen in the next chapter.

Record your predictions in the "Prediction" column, what actually happened in the "Confirmation" column, and document from the text the supporting evidence in the "Evidence" column. The supporting evidence should be a direct quote, so remember to use quotation marks and include the page number. Copy the following chart into your reading journal.

Prediction	Confirmation	Evidence

Making Connections

Good readers think about their own experiences as they read. They relate new text to their prior world knowledge, personal experiences, and/or other books they have read. These connections take three different forms:

- text-to-self connections
- text-to-text connections
- text-to-world connections

Text-to-self connections

When the pictures or the story remind you of your own life, you are making a text-to-self connection.

Text-to-text connections

Readers who relate parts of the text or pictures to another book they have read are making text-to-text connections.

Text-to-world connections

When your world knowledge contributes to the understanding of a book you are reading, you are making a text-to-world connection.

Directions: As you read, keep track of the connections you make in your reading journal. Be sure to mention the specific part of the text your connection relates to, note the page numbers, and specify the type of connection you made.

Analyzing Vocabulary

Directions: As you read, record two vocabulary words that you found interesting, difficult, unusual, and/or relevant to the story. Complete the following tasks required for each new vocabulary word. This form will help guide you as you record this information in your reading journal.

Vocabulary word: _____

Definition: _____

_____

Source used (dictionary, text) _____

Use a thesaurus to find three synonyms for the word. _____

_____

_____

Part of speech: _____

Page number: _____

Original sentence: _____

_____

Discussion Questions

Reading for meaning is a collaborative process. As we discuss it with others, we deepen our own understanding of a story. Your assignment is to create a minimum of three open-ended questions to present to your group as discussion prompts based on the assigned readings. The following are good examples of open-ended questions you are encouraged to include.

- What might happen if...?
- How is ... like ...?
- What do you think will happen after...?
- Do you agree with ... and why?
- What feelings did you have when...?
- What was your first reaction to...?
- What did you consider to be the most important word or phrase within this assigned group of readings? Support with details from the text.
- Would you be friends with...? Why or why not? Be very specific. Support your opinion with details from the text.
- I like the way ... said ... or did .... How do you feel?
- How do you think ... felt when...?
- What would you do if you were in the same situation as ... on page...?

The following question examples are NOT good discussion starters. Do you know WHY?

- Who was the main character?
- Where does this story take place?
- What is the name of...?
- Do you like...?

Summarizing

When good readers read large chunks of a story or challenging text, they usually summarize what they have read.

Directions: In your reading journal, write a brief summary of the text you have just read. Think about the main events and characters who are most important in the story. You may want to use the summarizing graphic organizer to help you organize the main events.

Secondary Reading Strategies

As students move to upper elementary and middle school, they are assigned content reading for classwork or homework with increasing frequency. One dilemma in assigning independent content reading is that the students often read the words as instructed; however, they are unable to extract the information they need from the reading. Successful content reading requires that we teach students specific strategies that allow them to extract important learning from the text. A second dilemma is when we assign content reading for homework. It is often difficult for teachers to determine which students have and have not completed (and comprehended) the assignment without administering quizzes and/or long sessions of recall question-and-answer periods that use up a great deal of class time. The following strategies are used by middle and high school teachers to increase students' comprehension of content-area reading. Several of these are also good techniques for monitoring students' completion of the content reading when it is assigned for homework.

Graphic Organizers

During units on short stories or other such fictional reading, we assign our students to read a short story for homework and also to fill out the blank plot curve as they read. As you can see in the following example, the blank plot curve leaves room for students to fill in information about the plot's rising action, climax, falling action, resolution, conflict, and main characters. We collect the plot curves at the beginning of class on which the assigned reading is due, not only as a means of ensuring that our students are doing their homework, but also to better determine which students understood the story and which struggled with comprehension. These plot curves may also serve as useful study aids for an end-of-unit test or to help in locating particular quotations from the text for an essay assignment. The following is a sample of a **plot curve graphic organizer**.

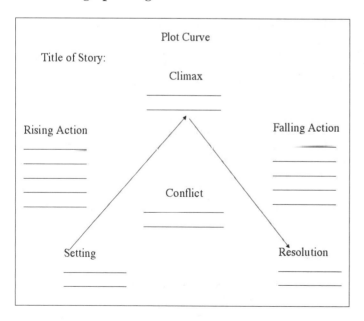

Guiding Questions

For a harder work, such as Shakespeare's *Romeo and Juliet*, we give our students a sheet with six or seven plot-based questions to answer as they complete a night's reading. As with the graphic organizers, our goals are threefold: (1) to hold our students accountable for their assigned reading, (2) to give us a means of seeing which students are struggling with comprehension, and (3) to provide checkpoints for keeping our students on track as they read. Chapter 5 gives a comprehensive explanation of questioning techniques. The following are questions related to a *Romeo and Juliet* reading assignment for Act II, scene iii.

Freedman   *Literature Section*

Romeo and Juliet
Act II, scene iii

Summary:

Vocabulary Words: _____ ,

_____ , _____

Discussion Questions:

1.   What is the Friar collecting?

2a. What does the following mean?

For naught so vile that on earth doeth live,
But to the earth some special good doth give:
Nor aught so good but, strained from that fair use,
Revolts true birth, stumbling on abuse.

(lines 18–21)

2b. What example does the Friar give of this principle?

2c. Where, besides in plants, does Friar Lawrence say this principle applies?

3.   What does the Friar mean when he says,

Within the infant rind of this small flower
Poison hath residence, and medicine power.
For this, being smelt, with that part cheers each part
Being tasted, slays all sense with the heart.

(lines 25–28)

4. What does the Friar guess about Romeo?

5. Whom does the Friar guess Romeo has been with?

6. How does Romeo respond to this guess?

7. What does Romeo want the Friar to do for him?

8. Why does the Friar criticize Romeo?

9. Why does the Friar agree to do what Romeo asks him to do?

10. What is the difference between Rosaline and Juliet
    a. according to Romeo?
    b. according to Friar Lawrence?

11. What is the Friar's final piece of advice to Romeo? What does it mean?

Note-Taking

In college, students will be able to take notes in the margins of their assigned reading. In high school, however, we sometimes provide students with "sticky notes" on which to take notes. This allows them to make their notes right on the page from which the notes came. This method is particularly useful if students have been assigned to look for certain literary devices as they read. Students might jot down the term foreshadowing on the sticky note, with an arrow directed at the paragraph in which they spotted the foreshadowing. The sticky notes technique may also be useful for students who are assigned essays or other writing assignments that are due upon completion of

the book. As students read, they may mark scenes, quotations, and incidents that they think might be useful as evidence for their papers. Toward this end, students might jot down one to two sentences noting why a page's text might be useful. Students might even draw an arrow directing their attention to the specific paragraph or sentence on the page that caught their attention.[7] (See the following example.) It should be noted, however, that students with poor handwriting might find it frustrating to be asked to take notes on such a small surface area.

Pre-Discussion

Before assigning students a short story or essay to read for homework, we often work with our students on some pre-reading brainstorming to activate their thinking about what they will read that night. For example, we might ask, "What does the title of the story make you think that this story might be about?" At the start of a new book, we might ask, "What does the cover of the book give away about the book's plot?" While students are working their way through a novel, we might ask, "What do you think is going to happen in the next chapter?" We then put our students' predictions on flipchart paper and begin class the next day by comparing their predictions to what actually occurred in the previous night's reading. By making predictions with our students, we are creating some "mental checkpoints" for them to consider as they read. Ideally, we want our students to be thinking as they read, "Oh, that's just like I predicted" or, "Oh, that's not what I expected at all."

Differentiated Reading Assignments

To best support classes with heterogeneous reading levels, we often assign **semi-independent reading projects**. For these projects, we choose four different

---

7   At the end of Chapter 3 is a brief article about reading for understanding. This article contains a procedure teachers can use to efficiently and effectively check assigned reading in the various content areas.

Romeo and Juliet, III, iii, 30–33   *Sticky Note*

Romeo: 'Tis torture and not mercy. Heaven is here
       Where Juliet lives, and every cat and dog
       And little mouse, every unworthy thing,   ←——— Hyperbole
       Live here in heaven, and may look on her
       But Romeo may not.   Romeo is exaggerating when he
                                                         says every little mouse gets to
                                                         look at Juliet.

books from our school's multiple-copy book collection and bring approximately 10 copies of each book to class. We describe each of the four books to the students, giving a brief description of plot, page length, and overall difficulty. Students are allowed to choose which of the four they want to read. Students write their choices on slips of paper, which they turn in. On the next day, we privately consult with students who we feel may have chosen a book that is either too challenging or not challenging enough. For the next few weeks, lessons are designed on literary elements, which students are then responsible for finding within the particular book that they have chosen to read. Concepts like *foreshadowing, tone, foil, antagonist, falling action*, and *internal conflict* are studied in class, and then students look for these elements in their respective books while reading for homework. The note-taking described previously is a good way for students to identify the elements in the book as they read so that they are prepared to talk about these elements the next day in class. For more information on differentiating instruction, see Chapter 6.

Choosing Good Material

Reading projects are unquestionably more successful when students are reading books and stories that genuinely interest them. A teacher of a twelfth-grade English class, for example, discovered that his students were absolutely fascinated by an autobiography written by a formerly homeless teenager who described living in New York's Grand Central Station (*Living at the Edge of the World*, by Tina P.). His students loved reading a book written by a teenager and were fascinated by her tales from the tunnels of Grand Central Station. Students who claimed they'd never actually completed a book in high school reported they'd bought their own copies of the memoir so they could read it again.

Teaching the Strategies for Reading Content-Specific Material in All Classes

Math, science, and social studies teachers sometimes believe that teaching students reading strategies should be left to the English and reading teachers; however, each of these disciplines requires its own type of reading. For mathematics, for example, standardized assessments in most states and provinces test students on lengthy word problems. Students need to practice reading these types of problems. They need to practice figuring out what the question is asking of

them and how to draw out the relevant information. Different math teachers favor different strategies for guiding students in this type of reading. Some math teachers prefer students to underline the relevant information provided in a word problem, while others encourage students to note this information in a table on a separate sheet of paper. Social studies teachers who expect students to do Internet research for projects and papers need to work with students on how to read material they come across over the Internet. For example, they should teach their students to ask, "Who is the author of this source?" and, "How credible is this source of information?" Finally, science teachers often assign reading in more traditional textbooks. For this type of assigned reading, students may be taught the **SQ3R method** (Robinson 1970) of (1) examining the bold-print section headings prior to reading a section, (2) mentally formulating a question that they believe this section of reading will attempt to answer, and then (3) using this question as a mental checkpoint as they go on to read and consider the section's content. English and reading teachers may support their colleagues in improving their students' reading, but to some degree *all* teachers need to teach reading as it relates to their specific content areas.

Book Pals

A way in which one teacher managed to sneak in some extra reading practice for students was by creating a partnership with a third-grade class in a nearby school. Once a week, this teacher's students would travel to the third-grade classroom and pair up with a "book pal," with whom they would read a story for approximately one half-hour. The high school students enjoyed working with their third-grade counterparts and, in the process of modeling good reading skills, unquestionably improved themselves.

Encourage Outside Reading

As people passionate about the subject matter we teach, the majority of us have shelves and shelves (or Kindles) full of books about or related to the courses we teach. If you feel comfortable doing so, bring in your books and fill up a bookshelf in the back of your classroom with a sign-out sheet for students, or direct students to the relevant section of their school or public library. Keep a list of URLs to readings on the Web on a wide array of topics. Offer students extra credit for reading one of these books or Web articles on their own and then coming to discuss it with you after school or during lunch. If your class load or teaching schedule precludes such an arrangement, consider asking students to record audio or video of themselves describing the book or article to a friend, sibling, or parent and answering their questions about the book. Provide guidelines about the expected length of the conversation and questions that the friend, sibling, or parent might be likely to ask. Perhaps you might start off each school week by profiling one of these books for the class, in a presentation similar to a coming attraction teaser for a recently released film.

Summer reading has been shown to be a significant factor in student reading ability. In their article, "Got Books?" Richard Allington and Anne McGill-Franzen (2008) show the dramatic impact that a lack of summer reading has on children from low-income families. They cite the work of Hayes and Grether (1983), and more recently Alexander, Entwisle, and Olson (2007), which indicates, "Summer [reading] setback explains approximately 80 percent of the reading achievement gap between poor and non-poor students at age 14." This problem is due in part to the lack of books available to these students during summer. Neuman and Celano (2001) "found roughly 10 times greater access to reading material in higher-income neighborhoods than in lower-income neighborhoods in the same large urban center" (p. 46). The article goes on to describe a number of ways in which school districts have successfully provided low-income families with books during and summer and encouraged reading among those students. Some examples include the following:

> *Summer [reading] setback explains approximately 80 percent of the reading achievement gap between poor and non-poor students at age 14.*

- at different intervals during the summer, mailing students books that they have selected , with postcards encouraging reading
- in the last two weeks of school (prior to summer vacation), teachers instructing students in comprehension and paired-reading skills
- opening school libraries in low-income neighborhoods during the summer months
- providing students with a selection of books from popular culture (It was found that students were more likely to read books that were about people and subjects in popular culture that were important to their lives. Books about people in the media [e.g., child TV stars] and other topics of daily interest were most likely to cause students to read during the summer.)

Developing Proficient Mathematical Problem Solvers

Unfortunately, many students have the misconception that they are poor math students and will always be "bad" at math. As teachers, it is our job to instill confidence in children so they feel as though they are able to solve a variety of mathematical problems. In order to do so, we must equip students with tools to use: that is, strategies they may use to better understand and solve such problems.

To begin teaching students about problem-solving, it is important to first understand what they believe problem-solving is all about. As a class, create a problem-solving web, and elicit students' prior knowledge about this topic. If necessary, teachers may need to prompt students with questions such as

"Is there one right way to solve mathematical problems? Explain."
"Is there always one right solution? Explain."

After brainstorming about problem-solving, highlight the important points with regard to it. The different problem-solving strategies should be introduced and explained at this point. Each week, teachers may want to emphasize a different strategy until all strategies have been covered. Teachers will want to post a sign with the following strategies in the classroom:

- Look for a pattern.
- Write an equation.
- Draw a picture.
- Make a chart, table, graph, or diagram.
- Make an organized list.
- Act it out.
- Use manipulatives.
- Guess, check, and revise.
- Work backwards.
- Solve a simpler or similar problem.

The following format may be used to teach students how to systematically solve problems.

Problem-Solving Format

Please use this format as a guide when you solve the Problem of the Week. Remember to use your POW journal to record your work.

Title of Problem:

Thought: Write a sentence that retells what the problem asks you to do.
The problem is asking me...

Information: Highlight the important information in the problem. Next, write a sentence that lists the important information in the problem.
The information tells me...

Plan: Choose a strategy that you plan to use. Remember, you may need to use several different strategies to help you solve the problem.
I plan to solve the problem by...

Steps to Solution: Show and label your work clearly and neatly. (Step 1...Step 2...Step 3...) Include visuals such as charts, graphs, pictures, or tables. Clearly explain, in order, each step to the solution.

Solution: Label your answer. Be sure to ask yourself, "Does this answer make sense?" Check your work.
My answer is...

Self-Assessment: Read over your work. Are your steps clearly written? Did you proofread carefully and make appropriate changes? Does your solution make sense? Did you remember to include all of the above parts?

I feel I deserve a _____ because...

Created by Jenny Deane and Laurie Levin.

Teachers should model the process of solving mathematical problems for students using the format described previously. Before solving a problem together as a class, share the rubric that will be used to evaluate their work.

Begin by choosing a problem in which all students will be able to grasp the mathematical content fairly easily. Read the problem together, and have students highlight or underline the important information, including what the problem is asking them to do.

Next, as a class, use the format to write a sentence that retells what the problem is asking students to do. Although this step seems straightforward, students often have difficulty determining what they are being asked to do, particularly with multi-step problems.

Then, as a class, write the important information in the problem. Be sure students are able to give reasons why the selected information is important. Students often tend to include irrelevant information, so it is important to discuss the difference between interesting information and information that is critical to solving the problem.

The next part of the process entails choosing a strategy and developing a plan to solve the problem. At this point, brainstorm a variety of strategies that might be used to solve the problem. Be sure to emphasize that a combination of strategies might be necessary and that sometimes the initial plan does not work. Students should also understand they should always use what they know to find out what they don't know.

After a plan is formulated, begin solving the problem as a class. As you solve the problem together, show and label all work. Keep track of the steps you take by recording each step in an organized manner. After the problem has been solved, check to make sure the solution makes sense. Reread your steps to solution, and add any necessary details.

At this point, share the following checklist with the students. They should use this form after completing a problem to ensure that they have completed all parts of the problem.

Assessing Open-Response Questions

Are all parts of the question answered?
Are all directions followed?
Are all parts and answers labeled?
Is the explanation clear for the reader?
Does the explanation include a combination of pictures, numbers, and words?
Are appropriate math vocabulary and symbols included in the response?
Is the work organized, neat, and spelled well enough to be understood by the reader?

Finally, students should assess their work and give specific reasons for giving themselves a particular score. Have them refer to the rubric when they assess their work. The rubric for this activity can be found in Chapter 4.

This problem-solving process should be modeled and practiced by students with guidance before they begin working independently. At times, you may wish to have students work in pairs or small groups. In this way, students may benefit from understanding others' perspectives and may experience firsthand how different strategies may be used to solve the same problem.

The problem-solving process may be used with both lower and upper elementary grade levels; however, the format that was outlined previously is most appropriate for grades three through five. Teachers of lower elementary grades may wish to modify and simplify this format for their students.

The form is used by one high school teacher to aid students in solving mathematics problems in a similar way.

Providing students with the necessary tools to use—that is, an organized process and an understanding of possible strategies—is imperative in order to help children develop the confidence and skills needed to solve higher-order mathematical problems. All students have the ability to solve open-ended, complex mathematical problems. It is our responsibility as teachers to ensure that they are equipped to do so!

Problem #	Problem Illustration(s): Add explanation.	Equation: Show all your attempts.	Solution: Show the final equation and the answer.

Conclusion

Bob and Joe were educated at a time when the concepts discussed in this chapter were not known to educators. In both low-socioeconomic circumstances like Bob and Joe's or in homes with the advantages that come with more financial resources, there are students who lack motivation in the school setting. Today, more and more educators are aware of the powerful impact that they may have on developing the motivation of their students. Motivating students requires that we address all seven components: connecting the curriculum, teacher enthusiasm, engaging teaching, differentiating instruction, interpersonal relationships, teacher-student beliefs about the nature of intelligence, and nutrition. Educators, with the right professional development and tools for instruction, may significantly increase student motivation and the likelihood that all students will reach high levels of success in school and in life.

References

Alexander, K.L., Entwisle, D.R., and Olsen, L.S. "Lasting Consequences of the Summer Learning Gap." *American Sociological Review* 72, no. 2 (2007): 167–180.

Allen, M. and Morrison, G. "Promoting Student Resilience in School Contexts." *Theory into Practice: Journal of the Ohio State University's College of Education* 46, no. 2 (Spring 2007): 62–169.

Allington, R. and McGill-Franzen, A. "Got Books?" *Educational Leadership* 65, no. 7 (April 2008): 20–23

Barron, J. "Intelligence and General Strategies. In *Strategies in Information Processing*, ed. Underwood, G., pp. 403–450. London: Academic Press, 1978.

Binet, A. *Modern Ideas about Children.* Translated by Suzanne Heisler. Menlo Park, CA: Suzanne Heisler, [1984] c. 1975..

Bloom, B. *Developing Talent in Young People.* New York: Ballantine, 1985.

Danforth, S., and Smith, T. *Engaging Troubling Students: A Constructivist Approach.* Thousand Oaks, CA: Corwin Press, 2005.

Devlin, B., Fienberg, S., Resnick, D., and Roeder, K. "Heredity, Environment, and the Question of 'How?'" *Psychological Review* 65 (1994): 197–208.

Devlin, B., Fienberg, S., Resnick, D., and Roeder, K. *Intelligence, Genes, and Success: Scientists Respond to the Bell Curve.* New York: Springer-Verlag New York, Inc., 1997.

Dermody, J. "Going for Growth." *Educational Leadership* 70, no. 1 (September 2012): p. 2.

Diala, C.C., Muntaner, C., and Walrath, C. "Gender, Occupational, and Socio-Economic Correlates of Alcohol and Drug Abuse among US Rural, Metropolitan, and Urban Residents." *American Journal of Drug and Alcohol Abuse* 30, no. 2 (2004): 409–428.

Duckworth, A. and Seligman, M. "Self-Discipline Outdoes IQ in Predicting Academic Performance of Adolescents." *Psychological Science* 16, no. 12 (2005): 939–944.

Duckworth, A., Peterson, C., Mathews, M., and Kelly, D. "Grit: Perseverance and Passion for Longer-Term Goals." *Journal of Personality and Social Psychology* 92, no. 6 (2007): 1087–1110.

Duckworth, A. and Seligman, M. "Self-Discipline Gives Girls the Edge: Gender in Self-Discipline, Grades, and Achievement Test Scores." *Journal of Educational Psychology* 98, no. 1 (2006): 198–208.

Dweck, C. (2000) *Essays in Social Psychology: Self Theories.* Philadelphia, PA: Psychology Press of Taylor and Francis Group, 2000.

Dweck, C. *Mindset: The New Psychology of Success.* New York: Random House Publishing Group, 2008.

Ericsson, K.A., Krampe, R., and Tesch-Romer, C. "The Role of Deliberate Practice in the Acquisition of Expert Performance." *Psychological Review* 100, no. 3 (1993): 363–406.

Fraser, S. *The Bell Curve Wars: Race, Intelligence, and the Future of America.* New York: Perseus Books, 1995.

Galea, S., Ahern, J., Tracy, M., and Vlahov, D. "Neighborhood Income and Income Distribution and the Use of Cigarettes, Alcohol, and Marijuana." *American Journal of Preventive Medicine* 32, no. 6 (June 2007): 195–202.

Gardner, H. and Walters, J. Excerpts from "The Development and Education of Intelligences." In *Essays on Intellect*, pp. 1–13. Washington, DC: Association for Supervision and Curriculum Development, 1985.

Gershoff, E.T. "Living at the Edge: Low Income and Hardship among America's Kindergarteners." *National Center for Children in Poverty Research Brief No. 3.* http://www.nccp.org/publications/pub_530.html.

Goleman, D. *Emotional Intelligence.* Washington, DC: PBS video, 1999.

Golemen, D. *Focus: The Hidden Driver of Excellent.* New York: Harper Collins, 2013.

Gould, S. "Curveball." *The New Yorker,* November 28, 1994.

Hager, E.R, Quigg, A.M., Black, M.M., et al. "Development and Validity of a Two-Item Screen to Identify Families at Risk for Food Insecurity." *Pediatrics* 126 (2010): 26–32.

Hanushek, E. "The Economics of School Quality." *German Economic Review* 6, no. 3 (2005): 269–286.

Harmon, A. "The DNA Age: In DNA Era, New Worries about Prejudice." *New York Times,* November 11, 2007.

Hart, B. and Risley, T.R. "The Early Catastrophe: The 30 Million Word Gap by Age 3." In *Meaningful Differences in the Everyday Experiences of Young American Children.* Reproduced in *American Federation of Teachers,* Spring 2003. https://www.aft.org/sites/default/files/periodicals/TheEarlyCatastrophe.pdf.

Hattie, J. *Visible Learning: A Synthesis of over 800 Meta-Analysis Relating the Achievement.* New York: Routledge, 2008.

Hayes, D.P. and Rether, J. "The School Year and Vacations: When Do Students Learn?" *Cornell Journal of Social Relations* 17, no. 1 (1983): 56–71.

Hernstein, R. and Murray, C. *The Bell Curve: Intelligence and Class Structure in American Life.* New York: The Free Press, 1994.

Hunter, M. "'If at First…': Attribution Theory in the Classroom." *Educational Leadership* (October 1987): 50–53.

Jacobson, L. "IQ Study Weighs Genes and Environment." *Education Week* XXIII, no. 2 (September 2003).

Jacobson, M. "Afraid of Looking Dumb." *Educational Leadership* 41 (September 2013): 40–43.

Jensen, E. "How Poverty Affects Classroom Engagement." *Educational Leadership* 70, no. 8 (May 2013): 24–30.

Jensen, E. *Engaging Students with Poverty in Mind: Practical Strategies for Raising Student Achievement.* Alexandria, VA: ASCD, 2013.

Jones, S.M., Bouffard, S.M. and Weissbourd, R. "Educators' Social and Emotional Skills Vital to Learning." *Phi Delta Kappan* 94, no. 8 (May 2013): 62–65.

Kelves, D.J. *In the Name of Eugenics: Genetics and the Uses of Human Heredity.* New York: Alfred A. Knopf, 1985.

Kosfeld, M., Heinrichs, M., Zak, P.J., Fischbacher, U., and Fehr, E. "Oxytocin Increases Trust in Humans." *Nature* 435, no. 2 (2005): 673–676.

Melville, N.A. "Child Poverty: Negative Impact on Brain Development." *Medscape.* July 28, 2015. http://www. medscape.com/viewarticle/848725.

Morgane, P.J., Mokler, D.J., Galler, J.R. "Effects of Prenatal Protein Malnutrition on the Hippocampal Formation." *Neuroscience and Biobehavioral Reviews* 26, no. 4 (June 2002): 471–483.

Murray, C. *Real Education: Four Simple Truths for Bringing America's Schools Back to Reality,* New York: Three Rivers Press, 2009.

Murray, C. and Pianta, R. "The Importance of Teacher-Student Relationships for Adolescents with High-Incidence of Disabilities." *Theory into Practice: Journal of the Ohio State University's College of Education* 46, no. 2 (Spring 2007): 105–112.

National Center for Children in Poverty. *Parental Employment in Low-Income Families,* 2004.

National Center for Education Statistics. *Parent and Family Involvement in Education: 2002–2003,* 2005.

Neuman, S.B. and Celano, D.C. "Access to Print in Low-Income and Middle- Income Communities." *Reading Research Quarterly* 36, no. 1 (2001): 8–26.

Nunley, K.F. "Active Research Leads to Active Classrooms." *Principal Leadership* (March 2002): 53–61.

Perkins, D. *Outsmarting IQ: The Emerging Science of Learnable Intelligence.* New York: The Free Press, 1995.

Robinson, F. *Effective Study,* 4th ed. New York: Harper and Row, 1970.

Seider, S. "Effort Determines Success at Roxbury Prep." *Phi Delta Kappan* 94, no. 2 (October 2013): 28–32.

Simon, H. and Chase, W. "Skill in Chess." *American Scientist* 61 (1973): 394–403.

Sullo, B. *Activating the Desire to Learn.* Alexandria, VA: ASCD, 2005.

Sullo, B. *The Inspiring Teacher: Making a Positive Difference in Students' Lives.* Livingston, NJ: Funderstanding LLC, 2013.

Terman, L. "Were We Born That Way?" *World's Work* 44 (1922): 660.

Theobald, M. *Increasing Student Motivation: Strategies for Middle and High School Teachers.* Thousand Oaks CA: Corwin Press, 2006.

Urban Child Institute. "Nutrition and Early Brain Development." March 2011. http://www.urbanchildinstitute .org/articles/updates/nutrition-and-early-brain-development.

Related Readings

Allan, S.D. and Goddard, Y.L. "Differentiated Instruction and RTI: A Natural Fit." *Educational Leadership* 68, no, 2 (October 2010).

Armstrong, T. *Neurodiversity in the Classroom: Strength-Based Strategies to Help Students with Special Needs Succeed in School and Life.* Alexandria, VA: ASCD, 2012.

Berger, R. "Classes in Courage." *Phi Delta Kappan* 95, no. 2 (October 2013): 14–18.

Cook J.T. and Frank, D.A. "Food Security, Poverty, and Human Development in the United States." *Annals of the New York Academy of Sciences* 1136, no. 1 (2008): 193–209.

Davis, K., Christodoulou, J., Seider, S., and Gardner, H. "The Theory of Multiple Intelligences." In *Cambridge Handbook of Intelligence*, eds. Sternberg, R. and Kaufman, S. pp. 485–504. Cambridge, UK: Cambridge University Press, 2011. http://people.bu.edu/seider/Consolidated%20papers/MI%20Chapter%20for%20Cambridge%20Handbook%20Most%20Updated%20Word%20Document%2011-22-2010.pdf.

DeLong, R.G. "Effects of Nutrition on Brain Development in Humans." *American Journal of Clinical Nutrition* 57 (1993): 286S–290S.

Dermody, J.H. "Going for the Growth." *Educational Leadership* 70, no. 1 (September 2012).

Dweck, C.S. "Even Geniuses Work Hard." *Educational Leadership* 68, no. 1 (September 2010): 16–20.

Ferlazzo, L. "Eight Things Skilled Teachers Think, Say, and Do." *Educational Leadership* 70, no. 2 (October 2012).

Gardner, W. "The IQ Debate." *Educator Week* blog, February 25, 2013. http://blogs.edweek.org/edweek/walt_gardners_reality_check/2013/02/the_iq_debate.html.

Golemen, D. *Focus: The Hidden Driver of Excellence.* New York: Harper Collins, 2013.

Innis, S.M. "Dietary (n-3) Fatty Acids and Rain Development." *Journal of Nutrition* 137 (2007): 855–859.

"It's OK—You're Just Not Good at Math." *Educational Leadership* 70, no. 1 (September 2012): 8–9.

Mann, D. "Does IQ Test Really Measure Intelligence?" *WebMD.* December 12, 2012. http://www.webmd.com/brain/news/20121218/iq-test-really-measure-intelligence.

Mieliwocki, R. "Focus: Teaching Middle School English." *GoTeach.* March 15, 2013. http://www.futureeducators.org/goteach/2013/03/15/focus-teaching-middle-school-english/.

Miller, D.L. "Got It Wrong? Think Again. And Again." *Phi Delta Kappan* 94, no. 5 (February 2013): 50–52.

Nakkula, M. "A Crooked Path to Success." *Phi Delta Kappan* 94, no. 6 (March 2013): 60–63.

Nord, M., Coleman-Jensen, A., Andrews, M., et al. "Household Food Security in the United States, 2009." *US Department of Agriculture Economic Research Report 108.* 2010. http://www.ers.usda.gov/Publications/ERR108.

Park, K., Kersey, M., Geppert, J., et al. "Household Food Insecurity Is a Risk Factor for Iron-Deficiency Anaemia in a Multi-Ethnic, Low-Income Sample of Infants and Toddlers." *Public Health Nutrition* 12 (2009): 2,120–2,128.

Perkins-Gough, D. "The Significance of Grit: A Conversation with Angela Lee Duckworth." *Educational Leadership* 71, no. 1 (September 2013): 14–20.

Phillips, V. and Popovik, Z. "More than Child's Play: Games Have Potential Learning and Assessment Tools." *Phi Delta Kappan* 94, no. 2 (October 2012): 26–30.

Rosales, F.J., Reznick, J.S., and Zeisel, S.H. "Understanding the Role of Nutrition in the Brain and Behavioral Development of Toddlers and Preschool Children: Identifying and Addressing Methodological Barriers." *Nutritional Neuroscience* 12, no. 5 (2009): 190–202.

Sparks, S.D. "Studies Link Student Boredom to Stress." *Education Week* 32, no. 7 (October 10, 2012): 1, 16. http://www.edweek.org/ew/articles/ 2012/10/10/07boredom_ep.h32.html.

Sullo, B. *Inspiring Teacher: Making a Positive Difference in Students' Lives.* Livingston, NJ: Funderstanding LLC, 2013.

Thiers, N. "EL Study Guide." *Educational Leadership* 68, no 3 (November 2010).

Von Frank, V. "Group Smarts: Elevate Collective Intelligence through Communication, Norms, and Diversity." *The Learning System* 8, no. 4 (Summer 2013): 1, 4–5.

Weissglass, J. "Listen First, Then Teach." *Phi Delta Kappan* 93, no. 6 (March 2012): 29-33.

Wight V.R., Thampi, K., Briggs, J. "Who Are America's Poor Children? Examining Food Insecurity among Children in the United States." National Center for Children in Poverty, 2010. http://www.nccp.org/publications/pdf/text_958.pdf.

Wiliam, D. "Feedback: Part of a System." *Educational Leadership* 70, no. 1 (September 2012): 30–34.

Winerman, L. "Smarter than Ever?" *Monitor* 44, no. 3 (March 2013): 1–4. http://www.apa.org/monitor/2013/03/smarter.aspx.

Students with Disabilities: Intelligence and Motivation

The focus on intelligence and motivation in this chapter is a very common area of discussion regarding supporting students with disabilities. These are two areas where assumptions are often made very early regarding them. Often, prior to a student being identified as having a disability, many people assume that they are not as intelligent as other students or that they lack the motivation to learn like other students. Component 6 described in this chapter shows the close relationship between intelligence and motivation or what a student believes about his or her intelligence and their level of motivation. This is very intriguing, since much of the basis of special education identification has been founded on intelligence or intelligence quotient (IQ).

In working with students with disabilities, IQ tests can be beneficial in helping teachers understand the type of instruction the student will best respond to or the accommodations that are needed to support the student with accessing the curriculum. IQ tests measure the multiple problem-solving abilities that are affected by a number of specific cognitive processes. While the measure itself is important, it is even more important to have the expertise of a psychologist or assessment specialist (e.g., speech/language pathologist) to determine the student's specific cognitive strengths and areas of need (Holdnack 2015). For example, a student may have poorly developed vocabulary and

limited world knowledge, but have strong auditory and visual perception skills. The student also may be able to repeat the information told to him or her, but not comprehend its meaning to use the information appropriately. The variance between the student's strengths and limitations could make the teacher think the student is ignoring the verbal directions when, in fact, the student is unable to comprehend and apply the information appropriately (Holdnack 2015). Given this information, the teacher can refrain from making assumptions about the student, and also use strategies of prompting and modeling to support the student in learning to apply the information appropriately. An important caution to teachers is to not focus so much on the quantitative IQ measure, but rather the specific strengths and limitations. Using the expertise of the person who interprets the evaluation will help identify the specific strength areas that can be built upon. There are many examples of students who have had low-average or below-average intelligence and learning challenges who have gone on to have many successes and accomplishments. Some of these people include Richard Branson, business investor and founder of the Virgin Group; Jamie Oliver, chef and restaurateur; and Danny Glover, actor—just to name a few.

The work of Carol Dweck on growth mind-set,

noted in this chapter, is very important and relevant to working with students with disabilities. Many students who have disabilities struggle with their confidence and feelings regarding their intelligence. For many of them, this starts very early in their school life. Understanding attribution theory and applying Dweck's work and research on developing a growth mind-set in students can support students with disabilities in building their confidence and understanding of increasing their intelligence. The "Growth Mindset 2015" states that in a growth mind-set school, teachers collaborate with their colleagues and instructional leaders, they strive to strengthen their practice, and believe that all students can learn and achieve and show results of that. For example, when working with students with disabilities, a teacher in a growth mind-set school would collaborate with the specialist to plan and refine the accommodations and strategies that work best for each student. The classroom teacher would agree to share lesson plans in advance with the special educator, and the special educator would agree to return sample accommodations to him or her to implement in the class for the lesson shared. Finding time to collaborate is often a barrier for teachers; however, using technology such as Google Hangouts and Google Docs can help diminish those challenges. Google Hangouts is a free, web-based video conferencing application that teachers could use to share videos of sample strategies or a model of implementing strategies or accommodations to support students with disabilities in the lesson shared. Google Docs is also free, and is a web-based platform for saving and sharing documents. While face-to-face planning is the best, these are very good and easy-to-use alternatives when time is a barrier.

Messaging to students with disabilities is extremely important; they often think or believe they are the only one who is experiencing or have experienced the challenges they often face. As noted in this chapter, using messages posted on the classroom walls and embedding stories about others who have succeeded in the face of challenges similar to those the students face can support students in believing that their intelligence can grow. Using real examples from past students and pointing out specific areas where they persevered and worked hard makes it more relatable to the student. In addition, the praise strategies that are used can make a difference for students with disabilities. Pointing out specifics and celebrating what the student has done well regarding their learning, rather than vague praises, help students with disabilities reshape their thinking and build their confidence in the effort they put into their work, which leads to improved motivation.

Once students with disabilities have experienced multiple negative interactions regarding their school performance, it is a challenge to turn it around; however, it is not impossible. Strategies shared in this chapter can support you in reaching your student before he or she has multiple negative interactions in his or her school performance. Designing a classroom that reinforces the belief that students' effort and perseverance matters will make the difference for students with disabilities. The following websites may be helpful in creating examples for students with disabilities who have faced challenges and have overcome them:

http://www.disabled-world.com/artman/publish/article_0060.shtml

http://healthresearchfunding.org famous-people-intellectual-disabilities/

References

Holdnack, J.A. "Defining the Role of Intellectual and Cognitive Assessments in Special Education." *The Psychological Corporation*. http://images.pearsonclinical.com/images/pdf/wisciv/definingtherole.pdf.

Langtree, I. "Famous People with Disabilities." *Disabled World*, November 1, 2005. http://www.disabled-world.com/artman/publish/article_0060.shtml.

"The Science: The Growth Mindset." *Mindset Works, Inc.* http://www.mindsetworks.com/webnav/whatismindset.aspx.

English Language Learners: Motivating Linguistically Diverse Learners

Gathering Relevant Data

Motivating linguistically diverse learners to fully participate in all content and curriculum activities requires gathering and using data to plan engaging lessons. During the registration process, valuable information is collected on an English language learner's proficiency and educational history in English.

Schools and districts have learned from the wait-and-see approach that English learners lose critical time spent on actual learning when the need for English language or other academic support is unclear at the time of registration. English learners cannot afford the time it takes to acquire the English proficiency level needed for teachers to accurately assess previously learned knowledge and skills. To develop lessons in which ELLs can immediately and fully participate, general education teachers should review the ELL's cumulative records file, if available, and communicate with the ESL teacher about the results of any current or previous English proficiency testing. Every teacher will need to be familiar with their ELLs' proficiency levels in each of the four language domains before selecting support strategies and materials. Teachers also have the responsibility of consistently measuring ELLs' progress in acquiring English and content knowledge and skills with appropriate assessment tools, and the duty to review and offer feedback on student work. Support offered to other students, such as small-group instruction for math or literacy, should also include English learners if and when they appear to struggle.

Understanding Why and How Linguistically Diverse Students Struggle

The information gathered during registration and from the list of questions from the essay at the end of Chapter 2 will provide insight into the life and experience of English learners, but teachers then must ask, "What do I do with this information to teach the child?" The ven components for increasing student motivation in this chapter will also increase the English learner's motivation, as long as messages and motivators are communicated in a way that students (and their parents) understand. However, some factors that cause low internal motivation will be unique to English learners. Below are samples of student voices that demonstrate circumstances unique to linguistically diverse students.

Kindergarten student: *"No me siento bien (I don't feel well). No escuché al cuento (I didn't listen to the story) porque tengo sueño (because I am tired) y me duele el diente (and my tooth hurts). Me quiero ir pa' mi casa (I want to go home). I want mámi."*
Analysis: This child does not participate in a read aloud because of physical pain, possibly caused by poor dental care. A child's socioeconomic status is private information and free lunch lists are prohibited from being shared. However, most teachers recognize signs of poverty because they are with students every day and notice habits, physical appearance, and frequency/quality of home/school communication. Economic, health, and nutritional issues are not unique to linguistic-minority students, but providing families with access to support is challenging when there is a language barrier. This is especially complicated if the family speaks a less commonly spoken home language like Spanish and interpreters are difficult to locate.

Recommendation: The teacher's nurturing personality may not be enough to comfort this child and provide the support he needs. The general education and ESL teachers communicate with the nursing staff and administrators to facilitate access to various educational, community, and medical resources. One-on-one attention and support from the ESL teacher, counselor, and the general education teacher will communicate messages that he is safe in school, the adults will take good care of him, and he is just as intelligent as every child in the class.

Third-grade student: *"My old school closed and I had to stay at home. I didn't get to read books, so I got kinda dumb. Here, we studied Helen Keller. Everyone thought she was dumb too, but she wasn't. She just couldn't understand what everyone was saying and couldn't tell them how smart she was. I know how she felt."*
Analysis: This student has had an interruption to her education most likely due to circumstances of poverty, political violence, or natural disaster. She is acutely aware of her interrupted learning and this has negatively influenced her motivation to learn and the

concept of her own intelligence. These students usually arrive after second grade with two or more years less schooling than their peers. They are likely to have suffered significant trauma in addition to other life experiences seldom experienced by average American students.

Recommendation: The ESL teacher, general education teacher, counselor, nurse, and principal collectively determine the type and frequency of English language support. The team may also recommend small-group or one-on-one intensive literacy/numeracy support, an in-school social group, outside counseling, and community resources for refugee and resettlement families. If the child has been adopted, counseling and/or nursing staff can locate support for families who adopt international children. Professional development on serving students with limited or interrupted formal education is recommended for all professional staff who work with this child.

Sixth-grade student: *"My family came here to have a better life. We wait a long time, so I try and be happy. I miss my friends and grandma. I feel sad when I sit in class or cafeteria. Is so loud. I don't know why they look at me, and I don't ask someone to help me. I don't want no one to sit next to me."*

Analysis: This child may have come from a bilingual program in an American school or may be new to the country. Children don't choose to move their family and often have difficulty seeing how a new place will be better for them. Not understanding social language isolates English learners when they are new to a school. Teachers and the student's peers may be unaware of their own lack of cultural understanding or their own preconceived ideas of newcomers. Some may make assumptions about students' past experience, socioeconomic situation, or immigration status/documentation. This can have a very negative effect on student learning.

Recommendation: Teachers use relationship-building strategies that demonstrate positive messages and facilitate all students to develop socio-linguistic competence and cultural proficiency. Recognizing obstacles can reassure struggling ELLs, but a welcoming atmosphere with appreciation for diversity will make all students feel more confident in school. Professional development on teaching diverse learners and developing cultural proficiency is also recommended.

Eighth-grade math student: *"Yeah, I'm mad. The teacher marked my answers wrong. She said I didn't understand the math. I didn't understand the words of the problem, but I do know how to do math. I got A's in my old school. I don't say anything, because I don't know how to explain my math in English, and I don't want to be disrespectful."*

Analysis: While this student has a good sense of his own skills, his motivation will decline because he does not have enough English proficiency to understand the linguistic complexity of word problems or to communicate with the teacher about what he knows in math and how he has been successful in the past. Talking to the teacher about his learning seems culturally inappropriate.

Recommendation: This student will benefit from participating in less print-dependent activities. The math and ESL teachers should communicate to understand why this student may be struggling, decide on how to assess what he does know about math concepts, and provide lessons and activities in which all students can demonstrate number sense and skills. Word problems can be acted out or modeled by students. Older students can write and/or perform dialogues that show a realistic word problem.

High school history student: *"Everyone thinks I am dumb. I know why they laugh at me, because when I talk my answers are wrong. My words are wrong. I see the teacher roll his eyes. I already know English and I don't want to do this. Everyone is smarter than me. I don't get it. I get it when we talk about it in class, but the text is too hard to read by myself."*

Analysis: This is typical of what a long-term English learner might say. A long-term English language learner has been in US schools for several years and has not yet met the district's criteria to exit English-language support programs. This student struggles with literacy and independently reading grade-level academic texts. Her success and motivation diminish because she cannot keep up with the demands of high school homework and reading assignments related to content. She is likely to act out in class to avoid her peers' judgment of her in-class participation.

Recommendation: The history teacher capitalizes on this student's strength: she "gets it" when they talk about it in class. This means that she understands and benefits from in-class discourse and relies on her oral-language proficiency to decipher, analyze, and interpret historical and political concepts. Recorded dialogues, text on tape, and graphic organizers facilitate this student's comprehension of content (see bullets below on techniques to facilitate academic language). This student may have been a victim of the "wait-and-see" period in which a learning issue other than

English proficiency was missed in her earlier educational experience. Small-group work, project-based assessment, intensive literacy instruction, and frequent progress monitoring are recommended.

Oral Fluency and Academic Language

The achievement gap widens quickly when ELLs do not have meaningful participation in content lessons. Effective approaches with the general education population are generally good for English learners, but English learners also require other types of instructional support (Goldenberg 2013, p. 5) and will become more engaged in literacy activities when there are connections to home and community (Goldenberg 2013, p. 8). Assessment of student knowledge or progress will be obscured when a teacher relies too heavily on the child's literacy skills. Expected and often scripted oral responses or definitions also challenge an English learner to demonstrate his or her learning, and will increase anxiety about learning and understanding English.

Over the last decade, research (August and Shanahan 2009) has also shown that some aspects of successful literacy instruction for native English speakers also benefit English learners; however, reading skills without intensive instruction for oral-language development is not sufficient (August and Shanahan 2006, p. 4). Without oral fluency, students will be unable to clearly demonstrate their comprehension (August and Shanahan 2009, p. 435) at the expected level of their native English-speaking peers. Most educators would probably agree that dialogues and conversations about texts, subject matter, and tasks are good for all students and promote analytical thinking skills. What teachers may not be aware of is how interaction and discourse are essential to the English learner's deeper comprehension of texts. Developing oral fluency also assists the ELL in the simultaneous tasks of acquiring content skills and knowledge while learning English.

Gottlieb and Ernst-Slavit's work explicitly informs educators on the ways in which oral language is a vehicle for promoting academic language development. The authors insist that teachers must evolve their own awareness of how academic language promotes academic thinking, and teachers need to become experts on ways to develop all students' receptive- and expressive-language skills (Gottlieb and Ernst-Slavit 2014, p. 4). Not only do English learners need to engage in oral discourse during lessons, but that discourse must also be supported with scaffolding techniques that develop specific language needed to understand information, complete tasks, and demonstrate comprehension.

- *Turn and talk:* The teacher pauses instruction and asks pairs or small groups of students to discuss a question, retell a story or fact, give an example, or brainstorm a list.

- *Analyzing words and phrases:* The teacher leads the class in asking, "What's in a word?" and then demonstrates ways to break up a word into its parts (i.e., root word + affix) or to look for cognates or links to words in students' home languages. The teacher can also demonstrate how to find the etymology of a word or origin of a phrase/idiom by preparing an online search.

- *Sentence frames* (also resemble rehearsed cloze responses): These are scripted phrases or sentences with blanks that allow a student to focus on a one- or two-word response while implicitly practicing academic English-language structures. Students newer to English will need a word bank to complete the sentence frames. Here are a few examples of sentence frames:
  - The butterfly uses _____ to protect itself from _____.
  - In my opinion, the author used _____ as a literary technique to make the reader _____.
  - The expected chemical response (did) (didn't) take place because the _____ of the independent variable _____.

- *Pre-, simultaneous-, and post-task prompts*: These are questions to discuss in pairs or small groups before, during, and after an assignment, project, experiment, or assessment.

- *Discuss parts of a whole*: In groups or pairs, students discuss a short passage, observe a tool, interpret a chart, or explain an opinion. They then present it to the class, and the whole group discusses how "pieces" are related to the whole topic.

- *Read alouds*: Boost students' interest in a topic, build background, and promote academic language learning (Gottlieb and Ernst-Slavit 2014, p. 18).

- *Students teach*: Leading students to ask and answer questions allows them to own the direction of discourse, think critically about what matters, and decide what information ought to be challenged or authenticated. Student pairs or groups can discuss and create questions for assignments, homework, or tests.

Embracing Home Languages and Cultures

Recognizing an English learner's skills and knowledge will motivate them to develop a sense of confidence and encourage them to be resourceful and to use whatever background resources they have in order to do well in school (Cloud, et al., p. 9). English learners are resourceful and have extraordinary life experiences and talents that ought to be celebrated and utilized during instruction, text exploration, and project work. Respectfully using students' cultural and linguistic backgrounds brings teachers and other students to a greater understanding of diversity and fosters pride of one's self and history.

• Student-centered self-studies or heritage projects are useful ways for teachers to learn about their students' cultures, and to convey the message that diversity is a good thing and that every student's voice is important and valued.

• Having students translate their own poems and record them bilingually or perform them for their classmates showcases a sometimes "buried skill" and assists native English speakers in understanding that everyone is fluent in at least one language. When schools celebrate heritage languages, they convey another message that speaking more than one language is a benefit, demonstrates intelligence, and is not something that should be repressed or hidden.

• Selecting multicultural literature allows students to have a "like me" experience with characters and authors. Learners whose ancestral heritage is similar to that from a poem, story, or novel can become the experts to explain or clarify aspects of culture, language, setting, or traditions. Students can drive an authentication process that challenges and validates whether a text has accurately told a story or portrayed a culture. Donna E. Norton provides a structured method for authenticating multicultural literature in her work, *Multicultural Children's Literature: Through the Eyes of Many Children* (2012).

• Positive and powerful experiences take place when students invite their family, relatives, or familiar community members to participate in any of the above-mentioned learning activities. Guest speakers and visitors facilitate cultural proficiency for all students when they read or tell a story; present a tradition; share an artist's work; or demonstrate culturally related talents, such as script or character writing, textile skills (knitting, crocheting, or weaving), dances, pastimes, games, sports, or musical instruments.

References

August, D. and Shanahan, T. *Developing Literacy in Second-Language Learners: Report of the National Literacy Panel on Language-Minority Children and Youth.* Mahwah, NJ: Lawrence Erlbaum Associates, 2006.

August, D. and Shanahan, T. "English Language Learners: Developing Literacy in Second-Language Learners—Report of the National Literacy Panel on Language-Minority Children and Youth." *Journal of Literacy Research* 41, no. 4 (December 2009): 432–452.

Cloud, N., Genesee, F., and Hamayan, E. *Literacy Instruction for English Language Learners: A Teacher's Guide to Research-Based Practices.* Portsmouth, NH: Heinemann, 2009.

Echevarria, J., Vogt, M., and Short, D. *Making Content Comprehensible for English Learners The SIOP Model.* Boston: Pearson, 2014.

Goldenberg, C. "Unlocking the Research on English Learners: What We Know—and Don't Yet Know—about Effective Instruction." *American Educator*, 37, no. 2 (Summer 2013): 4–38.

Gottlieb, M. and Ernst-Slavit, G. *Academic Language in Diverse Classrooms: Definitions and Contexts.* Thousand Oaks, CA: Corwin, 2014.

Individuals with Disabilities Education Improvement Act of 2004. Pub. L. No. 108-446, 108th Congress.

US Department of Education. "Tools and Resources for Identifying All English Learners." 2015. https://www2.ed.gov/about/offices/list/oela/english-learner-toolkit/chap1.pdf.

The Brain and Student Learning

Introduction

In recent years, developments in the field of mind and brain education (MBE) have brought us to new understandings about how learning happens in the brain. Whereas classroom teachers were previously known as troubleshooters who often relied on their intuition to develop best practices (usually based on past experiences or maxims), today we have a growing body of research that tells us more specifically how learning occurs from neurobiological, developmental, and psychological perspectives. Armed with new knowledge about the brain, it is encouraging to know that we teachers might now begin to craft our classroom lessons in ways that are more developmentally appropriate and neurologically sound. In other words, **with more technical knowledge about how the brain works, we can waste less time on ineffective practices and instead adopt empirically tested, evidence-based classroom solutions that are more likely to yield success.**

Imagine for a moment this typical scenario:

Ms. Johnson, a fourth-grade teacher, has struggled each year with getting her students to show mastery application of basic multiplication. Although most of them can compute single-digit algorithms with ease, many seem to have a hard time with applying their knowledge of multiplication to word problems. Not realizing that different representations of a particular number—for example, the word five vs. the numeral 5—are processed by the brain in very different ways or that some of her students' brains may have difficulty decoding the linguistic patterns of math, Ms. Johnson continues to have her students practice the multiplication

Objectives for the Chapter

After reading the chapter, the reader will be able to

a. explain the basics of brain anatomy and how the brain functions

b. explain the processes of memory creation and learning and how they are connected

c. explain how the brain functions in relation to learning math

d. explain how the brain functions in relation to reading and learning how to read

e. explain how the brain functions in relation to the arts and how the brain specifically benefits from arts engagement

f. distinguish between common neuro myths and research-backed findings about the brain

g. use knowledge of learning and memory processes to optimize classroom experiences in all subject areas

table with baited breath, hoping that one day it will all just "click."

Ms. Johnson, like many teachers, has not had the experience of considering the cognitive implications of her work. The brain is a complex organ, and because of its complexity, many people shy away from a deeper understanding of its processes. What we aim to do in this chapter is simple: provide you with a basic understanding of the brain and how it works; impart best practices for maximizing student achievement, informed by what we now know about the brain; and, finally, bring to light some of the implications of mind and brain education for our classrooms and schools. In the case of Ms. Johnson, improved practice may mean that she needs to incorporate math manipulatives as part of her daily math lesson because "manipulatives bridge the conceptual links between concrete number knowledge and the more abstract symbolic understanding of letters and numerals" (Tokuhama-Espinosa 2011, p. 188). For you, it may be an altogether different tool or understanding.

In books such as this one, there is often a temptation for us as educators to flip directly to the chapters on perennial challenges such as classroom management and lesson planning, while giving short shrift to the chapters covering more abstract topics such as this one on the brain and student learning. We urge you to resist this inclination, as we have found through our own experiences as classroom teachers that gaining a deeper understanding of what *learning* actually means and what precisely is happening in our students' brains when we say that learning is taking place are both crucial to using and benefiting from the strategies laid out in this book's other chapters.

Mind and brain education is a growing field. Over the past couple of decades, hundreds of books and articles have been published for educators about the importance of brain-based education, brain-compatible classrooms, brain-compatible learning, and so on. What researchers have found is that the acquisition of basic and higher-order thinking skills involves a variety of brain regions that must effectively be activated and allowed to communicate with each other via developed neural pathways. This can be enhanced by practices that take into account neurological functioning. Additionally, "classroom discipline, learning problems, instructional practices, and evaluation methods (among other teacher-learning issues) can now be approached in an innovative way using the multiple viewpoints pro-

> *The acquisition of basic and higher-order thinking skills involves a variety of brain regions that must effectively be activated and allowed to communicate with each other via developed neural pathways.*

vided by the new science to teaching and learning" (Tokuhama-Espinosa 2011, p. 7). Convincingly, there is much to be gained from knowing more about how the brain works.

Nuts and Bolts of the Brain

The brain weighs approximately three pounds and is divided into two mirror-image hemispheres: the right and the left. The front of the brain is called the *anterior region*, and the back of the brain is called the *posterior region*. Each hemisphere is made up of four sections (also called lobes): frontal, parietal, temporal, and occipital. Together, these four lobes make up what is referred to as the *cerebral cortex*.

As you can see in Figure 8.1, the **frontal lobe** is in the anterior (front) section of the brain, the **occipital lobe** is in the posterior (back), and the **parietal** and **temporal** lobes lie between the two previously mentioned lobes. It is important to remember that, as the right and left hemispheres of the brain are mirror-images of each other, each hemisphere contains its own frontal, parietal, temporal, and occipital lobe.

What role does each of these sections of the brain play in student learning? While the processes of learning and memory will be examined in more detail in the next section of this chapter, we can note here that the frontal lobe is used for higher-order thinking and fine motor skills, the occipital lobe for processing visual information, the temporal lobe for processing auditory information, and the parietal lobe for sensory information and spatial awareness.

The visual, auditory, and sensory information processed by the various sections of the brain comes from the body's five senses and reaches the various lobes of the brain through the spinal cord and brain stem (see Figure 8.1). In addition to serving as a conveyor of sensory information, the brain stem controls the body's heart rate, blood pressure, and breathing. Behind the brain stem (and beneath the occipital lobe) is the **cerebellum**, which controls the body's motor coordination and motor learning.

Two other fundamental areas of the brain are **Broca's area** and **Wernicke's area**. Located in the frontal lobe and temporal lobes, respectively (see Figure 8.1), these two areas of the brain are named for the doctors who discovered that these regions work together to produce and understand speech. People

Figure 8.1

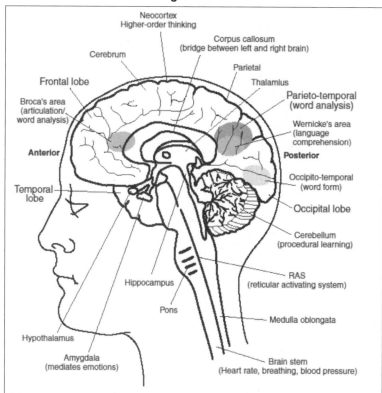

who experience brain damage in Broca's area are able to understand the speech of others but cannot speak comprehensibly themselves. In contrast, people who experience brain damage in Wernicke's area are able to speak (and, in fact, blather uncontrollably) but cannot understand the language of others.

Located in the middle region of the brain (primarily in the temporal lobe) are the **hippocampus, thalamus, hypothalamus,** and **amygdala** (see Figure 8.1). This area is sometimes referred to as the *limbic area* or the *limbic system*, and it controls body functions such as eating, drinking, sleeping, and processing emotions.

Finally, the brain's right and left hemispheres are primarily connected by a bundle of nerve fibers called the *corpus callosum* (see Figure 8.1). Neuroscientists refer to the corpus callosum as the brain's "information superhighway" because it allows for communication between the two sides of the brain and for information collected in one hemisphere to be conveyed to the other. The corpus callosum is a key tool for allowing the brain to coordinate all of its different functions. In the 1960s, studies by Sperry, Bogen, and Perry of people whose corpus callosum had been severed revealed that these people had difficulty performing certain tasks. For example, when subjects were blindfolded and an object such as a pencil was placed in their right hands, they could name and describe what they were holding. When the object was placed

in their left hands, however, the subjects were unable to name or describe the object they were holding (Wolfe 2001). While we will delve more deeply into the topic of left brain functions versus right brain functions in an upcoming section of this chapter, it is sufficient to note here that the severing of the corpus callosum prevented the two hemispheres of the various subjects' brains from working together to successfully identify and name an object using the sense of touch instead of sight.

The Brain and Learning

In order to explain what is actually happening in the brain when learning is taking place, we first need to give you one final lesson on the anatomy of the brain—namely, all of the different parts of the brain described in the previous section are composed of brain cells known as *neurons*. There are approximately 100 billion neurons in the brain, and each of these neurons is made up of three parts: the cell body, the dendrites, and the axons. The **cell body** (or **soma**) contains the neuron's DNA, while the **axons** and **dendrites** serve as "output fibers" and "input fibers," respectively. More specifically, a neuron's axons send information from the neuron to neighboring neurons, while the dendrites accept information from those neighboring neurons. The tiny space between two neurons is referred to as the *synapse*. When one neuron passes information through its axon across a synapse to the dendrites of another neuron, we say that the cells have "fired" across the synapse.

As you can see in Figure 8.2, one way to describe a neuron is by comparing it to a tree. The trunk of the tree represents a neuron's cell body. The tree's branches are analogous to a cell's dendrites, and the tree's roots represent the neuron's axons.

In short, **learning is the result of the firing of cells across synapses. The reason that we become more skilled at doing a particular task the more we practice it is that the neurons involved in that particular task actually get "better" at communicating with each other, or firing, across their synapses.** To have successfully learned something means that the neural pathways forged through practicing a particular task have strengthened so that firing can happen with little effort. Practice does make perfect (or at least it more perfectly facilitates learning). For example, if someone asks you to produce the answer

Table 8.1

Section	Location	Function
Frontal lobe	Anterior cerebral cortex (left and right hemispheres)	Higher-order thinking and fine motor skills
Parietal lobe	Mid-cerebral cortex (left and right hemispheres)	Sensory information and spatial awareness
Temporal lobe	Mid-cerebral cortex (left and right hemispheres)	Processing auditory information
Occipital lobe	Posterior cerebral cortex (left and right hemispheres)	Processing visual information
Brain stem	Base of brain	Controls heart rate, blood pressure, and breathing
Cerebellum	Base of brain, behind brain stem	Controls motor coordination and motor learning
Broca's area	Frontal lobe	Produce speech
Wernicke's area	Temporal lobe	Understand speech
Limbic area	Temporal lobe	Controls eating, drinking, sleeping, and processing emotions
Corpus callosum	Beneath the cerebral cortex, between left and right hemispheres	Allows communication between brain hemispheres

to 7 x 8, chances are the number 56 will immediately pop into your head. Now, if that same person challenges you to multiply 15 by 16, it may take you a little longer to produce an answer. Perhaps you would grab a piece of scratch paper and a pencil to do the calculation. This is probably because most of us only practiced and committed to memory the multiplication table up to 12 in elementary school. To calculate the products of numbers greater than 12, one might need to instead call on specific skills that assist with the process of multiplying, and these skills will likely have been committed to memory through sustained practice. While on the topic of learning, it is probably worth mentioning here that memorization does not wholly equate to learning; we know that people are fully capable of "figuring things out" through logic, reason, and/or creativity. But knowledge builds on knowledge. In figuring something out, we connect new ideas to what we already know. And once new ideas, concrete or abstract, are developed, recalling them for new connections can only be strengthened with practice.

This brings us to the concept of potentiation. As Barbara Given (2002) explains, "Scientists have learned that neurons that fire frequently remain active. This consistent state is called *potentiation*, which causes neurons to ... develop additional dendrit-

The brain operates on a "use-it-or-lose it" system. Individuals need to continue learning and practicing in order to keep their neural pathways and to keep them operating effectively and efficiently.

ic branches. Thus, [neurons] increase their ability to collect more information as learning occurs" (p. 69). To go back to the analogy of the neuron as a tree, when a student is first taught the definition of a preposition, for example, synapses fire in the student's brain, connecting the neurons necessary to process that information. If that student then goes home and completes a homework assignment asking him or her to identify 25 prepositions, the dendrites of the particular neurons that process information about prepositions actually *grow*. Imagine a tree's branches expanding before your eyes; that is what happens to the neuron's dendrites when new learning is practiced and applied in different ways. When the neurons' dendrites grow "bushier," information passes between them faster and more easily. Thus, the student becomes faster at identifying prepositions in a sentence. The neurons necessary for identifying prepositions are actually firing more efficiently than they were when this student first learned about prepositions in class earlier that same day. And the more he or she practices, the bushier the neuron's dendrites will get and the better those connections will be along that particular neural pathway. As Usha Goswami (2004) explains, "Successful teaching directly affects brain function by changing connectivity"; as learning occurs, the connections between neurons are strengthened (p. 75). The strengthening of fiber connections and synapses between neurons is referred to by neuroscientists as *synaptogenesis*.

According to Goswami (2004), the average individual's brain quadruples in size between birth and adulthood. This increase in size is due *primarily* to the "proliferation of connections" (p. 176), not the creation of new cells. An infant is born with nearly all of the "neurons of an adult, but the neural networks are not mature yet" (Carter 2009, p. 3). According to James Zull (2006), a recent study of people learning to juggle found that as these individuals

Figure 8.2

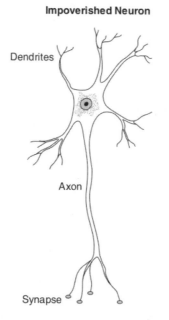

Impoverished Neuron

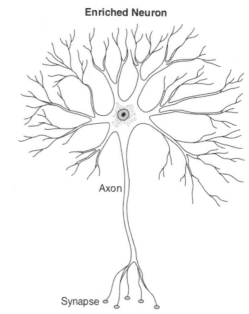

Enriched Neuron

learned to juggle, the region of their neocortex that senses movement increased in density. Scientists cite this study as a clear example of the brain's growth as a result of learning. Interestingly, however, when time passed and these individuals lost some of their juggling skills, the density of this region of the neocortex decreased. As we will discuss in more detail later in this chapter, the brain operates on a "use-it-or-lose-it" system. Individuals need to continue learning and practicing in order to keep their neural pathways and to keep them operating effectively and efficiently.

One way that neuroscientists sometimes describe this process of dendrites growing bushier is by comparing the dendrites' growth to that of an athlete's muscles growing stronger when the athlete lifts weights. Just as an athlete who regularly activates his or her muscles by following a consistent exercise regimen will increase the strength of these muscles, neurons along a particular neural pathway will become better at communicating with each other the more that they are activated.

A final point concerning the nuts and bolts of the brain relates to a fairly recent discovery about brain growth and adolescence. Prior to the late 1990s, the conventional wisdom concerning brain growth was that no *new* neurons developed in the brain after a child reached between 18 months and 2 years of age. Even earlier in this section, we mentioned that brain growth past infancy was largely due to the establishment of new neural connections and not the birth of new cells. Research tells us, however, that there are some exceptions. According to Dr. Jay Giedd, a

scientist with the National Institute of Mental Health, recent studies have revealed that some parts of the brain continue growing long after early childhood. For example, the cerebellum continues growing into a person's twenties (Spinks 2002). Moreover, the periods of pre-adolescence directly before puberty and the period of adolescence itself represent times of significant growth for the brain's prefrontal cortex. As was described in the previous section on the nuts and bolts of the brain, the prefrontal cortex is the area of the brain in which the mechanics of thinking and emotion occur. For this reason, **it is particularly important that all children, particularly adolescents, are exposed to a challenging school curriculum that pushes them to fully develop their cognitive skills in ways that engage both thinking and emotion.** Remember that, in the preceding paragraph, we compared the constant activation of neural pathways to an athlete's increasing his or her muscle mass by lifting weights. Unfortunately, the reverse analogy is true as well. Just as the muscles of an athlete who stops exercising will gradually lose strength and become weaker, a neural pathway that is not regularly activated through use will become slower and less efficient. As Dr. Jay Giedd explains, the brain's system of "use it or lose it" means that neural pathways not receiving sufficient use may be rendered inactive (Spinks 2002). For example, someone who played the violin throughout grade school and then stopped in early adulthood would not typically be able to pick up a violin at age 40 and resume playing with the same level of skill. Thus, it is particularly important for children to participate in activities that activate as many neural pathways as possible in order to allow their brains to grow to their full potential and then continually exercise those pathways so that connections remain strong. To shift for a moment to another demographic, it is precisely because of the brain's use-it-or-lose-it system that doctors have begun emphasizing the importance of senior citizens' continuing to exercise their brains by reading, playing card games, and taking classes. Senior citizens who *use* their neural pathways by participating in such activities are able to maintain their intellectual capacities significantly longer than those who do not.

The Brain and Memory

It makes sense to follow up our discussion of learning with a discussion of memory because, of course, the two processes are interconnected. Memory, broadly, is a recalled event that is drawn up by refiring the neurons involved in the original experience (Carter 2009). As teachers, we know that there is little value in our students learning a skill or concept if they are unable to remember that skill or concept a day, week, or month later. Cognitively, learning and memory are interconnected as well. As Barbara Given (2002) explains, "There is no single storage area for records of the past. …Memory is not a 'thing' but a process of neuronal network activation" (p. 74). This description of what memory "looks like" in the brain should strike you as similar to our earlier description of what learning looks like in the brain. That is because the two processes are effectively the same. If *learning* a particular skill or concept results in the firing of neurons along a particular neural pathway, then *remembering* that skill or concept means that the neurons along that pathway communicate so effectively with each other that the brain can easily recall the particular skill or concept upon request.

Here is an example of this process playing out in the classroom. Imagine that a Spanish teacher is teaching her students how to conjugate a particular verb. Inside her students' brains, *learning* these six verb forms involves activating a particular neural pathway inside the temporal lobe on the left side. As students practice reciting the various forms of this verb, the dendrites of the neurons along this neural pathway grow bushier, allowing these neurons to communicate with each other more quickly. With enough practice,

Stimuli or information entering the brain is more likely to become part of the brain's long-term memory if that stimuli or information can be connected to knowledge already held in long-term memory.

the communication of the neurons along this pathway becomes so efficient that the students can quickly *remember* the different conjugations of this particular verb. The teacher's goal, of course, is for her students to remember these verb forms well enough to instantly identify and utilize the correct form in conversation. Such automatic memory is achieved through practice.

While there is no single spot or system of neurons in the brain responsible for *all* memories, researchers have been able to determine the different locations in the brain in which various types of memories are stored. Eric Jensen (1998) explains that memories of sound are stored in the **auditory cortex**. The **hippocampus** stores memories related to speaking and reading, and the **amygdala** stores negative emotional events, such as an encounter with a bully. Memories of names, nouns, and pronouns are stored in the **temporal lobe**. Information regarding vital life functions is stored in the **brain stem**. The **cerebellum** is responsible for recalling basic muscle movements, such as pouring chemicals into a beaker.

Another expert in brain-based education, Marilee Sprenger (1999), breaks down the storing of memory in the brain as shown in Table 8.2.

Specific strategies for using each of these different aspects of our students' memories will be discussed later in this chapter.

Carter (2009) and Tokuhama-Espinosa (2011) recognize an additional type of memory, *working memory*, which holds special relevance to the classroom. Working memory, one of the ways that the brain multitasks, is a system that is activated when one part of the frontal lobe holds a plan of action while simultaneously retrieving information from other parts of the brain (Carter 2009). Tokuhama-Espinosa (2011) says, "Being able to maintain information in one's mind long enough to perform a task is the definition of good working memory" (p. 160). For example, a student engaged in a classroom debate on global warming might access her working memory to retain facts for a point she'd like to make in a planned rebuttal, while simultaneously listening to and processing her opponent's arguments.

So what, specifically, can teachers do to maximize their students' use of working memory? For starters, it's important to note that working memory development occurs throughout childhood, but the most substantial growth happens in the first 10 years of life, with peak working-memory capacity reached at

Table 8.2

Type of Memory	Definition	Section of the Brain in Which It Is Stored
Semantic memory	Information learned from words, such as a teacher's lecture or hand-out	Hippocampus (temporal lobe)
Episodic memory	Memory involving locations (such as the decorations on the walls of the classroom) in which learning occurs	Hippocampus (temporal lobe)
Procedural memory	Processes that the body does and remembers, such as the various steps of a cheerleader's routine	Cerebellum
Automatic memory	The body's conditioned responses, such as recalling the multiplication tables well enough to recite an answer instantly	Cerebellum
Emotional memory	Emotional information, such as excitement over a fascinating lesson or anxiety for an impending exam	Amygdala

Sprenger (1999)

age 25. (By *capacity*, we mean the space of working memory, or the number of items one can hold in the working memory at a time.) This is an amount that varies depending on one's age. For example: "The average five-year-old can hold one item in mind (list of words, instructions, etc.), a seven-year-old can remember two items, a 10-year-old can remember three items, and a 14-year-old can remember four items" (Alloway 2011, p. 2). This *space* or capacity of the working memory is but one of three potential impacts on working memory development in the classroom. Alloway (2011) suggests that teachers should always remain aware of space—what is developmentally appropriate with regard to working memory, and not give students too much or too little—to hold in their working memories at one time. Teachers should also pay attention to the amount of *time* spent in giving instructions or other information. A teacher who instructs quickly may not be able to effectively utilize and develop students' working memories. And, finally, teachers, knowing their students' abilities, should be mindful of the amount of *effort* required to hold specific information in the working memory. "Students with poor working memory have to use a lot of effort when they have to juggle two or more things. If they are asked to remember a sentence...and count the number of words the sentence contains, they find it too effortful" (Alloway 2011, p. 7).

There is yet one more aspect of memory that warrants attention. In our discussion of various teaching strategies in Chapters 2 and 5, we note that students are better able to remember information they are taught when that information is connected to knowledge already stored in their long-term memories. In

Accessing the General Curriculum, Victor Nolet and Margaret McLaughlin (2005) describe how long-term memory and new knowledge are linked:

> When something is stored in memory, it becomes part of a network in which various types of information (facts, propositions, concepts, and relationships) constitute "nodes." The more nodes and the more connections among nodes learners have, the better they will be at thinking, learning, recalling, and problem solving. ... As [new] information from the environment is detected through one of the senses, it is held briefly until it can be analyzed. This analysis involves matching to the incoming stimulus with a recognizable pattern already stored in memory (pp. 33–38).

To put it simply, stimuli or information entering the brain is more likely to become part of the brain's long-term memory if that stimuli or information can be connected to knowledge already held in long-term memory. For example, a student in a geometry class who has already committed definitions of *triangles* and *quadrilaterals* to his or her long-term memory will find it much easier to learn and remember the definition of *hexagon* than a student who holds no prior knowledge of polygons will. Why is this? Remember that, in cognitive terms, learning and memory both consist of laying down neural pathways by the firing of neurons across synapses. When a person is able to link new information to previously held knowledge, his or her brain is effectively linking that new information to neural pathways that have already been laid out. In contrast, new information unconnected to anything in a person's existing long-term memory necessitates the creation of a new neural pathway and the firing of synapses across neurons whose dendrites have not yet had the opportunity to become bushy, efficient communicators with each other. It is for this reason that in Chapters 1 and 2 we emphasize the importance of teachers planning with mastery objectives in mind and then giving students the mastery objectives at the outset of the learning. When we do this, we build a context for the upcoming learning in the long-term memory to which the new learning may connect.

The process of learning how to read is not innately wired into our brains, and this could be a part of the problem.

The Brain and Reading

Developmental psychologist Maryanne Wolf points out that human beings have only been able to read for a few thousand years. While children instinctively learn to understand and express oral language, they must be explicitly taught how to read. Wolf (2007) writes that children learning to read typically pass through five stages: emerging pre-reader, novice reader, decoding reader, fluent comprehending reader, and expert reader. Distressingly, results from the National Assessment of Education Progress (NAEP) exam in 2013 revealed that 60 percent of American fourth graders were below grade level in reading ability. Wolf describes statistics like this as the "great black hole of American education" (p. 136).

The process of learning how to read is not innately wired into our brains, and this could be a part of the problem. Unlike speech, which develops in much the same way across cultures and uses specific processes and brain structures, "reading is a complex, rule-based system that must be imposed on biological structures that were designed or evolved for other reasons" (Frey and Fisher 2010, p. 104). Despite the fact that reading instruction is perhaps the most researched area in the field of education, it is only recently that brain imaging technology has become advanced enough to allow scientists to observe what is going on inside the brain when a student is reading. This technology has provided scientists with a deeper understanding not only of the cognitive processes that occur during reading, but also of what is happening inside the brains of those students who have difficulty learning to read. One of the most important findings concerning reading and cognition is that there are actually two different neural pathways for reading: "one is for beginning reading, for slowly sounding out words, and another that is a speedier pathway for skilled reading" (Shaywitz 2003, p. 78). Both pathways involve multiple regions of the brain because reading involves both processing the visual information on the page and transforming this visual information into sounds and meaning (Shaywitz).

A child just learning to read uses the **parietal and temporal lobes** when reading. Called the parieto-temporal system and located in the middle of the brain, this system helps a child to recognize the different letters that make up a word and then to attach the appropriate sounds to these letters (Shaywitz 2003). It is for this reason that a child learning to read may be heard very slowly sounding out each word on the page.

When a child becomes a more fluent reader, the area of the brain activated during reading shifts from the mid-brain to the lower brain—specifically, the **occipito-temporal area**. Why does this shift occur? Dr. Sally Shaywitz (2003) explains that after the child has read a particular word several times, he or she "forms an exact neural model of the specific word [in the lower brain]...reflecting the word's spelling, its pronunciation, and its meaning" (p. 79). As a result, the child can now automatically read the entire word upon seeing it in print in about a tenth of a second. In contrast, the child who is still relying upon the mid-brain for reading must mentally divide the word into separate letters, sound each letter out and then recombine the sounds into a single word. Later in this section, we will offer some strategies for supporting children in achieving reading fluency.

One reason these new insights about reading and the brain are so important is that they provide us with a deeper understanding of what is occurring inside the brains of children who have difficulty becoming fluent readers. Shaywitz (2003) suggests that there are two major groups of poor readers: children who are dyslexic and children who are poor readers due to lack of experience. **Dyslexia** is a learning disability found in children of normal intelligence that impairs their ability to read fluently and accurately

While approximately one in five children are estimated to be dyslexic, it is only in the last few years that researchers have come to understand the "glitch" in the brains of dyslexic children and adults. Specifically, children and adults with dyslexia have a glitch in the lower region of the brain that forces them to continue to rely on the mid-brain when reading, in contrast to other readers who transfer control of reading to the lower brain. Since we know that the mid-brain supports reading by breaking words into pieces, sounding them out, and rejoining these sounds, while the lower-brain allows for nearly instantaneous sight-reading, Shaywitz (2003) suggests that children and adults with dyslexia are effectively forced to continue using a "manual" reading system when their non-dyslexic peers have shifted to "automatic." In other words, a child with dyslexia attempting to read a word such as *hamburger* will need to divide this word into syllables, sound out each syllable, and then combine these sounds to form a single word. As Shaywitz and Shaywitz (2004) observe, "This strategy enables them to read but much more slowly and with greater effort than their [non-dyslexic] classmates" (p. 9). In contrast, a non-dyslexic child who has come across the word *hamburger* previously will automatically activate the neural pathway in his or her lower brain in which this word's meaning and pronunciation are stored, allowing the word to be read fluently. Dyslexia, then, is not something that a child grows out of as an adult; however, in Shaywitz's book, *Overcoming Dyslexia* (2003), she lays out many strategies that children and adults with dyslexia can use to strengthen their manual reading systems. For example, Shaywitz explains that dyslexic children may benefit from "fluency training," which involves students reading and rereading a particular passage until they can read this passage with a high degree of accuracy. Shaywitz compares this approach to athletic training in which one practices a particular dance move or jump shot until the movement is ingrained in one's neural pathways (p. 269).

In contrast to dyslexics who literally have a glitch in the lower region of the brain, the brains of children with poor reading skills have working systems in place that have not been activated appropriately. For these children, the often-cited quote of one of our old tennis coaches comes into play: "Learn the rules. Play the game. Practice! Practice! Practice!" As Shaywitz (2003) explains, "New brain-imaging technology shows the powerful positive effect of practice in creating neural circuits related to the development of what scientists call expertise or skill. Basically, the brain learns by practice" (p. 188). As is the case with other types of learning, reading practice strengthens the speed with which synapses fire along the neural pathways in children's parieto-temporal and occipito-temporal regions. **Achieving reading fluency means that the neural pathways have been exposed to a particular word enough times to process the word,**

> *Children and adults with dyslexia are effectively forced to continue using a "manual" reading system when their non-dyslexic peers have shifted to "automatic.*

decode it, and attach it with meaning in less than a heartbeat. In *Overcoming Dyslexia* (2003), Shaywitz describes a number of early-intervention reading programs that have been effective in helping poor readers achieve this level of fluency. She notes that common threads that run through each of these reading programs are systematic and direct instruction in phonics, fluency training, and enriched language experiences, such as listening to and telling stories. The reading fluency of young children can, of course, also benefit from exposure to books, as "being read to builds the neural pathways critical to written language comprehension and production" (Frey and Fisher 2010, p. 105).

Finally, one of the most important studies of dyslexia was the Fast ForWord Language Study carried out in 2003. According to Patrick Tucker (2007), this study of dyslexic readers turned up the surprising finding that reading difficulties were connected to the "portion of the brain associated with hearing and processing sound" (p. 1). As a result of this finding, researchers designed a reading curriculum that focused on visual rather than auditory activities. After eight weeks, the dyslexic students who participated in the curriculum showed significant improvement on standardized reading tests. This finding was in line with other research that supports the idea that the brain prioritizes vision over other senses (Frey and Fisher 2010). **When the brain receives multiple stimuli, what is seen is most likely to be processed, stored, and later retrieved. Interestingly, it is typically pictures, not written words, to which the brain gives precedence.** This has significant repercussions for our text-based classrooms. If comprehension and retention are more successfully facilitated when illustrations are present, should we consider routinely pairing text with illustrations? Frey and Fisher (2010) believe that we should: "As brain researchers focus on the human visual system, a growing body of evidence suggests that text should be paired with illustrations" (p. 107). These findings seem to offer a glimpse of the potential for advances in cognitive neuroscience to help researchers and educators design effective interventions for both learning-disabled and non-learning-disabled students who have not reached reading fluency.

Other researchers have focused on the reading skills of English language learners. Usha Goswami (2004) reports that studies of non-native English speakers have found that "when English is acquired late due to auditory deprivation or late immigration to an English-speaking country, syntactic abilities do not develop at the same rate or to the same extent" (p. 178). What is particularly interesting about these studies is that non-native English speakers seem to have far more difficulty understanding the grammatical structures of English than acquiring a proficient English vocabulary. In other words, non-native speakers have an easier time learning words than grammatical constructions. For this reason, Goswami notes that "children acquiring English as a second language may thus need extra support with grammatical aspects of their second language, compared to support for basic vocabulary learning" (p. 178).

It doesn't matter, ultimately, whether a particular problem is solved. Rather, the dendrites grow as a result of the process of solving the problem, not as a result of determining the solution.

The Brain and Mathematics

In recent years, cognitive scientists have learned more about what mathematics looks like inside the brain. In the vignette that introduced this chapter, we alluded to the fact that different types of mathematics seem to activate different areas of the brain. For example, the act of comparing two numbers or amounts seems to lead to increased activation in the brain's parietal lobe. Simple calculations, such as finger-counting, seem to activate a parietal-premotor area, while more complex calculations activate visuo-spatial regions of the brain. Interestingly, cognitive scientists have come to believe that some numerical knowledge is stored in the brain as language rather than numerals, so it makes complete sense that children often present with both language and math problems simultaneously. According to Tokuhama-Espinosa (2011), this is due to overlapping neural systems in the brain. Evidence of how these systems overlap is apparent in how sometimes "number facts," such as the multiplication tables, "are so overlearned, at least by adulthood, that they may be stored as linguistic knowledge" (Goswami 2004, p. 179).

In terms of drawing on knowledge of the brain to improve mathematical ability, the Third International Mathematics and Science Survey (TIMSS) reported that American schoolchildren studying mathematics are handicapped by curricula that emphasize quantity over quality. As Bransford, Brown, and Cocking (1999) note in *How People Learn*, "Research on expertise suggests that superficial coverage of many topics in the domain may be a poor way to help students develop the competencies that will prepare them for future

learning and work" (p. 5). They also express concern that too often students' knowledge of mathematics is conditional, meaning that they can solve a particular problem when it appears on a structured worksheet with similar problems but are unable to identify when and why to apply various problem-solving techniques when faced with randomly presented problems. For example, can an elementary school student who has learned the concept of perimeter and completed a worksheet with questions testing this concept then successfully find the perimeter of his or her classroom upon being handed a tape measure? In Chapter 1 of this book, we refer to this process of applying problem-solving techniques in unfamiliar settings as *application mastery*.

In contrast, Bransford, Brown, and Cocking (1999) report on research findings that "mathematics experts are able to quickly recognize patterns of information such as particular problem types that involve specific classes of mathematical solutions" (p. 3). How can we, as educators, support students in their path toward attaining the skill level of such experts? Both researchers and educators suggest that mathematics curricula require an increased emphasis on application mastery, the application of learned skills to unfamiliar problems. Eric Jensen writes in *Teaching with the Brain in Mind* (1998) that "the single best way to grow a better brain is through challenging problem-solving. This creates new dendritic connections that allow us to make even more connections" (p. 35). An example of such a problem might be asking elementary school students who have recently learned how to add and subtract decimals to provide the appropriate change to a customer who pays for three glasses of lemonade (each class costing 60 cents) with a $5 bill.

Interestingly, Jensen (2008) notes that, as far as a student's brain is concerned, it doesn't matter, ultimately, whether a particular problem is solved. Rather, the dendrites grow as a result of the process of solving the problem, not as a result of determining the solution. In other words, it is the processes of reasoning and thinking about a problem that activate the neurons along a particular neural pathway, not the final step of achieving a solution. As long as the steps a student takes toward arriving at an answer are logical and reflective, the neuron activation inside that student's brain is the same whether the final answer is correct or not. For this reason, one might argue that there is a cognitive rationale for giving students partial credit when they complete several steps of a problem correctly but make a careless error that renders their final answer incorrect.

Finally, in *A Toolkit of Brain-Compatible Strategies* (2010), Patricia Wolfe suggests that teachers consider helping students to develop their own word problems. As she explains, "The purpose of instruction in mathematics is to give students the skills they need to solve real-life problems involving numbers. Texts typically include word problems to provide practice in problem-solving. Too often, however, these problems are abstract and meaningless. When students write their own word problems for others in the class to solve, the problems have more meaning and can be a lot of fun" (p. 201). For example, after students have been asked to determine the perimeter of their classroom, a teacher might assign as homework for students to choose a room in their house, measure its dimensions, and then create a word problem with an accompanying diagram of the chosen room for other students in the class to solve. The next day in class, students will enjoy the opportunity to apply their problem-solving skills to the "real life" rooms in their classmates' homes. More information about the value of drawing problems from real life and other types of authentic assessments can be found in Chapter 2.

In an earlier edition of her book, Wolfe (2001) suggests that teachers ask students to reflect in writing about the mathematical skills that they are acquiring. She asserts, "Writing about what they are learning in math helps students make sense of the information by putting the ideas and methods they are using into their own words" (p. 7) For example, the students in the earlier example, who applied their knowledge of decimals to solve a problem involving the purchase of lemonade, might be asked to write about the different situations in their current and future lives in which an understanding of how to add and subtract decimals might prove useful. In answering this question about when a learned skill might come in handy, students strengthen their procedural and conditional knowledge. **Procedural knowledge is knowledge about *how* to do something, and *conditional knowledge* is knowledge about *when* to apply a particular skill or concept.** Nolet and McLaughlin (2000) note that it is these types of knowledge—procedural and conditional—in which mathematics experts tend to far outstrip novices. Incorporating problem-solving and reflective writing into a mathematics curriculum, then, may be an important step in guiding students

toward mastery of the content and skills they will need to succeed in their future learning and chosen careers.

The Brain and the Arts

Our oft-repeated brain mantra, "use it or lose it," implies that the brain is under continual development and that neural connections are regularly reinforced or altered through brain activity. The arts, whether through creation, performance, or appreciation, provide the brain with opportunities to develop in multiple ways. Unlike MBE research findings involving reading and mathematics that show how activities of brain regions overlap, it has been proven that each form of art enlists a specific brain network. For example, visual arts like painting and sculpture activate the occipital and temporal lobes. Linguistic arts, such as poetry, enlist Broca's and Wernike's areas. (If you recall, these are the sections of the brain responsible for understanding and producing speech.) Finally, the motor cortex is involved in dance and other movement arts, and the auditory cortex is activated by music engagement.

The arts, whether through creation, performance, or appreciation, provide the brain with opportunities to develop in multiple ways.

Brain plasticity—the ability of the brain to change how its neurons are organized in response to various stimuli—has been most researched in the domain of music. Hinton et al. (2012) cite numerous studies that illuminate the profound effects that even short-term musical training can have on brain plasticity. As brain plasticity has been found to be helpful in enabling students to overcome even severe learning challenges (2012), it is worth considering the cognitive benefits of music, especially as they relate to student learning and achievement. Researchers agree that actions of listening to music and creating music are handled differently in the brain, with music creation seemingly imparting greater cognitive gains, "Although passive listening to music does have some therapeutic and short-term educational benefits, the making of music seems to provide many more cerebral advantages. ... For example, the auditory cortex, the motor cortex, the cerebellum, and the corpus callosum are larger in musicians than in non-musicians" (Sousa 2011, p. 228). For those who are not musicians and may be inclined to believe that musical talent is an inherited trait, you will be relieved to know that the more developed brain areas found in some musicians is likely due to training and not genetics, so it's never too late to reap the benefits of brain plasticity.

In terms of how musical training can specifically benefit students' classroom performance, one only needs to look to these findings as evidence: a study done by George and Coch (2011) found that musicians had superior performance on tests of working memory that involved executive, phonological, and visual memory. Several functional magnetic resonance (MRI) imaging studies have proven that musical training activates areas of the brain involved in mathematical processing (Sousa 2011). Additional studies highlight the positive effects of music training and performance on reading and verbal memory (2011).

The benefits of arts engagement are wide-ranging and, of course, not limited to music. There are obvious connections between various forms of arts instruction and the development of creative minds. In getting children to think creatively, we implore their brains to communicate "among brain regions that do not normally interact with each other during noncreative thinking" (Sousa 2011, p. 220). As there is no one brain area where creativity occurs, a student who seeks a creative solution to, say, a mathematics problem would build synaptic connections between multiple brain regions that may not under different circumstances be exercised. In the preceding section, we touched upon a held criticism of American students that their mathematical knowledge was limited due to a superficial understanding of concepts and an inability to apply what is known to varied contexts. Although some people may believe that creativity cannot be taught, this is actually not true. There is a growing body of research that shows that though creativity may come more naturally to some individuals, it is something that can be cultivated (Sousa 2011). Training in creative thinking through arts instruction may be just what is needed in our schools to get students to be able to think outside the box and apply what they know to varied contexts.

For budget reasons, many schools have limited exposure to the arts. If your school lacks art programming, there are still ways that you can have your students reap some of the brain benefits of exposure to the arts. One simple way is by playing calming, non-distracting background music while students are working. In a study of surgeons conducted by Siu et al. (2010), it was found that background music enhanced surgical performance, alertness, and ability to concentrate while working on patients. Comparable benefits

Several functional magnetic resonance (MRI) imaging studies have proven that musical training activates areas of the brain involved in mathematical processing. Additional studies highlight the positive effects of music training and performance on reading and verbal memory.

are likely for students. Additionally, "researchers have known for a long time that music can directly influence blood pressure, pulse, and the electric activity of muscles. Newer evidence shows that music may even help build and strengthen connection between brain cells in the cortex" (Sousa 2011, p. 227).

Creativity-fostering instructional practices can and should be built into lessons, as they not only bestow cognitive and other health benefits, but also give teachers an opportunity to address some of the multiple intelligences that exist in their classrooms. We'll talk more about multiple intelligences later in this chapter, but as a quick example of how you could easily bring art-inspired practice into the classroom, you might have younger middle school science students pantomime or act out the movements of various unicellular organisms and have their classmates try to guess what they represent. This activity is effective because it not only gets kids up and moving, but it also actually reinforces their knowledge of the properties of these organisms and how they behave. Further, using creative movement in the classroom has been shown to have valuable effects on learning and memory; it engages the cerebellum, which "plays an important role in attention, long-term memory, spatial perception, impulse control, and the frontal lobe's cognitive functions—the same areas that are stimulated during learning" (Sousa 2011, p. 237).

Left Brain vs. Right Brain: A Neuro Myth

One of the first things that most of us learned about the brain as students is that the left hemisphere of the brain controls the right side of the body and vice versa. This is generally true; however, virtually every book written about the brain in the past decade goes to great pains to note that many misconceptions exist about the activities controlled by the brain's right and left hemispheres. Jensen (1998) writes, "While each side of the brain processes things quite differently, some earlier assumptions about the left and right brain are outdated....The old biases about music and arts being 'right-brained frills' are outdated" (p. 8). Marilee Sprenger (1999) concurs, "Perhaps you have heard stories about 'right-brained' people and 'left-brained' people. These are simply that—stories. People are not 'right brained' or 'left brained,' unless, of course, they have had a hemisphere removed" (p. 41). Thus, a passing fad in the education world in the late 1970s and early 1980s of teachers directing their instruction toward one hemisphere of the brain or the other has rightly faded off the radar screen.

All that said, the right and left hemispheres of the brain do not operate identically. For example, Given (2002) reports that "the right side of the brain is associated with controlling negative emotions, whereas the left hemisphere is associated with positive emotions" (p. 25). In school, a student's right hemisphere might be activated by the disappointment of receiving a low test grade, while this same student's left hemisphere might register the pleasure activated by the teacher's offer of a retest. Moreover, the left hemisphere seems to play a primary role in producing and comprehending language, while the right hemisphere seems primarily responsible for processing visual, auditory, and spatial information. This means that a French teacher who is holding up various objects for his students to describe in French is activating both sides of his students' brains. The right hemisphere controls the process of students' seeing and recognizing the objects, and the left hemisphere controls the process of students' orally naming the objects and describing their characteristics.

Sprenger (1999) explains that "the left hemisphere is able to analyze; it deals with parts. The right hemisphere deals with wholes.... Analyzing music would occur in the left hemisphere and enjoying it in the right" (p. 42). In other words, a student in a music theory class might be asked to both identify the various types of chords and notes found in a particular piece and to explain what emotions the piece instills in its audience. The student might use his or her left hemisphere to recognize the chords and notes of which the piece is composed, and then use his or her right hemisphere to identify the different emotions that the song as a whole instills in its audience. This explanation of how the right and left hemispheres differentiate helps to explain the research cited by Eric Jensen (1998) that beginning chess players and mathematicians show intense left-hemisphere activity during these activities, while master chess players and mathematicians experience greater right-hemisphere activation during these activities. The novice chess players and mathematicians are regarding their activities move by move or step by step, whereas the experts examine the chessboard or math problem more holistically. More information on novice and professional chess players

can be found in Chapter 7. Readers may want to re-read this section to get a better understanding of the reason for their different levels of performance.

In closing, there are some clear differences between the way in which the right and left hemispheres of the brain operate. Patricia Wolfe (2001), however, seems to best express the point made by various researchers and brain-based educators that "although it now seems clear that our hemispheres each have their specialties ... the responses of the two hemispheres are so closely connected that they produce a single view of the world, not two" (p. 47). Usha Goswami (2004) concurs, "There are massive cross-hemisphere connections in the normal brain," and "both the 'left brain' and 'right brain' are involved in all cognitive tasks" (p. 180). To return to the example of the French teacher holding up objects for his students to identify and describe, both hemispheres of the brain are necessary to successfully carry out this activity. The right hemisphere allows students to process the visual information regarding these objects, and then the left hemisphere allows students to find the language to put this visual information into words.

Critical vs. Sensitive Learning Periods: A Neuro Myth

Another myth about the brain is that there are certain critical periods during which the brain is receptive to certain types of information and that, therefore, learning this particular information can only occur during a particular "critical period." One example that is often raised is the idea that language can only be learned fluently in early childhood.[1] While it is unquestionably true that early childhood represents an "optimum period" for language acquisition, during which individuals may acquire language skills with relative ease, it should also be noted that adolescents and adults are capable of achieving fluency in a foreign language as well. Thus, it is important to distinguish between the myth of "critical periods" of learning and the reality of "sensitive" periods of learning. This distinction holds important implications for educators who may falsely hold a now-or-never perspective on various types of learning.

---

1 Early childhood is when children are less inhibited or self-conscious with regard to trying and practicing the new language than older people. This makes learning a new language easier for young children that for adolescents or adults.

Gender, Cognitive Science, and Schooling: A Neuro Myth

As we move deeper into the twenty-first century, there is something of a movement afoot regarding the academic achievement of boys. Concerns are abound that boys are in "crisis," and in fact the research does seem to suggest that more girls than boys are graduating from high school, going on to college, and, for the first time in American history, girls outnumber boys in our nation's law schools and medical schools. It is, first of all, important to recognize that there is a cyclical nature to these gender wars and education. In the early 1990s, the American Association of University Women published a report on *How Schools Short-Change Girls*. Just a decade later, the reverse sorts of books, articles, and reports are coming out on the ways in which schools "shortchange" boys. One of the louder cries of late has been that the design and structure of schools are more amenable to girls' brains than to boys' brains. Educators have suggested that schools should use more manipulatives to draw on boys' superior spatial abilities and offer more recess and breaks so that energetic boys will have the opportunity for physical exertion. Cognitive scientist Daniel Willingham acknowledges that researchers have discovered some differences between the male and female brains. The region of the brain known as the hippocampus seems to be, on average, larger in the female brain than in the male brain. Males seem to have a slight advantage in certain spatial tasks and mathematical reasoning, while females seem to have an equally slight advantage in various memory tasks and mathematical calculation. Willingham (2006) explains, "Researchers who do this work debate whether these differences are very modest or moderate—but no researcher claims that they are large" (p. 4). For this reason, Willingham concludes that, as of now, "The neuroscience behind gender differences... doesn't add any practical knowledge that can be applied in the classroom" (p. 4). This doesn't mean that there are no differences between the male and female brain or that, at some point in the future, neuroscience will not have more to contribute to our understanding of how boys and girls learn differently. At the present time, however, educators should be cautious about boys and girls being educated differently *due to differences in their brains.*

> *Educators should be cautious about boys and girls being educated differently due to differences in their brains.*

Multiple Intelligences Theory

In 1983, Howard Gardner published a work entitled *Frames of Mind The Theory of Multiple Intelligences.* In this work, Gardner laid out his **theory of multiple intelligences**—namely, that intelligence is better conceived of a multiple rather than a unitary construct. In other words, Gardner argued that the traditional conception of intelligence is overly broad and that, in fact, different people are intelligent in different ways. Gardner suggested that there were seven different types of basic "intelligences": linguistic, logical-mathematical, spatial, bodily-kinesthetic, musical, interpersonal, and intrapersonal. In 1999, Gardner added an eighth intelligence—naturalist intelligence.[2] Chapter 7 gives a brief description of some of these intelligences.

While Gardner's theory remains controversial in the psychology world, his theory of multiple intelligences is invaluable to educators in that "MI theory" reminds us to design both learning experiences and assessments that play to the strengths of the various types of learners within our classroom. As Laura Erlauer (2003) explains, "Success in learning is heightened when a student learns through his or her preferred learning style or multiple intelligence" (p. 63). She argues that, too often, schools value only the linguistic and logical-mathematical intelligences and, as a result, shortchange the students whose strengths lie in one or more of the other intelligences identified by Gardner. In an elementary school class studying energy, then, a teacher committed to planning activities and assessments that address all eight intelligences might ask students to perform the following types of activities.

- Write a journal entry about a memorable experience that involved mechanical energy (*linguistic intelligence*).
- Solve math problems that relate to the amount of radiant energy provided by the sun (*logical-mathematical intelligence*).
- Design a map that shows which regions of the United States experience the most yearly sunlight and which regions experience the greatest number of thunder and lightning storms (*spatial intelligence*).
- Choreograph a dance routine that represents

---

2 In recent years, Gardner has also discussed—but not committed to—the idea of a ninth intelligence, existential intelligence, which deals with fundamental questions of existence, for example: Why do we live? Why do we die? Where do we come from?

the impact of lightning on our lives during a thunder and lightning storm (*bodily-kinesthetic intelligence*).

- Write or listen to a song or rap describing the effects of the different types of energy (*musical intelligence*).
- Interview a person whose work involves the use of mechanical or chemical energy (*interpersonal intelligence*).
- Ask students to reflect on the strength of their commitment to conserving energy both now and as an adult (*intrapersonal intelligence*).
- Prepare a report on an animal, such as the electric eel, that can actually produce its own energy (*naturalist intelligence*).

Each of these activities is specifically designed to address a specific type of intelligence; however, these activities also activate different areas of the brain. For example, writing a journal entry or interviewing a person whose work involves energy activates the brain's temporal lobe. Solving a math problem activates the frontal lobe. Listening to a song about energy involves the occipital lobe, and building a gadget that converts energy from one form to another activates the parietal lobe. "Teachers should be aware that by instructing information in different ways—through discussion, readings, videos, debates, projects, etc.—there is a greater possibility of student retention and learning because the information will be input in different (though sometimes overlapping) neural pathways" (Tokuhama-Espinosa 2011, p. 164). It is in this way that Gardner's work on multiple intelligences relates to a cognitive understanding of the brain's functions. More information about Gardner's theory of multiple intelligences can be found in Chapter 7.

Learning Systems Theory

Another theory through which the brain and learning may be viewed is the learning systems theory espoused by researchers such as neurobiologist Robert Ornstein, psychiatrist Richard Restak, clinical psychologist Daniel Goleman, and education professor Barbara Given. As Given (2002) explains, "Current knowledge [of the brain and learning]... has moved beyond the left/right dichotomy to a broader view of five different learning systems—emotional, social, cognitive, physical, and reflective—and their numerous often overlapping subsystems that reflect specific neurobiological brain structures and functions" (p. 4). A short description of each of these five different systems follows.

1. **The brain's emotional system.** The limbic area of the brain (described earlier in this chapter) is the primary controller of a person's emotions. The emotional system determines likes, dislikes, goals, desires, and reactions to different interactions and occurrences (Given 2002). In a classroom, a student's emotional system might be activated upon receiving an upsetting note from another student in the class or a teacher's compliment for excellent work on a homework assignment.

2. **The brain's social system.** The social system of the brain controls social interactions and social emotions (romantic, maternal, friendly, etc.) and is perhaps the least understood of the five systems. Researchers believe that the right hemisphere may be more important than the left for social interactions and that the orbito-frontal cortex may play a primary role in determining one's social judgments (Given 2002). When students are assigned to work in groups to complete a task, the social system plays a role in influencing different students' abilities to interact respectfully with their group members, divide up the work to be done, and work effectively together to carry out this work.

3. **The brain's cognitive system.** The cognitive system processes information received by the brain. The cognitive system may be found throughout the neocortex (the four lobes of the brain). As you may recall from the opening section of this chapter, each lobe is responsible for processing a different type of information: visual, auditory, sensory, higher-order, etc. The cognitive system is activated whenever a teacher plays a song, shows a video, writes on the chalkboard, or passes around an object for students to touch.

4. **The brain's physical system.** The physical system draws information from a person's physical environment. It is situated primarily in the brain stem and cerebellum (Given 2002). A science teacher activates a student's physical system when teaching the steps necessary to transfer microscopic organisms from a petri dish to a slide underneath a microscope.

5. **The brain's reflective system.** The reflective system controls the brain's higher-order thinking and problem-solving. This system takes the longest of the five systems to develop. It is primarily situated in the frontal lobe of the neocortex. The reflective system is activated when a teacher asks students to draw an inference about the narrator's

background in a particular short story or to apply a mathematical concept learned in class to a real-life situation.

While the five learning systems—emotional, social, cognitive, physical, and reflective—are described as separate entities, they are always working together. For example, imagine a teacher instructing her students to pair up and edit each other's essays on *Romeo and Juliet*. A student's emotional system is activated if he or she is paired with a student with whom he or she has argued in the past. Perhaps he or she experiences dismay at having to work with this student once again. This student's social system is activated when the pairs of students meet to exchange essays. Perhaps the student treats his or her partner collegially despite their prior tension. The partners may nod at each other respectfully or even shake hands. A student's physical system is activated when he or she lifts up his or her desk to slide it closer to his or her partner's. As he or she then reads his or her partner's essay and considers whether the point about *Romeo and Juliet* his or her partner is trying to make is a logical one, the reflective system is hard at work. Here, then, one may see how the relatively simple act of pairing up students to edit each other's work invokes all five of the learning systems.

What is the value to us as educators of learning systems theory? Given (2002) writes, "At any one moment, all systems simultaneously vie for attention and control" (p. 79). Many schools and teachers tend to focus primarily on a student's cognitive and reflective learning systems, as made evident by the fact that subjects such as health, physical education, art, and music and positions such as guidance counselor and school psychologist are in short supply. Research has revealed, however, that the emotional, social, and physical learning systems all have the capability of overriding these more *academic* systems. For example, if a student of ours got into an upsetting argument with her mother prior to leaving for school, this student's cognitive system will be unlikely to focus on our description of the quadratic formula. Her emotional and social learning systems are taking priority in her brain. Moreover, even if she puts the argument behind her, she will be equally unlikely to use her reflective system to solve a quadratic equation if the argument precluded her from eating breakfast before leaving for school. In this case, her physical system takes priority over the reflective system. In short, then, it seems that we, as educators, simply need to be aware of and attend to our students' emotional, social, and physical learning systems because of their impact upon our students' cognitive and reflective learning systems. If we sense that a student is distracted by some type of emotional or social issue, we may be better served by quietly sending this student to speak to his or her guidance counselor rather than keeping the student in class for fear that he or she will miss out on too much content. The ability of the emotional and social learning systems to override the cognitive and reflective learning systems renders it unlikely that this distraught student will benefit from remaining in class.

Strategies for Brain-Compatible Learning

Having spent the first half of this chapter describing the different components of the brain, what learning and memory look like from a cognitive perspective, and the theories of multiple intelligences and learning systems, we turn now to the more practical matter of how we can use this information to inform our work as classroom teachers. We have chosen to divide the remainder of this chapter into two sections: structural strategies for brain-compatible learning and instructional strategies for brain-compatible learning. In the first section—*structural strategies*—we will discuss structures and routines based on recent advances in our understanding of the brain and learning that may be used in either our own classrooms or in the school as a whole to support student learning. In the second section—*instructional strategies*—we will focus on pedagogical strategies that apply new discoveries about the brain and learning to our work as teachers. Please note that our placement of these strategies in either the structural or instructional camp is neither perfect nor neat. Many brain-compatible strategies are beneficial for both structure and instruction, and this is why you may notice that these categories sometimes overlap. If it makes sense to you to optimize prime learning periods within a classroom day to build your daily schedule and boost your instruction, then by all means take advantage of that and all else that this section has to offer.

> *We, as educators, simply need to be aware of and attend to our students' emotional, social, and physical learning systems because of their impact upon our students' cognitive and reflective learning systems.*

Structural Strategies for Brain-Compatible Learning

Attention Span

In the mid-1980s, research studies revealed that adult workers need five- to 10-minute breaks for every one to two hours that they work (Erlauer 2003). In 1995, David Sousa reported in *How the Brain Learns* that school-aged children cannot pay attention to a single subject for spans longer than 20 minutes. After 20 minutes of focus on a particular topic, the brain shifts its attention to something else. We have all experienced our minds wandering after a period of sustained focus on a particular activity. In discussing this finding, Laura Erlauer observes that this insight about children's attention spans does not require teachers to completely change the class's topic of study at 20-minute intervals, but **the type of activity or means through which the students are learning** *should* **shift in some way after approximately 20 minutes.** In other words, a teacher who has been lecturing to his or her class would be well served by transitioning after 15 or 20 minutes into an activity that allows students to reflect in writing about the information that has been conveyed or to shift into groups to carry out an activity related to this direct instruction. If we, as educators, don't factor our students' natural attention spans into our lesson designs, we virtually guarantee losing our students' attention over the course of a lesson. Shifting students' attention to a different activity every 15 or 20 minutes allows them to exercise different brain regions in grappling with a concept, reinforcing neural pathways, and making new synaptic connections. Further, it gives teachers an opportunity to engage the multiple intelligences that make up individual classrooms by tailoring these activities in ways that address students' diverse learning needs. A last consideration is what Tokuhama-Espinosa (2011) calls teachers' "obligation to help students become more conscientious about how the brain deals with conflicting stimuli and how to control and prioritize them" (p. 155). Teachers must take the responsibility of making students aware of certain brain processes and pitfalls so that they can begin to develop personal strategies for managing how they focus on tasks.

The Brain and Prime Learning Periods within a Class or Lesson

The work of neuroscientists has also given educators a deeper understanding of the way in which students'

The first 10 minutes of a class or lesson is the period during which the potential for student learning is highest.

capacity for learning changes over the course of a single class period or lesson. According to research conducted in the late 1990s, the *first 10 minutes* of a class or lesson is the period during which the potential for student learning is highest (Erlauer 2003). For this reason, it is imperative that educators use activities such as activators (described in Chapter 2) to fully capitalize on these opening minutes of class. Teachers who spend those 10 minutes passing back papers, taking attendance, or chatting with students are wasting their students' peak period for learning.

Though the first 10 minutes of class represent the period during which students are most likely to focus, comprehend, and commit to long-term memory the information they are taught, a second (and almost as) prime period for learning occurs during the *final 10 to 15 minutes* of a lesson or class (Erlauer 2003). For this reason, activities such as summarizers (described in Chapter 2) that review the content covered during a class period may be invaluable for ensuring that this content will become part of students' long-term memory. Whether through summarizers or another type of activity, using the final 10 minutes of class time for review greatly increases the likelihood that students will understand and remember a lesson's content.

If the opening and closing moments of a lesson or class period represent the times during which students' potential for learning is greatest, then it should be noted that the *middle stage* of a class period typically represents the low point for student learning. Erlauer (2003) encourages teachers to recognize that such a low point exists and to try to compensate by switching from one activity to another or by getting students up and moving in the middle of the class period or lesson. Such strategies may mitigate the natural lull in attention and focus that occurs in students' brains.

Prime Learning Periods within a School Day

Interestingly, the peak and low periods for student learning over the course of the school day follow a pattern similar to that of a single class period. In other words, students tend to be the most alert during the *first two hours* and *last two hours* of their day; on the flip side, "halfway between the time you wake up and the time you usually go to sleep is your low point in terms of energy and alertness" (Erlauer 2003, pp. 89–90). This finding suggests that **the low point of our students' day in terms of energy and alertness** occurs in the afternoon right after lunch period. For this reason, teachers whose classes fall during this afternoon period might be well served by using hands-on activities, cooperative learning activities, and activities that get students up and moving. These are the activities that may best combat the midday energy and attention lull that students experience.

It also seems worthwhile to point out here that the structure of your school's master schedule may have a significant impact on student learning. More specifically, a school that uses a schedule in which each class meets at the same time every day is likely to encounter situations in which the Algebra II class that meets first period (8:00–8:56 AM) finishes the year far ahead of the Algebra II class that meets fifth period (1:15–2:04 PM). Such a school might consider shifting to a rotating master schedule in which the time of day during which each class meets rotates to ensure that Algebra II doesn't always meet in the morning or always meet in the afternoon. If a schedule change is not feasible, then it becomes all the more important for us as teachers to consciously vary our instructional techniques over the course of a class period in order to maintain our students' attention.

The children in our classes who arrive at school without having eaten breakfast are starting the day at a cognitive disadvantage compared to their classmates.

The Brain and Technology

In the past 15 to 20 years, the Internet and mobile technologies have played an increasingly prominent role in our lives and in the lives of our students. With information readily at our fingertips, ever-expanding social networks, and the ability to connect person to person in real time, it is impossible not to wonder about the impacts of increased exposure to technology on the brain. While there are, of course, numerous educational benefits provided through web-based technologies (many teachers make good use of technology to facilitate teaching and learning), the implications of students' heavy reliance on computers should not be ignored.

Brain researchers have identified a number of ways that technology may impede memory and the process of learning. We already know that when it comes to acquiring new information, the brain typically needs multiple encounters with a concept in order to develop and enrich neural pathways. We also know that learning and memory are interconnected—remembering something is simply a function of synaptic firing along already established neural pathways.

In a 2006 study by Sparrow, Liu, and Wegner, it was found that use of web-based tools like Google can actually have a negative impact on memory and learning when compared with the use of more traditional sources of information like books. Reliance on information technology while learning "causes information processing in the brain to be shallow rather than deep, thereby preventing from [sic] information to be understood and encoded" (Spitzer 2014, p. 83). **Knowing that answers are readily accessible, that information can just be Googled on demand, your students' brains may be less likely to encode and retain new information.** The same logic can be applied to calculator use in young children who have not yet committed the multiplication table to memory. If a second grader habitually relies on a calculator to compute basic multiplication problems, he or she will be less likely to develop heightened levels of mastery when it comes to multiplication down the road. This is evidence of the importance of varied opportunities for students to engage with content. As dendrites, like muscles, are prone to atrophy when in disuse, it is also important to remember the significance of having your students think and perform tasks for themselves and not rely extensively on technology.

The Brain and Nutrition

While it may be difficult for us to influence our students' eating habits, these habits unquestionably affect the process of teaching and learning. Neuroscientists have determined that the foods our students eat (and do not eat) affect the functioning of their brains. As Barbara Given explains in *Teaching to the Brain's Natural Learning Systems* (2002), "It remains clear that children require sufficient intake of protein and complex carbohydrates to function effectively, mentally, and physically" (p. 88). Thus, the children in our classes who arrive at school without having eaten breakfast are starting the day at a cognitive disadvantage compared to their classmates. Today, many schools in the Boston area have chosen to address this issue by starting each school day with a light breakfast provided free of charge to its students. While some may criticize the use of limited resources on food rather than instructional supplies, these schools recognize that without providing food, a high percentage of these students would begin each school day on empty stomachs. An understanding of brain-based learning would lead one to the conclusion that providing students with breakfast supports their learning as much or more than new lab supplies or textbooks would. Better that they begin classes alert and focused with older textbooks than drowsy and distracted with new textbooks.

While students need to eat food with protein and complex carbohydrates in order for their brains to function effectively, there are also foods they eat that negatively impact their brain's capacity for learning during the school day. As Given (2002) explains, "Simple sugars can be devastating to learning because they create a rapid increase in insulin and a 'sugar high' that is quickly followed by an overwhelming sense of sleepiness and foggy thinking" (p. 97). In a previous section, we discussed the fact that the school periods that come directly after lunch and in the early afternoon represent a low point in students' capacity for learning. Those of us whose classes fall during these times must work hard to maintain our students' attention and focus. Compounding this challenge for teachers is that the foods many of our students eat for lunch are the sugary junk foods that lead to "sleepiness" and "foggy thinking." Is this challenge completely out of our hands? Well, yes and no. While we certainly don't have complete control over our students' eating habits, the clear link that researchers have established between what students eat and how they think suggests that it behooves us, as educators, to take the time to make sure that our students understand this connection as well. Ideally, such learning about health and nutrition might take the form of an extended unit or several units in a health or physical education class. But in an era when high-stakes testing and budget cutbacks have led to the reduction or even the outright elimination of these programs, the responsibility seems to fall on all educators to convey some important lessons about nutrition to our students. Of course, this is not necessarily a bad thing. In Chapters 2 and 7, we discussed the fact that students are more motivated and engaged learners when they feel the content that they are learning is "real." Toward this end, a math teacher teaching his or her students about fractions might ask students to find the percentage of fat in foods eaten during lunch time. This lesson serves the dual purpose of educating students about nutrition while simultaneously increasing the likelihood that they will remember the mathematical concepts they are using.

It may also behoove us as educators to remind our students' parents about the importance of nutritious breakfasts and lunches. Much of what we now know about the link between nutrition and learning

As far as the brain is concerned, sleep plays a significant role in neurogenesis (the creation of new neurons) and the encoding of information into long-term memory.

has come about in the time period since our students' parents finished their own schooling. The importance of nutritious meals for alert, focused thinking may be conveyed in a respectful and helpful manner on parent night. Alternatively, more and more schools are developing and using "school-home compacts" that explicitly lay out the responsibilities of the teacher, administrator, student, and caregiver for supporting a student's learning. Such a document should explicitly include nutritious meals as a responsibility that a student's caregiver must assume.

Finally, there may be some value in a school faculty or school district examining the quality of the meals provided by its own food-service provider. Many schools—although this number is diminishing—sell candy, cookies, and ice cream during lunch as a way of raising funds to be spent in other areas. While such a strategy is understandable, this strategy may actually be counterproductive if the snacks students are purchasing at lunch are reducing their capabilities as learners for the second half of the school day. Some schools are seeking out ways to provide their students with healthy, organic food options. The Berkeley Unified School District in California initiated a partnership with the Alice Waters' Chez Panisse Foundation to "create a formal curriculum that weaves organic gardening, cooking, and eating healthy lunches into the educational experience of the district's 9,000 students" (Severson 2004, p. 1). Such a partnership represents an impressive example of a school system not only recognizing the importance of nutritious lunches to student learning, but also realizing that the production of these meals represents a powerful learning opportunity as well. Although it has grown to be a politicized topic, federal school lunch programs have over the last few years attempted to adopt healthier standards to reduce the amount of unhealthy fats, sugar, and sodium found in American school lunches and replace them with more fruits, vegetables, and whole grains. It is clear that many, even at the higher levels of the government, understand the positive impacts that a nutritious diet can have on student learning.

The Brain and Sleep

Sleep is important for both the body and the brain. As far as the brain is concerned, sleep plays a significant role in neurogenesis (the creation of new neurons) and the encoding of information into long-term memory. Experts say that most young people need about nine hours of sleep each night, but, unfortunately, insufficient sleep is a disturbing phenomenon that affects a growing number of students. Many children do not have regular bedtimes that would support their cognitive development, or they may have their sleep interrupted for a variety of reasons. For example, some children have televisions in their bedrooms or are up late into the night playing video games or interacting with social media on their cell phones. Quite naturally, when students are sleep-deprived, the cognitive effects extend to their learning and behavior in the classroom. Some negative consequences include difficulty with activities that enlist the prefrontal cortex, which is known to be sensitive to sleep. Higher-order thinking tasks, creativity, and abstract reasoning are also negatively affected. Several studies point to the effects of sleep deprivation on student grades, asserting that students who get sufficient sleep each night receive higher grades on average than students who get less sleep (Sousa 2011). It is clear that, as a nation, we seem to be moving more and more toward becoming a sleepless society. A recent Gallup poll (2013) found that Americans currently average 6.8 hours of sleep per night, one hour less than was the average in 1942. Sleepiness, of course, affects memory and attention, as well as general alertness in the classroom. If it is becoming part of our national culture to sleep less, teachers must approach students and parents to spread a message that promotes healthy sleep habits. If you notice that your students may be suffering the effects of a lack of sleep, encourage an early bedtime in an electronic-device-free sleeping environment to promote improved health and school performance.

Emotional Wellness

In an earlier section of this chapter, "Learning Systems Theory," we discussed the fact that if the brain's emotional learning system becomes distressed, such distress may limit the ability of the brain's cognitive and reflective learning systems to function properly. In other words, if a student is concerned about an earlier interaction with a bullying classmate, he or she may be unable to focus on the day's lesson. As a result, there is an important educational reason for us to pay attention to the social and emotional wellness of our students; namely, the state of these learning systems has a direct impact on our students' cognitive

There is an important educational reason for us to pay attention to the social and emotional wellness of our students; namely, the state of these learning systems has a direct impact on our students' cognitive and reflective learning systems.

and reflective learning systems. In earlier chapters of this book on classroom management (Chapter 3) and questioning practices (Chapter 5), we discussed the importance of and strategies for creating a safe, respectful classroom environment. While there is no need to repeat our discussion of those strategies here, it seems important to point out that our discussion in this chapter of the interaction between the brain's different learning systems provides a cognitive rationale for investing the time necessary to create a classroom and school environment in which students feel physically and emotionally safe. Such an environment is a prerequisite for maximizing student learning.

The Brain and Physical Activity

Like arts education, physical exercise in schools has suffered greatly as the focus is now placed on raising test scores in high-stakes content areas like mathematics and reading. This is unfortunate, given the powerful effects of physical exercise on cognition, brain physiology, and mood. Although the US Department of Health and Human Services recommends that children ages 6–17 engage in at least 60 minutes of exercise each day, it was found that only 27.1 percent of high school students reach this benchmark (CDC 2014). Sadly, recess is no longer a standard feature of many elementary schools, and physical education classes are in many schools only weekly engagements.

Among the many benefits of exercise on the brain, perhaps the most important has to do with oxygen. Exercise increases oxygen levels that reach the brain, and this has a direct, positive correlation with improved cognition and task completion. In reflecting on the importance of oxygen to brain functioning, Sousa (2011) reports, "Higher concentrations of oxygen in the blood significantly enhance cognitive performance in healthy young adults. They are able to recall more words from a list and perform visual and spatial tasks faster. Moreover, their cognitive abilities vary directly with the amount of oxygen in the brain" (Sousa 2011, p. 238). Students' long-term memory also benefits from increased blood flow, as the hippocampus functions more efficiently under these conditions. Lastly, the brain-beneficial protein BDNF, which supports the health of new neurons and promotes the generation of new ones, is optimized in the presence of increased hippocampal oxygen.

In the face of limited opportunities for students

to engage in school-based physical activities, such as recess and gym, you may want to consider ways of building physical activity into your lessons. These could take the form of physical activity breaks, where students simply get up and do stretching routines for a few minutes at the beginning, middle, or end of a class. Or you might implement a classroom-based physical activity that serves as an introduction to or reinforcement of the content. For example, in a large enough classroom, a high school English teacher might have students, in groups of two or three, "take a walk" around the room for five minutes to discuss the relationship between George and Lenny in Steinbeck's *Of Mice and Men*, then have students report what they discussed back to the class. As you can see, the physical activities that you adopt do not have to be strenuous or elaborate, so there is no need to be apprehensive about getting your students moving.

Instructional Strategies for Brain-Compatible Learning

Practice, Practice, Practice

Earlier in this chapter, we mentioned a tennis coach who used to provide his team with the following recipe for success: "Learn the rules. Play the game. Practice! Practice! Practice!" Whether or not he knew it at the time, this advice is directly in line with what we know about brain-compatible learning. More specifically, repeated practice allows concepts, skills, or ideas to become more deeply ingrained in a person's long-term memory by increasing the speed with which synapses fire along a particular neural pathway. As Marzano, Pickering, and Pollock note in *Classroom Instruction That Works* (2001), "After four practice sessions, students will reach a competence level of 47.9 percent of complete mastery. It will take students 20 more practice sessions, about 24 times in all, to reach 80 percent competency" (p. 67). In *How People Learn* (1999), Bransford, Brown, and Cocking explain that world-class chess players typically require between 50,000 and 100,000 hours of practice to achieve a ranking of master or grand master (p. 4).

What kind of practice is most useful? In *Accessing the General Curriculum* (2000), Nolet and McLaughlin note that there are two different types of practice: massed practice and distributed practice. **Massed practice** "involves longer sessions of intense practice at irregular intervals," while **distributed practice** "refers to regularly scheduled practice sessions that may be shorter and less intense" (p. 38). "Cramming"

for a final exam by staying up until 2:00 AM the night before the exam would be an example of massed practice. In contrast, a high school junior who learns 10 new vocabulary words each week for the six months leading up to the SATs would be an example of distributed practice. As is probably no surprise to those of us who have used both methods in different situations, distributed practice is a significantly more effective strategy for transferring new information into a person's long-term memory. Distributed practice allows the dendrites of neurons along neural pathways the time to develop and grow bushier and for communication along this neural pathway to become faster and more efficient. In contrast, cramming the night before a big exam provides little opportunity for such processes to occur.

20-2-20

A strategy for teachers to consider in terms of the pacing of practice and review is the "20-2-20" rule offered by Laura Erlauer in *A Brain Compatible Classroom* (2003). **20-2-20** means that within 20 minutes of a lesson, students explain what they have learned. Within two days, students review and apply this new information. And within 20 days, students reflect on what they have learned. Such a system allows students to receive the distributed practice necessary to commit a skill or concept to their long-term memories. It should also be noted that Erlauer's suggestion that the initial review take place within 20 minutes of the original learning coincides with the research described earlier about students' peak learning times within a single class period or lesson. Because the final 10 minutes of a lesson represent a peak window for student learning, following up a 20- to 30-minute lesson with a short review is an important tool for helping students commit this lesson to their long-term memories.

Higher-Order Thinking

When the brain engages the prefrontal cortex and works to make connections between various concepts and ideas, or between past and new learning, this process is known as *higher-order thinking*. Contrasted with rote memorization, higher-order thinking "creates new [neural] pathways, strengthens existing pathways, and increases the likelihood that new learning will be consolidated and stored for future retrieval" (Sousa 2011, p. 266). There is a clear link to higher-order thinking and long-term memory formation. In *Classroom Instruction That Works* (2001), Marzano, Pickering and Pollock explain that, in order for students to learn a skill, concept, or idea well enough to recall and apply that knowledge at a future time, they must gain a conceptual understanding of this information. In other words, our students will have a far easier time remembering and applying the Pythagorean theorem ($A^2 + B^2 = C^2$) if we take the time necessary to help them understand how the equation is derived, and this understanding can most easily be facilitated by having them engage in higher-order thinking tasks. Toward this end, Laura Erlauer (2003) suggests, "It is usually far better to cut out about two-thirds of the simple, rote practice time in exchange for the more valuable synthesis, reflection, and application time of that same new knowledge" (p. 83). In other words, if students are learning to identify prepositions, we should avoid giving them three pages of sentences for homework with the instruction to circle the prepositions in each sentence. Rather, we might give them one page of sentences in which to find the prepositions and then ask them to write 10 sentences of their own that use prepositions correctly. We might also ask them to cut out an article from the daily newspaper and circle the five most interesting prepositions in the article. Through assignments like these, we are pushing students to apply the concept they are learning, rather than simply to identify its use.

Classroom Environment

In *Teaching with the Brain in Mind* (1998), Eric Jensen reports that studies have found that classrooms decorated with classroom wall displays, such as educational posters, student work, affirmations, etc., may have a positive impact on learning. These stimuli serve to "feed the brain." For foreign language teachers and elementary school teachers in grades K–2, simply labeling the names of all of the objects in the classroom may have a positive effect on students' reading levels (Erlauer 2003). For other teachers, similar strategies make sense, as well. Earlier on, we noted that students (and adults) are unable to focus on a single topic for more than 20 minutes. At various points in a school day, students' attention will drift. If these students shift their attention to the student work, mathematical rules, and sayings decorating their classroom walls, they may learn even as they are "spacing out" because their brains are absorbing information.

> *The act of combining our verbal lesson with a visual aid will better enable our students to commit the entire lesson to their long-term memory. This may be especially true for learning that involves text.*

The Brain and Responding to and Correcting Student Work

As we described in detail in earlier sections of this chapter, from a cognitive perspective, learning is the act of creating neural pathways in the brain and increasing the speed with which the neurons along this pathway convey information from one neuron to the next. While we have discussed this process in terms of learning a useful skill, concept, or idea, it is also possible, of course, for a student to lay down neural pathways for incorrect information. Unfortunately, such information may be difficult to "unlearn." Consider your own life. Have you ever misheard a lyric from a popular song and thus learned the song incorrectly? Even after someone explains the actual lyric to you, isn't it extremely difficult to get that incorrect lyric out of your head each time you hear the song played? Students face the same challenge if they learn a skill or concept incorrectly. For this reason, it is crucial that we as teachers assess and return assignments to our students in a timely fashion. While keeping up with grading is one of the more challenging (and often mundane) aspects of teaching, it is important that we quickly diagnose our students' misperceptions and misunderstandings in order to correct these mistakes before they grow more deeply embedded in our students' brains.

Pictures Are Worth a Thousand Words

Several years ago, a special education teacher with whom we work gave us an invaluable piece of advice for helping students to learn vocabulary. She suggested that students create flashcards with the word to be learned on one side of the index card and the definition of the word on the other side. She also suggested instructing our students to draw a small picture of something that they connected with this word's meaning on the same side of the index card as the word's definition. This practice had an unquestionably positive impact on our students' ability to learn and remember the assigned vocabulary. Though we did not know it when we first began employing this strategy, the reason behind this strategy's success was brain-based. You may remember that in the section of this chapter devoted to reading and the brain, we mentioned that visual stimuli were much more likely to be stored in the memory and later retrieved than other types of stimuli. As Bransford, Brown, and

Cocking explain in *How People Learn* (1999), "Comparisons of people's memories for words with their memories for pictures of the same objects show a superiority effect for pictures. The superiority effect of pictures is also true if words and pictures are combined during learning" (p. 13). Of course, this understanding of the brain and memory has implications far beyond simply memorizing vocabulary words. If we understand that our students are better able to learn and remember information when it is conveyed in pictures, we may purposely include visual aids during periods of direct instruction. For example, in discussing the route that Columbus took from Spain to the New World, we are well served by taking the additional few minutes necessary to pull down the map of the world in the front of our classroom and literally trace the route with a wooden pointer or pencil. Even if we don't feel it to be particularly important for students to be able to trace Columbus's route across a map, the act of combining our verbal lesson with a visual aid will better enable our students to commit the entire lesson to their long-term memory. This may be especially true for learning that involves text. Frey and Fisher (2010) remark, "As brain researchers focus on the human visual system, a growing body of evidence suggests that text should be paired with illustrations. This has implications for the Internet, picture books, and the comprehension strategy of visualizing" (p. 107).

> *When students enjoy the lesson or activity in which they are participating, their brain actually releases chemicals that increase their ability to remember the content they are learning.*

Short Answer vs. Multiple Choice

Beginning in 2006, Professor Henry Roediger and colleagues at the University of Washington in St. Louis carried out a study on test-enhanced learning in the classroom. Their goal was to investigate if particular types of testing best facilitated students' abilities to learn and retain information. According to Debra Viadero (2006), what they found was that "the learning benefits are greatest when the tests are composed of short-answer rather than multiple-choice questions" (p. 1). Several other studies have confirmed this finding. The thinking is that students are better at remembering information that they are forced to write down themselves than right answers that they simply find among a series of choices.

The Brain and Making Work Enjoyable

As teachers, of course, we always *want* our students to find learning enjoyable, but now there is brain research suggesting students learn better when they enjoy their learning. Judy Willis (2007) explains that recent neuroimaging studies have found increased levels of dopamine in people's brains during pleasurable and positive experiences. As Willis explains, "Because dopamine is the neurotransmitter associated with attention, memory, learning, and executive function, it follows that when the brain releases dopamine in expectation of pleasurable experience, this dopamine will be available to increase the processing of new information" (p. 71). In other words, when students enjoy the lesson or activity in which they are participating, their brain actually releases chemicals that increase their ability to remember the content they are learning.

Reducing Stress

We live in a society that often glorifies individuals who can "rise to the occasion" and perform effectively during periods of great stress. As teachers, we sometimes tell ourselves that final exams and high-stakes tests are important opportunities for students to cope with pressure and stress. While it is unquestionably important for individuals to learn how to manage stress, research on the brain suggests that high stress levels can impede learning. According to Willis (2007), **during periods of stress, the amygdala—the area of the brain that regulates emotion—becomes so overactive that it blocks activity in other parts of the brain.** As a result, MRI results have found that individuals going through high-stress situations show reduced activity in the "higher cognitive centers" of the brain. As a result, Willis explains, "New information coming through the sensory intake areas of the brain cannot pass as efficiently through the amygdala's effective filter to gain access to the brain's cognitive processing and memory storage areas" (p. 71). In short, then, placing students in high-stress situations has been found to reduce the efficiency with which students' brains can process and analyze new content. Clearly, there are situations and scenarios in which high stress is unavoidable; however, to the extent possible, we don't want our students learning in such conditions.

Using Different Types of Memory

You'll recall from an earlier section of this chapter on memory that brain-based education expert Marilee Sprenger breaks down the storing of memory in the brain into the following categories: semantic, episodic, procedural, automatic, and emotional (see Table 8.2 earlier in this chapter).

In *Learning and Memory: The Brain in Action*, Sprenger suggests a number of specific strategies for effectively using the strengths of these different types of memory.

Semantic Memory

In order to use students' semantic memory, Sprenger (1999) suggests that teachers use graphic organizers, peer teaching, summarizing, role-playing, debates, outlining, timelines, practice tests, paraphrasing, and mnemonic devices. Each of these strategies—many of which are described in detail in other chapters of this book—involves students learning from either written or spoken words. For example, paraphrasing asks students to put information they have recently learned into their own words. Likewise, a mnemonic device is a play on words that may help a student to commit information to long-term memory. Many science teachers help their students to remember the classification system of living things by using some variation of the phrase, "**K**ing **P**hillip **C**ame **O**ver **F**or **G**reat **S**paghetti!" The first letter of each word in this sentence corresponds to the different levels of classification: **k**ingdom, **p**hylum, **c**lass, **o**rder, **f**amily, **g**enus, and **s**pecies. Such a phrase utilizes students' semantic memory to help them remember the classification system of living things.

Episodic Memory

Because memory can be episodic, researchers have discovered that *where* a student learns a particular skill or concept and *where* a student is expected to apply this learning may have an impact on his or her ability to recall and use this information. More specifically, Sprenger (1999) explains, "Students who learn information in one room and take a test in another consistently underperform. Episodic memory has an important component called 'invisible information.' Students have more trouble solving math problems in English class than they do in their math classroom. Why? The walls, desks, overheads, chalkboards, and even the math teacher are covered with invisible information. The content of the room becomes part of the context of the memory" (p. 52). This finding has enormous implications for educators. Particularly in the current climate of high-stakes testing, it is important to recognize that students will perform better on

Particularly in the current climate of high-stakes testing, it is important to recognize that students will perform better on a science test if they take the test in the same room in which their learning about science has occurred.

a science test if they take the test in the same room in which their learning about science has occurred.

Of course, this understanding of episodic memory has applications beyond high-stakes testing as well. For example, one way in which a teacher may physically signify the end of one unit and the start of the next is by changing students' seating assignments or even the entire layout of the classroom. A less dramatic change would be replacing the information on the classroom bulletin boards with content about the upcoming unit. These physical changes will help students' minds to differentiate between the previous unit and the current unit and create physical associations with the new learning that will occur. In short, helping students to connect their learning to a particular type of physical space works in much the same way as connecting student's learning to pictures, described in the preceding section.

Procedural Memory

Procedural memory involves the processes that the body does and remembers. For classroom teachers, Sprenger (1999) suggests having "students move in some way as they learn" (p. 74). This movement creates muscle memory that, as with pictures and episodes, leads students to associate the content they are learning with their motion at the time the learning is taking place. For example, consider asking students to stand up or move to a new seat for a mini-lesson set within a larger class period. Ask students to clap their hands if they understand your explanation of a particular idea. Integrating such procedures into classroom instruction will better enable your students to recall the learning that has taken place.

Automatic Memory

Automatic memory is just that—information that can be recalled immediately without perceptible pause for thought. Most of us as elementary school students were expected to commit the multiplication tables to automatic memory. Automatic memory tends to require large amounts of practice, developing strong associations, or both. For example, one of us recalls our third-grade teacher asking us every night for homework to write out the multiplication tables for a particular number six times. Others remember endlessly practicing with flashcards. Repetitive drills such as these are par for the course for committing information to automatic memory. Sprenger (1999) also suggests working to develop associations between a particular type of information and something more easily remembered. For example, the vast majority of us do not have the 50 states of the United States committed to automatic memory. And yet some of our students have learned a song in which they literally rattle off the 50 states in perfect harmony. Much as young children first learn the alphabet through song, these students have committed the 50 states to automatic memory by successfully associating these states with a tune.

Emotional Memory

Perhaps the type of memory that we, as teachers, make the least use of is emotional memory. Just as our students are more likely to remember information that is connected to pictures, places, or movement, they are also better able to remember information linked with a particular emotion or feeling. How does this work? Imagine that we complete a unit with our first graders on the Thanksgiving holiday by actually holding a "practice" Thanksgiving meal (perhaps on the final day of school before the Thanksgiving break). Students create decorations and are responsible (with the help of their parents) for bringing in a type of food that might have been eaten at the first Thanksgiving. The excitement and pleasure that students experience while participating in such a hands-on (and tasty) activity greatly increase their ability to learn and commit to long-term memory the historical background of the Thanksgiving holiday.

Moreover, the emotion that can help students better remember a skill, concept, or idea does not always have to be their own. At the conclusion of Chapter 2 of this book, we explained that students are more likely to be engaged, active learners when they recognize their teacher's passion and enthusiasm for the material they are being asked to learn. We suggested that such a display of enthusiasm piques students' interest in understanding the relevance of the particular topic or skill to their own lives. There is also a brain-based rationale for teachers' expressing their enthusiasm for a particular topic of study; namely, students are better able to commit a particular piece of information or content to their long-term memory when they can link this information to the emotions expressed by their teacher at the time of instruction. For example, John Donne's "A Valediction Forbidding Mourning" is an example of a poem for which higher-order thinking questions might be used. This poem is a challenging one to understand, and when teaching this poem to our students, we

typically begin by describing our own introduction to the poem. We describe struggling to understand the poem and feeling our own frustration level mounting—and then, suddenly, right when we were ready to give up, an epiphany occurred, and it was almost as though a lightbulb turned on directly over the poem, illuminating its beauty. Such an introduction is meant not only to prepare our students for the challenging reading ahead (and to exhort them not to give up), but also to allow them to link the poem's content with the emotions described by their teacher—frustration transforming into illumination. By linking content and emotion, our students are far more likely to integrate the poem's content into their long-term memory than they would be if we simply handed out copies of the poem and began reading. This is an example of the strategic use of emotions to facilitate learning. However, knowing that emotions are not always felt or expressed in a deliberate way, we urge you to also consider the impact of negative emotions on learning. Memory consolidation (linking an emotional feeling with a particular memory) also happens in negatively charged learning situations and creates mental patterns that are difficult to break. For example, a student's bad experience with a sixth-grade math teacher may induce a fear of math that prevents his or her future learning of the subject and lasts for the rest of his or her life. Tokuhama-Espinosa (2011) cautions teachers to "understand that emotional memories 'override' memories of conceptual knowledge...[and] be more careful in how [you] interact with students in class and the type of feedback used" (p. 161).

Providing Structure

In previous sections of this chapter, we examined what learning and memory look like inside the brain. You will recall that students are better able to transfer new information into long-term memory if they connect this new information to knowledge they already possess. For new information *unconnected* to previously held knowledge, one strategy described in Chapter 2 was "chunking." This is the practice of grouping individual pieces of information into larger groups. For example, in *How the Brain Learns* (1995), David Sousa notes that it is difficult for students to commit seven random numbers to memory, but adding a dash between the third and fourth digit turns those seven numbers into a "phone number." Since this grouping of numbers is more meaningful than seven random numbers in a line, these numbers are then more easily committed to long-term memory. This strategy of chunking works because the human brain is better at encoding information into long-term memory when that information is received in an organized, categorized form than when it is simply individual, unconnected pieces of information. In various studies on the way in which experts in a particular field learn new information, researchers have discovered that "experts are able to analyze and remember larger chunks of information because they store information in categories rather than as separate bits" (Nolet and McLaughlin 2005 p. 35).

With this understanding of learning and memory in mind, there are several strategies that teachers may employ to support their students' learning. First, teachers should utilize curricula and develop units that base students' learning around "organizing ideas" (Bransford, Brown, and Cocking 1999). Essential questions (described in detail in Chapter 2) may be helpful in this regard. For example, a social studies unit on the Revolutionary War will better serve students if the teacher focuses the unit around two to three organizing ideas rather than simply leading students chronologically through the various battles, dates, and important events. Much more useful for students is an organizing idea (in the form of an essential question), such as, "What factors led the colonists to decide that they could no longer live under British rule?" Organizing the unit around this and one to two other organizing ideas will lead students to process the information they learn about the Revolutionary War in a structured, categorized way, enabling them to more easily transfer this information to their long-term memories.

Nolet and McLaughlin (2000) touch on a second strategy for supporting student learning when they write that "teachers may help their students employ more expert storage strategies when they are clear about the kind of information they want their students to learn and the manner in which students will be asked to use the information" (pp. 40–41). By this, they mean that the type of knowledge teachers expect students to learn may be divided into three categories: declarative knowledge, procedural knowledge, and conditional knowledge. **Declarative knowledge** takes the form of basic facts. **Procedural knowledge** is *how* to do something. And **conditional knowledge** takes the form of knowing *when* to apply a skill or concept. For example, the Pythagorean theorem itself is an example of declarative knowledge, but understanding how to use this formula to find the length of

Declarative knowledge takes the form of basic facts. Procedural knowledge is how to do something. And conditional knowledge takes the form of knowing when to apply a skill or concept.

the third leg of a right triangle requires procedural knowledge. Finally, recognizing the various situations when applying the Pythagorean theorem will be useful requires conditional knowledge.

A second example of these different types of knowledge can be seen in a lesson for elementary school students about the use of question marks and exclamation points. In this case, declarative knowledge takes the form of the definition of these two types of punctuation—namely, that question marks are used to show that someone is asking a question and that exclamation points are used to express excitement. However, understanding *how* to use these punctuation marks requires procedural knowledge and *when* to use these punctuation marks requires conditional knowledge. Demonstrating these types of knowledge would require students to create properly punctuated interrogative and exclamatory sentences or to read a paragraph in which all punctuation marks have been removed and correctly insert question marks and exclamation points at the appropriate intervals.

Nolet and McLaughlin (2000) suggest that students are better able to commit newly learned information to long-term memory when they are told at the outset of the lesson which type of knowledge they will be expected to learn and the way in which they will be expected to utilize this knowledge. In Chapter 5, we discussed the strategy of providing students with a unit's final assessment or project *at the start of the unit.* In Chapters 1 and 2, we discussed the importance of giving the students the mastery objectives at the outset of the learning. Here, we have the cognitive explanation for why such strategies promote higher levels of learning.

Using Color

In this section, we have discussed ways in which teachers may better organize the content that they convey to students. Two other strategies that come up in the literature on brain-based education involve the use of color. First, Eric Jensen suggests, in *Teaching with the Brain in Mind* (1998), that teachers may increase their students' memory retention by using different colored chalk or markers to categorize information they are writing on the blackboard or flipchart paper. For example, a science teacher educating his or her students about the concept of different species might choose to write all of the examples of mammals in red marker and all of the examples of amphibians in green marker. Using these colors will better enable students to remember the examples of these two species because the information is entering their brains in a structured, categorized way. Similarly, in *Learning and Memory the Brain in Action* (1999), Marilee Sprenger recommends using a single color of paper for all handouts related to a particular topic. For example, in one of our ninth-grade English classes, we ask students to keep grammar and literary terms sections in their notebooks. All of the handouts that go into their literary terms section are printed on light blue paper, and all of the handouts for their grammar sections are printed on pink paper. In this way, we work to connect the handout we are examining with the previous handouts they have received on a related topic.

Mind and Brain Education and the Future

In 1997, John Bruer, president of the James S. McDonnell foundation in St. Louis, made the controversial declaration in an article for *Educational Researcher* that the gap between brain research and education was a "bridge too far" to be crossed effectively. Until recently, Bruer seemed to have been right. As recently as 2006, Lynn Okagaki, of the Institute of Educational Sciences, observed, "Over the past 30 years, we have learned an enormous amount through the cognitive sciences about how people think or process information, and how we learn new information…[but] for the most part, the knowledge that has been gained has not made it into classroom practice" (p. 1). In recent years, however, many researchers and educators have been working to bridge that gap. In 2000, the Harvard Graduate School of Education began offering a program in "Mind, Brain, and Education," and Harvard's Peter Blake and Howard Gardner (2007) report that "similar programs have [subsequently] appeared across the country and abroad" (p. 63). In 2007, cognitive scientists from Harvard, the University of Northern Colorado, the University of Southern California, the Swiss Federal Institute of Zurich, and the National Academy of Education in Argentina joined together to launch a new journal, *Mind, Brain, and Education*, the first academic journal dedicated exclusively to the impact of brain-based research on education. In their inaugural edition, researchers from these five institutions

declared, "The discovery of powerful brain-imaging tools; the remarkable, burgeoning discoveries that are transforming genetics; and the growing power of methods for assessing cognition, emotion, and learning make possible an alliance that can illuminate human learning and development" (Fischer et al. 2007, p. 1).

So how will neuroscience affect education in the years ahead? Already, we see greater attention being paid to the workings of the brain and its relationship to learning. Many teacher preparation programs, even those that do not have a specific mind-and-brain education concentration, have begun to incorporate an understanding of how the brain functions in their courses. Books aimed at teachers, such as this one, increasingly draw from neuroscience findings to instruct on best practices. And school-based professional development programs are dedicating more attention to this area (Sousa 2011). According to neuroscientist Uta Frith (2005), by the year 2020, educators will "know about sensitive periods that could be used to make learning super-efficient" (p. 289). Additionally, she predicts that we will have a much deeper understanding of what learning difficulties look like in the human brain, "and there will probably be novel means of overcoming them" (p. 289). Finally, Frith predicts that education in 2020 will be more tailored to the needs of individual children. She suggests that "neuroscience techniques will be available to track the effects of learning in the developing brain of individual children. We will be able to decide which teaching method, or indeed which teacher, is best suited to each child" (p. 290).

In addition to cognitive science, many educational researchers predict that genomics—the study of the interaction of genes and the environment—will also have a strong influence on education in the years ahead. Elena Grigorenko (2007) explains that the human genome project has unequivocally revealed that individuals are born with a "genetic script," but it is the environments in which they live that lead "every individual to play out his or her genetic script in a unique way" (p. 21). Grigorenko notes, "The school environment has always been and will always be a major player in modifying children's gene expression" (p. 21). She predicts that, in the years ahead, genomics will play a role in "finding the best possible interventions for children with special needs" (p. 21). For this reason, she suggests that teacher preparation programs and school systems should "start preparing [educators] for the infusion of genomic knowledge into their everyday practice" (p. 23). Grigorenko and other researchers recognize that it is unrealistic to ask classroom teachers to become experts in cognitive science and genomics while still remaining experts in their own content areas. Instead, they look ahead to a day when teachers, administrators, and cognitive and genomic specialists will work together in teams to chart out the best educational pathways for individual students. That day may not be so far in the future.

We can be certain that the years ahead promise increased and deepening linkages between education, neuroscience, and genomics; however, there is also cause for caution. As Kurt Fischer warns in "The Myths and Promises of the Learning Brain" (2004), "The field [of neuroscience] is still in its infancy; much of the data in cognitive science, neuroscience, and genetics is incomplete. Far too often, new findings are misunderstood and disseminated by the press and other media—setting in motion a series of chain reactions and the establishment of some myths that are sometimes both entertaining and damaging" (p. 1). Fischer offers as an example a finding in the early 1990s by researchers that college students who studied while listening to Mozart did slightly better than their peers on certain problem-solving tasks. Unfortunately, this verifiable but small finding was exaggerated by the media and politicians and had some costly, ineffective results. For example, the governor of Georgia spent hundreds of thousands of dollars of state money mailing Mozart CDs to all expectant mothers in the state of Georgia, and state-run daycare centers in Florida began piping in classical music (Fischer 2004). Both of these steps were an overreaction to a small, preliminary finding. While educators would be wrong to turn their backs on the important findings that are beginning to emerge from our newfound understanding of the brain, it would be equally wrong to make massive curricular or structural changes in response to early findings. As the road sign warns us, we must proceed with caution!

Conclusion

In this chapter, we have endeavored to take advantage of recent advances in the field of neuroscience to bring you a more thorough understanding of what is occurring in our students' brains than any previous generation of educators has ever been afforded. We have tried to balance explanations of what learning and memory look like inside the brain with pedagogical strategies used by ourselves and recommended by doctors, psychologists, and scientists, based on their deepening understanding of the brain and learning. We have placed this chapter in the latter half of the book, recognizing that teachers might regard chapters on behavior management, assessment, and standards-based teaching with a greater sense of immediacy than a focus on the brain and learning. As you have now read this chapter on the brain and learning, however, we recommend you take time to look back over those previously read chapters. Reread the paragraphs you have highlighted or marked as particularly helpful. Strategies that have been offered throughout this book for maintaining an orderly classroom, generating activities that allow a class full of heterogeneous students to work to their potential, and using questions to strengthen students' higher-order thinking skills may now be viewed through the lens of the brain and learning. We believe you will find that rereading the strategies presented throughout this book with a heightened understanding of the impact of these strategies on the brain and learning will strengthen your ability to implement these ideas in your own classroom. As more and more research has been published on the brain and learning, we know that we have had the fascinating experience of more deeply understanding why and how various strategies we have employed for years in our classrooms actually work to support our students' learning. This deeper understanding has unquestionably increased our expertise as educators, and we hope that you feel a similar benefit to understanding the nuts and bolts of learning and the brain.

References

Alloway, T.P. *Improving Working Memory: Supporting Students' Learning*. London: SAGE, 2011.

Ansari, D. "Culture and Education: New Frontiers in Brain Plasticity." *Trends in Cognitive Sciences* 16, no. 2 (2012): 93–95. doi:10.1016/j.tics.2011.11.016.

Armstrong, T. *Multiple Intelligences in the Classroom*. Alexandria, VA Association for Supervision and Curriculum Development, 2000.

Battro, A.M. and Fischer, K.W. "Mind, Brain, and Education in the Digital Era." *Mind, Brain, and Education* 6, no. 1 (2012): 49–50. doi:10.1111/j.1751-228X.2011.01137.x.

Blake, P. and Gardner, H. "A First Course in Mind, Brain, and Education." *Mind, Brain, and Education* 1, no. 2 (2007): 61–65.

Bor, D., Duncan, J., Wiseman, R.J., and Owen, A.M. "Encoding Strategies Dissociate Prefrontal Activity from Working Memory Demand." *Neuron* 37, no. 2 (2003): 361–367. doi:10.1016/S0896-6273(02)01171-6.

Bransford, J., Brown, A., and Cocking, R. *How People*

Learn: Brain, Mind, and Experience at School. Washington, DC: National Academy Press, 1999.

Carter, R. *The Human Brain Book.* London: DK Pub, 2009.

Chomsky, N. "A Review of B.F. Skinner's Verbal Behavior." In *First Language Acquisition: The Essential Readings,* eds. Lust, C. and Foley, C., pp. 25–55. Malden, MA: Blackwell Publishing, 2004.

Cole, M.W., Bagic, A., Kass, R., and Schneider, W. "Prefrontal Dynamics Underlying Rapid Instructed Task Learning Reverse with Practice." *Journal of Neuroscience* 30, no. 42 (2010): 14245–14254. doi:10.1523/JNEUROSCI.1662-10.2010.

Curcio, G., Ferrara, M., and Degennaro, L. "Sleep Loss, Learning Capacity, and Academic Performance." *Sleep Medicine Reviews* 10, no. 5 (2006): 323–337. doi:10.1016/j.smrv.2005.11.001.

Cummins, J. "Age on Arrival and Immigrant Second-Language Learning in Canada: A Reassessment." *Applied Linguistics* 2 (1981): 132–149.

Cummins, J. Language, *Power, and Pedagogy: Bilingual Children in the Crossfire.* New York: Multilingual Matters Ltd., 2000.

Erlauer, L. *The Brain-Compatible Classroom: Using What We Know about Learning to Improve Teaching.* Alexandria, VA: ASCD, 2003.

Dewald, J.F., Meijer, A.M., Oort, F J., Kerkhof, G.A., and Bögels, S.M. "The Influence of Sleep Quality, Sleep Duration, and Sleepiness on School Performance in Children and Adolescents: A Meta-Analytic Review." *Sleep Medicine Reviews* 14, no. 3 (2010): 179–189. doi:10.1016/j.smrv.2009.10.004.

Donnelly, J.E. and Lambourne, K. "Classroom-Based Physical Activity, Cognition, and Academic Achievement." *Preventive Medicine* 52 (2011): S36–S42. doi:10.1016/j.ypmed.2011.01.021

Durisko, C. and Fiez, J.A. "Functional Activation in the Cerebellum during Working Memory and Simple Speech Tasks." *Cortex* 46, no. 7 (2010): 896–906. doi:10.1016/j.cortex.2009.09.009.

Fink, A., Benedek, M., Grabner, R., Staudt, B., and Neubauer, A. "Creativity Meets Neuroscience: Experimental Tasks for the Neuroscientific Study of Creative Thinking." *Methods* 42, no. 1 (2007): 68–76. doi:10.1016/j.ymeth.2006.12.001.

Fischer, K. "The Myths and Promises of the Learning Brain." *Harvard Graduate School of Education.* December 1, 2004. https://www.gse.harvard.edu/news/ed/04/12/myths-and-promises-learning-brain

Fischer, K., Daniel, D., Immordino-Yang, M., Stern, E., Battro, A., and Koizumi, H. "Why Mind, Brain and Education? Why Now?" *Mind, Brain, and Education* 1, no. 1 (2007) 1–2.

Frey, N. and Fisher, D. "Reading and the Brain: What Early Childhood Educators Need to Know." *Early*

Childhood Education Journal 38, no. 2 (2010): 103–110. doi:10.1007/s10643-010-0387-z.

Frith, U. "Teaching in 2020: The Impact of Neuroscience." *Journal of Education for Teaching* 31, no. 4 (2005), 289–291.

Gardner, H. *Frames of Mind: The Theory of Multiple Intelligences.* New York: Basic Books, 1983.

Gardner, H. *Multiple Intelligences: New Horizons in Theory and Practice.* New York: Basic Books, 2006.

George, E.M. and Coch, D. "Music Training and Working Memory: An ERP Study." *Neuropsychologia* 49, no. 5 (2011): 1083–1094. doi:10.1016/j.neuropsychologia.2011.02.001.

Given, B. *Teaching to the Brain's Natural Systems.* Alexandria, VA: ASCD, 2002.

Goswami, U. "Neuroscience, Education, and Special Education. *British Journal of Special Education* 31, no. 4 (2004): 175–183.

Grigorenko, E. "How Can Genomics Inform Education?" *Mind, Brain, and Education* 1, no. 1 (2007): 20–27.

Hattie, J. *Visible Learning for Teachers: Maximizing Impact on Learning.* London: Routledge, 2012.

Heilman, K.M., Nadeau, S.E., and Beversdorf, D.O. "Creative Innovation: Possible Brain Mechanisms." *Neurocase* 9, no. 5 (2003): 369–379. doi:10.1076/neur.9.5.369.16553.

Hinton, C., Fischer, K., and Glennon, C. "Students at the Center: Teaching and Learning in the Era of the Common Core." www.jff.org, n.d.

Jensen, E.P. "A Fresh Look at Brain-Based Education." *The Phi Delta Kappan* 89, no. 6 (2008): 408–417. http://www.fasa.net/upload_documents/neuroplasticity10.29.pdf.

Jensen, E. *Teaching with the Brain in Mind.* Alexandria, VA: ASCD, 1998.

Johnson, S.B., Blum, R.W., and Giedd, J.N. "Adolescent Maturity and the Brain: The Promise and Pitfalls of Neuroscience Research in Adolescent Health Policy." *Journal of Adolescent Health* 45, no. 3 (2009): 216–221. doi:10.1016/j.jadohealth.2009.05.016.

Jones, J. M. "In US, 40% Get Less Than Recommended Amount of Sleep." *Gallop.com.* December 19, 2013. http://www.gallop.com/poll/166533/less-recommended-amount-sleep.asx.

Kelly, A.C., Hester, R., Foxe, J.J., Shpaner, M., & Garavan, H. "Flexible Cognitive Control: Effects of Individual Differences and Brief Practice on a Complex Cognitive Task." *NeuroImage* 31, no. 2 (2006): 866–886. doi:10.1016/j.neuroimage.2006.01.008.

Kopasz, M., Loessl, B., Valerius, G., Koenig, E., Matthaeas, N., Hornyak, M., Kloepfer, C., Nissen, C., Riemann, D., and Voderholzer, U. "No Persisting Effect of Partial Sleep Curtailment on Cognitive Performance and Declarative Memory Recall in Adolescents." *Journal of Sleep Research* 19, no. 1, Part 1 (2010): 71–79. doi:10.1111/j.1365-2869.2009.00742.x.

Krashen, S. *The Input Hypothesis Issues and Implications*. New York: Longman, 1985.

Krashen, S. and Terrell, T. *The Natural Approach: Language Acquisition in the Classroom*. San Francisco, CA: The Alemany Press, 1983.

Marzano, R., Pickering, D., and Pollock, J. *Classroom Instruction That Works: Research-Based Strategies for Increasing Student Achievement*. Alexandria, VA: ASCD, 2001.

McCoog, I.J. "The Existential Learner." *The Clearing House* 83, no. 4 (2010): 126–128. doi:10.1080/00098651003774828.

McGeehan, J.R., ed. *Transformations Leadership for Brain-Compatible Learning*. Kent, WA: Books for Educators Inc., 1999.

Monk, C.A., Trafton, J.G., and Boehm-Davis, D.A. "The Effect of Interruption Duration and Demand on Resuming Suspended Goals." *Journal of Experimental Psychology: Applied* 14, no. 4 (2008): 299–313. doi:10.1037/a0014402.

Moriguchi, Y. and Hiraki, K. "Neural Basis of Learning from Television in Young Children." *Trends in Neuroscience and Education* 3 (2014): 122–127.

Nolet, V. and McLaughlin, M. *Accessing the General Curriculum*. Thousand Oaks, CA: Corwin Press, 2005.

Nunley, K.F. "Active Research Leads to Active Classrooms." *Principal Leadership: High School Edition*. March 2002. http//www.help4teachers.com/activeresearch.htm.

Ornstein, R. *The Right Mind: Making Sense of the Hemispheres*. New York: Harcourt Brace, 1997.

"Physical Activity Facts." October 7, 2014. http://www.cdc.gov/healthyyouth/physicalactivity/facts.htm

Price, G.R., Mazzocco, M.M., and Ansari, D. "Why Mental Arithmetic Counts: Brain Activation during Single Digit Arithmetic Predicts High School Math Scores." *Journal of Neuroscience* 33, no. 1 (2013): 156–163. doi:10.1523/JNEUROSCI.2936-12.2013.

Sakai, K.L. "Language Acquisition and Brain Development." *Science* 310 (November 2005): 815–819.

Schneider, D. "The Dan Schneider Interview 4: Steven Pinker" (August 25, 2007). *Cosmoetica.com*. http//www.cosmoetica.com/dsi4.htm.

Severson, K. "Academic Credit for Lunch with Program Combining Cooking, Organic Gardening." *The San Francisco Chronicle*, July 2, 2004.

Shaywitz, S. *Overcoming Dyslexia: A New and Complete Science-Based Program for Reading Problems at Any Level*. New York: Alfred A. Knopf, 2003.

Shaywitz, S. and Shaywitz, B. "Disability and the Brain." *Educational Leadership* 61 (March 2004): 7–11.

Shaywitz, S. and Shaywitz, B. "Paying Attention to Reading: The Neurobiology of Reading and Dyslexia." *Development and Psychopathology* 20, no. 4 (2008): 1329–1349. doi:10.1017/S0954579408000631.

Siu, K., Suh, I.H., Mukherjee, M., Oleynikov, D., and Stergiou, N. "The Effect of Music on Robot-Assisted Laparoscopic Surgical Performance." *Surgical Innovation* 17, no. 4 (2010): 306–311. doi:10.1177/1553350610381087.

Skinner, B.F. *Verbal Behavior*. New York: Appleton-Century-Crofts, 1957.

Sousa, D. *How the Brain Learns*. Reston, VA: National Association of Secondary School Principals, 1995.

Sousa, D. *How the Brain Learns*, 4th ed. Thousand Oaks, CA: Corwin Press, 2011.

Spinks, S. "Inside the Teenage Brain," television series episode. *Frontline*. New York and Washington, DC: PBS, 1999.

Spitzer, M. "Information Technology in Education: Risks and Side Effects." *Trends in Neuroscience and Education* 3 (2014): 81–85.

Sprenger, M. *Learning and Memory: The Brain in Action*. Alexandria, VA: ASCD, 1999.

"Statistics about Education in America" (October 2, 2014). https://www.studentsfirst.org/pages/the-stats.

Tatsuno, Y. and Sakai, K.L. "Language-Related Activations in the Left Prefrontal Regions Are Differentially Modulated by Age, Proficiency, and Task Demands." *The Journal of Neuroscience* 25 (February 2005): 1637–1644.

Tokuhama-Espinosa, T. *Mind, Brain, and Education Science: A Comprehensive Guide to the New Brain-Based Teaching*. New York: W.W. Norton, 2011.

Tsujimoto, S. "The Prefrontal Cortex: Functional Neural Development During Early Childhood." *The Neuroscientist* 14, no. 4 (2008): 345–358. doi:10.1177/1073858408316002.

Tucker, P. "The Rise of Brain-Focused Teaching." *The Futurist* 41, no. 3 (May/June 2007): 1–2.

Viadero, D. "Cognition Studies Offer Insights on Academic Tactics." *Education Week* 12 (August 30, 2006).

Willingham, D. "Ask the Cognitive Scientist: Brain-Based Learning More Fiction Than Fact." *American Educator* (Fall 2006): 1–9.

Willis, J. "The Gully in the Brain-Glitch Theory." *Educational Leadership* 65 (February 2007): 68–73.

Wolf, M. *Proust and the Squid: The Story and Science of the Reading Brain*. New York: Harper Collins, 2007.

Wolfe, P. *Brain Matters*. Alexandria, VA: ASCD, 2010.

Wolfson, A.R. and Carskadon, M.A. "Understanding Adolescent's Sleep Patternsand School Performance: A Critical Appraisal." *Sleep Medicine Reviews* 7, no. 6 (2003): 491–506. doi:10.1016/S1087-0792(03)90003-7.

Wong, P.C.M., Warrier, C.M., Penhune, V.B., Roy, A.K., Sadehh, A., Parrish, T.B., and Zatorre, R.J. "Volume of Left Heschl's Gyrus and Linguistic Pitch Learning." *Cerebral Cortex* 18, no. 4 (April 2008): 828–836.

Worden, J.M., Fischer, C., and Fischer, K.W. "What Does the Brain Have to Do with Learning? Ignoring Important Findings from Educational Neuroscience Can Be Just as Dangerous as Uncritically Embracing 'Brain-Based' Products or Interventions." *Phi Delta Kappan* 92, no. 8 (May 2011): 8–13.

Zull, J. "Key Aspects of *How the Brain Learns*." *New Directions for Adult and Continuing Education* 110 (Summer 2006): 3–9.

Students with Disabilities: Brain Function

The research of neuroscience in exploring the function of the brain in learning has become an important area for educators to give attention to, with regard to teaching practices and creating classrooms where all students can learn. In this chapter, we give a very in-depth look into the brain function in many areas, but specifically for students with learning disabilities, reading and mathematics stand out. They stand out because they are two of three primary areas of specific learning disabilities that teachers recognize in their students. According to the National Center for Educational Statistics (2012), one in every five students is diagnosed with a specific learning disability. A *specific learning disability* is defined by the Individuals with Education Act as "a disorder in one of the basic psychological processes involved in using language spoken or written, which the disorder may manifest itself in the imperfect ability to listen, think, speak, read, write, or do mathematical calculations." A very common understanding is that a student has a learning disability in at least one of three areas: reading, writing, or mathematics. Everything regarding a specific learning disability is tied to the function and processes of the brain.

One of the primary areas affected by a specific learning disability is reading. One of the most prevalent and recognized learning disabilities in reading is dyslexia. Dyslexia affects approximately one in every five people (National Center for Learning Disabilities 2014). Research in the area of dyslexia started over 100 years ago; however, the research has become more sophisticated as science has evolved over the past 20 years. Dyslexia is a reading disorder that is characterized by phonological processing problems. People with dyslexia have trouble manipulating language, not seeing language—they see words the same as everyone else. Persons with dyslexia use the right side of their brain (where music, art, and creativity live) and the frontal lobe more than those without it. Those without dyslexia use the left side of the brain (where language, reading, science, and logic live). In a dyslexic person's brain, it takes longer for a word to take a trip through the brain because it comes from the right side, and is delayed in the frontal lobe before reaching the lower brain, where words typically form and are connected to read. Dyslexia can be overcome by reprogramming the brain with the use of multi-sensory approaches to reading, through which the student is taught to decode words in the left side of his or her brain to read more fluently. Multi-sensory approaches use all of the senses, including hearing, seeing, smelling, tasting, and touching, to teach the student to read (Sandmon-Hurley 2014). Using such approaches helps the student process words through the brain quicker and via multiple modes.

In an everyday classroom that includes students with dyslexia, a teacher may see a student who has trouble breaking words down into smaller syllables or sound units called *phonemes*. For example, a teacher may have a student that is able to hear the word fine and participate by repeating the word, but will have trouble explaining or demonstrating how to separate the sounds that make the word. For younger students, a teacher may notice a student having difficulty matching the sound with the letters. In addition, a student may struggle with rapid automatized naming. This could look like a student who has shown mastery in naming colors or numbers, but when asked to do it on cue, quickly, he or she will not be able to perform (Semrud-Clikeman 2015).

Some things that are helpful for a teacher to know and understand is that boys are often identified with dyslexia quicker and more often than girls, because boys tend to present as behavioral challenges in the classroom while girls will be quiet and compliant so not to draw attention to themselves. The use of some of the questioning techniques outlined in Chapter 5 and some of the assessments outlined in Chapter 4 can be helpful in recognizing early warning signs of dyslexia. Letter reversals are common in young learners and may not be an indicator that the learner has dyslexia; however, as discussed earlier in this essay, if a student struggles to breakdown words, match sounds to letters, spell words phonetically, or even process language appropriately in social situations, this could be a sign that a student has dyslexia. As teachers, we are often concerned with motivating our students or their internal motivation to learn. Dyslexic students' inability to read is not tied to motivation (Sandmon-Hurley 2014). They benefit more when we know and understand that traditional reading and language instruction will not be effective for their ability to show sustained progress in reading. This is where collaboration between the general and special education teacher benefits the student greatly. The student needs not only core reading instruction, but also intensive instruction and intervention to reprogram their brains. Effective core reading instruction from the general education teacher involves using strategies that incorporate all of the senses, such as tactile letters and audio books. The special educator will work specifically on teaching the student strategies that reprogram his or her brain.

Dyslexia Strategies

The main focus of teachers at any grade level and content area is ensuring that the dyslexic student accesses the content curriculum. Below are specific strategies that can assist any teacher in supporting his or her dyslexic student:

- Give only one or two verbal instructions at a time.
- Allow the student to wear headphones to create a quiet environment so he or she can focus.
  - Incorporate multisensory approaches by using three learning pathways: tactile/kinestic, auditory, and visual.
  - Example: In science class, the science teacher can provide the textbook reading in advance through audio access, use picture prompts as an accommodation during the lecture, and then allow the student(s) to use models or a hands-on manipulative during group or independent work time.
- Highlight essential information for those who are able to read in the textbook.
  - Example: In history class, the history teacher

can provide notes from the textbook reading, with essential information that will be the focus of the lesson highlighted for the student. Also, providing a glossary of terms is essential for students to comprehend the reading and the notes provided.

- Use mnemonic devices or instruction to assist students.
  - Example: In geography class, the geography teacher can use a mnemonic device to help students remember essential information, such as the Great Lakes. You can have the student write the word *HOMES* vertically down the left side of their paper and write out the lake that corresponds with each letter. *H* is for Lake Huron, *O* is for Lake Ontario, *M* is for Lake Michigan, *E* is for Lake Erie, and *S* is for Lake Superior. Also, as a geography teacher, using visuals with mnemonic devices creates even stronger connections for students. For example, you can show the students a map of the world, have them trace each continent with their finger for the shape, and then give them this mnemonic for the six continents: *SEA NAA*. *S* is for South America, *E* is for Europe, *A* is for Africa, *N* is for North America, *A* is for Asia, and *A* is for Australia.
- Use wait time to allow additional processing time for dyslexic students.

Another area that is affected by a student with a specific learning disability is mathematics. Dyscalculia is the most common form of a learning disability in mathematics. A person with dyscalculia has trouble performing math calculations or solving math problems. It also includes difficulty or the inability to learn basic math operations, such as addition, subtraction, multiplication, and division. The research on dyscalculia is still fairly new, less than 20 years old, in comparison to dyslexia. As with dyslexia, neuroscientists have begun to study the brain of people with dyscalculia. The most extensive research has been with special populations, such as persons with Turner syndrome, fetal alcohol syndrome, or low birth weight. However, most recently, there have been small studies specific to children with dyscalculia. The results are interesting in that they show that regardless of whether it was the group with dyscalculia only or one of the special populations, their brains showed either less gray matter (brain cells) or less brain activity in the area of the brain that processes mathematics (the intra-parietal sulcus or parietal lobe) (Horowitz 2014). The key to addressing and overcoming dyscalculia is changing the brain functions. The plasticity of the brain is very important in order to do this. *Plasticity* refers to changes in neural pathways or synapses due to changes in behavior, environment, neural processes, thinking, or emotions. The younger the brain, the more likely new pathways can be created. In regards to dyscalculia, those new pathways change the way learning math occurs. Dyscalculia can stand alone; however, it often co-occurs with other learning difficulties such as dyslexia, dyspraxia (neurological disorder throughout the brain that results in lifelong impairments of memory, motor, judgment, processing, and other cognitive skills), attention deficit hyperactivity disorder, or language impairment (Wilson 2015). There are some common characteristics of students with dyscalculia, such as delayed counting. Five to seven year olds with dyscalculia show less understanding of basic counting principles than their peers. Students may also show delays in using counting strategies for addition. They tend to use inefficient strategies for calculating addition facts, compared to their peers, such as using their fingers or drawing pictures or lines. Memorizing arithmetic facts are also difficult for students with dyscalculia. They have great difficulty with addition, subtraction, and multiplication facts that persists up to at least 13 years of age. Lastly, they lack basic number sense or the fundamental understanding of quantity. They often may be slower at even simple quantity tasks, such as comparing simple numbers or identifying how many items there are in groups of one to three objects (Wilson 2015).

There are some basic strategies that teachers can use in their classrooms to support students who have dyscalculia. Students with dyscalculia know very early that math is an area they struggle with and will often attempt to avoid math tasks. Therefore, start by giving them work tasks at their exact level when they are working independently. The students are more successful when you preview the skills in advance of them being taught to the whole class or for group activities. Previewing can take place during the time students are working on the sponge activity at the start of class. Since students with dyscalculia struggle with basic

number sense and math facts, they would benefit from having extra time to complete in-class assignments or shortening the assignment, as long as the problems they are assigned reflect content standards that have been covered. Lastly, as long as the student does not struggle with dyslexia, use written instructions and questions, versus verbal instructions and questions, to lessen the "brain strain." This allows the student to save his or her mental energy for the work task, versus the instructions and practice problems.

The more we as teachers begin to understand about brain functioning and its impact on learning, the more we are able to use already learned approaches and strategies to meet the unique learning needs of our students.

References

Cortiella, C. and Horowitz, S.H. "The State of Learning Disabilities," 3rd ed. New York: National Center for Learning Disabilities, 2014. http://www.ncld.org/wp-content/uploads/2014/11/2014-State-of-LD.pdf.

"Fast Facts: Students With Disabilities" *National Center for Educational Statistics*, 2015. https://nces.ed.gov/fastfacts/display.asp?id=64.

Horowitz, S. "What Is a Specific Mathematics Disability?" May 5, 2014. *Understood.org*. https://www.understood.org/en/learning-attention-issues/child-learning-disabilities/dyscalculia/what-is-a-specific-mathematics-disability.

"IDEA." *LD Online: The Educator's Guide to Learning Disabilities and ADHD*. http://www.ldonline.org/features/idea2004.

Sandmon-Hurley, K. "Video: Inside the Dyslexic Brain." *Understood.org*. April 10, 2014. www.understood.org/en/learning-attention-issues/child-learning-disabilities/dyslexia/video-inside-the-dyslexic-brain.

Semrud-Clikeman, M. "Research in Brain Functioning and Learning." *American Psychological Association*. http://www.apa.org/education/k12/brain-function.aspx.

Wilson, A.J. "About Dyscalculia: Causes." *AboutDyscalculia.org*. http://www.aboutdyscalculia.org/causes.html.

English Language Learners: The Brain and Language Acquisition

Brain Studies and Language

Linguists have identified general developmental stages experienced by most infants, toddlers, and children in the process of acquiring their first language(s): cooing, babbling, one-word utterances, two- to four-word phrases, and oral fluency. The observation and analysis of human behavior, and the habits of babies and young children, have led linguists to develop theoretical hypotheses. In behavior studies linked to physiological studies, neuroscientists seek to explain why and how language is delayed, interrupted, or, in certain circumstances, lost. Parts of the brain that control language reception and production have been identified by examining individuals who have experienced a delay or loss of language, such as those identified with speech and/or language communication disorders (e.g., aphasia, dysnomia, or expressive language disorder). Sometimes this is done during brain surgery with an electrical stimulation procedure called **cortical stimulation mapping**. Patients are asked questions during procedures so as to locate and protect areas of the brain that are responsible for understanding and producing language.

As a result of the research done by Paul Broca, Carl Wernicke, and Korbinian Brodmann in the mid-1800s to the early 1900s, physicians learned that language function was generally a left-brain function. Loss of speech was associated with damage to the left hemisphere. Research since then has shown that other, specific parts of the brain are also responsible for language, including parts of the right brain. For example, understanding complex semantics and ambiguous sentences has been associated with the right part of the brain (Mohr, DiFrancesco, Harrington, Evans, and Pulvermuller 2014). Neuroscientists continue to identify very specific areas of the brain responsible for understanding syntax, phonology, lexico-semantics, sentence comprehension, and variations in grammatical structures and patterns (Sakai 2005). Results from magnetic resonance (MRI) imaging are used to compare the processes first language (L1) with learning additional languages (L2). One study (Sakai, Nauchi, Tatsuno, Muraishi, Kimura, Bostwick, and Yusa 2009) found that in the process of second-language acquisition, different parts of the left inferior frontal gyrus were activated for in the acquisition of past-tense verbs. In this study of 13- and 19-year-olds, when L2 proficiency level increased, activation in one part of the brain decreased; there was, however, an increase of use in another part of the brain. This may indicate that some brain areas are used for initial language acquisition, but as language skills increase, other areas become activated. The study also identified how developmental age and the age of first exposure to language influence which parts of the brain get activated differences in brain part activation, which varied according to developmental age and age of first exposure. While some common parts of the brain have been identified for acquisition of both first- and second-language learning, further studies are still necessary to examine distinct areas of the brain responsible for acquiring additional languages and which parts are used for specific language tasks.

Patrick Wong, a neuroscientist at Northwestern University, and his team found a connection between a small part of the brain called *Heschl's Gyrus* (HG) and the ability to learn tonal languages (Wong 2008). Tonal languages, such as Chinese dialects, are ones that requires vowels, consonants, pitch, and stress to pronounce different words, whereas non-tonal languages, such as English, use only consonants, vowels, and sometimes stress on these sounds. Even though Wong's study was small (17 adult participants), he was able to conclude that the size of the right HG and the volume of the white and grey matter predetermined a biological ability to learn tones. A positive correlation was made between participants who studied music at an early age and success in identifying tones in language. This may tell us that exercising these skills will increase the size and density of the right HG. While the conclusions of this study did make a connection between brain composition and identifying tones, they did not suggest that adults with smaller right HG were unable to learn tonal differences in languages or second languages in general. There is, however, further evidence that bilingualism also develops in certain areas of the brain. In 2012, Volker Ressel's team showed that the average bilingual Spanish-Catalan speaker had a larger HG than monolinguals. These scientists determined that "learning a second language is a causal factor in the increased size of the auditory cortex" (Ressel et. al 2012).

Psycholinguistics

Two widely known psycholinguists of the twentieth century are B.F. Skinner and Noam Chomsky. Skinner claimed that humans learn language through conditioning (Skinner 1957). One can apply Skinner's theory to explain how output correction, through positive or negative feedback, causes the speaker to use and apply patterns or change to irregular forms. For example, a child who learns "I play a lot" and then acquires "Yesterday I played" will apply the same past-tense pattern to say, "I wave bye-bye when Mommy goes to work" and "I waved to Daddy today." Unless the listener expresses confusion or corrects the child, the child has experienced positive feedback and will continue to apply the same language pattern. Negative feedback, like the listener's expression of confusion and/or output correction, can lead to correct variation in syntax. So when the child learns "I go to Grandma's house," she might try "We goed to the store"; the latter is either misunderstood or corrected, usually by the caretaker, sibling, teacher, or peer. Eventually, the experience of the negative reaction will cause the child to self-correct and use *went*.

Chomsky challenged Skinner's conditioning hypothesis and argued that humans have an innate language-acquisition ability and that our brains have a mechanism that enables us to quickly learn any first language in which we are immersed from infancy to age five or six. Younger children also pick up second languages with ease. It is this ability that explains why "children of immigrant parents may learn a second language in the streets, from other children, with amazing rapidity, and why their speech may be completely fluent and correct to the last allophone" (Chomsky 2004, p. 36). Chomsky defended his theory by examining how quickly children acquire their first language and pick up structural patterns through listening and without learning the rules of grammar. This development is important to understanding how English learners learn because language theorists claim that the process of acquiring an additional language closely mirrors that of learning the primary language. With this in mind, teachers of English learners facilitate a natural language-acquisition process as they plan lessons that depend on peer interaction and use activities that require both basic communication practice and academic discourse.

Psycholinguists and anthropologists have used Chomsky's ideas to identify psychological and emotional factors that influence language learning. Steven Pinker, a cognitive psychologist and researcher, ex-tends Chomsky's theories as he states "that we as humans have to be equipped with an instinct to use and learn language" (Schneider 2007). Stephen Krashen also uses Chomsky to define his theories on second-language acquisition and how an individual's emotional comfort level can help or hinder second-language development (Krashen 1985). Krashen has gone on to defend the idea that language is not learned in a stimulus-response mode such as that identified by Skinner. Instead, he maintains that it is acquired and that grammar, vocabulary, and structures are best learned by exposure to comprehensible language input (Krashen 1985). This means that teachers of English learners should be mindful of using multisensory (act outs, chants, raps, gestures) and graphic representation (tables, charts, semantic maps, diagrams) to support complex structures, advanced vocabulary, and new concepts. Teachers can create natural-language learning situations as they plan communicative activities during which English learners listen to peer language, negotiate, and express needs, wants, and opinions.

Conversational and Academic Language Proficiency

Generally speaking, linguists and second language educators have accepted the idea that second language fluency is composed of conversational language and academic language. James Cummins identified these two areas in 1979 as Basic Interpersonal Communication Skills (BICS) and Cognitive Academic Language Proficiency (CALP). According to Cummins, the average second (or additional) language learner needs approximately two years to establish conversational fluency. At this level, students may be able to express all their needs and wants with few, if any, structural errors. However, students who are still acquiring cognitive academic language proficiency often have difficulty mastering content objectives appropriate for their grade levels and perform poorly on standardized tests. Performing well on content objectives requires what has become known as academic language proficiency. This is the language of tests, textbooks, and science labs. Academic language involves complex structures needed to think critically and demonstrate one's understanding of abstract ideas and complexity (Gottlieb and Ernst-Slavit, p. 5). Cummins explains that academic language proficiency usually takes at least five years for most language learners (1981). Cummins' Common Underlying Proficiency (CUP) theory explains how knowledge in the first language can be drawn on to learn an additional language, and that there is an interdependence of knowledge in the first and second/additional language (2000).

With these theories in mind, teachers should be cognizant of the development of students' first languages and how to use the first-language knowledge to acquire academic English proficiency. Teachers can research cognates and English words borrowed from students' first languages for use in word analysis. During task-based lessons, teachers might inquire and help students make connections by doing a linguistic check-in. For example, a science teacher may facilitate partner work to complete a three-dimensional model that represents Earth's rotation on its axis and revolution around the sun. The science teacher may ask a student, "Is this topic familiar?" or, "Show me what you already know about this," or, "Have you learned/seen this before?" Teachers can also provide opportunities to develop conversational skills and expose English learners to cognitively challenging (a.k.a. academic) tasks and vocabulary. However, when students begin to demonstrate a high level of conversational language, they may still struggle with understanding texts, lectures, and tasks that require academic language proficiency. States and Canadian provinces provide guidance on developing K–12 curriculum documents for teaching communicative and academic language in the general education or mainstream classrooms. Increasingly, regular classroom teachers who have English learners in their classes are becoming English language teachers and taking on more responsibility for creating lessons that facilitate both conversational and academic language.

Strategies for English Learners Related to Brain Study and Language Acquisition Theory

Make Content Comprehensible with Contextualized Practice

- Elementary English learners who encounter new content vocabulary will need more visual support and contextualized use of words. For example, among elementary students studying habitats and animal survival, beginning English learners may need prior exposure to everyday words like *home* and *hide* before encountering words like *habitat* and *camouflage*. The content-specific words become more comprehensible when matched with visuals like pictures and photographs. Heterogeneous groups of students in the general education classroom can also contextualize content vocabulary by performing an act-out, drama, or task, such as building a habitat, categorizing habitats, or camouflaging themselves or an object in the classroom. (See Chapter 5 for more information on vocabulary and language demand of content areas.)

- Middle and high school students who read a passage on cells may struggle with key vocabulary. English learners at various levels of proficiency will benefit from previewing, highlighting, and contextualizing these words before reading. The science teacher can create a reference page that uses visuals, diagrams, or less-demanding language to explain a concept. The English as a Second Language (ESL) teacher can provide more opportunities to use and study challenging vocabulary in lessons that involve a comparative study of the first language(s), as well as examining word parts and affixes that may change the word for specific purposes. Multiple exposure to and analysis of vocabulary will make the text more comprehensible and offer all learners support to read, understand, and use academic vocabulary in dialogue and writing.

Provide Choral Response to Lower Anxiety

When the class responds chorally, students have a choice of responding or remaining silent and listening to peers. Instead of asking individual students questions, teachers can direct questions to cooperative groups or to the whole class.

Example 1. The teacher presents a question to a pair or cooperative group and tells the students she will revisit the team for the answer in two minutes. The students are to discuss the problem, agree on the answer, practice the answer, and respond in unison when the teacher returns to re-ask the question.

Example 2. First, the teacher prompts the whole class by asking for a "shout out" on the count of three. Second, she asks the question and sees what answers come up. The teacher then facilitates a class discussion as students defend their answers.

Example 3. This is similar to a "call and response" in music. The teacher gives groups of students the questions and answers in a script. Students choose a leader to "call" the question or prompt. The rest of the students provide the "response" or answer in unison. The teacher then leads the whole class in the call and response. To add an element of interaction, student groups can then create and teach their own call and response scripts. Other forms of choral response may include student-created chants, poems, or raps for content concepts like math facts, scientific procedures, or historical events.

Demonstrating Structures in Extended Dialogues

It can be difficult for a fluent speaker to avoid correction of language structures, pronunciation, or syntax when listening to an English learner. Correction is something that can also increase anxiety and imply that the way a student responds is more important than the response itself. Affirming the message, engaging in extended discourse, and modeling the appropriate English structure is a way for the English learner to hear correct forms without feeling as if his or her message was ignored or not heard. While self-correction (see example 2) is the long-term expectation, the immediate goal is for the English learner to hear the language model and acquire structures without overthinking them.

Example 1 Student: My mom **sign** my permission slip.
Teacher: Oh good. She **signed** your permission slip? I'm glad she signed it.
Student: Yeah. Now I can go on the field trip.
Teacher: Yes. She **signed** it and you can go to the aquarium. Good job!

Example 2 Student: She **drawed** on my paper!
Teacher: She **drew** on your paper? Where?
Student: Right there. She **drew** on it.
Teacher: I don't know why she **drew** a flower on your paper. Let's talk to her.

Example 3 Student: This microscope **not work**.
Teacher: You're right. This microscope **is not working**. Let's fix it. The illuminator needs a new bulb. Here's one.
Student: Thank you. **It working** now?
Teacher: You try it. I think **it's working**. You tell me.
Student: Yes. **It's working** now.

Find a Friend to Facilitate Problem-Solving and Natural Peer-to-Peer Dialogue

During one-on-one conference time, students share their work with the teacher, and the teacher usually offers warm and cool feedback. As part of the feedback, the teacher can prompt students to "find a friend" to get an answer, fix an error, reread directions, or proofread. This promotes peer dialogue and can be done with ease in a respectful class culture. Some direct instruction may be needed for the English learner to ask for help in an appropriate way and for the peer to offer feedback in a respectful way. Encouraging students to practice saying the answers aloud will provide an opportunity to practice structures with a proficient peer.

Transition-Time Chatter to Provide Authentic Dialogue and Sociolinguistic Competence

During transition time, anchor activities, or cooperative group work, off-task conversation is usually undesirable. Teachers feel compelled to refocus students' attention. However, English learners require some time spent chattering (or babbling), imitating, and listening to colloquial expressions and peer discourse. This can happen as students use materials or props to solve problems during cooperative groups. Also, teachers can allow for a "one-minute talk time" as they establish norms and class expectations. Setting a one- or two-minute timer for a "brain drain" is one way to set parameters on chatter without compromising actual learning time.

References

Chomsky, N. "A Review of B. F. Skinner's Verbal Behavior." In *First Language Acquisition: The Essential Readings*, eds. Lust, B. and Foley, C., pp. 25–55. Hoboken, NJ: Wiley-Blackwell, 2004.

Cummins, J. "Age on Arrival and Immigrant Second Language Learning in Canada: A Reassessment." *Applied Linguistics* 2, no. 2 (1981): 132–149.

Cummins, J. *Language, Power and Pedagogy: Bilingual Children in the Crossfire*. New York: Multilingual Matters Ltd, 2000.

Díaz-Rico, L.T. and Weed, K.Z. *The Crosscultural, Language, and Academic Development Handbook: A Complete K-12 Reference Guide*. 4th ed. Boston: Allyn and Bacon, 2010.

Gottlieb, M. and Ernst-Slavit, G. *Academic Language in Diverse Classrooms: Definitions and Contexts*. Thousand Oaks, CA: Corwin, 2014.

Krashen, S. and Terrell, T. *The Natural Approach: Language Acquisition in the Classroom*. San Francisco, CA: Alemany Press, 1983.

Krashen, S. *The Input Hypothesis: Issues and Implications*. New York: Longman, 1985.

Mandal, A. "Language and the Human Brain." *News Medical*. Accessed August 15, 2015. http://www.news-medical.net/health/Lan guage-and-the-Human-Brain.aspx.

Mohr, B., Difrancesco, S., Harrington, K., Evans, S., Pulvermüller, F. "Changes of Right-Hemispheric Activation after Constraint-Induced, Intensive Language Action Therapy in Chronic Aphasia: fMRI Evidence from Auditory Semantic Processing." *Frontiers in Human Neuroscience* 8 (November 2014). http://dx.doi.org/19.3389/fnhum.2014.00919.

Ressel, V., Pallier, C., Ventura-Campos, N., Díaz, B., Roessler, A., Ávila, C., and Sebastián-Gallés, N. "An Effect of Bilingualism on the Auditory Cortex." *The Journal of Neuroscience* 32, no. 47 (November 2012): 16,597–16,601.

Sakai, K.L. "Language Acquisition and Brain Development." *Science* 310 (November 2005): 815–819. http://mind.c.u-tokyo.ac.jp/Sakai_Lab_files/Papers/SakaiLab_Science_2005.pdf.

Sakai, K.L., Nauchi, A., Tatsuno, Y., Hirano, K., Muraishi, Y., Kimura, M., Bostwick, M., and Yusa, N. "Distinct Roles of Left Inferior Frontal Regions That Explain Individual Differences in Second Language Acquisition." *Human Brain Mapping*, 30, no. 8 (August 2009): 2,440–2,452.

Schneider, D. "The Dan Schneider Interview 4: Steven Pinker." *Cosmoetica.com.* August 25, 2007. http//www.cosmoetica.com/dsi4.htm.

Skinner, B.F. *Verbal Behavior*. New York: Appleton-Century-Crofts, 1957.

Tatsuno, Y. and Sakai, K.L. "Language-Related Activations in the Left Prefrontal Regions Are Differentially Modulated by Age, Proficiency, and Task Demands." *The Journal of Neuroscience* 25 (February 2005): 1,637–1,644.

Wong, P.C.M., Warrier, C.M., Penhune, V.B., Roy, A.K., Sadehh, A., Parrish, T.B., and Zatorre, R.J. "Volume of Left Heschl's Gyrus and Linguistic Pitch Learning." *Cerebral Cortex* 18, no. 4 (2008): 828–836. http://cercor.oxfordjournals.org/content/18/4/828.full.

9

Working Effectively with Parents and Guardians

With a Section on Working with Families from Poverty

Objectives for the Chapter[1]

After reading this chapter, the reader will be able to

a. use proactive communication to establish positive relationships with parents and guardians

b. conference effectively with parents and guardians

c. deal effectively with aggressive/overly assertive parents/guardians

d. maximize the engagement of uninvolved parents/guardians from poverty in their children's education

e. conduct a successful curriculum-night presentation

---

1   From this point forward in the chapter, we will refer to *parents/guardians* for the purpose of an easier flow for the reader. However, in every instance, we intend this chapter to also include grandparents, foster parents, and other guardians.

Educators have become extremely aware of the importance of working effectively with parents and the value of teacher training in this area. The 2011 "MetLife Survey of the American Teacher" (p. 52) reports that "teachers with high job satisfaction also receive more preparation and support to engage parents effectively. They are more likely to rate their professional development since becoming a teacher and their pre-service training as *excellent* or *good* in preparing and supporting them to engage parents effectively (82 percent vs. 67 percent, and 76 percent vs. 61 percent)." Preparing teachers to work effectively with parents is important to both students *and teachers*.

Research (Bryk, Sebring, Allensworth, Luppescu, and Easton 2010 in Henderson and Whipple 2013) shows that strong ties with family and community can make it four times more likely that your students will make major gains in math and reading.

Families come in a wide range of configurations and with a wide array of needs and expectations. Some parents/guardians are extremely aggressive consumers of their children's education. We will talk soon about these parents/guardians, who have come to be dubbed "helicopter parents." Other parents/guardians take no or little part in their children's education and may, at times, be detrimental to it. Most parents/guardians fall somewhere in between these two groups.

The "typical" school family unit has changed to the point where there is no typical family unit. Freeman-Loftis (2011) tells us that 31 percent of all families are now single-parent families. In 1970, fathers accounted for 1 percent of single parents. By 2000, they accounted for 17 percent (Cunningham and Knoester

2007; Grail 2009). The US minority population, now at 30 percent, is expected to exceed 50 percent by 2050 (Kotkin 2010).

Further compounding the situation is the increasing incidence of homeless students. Murphy and Tobin (2011) cite numerous studies that estimate the growth of homeless children.

> Homeless families with children and unaccompanied youth represent the fastest-growing category of homeless (National Center on Family Homelessness 2009)…. Homeless families grew from almost nothing in the 1950s to 1960s to about 25 percent of the total homeless population by the 1980s, to about 33 percent in the 1990s, and to about 40 percent in the 2000s, with perhaps as much as 50 percent in the nation's urban centers (Burt, et al. 2001; Better Homes Fund 1999; and National Alliance to End Homelessness 2007). The National Alliance of Homelessness (2007) estimates the total number of homeless children in the United States is 1.5 million.

In order to be successful, we must be able to work well with all types of parents/guardians and family structures. As with any area for which we do not receive adequate training, we often revert to familiar models and personal experiences for guidance on the best way to proceed. This tendency leads many of us to the explicit or implicit belief that good parenting is the way in which we parent/guardian our own children or the way in which we were parented. The reality is that effective parenting comes in many forms. It is shaped by factors such as the way the parents/guardians were parented, religious beliefs, cultural norms, number of children in the family, children's birth order, community norms, work schedules, availability of child care,[2] family financial resources, and various other factors. For many teachers, working with parents/guardians is one of the hardest parts of their jobs.

Homeless families with children and unaccompanied youth represent the fastest-growing category of homeless.

Help from Colleagues

Colleagues in the school who have worked successfully with parents/guardians may be among the most effective supports for learning new strategies. "Remember, you can't change toxic parents/guardians, principals, or fellow colleagues, but you can learn to cope with them and neutralize their impact in your life" (Moore). Having a broad repertoire of strategies can dramatically increase the possibility of positive interactions and the most beneficial outcomes. Colleagues have already learned (sometimes the hard way) many of the "dos and don'ts" related to establishing and maintaining effective parent/guardian communication and relationships. In addition to knowing generic strategies for working with parents/guardians, colleagues also know the culture of the community. The family demographics in each school may often influence the level of parent/guardian involvement (or lack thereof) and parent/guardian consumerism.

For example, a research study presented at the 2002 American Sociological Association meeting indicated that **the education level of mothers has a direct correlation to the number of activities in which the child is involved**. The study reports that "a child whose mother has at least a bachelor's degree is predicted to spend about two and a third more hours participating in organized activities (per week) than a child whose mother did not earn a degree" (Weininger 2002).

A colleague who has worked with the school's parent/guardian population successfully knows what strategies work best. He or she also knows the history of the hot-button issues in the community and may help other teachers to navigate those issues.

Schools with High Parent/Guardian Involvement

Schools with high parent/guardian education levels typically have a higher level of parent/guardian consumerism than other schools. However, it is important to note that even in low-socioeconomic status (SES) schools, some parents/guardians will operate as helicopter parents whatever their family socioeconomic level may be. This creates a different (but no less challenging) task for teachers. One experienced fifth-grade teacher in his first year in a district described the day before the first day of school in the following way:

---

2   A 2002 article in *Education Week* described a day-care center in Milwaukee that had extended its hours from 7:00 am to 6:00 pm to new hours from 5:30 am to 1:30 am. The hours were extended in recognition of the fact that many parents/guardians worked in service-sector jobs that required them to work early morning and/or night shifts.

Since I was new to the school and the district, the parents were invited to meet me at a coffee the day before the students returned from summer vacation. This was a school in which the parents had a reputation for being very involved and having very high expectations for teachers. The principal was concerned parents would be coming in the last two weeks in August to check me out and interrupt my work in planning and preparing the classroom. He scheduled the coffee as a way to bring them all in at the same time and limit the disruption to my planning. The plan worked. Few parents came during the last two weeks in August, and 100 percent of the families attended the coffee.

I had taught for five years and so had practice giving presentations to parents. However, my experience had been in a district in which parent/guardian involvement was far less than in this school. I planned a brief explanation about my background and the curriculum, followed by some time for questions. I had just finished my explanation about language arts and was beginning to talk about math when a parent/guardian raised his hand and asked, "Will you be spending much time teaching multiplication and division algorithms? Our children don't know these as well as they should." I answered that I intended to begin the year assessing students' mastery of various algorithms and teaching them to the extent the assessments indicated the teaching was needed. A second parent raised her hand and said, "I disagree with Mr. [the other parent]. I think you need to focus on math processes and problem-solving. I don't want you to spend a lot of time teaching algorithms at the start of the year." Before I could respond, a heated debate ensued between those parents who wanted more emphasis on the teaching of the algorithms and computation and those parents/guardians who wanted me to de-emphasize the algorithms so there could be greater emphasis on math processes and problem-solving. For the next 30 minutes, parents debated among themselves. The principal stopped in at this time and was able to quell the debate. Shortly thereafter, the ending time of the coffee was upon us, and the principal thanked the parents for coming and ended the coffee.

I learned afterwards that the district was entering its third year of a new mathematics curriculum. There had been considerable controversy among parents and the staff about the new curriculum.

Some believed it was a very exciting move toward teaching children to be math thinkers. Others believed it lacked rigor and did not adequately teach the basics.

One may see from this example the advantage this teacher would have had if he had been briefed on the mathematics curriculum.

Another teacher from a low-socioeconomic status school described the grandmother in a homeless family who had decided to "take charge" of the education of her grandchildren when she felt the school did not adequately support the children's needs, given their situation.

As soon as the period ended, she stormed into my classroom. She was angry that her grandchild was failing my class. She demanded to know what I was doing to help the student succeed. She informed me that the children's parents didn't care enough about education, and she would make sure her grandchildren got a good education and went to college. I closed the door so students wouldn't walk in, and calmed her enough to get her to agree to a conference after school the next day. It was clear to me that her angry outburst toward me was fueled by her fear for the future of her grandchild, not just about me.

Uninvolved Parents/Guardians

The same situation applies to the teacher working with *uninvolved* parents/guardians. By uninvolved, we mean parents/guardians who, for whatever reason, do not actively interact with the school about their children's education. It could be because they won't take the time, they don't know how to be productively involved, they don't have the time, they are afraid of the school, or various other reasons. Parent/guardian engagement strategies must again be targeted to the school's specific demographic. For example, in many high-SES schools, parents/guardians are able to provide children with intellectually stimulating summer experiences. Education vacations, summer reading, and intellectually stimulating camp experiences all maintain or enhance what was learned during the school year.

Families living in poverty[3] often do not have the ability to provide similar experiences or may not even understand the importance of such experiences. This creates what has become known as the **summer slide**

---

3 The poverty rate in 2014 for children under age 18 was 21.1 percent.

in student learning. In her 2011–2012 article, Lorna Smith identifies the significant gap that occurs between children who have academically stimulating summers and those who do not.

Johns Hopkins University researchers Karl Alexander, Doris Entwisle, and Linda Olson (2007) conducted a longitudinal study tracking Baltimore students from first grade through age 22. Although low-income children in the study made as much progress in reading during the academic year as middle-income children did, the poorer children's reading skills slipped away during the summer months. The researchers concluded that two-thirds of the ninth-grade reading gap can be explained by unequal access to summer learning opportunities during elementary school.

Budget restrictions have put the primary burden for summer learning on parents/guardians. Programs that engage these parents/guardians in the process of educating their children are often the only tool we have for limiting the summer slide.

For example, Joanna Cattanach (2013, p. 20) describes several schools in Texas that have developed parent/guardian-involvement programs specifically designed to address the specific characteristics of Mexican-American Latino families in those schools. The increase in parent/guardian involvement has led to significant student achievement gains. For example, 90 percent of the students whose parents completed the parent/guardian education programs between 2002 and 2009 graduated from high school, and 78 percent of the students completed at least one year of post-secondary education.

During the last 20 years, the authors of this book have had frequent opportunities to work with teachers in all settings, from affluent suburbs to urban schools with one dominant racial or ethnic group—such as African American students, Southeast Asian students, or Latino students—to rural schools in economically advantaged or depressed communities where the families of poverty were primarily white. In most cases, the teachers had had very little training for working with families. They were ill-prepared for working with either the uninvolved parent/guardian or the overly aggressive parent/guardian.

The researchers concluded that two-thirds of the ninth-grade reading gap can be explained by unequal access to summer learning opportunities during elementary school.

Strategies for Working Effectively with Parents/Guardians[4]

The next part of this chapter looks at strategies teachers have used to work with aggressive/overly assertive parents/guardians and uninvolved parents/guardians. The following ideas for working effectively with parents/guardians are based on research about parent/guardian-to-teacher communication and relationships, and on the authors' years of experience both as teachers and in training teachers to work effectively with parents/guardians and helping parents/guardians to work effectively with teachers.

Strategies for Increasing Success in a Difficult Parent/Guardian Conference

The Parent/Guardian Conference

Conferencing with parents/guardians is an area in which few teachers have received training. The following list of ideas for conferencing combines research on effective communication skills with suggestions from actual teachers and parents/guardians interviewed on the topic of parent/guardian-teacher conferences. This section is written to include ideas about all types of parents/guardians. Not all the ideas will be implemented in every conference. Later in the chapter, we explain how you take a conference through its various phases. At that time, you will better see how and when you can apply the strategies below within actual conferences.

1. Being proactive. We should obtain all the information we can about the parent/guardian and child in preparation for the first conference about the student. Conferencing with the child ahead of time may often give us the information we need to be well prepared for the parent/guardian meeting. Many teachers make contact with parents/guardians early in the year, asking them for information about their children. Examples of this strategy include asking parents/guardians to

---

4 Reminder: We continue to talk about "parents" in the chapter because some studies and quotes use only the term parent. But in every case, we intend the term parent to also mean legal guardians of all types. We use just *parent* to maintain accuracy from our sources.

write a letter telling the teacher about their children, sending home a questionnaire, calling them during the first week of school, and scheduling a brief "tell me about your child" conference during the first month of school. It is important to remember that some of these information-gathering strategies will not work well in some classrooms where there are high incidences of English language learners or poverty. Many parents/guardians living in poverty are either too busy working two jobs or are reluctant to write a letter because of their poor writing skills. For those parents/guardians, a checklist or face-to-face meeting may be best. You can also provide them with options so they can pick the way they are most comfortable communicating. For ELL parents/guardians, conference calling with an interpreter may be more effective.

2. Location. We should choose the location and setup that provides the best atmosphere for the conference. Should the conference be in our classroom? If so, do we want the doors open or closed? Is there another location that is better, such as the guidance office or a conference room? Do we want to sit at a table or at your desk, or should we set the chairs so there is no object between the parents/guardians and us? Be sure the location is tidy and well organized and that classroom rules and routines are posted (if you are meeting in the classroom) in view.

3. Time. Most districts have a set period of time for each parent/guardian conference; however, for those conferences we anticipate will be difficult, we should be sure to schedule enough time. In these cases, allowing an extra 10 or 15 minutes of conference time may save us a great deal of time and angst over the course of the year. It is also helpful to schedule "buffer time" in these instances. Be sure to begin and end conferences on time. It is helpful to post a schedule on the outside of your door or in the hallway so that parents/guardians can refer to it while waiting. Try not to speak too fast or appear overly frenzied due to time constraints. Oftentimes, less is more in terms of quality and focused content during the conference time frame.

4. Getting the parent/guardian talking about the child. We should use active listening and acknowledging responses (applying the stages of listening presented later in this chapter) to give the parent/guardian the message that we are hearing what he or she has to say. We should look for "hooks" in the parent/guardian's words that you might use later to

start a discussion about areas that need improvement. **Hooks** are words or statements that enable you to attribute the area of discussion to the parent/guardian's agenda, even if it was on your own. For example, the parent/guardian may talk about the child's strong verbal skills. This may give us the hook we need to open the conversation that you wanted to have with the parent/guardian about the student's talking out without raising his or her hand.

5. Being positive. "No matter how difficult the student is in our class, and no matter how serious the problems are, we should always find positive things to say. Parents/guardians want to hear something good, even though their children may be struggling. It gives them the strength to deal with the areas of difficulty" (Ribas 1991). Also, please keep in mind that no one knows a child like a parent/guardian, so there is always something to learn about a child from his or her parent/guardian.

6. Giving concrete examples from your observations of the child to support any statements of judgment. Samples of the student's work or specific descriptions of interactions are much more helpful to a parent/guardian's understanding than generalized comments. One second-grade teacher shared a time when he was having difficulty getting a student's parents/guardians to believe their daughter was having a hard time with decoding words. The teacher had a practice of periodically audiotaping all the students reading orally as a way for them to hear their own growth as readers. The students loved listening to themselves read. At one conference with these parents/guardians, the teacher played the tape of their child reading. The parents/guardians immediately recognized the decoding problems that the teacher described. No further persuasion was needed to get the parents/guardians to accept reading support for their daughter.

7. Thinking carefully about how to phrase negative information. The difficult balance here is in trying to phrase an area of student need in a way that is not only clear and honest, but also limits the "bite." See the stages of listening later in this chapter for help in this area. As stated previously, you may find examples or a good opening statement in the parent/guardian's own words if we give them an opportunity to speak early in the conference. Make sure to remain nonjudgmental and not to use educational jargon in your delivery, such as "emerging" or "at risk."

8. Knowing the child as a person. Indicate to the parent/guardian that you know—or are getting to know—his or her child as a person, not just as a student. Parents/guardians always worry about this and ask themselves, "Does this teacher really know my child? Does this teacher like my child?" Try to illustrate to the parents/guardians that you know and appreciate the child's strengths, as it is ultimately these strengths and your navigation of these strengths that will improve areas of weakness. An additional recommendation is to showcase your classroom as a respectful and safe community that meets the intellectual, social, and emotional needs of every student. One-on-one conferences with students, student questionnaires, learning-style inventories, surveys, student-designed rubrics, learning logs, flexible groups, contracts, and a zero-tolerance policy for bullying and harassment are all ways for teachers to get to know students. If you respect students, they in turn will respect you. Respect is a reciprocal and learnable characteristic.

Indicate to the parent/guardian that you know—or are getting to know—his or her child as a person, not just as a student.

9. Checking your emotions throughout the conference. We should resist the **fight/flight/freeze response** when involved in a confrontation with an aggressive or overly assertive parent/guardian. Brain researchers tell us that when humans and other animals feel threatened, the blood rushes from other parts of the brain to the brain stem. This is an evolutionary response designed to help us fight or flee from danger. The freeze response is the inability to react, or, as it is commonly called, "the deer in the highlights" reaction. Unfortunately, when blood is leaving the parts of our frontal lobes that foster problem-solving and higher-order thinking, these are the skills we need most at this time. Check your body language as well so that professionalism is modeled at all times.

10. Delaying your response until you have had sufficient information and time to think. The line, "I'll have to get back to you later on that question," gives us some time to think and gather more information before giving the best response. Make sure you write it down thoughtfully so you can refer to it after the conference. (Be forewarned that whatever you record, parents/guardians can ask to see.) Also, try to develop a comfort level with wait time. It is far better to say nothing than to say something that you will regret later on. In many heightened instances, what you don't say is more important than what you do say.

11. Attending to the feelings and emotions behind the words and behavior. (See the case study activities later in this chapter.) Disagreements sometimes have more to do with what a person is feeling than with what he or she is saying. A parent/guardian who is feeling overwhelmed, embarrassed, or frustrated may verbally attack in the conference, when what he or she really needs is help with the child. Try to keep the child at the center of the conversation and to redirect the emotions back to the needs of the child so that you become less of a focus. For example, in order to deflect the criticism, ask about the child's strengths, relay a recent academic accomplishment, or ask what would be most helpful in order to change the course of the conversation in the direction of the child, not the teacher. Mastering this level of finesse will take practice and will develop over time.

12. If deadlocked, consider using an objective third party. The third party might be an administrator, a resource room teacher, an interpreter, or another person you and the parent/guardian trust. Later in this chapter is a protocol that can be used for three-way conferences that include a third party.

13. If deadlocked, see if there is some small, workable piece you might give the parent/guardian so that he or she feels successful in advocating for the child. This is something that you might want to think about and plan for before the conference, so you choose an appropriate piece that you can follow through with.

14. Checking the names of the parents/guardians. For a variety of reasons, children often have last names that are different from those of their parents or guardians.

15. Identifying potential issues ahead of time. One high school teacher conducts the following activity at the end of each marking term, prior to parent/guardian-teacher conferences:

Hand out an index card to each student in the class. Ask the students to write their names on the cards and the grades they believe they earned for the term. Then, collect the cards and take five minutes to read each name and give each student a "hint" as to how close he or she is to the teacher's assigned grade, using words and phrases such as,

"Right on the money, Joe!" or, "One letter grade higher." If you come upon a student whose "guess-timated earned grade" is far superior to the one in your grade book, you know that a longer conference will be needed with the student to assess and problem solve the discrepancy. Make a note to review that file, just in case the student has led the parents/guardians to believe that he or she is doing better than he or she actually is.

An extra step to this activity is to have the students write a brief assessment of their work for the term, noting the factors that contributed to the grade. Students are generally very honest on such assessments, often stating that factors like lack of homework or test preparation led to poor grades. These assessments are good to have on file during parent/guardian-teacher conferences, and they can serve as firsthand "evidence" for parents/guardians who question a grade. It is advised to not change a grade during a parent/guardian conference. Changing a grade is an important decision that you need to take time to consider carefully.

We should be able to explain how we arrived at a grade.

It is important to make sure that the conference is not the first time a parent/guardian is receiving negative news that a grade has significantly dropped or that there are several missing homework assignments. This is also the case for a decline in a student's behavior or attitude. Teachers should have a communication system in place, which may include the following: phone calls home at early onset of problem; parent/guardian signatures on tests; and quizzes, self-assessments, and grades posted on websites.

16. Acting the part. To add a professional quality to a meeting, we should act the part by dressing professionally, smiling confidently, and shaking the parent/guardian's hand. We should introduce ourselves using the title of Ms., Mr., etc., and address the parent/guardian with the same courtesy. Acting the part sets professional boundaries and creates an atmosphere of respect.

17. Sending a copy of your grading policy, homework policy, and syllabus home at the beginning of the year. We should have parents/guardians sign off to make sure they have received and read important grading and homework information from school. There should be no surprises when it comes to grading or homework expectations! Chapter 3 provides examples of homework policies and pro-

cedures. Parents/guardians should be notified at the early onset of declining grades and missing assignments so that there is enough recovery time for the student to improve.

18. Knowing your grading policy and being prepared to explain it in clear, simple terms. We should be able to explain how we arrived at a grade. Keep in mind that not every parent/guardian is a math major. The simpler our policy is, the better! We should practice grading justification by explaining to a colleague how we arrived at a grade and seeing if he or she can follow our reasoning. Remember that consistency in grading and timely return of work are key so that students can improve their levels of mastery. Parent/guardian signatures on tests, quizzes, and project grades ensure that parents/guardians are informed about their child's performance as well as familiar with your grading policy.

19. Asking what parents/guardians would like to see in terms of change. Asking if there is anything we can do to make things easier lets the parents/guardians know that we are willing to help and are open to their ideas. It may be that parents/guardians are only seeking small accommodations, such as a seat change, a weekly progress report, etc. These types of accommodations are easy to implement and have the potential to make a big difference.

20. Not letting the conference be the first time parents/guardians hear that their child is not doing well. We can't expect parents/guardians to do something about a child's grades or behavior if we have not contacted them. In addition, we should document our efforts by keeping an index card or electronic document with notes for each student and by making notes about dates/times of phone calls and correspondence and general notes about any conversations. Having this information ready can help if we get flustered when a parent/guardian wants "evidence/justification" of grades. Remember to contact parents/guardians at early onset of declining grades and/or behavior so that there is sufficient recovery time for the student to improve.

21. Knowing our school's resources. Academic trouble can often be coupled with social difficulties. Sometimes a conference may be difficult because parents/guardians feel overwhelmed by their child's behavior. Oftentimes, they are seeing the same behavior in the home. Our job as the teacher is not to give off-the-cuff advice but, rather, to be a source of information for parents/guardians. We should know what the school has to offer in terms of social services, such as a school nurse, guidance counselor, social worker, or adjustment counselor. We should have their phone numbers and contact information ready to distribute if asked. It is advised to know school protocols in terms of accessing these resources.

22. Asking questions that show curiosity, but are not accusatory. Instead of asking parents/guardians if their child is having difficulty *in all* of his classes, keep questions open-ended: "How is John doing overall?"

23. Keeping the big picture in mind. We and the parents/guardians have the same goal in mind: to see the child succeed and reach his or her potential. Reminding ourselves of this goal and keeping the child in the center will help steer us away from or defuse a situation that could result in a "battle of the wills" between parent/guardian and teacher.

24. Keeping students' work. Many students never bring papers home, particularly if there is a less-than-desirable grade written on the top. We should keep a folder for each student that contains all written work from the term. These folders should go home frequently for parents/guardians to review and sign, indicating they have reviewed the work. The folder and work are then returned to the teacher until the end of the term. When a parent/guardian asks about his or her child's performance, we will be able to pull a variety of samples from the folder and show concrete examples of the student's work. Moreover, we can use this as an opportunity to discuss the assignments for our class and how they tie in to state or school learning goals and standards. Keeping a folder also protects us in another way. If there is ever a question about a child completing an assignment, all we need to do is check the folder. Some teachers like to require students who do not complete assignments to turn in papers that state the date, the title of the assignment, and the fact that they did not complete it.

25. Sharing resources. Is there an article that might be interesting to a parent/guardian? Or is there something that relates to the parent/guardian's

> *One strategy teachers have used to disengage with a parent/guardian who doesn't know when to stop is to schedule this parent/guardian at a time when there are conferences before and after the appointment. This ensures a finite amount of time for the conference.*

career, hobby, or culture that you can learn from or share with the class? This can open the door to discussion about student achievement and ways to help students succeed. It can also increase parent/guardian involvement and draw on parent/guardian resources.

26. Communicating with others when, at early onset, there is a problem with a student. We should make sure that the administration knows about the situation so that they are not blindsided if the parent/guardian makes a beeline for the office. Many explosive situations can be defused if we give a heads up to the administration. Again, anticipate and be proactive!

27. Not being offended or taking remarks personally. We should remember that each child is somebody's "baby," even if that child is in the eleventh grade. It is natural for parents/guardians to want to go to bat for their children. We should acknowledge this and put a positive spin on it: "It is nice to see parents/guardians who take such an interest in their child's education." It is advantageous to be open to learning from the parent/guardian and to remember that no one knows a child like a parent/guardian.

28. Disengaging from the endless conference. Some parents/guardians have so much they want to say that it is difficult to end the conference once we have completed our agenda. The first thing to ask ourselves is whether we are better off taking more time than expected now because it will pay dividends down the road. If this is a difficult child or parent/guardian and the time continues to be productive, we may want to continue the meeting. At other times, the conference may be past its productive point and we need an exit strategy from the parent/guardian conference that does not offend the parent/guardian. One strategy teachers have used to disengage with a parent/guardian who doesn't know when to stop is to schedule this parent/guardian at a time when there are conferences before and after the appointment. This ensures a finite amount of time for the conference. Another strategy is to have someone call us or come to get us at a specific time. In each of these cases, it is important to let parents/guardians know in advance how much time is available for the conference, so they are not surprised when the time has passed. Statements such as the following signal to parents/guardians that we are near the end of the conference time and may help to end the conference:

> "We are near the end of our time, and you are making an interesting point. Let's both think some more about what has been said. Please send me a note with your additional ideas."

> "We've covered a great deal so far. Let's focus on doing what we have said thus far before moving on to other ideas."

Nonverbal behaviors by themselves or combined with closing statements may be successful. For example, moving forward in our chair to a position that indicates we are preparing to stand, while also maintaining eye contact, sends the message that we are interested but are out of time. Or, at an appropriate break in the conversation, we might thank the parent/guardian for his or her time while extending our hand to shake hands. Placing our watch on the desk at the start of the conference may be a signal to the parent/guardian that there is a finite amount of time for the conference. Doing this also makes it easier for us to monitor the time without breaking our eye contact with the parent/guardian. We should take advantage of the insights of our colleagues, who may have other strategies and suggestions to share.

Three-Way Conferences

An option that may be useful in some situations is the three-way conference. Three-way conferences are conferences in which the teacher, a third party like a colleague or supervisor/administrator, and the parent/guardian meet together to discuss the facts of a specific situation. The primary goal of the vast majority of three-way conferences is to resolve the issue at hand. Consider parents/guardians who ask to conference with a teacher about their child's temporary loss of mobility and its impact on the child's participation in an upcoming field trip. With the agreement of the parents/guardians, the teacher can ask another school professional to join the conference to help strategize workable solutions. In this example, the colleague or administrator serves as an independent resource in the meeting. Another example of the way a colleague or supervisor may participate in a three-way conference is when the colleague's or supervisor's previous or current experience with the child and/or family can be used to help craft a solution for an issue in which the teacher and parent/guardian are in disagreement. In addition to these examples, a colleague or supervisor might also help the teacher to prepare

and rehearse for three-way conferences in which the parent/guardian and the teacher's supervisor will be involved.

Keeping in mind that the role of three-way conferences is primarily to resolve the issue at hand, we offer the following protocol for conducting three-way conferences. This protocol can be used when a colleague or supervisor (objective third party) is part of the three-way conference, as well as in conferences in which the colleague or supervisor assists the teacher to prepare for a three-way conference. Parts of this protocol were adapted from an article by a Kentucky high school principal (Elmore 2008).

Preparing for the conference—It is important, prior to the conference, for the third party to gather all the information possible about the situation. He or she can then begin to think about the situation and be ready with questions or comments that may help resolve the issue. In some circumstances, this will enable the third party to bring additional information that may be helpful in resolving the conflict.

Introduction—The teacher or the third party does a greeting and makes introductions if there are participants who haven't met previously. This little bit of small talk may help to lower the tension level. The small talk enables the parties to interact about a topic that is not emotionally charged and view one another in a different, positive light. This is also the stage during which the third party can explain the steps that the conference will follow (e.g., who will speak first, etc.). The third party also suggests some ground rules if necessary and may state the objective of the conference. It is often valuable for the teacher or the third party to frame the issue to keep the discussion focused on solving the problem at hand.

Presentation—The person whose issue is at stake (or his or her advocate) is asked to present the issue as clearly, factually, and calmly as possible (e.g., a parent/guardian expresses concern about the way a particular situation impacts a child, such as how a child will navigate a field trip with a temporary loss of mobility). During the presentation, the third party ensures that the speaker gets to make his or her case without interruption. At the conclusion of the presentation, the third party may also ask questions to gather additional information or to obtain clarification on a point.

Response—Once the issue is on the table, the other party presents information from his or her point of view. "Managing the response stage well—responding calmly and professionally—is essential to preventing the meeting from degenerating into an argument" (Elmore 2008). It is again important that the third party enables the speaker to present his or her information without being interrupted. At the conclusion of the response, the third party also may ask questions to gather additional information or to obtain clarification of a point.

Understanding—The third party suggests each side restate the other side's information in a way that shows that he or she heard and understood the issue. In some circumstances, the parties are not comfortable with restating what the other has said. In those circumstances, the third party can restate what has been said by both parties. Before moving to the next step, the third party ensures that all the information has been stated and that each party's position has been understood by all.

Generating solutions—The third party opens the discussion to both parties to begin to suggest possible solutions. As ideas are expressed, the third party may repeat or paraphrase to ensure that everyone has the same understanding. He or she may also suggest solutions.

Best options—Once some possible solutions are on the table, participants usually begin to feel less tense and discuss the solutions, working toward consensus on the one that will work best. At the end of this stage, an agreement can be put in writing. In some situations, it may be beneficial to have all parties sign the agreement before the meeting ends. In circumstances in which this is not possible, it is important to have the agreement written up and emailed or sent as a hard copy to all the parties as soon as is practicable. The more time that passes, the greater the likelihood that recollections of what was agreed to may change, or one party may change his or her mind.

Ending—At the close of the meeting, it is important for the third party to bring closure to the meeting by thanking everyone for coming and dispersing them promptly. The end of the meeting is often what Elmore calls *the danger zone*: "As participants relax, chat, or recap, there is a high chance that someone will misinterpret what is being said or begin to revisit the issue. When this occurs, the meeting that should be ending quickly circles back to the presentation and response stages. The hostility returns and the participants are likely to distrust the outcome of the meeting. The longer

the meeting stays in the danger zone, the more difficult it becomes to implement a solution" (Elmore 2008).

Follow up—It is important for the third party to ensure that what was agreed to is, in fact, implemented. Every solution requires a certain level of compromise by both parties. Each party may have agreed to one or more things that they were (or are) somewhat reluctant to do. Reluctance may cause a subconscious delay in following through. Lack of timely follow-through may result in the resurfacing of the tension between the parties and may undermine the agreement.

Three-way conferences also offer excellent opportunities for teachers to acquire or hone their communication skills. The third party is able to observe how a teacher handles challenge and discord. At times, he or she is able to identify behaviors that cause a teacher to have less successful interactions with others.

Study Guides for Tests and Quizzes

In the above section on conferencing, we included a number of strategies that are also important "standalone" strategies. By this we mean effective parent/guardian engagement strategies that aren't just associated with conferencing. These include sending parents/guardians homework policies and procedures, sending your classroom grading policy, providing information on the best way to contact you (the teacher), communicating a positive comment about the student early in the year, and communicating issues as they arise (as soon as possible) and in a sensitive manner. Another important practice is providing study guides for tests and quizzes. We have always been aware of how important study guides are for student success. In addition, they also give parents/guardians important information about the curriculum and enable them help their child at home. Equally important are the written descriptions we give students related to projects and papers they are expected to complete. It is important to let parents/guardians know that you give these written instructions to students so they know to ask their child to see this information.

Involving the Uninvolved Parents and Guardians

As stated previously, we must be careful about our assumptions regarding parents/guardians who are not involved in their children's education or (as stated in

Chapter 7) making assumptions about low-SES families.

There are many reasons why parents/guardians do not take as much of a role in their children's education as we would like or as, the research tells us, would be beneficial to their children. These include long commutes and/or work hours, high work stress, high family stress, abuse in the home, ill health, single-parent/guardian homes, low parent/guardian-education level, embarrassment about their grasp of the language, embarrassment about their lack of "appropriate clothes," not being aware of parent/guardian events because of their limited English, cultural belief that deems it disrespectful to question a teacher, drug and alcohol use, lack of transportation, lack of child care, religious restrictions, and a number of other factors. The parents/guardians may also have received poor parenting and lack parenting training, or the children may not want them at school, so the parents/guardians acquiesce.

It is the extremely rare case that a parent/guardian doesn't love his or her child. It is the case that some parents are unable to do what is best for their child because of life circumstances or emotional issues. If we believe this, then we are left with trying to figure out what factors cause a parent/guardian not to attend conferences, return phone calls, ensure that the student comes to school, or confirm that the student completes homework. We have little power to influence some of these factors. With other factors, we have significant power to change the dynamic. According to Joyce Epstein, a Johns Hopkins University sociologist, the greatest impact on student achievement comes from family participation in well-designed at-home activities, and this is true "regardless of the family, racial, or cultural background or the parents/guardians' formal education." One parent/guardian-involvement strategy with proven effects on student achievement over the long term is interactive homework that allows students to show, share, or demonstrate what they're learning in class. For example, parents/guardians can listen to a first grader read aloud or can talk with an eighth grader about the viscosity of products on the pantry shelf. Consequently, when trying to engage uninvolved parents, a priority is what kind of homework is given rather than how much homework. Teachers need to design and use homework that successfully engages families, parents, and guardians of low-SES students (Johns Hopkins 2003).

The following section presents ideas gathered

Make a home contact early in the year with positive information about the child.

from teachers who have successfully engaged uninvolved parents/guardians in their children's education. The key is, as Yale University child psychiatrist Dr. James Comer puts it, bringing parents/guardians into schools for activities that are "not frivolous but purposeful." Schools should use concerts, recitals, and drama productions as opportunities to distribute information, offer tours of the building, and begin discussions about their children's work (Jones 1999).

Strategies for Engaging Uninvolved Parents and Guardians

1. **Make a home contact early in the year with positive information about the child** (e.g., phone call, note, or email). For many uninvolved parents/guardians (both as adult parents/guardians and when they were students), the school has only contacted home when there was a problem. It is for this reason that many parents/guardians consciously or subconsciously avoid such contact.

2. **Send a written reminder home to parents/guardians and make sure it is translated** so that all students' parents/guardians feel welcome to attend the conference.

3. **Call home and request a specific appointment; have several dates and times in mind so that the parent/guardian has options.** A parent/guardian will be more likely to show up if he or she makes a commitment.

4. **Use the stages of listening** explained later in this chapter to encourage the parents/guardians' active participation in phone calls and meetings.

5. **Remember that some uninvolved parents/guardians who are also living in poverty may not have access to the Internet or email on a computer or phone.** Many schools are relying more and more on email and the Internet to communicate with parents/guardians. We cannot always assume that these tools are available to all parents/guardians.

6. As mentioned earlier, **study guides are an important tool for involving parents/guardians.** In the case of uninvolved parents/guardians who are low SES, it is important to remember that they may not have access to these online in their home.

7. **In meetings that include more teachers than parents/guardians, parents/guardians can feel**

"ganged up on." In these instances, it can be helpful and welcoming to designate a teacher to greet the parent/guardian five minutes before the meeting to share who will be at the meeting as well as what is likely to happen at the meeting.

8. **Have suggestions for positive changes, and be open to the parent/guardian's response and suggestions, when informing a parent/guardian about an issue.** Many of the remediation strategies that work with the majority of families may not be appropriate for a particular family situation for reasons they do not want to readily share (e.g., lack of their own education, problem spouse or sibling in the home, multiple jobs held by a single parent/guardian, or serious illness).

9. **Show the parent/guardian any notes you take during the conference.** You should also be open to the fact that the parent/guardian may not want teachers to take notes during some parts of the conference. Note-taking by the teacher is often reassuring to assertive, educated parents; however, uninvolved parents/guardians may often be worried about how the notes will be used, causing them to speak less freely. Remember, some of our recent immigrant parents/guardians come from countries in which the notes taken by an official (in this case, the teacher) during a meeting are often used to justify punishments of citizens.

10. **Follow through on what you say you will do, in a timely manner.** Many uninvolved parents/guardians feel they are inferior to the professionals in their lives and are accustomed to being considered low priorities by professionals. Your quick follow-up signals that you value them as people and appreciate their participation in the process.

11. **Be aware of cultural differences, particularly those of parents/guardians who are first-generation Americans.** For example, in their article, "Bridging Cultures with a Parent/Guardian–Teacher Conference," Quiroz, Greenfield, and Altchech (1999) describe the lessons they learned in working with the immigrant Latino community in the Los Angeles Public Schools. They quote one Mexican American mother's confusion after a parent/guardian-teacher conference as follows:

> I couldn't understand what the teacher was trying to communicate when she comments on my daughter's performance. I particularly recall two confusing comments that this teacher made: "Your daughter is very sociable" and "Your daughter is outstanding in . . ." My tendency as a Mexican

mother was to feel very happy she was sociable; after all, that was what I was fostering. However, I did not know what to do about her being "outstanding." I had tried to show my daughter not to "show off," but it seemed that it was not working.

One fifth-grade teacher we worked with described his work with a child from a Chinese immigrant family. The child worked diligently on class and homework assignments. The child was always attentive and never talked with other students when the teacher wanted their attention; however, the child never answered questions in class. When the teacher described this to the parents, they seemed confused by the fact that the teacher wanted the child to answer questions and give opinions. Both the parents' school experiences and the previous school experience of their child had never included opportunities for students to answer questions or give their opinions.

One district identified a gap between the perspectives of teachers and parents/guardians regarding parent/guardian-teacher communication and parent/guardian's involvement. The teachers initially were frustrated by what they perceived as the parents/guardians' lack of interest and involvement in their children's education. It was learned through outreach that the parents/guardians perceived their involvement as infringing on the teachers' professional domain. The district addressed this issue by developing two workshops. One workshop was for teachers, and it described the cultural perspective of the parents/guardians. The other workshop was for parents/guardians, and it described the school culture and its expectations related to parents/guardians' involvement in their children's education. After participating in these workshops, both groups better understood the other and were able to bridge the gap between their cultural perspectives (Colombo 2004).

12. **Check to see if you will need a translator at the conference.** Many students come from homes in which the primary language is one other than English. In many recent immigrant families, the parents/guardians speak less English than their children, and this lesser fluency may keep the parents/guardians from attending the conference. If a translator will be present, let the parent/guardian know ahead of time.

13. **Make meeting times and materials user-friendly.** In one district in which we worked, the third-grade teachers were struggling with trying to get the parents/guardians to work with their children at home on math facts. Most of the families were recent immigrants and both parents worked, often at two jobs.

One year, the teachers decided to hold parent/guardian meetings to explain how parent/guardians might help their children by quizzing them just 10 to 15 minutes each afternoon or evening on the math facts. The teachers planned and executed informational meetings for parents/guardians at two different times during the day. They planned a meeting during the day for the parents/guardians who worked nights and another one during the evening for the parents/guardians who worked during the day. The school did significant outreach, and a high percentage of parents/guardians came to the meetings. Unfortunately, after the meetings, the teachers found that the parents/guardians had disposed of many of the handouts on their way out the door. Upon talking with some parents/guardians, the teachers learned that many of the parents/guardians were overwhelmed by the amount of information given in the meeting and the comprehensiveness of the handout packet. They also learned that the only time during the day when the students sat with one or both of their parents/guardians was either at breakfast or dinner time.

Rather than giving up, the teachers used this data to plan better the next year. They again scheduled meetings for parents/guardians at two convenient times. The school again did considerable outreach that brought many parents/guardians to the meetings; however, the teachers changed the program in two ways. First, they scaled back the number of concepts they asked parents/guardians to practice with the students. Second, they put all the concepts they wanted parents/guardians to use on laminated placemats. They included specific facts and games the parents/guardians might play with their children at the dinner table. In the parent/guardian meeting, the teachers role-played a typical meal and how parents/guardians might incorporate math practice into the mealtime. After the parent/guardian meetings, the teachers checked the garbage but did not find one placemat thrown away. More important, the parents/guardians used the placemats with their children, and the students' math skills improved.

14. **Resist the urge to judge.** A judgmental demeanor will only exacerbate the problem and further alienate the parent/guardian.

15. **Know that parent and guardian involvement comes in many forms.** The "uninvolved" parent/guardian who does not show up for conferences might

Door opener is a technique used to indicate that we want to have a two-way conversation about the child and don't just want to tell the parent/guardian what we know about his or her child.

be working an extra job to raise money so that his or her child can enroll in a test-prep class or take violin lessons, or to make "ends meet." It does not mean that the parent/guardian does not care about or value his or her child's education. How can we follow up with these parents/guardians and find alternate ways to increase involvement?

Using the Stages of Listening to Increase Parent/Guardian Involvement

A good way to plan for a meeting with a parent is to think about the stages of the meetings. Planning for the stages below doesn't take much time. In fact it can be done on the commute to or from school.

Stage I: Preparation

Think about the parent/guardian(s) and the child related to each conference. What do you anticipate will be difficult issues in the conference? What materials should you have ready for the conference? Have you allocated sufficient time for the conference? If you anticipate this will be a conference that will be difficult from which to disengage, what plans have you made to help disengage? Will there be language issues? If so, how will you deal with this?

Stage II: Conference Location

Choose the best location/setting for the conversation. The best setting is situationally determined. For example, most parents/guardians will prefer complete privacy when we are addressing areas their child needs to change or when we are informing them of difficulties their child may be experiencing. In these cases, a room with a closed door is probably the best place.

Stage III: Statements That Open the Door to a Productive Discussion

Door opener is a technique used to indicate that we want to have a two-way conversation about the child and don't just want to tell the parent/guardian what we know about his or her child. This impression is best achieved by asking questions that encourage the parent/guardian to talk about those aspects of the child's personality and experiences that will be helpful for us to know. At this point, the questions should be open-ended to get the parent/guardian talking and thinking.

Some door openers include the following questions:

- What does your child tell you about school?
- What does he or she like best? What does he or she like least?
- When does he or she feel successful?
- Are there times in school when he or she does not feel successful?
- Whom does he or she identify as his friends?
- What do you think are your child's academic strengths?
- What types of hobbies or activities does your child enjoy outside of school?

Stage IV: Using Wait Time

Parents/guardians need wait time. It allows them to think about your questions and to formulate answers. Some may need time to translate the questions and answers because English is not their primary language. Others might be worried about not sounding "smart" and, therefore, are careful in formulating their answers.

Stage V: Passive Listening

Passive listening is a technique used to create an environment in which the parent/guardian feels that he or she may talk freely.

- Once the parent/guardian starts talking, the most important thing to do is "bite your lip and listen." Resist the urge to break in with comments or advice too soon. It may be quicker (and more gratifying to us) to give the parent/guardian advice and comments than to wait for him or her to fully answer the question. However, the purpose of the conference is better met if we give the parent/guardian time to fully answer the question.
- We should use body language that indicates openness to hearing what the parent/guardian has to say. *Body language* includes both body position and facial expressions. Listening carefully and using appropriate body language signals to the parent/guardian that what he or she is saying is important to you.

Stage VI: Acknowledgement Responses

Eye contact, nodding, comments such as "I hear you" and "I understand," and paraphrasing the parent/guardian's statements all send the message that you are listening. Remember that acknowledging is not agreeing! There will be ample opportunity to discuss areas of disagreement at the appropriate time later in the conference.

Stage VII: Active Listening

Active listening gives the speaker tangible evidence of the listener's understanding. For example, the listener labels the parent/guardian's feelings about the situation (e.g., anger, excitement, pride, frustration, fear, or confusion). The listener asks clarification questions and follow-up questions to gather additional information.

Ideas that the parent/guardian discovers about how to best help a child are far more likely to be implemented than those we give as advice that is not requested. Harry Truman said it best: "There is no limit to what you can achieve when you don't care who gets the credit." Active listening helps to lead the parent/guardian to his or her own solutions.

Stage VIII: Closing the Gap between the Teacher's and the Parent/Guardian's[5] Perceptions of Performance

Rarely does a year pass that we don't have at least one parent/guardian with whom there is a disagreement about some aspect of the child's education. In those circumstances, we identify differences between our perception and the parent/guardian's perception of the situation and generate options that sound reasonable to both parties. We ask questions that help the parent/guardian discover inconsistencies between his or her perception of the child's situation and a more holistic view. We want the changes parents/guardians make to "stick." The more the parent/guardian buys into the change, the more likely he or she will be to permanently change his or her practices.

- We should be open to the idea that we may not be completely correct in our perceptions. We should listen and consider the parent/guardian's rationale before making a final judgment.
- We should make an internal check of our frustration/defensiveness meter. If our frustration and defensiveness are growing faster than the progress we are making in closing the gap between our perception and that of the parent/guardian, it might be best to end the discussion and schedule a time to get together again in the near future. This will keep us from making a nonproductive statement. It will also give us time to reflect and decide whether there are other ways to word your con-

---

5   Please be reminded that when we use the term *parent*, we are referring to all legal guardians. We have kept *parent* in cases where that is the term used by the source. We intend that all discussion includes guardians as well as parents.

cerns that will better enable the parent/guardian to hear and "own" those concerns.

Stage IX: Concluding the Discussion

- We should generate options for next steps and decide as specifically as possible what each person will do and the deadlines for completing each task.
- We should summarize the conclusions reached in the conference.
- In situations in which we want the parent/guardian to follow up, we should set a date, time, location, and tentative agenda for the follow-up discussion or any follow-up activities.

The previous framework must always be considered within the context of the individual with whom we are meeting. Some parents/guardians prefer that the teacher "cut to the chase" if they believe the teacher is working up to a difficult area to discuss. Most, however, prefer that the teacher work through the stages and do appreciate the give-and-take this type of discussion provides.

Case Studies of Difficult Parent/Guardian Conferences

As mentioned earlier, few teachers ever receive pre-service or in-service training in strategies for working effectively with parents/guardians. The following case studies are from actual teachers' experiences in conferencing with aggressive or overly assertive parents/guardians. The cases are followed by exercises designed to help in analyzing each situation. For two reasons, it is important for teachers to study cases like this prior to being confronted with a difficult parent/guardian conference situation. The first reason is so the teacher may better understand the reasons and emotions that cause parents/guardians to be aggressive or overly assertive in a conference. For example, Wikipedia defines a *helicopter parent* as a person who pays extremely close attention to his or her child or children, particularly in educational institutions, and who often rushes to prevent any harm or failure from befalling their children. A helicopter parent appears to cross racial, ethnic, and socioeconomic lines. Experts say children need to learn how to cope with adversity in order to be effective in life. Anne Henderson, a senior consultant with New York University's Institute for Education and Social Policy, says what parents/guardians do with their children outside of school is the most important factor in teaching children how

to cope with adversity (2007). An extension of the helicopter metaphor, the term *Black Hawks* has been coined for those who cross the line from a mere excess of zeal to unethical behavior, such as writing their children's college admission essays. More and more, parents/guardians see themselves as purchasers of public education with a right to demand from schools individualized services. Once a teacher understands this, it makes such behavior easier to accept and deal with in a professional manner. We must remember that we are the professionals in the situation. Because we are the professionals, we need to hold ourselves to a high standard of behavior, even if the parent/guardian is acting in an irrational manner. Because we are the professionals, we also need to learn and practice strategies to use during a conference with a parent/guardian whose behavior is aggressive.

Secondary School Case Study

The student is from an upper-middle-class family living in a large house in an expensive neighborhood. The father is an executive for a local company, and he travels extensively and is away from home for long periods of time. The mother, who is not working at the present time, has recently started to travel with her husband on some business trips, leaving their two children with a babysitter–housekeeper. The oldest son has a history of being a successful student and is an excellent athlete. He is 15 years old and has an 11-year-old brother. The oldest son has been acting out recently by coming late to class and not working to his potential in math (and other subject areas). His math performance in middle school and freshman year in high school was in the top quarter of his class. He consistently received grades of B+ and A– in math during those years. His first-quarter grade in honors math during sophomore year was a C+, and the second-quarter grade had dipped to a C–.

The parents are asked to come in to meet with the math teacher and the guidance counselor to discuss the change in performance. The information is reviewed with the parents at the conference. The mother listens for the first 10 minutes while the teacher describes the student's performance, but she folds her arms and crosses her legs about five minutes into the explanation. Suddenly, she gets very angry and accuses the teacher of not telling them (the parents/guardians) soon enough about the dip in performance, not understanding her child, not motivating her child, and not liking her child. She says this would not be an issue if the class were more interesting. In a fit of anger, she states that her property taxes equal half the teacher's salary and that she should be getting more from the school and the teacher for her child.

Elementary School Case Study

It is November and the teacher's first conference with this particular parent. The parent is the father of one of the top three math students in her second-grade class. Dad is a successful attorney in his early forties. The teacher had no indication prior to the conference that the parent had concerns. The teacher begins by explaining how the child is doing in each subject area. Dad quietly sits through the language arts explanation. When the teacher begins to explain the math, the father shifts in his chair. He sits back and folds his arms. After about a minute, the father interrupts to say that Jimmy is bored in math. He states that he (the father) knows where Jimmy is in math because he does math problems with Jimmy on the weekend. Dad states further that the class is doing addition and subtraction, and Jimmy has known these operations since the beginning of first grade. Dad reports that he is doing multiplication and division with Jimmy and asks the teacher to do multiplication and division with Jimmy. Dad says he doesn't want Jimmy to do any cooperative learning because Jimmy knows more math than most of the other kids in the class. He doesn't learn anything from the other kids. As Dad talks, his voice gets louder, his face turns red, and he speaks faster. He tells the teacher that this has been a wasted year so far in math, and he won't let it continue to be a wasted year. He goes on to say he has heard from other parents/guardians that second graders in other schools do multiplication and division, and he can't understand why his son can't do it in this class. Dad goes on to say that he is *not* the only second-grade parent/guardian who feels this way and asks the teacher what she plans to do.

Secondary School Case Study

It is the English teacher's very first parent/guardian-teacher conference night. Danielle's mother rushes in five minutes before the night is about to end, heels clicking all the way down the corridor and into the teacher's classroom. Plopping down into a chair and bending over to dig through her purse, she pulls out a crumpled report card and sighs. Smoothing out the report card on the desk in front of her, Danielle's mom sighs again and in a shrill voice tells the teacher that the she has kept "her Danielle" off the honor roll. Before the teacher can get a word in, Danielle's mother informs the teacher that her daughter loved English class in middle school and now hates the class. Danielle's mother demands to know what is going on in this English class to make her daughter hate it so much. The tone in her voice tells the teacher that she is questioning the teacher's ability to teach English.

Secondary School Case Study

Mariel is one of the teacher's favorite students. She is responsible, hardworking, and articulate. One day, while the teacher is in the hallway directing students to class, Mariel stops by to chat. She looks tired and complains to the teacher that she didn't sleep well the previous night. She goes on to say that she doesn't have time to do homework because her parents/guardians expect her to babysit her three younger brothers and sisters. Helping them with homework, making dinner, and getting them ready for bed are just a few of the tasks Mariel has taken on. The teacher listens as sympathetically as she can in the chaotic hallway. She asks Mariel if her parents/guardians will attend the upcoming conference, but Mariel just shrugs, mumbles something about a late shift, and hurries off to her next class.

After reading each case study, consider the following questions:
1. What emotions or other factors are causing the parent/guardian behavior described in the case?
2. What are some emotions the teacher is likely to be experiencing?
3. If you were this teacher, what would you do next?
4. What are other situations that lead to difficult conferences?

Think of a difficult conference you have had.
1. What were the difficult parent/guardian behaviors that were evident during the conference?
2. What emotions or other factors caused these parent/guardian behaviors?
3. What strategies did you use (or could you have used) to better manage the conference?

Parent/Guardian Conference Tips for the Parent or Guardian

Here are some helpful "Tips for Parents/Guardians" as they prepare for the first parent/guardian conference of the year. Perhaps these tips could be inserted in a school newsletter or posted on the school website at the beginning of the school year so that parents/guardians are informed about and comfortable with the process.

1. **The most important thing is to be there on time and plan not to run over the amount of time that has been set aside.** Remember to work together as partners with your child's teachers.

2. **Get to know your child's teacher/teachers before the first conference if possible.** Express your desire to be informed of your child's progress throughout the year, not just when report cards are issued, says Becky Fleischauer, education consultant in Alexandria, VA, who stresses the importance of establishing early parent/guardian-teacher rapport (2005).

3. **Don't be timid.** No one knows your child better than you—the parent/guardian—and teachers benefit greatly from your insights. Sharing what's happening with your child at home and what interests and motivates him or her gives teachers a valuable perspective. "Really fill that teacher in on the good and the not-so-good," urges Anne Henderson, parent/guardian involvement expert and author of *Beyond the Bake Sale*. "Then if your child does stumble, the teacher feels she can contact you and won't be afraid of the kind of reception she will get" (2007).

Conversely, **if you know you have a tendency to be overly assertive, be sure you temper this behavior.** Work to make this a collaborative discussion about your child. Remember, the teacher has to work with your child in the context of a full class of children. Your child's behavior in that context may be different than what you see at home.

4. **Keep in mind that the teacher is apt to be apprehensive, too.** "Even though it seems like the person who should be more intimidated is the parent/guardian, since the teacher is the expert, s/he is likely to be just as nervous as you are. Many teachers are worried that the parents/guardians will be angry or overbearing" (Henderson 2007).

5. **Talk with your child before the conference.** Ask your child how she or he thinks the school year is going. Find out what is going well, what isn't going well, where she or he may need extra help or additional challenge, and whether there are issues you should raise with the teacher. Ask your child if there is anything he or she would like you to talk about at the conference. This not only provides valuable information to share in the conference, but also opens an important line of communication with your child and sends a message that you value education as well as want to help your child succeed in school.

6. **Make a list and prioritize.** The average parent/guardian-teacher conference lasts only 20 minutes, so in order to make every minute count, write a list of questions that you have and note any issues or concerns that you want to cover during the conference. Put the most crucial items at the top of the list so that you have enough time to cover them without feeling rushed.

7. **Keep the focus on what and how your child is learning.** Often, the conversations at conferences will revolve around behavior, but it's important to ask questions about learning. "Is my child performing at grade level? What are my child's strengths? Areas of weakness? What skills need reinforcing? How can we assist at home in remediating or extending our child's learning?" Ask to see samples of your child's work as well.

8. **Share good news about your child's school year or life with your child's teacher.** Specific praise goes a long way and means a great deal to teachers. Send in a positive note or email to the teacher or make a brief "compliment call." One veteran educator has saved every positive note, card, and letter from students' parents/guardians in a file, reporting that these tributes are the gifts that she has treasured throughout her 20 years of teaching.

9. **After the conference, share highlights with your child at home, including any action plan that you have agreed to with the teacher.** Make sure that your child knows that you and the teacher are working together as a team.

10. **Keep working with the teacher as needed.** Stay in regular touch with the teacher to discuss the progress that your child is making. Always avoid negative talk about the teacher in front of your child. Attend classroom and school events whenever possible in order to build strong home-school partnerships (Fleischauer 2005).

Year-Round Learning

In one of the longest-running studies of what is called the *summer slide for economically disadvantaged students* (low-SES students) or the summer *brain drain*, Johns Hopkins University sociologists Karl Alexander and Doris Entwisle have followed 790 randomly selected Baltimore students since they entered first grade in 1982. Alexander and Entwisle compared changes in test scores during the school months to changes that occurred in the summer months. Gains or losses during the school months can be primarily viewed as the school's contribution, while gains or losses that occur during the summer months are more likely the contributions of the family, economic, and neighborhood circumstances. Alexander and Entwisle learned that children in Baltimore's poor neighborhoods were learning at the same rate as middle-class students during the school year but fell much further behind during the summer. Children from more affluent families tended to enroll in summer camps or music or art lessons and were encouraged to attack summer reading lists. Poorer children had less to do in the summer and tended to forget what they had learned during the previous school year (Alexander and Entwisle 2007).

The Hopkins sociologists found that when low-SES students returned to school, they would again learn at the same rate as their more affluent peers. However, the summer slide created wider and wider learning gaps with each year. Due to the summer slide, each fall teachers typically spent up to six weeks reviewing material their students had been taught the previous school year. By the end of fifth grade, the difference in verbal achievement between poor and non-poor students was more than two years; in math, it was a year and a half. Alexander and Entwisle have shown that the cumulative effect of summer learning differences is a primary cause of widening achievement gaps between students of lower and higher socioeconomic levels.

The data shows that kids need to be actively engaged in learning over the summer. Reading is Fundamental (RIF), the nation's oldest and largest children's literacy organization, believes there is no better time than the summer to bridge the gap in learning between the end of one school year and the beginning of the next one. "Motivating children to read throughout the year is essential to building lifelong readers," says Carol H. Rasco, president and CEO of RIF. Research shows that reading just six books during the summer may keep a struggling reader from regressing. When choosing the six books, make sure that they are just right, not too hard and not too easy. Also, make sure that all children have access to books during the summer, which may mean rethinking student access

The Hopkins sociologists found that when low-SES students returned to school, they would again learn at the same rate as their more affluent peers.

to school library and classroom book collections over the summer, as they are often inaccessible (Allington 2008). Kids should also practice math skills every day over the summer. Suggested activities include cooking, measuring, tracking temperature, and playing educational games. According to Ron Fairchild, the executive director of the Center for Summer Learning, the trick is making this fun and motivating while giving children serious opportunities to learn the skills they need.

Top 10 List, or How Can I Help My Child Keep Learning This Summer?

Number 10: Let your child see *you* read!

Number 9: Take your child to the library to get his or her own card. Linger and attend summer library programs.

Number 8: Take home lots of books from the library. Make a special place for your child to keep his or her books.

Number 7: Make sure your child reads books independently for at least 20 minutes every day.

Number 6: Read a zillion picture books (both fiction and non-fiction) to your child. Picture books are not just for "babies" anymore. They usually offer eloquent literature accompanied by exquisite pictures. Non-fiction books offer clear overviews of interesting topics. They are extremely good for developing background information.

Number 5: Read your child's favorite books to him or her over and over and over.

Number 4: Encourage your child to read fairly easy books more than once because this will aid fluency (speed and accuracy).

Number 3: Discuss books at the dinner table or in the car.

Number 2: Listen to books on tape in the car.

Number 1: Help your child develop background information on curriculum topics that will be presented in September. Remember, picture books are good for this purpose. The idea is that new information is more easily organized, remembered, and recalled if the person already has some knowledge about the topic (Cooper and MacIver 2006).

In essence, all teachers are teachers of reading. They need to infuse year-round reading logs into their practice as well as math logs. Many teachers provide reading incentives during the summer months and vacations in order to reduce "summer slide" and to model that learning is ongoing. One teacher sends writing prompts via the computer to her fourth-grade students with prizes as incentives. Another school system provides summer reading logs and math calendars, in which students do a math activity each day during the summer in order to practice math skills. Summer reading and summer math celebrations are then held for the students in the fall. Libraries often run summer reading programs that motivate kids to read, so schools and parents/guardians can find out what's available in their area. Parents/guardians can encourage their children to continue learning over the summer as well and provide a variety of literacy and mathematics experiences. Parents/guardians can also investigate high-quality, low-cost summer learning programs, such as YMCA and Boys and Girls Clubs.

This also means that teachers need to weave this philosophy of year-round learning into their communication with parents/guardians. This can be done in parent/guardian conferences; classrooms and school newsletters; websites; open houses; class breakfasts; and music, art, drama, and athletic events. Teachers can help shift the thinking from "vacations, weekends, and summers mean respite from learning" to "learning needs to occur year-round." This shift also places responsibility for some of the learning after school, on weekends, and during the summer on students and their families. Consequently, effective home-school partnerships will strengthen year-round learning.

Thanksgiving Letter Sent Home with Students

Dear Student,

Here are some activities you may want to do over the break:
 See how many words you can make out of the letters in *Thanksgiving*.
 Try some online games!

http.www.hellam.net/maths/factmult.html
http://www.interactivestuff.org/sums4fun/noose.html
http://www.homeschoolmath.net
http://www.starfall.com/
http://www.mathfactcafe.com/games/
http://www.scholastic.com/kids/index.asp
http://www.aimsedu.org/aimskids/ipuzzles/farmer/index.html

Enjoy your holiday, family, friends, and long weekend! I look forward to seeing you on Tuesday.

Oh, and thanks for making 4T such a special place.

Love,
Ms. Teahan
Teahan 2006

Tips for Successful Curriculum Nights for Parents/Guardians

Parents' Night

Mary Burchenal

One by one the tidy classrooms across the courtyard
are going black. Parents filter out toward their cars
and headlights flicker across the windows.
But there she is at my desk, smiling out of a shapeless coat.

It isn't just the heavy Russian accent that makes it hard.
I lean my head toward what she has to say
about her daughter Sonya, with, I see now, the same shy smile—
her daughter Sonya who, too, lingers at my desk after class.

She burns a trail of smoky words: Sonya loves reading very much,
she has problem with hearing—she wants to write like Tolstoi—
she liked so much last year's English teacher—
I thank him for the rest of my life.

When she breaks off, eyes eager at my face,
I pull my head back, clearing for a smooth landing,
but the sentences I pave out about the course, about Sonya's progress
somehow crumble and fall away

Her forehead wrinkles; she veers sideways and lifts off again,
circling back over the territory, words thick and halting.
I watch but cannot follow
though I try until the halls are dark.

On the drive home the mother's words are large winged moths
that brush soft bodies against my hair
and flutter thinly at the windshield.
Suddenly I see the nonsense of my replies

"Please," she'd been saying, racing against the custodian
rattling his keys as he came, snapping off lights.
"Please," she had said, those keys jangling toward my door—
"Can you love my child?"

Poem author's note: I have a long way to go as far as listening is concerned. In the classroom (as elsewhere), I can become much too fascinated with what I'm saying or about to say. When a student complains, "But Mrs. Bellow's class isn't having an exam. It's unfair," it's easy to get annoyed or to come up with a very articulate and rational response about the importance of exams, instead of putting energy into understanding that the student might be saying, "I'm panicked about the exam. Help!" I wrote this poem partly, I suppose, as an apology to students and parents I haven't listened to hard enough.

Tips for Successful Curriculum-Night Presentations for Parents/Guardians

It has many names: *Curriculum Night, Back-to-School Night, Meet-the-Teacher Coffee,* and others. It is a meeting, morning or evening, early in the school year when parents/guardians[6] are invited to come as a group to hear the teacher explain the classroom plans for the year. In many schools, the new generation of parents/guardians is older, busier, better educated, and more assertive consumers of their children's education. Expectations for the quality and quantity of the information they receive at these meetings have increased dramatically. The curriculum night creates the parents/guardians' first impression of their children's teacher for that year. If the end result is a parent/guardian who feels confident that the child will experience academic and emotional success, a strong foundation is laid for a positive parent/guardian-teacher relationship throughout the year. If a parent/guardian leaves the meeting doubting the child will have a successful year, this self-fulfilling prophecy might make for a long and contentious year between teacher and parent/guardian. For all teachers, it is the most important meeting of the year. As the saying goes, "You don't get a second chance to make a first impression."

Few of us chose teaching as a career because we enjoy making presentations to adults that might affect our entire work year. There are teachers who look forward to curriculum nights as opportunities to meet parents/guardians and share with them the yearly plans; however, others dread the meeting and view the ultimate objective as *survival.* Most reactions fall somewhere in between. All teachers want the meeting to be successful and want to make a positive first impression on parents/guardians. Unfortunately, preservice and in-service programs rarely provide us with help for improving the quality of our presentations. Trial and error is the primary means of acquiring these skills, and we are left on our own to find the means to success.

The authors have spoken with hundreds of teachers and principals about the techniques or "tricks"

> *Few of us chose teaching as a career because we enjoy making presentations to adults that might affect our entire work year.*

that teachers have learned for giving successful group presentations to parents/guardians. The following are strategies and ideas collected in individual interviews and group meetings with kindergarten to high school teachers and administrators.

The following list should be viewed as a menu, not a checklist. It is designed to provide us with an opportunity to pick and choose strategies and implement them at a comfortable rate. The most important prerequisite to improving success in parent/guardian presentations is to increase your confidence level. The following strategies provide the tools to be successful, if we implement them at a rate that allows each of us to gain a reasonable comfort level with each strategy. Otherwise, the stress of worrying about properly implementing the strategies will reduce your ability to project an image of calm and confidence at the meeting.

1. **Have a handout or outline on the desk for parents/guardians when they arrive.** The handout serves three important functions. First, much of what parents/guardians are told at curriculum night meetings will be forgotten. Written material, which parents/guardians may refer to periodically after they go home, will save us from answering the same questions in the future. Second, the handout will also help us stay organized and on schedule throughout the presentation. Third, and most important for those of us who have a fear of speaking to groups of adults, it will focus the parents/guardians' eyes on the handout and reduce the number of pairs of eyes staring at you throughout the presentation.

2. **Provide a syllabus that outlines the material you will teach.** An outline that provides weekly topics and titles of literary works, for example, will inform parents/guardians of your classroom activities and enable them to check on their children to see if they are keeping up with their studies.

3. **Ask colleagues for samples.** Looking at how other teachers organize their presentations will give valuable tips.

4. **Tell parents/guardians how (e.g., note, email, phone, or drop-in) and when (e.g., before school, at lunch time, or at home) you prefer that they contact you when they have a question.** Teachers often have very different preferences. Parents/guardians are usually unaware of how "their" teacher wishes to be contacted. If we tell parents/guardians what we

---

6   Please be reminded that when we use the term "parent/guardian" that we are also referring to all legal guardians.

prefer, most will cooperate. You might include this information in your handout. We once interviewed two teachers who taught the same grade side by side. One liked to have brief conferences with parents/guardians who showed up at the door in the morning, so she might quickly dispense with the business and avoid large numbers of afternoon and evening phone calls. The other teacher found parents/guardians who dropped in very disconcerting and preferred a note or email from parents/guardians asking for a call in the afternoon or evening. These were two equally experienced and successful teachers with very different preferences. If your preferred method is email, you should be sure to have an alternative for those parents/guardians who do not have access to email. Increasingly, more and more parents/guardians have access to email; however, the ones who don't may be the parents/guardians with whom we need the most contact (e.g., recent immigrant who doesn't speak English, homeless, etc.). It is also helpful to send out reminders of your preferred contact information during the school year.

5. **Tell parents/guardians again about your homework policy and routines if you are not getting the type of response you need.** Chapter 3 in this book includes sample letters to send to parents/guardians explaining the policies. In many instances, the homework routines are successfully established well before this meeting. In those circumstances, we need not review the policy again.

6. **Check the parent/guardian handbook or any other information parents/guardians may have received from the school or district about curriculum or procedures.** It usually gives a good synopsis of the program and may save us time in preparing remarks. More importantly, though, it will help us to use consistent terminology and avoid difficult questions from parents/guardians who perceive what we say as different from what was written. We may be sure that at least some of the parents/guardians will have read the written description carefully. It is helpful to have additional copies of parent/guardian handbooks available for parents/guardians.

7. **Have a sign-up sheet available, if your school has fall conferences, to help deter parents/guardians from attempting to have "short" conferences about their children after your presentation.** A scheduled conference date does much to quell a parent/guardian's burning need to know, "How is my child doing?" Our favorite example of this is a husband and wife; the husband was an elementary principal and the wife an elementary teacher. When they attended their first parents/guardians' night in the role of parents/guardians, they had a combined total of 25 years of teaching and administration experience that included conducting innumerable parents/guardians' nights. At the end of the teacher's presentation, the school's principal announced the evening was over and the husband went to warm up the car. His wife said she would be out in a minute. After 10 minutes, though, the wife did not appear. The husband went to look for her and found her in the room with five other parents/guardians lined up trying to have a "brief" conference about their children with the teacher. The wife was third in line. She smiled with embarrassment when she saw her husband. *She was embarrassed, yes, but she never left her place in line!*

8. **Be organized, clear, concise, and cordial.** Parents/guardians will assume that the way you conduct the presentation is how you teach their children's classes. The curriculum night is an opportunity to build the parents/guardians' confidence in your capacity as a skilled, organized, and knowledgeable professional. Be sure to speak slowly, and never share any information about individual students or families in your presentation. Also, try to have some eye contact with your audience. Some teachers like to greet parents/guardians at the door and/or shake hands with them as they leave.

9. **Fight the urge to talk about what you *can't* do when parents/guardians make unrealistic suggestions.** Parents/guardians often lack the perspective of dealing with a group of more than 30 children at once. This inexperience may cause them to make suggestions about classroom operation that we know are not feasible. As teachers, we should focus our answers on what we can do. Watch the next presidential press conference, and you will see questions focused on what the administration is *not* doing refocused with answers about what related action is taking place.

10. **Leave some time at the end of your presentation for questions (but not too much time).** Many parents/guardians in our schools today are accustomed to questioning the professionals in their lives. They question (and disagree with) their pediatrician, clergy person, boss, and each other. Scheduling time at the end of the meeting (and informing parents/guardians early on about the schedule) avoids questions that will interrupt the flow of your presentation. If we anticipate our presentation will lead to many questions,

then we might have a note card for each parent/guardian. We might ask parents/guardians to write their questions on the note cards as they arise during your presentation. We might then select several to answer during the time we have for questions. Those that are not answered may be addressed through a newsletter if several parents/guardians have the same question, or by note, phone call, or email if the question is personal to the parent/guardian. This follow-up should be timely, as it will assist in building strong parent/guardian-teacher relationships.

11. **Give each parent/guardian a note card if the presentation time is insufficient to allow for answering questions.** We might have the parents/guardians write their questions on the cards, with the understanding that we will get back to the parents/guardians with the answers. This plan is also useful if there is a particularly hot topic that might generate controversial discussion if we open it up for questions. See the next item for more information about hot topics. Again, timely follow-up is important.

12. **Anticipate the difficult questions and prepare responses.** We might take a few minutes to discuss the class with a colleague and try to think of all the questions we hope parents/guardians *won't* ask. Some difficult questions that typically arise include:

- inquiries about physically or behaviorally challenged children in your classroom. The question may be asked in a variety of ways, but the concern behind the question is, "How are you going to ensure that this child's (or children's) needs don't detract from my child's experience?"
- "How will the most able students be challenged?" In recent years, most schools have eliminated or dramatically decreased ability grouping and gifted-and-talented programs. This has led to increased concern on the part of parents/guardians who perceive their children as having the ability to work above grade level.
- "What is the homework policy, and what is the role of parents/guardians in the completion of homework?" Homework is increasingly an area of discussion and controversy in education and in the media. If you are new to the district, you will want to discuss your policy for homework to be sure it is consistent with that of the school and that of the other teachers in the grade or department. See Chapter 3 for more information on establishing effective homework routines.

You might consult with the principal or another colleague if there are questions for which you are having trouble coming up with answers.

13. **Avoid panicking if you are confronted with a parent/guardian question or statement designed to get you into a debate.** The following statements are designed to deal with this situation, without getting into a public confrontation:

- "That is a good (or interesting) question/point, and I need to think about it more. Please call me (or send in a note), and we'll set up a time to talk." Note that the onus for initiating the next communication is on the parent/guardian. Often, your acknowledgement of the point is sufficient. Later, when thinking about it at home, the parent/guardian is less likely to pursue further discussion, giving *us* the option to drop it or seek a conference.
- "I understand your point of view and know that others think similarly." When we acknowledge that the parent/guardian is not the only one who thinks something, he or she feels validated, thereby decreasing the need to prove the point is valid with a debate. We should remember that validating and agreeing are two different things. Validating a point with which we disagree and withholding our disagreement until a more appropriate time is diplomacy, not surrender. You can then go on to a new topic.
- If you feel you must make it clear that you disagree with a statement, you might start by pointing out the areas of agreement. We might then say, "We obviously differ on some points, and I would be happy to discuss this issue with you further at another time." You may want to leave it with this statement or, as suggested previously, invite the person to contact you to set up a time to talk.

14. **Don't be embarrassed to practice in front of the mirror, a colleague, a friend, or your spouse.** You may find it helpful to practice your speech with a colleague. A typical rehearsal time for a nationally televised 30-minute presidential speech is from four to ten hours. And remember, this is after a team of writers has taken weeks to write the speech!

15. **Discuss your presentation with the colleagues in your building who teach the same grade or classes.** Coordinating presentations is difficult for some teachers, both for personal and logistical reasons; however, like it or not, parents/guardians are bound to make comparisons. They just can't help it. Coordi-

nating or at least sharing information with colleagues will reduce and/or prepare us for the inevitable comparisons. Increasingly, teachers and their grade-level colleagues or departments are choosing to make joint curriculum night presentations on curriculum nights to limit the amount of comparing that takes place.

16. **Have the students in elementary schools (and some middle schools) write letters to their parents/guardians.** The letter tells the parents/guardians those things the students want the parents/guardians to be certain to see while they are visiting. Parents/guardians are encouraged to write back to their children. In cases in which all but a few parents/guardians come, the teacher writes a note back to the children whose parents/guardians did not come. This, of course, would not be possible if the majority of parents/guardians did not come.

Teachers continue to try new and innovative methods for improving their parent/guardian presentations. Some use slideshows, PowerPoint, and video presentations. Media programs are time-consuming to prepare, but are effective ways to tell and show parents/guardians what the classroom program is about. Some teachers find that prerecording a program enables them to say what they want to say, the way they want to say it, without the fear of making a mistake due to "stage fright." One school district has its own television studio designed so that one person can record a production similar to a nightly news broadcast. Teachers are able to videotape their presentations, complete with pictures of the class participating in various activities. Other visual aids may also be included. The video is played for parents/guardians on curriculum night, and questions are answered at the end. Always make sure that you have a parent/guardian's permission to photograph students.

In most schools, teachers range widely in their ability and confidence in giving presentations to parents/guardians. The strategies described above are tools to help teachers increase their confidence and success. Most teachers find that as their skill in making these presentations increases, confidence increases, leading to improved presentations and even more confidence, and so on (Ribas 1998).

Social Media and Texting

Some teachers have begun to use social media as a way to communicate classroom information to families. As of the writing of this book, Facebook and Twitter are the most popular platforms. However, the social media frontier is changing rapidly. New products are coming out each year. It is impossible to predict what will be available in the future.

Another vehicle teachers are using with parents is text messaging. This has been found particularly effective with parents who are limited English speakers. The parent is able to take the time to translate on his or her own or have a friend (or the child) translate and respond. Many low-income parents working two jobs don't have access to using their cell phones at mutually convenient times. Texting allows both the teacher and parent/guardian to communicate without the hassle of finding a mutually convenient time.

Sample Newsletters and Websites for Parents/Guardians

Many teachers use parent/guardian newsletters (paper or email) and websites to keep parents/guardians informed about the curriculum and class activities. Teachers often find that these modes of communication decrease the number of phone calls, drop-in conferences, and other contacts we receive from the more assertive parents/guardians. Teachers who use these modes also report an increase in student completion of home assignments. Parents/guardians find well-written newsletters informative and comforting. It is true that newsletters or websites will not be read in some homes, and, in some cases, these are the homes in which they may be the most valuable. For the most part, teachers and parents/guardians find newsletters or websites with necessary translations to be helpful means of communication. The following are samples of classroom newsletters and classroom websites.

Grade 4M Newsletter—October 24, 20--

On a personal note, I would like to thank you all for the notes, cards, and words of sympathy regarding the loss of my grandfather this past week. It has been a very difficult time and coming back to such support and kindness made an enormous difference. Again, thank you.
Best wishes,
Ms. M

Curriculum Corner

Math: This month, the children will be continuing with practicing and gaining proficiency in their math facts, including multiplication and division. We have covered all facts up through 12, and all math facts should be practiced nightly. In addition, we will continue our study of large numbers. Looking for patterns, being able to estimate and predict math sentence solutions, and, finally, the addition and subtraction of large numbers (three digits) will be other components of the math program. This will lead us into our unit on place value, which will begin within the next two weeks.

Language Arts: We have been continuing to concentrate on comprehension with short stories from our Junior Great Books. These have also given the children a chance to begin writing essays. We continue to practice using the components of a good paragraph. We are continuing to implement our Writer's Workshop process using revising (content) and editing (mechanics—punctuation, capitalization, spelling, etc.). Children have had more opportunities for free writing this month. This gives them a greater sense of ownership of their writing, which will inspire them to see those pieces through to the publishing stage.

Social Studies: We have finished the archaeology unit and have started our study of map skills. Maps are on the way! We will also take some time during this unit to discuss our various heritages, as we look at the location of the different countries on our mini-maps.

Science: We have begun the hands-on explorations! We started with observing our own shadows at different times of day. We then moved on to the "straws in clay" experiment. Using flashlights, students used different techniques to change the length and position of their straw shadows; they then recorded their results and made written observations and hypotheses. We will continue this unit with the study of shadows on spheres, so please keep those flashlights handy!

Fourth Grade Forum

Student Council: Congratulations go out to our two newly elected Student Council Representatives!

Erik and Courtney were elected this week in a contest that proved (in case we weren't already certain) what an incredible group of people we have in this class. All of the candidates delivered well-written and well-spoken speeches, and each of them would have made a wonderful addition to our school council. All students handled both pre- and post-election time with grace and class. Needless to say, I was extraordinarily proud of each of them.

Correspondent: One of our correspondents was Jennie, who also used her position to reach out and thank members of the community. She wrote a wonderful letter to the members of the Sample District Fire Department expressing her sadness over the events of September 11 and sharing with them her favorite things about our class. Nice work, Jennie! We have received responses from both the Sample District Fire Department and the Sample District Police Department, which are hanging on our Correspondent's Row. Feel free to stop in and read them!

Other Notes

Teacher for a Day: Well, at least an hour anyway! Now that we are off and running, I would like to offer each of you the opportunity to personally enrich this class. How is this done? Well, it is my hope to have a parent/guardian/grandparent/aunt/uncle/etc., of each of the students come in and share with us! Your sharing can focus on your culture, career, or hobbies. Children need real-life connections to what they are learning each day, and this is a wonderful way to help provide that. It would involve a presentation and—depending on the culture, career, or hobby— a demonstration of some kind that will help bring your subject to the classroom. You would also need to come prepared to answer questions the children may have. You should plan to spend at least 30–45 minutes in the classroom. We will need to meet before

continued on next page

your presentation day for about 15–20 minutes, either after or before school, to discuss the details and how, if needed, I can help you in any way. If you (or someone else in your child's family) are interested, please send in a note letting me know what you would like to do and when you will be available. If you are not able to join us in the classroom during the day, I can make arrangements for a flip camera to be sent home with your child for an evening so you can videotape your presentation. Another option would be for us to speak by phone and to have your child bring the materials you wish to share to school on a mutually arranged date. Looking forward to having you here!

Wish List: I have had parents/guardians ask me what we need for the classroom. In response, I have put together a classroom Wish List. Thank you again to all of the families who have already given so much; you have made the transition into a new space much easier!

   globes
   small supply bins
   old tennis balls (44 to be precise—they have
      made such a difference!)
   books (old or new)
   Other teachers in our grade request: tissues,
      markers, colored pencils

Book Orders: I have sent home today two optional special book orders. I would like to send the order in by November 14 so the books arrive in plenty of time for the holidays! There are many wonderful books available in these catalogs, but, unfortunately, they don't count toward the free book picks available in our regular monthly order. Please note this opportunity is an option for children and not a requirement. If you would like to support another child's book purchase in addition to your own, we would welcome that kindness.

The "Write" Stuff

My Poem
by Kayla

John Adams School is so fun
Because I like to share with everyone.
I like doing math, reading, and social studies
And I like spending time with our first grade
   buddies.
We have fish and five computers
And I'm thankful for all our Martha Jones tutors.
So far we have been studying the moon
And J.T. and Hayley's birthdays are in June.
My teacher Ms. M likes to walk in the park
And her dog Remington just has a new thing—
   to bark!

Ms. Moran's Class
by Jennie

Hi! I am writing an article to tell you what is going on in Ms. M's class. First of all, we are voting for student council. There were a lot of really good speeches! In P.E., we are playing Ultimate Frisbee. In math, we are making 1,000 books made out of blank 100 charts. We have a book report every month. We also have Weekly Spotlight every week. If you do all of your homework and bring it in on time, you get a 10-minute choice time coupon. If you bring in your Book Log every day with initials, you get perfect Book Log, which also earns a 10-minute choice time coupon. In my opinion, this is the best class ever!

Fourth Grade
by Rachel

Fourth grade is terrific! Art is terrific because we get to make sculptures. Ms. M is a very nice teacher. Writing is really exciting because we get to write a story or a poem or an article for the Newsletter. During reading we get to read fiction, nonfiction, and historical fiction books. Pioneer Sisters was my favorite book so far. Recess is fun because there are lots of things to do like play with chalk, play ball, play games, or play pass with the football.

Newsletter — January 14, 20--

Dear Families,

I hope this New Year finds you all healthier and happier! I had a wonderful visit with my family and a quiet holiday. We are now back into the full swing of January and, with state testing looming on the horizon, test preparations have begun. You will be seeing items coming home marked with a red star; these are pieces that I need the children to complete absolutely independently. This means that no matter how small the question may seem, they need to handle it alone. While this test is by no means the main focus of our school day, I want our children to have all of the tools necessary to sit down to the test fully prepared.

Thank you for your continued support and, as always, please feel free to contact me with any questions!

Best Wishes,

Ms. Moran

A Curriculum Corner

Science: We are continuing our study of shadows with a unit on spheres. This gives children a more concrete example of how shadows on the surface of the Earth vary depending on its position. We will be doing more with our own shadows outdoors as the unit progresses.

Math: We are on our way with "Arrays and Shares." This unit will strengthen the students' understanding of the concepts behind multiplication and division. Their strong fact base will make this unit even more meaningful. The children will continue practicing and gaining proficiency in their math facts (including multiplication and division). We have covered all facts up through 12, and all math facts should be practiced nightly.

Language Arts: We are taking the opening steps toward long compositions. Early in the year, we started working on focused paragraphs. The children will continue honing this skill and will begin to link paragraphs together, along with introductory and concluding paragraphs, to form complete compositions.

We will begin a unit on biographies. Each child will have the opportunity to study a person of his/her choice and then write a biography. This unit will take children through the research process step by step. It will also help them to understand the importance of character development in their writing.

Social Studies: We have begun a mini-unit on Civilizations, beginning with the story "Weslandia" by Paul Fleischman. The children read this story aloud and were given materials to create their own civilizations. This unit has them focusing on the basic needs of a civilization, which will reinforce what they studied in the previous unit.

Fourth-Grade Forum

Student Council: Movie Night will be on January 23 at 6:30 pm. Tickets will be sold in advance for $2.00, and there will be refreshments for sale as well. The Student Council is looking for parents/guardians to donate refreshments for this event. If you are interested, please send in a note indicating what you would be willing to make. All proceeds go directly to the Sam Adams Student Council.

Other Notes

Teacher for a Day: The children had a wonderful opportunity to get up close and personal with a member of the law enforcement community. Mr. Ortiz came in last week to share his career as a sergeant with the Boston Police Department. He helped to dispel some of the myths about law enforcement fostered on television and in movies. Children gained a clearer understanding of the many facets of police work and how they all support the goal of safety within the community.

Thank you again to Mr. O. We are still looking for more parents/guardians to come in. Remember that the children find all careers interesting, and having parents/guardians take the time to come in means so much.

Winter Wear: With the winter weather in full swing, I would like to encourage all families to send in a "wet weather bag." This bag should contain one pair of sneakers or shoes, one pair of socks, and a pair of pants (sweatpants or leggings are fine) that can stay at school. This will ensure that none of the children spend an afternoon in wet clothes. Thank you!

Wish List: The children have voted and demonstrated great amounts of responsibility in the classroom, so within the next few weeks we will be adopting a pair of rats for the class. They come highly recommended

continued on next page

for classroom pets, as they are very intelligent and gentle. We already have a home for them, but we will need wood shavings, a water bottle, food dishes, toys, bedding, and food before we can get them. Any literature on domestic rats would also be wonderful. If any families have an objection to the animals being in the room, please do not hesitate to let me know.

Two large "body pillows" were very graciously donated by a parent/guardian. Unfortunately, they are not covered and need to be before I can put them out for the children. I am all thumbs when it comes to sewing, so I am hoping that there is a parent/guardian out there with a sewing machine and a little time to put together some covers. Thank you!

Other wish list items are:

old tennis balls (20 to be precise—we're almost there!)
books (old or new)
milk/juice caps (the plastic kind that you have to pull the tab off first)

Book Responses: The next Book Response is due on January 31. If there are any parents/guardians interested in attending the presentation portion, please let me know. I will let you know the dates and times.

The "Write" Stuff

Anna Ribas
I sit on the beautiful shore
Watching the waves crash on each other
I feel like a rich queen
Holding shiny sea glass
That looks like jewels

THE SAMPLE HIGH SCHOOL
115 Main St.
Sample, CA 01111
Phone: 403-713-5365
Fax: 403-713-5180

Science Department
August 28, 20--

Dear _____,

Welcome to SHS Conceptual Biology. I am delighted that you will be in my class and would like to share a little about the course, the class, and what we will be doing this year.

SHS Biology is a course that will encourage you to ask questions and to reflect on your observations of the natural world. Its emphasis on thoughtful inquiry and decision-making will encourage you to view biology as an approach to learning as well as an ever-changing body of scientific knowledge. You will come to understand and appreciate the major theories that help to explain the natural world and the relevance of biology to your life. The course will engage you in active learning and problem-solving through hands-on and minds-on activities. For example, one of the activities will require you to work as a member of a fictitious community, the Tri-Lakes Region, to study data, do experiments, and learn about some organisms that live in the lakes. You will also examine the different factors that affect the fish population in these lakes over time.

This year, there are eight different sections of this course. There are three teachers who have been working together this summer to improve the course based on information from last year's students. We are very excited by the opportunity to teach this course and to have you as our student. Students who elect this college preparatory course may take it for honors or standard credit. In the first week of school, you will receive information about the expectations for each level of the course. You will need to discuss these expectations with your parent/guardian(s) and, should you desire to receive honors credits, you will be given a contract that will require the signatures of your parent/guardian, your guidance counselor, and you by Friday, September 13.

If you want to get a head start on supplies for this course, you may purchase a 1.5-inch, three-ring binder with paper and dividers and a spiral-bound, three-hole-punched notebook (to be used as a lab notebook). Finally, if you wish to learn more about the course and upcoming assignments, please visit my website at http://placemark.tomsnyder.com/teachers/20719/. Click on *SHS Weekly Planner* to get to the SHS Weekly Planner web page for the first week of school. This web page will be updated weekly to give you your assignments and news of other upcoming events in the class.

In the meantime, enjoy the rest of your summer. See you on September 6 in room 360.

Sincerely,
Susan Plati

SHS Biology Weekly Planner Online
September 3–9, 20--

Mrs. Plati

Issue # 1-1

Welcome to SHS Biology!
An Introduction to the SHS Biology Weekly Planner Online

Welcome back to school! And welcome to the SHS Biology Weekly Planner Online! The online version of the weekly planner will be issued every Saturday or Sunday preceding the upcoming school week. You will get a printed copy during the first meeting of your class each week. Your assignments, explanations of these assignments, upcoming projects, tests, quizzes, and some extra-credit assignments will be present in both versions of the planner. The online version will also have some additional extra-credit assignments ("extra credit online") as well as some websites that may help you to learn more about the topic that we are studying in biology. If you consult your weekly planner every day, it will help you to stay organized and prepare for class.

Weekly Assignments
Date Due

Assignment

Friday, September 5, 20--
Welcome to your first biology class. See you in room 360!

Monday, September 8, 20--
1. Bring in 1½-inch, three-ring binder with college-ruled paper and dividers.
2. Bring in a spiral-bound college-ruled notebook that will fit inside your binder. This will be used as your lab notebook.
3. Read handouts given out in Friday's class.

Tuesday, September 9, 20--
Your assignments will be posted in this section each week. Usually, there will be a different section for each class. Please make sure you check the right class.

Some Information about Biology
And Some Specific Information about the SHS Course

SHS Biology is a course that will encourage you to ask questions and to reflect on your observations of the natural world. Its emphasis on thoughtful inquiry and decision-making will encourage you to view biology as an approach to learning as well as an ever-changing body of scientific knowledge. You will come to understand and appreciate the major theories that help to explain the natural world and the relevance of biology to your life. The course will engage you in active learning and problem-solving through hands-on and minds-on activities. For example, one of the activities will require you to work as a member of a fictitious community, the Tri-Lakes Region, to study data, do experiments, and learn about some organisms that live in the lakes. You will also examine the different factors that affect the fish population in these lakes over time.

Long-Term Assignments and Other Things to Plan For

Check this section regularly to find out when tests, quizzes, and other special assignments are due.

Happy Birthday to You!

Birthdays will be announced in this section
Make sure you have filled out the student information sheet and turned it in so that we can celebrate your birthday. (Maybe we'll dedicate a lab to you!)

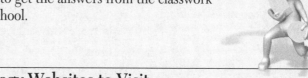

Extra Credit Online—Acid Rain

Answer the questions below and submit answers online for extra credit. This assignment is due on Friday, September 12. You should be able to get the answers from the classwork that you will be doing during the first full week of school.
1. What is acid rain and what is its cause?
2. Why are scientists concerned about acid rain?

Biology Websites to Visit

The Croak Mystery—Access Excellence Web Page

Here's a chance for you to be a biological detective! This is an interactive mystery about frogs and their disappearance from a certain environment. Read all the clues, and record information as you go. When you think you have solved the mystery, you can submit your answer online and you'll get a response from the people at the website. You may wish to work with a partner on this one. If you submit to me your solution and the response that you got from the people at the Access Excellence website, I'll give you extra credit for this.
URL: http://www.accessexcellence.org/croak/

Have a Great School Year!

Bring in lots of questions and be prepared to work with your classmates to learn the answers to these questions.

We'll begin the year with a case study of the "Tri-Lakes Region." You'll be students at Tri-Lakes High School and will work with your lab group to analyze data that will help you solve this problem.

Our first major unit will be *ecology*. We'll look at how organisms interact with each other and their environment. You'll build ecosystems in soda bottles to help you learn this material.

Our next unit is *evolution*. We'll compare human primates to non-human primates. You'll study differences and similarities in brain structure. You'll learn about Charles Darwin and the evidence that led to his theory of evolution by natural selection. And you'll learn about the diverse forms of life that exist on Earth.

You'll learn how living things reproduce and develop and how they pass on their genes to the next generation. You'll also learn how genes express themselves—what determines your blood type and hair and eye color. You'll learn how DNA (the material that comprises genes) functions in a living organism.

In the *homeostasis* unit, you'll learn how our cells function, how our blood and lungs work, and how we regulate our temperature and control water balance.

In the *energy* unit, we will study how all living things get their energy. You'll learn about the chemical reactions that take place inside living cells to help utilize this energy.

You'll do lots of lab work, and your lab notebook is very important in determining your term grade.
email: Susan_plati@sample.usa.edu
http://placemark.bigsur.com/teachers/20719/

continued on next page

SHS Bio Weekly Planner–BC1, Mrs. Plati, October 1–7, 20--

On the Web at http://placemark.tomsnyder.com/teachers/20719/

Weekly overview. This week you will study the predator-prey interactions between goldfish and brine shrimp in Lab 4—A Jar Full of Interactions. You will learn more about population growth during a class activity in which you'll observe data on populations of bacteria and humans in Lab 5—Potential Population Growth. You'll have an 80-point "quest" on Wednesday that will cover all the work that you've done since the beginning of the year.

Date Due	Assignment
Monday, Oct. 1, 20--	**Pre-lab #4—*A Jar Full of Interactions***
	1. Read E234–E237—*Growing, Growing, Grown* (back to book)
	2. Finish JE 2—*Reindeer on St. Paul Island*, pp. 323–328

Parts A and B were begun in class. Make sure that you have answered the procedural questions for Part A and completed the table and graph for Part B. You must complete the analysis questions for each part. Analysis Qs 1–5 Part A are on page 327.
Analysis Qs 1–3 for Part B are on page 328.

Date Due	Assignment
Wednesday, Oct. 3, 20--	**1. Answer the review questions to help you prepare for the "quest." Bring the completed questions to class. They'll be collected before you take the quest.**
	2. Prepare your index card of information that you may use during the quest.
	3. Eighty-point "quest" on all work done since the beginning of the school year.

Labs 1, 2, 3—Effect of pH and temperature on gammarus and daphnia, pH lab, and bottle ecosystem
Engage p. 1–13, Tri-Lakes packet
You should know what pH is and what the pH scale means. What is an acid pH? What is a base? What are some of the sources of pollution? What is the cause of acid rain? How are gammarus and daphnia important to the ecological balance of the lake? What is eutrophication?

Date Due	Assignment
Thursday, Oct. 4, 20--	**1. Read E-237–238 *Inquiring Minds*—information about population dynamics.**
	2. Read E-238k-241—*Endless Interactions*
Friday, Oct. 5, 20--	**1. Pre-lab #5—*Potential Population Growth***
	2. Write up Lab 4—*A Jar Full of Interactions*
Monday, Oct. 8, 20--	**1. Read the lab directions for Lab 6—*Using Owl Pellets to Become a Food Chain Detective* and bring to class.**
	2. Read E-136–E-141—*Food Chains, Webs, and Pyramids*

Long-term assignments and other things to plan for:
1. Keep working on your ecology vocabulary list this week. Each time you come across one of the words in class or in your reading, you should write the definition of the word in the space on the sheet of terms.
2. Don't forget to visit the weekly planner online for extra-credit assignments. There will be at least one new extra-credit assignment each week.
3. Remember that it is your responsibility to make up any work missed because of absence. Labs must be made up before the next double lab period so that the analysis can be completed and turned in on time.

Full period text on Ecology—Friday, October 17
Lab books due for the term grade on Tuesday, October 21

<u>Honor Assignments: Must be done by all students taking this course for honor credit (may be done for extra credit by any student)</u>
Make sure that you have turned in the "croak mystery" solution and your notes that you used as you solved the mystery.

Your first newspaper article review was due last week.
Your next one will be due on Oct. 12.

Student Portfolios as a Means of Communicating to Parents/Guardians

Sharing students' portfolios during conferences is an effective way to show parents/guardians the progress their children have made over time. Parents/guardians may celebrate their children's successes and growth. As parents/guardians look at their children's work and are able to more clearly understand areas of weakness, they will be better able to support their children's learning at home.

Student portfolios are also an excellent means for communicating to parents/guardians the type of work students are doing in class. It is important, however, to provide the parents/guardians with some guidance on the best way to review a portfolio. One middle school parent/guardian whose child had been keeping a portfolio all year remarked that he only knew to look at the portfolio because he was a teacher. At no point did the teacher or the child share with the parent/guardian that this excellent example of the student's work existed and that the parent/guardian should occasionally review it for information about the class's work. Some teachers are now placing signature sheets in the front of the portfolio and asking parents/guardians to review the portfolios at the end of each month and to sign the sheet to indicate that they did so.

Portfolios in the Secondary Classroom

While portfolios are used at the high school level in much the same way as described for the elementary school level, there are a few distinctions. Rather than students creating a single, large portfolio that includes material from each of their different subjects, high school students are typically asked to create a portfolio for each of their core academic subjects (one for English, one for science, etc.). These portfolios tend to consist of the same types of student work as described for the elementary school level, but—especially in the case of term papers and other types of writing assignments—students are generally expected to include the various brainstorming activities and drafts that helped them to ultimately put together the final products. The last item that high school students typically place into a portfolio is a piece of reflective writing about the various pieces of work that they have included. Generally, such a reflection activity asks students to page through their own portfolios, looking for areas in which they may see their own progress as learners as well as areas in which they recognize a need for

continued improvement. Although this assignment is generally the last piece of student work added to the portfolio, it is placed at the very front in order to provide the portfolio's reader with an overview of the work it comprises.

Effectively Using Email for Parent/Guardian Communication

Email is increasing the ease with which there is communication between home and school. General guidelines for email include

- Assume anything you write in an email may get forwarded and be read by someone else, so make sure the content of your emails is professional and grammatically correct.
- Keep emails focused on logistics and impersonal in nature, and keep your emotions in check. It is far better not to send email or to wait and meet with a parent/guardian in person than to regret email correspondence later. Liza Lee, head of the Columbus, Ohio, School for Girls (Mosle 2013), cautions that "conflicts often escalate in email in ways they never do face to face." Emotionally charged issues are often best addressed by phone or face to face when feasible.
- Remember at all times that you, the teacher, are the professional and must act accordingly.

In one author's own classes, he has utilized email in two different ways to facilitate parent/guardian communication. First, email may be useful when working with students who have trouble completing their homework assignments on a consistent basis. The first time a student fails to complete his or her homework assignment, he might simply give the student a warning; however, if the student neglects his or her homework again, he typically places a phone call home to the students' parents/guardians. For the parents/guardians who explain that whenever they ask their children about homework, the child invariably replies that no homework was assigned, email may provide a useful solution. Either nightly or at the beginning of the week, the teacher simply emails these parents/guardians the homework assignments that their children will be expected to complete for his class. In this way, the parents/guardians are clued in about precisely what their children should be working on.

Email may also be useful for providing parents/

guardians with weekly reports on their children's academic or behavioral performance. For a child who is either disruptive in class or not working to his or her potential, we will sometimes follow a parent/guardian conference with an agreement to send a brief email at the end of each week. The email fills in this child's parents/guardians about their son's or daughter's in-class behavior. Perhaps an agreement may be worked out such that the child's weekend privileges—watching TV, going out with friends, or using the car—are contingent upon a positive report via email from the teacher.

While both of these uses for email may initially appear to be time-consuming, the advantage of email is that we as teachers may make a decision about when to take the time to initiate this communication. It is important that teachers communicate with parents/guardians when they read and respond to emails. For example, one fourth-grade teacher tells parents/guardians that she reads and responds to emails after school (note: *not* during the school day). With email, teachers don't have to wait for a time that is convenient for a child's parents/guardians to take a phone call. Moreover, with email, we don't risk being drawn into a 45-minute conversation with a child's parents/guardians. Instead, we may simply send email whenever we are able to find a few free minutes. If the plan we have worked out with the student's parents/guardians is working correctly, the time that we invest in emailing about the student's progress should result in more diligent homework completion, better in-class behavior, etc. In other words, the time we invest in emailing is an investment from which we expect to see a return.

Working with parents/guardians can be both enriching and challenging. The process of honing your communication skills is a professional goal and the work of a lifetime.

Conclusion

As noted in this chapter, learning to work effectively with parents/guardians has many benefits for the teachers and students. These benefits include higher student achievement, higher teacher job satisfaction, and increased community confidence in the school and district. The most current teacher performance and licensure standards have made parent/guardian communication an important standard for measuring teacher performance. Unfortunately, teachers typically receive little training in how to work effectively with parents/guardians in their pre-service and in-

service training. It is our hope that this chapter helps fill that void.

References

Alexander, K. and Entwisle, D. "Lasting Consequences of the Summer Learning Gap." *American Sociological Review* 72, no. 2 (April 2007): 167–180.

Allington, R.L., McGill-Franzen, A.M., Camilli, G., Williams L., Graff, J., and Zeig, J. "Ameliorating Summer Reading Setback among Economically Disadvantaged Elementary Students." Paper presented at the American Educational Research Association, Chicago, 2007.

Barton, D., and Cardosa, N. "Helping Students Develop Their IEPs: Making It Accessible to Every Student," 2003. http://www.nichcy.org.

Better Homes Fund. "America's Homeless Children: New Outcasts." 1999. http://eric.ed.gov/?id=ED442897.

Bryk, A.S., Sebring, P.B., Allensworth, E. Luppescu, S., and Easton, J. Q. *Organizing Schools for Improvement: Lessons from Chicago*. Chicago: University of Chicago Press, 2010.

Burchenal, M. "Parents' Night." *Voices* XII, no. 6 (November/December 1997).

Burt, M., Aron, L., Lee, E., and Valente, J. *Helping America's Homeless: Emergency Shelter or Affordable Housing?* Washington, DC: The Urban Institute, 2001.

Cattanach, J. "Support Parents to Improve Student Learning." *Phi Delta Kappan* 94, no. 6 (March 2013): 20–25.

Colombo, M. "Family Literacy Nights: A Community Builds a Bridge between Teachers and Culturally Diverse Parents." *Educational Leadership* (May 2004): 48–51.

Cooper, J., and MacIver, A. "Recommendations for Summer and Beyond" (internal school document). Brookline, MA: 2006.

Cunningham, A.M. and Knoester. C. "The Psychological Well-Being of Single Parents." In *Focus on Single-Parent Families: Past, Present, and Future*, eds., Yarber, A.D. and Sharp, P.M., pp. 136–155. Santa Barbara, CA. Greenwood Publishing Group, 2007.

Elmore, M. "Effective Parent Conferences." *Principal Leadership* 8, no. 6 (February 2008): 7–8.

Fairchild, R. "Adventures in Summer Learning." 2005. http://www.readingrockets.org/shows/launching/summer _reading/.

Fege, A. "From Fund-Raising to Hell-Raising: New Roles for Parents." *Educational Leadership* 57, no. 7 (April 2000): 39–45.

Fleischauer, B. "Parent-Teacher Conference Tips: Aiming for a Win-Win Situation." *Washington Parent*, Washington, DC (October 2004).

Freeman-Loftis, B. "How to (Really) Listen to Parents." *Educational Leadership* 68, no. 8 (May 2011).

Grail, T. *Custodial Mothers and Fathers and Their Child Support: 2007*, P60-237 Washington, DC: US Census Bureau. November 2009. www.census.gov/prod/2009pubs/p60-237.pdf.

Hart, P.D. "All for All: Community Involvement." Survey conducted by Hart Research Association for the Public Education Network, 1999. http://www.publiceducation.org/pdf/publications/National_Poll/November_2000_All_for_All.pdf.

Henderson, A. *Beyond the Bake Sale: The Essential Guide to Family/School Partnerships*. New York: The New Press, 2007.

Henderson, A.T. and Whipple, M. "How to Connect with Families." *Educational Leadership* 70 (June 2013): 44–48.

Individuals with Disabilities Education Act (IDEA), 20 U.S.C. 1400 (2004).

Johns Hopkins University, "Education Researcher Joyce Epstein Comments on Homework Studies." *Ascribe Higher Education News Service*, October 3, 2003.

Jones, R. "How Parents Can Support Learning." *American School Board* 188, no. 9 (September 2001): 18–21.

Kotkin, J. "The Changing Demographics of America. *Smithsonian*, August 2010. http://www.smithsonianmag.com/40th-anniversary/the-changing-demographics-of-america-538284/.

Kupper, L. and McGahee-Kovac, M. *Helping Students Develop Their IEPs: Technical Assistance Guide*. 2nd ed. National Information Center for Children and Youth with Disabilities, January 2002.

Martin, J.E., Huber, M., Marshall, L., and Sale, P. "A 3-Year Study of Middle, Junior High, and High School IEP Meetings." *Exceptional Children* 70 (2004): 285–297.

Mason, C.Y., McGahee-Kovac, M., and Johnson, L. "How to Help Students Lead Their IEP Meetings." *Teaching Exceptional Children* 36, no. 3 (January/February 2004): 18–24.

McGahee-Kovac, M. *A Student's Guide to the IEP*. National Information Center for Children and Youth with Disabilities, 1995 (rev. ed., 2011). http://nichcy.org/wp-content/uploads/docs/st1.pdf.

Moore, M. "Tips: Dealing with Difficult Parents." *Inspiring Teachers*. http://www.inspiringteachers.com/classroom_resources/tips/parent_communication/dealing_with_difficult_parents.html. Accessed November 29, 2011.

Mosle, S. "The Dicey Parent-Teacher Duet." *The New York Times* (blog), January 11, 2013. http://opinionator.blogs.nytimes.com/2013/01/11/the-dicey-parent-teacher-duet/.

Murphy, J.F. and Tobin, K.J. "Homelessness Comes to School: How Homeless Children and Youths Can Succeed." *Phi Delta Kappan* 93, no. 3 (November 2011): 32–37.

Myers, A. and Eisenman, L. "Student-Led IEPs: Take the First Step." *Teaching Exceptional Children* 37, no. 4 (March/April 2005): 52–58.

National Alliance to End Homelessness. *Fact Checker: Family Homelessness*. 2007.

National Association of State Directors of Special Education, Inc. *NASDSE: 1998–1999 Satellite Series:* "Creating School Environments Conducive to Learning: Developing Quality IEPs." Biography of speakers.

The National Center on Family Homelessness. "America's Youngest Outcasts: State Report Card on Child Homelessness." 2009. http://www.canatx.org/CAN-Research/Reports/2009/rc_full_report.pdf.

Quiroz, B., Greenfield, P., and Altchech, M. "Bridging Cultures with a Parent-Teacher Conference." *Educational Leadership* (April 1999): 68–70.

Ribas, W. "An Analysis of the Communication that Occurs between Parents and Teachers." PhD diss., Boston College, 1991.

Ribas, W. "Helping Teachers Communicate with Parents." *Principal* 72 (November 1992): 19–20.

Ribas, W. "Tips for Reaching Parents." *Educational Leadership* (September 1998): 83–85.

Smith, L. "Slowing the Summer Slide." *Educational Leadership* 69, no. 4 (December 2011/January 2012): 60–63.

Teahan, J. Marblehead Public Schools internal document. Marblehead, MA, 2008.

Tingley, S. "Tips for Teachers Working with Difficult Parents." http://www.education.com/reference/article/Ref_Working_Difficult/. Accessed November 29, 2011.

Van Dycke, J.L., Martin, J.E., and Lovett, D.L. "Why Is This Cake on Fire? Inviting Students into the IEP Process." *Teaching Exceptional Children* 38 no. 3 (January/February 2006): 42–47.

Weininger, E. and Lareau, A. "Children's Participation in Organized Activities and the Gender Dynamics of the 'Time Bind.'" Paper presented at the meeting of the American Sociological Association, Chicago. August 16–19, 2002.

Zehr, M. "Late-Night Child Care Meets Needs of Milwaukee Families." *Education Week* (December 11, 2002): 6–7.

Related Readings

Baeder, A. "Stepping into Students' Worlds." *Educational Leadership* 67, no. 5 (February 2010): 56–60.

Barnwell, E. "Parent Outreach for Busy Leaders." *Responsive Classroom* newsletter (Winter 2013). http://www.responsiveclassroom.org/article/parent-outreach-busy-leaders.

Cavanaugh, S. "Standards Backers Seek Out Support of Parents." In *Education Week Spotlight on Parent and Community Involvement*, 3-4. Bethesda, MD: Editorial Projects in Education, Inc., 2013.

Centers for Disease Control and Prevention. *Parent*

Engagement: Strategies for Involving Parents in School Health. Atlanta, GA: US Department of Health and Human Services, 2012. http://www.cdc.gov/healthyyouth/protective/pdf/parent_engagement_strategies.pdf.

Crew, R. "Supply Parents, Demand Parents." *Educational Leadership* 68, no. 8 (May 2011).

Cushman, C. "School Safety, Climate Hinge on Communication." In *Education Week Spotlight on Parent and Community Involvement*, 11–12. Bethesda, MD: Editorial Projects in Education, Inc., 2013.

Fairchild, R. "Summer Is Prime Time for Building School-Community Partnerships." *ASCD Express* 5, no. 21 (2010). http://www.ascd.org/ascd-express/vol5/521-fairchild.aspx.

Ferlazzo, L. "Involvement or Engagement?" *Educational Leadership* 68, no. 8 (May 2011).

Ferriter, W.M. "Digitally Speaking/Becoming Digitally Resilient." *Educational Leadership* 68, no. 6 (March 2011): 86–87.

Ferriter, W.M. "Digitally Speaking/Drop.io: One-Stop Sharing." *Educational Leadership* 68, no. 1 (September 2010): 86–88.

Fleming, N. "Districts Deploy Digital Tools to Engage Parents." In *Education Week Spotlight on Parent and Community Involvement*, 6–7. Bethesda, MD: Editorial Projects in Education, Inc., 2013.

Hoerr, T.R. "*Principal* Connection/What Are Parents Thinking?" *Educational Leadership* 69, no. 4 (December 2011/January 2012): 90–91.

Jensen, E. *Engaging Students with Poverty in Mind: Practical Strategies for Raising Achievement*. Alexandria, VA: ASCD, 2013.

Jensen, E. "How Poverty Affects Classroom Engagement." *Educational Leadership* 70, no. 8 (May 2013): 24–30.

Jeynes, W. "Help Families by Fostering Parental Involvement." *Phi Delta Kappan* 93, no. 3 (November 2011): 38–39.

Kelly, A.P. and McGuinn, P. "Mobilizing Parent/guardian Power for School Reform." In *Education Week Spotlight on Parent and Community Involvement*, 10–11. Bethesda, MD: Editorial Projects in Education, Inc., 2013.

Kohn, A. "What Parents Aren't Asked in School Surveys—and Why." *HuffPost Education* (blog), May 23, 2011. http://www.huffingtonpost.com/alfie-kohn/what-parents-arent-asked-_b_864908.html.

Maxwell, L.A. "'Gateway' Districts Struggle to Serve Immigrant Parents." In *Education Week Spotlight on Parent and Community Involvement*, 8–9. Bethesda, MD: Editorial Projects in Education, Inc., 2013.

Molnar, M. "Boston Leader Connects Parents to Learning." In *Education Week Spotlight on Parent and Community Involvement*: 4–5. Bethesda, MD: Editorial Projects in Education, Inc., 2013.

Myers, M. "Finding Common Concerns for the Children We Share." *Phi Delta Kappan* 94, no. 8 (May 2013): 40–44.

Neuman, S.B. "The American Dream: Slipping Away?" *Educational Leadership* 70, no. 8 (May 2013): 18–22.

Reeves, J.E. and Rodriguez, L.O. "From Breakfasts to Backpacks." *Educational Leadership* 68, no. 8 (May 2011).

Smith, S. "Would You Step Through My Door?" *Educational Leadership* 70, no. 8 (May 2013): 76–78.

Stock, E. and Fisman, R. "Home Computers and Student Achievement." *Education Week*, October 11, 2010. http://www.edweek.org/ew/articles/2010/10/13/07stock.h30.html.

Strauss, V. "Answer Sheet: Is Parent Involvement in School Really Useful?" *The Washington Post* (blog), February 6, 2013. http://www.washingtonpost.com/blogs/answer-sheet/wp/2013/02/06/is-parent/guardian-involvement-in-school-really-useful/.

Turner, J.S. "The Right Conversation Can Extinguish Anger and Strengthen Parent-Teacher Relationships." *Journal of Staff Development* 31, no. 1 (February 2010): 65–66.

Students with Disabilities: Student Involvement in the Process

Some districts have been moving toward student-led Individualized Education Plan (IEP) meetings. With proper training and age-appropriate involvement, educators report student-led meetings are an important part of the process of developing the self-advocacy skills students will need in life.

In an ideal world, students would begin receiving self-advocacy and self-determination instruction in elementary school and would experience significant participation in IEP meetings before high school. It is, perhaps, easiest for teachers to envision students in high school preparing to leave school as IEP team leaders. People have had success implementing student-led IEPs with students as young as six years of age. The vocabulary is different, and the degree of responsibility is different; however, the concept of leadership is maintained through the emphasis that is placed on asking the child about what is important to him or her, and then using that information in planning goals.

How can elementary school students participate in their IEP meetings? The following is adapted from *Technical Assistance Guide: Helping Students Develop Their IEPs* (2002), a guide published by the National Information Center for Children and Youth with Disabilities. There are many ways elementary school students can be taught to participate. For instance, they may be shown how to send an invitation and a reminder letter to the team members. With support, they may be able to create a list of their academic strengths as well as the areas of the curriculum that they find hard to do. Certainly, all elementary-school-age children with special needs are able to brainstorm a list of their interests both in and outside of school and say what they want to be when they grow up. Some may even be able to name ways the teacher can help to make learning easier for them during class. Students this age may also be taught to welcome people to their meetings and to introduce their parents or guardians to the members of the team, who usually consist of people the student already knows: the classroom teacher, a special educator, related service providers (speech and language, physical therapist, occupational therapist, English language learner [ELL] tutor, or school psychologist), as well as the meeting chairperson. Finally, at the end of the meeting, the student can be taught to thank the team members for coming and for being a part of his or her IEP meeting. If the

student is capable of speaking to such a formidable group, then he or she should be encouraged to do so. Those who feel intimidated by the prospect of speaking in person could be helped to create a PowerPoint presentation, a picture book, a video presentation, or an IntelliKeys overlay with picture communication and/or voice augmentation. Numerous other audio/visual options are available to be used in lieu of or to aid the student presenter (Kupper and McGahee-Kovac 2002).

Middle school students are also able to be instructed on ways to be involved in the IEP process and to contribute at their meetings. From this grade level forward, if not sooner, students should be familiar with what an IEP is, its function, key parts of the IEP document, and the purpose of the IEP meeting. Students at this age may be ready to name their disability and describe how it affects them both in and out of school. They may be able to provide input or even write their present level of performance (PLEP), and discuss what goals and objectives they feel are important to address, as well as ways to measure their progress. Some middle school students may be able to identify the need for any related services, and state when and where the services will be provided. In the event that a student will not participate in a part of the regular education curriculum, perhaps he or she could state the reason why. Finally, as the mean age of eighth-grade students is 14—the age at which the law states that they should be invited to their IEP meetings—some may be able to verbalize their post-high school plans in order to begin transition planning discussions from school to work, vocational training, or post-secondary education. Students are encouraged to be a part of the IEP process to the greatest extent possible, given their abilities and willingness to participate.

By high school, there is an expectation that students will begin to take on even more responsibility. In addition to all the roles described for elementary and middle school students, high school students with special needs can be taught their legal rights. Students in this age group should also be familiar with their own IEPs and their component parts. They should have readily available evidence that demonstrates their progress toward meeting their current IEP goals. With guidance, they may be able to identify the focus of new goals and objectives. At this age, a discussion of their course of study, as it relates to their future plans upon graduation from high school, is appropriate. If properly trained and prepared through direct instruction over the years, high school students should be ready to help draft new IEPs and assume responsibility for leading their IEP meetings. Furthermore, at the age of 17, students are informed of and should understand the transfer of rights at the age of majority. This means that students are now at the legal age to make their own decisions and to sign their own IEPs, unless they choose to transfer that responsibility to parents or guardians. Ultimately, high school students who have been actively engaged in the IEP process may become excellent peer tutors. (Mason et al. 2004) One benefit of the student-led parent-teacher conference is that the student is responsible for and plays a vital role in the IEP development meeting. Instead of being an indifferent or passive member of the team, the student is now fully and actively engaged. The student-led parent-teacher conference is an authentic form of assessment that requires the student to reflect on his or her growth as a learner and to set goals for future learning and instruction. Furthermore, in the process of taking ownership of this leadership role, the student learns valuable life skills, such as pragmatisms, self-advocacy, self-reflection, self-assessment, goal setting, and presentation skills (Barton and Cardosa 2003). This form of assessment helps the student connect what he or she is learning in school with real-world skills, such as going on college and job interviews. Giving students a voice in their educational planning is empowering, and forces students to think about themselves as learners with the ability to assess their progress and set their own goals.

Research has found that training students to lead their IEP meetings resulted in students knowing more about their disabilities, legal rights, and accommodations. Students grew in self-confidence and were more comfortable speaking on their own behalf. Over the course of the year, parent participation at IEP meetings was 100 percent (Mason et al. 2004). The parents found this type of student-led conference more meaningful and user-friendly, and teachers enjoyed getting to know more about their students (Myers and Eisenman 2005). In the article "Inviting Students into the IEP Process," the authors say, "Parents understood the reason for the meeting better, felt more comfortable saying what they thought, understood more of what was said, and knew better what to do next" (Martin, Huber, Marshall, et al. pp. 291–293). Follow-up surveys with students who participated in two to four years of student-led IEP meetings reported

that the process was beneficial (Mason, et al. 2004). Teachers like the idea of the student taking ownership, rather than the team making IEP decisions for the student without the student's input. Martin, et al., conducted a study in which, after giving 65 students IEP leadership instruction, they observed students' meeting contributions increased from 3 percent to 12 percent. They (Martin, Van Dyke, Christensen, et.al. 2006) also found that student participation improved in the following ways: introducing themselves and team members, stating the purpose of the meeting, reviewing past goals and progress, and expressing options and goals. Results point to the fact that not only should students be invited to attend their IEP meetings, but they should also be properly prepared and encouraged to share their thoughts.

There are some disadvantages to the student-led parent-teacher conference, however. The disillusioned, disenfranchised student may not be willing to take the process seriously or participate at all. It may be viewed as something else to fail in. From the parents' point of view, there are some topics that they prefer to discuss with the team without the student being present. Some parents may be uncomfortable discussing family issues or social issues in the presence of their child. The student-led conference does not lend itself to this type of conversation. To address this, meetings can be divided into the student-attended time and the part at which only the adults are in attendance, or another meeting could be scheduled to address such issues when necessary. Special educators have concerns about when they will find the time to instruct the student (Myers and Eisenman 2005). The time will have to be taken from valuable classroom time—and not just from that particular student, but also from the other students with whom the teacher works. Some teachers reported not knowing how to go about talking to students about their disabilities in terms that the student would understand and accept (Myers and Eisenman). Professional-development time or action-research time would have to be used to teach the teachers how to implement the process.

There are many aspects of the student-led parent-teacher conference model that lend themselves to peer reflections teams, which will be discussed in Chapter 11.

Students with Disabilities, Part I: Autism and Communicating with Parents

Effective collaboration and communication with parents of disabled students is a very important part of ensuring their school success. As more students with disabilities are being included in the general education classroom, the number of interactions between general education teachers and parents/families of students with disabilities on a daily basis is increasing. While the special education teacher often acts as a liaison regarding specialized services and supports and the IEP process, families desire to engage with general educators just as any other family of students without disabilities would. Special education can be a complicated process for both general education teachers and families; therefore, it is important to be mindful of generalizations, misunderstandings, and miscommunication regarding the impact of a student's disability on his or her education. These discrepancies can threaten productive home-to-school relationships.

There are many factors involved when working with parents of students with disabilities. Some of these factors are the type of disability the student has, the severity or the severity of the impact of the disability on the student, the age of the student, how long the family has been aware of their child's needs, and past interactions with teachers and school staff. These factors play out in all disability areas; however, those students with autism spectrum disorder (ASD or autism) often have some of the most challenging, complicated, yet rewarding outcomes when working with their families. The nature of ASD as a spectrum disorder is the reason for the challenges. *Spectrum* refers to a wide range of symptoms, skills in levels of impairment, or disabilities (NIMH 2015).

ASD affects one in 68 children. The number of children with autism has steadily increased over the past 10 years. One reason for the increase is the improvements in the criteria for autism and improvements in early identification. At one time, persons suspected of having autism could be identified under four separate disorders: autistic disorder, Asperger's disorder, childhood disintegrative disorder, and pervasive developmental disorder not otherwise specified (PDD-NOS). However, due to the inconsistent ways that each of these diagnoses were applied across different clinics and treatment centers, researchers created a new, more accurate, and medically and scientifically useful way of diagnosing individuals with autism-related disorders. In the most recent *Diagnostic and Statistical Manual of Mental Disorders* (DSM-5), all four previous disorders are now categorized as ASD. This does not mean that there are not still students who have characteristics of the previous four diagnoses; it means that all of the characteristics of those diagnoses now fall under one disorder instead of four (American Psychiatric Association 2013).

Students with autism have deficits in social communication and social interactions across varied contexts. This means that they may be unable to carry on a general, light conversation with peers, understand jokes, or be aware of personal space and proximity. They also have restricted, repetitive patterns of behavior, interests, and activities, such as being overly dependent on routines or highly sensitive to changes in their environment, or a fixation on a certain toy or object that may not be age appropriate. As teachers at all levels, we may have students with autism in our classrooms who may have toys even at the middle and high school level. They may even become upset or hysterical if that toy or object is touched, lost, or taken away. Scientists have yet to identify a specific cause of autism; however, research does suggest that genetics and environment both play a role. In regards to environmental factors, this could include anything outside the body, such as the air that we breathe, water that we ingest or use, food we eat, or medicines we take. It also includes the surroundings in the womb prior to the birth of a child (NIMH 2015). Environment also includes events before and during birth, including advanced paternal age of both parents, illnesses of the mother during conception and birth, extreme prematurity at birth, and difficulties during birth, such as oxygen deprivation to the baby's brain (Autism Speaks 2015). It is important to know that when working with parents of students with autism, not knowing the cause of why their child has autism greatly affects their lives. Families report feelings of loss, internal blame, and confusion, especially early in the diagnosis of their child. They have shared that, over time, they learn to cope just as any family of a child with a disability. Families of children with autism often remain in "fight mode," especially when advocating for their children. This "fight mode" is a result of battles they often began engaging in early in their children's life due to debates with insurance companies for treatment or schools for specialized services.

Persons with ASD also can have sensory problems, sleep problems, intellectual disabilities, and other mental disorders like anxiety, ADHD, and depression. Persons with ASD are at a higher risk of mental health disorders than those who do not have ASD.

The intensity of the impact of ASD coincides with the impact or existence of other mental disorders and other associated problems. Age also plays a factor in the presence of some of the mental health disorders. Teens with ASD often have higher levels of anxiety and depression, as they become more aware of their differences between them and their peers without ASD. Teens with ASD are also at a greater risk of social isolation. This is often a result of the structure of high school and reduced teacher involvement in creating social relationships between the students.

For this essay, I surveyed families of students with disabilities and received responses from 15 families. A few responses are included below for each of the five survey questions:

- What do you want general education teachers to know about your child who has a disability?
  - *"She's a child first."*
  - *"He is our typical child. What does typical mean, anyway?"*
  - *"He can do it."*
  - *"Yes, she is different than other children, but aren't we all?"*
  - *"He does care, even though he may not always act like he does."*
  - *"Change is really hard for him. I know everyone is going to a different group of teachers next year, but it is harder for him because he has autism. It is important to begin preparing him now and he knows who his teachers are for next year so we can help him prepare for the change."*
  - *"I would like his PE teacher to recognize that he is not good at sports or competitive activities, and make accommodations or adaptations for him when there are team sports so that he is not bullied or made to feel bad by the other kids."*

- What kind of information would you like to receive from your child's general education teacher?
  - *"We would like to know about our son and not always about how he is performing against his peers."*
  - *"I want to know real information about how my daughter is doing in her class—not just the numbers and the data, but also more of, 'When we worked on math, she was able to do these type of problems. But when we worked on fractions, she did not know the difference between halves and fourths.' I sometimes don't know how to help at home when I only know that she got a certain score on her benchmark test."*

  - *"Our son has ADHD; we know he gets off task. We want to know what was done to get him back on task to finish his work or that he was off task and did not complete his work before his interim report comes out."*
  - *"Our son's teacher is very good about writing notes and calling. We have a good relationship. She cares a lot and tries really hard."*

- What causes you the most concern when working with general education teachers regarding your child?
  - *"In elementary school, she was with her teacher mostly all day. But now in middle school, she has different teachers every period, and I don't know that she has a strong relationship with anyone specifically. I want to know who helps take care of her."*
  - *"They may have too much on their plate and not be able to help my child."*
  - *"I'm concerned about all of the teachers when it comes to him being independent, especially when he goes to high school."*
  - *"This is the most he's been included since kindergarten, and I don't know if he is really considered a part of the class."*

- Why do you want your child educated in general education?
  - *"It's more like what the real world will be like."*
  - *"We don't want him treated special or differently. High school is hard enough without going to a special ed room all of the time."*
  - *"We want her to be like the other children and have friends."*
  - *"He is very smart and can do the work. He just needs more help than some of the other kids."*
  - *"Honestly, I don't know that I do, but I trust his teachers who say that he should be in gen ed."*

- What are some things teachers should never say to a parent of a child with a disability?
  - *"He's smart, but…"*
  - *"'She is so pretty and nice,' and that is all you can say about her."*
  - *"I'm sorry, but he will never…"*
  - *"I don't know how to teach her/him."*
  - *"I've done everything I can do."*

Working with parents/families of students with disabilities is really not very different from working with any other family. However, understanding the perspective and experiences that the parents of students with disabilities come from is helpful to teachers in having effective working relationships with parents/families. Below are some simple strategies and things to consider when working with families of students with disabilities:

• Be mindful that parents of students with disabilities often attend more meetings than the average family. Working collaboratively with the student's other teachers and special education service providers to align the meetings, and possibly prevent the family from coming to meet with different people on different days, will make a big difference and show care and empathy for the parents. This is especially true around parent/teacher conference time: be aware of an IEP meeting that may have already taken place or that is scheduled within a week or two before or after conferences. Acknowledge this, and give the family the option to come in more than once in a week or two.

• Use the IEP meeting as an opportunity to share about the content standards and how their child is progressing in alignment with the IEP goals in the content standards, and be specific about the accommodations that are being used to ensure the student's success. Parents often feel that general education teachers are not really active participants in the IEP meeting, especially with students who have more significant disabilities. Talk to the IEP team chairperson about being active in the IEP meeting to talk about your hopes for the student and what you are doing to actively support the student to success in general education. Give clear examples to parents, such as, *"We are working on listening and speaking skills by students giving oral presentations of the projects they have been working on this semester. I know that David has a challenge with speaking in front of his peers due to his autism, so I am working with him on creating a video to use for his presentation. You can also brainstorm with him at home about different ways he would like to present his project."*

• Before making any assumptions, get to know the family first. Even if you have worked with other students with the same or similar disability, do not assume that the parents will interact or respond the same. Be an attentive listener early in the school year, and do not be afraid to ask difficult questions about their needs regarding their child. For example: *"I have taught several students with ADHD before. A few struggled with organization, and others became very anxious. Tell me more about your son, specifically. What have been some things that have been*

successful for his teachers who have worked with him before? What are some things that may have caused some challenges for him?"

• Empathize rather than sympathize with parents of students with disabilities. Empathy acknowledges that there are challenges that they face along with their child and you will support them through it, while sympathy sends a message that something is wrong and that you are not able to help them.

The effectiveness of the collaboration and relationship between teachers and parents is important for every student, but for students with disabilities, the effectiveness of these relationships can change the academic, social, and emotional outcomes for students and their families. Using strategies shared in this chapter can assist in developing foundational skills and practices that support strong school-to-home connection.

Students with Disabilities Part II: Understanding Autism Spectrum Disorder

Autism Spectrum Disorder

For many years, the occurrence or diagnosis of autism spectrum disorder (ASD) was very rare, occurring only in five out of every 10,000 children. With advancements in research and clearer guidelines related to the criteria for determining the disorder, today autism is diagnosed in one in 68 children. Autism is more prevalent in boys than in girls, with one in 42 boys having ASD versus one in 189 girls. There is not one specific cause of ASD, just as each individual person with autism is unique. The criteria for determining autism changed in 2013 with the revision of the *Diagnostic and Statistical Manual of Mental Disorders*, 5 ed., (DSM-5), where instead of autism being categorized as four separate disorders—autistic disorder, childhood disintegrative disorder, Asperger's disorder, and pervasive developmental disorder not otherwise specified (PDD-NOS)—its authors have now aligned the criteria to include all four disorders as one broad umbrella of autism spectrum disorder, as well as one related disorder, social (pragmatic) communication disorder. This is important to teachers because while students will fall under the broad category of autism spectrum disorder, their needs are very specific, with specific characteristics of each of the former subcategories. While there are common strategies that teachers can use for any student with autism, there are certain strategies specific to those who have unique characteristics, such as those students who were once categorized as having Asperger's syndrome. As a teacher, you will often hear the phrase *on the spectrum*. This means that persons with autism have an array of exceptionalities and needs that are characterized based on the intensity of that exceptionality or need. For example, many individuals with autism have exceptional ability in the visual arts, music, and academics while about 40 percent have an intellectual disability (IQ less than 70). Sixty percent have average to above average intellectual ability (70–85 being low average, 85–100 average, and 100–115 above average). The spectrum means that each student can have varying levels of intensity of needs and exceptionalities (Autism Speaks 2015). There are some students with autism who have limited cognitive ability but have exceptional music ability. Hence, the term *on the spectrum*.

Symptoms

The types and severity of symptoms vary greatly among persons with autism. Symptoms are categorized across the three core areas that are affected by autism:

- social interactions
- communication challenges
- repetitive behaviors

The symptoms across all three areas of impact may be mild for someone whose needs and impact of ASD are less intense. These persons may be referred to as *high functioning* or *at the higher end of the spectrum*. For others, the combined symptoms across all three areas of impact may be more severe. Their behavior and language may be affected more. These persons may be referred to as *lower functioning* or *at the lower end of the spectrum*. When working with students and families who have autism, it is best to refer to the student by who they are and be explicit in describing their needs or the intensity of their needs and support, rather than by their functioning level. The symptoms are connected to the three core areas, and are categorized as neurological or physical:

Neurological Symptoms (characterizes social and communication areas)

- sleep deficits
- mood swings/disorders
- anxiety disorder
- attention problems
- seizures
- hyperactivity

- language disability
- intellectual disability

(Characterizes repetitive-behavior area)

- irritability
- tantrums
- self-injurious
- aggression
- hyperactivity
- anxiety

Physical symptoms

- immune dysfunction
- gastrointestinal disorders
- food allergies/sensitivities

As a teacher, you may have students with autism who one day may be in a happy mood at the beginning of the day but by mid-day, they may experience a change in mood and seem sad or melancholy. If you have a student with ASD that this happens to, it is important to note the time of day this occurs and see if there is a pattern in mood changes. If you notice a pattern, such as daily or even weekly, it is important to make his or her parents aware. For students who may not have a lot of language or who struggle to express their thoughts either verbally or in writing, you can use smiley faces to show examples of various moods. If you are a middle or high school teacher, texting is a great way to use the smileys and is very appropriate for this age of student. You can text your student at the beginning of the day and allow them to text you a smiley of what their mood is; you can also do this at another time of the day. While there may be school rules against cell phone use, this is an appropriate accommodation to use as long as everyone agrees and understands the purpose of the student's phone. Also you can use it with an instant messaging application on a computer or tablet. Many persons with ASD often take medication for mood and anxiety disorders, so it is important to keep open and consistent communication with their families in case there is a need to visit their doctor.

Children with autism have difficulty engaging in the everyday give and take of human interactions. Parents of children with ASD notice symptoms at various times. Some parents have recognized early symptoms as young as eight to 10 months of age. While other children that age are responding to sounds and their names or beginning to babble and giggle, they are also touching and feeling the face and mouth. Children with ASD, however, may fail to respond to their names and show little or no interest in people; they will not make or imitate sounds or babbling. Parents who have toddlers with ASD have reported that their children have difficulty or a lack of interest in social games and imitating actions, and they prefer to play alone on the playground. This is the time that many toddlers display affection, such as hugging and kissing their parents or siblings, but children with ASD fail to respond or display affection or any emotion, including anger. Most children with ASD are diagnosed between the ages of two and four. For students who have more severe symptoms and impact of ASD, they are diagnosed much earlier, as early as 12 to 18 months old.

Children and adults with ASD often do not notice, understand, or respond to subtle social cues such as a smile, wave, grimace, or scowl. They often do not respond to social cues of others, especially regarding space and proximity. They may either stand too close or too far away. They may lack the ability to interpret the gestures of others, such as facial expressions; typically an individual may smile or frown at a comment while the person with autism will be confused or not notice the expression. As students get older, this causes their social world to become more isolated. As social isolation occurs, the impact of the other symptoms can become more intense, such as greater anxiety or irritability. Persons with ASD often seem immature because they struggle to regulate their emotions. They may cry or have outbursts of anger or aggression in inappropriate situations. For example, a sixth-grade student with autism may be working in a collaborative group with two other students and required to take turns with the roles in the group. The student with autism only likes to be the timekeeper and refuses to switch roles; he or she may begin to cry when the teacher prompts him to switch roles. To avoid this type of outburst, you can use a timer and prompt before the activity starts to let the student know that he or she will be the timekeeper and the note taker, as well as when this transition will occur. Often, the outbursts are a result of an unanticipated change. For students without ASD, understanding the instructions to switch roles may not be a big deal, but for students with ASD, they need to know when changes are required and will happen, and have those changes planned out for them.

Repetitive behaviors are common in students with ASD. Students with ASD often struggle with being able to engage in restricted ranges of activities. Therefore, they exhibit repetitive behaviors like hand flapping, "stimming," rocking, jumping, twirling, arranging or rearranging objects, repeating sounds or phrases, or repeating what others say. The repetition of sounds, phrases, or what others say is called *echolalia*. Repetitive behaviors can also be a result of sensory processing problems or sensory overload. Students may require a sensory break when they experience sensory overload, when you may see them flap their hands or rock, or they are constantly moving. A sensory break can be taken in the classroom as the student disengages from the activity and engages in a sensory activity. Some students may use a fidget tool, clay, sensory brushes, or sensory exercises that the occupational therapist recommends. Any of these would be specific to the individual student, appropriate for them, and outlined in their IEP. For most students, once a routine and expectation is established, they are able to do this on their own without direction from the teacher.

In your classroom, you may see your student with ASD become preoccupied or fixated on numbers, a certain discussion topic, or book. This fixation can be both good and not so good. It is good when the student with ASD is actively participating with other students, but not so good when they are unable to transition to a new topic or activity. The reality is that the student with ASD may never move past his or her fixation; however, you can use the fixation as a motivator or incentive to get the student to engage in other activities. For example, you can trade a non-preferred activity for a preferred activity. In a tenth-grade English class, you are studying poetry, but the student with ASD is fixated on reading non-fiction books. You can trade 20 minutes of reading poetry and working on a poetry activity for 10 minutes of uninterrupted time reading a preferred non-fiction book. As a teacher, you may be concerned about the student missing 10 minutes of classwork or time on task with the other students, but this is a fair trade to ensure that the student with ASD is able to engage with the curriculum at the appropriate time. While free choice is a strategy often used in the elementary grades, you can create structured free choice within your high school classroom that allows flexibility for students to take more ownership of the learning based on their interest. This can be beneficial for any student, especially those who disengage quickly.

Autism: Common classroom strategies:

1. Use language that is clear, simple, and concrete. Use as few words as possible.
   a. Example: Get up, go to your table group, and wait for directions.
   b. Not Recommended: Today, we are going to be

working in our table groups. In five minutes, we will move to those groups, and you will go to your table and wait for further directions.

2. Provide explicit social skills instruction several times per week.

   a. Example: During the 10-minute warm up at the start of class, you can teach a three-minute mini-lesson on social distance: the distance that one should stand or sit while having a conversation. The lesson should give the rationale and also leave time for the students to practice with one another. This is a great community builder. You can change the theme, based on the needs of the students in your class. You can also use video models for these interactions for students who require more specificity.

3. Use task analysis. Task analysis is focusing on the small discrete steps in a task or activity.

   a. Example: Teaching journal writing with illustrations

      i. Take out your journal.

      ii. Take out your pencil and colored pencils.

      iii. Close your eyes and think about your favorite summer activity.

      iv. Open your eyes.

      v. Write a paragraph about your favorite summer activity and why this is your favorite activity.

      vi. On the next page in your journal, draw a picture that is an illustration of the paragraph you just wrote.

      vii. Use your colored pencils to make it neat and nice.

      viii. Bring your journal to me when you are finished.

4. Give fewer choices.

   a. Example: Never leave assignments as an open decision for students with ASD; it is better to give choices. If students are required to choose a book, complete a book report, and present their report, then you should give the student with ASD two or three choices of how to present their report and how they can complete their report. "OK, Matt, I see you are reading a science-fiction book for your book report. You can either write your report by hand, or you can voice record yourself retelling the story and submit it to me. When you get ready to present your report, you can stand in front of the class, or you can have your parents video-record you presenting your report to them and we can play it for the class."

5. Avoid using sarcasm and idioms. Remember, students with ASD are often very literal; therefore, they do not understand or are unable to relate to the use of sarcasm or idioms.

   a. Example: "I need you to use your brains and your best thinking to answer this one."

   b. Not Recommended: "Put your thinking caps on."

   c. Not Recommended: A student is acting up and disrupting the classroom, and you respond, "James, thank you, for being such a *great* example to your classmates."

6. Use visuals or a timer to signal a transition or change is about to occur.

7. Address students with ASD directly. They may not always realize that an instruction is meant for them. Use their names when giving directions so they know that the direction is meant for them.

8. Never take anything personally. Sometimes, students with ASD can seem rude or abrupt, especially when they experience stress or anxiety.

   a. Example: The student is obsessed with sitting at a table by the window. On a particular day, you were grading papers before school at that table and the time got away from you. When the student enters, he pushes all of the papers and your materials to the floor. Recognize that the student was not doing this to be rude and disregard your work, but rather was fixated on sitting at his table, and your materials were in his way.

9. Embed technology into the classroom as much as possible, and encourage the student to use computer technology and other applications throughout the class, especially with challenging tasks or activities like writing or presenting in front of the group.

10. Use peer models often. The benefit of peer modeling has both an academic and social impact. Students with ASD struggle socially, and a typical peer model that exhibits strong social behaviors can support a student with ASD in replicating those behaviors. This is very good when teaching students presentation skills, where a student needs to learn proper eye contact or projecting his or her voice. It is also very good when teaching students about cooperative groups and how to conduct themselves in those groups. They can model taking turns in conversation, eye contact, and appropriate proximity (Hensley 2015).

Asperger's Syndrome

As noted before, in the most recent *DSM-5*, all categories of autism are now categorized under ASD. However, due to the reality of today's classroom, it is important for teachers to know that while Asperger's syndrome does not have its own separate category and diagnosis any longer, the characteristics are still the same.

Asperger's syndrome is considered to be on the higher end of the autism spectrum. Students who would have been categorized as having Asperger's syndrome typically do not have delays in language or cognitive development, while the other symptoms noted for students with ASD are the same for this group of students. Students on the higher end of the spectrum are those who are most likely included in the general education classroom. The students have very high cognitive skills in several areas, while often displaying a very extensive vocabulary. Some characteristics that may be different from other students with ASD are the robotic or repetitive speech and their fixation on themselves. They tend to discuss themselves rather than others, their conversations can often seem one-sided. As with other students with ASD, they often lack making eye contact or reciprocal conversation. The common classroom strategies are appropriate to use with any student with ASD. Students have considerable academic strengths and require different teaching strategies to help capitalize on those strengths (*OAR* 2015).

Asperger's Classroom Strategies

1. Time is essential. Students often need additional time to complete assignments. You should expect a level of competency regarding an assignment or task; however, you should be flexible with how much of the assignment or task is completed. It takes students more time to adjust and plan for change, transition, or to orientate themselves to the transition.
2. Avoid sudden changes to schedule or routines. If there is a need to change the routine, the student(s) should be made aware of the change and given explicit directions about what to do to adjust to the change.
   a. Example: We are going to have a fire drill today. The alarm will be loud. When the alarm goes off, we will have to go outside and stop what we are doing. You should stay with your peer buddy, Andy. When we get outside, we will have to wait for about 15 minutes before coming back inside.

3. Give praise often. Students with Asperger's need consistent and frequent praise. You should take time throughout the class to tell your student what he or she has done well and encourage them to keep it up. You should also praise his or her efforts for attempts that were made at various tasks or activities. You should be specific in what you are pleased with and why you are pleased.
   a. Example: "Daniel, I noticed that you were looking at Jason when you were working in groups today. This is good because eye contact is important when working with others."
   b. Example: "Daniel, I am very proud of the way you tried to keep up with taking notes during the lecture before you picked up a copy of the notes from my desk. Learning how to take notes will be an important skill for you when you go to college in a couple of years."
4. Use frequent check-ins. Students with Asperger's can become irritable and stressed with tasks that others view as simple. Embed check-in time throughout the class to monitor the student closely and proactively address any areas of potential problems.
   a. Example: You can plan to check-in with the student every 15 to 20 minutes throughout the class. If you do this, there will be at least three times in an hour-long class that a student has been monitored closely.

Please refer to the resource list below for more comprehensive information and strategies for working with students with ASD, including those formerly known as having Asperger's syndrome:

www.autismspeaks.org
www.researchautism.org

References

Organization for Autism Research. "6 Steps to Success for Asperger Syndrome." http://www.researchautism.org/educators/aspergersteps/index.asp.

"Autism Spectrum Disorder." *American Psychiatric Association.* 2013. http://www.dsm5.org/Documents/Autism%20Spectrum%20Disorder%20Fact%20Sheet.pdf.

National Institute of Mental Health. "Autism Spectrum Disorder." https://www.nimh.nih.gov/health/topics/autism-spectrum-disorders-asd/index.shtml.

"Autism Spectrum Disorders in Children and Teens." School Psychiatry Program and MADI Resource Center, Massachusetts General Hospital, 2010. http://www2.massgeneral.org/schoolpsychiatry/info_autism.asp.

Hensley, P. "22 Tips for Teaching Students with Autism Spectrum Disorders." *Teaching Community.* http://

teaching.monster.com/benefits/articles/8761-22-tips-for-teaching-students-with-autism-spectrum-disorders.

Autism Speaks. "What Is Autism?" https://www.autism speaks.org/what-autism.

Kupper, L. and McGahee-Kovac, M. *Helping Students Develop Their IEPs. Technical Assistance Guide*. 2nd ed. National Information Center for Children and Youth with Disabilities. January 2002.

Kupper, L. and McGahee-Kovac, M. *A Student's Guide to the IEP*. 2nd ed. National Information Center for Children and Youth with Disabilities, 2002.

McGahee-Kovac, M. *A Student's Guide to the IEP*. Washington, DC: National Dissemination Center for Children with Disabilities, reprinted in *LD Online*, 2002. http://www.ldonline.org/article/ A_Student's_Guide_to_the_IEP/5944.

Martin, J.E., Huber Marshall, L., Hughes, W.M., Jerman, P.A., and Maxson, L. *Choosing Educational Goals*, video and instructional material. Longmont, CO: Sopris West, Inc., 2000.

Martin, J.E., Van Dycke, J.L., Christensen, W.R., Greene, B.A., Gardner, J.E., and Lovett, D.L. "Increasing Student Participation in Their Transition IEP Meetings: Establishing the Self-Directed IEP as an Evidenced-Based Practice." *Exceptional Children* 72 (2006): 299-316.

Mason, C.Y., McGahee-Kovac, M., and Johnson, L. "How to Help Students Lead Their IEP Meetings." *Teaching Exceptional Children* 36, no. 3 (2004): 18-25.

Mason, C.Y., McGahee-Kovac, M., Johnson, L., and Stillerman, S. "Implementing Student-Led IEPs: Student Participation and Student and Teacher Reactions." *Career Development for Exceptional Individuals* 25, no. 2 (2002): 171-192.

Myers, A, Eiseman, L. "Student Led IEPs: Take the First Step." *Teaching Exceptional Children* 37, no. 4 (March/April 2005).

Technical Assistance Guide: Helping Students Develop Their IEPs. 2nd ed. National Information Center for Children and Youth with Disabilities, 2002

English Language Learners: Home-School Communication

During the launch of the school year, linguistically diverse families will experience a few additional obstacles as they navigate through the flurry of events. They get to know new schedules, listen to open house speeches, and receive written communication about conduct, schedules, and academics in a language that is not their own. Additionally, they must negotiate cultural factors related to school that may be different from what they have experienced as learners. The role of teachers, expectations for student behavior, approaches to teaching and learning, and assessment strategies may be different from what they consider customary.

Providing translation services is a strong start to developing effective communication between and school and home. In the initial registration process, schools commonly have an interview or a form, such as a home-language survey to identify which families need interpreters for meetings and translated information. A designated team of professionals—such as an English as a Second Language (ESL) teacher, classroom teacher, parent-outreach worker, and administrator—can create a list of essential documents and have them translated into commonly spoken home languages. These documents usually include student handbooks, report cards, progress reports, welcome letters, field trip information, curriculum outlines, extracurricular activities, and forms related to health and emergency procedures.

Documents like lunch menus, weekly teacher notes, homework messages, and other informal communications may not be considered "essential," but will benefit students and increase awareness when communicated with parents in a comprehensible language. If there is no bilingual outreach professional, these translations can be done by bilingual parents, qualified community volunteers, or by high school students who have demonstrated successful bilingual literacy skills. When families receive and understand a school's messages, they will be more likely to respond by returning signed forms and attending events that help them become connected to their children's academic environment.

Making a Personal Connection: Face-to-Face Meetings

Building a school community in which linguistically diverse parents and guardians feel welcome and wanted in their children's learning processes takes time and relies on consistent two-way communication. As important as it is for schools to speak about routines and send home information, it is of equal value to engage in conversations with families about the academic goals they have for their children, talents each child brings to school, and expectations of learning activities. Larry Ferlazzo explains, "Effective family engagement requires the school to develop a relationship-building process focused on listening," (2011, pp. 10–14). When linguistically diverse families share stories, opinions, and ideas, it allows teachers and staff to gain cultural insights beyond holidays, recipes, and folklore. Educators will gain a deeper understanding of belief systems, values, and linguistic factors that could affect children's academic success.

A Fourth-Grade Teacher's Home Visit

"When we arrived, Mrs. Luriana greeted us with hugs and kisses. We went up to the second-floor apartment. She explained that her parents owned and lived in the first-floor apartment and her brothers lived in the building across the street. When I called her "Mrs. Luriana," she laughed at my formality and told me to call her by her first name, Kaltrina. We sat on couches in the living room and she offered us Turkish coffee, which 10-year-old Lila made in a little copper pot over an open gas flame. Lila also served us her homemade yogurt. She told us one of her chores is to make the yogurt, because she is exceptionally good at it, and her mother confirmed this with a smile.

"We chatted about school, Mrs. Luriana's and Lila's struggles to learn English, what school was like in Albania, and foods they missed from their homeland. Mrs. Luriana told us about attending university classes in Albania to become a nurse and the story of how several of her family members fled the country because of violence in nearby Kosovo. She went on to explain how her Albanian-speaking parents have taught Lila and her older twin brothers how to read and write in Albanian. She also mentioned that one of her goals was to hire a bilingual tutor who could help Lila with reading and math, as her daughter seemed to struggle over the past few years.

"My visit provided me with invaluable insights on this mother's value of education, my student's role and responsibilities in the family, and how one family has struggled for a better life in a new world. What I experienced in this home profoundly affected my teaching in that I had made a personal connection to Lila's life. I just felt like I understood her better and could teach her in more meaningful ways."

Even though districts throughout the United States have embraced the practice of home visits, such as those involved in the research-based The Parent/ Teacher Home Visit Project, others may only encourage face-to-face meetings on the school's campus or in the teacher's classroom. Some families may also feel uncomfortable inviting school staff into their homes and choose to meet at another venue, such as a local restaurant or public library. It may be easier for elementary teachers to schedule a meeting time with each of their students' families, but middle and high school teachers will need help from guidance counselors, support staff, and ESL teachers.

Regardless of the venue, developing a partnership will rely on a friendly tone in which all parties are encouraged to share ideas and exchange opinions. When possible, teachers and staff can make this happen fluidly by pre-planning and working with interpreters who are familiar with the nuances of the home culture. These bilingual experts can help break down linguistic and cultural barriers as they explain and clarify differences or the subtleties in the following: social behavior and rules; gestures and body language; norms related to gender roles; the hierarchy of family structure; the role of the teacher versus the role of the student; and codes of school conduct. Not only will some associated factors be different, but they may even oppose and conflict with what is considered "normal" in standard American or Western schools.

Active Outreach

Sometimes parents and families need time to self-navigate before having a face-to-face meeting. One way a teacher can establish a gentle connection is simply by "being visible." This can be done during drop off, pick up, and at after-school activities. Since parents often get to know each other at these times, a teacher can help facilitate introductions and be introduced as well. This helps connect names with faces, and is an easy way to make an initial connection with minimal effort and without hiring an interpreter. Another way to initiate an in-person connection is to schedule "open gallery times" in which students can lead their parents to tour the classroom(s), see their desk/locker, and view portfolio work. The gallery tour can also be sent home through a student-created video or photo collage that can be posted on a teacher website, sent in an email, or printed and sent home. There are added benefits to having students involved in home-school connections such as the gallery tour: the child becomes the "expert" guide who uses the home language to communicate about the classroom and his or her work. This role gives students ownership of a mini-project and communicates a respectful and welcoming message about diversity and home culture.

It is not uncommon for linguistically diverse families to have low attendance at school events such as an open house, curriculum night, or social gatherings. When the goal is a respectful partnership, criticizing parents on how often they "show up" will hinder the process, while understanding and overcoming obstacles will help build the relationship. Low or no attendance may be due to a language barrier, limited means of transportation, scheduling with multiple job commitments, a lack of access to electronic communication, or conflicts with cultural or religious holidays and observations. Providing a bilingual invitation may not be enough to ensure successful attendance, and increased action on the school's part may be necessary. Outreach professionals and volunteers can gather parent input on best event days/times with a paper, phone, or electronic survey. A follow-up phone call or email that respectfully asks for their presence (done by an interpreter, if necessary) may inspire a parent to either make a schedule change or ask another family member to attend. If the child is presenting, teachers can mention this and offer a time span during which they can observe their child's involvement. If childcare is an issue, schools can hire babysitters or allow families to bring younger children. Posting signs inside and outside the school in visible, high-traffic locations is another subtle way to advertise events. Students can even make the signs to save teacher time and broaden ownership of responsibility.

Another way to initiate communication with linguistically diverse parents is to actively recruit or invite children to participate in an after-school program. There are a multitude of grant opportunities for extended-day or -year programs for culturally and linguistically diverse learners. Even if parents initially see it as free tutoring or childcare, an extended-day program can offer English learners an additional hour or two of practicing English, and a program can become a point of interest or lever for making face-to-face connections.

A Middle School Peer-Mentoring Program

"My colleague and I started a peer-mentor program on our K–8 campus when we received funding from a federal entitlement grant to provide extended-day/year support for English learners. First, we recruited bilingual students in grades six through eight to be mentors. Each mentor completed an application with teacher recommendations. Next, we had invitations for each English learner in elementary grades translated into five of the most commonly spoken languages. We stamped and mailed the invitations directly to families' homes. Our first year, the program consisted of five mentors and 10 English learners. Mentors attended training sessions with teacher facilitators to learn how to respectfully assist with homework help and teach new board games and physical activities, such as Simon Says, kickball, and tag.

"Each Tuesday afternoon, as parents came to sign their children out, we addressed parents by name and reported what activities their child successfully completed during the program: 'Hi, Mrs. Robles. Edwin finished his math homework and learned a new game with his mentor, Jacob.'

"Even if we didn't see parents at pick up, every child had either a parent or adult family member present for the end-of-the-program party and award ceremony. Parents and guardians showed how happy they were with the program by sending thank-you notes, and by spreading the word spread to the bilingual communities about free homework help and how kind the bilingual role models were. All of the mentors and mentees returned the second year and the program doubled in number. By the end of the third year, there were over 50 children involved in the program and a group of adult family members of the program partnered with teacher facilitators to form a school-based action and advocacy committee for cultural and linguistic diversity. We are proud of the growth of our after-school program and know that parent involvement started with a simple 'hello' and a few positive comments."

Curricular Connections to Home

When bilingualism and diversity are seen as assets, then pride, confidence, and cultural expertise replace English learners' feelings of shyness and isolation. Educators can validate and capitalize on the cultural and linguistic resources students bring to school by learning about and using students' experiences and knowledge in the classroom. Finding and using materials, texts, and approaches that reflect home languages and cultures shows respect for students' familial experiences, builds a positive sense of self, and develops all students' global understanding. Using multicultural literature is not a new practice, but the study, analysis, and authentication of cultural accuracy in literature has developed considerably over the past 20 years. Donna Norton's work discusses how "positive multicultural literature has been used effectively to help readers identify cultural heritages, understand sociological change, respect the values of minority groups, raise aspirations, and expand imagination and creativity." (2013, p. 2).

While many English learners may feel socially isolated or judged academically because of their developing English language skills, they can be drawn closer to content when they are seen as experts. Teachers can use what students know and can do to teach curriculum objectives, rather than creating an environment where students feel the need to hide or mask their home cultures and language skills. For example, when the sixth-grade social studies teacher designs units for studying world history, he designs a series of cooperative projects in which student groups examine the history, culture, and contributions of their heritage countries. The English learners become experts in that they, their parents, or grandparents have recently arrived from their home countries. They offer firsthand knowledge of climate, clothing, history, language, and traditions.

Sonia Nieto (2003) has warned educators, though, not to diminish expectations of culturally and linguistically diverse students, and that in using multicultural approaches to teaching, teachers must continue to "give all students of all backgrounds an equal chance to learn." (pp. 6–10). Likewise, expectations for and access to grade-level curriculum standards must be upheld for English learners regardless of proficiency level. The rigor of the twenty-first-century curricula remains, but the materials for and methods of delivery need to connect to the lives, linguistic abilities, and what students know about the world. Including students in projects that build home-school connections can create a highway of information between families and the classroom. Engaging in project-based activities, such as those listed below, can support English learners in the general education classroom and engage families of all learners in teaching and learning.

- Create a home-school journal to make cultural connections to characters, settings, informational themes, and geographical locations.
- Allow students to interview family members to authenticate historical data or styles of music, art, architecture, clothing, and food preparation.
- Invite parents on community field trips (e.g., to the library to get a library card).

- Send a recording device home to have students capture a folktale or famous family story told by an elder family member in the home language. Then have students retell or summarize in English and illustrate stories.
- Invite parents/family members to the classroom to share an artifact of the home culture or language, or demonstrate a skill like kneading dough, knitting, weaving, or writing script or characters. Use these experiences for creating writing prompts.
- Guide students to conduct a survey of heritage languages in the school and/or community and analyze if and how it has changed over the past decade.
- Ask what home city or country families come from, and have students use the names/locations for writing graphing or distance word problems.
- Use statistics related to home culture demographics or population shifts.
- Lead (high school) students in an inquiry-based study to authenticate validity of themes or stereotypes of cultures in fiction, non-fiction, current events, and in the media.

References

Breiseth, L., Lafond, S., and Robertson, K. ¡Colorín Colorado! A Guide for Engaging ELL Families: Twenty Strategies for School Leaders. Washington, D.C.: AFT and the US Department of Education's Office of Special Education Programs, 2011. Retrieved on June 6, 2015. http://www.colorincolorado.org/pdfs/guides/En gaging-ELL-Families.pdf.

Castelluccio, J. "To Build Better Relationships, Bentley School Teachers Visit Their Students at Home." Salem Evening News, March 4, 2015. Retrieved June 6, 2015, from: http://www.salemnews.com/news/local_news/to-build-better-relationships-bentley-school-teachers-visit-their-students/article_fa120ed2-f969-5dc2-ba12-73090ba683cd.html.

Ferlazzo, L. "Involvement or Engagement?" Educational Leadership, 68, no. 8 (May 2011): 10–14.

Ferlazzo, L. and Hammond, L.A. Building Parent Engagement in Schools. Santa Barbara, CA: Linworth, 2009.

Hall, E.T. Beyond Culture. New York: Anchor Books-Random House, Inc., 1989.

Mathis, W. Research-Based Options for Education Policymaking, English Language Learners and Parental Involvement. Boulder, CO: National Education Policy Center, 2013. Retrieved August 6, 2015. http://great lakescenter.org/docs/Policy_Briefs/Research-Based-Op tions/07-Mathis-ParentalInvolvement.pdf

Nieto, S. "Profoundly Multicultural Questions." Educational Leadership 60, no. 4 (December 2002–January 2003): 6–10.

Norton, D.E. *Multicultural Children's Literature: Through the Eyes of Many Children*. Boston: Pearson, 2013.

Parent-Teacher Home Visits. http://www.pthvp.org/.

"Seven Steps for Building an Engaged Community." Toronto, Ontario. Retrieved June 6, 2015. People for Education. http://www.peopleforeducation.ca/how-does-education-work/parent-and-school-council-resources/training-and-resources/7-steps-for-building-an-engaged-community/.

10

Co-Teaching: Developing High-Performing Teams

Objectives for the Chapter

After reading the chapter the reader will be able to:

a. identify and describe each of the models of co-teaching

b. identify the strengths and challenges of each co-teaching model

c. list the observable behaviors that identify successful co-teaching

d. explain how co-teaching brings added value to the classroom

e. develop a plan with a co-teacher for supporting partnership and professional growth as educators in their use of data, their instruction, and their impact

f. develop a year-long plan and individual weekly lesson plans for co-teaching that select and use each teacher's capacity effectively, and that select models and instructional activities that support students' needs

g. develop a lesson plan with clear objectives for learning

h. explain the administrative support needed for co-teaching to the principal

i. develop a plan with a paraprofessional for working together for the year

What Is Co-Teaching?

Co-teaching has evolved since its origin as a part of a progressive movement in education in the 1960s. In the 1970s, the model was adopted to include a special educator in a general education class to provide education to all students "in the least-restrictive environment." The co-teaching model replaced the "pull-out" model for special education students to create a more inclusive learning environment and to provide equal access to the curriculum for all students, as required by the Individuals with Disabilities Education Improvement Act of 2004. The Education Reform Movement then increased pressure on schools and teachers to improve student achievement. Recently, as the student population has become more diverse, the co-teaching model has been further expanded to include English language teachers and speech pathologists, gifted and talented specialists, and multiple paraprofessionals.

Essentially, **co-teaching refers to two educators who share equally in the planning, instruction, assessment of, and accountability for a class with diverse populations.** Chapman and Hyatt, in their 2011 book *Critical Conversations in Co-Teaching: A Problem-Solving Approach*, describe it as

> an effective, evidence-based instructional strategy in which two or more caring professionals share responsibility for a group of students and work collaboratively to add instructional value to enhance their efforts (Chapman and Hyatt 2011, p. 8).

Co-teaching can provide many positive changes to the shared general education classroom, including (1) decreased student-teacher ratios and more

467

opportunities for students to interact with teachers, (2) increased cooperative group work and more chances for students to interact with one another, (3) more authentic applications of students' learning, and (4) an increased use of research-based practices, including standards-based curriculum design that uses essential questions and big ideas, differentiated instruction, and direct instruction in learning strategies (Murawski and Goodwin 2014, p. 292). In addition, co-teaching often supports school and district initiatives that may include response to intervention (RtI), multiple tiered systems of support (MTSS), and inclusion, higher expectations for all students, data-based decision-making (DBDM), flexible grouping, and differentiated instruction (DI).

In addition, when a co-teaching team is effective and functions well, the collaborative relationship adds value beyond simply having two teachers present in one room. Their synergistic partnership can enrich the classroom and the whole school.

This chapter provides a step-by-step process that will support two educational professionals as they become a value-added team. Planning documents provide guidance for new and established teams from the first meeting—when the two teachers establish their partnership—to their weekly planning sessions as they address the ongoing development of their partnership (Chapman and Hyatt 2011).

Research Base for Cooperative Teaching (Co-Teaching)

Research on the effectiveness of co-teaching has been primarily qualitative and anecdotal, though a meta-analysis found that it resulted in moderately positive effects; however, the results were limited to the narrative descriptions in qualitative studies and included very few quantitative studies (Swanson 2001, pp. 258–259). Quantitative research has been complicated by the variations in co-teaching components. Jennings describes the difficulty of getting clear results: "The criteria for effective teaching teams are not discrete and easily identifiable; in fact, they are intertwined and often as hard to untangle as the backlash on a fishing reel" (Jennings 2007, p. 45). Successful teams may attain identical goals using different methods, and a successful technique may not be as effective when it is used in a different group (Jennings 2007).

Students in co-taught classrooms often develop more positive attitudes about themselves and their academic and social skills.

Yet, Jennings concludes, based upon a review of quantitative research on student achievement, generally if the appropriate level of supports and services are provided, students' achievement as well as their attitudes improve.

The qualitative research studies have found that students in co-taught classrooms often develop more positive attitudes about themselves and their academic and social skills because students who were formerly educated in separate classrooms worked instead in a general classroom along with their peers. Because the ratio of teachers to students is increased with the co-teaching, students have more opportunities for interaction with teachers and with their peers in smaller groups. Also, differentiated instruction and flexible grouping techniques are easier to support with two educators in the room.

Many co-teachers have reported in qualitative studies that the co-teaching partnership has had a positive impact on their experience of teaching. They say that co-teaching has given them an opportunity for professional growth and increased engagement because they are sharing their teaching with another professional (Villa, Thousand, and Nevin 2013, p. 18).

Co-teaching proponent Marilyn Friend sees the potential of co-teaching as an intervention that can address the multiple needs of a diverse classroom that includes at-risk students. She says,

> Most students with disabilities or other special needs can meet the high standards being set in today's schools, but professionals have to find ways to tap their potential. Co-teaching is one way to do this while bringing out the best in teachers and providing them with ongoing collaborative support as they meet the many challenges of contemporary public education (Friend 2007, p. 51).

The development of the co-teaching team requires ongoing support from administration as co-teachers expand their individual and team-based repertoire and expertise. This is achieved by sharing their respective expertise and actively seeking out research-based techniques that support their diverse student population.

One research-based teaching technique that is often a major part of the co-taught classroom is co-operative learning. This teaching technique has hard data to support its use if it is carefully planned, implemented, and assessed, as described in *Inclusion Strategies That Work!* (See the section on effective group work found in Chapter 3 of this book.)

Research about cooperative learning affirm[s] that it confers both social and academic advantages (Jenkins, Antil, Wayne, and Vadasy 2003; Johnson and Johnson 1975; Kagan 1994; and Slavin 1990). Socially, positive interactions increase as students work collaboratively toward a common goal. Academically, students are willing to spend more time learning from each other rather than from the teacher, resulting in better products with often challenging curricula. ... Team skills, increased self-esteem, improved peer interaction, and higher task completion with learning assignments are some of the benefits that are yielded when structured cooperative groups heterogeneously work together in classrooms. Overall, cooperation is a functional skill for educators and peers in inclusive classrooms to repeatedly foster and model (Karten 2010, p. 17).

In addition to cooperative learning, other research-based techniques, including response to intervention, Universal Design for Learning, and differentiated instruction can have a positive impact on student achievement in the co-taught classroom (Beattie, Jordan, and Algozzine 2006; Damasio 2003; Karten 2007; LeDoux 2002; McNary, Glasgow, and Hicks 2005; and Sousa 2007).

Despite the fact that co-teaching has existed for more than 50 years, its purposes have changed many times. Because of the changes, often the required components that make up co-teaching differ from state to state and from school to school. Because of the confusion about precisely what makes up a co-teaching team, researchers consider the study of co-teaching and its impact on student learning to be in the formative stage.

Many quantitative studies have results that cannot be generalized because of the varied circumstances of co-teaching teams. In Murawski's article, "Inclusive Schools and the Co-Teaching Conundrum," she attributes the conundrum to three C's: (1) confusion in precisely what makes up co-teaching, (2) contradictions in the research because an unclear definition of the components of co-teaching, and (3) "cautious optimism" based on the clearly positive impact of effective co-teachers (Murawski and Goodwin 2014, p. 293).

Clear quantitative data is rare because researchers are challenged in trying to compare co-teaching results when critically important elements of co-teaching may not be present in all classes. The vari-

The critical factor for co-teaching is the professional partnership and the teachers' commitment to the team's ongoing development.

ations include: ages of students, rigor of curriculum, differences in the number of days the teachers work together in the classroom, the time that they have to co-plan, school culture and climate, professional development availability, instructional practices of each co-teacher, and administrative support. Zigmond and colleagues say

co-teaching may be a service, but it is not a "treatment" that can be imposed with fidelity on an experimental group and withheld with equal fidelity from a control group (Zigmond and Magiera 2013, p. 116).

To improve student achievement, researchers recommend that the co-teachers focus on the development of the co-teaching partnership and contend that the co-teaching team can provide added value and increased student achievement when that team becomes a high-performing team that uses a variety of research-based teaching techniques, collaborates to plan the curriculum and lessons carefully, sets clear goals and learning objectives for all students, and uses data to chart the progress of all students (Chapman and Hyatt 2011). See Chapters 1 and 6 for information on effective planning and Chapters 4, 5, and 11 for information on effective assessment and the analysis of assessment data.

What Co-Teaching Is Not

When the role of the second educator or paraprofessional is limited to that of an untrained assistant or volunteer, this is not a collaborative teaching partnership. Duties that include duplicating materials, correcting objective exams, or other jobs that do not require training are not included as appropriate responsibilities in the true co-teaching relationship. In addition, if the second person provides educational services exclusively to one student—for example, a special educator who serves as a tutor for a specific student or a behavior specialist who observes specific students—this is also not co-teaching.

The second professional must be a partner in teaching the entire class. Thus, co-teaching requires equal participation of two educators whose partnership and shared leadership result in providing a more effective model as they both plan, instruct, and monitor the progress of all students than either could have accomplished alone. Again, the critical factor for co-teaching is the professional partnership and the teachers' commitment to the team's ongoing development.

A Value-Added Partnership

Chapman and Hyatt call this synergistic partnership a *value-added* relationship "that can serve as a means to better meet the increasing demands on schools to improve student achievement" (Chapman and Hyatt 2011, p. 8). To achieve this goal, the partners need to work to improve each of the essential components of the co-teaching partnership. Protocols and checklists for continual improvement are provided in this chapter. In addition, to become a high-performing team, the co-teachers need to share equally in making ongoing decisions about the classroom, the students, the models, assessments, and instructional strategies, and they need to work on what is sometimes called *distributed leadership* throughout their work together.

Essential Elements for Co-Teaching[1]

Many factors have an impact on the co-teaching team's success. The relationship between the teachers, the values of the entire school, administrative support for this intervention, and a classroom climate that supports inclusion are necessary for sustained success within the classroom. The essential elements include the following 10 qualities:

The Partnership of the Co-Teaching Teams

1. **Collaborative relationship**: The co-teachers have an open, collaborative relationship and share decision-making.
2. **Expertise of co-teachers**: Each teacher brings different areas of expertise: content, standards, differentiating instruction, modification, scaffolding, monitoring student progress, and teaching techniques.
3. **The partnership has equity**: Both teachers share in the planning, assessment, and instruction of the class.
4. **The partnership has a plan to resolve conflict:** They have set norms for their behavior toward one another and have a process for solving problems and conflicts within the classroom and between themselves.
5. **Time** is allocated for planning and collaboration.

> *Each teacher brings different areas of expertise: content, standards, differentiating instruction, modification, scaffolding, monitoring student progress, and teaching techniques.*

The Co-Taught Classroom

6. **The classroom climate supports co-teaching practices**, including flexible grouping, differentiating instruction, and supporting the achievement of all students.
7. **The classroom is heterogeneous**: No more than 30 percent[2] target students are clustered in the class.
8. **The classroom has appropriate space and materials**: These are provided for flexible grouping and re-grouping during class and for differentiating instructions to address the needs of all students. Space is provided so that co-teaching models can be varied and based on the needs of the students.
9. **The co-teaching models are varied** to support student needs. Whole-class and group models are selected to provide the best learning environment for students.

The Whole-School Climate

10. **The whole-school climate supports co-teaching, inclusion, and teaching all students**. Ongoing professional development is provided for co-teachers with the expectation that the team will evolve over time (Beninghof 2012; Chapman and Hyatt 2011; and Perez 2012). The team works in a school that supports co-teaching as an effective practice and intervention; is committed to educating all students to high standards; and supports inclusion with time, materials, and professional development.

Table 10.1 describes what each element looks like in the classroom and the consequences to the classroom, to students, and to the co-teachers if this element is missing.

Each component of the essential elements of co-teaching is supported in a step-by-step process in the "Planning for Co-Teaching" section found later in this chapter.

The Three Major Models of Co-Teaching

In the classroom, co-teaching generally follows four different models, based on how the classroom is grouped and the differential functions of the second teacher. Effective co-teaching teams will vary their use of the following models, based on the needs of their students.

---

1   These essential elements are a synthesis of the work of Beninghof (2012); Chapman and Hyatt (2011); Perez (2012); Villa, Thousand, and Nevin (2013); Murawski and Goodwin (2014); and Taylor (2008).

2   This percentage is a recommendation that is often given by experts in the field, but it is not based on specific research.

The Supportive Model (Whole-Group, Unequal Partners) is used when the first teacher delivers the direct instruction and the second teacher moves throughout the class to provide individual support for students when needed. This model requires the least amount of planning or collaboration.

In the **Parallel Model (Small Group)**, both teachers work with separate smaller groups of students within the classroom. The teachers may swap groups. At times, the general education teacher teaches content and the special education or specialist teaches techniques for learning. Also, each teacher may teach the same lesson but to different groups which may be divided by readiness, interest, or learning style. This model requires collaboration and careful planning.

Complementary or the **Side-by-Side Co-Teaching (Whole-Group Equitable Partners)** makes use of the expertise of each educator. The general education teacher provides knowledge of the content and

Table 10.1 Essential Co-Teaching Elements and Consequences When Absent

Essential Element	Co-Teaching Is Present	Consequences to Co-Teachers Co-Teaching Is Absent	Consequences to Students Co-Teaching Is Absent
The Partnership: Collaborative Relationship	Co-teachers spend time together planning, sharing responsibilities, and reflecting on their practice. The "interdependence" of the co-teachers is recognized.	Teachers do not meet, and the specialist plays a limited role and may be seen as having limited useful expertise.	The specialist can be seen as an unimportant part of the classroom with his or her support limited to a few students. Support by this specialist can be seen negatively as remediation instead of teaching. General education students may not want to work with this educator.
The Partnership: Expertise of Co-Teachers	The content expertise and the instructional expertise of each teacher is fully used to teach all students.	One teacher dominates; the second teacher has a diminished role in the class, and her expertise may be underutilized.	The specialist can be seen as an unimportant part of the classroom with his or her support limited to a few students. Support by this specialist can be seen negatively as remediation instead of teaching. By not including the special education teacher's expertise, the classroom may lack differentiation, modification, and scaffolding, and may depend on whole-class teaching.
The Partnership: Has Parity	The co-teachers are equal in the relationship as they make decisions and in the classroom as they teach.	The general education teacher may dominate and the special education teacher may only assist his or her targeted students.	The specialist can be seen as an unimportant part of the classroom with his or her support limited to a few students. Support by this specialist can be seen negatively as remediation instead of teaching. General education students may not want to work with this educator.
The Partnership: Has a Plan to Resolve Conflict	As the two teachers try to merge their teaching styles, beliefs, processes, and procedures, they may encounter differences. As they begin their partnership, they need to plan for how they will make decisions when they do not agree.	One teacher's style may dominate, and the second teacher would have no voice in decisions.	Students will see that one teacher is in control of the class, and the co-teacher's status in the class will be diminished.
Time for Collaboration Is Provided	The expertise of both teachers is provided to all students because they can plan and work on improving their partnership.	The general education teacher plans the class, and the special education teacher can provide support only when the opportunity arises from a student question, for example.	As a result of the special education teacher being unable to plan, these services become ad hoc, and because they are not thoroughly planned as part of the goals of the classroom, they can be superficial. *continued on next page*

Essential Element	Co-Teaching Is Present	Consequences to Co-Teachers Co-Teaching Is Absent	Consequences to Students Co-Teaching Is Absent
The Classroom Climate Supports Co-Teaching Practices	The classroom provides a variety of ways for all students to learn from two educators who are responsible for all students' success. Individual differences among students are valued and supported in a variety of ways, from re-teaching to having greater challenges. Flexible grouping supports the multiple purposes of small groups, which may include readiness, interest, learning preferences, and needs.	Whole-class teaching may predominate. or When students are grouped, they are always separated into general education and target students.	The needs of the students, if met, are not carefully planned and only occur ad hoc. or The class functions as two separate classes.
The Classroom Is Heterogeneous	General education and target students work in whole-class and flexible groups to achieve academic and social-emotional goals set for the entire class.	If the target population exceeds 30 percent, academic and behavioral role models are missing and the class becomes remedial.	Without role models in homogeneous groups or classrooms, both academic and behavioral expectations may be lowered because of the missing positive role models.
The Classroom Has Appropriate Space and Materials	The class has flexible groups, uses stations or centers for learning, and learning is differentiated to ensure the success of all learners. Materials are provided to support these tasks.	The whole-class model may predominate.	If space and materials are limited, the whole-class model may be used most of the time, which limits opportunities to differentiate instruction and support the needs of all students.
The Classroom: The Co-Teaching Models Are Varied	Students work as a whole class and are flexibly grouped for different purposes based on their readiness, interests, learning preferences, and needs.	The class is divided into general education students and special education (or target) students, and it functions as if the teachers were teaching in separate classes.	When one model is used most of the time or groups are always separated into general education and the target students, the class becomes two classes—a general education class and special education class—without the positive impact that double the expertise can provide to all students.
The Whole-School Climate Supports Co-Teaching, Inclusion and Teaching All Students.	All educators recognize their responsibility for all students. Classroom collaboration between the general education teachers and specialists is seen as a necessary part of helping all students succeed. Professional development for teaching all students is provided to the whole school and to the co-teachers.	Specialists are seen as separate from general educators, with expertise only in their specialty and for use only with their target population. Dysfunctional teams may use the special education teacher as an aide or volunteer, may function as two separate classrooms, or may leave the specialist to provide only ad hoc support.	The specialist is seen as having expertise limited only to target, at-risk, special education students. His or her understanding of teaching techniques or of alternative ways of teaching is not fully used in the general education classroom to teach all students. Without the expectation for growth, unsuccessful or ineffective teams may continue year after year without addressing problems. As a result, the students do not have the value-added expertise of two educators working synergistically.

of the literacies necessary in the content area. This educator may be more responsible for setting mastery objectives while the specialist may provide the supports necessary to help all students attain mastery. Generally, the specialist provides the unique support based on his or her expertise, and he or she may scaffold the learning for some or all students. He or she may model the use of graphic organizers, demonstrate note-taking techniques, or ask questions that he or she can see some students have.

In the high-performing team model, **Team Co-Teaching/The Duet Model (Whole-Class and Small Groups and Equitable Partners)**, teachers are both equal in expertise and have developed their capacities in multiple interventions that may include differentiating instruction, Response to Intervention strategies, Universal Design for Learning, and ongoing data analysis. Both educators teach content and supportive techniques and are equal partners in the planning, delivery, and assessment of the course, as well as for supporting their professional growth as a team. The last category, with shared leadership, is a value-added model based on the work of Carrie Chapman and Cate Hart Hyatt in their 2011 book, *Critical Conversations in Co-Teaching: A Problem-Solving Approach.*

The Parity of Each Co-Teacher

A concern that applies to all models that must be addressed throughout each aspect of the co-teaching relationship is parity. According to Sonya Keieman Kunkel, **parity is "the ability to show your students that both adults are in charge of the classroom"** (Kunkel 2012, p. 12). This balanced, equal relationship needs to be clearly established if the team is to be successful (Kunkel 2012). Parity needs to be addressed in four areas:

1. **Physical parity**, the physical space that each teacher uses or does not use, can represent equal or differential power.
2. **Logistical parity** is based on the tasks assumed by each teacher.
3. **Instructional parity** is based on whether one teacher always leads or follows.
4. **Disciplinary parity** is based on who manages behavioral problems.

Without parity, one co-teacher can be seen as unimportant or as playing a subordinate role, with the result that his or her impact on student's learning can be diminished. Students may feel embarrassed to work with the "subordinate" or "remedial" teacher or may not see this teacher as having the knowledge necessary to assist.

Table 10.2 Parity Types When Present and Absent

Parity Type	Demonstrates Equality	Lacks Parity
Physical	Both teachers stand at the front of the class and work individually with students.	One teacher stands at the front of the class while the second teacher works only with individual student questions and stands at the side or back of the class.
Logistical	Both teachers are involved in all classroom tasks, although one teacher may be the content teacher and the other the expert in teaching techniques.	One teacher gives grades while the other corrects only multiple-choice tests or duplicates papers.
Instructional	Both teachers instruct, sometimes at the same time and alternate at others.	One teacher provides direct instruction and directions; the other teacher supports the first teacher's lesson with individual students.
Disciplinary	Both teachers handle classroom problems and share this responsibility equally; both meet with parents when conferences are scheduled.	One teacher makes classroom decisions about behavior and handles them on his or her own.

Co-Taught Classroom Essentials

Although elementary, middle school, and high school classrooms will vary, the following list by Karten, in *Inclusion Strategies That Work!*, captures what a co-taught class might look like:

- Both teachers are in the classroom, with one teaching (the general educator or special educator) and the other one assisting by verbally or physically supporting instruction.
- Teachers can also be teaching separate groups within the same classroom or simultaneously rotating among them to support learners while providing clarification to students completing individual assignments.
- Both teachers are responsible for the planning, instruction, and assessment for all students.
- Students work independently and cooperatively under teachers' auspices and modeling at their learning level.
- Centers with ongoing projects are available to students.
- Teachers keep anecdotal records and document modifications and accommodations. Nothing elaborate is necessary; even a composition book with the dates entered by hand works.
- Classroom reflection exists for students, teachers, and administration.
- Co-teachers communicate with next year's teachers to bridge learning and behavioral objectives (Karten 2010, p. 148).

The Models of Co-Teaching: Strengths and Challenges

The following models of classroom organization describe (1) the grouping (whole-class or small group) and (2) the function of the co-teachers. Each co-teaching model described below can provide support to students. Some models require time for co-planning, others may work without planning if time is not allocated to the team. The strengths and challenges for each model are described within each section. Note: *GET* represents the general education teacher and *ST* represents the specialist teacher. Often the specialist is the special education teacher, but it could also be a literacy specialist, a speech and language specialist, or an English language specialist. In the case of interdisciplinary teachers, both are general education teachers because each teaches English, mathematics, history/social studies, foreign/world language, or science.

Model I: Supportive Co-Teaching (Whole Group) Strengths and Challenges

Essentially, Model I Supportive Co-Teaching is focused on variations on the whole-class model, with a general educator leading the class and with the specialist supporting the GET. The first three variations describe the roles of each teacher, with the GET listed first and the ST listed second. In the last variation, the specialist adapts his or her curriculum for the target group.

- one teaches/one observes
- one teaches/one drifts
- one teaches/one assists or supports
- adapting curriculum

These four whole-class models do not require extensive collaborative planning, but may not always use the full capacity of the second educator. The strengths and challenges of each of the Model I variations are listed below each model.

Model I: Supportive Co-Teaching (Whole Group One Teaches/One Observes)

Strengths

- This supportive model is good to use as the co-teachers begin a new co-teaching relationship to allow a new co-teacher to observe the classroom of his or her colleague.
- This model can be used *occasionally* to focus on a specific aspect of the class or a specific student with a planned sharing of observations to consider possible instructional interventions or modifications. Those interested in learning more about effective peer observation may wish to read the peer observation section found in Chapter 11 of this book.
- Co-teachers can alternate the teaching and observing roles to gain better understandings of the class and its individual students as well as of the teaching style, strengths, and expertise of their co-teacher.
- Co-teachers can use this model to observe one another and provide valuable feedback on their teaching. Those who wish to learn more about peer observation should read the peer observation section in Chapter 11.

Challenges

- Unless these two leading and supporting roles are reversed, the ST can become more of an instructional aide.

- If this method is used because of a lack of co-planning time, the ST may not clearly understand the goals of the class.
- This model may become an ad hoc partnership that lacks long-term shared goals and, as a result, lacks depth.
- The skills of the second teacher may not be fully used throughout the class and may be limited to his or her target students or students who ask for assistance.

Model I: Supportive Co-Teaching (Whole Group One Teaches/One Drifts

Strengths

- This whole-class model is useful as the co-teachers are establishing a co-teaching relationship and the new co-teacher observes the classroom.
- This model can be used *occasionally* when one teacher is directly teaching and the other gathers data and assists students throughout the lesson.
- Co-teachers can alternate the teaching/drifting role to signal shared responsibility for teaching all students.

Challenges

- If this model is the favored model for co-teaching, it can indicate that direct teaching is the primary instructional method.
- Unless these two leading and supporting roles are reversed, the ST can become more of an instructional aide.
- If this method is used because of a lack of co-planning time, the ST may not clearly understand the goals of the class.
- This model may become an ad hoc partnership that lacks long-term shared goals and lacks depth.
- The skills of the second teacher may not be fully used throughout the class and may be limited to his or her target students or only students who ask for help.

Model I: Supportive Co-Teaching (Whole Group One Teaches/One Assists or Supports)

Strengths

- This model is often the "default" model when the team does not have time to co-plan.
- This model is typical when a content teacher teaches and plans in isolation and a special educator supports students at times without taking part in planning or goal-setting.

- This can be a useful model when the co-teachers have limited planning time or the specialist does not work in the classroom every day.
- After the direct teaching is concluded, both teachers assist and support students.
- The assisting teacher can provide the teacher who is teaching with misconceptions or questions that students may have.
- The assisting teacher can take notes or fill in a graphic organizer on the overhead while the other teacher teaches the lesson.

Challenges

- This model may become an ad hoc partnership that lacks long-term shared goals and lacks depth unless the team has time to collaborate.
- The assisting teacher can have a relatively passive role.
- The skills of the second teacher may not be fully used throughout the class and may be limited to his or her target students or those who ask for help.

Model I: Supportive Co-Teaching (Whole-Group Adapting Curriculum Approach)

Strengths

- One teacher takes the lead and the other makes modifications as the occasion presents itself, perhaps because of a student's look of confusion or a specific question.
- Co-teachers may develop a tool kit that can be used to support needed adaptations or modifications for specific students, which may include sticky notes, index cards, manipulatives, highlighters, a calculator, and a spell-checker, for example.
- The model requires very little planning time.
- Roles are clearly defined, with a lead teacher doing the majority of the teaching and a support teacher providing assistance only.
- The method provides accommodations, and the specialist is focused on his or her area of expertise.

Challenges

- This model may become an ad hoc partnership that lacks long-term shared goals and lacks depth.
- The skills of the second teacher may not be fully used throughout the class and may be limited to his or her target students.

Model II: Parallel Co-Teaching (Small-Group Instruction)

In the Parallel Co-Teaching Model, both educators teach students at the same time. The activity within the groups distinguish each model.

1. In **Station Teaching**, student groups move through two or more learning stations—two of which are taught or facilitated by one of the co-teachers. If the classroom has more than two stations, students will be able to navigate the independent tasks without teacher direction either because the station is part of a familiar classroom routine of the task is clearly explained by the instructions at the station. For example, the station could be a computer or group of computers and the student group could work through a program on which they have had prior experience, or the station could be a video that the student group views and takes notes about its content.

2. In the **Parallel Teaching** model, each educator teaches a different lesson to a group.

3. In **Alternative Co-Teaching** one group is smaller and is generally taught by the specialist, whose lesson is focused on specific targeted students.

4. **Skill Group Co-Teaching** is generally grouped for small-group re-teaching of skills.

5. The **Learning-Styles Approach** may divide the class according to students' learning preferences (auditory, visual, and kinesthetic) or to provide reinforcement for students who need further visual, auditory, or kinesthetic experiences to learn thoroughly. Groups may also be divided by the differentiated instruction categories: interest, process, or product as well as by readiness and interest, as discussed in the Chapter 6.

Model II: Parallel Co-Teaching (Small-Group Instruction Station Teaching)

Strengths

- Learning centers are used to organize the classroom. Students are divided into groups of from two to six and they rotate through the centers, working at times with a teacher teaching or facilitating, or working independently and receiving support when needed. For example, a third-grade class might be working on writing a summary based on informational text. At one station, a co-teacher could read a short passage that students collaboratively summarize. A second co-teacher might work on a longer passage, and teams of two students might summarize a different paragraph and share their summary with the rest of the group. A third station might have an informational passage already on a bank of two computers, and students, working in pairs, summarize the paragraph. Finally, a group of students might read an example summary and evaluate it using a rubric.

- Each center focuses on a skill or on content that may have multiple levels or alternatives for response for differentiation among the groups.

- Each center can provide differentiated and focused learning for support, reinforcement, or acceleration.

- This model can provide access for all students to curriculum through differentiation of the centers.

- The stations must be carefully planned.

- The stations can be self-directed by individual or groups of two students working together. If all of the stations are self-directed, teachers may circulate to provide support when it is needed. Thus, teachers' roles vary in station teaching and each teacher may facilitate a specific center, provide requested support, or circulate among all groups.

Challenges

- If centers are provided for at-risk students only, centers may appear to be remedial and not a kind of differentiation for all students.

- This method is time-intensive in the preparation of materials and the planning for the needs of all students.

- If these centers are developed separately, one for general education students and the other for special education students, the co-teachers may be teaching two classes, but in one classroom. As a result, there may not be a real partnership between the teachers if the groups are not co-planned and are always divided into general education and special education students.

Model II: Parallel Co-Teaching (Small-Group Instruction Each Teacher Teaches a Group)

Strengths

- The class is carefully divided into two groups either heterogeneously or homogeneously based on need—for example, in a middle school mathematics class, students who are having difficulty with ratios might be in one group while another group may be focusing on solving word problems about ratios.

- The same collaboratively planned content is taught by each co-teacher, possibly with each lesson taught on different levels of difficulty.

- The small groups provide for more student and teacher interaction.
- The model requires equal expertise if both co-teachers are teaching the same material.

Challenges

- This model may actually function as two separate classrooms held in one class if the groupings are always based on readiness or level of challenge or if general education and special education students are always in separate groups.
- There may not be a real partnership between the teachers if they plan separately for their special education or general education students all of the time.

Model II: Parallel Co-Teaching (Small-Group Instruction): Alternative Co-Teaching

Strengths

- Generally, the class is divided into a larger and a smaller group, with the smaller group generally needing more intensive support. For example, a small group of students may need re-teaching. The larger group may be going more deeply into a concept.
- For example, in a middle school English class that just finished writing an argument, the students who had difficulty with their conclusions might be in a small group looking at samples of good conclusions and working collaboratively to improve their own essays. Meanwhile, the larger class might use the class rubric to assess sample papers and then to work collaboratively to improve their essays.
- Both teachers may work with each group alternatively, in which case each educator teaches his or her unique content or each teacher may stay with one group.
- The smaller group participants change for different purposes including pre-teaching, re-teaching, and enrichment.
- This model is generally used for a short period of time.

Challenges

- This model may actually function as two separate classrooms held in one class if the groupings are always based on readiness or level of challenge, or if all of the students are divided into general education and special education students.
- There may not be a real partnership between the teachers if this type of lesson is planned separately.

Model II: Parallel Co-Teaching (Small-Group Instruction): Skill Group Teaching

Strengths

- Students are grouped according to their need in specific skills and could be taught by either co-teacher.
- At times, this model is based on a two- or three-day co-teaching model when the ST reteaches skills not yet mastered. In this case, the roles of the co-teachers would be unbalanced because the specialist would work with only part of the class.
- This method saves time, especially if specialist is not in the classroom daily.
- Multiple ability levels are addressed by dividing the groups into skills.

Challenges

- This model may actually function as two separate classrooms held in one class if the groupings are always based on readiness or level of challenge.
- There may not be a real partnership between the teachers if the specialist is only planning for the target students.

Model II: Parallel Co-Teaching (Small-Group Instruction): Learning-Styles Approach

Strengths

- Both teachers support effective learning by providing re-teaching using multiple modalities—for example, hands-on or visual re-teaching.
- All learning modalities are included: visual/auditory and tactile/kinesthetic.
- This model is generally used occasionally.

Challenges

- If this model is the usual model, the classroom may actually function as two separate classrooms if the modalities address only the re-teaching of the target students.
- There may not be a real partnership between the teachers if this is the only method used.

Model III: Complementary or Side-by-Side Teaching

In the following two models, the teachers work together as equals. In the Speak and Add Model, the second teacher may provide support and take notes on a smart board, provide scaffolding for the whole class, or they may ask questions that students might have. Also, teachers may switch roles. In addition, the second teacher may be a second content teacher in an interdisciplinary class who adds his or her content to the content of the co-teacher. In the Duet or Team Co-Teaching Model, both teachers are master co-teachers and function as a high-performing team. Each teacher is able to provide both content and support to all students. The Duet or Team Co-Teaching form of co-teaching requires planning time.

The difference between the two forms of Model III is the level of expertise in co-teaching of the teachers of the two models. In the former Speak and Add Model, generally teachers are teaching the whole class together as equals. Interdisciplinary teachers may use this model when most of their teaching is direct teaching. On the other hand, the Speak and Add co-teachers may be just beginning to co-teach or they may have been working together as co-teachers for a long period of time.

The high-performing Duet or Team Co-Teaching Team does not just use the whole-class model. It also uses all of the models: whole group, small group, and complementary. The Duet or Team Co-Teaching Model is called *high performing* because it is the most intensive of all of the models. It requires time for co-planning and for communication. It also provides the most support for students.

Model III: Complementary: Speak and Add Model (Whole Class)

Strengths

- One teacher takes the lead and the other teacher adds to the lesson with graphic organizers, examples, questions, ongoing assessment, and support.
- In an interdisciplinary co-teaching class, each teacher may contribute his or her content-area knowledge.
- This model can be used as a beginning stage of co-teaching while the specialist gains knowledge of the content and the GET's style.
- This method takes little time in co-planning and is easy to implement.

Challenges

- This model can underutilize the second teacher (specialist) if this teacher is always "adding."
- This model may become an ad hoc partnership that lacks long-term shared goals and lacks depth.
- The skills of the second teacher may not be fully used throughout the class and may be limited to his or her target students.

Model III: Complementary: Duet or Team Co-Teaching, A High-Performing Team

Strengths

- Duet teachers co-plan and make instructional decisions to work with small groups, individuals, or the whole class, based on ongoing assessments throughout the class.
- Both educators employ general and special education techniques to support the progress of all students.
- This model is the most completely integrated for students and fully uses all expertise of both co-teachers (Beninghof 2012, p. 52).
- This method is the most time intensive because extensive planning and communication is essential.
- This method provides the most support for students.
- The roles of the GET and ST are indistinguishable (Beninghof 2012, pp. 55–58).
- Chapman and Hyatt call this method "walking the talk" because all of the models are used as appropriate for the class (Chapman and Hyatt 2011, p. 29).
- Teachers facilitate whole and small groups, have stations that are independent and facilitated, and they differentiate instruction for all learners.
- This model's organization is based on student goals and needs.

Challenges

- The model takes time for planning, time for balancing the two teachers' relationship, responsibility, and trust; and it requires interdependence.
- The model needs administrative and whole-school support and a school-wide commitment to both inclusion and to high expectations for all students.
- This method puts the greatest stress on the relationship.

Table 10.3 summarizes the strengths and challenges of each of the models and describes each teacher's role in this model.

Table 10.3 Summary of the Three Models

Model I: Supportive Co-Teaching is generally whole-class teaching by one teacher and supportive teaching as needed by the second teacher.					
Category of Model	Model Type	Teacher A	Teacher B	Strengths	Challenges
Model I: Supportive Co-Teaching Models (Whole-Class Teaching; one teacher is generally the lead teacher; the specialist plays a supportive role.)	One teaches/one observes	Directly teaches the whole class	Observes	Good for the beginning of the co-teaching partnership	If this method is used as the main model, Teacher B may not have an equal voice in the partnership. Can be used to develop data for the course.
	One teaches/one drifts	Directly teaches the whole class	Drifts: May be gathering data or supporting students as the needs present themselves	Saves planning time if there is no common planning time.	Direct teaching to the whole class may become the dominant instructional model.
	One teaches/one assists or supports	Directly teaches the whole class	Assists and supports May have developed a "support kit"	Saves planning time B provides feedback about specific concerns.	A and B can alternate roles to provide a balance in the relationship.
Model II: Parallel Co-Teaching: Small-Group Instruction is generally group work with flexible or static groups, each one taught by a co-teacher.					
Category of Model	Model Type	Teacher A	Teacher B	Strengths	Challenges
Model II: Parallel Co-Teaching (Small-Group Instruction by Each Teacher)	Parallel Co-Teaching Small-Group Instruction	Parallel teaches a heterogeneous group	Parallel teaches a heterogeneous group	Provides smaller group Equal responsibility for xcontent and support	If this is the only model used or if teachers do not change groupings, students see only one teacher's strengths.
	Station Teaching	Station teaching: teaches a station	Station teaching: teaches a station	Provides smaller group Equal responsibility for content and support	If this is the only model used or if teachers do not change groupings, students see only one teacher's strengths. Teacher A and B may not know the effectiveness of the other group.
	Skill Group Teaching	Teaches a skill group, differentiated by readiness, interest, or learning style	Teaches a skill group, differentiated by readiness, interest, or learning style	Provides smaller group The responsibility may be equal unless the specialist always teaches the less ready group.	If this is the only model used or if teachers do not change groupings, students see only one teacher's strengths. Teacher A and B may not know the effectiveness of the other group.

continued on next page

Category of Model	Model Type	Teacher A	Teacher B	Strengths	Challenges
Model II (continued)	Alternative Teaching	Teaches the same lesson or a complementary lesson (then swaps groups)	Teaches the same lesson or a complementary lesson (then swaps)	Provides smaller group When groups are swapped, students see the strengths of each teacher.	Provides higher adult-to-student ratio. Teachers A and B may not know the effectiveness of the other group.
	Adapting Curriculum Teaching	Teaches larger general education group and provides more challenges	Teaches smaller group (usually at-risk or target group) and provides scaffolding	Provides smaller group Little co-planning time is needed. Each teacher can prepare separately.	There may be an imbalance in the relationship with Teacher A always in the lead. Teacher A and B may not know the effectiveness of the other group.
	Learning Styles Approach	Re-teaches using learning style to define group	Re-teaches using learning style or modality	Provides smaller group Provides hands-on or visual re-teaching	When used occasionally, this provides targeted support. If it serves as the usual model, the classroom becomes two separate classrooms.

Model III: Complementary (Side-by-Side) Co-Teaching is generally when teachers work together, with one teacher providing content and the second teacher providing whole-class access or scaffolding by modeling note-taking, providing visual support, and asking questions that anticipate misconceptions.

Category of Model	Model Type	Teacher A	Teacher B	Strengths	Challenges
Model III: Complementary or Side-by-Side Model (equal partners)	Speak and Add	Teacher A speaks.	Teacher B adds visual or kinesthetic supports to direct teaching.	Little co-planning time is needed. Each teacher can prepare separately.	There may be an imbalance in the relationship with Teacher A always in the lead.
	Duet Model Sometimes called *Team Co-Teaching* Described as a "high-performing" team	Teaches and supports	Teaches and supports	Requires time for comprehensive co-planning, co-instructing, co-assessment, and co-teaching professional development.	Uses all of the skills of each educator. Often this capacity is a result of working and learning together over a period of time.

Co-Teaching Models for Specialists and Interdisciplinary Teams

All of the co-teaching models can be used effectively by a variety of educators. Recently, as the pressure has increased for higher student achievement and for less restrictive environments, more specialists who once exclusively taught in pull-out classes or in separate groups at the back of the classroom are now co-teaching. In many cases, however, these specialists often work in more than four classrooms, which often makes providing time for co-planning challenging. See Table 10.4 (p. 483) for suggested models that specialists and interdisciplinary teams can use and the rationales for their use.

Special Educator[2]

- The Duet or Team Co-Teaching Model is the highest-performing model and can be accomplished with co-teachers who have strong administrative support and adequate planning time. However, often special educators have to co-teach in three or more classrooms. Some researchers believe that four different teachers or courses is the maximum workload if planning is required (Friend 2007). Without planning time, the ST must often support students without having adequate time to prepare with the second teacher. Co-teaching models described above include models that require little planning, but the consequence of using them is that, at times, the full capacity of the special educator is not used because he or she does not participate in goal-setting, planning, and assessment decision-making.
- The Skill Groups Model or the Complementary Skills Model provide the student with special education modifications and strategies in the general education classroom.
- The Speak and Add can also provide support for students even though support is often unplanned and, possibly, can be provided only on a superficial basis.
- The Learning Style Model can provide support in the modalities with tactile, kinesthetic, and hands-on activities provided by the special educator.

Speech and Language Pathologist (SLP)

- Formerly trained in a medical model, SLPs have historically delivered services in a pull-out environment. Recently SLPs have begun to seek out literacy training because it became clear that students who need speech and language services need to interact with language with their peers in authentic settings.
- Provide speech and language practice in social contexts
- Because the SLP probably is working in more than five different classrooms on more than five different teams or five different courses (too many to co-plan together, according to some researchers), the Complementary Skills Model is often used so that the SLP can provide access to the curriculum to his or her students.
- The Station Teaching Model can also be used so that centers can target specific students' needs.
- The Adaptive Teaching Model can be used when the SLP works with his or her students.

The Gifted Specialist

- The Complementary Skills Model, the Skill Groups Model, and the Stations Model provide a small-group setting for students to work with the specialist and for the specialist to support all students with appropriate challenges.
- Often, the gifted specialist works in multiple classrooms and has little opportunity for co-planning.
- Often, there are many misconceptions about what constitutes giftedness and the needs of gifted students, including the belief that gifted students will continue learning on their own in the general education classroom.

Occupational Therapist (OT) or Physical Therapist (PT)

- Historically, OTs and PTs were trained in a medical model in which students received services outside of the classroom. Recently, to provide the least-restrictive environment when "the use of supplementary aids and services are not required," OT/PT specialists have begun to bring their services into the general education classroom.
- Skill Groups, Station Teaching, and the Parallel Model can provide a small-group setting in which the OT/PT educator can work with the targeted students in the general education classroom.
- These therapists often move from class to class, and even from school to school, because of the low incidence of each type of intervention. This makes determining a regular planning time challenging for these educators.

---

2   The descriptions of the roles of specialists, paraprofessionals, and interdisciplinary teachers are based on the work of Beninghof (2012) and Chapman and Hyatt (2011).

Literacy Specialist

- The Skills Group Model would be appropriate if the literacy specialist works only with targeted students; however, the Complementary Skills Model or Speak and Add could work to improve the literacy for all students.
- Often, the literacy specialist takes on the additional roles of coach, teacher, consultant, assessor, curriculum specialist, and staff developer, along with being a co-teacher and, thus, has little time for co-planning.
- Acceptance of the literacy specialist's expertise requires that he or she use research-based and carefully selected activities in the general education classroom (Beninghof 2012, p. 190).

English Language Learner (ELL) Specialist

- To provide access to the curriculum to English learners, the best model is the Duet Model in which the general education teacher and ELL specialist co-plan every part of the lesson.
- If the specialist is in three to four different teachers' classrooms, the Speak and Add Learning Style and Adapting Models allow the specialist to make "just in time" changes and additions. The ELL tool kit (Beninghof 2012, p. 190) might include a tablet with Internet access for pictures of realia, words defined by real-world pictures or illustrations, highlighters, thesauruses, and sentence strips, for example.
- The major challenges for the general education teacher are language and cultural differences. For the English learner, the students' conversational fluency may mask their continued need for support as they acquire academic expertise and an adequate academic vocabulary.

Technology Specialist

- Co-teaching may bridge any gaps in the general education teacher's knowledge of technology.
- The recommended model is the Complementary Skills Model and the use of the gradual release of responsibility as the general education teacher becomes more capable with technology so that he or she becomes capable of teaching with technology independently.
- Initially, the Speak and Add Model can be used with general education teacher, rather than the specialist, as the teacher who provides support.
- Beninghof (p. 190) recommends the use of project-based scheduling—that is, scheduling for daily co-teaching during a project—when working with the technology specialist, instead of having a one-day-a-week schedule throughout the year, which is often typical for specialists.

Interdisciplinary Teams

- Often, the Duet or Team Teaching Model is used by the co-teachers.
- Time is essential for careful co-planning so that the course is truly interdisciplinary and provides not only mutually developed goals, but also provides the students with two voices that may not always agree with the other's interpretation of the content.
- Chapman and Hyatt recommend that interdisciplinary teams study student work together to determine "better ways to meet the needs of struggling students" and to use the data for planning (p. 48).

Working with Para-Educators or Instructional Assistants

Working with para-educators introduces additional challenges for the classroom teacher or for the co-teaching team. In this team, the classroom teacher must be a part of the supervision of the para-educator. Beyond this, the para-educator may have responsibilities to and expectations from other administrators, including the principal, the special education director, the English language supervisor, and content-area coordinators.

The expectations described in each para-educator's job description may vary greatly between different states, provinces and districts. In some instances, a para-educator functions encompass a wide range of tasks, including clerical work, direct instruction, one-to-one tutoring, facilitating groups, behavior management, preparation of classroom materials, charting students' behavior, and even bilingual support. Some states or provinces may restrict the para-educator's role by precluding them from taking part in assessment, parent conferences, or lesson planning unless these tasks are under the supervision of the co-teacher. Para-educator's roles have evolved from mainly clerical to primarily instructional since the 1950s. Because they may serve as a solution to the drive toward higher student achievement and decreasing the achievement gap between general education students and special education students, para-educators outnumber special educators in most states (McDonnell and Jameson 2014).

Table 10.4   Co-Teaching Models and Specialists

Specialist	Models	Rationale
Varied Specialist	• Models and Purposes • Supportive Model (whole class) • Parallel Model (small groups) • Complementary/Side-by-Side (whole class) • Duet/Team (high-performing, each teaches and supports)	Ultimately, the co-teachers may become a high-performing Duet.
Special Educator	• Model I: Supportive Model (whole class) • Model II: Parallel Mode (small groups) • Model III: Complementary/Side-by-Side (whole class) • Model III: Duet/Team (high-performing, each teaches and supports)	Initially, the Supportive Model requires the least amount of planning and gives the second teacher time to observe, gather data, and support students. As the partnership grows, the Parallel model will probably become more common as the teachers work in small, flexible groups. Ultimately, they may become a Duet.
Speech and Language Specialist	• Model II: Parallel Model (small groups) • skills • adaptive • station	In most cases, the SLP will not be in the classroom every day; these small groups provide a way for him or her to work with students on • skills • speech • possibly multiple stations created for his or her specific students • At times, the SLP teacher may be able to work with the classroom teacher and the whole class to demonstrate his or her expertise.
Gifted Specialist	• Model II: Parallel Model (small groups) • skills • adaptive • station	In most cases, the gifted specialist will not be in the classroom every day; these small groups provide a way for him or her to work with students on • skills • projects • possibly multiple stations created for his or her specific students • At times, the gifted specialist teacher may be able to work with the classroom teacher and the whole class to demonstrate his or her expertise.
Occupational Therapist and Physical Therapist	• Model II: Parallel Model (small groups) • skills • adaptive • station	In most cases, OT/PTs will not be in the classroom every day; these small groups provide a way for him or her to work with students on • skills • adaptive OT/PT • possibly multiple stations created for his or her specific students • At times, the OT or PT may be able to work with the classroom teacher and the whole class to demonstrate his or her expertise.

continued on next page

Specialist	Models	Rationale
ELL Specialist	• Model I: Supportive Model (whole class) • Model II: Parallel Model (small groups) • skills • adaptive technology • station	In most cases, the ELL specialist will not be in the classroom every day; these small groups provide a way for him or her to work with students on • skills • adaptive technology • possibly multiple stations created for his or her specific students • At times the ELL teacher may be able to work with the classroom teacher and the whole class to demonstrate his or her expertise.
Technology Specialist	• Model I: Supportive Model (whole class) Note: The Specialist leads the class, and the classroom teacher supports the technology specialist.	In this supportive relationship, the general education teacher is supportive, and the technology specialist gradually gives the responsibility for running the class back to the classroom teacher.
Interdisciplinary Team	• Model II: Parallel Model (small groups) • Model III: Complementary/Side-by-Side (whole class) • Model III: Duet/Team (high-performing, each teaches and supports)	Generally, the two content teachers have parity and work both with the whole class and with flexible groups. Ultimately, they may become experts in both content areas.
Paraprofessionals	• Model I: Supportive Model (whole class) • Model II: Parallel Model (small groups)	Generally, paraprofessionals work in a supportive role. With training, para-educators could run small groups in each of the parallel models.

Villa reports that, in recent years, because paraprofessionals provide a supportive role in co-teaching, many now have capacity beyond their clerical responsibilities. Additionally, through professional development and training at times supported by districts, they have

learned a variety of techniques, such as direct instruction in reading and math, cooperative group learning, hands-on teaching, computer-assisted instruction, educational games from Internet websites, and community-based instruction (Villa, Thousand, and Nevin 2013, p. 79).

Thus, this extra pair of hands may have a multiplicity of skills, and the co-teachers or the classroom teacher need to have a clear understanding of the job description, training, and expectations of the para-educator in order to incorporate him or her in their goals, plans, and their team.

Supervision of the Paraprofessional

One of the greatest challenges for the co-teaching partnership or for the general education teacher with a para-educator is taking on a supervisory role. The classroom teacher or co-teachers need to have a clear understanding of the para-educator's job description in order to plan for optimally supporting the students and clarifying expectations for the para-educator.

Planning for a Paraprofessional

A meeting with the principal, para-educator, co-teacher and other supervisors needs to take place to develop a clear communication and supervision plan.

Initial Administrative Planning Meeting with the Paraprofessional

This meeting could take many different forms. It could be a meeting with the principal or another administrator and all teachers and paraprofessionals who work together, along with any other administrator who could have a supervisory or evaluative relationship with the paraprofessionals. Another option might be to have the director of special education run this meeting. The agenda needs to address the following:

• **School-wide initiatives and vision for inclusion and para-educators**: to provide the big picture and how the goals, vision, and initiatives are expected to work for this school year
• **Job description and contractual provisions**: the principal's and the other administrators' expecta-

tions as well as the job descriptions and contractual descriptions

- **Expectations for the different roles paraprofessionals may play**: when they work one to one, every day in a classroom, some days in the classroom, etc.
- **Confidentiality**: Para-educators need to realize that the information that they may have about students cannot be discussed outside of the classroom with colleagues. Unless a teacher is present, generally the paraprofessional does not discuss his or her work with parents.
- **Schedules**: for support and for meeting times (if they are supported by the school)
- **The role of the classroom teacher**: developing a whole-year, weekly, and daily plan for working together; the degree of supervision or evaluation expected by the school; an accounting of the results of the paraprofessional's work (for example, does this teacher/para team need to track social-emotional or academic progress? Or does the classroom teacher need to use a rubric to provide feedback to the paraprofessional and the principal to evaluate the paraprofessional?)

Administrative Support for the Paraprofessional with the Whole School

In addition, McDonnell and Jameson recommend the following five programmatic supports that administrators need to make clear to the entire faculty so that the para-educator's role in the school is clear:

1. Paraprofessional work is an important part of a school-wide initiative to support inclusion. Paraprofessionals working with students actively support education for all students and demonstrate how the school values and supports a diverse student population.
2. The IEP or 504 Plan may be used to define the paraprofessional's role, although the team process makes the decision about exactly what services the paraprofessional provides.
3. Paraprofessionals supplement the classroom teacher's work.
4. Paraprofessionals are directed by teaching and behavioral planning as well as by the classroom teacher or co-teachers.
5. They are evaluated based on student achievement or improvement in student behavior (McDonnell and Jameson 2014, p. 5).

The Initial Meeting with the Paraprofessional

At this initial meeting, preferably before the school year begins, the teacher(s) need to make their expectations for the year and for every class clear. Explaining how the paraprofessional fits into the classroom routines, what kind of professional development or training he or she can expect, and what will happen from the first day are essential, since the skills of paraprofessionals often vary. The classroom teacher or the co-teachers should begin the discussion with the following:

- **Classroom routines**: an overview of the policies, procedures, and routines of the classroom, including attendance, make-up work, handing out and collecting work, schedules, calendars, etc.
- **Planning together**: In some cases, the para-educator will not have time. In this case, the routines need to be discussed so that he or she will understand his or her role. If there are scheduled meeting times, develop a schedule for the year for these meetings. Beninghof recommends allotting common planning time for the para-educator, which can be made possible by the use of flex time in which the para-educator arrives at school early or stays late for common planning and then is allowed to leave early one day a week (Beninghof 2012).
- **Working with individual students, small groups, and assisting with the whole class** and the way in which he or she will work within the classroom in groups and with specific students if that is part of the expectation.
- **Confidentiality**: Because teachers and paraprofessionals may have conversations about students, it is essential to remember that students' information is not to be shared.
- Table 10.5, The Respective Roles of the Para-Educator and the Classroom Teacher or Co-Teachers, and Table 10.6, "A Survey of the Para-Professional's Experience," provide a series of areas that can be discussed with the para-educator to begin the year with clear expectations.

Table 10.5 describes the differential roles of the co-teachers and the para-educator, and it can be used to clarify expectations for all of the team members in the classroom in the areas of instruction, planning, classroom management, accommodations, and assessment (Gerlach 2010).

Table 10.5 Respective Roles of the Para-Educator and the Classroom Teacher or Co-Teachers

	Classroom Teacher or Co-Teacher Responsibility	Para-Educator Role	Materials, Supports for Para-Educator
Instruction	Plan all instruction for whole class and small groups. Teach whole class and small groups.	Work with small groups of students on specific tasks, including review or re-teaching of content. Discuss specific classroom instruction plans that may have an impact on the paraprofessional.	• Para will be trained in all routines and ways necessary for working with students. • This may have to be a gradual process that will change when the students and paras are prepared for the next step. • All materials will be provided with directions and answers, at least initially.
Curriculum and Lesson Plan Development	Plan for year, week, and daily instruction Lead (or work with co-teacher) to teach whole class and groups.	Provide assistance in development of classroom activities, retrieval of materials, and coordination of activities as the year goes on. Discuss specific curriculum and instruction plans that may have an impact on the paraprofessional.	• Plans and materials will be reviewed. • New techniques will be modeled and discussed before the para is responsible.
Classroom Management and Classroom Climate	Provide classroom rules, norms, and consequences. When there are individual behavior plans, they will be discussed with the para-educator.	Assist with the implementation of class-wide and individual behavior management plans. Discuss all classroom management concerns that may have an impact on the paraprofessional.	• Teachers discuss classroom rules, processes and procedures. • Individual behavior plan processes will be discussed.
Accommodations and Modifications	Responsible for all accommodations and modifications	When necessary, provide appropriate accommodations to material (enlarged print, taking notes, or reading material aloud). Discuss all accommodation and modification concerns that may have an impact on the paraprofessional.	• Purpose of accommodations and modifications will be discussed. • Para-educator may need to provide feedback about the impact of modifications on the students.
Assessment	Develop, analyze, modify, and use assessment results to plan classes.	Provide accommodations (separate location, for example), read materials, etc., when asked. Assist in giving assessments. Discuss all classroom assessment issues that may have an impact on the paraprofessional.	• Training and modeling of all expectations will be provided.

Communication	Discuss how you will communicate, plan, and solve any problems that arise. Provide a plan for discussing concerns. Schedule meetings. Specify method(s) of communication; that may include email, instant messaging, notes, etc.	The para-educator needs to discuss any concerns that he or she has about his or her role and relationship with the classroom teacher or co-teachers, or with individual or groups of students.	• Schedule meeting times and specify what will be discussed. • Develop a communication plan to provide lessons and discuss concerns.
Supervision/ Evaluation	Discuss these responsibilities as defined by the school.	If there are rubrics, forms, processes, and procedures, each should be discussed with the paraprofessional.	• Develop a plan or schedule if this is part of your role with the paraprofessional.

The Paraprofessional in the Classroom

Historically, the para-educator has provided services to students in the style of Model I: Whole Group Instruction Model: One Teaches, One Assists or Supports. More recently, other models have been added, including the Complementary: Speak and Add Model. For example, the para-educator might type notes for the targeted student and class notes might be projected for the entire class or shared with some students in the class. In addition, Small Group Instruction: Skill Group Teaching, Station Teaching, and the Parallel Model could be facilitated by a paraprofessional if he or she receives professional development, modeling, training, and support from co-teachers or professional development.

Paraprofessional Initial Meeting Survey

Because of the variations in the experience, job descriptions, and contractual agreements, it is important to begin the year with a clear understanding of your expectations and the para-educator's expectations. The following table can be used to further clarify the para-educator's experience and teaching skills.

Table 10.6 Paraprofessional Initial Meeting Survey

Directions: The purpose of the survey is to make sure that we start our year working together smoothly. Our expectations are that by knowing what you already feel secure in and those areas that you're not as secure in doing, we'll be able to plan for successful work with our students and provide training or other supports to make sure this year is a successful year for us as educators and particularly for the students.

	Major strength	Some strength	I could learn something about	A challenging area that I could learn about
Experience in GE classroom				
Experience in SE classroom				
Experience with co-taught classrooms				
Facilitating small groups				
Re-teaching				
Technology				
Communicating about plans using lesson plans or technology (email, phone, IM, etc.)				
Content area of class				
Professional Development/Training/ Experience in learning difficulties				
Successful experiences you've had in education				
Comments or questions:				

Becoming a Value-Added High-Performing Co-Teaching Team

To attain the level of a high-functioning team and to improve student achievement, both teachers must be equal in expertise and must have parity both inside and outside the classroom. It is important to note that this level of partnership needs to be developed by all two-teacher teams, even if one or both teachers are experienced with co-teaching, because working as a smoothly running twosome in one space is a complex process.

Both "Model III: Duet" or "Team Co-Teachers" teach content and support students, and they share equal responsibility in the planning, delivery, and assessment of the classroom. Beyond these traits, in order to "walk the walk" and become a high-performing team that brings value beyond what each teacher can provide independently, the two teachers must work on their professional growth as instructors, assessors, and planners. Value-added co-teaching builds on the strengths each co-teacher brings to the partnership. "Having critical conversations can transform the way you plan and teach together," say Chapman and

Hyatt who maintain that true collaboration, "continual questioning and challenging of one another" (Chapman and Hyatt 2011, p. 4) in critical conversations, protocols, and reflective practice sessions can forge two teachers into a high-performing team that consistently works on the collaborative partnership, examines student data, and works to enhance instruction.

In addition to the time spent planning for the classroom, the partners need to spend time on their partnership and its development. According to Chapman and Hyatt, co-teachers need to have four ongoing critical conversations about their relationship and their classroom. These conversations should be sustained throughout the co-teaching partnership. Co-teachers need to consistently revisit and reflect on how they

1. **Define the partnership**. Partners develop a shared vision, establish roles and responsibilities, and lay the collaborative foundation that may need adjusting throughout the year.
2. **Examine data**. Together they focus on results, use data about students to make instructional improvements, and become more adept at adjusting materials and instruction to support each student.
3. **Enhance instruction**. They focus on ways to provide more value as a twosome than one teacher

could do alone and continue to learn together about research-based methods that work for their students.

4. **Expand impact**. They recognize that they are part of a school system and need administrative support for their work together and professional development, which will support the school and the team's capacity for improving instruction (Chapman and Hyatt 2011, pp. 10–11).

According to Chapman and Hyatt, models need to be addressed, but the true value-added component of co-teaching comes from the partnership's growth, which will take place over time as the four areas listed above are consistently considered, critically and reflectively, during the co-teaching meetings and in the classroom.

Parity of the Co-Teaching Team

Without parity between the two co-teachers, the partnership will not evolve. Villa, in his *Guide to Co-Teaching*, recommends both co-teachers agree to work toward six important goals to support their partnership:

1. Coordinate their work to achieve at least one common, publicly agreed-on goal (e.g., improved student outcomes)
2. Use their planning time efficiently and purposefully
3. Share a belief system that supports the idea that each of the co-teaching team members have unique and necessary expertise
4. Demonstrate parity by alternatively engaging in the dual roles of teacher and learner, expert and novice, and giver and recipient of knowledge or skills
5. Use a distributed functions theory of leadership in which the task and relationship functions of the traditional lone teacher are distributed among all co-teaching team members
6. Use a cooperative process that includes face-to-face interaction, positive interdependence, interpersonal skills, monitoring co-teacher progress, and individual accountability (Villa, Thousand, and Nevin 2013, p. 6). The initial planning sessions and the weekly planning sessions included in the sections that follow provide specific, adaptable forms for co-teachers that support equity in the relationship and ongoing focus on the essential elements in successful co-teaching teams.

Overview of the Stages in the Development of a Co-Teaching Team

New partners need to recognize that developing a truly collaborative relationship in one classroom is a complex and challenging task. Chapman and Hyatt, in *Critical Conversations in Co-Teaching Problem-Solving Approach* (Chapman and Hyatt 2011, p. 34), say that each partner should "expect to be 'disturbed'" and to realize that, over the course of their work together, possibly significant changes will be necessary in their shared classroom to account for the combined capacities and needs of both teachers and students. They recommend that teachers use their "passions as motivation," as well as their creativity, to provide the energy and alternatives to meet the needs of the partnership and the students. The co-teachers need to plan carefully by crafting their vision and final expectations and setting realistic goals for the year. If they then meet, plan, and reflect week by week and, as Chapman and Hyatt suggest, "ask tough questions of one another," they will be on their way to having a greater impact on students than either teacher could have achieved alone. Chapman and Hyatt emphasize that the need to collect, use, and analyze data is critically important, and they suggest that teachers consciously "add value every day and find qualitative and quantitative ways to show . . . [the] added value [of their partnership]" (Chapman and Hyatt 2011, pp. 34–35). The complex interpersonal, professional, and educational demands of co-teaching make it essential that throughout the year teachers actively work to improve their partnership, their ability to meet the students' needs and goals, planning, ongoing assessment, and their development as professionals.

Planning time is often described as the greatest barrier to effective co-teaching by co-teaching teams. Planning time may be part of the schedule in some schools. Other possibilities for providing time include hiring substitutes, professional development days scheduled in the school calendar, and using the summer for planning goals and the major units of curriculum to decrease the amount of time needed for planning during the year (Murawski 2014, p. 300). While common planning time is ideal, technological support— phone calls, weekly summary of the intended content, email, cloud sharing programs such as Evernote, Dropbox, or Google Docs, and curriculum mapping software—can support the co-teachers. The least effective method for teaching all students is ad hoc planning when the co-teacher has to respond to student needs without preparation. In this case, the lack of time may prevent the team from working on shared goals daily and using formative data to design the lessons for each day, and it generally puts the specialist and his or her expertise exclusively in a supportive role. Thus, the lack of time may prevent the two teachers from establishing an effective educational partnership.

Villa, in his book *A Guide to Co-Teaching*, describes the four stages of development of a team. At each stage, Novice, Developing, Proficient, and High Performing, he specifically describes the quality of the developing communication between the co-teachers over time (Villa, Thousand, and Nevin 2013).

Novice Stage

The first stage in becoming a team requires that the new partners begin to communicate to one another in appropriate ways and recognize that behaviors in and outside of the class can have an impact on their effectiveness as co-teachers. The partners need to establish their accountability to one another and their support of their work and their partnership.

Developing Stage

In the second stage, as the partnership begins to develop, the two educators need to continue to make mutual respect and accountability clear and address communication concerns more directly. They can begin to make suggestions about instruction and voice their concerns, but they need to support one another at all times. In their expanding instructional practice, they can begin to use student work to develop flexible groups.

Proficient Stage

In the third stage, the relationship has matured, yet the educators continue to need to work on clearly communicating, asking clarifying questions, and suggesting different solutions. They also need to ask questions to delve into their partner's expertise more completely. They will be using many of the models and will have determined which model works best for specific sets of circumstances.

High-Performing Team Stage

At the last and highest level, both teachers function at capacity and they can see that by working together, they add value to the classroom. They are more and more able to disagree without seeming negative or without disturbing their co-teacher. Their classroom functions well and they monitor their students' progress in their frequent planning sessions. They have

expanded their team beyond their classroom and may invite other experts to support their work and to help them solve problems. They are ready to seek out professional development for themselves as professionals and to contribute to the professional development of their school.

Only by working on all of the facets of their partnership will the co-teachers progress through these levels and become a high performing co-teaching team. This process may take multiple years.

Committing to Ongoing Improvement

To support the team's attainment of a high-performing team, Chapman and Hyatt recommend that co-teachers maintain a reflective journal grounded in the four major elements of co-teaching: (1) developing each co-teacher's capacity, (2) examining data, (3) enhancing instruction, and (4) expanding the impact of the co-teaching team to the school (Chapman and Hyatt 2011, pp. 48–52).

Planning for Co-Teaching

As the year begins, the co-teachers need to establish their intention to use their often limited meeting times effectively.

The following planning documents are provided to support co-teachers throughout the year.

1. Initial meeting documents
    - the teacher strength survey
    - the roles and responsibility matrix
    - agenda format
    - daily lesson planning form
    - weekly lesson planning form
2. Weekly lesson planning meetings
    - the Co-Teaching Progress Rubric/Tracker
    - agenda
    - weekly lesson outline form

The Co-Teaching Progress Rubric/Tracker is a rubric that can be used to make sure to keep the focus on the essential elements necessary to become highly effective co-teachers.

The teacher strength survey helps a new co-teaching team become acquainted with one another's strengths and with areas that they need to work on as a team or as individuals.

The Roles and Responsibilities Matrix can help a new co-teaching team talk over how the everyday routines and duties will be shared between the two co-teachers.

The Agenda Format includes the time that will be spent on each agenda item to help the co-teachers use their time effectively. A mutually agreed upon agenda that specifies how time will be spent and the general topics that are routinely discussed can provide structure and focus to the meetings.

The Daily Lesson-Planning Form provides a detailed and specific format to think through how the teachers will share their teaching.

The Weekly Lesson-Outline Form provides a condensed format for planning for the week.

Initial Planning Meeting: The Co-Teaching Progress Rubric/Tracker

The Co-Teaching Progress Rubric/Tracker is a tool that can be used throughout the year to assess the team's evolution and growth. Co-teachers need to remember that their partnership will take time and hard work, and it may involve more than a year of co-teaching to attain the highest levels of effectiveness. The critically important areas of concern are listed in the "Essential Criteria" in the left column below. The rubric needs to be revisited consistently to monitor progress and to maintain a focus on all of the priorities necessary for being highly effective as a team. The rubric is adapted from the work of a number of sources, including Chapman and Hyatt (2011), Kunkel (2012), and Villa, Thousand, and Nevin (2013).

Sample entries for the Co-Teaching Progress Rubric/Tracker are provided in Table 10.7 in italics. Attaining "High-Performing Team" in all categories is a multi-year process that depends upon time, support, and the engagement of the co-teachers and their school.

Put aside at least five minutes at each weekly meeting to address the rubric and your progress and at least 20 minutes to address your progress at the beginning of the year and at the end of each quarter.

Table 10.7, "Sample Co-Teaching Progress Rubric/Tracker" (p. 492), demonstrates the way in which the co-teachers can annotate the rubric throughout the year. Notice that the Table 10.7 sample rubric has only three categories.

Table 10.8, "Complete Co-teaching Progress Rubric/Tracker" (p. 494) has all the categories and provides a blank column on the far right for co-teachers to note their next steps throughout the year..

The Rubric/Tracker 10.8 provides the research-based essentials for developing a high performing team. The Rubric/Tracker should be used monthly by co-teachers to maintain focus on all of the important elements of co-teaching, from daily concerns to year-long goals.

Note that descriptive words such as begin, generally, and consistently are listed beneath each category to emphasize growth.

The length of time required for the co-teachers to move through the four levels from Novice to High Performing Team is at least two to four years.

Table 10.7 Sample Co-Teaching Progress Rubric/Tracker for a full year.

The sample includes three of the eight essential criteria.

Criteria Essential to Become a High-Performing Team	Novice *Begin Develop*	Developing *Fairly Generally Mainly*	Proficient *Generally, Consistently Generally, Effectively Generally, Reliably*	High-Performing Team *Consistently Mutually Wholly Naturally*	NOTES BY CO-TEACHERS Include: **Next Steps** **NOTE:** Date each comment
Partnership **SAMPLE** Level Achieved (write date)	*Begin* to set goals using Co-Teaching Progress Rubric/Tracker. *Begin* to clarify roles and responsibilities using teacher skills survey. *Begin* to set standards for classroom routines, behavior using the roles and responsibilities matrix. *Develop* daily/weekly communication plan. **Other** *Co-Grading Sept. 28: Novice*	Measure progress on goals *fairly* often and adequately. Roles and Resp. are *getting* clarified. Norms are *generally* observed. Meetings are *mainly* effective. Problem-solving protocol *mainly* works. Daily/weekly communication plan *mainly* works. **Other** *Co-grading went well.* *We both met with all parents on Parents and Curriculum Nights.* *Nov. 23: We are on our way!* *Mar 20: Not proficient yet.* *June 30: Almost proficient?*	Measure goal progress *generally, consistently.* Roles and Resp. are *generally, consistently* clarified. Norms are observed *generally, consistently.* Meetings *generally* are effective. Problem-solving protocol works *generally effectively.* Daily/weekly communication plan *generally* works *reliably.* **Other** *Year 2: Worked together for 3 full days in the summer to develop units and goals* *Began the year proficient.*	Goals are *mutually* shared and measured by each teacher and team *consistently.* Roles and Resp. are *consistently* clarified. Norms are observed *consistently.* Meetings are *consistently* effective. Problem-solving protocol works well *consistently.* Daily/weekly communication plan *consistently* works efficiently. **Other**	***August 28:*** *We spent most of our first meeting on this rubric setting goals, etc. We realized that although we need to do so many other things to be effective teachers, without the partnership, we won't do as well.* *November 23: Struggling with using planning time well* *March 20: We've survived one difficult conversation.* *June 30: We survived and think we'll make it to proficiency and beyond next year!*

Daily and Weekly Co-Planning	*Begin* to plan for full year's meeting schedule. Agree on agenda format. Agree on lesson plan format (long form). Agree on weekly lesson plan format (short form). *August 29: Agenda, planning documents, lesson plan all done and run off. Posted to Google Docs so that we can plan together and see each another's notes and changes*	The full year's meeting schedule *mainly works.* The agenda format *mainly works.* Lesson plan format (long form) *mainly works.* Weekly lesson plan format (short form) *mainly works.* *Nov 23: Planning and communicating it is still taking a lot of time. Routines are starting to work. The lessons are starting to take shape. March 20: Time to plan is a problem. Google Docs helps. June 30: We hope next year is easier!*	The full year's meeting schedule generally works *effectively and consistently.* The agenda format generally works *effectively and consistently.* Lesson plan format (long form) generally works *effectively and consistently.* Weekly lesson plan format (short form) generally works *effectively and consistently.* *Year 2: Planning takes less time and technology helps plus a year of working together*	The full year's meeting schedule works effectively and *consistently.* The agenda format works effectively and *consistently.* Lesson plan format (long form) works effectively and *consistently.* Weekly lesson plan format (short form) works effectively and *consistently.*
Co-Teaching Models DI, etc.	Models used are highlighted. Whole Class: • One teaches/One observes • One teaches/One drifts • One teaches/One assists or supports • One teaches/One adapts the curriculum Small Group • Parallel Teaching • Alternative • Skill Group • Learning Styles • Stations Duet • All models *First Quarter: We flipped roles occasionally, but didn't have time to develop stations.*	Models used are highlighted. Whole Class: • One teaches/One observes • One teaches/One drifts • One teaches/One assists or supports • One teaches/One adapts the curriculum Small Group • Parallel Teaching • Alternative • Skill Group • Learning Styles • Stations Duet • All models Began grouping	Models used are highlighted. Whole Class: • One teaches/One observes • One teaches/One drifts • One teaches/One assists or supports • One teaches/One adapts the curriculum Small Group • Parallel Teaching • Alternative • Skill Group • Learning Styles • Stations Duet • All models	Models used are highlighted. Whole Class: • One teaches/One observes • One teaches/One drifts • One teaches/One assists or supports • One teaches/One adapts the curriculum Small Group • Parallel Teaching • Alternative • Skill Group • Learning Styles • Stations Duet • All models • All models used effectively We know which models to use for what purpose.

Table 10.8   Complete Co-Teaching Progress Rubric/Tracker with Space for Next Steps

Criteria	Novice *Begin* *Develop*	Developing *Fairly* *Generally* *Mainly*	Proficient *Generally, consistently* *Generally, effectively* *Generally, reliably*	High-Performing Team *Consistently* *Mutually* *Wholly* *Naturally*	Next Steps for HIGH priority Selecting NOTE: Date each comment
Partnership	*Begin* to set goals using co-teaching progress rubric/tracker. *Begin* to clarify roles and responsibilities using teacher skills survey. *Begin* to set standards for classroom routines, behavior using the Roles and Responsibilities Matrix. *Develop* daily/weekly communication plan.	Measure progress on goals *fairly* often and adequately. Roles and resp. are getting clarified. Norms are *generally* observed. Meetings are *mainly* effective. Problem-solving protocol *mainly* works. Daily/weekly communication plan mostly works. **Other** Co-grading went well. We both met with all parents on Parents Night Nov. 23: We are on our way! Mar 20: Not proficient yet. June 30: Almost proficient?	Measure goal progress *generally consistently*. Roles and resp. are *generally*, consistently clarified. Norms are observed *generally consistently*. Meetings *generally* are effective. Problem-solving protocol works *generally effectively*. Daily/weekly communication plan *generally* works *reliably*. **Other**	Goals are *mutually* shared and measured by each teacher and team *consistently*. Roles and resp. are *consistently* clarified. Norms are observed *consistently*. Meetings are *consistently* effective. Problem-solving protocol works well *consistently*. Daily/weekly communication plan *consistently* works efficiently. **Other**	
Co-Planning	*Begin* to plan for full year's meeting schedule. *Develop* agenda format. *Develop* lesson plan format (long form). *Develop* weekly lesson plan format (short form).	The full year's meeting schedule *mainly* works. The agenda format *mainly* works. Lesson plan format (long form) *mainly* works. Weekly lesson plan format (short form) *mainly* works.	The full year's meeting schedule *generally* works *effectively* and *consistently*. The agenda format *generally* works *effectively* and *consistently*. Lesson plan format (long form) *generally* works *effectively* and *consistently*. Weekly lesson plan format (short form) *generally* works *effectively* and *consistently*.	The full year's meeting schedule works effectively and *consistently*. The agenda format works effectively and *consistently*. Lesson plan format (long form) works effectively and *consistently*. Weekly lesson plan format (short form) works effectively and *consistently*.	

Co-Teaching	Models used are highlighted. **Whole Class:** • One teaches/One observes • One teaches/One drifts • One teaches/One assists or supports • One teaches/One adapts the curriculum **Small Group** • Parallel Teaching • Alternative • Skill Group • Learning Styles • Stations **Duet** • All models First quarter: All whole group. We switched roles. *First quarter: We flipped roles occasionally, but didn't have time to develop stations.*	Models used are highlighted. **Whole Class:** • One teaches/One observes • One teaches/One drifts • One teaches/One assists or supports • One teaches/One adapts the curriculum **Small Group** • Parallel Teaching • Alternative • Skill Group • Learning Styles • Stations **Duet** • All models Second quarter: Began differentiating. *Third quarter: More DI, but it takes time to do well*	Models used are highlighted. **Whole Class:** • One teaches/One observes • One teaches/One drifts • One teaches/One assists or supports • One teaches/One adapts the curriculum **Small Group** • Parallel Teaching • Alternative • Skill Group • Learning Styles **Duet** • All models *Last quarter: We did some small group work as a year-end project and it went well.*	Models used are highlighted. **Whole Class:** • One teaches/One observes • One teaches/One drifts • One teaches/One assists or supports • One teaches/One adapts the curriculum **Small Group** • Parallel Teaching • Alternative • Skill Group **Learning Styles** • Stations **Duet** • All models
Co-Assessing and Co-Grading	Begin to assess students' work together and to set mutually agreed upon standards. Begin to develop rubrics and scoring sheets together.	Assess all major assignments together. Use mutually developed rubrics. Rubrics can include modified work. Do report cards and progress reports together and mainly agree	Assess together. Use common rubrics. Grade report cards and progress reports together. Use results to plan for the next week or unit.	Assess together with rubrics that are *mutually* created. Grade together. Use classroom results to develop flexible groups and to modify instruction for the week and for the year.
Using Data	Examine standardized assessments, IEPs, and previous grades together. Use these assessments to set goals and plan for year.	Student work is used at the end of each marking period to assess the effectiveness of teaching and to set goals for the next quarter.	*Consistently* use classroom assessments formatively to modify groups and plans to differentiate instruction. Begin to track at-risk students' progress.	Data (qualitative and quantitative) from observations, behavior, and classroom assessments is used *consistently* and effectively to plan and to monitor student progress throughout the year.

continued on next page

				Universal Design for Learning, differentiated instruction, Response to Intervention, and other local or team-based PD *consistently* support effective teaching and progress monitoring for all students.
Improving Practice	This rubric is used to assess the present state of and growth in differentiating instruction, *developing* group work, formative assessment of student work to adjust curriculum, IEP goals, UDL, RtI and/or self-selected professional development initiatives using the co-teaching progress rubric.	Differentiated instruction is begun in parallel groupings and includes flexible groups that reflect needs, interests, self-selection, learning styles, stations, etc. Co-teachers have begun to work on professional development as a team or individually.	The DI groupings are varied as need is demonstrated in the class. UDL, RtI, and/or specific local initiatives are *generally* employed in planning and teaching.	
School-Wide Inclusion	Co-teachers look at the status of school-wide inclusion: principal support, teacher attitudes, teacher support, time allotted, progress, and needs.	Co-teachers *begin* to discuss the status of school-wide inclusion with administrators and teachers.	Co-teachers provide regular feedback to administrators and teachers about the status of inclusion. They may provide workshops in the school.	Co-teachers advocate for inclusion and provide regular feedback to administrators and teachers about the status of inclusion. They may provide workshops in the school.

Initial Planning Session: Teacher Skills Survey

At their first meeting, the partners need to establish the parity of their relationship and define what each teacher brings to the classroom. The teaching skills survey in Table 10.9 can be used at their first meeting to answer the following two questions:

1. What two major strengths do I bring to this team?
2. What two areas would I like to learn more about? By using this very simple initial focus with the teaching skills survey, each teacher acknowledges his or her skills as well as areas for growth.

Directions: Take this survey to share the results with your co-teacher. The survey is meant to discuss what each co-teacher brings to the partnership. This form is part of the initial planning meeting.

Setting the Agenda for the Year

The detailed agenda in Table 10.11 could provide a starting point for planning weekly meetings and making sure that the time is focused and well spent. It is based on multiple models from a variety of co-teaching experts: Perez (2012, p. 76); Villa, Thousand, and Nevin (2013); Chapman and Hyatt (2011); and Beninghof (2012).

Table 10.9 Teacher Skills Survey

	Major Strength	Some Strength	I could learn something about	A challeng-ing area that I could learn about
Content areas of classroom				
Flexible grouping, cooperative learning				
Making groups accountable				
Teaching reading, writing, or specific skills				
Developing a positive classroom environment				
Routines for classroom (attendance, bathroom passes, transitions, passing out paper, make-up work)				
High expectations for all				
Grading with another teacher				
Modification of lessons for specific needs				
Designing scaffolds to support specific learner needs				
Differentiating for different learners				
Developing challenging and engaging units				
Positive behavior supports				
IEP goals and progress monitoring				
Creating a challenging yet safe environment for learning				
Using data to make decisions about curriculum, instruction, assessment, and specific students				
Specific district or school initiatives, such as project-based teaching, Response to Intervention, data analysis, curriculum based assessment, etc.				
Technology: databases, assessment, web-site design, behavior software				

Table 10.10 Roles and Responsibilities Matrix

	Teacher A	Teacher B	Shared	Concerns, Notes
Planning for the year				
Planning for the week				
Preparing materials				
Grading tests, quizzes, classwork, homework				
Collecting, organizing, and analyzing data				
Classwork, homework, observations, formative and summative data				
Classroom routines (attendance, make-up work, passes, behavior problems, meetings, schedules, IEPs, team meetings)				
Our two professional development goals for the year				
Our scheduled meeting days/times for the year				

Table 10.11 Agenda Form

Meeting date	People present
Minutes recorded by:	Follow-ups necessary:
AGENDA	

Time	
5 min	Review Agenda and Positive Results since the last meeting
5 min	Review the Co-Teaching Progress Rubric/Tracker to make sure you keep all of your priorities in focus
5-10 min	Review student needs, student work, student data
30 min	Plan for the next week using agreed-upon weekly lesson planning document or daily lesson planning document (see "Weekly Lesson Outline and Daily Lesson Planning" in Chapters 1 and 6.)
10 min	Review tasks for participants for the next week
5 min	Plan for next meeting: time, place, participants, topics

Weekly Lesson Planning

During the weekly meeting, the following form can be used to map out the week's goals for students, the responsibilities of each teacher, as well as the teaching models that will be used. At the beginning of the year, the more detailed daily lesson-planning form may be necessary to support the co-teachers as they consider the needs of the students and the specific groupings, instructional methods, and assessments.

Table 10.12 Weekly Lesson Outline Form

Day of Week/ Content	Whole Class • One teaches/ One observes • One teaches/ One drifts • One teaches/ One assists or supports • One teaches/ One adapts the curriculum	Small Groups • Parallel teaching • Alternative • Skill group • Learning styles • Stations	Materials, Tasks Teacher A	Materials, Tasks Teacher B
Monday Content:				
Tuesday Content:				
Wednesday Content:				
Thursday Content:				
Friday Content:				

The sample lesson plan in Table 10.13 uses the Reader's and Writer's Workshop models to develop flexible groups that allow for individual student work, working in small groups, whole-class mini-lessons, and individual conferences with each teacher. In this hero unit, students are writing their own graphic novel collaboratively and presenting it to the class, which uses a rubric to evaluate the group's work. In addition, students are reading literature about heroes, but the novels have varying levels of difficulty. In literature circles, students generally have the option of selecting the novel.

Table 10.13 Sample Middle School ELA Teacher and Special Educator Weekly Lesson Outline Form

Day of Week/ Content	Whole Class: • One teaches/ One observes • One teaches/ One drifts • One teaches/ One assists or supports • One teaches/ One adapts the curriculum	Small Groups • Parallel teaching • Alternative • Skill group • Learning styles • Stations	Materials, Tasks Middle School ELA Teacher	Materials, Tasks Middle School Special Educator
Monday Content: **Creating a graphic novel about the Hero**	Writer's Workshop Hero Graphic Novel writing in groups of four Roles: Plotter, Storyboard drawing, Dialogue, Publisher Small group models		Mini-Lesson: Storyboard examples Conference with Group ABC about plot and visuals	Conference with Group DEF about plot and visuals
Tuesday Content: **Creating a graphic novel about the hero**	Writer's workshop Drafts due		Conference with Group ABC about rubrics	Mini-lesson: Final product: example use rubric Conference with Group DEF about rubrics
Wednesday Content: **Reading hero novels**	Literacy Circles: Hero Theme		Mini lesson in group G the hero's journey Reading more challenging book	Mini lesson in group H the hero's journey Reading easier book
Thursday Content: **Reading hero novels**	Literacy Circles Hero Theme		Mini lesson in group G (Reading more challenging book)	Mini lesson in group H the hero's journey (Reading easier book)
Friday Content: **Present and evaluate writing on heroes**	Whole Class Present Six groups share graphic novels Shared Rubric Carousel—Using rubric Awards for Best of Criteria of Rubric: Best Plot, Best Story Board, Best Dialogue, Best as whole		Demonstrate Rubric/ Voting on Comic	Demonstrate How Carousel works Class Norms • Positive comments • We're all learning • Appreciate the strengths of one another • Grade—Best in gets "prize" from classroom box • Grade—Based on rubric

Table 10.14 Sample Elementary Classroom Weekly Lesson-Outline Form: Part-Time Specialist and Para-Educator

Day of week/ Content	Co-Teaching Models • Supportive Model (Whole Class) • Parallel Model (Small Groups) • Complementary/ Side-by-Side (Whole Class) • Duet/Team	Materials, Tasks Classroom Teacher	Materials, Tasks Special Educator	Materials, Tasks Para-Educator
Monday Content:	Classroom Teacher alone	Introduces addition of double-digit numbers using number line and manipulatives. Students' usual seats are in groups of four		
Tuesday Content:		Mini-lesson whole class on adding Then three groups Group A: word problem solved in twos	Re-teach Monday's lesson to small at-risk group	Students at computers work through program on adding Group C: at standard
Wednesday Content:		Works with group C on problem solving.	Problem solving with group B	Group A on computers
Thursday Content:		Group C: very challenging	Group B: at standard	Math Puzzler problem solving Group B: at standard
Friday Content:	Teacher alone	Math Read Aloud Back to usual seats to illustrate math read aloud new problem		

Daily Lesson Planning

After the weekly lesson planning, the following form can be used to map out the lesson more specifically by each co-teacher, although, at the earliest stages of the co-teaching team development, each day may need to be planned collaboratively and with the level of detail provided in the Daily Lesson-Planning Form. This kind of planning is time-consuming and may be necessary for a beginning co-teaching team. The Daily Lesson-Planning Form calls for specific detailing of the lesson purpose, student mastery objectives and standards, assessments, sequencing of the learning design, flexible group membership, accommodations, modifications, and assessment of progress.

Many teacher teams would not have time to do this careful planning daily, but co-teachers, if they want to use more than the whole-class model and include flexible grouping and differentiated instruction, need

to consider differentiating instruction with flexible grouping. In some districts, teachers plan the major goals for the whole course and for each unit during the summer months. Some districts support this planning as curriculum work. In this way, both teachers have the big picture established before school starts, with some time carved out—with administrative support—which may include being released from all or some duties, or time from release/professional development days. Some schools have teachers co-teach four days and provide the fifth day for planning together. Other schools will bring in substitutes for one day a week to release co-teachers for time to work. Also, after working together and with organization, sending hard copies of the week's lessons via email, instant messaging, or communicating via Skype, using curriculum mapping software, teachers may be able to create some efficiencies so that they have some collaborative time.

Table 10.15 Daily Lesson-Planning Form

Unit/Lesson	
Standard(s) (District or State)	
What students will know and be able to do at the end of the unit/lesson	
Assessments: Formative: observation, conference, quizzes, group work, rubrics Summative: test, performance-based task, etc.	
Sequence of lesson/activities: How will you support and scaffold students' learning as they move toward mastery? 1. Whole class introduction/mini-lesson, etc.: 2. Flexible group activities: 3. Wrap-up/Evaluation (exit slip, hand in work, observation, quiz, etc.):	
Co-Teaching Model • Supportive Model (Whole Class) • Parallel Model (Small Groups) • Complementary/Side-by-Side (Whole Class)	
Teacher A Responsibilities	**Teacher B Responsibilities**
Grouping Strategies (Seating Arrangements)	
Group A Students (identify by table, group, name)	Group B Students (identify by table, group, name)
Paraprofessional Role (Optional)	Paraprofessional Materials (Optional)
Accommodations, Modifications, and Materials for This Unit/Lesson	Accommodations, Modifications, Materials for This Unit/Lesson
Evaluation of Group A	Evaluation for Group B
Follow-Up Notes to Share with Co-Teacher	Follow-Up Notes to Share with Co-Teacher

Sample Elementary Co-Taught Lesson

In this section, an elementary co-taught lesson is **described and then outlined using the lesson planning form.**

Jane and Richard co-teach an inclusive class in English language arts in their third-grade classroom. Jane is the general educator and Richard is the ELL specialist. They want the students to expand their vocabularies and begin to collect a journal called "My A-Z Favorite Words." To begin this unit, they have selected a read-aloud picture book, *The Boy Who Loved Words* by Roni Schrotter. The first lesson is a whole-class lesson with all of the students sitting on the rug and listening and looking at this picture book about a boy who collects words. After the read aloud, students go to their heterogeneously grouped tables (four to a table) and are given two pages from the picture book to explain to others in the class. They work together to explain (1) what happened, (2) where it happened, (3) to whom,

and (4) what this shows about the boy who loved words. They work together, then use the digital camera to show their page and their explanation on day one. At the end of the day, they see that this boy has collected words for many different purposes (stopping people from fighting, joining with a girl named Melody to bring people "just the right word," or to remind them of melodies). On the second day, they begin their journals and letter them from A to Z as a whole group. As a group, they nominate words to go in their journals from this book as words they like and words that have power. They then divide into five groups of four. One of the groups is made up of ELL students. They had all read stories that they had selected. They are asked to "collect" four words from their favorite stories and write them in their journal. They share their words with their tables. The tables pick four favorite words and record them on post-its or oak tag for the classroom's word wall of powerful words.

In this first lesson, the teachers initially co-taught the whole class together—each teaching, each coaching—using the Model III: Duet or Team Co-Teaching Model. Then, they circulated throughout the room to the table groups (Model II); then, the class reassembled as a whole group. On the second day, the whole class selected favorite words, then students went to groups based on the books they had been reading with different levels of challenge. The ELL students were in one group. Students selected and shared words, then went back to a whole class discussion to share their words for the class's word wall. The added value in this lesson was that ELL students were able to participate with their peers in whole-class work and able to read materials that support their growth in language in small-group work. All of the smaller groups supported different levels of challenge. Students cannot learn if the complexity of the text is at the students' frustration level. ELL students' need for vocabulary building is important, but that is also true for all third graders. Eventually, students would use these words in writing a story for museum exhibit about a person who loved (and collected) something. They would do research on that area to build their vocabulary.

Table 10.16   Daily Lesson-Planning Form: Elementary Sample

Unit/Lesson
Character traits and adjectives leading up to writing a paragraph about a character
Standard(s) (District or State)
Common Core Reading Literature (RL), Speaking and Listening (SL), and Writing (W) standards:
SL 3.2 Determine the main ideas and supporting details of a text read aloud or information presented in diverse media and formats, including visually, quantitatively, and orally.
W 3.10 Write routinely over extended time frames (time for research, reflection, and revision) and shorter time frames (a single sitting or a day or two) for a range of discipline-specific tasks, purposes, and audiences.
L 3.4 Determine or clarify the meaning of unknown and multiple-meaning word and phrases *based on grade three reading and content,* choosing flexibly from a range of strategies.
What students will know and be able to do at the end of the unit/lesson:
Retell part of a read-aloud story when they're given the text. Share their story with the class.
Collect powerful vocabulary words that they want to use in their writing.
Create a museum collection and list the words that a collector would need to know.
Assessments:
Formative: observation, conference, quizzes, group work, rubrics
Summative: test, performance-based task, etc.
Sequence of Lesson/Activities: How will you support and scaffold students' learning as they move toward mastery?
1. Whole class introduction/mini-lesson, etc.: Jane reads a story. Richard gives instructions for group work and models how to write a summary of a selected part of the text to share.
2. Flexible group activities: The students move to a second group and read a two-page passage closely and work together to create a summary to share.
3. Wrap-up/Evaluation (exit slip, hand in work, observation, quiz, etc.): Students hand in their summaries.
Day 2 Students begin their collection journals as a class. They select words they liked from *The Boy Who Loved Words* and Richard posts them on the class word wall for powerful words. Students begin their journals then break up into groups based on books that they are reading. The ELL group is together. Students select words from their books and enter them into their journals. They select four words to share with the class. Each student in the group picks his or her favorite word. The whole class meets and each student contributes a word for the powerful word collection.
Co-Teaching Model
● Supportive Model (Whole Class)
X Parallel Model (Small Groups)
● Complementary/Side-by-Side (Whole Class)

Jane's Responsibilities	Richard's Responsibilities
1. Read story to whole class.	1. Model "My A to Z Favorite Words"
2. Circulate among groups.	2. Work with all groups on day 1
Day 2: Co-Lead group as they collect favorite words from *The Boy Who Loved Words*	Day 2: Show students how to add words to their journal
Work with book groups	Work with book groups
Whole class: Co-lead and collect each student's powerful word.	Whole class: Write powerful words
Grouping Strategies (Seating Arrangements) Whole Class Table-Groups (Typical home-room seating, heterogeneous) Book Groups based on the specific book they are reading (homogeneous).	
Group Students (identify by table, group, name) Homeroom heterogeneous grouping Flexible Reading Group based on book and level. One group is made up of ELL students.	Group Students (identify by table, group, name) Homeroom heterogeneous grouping Flexible Reading Group based on book and level. One group is made up of ELL students.
Accommodations, Modifications, and Materials for this unit/lesson Journals for all students Leveled books for book groups	Accommodations, Modifications, Materials for this unit/lesson Document camera for read aloud and for student presentations of their summaries on day one and their words on day two. ELL book group materials
Evaluation of Group A Journals, small group work, whole-class work	Evaluation for Group B Journals, small group work, whole-class work
Follow-up Notes to Share with Co-Teacher Most were successful. HH did very well considering he missed a week of school. The kids liked the story.	Follow-up Notes to Share with Co-Teacher Students did very well, and the ELL students really liked that they had some really powerful words to share with classmates.

The rubric below (Table 10.17) can be quickly marked by putting a check in the appropriate level: Not Yet, Nice Job!, and You Went Above and Beyond. The Fishbone Rubric can be used to give quick feedback to all students and maintain high standards. It allows each teacher to organize a quick, flexible group for the Not Yets on the next day of class.

Table 10.17 Elementary "My A-Z Powerful Words Journal" Rubric

Fishbone Rubric	Not Yet, Keep Going!	Nice Job, You Did It!	You Went Above and Beyond!
Completion of work	You have some more work to do.	Your work is complete.	You completed the Fishbone and added more details.
Your powerful words are a good beginning for your collection.	You need at least four words from your book.	You have all of your powerful words.	Your powerful words come from the shared book, your group book, plus other books that you have enjoyed.
The words show you are paying attention to your spelling and editing (after you finished thinking).	Check your spelling on your own or with help in class tomorrow.	Careful checking	You have used some of our challenge words. You went beyond what was asked of you.

Sample High School Co-Taught Lesson

A second example from a high school class follows. Following the lesson and the discussion is a lesson plan using the Daily Lesson Planning template.

During a ninth-grade interdisciplinary unit on the French Revolution, as part of their units on "War: Causes and Effects" in their block-scheduled American Studies class, co-teachers John and Dana divided their students into three groups. One group worked with John to explore the demographics and living conditions of the poor in France, using primary sources. Dana led her smaller group in a discussion about the conditions of the aristocratic class, using excerpts from *Les Miserables*. The third group of students watched a short video of the stage adaptation of *Les Mis*, watching the storming of the Bastille and taking notes on the cause of the revolution based on their observations of how the poor and the aristocracy are represented in this popular musical. Every 25 minutes, the groups rotated so that all students participated in all the activities during the class period. The teachers spent the last few minutes of class leading a whole-class discussion of what students had learned about revolutions and their causes, as well as the point of view of the writer and its impact on the message.

In this example, the co-teachers used the Parallel Model and Small Group Instruction, using Station Teaching for each of the three groups. The class was divided into three groups, which rotated into three activities, two of which were taught by the co-teachers. The third was done independently by students. The value added by the second teacher is that students were able to work in a small group with a teacher who had expertise in either history, in the case of John, and in literature, in the case of Dana. The students were also able to debrief with two teachers who had different perspectives on the era: one historical, the other literary. Students also have the opportunity to be exposed to the popular musical on their own and to critique the facts versus the fiction of war in preparation for their group projects in which they must represent the views of the views of the poor and aristocrats, as well as present the "fact finder" truth about the French Revolution.

Table 10.18 Sample Daily Lesson-Planning Form: High School Example

Unit/Lesson: World Studies (Interdisciplinary) War: Causes and Effects: The French Revolution

Standard(s) (District or State)
HSS: Massachusetts History Curriculum World History
WHII.3 Summarize the important causes and events of the French Revolution. (H, C, E)
Causes:
A. the effect of Enlightenment political thought
B. the influence of the American Revolution
C. economic troubles and the rising influence of the middle class
D. government corruption and incompetence

Events:
A. the role of the Estates General and the National Assembly
B. the storming of the Bastille on July 14, 1789
C. the 1789 Declaration of the Rights of Man and the Citizen
D. the execution of Louis XVI in 1793
E. the Terror
F. the rise and fall of Napoleon
G. the Congress of Vienna

World History II.4 Summarize the major effects of the French Revolution. (H)
A. its contribution to modern nationalism and its relationship to totalitarianism
B. the abolition of theocratic absolutism in France
C. the abolition of remaining feudal restrictions and obligations
D. its support for the ideas of popular sovereignty, religious tolerance, and legal equality

Common Core for English Language Arts and History/Social Studies Literacy

MA. Reading and Literature, 9-10. 8. A.

Analyze a work of fiction, poetry, or drama using a variety of critical lenses (e.g., formal, psychological, historical, sociological, feminist).

MA. Reading and Literature 9-10 History

Compare the points of view of two or more authors for how they treat the same or similar topics, including which details they include and emphasize in their respective accounts.

Assessments:

Formative: observation, conference, quizzes, group work, rubrics

Observation: Discussion at the end of class on point of view, primary documents, literature, and popular plays and point of view.

Formative: Hand in the notes from the musical: how the poor and the aristocrats were represented

Observation by each teacher: Discussion and activities when they met with each of the three groups

Summative: (test, performance-based task, etc.) They will present the French Revolution from three points of view: the poor, the aristocrats, and the "fact finders."

Sequence of Lesson/Activities: How will you support and scaffold students' learning as they move toward mastery?

1. Whole class introduction/mini-lesson, etc.: Whole class description of the three groups and their responsibilities.
2. Flexible group activities: Students move from group to group every 25 minutes.
3. Wrap-up/Evaluation (exit slip, hand in work, observation, quiz, etc.)

Final discussion.

Co-Teaching Model

*   Supportive Model (Whole Class)
    X Parallel Model by-Side (Whole Class)

John's Responsibilities	Celeste's Responsibilities
1. Co-Explain the three groups	1. Co-Explain the three groups
2. Materials for primary source about the poor activity	2. Materials for novel activity
3. Co-Lead final discussion	3. Co-Lead final discussion
4. Collect students' notes	4. Collect students' questions

Grouping Strategies (Seating Arrangements)

Random grouping: Count off by threes and move from group to group every 25 minutes and gather together at the end of class to discuss the three activities.

Group A Students Random	Group B Students Random	Group C Students Random
Modifications None	Modifications None	Modifications None
Assessment Observation in HSS or ELA group and at end of class Evaluate quality of questions using rubric	Assessment Observation in HSS or ELA group and at end of class Evaluate quality of questions using rubric	Assessment Observation in HSS or ELA group and at end of class Evaluate quality of questions using rubric
Follow-up Notes to Share with Co-Teacher		Follow-up Notes to Share with Co-Teacher

The World Studies rubric below (Table 10.19) can be used to give quick feedback to students after they have worked in multiple groups. The Not Yet group could be asked to make up this work or could work in a small group with a teacher's support to finish it. The rubric is a quick formative assessment that can communicate the high standards for class participation and scaffold further work by students.

Table 10.19 High School Rubric for World Studies

Category	Not Yet	You Get It!	You've Gone Above and Beyond
Your notes indicated that you understand how point of view can result in different descriptions of an event.	Incomplete or hastily done	Your understanding is clear.	Wow! You understand and bring a unique perspective to the class.
Your notes indicated that you understand the question of point of view in literature and in history.	You did not see the bias in each resource.	You saw bias in the three sources.	Wow! You have gone beyond mere description of bias and have seen many differences and nuances in the three different texts.
Your work demonstrates your understanding of the purpose of the activity.	You can make this work up.	You get it! You can see the impact of beliefs and values on what is seen.	Your work shows your insightful understanding of the intention of the work on point of view.

Planned vs. Taught Curriculum

When a class is taught, the lesson that a particular class experiences can differ from the original lesson plan because of the needs and responses of students. To assure that lessons are of high quality, despite modifications, both teachers can address the following themes based upon Wilson's research on evaluating co-teaching.

Theme 1: Meaningful Roles for Each Teacher

1. What did I do during the class? E.g., directly teach, tag-team teach, passively watch, or provide support to students (Karten 2010 and Villa, Thousand, and Nevin 2013).
2. What is my relationship to all of the students in the class? Are there some that I exclude, favor, or do not support?

Theme 2: Strategies to Promote Success for All Students

1. Which strategies did I use? (Scaffolding, higher-order questioning, modeling thinking out loud, the gradual release of responsibility, differentiating instruction, etc.)
2. Which strategies might be helpful?

Theme 3: Evidence for Success

1. What assessments or behaviors demonstrate that all students are learning? (Wilson 2005, p. 275)
2. Does this evidence include every student? (Wilson 2005)

Sharing Decision-Making Power

It is clear from these planning documents that sharing responsibilities is essential for the team's success. Distributed leadership has a positive impact on student learning when co-teachers have a thoroughly equal partnership in all areas. Based on the "Distributed Functions Theory of Leadership" developed by Spillane, et al., this shared leadership means that the co-teachers make all major decisions about the classroom, the students, the models, assessments, and instructional strategies in a collaborative manner (Spillane, Halverson, and Diamond 2001). In recent research, Erika Engel Small and Joan R. Rentsch describe shared leadership as an "emergent team process" in co-teaching (Small and Rentsch 2010, p. 203) and found that the level of cooperation when making decisions and sharing power was positively related to team performance. Just as important a finding was that the longitudinal analysis of students' performance over time clearly showed that shared leadership "increased over time," and its increase was directly related to both trust and a commitment by both teachers for parity (p. 210).

What Does Administrative Support Really Mean for Co-Teaching Teams?

Based upon Billingsley and McLeskey's research on the principal's role in an inclusive school (Billingsley and McLeskey 2014), principals are key in leading the change process toward both maintaining high standards and educating all students. Principals do not have to lead each part of the initiative, but they may distribute some of the leadership to teams of teachers or teacher leaders.

The principal's major role is to provide his or her school with a clear vision that the purpose of inclusion is to meet the needs of all students. The principal also needs to support the co-teaching team and the whole faculty with time to work collaboratively toward this goal. Professional development may include having outside experts work periodically with the whole faculty to support their growth in understanding inclusion, learning disabilities, effective teaching practices, and the roles of specialists.

The organization of the school may need to be redesigned to support inclusion. This includes the practical needs for space to work in groups, the organization of time to support a collaboration school culture, and the redefining of roles in some schools (for example, if coaches are added to the faculty).

The principal needs to support and monitor progress of inclusion while balancing inclusion with the mandates and drive for student achievement (Billingsley and McLeskey 2014).

Conclusion

The complexity of the skills essential for teaching effectively are compounded in co-teaching by the necessity of having two teachers work collaboratively both in and out of the classroom. Building this relationship is critically important if the co-teachers want to add value beyond that of teaching separately. The process for developing this relationship is demanding and requires regular meetings, as well as increasing each partner's capacity through dialogue, reflection, and a variety of professional development. Partners need to become adept at working with another adult to solve problems, improve teaching techniques and use of data, and to gain an awareness that in order to be successful the school needs to be a supportive environment for their work.

Without a value-added partnership, co-teaching provides many positive advantages. By providing a lower adult-to-student ratio, students receive more individual feedback. The use of a variety of groups to support the multiple needs of the students provides opportunities for all students to learn. Truly including at-risk students in a general education classroom, in which they are respected members with expectations that equals that of the general education students, provides opportunities for general education students and "target" students to appreciate the diversity of others. Research has shown that students gain from inclusive classrooms in terms of attitudes and interpersonal understanding.

However, student growth and increased scores are not always the result of co-taught classes. For students to learn more than they would have learned in separate classrooms, teachers need to develop their teaching, collaboration, and assessment skills to add value to provide the support needed for all students to improve. To achieve these high standards, this chapter has provided adaptable forms and rubrics to support teachers' growth on a step-by-step basis. Co-teachers are provided with concrete processes and procedures to begin their partnership well, plan carefully throughout the year, and improve professionally throughout the time they are working together.

References

Beninghof, A.M. *Co-Teaching That Works: Structures and Strategies for Maximizing Student Learning, Grades K-12*. San Francisco, CA: Jossey-Bass, 2012.

Billingsley, B. and McLeskey, J. "Chapter 6: What Are the Roles of Principals in Inclusive Schools?" In *Handbook of Effective Inclusive Schools: Research and Practice*, eds. McLeskey, J. and Waldron, N. London: Routledge, 2014.

Brown, N., Breyers, C., Howerter, S., and Morgan, J.J. "Tools and Strategies for Making Co-Teaching Work." *Intervention in School and Clinic: A Journal of the Hammill Institute on Disabilities* 49, no. 84 (2013): 84–91.

Chapman, C. and Hyatt, C.H. *Critical Conversations in Co-Teaching: A Problem-Solving Approach*. Bloomington, IN: Solution Tree Press, 2011.

Fattig, M.L. and Taylor, M.T. *Co-Teaching in the Differentiated Classroom: Successful Collaboration, Lesson Design, and Classroom Management, Grades 5-12*. San Francisco, CA: Jossey-Bass, 2008.

Friend, M. "The Co-Teaching Partnership: Improving Instruction for Students with Learning Needs." *Educational Leadership* 64, no. 5 (February 2007): 48–51.

Friend, M. and Cook, L. *Interactions: Collaboration Skills for School Professionals*. 4th ed. New York: Longman, 2003.

Gerlach, K. *The Paraprofessional and Teacher Team: Strategies for Success*. Seattle, WA: Pacific Training Association, 2010.

Jennings, M. "Understanding Inclusion Teaching Teams." In *Leading Effective Meetings, Teams, and Work Groups in Districts and Schools*. Alexandria, VA: Association for Supervision and Curriculum Development, 2007.

Karten, T.J. *Inclusion Strategies That Work!:Research-Based Methods for the Classroom*. 2nd ed. Thousand Oaks, CA: Corwin Publishing, 2010.

Karten, T.J. *More Inclusion Strategies That Work! Aligning Student Strengths with Standards*. Thousand Oaks, CA: Corwin, 2011.

Kunkel, S.H. *Advancing Co-Teaching Practices: Strategies for Success*. Cromwell, CT: Kunkel Consulting Services, 2012.

McCray, E.D., Butler, T.W., and Bettini, E. "What Are the Roles of General and Special Educators in Inclusive Schools?" In *Handbook of Effective Inclusive Schools: Research and Practice*, eds. McLeskey, et al. London: Routledge, 2014.

McDonnell, J. and Jameson, M. "What Are the Roles of Paraprofessionals in Inclusive Schools?" In *Handbook of Effective Inclusive Schools: Research and Practice*, eds. McLeskey, et al. London: Routledge, 2014.

McDuffie-Landrum, K. *Academic and Behavior Response to Intervention*. University of Louisville, 2011.

Murawski, W.W. and Goodwin, V. "Effective Inclusive Schools and the Co-Teaching Conundrum." In *Handbook of Effective Inclusive Schools: Research and Practice*, eds. McLeskey, et al. London: Routledge, 2014.

Murawski, W.W. and Swanson, H.L. "A Meta-Analysis of Co-Teaching Research: Where Are the Data?" *Remedial and Special Education* 22, no. 5 (2001): 258–267.

Nevin, A., Cramer, E., Voigt, J., and Salazar, L. "Instructional Modifications, Adaptations, and Accommodations of Co-Teachers Who Loop." *Teacher Education and Special Education* 31, no. 4 (2008): 283–297.

Perez, K. *The Co-Teaching Book of Lists*. San Francisco, CA: Jossey-Bass, 2012.

Russo, C., Tiegerman, E., and Radziewicz, C. *RTI Guide: Making It Work, Strategies=Solutions*. Naples, FL: National Professional Resources, 2009.

Small, E.E. and Rentsch, J.R. "Shared Leadership in Teams: A Matter of Distribution." *The Journal of Personal Psychology* 9, no. 4 (2010): 203–211.

Spillane, J., Halverson, R., and Diamond, J. "Investigating School Leadership Practice: A Distributed Perspective." *Educational Researcher* 30, no. 3 (2001): 23–28.

Villa, R.A., Thousand, J.S., and Nevin, A.I. *A Guide to Co-Teaching: New Lessons and Strategies to Facilitate Student Achievement*. 3rd ed. Thousand Oaks, CA: Corwin Press, 2013.

Villa, R.A., Thousand, J.S. and Nevin, A.I. *A Guide to Co-Teaching: Practical Tips for Facilitating Student Learning*. 2nd ed. Thousand Oaks, CA: Corwin Press, 2013.

Volonio, V. and Zigmond, N. "Promoting Research-Based Practices Through Inclusion." *Theory into Practice* 46, no. 4 (2007): 291–300.

Wilson, G.L. "This Doesn't Look Familiar! A Supervisor's Guide for Observing Co-Teachers." *Intervention in School and Clinic* 40, no. 5 (2005): 271–275.

Zigmond, N., Simmons, R., Volonino, V., and Magiera, K. "Strategies for Improving Student Outcomes in Co-Taught General Education Classrooms." In *Research-Based Strategies for Improving Outcomes in Academics*, eds. Cook, B.G. and Tankersley, M. Upper Saddle River, NJ: Pearson, 2013.

Students with Disabilities: Co-Teaching

Co-teaching as a service-delivery option for special education services has been around for many years. However, as the needs of students in the general education classrooms are becoming more pervasive, the popularity and desire to co-teach is becoming more prevalent. While there are many categories of disability present in our classrooms, there are two that often go undiagnosed that cause concern among teachers for both the students and their own ability to meet the students' needs. Over the past several years, the number of children and youth in our schools who have diagnosed and undiagnosed attention deficit hyperactivity disorder (ADHD) and anxiety disorders has risen and is affecting students' ability to progress successfully in schools. Co-teaching is an approach to teaching and learning that can support these students.

DHD is the most common childhood brain disorder that continues through adolescence and adulthood. An individual with ADHD is marked by difficulty staying focused and attentive, as well as controlling behavior. They also exhibit hyperactivity. ADHD can impact school success, personal and social relationships, and task completion at home and at school. Since ADHD has been around for such a long time, there has been quite a bit of research in the area. Most recent brain research has revealed that those persons with ADHD have a delay in their brain function that controls thinking, attention, and planning. Most common symptoms that teachers recognize in the classroom are inattention, hyperactivity, and impulsivity. Regardless of your level of knowledge of ADHD, you should be cautious of myths.

- Myth: Girls have lower rates of and less severe cases of ADHD than boys.
  - Truth: Girls are less likely than boys to receive a diagnosis of and treatment for ADHD. Girls tend to experience a greater impact on cognition and lower rates of hyperactivity than boys, but both show the same similarities and differences in treatment and needs. Conduct problems are not as severe in girls as in boys with ADHD, which accounts for the lower rates of identification ("About ADHD and ADD" 2015).

Overall, one in 11 school-aged children are diagnosed with ADHD. For teachers, it is important to note that more middle- and high-school-aged students have ADHD than elementary-school-aged students. The following statistics represent the average rate of occurrence by the age span:

- One in 15, ages 4–10 years (elementary school)
- One in nine, ages 11–14 years (middle school/ grades)
- One in 10, ages 15–17 years (high school) ("About ADHD and ADD" 2015)

Co-teaching, as discussed in this chapter, refers to two educators who share equally in the planning, instruction, assessment, and accountability for a class with diverse populations. Regarding special education, co-teaching is a means for providing specialized instruction to students who have a disability and are being educated in the general education classroom (Friend 2008). For students with ADHD, co-teaching is an effective service-delivery model to use for ensuring the success of the students in the general education classroom. Students with ADHD benefit from minimized distractions in the classroom. A common accommodation for teachers is to use proximity and be intentional about the seating arrangement in order to minimize the distractions for the students. In the supportive model, the co-teachers should plan that every eight to 10 minutes, either teacher would move in close proximity of the student to ensure the student is on task, and also to redirect as needed. It is important that the special education teacher is not always the person who does this. Using the parallel model ensures that the student with ADHD is put in a small group with fewer distractions and is seated near the teacher.

Students with ADHD struggle with keeping up, due to their inattentiveness. They often fall behind and are unable to complete their assignment or task. As a teacher, I often worried about how I could not only support my students with ADHD, but also teach them independence and accountability. Becoming a co-teacher and using the co-teaching models helped address my concerns.

One essential element of co-teaching that is discussed in this chapter is the partnership and collaborative relationship between co-teachers. Planning is a large part of this. During the co-teachers' planning time, they can develop outlines for students with ADHD to use for note-taking, which will guard against them falling behind during class and also ensure their independence. Organizing the lesson content so that you teach the most difficult part of the lesson or content early in the class if you are a middle or high school teacher, and early in the day if you are an elementary teacher, ensures students' independence in learning. Students with ADHD are able to sustain their focus better during the early onset of a task or class.

During classroom instruction, co-teachers can use the complementary or side-by-side co-teaching model so that the special educator can model the use of pointers and bookmarks for tracking during reading assignments. In addition, this model can be helpful during any content lesson when the general education teacher is introducing a new concept, and when the special educator is at the Elmo or whiteboard modeling the steps to solving a problem and using the strategies the general education teacher is explaining. Another model that is good to use with students with ADHD is station teaching, which is one of the parallel models. The use of this model ensures the student has consistent teacher contact as well as movement breaks when transitioning between stations. Teachers design learning stations and plan for each teacher taking a station and delivering direct instruction or reteaching skills. Meanwhile, one station remains as an independent technology station where students can still access the curriculum on their own without a teacher. You can use interactive sites for online simulations for math and science or for Public Broadcasting Service (PBS) learning media for social studies or history. You can also modify the station-teaching model and have four stations, with the fourth station being a peer-modeling or peer-collaboration station. At this station, students come together, share their thinking, and model their thinking for one another. This is helpful to students with ADHD, but also to those with non-academic challenges, such as students who have low self-esteem or trouble making connections with peers.

Anxiety is a natural safety and defense mechanism that we all have. It helps us get out of harm's way and prepare for important events. But when one experiences anxiety that is persistent, uncontrollable, and overwhelming, or becomes excessive, irrational, and debilitating to daily activities, this is considered an anxiety disorder. The term *anxiety disorder* encompasses generalized anxiety disorder (GAD), panic disorders, and social anxiety disorders.

As with ADHD, the number of students diagnosed with anxiety disorders is also increasing and becoming more prevalent in our schools and classrooms. According to the School Mental Health Organization (2015), one in every 10 young people suffers from an anxiety disorder. Anxiety disorders are the most common childhood mental health issue. Of the children and youth who have an anxiety disorder, 50 percent have second anxiety, mental health, or behavior disorder like depression ("SMH Connection Home" 2015).

Generalized anxiety disorder is one category of anxiety disorders marked by constant worry about everything. They worry every day, mostly all day. People with GAD experience exaggerated worry and tension, always expecting the worse when there is no apparent threat or reason for concern. They often anticipate disaster and are overly concerned about family, money, health, school, or work. A person is diagnosed with GAD when he or she worries excessively about a variety of everyday problems for at least six months.

A panic disorder is another category of anxiety disorders, marked by sudden and repeated panic attacks and the fear of recurring panic attacks. Panic attacks can occur when a person, even one without a panic disorder, is under a lot of stress. However, recurring panic attacks in non-stressful situations are uncommon. When a panic attack occurs, there is an abrupt onset of intense fear or discomfort that reaches a peak within minutes and includes at least four of the following symptoms:

- palpitations, pounding heart, or accelerated heart rate
- sweating
- trembling or shaking
- sensations of shortness of breath or smothering
- feelings of choking
- chest pain and discomfort
- nausea and abdominal distress
- feeling dizzy, unsteady, light-headed, or faint
- chills or heat sensations
- numbness or tingling sensations in limbs
- feeling of non-reality or being detached from one's self

- feelings of losing control or going crazy
- fear of dying

People who have a panic disorder experience panic attacks daily or throughout the course of the day. There is a fear of disaster or losing control when there is no real danger.

One last category of anxiety disorders is social anxiety disorder, which is also referred to as *social phobia*. Social anxiety disorder is a fear of being around, scrutinized, judged by, or embarrassed by others in social or performance situations. People who suffer from social anxiety disorder have few or no social relationships, including adult sufferers who will not have romantic relationships although they may desire them. The absence of social relationships makes them feel powerless, alone, or even afraid. The typical age of onset is around 13 years old. Social anxiety disorder causes debilitating fear of being embarrassed, to a point that it can prevent a student from being able to attend school. Approximately 36 percent of people with social anxiety disorder report suffering 10 years or more before seeking help. Therefore, it is very likely that children will begin to show mild warning signs prior to the age of onset, such as extreme shyness, that never fades. Regardless of how familiar they become with people or how much they desire to have friends and play, they are unable to will themselves to play or make friends with others because of fear.

Anxiety disorders can strike any student at any age; however, middle and high school teachers are more likely to have more students diagnosed with an anxiety disorder, with 25.1 percent of childhood anxiety being diagnosed in youth ages 13 to 18. Girls (6.6 percent) are at a higher risk of social anxiety disorder than boys (4.5 percent).

Students who suffer from one of the categories of anxiety disorders require a classroom where teachers understand the impact of their specific anxiety disorder on learning. Co-teaching is a model that can create a responsive classroom for students who suffer from anxiety. Students who have an anxiety disorder often need focused attention at some of the most critical times in a classroom, such as during the delivery of instruction or when a teacher is administering a test or assessment. Using the supportive co-teaching model creates a structure of embedded support for students during times when they are affected most by their anxiety disorder.

Students who suffer from anxiety crave predictability. They become most anxious in their classrooms when they are not able to predict what will happen next. Using posted agendas and the mastery objectives for the day, as discussed in Chapter 2, supports students by allowing them to know what will occur throughout the classroom. Using the supportive co-teaching model enables one of the co-teachers to prompt the student prior to a transition happening in the class. Students who require predictability will sometimes act out in class because they know what will happen when they act out; therefore, communicating the learning expectations will help decrease acting-out behaviors. As co-teachers plan, they should plan to decide who will preview the lesson with students and give deeper explanation of information taught. Using the parallel co-teaching model ensures these opportunities are embedded in the structure of the class and lesson delivery.

A great strategy to use with students who suffer from an anxiety disorder is to create a calming corner or a break space within your classroom. A calming corner or a break space is a small, comfortable area in the classroom that is separate from the other students so that students can practice calming techniques, such as deep breathing, meditation, or yoga. A calming corner or break space will have items like pillows, headphones, a CD player with calming music to play, and a folder containing examples of calming techniques with pictures that model those techniques. For middle or high school students, a break space can be set-up like a multimedia center where there are tech devices, such as a tablet, along with tech accessories and various applications, including meditation applications to use with the devices. It is important that, for middle and high school students, the break space is introduced to the entire class as a space for brain breaks or thinking breaks that can be used by anyone in the class, as they may need. Initially, when introducing the calming corner or break space, one of the co-teachers should go to the calming corner or break space with the student and model the techniques with the student until he or she learns the strategies.

Below are directions for calming techniques to use with your students:

Partner Breathing

Directions for partner breathing:
- Sit back-to-back with a partner.
- Close your eyes.
- Take a deep breath in through your nose.
- Hold it.
- Take a deep breath out through your mouth.
- Repeat several times.

Meditate

Meditation directions:
- Place headphones over your ears.
- Close your eyes.
- Focus on a calming thought in your mind.
- Breathe in and out lightly.
- Focus totally on the sound of your breath when breathing.

Students who have ADHD and anxiety disorders have the ability to be successful in the general education classroom when the conditions are created that ensure success. The various strategies outlined are proven to ensure the success of such students. Co-teaching is an effective model to use with these strategies to support students with disabilities who have these needs.

References

"About ADHD and ADD." *National Resource Center on ADHD: A Program of CHADD.* http://www.help4adhd.org/Portals/0/Content/CHADD/NRC/Factsheets/aboutADHD.pdf.

Friend, M.P. *Co-Teach!: A Handbook for Creating and Sustaining Effective Classroom Partnerships in Inclusive Schools.* Greensboro, NC: Marilyn Friend, 2007.

"Obsessive-Compulsive Disorder (OCD)." Anxiety and Depression Association of America (ADAA). http://www.adaa.org.

"SMHConnectionHome." SMHConnectionHome. http://www.schoolmentalhealth.org/index.html.

English Language Learners: Co-Teaching as a Response to the Rise in Their Population Numbers

The need for cooperative teaching for linguistically diverse learners has grown exponentially over the past few decades, and the network of accountability has reached far beyond the English as a Second Language (ESL) teacher and pull-out programs. Since 1990, the United States' English-learner population over the age of five has increased by more than 80 percent, and English learners account for about 10 percent of the total school-age population. Canada's 2011 National Household Survey reported the population that speaks both English and a language other than French at home grew by nine percent over the previous year. English learners are populating classrooms beyond bilingual programs and contained ESL lessons, and are expected to fully participate in mainstream and general-education classrooms.

To prepare for increasing populations of linguistically diverse students, government education agencies in states and provinces provide specific, research-based guidance on identification, program development, and assessment for English learners. This guidance is updated consistently and includes an "English Learner Tool Kit" created by the US Department of Education. A library of resources supports English and bilingual language-education programs with combined content-based ESL/language instruction and differentiated, also known as *sheltered content*, instruction. Districts and schools have adopted teaching tools related to the Sheltered Instruction Observation Protocol (SIOP) model (Echevarria, Vogt, and Short 2013) and the World-Class Instructional Design and Assessment (WIDA) framework to support collaborative teaching approaches based on an interdisciplinary partnership of general-education teachers, ESL teachers, and other support staff, such as reading specialists and special-education teachers. Sheltered content aligned with general-education curriculum standards are the focus of co-teaching for English language learners in this essay.

Developing a Shared Vision for Success

When administrators designate and protect shared time for collaboration among teachers, it sends a positive message about planning differentiated instruction for all learners. Initial planning for co-teaching with ESL/ bilingual teachers will involve sharing each co-teacher's professional knowledge and discussion of teacher roles in various learning scenarios. Since ESL and bilingual teachers have studied linguistics, their expertise will focus on the language acquisition process and culture. They can provide information on English learners' English proficiency levels, prior schooling experience, and social/cultural needs. For instruction, the ESL teacher will also share insights and suggestions for using language objectives, students' first culture and home language, tasks for peer-to-peer interaction, and activities for the successful development of academic vocabulary, sentence structures, and extended discourse.

ESL and bilingual teachers may be less familiar with content curriculum objectives, daily routines of the grade or classroom, benchmarks for grade-level skills, and general-education assessments. The classroom or content teachers will share expertise on curriculum materials, instructional approaches for teaching content, and clarification of texts and assessments that have been designed for measuring progress in math, content knowledge, and literacy. Reading and math specialists offer the co-teaching team expertise in research-based instructional practices and activities that promote skill building. Each member of a co-teaching team will consistently distribute data collected so that instruction and assessment strategies can be adjusted or modified for academic achievement and language-development levels.

Instructional Grouping for Co-Teaching English Learners

Placing English learners in classes with English-speaking peers will create authentic contexts that can be intentionally used for teaching both language and content. When a student leaves the classroom, he or she loses out on a common social and academic experiences shared by the rest of the class. He or she may also miss observing, listening to, and engaging in their peers' discourse related to academic tasks in lessons that use modeling, hands-on activities, and cooperative group work. When the ESL and general-education teachers co-teach, they facilitate English learners' participation in content curricula and provide the appropriate support needed to develop listening and speaking skills related to school topics.

States and provinces provide guidance on the

actual amount of time English learners need at each proficiency level (with a licensed ESL teacher). Students new to English may still need to leave the classroom during content instruction for intensive English "survival language," or lessons with the ESL/bilingual teacher that focus on adapting to a new learning culture, developing everyday vocabulary, and acquiring basic communication skills. Through the common planning time, ESL/bilingual teachers can align pull-out lessons with content and themes for English learners to become familiar with topics and discussions when they return to the general-education classroom. Students of like proficiency levels in one grade level should be grouped together because they will need similar support and have approximate language goals. Generally, students with less English proficiency will need more time in co-taught classes with the ESL/bilingual teacher present, and students with higher proficiency levels will benefit from co-taught lessons with either the literacy specialist or ESL/bilingual teacher present. Students who are recovering from the effects of trauma, coming to the classroom with limited or interrupted formal education, or living with diagnosed disabilities will benefit from flexible learning time so that support personnel such as special-education teachers, social workers/counselors, speech and language pathologists, and literacy specialists can be present to offer specialized scaffolding.

The most influential factor in the stability of the ESL/bilingual teacher's role in co-teaching will be scheduling. This will increase in difficulty with the number of grade levels, classrooms, and schools in which these language teachers work. Some teacher teams find it effective to choose one co-taught subject area to provide consistency and momentum for activating prior knowledge, teaching grade-level skills, and applying academic language. On the average, educators in lower grades tend to co-teach during literacy blocks to provide small group and individual support for decoding, background building, and comprehension strategies. In higher grades, lessons in social studies might be co-taught, because the schema and text density are challenging for most learners, and topics tend to be far-removed from English learners' academic experience and literacy levels in English.

Early Childhood

For English learners in junior or pre-kindergarten and kindergarten, lessons can be co-taught with minimal pull-out lessons for newcomers. While the nature of early childhood curricula is rooted in communicative activities that nurture language acquisition, English learners in early childhood classes still require language support, and research continues to back the theory that "oral language production in English at kindergarten entry has an important independent effect on later achievement for language minority children." (Galindo 2010, p. 48). With ESL/bilingual teachers whose caseload of students allows more time in the classroom, teachers may co-plan Duet Model lessons with specific language objectives for English learners. Both teachers would provide explicit modeling of academic discourse and contextualized vocabulary support with actions, picture books, and realia, or real-life objects in the classroom. When ESL/bilingual teachers are unable to co-teach in more than one content class, teachers can plan to target specific skills and language for the Speak and Add model. During the common planning time, they can create a list of multi-sensory or technology support materials for the ESL/bilingual teacher to bring to enrich lessons and clarify concepts (e.g., a tablet with digital pictures that illustrate new words or settings in stories).

Early Elementary

It is common practice for a team of support staff to co-teach during the literacy blocks in lower grades. Since many schools have adopted systematic approaches to teaching decoding skills, ESL/bilingual teachers will need to become familiar with and, when possible, attend professional development workshops about the literacy program. English learners do benefit from explicit instruction for foundational reading skills necessary for decoding text (August and Shanahan 2006, 2008), but they also need to make meaning from what they read. The ESL/bilingual teacher's role during co-teaching in the literacy block is to provide support for English learners to connect with and make meaning from text. For example, in the Parallel Co-Teaching Model, the ESL/bilingual teacher may lead a text-talk center or station with four to six heterogeneously grouped students. The dialogue can include a picture walk of the story or informational text that targets pre-selected vocabulary for the ESL/bilingual teacher to contextualize and pre-teach. English learners with emergent and higher-level proficiency can discuss answers to questions such as, "What does this picture show?" or "Why do you think the author included ___?" or "This phrase says ___. Have you heard of the word ___ before?"

In a more complementary co-teaching model, the ESL/bilingual teacher might provide one-on-one or small-group targeted assistance for English learners during independent writing practice. Through the use of word banks, graphic organizers, a talk-and-write approach, or sentence frames, the ESL/bilingual teachers assist English learners to tell a story or demonstrate knowledge through writing. This small grouping may include one or two struggling English-proficient children who need writing support but who also offer English learners a model of language fluency during think-aloud or talk-and-write time. In this model, the ESL/bilingual teacher may consult with or co-teach with the literacy specialist or special-education teacher, when appropriate.

Upper Elementary and Middle School

By third and fourth grades, co-teaching for English learners will need to consider best approaches for students who continue to need literacy support for foundational skills, vocabulary development, and comprehension. Intentional, content-based text selection can serve as a medium for the ESL/bilingual and reading teachers to use for developing skills. Whenever possible, ESL/bilingual teachers should be included in professional development for administering and analyzing reading and math assessments. This will nourish a common dialogue among general-education and support staff when they rely on data to drive instruction. For English learners reading below grade level, the ESL/bilingual teacher can assist in searching for and providing high-interest reading selections for on-level independent reading (IR or Drop Everything And Read/DEAR time).

Flexible grouping for literature circles will allow the ESL/bilingual teacher to lead text analysis with oral language and extended discourse. This practice will contextualize vocabulary, study characters' motivation, summarize events, or collect facts about a topic. Relying on easy English texts is not recommended, as English learners need to engage in age-appropriate academic language found in grade-level chapter books, textbooks, and informational texts. Margo Gottlieb recommends building in instructional time for pairs and groups of students to "collaborate, interact with each other, and engage in academic conversations" (2013, p. 18). ESL/bilingual teachers and general-education teachers can co-plan activities and projects that address curriculum standards, and rely on peer-to-peer interaction, such as school newspapers or newscasts, interviews, inquiry-based experiments, informational surveys, and role play for historical events.

Secondary School and High School

ESL for high school students is usually a credit-bearing class that satisfies required hours for English language arts. English learners continue to be grouped according to proficiency level, but they are separated from English-speaking peers for explicit and direct language instruction. The district or school's English language proficiency curriculum may include a computer-assisted language lab, literature-based approaches, or a contained program with materials purchased by the school or district. The opportunity for co-teaching may be limited, but teachers' common planning time can create connections between content classes and English language development. ESL teachers can use subject-matter knowledge and skills to teach vocabulary, sentence structure, and discourse, while content teachers can use multisensory or project-based experiences and approaches to stimulate academic conversations. The ESL teacher might also assist content teachers in scaffolding materials for proficiency levels (e.g., graphic organizers, illustrated glossaries, content-specific sentence frames, expected dialogues, and digital presentations). When a high school's language-support program is designed for the ESL and content teachers to co-teach, they can co-plan for a supportive co-teaching model. The ESL teacher will need to become familiar with the topics and texts to assist in making content comprehensible for various English proficiency levels and to prepare for in-class clarification as well as individual and small-group support.

Resources

August, D. and Shanahan, T. *Developing Literacy in Second-Language Learners: Report of the National Literacy Panel on Language-Minority Children and Youth.* Mahwah, NJ: Lawrence Erlbaum Associates, 2006.

August, S. and Shanahan, T. *Developing Reading and Writing in Second-Language Learners: Lessons from the Report of the National Literacy Panel on Language-Minority Children and Youth.* New York: Routledge, 2008.

Bunch, G.C., Kibler, A.K., and Pimentel, S. "Shared Responsibility: Realizing Opportunities for English Learners in the Common Core ELA and Disciplinary Literacy Standards." In *Effective Educational Programs, Practices, and Policies for English Learners*, ed. Minaya-Rowe, L. Charlotte, NC: Information Age Publishing Inc., 2015.

"Developing Programs for English Language Learners: Services." *US Department of Education.* Retrieved July 2015. http://www2.ed.gov/about/offices/list/ocr/ell/services.html.

Echevarria, J., Vogt, M., and Short, D.J. *Making Content Comprehensible for English Learners: The SIOP Model.* 4th ed. Boston: Pearson, 2013.

Galindo, C. "English Learners' Math and Reading Achievement Trajectories in the Elementary Grades." In *Young English Language Learners: Current Research and Emerging Directions for Practice and Policy*, eds. Garcia, E.E., and Frede, E.C. New York: Teachers College Press, 2010.

Gottlieb, M. and Ernst-Slavit, G. *Academic Language in Diverse Classrooms: Definitions and Contexts.* Thousand Oaks, CA: Corwin, 2014.

Honigsfeld, A. and Dove, M.G. *Collaboration and Co-Teaching for English Learners: A Leader's Guide.* Thousand Oaks, CA: Corwin, 2015.

"Linguistic Characteristics of Canadians. Language, 2011 Census of Population." *Statistics Canada.* Ottawa, ON: Statistics Canada Catalog no. 98-314-X2011001. Retrieved July 2015. http://www12.statcan.ca/census-recensement/2011/as-sa/98-314-x/98-314-x2011001-eng.cfm#a2.

US Department of Education, Office of English Language Acquisition. *English Learner Tool Kit.* Retrieved July 2015. http://www2.ed.gov/about/offices/list/oela/english-learner-toolkit/index.html.

World-Class Instructional Design and Assessment (WIDA) Consortium. *The English Language Learner Can Do Booklet: Grades 3–5.* Madison, WI: Board of Regents of the University of Wisconsin System, 2012.

Job-Embedded
Professional Development
Teacher-Led Collaborative Inquiry Groups and
Professional Learning Communities (PLCs)

Objectives for the Chapter

After reading the chapter, the reader will be able to work effectively within a collaborative group to improve teaching and learning by

a. working in a highly effective group that works collaboratively and establishes its group norms, sets collaborative goals, collects and analyzes data, and researches and employs best practices

b. participating in a cycle of ongoing improvement

c. collaboratively solving classroom, curricular, school-based, and district-based concerns using a job-embedded and collaborative inquiry group, including[1]

- a learning community or professional learning community (PLC)
- data teams
- peer reflection teams, including mentoring and coaching
- peer-facilitated action research
- peer observation of teaching
- a lesson study group
- common assessments
- collaboratively assessments of student work (CASW)
- study groups for professional reading and research

---

1 Chapter 10 addresses co-teaching, so it is not addressed in this chapter.

Chapter 10 provided information about how two teachers could work together effectively in a classroom and how their partnership, with work and time, could evolve into a value-added team to provide improved conditions for teaching and learning.

This chapter looks at collaborative groups in which teachers work to improve their school. Examples of the groups described in this chapter range from two teachers in a coaching or mentoring relationship to a grade-level, department-wide, or a whole-school data team. They organize their work into a cycle of ongoing improvement that looks at both professional practice and student achievement. The group collaboratively determines the problem to be investigated and works together to set, implement, and measure the attainment of their goals.

These job-embedded inquiry groups have many labels, including *professional learning communities (PLCs)*, *lesson study groups*, *action research*, **and** *data teams*, to name a few familiar examples. In addition, these groups often seek out experts from within or outside of their team and online or in professional literature for further professional development.

This chapter will review the essential components of job-embedded professional development and their basis in research, including the importance of the groups:

- job-embedded
- collaborative
- focused on specific research-based teaching and learning goals
- following a cycle of ongoing improvement
- using protocols and norms to maintain a focus on results

517

- sharing a collective responsibility for educating all students

In addition, we will look at the commonalities among the groups that support their effectiveness:
- the typical steps in the cycle of inquiry
- the development of norms
- the use of protocols
- the use of data

This chapter will examine the many types of job-embedded inquiries and school-based problems that teachers working collaboratively address in groups. These groups may have a generic focus of improving teaching and learning across the school, as seen in action planning groups or learning communities (sometimes called *professional learning communities*), or they may have a very clear and limited focus, as seen in lesson study groups or peer observation. Lesson study is focused on the curriculum, and peer observation is focused on instruction. Figure 11.1 is a list of the major areas of inquiry for these teacher groups:

Figure 11.1 Focus of Inquiry and Possible Group Name

Focus of Inquiry	Possible Concerns	Possible Job-Embedded Activity or Group Name
Curriculum	• quality of the documented, taught, or written curriculum	lesson study assessing student work (CASW) action research data team learning community or PLC
Instruction	• quality of instruction and its impact on student learning • the quality of the tasks given to students	peer observation action research data team learning community or PLC
Assessment	• performance level of students, as demonstrated in their work • quality of assessments, including rigor, authenticity, validity, calibration, and reliability	creating common assessments CASW action research data team learning community or PLC
Whole-School or Whole-District Focus	• improving the learning of all students • discovering root causes of learning gaps	data teams action research learning community or PLC

Both Chapters 10 and 11 emphasize the power of (1) groups and teams of teachers working collaboratively and of (2) colleagues learning together to improve their practice and support the growth of all of the learners in their classroom. **This job-embedded work is essential when teachers are committed to ongoing improvement.**

The Power of Collaboration

For years, professional development was an individual pursuit focused on developing individual skills and knowledge. Carrie R. Leana, in "The Missing Link in School Reform," has found in her research that professional development also needs to focus on the entire group and its interactions as well as on the individual teacher. Based on her longitudinal study of educators, she distinguishes between "human" capital—that is, what the individual educator brings to the school, based on education, skills, and experience—and "social" capital, that is, the interactions among educators. She found in her research that to improve, a school or district needs to support a collaborative environment. She says,

> When the relationships among teachers in a school are characterized by high trust and frequent interaction—that is, when social capital is strong—student achievement scores improve (Leana 2011, p. 34).

The increase in social capital, as Leana uses the term, results in an increase in the capacity of the entire school or team. One teacher described this increased capacity: "With collaboration, you are exposed to other teachers' priorities and are better able to incorporate them to broaden your own approach in the classroom" (Leana 2011, p. 35). While one teacher may emphasize relationships and another might deeply understand assessment, and a third might focus on computation, all of these perspectives are important in the classroom.

Leana found that the combination of the human capital of individual teachers and the social capital of open communication provide improved student growth. She says,

> If human capital is strong, individual teachers should have the knowledge and skills to do a good job in their own classrooms. But if social capital is also strong, teachers can continually learn from their conversations with one another and become even better at what they do (Leana 2011, p. 34).

The impact of teacher collaboration on student achievement has been linked in Bolam, et al.'s research on 11 empirical studies of learning communities. Effective groups share the following seven characteristics (Bolam, McMahon, Stoll, Thomas, and Wallace 2005).

1. Collective focus on improving student achievement
2. Shared values that all children can learn
3. Ongoing learning among all members of the group about curriculum, instruction, student learning, and their own practice
4. "De-privatizing" practice so that all educators and teachers are included in the inquiry
5. The process is collaborative
6. The dual purpose: changing teacher practice and improving student achievement
7. Group, as well as individual, learning is promoted

Importantly, according to Bolam et al. (2005), these groups must be a community "with the capacity to promote and sustain the learning of all professionals in the school community, with the collective purpose of enhancing student learning" (p. 145). According to Cochran-Smith's research, PLCs at their best are grounded in generation of "knowledge of practice."

It is assumed that the knowledge teachers need to teach well is generated when teachers treat their own classrooms and schools as sites for intentional investigation at the same time that they treat the knowledge and theory produced by others as generative material for interrogation and interpretation (Cochran-Smith and Lytle 1999, p. 272).

Collaboration refers to a team of teachers that has a common goal, actively negotiates this goal, and tries

One teacher described this increased capacity: "With collaboration, you are exposed to other teachers' priorities and are better able to incorporate them to broaden your own approach in the classroom."

to come to a solution. Teacher collaboration can have several advantages. Handelzalts summarized several of them (Handelzalts 2009):

- contributes to building a culture of collaboration and deliberation (i.e., leads to increased communication and interaction between teachers)
- redistributes authority (i.e., increase in decision-making in different levels of the school, which gives access to new ideas and encourages a sense of ownership)
- leads to an increased sense of efficacy, because through interaction about teaching, teachers can improve their practice and gain a better sense of efficacy (i.e., a crucial element in improving teaching)
- leads to greater collective responsibility for teachers' learning because, through interaction and collaborative work, the common goals are strengthened (i.e., causing a powerful effect on school performance)

Diaz-Maggioli (2004) and Drennon and Foucar-Szocki (1996) further explain the power of collaboration. "Practitioners working with groups of colleagues have the benefit of immediate feedback on their ideas from peers. **Learning is enriched as group members draw on the skills and perspectives each brings. As individuals learn, so does the entire group.** ... Authority shifts from outside experts to practitioners inside the program who come to develop and articulate theories grounded in their real-world experience" (p. 72). The stakes are so high today and the professional demands so great that, in order to be successful, educators must begin to work together.

In addition, when a group works collaboratively, its collective intelligence raises the decision-making ability of the individuals. According to Robert Garmston and Valerie von Frank in *Education Week*:

> The group is (almost) always smarter than its members. Working together in groups, humans have a collective intelligence that exceeds the intelligence of the smartest member or the average of the group members' intelligence, according to research. The idea of collective intelligence, the wisdom of the group, has gone from folklore (two heads are better than one, the wisdom of the crowd) to scientific inquiry with researchers from MIT and the nation's leading universities studying its existence (Garmston and Von Frank 2013).

The Power of Job-Embedded Practice

New teachers with master's degrees in education begin their teaching careers with substantial theoretical knowledge. However, in Green's historical study of how good teaching can be realized, *Building a Better Teacher* (Norton 2014), she contends that great teaching is based less on generalized theory than on the specific, specialized knowledge and skills that are developed through the act and experience of teaching students in a school environment. Content and pedagogical theories provide one important level of a teacher's effectiveness, but Green maintains that on-the-job professional development that centers on student growth and improving teacher practice in the school context are both essential for a formally educated professional to become a highly effective teacher in a real classroom.

Thus, the need for ongoing, job-embedded learning continues throughout all teachers' careers. Conditions, curricula, and student needs change, and, as a result, each teacher needs to learn the specifics of teaching in his or her grade level or specialty. For example, a new teacher with a master's degree in teaching mathematics will need to learn specific content and skills in order to teach all of his or her students in a fifth-grade classroom effectively. He or she needs to know how to ensure that all students learn, as well as how to measure growth based on the school's curriculum standards, using the materials and technology provided by the district and adjusted to support all of the students in his or her classroom. Thus, each teacher needs to continue to develop his or her knowledge, teaching techniques, and context-specific skills as schools, curricula, and technologies evolve. Teaching effectiveness, thus, needs ongoing, "on-the-job" inquiry and learning, which can be provided in-house through teacher collaboration.

Professional Learning Standards

Researchers have found that there are specific essential components that ensure the effectiveness of the collective work of teachers in their department, grade level, school, or specialized group. The Standards for Professional Learning developed by Learning Forward, in collaboration with 40 learning associations, including ASCD, colleges, and national teacher associations, describe the conditions for adults.

The standards make explicit that the purpose of professional learning is for educators to develop the knowledge, skills, practices, and dispositions they need to help students perform at higher levels. The standards are not a prescription for how education leaders and public officials should address all the challenges related to improving the performance of educators and their students. The standards focus on one critical issue—professional learning (Learning Forward 2011, p. 11).

Described in the next section are commonly used norms and protocols that can help groups create an environment that supports collaboration and teacher learning.

High-Performing Inquiry Teams: A Further Shift in the Emphasis of Professional Learning

The criteria for high-performing teams are listed in Figure 11.2 and include (1) data use throughout the entire inquiry process, from setting goals to defining successful results, (2) collaboration among all of the educators on a team, (3) student equity as a value held by the entire team, that is, the expectation that all students will learn, and (4) knowledge and use of educational research and best practices by the team. To achieve high levels of performance, shifts in values and practices need to take place. The present status of data, collaboration, student equity, and best practices are described in the middle column. The needed shifts are described in the column to the right. Research into effective teams and learning communities demonstrate the need of shifts to more data use as feedback and as a guide to decision-making, toward shared inquiry and collaborative values, to more culturally appropriate responses to student differences in ability and background, and to use research as well as their own experiences to design their professional learning goals to improve their own professional practice and teaching, as well as their students' learning (White and McIntosh, 2007; Miller, 2009; Armstrong and Anthes 2001; Nunnaley 2013; and Unger 2013).

Principles for Success: Group Interdependence

In addition to the high expectations for high-performing teams to effect change in their schools, they also need to coalesce as a group of individual educators. The following principles for successful collegial groups working well together are synthesized from the work of Cohen (1994); Jacob, Power, and

Figure 11.2 Shifts in Professional Group Practice Table

Element	Less emphasis on	More emphasis on
Data Use	• using data to punish or reward schools and sort students • infrequent use by the school community to inform action	• using data as feedback for continual improvement and to serve students • frequent and in-depth use by entire school community
Collaboration/ Interdependence	• teacher isolation • top-down, data-driven decision-making • no time or structure for collaboration	• shared norms and values • ongoing data-driven dialogue and collaborative inquiry • time and structure for collaboration
Equity for Students (All Students Can Learn)	• belief that only the "brightest" can achieve at high levels • talk about race and class is taboo • culturally destructive or color-blind responses to diversity	• belief that all children are capable of high levels of achievement • ongoing dialogue about race, class, and privilege • culturally proficient responses to diversity
Research and Best Practices	• decision-making based on instinct and intuition • continuing past practices that yield little or no results	• using findings from research and best practices in conjunction with previous experiences to inform instructional decisions • making changes in classroom practices and monitoring results and impact

Adapted from: Love, N., Stiles, K., Mundry, S., and DiRanna, K. *The Data Coach's Guide to Improving Learning for All Students.* Thousand Oaks, CA: Corwin Press, 2008.

Wan Inn (2002); Johnson and Johnson (1984); Kagan (1994); and Diaz-Maggioli (2004).

• "Cooperation is a value." In a truly collaborative culture, teachers share their expertise with other educators and offer support and encouragement. Other means by which educators seek to make contributions to team members are sharing assessments, posing thought-provoking questions, and jointly problem-solving.

• "Teams are more often heterogeneous than homogeneous." Heterogeneous teams encourage individual team members to share their different areas of expertise, thus capitalizing on the strengths of the educators within the group. For example, elementary school teachers may come with strengths in different subject areas. A teacher who happens to be particularly strong in math can share instructional strategies that have improved student learning in this area, while a teacher who has a passion for reading can share strategies that improve student learning in this area. High school teachers may work in cross-disciplinary teams, examining group and partner work norms to ensure that students are receiving common expectations for working in groups and with partners across the departments. In doing so, the teachers also become more familiar with one another's curriculum and are better able to make connections across the disciplines. It is important to note, however, that not all heterogeneous teams are successful, and caution should be taken when forming teams. There are times when homogeneous teams can be effective. However, a reliance on homogenous teams leaves us talking to people just like us and does not provide us with a diversity of viewpoints and expertise.

• "Team members are interdependent." Jacob, Power, and Wan Inn (2002) assert that: **The principle of positive interdependence is the most important principle in cooperative learning. Positive interdependence represents a feeling among group members that what helps one group member benefits all the members and what hurts one member hurts them all"** (pp. 31–32).

• "Team members are individually accountable." Giving individual responsibility fosters team cohesion yet keeps individual members productive.

• "Team members interact simultaneously." Schools are interrelated, so the individual needs of the teachers should be met at the same time, not sequentially.

• "All team members should have the chance for equal participation." Learning is maximized when all participants, both novices and experts in a particular area, have the same opportunities to engage in the team activities. It is important to note, however, that teachers may not always participate equally in every activity.

• "Team members need to learn the core cooperative skills that will help them succeed." One of these skills is developing group norms that all members of the group should be expected to follow. Figure 11.3 provides examples of norms a team might establish. Just as students need to learn how to work collaboratively through modeling and practicing such skills, so do adults.

Figure 11.3 Sample Group Norms

**Collegial Professional Development Groups:
Sample Group Norms**

• We will respect our team members and keep a positive attitude during our meetings.

• We will stay focused on the task and refrain from inappropriate, irrelevant comments.

• We will listen carefully to our team members and aim to understand their perspective.

• We will respect the confidentiality of team members as they share their teaching vulnerabilities.[2]

• Meetings will begin and end on time, and team members will arrive promptly.

• The team's effectiveness will be assessed at least twice a year.

In addition, teams evolve in their development. Figure 11.4 outlines the stages most teams go through as they begin their collaborative work. It is important to keep in mind that all teams may not progress through each stage in a linear fashion and that some teams may never attain the final stage. "School culture, leadership styles, and individual personalities have a profound effect on whether a team succeeds or not" (Diaz-Maggioli 2004).

Although developing an effective, functioning collaborative team requires a strong commitment from all participants, the hard work is worth the core benefit: increased student achievement.

Figure 11.4

Collegial Professional Development Groups: Stages of Group Growth

Stage 1	Members are uncertain of their roles and their expected level of dependence on team leaders. Teaching is a profession in which we have historically worked alone, one teacher with his/her students. For many, the only in-depth analysis of our teaching we have done with another educator is with a supervisor during the supervision and evaluation process. When analyzing our work with our peers, it often takes time before we feel comfortable in this new role.
Stage 2	Members compete to assert their individuality within the team. Part of increasing our comfort level with these models is moving from feeling competitive with our peers to feeling collaborative. It is important to note that this process is different for each member of the team. Some come to the experience with a fully collaborative and noncompetitive attitude. Some come to the experience with a primarily competitive attitude and need to work toward shifting those feelings and behaviors to an attitude that is more collaborative in nature.
Stage 3	Members renew their commitment to team objectives and develop trust in one another. Stages 1 and 2 are processes individuals and groups evolve through to get to this stage. We must keep in mind that, as with any process, the speed with which the group or individuals within the group move to this stage will vary.
Stage 4	Teams achieve their goals by becoming more cohesive and focused on the tasks at hand. They value the individual contributions of members. As with all teams, there are times when we work at high levels of focus and cohesion. At other times, we may find ourselves temporarily slipping back into one of the earlier stages. This is typical. When this happens, it is important to recognize this "slip" and talk about what we need to do to get ourselves back into this stage.

Based on Diaz-Maggioli (2004) in *Teacher-Centered Professional Development*.

Setting Norms

Bringing changes in practice is challenging in education because of the centuries of traditions that still exist in everyday practices and long-standing beliefs. Even if research reveals that a long-held practice is

---

2   Later in this chapter is a sample confidentiality statement that is used by some teams to ensure that people feel safe to share openly those areas of their teaching in which they are struggling.

unproductive, change is not automatic. Conditions necessary for facilitating change and supporting collaboration, according to Robert Garmston in *Unlocking Group Potential to Improve Schools,* include that group participants

- see that others' ideas could be useful to them
- are assured that all participate
- listen to others and build on their ideas
- feel free to disagree about ideas but do not personalize these differences (Garmston and von Frank 2012).

To begin, groups of educators need to develop norms for behavior toward one another. Figure 11.5 can be used to support the discussion and development of norms.

Norm-Setting Directions for Figure 11.5

1. In the first column, brainstorm areas of concern about meetings as a group, using the topics and questions below to prompt suggestions. In a think-pair-share, brainstorm "bad meeting" conditions and add those areas to those listed below.
2. In the second column, begin to draft possible group norms.
3. Once the group has a list, hone the norms down to a relatively brief series of expressions. The following format can be used.

During our meetings, we agree to
- follow the agenda, which focuses on our goals and our students' learning
- start and end on time
- work constructively to address the agenda's concerns and issues
- welcome others' ideas, even if we do not agree
- solve problems through consensus
- respect confidentiality of students and colleague

Sample District Confidentiality Agreement

The issue of confidentiality within any group or team relationship is as sensitive as it is important. **To create an environment based on trust and safety, teams need to create standards for the confidentiality of its members, such as the following**: Peer-reflection teams will not discuss their teammates' performance with anyone, including school or district administrators, other administrators, or other teachers, *except under the following conditions:*

a. The peer-reflection team, with the teacher's knowledge, may discuss the teammates' performance if the teacher gives his or her peer-reflection teammates unequivocal permission to talk with a specific person or group of people.

b. The peer-reflection team, with the teacher's knowledge, may discuss the teammate's performance with appropriate administrators if, in the team's professional judgment, the physical safety or emotional well-being of the students or other members of the school community is at risk.

Figure 11.5 **Norm-Setting Areas**

Areas for Norms	Possible Norms
Agenda, Minutes, Communication When sent? Who contributes? Is there a time limit? Are there minutes? How are the topics determined?	*A detailed agenda will be posted at least a week before the meeting; the minutes posted two days after the meeting.*
Participation, Air Time, Listening Who talks? Consider cell phones, talking over others	
Problem-Solving, Consensus, Conflicts How will decisions be made? In what way do people disagree?	
Violation of Norms What are the consequences?	
Norm Reminders, Review, Additions to, Modifications of	
Other:	

Using Protocols to Achieve Specific Goals

Education has often been called the "culture of nice" because of the long-standing tradition of avoiding conflict. In order for a group to collaborate and to examine diverse views fairly—which may include looking at other practitioners' teaching or their students' work—disagreement, or at least feedback, that is not perfectly "nice" is essential. Protocols can facilitate an environment that allows for disagreement but also one that creates guidelines and rules to focus on improvement for everyone, not personalizing differences. Protocols are prescribed, step-by-step processes in which the time, the goals and activity, and the roles of participants are clearly defined.

In his book, *The Power of Protocols: An Educator's Guide to Better Practice*, Joseph McDonald stated that protocols are "prearranged constraints designed to sharpen communication, enhance collective thinking, and build knowledge" (McDonald et al. 2012).

As McDonald says,

> Protocols force transparency. By specifying, for example, who speaks when and who listens when, protocols segment elements of a conversation whose boundaries otherwise blur. They make clear the crucial differences between talking and listening, between describing and judging, or between proposing and giving feedback. In the process, they call attention to the role and value of each of these in learning, and make the steps of our learning visible and replicable (McDonald et al. 2012, p. 5).

Thus, protocols provide structure and delay our quick-to-judge responses to help people see more objectively than is typical in everyday conversation. Protocols can create a safe place for the quiet and reflective group member, and they can create conditions that ask group members to delay judgment and to spend more time on everything that they see in student work or tables of standardized assessments.

An annotated example of a protocol for looking at student work is in the table below. It is adapted from one of the National Staff Development Council's Looking at Student Work Protocols (National School Reform Faculty 2014).

> *Protocols can facilitate an environment that allows for disagreement but also one that creates guidelines and rules to focus on improvement for everyone, not personalizing differences.*

Determining the Type of Inquiry Group to Achieve the Group's Goals

As Bradley A. Ermeling and Ronald Gallimore found in their research on learning communities, most districts have created learning communities, data teams, or have engaged in the work of learning communities by creating common assessments or examining student work. However, Emerling states that the present challenge for learning communities is that "schools and districts need implementation models flexible enough to adapt to local conditions but sufficiently specific that educators aren't reinventing the wheel" (Ermeling and Gallimore 2013, p. 44). In addition, their research recommends that the next generation of professional learning communities "need to develop and offer fully specified implementation models that emphasize instruction" (Ermeling and Gallimore 2013, p. 41).

A Focus on Teaching and Learning

Lois Brown Easton says, "Every system needs an orientation towards results, both interim and, ultimately, related to student achievement" (Easton 2013). All of these inquiry groups are focused on improving student growth or achievement and, at the same time, those instructional techniques that support this improvement.

Improving Teaching and Learning: The Research

Once the models are selected, the team needs to determine the best practices for curriculum, instruction, assessment, and school culture that are based on the best research. Easton, whose studies include American and international staff development, says, "Educators desperately need more professional learning, but they need high-quality and effective professional learning" (Easton 2013). However, the content of professional development can be conceptualized clearly because

- What's known about effective teaching can be learned.
- What's known about what works in terms of high-quality professional learning can be implemented.
- What's known about school- and system-level conditions that provide high-quality professional learning can be achieved (Easton 2013).

Within the first chapters of this book, best practices based on research for professional practice are clearly outlined. Thus, this text can serve as the resource to initiate research to consider all of the planning, instructional, and assessment areas essential for effective professional practice and that result in improved student achievement for all students.

What's known about school- and system-level conditions that provide high-quality professional learning can be achieved.

4. **Examine progress at intervals and modify the plan, if necessary.**
5. **Stop to examine progress, reflect, and refocus or continue**. Celebrate success; determine needs. Return to step 1.

Determining the Area of Inquiry

All of the inquiry groups focus on improving teaching and learning. In Figure 11.7 (next page), the second row provides a list of possible areas for investigation. In the third row, the area of inquiry is matched with a possible group dedicated to this particular concern. So, for example, if curriculum is a problem, a lesson study group could be formed to do in-depth study of this area. If state exam results are a concern, assessment is the area of investigation and a data team may be formed. Learning communities or PLCs are listed under each area of inquiry because in their search for ways to improve instruction and student achievement, any of these areas may be investigated.

Improvement Cycle for All Collaborative Inquiry Groups

In addition to norms and protocols, collaborative inquiry groups follow a series of steps similar to the ongoing improvement cycle, described below and in Figure 11.6.

1. **Determine the focus of the teaching/learning work**: Teams begin by analyzing local data to determine the primary area of need for investigation, such as curriculum, instruction, or assessment, that directly connects with both teaching all students and improving practice. Data teams, peer observation groups, and learning communities begin with an analysis of their school's or team's primary need.

2. **Establish norms, determine the problem of practice for their inquiry, and select the inquiry group for the work.** Once the team's membership is determined, they gather to set their norms to begin researching best practices to determine the model they will use for their inquiry to examine the curriculum, instruction, assessment, or school culture.

3. **Develop an action plan with SMART goals[3] for both teaching and learning.** The team will set goals, timelines, and determine the people responsible, as well as interim and final measures of progress.

Figure 11.6 Ongoing Improvement Cycle

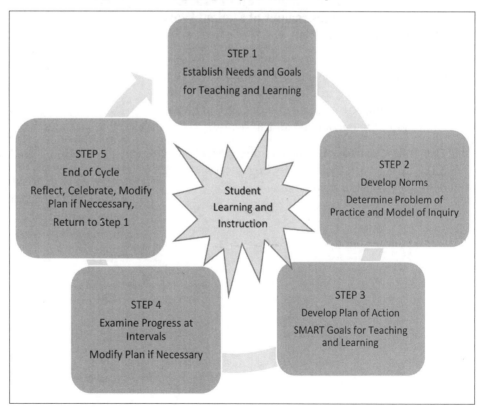

---

3 See later in this chapter for an example of the SMART goal-setting process, which requires specific, measurable, actionable, results-oriented, and time-specific goals in the development of an effective action plan.

Figure 11.7　Inquiry Groups and Problems Each Investigates

Area of Inquiry	Curriculum	Instruction	Assessment	School/Class-room Culture	Other Factors
Possible Problems	• curriculum alignment • curriculum mapping • vertical alignment within or between schools • defining mastery objectives, essential questions	• new techniques (differentiating instruction, for example) • new program (literacy or math, for example) • need for formative assessment • need for higher expectations	• student achievement • benchmarking • assessing growth • formative assessment and checking for understanding needed	• loss of students for school choice • low morale for: 　○ students 　○ teachers	• excessive absences • excessive disciplinary incidents • low college enrollment • low college perseverance
Type of Inquiry Group	• lesson study • collaboratively assess student work (CASW) • learning community or PLC	• peer observation team(s) • lesson study group • coaching • mentoring • learning community or PLC	• data team • CASW • lesson study • learning community or PLC	• data team • study group to look at professional literature • learning community or PLC	• data team • learning community or PLC

Sample Inquiry Group Activity: Short Protocol for Collaborative Assessment of Student Work (CASW) with Action Plan

Figure 11.8 is a summary of the process that an inquiry group focused on improving student work might use. As you will see from the table above, its primary concern is improving student work and its focus includes both the curriculum and student work.

The H-M-L protocol: Teachers often use the High-Medium-Low Protocol as they begin to monitor student work collaboratively.

Overview of the process: The teachers from a team, grade level, or department are asked to bring in two or three samples of high, average, and low student work from a mutually agreed upon prompt or assessment. They describe the traits of each level of work. Then they work to develop an appropriate next step for each level of performance and plan to provide interventions for their students after their whole class has been assessed using this group's descriptors. See Figure 11.9 for an example of this process.

NOTE: If teachers are limited to shorter periods of time, teachers can do the first five steps, then return with their comments from step 5 and continue through steps 6–8 and develop an action plan.

Figure 11.8 High-Medium-Low Protocol for Examining Student Work and Developing an Action Plan

Time	Process	Notes on the Process
2 min.	1. Before looking at the student work • Choose a facilitator. • Choose a timekeeper. • Choose a recorder.	*Facilitator:* keeps the group on task *Timekeeper:* warns that the end of the time segment is within two minutes and then one minute. This warning can be a simple hand gesture. *Recorder:* takes notes of the meeting on chart paper or projected on a screen
10 min.	2. High-Medium-Low sorting • Without consulting other group members, each person sorts student work into High, Medium, and Low piles. • After everyone has sorted the work, each member briefly shares general observations about student performance.	*Facilitator:* ask teachers to place their papers in one of three piles. Tell them that the piles may be subdivided if any one seems to have more than a single level of performance.
5 min.	3. Developing a rubric (or a general list of criteria) • Each member writes general descriptors for each level: H, M, and L. This can be done in sets of two or three if there is a large group.	*Facilitator:* based on the size of the group, give each group one level of papers to describe. Teachers can work in sets of two, three, and four.
15 min.	4. Each level shares descriptors and agrees on a group rubric (or, less formally, a simple list of criteria that participants used to sort the work into piles).	*Groups report out and describe the papers at each level.* *Recorder:* record descriptors on chart paper for the whole group.
10 min.	5. Summarize for three minutes and discuss for seven. • What have you found in the student work? • What was notable or surprising about the criteria your group used to sort the work? • What was notable to you about the students' understanding?	*Facilitator:* give the group three minutes to reflect on the descriptors. Then lead a discussion. End with the question, "What are the next steps for each group?" **NOTE:** there will be variations within each category; the purpose of the sort is to develop a plan for a flexible group.
15 min.	6. Consider the next steps individually (five minutes), then with the group. What are the next steps for teaching the students in the High, the Medium, and the Low groups?	*Facilitator:* give the group five minutes to consider the next steps for each group. Then lead a discussion. *Recorder:* record the action plans under each descriptor.
10 min.	7. Decide on the next step that all of the members of the group will take with each level of performance.	*Facilitator:* discuss the next steps and ask all participants to bring the next set of papers produced to the meeting after the interventions. Decide on a prompt, if necessary. *Facilitator:* ask the group to select exemplars for each level which teachers can use in their classroom. **NOTE:** ask teachers to assess all students using these descriptors and to differentiate instruction based on their performance. (See sample descriptors and action plans below.)

continued on next page

| 5 min. | 8. Reflect on the protocol on a note card or half a piece of paper:
• What did you gain by using this protocol?
• In what ways did the structure of this protocol help you and your group understand student thinking?
• How could using this protocol to look at student work improve student learning, your classroom practice, and your work with peers? | *Facilitator:* make sure that all group members record and hand in their reflections as exit slips (anonymously). |

This protocol is an adaptation of the High-Medium-Low protocol to be used in a workshop environment. See http://www.nsrfharmony.org/free-resources/protocols/a-z.

Figure 11.9 Descriptors and Action Plans from Examining Student Work

High-Level Writing	Medium-Level Writing	Low-Level Writing
***Advanced* Descriptors**	***Proficient* Descriptors**	***Needs Improvement* Descriptors**
• rich topic and idea development • careful organization • subtle organization • effective details • effective use of language • demonstrates control over spelling and grammar • few, if any, distracting grammar, spelling, or usage errors	• complete topic and idea development • logical organization • good details • appropriate use of language • The grammar, spelling and usage are adequate, though there may be more than a few errors.	• Topic is not completely or clearly developed. • some adequate details or few adequate details • Language is limited and very simple. • Grammar, spelling, and usage may be inadequate and may distract from the message.
Action Plan for High	**Action Plan for Medium**	**Action Plan for Needs Improvement**
• Read best examples from the advanced group. • Read a professional model of this kind of essay. • Have students describe what is good about the writing in each example. • Revise their papers using at least two of the ideas from the student exemplars.	• Provide scaffolding that links the topic to the examples. • Provide exemplars and a professional sample. • Ask students to highlight and describe what is good about the writing (in pairs or groups). • Model an example of how a topic can be developed more deeply using a graphic organizer with a column for "Topic" and boxes for examples, with space below each for their explanations of the examples. • Have students revise their essays with a partner.	• Let students work in pairs to write a topic and to collect examples from the text. • Model, using the students' words, how to clarify and strengthen their topics. • Model quoting from the text. • Have students write their explanation of what each quoted section means in answering the question. • Provide some good examples, perhaps from other class members' work. • Have students rewrite the original or develop a new essay.

Classroom Follow-Up of High-Medium-Low Protocol

Step 1: Students to use the descriptors/rubrics. After working with your colleagues, bring three anonymous examples of High, Medium, and Needs Improvement work to your classroom. Ask the students to use the descriptors to sort the papers based on the three levels of performance. Students' writing will improve when they apply rubrics to others' papers.

Step 2: Students revise their writing based on your analysis. Work with the three differentiated action plans on the writing tasks that you have developed with your colleagues. Ask students to work with a peer from their differentiated group to revise their papers. Then, have students re-assess their work using the descriptors/rubrics to see in what ways their work has improved.

Step 3: As a further possible follow-up, have students write a second essay. Ask them to self-assess their essay and then ask them to work with a partner after they have finished their first draft to revise and edit. Ask each student pair to assess their work.

Step 4: Return to your collaborative team the samples of the new H, M, and L examples of this work to your next session to CASW and discuss what worked well and what did not.

Possible Areas for Group Inquiry

It is important to note that the scope of this book does not provide the opportunity to fully describe the richness of a professional learning community and other peer-facilitated professional development. We instead seek to give an overview of these models and provide teachers with examples of concrete tools with which to work within these models. We encourage readers to seek out the references referred to in this chapter to learn more about these models.

Professional Learning Communities: Three Big Ideas to Guide the Implementation of PLCs

Richard DuFour's professional learning communities (PLCs) were established as a school- or district-wide response to school improvement. Unfortunately, often other groups of teachers are called PLCs when they are not following the DuFours' three major principles:

1. All students must learn essential skills and concepts.
2. Focus on what students learned, not what was taught.
3. Focus on results of student achievement.

I. All Students Must Learn Essential Skills and Concepts

According to DuFour (2005), three big ideas define professional learning communities. The first big idea is that educators make sure all students learn the essential skills and concepts. Focusing on what students have learned, rather than on what they have been taught, may require a shift in our thinking and practices. The following questions can be used to guide educators as they work to ensure that all students master the content that has been set forth in the standards:

- **What do we want each student to learn?**
- **How will we know when each student has learned it?**
- **How will we respond when a student experiences difficulty in learning?** (DuFour 2005, p. 33)
- **How will we respond when a student already knows it?** (DuFour 2006, p. 2)

Many schools do not yet have a uniform response to students who do not master the necessary content in the established time frame. Although some teachers may effectively differentiate instruction to meet the needs of these learners, others may lower expectations for such students or simply let them fail. When a school culture becomes that of a professional learning community, teachers work together to design systemic and system-wide strategies for the struggling learners (DuFour 2005). In addition, educators respond in a timely manner, quickly identifying the learners who need additional time and help. The intervention plan provides students who need it with immediate help, rather than wait for summer school or remedial help. This plan also requires struggling students to receive additional support services until they have mastered the necessary skills and concepts (DuFour 2005).

II. Focus on What Students Learned, Not What Was Taught

DuFour also suggests that certain "barriers to success" be removed before a truly collaborative culture can be established. DuFour asserts that although many schools spend a lot of time designing the intended curriculum, they fail to devote much time to the implemented and attained curriculum (DuFour 2005 and Marzano 2003). He maintains that schools must also spend more time looking carefully at state and district standards. In addition, "Teacher conversations must quickly move beyond, 'What are we expected to teach?' to 'How will we know when each student has learned?'" (DuFour 2005, p. 39). In other words, how much students learn is more important than how much we teach.

One of the most critically important data literacy skills is the ability to communicate the narrative told by the data to others in the schools, district, and community.

III. Focus on Results of Student Achievement

The third big idea DuFour (2005) discusses is that professional learning communities focus on the results of student achievement. In a professional learning community, all teachers work together toward the common goal of improving student achievement. Teachers are constantly evaluating the current status of their students' achievement, setting goals to improve achievement results, working together to attain the established goals, and frequently monitoring progress through formative assessments. Using common formative assessments[4] is an effective way for teachers to compare the progress of their students. In this way, teachers can utilize the expertise of their colleagues to help identify and address areas of concern.

PLC Success Depends on Educator Commitment

Finally, DuFour tells us, "The rise or fall of the professional learning community concept depends not on the merits of the concept itself, but on the most important element in the improvement of any school—the commitment and persistence of the educators in it" (2005, p. 42).

Data Team Inquiry Groups

A data team can be a school-based or a district-based group of educators. Its general focus is the improvement of teaching and learning by using data to discover trends and patterns in teacher instruction and student learning. This data is plentiful and ranges

from national and state assessments to local demographics to attendance, curriculum, instruction, and student work. The first step in establishing a data team is to train all members so that they are data literate. The following steps are a synthesis of the following authors' writing about data teams (Boudett, City, and Murname 2011; Love 2008; Peery 2011; Bambrick-Santoyo 2010; and Venables 2014).

Step 1: Data Literacy

Data team members need to understand how to generate data through questionnaires and surveys; and collect data from local, state, and national sources;and how to analyze both qualitative and quantitative data. One of the most critically important data literacy skills is the ability to communicate the narrative told by the data to others in the schools, district, and community. Figure 11.10 provides a qualitative description of the changes from beginning to secure data literacy. Figure 11.11 provides an example of quantitative data for which the data team needs to communicate an explanation or narrative.

Step 2: Develop a Shared Mission and Goals

Goals must be focused on student learning and teacher development, maintaining high expectations for all students. Develop norms for communication within the data team.

Provide protocols for data analysis to the teams and for when data is communicated to the school.

Step 3: Define Focus or Goal of the Data Team

Once a data team is created, the team needs to define its focus and to assure that the goal is SMART: specific, manageable, actionable, results-oriented, and time-specific and, of course, is focused on an aspect of teaching and learning. The goals may focus on developing an annual assessment calendar for the data team's school, analyzing the results of these assessments (which may include benchmark, formative, and summative common assessments[5]), classroom observations by evaluators or peers, and communicating the results to all educators in the school through student work samples, tables, and graphs that communicate the trends, improvements, gaps, and successes in the school.

---

4 By common formative assessments, we mean assessments that teachers create together for a particular unit of study to identify "(1) individual students who need additional time and support for learning, (2) the teaching strategies most effective in helping students acquire the intended knowledge and skills, (3) areas in which students generally are having difficulty achieving the intended standard, and (4) improvement goals for individual teachers and the team" (DuFour 2006, p. 14).

5 See Chapters 4 and 5 for discussions about assessments, including formative, benchmark, and summative.

Figure 11.10 Self-Assessment Data Literacy Rubric from Massachusetts Department of Education

Self-Assessment	Beginning Assessment Literacy	Developing Assessment Literacy	Secure Assessment Literacy
Directions: Highlight each bullet that describes you/your school's/your team's literacy. The level with the highest number of highlighted bullets indicates the level of assessment literacy.	• Our educators need significant support to determine which assessment data should be used day to day within semester/year, or cross-year instructional planning and decision-making. • Our educators need significant support to determine how to translate assessment data into instructional changes in practice. • The assessment process is mostly teacher-driven.	• Our educators need some support to determine which assessment data should be used day to day within semester/year, or cross-year instructional planning and decision-making. • Our educators need some support to determine how to translate assessment data into instruction changes in practice. • Our educators make some attempts to draw students and parents into the assessment process; students and parents receive information of inconsistent quality or quantity about expectations, assessments, and results.	• Our educators consistently select which appropriate assessment data should be used day to day within semester/year, or cross-year instructional planning and decision-making, and they help other educators select appropriate data. • Our educators successfully translate assessment data into instruction and help other educators interpret and apply data. • Students and parents are involved as partners in the assessment process; educators provide clear and concrete information to students on expectations, assessments, and results.

Step 4: Implement an Ongoing Improvement Cycle for Data Analysis

The data team will collect, analyze, and communicate the data trends with data that facilitates teacher-level planning.

Plan for the First Meeting

☐ Take attendance; review minutes.
☐ Develop a consistent meeting format and communication process.
☐ Finalize the assessment inventory.
☐ Develop an annual calendar.
☐ Include formative assessment schedule.
☐ Look at gaps in knowledge about students.
☐ Look at assessment results (using four-step process).
☐ What are the priorities for this year?
☐ How will you measure the change in students' knowledge and the teaching techniques that teachers will use?
☐ Develop SMART goals for students and teacher practice.
☐ How will you see the early impact of these measures?
☐ How will you communicate this to the school?

☐ How will you collaboratively assess student progress?
☐ See protocols for CASW at http://www.nsrfharmony.org.

Checklist for the First Few Data Team Meetings

☐ Review with the team members the key concepts in your school's and district's goals.
☐ Take attendance.
☐ Designate a note-taker for minutes.
☐ Develop norms for the group.
☐ Hand out the assessment inventory (see sample below).
☐ Review the four-step process for looking at data. Begin to look at your school's data.
  ○ Step 1: What do you anticipate that you will see?
  ○ Step 2: Develop tables, graphs, and charts.
  ○ Step 3: Analyze what you see.
  ○ Step 4: Infer questions.
☐ How will you communicate your work to the school? To the district office?

In the chart below, the district's percentage for correct answers in the state test is compared to the state's percentage. Which numbers stand out? Which numbers are puzzling? What other information would you seek after looking at this table?

Figure 11.11 State and District Results for Grades 4–High School

Grade and Subject	District %	State %
GRADE 04 - English Language Arts	49	54
GRADE 04 - Mathematics	68	62
GRADE 05 - English Language Arts	56	60
GRADE 05 - Mathematics	73	74
GRADE 05 - Science and Tech/Eng	50	53
GRADE 06 - English Language Arts	68	66
GRADE 06 - Mathematics	91	81
GRADE 07 - English Language Arts	78	75
GRADE 07 - Mathematics	70	70
GRADE 08 - English Language Arts	81	79
GRADE 08 - Mathematics	52	60
GRADE 08 - Science and Tech/Eng	65	57
GRADE 10 - English Language Arts	88	83
GRADE 10 - Mathematics	81	72
HS - Introductory Physics	48	52
HS - Technology / Engineering	71	38
ALL GRADE - English Language Arts	71	70
ALL GRADE - Mathematics	72	70
ALL GRADE - Science and Tech/Eng	56	56

Collaborative Inquiry Groups: Peer-Reflection Teams

Peer Coaching, Mentoring, and Teaming

Peer-reflection teams consist of pairs, small groups, or large groups of teachers working together to help one another examine and improve their practice. **The term *peer-reflection team* encompasses the full range of experiences in which teachers work with one another to examine their practice.** It can be as small as one teacher sharing the results of his or her action research with a single colleague, or it can be as broad as an entire school district examining the achievement gap, using the professional learning community's model.

Much of what has been written previously about teachers developing their practice by working with colleagues in this way has become commonly known as peer coaching. Peer coaching describes the relationship between an experienced mentor teacher and a novice teacher (or a highly skilled teacher working with a less-skilled teacher). In this case, the mentor has more experience and knowledge about the district

and/or the practice of teaching and serves as a coach for the newly hired teacher. In some districts, peer coaching takes place when a specially trained group of teachers helps other teachers with their guided practice of newly learned teaching strategies. These coaches typically have received significant prior training and practice, and they have mastered the strategies that they are coaching at a higher level than the other staff members.

In contrast, peer-reflection teammates have a different kind of relationship. It is the relationship that exists between two professionals of equal status who have skill levels that enable each to learn from the other. The term reflection is used because it denotes the improvement of one's practice by examining one's own practice. This *reflection* is done within the context of the knowledge base of effective teaching created through well-structured research and confirmed through actual classroom application. Teammates serve to help their peers reflect more clearly and more deeply on their practice.

In Chapter 10, we looked at ways we can practice structured self-reflection to improve our teaching performance. During structured self-reflection, professionals ask themselves the following questions:

1. What data do I need to determine if the lesson went well?
2. What part of the lesson does the data indicate went well?
3. Why did that part of the lesson go well?
4. How can I use that information to further improve an area of my teaching that is not going as well?
5. What part of the lesson does the data indicate did not go as well as I would have liked?
6. Why didn't that part go well?
7. What can I do differently next time to improve the lesson?
8. Who can I go to for ideas about how to do it differently the next time?

As noted above, professional literature supports the practice of consulting a trained colleague. Research indicates that reflecting on practices and learning from a colleague can be an effective means of professional development. The reasons for effectiveness are the following:

1. Teachers know teaching, and they have an enormous storehouse of knowledge about what works and what doesn't work in the local context, based on the hundreds of situations teachers confront each day in the classroom.

2. It is often easier to be honest with a colleague about the areas of performance in which we are less successful than it is to discuss them with a supervisor, although the supervision and evaluation process, when done well, can be very helpful in developing our practice.

3. Our own self-reflection can be more effective by collaborating with knowledgeable teammates. The act of verbalizing the classroom problem that a teacher may be grappling with often helps expand partially developed ideas or to see the issue more clearly.

4. Peer-reflection teammates may help a teacher look with greater depth at a classroom issue by asking questions that expand thinking. For example, a teacher may be frustrated by the behavior of the entire class. A peer-reflection team, through skillful and patient questioning, may help a teacher to be more objective about the problem. The team's questions may help isolate those times when the behavior is appropriate and those times when it is not. The team's questions may help identify which students are behaving appropriately, which students are acting out, and which students are not acting out but reinforcing the acting-out behavior of others. With this information, the teacher would be in a much better position to put a plan in place that diminishes the problem.

5. Peer-reflection teams can provide objective data that one teacher may not be able to gather alone either because the teacher is too close to the problem or because the teacher cannot gather the information alone while in the midst of teaching. For example, when a teacher is developing a rubric for an assignment, an excellent way of determining whether the rubric is as specific and complete as it needs to be is to give the assignment to the students and then ask a colleague to assess the student's papers based solely on the information in the rubric. If another teacher is having difficulty understanding the criteria for success in the rubric, then it is very likely that students will have trouble as well.

6. The peer-reflection team has one primary goal: helping to improve a teammate's teaching in an area in which the teacher has asked for help. Supervisors often have this goal as well; however, they are also required by law to make summative judgments about a teacher's performance and, ultimately, employment decisions about the teachers they supervise. For this reason, it may be difficult for us to be truly honest

> *Teammates serve to help their peers reflect more clearly and more deeply on their practice.*

about our areas of weakness, even with supervisors with whom we have excellent relationships.

7. Peer-reflection teams may observe a teacher and provide valuable data prior to, during, and/or after we have implemented an intervention. It is sometimes difficult to assess whether something is working in a classroom. Observations by our peer-reflection teammates may provide an objective second set of eyes. When teachers are being observed by their teammates, they generally determine what data to collect. This specified data gathering is sometimes called focused observation. There are times, however, when teammates are asked to observe and gather all the data they can without a focus. The teammates then analyze the data together to determine the areas for future growth and development. This process is known as a comprehensive observation. Later in this chapter, we explain the process for observing peers.

DuFour and other researchers have found that higher levels of collegial interaction in a building improve teacher morale and student performance.

Choosing a Topic for Collaborative Work

It is important at the outset of choosing a focus that the team is realistic about its goals. Often, teams begin with broad concepts (e.g., improving teaching and learning), but they need to be broken into the component parts so that they are manageable (e.g., examining student work from the new mathematics program). Another example of a larger concept could be the development of students' higher-order thinking skills. Examining our use of questions to develop higher-order thinking is a manageable chunk that may be the goal initially addressed in the group's inquiry.

Realistically, the final goal should not be to fully solve or eliminate a broad issue. Instead, the team should set measurable and achievable goals within the broader concept. Typically, the result of the work will be that the identified classroom issues become less prevalent. Or, in the case of improving achievement, the students do better than they did prior to our interventions. The following are the typical steps that can be taken to identify and solve a school-based or classroom-based issue or question.

1. Clearly state the issue or the question for which data will be used to answer. For example, has writing improved with the use of the new writing program?

2. Write a research question. For example, using the same writing prompt for narrative writing, the CASW group will compare students' achievement in September and January using the district's rubric. From that data, the team will create a plan to improve students' narratives from January to April when their writing will be assessed again.

3. Be clear exactly how this project affects student learning. If we are unsure of how it affects student learning, then we may need to identify a new topic or revise the question for our original topic.

4. Some schools and districts require that the question or issue addressed be directly connected to the district's goals or the school's goals.

5. Be sure the issue or question is one for which the group can control enough of the variables to make a change.

6. Be sure the issue or question is worded in such a way that the group can gather objective data both to study the issue and to measure the impact of interventions.

7. Determine what data will help the team better understand the issue and the method of gathering that data.

8. Determine as a group the method the team will use.

The steps above are done prior to beginning the data gathering. The steps below are those done after the initial data gathering is completed.

9. Analyze the data.

10. Generate one or more interventions to improve the situation.

11. Set reasonable and measurable goals for improvement.

12. Implement the intervention(s).

13. Gather data to determine whether there has been a change in student behavior.

14. Analyze the data to determine the impact of the intervention(s).

15. Based on the impact, determine our next steps. One next step can be to continue the work on the same issue or question. If this is the direction, first check to be sure the research question (see No. 2 above) is still valid. If necessary, we revise the question. We then follow steps 2–15 once again. Another next step can be to choose a new classroom issue or question to address. If that is the direction we choose, then we repeat steps 1–15.

Effective peer-reflection teams don't happen on their own.

Characteristics of Effective Peer-Reflection Teams

Effective peer-reflection teams don't happen on their own. They require training and careful planning. There are specific skills peer-reflection team members need to assist one another with their classroom teaching. The following is a list of characteristics that lead to effective peer-reflection teams.

1. **The most effective peer-reflection teams are made up of successful teachers.** This doesn't mean that the teachers must have achieved awards or demonstrated an inordinate level of proficiency. It does mean that the teachers should have been evaluated as being at or above the district standard. It can be helpful for a struggling teacher to be placed on a team with more successful teachers. However, teaming several struggling teachers together will typically not yield good results.

2. **Peer-reflection teams need a common language for discussing teaching.** One of the objectives of this book is to provide teachers with a common language with which to discuss and analyze our own teaching. In this chapter, we talk about how that common language can be used by teachers to discuss and analyze teaching with one another. For example, in Chapter 1, we describe the levels of mastery as introductory, guided practice, immediate mastery, mastery, immediate application mastery, and application mastery. Each term is defined, and examples are given to describe each term. These common terms enable peer-reflection teammates to discuss student achievement in a way that ensures all members of the team understand one another when a reference is made to a student's level of mastery.

3. **Peer-reflection team members need to be sensitive to the fact that there are many "right" ways to teach a lesson or unit.** We all feel passionately about our teaching. We all try to teach in ways that provide the maximum success for our students. What works for us, however, may not work for another teacher, given his or her style and particular group of students. It is important that we constantly remind ourselves of this when we are working with our peer-reflection partners. Our objective is not to have our peer-reflection partners teach just like we would. Our objective is to help them more effectively teach like they would. To do this, peer-reflection partners need to be able to objectively gather and analyze data about their partner's teaching and the performance of their

partner's students. This is particularly true when we gather the data through a classroom observation of our teammates. Later in this chapter, we provide examples of ways in which we gather and analyze data.

4. **Peer-reflection teams need to be able to conference together in a respectful, sensitive, and effective manner.** As previously stated, we all feel passionately about our teaching. It is important that peer-reflection team members obtain the skills needed to discuss their partners' teaching in clear and concise yet non-threatening ways. Administrators often receive such training for their work with teachers. Teachers seldom receive this training, and it would be beneficial for districts moving toward professional learning communities using peer-reflection teams to provide such training for their teachers.

It is important that the second and third areas be addressed thoroughly. It is at this point that we emphasize the complexity of teaching and the estimated hundreds of decisions a teacher makes on an average day. When training teachers, we often illustrate this point with the story of the high school math class in which a student raises his hand to go to the bathroom. We talk about all the questions the teacher is asking himself or herself when this hypothetical student, "John," first raises his hand and asks to go to the bathroom.

1. Is John the student who will be completely lost when he returns from the bathroom? If so, and I let him go, how will I catch him up and keep the rest of the class going?
2. Will John disrupt the other students when he comes back because he does not understand what is happening?
3. Is John the student who will saunter to the door, smacking his friends on the head, flipping over the pages in their notebooks, or exhibiting a myriad of other distracting behaviors?
4. Is John the student who will leave for 20 minutes or maybe leave school altogether?
5. Is John the student who will leave my room just fine but, as soon as he leaves my sight, will make faces and gestures to the students through the windows in each classroom door between my room and the bathroom?
6. Is John the student who has a confidential history I know as his teacher that indicates he might vandalize the bathroom if allowed to go alone? For the sake of making the decision easier, let's assume John is a student who will go straight to the bathroom, return in a timely and appropriate manner,

and be able to pick up the content with little difficulty. Three minutes ago, however, I did not allow Sandra to go to the bathroom because her IEP indicates she might vandalize the bathroom if left unattended. None of the students have this information about Sandra, so what will be their reaction if I let John go after saying no to Sandra? In this scenario, I am asking myself all these questions and making decisions based on the answers in a couple of seconds while continuing to teach mathematics concepts! This complexity makes it essential that a common language for discussion and sensitivity to our teammates be at the center of our work.

Peer-Facilitated Classroom Research

Below are some examples of peer-facilitation team projects. The first example (Figure 11.12) shows the entire first phase of the project with the actual data collected and the analysis of the data. It then goes into a second phase of the project (Figure 11.13), based on the findings. Examples B through G show project designs prior to the initial collection of data. See page 572 for two examples of completed special education projects. These examples are provided to help teachers design their own projects or as suggested projects if one of the designs fits a teacher's classroom need.

Example A—Figure 11.12

1. **The question I need data to answer**
   The same five students answer 90 percent of the questions in my class. How do I get more students to answer?
2. **Impact on student learning**
   When students don't ask or answer questions, I am unable to determine what they do not know and am therefore unable to reteach them the concepts.
3. **Method of data collection**
   One of my teammates will observe my third-period class on two occasions. I will give the observer a copy of the seating chart for the class. Each time I ask a question, my partner will put a slash on the seating chart square that represents each of the students who raises his or her hand. When I call on a student, the observer will cross the slash, creating an X. At the end of the observation, I will have accurate data on which students answer questions and which do not.

4. **Method of analysis**
   a. My team and I will review the data for any likely patterns (e.g., the boys ask or answer most of the questions, the Hispanic students ask or answer most of the questions, or the students who sit in the front of the room ask or answer most of the questions).
   b. My team and I will generate some suggestions for remedying the issue (e.g., using assigned seats, more wait time, or calling sticks).
   c. I will implement the strategies for two weeks.
   d. One of my teammates will come back, observe, and gather the data again.
   e. We will analyze the data to see if there has been a change. If so, we will discuss why the change has occurred. If not, we will discuss why it didn't occur and then try a new strategy.

   Figure 11.12 shows samples of seating charts after two observations by a peer-reflection teammate who is gathering data about who raised his or her hand and who was called on. The slash indicates a student raised his or her hand. The crossing of the slash (X) indicates a student who was called on by the teacher.

The results of our analysis of the data from the first two observations show the following:
   a. I have a tendency to call on students on my right.
   b. Hamid, Thomas, Damien, Cameron, and Edward did not raise their hands during either lesson.
   c. With the exception of Joseph, the students sitting near the front of the room raised their hands more often than the students sitting in the back of the room.
   d. In both observations, Jane, Margarita, Kim, and William raised their hands but were not called on.
   e. In the first observation, when he was sitting in the back of the room, Robert only raised his hand once. In the second observation, when he was sitting in the front of the room, Robert raised his hand five times.

5. **Conclusions and next steps**
   a. I will make an effort to call on more students sitting on my left side.
   b. I will increase my wait time to see if the additional processing time enables Hamid, Thomas, Damien, Cameron, and Edward to answer questions.
   c. I will try to call on students more evenly by ensuring that every student who raises his or

her hand gets called on at least once during the lesson.
   d. Based on Robert's increased participation when he was in the front of the room, I suspect my physical proximity to individual students influences how frequently they raise their hands. I will ask one of my teammates to observe once more, keep the question data, and also note where I stand during the lesson to see if this affects the level of student participation.

The next observation is the first observation after some of the interventions were implemented. The "p" noted noted in Figure 11.14 between Irina and Nomar is the location of a paraprofessional. The time notations show where the teacher was standing at the time of each notation. We see the following from this data:

1. Twenty-one students asked or answered questions. This is more than in either of the first two observations.
2. I spent most of my time near the front two tables. Every student at one of the front two tables asked or answered a question.
3. The six students who did not ask or answer a question sat at one of the back three tables.
4. Twenty-two students on my right side raised their hands to ask or answer a question. I called on 11 students on my right. Seventeen students on my left side raised their hands to ask or answer a question. I called on eight of the students on my left. In the previous two observations, I only called on students on my left side three times in the first observation and four times in the second observation.

Example B—Figure 11.13

1. **The question I need data to answer**
   How do I get students to more quickly and more completely clean up and put materials away at the end of the science laboratory periods?
2. **The impact on student learning**
   We are losing important instructional time because students do not efficiently and effectively clean up their lab spaces after a science lab. The result of students leaving their lab areas messy is that subsequent groups are unable to come into class and get right to work. Instructional time in the subsequent class is lost as students complain about sitting in the mess, and I have to either clean up myself or coax the next class to clean up the mess from the previous class.

Figure 11.14 Charting Student Responses

OBSERVATION 1:

White Board
Front of the Room

▌Door

Robert // XX	Jamal
Maria X /	Edward
Anna X / /	

Fernando / X	William /
Cameron	Jane / / /
Catherine / / /	Mary

Irina X / /	Pedro X /
Barry /	Nicole X X
Nomar	Thomas

Theodore / /	Margarita / / /
Hamid	Tyrone
Deborah X X	

Joseph X X / / /	Jennifer
Bonita	Kimberly /
Damien	

OBSERVATION 2:

White Board
Front of the Room

▌Door

Tyrone /	Jamal X
Maria X /	Edward
Anna X / /	Robert X / XX /

Fernando X / /	William /
Cameron	Jane /
Catherine / X /	Mary /

X Irina	Pedro / X X /
Barry /	Nicole X
Nomar X	

Theodore / X	Margarita / / /
Hamid	
Deborah X / /	Thomas

Joseph X X / /	Jennifer
Bonita X	Kimberly /
Damien	Robert

Figure 11.15   Observation 1: After the Interventions

1:00–1:45

Teacher's
Desk

Observation 1:

White Board
t1:39– 1:43

t1:45
Door

Front of the Room

t1:20
t1:18   1:16
t1:19   t1:15   t1:14

t1:21   t1:03
t1:08   t1:06   t1:04   t1:04
1:12   1:28   1:24   1:23
1:38   1:30

Robert	Jamal
//XX	/X
Maria	
X/	
Anna	Cameron
X//	/X

t1:09

t1:10
1:32

1:25t

1:26t

1:36t

Fernando	William
/X/	X
Edward	Nicole
/X	XX
Catherine	Mary
/X	X

t1:34   *t1:33*

t1:34   *t1:35*

Irina	Pedro
X//	X/
	Deborah
	XX
Nomar	Jane
	/X

1:20– 1:45P

Theodore	Margarita
//	X//
Hamid	Tyrone
	Barry
	/

Joseph	Jennifer
XX///	
Bonita	Kimberly
	X
Damien	Thomas
X	

Activity
Table

3. **Method of data collection**
   a. One of my teammates will observe the ending time of three science lab periods.
   b. The observer will keep track of the amount of time that passes from the point when I first ask students to clean up to the point when the bell rings for the end of class.
   c. The observer will note which students are still doing the lab after I tell them to clean up.
   d. The observer will note which of the students

   in each lab group are (or are not) doing their fair share of the cleanup.
   e. The observer will note what the students who are not helping are doing.
   f. The observer will note which of the students appear to be unaware of what they are supposed to do to clean up successfully.
   g. The observer will note which lab areas were clean at the end of class and which were not.

4. **Method of analysis**
   a. After the observations, the team and I will meet to review the data.
   b. We will determine which students are not helping with cleanup and why they are not helping.
   c. We will create a plan for increasing those students' level of participation in the cleanup.
   d. We will see which students continue to do the lab during cleanup time and why they continue working rather than cleaning up.
   e. We will create a plan[6] that will enable those students to begin the cleanup on time.
   f. I will implement the plan for one month.
   g. One of my teammates will return to my classroom once again to observe and gather data.
   h. We will compare the two sets of data to determine if there has been a change. If there has, we will discuss why the change has occurred. If not, we will discuss why there wasn't any change and consider other strategies.

Example C

1. **The question I need data to answer**
   On most days, 25 percent of the students do not bring their homework in on time. How can I increase the percentage of students who bring in their homework?[7]
2. **Impact on student learning**
   Students who do not complete their homework are less ready to move on to the new learning planned for the day's lesson. I also use homework as a way to check students' level of mastery. Without that data, I am less able to differentiate my teaching to address the varied levels of mastery of the concepts taught in the previous lesson.
3. **Method of gathering data**
   I will bring to our meeting four weeks of records that indicate which students bring their homework in on time and which do not.
4. **Method of analysis**
   a. We will categorize the students in the following way: those with all their homework completed, those missing one assignment, those missing two assignments, those missing three to five assignments, and those missing more than five assignments.

   b. We will examine the students on a case-by-case basis to see what is causing each one not to bring in his or her homework.
   c. We will create a plan with the intent of reducing the percentage of students without homework to 15 percent.[8]
   d. We will meet again in four weeks and repeat steps a through c to determine if the behavior changed.

Example D

1. **The question I need data to answer**
   During times when the students are doing seat work, how do I get them to use each other as resources rather than always needing the teacher when they get "stuck" on an assignment?
2. **Impact on student learning**
   The result of students not using peers for assistance is that I always have a line of students waiting to get help from me. While waiting, these students stop working. By the end of the seat work time, as many as 20 percent of the students are not working because they are "stuck."
3. **Method of gathering data**
   a. My partner will observe my class twice while the students are doing independent seat work.
   b. My partner will keep track of which students need the teacher's help and what help they need.
   c. My partner will keep track of the students who get help from friends and how they go about getting that help.
4. **Method of analysis**
   a. We will group the reasons students need help into two categories. The first category is problems only the teacher can solve. The second is problems other students or other resources could solve.
   b. We will develop a plan for teaching students when they should come to the teacher, when they should go to another student, and when they should access other resources.

Example E

1. **The question I need data to answer**
   How do I get students who master math concepts quickly to move to the Problem of the Day extension activity without teacher prompting and/or assistance?

---

6 A sample lesson plan for cleaning a science lab area can be found in Chapter 3.
7 In this first phase of the project, the teacher chose not to address the issue of the quality of the homework that was completed. Her plan was to get the completion percentage up and then follow this process to increase the quality of the completed homework.

8 See Chapter 3 for examples of classroom homework plans designed to increase the quantity and quality of the homework that is completed.

2. **Impact on student learning**

   The result of those students who finish early not transitioning to the Problem of the Day or other extensions is that they become bored and do not expand their learning. The time I use to get them to transition would be better used providing remedial assistance to those students who have not yet mastered the concept.

3. **Method of gathering data**

   a. My partner will observe my class twice during math.

   b. My partner will note which students finish the seat work and demonstrate mastery before the math period is over. My partner will specifically note those students who finish their independent work and go right to the Problem of the Day without prompting; those students who go to the Problem of the Day with teacher prompting; those students who go to the Problem of the Day with student prompting alone; and those students who do not go to the Problem of the Day, even with teacher or student prompting. She will also note the reason why this last group of students does not work on the Problem of the Day.

   c. My partner will also note the students who start the Problem of the Day and get help from other students when they get stuck. She will note how the students go about getting that help.

4. **Method of analysis**

   a. We will categorize the students in the following way: those who go right to the Problem of the Day without prompting; those who go to the Problem of the Day with teacher prompting; those who go to the Problem of the Day with student prompting alone; and those students who do not go to the Problem of the Day, even with teacher or student prompting.

   b. Of the students who start to solve the Problem of the Day, we will examine which students finish alone, which go to another student for help when stuck, which come directly to the teacher when stuck, and which give up when stuck.

   c. We will examine the students on a case-by-case basis to see why some students don't ever go to the Problem of the Day. We will examine the students on a case-by-case basis to see why the students who only go to the teacher when stuck choose not to use their peers or other resources.

   d. We will create a plan with the intent of reducing the number of students who don't move to the Problem of the Day, even with teacher or student prompting. We will create a plan with the intent of reducing the number of students who need teacher prompting to move to the Problem of the Day.

   e. In four weeks, my peer-reflection partner will observe again to gather data that will help us determine if there has been a change in behavior. We will then meet again to analyze the data, determine if the behavior changed, and if so, why there was a change.

Example F

1. **The question I need data to answer**

   How do I use current successful practice and research in the educational literature to increase the achievement of my African American and Hispanic students?

2. **Impact on student learning**

   Our district assessment data indicates that our African American and Hispanic students do not achieve as well as our white and Asian students. This learning gap reduces their readiness for meeting the challenges in the next level of their education. Since they start the next level "behind," the gap continues to widen.

3. **Method of gathering data**

   a. My team and I will examine the most recent standardized assessment for our students to determine the extent to which a gap exists between our white and Asian students and our Latino/Hispanic and African American students.

   b. My team and I will read the following articles:

      i. "Helping Young Hispanic Learners," by E. Garcia and J. Bryant, in *Educational Leadership*, March 2007.

      ii. "A Journey from the Bottom of the Class to Brain Surgeon," by B. Carson, in *ASCD Education Update*, June 2004.

      iii. "The Culturally Responsive Teacher," by M. Villegas and T. Lucas, in *Educational Leadership*, March 2007.

      iv. "Collective Efficacy Beliefs: Theoretical Developments, Empirical Evidence, and Future Directions," by R. Goddard, W. Hoy, and A. Woolfolk Hoy, in E*ducational Researcher*, April 2004.

   c. We will each make a list of the following:

      i. The statements in the articles we find particularly interesting and helpful in our efforts to close the achievement gap in our classrooms

ii. Any questions we each have related to the articles

iii. A list of strategies for implementing the concepts learned from the article in our classrooms

d. We will meet and share each of our lists and answer the questions we have generated. We will each choose a strategy (or strategies) to try in our classrooms. We will collect student work before and after the implementation of the strategy to use during our analysis.

4. **Method of analysis**

a. We will examine the student work and other evidence of change in student performance.

b. We will write a reflection on the impact of the strategies we tried. The reflection will include what went well and why and/or what did not go well and why.

c. We will meet to share our reflections.

d. We will generate a list of next steps we will take to improve the achievement of our African American and Hispanic students.

Example G

1. **The question I need to data to answer**
How do I get my students to perform better on open-response questions?

2. **Impact on student learning**
Our students perform poorly on open-response

questions on the district assessments. Since they are unable to demonstrate what they know through these questions, teachers lack the accurate information they need to inform and adjust their instruction to help students meet higher levels of mastery.

3. **Method of gathering data**
I will have my students answer a series of open-response questions that use the following words that are typically associated with open-response questions: *describe/discuss, explain, identify, illustrate, trace, compare/contrast, analyze, show cause/effect, argue,* and *criticize/evaluate.*

4. **Method of data analysis**

a. My team and I will meet to examine their responses.

b. For each student, we will identify those questions that were answered incorrectly.

c. I will plan a lesson teaching the meaning of each verb as it relates to open-response questions in standardized testing situations. See Figure 11.16 for open-response verb examples.

d. After the lesson, I will use the processing partner sheet below with my students for one month to embed the learning.

e. I will quiz the students each week with one or more open-response questions.

f. After one month, I will again give my students a series of open-response questions that use the verbs noted above.

Figure 11.16 Open-Response Question Terminology

If You Are Asked to...	Then You Are to...
describe / discuss	tell all you know
explain	tell how and why
identify	recognize and explain
illustrate	give examples with labels; explain briefly
trace	list (and label) chronologically
compare / contrast	find similarities and differences
analyze	separate into parts to explain
show cause / effect	tell what happened and why
argue	prove points by using facts
criticize / evaluate	find (and support) the strengths and weaknesses

Lesson Study Inquiry Group

Lesson study is a form of professional development that has been used in Japan for many years (Lewis 2002, p.1). It is a process in which a team of teachers work together to perfect the planning and teaching of a lesson. It is one of the techniques teachers can use for collaborative professional development.

A lesson study begins by selecting a lesson that will be studied by the group. The team may assist one teacher in planning the lesson, or the teacher may plan the lesson alone. Before the lesson is taught, the team reviews the lesson and the teacher makes any modifications the team believes will increase the success of the lesson. The team then decides what data will be helpful to gather during the lesson for the analysis of the lesson's level of success in the study session that follows. Each member of the team is assigned specific data to gather. For example, one team member may list the questions the teacher asks during the class. Another team member may track who raises his or her hand. A third team member may write down the names of the students who answer the questions and their responses.

After the lesson, the teachers analyze the data together. The data tells them what percentage of the questions were asked at recall, comprehension, and higher-order thinking levels; which questions worked best in formatively assessing the students' mastery of the concepts; which students, if any, dominated the discussion; which students, if any, did not participate adequately; and which students seemed to master the information and skills noted in the mastery objectives versus which did not.[9] The team then determines what impact the questioning portion of the lesson had on student achievement.

This data is then used, first, to modify the lesson for improved teaching in the future and, second, to modify the planning of upcoming lessons to make them more successful.

The lesson study process is then repeated with another teacher from the team as the focus. It is important to note that a confidentiality agreement is essential for this process. Those interested in learning more about lesson study can visit the website http://www.tc.columbia.edu/lessonstudy.

Before the lesson is taught, the team reviews the lesson and the teacher makes any modifications the team believes will increase the success of the lesson.

Sample Lesson Study

Figure 11.17 is a typical differentiated instruction lesson.[10] The lesson is followed by the questions a lesson study group chose to examine. The teacher who designed the lesson is looking for information that will help ensure that the lesson has a balance of whole-class work, guided group work, and independent work and that it is challenging, but not overwhelming, for students.

Lesson study partner 1: I will track the level of on-task behavior of the class by indicating on the seating chart the beginning and ending time for any student who is exhibiting off-task behavior.

Lesson study partner 2: When the students move into their differentiated instruction groups, I will observe the independent work of the groups at mastery to determine which students are sufficiently challenged, which students are not sufficiently challenged, and which students are overwhelmed by the assigned task.

---

10 The example below is an elementary example. Secondary teachers will want to go the end of Chapters 1 and 6 to find secondary lesson plans that can be used in the same way.

Figure 11.17
Lesson Study: Differentiating Instruction Lesson: Language Arts Grades 2 or 3

1. **What district curriculum standard (and/or benchmark) does this lesson address?** Students will demonstrate the correct use of simile in their writing assignments (standard 6A, benchmark 12).

2. **What do I want the students to know and be able to do by the end of the lesson (my mastery objectives)?** By the end of the lesson, students will be able to correctly give the definition of a simile and write at least three similes that describe themselves: I'm as _____ as a _____, and I'm as_____ as a _____ (modeled after _Quick as a Cricket_ by Audrey Wood).

3. **How will I formatively and summatively assess the students' level of mastery of these concepts?**

    a. **How will I pre-assess the students' level of knowledge?** _(If you are not planning to do a mini-lesson, go directly to differentiating, which is question 3b after this pre-assessment.)_ I will write the word _simile_ on the white board. Each student will be instructed to write the word _simile_ on his

---

9   See Chapter 1 for information about the process of planning lessons for mastery.

or her white board and to write a definition for the word *simile*. Students will hold up their white boards. I will then call on three students with correct definitions to share. I will also model similes that adhere to the *Webster's Student Dictionary* definition of *simile*, "a comparison using like or as."

b. **How will I formatively assess after the mini-lesson to determine each student's level of mastery?**
   - I will be able to monitor their progress using the colored cups.
   - I will be able to monitor the rate at which students are moving to mastery, based on their white board work. During independent work time, I will circulate around the room with the class list on a clipboard and observe the students working. I will write *i* (introductory), *g* (guided practice), *im* (immediate mastery), or *ap* (application mastery) next to each student's name.

4. **The sequence of events of the lesson**
   a. **What information and skills will I teach during the whole-class mini-lesson?**
      - I will read aloud *Quick as a Cricket* by Audrey Wood twice. This is a story that contains 22 captivating similes. The students will be instructed to listen for similes during the first reading. Then, the students will be instructed to recall similes orally after the second reading. The purpose is for students to see and hear similes in a vividly illustrated book.
      - I will then ask students to write at least three similes about themselves on a worksheet, using this model from *Quick as a Cricket*: "I'm as quick as a cricket and I'm as slow as a snail and I'm as small as an ant." Each student will have a copy of this model on his or her worksheet.
      - Students will work on the similes, using their colored cups to signal if they need assistance. Only those students who have completed all three similes may give help. No student may help more than two students. Students who finish early will be instructed to write more similes using the back of the worksheet. *Quick as a Cricket* contains 22 similes, so students can challenge themselves to write as many as 22 similes.

b. **After the mini-lesson, what activity will I use with the students who are at introductory level?** These students will come to the table area with the guided-practice students for more direct teaching of the definition and more experience with similes. At the table area, these students will choose two similes from *Quick as a Cricket* and write them on a white board, underlining the word *as*. The students and I will then read *Quick as a Cricket* aloud and in unison. We will then make a list on chart paper of the similes that are in the book.

c. **What activity will I use with the students who are at guided-practice level?** These students will come to the table area with the introductory students for more direct teaching of the definition and more experience with similes. (See the explanation above.)

d. **What activity will I use with the students who are at immediate-mastery level?** These students will write three more similes and check their work with another student at this level. If there are any errors, they will write the similes together correctly. If their similes are correct, they will move on to writing more similes. They may then illustrate their favorite similes. For further challenge, they can define *metaphor* (using a dictionary), and, using the same format, write metaphors to describe themselves.

e. **What activity will I use with the students who are at the immediate-application-mastery level?** These students will write six similes and move on to the following extension: define *metaphor* and *cliché* (using a dictionary), and, using the same format, write metaphors to describe themselves (using no clichés). As an option, these students may illustrate one metaphor.

5. **What other person can assist me in planning this lesson?** I will consult with the librarian and/or literacy specialist to see if there are additional copies of *Quick as a Cricket* by Audrey Wood as well as other picture books that contain examples of similes and metaphors.

Materials: I need dipsticking cups, worksheets, white boards, dry-erase markers, the class list, a clipboard, student dictionaries, drawing paper, markers, and *Quick as a Cricket* by Audrey Wood.

(This lesson was developed by Deborah Mercer of the Brookline Public Schools in Brookline, MA.)

Developing Thought-Provoking Lesson-Study Questions

One of the best resources we can use for developing thought-provoking questions to study teaching is to convert teaching performance standards for our district into lesson-study questions. For example, Appendix A at the end of this chapter contains the California Department of Education's Standards for the Teaching Profession. In the following section, we have converted the Standard for Assessing Student Learning into potential lesson study questions.

> *Data is gathered during the observation, but the judgments are made by the teacher being observed, not by the observer.*

1. How can I review and revise learning goals for each of my students in an effective and time-efficient manner?
2. Do the learning goals for my lesson reflect the key subject-area concepts, skills, and applications?
3. What other assessments can I use to determine what students know and are able to do?
4. Do the assessments I use reliably and validly assess what they are intended to assess?
5. Do the grades I give students accurately reflect what they know and are able to do?
6. How can I use standardized tests and other diagnostic tools to better understand the learning progress of my students?
7. How can I teach students to better assess their own work?
8. How can I better use classroom assessments to guide my planning?
9. How can I better communicate the results of classroom assessments to my students and their families?

Peer-Observation Inquiry Group

Observing teaching is a daily activity for most administrators. Teachers, however, seldom get the opportunity to observe other teachers or to be observed by other teachers. There are few things that can be done to relieve the feeling of anxiety often experienced when being observed. First, it is important to establish that these observations are not evaluative. Administrators observe for the purpose of evaluating teachers (and providing support). To do this, they gather data and make judgments based on that data. In contrast, teachers observe one another solely for the purpose of helping develop their practice in a safe, judgment-free environment. Data is gathered during the observation, but the judgments are made by the teacher being observed, not by the observer. Judgments are only given by the observer when they are requested by the observed teacher. Observation requires practice.

As human beings, we are often prone to make quick judgments. When observing our peers, we need to avoid this natural tendency. We need to force ourselves to focus on the data gathering and suppress the natural tendency to make judgments. Learning to do this can bring positive change to a school.

Peer observation can improve teaching and learning. As Ball and Cohen note, "Teaching occurs in particulars—particular students interacting with particular teachers over particular ideas in particular circumstances." These particulars make traditional approaches to professional development inadequate in cultivating instructional change. We can only get at these particulars effectively by embedding professional development in the classroom and by activating the voice too often absent in professional development efforts—the teacher's (Ball and Cohen 1999, p. 10).

There are two types of classroom observations. The first is a focused observation. **During a focused observation, the observer is gathering very specific types of data.** Focused observations may be about one or a few specifically identified areas of performance. In focused observations, the specific data to be collected is identified before the observation begins. The focused observation noted in the research examples in the peer-reflection partners section of this chapter is focused on one area of performance. The focused observation noted in the lesson study example is focused on several areas of performance.

The second type of observation is a comprehensive observation. Comprehensive observations gather data on the totality of the lesson. The observer gathers all the data that is available without discriminating as to what is important data and what is not. The subsequent analysis of the data by the teacher and his or her peer-reflection teammates leads to the identification of the areas of performance that were evident and those that were lacking in the teaching of the lesson. Most of the observations completed by teacher evaluators are comprehensive observations. Most of the observations completed by peer-reflection teammates are focused observations. However, a person might ask his or her teammates to conduct a comprehensive observation if he or she is at the guided-practice level of a newly implemented mathematics curriculum and wants the teammate to gather data on all aspects of the lesson. In this instance, the observer is trying to help the teacher determine all the areas he or she has mastered and all the areas that need reteaching or coaching. Also, peer observations are typically full-lesson observations, whereas administrators sometimes complete short (10- to 15-minute) observations.

Mentor teachers may also be expected to conduct comprehensive observations in addition to their focused observations. A teacher who is mentoring another teacher just out of college might complete a comprehensive observation early in the year to help the new teacher determine his or her areas of strength and those areas that are most in need of development. The mentor and the new teacher may then jointly decide on which areas they will address first. Subsequent observations would then be focused on the area or areas identified.

Gathering Data Prior to the Peer Observation

The primary objective when observing a peer is to gather data that will be helpful to the teacher in analyzing the classroom issue the teacher is trying to address. To best do this, the observer needs to have sufficient background information to observe with depth, which is often obtained in a pre-observation conference. In the following pre-conference, the teacher gives the observer the needed background data about the lesson and students. The questions are provided before the conference, which gives each teacher the opportunity to think about the information prior to the pre-observation conference and enables the observer(s) to ask questions during the conference that add to his or her information and perspective prior to the observation. Please note that these questions are similar to those presented in Chapter 1 and are designed to promote mastery thinking about teaching.

Figure 11.18 is information a third-grade teacher gave to her lesson-study team prior to the pre-observation conference about an upcoming science lesson.

Figure 11.18

1. **What is the district's curriculum standard and/or the benchmarks from which these concepts are derived?**
Grade-Three Curriculum Frameworks for Science, Technology, and Engineering Construction

   3.1 Parts of a structure
   3.2 Three major types of bridges and their appropriate uses
   3.3 The forces of tension, compression, torsion, bending, and shear affect the performance of bridges
   3.4 Effects of load and structural shape on bridges

Science Inquiry Questions
Students will be able to comprehend and respond to scientific information from a variety of sources.
- Ask questions and make predictions.
- Use common working vocabulary as it relates to the unit.
- List results from experiments as sources of information.
- Describe what would happen during an experiment, how, and why.
- Interpret findings by relating one factor to another.
- Come to conclusions based on observations, discussion with peers, and experimental results.

2. **What do you want the students to know and be able to do by the end of the lesson (your goals and/or mastery objectives)?**
By the end of the unit, the students will be able to
- work with a partner to build a three-dimensional structure that is at least three feet tall
- maximize the stability of their structures using triangle braces
- explain verbally and in writing how they built their structures
- explain verbally and in writing how they used triangles to increase the stability of their structures
- describe various types of structures (e.g., bridges, houses, garages, office buildings, dams)
- work with a partner in way that ensures that the work is equally divided

continued on next page

- work with a partner in a way that ensures that both partners know the same information
- resolve differences with their partners equitably and amicably
- work with a partner in a way that does not disturb the other students in the class

3. **How will you formatively and summatively assess the extent to which the students have mastered the objectives?**
   a. As I check in on each working group, I will ask the students to define *stability*.
   b. As I check in on each working group, I will ask students to show me and explain to me how they added a triangle or triangles to their structure to increase its stability.
   c. I will observe the students while they are adding triangles to their pentagon structures to increase the structure's stability.
   d. I will note their levels of mastery on the running record.
   e. I will assess the students' completed structures using the criteria described in the tall structures rubric.
   f. I will assess each student's written answers in his/her science journal.

4. **Describe the sequence of events in the lesson.**
   a. With the class sitting in a circle, I will activate the students' knowledge about structures, which were the topic of the previous class.
   b. I will use a student-made exemplar to demonstrate how one can make a pentagon figure more stable using triangle supports.
   c. I will ask questions that will lead the students to an understanding of how they can use triangle supports to increase the stability of their pentagon structures.
   d. I will ask questions to check student understanding.
   e. Students will work with a partner using straws and connectors to increase the stability of their pentagon structures.
   f. In the last 10 minutes, students will stop work and answer two questions in their science journals: What worked, and why did it work? What did not work, and why didn't it work?

5. **What is the classroom problem you wish to address?**
   I have been frustrated by the number of students who leave the circle area not remembering what they are supposed to do when they get with their partners or groups. In some cases, as many as a third of the students need me to remind them of the instructions. What can I do to get students to remember the directions and begin to work independently after they leave the circle?

6. **What was taught leading up to this lesson?**
   In the first lesson, students learned about various types of structures. We looked at pictures of famous structures, such as the Eiffel Tower, the Golden Gate Bridge, the Empire State Building, and the Pyramids. We looked at a set of the architect's plans for the new addition to the school. We then went on a field trip to the attic of the school to see the supports and other components of the school building. We learned how to make a pentagon figure using the straws and connectors they will use in the lab. We learned the vocabulary words *structure*, *supports*, *stability*, and *reinforce*. We then reviewed the tall structure rubric.

7. **What will be taught after this lesson?**
   We will start the next lesson by reviewing the tall structure rubric. Each pair will be asked to self-assess their work thus far using the rubric. Some volunteer student pairs will then explain how they built their structures. We will have a discussion about what is working for the different teams and what is not working. Each pair will then indicate their next steps in building their structure. The students will then continue to work in their pairs building a tall structure. Once a structure is completed, the students will assess the structure based in the rubric.

8. **What data will be most helpful to you?**
- writing down the questions I ask to check student understanding
- keeping track of how many seconds I give students to process the question before I choose someone to answer the question[11]
- writing down the names of the students who answer the questions and what they say
- keeping track of which students are listening during the explanation and which students are not
- noting what the students who are not listening are doing
- after I send them off to work in pairs, noting which students are able to work independently and which students need my help to get started
- of the students who need help, noting which part of the assignment they do not understand
- noting how much time I spend with each pair of students who need help.

---

11 For more information on wait time and its impact on student learning, see Chapter 5.

Gathering Data during the Observation

The observation follows the pre-observation conference. It is important to take copious notes during the observation. The objective of a focused observation[12] is to gather all the data that will be helpful in assessing the area(s) of performance identified for study. The objective of a comprehensive observation is to gather as much raw data as possible and analyze it for any and all information that could improve the lesson. It is the data that will be most helpful to our teammate in addressing the identified classroom question or challenge. We should resist the temptation to make judgments or recommendations while observing. We should only be focused on the getting the data—that which is seen and heard. There are four important reasons why we avoid judgments.

1. Teaching is a very complicated activity that involves literally hundreds of decisions in the course of a day. Good judgments cannot be made until it is understood why the teacher chose to say or do what was observed in the lesson. The post-observation conference provides an opportunity to ask these questions.
2. The best solutions to classroom problems are those that a teacher develops through thoughtful reflection and discussion about the data an observer has gathered.
3. Pausing to analyze the data to make judgments during the observation may result in missing important data.
4. Unless asked for judgments, the peer observer's role is solely that of the data gatherer. Giving unsolicited judgments can inhibit the trusting relationship that is critically important in a teacher's improvement. As the relationship builds, we often become more comfortable with our partners and begin to ask for their opinions and judgments. Each person comes to this level of comfort at his or her own rate. Therefore, it is important that observers stay in the role of data gatherer or provider unless and until asked to do otherwise.

There are a variety of techniques we use for gathering data during an observation. The best techniques to use are determined by the area of focus for the observation. Two-column note-taking, notations on seating charts, audio recordings, and video recordings can all be effective techniques for gathering data.

Two-Column Note-Taking

When gathering data with two-column note-taking, bring a pad and paper, laptop computer, or tablet on which to write notes. Divide the paper or screen into two columns as seen in Figure 11.19. This can be done easily on laptops or tablets using the table function of most word-processing programs. In the right column, note what the students say, what the teacher says, and what we refer to as *stage directions*. Stage directions are all the data that is not spoken. They include the arrangement of the classroom furniture, information on a black or white board, wall displays, the location of the students, and the location of the teacher.

In the left column, write the time,[13] any questions to ask the teacher after the observation, and any notes or reminders about the observation. Track the time because it may be useful to the teacher to know at what point a specific incident occurred in a lesson or to know how long it took to complete a certain part of the lesson. While teaching, teachers often lose track of the time. It is hard to gauge how long each part of the lesson took. Keeping track of the time is also helpful in determining the amount of time certain students are on task. The observer should note the time at least every five minutes and more frequently during transitions.

In the left column, also write down questions and personal notes. A class moves very quickly, and there is so much to note that a thought in the first three minutes of the class is typically forgotten five minutes later. Finally, the left column is used for analysis notes made after the observation. While the observer is busy gathering data, there isn't time to analyze it. The time spent in the classroom should be focused on getting as much data as possible.

The right column is used for teacher and student quotes as well as their movements (stage directions). For examples of two-column notes, see Figure 11.22.

Figure 11.19

Two-Column Notes	
1. Time 2. Questions or reminders to yourself 3. Questions for the teacher 4. Analysis and comments made after the observation	1. Teacher quotes 1. Student quotes 2. Stage directions

12 The "Self-Reflection: Educating ELLs" form found in the ELL essay at the end of this chapter can easily be adapted for use by a colleague observing in our class with a focus on performance of ELL students.

13 Some tablets and online note-taking forms in educator-evaluation platforms contain forms that have "time stamps." This feature is a button that can be clicked to automatically note the time in the notes document.

Figure 11.20 **Rubric to Assess the Development of Note-Taking Skills**

	Novice	Emerging	Proficient
Completeness of Notes	The notes contain sporadic words and short statements that do not make sense to you when reading them 24 hours after the observation.	The notes are becoming more comprehensive and complete. They make some sense to you when you go back to read them 24 hours later. Questions remain because of insufficient note-taking.	The notes have sufficient data for the observer and observed to make judgments about areas identified as the focus of the observation.
Note-Taker's Frustration Level	You experience very high levels of frustration because you either write notes and miss what is happening, or you watch what is happening and miss some notes.	You experience high to moderate levels of frustration because you either write notes and miss some of what is happening, or you watch what is happening and miss some notes.	You experience a low and decreasing level of frustration because you rarely miss what is happening while you write notes, or you rarely miss some notes while you watch what is happening.
Narrative vs. Literal Notes	The notes are primarily a narrative. The quotes are limited to single words or short phrases that don't make sense after revisiting them 24 hours later.	The notes include most of the quotes from the teacher in a form that makes sense when revisited 24 hours later. Observer narrative is less than 40 percent of the notes. Notes contain some student quotes. Your notes begin to note the arrangement of the room and the displays on the walls.	The notes include most of the important quotes from the teacher and the students. The observer narrative is reduced to brief stage directions, such as a description of the teacher's location in the classroom. The room arrangement and most of the displays on the walls that support the lesson are noted.
Labeling Based on the Knowledge Base of Effective Teaching	Some areas of performance are labeled with general terms from common language. Sporadically, effective teaching terminology is used.	After analyzing your notes, 50 percent of the areas of performance are labeled with specific terms from effective teaching found in the earlier chapters of this book. The rest of the notes are labeled correctly with common language and/or general terms.	After analyzing your notes, 80 percent or more of the areas of performance are labeled with specific terms for effective teaching. For example, the name of the specific routines or research-based techniques, such as *wait time*, are used.
Data Supports Labeled Areas of Performance	The data does not adequately or accurately support the labels given for the areas of performance.	The data adequately and accurately supports about 50 percent of the labels given for the areas of performance.	The data adequately and accurately supports 75 percent or more of the labels given for the areas of performance.

Time Notations	The notes do not contain time notations.	The notes contain time notations at least every 10 minutes.	The notes contain time notations at least every 3 to 4 minutes and at critical times, such as the beginning and the end of transitions, or the time it takes to get the learning started at the beginning of the class.
Listing Questions	After the initial analysis, there are at least two non-judgmental questions to ask the teacher at the post-conference.	After the initial analysis, there are up to four non-judgmental questions to ask the teacher at the post-conference.	After the initial analysis, there are more than four non-judgmental questions to ask the teacher during the post-conference
Resisting Judgments	During a 40-minute observation, you made eight or more judgments.	During a 40-minute observation, you made three to seven judgments.	During a 40-minute observation, you made two, one, or no judgments.
Data Describes Levels of Student Mastery of the Objectives	Data and labels are only sufficient to address classroom management, routines, and/or teacher preparation, but they do not show the levels of student mastery of the objectives.	Data and labels are sufficient to address classroom management, routines, teacher preparation, and the level of mastery of some of the students.	Data and labels address all of the areas identified for analysis. There is also ample data to determine the level to which most or all the students demonstrated mastery of the lesson objectives.

The following are three sets of notes from a comprehensive observation taken by observers at varying stages in their note-taking development. Note that in the places where the note-taker missed a part of the dialogue, the observer placed three dots to indicate that some information was missing. The note-taking process is typically quite frustrating for the novice; however, the quality of your notes improve with practice.

Below are some tricks note-takers use to get the most comprehensive notes.

1. Avoid analysis while observing. Analysis takes up intellectual time and energy needed for getting the most accurate notes.
2. Use lulls in the lesson, such as quiet student-work time, to fill in the missing notes.
3. When necessary, get up and move to be able to hear or see something that is taking place in another part of the room.
4. Arrive five minutes early and take down (write, photograph, or record video of) information such as the arrangement of the furniture and the wall and blackboard displays.

5. If you are gathering data about questioning practice, teacher physical proximity, or student behavior, bring a seating plan of the classroom with the students' names already written into each seat area.
6. Stay in the class for five or 10 minutes after the observation is over, and fill in the information that is not yet on the paper.
7. Give your partner a copy of your notes so that he or she may fill in any information you missed but that he or she remembers from the lesson.
8. Recognize that notes will never include everything. Try to get as much of what the teacher is saying as possible. You can then use the abbreviation "S..." as a place holder to show that a student spoke.
9. Use abbreviations or shorthand whenever possible. Below is a sample of abbreviations that one observer uses. Any abbreviation that helps gather data more quickly is fine.

Figure 11.21 Abbreviations for Two-Column Note-Taking

	Wherever possible, use pictures or video to replace written descriptions
Machiavelli= Mach	Once a name is used, the name can be abbreviated.
Circulate=circ	A word that is used frequently can be truncated.
Room=rm, higher-order thinking skills=hots	Words that are easy to remember can be written with letters omitted.
T	Teacher or, in the case of co-teaching, such as in an inclusion classroom, the regular classroom teacher or the first teacher.
T2	In a co-teaching arrangement, this is the second teacher in the room.
P	The paraprofessional or teacher assistant
S	Student, if you don't know the student's name. If you do know the student's name, then put the student's initials.
…	Missed data. Typically, the ellipsis is preceded by either a T or an S to indicate whether it was a student or the teacher whose statement was missed.
S…?	Student asked a question, but you didn't get the wording of the question.
T…?	Teacher asked a question, but you didn't get the wording of the question.
Wt	Wait time. This is usually followed by a number indicating the number of seconds the teacher waited. This abbreviation is used for both wait time I and wait time II.
( )	Words in parentheses are the observer's narrative or description; all other words, phrases, or sentences are quotes.
grp 1	Indicates the teacher is standing next to group 1. (A seating chart or a quickly drawn chart of the groups can also be helpful in showing where the teacher is standing in relation to the various groups of students.)
Grp 1 S	A student from group 1 is speaking.
R	Recall question
c	Comprehension question
h	Higher-order thinking question
ot	Students are off task. This is usually followed by a number that indicates the number of students off task. Some observers use a percentage. If the observer has a class-seating chart, the ot can be put at the spot of the student's seat, followed by the time to increase the specificity.
se	Student enters the class. This abbreviation is typically used for students who arrive late to the class.
sl	Student leaves. If the observer knows the student's name, the s can be replaced with the student's initials.
bl	Bored look. This is usually followed by a number that indicates the number of students looking bored or stating their boredom. Some observers use a percentage. If the observer has a class-seating chart, the bl can be put at the spot of the student's seat, followed by the time to increase the specificity.
cl	Confused look. This is usually followed by a number that indicates the number of students looking confused or stating their confusion. Some observers use a percentage. If the observer has a class-seating chart, the cl can be put at the spot of the student's seat, followed by the time to increase the specificity.

hr	Indicates the number of hands raised to answer or ask a question. The abbreviation is usually followed by the number or percentage of students with their hands raised. If the observer has a seating chart, he/she can put a slash each time a student raises his/her hand. The slash is then crossed to make an X when a student is called on by the teacher.	
op	Objectives are posted. If possible, the observer should write or take a photograph of the actual objectives as they are posted.	
os	Objectives are stated. If possible, the observer should write the actual objectives as they are stated. If the objectives are posted and stated, the observer need only write them once.	
ap	Agenda/itinerary is posted.	
as is	Agenda (*as*) and/or itinerary (*is*) is stated. If possible, the observer should write the actual agenda as it is stated. If the agenda is posted and stated, the observer need only write it once.	
csl	Connection to students' own lives or the real world	
cpl	Connection to previous learning	
rp	Classroom rules are posted. If possible, the observer should write the rules as posted.	
be	Behavior expectations are stated. If possible, the observer should write the behavior expectations as stated.	
am	Attention move	
ds	Dipstick	
sm	Students moved	
pr	Processing activity (individual, partner, or group)	
mm	This abbreviation followed by the students name means he/she is missing materials needed for class.	
tech	Teacher uses an LCD, document camera, or SMART/interactive white board.	
dr	Teacher uses document reader.	
go	Teacher uses a graphic organizer.	
v	Teacher uses a visual other than an overhead or graphic organizer.	
rb	Relationship-building statement or action	

Figure 11.22 (on the next page) shows three levels of two-column notes that range from proficient to novice. They are notes from a high school class that is studying the Renaissance. The first set of notes is from an observer whose note-taking is at the proficient level. In this example, the notes are from the full lesson. The second set of notes is from an observer at the emerging level. The final set of notes is from an observer at the novice level. In the emerging and novice set of notes, just the first 10 minutes of the class are shown for comparison purposes. The lesson plan for this lesson is in Chapter 1.

When reading these notes, please note the following:

1. There are many spelling and grammatical errors. When taking notes, your focus is on getting the data. Don't use extra time trying to ensure correct spelling or grammar. The only reader of the notes is the observer. When the notes are shared, the observer will be there to explain any questions about the notes.

2. One difference between the proficient notes and the novice notes is the number of literal quotes. The proficient notes have a larger number of literal quotes. The novice notes are more dependent on the observer narratives.

3. A second difference is the frequency of the time notations. The first set of notes has many more time notations.

4. A third difference between the proficient notes and novice notes are the notations in the left column. One of the areas this high school teacher wanted help with was getting students to work effectively in groups. In the proficient notes, the

observer has noted some questions for the teacher about the structure of the group in the left-hand column. These questions give the observer more data that will help the observer better help the teacher with the area he is working to improve. Some of these questions were noted during the observation; some of these questions were noted after the observation when the observer reviewed the notes, prior to meeting with the teacher who was observed. The teacher also wanted to know how well he tied the lesson to the students' own lives and the real world. The proficient version has notations about those connections in the right column.

Figure 11.22 Three Levels of Two-Column Notes

Proficient Level

8:26	T hurry back I'm going to start in just a min. (Desks arranged in groups to facilitate grop work desks were in rows for the previous teacher)
	(Ss sitting in classroom 5 minues before class-teacher is interacting with Ss in a joking manner prior to the lesson-is also geting his work ready for class)
	(on walls) map of the world agdnda on bl brd questions on blbd cahtedral architect plan poster
	(ap) Sit in your manor groups Self assessment Read Machiavelli selecxtion Answer questions Discuss connections to the world today
	(Questions on board) Why should a prince be concerned with warfare? Should a prince be cruel?Why or why not? How should a prince utilize fear? How should a prince regard property? Why did Mach write The Prince?
8:30	(16 students in class) T OK folkks sit in you r manor groups Sit in your manor groups you remember you manor groups
	let me just announc a couple of things I know you have some questions about the paper. Some other issues we will be in the linbrary tomorrow.. we are going to look at the schedule. I wil give yo some due dates
why so much time at group 1? 8:31	... (grp 1) S...

T right

tomorrow in the library .. we will have another resdearch day..

after that you are pretty much on your own

remember ... use the websites Mr. Kramer showed you how to use the website

T ... make sure you are doing that and I will check in more about that tomorrow

any questions about the essay at this point

S can you go online... can you use the URL... .org, .gove

T that is a great question...

.. in the blue packet I gave you at the start of the year there is a page in there about...

look at that. There is a page in theat blue packet about how to evaluatate a good website..

if it says.gove. .edu, it usually means it is a good website

...org .com mean

if so and so wnt to Germany and took pictures about Martin Luther

...

you are asking a great question because all

one other asnouncement before we get started

tomorrow night is the hunger banquet

...

I'd really like you all to go

8:34   ...you will get extra credit... V.I.P. tour

T Yes

S you can't bring a priest

T...you can't bring a priest S...

T. Ralph will definitely be there as pennacne

...

8:35 self assess-   I want to talk about poikties and pol theory in the renaissance and theis person named
ment connects   Nicolo Mach
to the students'   ...think about how a prince and the govt should act
own lives   before we start I want you t look at this.. self assessment

...indicate 1,2,3,4,5 next to the statement

one means you strongly disagree

five means you strongly agree with a statement take 3 or 4 mins to do that

.S...

T you are supposed to be sitting with your manor groups. if you are in a sit stay there

...

rember one if

five if... 3 if it is in the middle

8:37   T yes

S do we do this as if it is today

have the groups   T yes, do this as though it is you in 2004
been assigned   (SE)
jobs?   T why don't you sit there

(T circulates around the room)

T if everyone in the group is finished just choose one or two and tell...

tell how you answered the question and why

speak out loud

make some noise

8:39 (grp 1) do you agree with the statement of disagree
…. which one are you guys going to discuss
why don't you discuss number 5… what did you get for #5
S..
talk about why you skipped it, why did you skip it
S…
T…
Is it because sometimes it is true and sometimes it is not or depends on what

(grp 1) complicates the question for sure
S…
T what is that
S…
T sure absolutely…
Ok let's bring it toegher her
8:40 Let's start with …'s group
(grp 4) S…(gives a report on the group's discussion)…even if it means… it says that… and
we did not understand why people …
T… any one else wnat to comment on that
Any other groups want to say something about #8?

(grp 6).. S…
T… I guess I look at that as saying in order to get a secure socieity then…if you can guar-
antee safety over your property then…
T did anyone put a one or a two for
(grp 2) S…
T… let's take one from this group
(Grp 5) S…
T so what did you gyys thnk about that
S..
T so you totally…
S I feel that if the president cries every time he is hurt people whould think tat he is not
such a strong leader…
You can't just say during a crisit that I don't know the answer
…
(grp 5) S I disagree with because…
T someone else in the group who disagree with that
S…
yea
S…
yea
S…
T you want a little vulnerability, a little humanity
(Grp 5) S…
T Ok
(grp 6) S people don't need someone else to…

8:45 (grp 5) S2…
T mmm
S I don't think a president like that would…that is why I
personally gave it a 5…
I beleive it is his job to be strong
T Let's take a couple…we will be able to bring these

	questions back later
	(grp 4) S… I wold realy be botther by this..
	T. you want a leader to show strength and toughness but you don't always need to be tough…
	T let's take aontehr statement from the group here
	(grp 6) S I don't think… during the revolutionary war…
	sometimes.. like n Iraq.
Should students who answer tell their own answer or give a sum- mary of the group discussion?	T you neeed war to achieve peace…
	T..
	(grp 2) S…I think war is the opposite of peace… if you have war to get peace then you are cancelling it out
	T a couple more comments on that, interesteing
	(grp 3) S.. I think… the holocaust.. if it hadn't occurred then alot more people would have died..
	T I probalby want to hear more about when it is worth it and when it is not…
	T let's hear one more comment from Ellie
	grp 1 S..
	T let's put htis on hold for a minute and we'll come back to
	this. turn the page over and
	let's see what Mach had to say about these issue…
	we will get back to this
	…
8:51	Mach is ..in the 1500s and
	I want you think about these four questions (T reads the four questions from the balck board)
	T he was basically born in the late 1400 (goes on to give background about machiavelli)
8:52	T: read this in your groups. read it out loud, take turns, somebody read 1,2,3,and 4
	go ahead and read it an we will check in in a few minutes
8:54	(students round robin read orally in the group)
	(grp 1) T read the whole thing..
	(circulates around the room and checks in on group discussions)
	(grp 5)
	(grp 1)
	(grp 2)
	(grp 3)
	(grp 4)
	(grp 5)
	(grp 1) T fair treatment
8:56	(continues to circulate from grp to grp whicle students read)
	(grp 6) T…
	(grp 4) T…
	(grp 3)
	(grp 1) T why should a prince use fear
8:59	(speaks to all) T you are doing this according to Machiavelli
	(grp 6) T why should a prince…

　　　　T talk out loud folks. remember you answer these questions according to Mach- what is mach's view
(grp 3) – (T sits and discusses)
T rermember the Aztecs…it wa a way for males to climb the social ladder…any way keep going

9:01　　　(grp 4) T what did you get for number 2 should a prince be cruel?...
T meaning? what is…
S…
T go ahead
S…
T…

9:03　　　(to all) OK let's take a few more minutes on
this- you guys area doing a nice job- then we will come back and talk again
(grp 4)
(to all) Ok folks keep going folks make some noise here here…
(grp 2) T he had some personal ambition here. he want to impress some of the people in power. he want to get hired as an advisor… but what is he truly trying to get at there?
S…
T what is his view of power here… how should a prince…

S…
T he thinks….
S…
T luke to you agree or disagree
S…
T you were able to read part of this…what do you think his point is here… you are the prince. you are reading this book…even if it means being cruel?
S…
T … Cruelty should not allowed? … so be powerful but don't be cruel (continues to probe with Luke in grp 2)
S…
T to all, stay focused folks we are going to do about two more minutes
T do you agree with Luke (addressed to student who has not yet answered)

9:07　　　T let's bring it togeher here.. Let's get people who haven't spoken yet out loud to talk
T let's start with Segovia (grp 1) why should a prince be concerned about warfare that was…
S…
T what is this second think you are saying
S…
mmhm
S…
T so it is important for a prince to think …Segvia what do you think- should people fear presidents or prime ministers

S…
T don't be a person who inspires fear…
T do all People agree or disagree with Segovia…
S…
T let's just take it in your own opinion now…
T spencer. yea

	(grp 1) S… I think that… but when you are nice people don't generally have anything to fear so they will… you have to instill some fear so they won't betray you….
9:10	(grp 6) S… T you are saying don't be too nice. a ruler should always be suspicious that someone will want to replace him… S… T even if it means using some cruelty S… T what is mcahiavellis say in abour cruelty T Tobias (grp 5) S… machiavelli is saying T soe if the goal is to achieve a little cruelty along the way might be worth it T (grp 5) what do you think? S (first time this student speaks) S (tobias)… although more lives will be lossed.. T… if machiavelli is remembered for one thing it is that " the ends justify they means. (T writes this statement on the blk brd) .. what is all that about… anyone know what that means
9:14	S… T …. what is the real world example that this is OK Tobias: … when there is not end in sight. if it is going to go on indifiinitely then it is Ok to … to end it … if it cuts the loss of life short T to all .. if it looks like… let's take the war on terrorism. if it .. it is ok to use a little cruelty if it is going to end the war earlier (grp 1) S… S…? T she wants more claarification. what do you mean by that (grp 1) Ellen …. I do't hunderstand how that … but I think that if you.. the means cause. if your means are bing cruel then you have to factor in all the suffering you caused along the way with the ends and see if it is still justified T So at the end you look at all the Iraqis who died all the americans whodied… what happns if after that you decide it wasn't worth it… (Grp 6) S (give example of the sherman's March in civil war… the bombing of German cities in WWII)
9:18 **Starts to make** **a connection** **to the Iraq war**	unfortunately we are out of time. don't put all your stuff away just yet… how far do we go in Afgan. how far do we go in Iraq. do we go into North Korea. at what point do we say what we are doing is questionable… if we have some hardship in the end…. (end of class) bring your note cards tomorrow…do not forget your citation cards… if anyone needs to chat with me about the paper see my after class. (4 students come up to speak to the teacher) T try to get some specific ecamples,
Emerging Level	**The first 10 minutes of the class**
8:26	T hurry b ack I'm going to start in just a min. (Desks arranged in groups to facilitate grop work desks were in rows for the previous teacher) students sitting in classroom 5 minues before class-teacher is interacting with students in a positive relation ship manner prior to the lesson-is also geting his work ready for class (agenda on board)

8:30	T OK folkks sit in you r manor groups
	Sit in your manor groups
	you remember you manor groups
	…
	(grp 1)
	S…
	T right
	tomorrow in the library .. we will have another resdearch day..
	after that you are pretty much on your own
	remember … use the websites Mr. Kramer showed you how to use the website
	T … make sure you are doing that and I will check in more about that tomorrow
	any questions about the essay at this point
	S can you go online… can you use the URL… .org, .gove
	T that is a great question…
	.. in the blue packet I gave you at the start of the year there is a page in there about…
	…if so and so wnt to Germany and took pictures about Martin Luther
	…
	you are asking a great question because all
	one other asnouncement before we get started
	tomorrow night is the hunger banquet
	…
	I'd really like you all to go
	…you will get extra credit… V.I.P. tour
	T Yes
	S you can't bring a priest
	T…you can't bring a priest S…
	T. Ralph will definitely be there as pennacne
	…
	I want to talk about poiktics and pol theory in the renaissance and theis person named Nicolo Maciavelli
	…think about how a prince and the govt should act
	before we start I want you t look at this.. self assessment
	…indicate 1,2,3,4,5 next to the statement
	one means you strongly disagree
	five means you strongly agree with a statement take 3 or 4 mins to do that
	.S…
	T you are supposed to be sitting with your manor groups. if you are in a sit stay there
	…
	rember one if
	five if… 3 if it is in the middle

Novice Level	**First 10 minutes of class**
8:26	T (desks in groups of 4)
	(agenda on board and questions on the board)
	(Questions on board)
8:30	T (starts class)
	…
	(grp 1)
	S…
	T right
	(T explains about the work on the manor project they will be in the library tomorrow)
	T … make sure you are doing that and I will check in more about that tomorrow

any questions about the essay at this point
S (asks about using websites)
T … in the blue packet I gave you at the start of the year there is a page in there about…
… one other announcements (T explains about the hunger banquet)
…
…you will get extra credit… V.I.P. tour
T Yes
S (makes joke and T responds with a joke)
…
I want to talk about politics and policol theory in the renaissance … Machiavelli ….
(T explains how to use the self assessment
.S…
T you are supposed to be sitting with your manor groups. if you are in a sit stay there
…
rember one if
five if… 3 if it is in the middle

Video-Recorded Observations

It takes a great deal of practice to get comprehensive two-column notes. It is for this reason that some peer-reflection teams and lesson-study teams choose to record video rather than, or in addition to, taking handwritten notes. The advantage of recording video is that it is possible to get everything the teacher says. The disadvantage of recording video is that the camera often does not clearly pick up the students' comments. The camera (or tablet, laptop, or smartphone) is also limited in what can be seen, as it is following the teacher. It misses those things our human peripheral vision can observe, such as what the students who are not next to the teacher are doing, the displays on the walls, and other important data. It also takes good equipment and practice to record video of a classroom in a way that yields the maximum amount of information. **The ideal data-gathering situation is to have one teammate record video while another teammate takes two-column notes. This provides the benefits of both forms of data gathering.**

Figure 11.23 is a script of the first four minutes of the lesson that corresponds to the pre-observation conference information shown earlier in this chapter. It resulted from a single note-taker and a second person recording video of the lesson. The script shows the stages of development that note-takers pass through in building their competence to take copious literal notes. The rubric is followed by three sets of notes taken of the same classroom by note-takers at different levels of development.[14]

---

14 See the rubric on page 548 that describes the stages of development that note-takers pass through in building their competence to take copious literal notes.

Analyzing Your Notes Prior to the Post-Conference

The next stage of the process is to analyze the notes in preparation for the post-conference. As mentioned previously, it is good to have a partner fill in any missed data prior to our analysis. During the analysis, the notes are read from beginning to end with the objective of identifying the data that will address the issues and/or specific questions our partner raised in the pre-observation conference. Also, write additional questions that will be asked of the observed teacher in the post-conference. These are typically clarification questions about something we saw in the observation that was not clear to the observer.

Using Charts to Gather Data

Seating charts can be used to gather certain types of data. These charts are an effective means of gathering data about who raised their hands to ask a question and who was called on. They are also an effective means of gathering data about the teacher's physical proximity to various students during the class.

The Post-Observation Conference

The post-observation conference needs to be prepared for thoughtfully. Something as simple as deciding where to hold the conference can make a difference in the conference's effectiveness in meeting the needs of the teacher who was observed. For example, the best place to hold the post-conference is typically in the classroom of the teacher who was observed. This allows easy reference to any data in our notes that might be enhanced by something that is in the room, such as questions about some of the

Figure 11.23

3rd Grade	SCIENCE: STRUCTURES
	The students are seated in a circle. Some are seated on the floor and others are seated in chairs. The teacher is seated in the circle on a chair. Written on a poster on the wall is the definition of stability. 20 students
1:10	T: What I wanted to start with was, last week, we'd started with the word stable. Can you see that this shape is not stable? Does anyone remember the definition that we gave of stability? We did it with a structure, what was it? *wt< 1 second*
	Student: We said that squares aren't as stable as triangles.
Cody answers at least 25% of the questions. Does he always answer most of the questions?	T: Okay, we're going to get to that, and that's a good point. Remember the test for stability? If you were to push it, it needed to come back to its original position. And certainly with this, if that's the original position, if we were to push it, did that return to its original shape? *wt< 1 second*
	Ss: No.
	T: So that's why we say this is not stable. Now, one thing we did yesterday was we took a triangle and a square, and we added washers to it. Can somebody raise their hand and share what we learned from that, so that Chris will know what we did yesterday? *wt< 1 second*
	Sam: We said that the square wasn't as stable as a triangle.
	T: Yes, and we said it wasn't as strong or stable. And how many washers did the square hold? *wt< 1 second*
	Cody: 23
	Sarah: Yes, I can see that you're looking up there, and we did record it up there. And of course, how many washers did the triangle hold, everybody? *wt< 1 second*
	Ss: 110.
What would happen if you waited three to five seconds after asking a question before you called on a student to answer?	T: Yes, so one of the things we learned yesterday was the triangle was really a strong shape. All right, let's see what Emma's done. She took a pentagon, pent meaning 5, this is a 5-sided shape that wasn't very stable, and look at the straws that Emma has added to this, okay. Now let's do some stability tests on this. We're pushing in, and is it returning to its original shape? *wt< 1 second*
	Ss: Yes.
	Teacher: So she's added some straws to make it more stable. Do we see some shapes in here? What shapes do you see? *wt< 1 second*
	Sam: A triangle.
	T: Yes, we see our triangles, and of course, what did we learn about triangles? Triangles are strong. Now, we do have another shape down here. Now do you think maybe if you were going to add a straw, where would you add your next straw to make this just a little bit more stable? Do you have an idea? *wt< 1 second*
	S: The bottom.

1:14 How many of the students understood the concept of using triangles to increase stability before you sent them back to stabilize their pentagons?	T: Yes, and in fact, if you did that, we'll just use this straw as a demonstration. If she added one here, what is the shape you would see? wt< 1 second The triangle, right? So today, what we're going to do is, you're going to keep building with your shapes, your structures, building up, and I want you to think about the using the information we learned about triangles. Think about how to make things more stable, and keep building up.
	The students move to different parts of the room with their partners. They all know their partners and get in their partners quickly. The materials are all set out at each of the ten locations.
1:17	*At this point four of the groups have their hands raised looking for help. Six of the groups appear to be working. Sam's and Cody's groups are working. The teacher moves to the first group….*

wall displays. It is much easier to ask the questions and refer to the actual displays than to be in another space and try to describe the display. This is equally true with discussions about room arrangement, physical proximity, and other areas of performance that may be discussed.

Providing accurate data and asking good questions in the post-observation will be most helpful in improving teaching and learning. To do this, the observer needs to look at the data and think about our approach to the conference. There are typically three objectives for the post-conference.

1. Ask the clarification questions we need to obtain the data that fills in the gaps in the notes.
2. Ask questions that stimulate the teacher's self-analysis of the lesson.
3. Provide the teacher with data related to the target performances he or she has identified as areas to study.

In some cases, these three points can be mutually exclusive parts of the conference. More often, however, they are intertwined in the overall conference discussion.

Asking Clarification Questions

Clarification questions are used to obtain the data needed to better understand the context of the lesson. There may be pieces of learning observed in the lesson for which more context is needed about how these pieces fit with something that was taught earlier or how they will fit with what will happen in future lessons. Often, the observer has questions about individual students to better understand the behavior. Since, at times, the observer is observing a grade or

discipline different from the one the observer teaches, the observer may have a question about how the material in this lesson fits with the larger curriculum. Or the observer may not understand some of the lesson's content and may need an explanation of the content from the teacher. An effective observer *does not* need to be a person who teaches the same discipline or student age level. Often, an observer from another level or discipline can offer effective feedback. They look at the lesson with a different lens. Their questions are asked with less context and understanding, often giving the observed teacher more perspective as to how his or her teaching is perceived by the students in the class.

Giving Data about the Target Performances

Often, the only data provided in the post-conference is data about the target performance identified as an area for analysis. This is done by restating the target performance and then giving the teacher either the literal data or the analyzed data related to the target performance. The observed teacher then reflects on any gap that exists between the target performance and the data related to that performance. The observer then draws conclusions and makes recommendations how future teaching can be modified to meet the target performances more effectively. Below is a list of examples of target performances and the data that is typically associated with those target performances.

Target performance: Wait a minimum of three seconds after asking a question 90 percent of the time.
Data: You waited two seconds or less after 90 percent of the questions you asked.

Target performance: All groups will be on task at least 90 percent of the time.

Data: Group 5 was on task 60 percent of the time.

Target performance: At least 50 percent of the questions will be at the comprehension or higher-order-thinking skills level.[15]

Data: You asked 12 recall questions and one comprehension question.

Target performance: At least 60 percent of the students will ask or answer a question.

Data: Twenty percent of the students asked or answered a question.

Target performance: Teach in the target language (world languages class) at least 85 percent of the time.

Data: You spoke in the target language 50 percent of the time.

Target performance: The transition from morning circle will take less than two minutes.

Data: The transition from morning circle to the centers took five minutes.

Questions That Cause Self-Analysis

Recommendations to the teacher should be avoided. Instead, the observer should use thought-provoking questions to facilitate self-discovery. It is important that these questions sound like questions and not like judgments.

For example, one middle school teacher asked her peer-facilitation teammate during lesson study to observe her class to determine why most of the answers students gave during question-and-answer times were one- or two-word answers. She wanted the students to give more thoughtful and comprehensive answers. The data gathered during the observation indicated that the teacher asked 11 recall questions, five comprehension questions, and one higher-order thinking question. An example of a judgmentally worded question would be, "You only asked one higher-order thinking question. Why didn't you ask more?" An example of a thought-provoking way to ask the same question would be, "My notes show you asked the following questions and then received the following answers from students." (Show the teacher the observer's literal notes with the teacher's questions and the students' answers.) "Which of your questions resulted in answers with the level of thinking you were

With this type of questioning, the teacher can analyze her own practice and generate solutions for improvement.

looking to get from the students? Which questions resulted in inadequate answers?"

With this type of questioning, the teacher can analyze her own practice and generate solutions for improvement. The observer may also learn more about the thinking behind the teacher's classroom decisions. For example, the teacher might conclude that she needs to ask a greater number of higher-order thinking questions. Or she might conclude that the recall questions asked at the beginning of the lesson were needed for the students to have the foundation information needed to answer the comprehension and higher-order thinking questions that could have been asked later in the lesson. Or the actual conclusion might be that the questions asked in this lesson were correct but that, in the next lesson, the teacher should quickly activate the learning from the previous class and move right into asking higher-order thinking questions. If the best course of action is the latter, then asking the judgment question might have denied the teacher data that was truly needed to improve her instruction.

Peer observation is a very effective tool for gathering data that helps a teacher analyze his or her own teaching. However, it is important that teachers learn the skills above before observing a colleague. The result of observing without adequate preparation often makes the experience more negative than positive. For this reason, only after they receive adequate training and preparation should teachers observe one another.

Creating a Common-Assessments Inquiry Group

In order to collaboratively create common assessments, a teaching team needs a clear set of quality expectations from its district that includes the district's expectations for the following:

1. **Curriculum standards that are to be assessed.** The district may, for example, require that all of the major standards taught from the district's written curriculum are assessed. (See example below for a ninth-grade English midterm exam.)

2. **Assessment validity.** Does the assessment test what it taught? For example, if reading is assessed, are students reading an appropriate passage? If writing is being assessed, are students writing?

---

15 See Chapter 6, Figure 6.22, for a table with examples of the language used in higher-order-thinking skills questions.

3. **Rigor of the assessment.** The district may require, for example, that at least one question is on the application, analysis, and synthesis level of Bloom's taxonomy.

4. **Time-span of the assessment.** If this is a benchmark assessment, the district may expect it to be given in a specific month or to be given twice a year. If it is a high school assessment, it may take the form of a midterm or final.

5. **Grading/measurement of the assessment.** The district may expect a rubric, an answer key, or a scoring guide to assure that all assessors are calibrated in their grading.

6. **Calibration protocols.** Districts may expect that teachers will grade some or all of the assessments in a collaborative group following a protocol to assure calibration. The Low-Medium-High Protocol can be used to generate a local rubric, which can then be used to score all written assessments using this local rubric. Or, the district may use a commercially developed or state- or province-wide rubric.

7. **Data analysis.** The district may expect administrators or department heads to gather the results and provide a table and an analysis of the results of the common exam. These results may then be compared to the state or province assessment results or results from other standardized assessments.

Figure 11.24 Sample Grade 9 ELA Assessment

Standards Assessed	RL9-10.1 Reading Standards for Literature 6–12 [RL] The CCR anchor standards and high school grade-specific standards work in tandem to define college and career readiness expectations—the former providing broad standards, the latter providing additional specificity. **Grades 9–10 students:** 1. Cite strong and thorough textual evidence to support analysis of what the text says explicitly as well as inferences drawn from the text. **W.9-10.1 Writing Standards 6–12 [W]** The CCR anchor standards and high school grade-specific standards work in tandem to define college and career readiness expectations—the former providing broad standards, the latter providing additional specificity. **Grades 9–10 students:** Write arguments to support claims in an analysis of substantive topics or texts, using valid reasoning and relevant and sufficient evidence. a. Introduce precise claim(s), distinguish the claim(s) from alternate or opposing claims, and create an organization that establishes clear relationships among claim(s), counterclaims, reasons, and evidence. b. Develop claim(s) and counterclaims fairly, supplying evidence for each while pointing out the strengths and limitations of both in a manner that anticipates the audience's knowledge level and concerns. c. Use words, phrases, and clauses to link the major sections of the text, create cohesion, and clarify the relationships between claim(s) and reasons, between reasons and evidence, and between claim(s) and counterclaims. d. Establish and maintain a formal style and objective tone while attending to the norms and conventions of the discipline in which they are writing. e. Provide a concluding statement or section that follows from and supports the argument presented.
Validity	Students will read two passages aligned with district standards and will write an argument with claims, evidence, an introduction, and a conclusion.
Rigor	The assessment has students apply their knowledge of reading literature and writing arguments; they analyze two pieces of literature, and they write an argument with a thesis, which requires a synthesis of ideas.

continued on next page

Time Span	This is the ninth-grade midterm administered over two days of classes.
Assessment	The rubric will be the locally designed rubric that aligns to the state rubric standards for writing about literature.
Calibration Protocol	The ELA department will assess six exams using the rubric before each member of the English department uses the rubric independently to assess the work from another colleague's class. The department head will spot-check at least two essays per teacher for consistency.
Data Analysis	The department head will analyze the scores and provide them for the whole ninth grade and for each teacher's class. These results will be analyzed for strengths and weaknesses using the Low-Medium-High protocol, and each teacher will leave the department meeting with an action plan to support student growth.

The 10th-Grade Common Assessment Prompts and Paired Readings

Read the Frost poem "Nothing Gold Can Stay." Paraphrase the poem in your own words, then explain the meaning of the poem using at least two specific quotations from the text.

Read the last pages of *The Great Gatsby* again. In your own words, describe what Nick sees as he looks at Gatsby's empty house for the last time. Use at least two specific quotations from the text. For your argument, compare and contrast the poem and the novel's ending. How are their themes similar? How are they different? How are Fitzgerald's and Frost's writing alike? How are they different? Provide at least four quotations from the texts in your answer.

Study Groups: Student-Work Inquiry

Examining Student-Work Study Groups

There are many different models for examining student work. Some are large in scope and require extensive amounts of teacher meeting time. These models tend to take an open-ended look at the student work. The teacher who provides the work may give little or no direction to the group prior to the reviewers examining the work. The teachers in the group analyzing the work may then do so without context or specific direction and provide whatever productive comments arise from their review of the work. These models also tend to look at larger numbers of work samples.

The CASW model provided earlier in this chapter provides a highly structured protocol with limited time (one or two sessions) and limited samples of student work (each teacher brings a sample of a low-, moderate-, and high-performing piece of student work). All teachers have given the same assignment or this student work may be a common assessment, thus the context of the assignment is understood by all participants. In this case, no single teacher presents; instead, the group has a facilitator and the results are collaboratively developed.

Other models for examining student work are more defined in scope and can be completed in shorter blocks of meeting time. In these models, the teacher presenting the work provides a great deal of context about the work. The presenter then provides focus questions or statements that tell the reviewers what he or she hopes to learn as a result of their review of the student work.

The model in Figure 11.24 can be completed in the blocks of time typically available to teachers. The protocol in Figure 11.25 can be used in a single four-hour block; in two blocks of two hours on early release days; or in four 50-minute planning blocks. Those teachers who have more than an hour per session or more than four hours in total may wish to use this protocol with more complex pieces of work or larger numbers of student work pieces. For those who wish to look at some of the more comprehensive and time-intensive models, a good place to start your search is by looking at student work on the National School Reform Faculty website at lasw.org.

The Purpose of Examining Student Work

Chapter 1 demonstrated the importance of focusing on what students master or, specifically, what they learn, rather than on what is covered in the lesson. Student work is the ultimate reflection of what students have mastered, and the degree to which that occurs may vary in a classroom. Thus, student work is a method for understanding more clearly how what

Figure 11.25 Argument Rubric for 10th Grade

	Score of 4	Score of 3	Score of 2	Score of 1
Reading/Research x ___ = ___	The writing • makes effective use of available resources • skillfully/effectively supports an opinion with relevant and sufficient facts and details from resources with accuracy • uses credible sources*	The writing • makes adequate use of available resources • supports an opinion with relevant and sufficient facts and details from resources with accuracy • uses credible sources*	The writing • makes limited use of available resources • inconsistently supports an opinion with relevant and sufficient facts and details from resources with accuracy • inconsistently uses credible sources*	The writing • makes inadequate use of available resources • fails to support an opinion with relevant and sufficient facts and details from resources with accuracy • attempts to use credible sources*
Development x ___ = ___	The writing • addresses all aspects of the writing task with a tightly focused response • skillfully develops the claim(s) and counterclaims fairly, supplying sufficient and relevant evidence for each, while also pointing out the strengths and limitations of both in a manner that anticipates the audience's knowledge level and concerns	The writing • addresses the writing task with a focused response • develops the claim(s) and counterclaims fairly, supplying sufficient and relevant evidence for each, while also pointing out the strengths and limitations of both in a manner that anticipates the audience's knowledge level and concerns	The writing • addresses the writing task with an inconsistent focus • inconsistently develops the claim(s) and counterclaims fairly, supplying sufficient and relevant evidence for each, while also pointing out the strengths and limitations of both in a manner that anticipates the audience's knowledge level and concerns	The writing • attempts to address the writing task but lacks focus • attempts to establish a claim or proposal • supports claim(s) using evidence that is insufficient and/or irrelevant
Organization x ___ = ___	The writing • effectively introduces precise claim(s); distinguishes the claim(s) from alternate or opposing claims • effectively creates an organization that establishes clear relationships among claim(s), counterclaim(s), reasons, and evidence • skillfully uses words, phrases, and/or clauses to link the major sections of the text, create cohesion, and clarify the relationships between claim(s) and reasons, between reasons and evidence, and between claim(s) and counterclaims • provides an effective concluding statement or section that follows from and skillfully supports the argument presented	The writing • introduces precise claim(s); distinguishes the claim(s) from alternate or opposing claims • creates an organization that establishes clear relationships among claim(s), counterclaim(s), reasons, and evidence • uses words, phrases, and/or clauses to link the major sections of the text, create cohesion, and clarify the relationships between claim(s) and reasons, between reasons and evidence, and between claim(s) and counterclaims • provides a concluding statement or section that follows from and supports the argument presented	The writing • introduces the claim(s); however, may fail to distinguish the claim(s) from alternate or opposing claim(s) • has a progression of ideas that may lack cohesion (ideas may be rambling and/or repetitious) • inconsistently uses words, phrases, and/or clauses to link the major sections of the text, create cohesion, and clarify the relationships between claim(s) and reasons, between reasons and evidence, and between claim(s) and counterclaims • provides a sense of closure	The writing • identifies the claim(s) • has little or no evidence of purposeful organization

* See Delaware website for other writing rubrics at http://www.doe.k12.de.us/Page/508

was taught and the way it was taught influenced the level of student mastery of the information and skills in the curriculum.

Group Norms

Figure 11.3 (Diaz-Maggioli 2004) contains group norms that are important to follow when doing any peer-facilitated professional development. These norms are also relevant to our study groups. In addition to those norms, we add the following for examining student-work study groups.

1. Speak respectfully about the students whose work is being examined. Assume that the student has given his or her best effort.

2. Presenters should avoid feeling or acting defensive when listening to the discussions of the reviewers. Instead, they should listen carefully and ask themselves what they have learned from any statement that makes them feel defensive.

3. Each group should have a facilitator who does not serve as a presenter or reviewer during this session. The facilitator is typically a person who is a member of a different student-work study group.

Figure 11.4 contains an assessment the study group can use at the end of the session to assess the effectiveness of the group process.

Choosing and Preparing the Student Work for the Study

1. Choose work that does not have a single, finite answer and avoid multiple choice, true/false, and fill-in-the-blank assignments.

2. Choose assignments that are more open-ended yet may be reviewed in five to seven minutes. If longer assignments are used, then the time for the steps below should be extended. Some examples of possible assignments are

   - essay questions or open-response questions from a classroom assessment
   - open-ended homework assignment in any subject area
   - math problem of the day/week
   - journal entry (learning log entry)
   - models, artifacts, and other performance assessments (e.g., poster, wiring a house plug, map, art work, student-created musical instruments, video of a student shooting a foul shot)
   - video of student presentations; each student's presentation should be no more than seven minutes long.

- audiotapes of student performance assessments
- audio or video of students working in groups; these are used to determine the effectiveness of the student's group work. Chapter 3 contains a description of the components of effective group work.

3. To the extent possible, keep the students anonymous. When using written work, remove the students' names before copying the assignments.

4. Bring with the work the scoring guides (criteria sheets or rubrics), exemplars, anchor papers, and other guides used to communicate to students how to complete the assignment. If the students were given a timeline, checklist, or other scaffolds, bring those as well.

5. Copy the work prior to correcting the assignment. Bring copies of the work that does not display your assessment or comments on the quality of the work. After copying the work, assess the work prior to having it reviewed by your team.

6. Bring the work from three students. One student's performance should be at the high end of performance, one student should be in the middle range, and one student in the low range. The presenting teacher will decide on which student he or she wants the review to focus.

7. If the work is written, bring enough copies of all the materials for every member of the group.

Group Size

The recommended group size for this protocol is four people. This includes two teachers reviewing the work, the presenter of the work, and a facilitator. It is the discussion between the reviewers that is most valuable to the presenter. Groups larger than four will not give all three teachers (the facilitator is an objective third-party teacher who does not present with this group) an opportunity to present in the four-hour block set aside for this meeting. In circumstances in which more time is available, the group could be larger. Each additional group member adds about 50 minutes altogether to the four sessions.

As mentioned in the previous paragraph, the facilitator is typically an objective third-party teacher who does not present with this group. In some circumstances, it may not be possible to have a facilitator not from the group. For example, a middle school team of four teachers using this protocol during their team time may not have access to an independent facilitator. In such cases, it is acceptable to have the facilitator as one of the team members. In these cases, there are two options:

1. In cases in which the team members plan to use the protocol multiple times during the year, they may assign one person to act as the facilitator for the entire time. In this circumstance, the person will not be one of the three presenters. He or she will facilitate the presentations of the other three group members. It is understood that the next time the protocol is used, this person will be one of the presenters and another person will serve as the facilitator.

2. In cases in which the team will only be going through the protocol once, the facilitator can be rotated. In these cases, each of the four people will be a presenter and each will have an opportunity to be the facilitator. Please remember that if you have four presenters, you will need to increase the time needed to complete the full protocol by 40 or 50 minutes.

Once the groups have been set, the schedule has been made, and the work has been selected, you are ready to follow the steps of the protocol (Figure 11.26).

Figure 11.26 Protocol for Examining Student Work

Steps

The steps below are written with the assumption that the group has a full four hours of uninterrupted time to carry out the protocol. Modifications for use of this protocol during shorter periods of time (e.g., planning periods, team meetings, or early-release professional development days) are noted in *italic* lettering.

Step 1 (approximately five to seven minutes): Make sure each presenter has all the materials noted on the previous page. The facilitator reviews the group norms and the purpose of examining student work, and he or she ensures that everyone understands the norms and purpose. The facilitator briefly reviews each of the steps of the protocol. The facilitator reviews the survey of team norms (see Figure 11.3, which the group will use to collectively assess its work at the end of the session). The facilitator helps the group choose the order for the presentations. The facilitator keeps a check on the time for each step and moves the group along as needed. The first time the protocol is used, additional time should be allotted for explaining each step. It will also be important to allow time at the start of each step to review the expectations for that step.

[If the protocol is used in successive planning periods of 40 to 50 minutes, the first time the protocol is used the teachers may wish to reserve a full block to complete the activities noted in step 1. It typically takes more time because people are unfamiliar with the protocol and have questions about the steps. In subsequent uses of the protocol, when everyone is experienced in its use, that much time will not be necessary.]

Step 2 (approximately 10 minutes): The first presenter provides the reviewers with student work pieces, scoring guides, and other scaffolds noted on the previous page. The presenter explains the assignment directions to the reviewers in the same way he or she explained it to the students. The presenter provides the reviewers with focus questions that indicate what he or she wants to learn from this experience. The presenter should limit the focus to no more than two areas. Groups that have larger blocks of work time may be able to have more than two areas of focus. Some questions can include

*   How can I improve the clarity of the directions I give for the assignment?
*   How can I improve the scoring guide so it more clearly provides students with a road map for success when I'm teaching the assignment?
*   What is each student's level of mastery based on the scoring guide?
*   What is each student's level of mastery based on the lesson mastery objectives?
*   What does the work tell you about each student's learning style?
*   What kinds of mathematics problem-solving strategies does each student use?
*   What mathematical language, reflection, or evidence do you see each student using to demonstrate mathematical reasoning?
*   What kinds of science problem-solving and inquiry-based strategies does each student use?
*   What scientific skills and procedures does each student apply in his or her learning?

- What primary-source documents can I use to teach these concepts (social studies)?
- What social studies skills and procedures does each student apply in his or her learning?
- How can I connect this assignment to a context in the students' own lives or the real world?

Step 3 (approximately 10 minutes): The reviewers listen carefully to the assignment directions. They then review the scoring guides and other scaffolds. They ask the presenter any context questions that will help them understand the process for completing the assignment or the purpose of the assignment. Some examples of context questions include

- How much time did the students have to complete the assignment?
- Were there any parts of the assignment the students found particularly difficult?
- Was the assignment completed individually, with partners, or in a group?
- What mathematical skills and procedures did the student apply in his or her learning?

Step 4 (approximately 15 to 20 minutes): The reviewers review the assignment. This may involve reading a written assignment or viewing the videos of student presentations. After they have reviewed the student work, the reviewers discuss it with the objective of reaching consensus on how the assignment should be rated based on the scoring guide and generating ideas that address the teacher's focus questions. The reviewers should verbalize all their thinking for the presenter to hear. The reviewers may ask the presenter further context questions during this discussion. Other than answering context questions, the presenter should remain quiet throughout the reviewers' discussion. While listening, the presenter should note the following:

- what the presenter is learning that will help improve his or her teaching of the information and skills reflected in this assignment or similar assignments in the future
- how the presenter's assessment of each student's work differs from the consensus assessment of the reviewers and why it is different
- any questions the presenter has for the reviewers
- any additional context that the reviewers have not asked about

It is often recommended that any reference the reviewers make to the presenting teacher during the discussion be made in the third person as if the presenter were not in the room. This helps maintain the objectivity of the discussion. This part will take some practice, as it may seem awkward at first. The facilitator can help by reminding the reviewers when they slip into using the second person.

Step 5 (approximately 15 minutes): This is the step in which there is dialogue between the presenter and the reviewers. The presenter asks any questions he or she has written while listening to the reviewer. The purpose of these questions is to obtain additional information that will help the presenter teach and/or assess the information and skills in this assignment or similar assignments more effectively in the future. The presenter may also reiterate the focus questions he or she asked in step 2 to ensure he or she has extracted all the helpful information related to those questions. During this step, the presenter adds to the list of what he or she has learned that will help improve future teaching or assessing of the information and skills reflected in this assignment or similar assignments.

Step 6 (approximately 10 minutes): The presenter reads the list of ideas he or she has obtained for improving the teaching or assessment of the information and skills in this assignment or similar ones. Included in the list should be the learning obtained related to the focus questions given in Step 2. This should include concrete "next steps" the presenter will take to implement these ideas. Each next step should be specific and have a date by which the step will be taken.

[In circumstances in which the protocol will be used during successive planning or team periods of 40 or 50 minutes, Steps 2 through 6 are completed by one of the presenters during the period. In each of the next two time periods, another teacher presents his or her student work. In early-release professional development time periods of two hours, Step 1 and a single presenter can be completed in the first time period. The second and third presenter teachers present their student work in the second early-release period. Step 7 is completed at the conclusion of the second session.]

Step 7 (approximately 10 minutes): This step is completed after all three presenters have had their work reviewed. Each member of the group, including the facilitator, fills out the survey of team norms. The group members list ways in which they can improve their work as a group the next time they look at student work. The group members set a check-in meeting time when they can check in on how their next steps are progressing.

Step 8 (approximately 50 minutes): The meeting check-in should be scheduled far enough in advance for the members to implement some of their next steps. Each member of the group reviews the list of next steps he or she created during Step 6 of the work

session. The members report on the progress they have made in implementing the next steps. This is also a time for members to ask for help with any steps they are having difficulty implementing. This discussion may result in modifying a member's next steps. At the end of the meeting, the group either decides that the next meeting will be another check-in meeting or that they are ready to look at additional student work in another full work session.

Study Groups with a Focus on Research and Professional Reading

There are hundreds of books and articles about effective teaching that make for excellent reading by professional reading study groups. This book has been used by many schools for that purpose. Professional reading study groups seek to examine a piece of the professional literature for the purpose of implementing the concepts contained within it in their classroom. The following are guidelines for these study groups.

1. The norms found in Figure 11.3 should be followed by the group.
2. The reading should be broken into defined sections that can be discussed at a single meeting. Journal articles are typically a good length for study groups. Books, on the other hand, typically need to be broken up into chapters or sections.
3. All members of the group should complete the reading prior to the discussion meeting.
4. The type of analysis and some focus questions should be agreed upon prior to completing the reading.
5. The most interesting pieces to discuss tend to be those that enable teachers to immediately apply the concepts in the reading to their classrooms.

Types of Analysis

1. Text-to-text activities are designed to have teachers examine two pieces of reading and compare the components of each. For example, teachers may choose the "Working with Special Education Students" and the "Working with English Language Learners" essays at the end of this chapter in this book and discuss the ways in which the successful classroom practices for each group are the same and the ways they differ.

2. Text-to-self activities are designed to have teachers examine a piece and determine how the concepts in that piece apply to their own ideas about students and teaching. Activities such as Take a Sip, found at the end of Chapter 3, are used to examine the piece.

Conclusion

As discussed at the beginning of both Chapter 10 and 11, teachers are the best people to help other teachers become more effective practitioners and to investigate and solve problems for their specific context. Thoughtfully planned, job-embedded group inquiry improves teaching practice, increases collegiality, and improves student learning. It develops a culture of ongoing improvement, lifelong learning, and self-analysis among staff members that translates into continual growth for the entire school community, both educators and learners. These well-designed group inquiries send the message to teachers that their professional knowledge, voices, and experience are valued and important. The result is high student achievement and higher levels of teacher morale.

> *Teachers are the best people to help other teachers become more effective practitioners and to investigate and solve problems for their specific context.*

Appendix A: California Standards for the Teaching Profession

Standard 5: Assessing Students for Learning

Teachers apply knowledge of the purposes, characteristics, and uses of different types of assessments. They collect and analyze assessment data from a variety of sources and use that data to inform instruction. They review data, both individually and with colleagues, to monitor student learning. Teachers use assessment data to establish learning goals and to plan, differentiate, and modify instruction. They involve all students in self-assessment, goal-setting, and monitoring progress. Teachers use available technologies to assist in assessment, analysis, and communication of student learning. They use assessment information to share timely and comprehensible feedback with students and their families.

5.1. Applying Knowledge of the Purposes, Characteristics, and Uses of Different Types of Assessments

As teachers develop, they may ask, "How do I…" or "Why do I…"
- …become knowledgeable of the different types of assessments—and their uses, benefits, and limitations—that I draw on to inform my instruction?
- …select assessment strategies and instruments appropriate to the learning outcomes being evaluated?
- …use my knowledge of assessment concepts such as validity, reliability, and bias to choose assessments appropriate to my students?
- …design grading practices that draw on multiple sources of information and reflect student learning?

5.2. Collecting and Analyzing Assessment Data from a Variety of Sources to Inform Instruction

As teachers develop, they may ask, "How do I…" or "Why do I…"
- …keep a continual and comprehensive record of group and individual achievement?
- …select, design, and use assessment tools appropriate to what is being assessed?
- …collect, select, and reflect upon evidence of student learning?
- …work with families to gather information about all students and their learning?
- …use standardized tests, diagnostic tools, and developmental assessments to understand student progress?
- …use a range of assessment strategies to implement and monitor individualized student learning goals (including IEP goals)?
- …assess student behavior to support learning?
- …interpret data based on how an assessment is scored and what results it reports?

5.3. Reviewing Data, Both Individually and with Colleagues, to Monitor Student Learning

As teachers develop, they may ask, "How do I…" or "Why do I…"
- …review student assessment data with colleagues?
- …use assessment results to monitor my teaching and guide planning and instruction?
- …use assessment information to determine when and how to revisit content that has been taught?
- …use assessment data to eliminate gaps between students' potential and their performance?
- …use assessment results to plan instruction to support English learners?
- …use assessment results to plan instruction to support students' IEPs?

5.4. Using Assessment Data to Establish Learning Goals and to Plan, Differentiate, and Modify Instruction

As teachers develop, they may ask, "How do I…" or "Why do I…"
- …draw on assessment data to support development of learning goals?

- ...review and revise learning goals with students over time?
- ...ensure that student learning goals reflect key subject matter concepts, skills, and applications?
- ...use informal assessments to adjust instruction while teaching?
- ...use multiple sources of assessment to measure student progress and revise instructional plans?
- ...work to differentiate goals and plans based on assessed needs of my diverse learners?
- ...address the specific needs of English learners and students with special needs as I use assessments to inform my instruction?

5.5. Involving All Students in Self-Assessment, Goal Setting, and Monitoring Progress

As teachers develop, they may ask, "How do I..." or "Why do I..."
- ...make assessment integral to the learning process?
- ...make assessment an interactive process between teacher and student?
- ...model self-assessment strategies for all students?
- ...develop and use tools and guidelines that help all students assess their work and monitor their learning goals?
- ...provide opportunities for all students to engage in peer discussion and reflection of their work?
- ...provide opportunities for all students to demonstrate and reflect on their learning inside and outside of the classroom?

5.6. Using Available Technologies to Assist in Assessment, Analysis, and Communication of Student Learning

As teachers develop, they may ask, "How do I..." or "Why do I..."
- ...become familiar with and select technology resources that support assessment practices?
- ...use technology to analyze student learning and inform instruction?
- ...use appropriate technology resources to communicate students' learning to students and their families?

5.7. Using Assessment Information to Share Timely and Comprehensible Feedback with Students and Their Families

As teachers develop, they may ask, "How do I..." or "Why do I..."
- ...provide all students with information about their progress as they engage in learning activities?
- ...initiate regular and timely contact with families and resource providers about student progress?
- ...communicate assessment results to families in ways that are respectful and understandable?
- ...provide families with ways to use assessment information at home to improve student learning?

References

Bambrick-Santoyo, P. *Driven by Data: A Practical guide to Improve Instruction*. San Francisco, CA: Jossey Bass, 2010.

Ball, D.L. and Cohen, D.K. "Developing practice, developing practitioners: toward a practice-based theory of professional development." In L. Darling-Hammond and G. Skyes, eds. *Teaching as the Learning Professional: Handbook of Policy and Practice*. 3–32. San Francisco, CA: Jossey-Bass.

Barth, R., DuFour, R., DuFour, R., Eaker, R., Eason-Watson, B., Fullan, M., Lezotte, L., Reeves, D., Saphier, J., Schmoker, M., Sparks, D. and Stiggin, R. *On Common Ground: The Power of Professional Learning Communities*. Bloomington, IN: National Educational Service, 2005.

Boudett, K.P., City, E., and Murname, R. *Data Wise: A Step-by-Step Guide to Using Assessment Results to Improve Teaching and Learning*. Cambridge, MA: Harvard Education Press, 2011.

California Department of Education and the California Commission on Teacher Credentialing. "California Standards for the Teaching Profession (CSTP) (2009)" http://www.ctc.ca.gov/educator-prep/standards/CSTP-2009.pdf.

Cohen, E. *Designing Group Work: Strategies for the Heterogeneous Classroom*, 2nd ed. New York: Teachers College Press, 1994.

Diaz-Maggioli, G. *Teacher-Centered Professional Development*. Alexandria, VA: Association for Curriculum and Development, 2004.

DuFour, R., DuFour, R., and Eaker, R. *Professional Learning Communities at Work Plan Book*. Bloomington, IN: Solution Tree, 2006.

DuFour, R. "What Is a PLC?" In *On Common Ground: The Power of Professional Learning Communities*, eds. DuFour, R., Eaker, R., and DuFour, R., 31–43. Bloomington, IN: Solution Tree, 2005: pp. 31–43.

DuFour. R. "Professional Learning Communities: A Bandwagon, an Idea Worth Considering, or Our Best Hope for High Levels of Learning." *Middle School Journal* (September 2007): 4–8.

DuFour R. and DuFour, R. "What Might Be: Open the Door to a Better Future." *Journal of the National Staff Development Council* 28, no. 3 (Summer 2007): 27–28.

Easton, L.B. "What Professional Learning Looks Like Around the World." *Journal of Staff Development* 4, no. 3 (2013).

Ermeling, B.A. and Gallimore, R. "Learning to Be a Community: Schools Need Adaptable Models to Create Successful Programs." *Journal of Staff Development* 34, no. 2 (2013): 42–45.

Garcia, E. and Bryant, J. "Helping Young Hispanic Learners." *Educational Leadership* 64, no. 6 (March 2007): 34–39.

Garmston, R.J. and von Frank, V. *Unlocking Group Potential to Improve Schools*. Thousand Oaks, CA: Corwin Press, 2012.

Garmston, R.J. and von Frank, V. "Working Together, We Can Produce Genius." *Education Week*. http://blogs.edweek.org/edweek/finding_common_ground/2013/2/working_together_we_can_produce_genius.html.

Goddard, R., Hoy, W., and Woolfolk Hoy, A. "Collective Efficacy Beliefs: Theoretical Developments, Empirical Evidence, and Future Directions." *Educational Researcher* 33, no. 3 (April 2004): 3–13.

Handelzalts, A. "Collaborative Curriculum Development in Curriculum Development in Teacher Design Teams." PhD diss., University of Twente, 2009.

Jacob, G.M., Power, M.A., and Wan, I.L. *The Teacher's Sourcebook for Cooperative Learning: Practical Techniques, Basic Principles and Frequently Asked Questions*. Thousand Oaks, CA: Corwin Press, 2002.

Johnson, D.W. and Johnson, R.T. "Cooperative Small-Group Learning." *Curriculum Report* 14, no. 1 (1984): 2–7.

Kagan, S. *Cooperative Learning*. San Clemente, CA: Kagan Publishing, 1994.

Leana, C.R. "The Missing Link in School Reform." *Stanford Social Innovation Review* (Fall 2011): 30–37.

Lewis, C. *Lesson Study: A Handbook of Teacher-Led Instructional Change*. Philadelphia: Research for Better Schools, Inc., 2002.

Love, N. et al. *The Data Coach's Guide to Improving Learning for All Students*. Thousand Oaks, CA: Corwin Press, 2008.

McDonald, J., Zydney, J., Dichter, A., and McDonald, E. *Going Online with Protocols: New Tools for Teaching and Learning*. New York and London: Teachers College Press, 2–12.

National School Reform Faculty. "NRSF Protocols and Strategies…A to Z." 2014. http://www.nsrfharmony.org/free-resources/protocols/a-z.

Peery, A. *The Data Team Experience: A Guide for Effective Meetings*. Englewood, CO: Lead and Learn Press, 2011.

Unger, J. "Flex Your School's Data Muscles: Leadership Strategies Strengthen Data's Impact." *Journal of Staff Devlopment* 34, no. 4 (August 2013): 50–54.

Venables, D. *How Teachers Can Turn Data into Action*. Alexandria, VA: ASCD, 2014.

Villegas, M. and Lucas, T. "The Culturally Responsive Teacher." *Educational Leadership* 64, no. 6 (March 2007): 28–33.

Students with Disabilities: Transition Planning

One of the most important parts of the Individualized Education Plan (IEP) process for students with disabilities is transition planning. Transition planning is a requirement for students with disabilities, beginning at age 14. Effective transition planning has a strong focus on teaching students self-advocacy skills that are very important as students matriculate to college and pursue careers. Over the past several years, research has shown that students with learning disabilities and attention deficit hyperactivity disorder (ADHD) are attending college but are not earning degrees within a timeframe that is comparable with students without disabilities (Hamblet 2014). Many students with disabilities have reported difficulty in navigating the variances in disability accommodation systems and academic environments at the college level compared to their high school experience. In addition, the students have noted that their experiences in college fail to meet their overall academic expectations. The lack of knowledge about their learning profile also affects their ability to advocate for themselves (Hamblet 2014).

Many of the activities that are outlined in a student's transition plan take place in school and in the community. During transition planning and activities, all teachers and service providers are able to create opportunities in a supportive, non-threatening environment for students to practice the skills needed to be successful after high school. Transition planning is not only focused on a student's success academically after high school, but also on their ability to gain skills for independent living (Stanberry 2015).

As previously mentioned, helping a student gain skills in self-advocacy is a primary part of transition planning. Cultivating the skills necessary for self-advocacy for the student begins with helping them learn as much as they can about their disability and the impact that it has and will have on them in all areas of their life and development. It is also important to help the student self-advocate by teaching them about the rights that are afforded to them as persons with a disability and, as they transition to adult life, how their rights are protected by the Individuals with Disabilities Education Act (IDEA), the law that protects their rights in K–12 school. Likewise, they should also be taught about how they will be affected by changes to the Americans with Disabilities Act (ADA), the law that protects persons with disabilities post K–12 school (McNair and Solomon 2015).

Strategies for Elementary School Teachers

While transition planning for students with disabilities is not required until age 14, skills for independence and self-advocacy can begin as early as kindergarten. Below are several ways that elementary, middle, and high school teachers can support building these skills in students and create a strong foundation for their future.

• **"All about me"** units are not only a great way for students to explore their family, people, places, and interests, but also a great opportunity for teachers to encourage students to explore specific topics in school and learning that they like and are of interest to them. Teachers can also encourage students to talk about things in school and learning that are a challenge and how they seek help when they are challenged. Creating opportunities for students to share their strengths and areas of needed support also allows for them to learn to ask for help when needed, and it takes away the stigma of having a learning difference.

• **"Circle and center time"** provide natural opportunities in the classroom for students to learn independence and self-advocacy skills. During circle time, students gain skills for proper greetings, as well as how to ask and respond to questions from peers; these are all relevant to building the foundation of self-advocacy skills. For students with disabilities, teachers may initially need to use prompts to help them, but those prompts should fade as students' skills are gained over time. Center time is optimal for allowing students to make choices and work with peers both collaboratively and independently. Self-advocacy skills can begin very early with center time in the classroom. Learning to manage disagreements and collaborate with peers is also important for building self-advocacy skills, and centers are a natural mode of building a foundation for these skills.

• **Recess time**, when embedded in some guided or structured play, can become a great teaching tool for self-advocacy. Recess is a time when most conflicts occur and when students tend to have most of their disagreements. Some students never play with certain groups of students or certain playground equipment because they have difficulty speaking up or expressing their interest to their peers. Teachers can organize a short game during recess to support students who struggle in this area. Teachers can model how to ask to join a game and then encourage the student to do the same.

Strategies for Middle School Teachers

- During student advisory time, teachers should incorporate journal writing. Self-advocacy is very much about self-discovery. Journal writing helps the student keep a record of his or her personal history, choices, and growth.
- Use class projects to teach real skills that will help build independence and self-advocacy skills. For example, a math unit focused on budgets can incorporate a project for which the student has to search for an apartment, negotiate the rent, and plan for the move by getting a moving truck, rental insurance, etc.
- Use field trips as opportunities to visit local points of interest that have a connection with the disability community. In addition, invite guest speakers from organizations such as social service agencies, college disability services, or student support services, so that students may realize that there are community supports available to them when they graduate high school.

Strategies for High School Teachers

- Use interest inventories with students so that they begin to learn areas they are most interested in and their areas of strength. Once they receive the information from the inventories, use this in planning instruction and long-term projects with and for your students.
- Create opportunities for debate during classroom discussion in which students have to argue their point and persuade their classmates to agree with their viewpoint. This also allows students to practice advocating for their needs and preferences. It can give them a voice.

The following case study and action research conducted by teachers gives an example of how teachers' focus on their own professional growth leads to students with disabilities gaining stronger self-advocacy skills.

Special Education Peer-Facilitated Classroom Research Case Studies

Example 1

An interdisciplinary team of general education and special education teachers decided to form a professional learning community to further explore the concept of student self-advocacy in their high school. These teachers were all in agreement that self-advocacy is essential to academic success. They wanted to investigate ways to incorporate self-advocacy into the culture of their high school. For this study, however, they began with the question: "What do other teachers at our high school believe about self-advocacy?"

1. **The question we need data to answer**:
   What do other teachers at our high school believe about self-advocacy?

2. **Impact on student learning**:
   Self-advocacy is an important skill for students to learn both for their continuing education and as a life skill. In school, special-needs students (and other students as well) frequently have people such as parents and teachers who advocate for them. In college and in the workforce, this is typically not the case. After high school, students will need self-advocay skills to succeed in college and/or the work world.

3. **The method of data collection**:
   A questionnaire for their colleagues. The questionnaire asked three questions:
   a. What do you think are the best ways for students to engage in self-advocacy?
   b. How do you promote self-advocacy in your classroom?
   c. What do you think are the most significant impediments to self-advocacy for students at our school?

4. **Method of analysis**:
   The teachers will meet to collate the results. They will review the results together and generate recommendations.

5. **Results of the data analysis**:
   The responses from the teachers were as follows:
   a. What do you think are the best ways for students to engage in self-advocacy?
      i. Arrange to meet a teacher for extra help.
      ii. Raise hand and ask questions in class.
      iii. Use organizational strategies (assignment notebook, binders, calendars).

iv. Identify an adult advisor who will support and guide you.

v. Let the teacher know when and on what help is needed.

vi. Understand your learning style.

vii. Use available in-school resources (e.g. math seminar, writing lab).

viii. Review homework, quizzes, and tests.

ix. Know when, where, and from whom you can get help.

x. Meet with your teacher when you return from an absence.

xi. Access the help available.

b. How do you promote self-advocacy in your classroom?

i. Encourage students to ask questions.

ii. Promote a comfortable, safe environment.

iii. Provide extra help after school.

iv. Praise students when they go to the math seminar or writing lab and advocate for themselves.

v. Post teachers' schedules/availability.

vi. Provide one-to-one help during class.

vii. Use entrance/exit tickets (strategy) whereby students ask questions about things they do not understand (anonymously on a slip of paper upon entering or exiting the class for teachers to follow up on).

viii. Role-play scenarios for advocacy.

ix. Direct students to proper resources.

x. Direct students to my website, where they can keep track of their grades, assignments, and notes.

c. What do you think are the most significant impediments to self-advocacy for students at our school?

i. Students' beliefs about how they are being perceived by other students when they attempt to self-advocate. Students in a classroom situation are often intimidated by more self-confident peers.

ii. Teachers' belief that parents often take on the role of advocate for their children and, in doing so, enable students to avoid having to assume responsibility for themselves.

iii. Parents' efforts to help get students into the college of their choice motivates parents to intervene on behalf of the student.

iv. Teachers report they may be appearing unintentionally unapproachable at times.

v. Certain student traits such as shyness, disorganization, lack of motivation, disinterest, and low self-esteem were noted.

vi. Students often claim that their commitment to a sports team prevents them from going for extra help after school.

vii. Students' lack of knowledge of the benefits of self-advocacy.

viii. Students' lack of a sense of urgency to seek help in a timely manner

ix. Aides and other support staff may unintentionally be doing too much for students, rather than having students do for themselves.

x. Lack of teacher availability may discourage students.

xi. Students' lack of comfort level with teachers.

xii. A prior bad experience with a teacher may limit student contact with that teacher.

A random sampling of students was also given a brief questionnaire. The three questions asked were:

1. Do you seek help from your teachers?
2. What do your teachers do to encourage you to ask for help?
3. What gets in the way of your asking or going for extra help?

Students responses were as follows:

1. Do you seek help from your teachers?
Yes (26) No (6)

2. What do your teachers do to encourage you to ask for help?
- offer help (23)
- tell me to go to the math seminar or writing lab (8)
- warn me that I am failing (6)
- post their availability (5)
- create incentives (4)
- praise me when I seek help (3)
- learning center teacher makes me seek help (2)
- progress reports (1)
- teacher's website (1)
- write it in my assignment notebook (1)
- write "come see me" on a test (1)
- yell at me (1)
- nothing (1)

3. What gets in the way of your asking or going for extra help?
- teacher (23)

- sports/work/appointments after school (21)
- free blocks don't match up with teachers' schedules (8)
- feel unintelligent/pride (7)
- other homework or need to study for another class (6)
- nothing (5)
- grades good (3)
- friends/peers (3)
- class (2)
- problems at home (1)
- Learning Center helps me (1)
- too many people in math seminar room (1)

The questionnaires were tallied and analyzed. The interdisciplinary team of teachers came to the following conclusions about self-advocacy in their high school:

1. Some teachers are ambivalent about self-advocacy, and for others, the topic is an emotionally charged one.
2. Many students do not appear to know how to self-advocate effectively.
3. Students need to be taught how to self-advocate.
4. There are impediments to self-advocacy within our school culture and environment.
5. Students report that they meet with teachers more frequently than they actually do.
6. Some teachers are not as approachable and welcoming as perhaps they think they are or should be.
7. For many students, self-advocacy is not a priority.
8. Self-advocacy is not synonymous with asking for a break, a favor, or a way to avoid responsibility.
9. As adults, we can relate to having difficulty self-advocating with someone who is in a position of authority over us, such as our boss or supervisor. Students feel this way, too.
10. Certain categories of students may have a harder time self-advocating than others (e.g., students with special needs, students with a history of low achievement, English language learners, disenfranchised students).

The final thoughts of this action research group were that more discussion needed to take place on the topic of self-advocacy. They would like to see their high school adopt certain policies around self-advocacy as a way of changing the school culture so that going to see one's teachers during and after school is a more widely used and accepted practice among students of all grades. The chairperson of this professional learning community said, "We know that we are onto something here."

Example 2

1. **The question we need data to answer**:
   How can we improve reading comprehension across content areas?

2. **Impact on student learning**:
   a. Standardized test results show a disparity between students' comprehension of fiction and nonfiction.
   b. Classroom assignments of reading, reading instructions, and essay responses (open-response test items and document-based questions) show that students do not always understand what they are asked to read and to do.
   c. Notes taken from textbook reading assignments show that many students are not able to discern important information and to summarize it effectively.

3. **The method of data collection and analysis:**
   This group functioned as part peer-reflection team and part lesson-study team, with reading nonfiction as the underlying theme. Teachers in this group brought their classroom concerns to the group to be discussed. For example, a biology, a physics, and a chemistry teacher were concerned about students' comprehension and their skills at taking notes from the textbook. The special educator and English teacher in the group shared information about SQ3R (survey, question, read, recite, review) as a textbook-reading strategy. The content-area teachers had never heard of SQ3R or its many adaptations. Next, the special educator and English teacher introduced the Cornell note-taking method (explained below) to the group. The members of the team took a physics chapter and tried to apply SQ3R and Cornell notes to the chapter as a means of introducing these concepts to the teachers. It became clear that a third column was necessary for formulas.

   Both of the physics and chemistry teachers tried out the three-column Cornell note-taking adaptation in their classes. They reported back to the group that they found that a fourth column was, in fact, necessary for science. (They needed another column for formula examples.) So their final format was a piece of paper in landscape format divided into fourths. The teachers are in the process of standardizing this method of note-taking in their classes. They were thrilled with the results of this peer-reflection team that met just five times every other week.

To take Cornell notes, the student divides a piece of paper into a 2.5-inch column on the left side of the paper and a 6-inch column on the right side. On the left side, the student turns textbook headings into questions, and on the right side, the student writes the answer. A bold-print vocabulary word would go on the left side and its definition on the right side. The content-area teachers liked this systematic format for organizing notes.

Cornell Note-Taking Setup

Main Ideas	Notes from class discussion, lecture, or reading material
In this column, the student turns the textbook headings into questions and notes the main ideas derived from the content of the notes in the right column.	*This box contains the actual notes the student takes about the topic being studied. These notes can be obtained during a class discussion, a teacher lecture, group work, or completing an assigned reading.*
Summary	*At the conclusion of the note-taking, the student synthesizes what was learned in the notes and writes a summary of that synthesis.*

A biology teacher in the group found the Cornell note-taking system to be most effective for his use. It was suggested by those more familiar with the process that he use the following scaffold method to teach his students the technique:

1. Model the left and right sides of the note-taking system for the students.
2. Provide the questions on the left side, and have the students answer the questions on the right side.
3. Provide the answers on the right side and have students ask the appropriate question for the left side.
4. Provide a worksheet with some questions (left side) and some answers (right side) missing.
5. Have the students generate the entire set of notes on their own.

The biology teacher came to the realization that Cornell notes result in an excellent study guide and review for mid-year and final exams. He, too, gained value from his participation in the peer-reflection team.

Other possible questions for special education-related professional learning communities, reflection teams, lesson studies, or peer observations are:

1. How can teachers meet the needs of diverse learners in their classrooms?
2. How should teachers grade student-centered assignments for special education students while maintaining high standards?
3. How can teachers train special needs students to plan for and appropriately cope with stress?
4. How can I make my lesson(s) more multi-sensory?
5. What can I do to make outlining or webbing an automatic step in my students' writing process?
6. What can I do to make proofreading an automatic step in my students' writing process?
7. How can I get my special needs students to check their math answers?
8. How can I get my special needs students to keep their school papers organized?
9. What would motivate my special needs students to complete all of their homework nightly?
10. What's the best method of teaching summarization skills?
11. How do I manage interactive class discussions?
12. Is my wait time having an impact on responses to open-ended questions?
13. Do I ask more divergent or more convergent questions?
14. How can I improve the way students think critically/reflectively about what they are reading?
15. How can I improve my students' reading fluency, accuracy, or intonation?
16. What is the best way to help students who read well but don't remember what they read?
17. How can I infuse technology into my instruction?
18. Would a reading blog stimulate my unmotivated readers?
19. Would creating a teacher website containing student homework and grades reduce parent emails, improve homework completion, and/or motivate students to do well?
20. Why do students appear inattentive when I give directions?
21. What is the best method of helping students increase their reading speed?

22. How can I improve the social interactions of my special-needs students?
23. Are my instructional aides being used most effectively?
24. What are alternative ways of assessing students with pervasive development disorder (PDD) in the inclusive classroom?
25. How can I motivate my most resistant readers to read?

Teachers who take the time to reflect on their teaching practices and address their greatest questions and concerns will improve their teaching and maximize student achievement.

References

Hamblet, E.C. "Nine Strategies to Improve College Transition Planning for Students with Disabilities." *Teaching Exceptional Children* 46, no. 3 (January/February 2014): 53–59.

McNair, R. and Solomon, A. "A Practical Guide for People with Disabilities Who Want to Go to College." *Horizon House Employment Services.* http://tucollaborative.org/pdfs/education/College_Guide.pdf.

Stanberry, K. "IEP Transition Planning: Preparing for Young Adulthood." *Understood.org.* January 18, 2014. https://www.understood.org/en/school-learning/special-services/ieps/iep-transition-planning-preparing-for-young-adulthood.

English Language Learners Peer-Facilitation Research Project

1. **The question I need to answer:**
   After listening to oral directions for expected writing responses, English learners with intermediate fluency wait for a re-explanation, write off-topic information, or copy from the work of peers.

   What instructional strategies will ensure that English learners understand oral directions and participate in independent writing tasks related to challenging language and content objectives?

2. **Impact on student learning:**
   English learners with intermediate fluency struggle to independently complete written assignments to subject-matter knowledge and skills.

3. **Method of gathering data:**
   a. My partner(s) and I will collect and review three writing responses from English learners and accompanying rubrics. We will also critique descriptions of the directions we gave the class and share our reflective narratives explaining any modifications or adjustments for English learners. We will respectfully ask for English learners' oral feedback after they attempt writing tasks and record difficulties that each student had in understanding and completing the assignment.
   b. We will read, review, and reflect upon research-based strategies for English learners (see related essays in this chapter and previous chapters of this book), and choose three new approaches that rely on written responses to implement in our lessons.
   c. After implementing the new strategies, we will collect three more writing samples and again make notes on students' oral feedback about directions and completing the writing assignment. We will analyze these notes, our descriptions of the revised directions, rubric changes, and our own reflective narratives on how the strategies were implemented.

4. **Method of data analysis:**
   a. We will review the student work and determine if the new independent work has met the expectations as determined by the rubrics. We will examine student work to ascertain whether the changes we impacted student performance. We will analyze our adjustments to learn how they impacted the language demand in reading, writing, and listening.
   b. We will review our reflective narratives and student comments to gain insight on successes and continuing challenges.
   c. We will determine which new strategies were successful and whether it is reasonable to implement these strategies on a regular basis. In planning for students' increasing English proficiency level(s), we will decide when and how to decrease language support (offered to English learners but not to the general population of students).
   d. We will continue to attempt other strategies on a trial-and-error basis and use the same format for analysis. For eight weeks, we will collect artifacts that demonstrate successful strategies and present findings to the greater learning community.

Strategy Analysis for Teaching English Learners in Content Classes

Teacher Name(s):

Date:

Grade and Content Area:

Description of Project/Assignment:

English Proficiency Level of Student(s):

Pre-Production   *Early Production*   *Speech Emergent*   *Intermediate Fluency*   *Advanced Fluency*

Task	Notes
Strategy Implemented Choose a strategy from the outline that follows (or from previous chapters) and record.	
Student Feedback Describe how you collected student data to determine the level of success of the strategy.	
Language Demand Describe the strategy's impact on reading, writing, listening, or speaking.	
Reflection on Practice Record notes on whether it is reasonable to implement this strategy on a regular basis.	
Planning for Increasing Proficiency Describe how and when you will adapt this language support for an expected increase in proficiency.	

English Language Learners: Clarification Strategies for Teaching Content

Pre-Production–Early Production

- Refer to visual and graphic support used to teach vocabulary and content (pictures, graphs, photos, web images, or charts).
- Model skills and the use graphic organizers when explaining directions.
- List, practice, and review expected responses (e.g., short phrases with embedded content vocabulary).
- Plan interactive activities that use non-verbal demonstrations of knowledge and skills.
- Create cue cards that can be sorted, matched, ordered, patterned, and/or labeled.

- Use manipulatives and/or props to support content and academic language.
- Use themes that incorporate and validate students' culture and/or language experience.
- Send topics and/or visuals home for families to discuss in their primary language.
- Use technology to facilitate communication and demonstrate understanding (e.g., images, online activities, student blogs, or sound/video clips).

Early Production –Speech Emergent

- Use previous strategies when necessary.
- Create prompts for cooperative groups to preview vocabulary, repeat directions, and model skills.
- Use sentence frames to demonstrate and, for partners or groups, create dialogues with content vocabulary and phrases of increased difficulty.

- Plan interactive activities that evoke choral, yes/no, or one- or two-word responses.
- Use reference and response pages and graphic organizers that contain student and/or peer- created visuals that link vocabulary to print.
- Refer to and review previous relevant lessons or activities to explain new content, give directions, or model skills.
- Send home illustrated note cards that support vocabulary and academic phrases for students to share and study with a family member.
- Provide one-on-one checks for understanding, and write on index cards or sticky notes to clarify content or rewrite multi-step directions.

Speech Emergent–Intermediate Fluency

- Use previous strategies when needed.
- Encourage all students to ask a friend, repeat directions, and model skills.
- Create open-ended prompts for student groups to write and present extended dialogues that embed content vocabulary and phrases.
- Plan problem-solving activities that require students to explain in short phrases how they arrived at their conclusions.
- Refer to wall collages, word walls, visuals, apparatuses, or previous lessons when clarifying content and directions.
- Demonstrate the use of challenging content vocabulary and phrases when facilitating hands-on activities and asking questions.

- Check for understanding, and rephrase with less-demanding content vocabulary when necessary.
- Send translated monthly outlines with visuals that represent themes/topics for students to share with their families.
- Provide written directions with clarifying vocabulary, graphic support, or sample responses.

Advanced Fluency–Near Native English

- Use previous strategies when needed.
- Have each student write one "wh-" question (what, when, where, or why) about the directions, vocabulary, and/or skills modeled.
- Use specific journal prompts that ask students to reflect on their learning and understanding of content, skills, vocabulary, and academic dialogue.
- Incorporate students' evaluations of the level of difficulty of assignments into rubrics.
- Create a survey for students to suggest ways to make an activity/assignment easier or more challenging.
- Allow students to ask each other questions about the content and provide clarity.
- Send home easy English articles/texts that support content and themes.
- Provide some in-class time for reading/listening on tape, as necessary.
- Offer students highlighters, sticky notes, and index cards to use for outlining and asking questions.

Index of Topics and Names

Social and Emotional Learning
Examples of Teacher Questions That Develop Social and Emotional Learning Skills

Self-Awareness

Self-Awareness Behaviors in Classroom Management	Questions that develop self-awareness about transitions
Label and recognize own and others' emotions	You looked nervous when I announced the upcoming transition. Were you nervous about the transition? If so, why?
Self-Awareness Behaviors in Classroom Management	**Questions that develop self-awareness about conflict**
Label and recognize own and others' emotions	• How did it make you feel when he called you that name? • Why do you think he called you that name? • Why did you call him that name?
Analyze emotions and how they affect others	• How do you think he felt when you called him that name? • Did you want to make him feel that way? Why?

Self-Management

Self-Management Behaviors in Group Work	Questions that develop self-management when working on an academic project
• Set plans and work toward goals • Overcome obstacles and create strategies for more long term goals • Seek help when needed • Manage personal and interpersonal stress	• How will the waterwheel work when you finish it? • What is your first step? Second step?... • What do you anticipate will be the most difficult part? • If you get stuck how will you get help from another group? • When should you come to me for help? • If you disagree with someone in your group how will you resolve that disagreement?
Self-Management Behaviors in Cooperative Group Work	**Questions that develop self-management related to transitions**
• Set plans and work toward goals • Overcome obstacles and create strategies for more long term goals • Seek help when needed • Manage personal and interpersonal stress	• What can you do or I do to help reduce your anxiety before the transition? • Is there a way I can structure the transitions that will make you feel more confident?

Responsible Decision Making

Responsible Decision Making Behaviors When Setting up Classroom Routines	Questions that develop responsible decision making when setting up classroom routines.
• Identify problems when making decisions, and generate alternatives • Implement problem-solving skills when making decisions, when appropriate	• In what ways do these expectations help with the learning in this class (yours and that of the others)? • Are there any ways in which these expectations will detract from the learning? • If a student raises a way in which the expectations may detract from the learning a follow up question may be: What is an alternative set of expectation that better meets our goal of respectful behavior and maximum learning?

(continued on next page)

589

Relationship Skills

Relationship Skills in Cooperative Group Work	Questions that develop relationship skills in cooperative group work
• Exhibit cooperative learning and working toward group goals • Evaluate own skills to communicate with others	• When you are the leader how do you determine if someone is doing too much of the talking and not giving others adequate chance to speak? • If you see this happening what can you do to correct the situation?

Social Awareness

Social Awareness Behaviors Related to Classroom Presentations	Questions that develop the social awareness during classroom presentations (presenter)
• Identify social cues (verbal, physical) to determine how others feel • Predict others' feelings and reactions • Evaluate others' emotional reactions • Respect others (e.g., listen carefully and accurately) • Understand other points of view and perspectives	• When you were presenting what did you notice about the audience? • Were there parts of your presentation when you thought they were more interested than other parts? If so, what did you see that gave you that impression? • What do you think they were feeling at that time? • Were there parts of your presentation when you thought they were less interested? If so, what did you see that gave you that impression? • What do you think they were feeling at that time? • What do you think you could do differently to make more people interested more of the time?
Social Awareness Behaviors Related to Classroom Presentations	**Questions that develop the social awareness during classroom presentations (audience)**
• Predict others' feelings and reactions • Evaluate others' emotional reactions	• On which area of the audience rubric did you rate yourself the highest? • On which areas of the audience rubric did you rate yourself the lowest? What could you or the presenter do that would cause you to perform better on that area? • How do you think a person feels when you interrupt them and don't wait your turn to speak? • What impact do you think it has on others when you talk while someone is presenting?